American Foreign Relations

VOLUME 2

A History • Since 1895

SIXTH EDITION

Thomas G. Paterson

J. Garry Clifford

Shane J. Maddock

Deborah Kisatsky

Kenneth J. Hagan

HOUGHTON MIFFLIN COMPANY

Boston   New York

Editor-in-Chief: *Jean Woy*
Senior Development Editor: *Fran Gray*
Senior Project Editor: *Jane Lee*
Editorial Assistant: *Eddie Fournier*
Senior Art and Design Coordinator: *Jill Haber*
Senior Photo Editor: *Jennifer Meyer Dare*
Senior Composition Buyer: *Sarah Ambrose*
Senior Manufacturing Coordinator: *Priscilla Bailey*
Senior Marketing Manager: *Sandra McGuire*
Marketing Coordinator: *Ilana Gordon*

Cover Image: *After the Eleventh,* 2001 (acrylic on canvas on corrugated wood support) by P. J. Crook (b. 1945), © Courtesy of Theo Waddington Fine Art/Bridgeman Art Library.

Printed in the U.S.A.

Library of Congress Control Number: 2003110145

ISBN: 0-618-37073-0

5 6 7 8 9-MV-08 07

for

Colin Graham Paterson

Carol Davidge

Vera Low Hagan

Emily Rose Maddock

About the Authors

Thomas G. Paterson, professor emeritus of history at the University of Connecticut, graduated from the University of New Hampshire (B.A., 1963) and the University of California, Berkeley (Ph.D., 1968). He has written *Soviet-American Confrontation* (1973), *Meeting the Communist Threat* (1988), *On Every Front* (1992), *Contesting Castro* (1994), *America Ascendant* (with J. Garry Clifford, 1995), and *A People and a Nation* (with Mary Beth Norton et al., 2001). Tom has also edited *Cold War Critics* (1971), *Kennedy's Quest for Victory* (1989), *Imperial Surge* (with Stephen G. Rabe, 1992), *The Origins of the Cold War* (with Robert McMahon, 1999), *Explaining the History of American Foreign Relations* (with Michael J. Hogan, 2004), and *Major Problems in American Foreign Relations* (with Dennis Merrill, 2005). With Bruce Jentleson, he served as senior editor for the *Encyclopedia of American Foreign Relations* (1997). A microfilm edition of *The United States and Castro's Cuba, 1950s–1970s: The Paterson Collection* appeared in 1999. He has served on the editorial boards of the *Journal of American History* and *Diplomatic History*. Recipient of a Guggenheim fellowship, he has directed National Endowment for the Humanities Summer Seminars for College Teachers. He is a past president of the Society for Historians of American Foreign Relations. In 2000 the New England History Teachers Association awarded him the Kidger prize for excellence in teaching and mentoring. Besides visits to many American campuses, Tom has lectured in Canada, China, Colombia, Cuba, New Zealand, Puerto Rico, Russia, and Venezuela.

J. Garry Clifford teaches at the University of Connecticut, where he is a professor of political science and director of its graduate program. Born in Massachusetts, he earned his B.A. from Williams College (1964) and his Ph.D. in history from Indiana University. He has also taught at the University of Tennessee and Dartmouth College and has taught in two National Endowment for the Humanities seminars for high school teachers at the Franklin D. Roosevelt Library. For his book *The Citizen Soldiers* (1972), he won the Frederick Jackson Turner Award of the Organization of American Historians. With Norman Cousins, he has edited *Memoirs of a Man: Grenville Clark* (1975), and with Samuel R. Spencer, Jr., he has written *The First Peacetime Draft* (1986). He also co-authored *America Ascendant* (with Thomas G. Paterson) in 1995. Garry's essays have appeared in Gordon Martel, ed., *American Foreign Relations Reconsidered* (1994), Michael J. Hogan and Thomas G. Paterson, eds., *Explaining the History of American Foreign Relations* (1991 and 2004), Arnold A. Offner and Theodore A. Wilson, eds., *Victory in Europe, 1945* (2000), and in the *Journal of American History, Review of Politics, Mid-America, American Neptune,* and *Diplomatic History*. Garry has served on the editorial board of *Diplomatic History* as well as on the editorial board of the Modern War Series of the University Press of Kansas. He frequently participates in American professional conferences and has also lectured in Russia and Northern Ireland.

Shane J. Maddock is associate professor of history at Stonehill College in Easton, Massachusetts, where he also serves on the faculty of the Martin Institute for Law and Society. Born in North Dakota, he earned his B.A. from Michigan State University (1989) and his Ph.D. from the University of Connecticut (1997). He has also taught at the U.S. Coast Guard Academy. Shane has edited *The Nuclear Age* (2001) and has published in the *Journal of American History, International History Review, Pacific Historical Review, Presidential Studies Quarterly, Mid-America, Journal of Military History, American Jewish History, Canadian Journal of Latin American and Caribbean Studies, History in Dispute,* and *The Encyclopedia of U.S. Foreign Relations.* He has received fellowships from the Institute for the Study of World Politics, the U.S. Arms Control and Disarmament Agency, and the Hoover, Truman, Eisenhower, Kennedy, and Johnson presidential libraries. Shane has presented lectures and papers on his main research interests—U.S. nuclear nonproliferation policy and the intersection of popular culture and foreign relations. He is currently working on a book titled *The Nth Country Conundrum: The American and Soviet Quest to Halt the Spread of Nuclear Weapons, 1945–1970.*

Deborah Kisatsky is assistant professor of history at Assumption College in Worcester, Massachusetts. Born in Pennsylvania, she earned both her B.A. (1990) and her Ph.D. (2001) from the University of Connecticut. Deborah is the recipient of numerous awards and fellowships: the 1998–1999 Alexander von Humboldt Foundation Bundeskanzler (Federal Chancellor's) Scholarship for research in Germany, where she also served as a Junior Fellow of the Center for European Integration Studies, University of Bonn; the Myrna F. and Stuart L. Bernath Dissertation Grants of the Society for Historians of American Foreign Relations (1996 and 1999); a Franklin D. Roosevelt Library Lubin-Winant Fellowship (1996); and a Harry S. Truman Institute Research Grant (1996). She has published in *Intelligence and National Security, The Historian, Presidential Studies Quarterly,* and *The Journal of Interdisciplinary History,* as well as in the *Encyclopedia of U.S. Foreign Relations.* Deborah's book *Containment, Co-optation, Cooperation: The United States and the European Right, 1954–1955* will be published by Ohio State University Press.

Kenneth J. Hagan is an adjunct professor on the faculty of the U.S. Naval War College, Monterey Program, and professor emeritus of history and museum director at the U.S. Naval Academy, Annapolis. He previously taught at Claremont McKenna College, Kansas State University, and the U.S. Army Command and General Staff College. A native of California, he received his A.B. and M.A. from the University of California, Berkeley (1958, 1964) and his Ph.D. from the Claremont Graduate School (1970). Ken is the author of *This People's Navy: The Making of American Sea Power* (1991), a comprehensive history of American naval strategy and policy since the Revolution, and *American Gunboat Diplomacy and the Old Navy, 1877–1889* (1973). His scholarship also includes two edited collections of original essays: *In Peace and War: Interpretations of American Naval History, 1775–1984* (1984) and *Against All Enemies: Interpretations of American Military History from Colonial Times to the Present* (1986). He frequently contributes articles to the journal *Naval History* and lectures annually at the Canadian Forces College in Toronto. Besides regularly participating in panels at conferences in the United States, he has given papers on the history of naval strategy in Sweden, Greece, Turkey, France, and Spain. A retired captain in the naval reserve, he served on active duty with the Pacific Fleet from 1958 to 1963 and currently advises the Naval ROTC college program on its history curriculum.

Contents

Preface   xiii

1 *Imperialist Leap, 1895–1900*   1

Diplomatic Crossroad: The *Maine,* McKinley, and War, 1898   2

The Venezuela Crisis of 1895   5

Men of Empire   8

Cleveland and McKinley Confront *Cuba Libre,* 1895–1898   11

The Spanish-American-Cuban-Filipino War   16

Peace and Empire: The Debate in the United States   18

Imperial Collisions in Asia: The Philippine Insurrection and the Open
   Door in China   21

The Elbows of a World Power, 1895–1900   27

FURTHER READING FOR THE PERIOD 1895–1900   29

NOTES TO CHAPTER 1   30

2 *Managing, Policing, and Extending the Empire, 1900–1914*   33

**Diplomatic Crossroad: Severing Panama from Colombia
for the Canal, 1903**   34

The Conservative Shapers of Empire   38

Cuba's Limited Independence Under the Platt Amendment   42

The Constable of the Caribbean: The Roosevelt Corollary, Venezuela,
   and the Dominican Republic   44

The Quest for Order in Haiti and Nicaragua   46

The Mexican Revolution Threatens U.S. Interests   48

Japan, China, and Dollar Diplomacy in Asia   51

Anglo-American Rapprochement and Empire-Building   55

FURTHER READING FOR THE PERIOD 1900–1914   61

NOTES TO CHAPTER 2   64

3 *War, Peace, and Revolution in the Time of Wilson,*
1914–1920   **67**

     Diplomatic Crossroad: The Sinking of the *Lusitania*, 1915   68

     The Travails of Neutrality   73

     Submarines, Neutral Rights, and Mediation Efforts   76

     Wilson Leads America into World War   79

     The Debate over Preparedness   82

     The Doughboys Make the Difference in Europe   85

     Wilson Imagines a Better Future: The Fourteen Points
       and the Peace Conference   87

     Principle, Personality, Health, and Partisanship:
       The League Fight   91

     Red Scare Abroad: Bolshevism and Intervention in Russia   96

     The Whispering Gallery of Global Disorder   99

     FURTHER READING FOR THE PERIOD 1914–1920   102
     NOTES TO CHAPTER 3   103

4 *Descending into Europe's Maelstrom,*
1920–1939   **106**

     Diplomatic Crossroad: Roosevelt's Attempt to Extend America's
     Frontier to the Rhine, 1939   107

     "Prize Fighters with a Very Long Reach":
       The Independent Internationalists   110

     Economic and Cultural Expansion in a Rickety World   115

     Peace Seekers for a World Without War   120

     Cold as Steel: Soviet-American Encounters   122

     Hitler's Germany, Appeasement, and the Outbreak of War   125

     American Isolationism and the Neutrality Acts   129

     Roosevelt Shifts and Congress Balks on the Eve of War   131

     FURTHER READING FOR THE PERIOD 1920–1939   133
     NOTES TO CHAPTER 4   136

5 *Asia, Latin America, and the Vagaries*
of Power, 1920–1939   **139**

     Diplomatic Crossroad: The Manchurian Crisis, 1931–1932   140

     A Question of Power   142

     Facing Japan: The Washington Naval Disarmament
       Conference and China   144

Japan's Footsteps Toward a New Pacific Order   147

Making and Managing Good Neighbors in Latin America   151

Creating Dictators in the Dominican Republic, Nicaragua, and Haiti   156

Subverting Nationalism in Cuba and Puerto Rico   161

Compromising with Mexico: Oil and Nationalism   163

Pan Americanism and the Approach of the Second World War   165

FURTHER READING FOR THE PERIOD 1920–1939   167

NOTES TO CHAPTER 5   169

6   *Survival and Spheres: The Allies and the Second World War, 1939–1945*   172

Diplomatic Crossroad: The Atlantic Charter Conference, 1941   173

Juggling Between War and Peace, 1939–1941   176

Asian Collision Course: Japanese-American Relations, 1939–1941   181

The Big Three: Strategies and Fissures, 1941–1943   186

In Search of a China Policy   191

Bystanders to the Holocaust: Americans and the Murder of the Jews   195

Planning the Postwar Peace, 1943–1945   198

Compromises at the Yalta Conference   202

To Each Its Own: Allied Divergence and Spheres of Influence   206

The Potsdam Conference and the Legacy of the Second World War   210

FURTHER READING FOR THE PERIOD 1939–1945   213

NOTES TO CHAPTER 6   216

7   *All-Embracing Struggle: The Cold War Begins, 1945–1950*   221

Diplomatic Crossroad: The Atomic Bomb at Hiroshima, 1945   222

The Big Two and the International System: Sources of the Long War   228

Challenging the Soviet Sphere in Eastern Europe   231

Stiffening Up: Early Cold War Crises   235

The Truman Doctrine, Israel, and Containment   239

On Its Feet and Off Our Backs: The Marshall Plan, NATO,
    and the Division of Europe   243

Asian Allies: Restoring Japan and Backing Jiang in China   248

The People's Republic of China and U.S. Nonrecognition   252

A Cold War Culture Emerges   253

FURTHER READING FOR THE PERIOD 1945–1950   256
NOTES TO CHAPTER 7   261

8   *Global Watch: The Korean War and Eisenhower Foreign Relations, 1950–1961*   **265**

Diplomatic Crossroad: The Decision to Intervene in the Korean War, 1950   266

Korea, the Cold War, and the "Trojan Horse" of
    National Security   268

Ambivalent Cold Warrior: Dwight D. Eisenhower   275

John Foster Dulles, McCarthyism, and the New Look   279

The Glacier Grinds On: Khrushchev, Eisenhower,
    and the Cold War   282

Missile Race, Berlin, and the U-2 Mess   287

To the Brink with China; To the Market with Japan   291

The Third World Rises: Revolutionary Nationalism
    and Nonalignment   295

Stormy Weather: Nationalism in the Middle East
    and Latin America   300

Cultural Expansion and the Globalized Cold War   305

FURTHER READING FOR THE PERIOD 1950–1961   308
NOTES TO CHAPTER 8   311

9   *Passing the Torch: The Vietnam Years, 1961–1969*   **316**

Diplomatic Crossroad: The Tet Offensive in Vietnam, 1968   317

Vietnamese Wars Before 1961   321

John F. Kennedy and His "Action Intellectuals"   326

Nation Building   329

The Most Dangerous Area in the World: The Cuban
    Revolution and Latin America   335

Spinning Out of Control: The Cuban Missile Crisis   337

Laos, Vietnam, and the Kennedy Legacy   342

Nose to Nose: Lyndon B. Johnson and the World   346

"The Biggest Damned Mess": Johnson's Vietnam War   348

As the Doves Dissent, the Peace Efforts Fail   353

FURTHER READING FOR THE PERIOD 1961–1969   356

NOTES TO CHAPTER 9   359

10   *Détente and Disequilibrium, 1969–1977*   **364**

**Diplomatic Crossroad: Richard M. Nixon's
Trip to China, 1972**   365

Nixon, Kissinger, and Their Critics   368

Détente, SALT, and the Nuclear Arms Race   372

Regional Tails Wagging the Superpower Dogs:
The Middle East   377

Covert Action and Economic Relations in Latin
America and Africa   382

Economic Competition, Environmental Distress,
and the North-South Debate   386

Vietnamization, Cambodia, and a Wider War   391

The Jabberwocky Peace Agreement, Withdrawal, and Defeat   394

The Many Lessons and Questions of Vietnam   397

FURTHER READING FOR THE PERIOD 1969–1977   402

NOTES TO CHAPTER 10   404

11   *To Begin the World Over Again: Carter,
Reagan, and Revivalism, 1977–1989*   **408**

**Diplomatic Crossroad: The Iranian Hostage
Crisis, 1979–1981**   409

Zbigs and Zags: Carter's Divided Administration   414

The Panama Canal and High Voltage Nationalism
in Latin America   417

Carter's Activism in the Middle East and Africa   421

The Red Thread: SALT-II, Afghanistan, and the
Carter Record   424

Ronald Reagan's Mission to Revive Hegemony   431

Soviet-American Crises and Antinuclearism   436

The "Backyard": Central America and the Caribbean   442

Hornets' Nests in the Middle East, Africa, and Asia   447

Triumphs and Hazards: The Reagan Legacy   452

FURTHER READING FOR THE PERIOD 1977–1989   454

NOTES TO CHAPTER 11   457

12 *Imperial America: The United States and the World Since 1989* **461**

   Diplomatic Crossroad: 9/11 and After   462

   The Earthquakes of 1989–1991   467

   Indispensable Nation: Bush–Clinton–Bush
      and Post–Cold War Priorities   471

   Europe Transformed: Russian Disintegration, German Reunification,
      NATO Expansion, Balkan Hell   476

   Hope and Tragedy in Africa   482

   Markets, Invasions, and Implosions in Latin America   485

   Mideast Quagmires: Gulf Wars and the Arab-Israeli
      Peace Process   491

   Feuding and Trading with China, Vietnam, and Japan   496

   Global Bewilderments and Opportunities   499

   FURTHER READING FOR THE PERIOD SINCE 1989   509
   NOTES TO CHAPTER 12   512

Appendix: Makers of American Foreign Relations   **517**

General Bibliography   **521**

   General Reference Works   521

   Overviews of Relations with Countries, Regions, and Other Places of
      the World, Including Atlases and Gazetteers, Annual Surveys and
      Chronologies, Bibliographies, Biographical Aids, Chronologies, En-
      cyclopedias and Dictionaries, and Statistics   522

   Overviews of Subjects, Including Atlases, Annual Surveys,
      Bibliographies, Biographical Aids, Chronologies,
      Encyclopedias, and Statistics   533

Index   **545**

Maps and Graphs

The Great Powers in Asia, 1900   **26**

Panama Canal Zone   **36**

U.S. Interventions in the Caribbean and Central America   **47**

The *Lusitania* and *U-20*   **71**

The Outbreak of World War I: Summer 1914   **75**

Europe Reshaped by War and Peace   **92**

The Weight of the United States in the World Economy   **117**

The Contracting Spiral of World Trade   **118**

Japanese Expansion to 1941   **150**

The German Onslaught, 1939–1942   **179**

The Allies Push Japan Back, 1942–1945   **207**

Changes in Europe After World War II   **232**

Changes in Asia After World War II   **251**

The Korean War, 1950–1953   **269**

Africa in 1945   **296**

Africa in 2000   **297**

Southeast Asia and the Vietnam War   **352**

The Middle East   **378**

The United States and Latin America Since 1945   **419**

U.S. Dependence on Imports of Raw Materials, 1980   **423**

Transformations: Russia, the Former Soviet Republics, Eastern Europe, and Germany   **470**

World Arms Exports Shares, 1992–1994   **500**

Preface

Much has happened to challenge and to redirect American foreign relations since the fifth edition of this text appeared in 2000. The shocking attacks of September 11, 2001, the subsequent invasions of Afghanistan and Iraq, terrorist bombings in Spain and elsewhere, putative nuclear threats from so-called "rogue" states and terrorist networks, complaints from allies about America's behavior as a "hyperpower," continued debates about "globalization" and its myriad effects, increased alarm over fast-spreading deadly diseases and environmental decline, new definitions of national security and "homeland defense" that include preemptive war, anguished questioning as to why our enemies "hate" us—all have riveted attention on America's global travails and how and why they came to be. These urgent contemporary developments, along with the advance of scholarly literature and encouraging comments from instructors and students, have prompted us to revise *American Foreign Relations*. As before, in this sixth edition we engage influential approaches and interpretations, especially those articulated by younger scholars. We seek to explain foreign relations in the broadest manner as the many ways that peoples, organizations, states, and systems interact—economic, cultural, strategic, environmental, political, and more.

We continue to emphasize the theme of expansionism, explaining its many manifestations. We also show that on almost every issue in the history of American foreign relations, alternative voices unfailingly sounded among and against official policymakers. Americans have always debated their place in the world, their wars, their overseas commitments, and the status of their principles and power, and they have always debated the people of other nations about the spread of U.S. influence. We try to capture with vivid description and quotation the drama of the many debates.

A historical overview such as this one necessarily draws on the copious work of scholars in the United States and abroad. Their expertise informs this book throughout and helps lend it the authority instructors and students expect. Our "Further Reading" and "Notes" sections are one way to thank them for their books, articles, and conference papers. We have also appreciated their recommendations for text revisions and their suggestions for teaching the courses for which this book is intended. We thank them, too, for challenging us to consider the many different approaches and theories that have commanded attention in this field, including world systems, corporatism, dependency, culture, psychology and personality, medical biography, lessons from the past ("thinking in time"), bureaucratic politics, public opinion, executive-legislative competition, gender, national security and power, impact on recipients of foreign aid, the natural environment, and ideology. This book also presents the findings of our own ongoing archival research and writing as we discover and rediscover the past.

We are especially pleased to welcome two new authors to this edition, Deborah Kisatsky and Shane Maddock. These young scholar-teachers both received their Ph.D. from the University of Connecticut, have published widely in foreign relations history, and are dedicated teachers at small New England colleges. For further details, see the biographies on p. vi.

The traditional topics of diplomacy, war, economic intercourse, and politics remain central to our presentation of the foreign-relations story. As in the fifth edition, however, we have made this edition more comprehensive by extending our discussion of the cultural dimensions of foreign relations: race-based and gender-based images of other peoples that condition the decisionmaking environment; how the "reel" world of films reflects cultural myths and captures public perceptions of international events; the proliferation abroad of American mass culture (such as rock and roll and sports); the foreign responses to "Americanization"; travel and tourism that help create a pool of knowledge about foreign places that promotes an expansionist consciousness; and cultural transfer through "public diplomacy"—the presentation of a positive image of the United States abroad through, for example, propaganda, radio and television, and trade fairs.

We have also increased our coverage of the self-conscious expansion of American "empire" from its westward displacement of Native Americans in the eighteenth and nineteenth centuries to its overseas incarnations in the twentieth and twenty-first centuries. We add new details about "makers" of American foreign relations from presidents such as Thomas Jefferson and Harry Truman to diplomats such as Nicholas Trist and William C. Bullitt. We take note, for example, of recent scholarship that reveals the phrase "manifest destiny" not to have been coined by the oft-cited editor John L. O'Sullivan, but to have originated with the dashing journalist-publicist Jane McManus Storm Cazneau.

Issues that spring from human interaction with the natural environment and the international conferences convened to deal with damage to the environment also receive more space in this edition. The linkage between the civil rights movement and American foreign relations with the Third World in the 1940s through the 1960s receives added attention. New scholarship prompted by anniversaries—such as the Louisiana Purchase and Lewis and Clark Expeditions, the Spanish-American-Cuban-Filipino War, Cuban Missile Crisis, and Vietnam War, among others—have enabled us to bring fresh insights to these important events.

Equally important, with the Cold War International History Project providing scholars with a treasure trove of declassified documents from foreign archives (Russian, East German, Cuban, and Chinese among them), we have rewritten our treatment of Joseph Stalin's goals and tactics during and after World War II, the origins of the Korean War, Sino-American relations, Cuban policy toward Africa, the Soviet invasion of Afghanistan, the failure of détente in the 1970s, and the end of the Cold War in 1989-1991. Similarly, recently declassified U.S. government documents made available via "electronic briefing books" from the National Security Archive have added nuance to our coverage, for example, of the India-Pakistan War of 1971 and the Indonesian invasion of East Timor in 1976, as well as new evidence regarding Washington's Cold War initiatives toward the Soviet Union, the People's Republic of China, and Fidel Castro's Cuba. The declassification, duplication, and public release of presidential audio tapes from the Kennedy, Johnson, and Nixon years help to recapture their colorful language and reveal how the assumptions, styles, and emotions of these leaders influenced their decision-making.

In preparing this edition, we once again immersed ourselves in the memoirs, diaries, letters, speeches, recorded tapes, and oral histories of U.S. and international leaders. We often let them speak for themselves in the frankest terms, guarded and unguarded. We have sought to capture their anger and their humor, their cooperation and their competitiveness, their truths and their lies, their moments of doubt and times of confidence, their triumphs and setbacks. *American Foreign Relations,* in short, strives to capture the erratic pulse of international relations through peoples' struggles to plan, decide, and administer. We study not only the leaders who made influential decisions, but also the world's peoples who welcomed, resisted, or endured the decisions that profoundly influenced their lives. In this regard, we have drawn on the growing scholarship that studies non-state actors, including peace groups, African Americans, and international bodies such as the World Health Organization.

Each chapter opens with a significant and dramatic event—a "Diplomatic Crossroad"—that helps illustrate the chief characteristics and issues of the era. Three such "Crossroads"—on filibustering in the 1850s, war with Spain in 1898, and the seismic changes triggered by 9/11—are new to this edition. The introductory and concluding sections of each chapter set the themes. Illustrations—many of them new to this edition—from collections around the world, are closely tied to the narrative in image and caption description. The revised maps, graphs, and "Makers of American Foreign Relations" tables in each chapter provide essential information. The updated chapter bibliographies guide further reading and serve as a starting point for term or research papers. The "General Bibliography" at the end of the book is also a place to begin research or seek more information. The "General Bibliography" consists of three parts: first, general reference works, such as biographical dictionaries, atlases, statistics, encyclopedias, and bibliographies; second, overviews of U.S. relations with countries and regions, from Afghanistan to Zimbabwe; and, third, overviews of subjects, such as Air Force and air power, CIA and covert action, Congress, cultural relations, ethnic conflict, human rights, isolationism, Manifest Destiny, Monroe Doctrine, oil, refugees, slave trade and slavery, terrorism, and United Nations.

In the late 1970s, the People's Republic of China adopted a new system for rendering Chinese phonetic characters into the Roman alphabet. Called the Pinyin method, it replaced the Wade-Giles technique, which had long been used in English. Use of the Pinyin method is now common, and we use it in *American Foreign Relations.* Many changes are minor—Shantung has become Shandong and Mao Tse-tung has become Mao Zedong, for example. But when we have a possibly confusing Pinyin spelling, we have placed the Wade-Giles spelling in parentheses—for example, Beijing (Peking) or Jiang Jieshi (Chiang Kai-shek).

Instructors and students interested in the study of foreign-relations history are invited to join the Society for Historians of American Foreign Relations (SHAFR). This organization publishes a superb journal, *Diplomatic History,* and a newsletter; offers book, article, and lecture prizes and dissertation research grants; and holds an annual conference where scholars present their views and research results. Dues are very reasonable. For information, contact the SHAFR Business Office, Department of History, Ohio State University, 106 Dulles Hall, 230 West 17th Avenue, Columbus, OH 43210, or email to shafr@osu.edu.

Another informative web site is H-Diplo: Diplomatic History, found at www.h-net2.msu.edu/~diplo. Besides presenting provocative online discussions on foreign-relations history, this site also provides research and bibliographic aids and an extensive list of links to other useful resources, including journals, newspapers, archives and presidential libraries, research organizations such as the National Security Archive, and government agencies such as the Central Intelligence Agency and Department of State. Readers should also note our citations to relatively new scholarly journals in foreign relations history—*Cold War History, Journal of Cold War Studies, Diplomacy & Statecraft, International History Review, Intelligence and National Security, Journal of Military History,* among others. Such journals often publish fresh perspectives from younger scholars before they appear in book form.

Many colleagues, friends, students, and editors contributed to this edition of *American Foreign Relations* by providing research leads, correction of errors, reviews of the text, library searches, documents and essays, and editorial assistance. We give our heartiest thanks to Derick Becker, Mark Boyer, Michael Butler, Regina Egan, Robert H. Ferrell, David S. Foglesgong, Irwin Gelman, Robert E. Hannigan, Florencia Luengo, Jay Mullen, Arnold A. Offner, Larry Spongberg, Jennifer Sterling-Folker, and Sherry Zane. We also thank the following reviewers, who gave many helpful comments and suggestions for this new edition: Robert Buzzanco, University of Houston; Peter Hahn, Ohio State University; Kristin Hoganson, University of Illinois, Urbana-Champaign; William Mood, University of Maryland; Nicholas Evan Sarantakes, Texas A & M University-Commerce; Kevin Smith, Ball State University; and Stephen M. Streeter, McMaster University. Houghton Mifflin's talented team merits the highest of praise: Jean L. Woy, senior consulting editor; Frances Gay, senior development editor; Jane Lee, senior project editor; Linda Blundell, photo researcher; Chris Thornton, copyeditor; and Mary Kanable, proofreader.

We are also eager to thank the many people who helped us in previous editions: Philip J. Avillo, Jr., Richard Baker, Ann Balcolm, Michael A. Barnhart, Robert Beisner, R. Christian Berg, Kenneth J. Blume, Richard Bradford, Kinley J. Brauer, John Burns, Richard Dean Burns, Charles Conrad Campbell, Chen Jian, John Coogan, Alejandro Corbacho, Frank Costigliola, Carol Davidge, Mark Del Vecchio, Ralph Di Carpio, Justus Doenecke, Michael Donaghue, Xavier Franco, Paul Goodwin, James Gormly, Eric Hafter, Hope M. Harrison, Alan Henrikson, Gregg Herken, George Herring, Ted Hitchcock, Joan Hoff, Reginald Horsman, Michael Hunt, Edythe Izard, Holly Izard, Richard Izard, Leith Johnson, Burton Kaufman, Melville T. Kennedy, Jr., Thomas Lairson, Lester Langley, Thomas M. Leonard, Li Yan, Terrence J. Lindell, Martha McCoy, David McFadden, Charles McGraw, Elizabeth McKillen, Matt McMahon, Robert McMahon, Elizabeth Mahan, Paul Manning, Herman Mast, Dennis Merrill, Jean-Donald Miller, Carl Murdock, Brian Murphy, R. Kent Newmyer, Arnold Offner, John Offner, Marc O'Reilly, Chester Pach, Jerry Padula, Carol Petillo, David Pletcher, Salvadore Prisco, Stephen G. Rabe, Carol S. Repass, Wayne Repeta, Barney J. Rickman III, Michael Roskin, John Rourke, Kenneth E. Shewmaker, Kent M. Schofield, David Sheinin, Anna

Lou Smethurst, Elbert B. Smith, Thomas G. Smith, Kenneth R. Stevens, Mark A. Stoler, William W. Stueck, Jr., Duane Tananbaum, George Turner, Jonathan G. Utley, Thomas Walker, Wang Li, Kathryn Weathersby, Ralph E. Weber, Edmund S. Wehrle, Immanuel Wexler, Lawrence Wittner, Sol Woolman, and Thomas Zoumaras.

We welcome comments and suggestions from students and instructors.

T. G. P.
J. G. C.
S. J. M.
D. K.
K. J. H.

CHAPTER 1

Imperialist Leap,
1895–1900

***U.S.S. Maine** Entering Havana Harbor.*   *The gleaming white battleship, commanded by Captain Charles Sigsbee, arrived in Havana on January 25, 1898, ostensibly to protect American citizens caught up in the Cuban rebellion against Spanish rule. Because a few sailors had been swept overboard and drowned on earlier missions, the* Maine *had the reputation of being a "Jonah" or "Hoodoo" ship. (Courtesy National Archives—SC-94543)*

1

DIPLOMATIC CROSSROAD

✎⟡ *The Maine, McKinley, and War, 1898*

THE SLEEK U.S. battleship *Maine* steamed into Havana harbor on January 25, 1898. "A beautiful sight and one long to be remembered," reported the American consul-general Fitzhugh Lee, who had requested the visit ostensibly to protect the lives of Americans living in war-torn Cuba.[1] President William McKinley had sent the vessel to Havana hoping to calm tensions with Spain, then in its third year of attempting to suppress Cuban rebels fighting for national independence. The *Maine* was to stay three weeks and then depart for New Orleans in time for Mardi Gras. But at 9:40 P.M. on February 15, a "dull sullen" roar followed by massive explosions ripped through the 6,700-ton ship, killing 266 Americans.[2] McKinley, who had been taking drugs to sleep, awoke an hour before dawn for a phone call from Secretary of the Navy John D. Long. "The *Maine* blown up! The *Maine* blown up!" the stunned president kept muttering to himself.[3] Even though "the country was not ready" for it, the war with Spain that McKinley was laboring so hard to avoid would occur within three months.[4]

McKinley ordered an official investigation of the *Maine* disaster and tried diplomacy and threat to gain time. With no evidence but with considerable emotion, many Americans, such as Assistant Secretary of the Navy Theodore Roosevelt, assumed that the *Maine* had been "sunk by an act of dirty treachery on the part of the Spaniards."[5] In early March U.S. Minister Stewart L. Woodford protested strongly to the Spanish about the *Maine*. "End it at once—*end it at once—end it at once!*" Woodford exhorted Madrid regarding the war in Cuba.[6] On March 6 the president met with Joe Cannon, chair of the House Appropriations Committee, and asked for $50 million for war preparedness. "It seemed as though a hundred Fourths of July had been let loose in the House," a clerk noted, as Congress enthusiastically obliged three days later.[7] "The Ministry and press are simply stunned," Woodford reported from Madrid.[8]

In mid-March Senator Redfield Proctor of Vermont, a friend of McKinley reportedly opposed to war, graphically told his colleagues about his recent visit to Cuba. He recounted ugly stories about Spain's notorious reconcentration policy (the forced settlement of Cubans into fortified camps): "Torn from their homes, with foul earth, foul air, foul water, and foul food or none, what wonder that one-half died and one-quarter of the living are so diseased that they cannot be saved?"[9] Shortly after this moving speech, which convinced many members of Congress and business leaders that Spain could not restore order to Cuba, the American court of inquiry on the *Maine* concluded that an external mine of unknown origin had destroyed the vessel. A Spanish commission at about the same time attributed the disaster to an internal explosion. (More than a century later, after several more investigations, experts still disagree whether the *Maine* blew up because of "a coal bunker fire" or from an "undership mine.")[10] In 1898 vocal Americans pinned "the crime" squarely on Spain. "Remember the *Maine,* to hell with Spain" became a popular slogan.

A veteran Republican politician and deft manager of people, President McKinley had little desire for war. This decorated veteran of the Civil War once asserted:

"I have been through one war; I have seen the dead piled up, and I do not want to see another."[11] McKinley quietly explored the possibility of purchasing Cuba for $300 million—or some other means "by which Spain can part with Cuba without loss of respect and with certainty of American control."[12] But a jingo frenzy had seized Congress. Interventionist critics increasingly questioned the president's manhood, claiming, as did Teddy Roosevelt, that he "had no more backbone than a chocolate eclair."[13] One member of Congress called his policies on Cuba "lame, halting, and impotent," while another said of McKinley: "He wobbles, he waits, he hesitates. He changes his mind."[14] Following one stormy Senate session, Vice President Garrett Hobart warned McKinley: "They will act without you if you do not act at once." "Say no more," McKinley responded.[15]

On March 27, Washington cabled the president's demands to Madrid: an armistice, Cuban–Spanish negotiations to secure a peace, McKinley's arbitration of the conflict if there was no peace by October, termination of the reconcentration policy, and relief aid to the Cubans. Implicit was the demand that Spain grant Cuba its independence under U.S. supervision. As a last-ditch effort to avoid American military intervention, the scheme had little chance of success. Spain's national pride and interest precluded surrender. The Cubans had already said they would accept "nothing short of absolute independence."[16] Madrid's answer held some promise: Spain had already terminated reconcentration, would launch reforms, and would accept an armistice if the rebels did so first. Yet by refusing McKinley's mediation and Cuban independence, the Spanish reply did not satisfy the president or Congress. McKinley began to compose a war message in early April. On April 9, Spain made a new concession, declaring a unilateral suspension of hostilities "for such a length of time" as the Spanish commander "may think prudent."[17] Too qualified, the declaration still sidestepped Cuban independence and U.S. mediation. Any chance of European support for Spain faded when the British told Washington that they would "be guided [on Cuban issues] by the wishes of the president."[18]

On April 11, McKinley asked Congress for authority to use armed force to end the Cuban war. Since neither Cubans nor Spaniards could stem the flow of blood, Americans would do so because of the "cause of humanity" and the "very serious injury to the commerce, trade, and business of our people, and the wanton destruction of property." Citing the *Maine,* he described the conflict as "a constant menace to our peace." Conspicuously, he made no mention of Cuban independence, defining the U.S. purpose as "forcible intervention . . . as a neutral to stop the war." At the very end of the message, McKinley asked Congress to give "your just and careful attention" to news of Spain's recently offered armistice.[19]

As Congress debated a solution that the Cubans themselves rejected, McKinley beat back a Senate attempt to recognize the rebels. He strongly believed that Cuba needed American tutelage to prepare for self-government. And he wanted a Cuba subservient to the United States. Indeed, as the historian Louis A. Pérez, Jr., has argued, McKinley's decision for war seemed directed "as much against Cuban independence as it was against Spanish sovereignty."[20] Congress did endorse the Teller Amendment, which disclaimed any U.S. intent to annex the island. Even Teddy Roosevelt supported the amendment lest "it seem that we are merely engaged in a land-grabbing war."[21] On April 19 Congress proclaimed Cuba's independence (without recognizing

William McKinley (1843–1901). In one of his last speeches before his death in 1901, McKinley peered into the next century: "How near one to the other is every part of the world. Modern inventions have brought into close relations widely separated peoples . . . distances have been effaced. . . . The world's products are being exchanged as never before . . . isolation is no longer possible or desirable."

the Cuban junta), demanded Spain's evacuation from the island, and directed the president to use force to secure these goals. Spain broke diplomatic relations on April 21. The next day U.S. warships began to blockade Cuba; Spain declared war on April 24. Congress issued its own declaration the next day.

Because of the Teller Amendment, the choice for war seemed selfless and humane, and for many Americans it undoubtedly was. But the decision had more complex motives. Different people endorsed war for different reasons. McKinley cited humanitarian concern, property, commerce, and the removal of a threat. Politics also mattered. Senator Henry Cabot Lodge, among others, told the White House that "if the war in Cuba drags on through the summer . . . we [Republicans] shall go down to the greatest defeat ever known."[22] Important business leaders, initially hesitant, shifted in March and April to demand an end to Cuban disorder. Farmers and entrepreneurs ogling Asian and Latin American markets thought a U.S. victory over Spain might open new trade doors by eliminating a colonial power. Republican senator George F. Hoar of Massachusetts, later an anti-imperialist, could not "look idly on while hundreds of thousands of innocent human beings . . . die of hunger close to our doors. If there is ever to be a war it should be to prevent such things."[23] Another senator claimed that "any sort of war is better than a rotting peace that eats out the core and heart of the manhood of this country."[24] Christian missionaries dreamed of new opportunities to convert the "uncivilized." Imperialists hoped that war would add new territories to the United States and encourage the growth of a larger navy. "Warriors" differed from "imperialists" in that some people opposed empire and sincerely thought war would halt the protracted conflict in Cuba, whereas imperialists seized on war as an opportunity to expand the American empire.

Emotional nationalism also made an impact. The *Maine* and de Lôme (see page 16) incidents ignited what one educator called the "formidable inflammability of our multitudinous population."[25] Imperialist senator Albert Beveridge waxed ebullient: "At last, God's hour has struck. The American people go forth in a warfare holier than liberty—holy as humanity."[26] Excited statements by people such as Roosevelt, who regarded war as he regarded horseback riding and cowboying in the Dakotas—a sport, a game, fun—aroused martial fevers. War would surely redeem national honor and repudiate those "old women of both sexes, shrieking cockatoos" who made virile men "wonder whether" they lived "in a free country or not."[27] Newspapers of the "yellow press" variety, such as William Randolph Hearst's *New York Journal* and Joseph Pulitzer's *New York World,* sensationalized stories of Spanish lust and atrocities. Others proudly compared the Cuban and American revolutions. The American public, already steeped in a brash nationalism and prepared by earlier diplomatic triumphs, reacted favorably to the hyperbole.

Both Washington and Madrid had tried diplomacy without success. McKinley wanted "peace" and independence for Cuba under U.S. tutelage. The first Spain could not deliver because the Cuban rebels sensed victory and complete independence and Spanish forces remained weak. The second Spain could not grant immediately because ultranationalists might overthrow the Bourbon constitutional monarchy. When Spain promised to fight the war more humanely and grant autonomy, McKinley and Congress wanted more, and they believed they had the right and duty to judge the affairs of Spain and Cuba.

Critics said the United States might have been less haughty and let Cubans and Spaniards settle their own affairs. McKinley's actions in dispatching the *Maine* and asking Congress for $50 million probably encouraged the Cuban rebels to resist any compromise. He could have given Spain more breathing space. Spain, after all, did terminate reconcentration and approve an armistice; most important, Madrid did grant partial autonomy, which ultimately might have led to independence. Some critics said the president should have recognized the Cuban insurgents and covertly aided them. American materiél, not men, might have liberated Cuba from Spanish rule. By April 1898, an assistant secretary of state concluded that Spain had become "absolutely hopeless, . . . exhausted financially and physically, while the Cubans are stronger."[28] McKinley wanted to avoid war and chose it reluctantly only after trying other options. That he adamantly refused to recognize the insurgency or the republic indicates also that the president did not endorse outright Cuban independence. He probably had two goals in 1898: to remove Spain from Cuba and to control Cuba in some manner yet ill defined. When the Spanish balked at a sale and both belligerents rejected compromise, McKinley chose war—the only means to oust Spain *and* to control Cuba. A new and enlarged American empire was about to be created.

The Venezuela Crisis of 1895

Three years earlier, during the administration of an avowedly anti-imperialist president, a seemingly insignificant cartographic controversy in South America had served as a catalyst for empire. In July 1895, Secretary of State Richard Olney personally delivered a 12,000-word draft document to President Grover Cleveland on the Venezuelan boundary dispute. The president thought it "the best thing of its kind I ever read," suggested some "softened verbiage here and there," and directed that Olney send the document to London, which he did on July 20.[29]

What became known as Olney's "twenty-inch gun" was aimed at Great Britain, which for decades had haggled with Venezuela over the boundary separating that country from British Guiana. The British had drawn a line in the 1840s, but nobody liked it. In the 1880s, the discovery of gold in the region in question raised the stakes. Disputed, too, was control of the mouth of the Orinoco River, gateway to the potential trade of northern South America. Since the 1870s Venezuela had appealed to the United States over Britain's alleged violation of the Monroe Doctrine. Washington repeatedly asked the British to submit the issue to arbitration but met constant rebuff. London's latest refusal in December 1894 led to Olney's "twenty-inch gun" answer.

Why such high-level concern about the Venezuelan boundary? The Venezuelans had hired William L. Scruggs, a former U.S. minister to Caracas, to propagandize their case before the American public. His widely circulated pamphlet *British Aggression in Venezuela, or the Monroe Doctrine on Trial* (1895) stirred considerable sympathy for the South American nation. American sentiment soon congealed: The land-grabbing British were robbing a poor hemispheric friend of the United States. A unanimous congressional resolution of February 1894, calling for arbitration, underscored growing U.S. concern. Cleveland's Democratic party had lost badly in the 1894 elections, and Republicans were attacking his administration as cowardly for

"The Real British Lion."   A popular American depiction of the British global presence during the crisis over Venezuela. A few years later, President Cleveland himself recalled British behavior as "mean and hoggish." (*New York Evening World,* 1895)

not annexing Hawai'i and for doing nothing when the British briefly landed troops in Nicaragua in April 1895. Bold action might deflect criticism and recoup Democratic losses. As one Democrat advised Cleveland, "Turn this Venezuelan question up or down, North, South, East or West, and it is a 'winner.'"[30]

The global imperial competition of the 1890s, with the great powers carving up territories in Asia, the Near East, and Africa, also pushed the president toward action. The British, already holding large stakes in Latin America, seemed intent on enlarging them. Like the French intervention in Mexico a generation earlier, London's claim against Venezuela became a symbol of European intrusion into the hemisphere. The economic depression of the 1890s also caused concern. Many Americans, including Cleveland, thought that overproduction had caused the slump and that expanding foreign trade could cure it. The National Association of Manufacturers, organized in 1895 to encourage exports, chose Caracas as the site of its first overseas display of American products. Might the British close this potential new market?

Cleveland's style also colored his response. He did not like bullies. He had already rejected Hawaiian annexation in part because he thought Americans had bullied the Hawaiians. Now the British were arrogantly slapping the Venezuelans. Defense of the Monroe Doctrine became his and Olney's maxim. In unvarnished language, the "twenty-inch gun" of July 20, 1895, warned that European partition of Africa should not repeat itself in Latin America. The "safety," "honor," and "welfare" of the United States were at stake, and the Monroe Doctrine stipulated that "any permanent political union between a European and an American state [was] unnatural and inexpedient." The Cleveland–Olney message stressed that "the states of America, South as well as North, by geographical proximity, by natural sympa-

"If There Must Be War."   Lord Salisbury and President Grover Cleveland slug it out during the Venezuelan crisis of 1895. According to the historian Richard E. Welch, Jr., Cleveland's "innate talent to identify his personal judgment with righteousness and truth encouraged him to confuse compromise with surrender." (*Life,* 1896)

thy, by similarity of government constitutions, are friends and allies, commercially and politically, of the United States. To allow the subjugation of any one of them by a European power . . . signifies the loss of all the advantages incident to their natural relations with us." The forceful overriding theme of the note boldly addressed an international audience. "To-day the United States is practically sovereign on this continent, and its fiat is law upon the subjects to which it confines its interposition." And more: The United States's "infinite resources combined with its isolated position render it master of the situation and practically invulnerable as against any or all other powers."[31] Finally, the message demanded arbitration, threatened U.S. intervention, and requested a British answer before Cleveland's annual message to Congress in December.

Lord Salisbury, then doubling as British prime minister and foreign secretary, received the missive with some surprise and sent it to the Foreign Office for study. Distracted by crises elsewhere (especially in Africa), Salisbury saw no urgency. In the late nineteenth century American Anglophobic bombast was not unusual, especially before elections. Nor did he relish arbitrating any question that might weaken the British Empire. Thus the British reply did not arrive until after Cleveland's annual message, which was actually quite tame on Venezuela. Salisbury's note, which smacked of the "peremptory schoolmaster trying—with faded patience—to correct the ignorance of dullards in Washington," denied the applicability of the Monroe Doctrine and dismissed any U.S. interest in the controversy.[32]

On reading the note, Cleveland became "mad clean through."[33] Now what? War? Retreat? Cleveland's special message to Congress on December 17 rang the alarm bell: England must arbitrate; the United States would create an investigating commission to set the true boundary line; then American action would follow. The message seemed an ultimatum, with the danger of war lurking throughout.

The nation buzzed in anticipation. Congress quickly voted funds for the commission. Republicans and Democrats rallied behind the president, and New York City police commissioner Theodore Roosevelt boomed: "Let the fight come if it must; I don't care whether our sea coast cities are bombarded or not; we would take Canada."[34] With Irish-Americans volunteering to fight their ancient foe, the British ambassador reported: "Nothing is heard but the voice of the Jingo bellowing defiance to England."[35]

War fevers cooled rapidly in early 1896. Many bankers and business leaders grew alarmed when the stock market plummeted, in part because British investors were pulling out. The *New York World* put out a special Christmas issue with portraits of the Prince of Wales and Lord Salisbury under the headline "PEACE AND GOOD WILL," suggesting the irrationality of war with Britain, a country so close in race, language, and culture.[36] Critics pointed out how haughtily Cleveland and Olney had acted. Even the U.S. ambassador in London feared the president had been "too *precipitate*" in joining "the camp of aggressiveness."[37] But Cleveland never wanted war. He wanted peace on his terms.

What followed seemed anticlimactic. The British cabinet in early January 1896 decided to seek an "honourable settlement" with the United States.[38] Facing a new dispute with Germany over South Africa, England needed friends, not enemies. Formal talks continued until November 1896, when the United States and Britain agreed to set up a five-person arbitration board to define the boundary. Finally, in October 1899, the tribunal reached a decision that rejected the extreme claims of either party and generally followed the original line from the 1840s. The mouth of the Orinoco went to Venezuela, which came out of the dispute rather well, considering that neither the United States nor Britain cared much about Venezuela's national interest. In fact, both parties excluded Venezuela's duly accredited minister in Washington from the talks. When Caracas balked over the 1896 Anglo-American agreement, Olney curtly made one concession: Venezuela could name a single member of the arbitration board—so long as that person was not a Venezuelan. Lobbyist William Scruggs complained that the United States sought to "*bull-doze* Venezuela."[39] He had it right, but Washington's "sledgehammer subtlety" targeted others besides that South American nation.[40] The overweening theme of the "twenty-inch gun" merits repeating: "To-day the United States is practically sovereign on this continent, and its fiat is law upon the subjects to which it confines its interposition."

Men of Empire

The Venezuelan crisis and the war with Spain punctuated an era of imperialist competition when, as one senator grandly put it: "The great nations are rapidly absorbing . . . all the waste areas of the earth. It is a moment which makes for civilization and the advancement of the race."[41] Cleveland and McKinley helped move the United

Makers of American Foreign Relations, 1895–1900

Presidents	Secretaries of State
Grover Cleveland, 1893–1897	Walter Q. Gresham, 1893–1895
	Richard Olney, 1895–1897
William McKinley, 1897–1901	John Sherman, 1897–1898
	William R. Day, 1898
	John Hay, 1898–1905

States toward world-power status. As examples of forceful, even aggressive, diplomacy, both events accelerated important trends. Besides ignoring the rights and sensibilities of small countries and so-called lesser breeds, both episodes revealed a United States more sure of itself, more certain about the components of its "policy," and more willing to lecture and fight rivals. Both episodes stimulated what critics at the time called "jingoism." The Monroe Doctrine gained new status as a warning to European nations to curb their activities in the Western Hemisphere. Just as Cleveland went to the brink of war over Venezuela without consulting Congress, so McKinley, despite a jingo Congress and inflamed public opinion, preserved and extended presidential control over foreign policy.

In both crises Latin Americans learned again that the United States sought supremacy in the Western Hemisphere and would intervene when it saw fit. The United States had always kept an eye on the Caribbean, but the Venezuela crisis and the outbreak of revolution in Cuba in 1895 intensified North American interest, a significant dimension of which was economic. Coinciding with a severe economic depression at home, the potential loss of markets in Venezuela and Cuba brought more attention to the theory of overproduction as a cause of depression, which exports could allegedly cure. Commercial expansion, always a trend in American history, received another boost.

The discord with Britain over Venezuela helped foster Anglo-American rapprochement. Cooperation and mutual interest increasingly characterized relations between Washington and London. British diplomats cultivated U.S. friendship as a possible counterweight to growing German power, and Britain's support over Cuba and its subsequent deference to the United States regarding the Caribbean facilitated the emerging entente.

The chief way the United States could manage events in that area was through naval power. The Venezuelan crisis, joined by crises in Asia and the belief that naval construction would employ those idled by the depression, stimulated additional naval expansion. The Navy Act of 1896, for example, provided for three new battleships and ten new torpedo boats, several of which contributed to naval victories over Spain two years later.

By the end of the decade the United States had gained new U.S. colonies in the Pacific, Asia, and the Caribbean, a firm hold on independent Cuba, and Europe's

"Either Caesar or Nothing!"   Uncle Sam protests against imperialism but refuses to return to his cramped log cabin now that he has taken up "skyscraper" diplomacy, according to this German cartoon. (*Kladderadatsch,* 1899)

recognition of U.S. hegemony in the Caribbean. By 1900, too, the United States had pledged itself to preserve the "Open Door" in China; it had built a navy that had just annihilated the Spanish fleet and ranked sixth in the world; and it had developed an export trade amounting to $1.5 billion. Steel and iron production exemplified its industrial might, which almost equaled that of Britain and Germany combined. U.S. acquisition of new colonies after the Spanish-American-Cuban-Filipino War suggests that *only then,* about 1898, did the United States become an imperialist world power. But what actually happened, one scholar writes, was a "culmination" not an "aberration."[42] Having taken halting steps toward a larger empire before the depression of the 1890s, the United States then took the leap.

Assistant Secretary of the Navy Theodore Roosevelt described the anti-imperialists in 1897 as "men of a by-gone age" and "provincials."[43] Indeed, anti-imperialism waned through the late nineteenth century. Increasing numbers of educated, economically comfortable Americans made the case for formal empire (colonies or protectorates) or informal empire (commercial domination). Naval officers, diplomats, politicians, farmers, skilled artisans, business leaders, and clergy made up what political scientists call the "foreign-policy public." Better read than most Americans and having access to lecterns to disperse their ideas, this "elite" helped move America to war and empire. Neither "public opinion," nor the jingoistic "yellow press," nor the "people" in the 1890s compelled the United States to war. Rather, two key elements stand out: a McKinley administration very much in charge of its diplomacy through skillful maneuvering, and a majoritarian view within the articulate "foreign-policy public" in favor of a vigorous outward thrust.

Analysis of the phrase "public opinion" helps explain the *hows* as distinct from the *whys* of decisionmaking. One often hears that "public opinion" or "the man in the street" influenced a leader to follow a certain course of action. But "public opinion" did not comprise a unified, identifiable group speaking with one voice. Further, political leaders and other articulate, knowledgeable people often shaped the "public opinion" they wanted to hear by their very handling of events and their control over information—that is, leaders *led*. In trying to determine who the "people" are and what "public opinion" is, social-science studies demonstrate that in the 1890s the people who counted, the people who expressed their opinion publicly in order to influence policy, numbered no more than 1.5 million to 3 million, or between 10 and 20 percent of the voting public. This percentage—upper- and middle-income groups, educated, active politically—constituted the "foreign-policy public." As Secretary of State Walter Q. Gresham put it in 1893: "After all, public opinion is made and controlled by the thoughtful men of the country."[44] The "public opinion" the president heard in the 1890s did not come from the "people," but rather from a small, articulate segment of the American population alert to foreign-policy issues. Although this educated public counted anti-imperialists among them, including small numbers of women, "immigrant labor, and left activists," the "foreign-policy public" leaned heavily toward the side of imperialism.[45]

The president, as a consummate politician and good tactician, often dominates policymaking, even thwarting the advice of the "foreign-policy public" itself. President Cleveland, for example, successfully resisted pressure to annex Hawai'i and withdrew the treaty from the Senate, and he never let Congress or influential public opinion set the terms of his policy toward the Venezuelan crisis. Pressures from jingoes in Congress and a sensationalist press intruded in the 1890s, but the initiative in foreign affairs, unlike in the 1860s and 1870s, remained largely in executive hands, with Cleveland and McKinley "unabashed in their resistance" to "public opinion."[46] In most historical periods, the public *reacts* to *immediate* events; the executive *acts* and *manages* with *long-term* policy considerations.

Grover Cleveland (1837–1908). This portrait of the two-term president, overweight from frequenting saloons as a young man, exhibits the gruff American attitude toward Britain during the Venezuelan crisis. The historian Dexter Perkins wrote that Cleveland was "so honest, so brave, so independent . . . , but also so rigid and inflexible in his thinking, so unimaginative, so dogmatic." (Library of Congress)

Cleveland and McKinley Confront *Cuba Libre*, 1895–1898

The year 1895 brought momentous events. The Venezuelan crisis, Japan's defeat of China in the Sino-Japanese War, and the outbreak of revolution in Cuba—all carried profound meaning for U.S. foreign relations. The sugar-rich island of Cuba, since the close of its unsuccessful war for independence (1868–1878), suffered political repression and poverty. After that war Cuban nationalists prepared for a new assault on their Spanish overlords. From 1880 to 1895, the Cuban national hero José Martí plotted from exile in the United States. In 1892 he organized the Cuban Revolutionary party, using U.S. territory to recruit men and money. Martí's opportunity came when Cuba's economy fell victim in 1894 to a new U.S. tariff, which raised duties on imported sugar and hence reduced Cuban sugar shipments to the United States. On February 24, 1895, with cries of "*Cuba Libre,*" the rebels opened their drive for independence.

Cuban revolutionaries kept a cautious eye on the United States, well known for its relentless interest in the island, and thus feared an ultimate U.S. attempt to control their nation's destiny. José Martí's fifteen-year stay in the United States had turned him into a critic of what he called "the monster"—an "aggressive" and "avaricious" nation "full of hate" and "widespread spiritual coarseness." He asked rhetorically: "Once the United States is in Cuba, who will drive them out?"[47] On May 19 Martí died in action.

Cuban and Spanish military strategies produced destruction and death. Led by General Máximo Gómez, a veteran of the 1868–1878 war, the *insurrectos* burned cane fields, blew up mills, and disrupted railroads, with the goal of rendering Cuba an economic liability to Spain. "The chains of Cuba have been forged by her own richness," Gómez proclaimed, "and it is precisely this which I propose to do away with soon."[48] Spain, in turn, vowed to "use up the last peseta in her treasury and sacrifice the last of her sons" to retain Cuba.[49] Although outnumbered (about 30,000 Cuban troops fought 200,000 Spanish) and lacking adequate supplies, the insurgents, with the sympathy of the populace, wore the Spanish down through guerrilla tactics. By late 1896 rebels controlled about two-thirds of the island, with the Spanish concentrated in coastal and urban regions. That year, to break the rebel stronghold in the rural areas, Governor-General Valeriano y Nicolau Weyler instituted the brutal reconcentration program. He divided the island into districts and then herded a half-million Cubans into fortified camps, where frightful sanitation conditions, poor food, and disease contributed to the death of perhaps 200,000 people. Weyler's soldiers regarded any Cubans outside the camps as rebels and hence targets for death; they also killed livestock, destroyed crops, and polluted water sources. This effort to starve the insurgents and deprive them of physical and moral support, combined with the rebels' destructive behavior, made a shambles of Cuba's society and economy.

The Cleveland administration faced several alternatives. It could recognize Cuban belligerency. But such an act, Olney noted, would relieve Spain of any responsibility for paying claims filed by Americans for properties destroyed in Cuba. Cleveland and Olney found recognition of Cuban independence even less appetizing, for they believed the Cubans ("the most inhumane and barbarous cutthroats in the world") incapable of self-government and feared anarchy and even racial war.[50] That course might also arouse a Spanish declaration of war or force U.S. belligerency because, logically, a Spanish attempt to conquer an "independent" Cuba would constitute a violation of the Monroe Doctrine. Olney toyed with buying the island at one point. The Cleveland administration settled on a dual policy of hostility to the revolution and pressure on Spain to grant some autonomy. Diplomacy and lecturing to a foreign government seemed to work in the Venezuelan crisis; perhaps it would work with Cuba.

Prodded by a Republican Congress (it passed a resolution in April 1896, urging the president to recognize Cuban belligerency), by continued evidence of wholesale destruction, and by Spanish obstinacy in refusing reforms and adhering to force, Olney sent a note to Spain in April 1896. He urged a political solution that would leave "Spain her rights of sovereignty . . . yet secure to the [Cubans] all such rights and powers of local self-government as they [could] ask."[51] Spain should initiate reforms short of independence. Olney showed particular concern for the interests of Americans, not Cubans. With American property estimated at $50 million, the decline in sugar production wrought disaster to Cuban-American trade relations. In 1892 Cuba had shipped to the United States goods worth $79 million; by 1898 that figure had slumped to $15 million.

When Spain rejected Olney's advice, the Cleveland administration seemed stymied. It did not desire war, but it meant to protect U.S. interests. Congress kept asking for firm action. And in Havana, hotheaded Consul-General Fitzhugh Lee clamored for U.S. annexation. Cleveland did not feel he could fire Lee, nephew of General Robert E. Lee, because the incumbent president needed political friends at a time when Democrats were dumping him in favor of William Jennings Bryan. Consul-General Lee also warned that "there may be a revolution within a revolution," noting that Cuban insurgents vowed to redistribute property, which U.S. officials (and Creole elites) would not tolerate.[52] It further nettled Cleveland and Olney that Spain had approached the courts of Europe for diplomatic support, with the argument that the Monroe Doctrine threatened all European powers. Spain's appeal went unheeded, but leaders in Washington still worried about possible European intrusion in Cuba.

British ambassador to Spain H. Drummond Wolff accurately claimed that for Cuba the United States wanted "peace with commerce."[53] In December 1896, Cleveland reported that neither the Spanish nor the Cuban rebels had established their authority over the island. Americans felt a humanitarian concern, he said, and their trade and investments ("pecuniary interest") faced destruction. Further, to maintain its neutrality, the United States had to police the coastline to intercept unlawful expeditions. Spain must grant autonomy or "home rule," but not independence, to "fertile and rich" Cuba to end the bloodshed and devastation. Otherwise, the United States, having thus far acted with "restraint," might abandon its "expectant attitude."[54]

But Cleveland had more bark than bite. Through Olney he successfully buried a Senate resolution urging recognition of Cuban independence and contented himself with some limited Spanish reforms of February 1897. Thereafter he let the Cuban issue fester, bequeathing it to the incoming McKinley administration.

President William McKinley had defeated William Jennings Bryan in the election of 1896. The teetotaling Ohioan seemed a stable, dignified figure in a time of crisis. He projected deep religious conviction, personal warmth, sincerity, commitment to economic development and the revival of business, party loyalty, and support for expansion abroad. Yet McKinley often gave the appearance of being a pliant follower, a mindless flunky of the political bosses. One joke went: "Why is McKinley's mind like a bed?" Answer: "Because it has to be made up for him every time he wants to use it." Cartoonists often depicted him in women's dress and called him a

Uncle Sam—"All That You Need Is Backbone." This cartoon depicts a tall, erect Uncle Sam shoving a rifle down President McKinley's coat to provide him with a backbone. As the historian Kristin Hoganson points out in *Fighting for American Manhood* (1998), expansionist critics of McKinley often accused the president of being weak, flabby, and vacillating because he did not immediately leap into war with Spain. (*Chicago Chronicle,* in *Cartoons of the War of 1898 with Spain,* Chicago, 1898)

"goody-goody" man.[55] Such an image was created in large part by bellicose imperialists who believed that McKinley was not moving fast enough. Certainly a party regular and friend of large corporations, the president was no lackey. A manager of diplomacy, who wanted expansion and empire without war and a settlement of the Cuban question without U.S. military intervention, McKinley acted as his own man.

McKinley shared America's image of itself as an expanding, virile nation of superior institutions and as a major power in Latin America. He agreed that the United States must have a large navy, overseas commerce, and foreign bases. He believed strongly that America must export its surplus goods. As a tariff specialist, he favored high tariffs on manufactured goods, low tariffs on raw materials, and reciprocity agreements. Although McKinley uttered almost nothing about foreign issues in the campaign of 1896, the Republican party platform overflowed with expansionist rhetoric. It urged American control of Hawai'i, a Nicaraguan canal run by the United States, an enlarged navy, purchase of the Virgin Islands, and Cuban independence. Between election and inauguration, however, McKinley quietly joined Cleveland and Olney in sidetracking a Senate resolution for recognition of Cuba. He wanted a free hand, and he did not believe that Cubans could govern themselves. His appointment of the old and ailing Senator John Sherman as secretary of state suggested

The U.S.S. *Maine*. Part of the battleship was raised in 1911, investigated, and sunk at sea with flag flying. Because experts have never determined conclusively how and why the *Maine* blew up, the historian Louis A. Pérez, Jr., in *The War of 1898* (1998), notes that writers have found it convenient to depict the event as part of a narrative strategy in which war occurred as "a function of chance and happenstance, as an improvised response to an unforeseen circumstance." He suggests instead that the *Maine* served as "a pretext for war rather than a chance precipitant" and was "exploited by expansionist politicians to mobilize public opinion in behalf of a policy of territorial expansion." (National Archives)

further that McKinley would take charge of his own diplomacy. His inaugural address vacuously urged peace, never mentioning the Cuban crisis.

McKinley's first tilt with Congress came in March 1897. Resolutions on Cuba sprang up repeatedly, but the president managed to kill them. He did satisfy imperialists by sending a Hawaiian annexation treaty to the Senate. The president was preparing for his own nonpublic diplomatic assault on Spain. In June, Madrid received an American reprimand for Weyler's uncivilized warfare and for his disruption of the Cuban economy. Spain, however, showed no signs of tempering its military response to the insurrection. American citizens languished in Spanish jails; American property continued to be razed. Fitzhugh Lee, who remained at his post in Havana, bellowed for U.S. intervention. In July, McKinley instructed Minister Woodford to demand that the Spanish stop the fighting. Increasingly convinced that the Cuban *insurrectos* would not compromise, the president implored Spain to grant autonomy. A new Spanish government soon moderated policy by offering Cuba a substantial degree of self-government. Even more, it removed the hated Weyler and promised to end reconcentration. Such reforms actually encouraged intransigence, as Cuban leaders saw them as "a sign of Spain's weakening power and an indication that the end is not far off."[56]

McKinley's December 6, 1897, annual message to Congress discussed the Cuban insurrection at great length. Voicing the "gravest apprehension," McKinley rejected annexation as "criminal aggression." He argued against recognition of belligerency, because the rebels hardly constituted a government worthy of recognition. And he ruled out intervention as premature at a time when the Spanish were traveling the "honorable paths" of reform. He asked for patience to see if Spanish changes would work, but he hinted that the United States would keep open all policy options, including intervention "with force."[57]

By mid-January evidence had poured into Washington proving that the reforms had not moderated the crisis; in fact, insurgents, conservatives, and the Spanish army all denounced them. After antireform Spaniards rioted in Havana, McKinley sent the *Maine* to the Cuban city. On February 9, the State Department received a copy of a private letter written in late 1897 by the Spanish minister to the United States Enrique Dupuy de Lôme and sent to a senior Spanish politician touring Cuba. Intercepted in Cuba by a rebel sympathizer who forwarded it to the Cuban junta in New York City, the letter not only reached the State Department, but William Randolph Hearst's flamboyant *New York Journal* published it that day with the banner headline: "Worst Insult to the United States in its History." De Lôme labeled McKinley "weak," a "bidder for the admiration of the crowd," and a "would-be politician."[58] McKinley, along with most Americans, found de Lôme's remarks infuriating. The administration particularly resented another statement that suggested that Spain did not take its reform proposals seriously and would persist in fighting to defeat the rebels. Spain, it appeared, had tricked the United States. De Lôme's hasty recall hardly salved the hurt. Less than a week later the *Maine* blew up, setting in motion events and decisions that led to war and overseas empire for the United States.

The Spanish-American-Cuban-Filipino War

Americans flocked to recruiting stations and enlisted in what they trumpeted as a glorious expedition to demonstrate U.S. right and might. They were cocky. Theodore Roosevelt, who resigned as assistant secretary of the navy to lead the flashy but overrated Rough Riders, said that it was not much of a war but it was the best Americans had. It was a short war, ending August 12, but 5,462 Americans died in it—only 379 of them in combat. Most met death from malaria and yellow fever, as a surgeon wrote: "The pale faces, the sunken eyes, the staggering gait and the emaciated forms" marked some as "wrecks for life" and others as "candidates for a premature grave."[59] Camera operators for Thomas Edison and Biograph shot "moving pictures" of the war, as crowds flocked to see flickering images of battleships at sea, the wreck of the *Maine,* and triumphant victory parades.[60]

Led by officers seasoned in the Civil War and in campaigns against Native Americans, the new imperial fighters embarked from Florida in mid-June. Seventeen thousand men, clutching their Krag-Jörgensen rifles, crammed into the flotilla for a week. They ate hardtack and tasteless canned beef, drank bitter coffee, waited anxiously, and got seasick. On June 22 they landed on Cuban soil unopposed because Cuban insurgents had driven Spanish troops into the cities. Cubans and Americans cooperated warily.

Yet the big news had already arrived from the Philippine Islands, Spain's major colony in Asia. Only days after the American declaration of war, Commodore

"Cuba Reconciling the North and South." Captain Fritz W. Guerin's 1898 photograph depicted nationalism in the Spanish-American-Cuban-Filipino War. Golden-haired Cuba, liberated from her chains by her North American heroes, oversees the reconciliation of the Union and Confederacy in a splashy display of patriotism. Nevertheless, as the historian David W. Blight has written in *Race and Reunion* (2001), "national unity in foreign policy . . . gave the promoters of Jim Crow in the South a freer hand than ever in fashioning a segregated social system." (Library of Congress)

George Dewey sailed his Asiatic Squadron from Hong Kong to Manila Bay, where he smashed the Spanish fleet with the loss of one sailor. Slipping by the Spanish guns at Corregidor, Dewey entered the bay at night. Early in the morning of May 1 his flagship *Olympia* began to demolish the ten incompetently handled Spanish ships. With his laconic order, "You may fire when ready, Gridley," Dewey quickly became a first-line hero. Some people, ignorant of American interests in the Pacific, the beckoning China market, and the feebleness of Spanish rule over the Philippines, wondered how a war to liberate Cuba saw its first action in Asia. Although probably few Americans knew the location of the Philippines, naval officials had pinpointed them in contingency plans as early as 1896. Often credited alone with ordering Dewey on February 25, 1898, to attack Manila if war broke out, Assistant Secretary of the Navy Theodore Roosevelt actually set in motion preexisting war plans already known and approved by the president. After the war, when the Navy Department balked at revealing its advance preparations, Roosevelt was "naturally delighted at shouldering the responsibility."[61]

By late June, U.S. troops in Cuba had advanced toward Santiago, where dispirited Spanish soldiers manned antique guns. Joined by experienced Cuban rebels, the North Americans on July 1 battled for San Juan Hill. American forces, spearheaded by the Rough Riders and the black soldiers of the Ninth Cavalry, finally captured the strategic promontory overlooking Santiago after suffering heavy casualties. Two days later the Spanish fleet, penned in Santiago harbor for weeks by U.S. warships, made a desperate daylight break for open sea. Some U.S. vessels nearly collided as they hurried to sink the helpless Spanish craft, which went down with 323 dead. Its fleet destroyed, Spain surrendered – but only to the Americans. Cubans were forbidden from entering towns and cities to celebrate. "We feel as the patriots under Washington would have felt had the allied armies captured New York, and the French prohibited the entry of Americans and their flag," said one insurgent.[62]

U.S. troops also invaded another Spanish colony, Puerto Rico, which expansionists such as Roosevelt coveted as a Caribbean base for a proper navy and a strategic post that might help protect a Central American canal. In nineteen days General Nelson A. Miles, losing only three soldiers, captured the sugar- and coffee-exporting island. At least at first, the Puerto Rican elite welcomed their new North American masters as an improvement over their Spanish rulers.

Manila capitulated in mid-August, after the Spanish put up token resistance in a deal with Dewey that salvaged Spanish pride and kept Filipino nationalist Emilio Aguinaldo from the walled city. Washington soon ordered Aguinaldo and other Filipino rebels, who had fought against the Spanish for independence since 1896 and had surrounded Manila for weeks, to remain outside the capital and to recognize the authority of the United States.

In July, to ensure uninterrupted reinforcement of Dewey, the United States officially absorbed Hawai'i, where ships took on coal en route to Manila. From 1893 to 1897, when Cleveland refused annexation, politics in Hawai'i had changed little. The white revolutionaries clung to power. Once elected, McKinley proclaimed: "We need Hawai'i . . . a good deal more than we did California. It is manifest destiny."[63] After negotiating a new treaty with the white-led Hawaiian government, he adopted the ploy of asking for a joint resolution. On July 7, 1898, Congress passed the resolution for annexation by a majority vote (290 to 91 in the House and 42 to 21 in the Senate), thereby formally attaching the strategically and commercially important islands to the United States. Annexation was "not a change" but "a consummation," said McKinley.[64]

Peace and Empire: The Debate in the United States

Spain sued for peace, and on August 12 the belligerents proclaimed an armistice. To negotiate with the Spanish in Paris, McKinley appointed a "peace commission" loaded with imperialists and headed by Secretary of State William R. Day, friend and follower of the president's wishes. As negotiations continued into autumn, and after McKinley tested public opinion by touring the Midwest, he demanded all of the Philippines, the island of Guam in the Marianas, and Puerto Rico, as well independence for Cuba. Articulate Filipinos pleaded for their country's freedom but met a stern U.S. rebuff. Spanish diplomats accepted this American land grab after the United States offered $20 million as compensation. In early December, U.S. delegates signed the treaty and walked out of the elegant French conference room with the Philippines, Puerto Rico, and Guam.

"Hurrah for Imperialism." This anti-imperialist cartoon expressed the fear that the United States was walking blindly along a disastrous path of empire. Anti-imperialists lost the debate in part because Uncle Sam knew where he was going in adding new territories to the U.S. domain. (*Life*, 1898)

Anti-imperialists howled in protest. They had organized the Anti-Imperialist League in Boston in November 1898, but they never acted in unison. They counted among their number such unlikely bedfellows as the steel magnate Andrew Carnegie, the labor leader Samuel Gompers, the agrarian spokesman William Jennings Bryan, the Massachusetts senator George Hoar, Harvard president Charles W. Eliot, and the humorist Mark Twain—people who had often disagreed on domestic issues. Some anti-imperialists took inconsistent positions. Hoar, the most outspoken senator against the treaty, had voted for war and annexation of Hawai'i. An expansionist, Carnegie apparently would accept colonies if they could be taken without force. He even offered to write a personal check for $20 million to buy the independence of the Philippines. And the anti-imperialists could not overcome the *fait accompli,* possession and occupation of territory, handed them by McKinley. After all, argued the president, could America really let loose of this real estate so nobly taken in battle?

The anti-imperialists denounced the thesis that greatness lay in colonies. Some of them wanted trade too, but not at the cost of subjugating other peoples. The anti-imperialist David Starr Jordan, president of Stanford University, spoke of the "peaceful conquest" of Mexico by trade rather than by annexation.[65] Quoting the Declaration of Independence and Washington's Farewell Address, these critics recalled America's tradition of self-government and *continental* expansion. Some anti-imperialists insisted that serious domestic problems demanded attention and resources first. The racist South Carolina representative "Pitchfork" Ben Tillman opposed annexing ten million "barbarians of the lowest type," while another opponent claimed that "you can no more produce a white man . . . in the Tropics than

George F. Hoar (1826–1904).
Graduate of Harvard, this
Republican became a U.S.
senator in 1877. He urged Cuban
independence and opposed the
annexation of the Philippines. He
praised the Filipinos for their
written constitution and ability to
govern themselves. He compared
the lynching of African Americans
in the U.S. South to the "lynching"
of the Filipino people. (Library of
Congress)

you can a polar bear."[66] Mark Twain wrote a scathing parody of the *Battle Hymn of the Republic:* "Mine eyes have seen the orgy of the launching of the Sword;/He is searching out the hoardings where the strangers' wealth is stored;/He has loosed his fateful lightning, and with woe and death has scored;/His lust is marching on."[67]

Prominent women also participated in the debate, hoping to build a distinct foreign-policy constituency out of existing networks of women's clubs and organizations. The New Hampshire pacifist Lucia True Ames Mead pronounced it immoral for "any nation . . . which buys or takes by conquest another people, and dominates them without promise of granting them independence."[68] The social reformer Jane Addams saw children playing war games in the streets of Chicago. The kids were *not freeing Cubans,* she protested, but rather *slaying Spaniards* in their not-so-innocent play. Although unsuccessful in the fight against empire, tens of thousands of women became activists over the next decade. "Never before," writes the historian Judith Papachristou, "had American women involved themselves in foreign affairs in such a way and to such an extent."[69]

The imperialists, led by Senators Henry Cabot Lodge and Nelson Aldrich, Roosevelt, and McKinley, and backed strongly by business leaders, engaged their opponents in vigorous debate in early 1899. These empire builders stressed pragmatic considerations, although they communicated common ideas of racial superiority and national destiny to civilize the savage world. "We are a conquering race," boasted Senator Albert Beveridge, and "we must obey our blood and occupy new markets, and, if necessary, new lands."[70] The Philippines provided stepping-stones to the rich China market and strategic ports for the expanding navy that protected American commerce and demonstrated U.S. prestige. International competition also dictated that the United States keep the fruits of victory, argued the imperialists; otherwise, a menacing Germany or expansionist Japan might pick up what America discarded. Few believed that the United States should relinquish territory acquired through blood. National honor demanded retention, or so the annexationists argued. Roosevelt, countering the charge that no one had asked the Filipinos if they desired annexation to the United States, delighted in telling Democratic anti-imperialists that President Thomas Jefferson took Louisiana without a vote by its inhabitants. McKinley put it simply: "Duty determines destiny."[71] Duty, destiny, defense, and dollars became the alliterative imperialist litany.

Pro-imperialist Senator Lodge described the treaty fight as the "closest, most bitter, and most exciting struggle I . . . ever expect to see in the Senate."[72] Shortly before the upper house took action, word reached Washington that Filipino insurrectionists and American soldiers had begun to fight. The news apparently stimulated support for the Treaty of Paris. Democrats tended to be anti-imperialists and Republicans imperialists, yet enough of the former endorsed the treaty on February 6, 1899, to pass it, just barely, by the necessary two-thirds vote, 57 to 27. William Jennings Bryan, believing that rejection of the treaty would prolong the war and that the Philippines could be freed after terminating the hostilities with Spain, urged an aye vote on his anti-imperialist friends. The Republicans probably had enough votes in reserve to pass the treaty even if Bryan had opposed it. Eight days later, the tie-breaking vote of the vice president killed a Senate resolution providing for Philippine independence as soon as the Filipinos established a stable government.

Imperial Collisions in Asia: The Philippine Insurrection and the Open Door in China

Controlling, protecting, and expanding the enlarged U.S. empire became a major chore. The Filipinos proved the most obstructionist. By the end of the war, Aguinaldo and rebel forces controlled most of the islands, having routed the Spanish and driven them into Manila. Aguinaldo had arrived from exile in a U.S. warship and believed that American leaders, including Dewey, had promised his country independence if he joined U.S. forces in defeating the Spanish. Ordered out of Manila by U.S. authorities after the Spanish-American armistice, he and his cohorts had to endure racial insults, including "nigger" and "goo goo." American soldiers considered the Filipinos inferior, the equivalent of Indians and blacks at home. Although one Methodist missionary boasted that the Americans had found Manila "a pesthole, and made it a health resort," critics claimed that imperialism exported the worst in American life.[73] The Treaty of Paris angered the Filipinos, as did McKinley's decree asserting the supreme authority of the United States in the Philippines. In open defiance of Washington, Aguinaldo and other prominent Filipinos organized a government at Malolos, wrote a constitution, and proclaimed the Philippine Republic in late January 1899.

McKinley believed his new subjects to be ill fitted for self-government. In February 1899 the Filipinos began fighting better-armed American troops. After bloody

Emilio Aguinaldo (1869–1964). Of mixed Chinese and Tagalog ancestry, this Filipino nationalist was exiled by the Spanish from his country in 1897. He returned with American forces and later clashed with them when he declared independence for the Philippines. Captured in 1901, he then declared allegiance to the United States. During World War II, however, he favored the Japanese, who occupied the islands, and American authorities briefly imprisoned him in 1945 when they reestablished U.S. power over Manila. (Library of Congress)

William Howard Taft (1857–1930) and Animal. The first U.S. civil governor of the Philippines, Taft weighed more than 300 pounds. He once proudly reported to Washington that he had ridden twenty-five miles to a high mountain spot. Secretary of War Elihu Root replied: "HOW IS HORSE?" With regard to Filipino self-rule, Taft wrote revealingly in 1907: "The principles of the Declaration of Independence do not require the immediate surrender of a country to a people like this. If they did, then it would be utterly impossible to defend the rules which exclude women, . . . minors, . . . [and] ignorant and irresponsible male adults from the ballot." (U.S. Army Military History Institute)

struggles, Aguinaldo was captured in March 1901. Before the insurrection collapsed in 1902, some 4,165 Americans and more than 200,000 Filipinos died. One hundred twenty-five thousand American troops quelled the insurrection, which cost the United States at least $160 million. In Batangas province south of Manila, General J. Franklin Bell drove insurrectionists into the hills and killed their livestock. Then malaria-transmitting mosquitoes "were forced to get their meals from people" instead of cattle. The result: an "epidemiological catastrophe" wherein the Batangas population declined by 90,000 (one-quarter of the people) over a six-year period.[74] Andrew Carnegie caustically jeered the pacification of the Filipinos: "About 8,000 of them have been completely civilized and sent to heaven. I hope you like it."[75] The Harvard philosopher William James similarly mocked "Civilization" as "the big, hollow, resounding, corrupting, sophisticating, confusing torrent of brutal momentum and irrationality that brings forth fruits like this!"[76]

This savage contest saw both sides commit atrocities. After Filipinos massacred an American regiment on Samar and stuffed molasses into disemboweled corpses to attract ants, General Jacob Smith told his officers: "I want no prisoners. I wish you to kill and burn, the more you kill and burn the better you will please me."[77] With

"The Metamorphosis of a Bontoc Igorot." Dean Worcester, an American zoology professor who served as the U.S. secretary of the interior for the Philippines from 1900 to 1913, included these two photographs of "Pit-a-pit," a Bontoc Igorot, in his 1914 book to illustrate his conclusion that U.S. policies and programs had a civilizing effect on Filipinos. The two pictures were taken nine years apart. Worcester classified the islands' population of 8 million into eighty-four tribes, including the Bontoc Igorot. At the 1904 St. Louis World's Fair, the village of three Igorot tribes (Bontoc, Syoc, and Benguet) became one of the most popular exhibits, to which visitors flocked because of the popularized image of the Igorot as head-hunters and dog-eaters. As the historian Emily Rosenberg has noted, such images of "uncivilized" peoples produced "a generalized other against which Americans could imagine their own national virtues." (Dean Worcester, *The Philippines Past and Present* [New York: Macmillan Company, 1914], vol. 2, frontispiece)

"the judicious application of the torch," U.S. soldiers burned *barrios* to the ground, placing villagers in reconcentration camps like those that had defaced Cuba.[78] To get information, Americans administered the "water cure," forcing prisoners to swallow gallons of water and then punching the swollen stomach to empty it quickly. Senator Lodge defended such practices as legitimate responses to the "torture and castration of [U.S.] prisoners" by Filipinos.[79] Racist notions of white superiority surfaced. Army captain Frank R. McCoy could not comprehend the Muslim Moros who refused American medical treatment. "You mention Cholera to them," he wrote, "and they throw up their hands [saying,] 'God has given and God has taken away.'"[80] "Civilize 'em with a Krag" went a popular army song, as one officer urged the same "remedial measures that proved successful with the Apaches."[81] The civil governor of the Philippines from 1901 to 1904, William Howard Taft, put it less crudely when he described the American mission: to "teach those people individual liberty, which shall lift them up to a point of civilization . . . , and which shall make them rise to call the name of the United States blessed."[82] In fact, Taft administered a sedition act that sought to suppress criticism of the United States. His authorities censored newspapers and jailed dissenters.

For years, the Moros would not submit to American rule. One military expert predicted that "the Moro question will eventually be settled in the same manner as the Indian question, that is by gradual extermination."[83] In a June 1913 battle on the island of Jolo, U.S. forces killed 500 Moros. The army's premier "guerrilla warrior," General John J. Pershing, called that bloody encounter "the fiercest [fighting] I have ever seen."[84] Until 1914, moreover, the followers of Artemio Ricarte harassed the U.S. military with their hit-and-run tactics. Ricarte himself, imprisoned from 1904 to 1910 and then deported to Hong Kong and Japan, refused allegiance to the United States and set up a government-in-exile that demanded "immediate and complete independence and the equalization of wealth."[85]

The carrot joined the stick to pacify the Philippines. Local self-government, social reforms, and American schools, which taught Filipinos of all social classes English and arithmetic, helped win over elites ("*ilustrados*") and key minorities.[86] "We'll larn ye our language," said the inimitable Mr. Dooley, "because 'tis easier to larn ye ours thin to larn ourselves ye'ers."[87] A general amnesty proclaimed by President Theodore Roosevelt on July 4, 1902, also encouraged accommodation. By restricting suffrage at the outset to Filipinos with wealth, education, and previous government service, U.S. administrators successfully wooed Filipino elites, including former revolutionaries. American roads, bridges, port improvements, and sanitation projects soon followed. At the St. Louis World's Fair in 1904, a thousand Filipinos were put on display as "living exhibits," and photographs and dioramas depicted their "rapid social, educational and sanitary development" under "the kindly tutelage of the United States."[88] By 1911, Cebu City could boast an electric railway, telephone service, English-language newspapers, Fords and Buicks, movie houses, and a baseball park, but "the poor are still poor," as one Cebuano put it.[89] The Jones Act of 1916 promised eventual Philippine independence. It did not occur until 1946.

Proximity to China made the Philippines especially valuable to U.S. leaders who predicted lucrative markets for American products. In early 1898 business leaders organized the American Asiatic Association to stimulate public and governmental concern to protect and enlarge U.S. interests in China. Treasury official Frank Vanderlip typically lauded the Philippines as the "pickets of the Pacific, standing guard at the entrances to trade with the millions of China."[90] Although China attracted only 2 percent of U.S. foreign commerce, American traders had long dreamed of an unbounded China market, and missionaries romanticized a Christian kingdom. These ambitions remained dreams more than reality. Yet dreams spurred action, and during the 1890s the United States, despite limited power, sought to defend its Asian interests, real and imagined.

In that decade the European powers and Japan were dividing China, rendered helpless in 1895 after the Sino-Japanese War, into spheres of influence and establishing discriminatory trading privileges in their zones. The McKinley administration in early 1898 watched anxiously as Germany grabbed Jiaozhou (Kiaochow) and Russia gained a lease at Port Arthur on the Liaodong Peninsula. France, already ensconced in Indochina, leased Guangzhou Bay in southern China in April of that year. Japan already had footholds in Formosa and Korea. The British in March 1898 suggested a joint Anglo-American declaration on behalf of equal commercial opportunity in China. In the midst of the Cuban crisis, Washington gave little atten-

American Cigarettes in China.   An American soldier in China peddles cigarettes. After the invention of the cigarette machine in 1881, the tobacco tycoon James B. Duke asked to see an atlas. Leafing through the pages, he noticed China's large population of 430 million. "That," he said, "is where we are going to sell cigarettes." Nine years later came the first exports; by 1916 Duke and other American entrepreneurs were selling 12 billion cigarettes in China. (Edward J. Parrish Papers, Duke University Library)

tion to the request. Britain, which already had Hong Kong, then forced China to give up part of the Shandong Peninsula.

American economic and religious interests in China seemed threatened. The American Asiatic Association and missionary groups appealed to Washington for help. Drawing on recommendations from William W. Rockhill, adviser on Asian policy, who in turn consulted his British friend and officer of the Chinese customs service, Alfred Hippisley, Secretary of State John Hay tried words. Hay sent an "Open Door" note on September 6, 1899, to Japan, Germany, Russia, Britain, France, and Italy, asking them to respect equal trade opportunity for all nations in their spheres. It was, of course, a traditional American principle. Noncommittal replies trickled back, but Hay read into them what he wanted and proclaimed definitive acceptance of the Open Door proposal.

Although frail, the Open Door policy carried meaning. Americans knew they had less leverage than the other imperialists in Asia, but they also noted that a delicate balance of power existed there that the United States could unbalance. The European powers and Japan might hesitate to exclude American commerce altogether from China, for fear that the United States would tip that balance by joining one of the powers against the others. They also feared that a world war might erupt from

The Great Powers in Asia, 1900

RUSSIAN EMPIRE

Bering Sea

KAMCHATKA (Russ.)

L. Baikal

Trans-Siberian Railroad (built 1891-1917)

Amur R.

Sea of Okotsk

SAKHALIN (Russ.)

ALEUTIAN IS. (U.S.)

MONGOLIA   MANCHURIA

KURILE IS. (Jap.)

HOKKAIDO

Mukden • Vladivostok

⊛ Beijing • Tianjin (Tientsin)
• Lüshun • Wei-hai-wei   KOREA
Qingdao (Ger.)
Jiaozhou (Ger.)

Yellow R.

HONSHU

Tokyo ⊛

Japan Sea

CHINA

East China Sea

Yangtze R.

SHIKOKU
KYUSHU

J   A   P   A   N

TIBET

Shanghai •

PACIFIC

BONIN IS. (Jap.)

Fuzhou (Foochow) •   *Sansha Bay*
PESCADORES IS. (Jap.)

VOLCANIC IS. (Jap.)

Marcus (Jap.)

Canton • Amoy •
Macao HONG
(Port.) KONG (Br.)

FORMOSA (Jap.)

RYUKYU IS. (Jap.)

O   C   E   A   N

BURMA (Br.)

Hanoi •

Guangzhou Bay *Kwangchow (Fr.)*

HAINAN

Philippine Sea

Wake I. (U.S.)

Johnston I. (U.S.)

Mekong R.

FRENCH INDO-CHINA

SIAM
Bangkok ⊛

South China Sea

LUZON
Manila •

PHILIPPINE ISLANDS (U.S.)

MARIANIAS IS. (Ger.)

Guam (U.S.)

Gulf of Siam

PELEW IS. (Ger.)

C A R O L I N E   I S L A N D S
(Ger.)

MARSHALL IS.

(Ger.)

MINDANAO

BRUNEI (Br.)
NO. BORNEO (Br.)
SARAWAK (Br.)

MALAY STATES

• Singapore

BORNEO

EQUATOR

Nauru (Ger.)

GILBERT IS. (Br.)

CELEBES

INDIAN OCEAN

NETHERLANDS EAST INDIES

• Batavia   JAVA

NEW GUINEA
(Ger.)

Bismarck Archipelago (Ger.)

SOLOMON IS. (Ger.)

ELLICE IS. (Br.)

SUMATRA

TIMOR (Port.)

PAPUA (Br.)

SANTA CRUZ IS. (Br.)

(Ger.)

SAMOA (U.S.)

Coral Sea

NEW HEBRIDES (Fr. & Br.)

FIJI IS. (Br.)

AUSTRALIA

NEW CALEDONIA (Fr.)

LOYALTY IS. (Fr.)

(Inset map)

Mukden •

Yalu R.

Beijing (Peking) ⊛

C   H   I   N   A

Liaodong Pen. (Russ.)
Lüshun (Port Arthur) (Russ.)

KOREA

• Tianjin (Tientsin)

Yellow R.

Wei-hai-wei (Br.)

Yellow Sea

Shandong Pen. Qingdao (Tsingtao) (Ger.)

• Jiaozhou (Kiaochow) (Ger.)

competition in Asia. Americans hoped the Open Door policy would serve their goals in an area where they had little military power. The United States wanted the commercial advantages without having to employ military force, as it did in Latin America. The policy did not always work, but it fixed itself in the American mind as a guiding principle for Chinese affairs.

The Open Door note notwithstanding, the Manchu dynasty (1644–1912) neared death, unable to cope with the foreign intruders. Resentful nationalistic Chinese, led by a secret society called *Yihequan* ("Righteous and Harmonious Fists," or the "Boxers"), undertook in 1900 to throw out the imperialist aggressors. The Boxers murdered hundreds of Christian missionaries and their Chinese converts and laid siege to the foreign legations in Beijing (Peking). The foreigner "often treats the Chinese as though they were dogs," wrote the wife of the U.S. minister in Peking. "No wonder that they growl and sometimes bite."[91] To head off a complete gouging of China by vengeful Europeans and Japanese, McKinley, without consulting Congress, sent 2,500 American troops to Beijing from the Philippines to join 15,500 soldiers from other nations to lift the siege. And Hay, without consulting the Chinese government, issued another Open Door note on July 3, 1900. He defined U.S. policy as the protection of American life and property, the safeguarding of "equal and impartial trade," and the preservation of China's "territorial and administrative entity."[92] In short, keep the trade door open by keeping China intact.

Certainly these actions did not save China from continued incursion (it had to pay more than $300 million for the Boxers' damages). The United States itself even asked for a territorial concession in late 1900 at Sansha Bay, Fujian Province, but then shelved the request. Thereafter Washington buttressed its support for the Open Door by increasing the Asiatic Squadron to forty-eight warships and earmarking army forces in the Philippines for future emergency deployment in China. Even Buffalo Bill Cody extended America's frontier to China by reenacting the suppression of the Boxer Rebellion in his Wild West Show to depict the "triumph of Christian civilization over paganism."[93]

The Elbows of a World Power, 1895–1900

Venezuela, Cuba, Hawai'i, the Philippines, Open Door notes—together they meant an unprecedented set of commitments and responsibilities for the United States. Symbolic of this thrust to world-power status was the ascendancy of the imperialists' imperialist, Theodore Roosevelt, to the presidency in 1901. Peering into the twentieth century, Roosevelt warned Americans to avoid "slothful ease and ignoble peace." Never "shrink from the hard contests"; "let us therefore boldly face the life of strife."[94] Indeed, many diplomats looked back on the triumphs of the 1890s as a testing time when the United States met the international challenge and rightfully asserted its place as a major world power. Europeans watched anxiously. Some, especially Germans, spoke of the "American peril."[95] Russia, however, supported U.S. annexation of Hawai'i because it prevented this "Malta of the Pacific" from becoming Japanese.[96] The United States, European leaders pointed out, had become a factor in the "balance of power." With whom would the nation ally itself?

John M. Hay (1838–1905). The author of the Open Door notes graduated from Brown University and served as one of President Abraham Lincoln's secretaries. He became a newspaper editor and diplomat and, in 1897, ambassador to Great Britain. The following year McKinley named him secretary of state, a post he held until his death. Hay's support of the Open Door policy underscored the confidence Americans had in their ability to compete in the globalizing economy. Hay told Congress in 1902 that "the financial center of the world, which required thousands of years to journey from the Euphrates to the Thames and Seine, seems [to be] passing to the Hudson between daybreak and dark." (National Portrait Gallery, Smithsonian Institution)

Pears Soap advertisement.
This unusual mixture of commercial and diplomatic advertising salutes Anglo-American rapprochement. (*Life*, 1898)

The odds seemed to favor Great Britain, although the Anglo-American courtship would be prolonged and marriage something for the future. Ever since the eye-opening Venezuelan crisis, the British, in Colonial Secretary Joseph Chamberlain's words, had applauded Washington for "entering the lists and sharing the task which might have proved too heavy for us alone" and pursued what one historian has called the "great rapprochement."[97] Looking for support against an expansionist Germany, John Bull thought Uncle Sam a fit partner. During the Spanish-American-Cuban-Filipino War the British conspicuously tilted toward the American side and encouraged the subsequent U.S. absorption of Spanish colonies. U.S. leaders, in turn, compared the British suppression of the Boers in South Africa (1899–1902) with their own war against the Filipinos, saying that both peoples were equally "incapable of statehood."[98] Articulate Americans welcomed Britain's implicit acceptance of their imperialism. "Germany, and not England, is the power with whom we are apt to have trouble over the Monroe Doctrine," wrote Roosevelt in 1898.[99] England had "suddenly become a guiding star," one anti-imperialist complained in 1900, so that "conquest, extension of territory, subjugation of semi-barbarous peoples, [and] establishment of a Roman peace" had become common goals.[100]

Britain still ranked first in naval power, but in the late 1890s the United States was growing, standing sixth by 1900. In 1898 alone, spurred by the war with Spain, the United States added 128 vessels to its navy, at a cost of $18 million. At the 1898 American Historical Association meeting, Professor Edwin A. Grosvenor of Amherst College caught the new times in his address: "Barriers of national seclusion are everywhere tumbling like the great wall of China. Every nation elbows other nations to-day."[101] The steel magnate Andrew Carnegie boasted that "the old nations of the earth creep at a snail's pace," but the United States "thunders past with the rush of the express."[102] Many commentators reported that the United States, although still divided North and South on many issues, had united as never before. Southern racists and northern imperialists now had something in common: the need to keep inferior peoples in their place. Befitting their new imperial status, U.S. leaders often used gendered and age-based language that presumed superiority over peoples deemed "emotional, irrational, irresponsible, unbusinesslike, unstable, childlike."[103] If Americans played "the part of China, and [were] content to rot by inches in ignoble ease within our borders," warned Roosevelt, they will "go down before other nations which have not lost the manly and adventurous qualities."[104] Imperial annexation, bragged Senator Beveridge in 1900, "means opportunity for all the glorious young manhood of the republic, the most virile, ambitious, impatient, militant manhood the world has ever seen."[105]

The events of the 1895–1900 period further altered the process of decision-making. Both Cleveland and McKinley conducted their own foreign policies, often thwarting or manipulating Congress. "Expansion and disorder abroad equaled centralization at home," one historian has written.[106] Woodrow Wilson, then president of Princeton University, later noted that 1898 had "changed the balance of powers. Foreign questions became leading questions again. . . . Our President must always, henceforth, be one of the great powers of the world."[107] Wilson also welcomed the "primeval" Philippines as a new "frontier on which to turn loose the colts of the race."[108] From "a provincial huddle of petty sovereignties held together by a rope of sand," one editor boasted, "we rise to the dignity and prowess of an imperial republic incomparably greater than Rome."[109]

Indeed, the allure of empire seemed to offer an exceptionalist mission for the "most merciful of the world's great race of administrators," that of "teaching the world how to govern dependent peoples through uplift, assimilation, and eventual self-government."[110] Thus did the optimistic leaders of the "new world power" after 1900 see themselves as reforming an international system that seemed to be "working in their favor."[111] After 1900 the task of managing the expansive empire and the global responsibilities that came with it preoccupied U.S. leaders.

FURTHER READING FOR THE PERIOD 1895–1900

For the 1890s push for empire and the coming and waging of the Spanish-American-Cuban-Filipino War, see Ronald J. Barr, *The Progressive Army* (1998); Edward J. Berbusse, *The United States and Puerto Rico, 1898–1900* (1966); H. W. Brands, *The Reckless Decade* (1985); Richard Challener, *Admirals, Generals,* and *American Foreign Policy, 1898–1914* (1973); Graham A. Cosmas, *An Army for Empire* (1971); Ada Ferrer, *Insurgent Cuba* (1999); Robert E. Hannigan, *The New World Power* (2002); Kenneth E. Hendrickson, Jr., *The Spanish-American War* (2003); Sylvia Hilton and S. J. Ickringell, eds., *European Perceptions of the Spanish-American War* (1999); Kristin L. Hoganson, *Fighting for American Manhood* (1998); John M. Kirk, *José Martí* (1983); Gerald F. Linderman, *The Mirror of War* (1974); Ernest R. May, *Imperial Democracy* (1961); Joyce Milton, *The Yellow Kids* (1989) (journalists); Ian Mugridge, *The View from Xanadu* (1995) (Hearst); Ivan Musicant, *Empire by Default* (1998); John L. Offner, *An Unwanted War* (1992); Louis A. Pérez, Jr., *The War of 1898* (1998), *Cuba and the United States* (1997), and *Cuba Between Empires, 1878–1902* (1983); Hyman G. Rickover, *How the Battleship* Maine *Was Destroyed* (1976); Emily Rosenberg, *Spreading the American Dream* (1982); Thomas Schoonover, *Uncle Sam's War and the Origins of Globalization* (2003); Peggy Samuels and Harold Samuels, *Remembering the* Maine (1995); Angel Smith and Emma Davila-Cox, eds., *The Crisis of 1898* (1999); David F. Trask, *The War with Spain in 1898* (1981); David Traxel, *1898* (1998); and Warren Zimmermann, *First Great Triumph* (2002).

For U.S. leaders, see Howard K. Beale, *Theodore Roosevelt and the Rise of America to World Power* (1956); John Braeman, *Albert J. Beveridge* (1971); H. W. Brands, *T.R.* (1997); Charles W. Calhoun, *Gilded Age Cato* (1988) (Gresham); Kathleen Dalton, *Theodore Roosevelt* (2002); Gerald Eggert, *Richard Olney* (1973); Lewis L. Gould, *The Presidency of William McKinley* (1981); Nathan Miller, *Theodore Roosevelt* (1992); H. Wayne Morgan, *William McKinley and His America* (1963); Ronald Spector, *Admiral of the New Empire* (1974) (Dewey); Richard E. Welch, Jr., *The Presidencies of Grover Cleveland* (1988); and William C. Widenor, *Henry Cabot Lodge and the Search for an American Foreign Policy* (1980).

Anti-imperialism is treated in Robert L. Beisner, *Twelve Against Empire* (1968); Kendrick A. Clements, *William Jennings Bryan* (1983); Paolo E. Coletta, *William Jennings Bryan* (1964–1969); John C. Farrell, *Beloved Lady* (1967) (Addams); Amy Kaplan, *The Anarchy of Empire in the Making of U.S. Culture* (2002); Frank Ninkovich, *The United States and Imperialism* (2001); Thomas J. Osborne, *"Empire Can Wait": American Opposition to Hawaiian Annexation, 1893–1898* (1981); Hans L. Trefousse, *Carl Schurz* (1982); and Joseph F. Wall, *Andrew Carnegie* (1970).

The Open Door policy and Asia are discussed in Thomas A. Breslin, *China, American Catholicism, and the Missionary* (1980); Charles S. Campbell, *Special Business Interests and the Open Door Policy* (1951); Sherman Cochran, *Big Business in China* (1980) (cigarette industry); Paul A. Cohen, *History in Three Keys* (1997) (Boxers); Michael Hunt, *Frontier Defense and the Open Door* (1973) and *The Making of a Special Relationship* (1983); Thomas McCormick, *China Market* (1967); Valentin H. Rabe, *The Home Base of American China Missions, 1880–1920* (1978); and Marilyn Blatt Young, *The Rhetoric of Empire* (1968).

The Philippine rebellion and the American debate receive scrutiny in Teodoro Agoncillo, *Malolos* (1960); A. J. Bacevich, *Diplomat in Khaki* (1989) (General Frank McCoy); Kenton J. Clymer, *Protestant Missionaries in the Philippines, 1898–1916* (1986); John M. Gates, *Schoolbooks and Krags* (1973); Brian M. Linn, *Guardians of*

Empire (1997), and *The U.S. Army and Counterinsurgency in the Philippine War, 1899–1902* (1989) and *The Philippine War* (2000); Glenn A. May, *Battle for Batangas* (1991) and *Social Engineering in the Philippines* (1980); Stuart C. Miller, *"Benevolent Assimilation"* (1982); Resil B. Mojares, *The War Against the Americans* (1999); Daniel B. Schirmer, *Republic or Empire* (1972); Angel Velasco Shaw and Luis Francia, eds., *Vestiges of War* (1999); Peter Stanley, *A Nation in the Making* (1974), and ed., *Reappraising an Empire* (1984); and Richard E. Welch, *Response to Imperialism* (1979).

For the Venezuelan crisis and Anglo-American relations, see Stuart Anderson, *Race and Rapprochement* (1981); Charles S. Campbell, *From Revolution to Rapprochement* (1974); Judith Ewell, *Venezuela and the United States* (1996); Richard B. Mulanax, *The Boer War in American Politics and Diplomacy* (1994); R. G. Neale, *Great Britain and United States Expansion, 1800–1900* (1966); Thomas J. Noer, *Briton, Boer, and Yankee* (1978); Bradford Perkins, *The Great Rapprochement* (1968); Serge Ricard and Hélène Christol, eds., *Anglo-Saxonism in U.S. Foreign Policy* (1991); and Joseph Smith, *Illusions of Conflict: Anglo-American Diplomacy Toward Latin America, 1865–1896* (1979).

See also the General Bibliography, the following notes, and Robert L. Beisner, ed., *Guide to American Foreign Relations Since 1600* (2003).

For comprehensive coverage of foreign-relations topics, see the articles in the four-volume *Encyclopedia of U.S. Foreign Relations* (1997), edited by Bruce W. Jentleson and Thomas G. Paterson.

NOTES TO CHAPTER 1

1. Quoted in H. Wayne Morgan, *William McKinley and His America* (Syracuse: Syracuse University Press, 1963), p. 359.
2. Lt. Blandin quoted in David Traxel, *1898* (New York: Knopf, 1998), p. 102.
3. Quoted in Walter Millis, *The Martial Spirit* (Boston: Houghton Mifflin, 1931), p. 102.
4. McKinley quoted in Morgan, *McKinley*, p. 361.
5. Quoted in John L. Offner, *An Unwanted War* (Chapel Hill: University of North Carolina Press, 1992), p. 123.
6. Quoted in Louis A. Pérez, Jr., *The War of 1898* (Chapel Hill: University of North Carolina Press, 1998), p. 15.
7. Quoted in Offner, *Unwanted War*, p. 129.
8. Quoted in H. W. Brands, *The Reckless Decade* (New York: St. Martin's, 1995), p. 313.
9. *Congressional Record, XXXI* (March 17, 1898), 2916–2919.
10. Thomas B. Allen, ed., "What Really Sank the Maine?" *Naval History, XII* (March/April 1998), 38.
11. McKinley quoted in Warren Zimmermann, *First Great Triumph* (New York: Farrar, Straus and Giroux, 2002), p. 252.
12. Quoted in Louis A. Pérez, Jr., *Cuba Between Empires, 1878–1902* (Pittsburgh: University of Pittsburgh Press, 1983), p. 172.
13. Quoted in Edmund Morris, *The Rise of Theodore Roosevelt* (New York: Coward, McCann, & Geoghegan, 1979), p. 610.
14. Sen. George Turner and Rep. William Sulzer quoted in Kristin L. Hoganson, *Fighting for American Manhood* (New Haven: Yale University Press, 1998), p. 91.
15. Quoted in Pérez, *Cuba Between Empires*, p. 174.
16. Tomas Estrada Palma quoted in Pérez, *War of 1898*, p. 9.
17. *Foreign Relations, 1898*, p. 746.
18. Quoted in Walter LaFeber, *The American Search for Opportunity, 1865–1913* (New York: Cambridge University Press, 1993), p. 143.
19. *Congressional Record, XXXI* (April 11, 1898), 3699–3702.
20. Pérez, *Cuba Between Empires*, p. 178.
21. Roosevelt quoted in Brands, *Reckless Decade*, p. 336.
22. Quoted *ibid.*, p. 174.
23. Quoted in H. Wayne Morgan, *America's Road to Empire* (New York: Wiley, 1965), p. 63.
24. Senator Hernando de Soto Money quoted in Hoganson, *Fighting for Manhood*, p. 73.
25. Charles W. Eliot quoted in Frank Ninkovich, *The United States and Imperialism* (Malden, Mass.: Blackwell, 2001), p. 14.
26. Quoted in John Braeman, *Albert J. Beveridge* (Chicago: University of Chicago Press, 1971), p. 23.
27. Max O'Rell quoted in Hoganson, *Fighting for Manhood*, p. 35.
28. William Day quoted in Pérez, *War of 1898*, p. 12.
29. Quoted in Gerald G. Eggert, *Richard Olney* (College Park: Penn State University Press, 1974), p. 208.
30. Quoted in Ernest R. May, *Imperial Democracy* (New York: Harper and Row, [1961], 1973), p. 33.
31. *Foreign Relations, 1895*, Part I (Washington, D.C.: Government Printing Office, 1896), pp. 545–562.
32. Richard E. Welch, Jr., *The Presidencies of Grover Cleveland* (Lawrence: University Press of Kansas, 1988), p. 184.
33. Quoted in Robert L. Beisner, *From the Old Diplomacy to the New, 1865–1900* (Arlington Heights, Ill.: Harlan Davidson, 1986; 2nd ed.), p. 111.
34. Quoted in H. W. Brands, *T.R.* (New York: BasicBooks, 1997), p. 289.
35. Quoted in Stuart Anderson, *Race and Rapprochement* (Rutherford, N.J.: Fairleigh Dickinson University Press, 1981), p. 97.
36. Quoted in Joyce Milton, *The Yellow Kids* (New York: Harper and Row, 1989), p. 27.
37. Quoted in Allan Nevins, *Grover Cleveland* (New York: Dodd, Mead, 1932), p. 644.
38. Quoted in Joseph Smith, *Illusions of Conflict* (Pittsburgh: University of Pittsburgh Press, 1979), p. 207.
39. Quoted in George Young, "Intervention Under the Monroe Doctrine," *Political Science Quarterly, LVII* (June 1942), 277.
40. Lars Schoultz, *Beneath the United States* (Cambridge: Harvard University Press, 1998), p. 115.

41. Henry Cabot Lodge quoted in Fredrick B. Pike, *The United States and Latin America* (Austin: University of Texas Press, 1992), pp. 158–159.
42. Joseph A. Fry, "From Open Door to World Systems," *Pacific Historical Review*, LX (May 1996), 282.
43. Quoted in Richard E. Welch, Jr., *George Frisbie Hoar and the Half-Breed Republicans* (Cambridge: Harvard University Press, 1971), p. 209.
44. Walter Q. Gresham to Carl Schurz, October 6, 1893, Walter Q. Gresham Papers, Library of Congress, Washington, D.C.
45. Elizabeth McKillen, "Ethnicity, Class, and Wilsonianism Reconsidered," *Diplomatic History*, XXV (Fall 2001), 586.
46. Pérez, *War of 1898*, p. 74.
47. Quoted in Louis A. Pérez, Jr., *Cuba and the United States*, 2nd ed. (Athens: University of Georgia Press, 1997), p. 80; quoted in Pérez, *War of 1898*, p. 20; John M. Kirk, *José Martí* (Gainesville: University of Florida Press, 1983), pp. 52, 56, 58, 90, 118.
48. Quoted in Philip S. Foner, *The Spanish-Cuban-American War and the Birth of American Imperialism* (New York: Monthly Review Press, 1972; 2 vols.), I, 21.
49. P. M. Sagasta quoted in Angel Smith, "The People and the Nation," in Angel Smith and Emma Davila-Cox, eds., *The Crisis of 1898* (New York: St. Martin's, 1999), p. 165.
50. Olney quoted in Schoultz, *Beneath the United States*, p. 128.
51. Quoted in Offner, *Unwanted War*, p. 26.
52. Quoted in LaFeber, *American Search*, p. 132.
53. Quoted in Eggert, *Olney*, p. 265.
54. James D. Richardson, ed., *A Compilation of the Messages and Papers of the Presidents, 1789–1897* (Washington, D.C.: Government Printing Office, 1896–1899; 10 vols.), IX, 716–722.
55. *Atlanta Constitution* quoted in Hoganson, *Fighting for Manhood*, p. 90.
56. General Calixto Garcia quoted in Pérez, *War of 1898*, p. 9.
57. *Congressional Record*, XXXI (December 6, 1897), 3–5.
58. *Foreign Relations, 1898* (Washington D.C.: Government Printing Office, 1901), pp. 1007–1008.
59. Quoted in Frank Freidel, *The Splendid Little War* (Boston: Little, Brown, 1958), p. 295.
60. Amy Kaplan, *The Anarchy of Empire in the Making of U.S. Culture* (Cambridge: Harvard University Press, 2002), p. 147.
61. Quoted in John A. S. Grenville and George B. Young, *Politics, Strategy, and American Diplomacy* (New Haven: Yale University Press, 1966), p. 278.
62. Quoted in Ada Ferrer, *Insurgent Cuba* (Chapel Hill: University of North Carolina Press, 1999), p. 187.
63. Quoted in Walter A. McDougall, *Promised Land, Crusader State* (Boston: Houghton Mifflin, 1997), pp. 111–112.
64. Quoted in Ninkovich, *United States and Imperialism*, p. 29
65. Quoted in Robert L. Beisner, "1898 and 1968," *Political Science Quarterly*, LXXV (June 1970), 200.
66. Tillman quoted in David W. Blight, *Race and Reunion* (Cambridge: Harvard University Press, 2001), p. 354; senator quoted in Ninkovich, *United States and Imperialism*, p. 44.
67. Quoted in Hugh Deane, *Good Deeds & Gunboats* (San Francisco: China Books and Periodicals, 1990), p. 65.
68. Quoted in John M. Craig, "Lucia True Ames Mead," in Edward P. Crapol, ed., *Women and American Foreign Policy* (Westport, Conn.: Greenwood, 1992; 2nd ed.), p. 72.
69. Judith Papachristou, "American Women and Foreign Policy, 1898–1905," *Diplomatic History*, XIV (Fall 1990), 493.
70. Quoted in Anders Stephanson, *Manifest Destiny* (New York: Hill & Wang, 1995), p. 98.
71. Quoted *ibid.*, p. 87.
72. Quoted in H. Wayne Morgan, *William McKinley and His America* (Syracuse: Syracuse University Press, 1963), p. 422.
73. Quoted in Kenton J. Clymer, *Protestant Missionaries in the Philippines, 1898–1916* (Urbana: University of Illinois Press, 1986), p. 159.
74. Glenn A. May, *Battle for Batangas* (New Haven: Yale University Press, 1991), pp. 267, 291.
75. Quoted in Ronald J. Barr, *The Progressive Army* (New York: St. Martin's, 1998), p. 56.
76. *Boston Evening Transcript*, March 1, 1899.
77. Quoted in James Chace, "Tomorrow the World," *New York Review of Books*, November 21, 2002, p. 36.
78. General S. B. M. Young quoted in Brian McAllister Linn, *The Philippine War, 1899–1902* (Lawrence: University Press of Kansas, 2000), p. 220.
79. Lodge quoted in Kathleen Dalton, *Theodore Roosevelt* (New York: Knopf, 2002), p. 228.
80. Quoted in A. J. Bacevich, *Diplomat in Khaki* (Lawrence: University Press of Kansas, 1989), p. 29.
81. S. B. M. Young quoted in Linn, *Philippine War*, p. 211; quoted in John M. Gates, *Schoolboys and Krags* (Westport, Conn.: Greenwood, 1979), p. vii.
82. Henry F. Graff, ed., *American Imperialism and the Philippine Insurrection* (Boston: Little, Brown, 1969), p. 36.
83. Benjamin Foulois quoted in Linn, *Guardians*, p. 36.
84. Quoted in Donald Smythe, *Guerrilla Warrior* (New York: Charles Scribner's Sons, 1973), p. 198.
85. Quoted in Reynaldo C. Ileto, "Orators and the Crowd," in Peter W. Stanley, ed., *Reappraising an Empire* (Cambridge: Harvard University Press, 1984), p. 103.
86. Jean Heffer, *The United States and the Pacific* (South Bend: University of Notre Dame Press, 2002), p. 206.
87. Quoted in Karnow, *In Our Image*, p. 201.
88. Robert W. Rydell, *World of Fairs* (Chicago: University of Chicago Press, 1993), pp. 75–76.
89. Quoted in Resil B. Mojares, *The War Against the Americans* (Manila: Manila University Press, 1999), p. 211.
90. Quoted in Thomas J. McCormick, *China Market* (Chicago: Quadrangle, 1967), p. 119.
91. Sarah Pike Conger quoted in Carol C. Chin, "American Women Missionaries in China at the Turn of the Twentieth Century," *Diplomatic History*, XXVII (June 2003), 350.
92. *Foreign Relations, 1901* (Washington, D.C.: Government Printing Office, 1902), Appendix, p. 12.
93. J. G. Blair, "First Steps Toward Globalization," in Reinhold Wagnleitner and Elaine Tyler May, eds., *"Here, There and Everywhere": The Foreign Politics of American Popular Culture* (Hanover, N.H.: University Press of New England, 2000), p. 25.
94. Quoted in Beale, *Theodore Roosevelt*, p. 84.
95. Quoted in Fareed Zakaria, *From Wealth to Power* (Princeton: Princeton University Press, 1998), p. 133.
96. Mikhail Murav'ev quoted in Normal Saul, *Concord and Conflict* (Lawrence: University Press of Kansas, 1996), p. 438.
97. Quoted in Anderson, *Race and Rapprochement*, p. 127.
98. A. T. Mahan quoted in Paul A. Kramer, "Empires, Exceptions, and Anglo-Saxons," *Journal of American History*, LXXXVIII (March 2002), 1335.
99. Quoted in Edward P. Crapol, "From Anglophobia to Fragile Rapprochement," in Hans-Jürgen Schröder, ed., *Confrontation and Cooperation* (Providence, R.I.: Berg, 1993), p. 21.

100. J. W. Martin quoted in Kramer, "Empires," p. 1320.

101. American Historical Association, *Annual Report, 1898* (Washington, D.C.: Government Printing Office, 1899), p. 288.

102. Quoted in Smith, *Illusions of Conflict,* p. 40.

103. Emily S. Rosenberg, "Walking the Borders," in Michael J. Hogan and Thomas G. Paterson, eds., *Explaining the History of American Foreign Relations* (New York: Cambridge University Press, 1991), p. 33.

104. Quoted in Gail Bederman, *Manliness & Civilization* (Chicago: University of Chicago Press, 1995), p. 193.

105. Quoted in Cecilia Elizabeth O'Leary, *To Die For* (Princeton: Princeton University Press, 1999), p. 142.

106. LaFeber, *American Search,* p. 117.

107. Quoted in Arthur Link's essay in *Wilson's Diplomacy* (Cambridge: Schenkman, 1973), p. 6.

108. Quoted in Robert Hannigan, *The New World Power* (University Park: Pennsylvania State University Press, 2002), p. 282.

109. Henry Watterson quoted in Alan Brinkley, "The Concept of an American Century," in R. Laurence Moore and Maurizio Vaudagna, eds., *The American Century in Europe* (Ithaca: Cornell University Press, 2003), p. 8.

110. A. J. Beveridge quoted in Kramer, "Empires," p. 1351.

111. Hannigan, *New World Power,* p. xii.

CHAPTER 2

Managing, Policing, and Extending the Empire, 1900–1914

"The Thirteenth Labor of Hercules." *With this official poster by Perham Nahl, the Panama-Pacific Exposition in San Francisco in 1915 celebrated the opening of the Panama Canal. The artist commemorates the ten-year construction project using symbols that reflect the era's themes of empire-building and male hegemony: A powerful, muscular Hercules (the United States) forcibly parts the land (a yielding Panama) to make space for the canal. (Library of Congress)*

DIPLOMATIC CROSSROAD

❧ *Severing Panama from Colombia for the Canal, 1903*

"REVOLUTION IMMINENT" WARNED the cable from the American consul at Colón, a normally quiet Colombian seaport on the Atlantic side of Panama. Acting Secretary of State Francis B. Loomis bridled his curiosity for an hour. Then he fired off an inquiry to the U.S. consul at Panama City, on the Pacific slope: "Uprising on Isthmus reported. Keep Department promptly and fully informed." The response came back in four hours: "No uprising yet. Reported will be in the night. Situation is critical." Loomis's anxiety soon increased when he learned that an "important message" intended for the U.S.S. *Nashville* anchored at Colón had miscarried and troops of the Colombian government had landed in the city.

At the Department of State it was now 8:20 P.M., November 3, 1903. As far as Loomis knew, a revolution had not yet broken out on the isthmus. Nonetheless, he hurriedly drafted instructions for the consuls at Panama and Colón. "Act promptly" to convey to the commanding officer of the *Nashville* this order: "In the interests of peace make every effort to prevent [Colombian] Government troops at Colón from proceeding to Panama [City]." Loomis agonized for another hour. Finally, a new cable arrived in Washington, D.C.: "Uprising occurred to-night . . . no bloodshed. . . . Government will be organized to-night." Loomis had done his part to ensure success in the scheme to acquire a canal controlled by the United States.

November 3 was far more hectic for José Augustín Arango and his fellow conspirators in Panama. The tiny band of Panamanians and Americans living on the isthmus had actively plotted revolution since August, when the Colombian congress rejected the treaty that would have permitted the United States to construct an isthmian canal. By late October, they had become convinced that the North American colossus, frustrated in its overtures to Colombia, would lend them moral and physical support. Confident that U.S. naval vessels would be at hand, they selected November 4 as the date of their coup d'état. To their dismay, however, the Colombian steamer *Cartagena* disembarked about 400 troops at Colón early on November 3. Because the "important message" directing him to prevent the "landing of any armed force . . . at Colón" had not reached him, Commander John Hubbard of the *Nashville* did not interfere with the landing.

Forced to rely on their own wits, the conspirators made good use of the transisthmian railroad. They deviously separated the Colombian commanding general from his troops, lured him aboard a train, and sped him across the isthmus to Panama City. At 6:00 P.M. on the third, the revolutionaries arrested their guest, formed a provisional government, and paraded before a cheering crowd at the Cathedral Plaza. But the revolution would remain perilously unfinished so long as armed Colombian soldiers occupied Colón. Too weak to expel the soldiers by force, the insurgents gave the colonel in charge $8,000 in gold, whereupon he ordered his troops aboard a departing steamer. The U.S. consul at Panama City cabled: "Quiet prevails." At noon the next day, Secretary of State John Hay recognized the sovereign Republic of Panama.

The new Panamanian government appointed as its minister plenipotentiary a Frenchman, Philippe Bunau-Varilla, an engineer of an earlier failed Panama canal project. With Gallic flourish, Bunau-Varilla congratulated Secretary Hay for rescuing Panama "from the barbarism of unnecessary and wasteful civil wars to consecrate it to the destiny assigned to it by Providence, the service of humanity, and the progress of civilization."[1] John Hay thoroughly understood Bunau-Varilla's rhetoric and eagerly negotiated the treaty both men wanted. On November 18, 1903, less than two weeks after U.S. recognition of Panama, they signed the Hay–Bunau-Varilla Treaty, by which the United States would build, fortify, and operate a canal linking the Atlantic and Pacific oceans. Washington also guaranteed the "independence of the Republic in Panama," thereby ensuring against any threat from Colombia.[2]

Hay had at last achieved a goal set by his chief, President Theodore Roosevelt, several years earlier. "I do not see why we should dig the canal if we are not to fortify it," Roosevelt had remarked in 1900. If an unfortified, neutral canal had existed in Central America during the recent war with Spain, Roosevelt argued, the United States would have spent the war in "wild panic," fearful that the Spanish fleet would slip through the waterway and rush to the Philippines to attack Commodore Dewey. The obvious lesson: "Better to have no canal at all, than not give us the power to control it in time of war," Roosevelt expostulated.[3]

The Clayton-Bulwer Treaty of 1850, stipulating joint Anglo-American control of any isthmian canal, seemed to block the way. In December 1898, flushed with victory over Spain, President William McKinley had directed Secretary Hay to modify that agreement with the British ambassador, Sir Julian Pauncefote. The Hay-Pauncefote Treaty of February 1900 permitted the United States to build a canal but forbade its fortification, much to the dismay of Roosevelt, then governor of New York. He spearheaded an attack that defeated the treaty in the Senate, forcing renegotiation. On November 18, 1901, with Roosevelt now president, Hay and Pauncefote signed a satisfactory new pact.

Then began the complex process of determining the route. In November 1901, after a two-year investigation, the Walker Isthmian Canal Commission reported in favor of Nicaragua. The decisive criterion—cost—seemed exorbitant for Panama because of the obduracy of the New Panama Canal Company, a French-chartered firm that held the Colombian concession for canal rights. The company estimated its assets on the isthmus at $109 million—machinery, property, and excavated soil left by the defunct de Lesseps organization in 1888. Purchase of the company's rights and holdings would make a Panama canal prohibitively expensive if technologically easier. For these reasons, plus travel accounts that depicted Panama as "a hideous dung heap of physical and moral degradation," the House passed the Hepburn Bill in January 1902 authorizing a canal through Nicaragua.[4]

The New Panama Canal Company's American lawyer, William Nelson Cromwell, a partner in the prestigious New York law firm of Sullivan and Cromwell, schemed to sell the assets of his French client for the highest possible price. Lobbying hard, Bunau-Varilla even exposed the unsuitability of Nicaraguan terrain by deluging Congress with Nicaraguan postage stamps that depicted a belching volcano.

Theodore Roosevelt the Pirate. The Colombian minister called the United States a "pirate." When Roosevelt asked about legal precedents for his Panama policy, Attorney General Philander C. Knox replied, "Oh, Mr. President, do not let so great an achievement suffer from any taint of legality." Nonetheless, TR publicly avowed that "no one connected with this Government had any part in preparing, inciting, or encouraging the late revolution on the Isthmus of Panama." He lied. (Frank Nankivell, Swann Collection of Caricature and Cartoon)

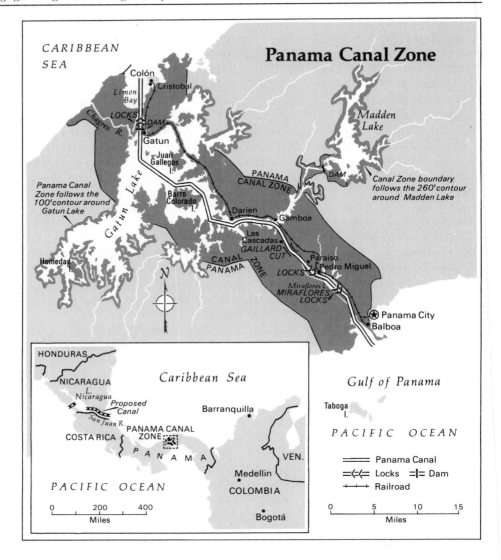

On January 18, 1902, the Walker Commission reversed itself and decided for the technologically preferable Panama passage, citing the company's willingness to sell out for the reduced sum of $40 million. Guided by Roosevelt and Cromwell, Congress five months later chose the Panama route. The State Department soon opened negotiations with Colombia. The annual rent became a stumbling block, which Hay removed only by delivering an ultimatum to the Colombian chargé d'affaires, Tomás Herrán, in January 1903. On January 22 he and Hay signed a treaty granting Colombia an initial payment of $10 million and $250,000 annually. The United States would control the six-mile-wide canal zone for one hundred years, renewable at the "sole and absolute option" of the North American republic.[5]

The U.S. Senate approved the Hay–Herrán Treaty on March 17, 1903, but the Colombian government attempted to extract a $10 million payment from the New Panama Canal Company for permitting the transfer of its assets to the U.S. government. Cromwell promptly cried foul, whereupon Hay bluntly announced that any payment to Colombia was "not permissible."[6] The Colombians next tried to raise the initial American cash payment from $10 million to $15 million. Roosevelt exploded against "those contemptible little creatures in Bogotá."[7] The president believed that "you could no more make an agreement with the Colombian rulers than you could nail currant jelly to the wall."[8] TR's intransigence and Hay's extraordinary intercession on behalf of a privately owned foreign corporation increased Colombians' resentment against U.S. infringement on their sovereignty over Panama. The Colombian congress unanimously defeated the treaty on August 12, 1903.

As early as March 30, U.S. minister Arthur N. Beaupré had warned that "without question public opinion is strongly against its ratification." Roosevelt then began to ponder undiplomatic alternatives.[9] In June the ubiquitous Cromwell had met with Roosevelt and then planted a story in the *New York World* reporting that, if Colombia rejected the treaty, Panama would secede and grant to the United States "the equivalent of absolute sovereignty over the Canal Zone," and that "President Roosevelt is said to strongly favor this plan."[10] By now the president was privately castigating Colombia for its "squalid savagery," combined with "the worst forms of despotism and of anarchy, of violence and of fatuous weakness, of dismal ignorance, cruelty, treachery, greed, and utter vanity."[11]

Roosevelt now considered two options: seizure of Panama by force, or instant recognition and support for any revolutionary regime in Panama. The president inclined sharply toward the latter course after a meeting with Bunau-Varilla on October 10, during which the Frenchman predicted an uprising. When Bunau-Varilla asked what the United States would do, TR replied: "Colombia by her action has forfeited any claim upon the U.S. and I have no use for a government that would do what that government has done."[12] One week later, on October 16, Secretary Hay informed Bunau-Varilla that American naval vessels were heading toward the isthmus. Calculating the steaming time, Bunau-Varilla cabled the revolutionaries on the isthmus that warships would arrive by November 2. Early that evening the U.S.S. *Nashville* dropped anchor at Colón as predicted. Although the *Nashville* landed troops to keep order *after* the Panamanian junta had gained control, a Colombian diplomat rightfully complained: "The Americans are against us. What can we do against the American Navy?"[13]

In his annual message to Congress after the Panamanian revolution, Roosevelt urged swift ratification of the Hay–Bunau-Varilla Treaty, claiming that Colombia had forced the United States "to take decisive steps to bring to an end a condition of affairs which had become intolerable."[14] When critics complained about his "Bowery-boy" behavior toward Colombia, Roosevelt denounced the "small body of shrill eunuchs who consistently oppose" his "righteous" policies.[15] On February 23, 1904, the Senate approved the treaty by a vote of 66 to 14. The treaty granted the United States "power and authority" within the zone "in perpetuity" as "if it were the sovereign of the territory."[16] Later, in 1911, TR reportedly boasted that "I took the Canal Zone and let Congress debate; and while the debate goes on the Canal does also."[17]

Panama Canal. The U.S.S. *Ohio* passes through the Culebra Cut (now called the Gaillard Cut) of the Panama Canal about a year after the canal opened to traffic—both warships and commercial vessels. "For the next seven decades," the scholar Lars Schoultz has noted, "the Panama Canal Zone stands as the most obvious legacy of the age of imperialism in United States policy toward Latin America." (Library of Congress)

Construction began in mid-1904, and the fifty-mile-long canal opened on August 15, 1914. During the first year of operation alone, 1,058 merchant vessels slid through the locks, while the Atlantic and Pacific fleets of the U.S. Navy freely exchanged ships. In 1922 the United States paid "conscience money" or "canalimony" of $25 million to Colombia but did not formally apologize for having taken the canal zone. Despite critics, most Americans have applauded Roosevelt's bold venture against Colombia. TR ranked it alongside the Louisiana Purchase and the acquisition of Texas. The canal, Woodrow Wilson later asserted, shifted "the center of gravity of the world."[18]

The Conservative Shapers of Empire

The taking of Panama symbolized the new activism characteristic of American foreign policy after the Spanish-American-Cuban-Filipino War, and construction of the canal ensured the United States virtual hegemony over Latin America. It also intensified Washington's participation in the global contest for empire among the great powers. "The United States will be attacked as soon as you are about to complete the canal," Germany's Kaiser Wilhelm II predicted in 1907, identifying Japan as the most likely culprit.[19] Britain, which had the power to challenge U.S. preeminence in the hemisphere, chose to acquiesce in the face of a growing political and naval threat from Germany. In turn, the vigorous German Empire, having expanded

Makers of American Foreign Relations, 1900–1914

Presidents	Secretaries of State
Theodore Roosevelt, 1901–1909	John Hay, 1898–1905
	Elihu Root, 1905–1909
	Robert Bacon, 1909
William Howard Taft, 1909–1913	Philander C. Knox, 1909–1913
Woodrow Wilson, 1913–1921	William Jennings Bryan, 1913–1915

its markets and investments in Central and South America to more than 2 billion marks by 1900, seemed "desirous of obtaining a foothold in the Western Hemisphere," as the General Board of the U.S. Navy put it.[20] The kaiser boasted: "We will do whatever is necessary for our navy, even if it displeases the Yankees. Never fear."[21] Revolutionary upheavals in Russia, China, and Mexico produced further shifting in the international balance of power. As European alliances consolidated and lurched toward a world war, President Roosevelt and his successors had to defend, develop, and enlarge the new U.S. empire in an era of tumultuous transformation.

In the late nineteenth century, Roosevelt had associated closely with the most vocal pressure group agitating for an American canal, the uniformed "professors of war" at the Naval War College.[22] He corresponded regularly with Alfred Thayer Mahan, the navalist who tirelessly touted the strategic advantages of a canal. During the war of 1898, the warship *Oregon* dashed at full speed from San Francisco around South America to Cuba in time to help destroy the Spanish fleet off Santiago. The race of more than 14,000 miles fired American imaginations, but it also consumed sixty-eight days and underscored the need for an interoceanic canal across Central America.

Roosevelt's sense of isthmian strategic necessity reflected a broad worldview he shared with many "progressives" in the early twentieth century. A conservative patrician reformer motivated by noblesse oblige, he "feared that unrest caused by social and economic inequities would impair the nation's strength and efficiency."[23] He saw a similar danger in unrest abroad, and he sought to exert U.S. influence to create order on a global scale through "proper policing."[24] A quintessential chauvinist, Roosevelt talked about doing the "rough work of the world" and the need to "speak softly and carry a big stick."[25] Imbibing Darwinist doctrines of "natural selection," Roosevelt proclaimed "our duty toward the people living in barbarism to see that they are freed from their chains, and we can free them only by destroying barbarism itself."[26] Anglo-Saxon superiority was best expressed in war. "All the great masterful races have been fighting races," TR lectured.[27] Not all Progressive-era reformers joined Roosevelt in advocating a vigorous activism abroad. Wisconsin's Senator Robert M. La Follette, for example, opposed imperialism and contended that the same corporate monopolists they battled at home were dragging the United States into perpetual intervention overseas. Activists in women's organizations bemoaned the "present intoxication with the hashish of conquest" as they urged "women's values" on a male government so as to rein in the "champing steeds" of American militarism and expansion.[28]

Roosevelt vigorously debated his critics and added his unique personal characteristics to American foreign policy. Exuberant and calculating, he centralized foreign-policy decisionmaking, frequently bypassed Congress, and believed "the people" so ignorant about foreign affairs that they should not direct an informed president like himself. At the same time, he kept favorite journalists and other "intelligent observers sufficiently enlightened to prevent their going wrong."[29] Seeking world stability, Roosevelt advocated "minimizing the chances of war among civilized people" and "multiplying the methods and chances of honorably avoiding war in the event of controversy."[30] Indeed, he won the Nobel Peace Prize in 1906 for his mediating effort at the Portsmouth Conference (see pages 52–53). The robust president disliked pomp and ceremony and once broke up a state luncheon by demonstrating jujitsu holds on the Swiss minister. "The biggest matters," this progenitor of the imperial presidency later wrote, "I managed without consultation with anyone; for when a matter is of capital importance, it is well to have it handled by one man only."[31]

Roosevelt and other shapers of American foreign policy before World War I were members of an American quasi-aristocracy and sure-footed devotees of "order." They moved comfortably in the affluent, cosmopolitan, upper-class society of the Atlantic seaboard. Roosevelt, a graduate of Harvard College and prolific author, had served as assistant secretary of the navy and governor of New York. His successor, Ohioan William Howard Taft, a graduate of Yale, had served as a federal circuit court judge, governor of the Philippines (1901–1904), and secretary of war (1904–1908). Woodrow Wilson earned a Ph.D. from Johns Hopkins, wrote books on government and history, presided over Princeton, and governed New Jersey before entering the White House. Each president believed that "we owe to our less fortunate [international] neighbors that come under our guardianship the same degree of neighborly feeling and aid that a successful man in a community owes to his less fortunate fellow citizens."[32]

Their secretaries of state, with one exception, belonged to the same elite. John Hay, secretary from 1898 to 1905, was educated at Brown University. A poet, novelist, biographer, and editor of the *New York Tribune,* the wealthy Hay had served as Lincoln's personal secretary during the Civil War and later as McKinley's ambassador to Great Britain. A chief architect of the Anglo-American rapprochement, Hay regarded "a firm understanding with England" as the "indispensable feature of our foreign policy."[33] His successor, Elihu Root (1905–1909), graduated from Hamilton College, took a law degree at New York University, and became one of America's most successful corporation lawyers. As secretary of war from 1899 to 1904, he created mechanisms, such as the Platt Amendment for Cuba, for managing the American empire. Like TR, he believed that the "main object of diplomacy is to keep the country out of trouble" and maintain order abroad.[34] Philander C. Knox (1909–1913) followed Root. A corporation lawyer, Knox served as attorney general and U.S. senator before entering the State Department. He liked to play golf at Chevy Chase, spend summers with his trotters at his Valley Forge Farms estate, vacation in Florida in the winter, and delegate departmental work to subordinates. He advocated "dollar diplomacy" as a means of creating order in revolution-prone areas—that is, using private financiers and business leaders to promote foreign policy, and using diplomacy to promote American commerce and investment abroad. As his *second* secretary of state President Wilson named New Yorker Robert Lansing (1915–1920), a graduate of Amherst College, son-in-law of a former secretary of state, and practitioner of international law. Reserved and conservative, Lansing also abhorred disorder in the U.S. sphere of Latin America.

William Jennings Bryan, Wilson's *first* appointment (1913–1915), lacked such conservative elite status. The "boy orator" of Nebraska could mesmerize crowds by decrying the "cross of gold" on which eastern capitalists were crucifying western and southern farmers, but he could not win a presidential election (he ran in 1896, 1900, and 1908). The "Great Commoner" languished for years as the most prominent has-been of the Democratic party until Wilson named him secretary of state as a reward for support at the convention of 1912. The president let Bryan appoint "deserving Democrats" to diplomatic posts and indulge his fascination with "cooling off" treaties, but Wilson bypassed him in most important diplomatic decisions, even to the point of composing overseas cables on his own White House typewriter.

The conservative managers of American foreign policy believed that a major component of national power was a prosperous, expanding economy invigorated by a healthy foreign trade. The principle of the "Open Door"—to keep open trade and investment opportunities—became a governing tenet voiced globally, if often tarnished in application. Mahan saw commerce as the "energizer of material civilization," and Roosevelt declared that "America has only just begun to assume that commanding position in the international business world which we believe will more and more be hers."[35] In 1900 the United States exported goods valued at $1.5 billion. By 1914 that figure stood at $2.5 billion. Exports to Latin America increased markedly from $132 million at the turn of the century to $309 million in 1914. Investments there in sugar, transportation, and banking shot up. By 1913 the United Fruit Company, the banana empire, had some 130,000 acres in cultivation in Central America, a fleet of freighters, and political influence as well. By 1914 U.S. entrepreneurs dominated nickel mining in Canada and sugar production in Cuba, and total American investments abroad equaled $3.5 billion.

But those statistics meant more than contributions to pocketbooks. Americans believed that economic expansion also carried abroad positive values of industriousness, honesty, morality, and private initiative. Thus Yale University-in-China and the Young Men's Christian Association (YMCA) joined Standard Oil Company and Singer Sewing in China as advance agents of civilization. And Taft said about the Chinese: "The more civilized they become the more active their industries, the wealthier they become, and the better market they will become for us."[36] President Wilson, who added missionary paternalism to the quest for order, said simply that he would "teach the South American Republics to elect good men."[37] For some foreigners, however, "voracious, preachy, mercenary, and bombastically chauvinist" Americans already invited scorn.[38] One Venezuelan writer characterized "Yanquis" as "rough and obtuse Calibans, swollen by brutal appetites, the enemies of idealism, furiously enamored of the dollar," whiskey-soaked sots, "overwhelming, fierce, [and] clownish."[39] Whatever Americans' intentions, their compulsion to shape the lives of other peoples while denying any desire to dominate brought mixed results.

Cuba's Limited Independence Under the Platt Amendment

In December 1898, President McKinley rejected advice that the Cubans "are no more fit for self-government than gunpowder is for hell" and promised "free and independent" status for Cuba once the U.S. occupation had established "complete tranquility" and a "stable government."[40] To accelerate Cuban democracy and stability, he appointed General Leonard Wood the military governor of the island. A Harvard graduate with a degree in medicine, Wood favored outright annexation of Cuba, but he loyally carried out the administration's policy of patrician tutelage. During his tenure as military governor (1899–1902), he worked to eradicate yellow fever, Americanize education, construct highways, and formulate an electoral law. He even added "before" and "after" photos of public toilets in his reports. The general defined his objectives conservatively: "When money can be borrowed at a reasonable rate of interest and when capital is willing to invest in the Island, a condition of stability will have been reached."[41] Given the war-ravaged Cuban economy, only the North Americans had the resources for reconstruction. Those Cuban elites who spoke English and knew American ways could serve as local managers, traders, agents, and advisers. The occupation thus stressed English in public schools because "the Cuban people will never understand the people of the United States until they appreciate our institutions."[42]

Secretary of War Elihu Root began construction of a Cuban-American political relationship designed to weather the storms of independence. Working closely

"If General Wood is Unpopular with Cuba, We Can Guess the Reason."
General Leonard Wood (1860–1927) joined the army as a surgeon in 1886 and earned the Congressional Medal of Honor for helping to capture the Apache leader Geronimo. Wood commanded the Rough Riders at San Juan Hill before his appointment as the military governor of Cuba. As this cartoon suggests, he saw his role in Cuba as "paternalistic" supervision of a Cuban "race that has been steadily going down for a hundred years," as he put it. Later he served as governor general of the Philippines. (*Minneapolis Tribune* in *Literary Digest*, 1901)

with Senator Orville Platt, Root fashioned the Platt Amendment to the Army Appropriation Bill of 1901. By the amendment's terms, Cuba could not make a treaty with any nation that might impair its independence. Should Cuban independence ever be threatened, or should Cuba fail to protect "life, property, and individual liberty," the United States had the right to intervene. For these purposes, Cuba would cede to the United States "lands necessary for coaling or naval stations."[43]

Cubans protested. On Good Friday 1901, the front page of Havana's *La Discusión* carried a cartoon of "The Cuban Calvary" depicting the Cuban people as Christ and Senator Platt as a Roman soldier. Anti-imperialist critics charged that the amendment extinguished Cuban independence. Root piously denied any "intermeddling or interference with the affairs of a Cuban government," but Wood privately conceded that "little or no independence [was] left Cuba under the Platt Amendment."[44] A reluctant Cuban convention adopted the measure as an amendment to the new constitution on June 12, 1901, and the two governments signed a treaty embodying the Platt Amendment on May 22, 1903. That same year the U.S. Navy constructed a naval base at Guantánamo Bay; "Gitmo," as the marines christened it, was leased to the United States in perpetuity for a small annual fee. With North American investments pouring into capital-starved Cuba, extending control over sugar, tobacco (the new Tobacco Trust exported 90 percent of Havana cigars by 1902), mining, transportation, utilities, and cattle ranching, the Reciprocity Treaty of 1902 permitted Cuban products to enter the United States at specially reduced tariff rates, thereby further interlocking the two economies.

The first president of the Republic of Cuba, Tomás Estrada Palma, acted "more plattish than Platt himself."[45] Following his rigged reelection and second inauguration, discontented Cuban nationalists revolted. In September 1906, the U.S. consul general in Havana reported Estrada Palma's inability to "protect life and property."[46] President Roosevelt immediately ordered the cruiser *Denver* to Havana, whereupon a battalion of sailors landed at Estrada Palma's request. Roosevelt summarily ordered the men back aboard ship. "I am so angry with that infernal little Cuban republic," exploded the Rough Rider, "that I would like to wipe its people off the face of the earth." All he wanted was that the Cubans "should behave themselves."[47]

Into this turmoil stepped the portly secretary of war, William Howard Taft, sent by TR to mediate between the warring factions. Estrada Palma resigned, permitting Taft to establish a new government with himself as governor. Taft soon lectured students in Havana that Cubans needed a "mercantile spirit," a "desire to make money, to found great enterprises."[48] He returned home in mid-October, leaving behind a government headed by an American civilian, administered by U.S. Army officers, and backed by 5,000 American soldiers. For twenty-eight months Governor Charles E. Magoon attempted to reinstate Leonard Wood's electoral and humanitarian reforms, while Roosevelt worried that "those ridiculous dagoes would flare up over some totally unexpected trouble and start to cutting one another's throats."[49]

Under his successor Taft, and under Taft's successor Woodrow Wilson, U.S. policy toward Cuba reflexively supported existing governments, by force if necessary. Taft and Wilson made no serious effort to reform Cuba in the North American image. Through "dollar diplomacy," the United States sought order in Cuban politics and security for investments and commerce, particularly in sugar. The

$50 million invested by Americans in 1896 jumped to $220 million in 1913. By 1920 American-owned mills produced about half of Cuba's sugar. Cuban exports to the United States in 1900 equaled $31 million, by 1914 $131 million, and by 1920 $722 million, thus confirming José Martí's dictum that *"el pueblo que compra, manda"* ("the country which buys, commands").[50] U.S. entrepreneurs helped establish missionary schools (such as the Candler school in Havana, named after the founder of Coca-Cola) that, in effect, trained Cubans for employment in North American companies. When revolution threatened these interests, as in May 1912 and February 1917, marines went ashore. After Havana followed Washington's lead and declared war against Germany in April 1917, some 2,500 American troops went to the island, ostensibly to protect the sugar plantations that helped feed the Allied armies.

The Constable of the Caribbean: The Roosevelt Corollary, Venezuela, and the Dominican Republic

In his first annual message, on December 3, 1901, President Roosevelt called the Monroe Doctrine "a guarantee of the commercial independence of the Americas." The United States, however, as protector of that independence, would "not guarantee any state against punishment if it misconducts itself, provided that punishment does not take the form of the acquisition of territory by any non-American power."[51] If a Western Hemispheric country misbehaved toward a European nation, Roosevelt would "let the European country spank it."[52]

The president was thinking principally of Germany and Venezuela. The flamboyant Venezuelan dictator Cipriano Castro had perpetually deferred payment on $12.5 million in bonds held by German investors, once graphically showing contempt during negotiations by "breaking wind" against German diplomats, who reacted indignantly.[53] Britain also rankled at Venezuelan defaults to British creditors. In December 1902, after clearing the way with Washington, Germany and Britain delivered an ultimatum demanding immediate settlement of their claims, seized several Venezuelan vessels, bombarded two forts, and blockaded all ports. To all of this Roosevelt initially acquiesced, despite the doctrine of Argentina's Foreign Minister Luis M. Drago that "physical force cannot be used to compel the collection of public debt under any circumstances."[54]

In mid-January 1903, the German navy bombarded two more forts. This time the president delivered a quiet warning to desist. He also sent Admiral George Dewey on naval maneuvers in the Caribbean, which were intended, Dewey later boasted, as "an object lesson to the Kaiser."[55] TR worried that the "fuss-cat" kaiser might spark war through his "incessant hysterical vacillations."[56] Impressed by the U.S. reaction, the kaiser replaced his ill-informed ambassador with Hermann Speck von Sternburg, an old friend of Roosevelt. The president urged on him a quick settlement. Thereupon, Britain and Germany in February lifted the blockade and submitted the dispute to the Permanent Court at The Hague. Prime Minister Arthur Balfour calmed troubled waters by announcing that "the Monroe Doctrine has no enemies in this country."[57] Speck von Sternburg also averred that the kaiser "would no more think of violating that [Monroe] doctrine than he would of colonizing the moon."[58] When the Hague arbiters found in favor of Germany and England in early 1904, a State Department official complained that this decision put "a premium on violence" and made likely similar European interventions in the future.[59]

TR also fretted about the Dominican Republic, revolution-torn since 1899 and seemingly vulnerable to German interests. "I have about the same desire to annex it," Roosevelt said privately, "as a gorged boa constrictor might have to swallow a porcupine wrong-end to."[60] An American firm claimed damages of several million dollars, and European creditors demanded action by their governments. The president prayed that the Dominicans "would behave so that I would not have to act in any way." By spring 1904 he thought he might have to do "what a policeman has to do."[61] If he said "'Hands off' to the powers of Europe, then sooner or later we must keep order ourselves," he told Root.[62]

On December 6, 1904, Roosevelt described to Congress his conception of the United States as hemispheric policeman. "Chronic wrongdoing, or an impotence which results in a general loosening of the ties of civilized society," he proclaimed, "may in America, as elsewhere, ultimately require intervention by some civilized nation, and in the Western Hemisphere the adherence of the United States to the Monroe Doctrine may force the United States, however reluctantly, in flagrant cases of such wrongdoing or impotence, to the exercise of an international police power."[63] This "*trés* long message," in the French ambassador's words, meant that James Monroe "certainly would no longer recognize" his own doctrine because TR had transformed the ban on European meddling into a brash promise of U.S. hegemony over the Americas.[64]

The Rough Rider soon donned his constable's badge. He assigned a U.S. collector of Dominican customs. "The Constitution," Roosevelt later explained, "did not explicitly give me the power to bring about the necessary agreement with Santo Domingo. But the Constitution did not forbid me."[65] Yet "policing" and "civilizing" the Dominican Republic by presidential order provoked nationalist resentment from Dominicans who, as one naval officer reported in 1906, "are quieting their children with the threat 'There comes an American. Keep quiet or he will kill you.'"[66] Taft's secretary of state, Philander C. Knox, applauded the customs receivership in the Dominican Republic because it denied to rebels the funds they so eagerly "collected" through the capture of customshouses, thus curing "century-old evils."[67] The assassination of the Dominican president in November 1911 suggested that Knox spoke prematurely. And in 1912 revolutionaries operating from contiguous Haiti marauded throughout the Dominican Republic, forcing the closure of several customshouses. To restore order, Taft in September 1912 sent a commission backed by 750 marines. The commissioners redefined the Haitian-Dominican border, forced the corrupt Dominican president to resign, and avoided direct interference in a new election.

His denunciation of "dollar diplomacy" notwithstanding, Woodrow Wilson had written in 1907 that "concessions obtained by financiers must be safeguarded by ministers of state, even if the sovereignty of unwilling nations be outraged in the process."[68] No wonder that President Wilson's search for stability in Latin America retraced familiar steps. When, in September 1913, revolution again threatened the

Dominican government, Secretary Bryan promised "every legitimate means to assist in the restoration of order and the prevention of further insurrections."[69] When Wilson ordered naval intervention after further Dominican disorders in May 1916, he said: "If a man will not listen to you quietly in a seat, sit on his neck and make him listen."[70] As the 400 marines of Admiral William Caperton's landing force entered the city of Santo Domingo at dawn on May 15, they found empty streets, bolted doors, shuttered windows, and Dominican flags festooned with black crepe. A new treaty gave the United States full control over Dominican finances. In November, as U.S. participation in the European war became increasingly probable, Wilson proclaimed the formal military occupation of the Dominican Republic, ostensibly to suppress revolutionaries suspected of a pro-German bias. Despite an insurgency by peasants in the eastern region of the Dominican Republic, the U.S. Navy formally governed the country until 1922. The main legacy of the occupation, in the historian Bruce Calder's terse judgment, was "a strong anti-U.S. feeling" among the Dominican people.[71]

The Quest for Order in Haiti and Nicaragua

The Dominican Republic shares the island of Hispaniola with Haiti, where revolution became an increasingly popular mode of changing governments. American investments in Haiti were limited to ownership of a small railroad and a one-third share in the Haitian National Bank. Nationals of France and Germany controlled the bank, and disorder thus could give either European nation a pretext for intervention. After the outbreak of World War I, the Wilson administration worried about "the ever present danger of German control" of Haiti and its deepwater harbor of Môle Saint Nicolas.[72] The Navy Department, content with bases in Cuba and Puerto Rico, nonetheless remembered the German cruiser *Panther*'s sinking a Haitian gunboat in 1902. The State Department sought to buy the Môle "to take it out of the market."[73] To impose order on Haiti, Wilson pressed for an American customs receivership on the Dominican model.

The Haitians resisted successfully until July 1915, when the regime of Guillaume Sam fell in an orgy of grisly political murders. Wilson ordered the navy to "amicably take charge" of the "dusky little republic."[74] As 2,000 troops imposed martial law and seized the customshouses, one marine recorded that "the opaque eyes in the black faces were . . . as indifferent as the lenses of cameras."[75] Subsequent fighting between occupiers and native guerrillas, which critics perceived as "a racial war of extermination," killed more than 2,250 Haitians compared to 16 marine casualties.[76] Until the marines finally departed in 1934, U.S. officials noted "the intense feeling . . . practically everywhere against the American occupation."[77]

The United States also intervened, virtually at will, in Nicaragua. In 1907 Roosevelt and Mexico's president jointly proposed a peace conference to end the incessant warfare among Central American states. As Secretary Root explained, their conduct mattered because the Panama Canal put them "in the front yard of the United States."[78] When President José Santos Zelaya solicited funds to build a second interoceanic canal, especially from Germany (whose capital investments stood three times greater than U.S. properties in Nicaragua), Washington turned against a leader whom some Nicaraguans had compared to Roosevelt himself. For Zelaya's crime of seeking a "better economic position for Nicaragua outside the U.S. economic subsystem," the State Department labeled him "the most reprehensible ruler that ever oppressed an aspiring people."[79]

After Zelaya "yanked Mr. Taft by the ear" by executing two Americans for aiding rebels, Washington broke diplomatic relations in November 1909, sent a battleship for "moral effect," forced Zelaya into exile, and threatened to "knock heads together until they should maintain peace."[80] Secretary Knox then negotiated a treaty with the victorious conservatives led by Adolfo Díaz, providing for U.S. control of the customs service and an American loan. Instead of gratitude, "the natural sentiment of an overwhelming majority of Nicaraguans is antagonistic to the United States," the U.S. envoy reported.[81] Rebuffed by the U.S. Senate, Knox and a group of bankers simply went ahead without a treaty. In September 1912, the administration sent 354 marines into

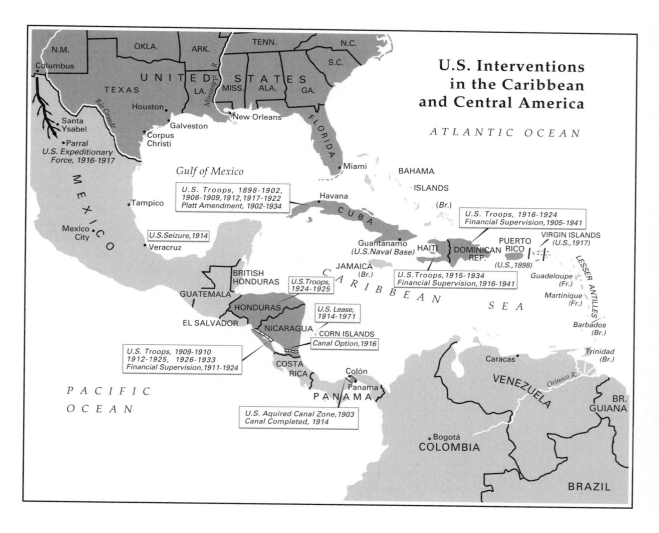

U.S. Interventions in the Caribbean and Central America

battle on behalf of the Díaz regime, which the State Department deemed representative "of an educated, property-owning and civilized small minority . . . , [and] the ablest people of the country."[82] After tipping the scales against the newest revolutionary army, the leathernecks returned home, leaving one hundred behind as a legation guard in Managua. The marines could prevent a coup d'état, but "*keeping* a surrogate in power in Central America was often as problematical as *putting* him in power."[83]

Bryan in spring 1913 dusted off a shelved draft treaty granting the United States a canal option in Nicaragua in exchange for $3 million. He hoped that this money would "give sufficient encouragement" to American bankers to lend Díaz more.[84] The secretary also added a clause similar to the Platt Amendment before sending the Bryan-Chamorro Treaty to the Senate. When the upper house balked, Bryan deleted the U.S. right of intervention. Ratification in February 1916 did help Nicaragua's finances. The treaty also effectively excluded European powers from naval bases in the Gulf of Fonseca, and to make that point stick, Wilson ordered U.S. warships to cruise offshore during the 1916 Nicaraguan presidential campaign. Although nominally independent, Nicaragua remained a U.S. protectorate until 1933.

The Mexican Revolution Threatens U.S. Interests

Mexico changed governments with uncharacteristic frequency after the outbreak of revolution in 1910. In 1911 Francisco I. Madero toppled Porfirio Díaz, the aged dictator who had maintained order, personal power, and a healthy environment for North American investments since the late 1870s. U.S. citizens owned more than 40 percent of Mexico's property, and Mexico had become the world's third largest oil producer, thanks to Standard Oil Company, Texas Oil Company (Texaco), and other firms. The revolution thus inevitably took on an anti-Yankee tinge. Despite the threat to American lives and property, Taft determined to "sit tight on the lid and it will take a good deal to pry me off."[85] In February 1913, U.S. ambassador Henry Lane Wilson encouraged one of Madero's trusted generals, Victoriano Huerta, to overthrow the revolutionary nationalist. Indeed, Huerta had Madero shot and then set about to consolidate his own power. The German ambassador called these events "the usual American policy of replacing hostile regimes with pliable ones through revolutions without taking official responsibility for it."[86] But one of the state governors, Venustiano Carranza, organized the "Constitutionalist" revolt on February 26. When American residents became caught in the crossfire, the departing Taft administration refused recognition until Huerta punished the "murderers of American citizens" and ended "discriminations against American interests."[87]

Appalled by Madero's murder, President Wilson vowed not to recognize a "government of butchers."[88] He denounced Huerta as a "diverting brute! . . . seldom sober and always impossible."[89] Seemingly unconcerned about private American properties in Mexico worth some $1.5 billion, Wilson refused to act as "the servant of those who wish to enhance the value of their Mexican investments."[90] When Ambassador Wilson continued to urge recognition of Huerta to protect those U.S. interests, the president recalled him in July 1913 for "treason, perfidy, and assassination

William Jennings Bryan (1860–1925), Woodrow Wilson (1856–1924), and Franklin D. Roosevelt (1882–1945), 1913. President Wilson, in white trousers and dark jacket, speaks while Secretary of State Bryan, to the president's right, and Assistant Secretary of the Navy Roosevelt, at the far right of the picture, look on. Wilson spoke proudly of his "missionary diplomacy," for he believed that "every nation needs to be drawn into the tutelage of America." To achieve this goal, Wilson sent more U.S. warships into more Caribbean harbors than did any other president. (Franklin D. Roosevelt Library)

in an assault on constitutional government."[91] The president thereafter treated with Mexico through special emissaries, only one of whom spoke fluent Spanish.

In August one such representative, John Lind, arrived in Mexico City. A rabid anti-Catholic and former governor of Minnesota without diplomatic experience, Lind delivered Wilson's proposal for an armistice between Huerta's federalist troops and all revolutionary groups, "an early and free election," and Huerta's promise not to run for president. In exchange, the United States pledged recognition and aid to "the administration chosen and set up . . . in the way and on the conditions suggested." With sublime arrogance, Woodrow Wilson wondered: "Can Mexico give the civilized world a satisfactory reason for rejecting our good offices?"[92] "Where in the hell does he get the right to say who shall or shall not be President of Mexico," wrote one Mexican after Wilson's "counsels" were rebuffed.[93] After this snub, Woodrow Wilson announced a restrained policy of "watchful waiting."[94]

Undeterred, Huerta in October dissolved an unruly legislature, arrested its members, and held a special election, which returned an entirely submissive congress ready to extend his presidency indefinitely. Wilson then turned to Carranza in northern Mexico, sending the same proposal Huerta's foreign minister had rejected in August. Equally nationalistic, Carranza contemptuously refused Wilsonian mediation and rejected any solution short of his own triumph. Wilson informed the other powers in November of his policy "to isolate General Huerta entirely . . . and so to force him out." If such pressure failed to induce Huerta's retirement, he promised "less peaceful means to put him out."[95]

Most European powers, especially Germany, had recognized Huerta in defiance of Wilson. "Good. Finally unity against the Yankee," the kaiser had noted in July 1913.[96] The British, however, their capital investments in Mexico ranking second only to those of the United States and their navy relying on Mexican oil, did not want to antagonize Wilson, with tensions mounting in Europe. The British Foreign Office therefore notified Huerta that it would not support him against the United States, and urged him to resign—all the while viewing Wilson's policies as "most impractical and unreasonable."[97]

With British compliance assured, Wilson lifted the U.S. arms embargo in February 1914 and permitted large quantities of arms to flow to both factions. As Carranza's resupplied forces pushed south, the president sent U.S. naval vessels to the oil-producing town of Tampico on the Gulf of Mexico. On April 9, at Tampico, Huerta's troops arrested several American sailors loading gasoline aboard a whaleboat docked provocatively near the Mexican outpost. The Mexican colonel in charge quickly disavowed the arrests, freed the sailors, and apologized orally. The hotheaded U.S. squadron commander, Rear Admiral Henry T. Mayo, demanded a formal twenty-one-gun salute because Mexico had insulted the flag. Using Huerta's rejection of the Mayo ultimatum as justification, the president on April 20 requested congressional approval to use armed force "to obtain from General Huerta and his adherents the fullest recognition of the rights and dignity of the United States."[98] Rather than protect American-owned oil fields at Tampico, Wilson ordered U.S. warships to the port of Veracruz to stop a German arms shipment intended for Huerta.

On April 21, 1914, 800 American sailors and marines landed. Huerta's troops withdrew, but cadets from the naval academy, joined by prisoners liberated from jails and other irregulars, put up a bloody resistance. Nineteen Americans and several hundred Mexicans died. An anguished Wilson bemoaned that "it was I who ordered those young men to their deaths."[99] Although calculated to undermine Huerta, "the capture of Veracruz nearly united Mexicans behind him . . . [because] Mexicans, believing their independence endangered, rushed to enlist in Huerta's army."[100] Rejecting advice from his military advisers, who wanted to march to Mexico City, Wilson accepted mediation when proposed by Argentina, Brazil, and Chile (the ABC powers) on April 25.

A month later, representatives of the United States, Huerta, and the ABC powers met on the Canadian side of Niagara Falls. Wilson refused to discuss the evacuation of Veracruz or Tampico, a major reason for convening the conference. He sought instead "the entire elimination of General Huerta."[101] On July 2 the jilted mediators adjourned, two weeks later Huerta fled to Europe, and on August 20 a triumphant Carranza paraded before enthusiastic throngs in Mexico City.

The Constitutionalist triumph did not last. One of Carranza's northern generals, Francisco (Pancho) Villa, soon broke from the ranks, marched south, and in December occupied Mexico City. Wilson saw Villa as "the only instrument of civilization in Mexico" whose "firm authority allows him to create order and to educate the turbulent masses of peons so prone to pillage."[102] Because Villa had not criticized the U.S. assault on Veracruz, the president eased arms exports to him and refused to recognize Carranza. To prevent a military clash with any Mexican faction, all American troops withdrew from Veracruz on November 23, 1914. Once again, Wilson watched and waited.

Relations remained tense during early 1915. Carranza's forces gradually drove Villa north, but in the process Mexico City became a no-man's-land, with bread riots and starvation threatening its inhabitants, including 2,500 Americans and 23,000 other foreign residents. Further complications arose along the Mexico-U.S. borderland, especially in southern Texas, where the massive influx of refugees and revolutionaries exacerbated local tensions between Anglos and *Tejanos.* The Plan of San Diego, an anarchist manifesto in early 1915, demanded return of all lands "robbed in a most perfidious manner," execution of every North American "over sixteen years of age," restoration of Indian lands, and sovereign territory for blacks.[103] The ensuing raids and counterraids turned south Texas into a war zone as vigilantes and Texas rangers killed at least 150 Mexicans. A new verb—"rangered"—described summary treatment of suspects by Texas authorities.[104] Preoccupied by the *Lusitania* crisis with Germany after May 1915 (see page 68), Wilson reluctantly concluded that "Carranza will somehow have to be digested."[105] With American oil fields under Carranza's protection, Wilson extended de facto recognition to the Constitutionalist regime in June 1915, permitted arms exports (while banning them to opponents), and beefed up the U.S. military presence along the border.

Egged on by German agents who envisaged a Mexican-American war as "a noose . . . to tie the United States to the American continent," Villa denounced *Carranzistas* as "vassals" of the United States.[106] In the predawn hours of March 9, 1916, Villa led a band of *Villistas* across the border into Columbus, New Mexico, initiating a battle that left seventeen Americans and more than a hundred Mexicans dead. Within hours of the attack, Wilson unleashed the Punitive Expedition of 7,000 soldiers, commanded by General John J. Pershing, which penetrated 350 miles into Mexico in a vain search for Pancho Villa. Even though, as Pershing reported, "the natives are not generally arming to oppose us," a clash with *Carranzista* troops occurred at Carrizal in June 1916.[107]

Carranza kept up drumfire demands for U.S. withdrawal, but Wilson hesitated for fear of appearing weak during a presidential election year. Just prior to Germany's resumption of unrestricted submarine warfare, however, Wilson ordered Pershing's troops to disengage; all left Mexico by February 5, 1917. In late February, the secret Zimmermann telegram, proposing an anti-American alliance between Germany and Mexico (and possibly including Japan), came into the hands of the State Department, courtesy of British intelligence. This German ploy accelerated Wilson's movement toward full diplomatic relations with Carranza's government. The United States extended de jure recognition on August 31, 1917, in order to ensure Mexican neutrality during the fight against Germany. After four futile years, Wilson had finally given up trying to tutor the Mexicans.

Francisco (Pancho) Villa (1878–1923). The intelligent, dedicated revolutionary nationalist bedeviled both Mexico and the United States. His daring raid on an American town was calculated to outrage President Wilson, whom he mocked as "an evangelizing professor of philosophy who is destroying the independence of a friendly people." (W. H. Horne postcard. Southwest Collection, El Paso Public Library)

Japan, China, and Dollar Diplomacy in Asia

Managing Asian affairs proved even more difficult. Secretary of State John Hay's Open Door notes did not prevent the further humiliation of China. During the Boxer Rebellion, Russia stationed 175,000 troops in Manchuria and demanded exclusive rights from China, including a commercial monopoly. Roosevelt and Hay acquiesced because the Open Door had "always recognized the exceptional position

"Spread-eagleism" in China. The missionary teacher Grace Roberts teaches a Bible class in 1903 in Manchuria. Americanism and religious work, flag and missionary, became partners. The mission force was feminized—the majority of missionaries were women. (By permission of the Houghton Library, Harvard University)

of Russia" in Manchuria and had merely sought the commercial freedom "guaranteed to us by . . . the whole civilized world."[108] Washington retreated because Roosevelt realized that the American people would not fight for nebulous principles of Chinese integrity in Manchuria. He thought it folly "to play the role of an Asian power without military power."[109]

Japan viewed the question quite differently. Russia blocked Japanese economic expansion into Manchuria, posed a potential naval menace, and endangered the Japanese position in Korea. Tokyo covered its flanks with an Anglo-Japanese Alliance in 1902 and prepared for war. On February 8, 1904, the Japanese navy destroyed Russia's Asian fleet in a surprise attack at Port Arthur. At first Roosevelt cheered privately, "for Japan is playing our game," but as the enormity of Japanese victories became apparent he hoped for peace "on terms which will not mean the creation of either a yellow peril or a Slav peril."[110] By spring 1905, Japanese soldiers had taken Mukden, where Russia lost 97,000 men. Revolutionary stirrings had hit St. Petersburg, and Admiral Nakagori Togo had sunk the Russian Baltic fleet. "The Russian bubble has been pretty thoroughly pricked," TR noted.[111] On May 31, Japanese envoy Kogoro Takahira requested Roosevelt "directly and entirely of his own motion and initiative to invite the two belligerents to come together" for direct peace negotiations.[112]

Hoping to balance the belligerents "so that each may have a moderate action on the other" and thus protect U.S. interests in the Pacific and Asia, Roosevelt invited Japanese and Russian diplomats to meet at Portsmouth, New Hampshire, in August 1905.[113] Japan demanded Russia's leasehold on the Liaodong Peninsula and the railroad running from Harbin to Port Arthur, evacuation of Russian troops from Manchuria, and Japan's control of Korea. The Russians quickly conceded these points but rejected demands for an indemnity and cession of the island of Sakhalin. Roosevelt broke the deadlock by proposing division of Sakhalin and agreement "in principle" on an indemnity. Tsar Nicholas II agreed to partition the island but "not a kopeck of compensation."[114] Japan yielded and in late August signed a peace treaty. Roosevelt had earned the Nobel Peace Prize.

The Roosevelt administration's search for equipoise in East Asia neither began nor ended at Portsmouth. As early as March 1904, TR had conceded to Japan a relationship with Korea "just like we have with Cuba."[115] Secretary of War Taft reaffirmed the concession with Prime Minister Taro Katsura on July 27, 1905. In the Taft-Katsura "agreed memorandum of conversation," Japan denied any designs on the Philippines, and Taft thereby put an American "seal on the death warrant of an independent Korea."[116] A year later the Japanese reopened southern Manchuria to foreign and American trade but discouraged foreign capital investments. Japan formally annexed Korea in 1910.

This studied attempt to balance interests augured well for continued Japanese-American cordiality, until a dispute in California abruptly undercut Rooseveltian diplomacy. On October 11, 1906, the San Francisco School Board created a special "Oriental Public School" for all Japanese, Chinese, and Korean children. Japan immediately protested, and TR denounced the "infernal fools in California" whose exclusion of Japanese from all other public schools was "as foolish as if conceived by the mind of a Hottentot."[117] Given existing federal-state jurisdictions, however, he could do little more than rail against the recalcitrant school board, apply political pressure to the California legislature to prevent statewide discriminatory measures, and propose legislation to naturalize Japanese residing permanently in the United States. Defending segregation, the *San Francisco Examiner* editorialized: "Californians do not want their growing daughters to be intimate in daily school contact with Japanese young men. Is this remarkable?"[118] Always the political realist, Roosevelt accepted what he personally disliked and sought accommodation with Japan. In February 1907, he reached a "Gentlemen's Agreement" with Tokyo, sharply restricting Japanese immigration on a voluntary basis.

Because "the Japanese jingoes are . . . about as bad as ours," the president shrewdly pressed for more battleships and fortification of Hawai'i and the vulnerable Philippines, now America's "heel of Achilles," so that the United States would "be ready for anything that comes."[119] He also dramatized the importance of a strong navy to Congress and to Japan by ordering the battle fleet in 1907 to the Pacific and around the world. An armada of sixteen battleships steamed out of Hampton Roads, Virginia. Germany's kaiser predicted that U.S. warships in the Pacific "will upset all British and Japanese calculations."[120] Just after the "Great White Fleet" visited Tokyo

Elihu Root (1845–1937).
Root served as secretary of state
(1905–1909). He helped devise
methods for managing the
American empire. (Library of
Congress)

in October 1908, Ambassador Takahira received instructions to reach an agreement with the United States recognizing the Pacific Ocean as an open avenue of trade, pledging the integrity of Japanese and American insular possessions in the Pacific, and promising equal opportunity in China. The ensuing Root-Takahira declaration of November 30, 1908, seemed to restore Japanese-American harmony.

Conflicting Japanese-American goals toward China spoiled the new epoch. Despite the Open Door notes, American commerce with China stalled during the Roosevelt era, in part because of resurgent nationalism. When Congress barred Chinese immigration in 1904, the Chinese staged a short-lived boycott of American goods. A protest song against "American Flour-Made Mooncakes" became popular in Chinese cities.[121] As the historian Eileen Scully has noted, moreover, prostitution flourished in China's treaty ports, conducted by "American sex workers and their male compatriots." This illegitimate China trade ("deeply corrupt, overtly predatory, transnational, transracial, conducted without regard to a 'national interest' ") undercut the gains of legitimate American commerce in China.[122] Because Roosevelt viewed the Chinese as passive and effete, "sunk in Oriental stagnation and corruption," he placed strategic interests first and refused to antagonize Japan over China.[123]

Taft thought otherwise. Instead of a decrepit China in decay, Taft envisaged expanded trade with a "young China, rousing from a centuries-old slumber and rubbing the sand of its past from its eyes."[124] During a 1905 trip to East Asia, Taft met the intensely anti-Japanese American consul general in Mukden, Willard Straight. Two years later Straight proposed the creation of a Manchurian bank, to be financed by the American railroad magnate E. H. Harriman. He condemned the Root-Takahira agreement as "a terrible diplomatic blunder," because it accepted Japan's exploitation of Manchuria.[125] Under Taft, Straight and the State Department quickly inspired several New York banks to form a combination, headed by J. P. Morgan, to serve as the official agency of American railroad investment in China. As acting chief of the department's new Far Eastern Division, Straight demanded admission of the American bankers into a European banking consortium undertaking construction of the Huguang Railway linking Beijing and Guangzhou (Canton). Straight then resigned from the State Department to become the Morgan group's roving representative.

In November 1909, Washington had proposed to Britain the neutralization of Manchurian railroads through a large international loan to China for the purchase of the lines. Britain, however, joined both Japan and Russia to reject the proposal. Instead of an open door in Manchuria, Secretary of State Knox had "nailed that door closed with himself on the outside."[126] In fall 1910, an agreement expanded the Huguang Railway consortium to include American bankers, but the Chinese Revolution broke out in May 1911 against the Manchu dynasty and foreign interests and delaying railroad construction until 1913. "Dollar diplomacy," Straight ruefully admitted, "made no friends in the Hukuang matter."[127]

Hoping to reap tangible benefits by dissociating from the other powers, President Wilson and Secretary Bryan repudiated American participation in the international consortium on March 18, 1913. Failure to cancel the loan, Wilson believed, would have cost the United States "the proud position . . . secured when Secretary Hay stood for the open door in China after the Boxer Uprising." Wilson extended formal diplomatic recognition to the Chinese Republic on May 6.[128] He had thereby renewed America's commitment to the political integrity of China, a goal pragmatically abandoned by Roosevelt, unsuccessfully resuscitated by Taft, and consistently opposed by Japan.

Events at home soon made Wilson's Asian policy resemble Taft's more than Roosevelt's. In April 1913, Democratic and Progressive politicians placed before the California legislature a bill denying residents "ineligible to citizenship" the right to own land. The measure struck directly at the 50,000 Japanese living in California. Racist passions erupted, with one farmer recoiling from the prospect of racial intermarriage: "What is that baby? It isn't a Japanese. It isn't white. It is a germ of the mightiest problem . . . that will make the black problem of the South look white."[129] Basically sharing the Californians' anti-Japanese prejudices, and sensitive to states' rights, Wilson nonetheless sent Bryan to Sacramento to beg for a less harsh statute. But the California legislature passed the offensive bill on May 3, 1913. When Japan protested the "unfair and intentionally racially discriminatory" measure, Wilson and Bryan lamely argued that one state's legislation did not constitute a "national discriminatory policy."[130]

Wilson's antipathy toward Japan reappeared in fall 1914 when Japan declared war on Germany, seized the German Pacific islands north of the equator, and swept across China's Shandong Peninsula to capture the German leasehold of Jiaozhou. "When there is a fire in a jeweller's shop," a Japanese diplomat theorized, "the neighbours cannot be expected to refrain from helping themselves."[131] Tokyo immediately followed with the Twenty-One Demands of January 18, 1915, creating a virtual protectorate over all of China. Despite stout resistance by Beijing, Japan emerged with extensive political and economic rights in Shandong, southern Manchuria, and Mongolia. Preoccupied with Mexico and the *Lusitania* crisis, the Wilson administration refused to recognize Japan's gains, which amounted to a repudiation of the Open Door policy.

Wilson's nonrecognition policy ran counter to secret treaties in which the European Allies promised to support Japan's conquests at the peace conference after World War I. The United States soon compromised. In an agreement with Viscount Kikujiro Ishii, signed November 2, 1917, Secretary Lansing admitted that "territorial propinquity creates special relationships between countries, and consequently . . . Japan has special interests in China," while Ishii pledged his nation's dedication to the Open Door and integrity of China.[132] The Wilson administration also revived the international banking consortium as the only way to check further unilateral Japanese economic penetration of China proper. The wheel had turned full circle for Wilson. Like Taft before him, Wilson failed to protect China's fragile sovereignty without conciliating or blocking Japan.

Anglo-American Rapprochement and Empire-Building

American policies toward Asia and Latin America often fell short of their proclaimed goals because of the pseudoscientific race thinking of the early twentieth century. Americans viewed Asians as "inscrutable and somnolent," depicted Latin Americans as black children or alluring maidens, imagined Africa as the "dark continent" of "savage beasts and beastly savages," and referred to Filipinos as "our little brown brothers,"

John Bull in Need of Friends. Battered by criticism over its war against the Boers in South Africa and challenged by a rising Germany, Great Britain found a new friend in the United States. Not all Britons embraced Anglo-American affinity. "Only 1/4 of the population of the United States are what you might call natives," wrote a British admiral in 1901. "The rest are Germans, Irish, Italians, and the scum of the earth! all of them hating the English like poison." (*Des Moines Leader* in *Literary Digest,* 1901)

and these biased stereotypes inevitably impeded statecraft and aroused resentment from Bogotá to Beijing, from Managua to Manila.[133] Yet such Darwinist racial attitudes also facilitated much closer relations between the United States and Great Britain. As the historian Michael H. Hunt has written about the ideology of the time, victory "in the international competition among the races . . . might not go to the refined and peaceful peoples but rather to the amoral, the cunning, the fecund, and the power hungry." Thus "Anglo-Americans might then need to cultivate a sense of solidarity and a capacity for cooperation."[134] Theodore Roosevelt certainly thought so when he predicted that the "twentieth century" would "still be the century" of "men who speak English."[135] So too did the British, as shown by their willingness to accept exclusive U.S. control of a canal in Panama. Also prompted by Britain's search for allies against Germany (evidenced in the Anglo-Japanese Alliance of 1902 and the Entente Cordiale with France in 1904), London's pursuit of "the most cordial and constant co-operation" with the United States led to a celebrated "great rapprochement."[136]

The new Anglo-American affinity, however, nearly dissolved in 1903 when the Alaska boundary controversy, which stemmed from Canadian claims to large areas of the Alaskan panhandle, strained relations. As the power responsible for the Do-minion's foreign relations (Canada did not establish a foreign office until 1909), Britain found itself backing Ottawa's dubious contention that much of the panhan-dle's coastline actually belonged to Canada. Roosevelt thought Canada had less right "than the United States did to Cornwall or Kent."[137] The president refused arbitra-tion and sent 800 soldiers to Alaska to awe his opponents. London finally agreed in January 1903 to an American proposal for a mixed boundary commission composed of six jurists, three from each side. Taking no chances, Roosevelt appointed Sena-tor Henry Cabot Lodge and Secretary Root, hardly disinterested judges, to the commission. He informally warned London he would run the line himself if the commissioners failed to agree. One British commissioner sided with the Americans, and on October 20, 1903, by a vote of 4 to 2, the commission officially decided for the United States. The British "made the inevitable choice to please a power ten times the size of Canada and with more than ten times the wealth."[138]

Canadian-American relations did improve with the Migratory Bird Treaty of 1916. Conservationists and scientists, alarmed by a decline in North American birds caused by reckless sport and commercial hunting, pressed for this agreement under the principle of "common property resources." The death of the last passenger pi-geon, in the Cincinnati Zoo in 1914, symbolized the crisis. Because the treaty re-stricted hunting, especially during the mating season, it sparked some opposition in the United States. Member of Congress John Tillman, a Democrat from Arkansas who defended duck hunting in gendered terms, cried that the accord "should be bedecked with skirts" because it "would feminize our boys."[139] The bird population increased, and such wildlife protection, also evident in the Inland Fisheries Treaty (1908) and the North Pacific Fur Seal Convention (1911), became landmarks in in-ternational environmental history.

Anglo-American entente also characterized the settlement of the North At-lantic fisheries dispute. Since 1782, American fishermen had insisted on retaining their pre-Revolutionary privileges off Canada's Newfoundland. Indeed, "a gilded wooden cod" still hung from the ceiling of the Massachusetts State House.[140] The modus vivendi of 1888, under which they had fished for several years, collapsed in 1905 when Newfoundland placed restrictions on American fishing vessels. Senator Lodge cried for warships to protect his constituents' livelihood. Instead, Roosevelt proposed, and London accepted, arbitration at The Hague Tribunal. In 1910 the tribunal ruled that Britain could oversee fishing off Newfoundland if it established reasonable regulations, that a fisheries commission would hear cases, and that Amer-icans could fish in large bays if they remained three miles from shore. This com-promise defused the oldest dispute in American foreign relations and symbolized London's political withdrawal from the Western Hemisphere.

The naval retreat had occurred earlier, when the Admiralty abolished the North Atlantic station based at Jamaica. After 1902 the Royal Navy patrolled the Caribbean only with an annual visit by a token squadron of cruisers. Admiral Sir John Fisher, who oversaw this historic retrenchment, wanted to concentrate his heavy ships in the English Channel and North Sea as monitors of the growing German navy. He regarded the United States as "a kindred state with whom we shall never have a parricidal war."[141]

Even the aggressive hemispheric diplomacy of Taft and Wilson did not undermine Anglo-American rapprochement. Britain criticized both dollar diplomacy in Latin America and Wilson's quixotic efforts to dislodge Huerta. But Foreign Secretary Sir Edward Grey tersely laid to rest all talk of a challenge: "His Majesty's Government cannot with any prospect of success embark upon an active counterpolicy to that of the United States, or constitute themselves the champions of Mexico or any of these republics against the United States."[142] In reciprocation, Wilson protected British oil interests and made it a "point of honor" to eliminate the one potentially dangerous British grievance inherited from his predecessor.[143] Late in the Taft administration, Congress had exempted American intercoastal shippers from payment of Panama Canal tolls. British opinion condemned this shifting of canal maintenance costs to other users. Because it unfairly discriminated against foreign shipping, Wilson persuaded Congress to revoke the law in June 1914.

In the end, rapprochement meant mutual respect for each other's empires. Roosevelt, for example, encouraged London to frustrate native aspirations for independence in India, while the British accepted the American suppression of the Filipinos and U.S. hegemony in Latin America. American leaders usually spoke favorably of independence for colonial peoples—but independence only after long-term tutelage to make them "civilized" enough to govern. In 1910 in Egypt, where Roosevelt applauded Britain's "great work for civilization," the ex-president even lectured Muslim nationalists about Christian respect for womanhood.[144] In unstable Liberia, where the United States in 1912 instituted a financial receivership in the African nation like that in the Dominican Republic, the British encouraged Washington to use a strong hand in what London called America's "protectorate."[145]

While building an empire, policymakers largely adhered to the tradition of aloofness from continental European political and military affairs. Even Roosevelt overtly tampered only once with Europe's balance of power. In 1904 France acquiesced in British control of Egypt in exchange for primacy in Morocco. A year later, Germany decided to test the solidity of the new Anglo-French entente by challenging France's claims in Morocco. The kaiser belligerently demanded a German political role in Morocco, which France at once refused. After a brief European war scare, in which Britain stood by its ally, Germany asked Roosevelt to induce France and England to convene a conference to settle Morocco's future. Worried about Kaiser Wilhelm's "violent and often wholly irrational zigzags," Roosevelt accepted the personal invitation only after assuring Paris that his "sympathies . . . at bottom [were] with France."[146] During the conference, held in early 1906 at Algeciras, Spain, Roosevelt devised a pro-French compromise and persuaded the kaiser to accept it. This political intervention isolated Germany and reinforced the Anglo-French entente, but it generated criticism at home. Roosevelt's successors made sure they did not violate the Ameri-

Naval Arms Race. The international naval competition in the early twentieth century was foreboding. Disarmament talks at The Hague Conferences and arbitration treaties did not curb the arms buildup. Roosevelt's decision to send the "Great White Fleet" around the world in 1907–1908 may have encouraged both Japan and Germany to speed up their naval programs. (*Detroit News* in *Literary Digest*, 1904)

can policy of nonentanglement with Europe during the more ominous second Moroccan and Balkan crises preceding the First World War.

Nonentanglement also doomed the sweeping arbitration treaties that Secretary Hay negotiated with several world powers. When the Senate attached crippling amendments, Roosevelt withdrew the treaties because they did "not in the smallest degree facilitate settlements by arbitration."[147] After 1905 Secretary Root persuaded Roosevelt to accept watered-down bilateral arbitration treaties, and Secretary Bryan later negotiated a series of supplementary "cooling-off" treaties by which nations pledged to refrain from war during international investigations of serious disputes. None of these arrangements, however, effectively bound signatories, and like the Permanent Court of Arbitration at The Hague, they represented a backwater in international diplomacy. Ambassador Whitelaw Reid compared U.S. participation in the Hague Peace Conference of 1907 to a farmer taking his hog to market: "That hog didn't weigh as much as I expected he would, and I always knew he wouldn't."[148]

The mainstream of American foreign policy between 1900 and 1914 flowed through the Panama Canal, a momentous political, military, and technological achievement. The United States became the unchallenged policeman of the

Caribbean region, empowering Washington, in Taft's words, "to prevent revolutions" so that "we'll have no more."[149] Although German authorities thought that the canal would shift American priorities to Asia and "today's Atlantic fleet will become the Pacific fleet," the United States still lacked the power to challenge Japan or Britain.[150] As Roosevelt understood, the Open Door "completely disappears as soon as a powerful nation determines to disregard it."[151] One military officer told Congress in 1910: "We have grown from a little frontier army to one spread all over the world—in America, Puerto Rico, Hawai'i, Alaska, the Philippines, and sometimes in Cuba—and we have not got the officers and men to do it."[152]

American insensitivity to the nationalism of other peoples became another imperial legacy. Filipino resistance to American domination, Cuban anger against the Platt Amendment, Colombian outrage over Panama, and Mexican rejection of Wilsonian intervention bore witness to the depth of nationalistic sentiments. Like the European powers who were carving up Asia, Africa, and the Middle East, the United States was developing its empire and subjugating peoples and compromising their sovereignty in Latin America and the Pacific. As a Panamanian diplomat later explained: "When you hit a rock with an egg, the egg breaks. Or when you hit an egg with a rock, the egg breaks. The United States is the rock. Panama is the egg. In either case, the egg breaks."[153] With the exception of the Virgin Islands, purchased from Denmark for $25 million in 1917 to forestall any wartime German seizure, the empire grew little from outright territorial gains. It was, instead, an informal empire administered by troops, financial advisers, and reformers who showed contempt for native peoples' culture, politics, and economies through a paternalistic discourse. The U.S. Army marching song—"The Monkeys Have No Tails in Zamboanga"—expressed soldierly disdain for the Filipino populace.

In contrast, Puerto Rico seemed the "good" territorial possession, as political cartoons portrayed the populace as a "polite schoolchild, sometimes female, in contrast to ruffian boys" in Cuba and the Philippines.[154] Under the Foraker Act (1900), Puerto Rico and its naval base on Culebra became a "new constitutional animal"—an "unincorporated territory" subject to the will of the U.S. Congress and governed by the War Department (until 1934).[155] In a series of decisions called the Insular Cases (1901–1904), the Supreme Court upheld the Foraker Act, providing Washington with a means to govern people it did not wish to organize as a state. In March 1917, Congress granted Puerto Ricans U.S. citizenship just in time for them to be drafted into the U.S. armed forces in the war against Germany. To this day, Puerto Rico remains a colony, or "commonwealth," and Puerto Ricans remain divided in their views about statehood, independence, and commonwealth status.

The adventures of American foreign relations under an imperial ideology and the male ethos in the years 1900–1914 attracted many capable, well-educated young men to diplomatic service. "It was TR's call to youth which lured me to Washington," the diplomat William Phillips recalled.[156] Career ambassador Joseph C. Grew first gained presidential favor by shooting a tiger in China. Several of these young foreign-service professionals, virtually all graduates of Ivy League colleges, including Phillips, Grew, Willard Straight, former Rough Rider Henry P. Fletcher, and soldier-diplomat Frank R. McCoy, lived in an exclusive bachelors' townhouse at

1718 H Street during their Washington service. Known among themselves as "the Family," these youthful professionals blended camaraderie with careers and "became the elite or legendary 'inner circle' of the State Department" for the next forty years.[157] The New York attorney Henry L. Stimson, himself a protégé of Elihu Root, served as secretary of war under Taft (1911–1913) and continued this tradition of recruiting some of the brightest public servants in a succession of high-level posts through the end of World War II.

Cultural, or public, foreign relations also flourished during these years. Just as Buffalo Bill Cody's Wild West Show had "hyped" American cultural myths abroad since the 1890s, Wilbur Wright's airplane tour of Europe in 1908 set records, thrilled crowds, and impressed military strategists.[158] The cruise of the "Great White Fleet" provided as much pageantry as statecraft—"a feast, a frolic, or a fight," as Admiral Robley D. Evans put it.[159] Colonial subjects became popular on college campuses, as anthropologists and ethnographers offered courses on "Savage Childhood" and "Peoples of the Philippines."[160] When academic exchanges with European universities expanded after 1900, Harvard University commemorated its new Germanic Museum by bestowing an honorary doctorate on Prince Henry of Prussia (the kaiser's brother)—"a simple, natural person who got used in a day to our troublesome democratic ways."[161]

Hundreds of thousands of U.S. tourists ("the world's wanderers") traveled abroad clutching their Baedeker guidebooks, spending American dollars, and sometimes acquiring foreign titles through marriage, as in the case of Jennie Jerome and Lord Randolph Churchill, whose son Winston valued Anglo-American partnership.[162] Civic leaders took pride in hosting the Olympic Games in St. Louis in 1904, hailed an American victory in the 1908 Round-the-World Automobile race, became weekend frontiersmen after organizing the Boy Scouts of America in 1910, and cheered the gold medals won by Native American Jim Thorpe at the Stockholm Olympics in 1912. Just as they seemed to take up the great game of empire from Great Britain, so too did Americans become proficient in that most diplomatic of athletic competitions, the royal and ancient Scottish sport of golf. For some Americans, true Anglo-American entente did not occur until young Francis Ouimet bested British champions Harry Vardon and Ted Ray in the U.S. Open at Brookline, Massachusetts, in 1913.

Yet beneath the glitter lurked danger. Winston Churchill later wrote of living in two different worlds: "the actual, visual world with its peaceful activities" and "a hypothetical world 'beneath the threshold' "—"a world at one moment utterly fantastic, at the next seeming to leap into reality—a world of monstrous shadows moving in convulsive combination through vistas of fathomless catastrophe."[163] Once the world started spinning around Sarajevo, Bosnia, it became impossible for the growing American empire to escape the maelstrom of world war.

FURTHER READING FOR THE PERIOD 1900–1914

See studies listed in the last two chapters and Michael C. C. Adams, *The Great Adventure: Male Desire and the Coming of World War I* (1990); A. J. Bacevich, *Diplomat in Khaki* (1989) (General Frank McCoy); William H. Becker, *The Dynamics of Business-Government Relations: Industry and Exports, 1893–1921* (1982); Gail Bederman, *Manliness & Civilization* (1995); Frances A. Boyle, *Foundations of World Order* (1999); Lester H. Brune,

The Origins of American Security Policy (1981); Richard D. Challener, *Admirals, Generals, and American Foreign Policy, 1898–1914* (1973); Kendrick A. Clements, *William Jennings Bryan* (1982); Kurkpatrick Dorsey, *The Dawn of Conservation Diplomacy: U.S.–Canadian Wildlife Protection Treaties in the Progressive Era* (1999); Lloyd C. Gardner, *Safe for Democracy: The Anglo-American Response to Revolution, 1913–1923* (1984); Robert E. Hannigan, *The New World Empire* (2002); Robert C. Hilderbrand, *Power and the People: Executive Management of Public Opinion in Foreign Affairs, 1897–1921* (1981); Cyrus Veeser, *A World Safe for Capitalism* (2002); Richard H. Werking, *The Master Architects* (1977) (foreign service); William C. Widenor, *Henry Cabot Lodge and the Search for an American Foreign Policy* (1980); and Mira Wilkins, *The Emergence of Multinational Enterprise: American Business Abroad from the Colonial Era to 1914* (1970).

Theodore Roosevelt is the subject of Howard K. Beale, *Theodore Roosevelt and the Rise of America to World Power* (1956); H. W. Brands, *T.R.* (1997); Richard H. Collin, *Theodore Roosevelt: Culture, Diplomacy, and Expansion* (1985); John M. Cooper, Jr., *The Warrior and the Priest: Woodrow Wilson and Theodore Roosevelt* (1983); Kathleen Dalton, *Theodore Roosevelt* (2002); Thomas G. Dyer, *Theodore Roosevelt and the Idea of Race* (1980); Raymond A. Esthus, *Theodore Roosevelt and the International Rivalries* (1970); Lewis L. Gould, *The Presidency of Theodore Roosevelt* (1991); Frederick W. Marks, *Velvet on Iron* (1979); Edmund Morris, *Theodore Rex* (2001); Natalie A. Naylor et al., eds., *Theodore Roosevelt* (1992); and William N. Tilchin, *Theodore Roosevelt and the British Empire* (1997).

For the Taft administration, see Paolo E. Coletta, *The Presidency of William Howard Taft* (1973); Ralph E. Minger, *William Howard Taft and American Foreign Policy* (1975); and Walter V. Scholes and Marie V. Scholes, *The Foreign Policies of the Taft Administration* (1970).

For Wilson policies, see the next chapter and Frederick S. Calhoun, *Power and Principle: Armed Intervention in Wilsonian Foreign Policy* (1986) and *Uses of Force and Wilsonian Foreign Policy* (1993); Kendrick A. Clements, *The Presidency of Woodrow Wilson* (1990); and Edward S. Kaplan, *U.S. Imperialism in Latin America* (1997) (on Bryan's policies).

U.S. relations with Latin America are examined in Laura Briggs, *Reproducing Empire* (2002) (Puerto Rico); José A. Cabranes, *Citizenship and the American Empire* (1979) (Puerto Rico); Bruce J. Calder, *The Impact of Intervention* (1984) (Dominican Republic); Raymond A. Carr, *Puerto Rico* (1984); Arturo M. Carrión, *Puerto Rico* (1983); Mark T. Gilderhus, *Pan American Visions* (1986) (Wilson); David Healy, *Drive to Hegemony* (1989) and *Gunboat Diplomacy in the Wilson Era* (1976) (Haiti); Warren G. Kneer, *Great Britain and the Caribbean, 1901–1913* (1975); Walter LaFeber, *Inevitable Revolutions* (1993) (Central America); Lester D. Langley, *Struggle for the American Mediterranean* (1976), *The United States and the Caribbean, 1900–1970* (1980), and *The Banana Wars* (2002); Lester D. Langley and Thomas Schoonover, *The Banana Men* (1995); Nancy Mitchell, *The Danger of Dreams: German and American Imperialism in Latin America* (1999); Dana Munro, *Intervention and Dollar Diplomacy* (1964); Thomas F. O'Brien, *The Revolutionary Mission: American Business in Latin America* (1996); Fredrick B. Pike, *The United States and Latin America* (1992); Brenda G. Plummer, *Haiti and the United States* (1992) and *Haiti and the Great Powers, 1902–1915* (1988); Mary Renda, *Taking Haiti* (2001); Emily Rosenberg, *Financial Missionaries to the World* (1999) (dollar diplomacy); Hans Schmidt, *The United States Occupation of Haiti, 1915–1934* (1971); Thomas D. Schoonover, *The United States in Central America, 1860–1911* (1991); David Sheinin, *Searching for Authority* (1998) (Argentina) and *Beyond the Ideal* (2000) (Pan Americanism); Lars Schoultz, *Beneath the United States* (1998); and Richard P. Tucker, *Insatiable Appetite* (2000).

For the Panama Canal, see Richard H. Collin, *Theodore Roosevelt's Caribbean* (1990); Michael L. Conniff, *Panama and the United States* (1992); and *Panama and the United States* (2001); James Howe, *The People Who Would Not Kneel* (1998); Richard L. Lael, *Arrogant Diplomacy* (1987); Walter LaFeber, *The Panama Canal* (1989); John Lindsay-Poland, *Emperors in the Jungle* (2003); John Major, *Prize Possession* (1993); David McCullough, *The Path Between the Seas* (1977); and Stephen J. Randall, *Colombia and the United States* (1992).

U.S. hegemony in Cuba is discussed in David Healy, *The United States in Cuba, 1898–1902* (1963); José M. Hernández, *Cuba and the United States* (1993); James H. Hitchman, *Leonard Wood and Cuban Independence, 1898–1902* (1971); Allan R. Millett, *The Politics of Intervention* (1968); and Louis A. Pérez, Jr.,

Cuba and the United States (2003), *On Becoming Cuban* (1999), and *Cuba Under the Platt Amendment, 1902–1934* (1986).

Relations with Mexico are treated in Jonathan C. Brown, *Oil and Revolution in Mexico* (1993); Jules Davids, *American Political and Economic Penetration of Mexico, 1877–1920* (1976); Jorge Domínguez and Rafael Fernandez de Castro, *United States and Mexico* (2001); Joseph M. Gilbert, *Revolution from Without* (1982); Mark T. Gilderhus, *Diplomacy and Revolution* (1977); Kenneth J. Grieb, *The United States and Huerta* (1969); John M. Hart, *Revolutionary Mexico* (1988) and *Empire and Revolution* (2002); Friedrich Katz, *The Life and Times of Pancho Villa* (1998) and *The Secret War in Mexico* (1981); Alan Knight, *U.S.–Mexican Relations, 1910–1940* (1987); Daniel Nugent, ed., *Rural Revolt in Mexico and U.S. Intervention* (1988); Ramón E. Ruíz, *The Great Rebellion* (1980); Karl M. Schmitt, *Mexico and the United States, 1821–1973* (1974); Joseph A. Stout, Jr., *Border Conflict* (1999); Paul J. Vanderwood and Frank N. Samponaro, *Border Fury* (1988); and Josefina Vázquez and Lorenzo Meyer, *The United States and Mexico* (1985).

For America's interactions with Asia and China, see William R. Braisted, *The United States Navy in the Pacific, 1897–1909* (1958) and *1909–1922* (1971); Jongsuk Chay, *Diplomacy of Asymmetry* (1990) (Korea); Warren I. Cohen, *America's Response to China* (2000); Daniel M. Crane and Thomas A. Breslin, *An Ordinary Relationship: American Opposition to Republican Revolution in China* (1986); Jonathan Goldstein et al., eds., *America Views China* (1991); Michael H. Hunt, *The Making of a Special Relationship* (1983); Akira Iriye, *Across the Pacific* (1967); Delber L. McKee, *Chinese Exclusion Versus the Open Door Policy, 1900–1906* (1976); Dennis L. Noble, *The Eagle and the Dragon* (1990); Noel H. Pugach, *Paul S. Reinsch* (1979); Eileen Scully, *Bargaining with the State from Afar* (2001) (Extraterritoriality); and Guanhua Wang, *In Search of Justice* (2002).

Japanese-American relations are studied in Burton F. Beers, *Vain Endeavor: Robert Lansing's Attempt to End the American-Japanese Rivalry* (1962); Raymond A. Esthus, *Double Eagle and Rising Sun* (1988) (Portsmouth) and *Theodore Roosevelt and Japan* (1966); Akira Iriye, *Pacific Estrangement* (1972); Walter LaFeber, *The Clash* (1997); Charles E. Neu, *An Uncertain Friendship* (1967) and *The Troubled Encounter* (1975); and E. P. Trani, *The Treaty of Portsmouth* (1969).

American missionaries, especially in Asia, are covered in Kenton J. Clymer, *Protestant Missionaries in the Philippines, 1898–1916* (1986); Gael Graham, *Gender, Culture, and Christianity* (1995); Patricia R. Hill, *The World Their Household* (1985) (women); Jane Hunter, *The Gospel of Gentility* (1984) (women in China); Xi Lian, *The Conversion of Missionaries* (1997); and James Reed, *The Missionary Mind and American East Asia Policy, 1911–1915* (1983).

U.S. relations with Europe and Great Britain, and rivalry with Germany, are discussed in Stuart Anderson, *Race and Rapprochement* (1981); A. E. Campbell, *Great Britain and the United States, 1895–1903* (1960); Charles S. Campbell, *Anglo-American Understanding, 1898–1903* (1957); David Dimbleby and David Reynolds, *An Ocean Apart* (1989); Holger H. Herwig, *Politics of Frustration: The United States in German Naval Planning, 1889–1941* (1976); Manfred Jonas, *The United States and Germany* (1984); B. J. C. McKercher and Lawrence Aronson, eds., *The North Atlantic Triangle in a Changing World* (1996); Bradford Perkins, *The Great Rapprochement* (1968); Hans-Jürgen Schröder, ed., *Confrontation and Cooperation* (1993) (Germany); and Frederick F. Travis, *George Kennan and the Russian-American Relationship, 1865–1924* (1990).

The peace movement and the role of The Hague are discussed in Peter Brock, *Pacifism in the United States* (1968); Charles Chatfield, *The American Peace Movement* (1992); Calvin Davis, *The United States and the First Hague Conference* (1962) and *The United States and the Second Hague Peace Conference* (1975); Charles DeBenedetti, *The Peace Reform in American History* (1980); Sondra R. Herman, *Eleven Against War* (1969); Charles F. Howlett and Glen Zeitzer, *The American Peace Movement* (1985); C. Roland Marchand, *The American Peace Movement and Social Reform, 1898–1918* (1973); and David S. Patterson, *Toward a Warless World* (1976).

See also the General Bibliography, the following notes, and Robert L. Beisner, ed., *Guide to American Foreign Relations Since 1600* (2003).

For comprehensive coverage of foreign-relations topics, see the articles in the four-volume *Encyclopedia of U.S. Foreign Relations* (1997), edited by Bruce W. Jentleson and Thomas G. Paterson.

NOTES TO CHAPTER 2

1. All quotations from U.S. Congress, *Diplomatic History of the Panama Canal*, Senate Doc. 474 (1914), pp. 345–363.
2. Quoted in John Major, *Prize Possession* (New York: Cambridge University Press, 1993), p. 45.
3. Elting E. Morison, ed., *The Letters of Theodore Roosevelt* (Cambridge: Harvard University Press, 1951–1954; 8 vols.), II, 1185–1187.
4. James A. Froude quoted in John Lindsay-Poland, *Emperors in the Jungle* (Durham: Duke University Press, 2003), p. 5.
5. *Diplomatic History of the Canal*, p. 261.
6. Quoted in Dwight C. Miner, *The Fight for the Panama Route* (New York: Columbia University Press, 1940), p. 275.
7. Quoted in Henry F. Pringle, *Theodore Roosevelt* (New York: Harcourt, Brace, 1931), p. 311.
8. Quoted in Howard K. Beale, *Theodore Roosevelt and the Rise of America to World Power* (Baltimore: Johns Hopkins Press, 1956), p. 33.
9. Quoted in David McCullough, *The Path Between the Seas* (New York: Simon & Schuster, 1977), p. 333.
10. *New York World*, June 14, 1903.
11. Quoted in Lars Schoultz, *Beneath the United States* (Cambridge: Harvard University Press, 1998), p. 164.
12. Quoted in Thomas Schoonover, "Max Farrand's Memorandum on the U.S. Role in the Panamanian Revolution of 1903," *Diplomatic History*, XII (Fall 1988), 505.
13. Quoted in Stephen J. Randall, *Colombia and the United States* (Athens: University of Georgia Press, 1992), p. 88.
14. Quoted in Lewis L. Gould, *The Presidency of Theodore Roosevelt* (Lawrence: University Press of Kansas, 1991), p. 98.
15. C. F. Adams to Moorfield Story, December 9, 1903, Moorfield Story Papers, Massachusetts Historical Society, Boston; Roosevelt quoted in H. W. Brands, *T.R.* (New York: BasicBooks, 1997), p. 487.
16. Quoted in Walter LaFeber, *The Panama Canal* (New York: Oxford University Press, 1989; updated ed.), pp. 225–226.
17. *New York Times*, March 25, 1911.
18. Quoted in Robert E. Hannigan, *The New World Power* (Philadelphia: University of Pennsylvania Press, 2002), p. 46.
19. Quoted in Wayne A. Wiegand, *Patrician in the Progressive Era* (New York: Garland, 1988), p. 120.
20. Quoted in Stephen R. Rock, *Why Peace Breaks Out* (Chapel Hill: University of North Carolina Press, 1989), p. 132.
21. Quoted in Holger H. Herwig, *Politics of Frustration* (Boston: Little, Brown, 1976), p. 67.
22. Ronald H. Spector, *Professors of War* (Newport, R.I.: Naval War College Press, 1977).
23. John Milton Cooper, Jr., "Progressivism and American Foreign Policy," *Mid-America, LI* (October 1969), 261.
24. Quoted in John Morton Blum, *The Republican Roosevelt* (New York: Atheneum [1954], 1973), p. 127.
25. Quoted in Beale, *Theodore Roosevelt*, p. 77; G. Wallace Chessman, *Theodore Roosevelt and the Politics of Power* (Boston: Little, Brown, 1969), p. 70.
26. Quoted in Frank Ninkovich, *Modernity and Power* (Chicago: University of Chicago Press, 1994), p. 6.
27. Quoted in Beale, *Theodore Roosevelt*, p. 140.
28. Quoted in Judith Papachristou, "American Women and Foreign Policy, 1896–1905," *Diplomatic History*, XIV (Fall 1990), 499, 501, 509.
29. Quoted in Frederick F. Travis, *George Kennan and the Russian-American Relationship, 1865–1924* (Athens: Ohio University Press, 1990), p. 266.
30. Quoted in Ninkovich, *Modernity*, p. 13.
31. Quoted in John Milton Cooper, Jr., *The Warrior and the Priest* (Cambridge: Harvard University Press, 1983), p. 75.
32. Taft quoted in Hannigan, *New World Power*, p. 282.
33. Quoted in Foster Rhea Dulles, "John Hay," in Norman A. Graebner, ed., *An Uncertain Tradition* (New York: McGraw-Hill, 1961), p. 24.
34. Quoted in Richard W. Leopold, *Elihu Root and the Conservative Tradition* (Boston: Little, Brown, 1954), p. 50.
35. Quoted in David H. Burton, *Theodore Roosevelt* (Philadelphia: University of Pennsylvania Press, 1968), p. 97; *Congressional Record*, XXXV (December 3, 1901), 82–83.
36. Quoted in Ralph E. Minger, *William Howard Taft and United States Foreign Policy* (Urbana: University of Illinois Press, 1975), p. 179.
37. Quoted in Ray S. Baker, *Woodrow Wilson* (Garden City, N.Y.: Doubleday, Doran, 1927–1939; 8 vols.), IV, 289.
38. Simon Schama, "The Unloved American," *The New Yorker*, LXXIX (March 10, 2003), 34.
39. Jesus Samprun quoted in David M. Pletcher, *The Diplomacy of Trade and Investment* (Columbia: University of Missouri Press, 1998), p. 393.
40. William Shafter quoted in Louis A. Pérez, Jr., *The War of 1898* (Chapel Hill: University of North Carolina Press, 1898), p. 29; *Foreign Relations, 1898* (Washington, D.C.: Government Printing Office, 1901), pp. lvi–lvii.
41. Quoted in David F. Healy, *The United States in Cuba, 1898–1902* (Madison: University of Wisconsin Press, 1963), p. 133.
42. U.S. Commissioner Robert P. Porter quoted in Louis A. Pérez, Jr., *Cuba and the United States* (Athens: University of Georgia Press, 1997, 2nd ed.), p. 127.
43. *Congressional Record, XXXIV* (February 26, 1901), 3036.
44. Quoted in H. Hagedorn, *Leonard Wood* (New York: Harper, 1931; 2 vols.), I, 362; Healy, *United States in Cuba*, p. 178.
45. Quoted in R. H. Fitzgibbon, *Cuba and the United States, 1900–1935* (New York: Russell & Russell, 1964), p. 112.
46. Quoted in Allan R. Millett, *The Politics of Intervention* (Columbus: Ohio State University Press, 1968), p. 72.
47. Quoted in Burton, *Theodore Roosevelt*, p. 106.
48. James D. Richardson, ed., *A Compilation of the Messages and Papers of the Presidents, 1789–1897* (Washington, D. C.: Government Printing Office, 1896–1899; 10 vols.), X, 7436–7437.
49. Quoted in Schoultz, *Beneath*, p. 201.
50. Quoted in Alistair Hennessy, "The Origins of the Cuban Revolt," in Angel Smith and Emma Davila-Cox, eds., *The Crisis of 1898* (New York: St. Martin's, 1999), p. 85.
51. Fred L. Israel, ed., *The State of the Union Messages* (New York: Chelsea House, 1967; 3 vols.), II, 2038.
52. Morison, *Letters of Roosevelt*, III, 116.
53. William Haggard quoted in Nancy Mitchell, *The Danger of Dreams* (Chapel Hill: University of North Carolina Press, 1999), p. 69.
54. Francis Anthony Boyle, *Foundations of World Order* (Durham: Duke University Press, 1999), p. 81.
55. Quoted in John G. Clifford, "Admiral Dewey and the Germans, 1903," *Mid-America, XLIX* (July 1967), 218.
56. Quoted in Kathleen Dalton, *Theodore Roosevelt* (New York: Knopf, 2002), p. 238.
57. Quoted in David Dimbleby and David Reynolds, *An Ocean Apart* (New York: Vintage, 1989), p. 38.
58. Quoted in Jonas, *United States and Germany*, p. 73.

59. Quoted *ibid.*, p. 420.

60. Quoted in Brands, *T.R.*, p. 524.

61. Quoted in Dexter Perkins, *The Monroe Doctrine, 1867–1907* (Baltimore: Johns Hopkins Press, 1937), p. 420.

62. Quoted in Warren G. Kneer, *Great Britain and the Caribbean, 1901–1913* (East Lansing: Michigan State University Press, 1975), p. 103.

63. Quoted in Cyrus Veeser, "Inventing Dollar Diplomacy," *Diplomatic History, XXVII* (June 2003), 314.

64. Jules Jusserand quoted *ibid.*, p. 320.

65. Theodore Roosevelt, *An Autobiography* (New York: Charles Scribner's Sons, 1926), p. 511.

66. Quoted in Richard D. Challener, *Admirals, Generals, and American Foreign Policy, 1898–1914* (Princeton: Princeton University Press, 1973), p. 142.

67. *Foreign Relations, 1912* (Washington, D.C.: Government Printing Office, 1919), p. 1091.

68. Quoted in Lloyd C. Gardner, *Safe for Democracy* (New York: Oxford University Press, 1984), p. 41.

69. *Foreign Relations, 1913* (Washington, D.C.: Government Printing Office, 1920), p. 426.

70. Quoted in Frederick S. Calhoun, *Uses of Force and Wilsonian Foreign Policy* (Kent, Ohio: Kent State University Press, 1993), p. 53.

71. Bruce Calder, *The Impact of Intervention* (Austin: University of Texas Press, 1984), p. 250.

72. Quoted in Dana G. Munro, *Intervention and Dollar Diplomacy in the Caribbean* (Princeton: Princeton University Press, 1964), p. 336.

73. Quoted in Brenda G. Plummer, *Haiti and the Great Powers, 1902–1915* (Baton Rouge: Louisiana State University Press, 1988), p. 188.

74. Quoted in Hannigan, *New World Power*, p. 49.

75. Franklin Wirkus quoted in Mary Renda, *Taking Haiti* (Chapel Hill: University of North Carolina Press, 2001), p. 85.

76. Alexander DeConde, *Ethnicity, Race, and American Foreign Policy* (Boston: Northeastern University Press, 1993), pp. 79–80.

77. Victor Hoiser quoted in Renda, *Taking Haiti*, p. 34.

78. Quoted in Munro, *Intervention*, p. 155.

79. Thomas D. Schoonover, *The United States in Central America, 1860–1911* (Durham: Duke University Press, 1991), p. 130; quoted in Hannigan, *New World Power*, p. 291.

80. Zelaya quoted in Lester D. Langley and Thomas D. Schoonover, *The Banana Men* (Lexington: University Press of Kentucky, 1995), p. 89; quoted in Emily S. Rosenberg, *Financial Missionaries to the World* (Cambridge: Harvard University Press, 1999), p. 67; Taft quoted in Alexander DeConde, *Presidential Machismo* (Boston: Northeastern University Press, 2000), p. 92.

81. Elliott Northcott quoted in Walter LaFeber, *The American Search for Opportunity, 1865–1913* (New York: Cambridge University Press, 1993), p. 219.

82. Quoted in John E. Findling, *Close Neighbors, Distant Friends* (Westport, Conn.: Greenwood, 1987), p. 61.

83. Langley and Schoonover, *Banana Men*, p. 114.

84. Quoted in Baker, *Wilson, IV*, 436.

85. Quoted in Paolo E. Coletta, *The Presidency of William Howard Taft* (Lawrence: University Press of Kansas, 1973), p. 176.

86. Quoted in Friedrich Katz, *The Secret War in Mexico* (Chicago: University of Chicago Press, 1981), p. 113.

87. *Foreign Relations, 1912*, p. 846.

88. Quoted in Howard F. Cline, *The United States and Mexico* (New York: Atheneum, 1963; rev. ed.), p. 144.

89. Quoted in Arthur S. Link, *Wilson: The New Freedom* (Princeton: Princeton University Press, 1956), p. 360.

90. Quoted in Arthur S. Link, *Wilson: Confusions and Crises, 1915–1916* (Princeton: Princeton University Press, 1964), p. 317.

91. William Bayard Hale quoted in Schoultz, *Beneath*, p. 240.

92. Quoted in Link, *Wilson: New Freedom*, p. 358.

93. Quoted in Elizabeth McKillen, "Wilsonian Internationalism Reconsidered," *Diplomatic History, XXV* (Fall 2001), 567.

94. Quoted in Kenneth J. Grieb, *The United States and Huerta* (Lincoln: University of Nebraska Press, 1969), p. 137.

95. Quoted in Link, *Wilson: New Freedom*, pp. 386–387.

96. Quoted in Katz, *Secret War*, p. 216.

97. Quoted in Grieb, *United States and Huerta*, p. 135.

98. Quoted in Mark T. Gilderhus, *Diplomacy and Revolution* (Tucson: University of Arizona Press, 1977), p. 11.

99. Quoted in Cary T. Grayson, *Woodrow Wilson* (New York: Holt, Rinehart and Winston, 1960), p. 30.

100. Ramón E. Ruíz, *The Great Rebellion: Mexico, 1905–1924* (New York: Norton, 1980), p. 395.

101. Quoted in Grieb, *United States and Huerta*, p. 160.

102. Wilson quoted in Hannigan, *New World Power*, p. 177.

103. Quoted in Douglas Monroy, "Fence Cutters, *Sedicioso*, and First Class Citizens: Mexican Radicalism in America," in Paul Buhle and Dan Georgakis, eds., *The Immigrant Left in the United States* (Albany: State University of New York Press, 1996), pp. 21–22.

104. Quoted in James A. Sandos, *Rebellion in the Borderlands* (Norman: University of Oklahoma Press, 1992), p. 92.

105. Quoted in Arthur S. Link, *Wilson: The Struggle for Neutrality, 1914–1915* (Princeton: Princeton University Press, 1960), p. 491.

106. Katz, *Secret War*, p. 560; Villa quoted in Friedrich Katz, "Pancho Villa and the Attack on Columbus, New Mexico," *American Historical Review, LXXXIII* (February 1978), 111, 114.

107. Quoted in Ana Maria Alonso, "U.S. Military Intervention," in Daniel Nugent, ed., *Rural Revolt in Mexico and U.S. Intervention* (San Diego: Center for U.S.–Mexican Studies, 1988), p. 217.

108. Morison, *Letters of Roosevelt, III*, 497–498.

109. Akira Iriye, *The Cold War in Asia* (Englewood Cliffs, N.J.: Prentice-Hall, 1974), p. 35.

110. Morison, *Letters of Roosevelt, IV*, 724, 761.

111. Quoted in Norman Saul, *Concord & Conflict* (Lawrence: University Press of Kansas, 1996), p. 496.

112. Quoted in Raymond A. Esthus, *Double Eagle and Rising Sun* (Durham: Duke University Press, 1988), p. 39.

113. Quoted in Brands, *T.R.*, p. 534.

114. Quoted in Saul, *Concord*, p. 504.

115. Quoted in Raymond A. Esthus, *Theodore Roosevelt and Japan* (Seattle: University of Washington Press, 1966), p. 101.

116. John Edward Wilz, "Did the United States Betray Korea in 1905?" *Pacific Historical Review, LIV* (August 1985), 252.

117. Quoted in Akira Iriye, *Across the Pacific* (New York: Harcourt, Brace & World, 1967), p. 107.

118. Quoted in Ian Mugridge, *The View from Xanadu: William Randolph Hearst and American Foreign Policy* (Montreal: McGill–Queen's University Press, 1995), p. 51.

119. Quoted in Walter A. McDougall, *Let the Sea Make a Noise* (New York: BasicBooks, 1993), p. 479; Morison, *Letters of Roosevelt, V*, 729–730, 761–762.

120. Quoted in Ute Mehnert, "German *Weltpolitik* and the American Two Front Dilemma," *Journal of American History, LXXXII* (March 1996), 1458.

121. Quoted in Guanhua Wang, *In Search of Justice* (Cambridge: Harvard University Press, 2001), p. 90.

122. Quoted in Eileen P. Scully, "Taking the Low Road" *Journal of American History, LXXXII* (June 1995), 63–64.

123. Anders Stephanson, *Manifest Destiny* (New York: Hill & Wang, 1995), p. 97.

124. Ninkovich, *Modernity*, p. 25.

125. Quoted in Herbert Croly, *Willard Straight* (New York: Macmillan, 1925), p. 276.

126. A. Whitney Griswold, *The Far Eastern Policy of the United States* (New Haven: Yale University Press, 1938), p. 157.

127. Quoted in Croly, *Straight*, pp. 392–393.

128. Quoted in Daniel M. Crane and Thomas A. Breslin, *An Ordinary Relationship* (Miami: Florida International University Press, 1986), p. 122.

129. Quoted in Roger Daniels, *The Politics of Prejudice* (New York: Atheneum, [1962], 1968), p. 59.

130. Quoted in Link, *Wilson: New Freedom*, pp. 300–301.

131. Quoted in Kendrick A. Clements, *The Presidency of Woodrow Wilson* (Lawrence: University Press of Kansas, 1990), p. 108.

132. *Foreign Relations, 1922* (Washington, D.C.: Government Printing Office, 1938; 2 vols.), II, 591.

133. Quoted in Michael H. Hunt, *Ideology and U.S. Foreign Policy* (New Haven: Yale University Press, 1987), pp. 69, 71, 79, 81.

134. *Ibid.*, p. 79.

135. TR quoted in Hannigan, *New World Power*, p. 270.

136. Herbert Asquith quoted in Rock, *Why Peace*, p. 51; Bradford Perkins, *The Great Rapprochement* (New York: Atheneum, 1968).

137. Roosevelt quoted in Frederick W. Marks, *Velvet on Iron* (Lincoln: University of Nebraska Press, 1979), p. 168.

138. Robert Bothwell, *Canada and the United States* (New York: Twayne, 1992), p. 8.

139. Quoted in Kurk Dorsey, "Scientists, Citizens, and Statesmen," *Diplomatic History, XIX* (Summer 1995), 426.

140. Mark Kurlansky, *Cod* (New York: Walker, 1997), p. 79.

141. Quoted in Arthur Marder, *From the Dreadnought to Scapa Flow* (London: Oxford University Press, 1961–1970; 5 vols.), I, 125.

142. Quoted *ibid.*, p. 201.

143. Quoted in Link, *Wilson: New Freedom*, p. 308.

144. Quoted in Burton, *Theodore Roosevelt*, p. 190.

145. Quoted in Emily S. Rosenberg, "The Invisible Protectorate: The United States, Liberia, and the Evolution of Neocolonialism, 1909–40," *Diplomatic History, IX* (Summer 1985), 194, 198.

146. Quoted in Tilchin, *Theodore Roosevelt*, p. 67; quoted in Hannigan, *New World Power*, p. 204.

147. Morison, *Letters of Roosevelt, IV*, 1119.

148. Quoted in Calvin Davis, *The United States and the Second Hague Peace Conference* (Durham: Duke University Press, 1975), p. 296.

149. Quoted in Minger, *William Howard Taft*, p. 106.

150. Quoted in Mehnert, "German *Weltpolitik*," p. 1461.

151. Quoted in Jerry Israel, *Progressivism and the Open Door* (Pittsburgh: University of Pittsburgh Press, 1971), p. 96.

152. General William Carter quoted in Brian Linn, *Guardians of Empire* (Chapel Hill: University of North Carolina Press, 1997), p. 62.

153. Quoted in Michael L. Conniff, *Panama and the United States* (Athens: University of Georgia Press, 1992), p. 3.

154. Laura Briggs, *Reproducing Empire* (Berklee: University of California Press, 2002), p. 2.

155. Raymond Carr, *Puerto Rico* (New York: Vintage, 1984), p. 36.

156. William Phillips, *Ventures in Diplomacy* (Boston: Beacon Press, 1952), p. 6.

157. Quoted in A. J. Bacevich, *Diplomat in Khaki* (Lawrence: University Press of Kansas, 1989), p. 48.

158. Emily S. Rosenberg, *Spreading the American Dream* (New York: Hill & Wang, 1982), p. 35.

159. Quoted in Robert A. Hart, *The Great White Fleet* (Boston: Little, Brown, 1965), p. 45.

160. Quoted in Franklin Ng, "Knowledge for Empire," in Robert David Johnson, ed., *On Cultural Ground* (Chicago: Imprint Publications, 1994), p. 135.

161. Charles W. Eliot quoted in Frank Trommler, "Inventing the Enemy," in Hans-Jürgen Schröder, *Confrontation and Cooperation* (Providence, R.I.: Berg, 1993), p. 101.

162. Quoted in Christopher Endy, "Travel and World Power," *Diplomatic History, XXII* (Fall 1998), 574.

163. Winston S. Churchill, *The World Crisis* (New York: Charles Scribner's Sons, 1927; 6 vols.), I, 18.

CHAPTER 3

War, Peace, and Revolution in the Time of Wilson, 1914–1920

Mass Grave of* Lusitania *Victims. *In Queenstown, Ireland, a large burial ground holds more than a hundred victims of the* Lusitania *disaster of 1915, which rudely brought World War I to American consciousness. (U.S. War Department, National Archives)*

DIPLOMATIC CROSSROAD

⚓ *The Sinking of the* Lusitania, *1915*

"PERFECTLY SAFE; SAFER than the trolley cars in New York City," claimed a Cunard Line official the morning of May 1, 1915.[1] Indeed, the majestic *Lusitania,* with its watertight compartments and swiftness, seemed invulnerable. The British government loaned Cunard the money to build this fast passenger liner, more than twice as long as an American football field. The British Admiralty dictated the coal-burning ship's specifications, so that the 30,396-ton vessel could be armed if necessary during war. "Lucy's" priority was pleasure, not war. Resplendent with tapestries and carpets, the luxurious floating palace dazzled. One impressed American politician found the ship "more beautiful than Solomon's Temple—and big enough to hold all his wives."[2]

A crew of 702 attended the 1,257 travelers who departed from New York's Pier 54 on May 1. Deep in the *Lusitania*'s storage area rested a cargo of foodstuffs and contraband (4.2 million rounds of ammunition for Remington rifles, 1,250 cases of empty shrapnel shells, and eighteen cases of nonexplosive fuses). The Cunarder thus carried, said a U.S. State Department official, both "babies and bullets."[3]

In the morning newspapers of May 1 a rather unusual announcement, placed by the German Embassy, appeared beside the Cunard Line advertisement. The German "Notice" warned passengers that the waters around the British Isles constituted a war zone wherein British vessels were subject to destruction. Only a handful of passengers transferred to the *New York,* ready to sail under the American flag that same day. The *New York* was slow and for the American "smart set" socially unacceptable. The State Department did not intercede to warn the 197 American passengers away from the *Lusitania.* Most Americans accepted the Cunard Line statement: "She is too fast for any submarine. No German war vessel can get her or near her."[4] During this very time, Secretary of State William Jennings Bryan was trying futilely to persuade President Woodrow Wilson that Americans should be prohibited from traveling on belligerent ships.

Captained by William T. Turner, the *Lusitania* steamed into the Atlantic at half past noon on May 1. Manned by an ill-trained crew (the best now on war duty), "Lucy" enjoyed a smooth crossing in calm water. Despite lifesaving drills, complacency about the submarine danger lulled captain, crew, and passengers alike. Passengers joked about torpedoes, played cards, consumed liquor, and listened to concerts on deck. On May 6, as the *Lusitania* neared Ireland, Turner received a warning from the Naval Centre at Queenstown: "Submarines active off south coast of Ireland."[5] The captain posted lookouts but took no other precautions, despite follow-up warnings. He had standing orders from the Admiralty to take a zigzag path, to steer a midchannel course, and to steam at full speed—all to make it difficult for lurking German submarines to zero in on their targets. But Turner proceeded straight ahead.

A beautiful day with unusually good visibility, recorded Lieutenant Walter Schwieger in his log on May 7. The young commander was piloting his *U-20* sub-

The *Lusitania* and *U-20*. The majestic passenger liner was sunk by German submarine *U-20* off the coast of Ireland on May 7, 1915. "Suppose they should sink the *Lusitania* with American passengers on board," King George V had mused to Colonel Edward M. House on that fateful morning. (Peabody Museum of Salem; Bundesarchiv)

marine along the southern Irish coast. That morning it had submerged because British ships capable of ramming the fragile, slender craft were passing by. Schwieger surfaced at 1:45 P.M. and soon spotted a four-funneled ship in the distance. Schwieger quickly submerged and set a track toward the *Lusitania*. At 700 meters the *U-20* released a torpedo. The deadly missile dashed through the water tailed by bubbles. A watchman on the starboard bow of the *Lusitania* cried out. Captain Turner, unaccountably below deck in those dangerous waters, did not hear the megaphone one minute before the torpedo struck. Had he heard the warning, the ship *might* have veered sharply and avoided danger. Turner felt the explosion as it

Captain William T. Turner (1856–1933). He commanded the *Lusitania* to disaster. (U.S. War Department)

Lieutenant Walter Schwieger (1885–1917). His *U–20* sank the *Lusitania*. (Bundesarchiv)

ripped into the *Lusitania*. Panic swept the passengers as they stumbled about the listing decks or groped in the darkness below. Steam whistled from punctured boilers. Less than half the lifeboats lowered; some capsized or embarked only partially loaded. Within eighteen minutes the "Queen of the Atlantic" sank, killing 1,198— 128 of them Americans. A survivor said that when the *Lusitania* went down, "it sounded like a terrible moan."[6]

President Wilson had just ended a cabinet meeting when he learned of the disaster. His special assistant, Colonel Edward House, then in London, predicted: "We shall be at war with Germany within a month."[7] The pro-British House had actually sailed on the *Lusitania* in February and had witnessed, much to his surprise, the hoisting of an American flag as the ship neared the Irish coast. Fearing war, Secretary Bryan told the president that "ships carrying contraband should be prohibited from carrying passengers. . . . it would be like putting women and children in front of an army."[8] Bellicose ex-president Theodore Roosevelt soon seared the air with his declaration that "this represents . . . piracy on a vaster scale of murder than old-time pirates ever practiced."[9] American after American voiced horror, but few wanted war. Wilson secluded himself to ponder a response to this ghastly event. Just months before, he had said he would hold Berlin strictly accountable for the loss of any American ships or lives because of submarine warfare. Thereafter, Wilson found himself trying to fulfill America's "double wish"—"to maintain a firm front . . . [toward] Germany and yet do nothing that might by any possibility involve us in war."[10]

Wilson spoke in Philadelphia on May 10. His words, much misunderstood, suggested he had no backbone: "There is such a thing as a man being too proud to fight. There is such a thing as a nation being so right that it does not need to convince others by force that it is right."[11] When former secretary of state Elihu Root

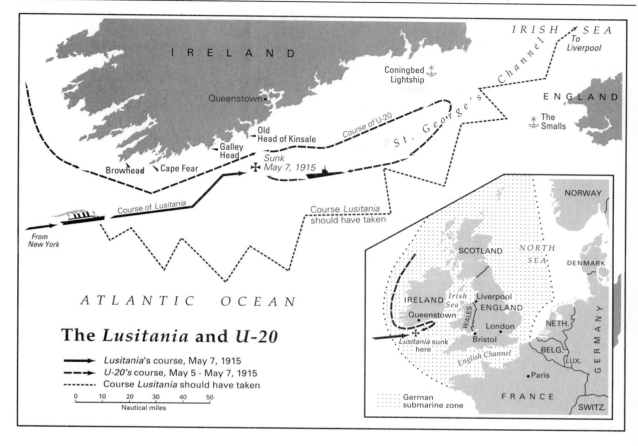

The *Lusitania* and U-20

→ *Lusitania*'s course, May 7, 1915
--→ U-20's course, May 5 - May 7, 1915
········ Course *Lusitania* should have taken

0 10 20 30 40 50
Nautical miles

called it "incredible" that Wilson could see "no greater moral question involved," the president regretted his impromptu words.[12] Preoccupied by his intense courtship of his future second wife, Wilson did "not know just what I said in Philadelphia . . . because my heart was in such a whirl."[13] The next morning he told the cabinet that he would send a note to Berlin insisting that Americans had a right to travel on the high seas and demanding a German disavowal of the inhumane acts of its submarine commanders. Bryan sadly approved this first "*Lusitania* note." Long upset about an apparent American double standard in protesting more against German than British violations of American neutral rights, the secretary pleaded for a simultaneous protest to London. But only one note went out on May 13—to Berlin: "The Imperial Government will not expect the United States to omit any word or any act necessary to the performance of its sacred duty of maintaining the rights of the United States and its citizens and of safeguarding their free exercise and enjoyment."[14] In short, end submarine warfare, or else.

The German government took much less pleasure than the German navy did in the destruction of the *Lusitania*. Chancellor Theobold von Bethmann-Hollweg had more than once chastised the navy for inviting war with the United States through submarine attacks on neutral or Allied merchant vessels. On May 28 he sent an evasive reply to Wilson's note. The *Lusitania* case could not be settled until they clarified certain questions. The German note claimed that the ship was armed, carried munitions, and had orders to ram submarines. Germany asked Washington to investigate. That same day, in a secret meeting with German ambassador Johann von Bernstorff, Wilson proposed that if Germany would settle the *Lusitania* crisis favorably, he would press the British to suspend their blockade and then call a conference of neutrals to mediate an end to the war on the following basis: "1. The status quo in Europe; 2. Freedom of the seas. . . . 3. Adjustments concerning colonial possessions."[15]

Wilson convened the cabinet on June 1. When one member recommended a strong note demanding observance of American rights, another suggested as well a note to England to protest British interference with American commerce. Debate became heated. A majority rejected simultaneous notes. Bryan called the cabinet pro-Allied. Wilson quickly rebuked him for "unfair and unjust" comments.[16] When Germany did not immediately reply to his mediation proposal, Wilson sent a second "*Lusitania* note" that vigorously demanded an end to warfare by submarine. Wilson rejected Bryan's plea for a warning to passengers and a protest note to England. Sensing that "this will destroy me," Bryan quietly resigned on June 8.[17] Wilson went to the golf links to free himself from the blinding headaches of the past several days. "He is absolutely *sincere*," the president said of Bryan. "That is what makes him dangerous."[18]

More correspondence on the *Lusitania* followed. The United States insisted that Germany admit it had committed an illegal act; but Germany, unwilling to abandon one of its few effective weapons against British mastery of the ocean, refused to admit wrongdoing and asked for arbitration. "Utterly impertinent," sniffed Kaiser Wilhelm II, who preferred victory to Wilson's mediation.[19] Eventually Germany sought compromise. On February 4 it expressed regret over the American deaths and offered to pay an indemnity (eventually paid in the early 1920s). Wilson accepted the German concession.

The horrible deaths from the *Lusitania* remained etched in American memories. The torpedoing of the magnificent Cunarder marked a turning point. The Germans suffered a "naval victory worse than a defeat," as Britons and Americans alike depicted the "Huns" as depraved.[20] The sinking also hardened Wilson's opinion of Germany. After Germany spurned his secret mediation offer, Wilson no longer made diplomatic life easier for the Germans by simultaneously protesting British infractions. The British were violating property rights, but the Germans violated human rights. He also refused to warn Americans away from belligerent ships. In short, if a U-boat attacked a British ship with Americans aboard, Germany would have to take the consequences. Wilson did not spell out those consequences, but the logical implication was war—just what Bryan feared. His resignation brought pro-Allied Robert Lansing to the secretaryship of state. After the *Lusitania* crisis, Lansing believed "that we would ultimately become an ally of Great Britain."[21] The sinking of the *Lusitania* pointed up, for all to see, the complexities, contradictions, and uncertainties inherent in American neutrality during the European phase of the First World War, 1914–1917.

The Travails of Neutrality

Woodrow Wilson acted virtually as his own secretary of state during those troubled years. "Wilson makes confidant of no one. No one gets his whole mind," an aide wrote.[22] British prime minister Lloyd George put it less kindly: Wilson "believed in mankind but . . . distrusted all men."[23] The president defined the overall character of American foreign policy—what historians call "Wilsonianism." Above all else, Wilson stood for an *open* world unencumbered by imperialism, war, or revolution. Barriers to trade and democracy had to come down, and secret diplomacy had to give way to public negotiations. The right of self-determination would force the collapse of empires. Constitutional procedures would replace revolution. A free-market, humanized capitalism would ensure democracy. Disarmament programs would restrict weapons. The Open Door of equal trade and investment would harness the economic competition that led to war. Wilson, like so many Americans, saw the United States as exceptional—"a sort of pure air blowing in world politics, destroying illusions and cleaning places of morbid miasmic gasses."[24] His "semi-divine power to select the right" blended with realism.[25] The president calculated the nation's economic and strategic needs and devised a foreign policy to protect them. Yet many Americans feared that his world-reforming efforts might invite war, dissipate American resources, and undermine reform at home. Wilson led a divided nation.

Few Americans, Wilson included, desired war. Most watched in shock as the European nations savagely slashed at one another in 1914. The progressive faith in human ability to correct wrongs, the belief that war belonged to the decadent past, the conviction that civilization had advanced too far for such bloodletting—all were ruthlessly challenged. Before 1914 the new machine guns, howitzers, submarines, and dreadnoughts seemed too awesome for leaders to launch them. The outbreak of World War I smashed illusions and tested innocence. The shock did not become despair, despite the news of poison gas, U-boats, and civilian casualties. The Progressive era exuded optimism, and Americans, particularly the crusading Wilson, sought to retrieve a happier past by assuming the role of civilized instructors: America would help Europe come to its senses by teaching it the rules of humane conduct. The war's carnage justified the mission. In 1915 alone France suffered 1.3 million casualties, including 330,000 deaths. Germany suffered 848,000 casualties, 170,000 of them deaths. Britain followed with 313,000 casualties, and 73,000 deaths.

Americans had good reason, then, to believe that Europe needed help in cleaning its own house. The outbreak of the war seemed so senseless. By June 1914, the

Makers of American Foreign Relations, 1914–1920

President	Secretaries of State
Woodrow Wilson, 1913–1921	William Jennings Bryan, 1913–1915
	Robert Lansing, 1915–1920
	Bainbridge Colby, 1920–1921

great powers had constructed two blocs, the Triple Alliance (Germany, Austria-Hungary, and Italy) and the Triple Entente (France, Russia, and Great Britain). Some called this division of Europe a balance of power, but an assassin's bullet unbalanced it. Between Austria and Serbia lay Bosnia, a tiny province in the Austro-Hungarian Empire. Slavic nationalists sought to build a greater Serbia—an independent Slavic state—by annexing Bosnia, which the Austro-Hungarian Empire had absorbed just a few years before, in 1909. A Slavic terrorist group, the Black Hand, decided to force the issue. On June 28 the heir to the Hapsburg Crown of Austria-Hungary, Archduke Franz Ferdinand, visited Sarajevo, the capital of Bosnia. As his car moved through the streets of the city, a Black Hand assassin gunned him down.

Austria-Hungary sent impossible demands to Serbia. The Serbs rejected them. Austria-Hungary had already received encouragement from Germany, and Serbia had a pledge of support from Russia, which in turn received backing from France. A chain reaction set in. On July 28 Austria-Hungary declared war on Serbia; on August 1 Germany declared "preventive" war on Russia and two days later on France; on August 4 Germany invaded Belgium, and Great Britain declared war on Germany. In a few weeks Japan joined the Allies (Triple Entente) and Turkey the Central Powers, and Italy entered on the Allied side the next year. Wilson's friend Colonel House, visiting Europe that May, had reported "jingoism run stark mad . . . there is some day to be an awful cataclysm."[26]

The Atlantic seemed at first an adequate barrier to insulate the United States. In early August, the U.S. ambassador to England, Walter Hines Page, wrote the president: "Be ready; for you will be called on to compose their huge quarrel. I thank Heaven for many things—first the Atlantic Ocean."[27] Wilson issued a Proclamation of Neutrality on August 4, followed days later by an appeal to Americans to be neutral in thought, speech, and action. Laced with patriotic utterances, the decree sought to cool the passions of immigrant groups who identified with the belligerents. America must demonstrate to a troubled world that it was "fit beyond others to exhibit the fine poise of undisturbed judgment, the dignity of self-control, the efficiency of dispassionate action."[28] A lofty call for restraint, an expression of America as the beacon of common sense in a world gone mad, a plea for unity at home—but difficult to achieve.

Few Americans proved capable of neutral thoughts and deeds. Loyalties to fatherlands and motherlands did not abate. German Americans identified with the Central Powers. Many Irish Americans, nourishing their traditional Anglophobia at a time when Ireland chafed under British rule and readied for rebellion, wished catastrophe on Britain. But Anglo-American traditions and cultural ties, as well as slogans such as "Remember Lafayette," pulled most Americans toward a pro-Allied position. Since the 1890s Anglophobia had weakened in the face of the calming Anglo-American rapprochement. Woodrow Wilson himself harbored pro-British sentiment, telling the British ambassador that "everything I love is at stake" and that a German victory "will be fatal to our form of Government and American ideals."[29] Wilson's advisers, House and Lansing, were ardently pro-British. Ambassador Page even wanted Americans "to hang our Irish agitators and shoot our hyphenates and bring up our children with reverence for English history and . . . English literature."[30]

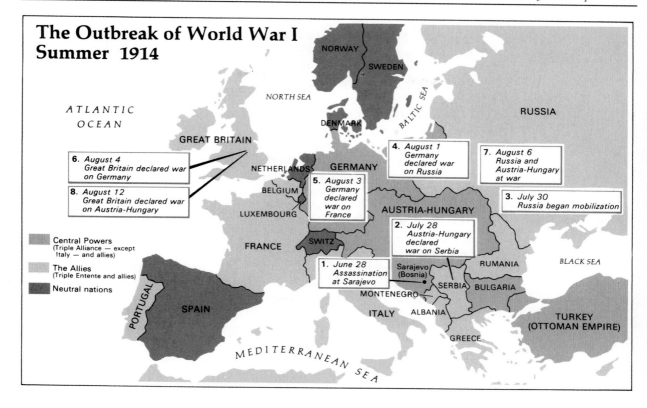

The Outbreak of World War I
Summer 1914

NORWAY

SWEDEN

NORTH SEA

BALTIC SEA

RUSSIA

ATLANTIC OCEAN

DENMARK

GREAT BRITAIN

6. *August 4*
Great Britain declared war
on Germany

8. *August 12*
Great Britain declared war
on Austria-Hungary

NETHERLANDS

GERMANY

4. *August 1*
Germany
declared war
on Russia

7. *August 6*
Russia and
Austria-Hungary
at war

5. *August 3*
Germany
declared
war on
France

BELGIUM

LUXEMBOURG

AUSTRIA-HUNGARY

3. *July 30*
Russia began mobilization

2. *July 28*
Austria-Hungary
declared
war on Serbia

FRANCE

SWITZ.

1. *June 28*
Assassination
at Sarajevo

Sarajevo
(Bosnia)

SERBIA

RUMANIA

BULGARIA

BLACK SEA

MONTENEGRO

Central Powers
(Triple Alliance — except
Italy — and allies)

The Allies
(Triple Entente and allies)

Neutral nations

PORTUGAL

SPAIN

ITALY

ALBANIA

GREECE

TURKEY
(OTTOMAN EMPIRE)

MEDITERRANEAN SEA

German war actions, exaggerated by British propaganda, also undermined neutrality. To Americans, the Germans, led by arrogant Kaiser Wilhelm II (once described by Wilson as a "bumptious . . . gentleman slenderly equipped with wisdom or discretion"), became symbols of the dreaded militarism and conscription of the Old World.[31] Germany, too, seemed an upstart nation, an aggressive latecomer to the scramble for imperialist prizes, and a noisy intruder in the Caribbean where the British had already acknowledged U.S. hegemony. Eager to grasp world power and encouraging Austria-Hungary to war, Berlin certainly had little claim on virtue. The European powers had guaranteed Belgium neutrality by treaty, but Bethmann-Hollweg dismissed it as a "scrap of paper."[32] On August 4, 1914, hoping to get at France, the Germans attacked Belgium and, angered that the Belgians resisted, ruthlessly proceeded to raze villages, unleash firing squads against townspeople, and deport young workers to Germany. One magazine called Belgium "a martyr to civilization, sister to all who love liberty, or law; assailed, polluted, trampled in the mire, heel-marked in her breast, tattered, homeless."[33] American hearts and hands went out in the form of a major relief mission headed by a young, wealthy, and courageous mining engineer, Herbert Hoover.

American economic links with the Allies also undercut neutrality. England had always been America's best customer, and wartime conditions simply intensified the relationship. The Allies needed both war matériel and consumer goods. Americans, inspired by huge profits and a chance to pull out of a recession, obliged. In 1914 U.S. exports to England and France equaled $754 million; in 1915 the figure shot up to $1.28 billion; and in 1916 the amount more than doubled to $2.75 billion. Comparable statistics for Germany reveal why Berlin believed the United States was taking sides. In 1914 exports to Germany totaled $345 million; in 1915 they plummeted to $29 million; and in 1916 they fell to $2 million. In 1914–1917 New York's banking house of J. P. Morgan Company served as an agent for England and France and arranged for the shipment of more than $3 billion worth of goods. In April 1915, Britain ordered shells from the American Locomotive Company costing $63.7 million, and that year Bethlehem Steel contracted for some $150 million in ammunition, to cite two examples. By April 1917, British purchasing missions were spending $83 million a week for American copper, steel, wheat, oil, and munitions.

Britain and France sold many of their American securities and liquidated investments to pay for these goods. This netted them several billion dollars. Next, in appeals to prominent American bankers and State Department officials, they also sought loans. In 1914 Bryan discouraged private American loans to the belligerents, because "money is the worst of all contrabands because it commands everything else."[34] Yet in early 1915 the Wilson administration did not object to a Morgan credit to France of $50 million. After Bryan's resignation, Robert Lansing argued that loans to the Allies would prevent "restriction of output, industrial depression, idle capital, idle labor, numerous failures, financial demoralization, and general unrest and suffering among the laboring classes."[35] Because U.S. industries "will burst their jackets if they cannot find a free outlet to the markets of the world," Wilson thus approved $2.3 billion in loans to the Allies during 1914–1917—a sharp contrast to loans of only $27 million to Germany.[36] Once it joined the war as a belligerent, the American economic powerhouse became even more the dispenser of munitions, food, and money to the Allies. Indeed, "the passing of hegemony from Britain to the United States . . . as the leading financial power can be seen occurring, step by step, in the negotiations between the British Treasury mission and the American government during 1917–18."[37]

Berlin protested such "unneutral" economic ties. Yet curbing trade with Britain, which ruled the seas, would have constituted unneutral behavior in favor of the Germans, for under international law a belligerent could buy, at its own risk, contraband and noncontraband goods from a neutral. Neutral or not, the United States had become the arsenal of the Allied war effort.

Submarines, Neutral Rights, and Mediation Efforts

To strangle Germany, the British invoked legal doctrines of retaliation and contraband without ever technically declaring a blockade. They mined the North Sea, expanded the contraband list to include foodstuffs and cotton, forced American ships into port for inspection, seized "contraband" from neutral vessels, halted American trade with Germany's neutral neighbors Denmark and Holland, armed British merchant ships, used decoy ships to lure U-boats into traps, flew neutral (often American) flags, and rammed whenever possible any U-boats that complied with international law by surfacing to warn a British merchant vessel of an imminent attack. The British "ruled the waves and waived the rules," so to speak. The Wilson administration issued protests, some mild, some tough, against these illegalities. The Foreign Office usually paid appropriate verbal deference to international law and went right on with its restrictive behavior. Britain sometimes compensated U.S. businesses for damages and purchased large quantities of goods at inflated prices. Americans thus came to tolerate the indignities of British economic warfare. Britain managed brilliantly to sever American economic lines to the Central Powers without rupturing Anglo-American relations.

Germans protested vehemently against American acquiescence in the British "hunger" or "starvation" blockade. To continue the war, Germany had to have imports and had to curb the flourishing Anglo-American trade that fueled the Allied war machine. The German surface fleet, bottled up in ports, seemed inadequate for the task, so German leaders hesitantly turned to a relatively new experimental weapon of limited maneuverability, the submarine. At the start they possessed just 21 U-boats, and at peak strength in October 1917 they had but 127. Only a third of this fleet operated at sea at any one time. On February 4, 1915, Berlin announced that it was retaliating against British strangulation by declaring a war zone around Britain. All *enemy* ships in the area would be destroyed. It warned neutral ships to *stay out* of the zone because of possible mistaken identity, a real prospect given the British practice of hoisting neutral flags. Passengers from neutral countries were urged, moreover, to *stay off* enemy passenger vessels. Six days later Wilson held Germany to strict accountability for the loss of American life and property.

The British continued to arm their merchant vessels, which thereby became warships and theoretically ineligible to take on arms or munitions in neutral ports. But Washington invoked a fine distinction between offensive and defensive armaments and permitted such "defensively" armed British craft to carry war supplies from American ports. Crying foul, the Germans also argued that old international law, which Wilson invoked, did not fit the submarine. Rules adopted during the sailing-ship era held that an attacking cruiser about to sink or capture enemy merchant vessels had to give adequate warning so as to ensure the safety of passengers and crew. Yet if a submarine surfaced in its sluggish fashion, the merchant ship's crew might sink it with a deck gun or even a hand grenade, or ram the slow-moving craft. Imagine the problem for Schwieger of *U-20* when he spotted the *Lusitania*. Had he surfaced to warn the ship, the *Lusitania* probably would have attempted to ram *U-20* or flee and would have sent distress signals to British warships in the vicinity. Even if the *Lusitania* had submitted to the warning, it might have taken an hour for passengers to get into lifeboats before Schwieger could torpedo the *Lusitania,* by which time British warships might have closed in. In short, from the German point of view, to comply with an international law that failed to anticipate the submarine was not possible. Wilson retorted that differences over international law could be "adjusted after the war," whereas Germany's "sheer acts of piracy on the high seas . . . might easily lead to actual hostilities."[38]

Secretary Bryan tried diplomacy in early 1915, asking Germany to give up use of unannounced submarine attacks in exchange for a British promise to disarm its

William Jennings Bryan (1860–1925). The great agrarian reformer went to Congress in 1890 as a Democrat from Nebraska. After several unsuccessful runs for the presidency, Bryan endorsed Wilson and became secretary of state in 1913. He favored the arbitration of international disputes, and he perpetuated U.S. interventionist policy in Latin America. Believing that Wilson was tilting toward the British after the *Lusitania* disaster of 1915, Bryan resigned in protest. A colleague called him "too good a Christian to run a naughty world." (National Portrait Gallery, Smithsonian Institution)

merchant carriers and permit food to flow to Germany. The Germans seemed interested, but London refused. At this point Wilson might have pressed the belligerents to alter their naval strategies or face the prospect of U.S. warships convoying America's neutral ships. Or he might have launched a vigorous diplomatic offensive to delay explosive events on the seas. Yet American armed convoys in the Atlantic could very well draw the country into a war it did not want. A diplomatic offensive, given the intensity of war fever in Europe, seemed a long shot. In March 1915, Wilson did send Colonel House to Europe to sound out possibilities for mediation, but to no avail. Nonetheless, Wilson failed to adjust or shelve ancient international law, which had no provision for the submarine. He accepted British alterations but not German ones, for reasons of both morality and economics.

Between February and May 1915, marauding submarines sank ninety ships in the war zone. One American, on the British passenger ship *Falaba,* died in the sinking of that vessel on March 28. Then came the *Lusitania* in May. Through Wilson's many protest notes, a U.S. posture took shape: uneasy tolerance of British violations of property rights and rejection of German violations of human rights. Despite secret German orders to submarine commanders to avoid a repetition of the *Lusitania* incident, on August 19 the *Arabic,* another British liner, was torpedoed with the loss of two American lives. A worried Ambassador Bernstorff publicly pledged that U-boats would now spare passenger ships.

In early 1916, calling the United States ideally suited as the "mediating nation of the world," Wilson tried to bring the warring parties to the conference table.[39] Colonel House talked with British officials in London but left with no promises for peace. He journeyed next to Berlin, where German leaders gave no assurances. Both sides would fight on. "Hell will break loose in Europe this spring and summer as never before," House informed Wilson.[40] House then traveled to Paris, where he rashly informed his skeptical French hosts: "If the Allies obtain a small success this spring or summer, the U.S. will intervene to promote a peaceful settlement, but if the Allies have a setback, the United States will intervene militarily and will take part in the war against Germany."[41] House did not report his prediction to the president.

Edward M. House (1858–1938). This Texas "colonel" served as Wilson's trusted emissary abroad. In the House-Grey Memorandum of 1916 he showed signs of the deviousness that led to his break with the president after the Versailles conference. President Wilson once identified House as "my second personality. He is my independent self. If I were in his place I would do just as he suggested." An opponent called House "an intimate man . . . even when he was cutting your throat." (National Portrait Gallery, Smithsonian Institution)

House returned to London to press Sir Edward Grey, British foreign secretary, to heed Wilson's call for a peace conference. The American envoy recorded their agreements in the House-Grey Memorandum of February 22, 1916, a document loaded with "ifs." The first paragraph read: "Colonel House told me that President Wilson was ready, on hearing from France and England that the moment was opportune, to propose that a Conference should be summoned to put an end to the war. Should the Allies accept the proposal, and should Germany refuse it, the United States would probably enter the war against Germany." The record of conversation also reported that House had said that the peace conference would secure terms "not unfavourable to the Allies" and that if the conference failed to achieve peace, "the United States would leave the Conference as a belligerent on the side of the Allies, if Germany was unreasonable."[42] Wilson pronounced the memorandum a diplomatic triumph, but he clouded its meaning all the more by inserting a "probably" before the word "leave" in the sentence quoted above. He took the document much more seriously than did the British or French, who shelved it, snubbed American mediation, and vowed victory over Germany.

As House moved among European capitals, Lansing informed the Allied governments that the United States sought a modus vivendi to defuse naval crises: The Allies would disarm merchant vessels, and the Germans would follow international law by warning enemy merchant ships. This suggestion revealed that Wilson understood the German argument that armed merchant vessels actually operated as offensive craft—that is, warships. The British and Colonel House protested when they received this news. The Germans seemed to endorse the proposal by declaring on February 10 that submarines would henceforth attack only *armed* merchant ships without warning. Suddenly Wilson reversed policy. He abandoned the modus vivendi in order to restore his standing with the British and sustain House's mediation efforts in London. Lansing announced, furthermore, that the United States would not ban its citizens from traveling on "defensively" armed merchant ships.

Wilson Leads America into World War

Why let one American passenger and a trigger-happy U-boat captain start a war? Why not keep Americans off belligerent ships and require them instead to sail on American vessels? From August 1914 to mid-March 1917 only three Americans (on the oil tanker *Gulflight,* May 1, 1915) had lost their lives on an American ship torpedoed by a U-boat. In contrast, about 190 Americans, including the *Lusitania's* 128, died on belligerent ships. After the *Falaba* was sunk, Bryan, still secretary of state, recognized that Americans had a right to travel on belligerent vessels, but he wanted Wilson to forgo that right. "I cannot see," Bryan wrote the president, "that he [an American on a belligerent ship] is differently situated from those who by remaining in a belligerent country assume risk of injury."[43] Wilson had, after all, urged Americans to leave war-torn Mexico. Ambassador James W. Gerard in Berlin wondered: "Why should we enter a great war because some American wants to cross on a ship where he can have a private bathroom?"[44]

In January 1916, member of Congress Jeff McLemore of Texas, a Democrat, introduced a resolution to prohibit Americans from traveling on armed belligerent vessels. In February, Senator Thomas P. Gore of Oklahoma, another Democrat, submitted a similar resolution in his chamber. Wilson, a firm believer in presidential supremacy, bristled at this challenge from Congress. He unleashed cabinet members with patronage muscle on timid legislators, suggesting that Gore-McLemore was a pro-German ploy. To halt American passage on belligerent ships, Wilson declared, would be to accept national humiliation and destruction of the "whole fine fabric of international law."[45] In short, he stuck with rigid, archaic concepts, refusing to adjust to the new factor of the submarine or to appreciate the impact on Germany of the obvious British violations of the same law. In early March, the Gore-McLemore resolution lost 68 to 14 in the Senate and 276 to 142 in the House. The resolution asked America to give up very little; it did not besmudge national honor. Wilson's message to Berlin rang loud and clear: Do not use your submarines.

In March 1916, another passenger ship, another U-boat, another torpedo, more American injuries: The French ship *Sussex,* moving across the English Channel, took a hit but did not sink. Aboard was a young American scholar, Samuel Flagg Bemis, later a renowned historian of foreign relations but then fresh from archival research

Woodrow Wilson (1856–1924). Scholar, professor, university president (Princeton), and Democratic governor (New Jersey), Woodrow Wilson was usually cocksure once he made a decision. "I would rather fail in a cause that will ultimately triumph than triumph in a cause that will ultimately fail," he once said. (*Cartoons,* 1912)

on Jay's Treaty. Bemis glimpsed the swirling wake of a torpedo. "The entire bow was blown off and with it the people who were in the dining room," he recalled.[46] Although four Americans sustained injuries, a wet Bemis escaped serious harm.

The *Sussex* attack violated the "*Arabic* pledge," even though the U-boat commander mistook the ship for a minelayer. Lansing wanted to break diplomatic relations with Berlin. Wilson decided instead on an ultimatum. He warned the Germans on April 18 that he would sever relations if they did not halt their submarine warfare against passenger and merchant vessels. With the unsuccessful German offensive at Verdun costing more than half a million lives, Berlin did not want war with the United States. In early May Germany promised (the "*Sussex* pledge") that submarines would not attack passenger or merchant ships without prior warning. The Germans also nagged Washington to stop British infractions of international law.

The British clamped down even harder on trade with the Central Powers. In July, London issued a "blacklist" of more than eighty American companies that had traded with the Central Powers. Even Wilson now fumed that he was "about at the end of my patience with Great Britain and the Allies."[47] He contemplated a ban on loans and exports to them, but he did little. Many Americans also condemned the brutal British smashing of the Irish Easter Rebellion in April 1916.

Shortly after his reelection in 1916, under the slogan "He Kept Us Out of War," the president boldly asked the belligerents to state their war aims. Neither Berlin nor London, still seeking military victory, welcomed Wilson's mediation. Germany coveted Poland, Lithuania, Belgium, and the Belgian Congo; Britain sought German colonies; France wanted Alsace-Lorraine. Wilson pointedly rejected such goals on January 22, 1917, when he called for a "peace without victory" because only through a peace founded on the "equality of nations" could a lasting world order be achieved. He regarded victory as "an intoxicant that fires the national brain and leaves a craving for more."[48] The French novelist Anatole France responded cynically: "Peace without victory is bread without yeast . . . , love without quarrels, a camel without humps, night without moon, roof without smoke, town without brothel."[49]

In early 1917 crises mounted quickly. On January 31 Berlin announced that German submarines would attack without warning and sink all vessels, enemy and neutral, found near British waters. This declaration of unrestricted submarine warfare expressed Germany's calculated risk that it could defeat England and France before the United States could mobilize and send soldiers overseas. The cocky German naval minister remarked: "From a military standpoint, America's entrance is as nothing."[50] German naval officers persuaded the kaiser that the U-boats, now numbering about one hundred, could knock Britain out of the war in six months. Army officers, bogged down in trench warfare, hoped to end their costly immobility through a bold stroke.

On February 3 Washington severed diplomatic relations with Berlin. According to Lansing, Wilson became "more and more impressed with the idea that 'white civilization' and its domination over the world rested largely on our ability to keep this country intact, as we would have to build up the nations ravaged by the war."[51] Yet Wilson had also committed himself to stand firmly against unrestricted submarine warfare. Allied ships carrying war supplies soon suffered increasing losses, and the few American vessels carrying contraband stayed in port or shifted to trade outside the European war zones. Goods stacked up on wharves. The U.S. economy seemed imperiled.

Next came an apparent challenge to U.S. security. Washington had already endured espionage and sabotage by German agents, most notably the explosions at the Black Tom munitions factories across from the Statue of Liberty in July 1916. In late February the British passed to Ambassador Page an intercepted telegram dated January 16 and sent to Mexico by German foreign minister Arthur Zimmermann. The message proposed a military alliance with the U.S. neighbor. And should war with the United States break out, Germany would help Mexico "reconquer" the territory lost in 1848. Zimmermann also suggested adding Japan to the alliance "at the moment war breaks out between Mexico and the United States."[52] Although the skeptical Mexican government never took up the German offer, Wilson now saw Germany as a "madman that should be curbed."[53] "This wd [would] precipitate a war between almost any 2 nations," Page confided to his diary.[54]

Wilson now asked Congress for authority to arm American merchant vessels. On March 1, to create a favorable public opinion for the request, he released the Zimmermann telegram to the press. But antiwar senators Robert La Follette and George Norris led a filibuster—a "little group of willful men," Wilson snarled—that killed the armed ship legislation.[55] Stubbornly ignoring the Senate, Wilson ordered the arming anyway. To no avail: during March 16–18 alone U-boats sunk the American ships *City of Memphis, Illinois,* and *Vigilancia.* Buttressed by the unanimous support of his cabinet, the president decided for war.

After several intense days writing his own speech with help from Colonel House, Wilson addressed a special joint session of Congress on the evening of April 2. He asked for a declaration of war against Germany—a war that Berlin had "thrust" on the United States. The "unmanly business" of using submarines, he asserted, constituted "warfare against mankind." Freedom of the seas, commerce, American lives, human rights—the "outlaw" U-boats challenged all. Economic self-interest, morality, and national honor compelled Americans to fight. He characterized the German government as a menacing monster striking at the "very roots of human life." The "Prussian autocracy" stirred up trouble through spies and the Zimmermann telegram. He also hailed the Russian Revolution of March, which made Russia "a fit partner for a league of honor" in a crusade against autocracy. Then came the memorable words: "The world must be made safe for democracy."[56]

Although the oration simplified issues and promised too much for American intervention, the moment evoked patriotic fervor. "It is [Kaiser] Bill against Woodrow, Germany against America, Hell against Heaven," proclaimed the evangelist Billy Sunday, as he demonized the enemy as "wolfish Huns, whose fangs drip with blood."[57] By votes of 82 to 6 in the Senate on April 4 (La Follette and Norris among the dissenters) and 373 to 50 in the House on April 6 (Majority Leader Claude Kitchin and nine of Wisconsin's eleven representatives among those voting nay), Congress endorsed Wilson's call for a war for peace. In a rebuke to feminist pacifism, one senator voted for war because it required "a courage both moral and physical, a mind free from trash and slush, flexed muscles and sinews that have not been debilitated, or degenerated by sensuality, security, and luxury."[58]

Jeannette Rankin (1880–1973). Native of Montana, Rankin, in 1916, became the first woman to be elected to the House of Representatives. A life-long pacifist, she voted against war in 1917, only to lose her seat the following year. In the interwar period she lobbied for peace and was again elected to Congress in 1940. Once again she cast the only vote against war in 1941. She later marched against the Vietnam War. Rankin took pride in being "the first woman who was ever asked what she thought about war [and] said 'NO.'" (Library of Congress)

Submarine warfare precipitated the American decision to enter the war. Had no submarine menaced American lives, property, and the U.S. definition of international law, no American soldiers would have gone to France. Critics have argued, however, that from the German perspective, the submarine became necessary because of the long list of unfriendly American acts: acquiescence in the British blockade, part of a general pro-British bias; huge munitions shipments to the Allies; large loans; an interpretation of neutral rights that insisted that American passengers could sail anywhere, even into a war zone. Take away those acts, which the Germans considered unneutral, and they might not have unleashed the U-boats. To dissenters it seemed wrong that American ideals and interests could depend so perilously on armed ships carrying contraband, heading for Britain, and steaming through a war zone. Yet Wilson and his advisers had so defined the problem.

Permeating Wilson's policies was the traditional American belief that others must conform to U.S. prescriptions and that America's ideals served as a beacon for the world. "We created this Nation," the president once proclaimed, "not to serve ourselves, but to serve mankind."[59] When the Germans defied America's rules, ideals, and property, and threatened its security through a proposed alliance with Mexico, they had to be punished. Here was an opportunity to protect both humane principles and commercial interests. When Wilson spoke passionately of the right of a neutral to freedom of the seas, he demonstrated the interconnections among American moral, economic, and strategic interests. Wilson sought the role of peacemaker and promised to remake the world in the American image—world order in which barriers to political democracy and the Open Door came down, in which revolution and aggression no longer threatened. As the philosopher John Dewey put it, war came at a "plastic juncture" in history in which Americans could fight to reshape the world according to progressive principles.[60]

The Debate over Preparedness

Berlin's assumption that U.S. soldiers could not reach France fast enough to reverse an expected German victory proved a gross misjudgment. American military muscle and economic power, in fact, decisively tipped the balance against Germany. Given the information available in early 1917, however, the German calculation does not seem so unrealistic. In April the United States had no capacity to send a major expedition to the western front. At that date the Regular Army counted only 130,000 officers and men, backed by 180,000 national guardsmen. Although some officers had been seasoned by interventions in Cuba, the Philippines, and Mexico, many soldiers lacked adequate training. Arsenals had meager supplies of such modern weapons as the machine gun. The "Air Service," then part of the army, did not have a plane of modern design with a machine gun, and some warships had never fired a gun.

An American "preparedness movement" had been under way for months, encouraged by prominent Americans such as General Leonard Wood, who overstated the case when he argued that America's military weakness invited attack, but rang true when he noted that the United States was not recognized as a top-notch military power. After 1914, Wood, Theodore Roosevelt, the National Security League, the Army League, and the Navy League lobbied for bigger military appropriations with the argument that "preparedness" offered insurance against war. When the hit pacifist song "I Didn't Raise My Boy to Be a Soldier" became "an icon of popular antiwar sentiment" in 1915, preparedness proponents countered with "I Didn't Raise My Boy to Be a Coward."[61] One propaganda film, *The Battle Cry of Peace* (1916), depicted spike-helmeted soldiers rampaging through New York City where an American mother killed her two daughters to spare them "a fate worse than death."[62] That same year a U.S. admiral claimed that a single hostile dreadnought could "knock down all the buildings in New York . . . , smash all the cars, break down all the bridges, and sink all the shipping."[63]

Convinced that "a great standing army" was "antidemocratic," Wilson belatedly sought moderate preparedness.[64] He asked for a half-billion-dollar naval expansion program in late 1915, including ten battleships. The new force would surpass Britain as "incomparably the greatest navy in the world."[65] He also urged that land forces be enlarged and reorganized.

Perpetuating the antimilitarist tradition of great numbers of Americans, Senator La Follette, Representative Kitchin, and prominent reformers such as William Jennings Bryan, Lillian Wald, and Oswald Garrison Villard spurred a movement against these measures. These peace advocates, especially the Women's Peace Party (representing "the mother half of humanity"), argued that war would interrupt reform at home, benefit big business, and curtail civil liberties.[66] Several peace leaders also joined the auto manufacturer Henry Ford in December 1915 as he sailed to Europe on his peace ship, *Oscar II,* to establish a Neutral Conference for Continuous Mediation—a quixotic attempt to end the war and get "the boys out of the trenches by Christmas."[67] The American Union Against Militarism agitated against preparedness with its papier-mâché dinosaur, "Jingo," whose collar read "ALL ARMOR PLATE—NO BRAINS."[68] Because his support of mediation, disarmament, and a postwar association of nations appealed to antiwar liberals and socialists ("progressive internationalists"), Wilson hoped that moderate preparedness would not alienate them. Chicago's famed social reformer Jane Addams remembered "moments of uneasiness," but she and others endorsed Wilson in the 1916 presidential campaign, for it seemed "at last that peace was assured and the future safe in the hands of an executive who had received an unequivocal mandate from the people 'to keep us out of war.'"[69]

In January 1916, Wilson set out on a two-month speaking tour, often criticizing members of his own party for their opposition to a military buildup. U-boat sinkings aided the president's message. In May 1916, Congress passed the National Defense Act, increasing the Regular Army to some 200,000 men and 11,000 officers, and the National Guard to 440,000 men and 17,000 officers. The act also authorized summer training camps, modeled after one held in Plattsburg, New York, in 1915 for the social and economic elite. Despite Jane Addams's query, "Why spend $45,000,000 for warships, when they will only be reduced to scrap heap after this war," the navy bill passed in August 1916.[70] Theodore Roosevelt thought the measures inadequate, but the anarchist Emma Goldman saw no difference between Roosevelt, "the born bully who uses a club," and Wilson, "the history professor who uses the smooth polished mask."[71] TR denounced pacifists as "active agents of the devil."[72]

Once in the war, after learning what the Allies "want and need is men, whether trained or not," Wilson relied on the Selective Service Act of May 1917.[73] National

Senator Robert M. La Follette (1855–1925). This *Life* magazine cartoon depicted the antiwar, progressive reformer as a traitor. La Follette wanted a referendum on the war, certain that the American people would vote no. Some Americans thought that he should be expelled from the Senate. Others claimed that he took orders from the German kaiser, here shown pinning medals on the Wisconsin senator. La Follette withstood the intolerance of dissent and continued to speak against organized power and for the powerless, who, he said, were the people destined to do the fighting and dying abroad. (State Historical Society of Wisconsin)

military service, proponents believed, would not only prepare the nation for battle but also instill respect for order, democracy, and sacrifice. Under the selective service system, 24,340,000 men eventually registered for the draft. Some 3,764,000 men received draft notices, and 2,820,000 were inducted (the others failed preinduction tests, never showed up, or claimed conscientious objector—CO—status). Over all, 4,744,000 soldiers, sailors, and marines served. The typical serviceman was a white, single, poorly educated (most had not attended high school) draftee between twenty-one and twenty-three years of age. Officer training camps turned out "ninety-day wonders," thousands of commissioned officers drawn largely from people of elite background. Although excluded from military combat, women became navy clerks, telephone operators in the Army Signal Corps, and nurses and physical therapists to the wounded and battle-shock cases.

Right after the U.S. declaration of war, the Allies begged for soldiers. General John J. "Black Jack" Pershing, now head of the American Expeditionary Force to Europe, soon sent a "show the flag" contingent to France to boost Allied morale. Neither Wilson nor Pershing, however, would accept the European recommendation that U.S. troops be inserted in Allied units. American units would cooperate in joint maneuvers with other forces, but the U.S. Army would remain separate and independent. National pride dictated this decision, but so did the realization that Allied commanders had for years wasted the lives of hundreds of thousands in trench warfare. Soldiers jumped out to charge German lines, also a maze of trenches.

Machine guns mowed them down; chlorine gas, first used by Germany in 1915, poisoned them. Nor did Wilson wish to endorse exploitative Allied war aims. Thus did the United States call itself an "associated" rather than an "allied" power in the war.

The Doughboys Make the Difference in Europe

On July 4, 1917, General Pershing reviewed the first battalion to arrive in France, as nearly a million Parisians tossed flowers, hugged the "doughboys" (apparently so-called because their buttons resembled dumplings made of dough), and cheered wildly. *"Lafayette, nous sommes ici!"* shouted Pershing's aide.[74]

To the dismay of American leaders, taverns and brothels quickly surrounded military camps. Alcohol and prostitution, of course, ranked as taboos in the United States during the Progressive era. "Fit to Fight" became the government's slogan, as it moved to close "red-light districts," designated "sin-free zones" around camps, and banned the sale of liquor to men in uniform. Government signs and flyers declared: "A German Bullet Is Cleaner Than A Whore."[75] The YMCA and the Jewish Welfare Board sent song leaders to camps. Movies, athletic programs, and well-stocked stores sought to keep soldiers on the base by making them feel "at home."

Success against venereal disease contrasted with a major flu epidemic, which first struck camps in spring 1918. The extremely contagious flu virus cut across race, gender, and class lines. At Camp Sherman, Ohio, one of the bases hit hardest, 1,101 people died between September 27 and October 13. Whereas about 51,000 soldiers died in battle during the war, some 62,000 soldiers died from diseases. "Doughboys" infected with the virus carried the flu with them to the European war, where it ignored national boundaries and turned into a global pandemic that killed more than 21 million people by spring 1919.

Approximately 400,000 African-American troops suffered racism and discrimination during this war "to make the world safe for democracy." Camps were segregated and "white only" signs posted. In 1917 in Houston, Texas, whites provoked blacks into a riot that left seventeen whites and two blacks dead. In the army, three out of every four black soldiers served in labor units, where they wielded a shovel, not a gun, or where they cooked or unloaded supplies. African Americans endured second-class citizenship and the contradiction between America's wartime rhetoric and reality. A statistic revealed the problem: 382 black Americans were lynched in the period 1914–1920. To little effect, Germany's propagandists added a separate unit for "American race problems" to target discontented blacks in the South.[76]

The first official American combat death in Europe came only ten days after Congress declared war—that of Edmund Charles Clinton Genet, the great-great-grandson of French Revolutionary diplomat Citizen Genet and member of the famed American volunteer air squadron, the Lafayette Escadrille. Despite Allied impatience, General Pershing hesitated to commit his green soldiers to full-scale battle. As it was, great numbers of troops shipped over in British vessels and had to borrow French weapons. Disease continued to stalk U.S. forces. American reformers hoped soldiers had enough social armor not to be tempted by "sin" overseas, but the venereal-disease rate spiraled up. French premier Georges Clemenceau offered licensed—health-inspected—prostitutes. When Secretary of War Newton Baker received the Gallic proposal, he exclaimed: "For God's sake . . . don't show this to the

Red Cross Postcard. Women served in many roles in the war. They became workers in weapons factories. They sold Liberty Bonds and publicized government mobilization programs as members of the Women's Committee of the Council of National Defense. In France, women nurses and canteen workers became envoys of the U.S. home front, representing the mothers, wives, and sisters left behind. As the historian Susan Zeiger has written, the government's sponsorship of these wartime roles for women cleverly blunted the feminist-pacifist claim that women were "inherently more peaceful than men and would oppose war out of love for their children." (Library of Congress)

President or he'll stop the war."[77] Prevention programs and the threat of court-martial eventually reduced the "VD" problem.

By early 1918 the Allies had become mired in a murderous strategy of throwing ground forces directly at enemy ground forces. German troops were mauling Italian forces, and the French army was still suffering from mutinies of the year before. In March, after Germany swallowed large chunks of European Russia through the Brest-Litovsk Treaty, Wilson warned of a German "empire of force" out to "dominate the world itself" and urged Americans to "arm and prepare themselves to contest the mastery of the world."[78] In April he called for "Force, Force to the utmost, Force without stint or limit."[79] Doughboys soon trooped into battle.

In March the German armies, swollen by forty divisions from the Russian front, launched a great offensive. Allied forces retreated, and by late May the kaiser's soldiers encamped near the Marne River less than fifty miles from Paris. Saint-Mihiel, Belleau Wood, Cantigny, Château-Thierry—French sites where U.S. soldiers shed their blood—soon became household words for Americans. In June at Château-Thierry the doughboys dramatically stopped a German advance. From May through September 1918 more than 1 million American troops went to France—2 million

First Division Troops Encounter German Gas Warfare, 1918. Near Soissons, France, U.S. soldiers attacked German lines through air contaminated with poisonous gas. The soldier in the foreground, wounded by fire, tore off his gas mask. Before U.S. intervention, President Wilson had deplored "this vast, gruesome contest of systematized destruction" and denied any "glory commensurate with the sacrifice of millions of men." (The Bettmann Archive)

by the November armistice. In mid-July the Allies launched a counteroffensive; nine American divisions fought fiercely near Château-Thierry, helping to lift the German threat from Paris. In the Meuse-Argonne offensive (begun in late September), more than 1 million American soldiers joined French and British units to penetrate the crumbling German lines. "The American infantry in the Argonne [Forest] won the war," German marshal Paul von Hindenburg later commented.[80]

On October 4, the German chancellor asked Wilson for an armistice. German troops had mutinied; revolution and riots plagued German cities; Bulgaria had left the war in September. Then Turkey dropped out in late October, and Austria-Hungary surrendered on November 3. Germany had no choice but to seek terms. The kaiser fled to Holland. On November 11, in a railroad car in the Compiègne Forest, German representatives capitulated.

Wilson Imagines a Better Future: The Fourteen Points and the Peace Conference

During the combat, President Wilson had begun to explain his plans for the peace. He trumpeted his vision most dramatically in his "Fourteen Points" speech before Congress on January 8, 1918. The first five points promised an "open" world after the war, a world distinguished by "open covenants, openly arrived at," freedom of navigation on the seas, equal trade opportunity and the removal of tariffs, reduction of armaments, and an end to colonialism. Points six through thirteen called for self-determination for national minorities in Europe. Point fourteen stood paramount: a "general association of nations" to ensure "political independence and territorial integrity to great and small states alike."[81] His Fourteen Points signaled a generous, nonpunitive postwar settlement. Pacifists felt that they had been "sent up into the very heaven of internationalism."[82] The Fourteen Points served too as effective American propaganda against revenge-fed Allied aims and Russian Bolshevik appeals for European revolution.

Leaders in France, Britain, and Italy feared that Wilson would deny them the spoils of war. In 1915 the Allies had signed secret treaties carving up German territories, including colonies in Africa and Asia. Dreaming of imperial expansion at Germany's expense, the Allies did not appreciate his attempts to slay the "dragons of reaction" in Europe.[83] In view of the comparative wartime losses, Europeans believed that Wilson "had bought his seat at the peace table at a discount."[84] When, in September and October 1918, Wilson exchanged notes with Germany and Austria-Hungary about an armistice, the Allied powers expressed strong reservations about the Fourteen Points. General Tasker Bliss, the U.S. representative on the Supreme War Council (established in fall 1917 to coordinate the Allied war effort), despaired that "the war will accomplish more than the abolition of *German* militarism while leaving *European* militarism as rampant as ever."[85] Wilson hinted that the United States might negotiate a separate peace with the Central Powers. The president might even publicize the exploitative Allied war aims. Also facing possible reduced American shipments to Europe, London, Paris, and Rome reluctantly accepted, in the armistice of November, peace negotiations on the basis of the Fourteen Points.

Wilson relished his opportunity. "For a brief interval," wrote the novelist H. G. Wells, "Wilson stood alone for mankind."[86] The United States could now claim a major role in deciding future international relations. The pictures of dying men dangling from barbed-wire fences and the battle-shock victims who staggered home persuaded many Americans of the need to prevent another conflagration. Wilson's call for a just peace commanded the backing of countless foreigners as well. Italians hoisted banners reading *Dio di Pace* ("God of Peace") and *Redentore dell' Humanità* ("Redeemer of Humanity") to welcome Wilson to Europe.

The president weakened his position even before the peace conference. Congressional leaders wanted him to stay home to handle domestic problems. Lansing feared that Wilson would lose his exalted image in the day-to-day conference bickering. The president would have only one vote, whereas from Washington he could symbolically marshal the votes of humankind. Wilson retorted that "England and France have not the same views with regard to peace that we have," so he had to attend personally to defend the Fourteen Points.[87]

Domestic politics soon set Wilson back. In October 1918, Wilson "hurled a brick into a beehive" by asking Americans to return a Democratic Congress loyal to him.[88] Partisan Republicans, resenting Wilson's attempt to identify himself and the Democratic party with the well-being of the nation, proceeded to capture the November election and majorities in both houses of Congress; they would sit in ultimate judgment of Wilson's peacemaking. The president also made the political mistake of not appointing either an important Republican or a senator to the American Peace Commission. Wilson, House, and Lansing sat on it; so did General Bliss and Henry White, a seasoned diplomat and nominal Republican. Some concessions to his political opposition, and to senatorial prerogatives in foreign affairs, might have smoothed the path later for his peace treaty.

On December 4, with great fanfare, Wilson departed from New York aboard the *George Washington*. He settled into a quiet voyage, surrounded by advisers and nearly 2,000 reports produced by "The Inquiry," a group of scholars who had studied issues likely to arise at the peace conference. Confident that "we can force" the Allies "to our way of thinking" because they will be "financially in our hands," the president had made few concrete plans.[89] After reaching France on December 15, Wilson basked in the admiration of enthusiastic Parisian crowds, and later thousands in Italy and England cheered him with near religious fervor. Wilson assumed that this generous outpouring meant that *his* peace aims were universally popular and that Americans "would be the only disinterested people" at Versailles.[90] He would soon discover that such "man-in-the-street" opinion did not impress David Lloyd George, prime minister of Britain, French premier Georges Clemenceau, or Italian prime minister Vittorio Orlando, his antagonists at the peace conference.

Germany and Bolshevik Russia (see page 98) were excluded from the conference of January–May 1919, but thirty-two nations sent delegations, which essentially followed the lead of the "Big Four." Most sessions worked in secrecy, hardly befitting Wilson's first "point." Clemenceau resented Wilson's "sermonettes" and preferred to work with the more compliant Colonel House. "The old tiger [Clemenceau] wants the grizzly bear [Wilson] back in the Rocky Mountains before he starts tearing up the German Hog," commented Lloyd George, who sought to build a strong France and to ensure German purchases of British exports.[91] A fervent Italian nationalist, Orlando concerned himself primarily with enlarging Italian territory. These leaders distrusted American power and sought bigger empires. Lloyd George complained of a chameleon-like Wilson—"the noble visionary, the implacable and unscrupulous partisan, the exalted idealist and the man of rather petty personal rancour."[92] Wilson, in turn, thought the Europeans "too weatherwise to see the weather."[93]

Much wrangling occurred over the disposition of colonies and the creation of new countries. "Tell me what's right and I'll fight for it," said Wilson as he appealed for self-determination, but the belligerents had already signed secret treaties of conquest.[94] After hard negotiating, the conferees mandated former German and Turkish colonies to the countries that had conquered them, to be loosely supervised under League of Nations auspices. Under the mandate system—a compromise between outright annexation and complete independence—France (with Syria and Lebanon) and Britain (with Iraq, Trans-Jordan, and Palestine) received parts of the Middle East. Japan acquired China's Shandong Province and some of Germany's Pacific islands. After Wilson's reluctant acceptance of the Shandong arrangement, the president deemed it "the best that could be accomplished out of a 'dirty past' " and planned to "let the League of Nations decide the matter later."[95] Outraged Chinese students in Beijing protested by launching the May Fourth Movement, an increasingly important anti-imperialist voice. Wilson also ignored a petition, "*Revendications du People Annamite,*" calling for self-determination in French Indochina and signed by, among others, Nguyen Al Quoc—later famous under the name Ho Chi Minh.[96] France gained the demilitarization of the German Rhineland and a stake in the coal-rich Saar Basin. Italy annexed South Tyrol and Trieste from the collapsed Austro-Hungarian Empire. Some 1,132,000 square miles changed hands. Newly independent countries also emerged from the defunct Austro-Hungarian Empire:

David Lloyd George (1863–1945). "America," said the British prime minister referring to the League of Nations, "had been offered the leadership of the world, but the Senate had tossed the sceptre into the sea." (Sketch by Anthony Saris, American Heritage Publishing Company)

Wilson in Dover, England, 1919. Wilson received flowers from English schoolchildren. The biographer Louis Auchincloss has written that "the ringing shouts in the streets and squares of the Old World must have made him [Wilson] feel like a messiah endowed with the vision to understand that the multitude was on the side of the merciful angels of a fair and lasting peace and that only a minority of stubborn old men wanted to crush the enemy to dust. He never learned that the only leader who can take advantage of the momentary enthusiasm of the common man is a dictator who can use its force to blast his way to power; a democrat must abide by the decision of those whom the common man has elected to represent him." (U.S. Signal Corps, National Archives)

Austria, Czechoslovakia, Hungary, Romania, and Yugoslavia. The Allies further exploited nationalism to recognize a ring of hostile states already established around Bolshevik Russia: Finland, Poland, Estonia, Latvia, and Lithuania, all formerly part of the Russian empire (see map on page 92). The mandate system smacked of imperialism, in violation of the Fourteen Points, but the new states in Europe fulfilled Wilson's self-determination pledge. To assuage French fears of a revived Germany, Britain and the United States signed a security pact with France guaranteeing its border, but Wilson never submitted it for Senate approval.

Reparations proved a knotty issue. The United States wanted a limited indemnity for Germany to avoid a harsh peace that might arouse long-term German resentment or debilitate the German economy and politics. "Our greatest error," Wilson predicted in March 1919, "would be to give her [Germany] powerful reasons for wishing one day to take revenge. Excessive demands would most certainly sow the seeds of war."[97] To cripple Germany, France pushed for a large bill of reparations. The conferees wrote a "war guilt clause," which held Germany responsible for all of the war's damages. Rationalizing that the League would ameliorate any excesses, Wilson gave in on both reparations and war guilt. The Reparations Commission in 1921 presented a hobbled Germany with a huge reparations bill of $33 billion, thereby helping to destabilize international economic relations for more than a decade.

The Allies played to Wilson's priorities: "Give him the League of Nations and he will give us all the rest."[98] Drafted largely by Wilson, the League's covenant provided for an influential council of five big powers (permanent) and representatives from smaller nations (by election) and an assembly of all nations for discussion. Wilson saw the heart of the covenant as Article 10, a provision designed to curb aggression and war: "The Members of the League undertake to respect and preserve as against external aggression the territorial integrity and existing political independence of all Members of the League." In case of aggression or threat, "the Council shall advise upon the means by which this obligation shall be fulfilled."[99] Wilson persuaded the conferees to merge the League covenant and the peace terms in a package. The League charter, then, constituted the first 26 articles of a 440-article Treaty of Paris. Wilson deemed the League covenant the noblest part of all—"It is practical, and yet it is intended to purify, to rectify, to elevate."[100]

The Germans signed sullenly on June 28 in the elegant Hall of Mirrors at Versailles. By stripping Germany of 13 percent of its territory, 10 percent of its population, and all of its colonies, and by demanding reparations, the treaty humiliated the Germans without crushing them. In one historian's words, the treaty contained "a witches' brew" with "too little Wilsonianism to appease, too little of Clemenceau to deter; enough of Wilson to provoke contempt, enough of Clemenceau to inspire hatred."[101] When Wilson died on February 3, 1924, the Weimar Republic in Berlin refrained from issuing an official condolence, and the German Embassy in Washington broke custom by not lowering its flag to half-mast.

Principle, Personality, Health, and Partisanship: The League Fight

Wilson spent almost six months in Europe negotiating the postwar peace. From February 24 to March 14, 1919, he returned to the United States for executive business. On arrival, he asserted that any U.S. failure to back the League "would break the heart of the world."[102] In Washington, Republicans peppered Wilson with questions about the degree to which the covenant limited American sovereignty. When Wilson spoke vaguely, Senator Frank Brandegee of Connecticut felt as if he had been "wandering with Alice in Wonderland and had tea with the Mad Hatter."[103] In early March, Republican senator Henry Cabot Lodge of Massachusetts engineered a "Round Robin," a statement by thirty-nine senators (enough to deny the treaty a two-thirds vote) that questioned the League covenant and requested that the peace treaty and the covenant be acted on separately. Many signers feared that the League would limit U.S. freedom to act independently in international affairs.

A defiant Wilson sailed again for France, determined that "little Americans," full of "watchful jealousies [and] of rabid antagonisms," would not destroy his beloved League.[104] Still, he was politician enough, and stung enough, to seek changes in Paris. He amended the covenant so that League members could refuse mandates, League jurisdiction over purely domestic issues was precluded, and the Monroe Doctrine was safeguarded against League interference. But he would not alter Article 10. When he returned to the United States in July, Wilson submitted the long Treaty of Versailles to the Senate on July 10, with an address that resembled an evangelical sermon: "The stage is set, the destiny disclosed. It has come about by no plan of our conceiving, but by the hand of God, who led us into this way."[105] Asked if

Boundaries of German, Russian, and
Austro-Hungarian Empires in 1914
Areas lost by Austro-Hungarian Empire
Areas lost by Russian Empire
Areas lost by German Empire
Areas lost by Bulgaria
Demilitarized zone
Boundaries of 1926

Europe Reshaped by War and Peace

he would accept senatorial "reservations" to the treaty, Wilson snapped: "Anyone who opposes me in that, I'll crush."[106]

Wilson, against strong odds, gained a good percentage of his goals as outlined in the Fourteen Points. Self-determination for nationalities advanced as never before in Europe, and the League ranked as a notable achievement. But Wilson did

Georges Clemenceau (1841–1929). Auguste Rodin's bronze aptly conveys the formidable stature of "The Tiger" from France, eager for revenge against Germany. "You seek to do justice to the Germans," Clemenceau told Wilson. "Do not believe that they will ever forgive us; they seek only the opportunity for revenge. Nothing will destroy the rage of those who wanted to establish their dominion over the world." (The Rodin Museum, Philadelphia)

compromise, especially when faced by formidable opposition such as that thrown up by Clemenceau. During the conference, too, both Italy and Japan had threatened to walk out unless they realized some territorial goals. Still, Wilson had so built up a case for an unselfish peace that when the conquerors' hard bargaining and harsh terms dominated the conference, observers could only conclude that the president had failed badly to live up to his millennial rhetoric. Critics said that Wilson should have left Paris in protest, refusing to sign, or that he might have threatened the Allies with U.S. economic pressure. Believing desperately that the League, with Article 10, would rectify all, Wilson warned Congress that without it, "the United States and every other country will have to arm to the teeth."[107]

He would not compromise at home, however. And he seldom provided systematic, technical analysis to treaty clauses. He simply expected the Senate dutifully to ratify his masterwork. Yet his earlier bypassing of that body and his own partisan speeches and self-righteousness ensured debate. Progressive internationalists protested that "the capitalists wanted the League as a superstate to protect their exploitative concessions in underdeveloped countries."[108] Henry Cabot Lodge asked a key question: "Are you willing to put your soldiers and your sailors at the disposition of other nations?"[109] Senator James Reed of Missouri feared racial peril from a League initially comprising fifteen white nations and seventeen nations of "black, brown, yellow, and red races," which, he claimed, ranked low in "civilization" and high in "barbarism."[110]

Article 10 seemed to rattle everybody. The article did not require members to use force, but it implied they should. Senator William Borah complained that "I may be

Henry Cabot Lodge (1850–1924). Wilson's partisan rival observed of the League Covenant that "it might get by at Princeton," Wilson's alma mater, "but certainly not at Harvard," where Lodge had earned a Ph.D. In a recent study of the League fight, the historian John Milton Cooper, Jr., has concluded: "For all their decency and intelligence, Wilson's opponents were wrong. For all his flaws and missteps, Wilson was right. He should have won the League fight. His defeat did break the heart of the world." (Library of Congress)

willing to help my neighbor . . . , but I do not want him . . . [to] decide for me when and how I shall act or to what extent I shall make sacrifice."[111] Senator Hiram Johnson of California claimed that Article 10 would "freeze the world into immutability and put it in a straightjacket," keeping "subject peoples . . . subject until the crack of doom."[112] The article seemed too open-ended. Without Article 10, which Wilson termed "the kingpin of the whole structure," the League "would be limited to dispensing aspirins to an international community in need of chemotherapy," according to one historian.[113]

Henry Cabot Lodge towered as Wilson's chief legislative obstacle. Chair of the Senate Foreign Relations Committee, nationalist-imperialist, author, Republican partisan, like Wilson a scholar in politics, Lodge packed his committee with anti-League senators, dragged out hearings for weeks, kept most Republicans together on treaty votes, and nurtured a personal animosity toward Wilson matched only by Wilson's detestation for Lodge. He attacked obliquely. He proposed "reservations" to the League covenant. Although in retrospect these reservations, intended to guard American sovereignty, do not appear to have been death blows to the League, at the time they stirred impassioned debate. They addressed the central question of American national interest—the degree to which the United States would limit its freedom of action, the degree to which the United States should engage in collective security. In fact, many of the fourteen reservations stated the obvious—that Congress would retain its constitutional role in foreign policy, for example. Another denied the League jurisdiction over American domestic legislation such as immigration laws. The reservation on Article 10 disclaimed any obligation to preserve the territorial integrity or political independence of another country unless authorized by Congress. For Wilson this meant "nullification of the treaty."[114]

The Senate divided into four groups. Wilson counted on about forty loyal Democrats called the Non-Reservationists. Another group, the Mild-Reservationists, led by Frank B. Kellogg, numbered about thirteen Republicans. The third faction, managed by Lodge, stood together as the Strong-Reservationists—some twenty Republicans and a few Democrats. The fourth group, consisting of sixteen Irreconcilables, ardently opposed the treaty with or without reservations. Most of them were Republicans, including La Follette, George Norris of Nebraska, and Hiram Johnson of California.

Wilson met individually with some twenty-three senators over two weeks, but he suffered a minor stroke on July 19, 1919. He thereafter rigidly refused to accept any reservations. He argued that a treaty ratified with reservations would have to go back to another conference for acceptance and every nation would then rush in with its pet reservations. This argument seemed hollow after the British announced that they would accept American reservations. In September 1919, Wilson set off on a 10,000-mile train trip across the United States. Growing more exhausted with each day, suffering severe headaches and nighttime coughing spells, and showing signs of what the medical historian Bert E. Park has diagnosed as dementia from hypertension and cerebrovascular disease, Wilson pounded the podium in forty speeches. He blasted his traducers as "absolute, contemptible quitters."[115] Comparing critics to radical Bolsheviks, he denounced Irish- and German-American opponents—"hyphens are the knives that are being stuck" into the treaty, he asserted.[116] He confused his audiences when he stated that Article 10 meant that the United States had a moral but not legal obligation to use armed force. Failure to join the League, he prophesied in St. Louis, would result in a war "in which not a few hundred thousand fine young men from America will have to die, but as many millions as are necessary to accomplish the final freedom of the peoples of the world."[117] On September 26, after an impassioned speech in Pueblo, Colorado, he awoke to nausea and uncontrollable facial twitching. "I just feel as if I am going to pieces," he said.[118] When his doctor ordered him to cancel the rest of his trip, Wilson wept.

After Wilson returned to Washington, a massive stroke paralyzed his left side. He lay flat in bed for six weeks and saw virtually no one except his wife and Dr. Cary Grayson. For months Mrs. Wilson ran her husband's political affairs, screening messages and banishing House and Lansing, among others, from presidential favor. If the president had resigned, as Dr. Grayson advised him to do, the Senate and Vice President James Marshall almost certainly would have reached some compromise agreement on admission to the League with reservations. As it was, his concentration hampered and his stubbornness accentuated by the stroke, Wilson adamantly refused to change his all-or-nothing position.

In November 1919, the Senate balloted on the complete treaty *with* reservations and rejected it, 39 to 55 (Irreconcilables and Non-Reservationists in the negative). Then it voted on the treaty *without* reservations and also rejected it, 38 to 53 (Irreconcilables and Reservationists in the negative). The president had instructed loyal Democrats not to accept any "reserved" treaty. In March 1920, another tally saw some Democrats vote in favor of reservations. Not enough, the treaty failed, 49 to 35, short of the two-thirds majority required for approval. When his wife urged him to accept reservations, Wilson admonished: "Little girl, don't you desert me. That I cannot stand."[119] Still a fighter, the president claimed that the election of 1920 would be a "solemn referendum" on the treaty. Other questions actually blurred the League issue in that campaign, and Warren G. Harding, who as a senator had supported reservations, promptly condemned the League after his election as president. In July 1921, Congress officially terminated the war, and in August, by treaty with Germany, the United States claimed as valid for itself the terms of the Treaty of Versailles—exclusive of the League articles.

The memorable League fight had ended. The tragic denouement occurred because of political partisanship, personal animosities, senatorial resentments, the president's failing health, adherence to traditional unilateralism, and disinterest and confusion in the public, which increasingly diverted its attention to readjusting to a peacetime economy. Progressive internationalists, many of them harassed by wartime restrictions on civil liberties and disappointed by Wilson's compromises with the imperial powers, no longer backed a president they thought reactionary. Then, of course, there was Wilson himself—stubborn, pontificating, combative, and increasingly ill. He might have conceded that the peace had imperfections. He might have provided more careful analysis of a long, complicated document. He might, further, have admitted that his opponents held a respectable intellectual position. Instead, he chose often shrill rhetoric and rigid self-righteousness. Most important, he saw the difference between himself and his critics as fundamental: whether it was in America's national interest to participate in collective security or seek safety unilaterally. As one critic put it, Wilson sought "collective security without forming an alliance." He wanted the "omelet" without "cracking the eggs."[120]

Although the League came into being without the United States as a member, none of the great powers wished to bestow significant authority on the new

Woodrow Wilson After His Stroke. Recent scholarly assessments of medical evidence reveal that Wilson had a long history of cerebrovascular disease. Wilson remained in the White House after his massive stroke in October 1919, while his wife and doctor tried to keep secret the severity of his physical incapacity. Dr. Edwin A. Weinstein, who has studied the relationship among Wilson's health, personality, and decisionmaking, has noted that the president could not maintain his train of thought and was prone to bursts of temper. (Library of Congress)

organization. Even if Washington had joined, it most likely would have acted outside the League's auspices, especially regarding its own empire in Latin America. No international association at that time could have outlawed war, dismantled empires, or scuttled navies. Wilson overshot reality in thinking that he could reform world politics through a new international body. Certainly the League represented a commendable restraint against war, but hardly a panacea for world peace.

Red Scare Abroad: Bolshevism and Intervention in Russia

"Paris cannot be understood without Moscow [Russia]," wrote Wilson's press secretary Ray Stannard Baker.[121] As he traveled to France aboard the *George Washington,* President Wilson depicted Bolshevism as "the poison of disorder, the poison of revolt, the poison of chaos."[122] Revolutionary and anticapitalist, the Bolsheviks, or Communists, threw fright into the leaders of Europe and America. At home and abroad the peacemakers battled the radical left. In the United States the Wilson administration trampled on civil liberties during an exaggerated "Red Scare," which sent innocent people to jail or deported them. The fluidity of events abroad prompted different opinions on "how we shall deal with the Bolsheviki"—from recognizing and taming them to overthrowing them.[123] Wilson himself seemed to think that "the only way to kill Bolshevism is . . . to open all the doors to commerce."[124] Only belatedly, after authorizing secret aid and espionage against the "Reds," did the president openly "cast in his lot" with the other powers in a futile attempt to destroy the new revolutionary regime.[125]

Most Americans applauded the Russian Revolution of March 1917, which toppled Tsar Nicholas II. Wilson himself viewed it as a thrust against autocracy, war, and imperialism. But when the moderate Provisional government under Alexander Kerensky fell to the radical Bolsheviks in October, Americans responded first with irritation and then anger in March 1918 after the Bolsheviks signed the Brest-Litovsk Treaty with Germany and ceded Ukraine and Finland, among other territories—a total of 1,267,000 square miles, 62,000,000 people, and one-third of Russia's best agricultural land. A necessary peace for a devastated Russia from the Bolshevik perspective, the treaty seemed a stab in the back for the Allies, a decisive victory for Berlin. Because German authorities had allowed Lenin to travel to Russia via Germany in 1917, some irate American officials even considered Bolsheviks pro-German. Others recoiled after Ambassador David Francis's testimony that Bolsheviks had "nationalized women."[126]

Lenin actually treated the United States as a special, favored case, and he consistently sought accommodation with Washington. Described by the Red Cross official Raymond Robins as "heavy set, deliberate, always cool . . . , steadfast, patient, utterly courageous, fanatical and confident," Lenin (and other Soviet officials) held a series of cordial conversations from December 1917 to May 1918 with Robins, a de facto U.S. representative.[127] They reached agreements on food relief, purchase of strategic materials, and exemption of American corporations from Bolshevik nationalization decrees. Prior to Brest-Litovsk, Robins urged prompt recognition of the Bolshevik government to keep Russia in the war, but President Wilson paid more heed to Francis's prediction that the Bolshevik regime would soon collapse.

ТОВ. Ленин ОЧИЩАЕТ

землю от нечисти.

"Comrade Lenin Sweeps the Globe Clean." Vladimir Ilyich Lenin (1870–1924) is shown in this Bolshevik art as a revolutionary ridding the world of monarchs and capitalists. But Lenin also craved Western trade and investment to spur his nation's economic reconstruction. As he said in 1919: "We are decidedly for an economic understanding with America—with all countries, but especially with America." (By Mikhail Cheremnykh and Victor Deni in Mikhail Guerman, comp., *Art of the October Revolution*, Leningrad: Aurora Art Publishers, 1979)

Although American officials in Russia engaged in propaganda and espionage and cooperated with Allied and "White" agents in anti-Bolshevik activities after November 1917, Wilson knew only broad outlines of this "secret war" when he sent U.S. troops to Archangel in northern Russia in August 1918. Ordered to avoid military action in the Russian civil war, they inevitably cooperated with British and French forces in attempts to roll back Bolshevik influence. Wilson said publicly that he authorized the expedition only to prevent German seizure of military supplies and a railroad, but he quickly approved $50 million in secret payments to White armies fighting the Bolsheviks. Wilson's motives, according to the historian David Foglesong, were "simultaneously anti-German and anti-Bolshevik."[128] Some 5,000 American troops eventually participated. They suffered through a bitter winter of fifty-below-zero temperatures. Their morale sagged; mutiny threatened. In December 1918, Senator Hiram Johnson introduced a resolution to withdraw them from Russia. It failed by one vote. U.S. soldiers did not leave Russia until June 1919. Two hundred twenty-two American soldiers died in what critics dubbed "Mr. Wilson's little war with Russia."[129]

Wilson claimed to be "sweating blood over the question of what is right and feasible . . . in Russia. It goes to pieces like quicksilver under my touch."[130] Pressure from the deeply anticommunist French and British and expansionist Japanese and his own anti-Bolshevism inclined him to send another expedition, this time to Siberia, where many envisioned the growth of a non-Bolshevik Russian bastion. In July 1918 he approved the expedition, later officially explaining to the American people that he was sending the troops (eventually numbering 10,000) to rescue a group of 70,000

A. Mitchell Palmer (1872–1936). When U.S. troops were intervening in Bolshevik Russia, Wilson's attorney general, A. Mitchell Palmer, was chasing suspected radicals at home. An architect of the "Red Scare," Palmer believed that the "blaze of revolution" was "eating its way into the homes of the American workmen, its sharp tongues of revolutionary heat . . . licking the altars of the churches, leaping into the belfry of the school bell, crawling into the sacred corners of American homes, burning up the foundations of society." In January 1920, the "Palmer Raids" put 4,000 people in jail. (Library of Congress)

Czechs stranded in Russia. Organized earlier as part of the Tsarist Russian army to fight for a Czech homeland in Austria-Hungary, the Czech legion was battling Bolsheviks along the Trans-Siberian Railroad in an effort to reach Vladivostok and possible transportation to the western front. Wilson's avowed purpose of evacuating the Czech legion derived also from his "friendly feelings" for Professor Thomas Masaryk and Czechoslovakia's independence, which Wilson soon recognized in October.[131]

Despite his disingenuous official explanation, Wilson believed that "a limited, indirect intervention to help the Russian people overcome domination by Bolsheviks and Germans would not contradict, but rather facilitate self-determination."[132] Yet intervention in Siberia became openly anti-Bolshevik because the Czechs were fighting Lenin's forces. Once Wilson found it impossible to evacuate the Czechs in time to fight in Europe, he reluctantly bowed to Allied pressure and gave support to the anti-Bolshevik White Russian leader Admiral A. V. Kolchak in the hope that he could form a pro-Western constitutional government. Despite money and supplies from the Allies, Kolchak faltered and his armies were routed before they could reach Moscow in June 1919. U.S. troops finally withdrew from Siberia in 1920, with one departing soldier noting that Vladivostok looked better in photographs because "the 'smell' ain't in the pictures or it m't be 'good night' when you opened the letter that contained them."[133]

At the Paris peace conference, the victors tried to isolate what they considered revolutionary contagion. The organization of the Third International in Moscow in early 1919 alarmed postwar leaders, as did communist Bela Kun's successful revolution in Hungary in March 1919, which lasted only until August. At Versailles, the conferees granted territory to Russia's neighbors (Poland, Romania, and Czechoslovakia) and recognized the nations of Finland, Estonia, Latvia, and Lithuania as a ring of unfriendly states around Russia. During the conference, besides the military interventions, the Allies imposed a strict economic blockade on Russia, sent aid to the White forces, and extended relief assistance to Austria and Hungary to stem political unrest.

Even though Wilson found the Soviets distasteful for their revolutionary, anticapitalist, anticlerical, authoritarian program, he never settled on a definitive, workable policy to co-opt or smash Bolshevism. Through "a reluctant, chaotic, and capricious process," the president allowed subordinates and circumstances to determine U.S. policy toward Russia.[134] His growing estrangement at Versailles from Colonel House, a conduit for pro-Soviet liberals, meant that the interventionist Allies and the rabidly anti-Bolshevik Secretary Lansing exerted greater influence.

Wilson's one serious effort to end the civil war in Russia through diplomacy came in January 1919 when he invited the warring groups to meet on Prinkipo (Prince's) Island off the Turkish coast. The Bolsheviks cautiously accepted the invitation, but the anti-Bolsheviks rejected any meeting. Next, in February, House helped arrange a trip by William C. Bullitt, a member of the U.S. delegation at Versailles, and Lincoln Steffens, the radical muckraking journalist, to Russia. Wilson envisioned a fact-finding mission. "Like white men encountering Indians," Bullitt "brought diplomatic pouches filled with cheap but much-welcomed canned goods and received heaps of caviar and box tickets to the ballet in return."[135] The ambitious envoy negotiated a proposal whereby the Allies would withdraw their troops, suspend military aid to White forces, and lift the economic blockade; in return the Soviets promised a cease-fire in which their opponents would hold the territories they occupied. Bullitt and Steffens returned to Paris convinced that their agreement would satisfy all parties. Lloyd George squelched it; Wilson ignored it. Bullitt resigned in protest.

The Allied counterrevolution proved costly. "It intensified the civil war and sent thousands of Russians to their deaths," the British official Bruce Lockhart later wrote. "Its direct effect was to provide the Bolsheviks with a cheap victory, . . . and to galvanize them into a strong and ruthless organism."[136] Although the Bolshevik emissary Ludwig Martens laid the foundations for future Soviet-American trade during the height of the Red Scare, Kremlin leaders nurtured long memories. "Never have any of our soldiers been on American soil," Premier Nikita S. Khrushchev lectured Americans as late as 1959, "but your soldiers were on Russian soil."[137] Participation by such young men as Allen and John Foster Dulles in Wilson's "secret war" against the Bolsheviks provided "the formative experiences that inclined [them] to rely on propaganda and covert action" when they later directed U.S. policies during the Cold War.[138] Such tactics ultimately backfired, as Wilson recognized before his death. "Bolshevism is a mistake," Wilson said. "If left alone it will destroy itself. It cannot survive because it is wrong."[139]

The Whispering Gallery of Global Disorder

More than 116,000 American soldiers died in World War I, which cost the U.S. government more than $30 billion. A third of the figure was paid through taxes; the other two-thirds represented borrowed money, which postwar generations would have to pay back. If one counts the long-term expense of veterans' benefits, the cost to the United States probably equaled three times the immediate direct costs. What President Dwight D. Eisenhower would later call the "military-industrial complex" had its origins in a high degree of government-business cooperation during the war; economic decisionmaking for the nation became centralized as never before; and the increased application of efficient methods in manufacturing contributed to U.S. economic power. The era of World War I witnessed other domestic events that impinged on foreign affairs: racial conflict, evidenced by twenty-five race riots in 1919; suppression of civil liberties under the Espionage and Sedition Acts, by which people who dissented from the war were silenced; the stunting of radical commentary (Socialist leader Eugene Debs and the pacifist Alice Paul, among others, went to jail for opposing the war) and hence the imposition of coercive consensus; and the withering of the reform impulse. Although Wilson tried to co-opt dissent by appointing labor leaders such as Samuel Gompers to war mobilization agencies, the negative response to the League of Nations among immigrants and industrial workers indicated "a revolt against corporatist wartime institutions."[140]

In foreign affairs, the White House assumed more authority in initiating policy and controlling execution. The State Department read diplomatic messages that Wilson had typed on his own machine. Wilson bypassed Congress on a number of occasions, failing to consult that body about the Fourteen Points, the goals at Versailles, and the intervention in Russia. He acted "like a divine-right monarch in the conduct of foreign relations."[141] The Senate finally rebelled by rejecting the League of Nations, but that negative decision did not reverse the trend of growing presidential power over foreign policy.

"We Are Making a New World."   The British painter Paul Nash rendered this gloomy commentary on the devastation wrought by World War I. The wartime ambulance driver Ernest Hemingway later wrote: "I had seen nothing sacred, and the things that were glorious had no glory and the sacrifices were like the stockyards at Chicago." (Imperial War Museum, London)

World War I took the lives of some 14,663,400 people—8 million soldiers and 6.6 million civilians (flu pandemic victims not included). Russia led with 3.7 million dead; Germany followed with 2.6 million; then came France with 1.4 million, Austria-Hungary with 950,000, and Britain with 939,000. One out of every two French males between the ages of twenty and thirty-two (in 1914) died during the war. It had been a total war, involving whole societies, not merely their armies. Never before had a war left the belligerents so exhausted, so battered. New destructive weapons made their debut—tanks, airplanes, poison gas, and submarines—"a preview of the Pandora's box of evils that the linkage of science with industry in the service of war was to mean."[142] The war reinforced American desires to avoid foreign entanglement. Captain Harry S. Truman of Missouri claimed that most soldiers "don't give a whoop (to put it mildly) whether Russia has a Red Government or no government and if the King of the Lollipops wants to slaughter his subjects or his Prime Minister it's all the same to us."[143] Disillusioned clergy regretted their participation in the "shrieking and hysterical patriotism."[144] As the amputee protagonist in the movie *The Big Parade* (1925) put it: "What the hell did we get out of this war? Parades—who the hell cares."[145] The war had ended "the artificial glow of past American idealism," wrote the novelist Ellen Glasgow.[146]

World War I stacked the cards for the future by bequeathing an unstable international system. Empires broke up—the Turkish, Austro-Hungarian, German, and Russian—creating new and weak nations. The Europe-oriented international order of the turn of the century fragmented and left, in Thomas Masaryk's words, "a laboratory atop a vast cemetery" that included several new states in central and eastern

Europe.[147] Nationalists in Asia, such as Mahatma Gandhi in British-dominated India and Ho Chi Minh in French-controlled Indochina, set goals of national liberation based in part on Wilson's ideal of self-determination. "Wilson's proposals, once set forth, could not be recalled," said Sun Zhongshan (Sun Yat-Sen) in 1924 as his China battled imperialist domination.[148] In Latin America, prewar European economic ties withered, inviting the United States to expand its interests there, where nationalists resented the greater North American presence. The rise of Bolshevism in Russia and the hostility it aroused around the world made an already fluid international system even more so. Because of fear of a revived Germany, leaders tried to strip it of power, creating bitter resentments among the German people. Facing reconstruction problems at home, the victors tagged Germany with a huge reparations bill that would disorient the world economy. Nobody seemed happy with the postwar settlement; many would attempt to recapture lost opportunities or to redefine the terms. Yet to blame World War II on Wilson's failures, as the historian Margaret MacMillan has noted, "is to ignore the actions of everyone—political leaders, diplomats, soldiers, ordinary voters—for twenty years between 1919 and 1939."[149]

World War I made the United States the world's leading economic power. As Wilson confidently put it: "The financial leadership will be ours. The industrial primacy will be ours. The commercial advantage will be ours."[150] During the war years, to meet the need for raw materials, American companies expanded operations in developing nations. Goodyear went into the Dutch East Indies for rubber, Swift and Armour reached into South America, tin interests tapped Bolivia, copper companies penetrated Chile, and oil firms sank new wells in Latin America and gained new concessions in the Middle East. Washington encouraged this economic expansion by building up the merchant marine, which by 1919 had grown 60 percent larger than its prewar size. By 1920, the United States produced about 40 percent of the world's coal and 50 percent of its pig iron.

Because the U.S. government and American citizens loaned heavily to the Allies during the war, the nation shifted from a debtor to a creditor, with Wall Street replacing London as the world's financial center. Whereas before the war Americans owed foreigners some $3 billion, after the conflict foreigners owed Americans and the U.S. government about $13 billion ($10 billion of which represented governments' debts). Americans had devised plans to seize the apparent economic opportunities given them by the war—the Edge Act to permit foreign branch banks, and the Webb-Pomerene Act to allow trade associations to continue to combine for export trading without fear of antitrust action, for example—but a key question remained: How could Europeans pay back their debt to the United States? The answer lay somewhere in a complicated tangle of loans, reparations, tariffs, and world trade.

Economic disorder and political instability thus became the twin legacies of global war. "The world is all now one single whispering gallery," Wilson asserted in September 1919. "All the impulses . . . reach to the ends of the earth; . . . with the tongue of the wireless and the tongue of the telegraph, all the suggestions of disorder are spread." More than most Americans, Woodrow Wilson understood that global interdependence exposed America to "disorder and discontent and dissolution throughout the world."[151] And "democracy has not yet made the world safe against irrational revolution," he admitted.[152]

FURTHER READING FOR THE PERIOD 1914–1920

Many of the works listed in the last chapter also explore the themes, events, and personalities in the era of World War I. See also Anthony Boyle, *Foundations of World Order* (1999); John W. Chambers, *The Tyranny of Change* (1992); Alan Dawley, *Changing the World* (2003); Robert E. Hannigan, *The New World Power* (2002); Ellis W. Hawley, *The Great War and the Search for a Modern Order* (1992); Clayton D. James and Anne Sharp Wells, *America and the Great War* (1998); Bernadotte E. Schmitt and Harold C. Vedeler, *The World in the Crucible, 1914–1919* (1984); Tony Smith, *America's Mission* (1994); David Stevenson, *The First World War and International Politics* (1988); and Spencer C. Tucker, *The Great War* (1998).

For Woodrow Wilson and his foreign-policy views, consult Lloyd E. Ambrosius, *Wilsonianism* (2002); Louis Auchincloss, *Woodrow Wilson* (2000); H. W. Brands, *Woodrow Wilson* (2003); Kendrick A. Clements, *The Presidency of Woodrow Wilson* (1990) and *Woodrow Wilson* (1987); John Milton Cooper, Jr., *The Warrior and the Priest* (1983); Thomas J. Knock, *To End All Wars* (1992); Phyllis Lee Levin, *Edith and Woodrow* (2001); Arthur S. Link, *Wilson* (1960–1965) and *Woodrow Wilson: Revolution, War, and Peace* (1979); Frank Ninkovich, *The Wilsonian Century* (1999); Jan Willem Schulte Nordholt, *Woodrow Wilson* (1991); and John A. Thompson, *Woodrow Wilson* (2001).

Wilson's health problems and their relationship to decisionmaking are examined in Robert H. Ferrell, *Ill-Advised* (1992), and Edwin A. Weinstein, *Woodrow Wilson: A Medical and Psychological Biography* (1981). See also the essays by Dr. Bert E. Park in volumes of Arthur S. Link et al., eds., *The Papers of Woodrow Wilson*, and Park's *Ailing, Aging, and Addicted* (1993) and *The Impact of Illness on World Leaders* (1986).

Central actors in the period's drama are presented in LeRoy Ashby, *William Jennings Bryan* (1987); Kendrick A. Clements, *William Jennings Bryan* (1982); Paolo Coletta, *William Jennings Bryan* (1956–1969); John Milton Cooper, Jr., *Walter Hines Page* (1977); Ross Gregory, *Walter Hines Page* (1970); George H. Nash, *The Life of Herbert Hoover* (1996); Ronald Steel, *Walter Lippmann and the American Century* (1981); David P. Thelen, *Robert M. La Follette and the Insurgent Spirit* (1976); and William C. Widenor, *Henry Cabot Lodge and the Search for an American Foreign Policy* (1980).

For European questions and the neutrality issue on the U.S. road to World War I, see Thomas A. Bailey and Paul B. Ryan, *The Lusitania Disaster* (1975); Henry Blumenthal, *Illusion and Reality in Franco-American Diplomacy, 1914–1945* (1986); John W. Coogan, *The End of Neutrality* (1981); David M. Esposito, *The Legacy of Woodrow Wilson* (1996); Robert H. Ferrell, *Woodrow Wilson and World War I* (1985); Ross Gregory, *The Origins of American Intervention in the First World War* (1971); Ernest R. May, *The World War and American Isolation, 1914–1917* (1959); Diana Preston, *Lusitania* (2002); and David Ramsey, *Lusitania* (2002).

The German-American relationship is spotlighted in Reinhard R. Doerries, *Imperial Challenge* (1989); Manfred Jonas, *The United States and Germany* (1984); Hans-Jürgen Schröder, ed., *Confrontation and Cooperation* (1993); and Barbara Tuchman, *The Zimmermann Telegram* (1958).

The Anglo-American relationship is featured in Kathleen Burk, *Britain, America, and the Sinews of War, 1914–1918* (1985); G. R. Conyne, *Woodrow Wilson: British Perspectives, 1912–21* (1992); and Joyce G. Williams, *Colonel House and Sir Edward Grey* (1984).

For the peace movement, see works cited in the previous chapter and Charles DeBenedetti, ed., *Peace Heroes in Twentieth-Century America* (1986); Allen F. Davis, *American Heroine* (1974) (Addams); Frances H. Early, *A World Without War* (1997); Barbara S. Kraft, *The Peace Ship* (1978); Kathleen Kennedy, *Subversive Mothers and Scurrilous Citizens* (1999); Erika A. Kuhlman, *Petticoats and White Feathers* (1997); and Ernest A. McKay, *Against Wilson and War* (1996).

America's preparedness and warmaking experiences are discussed in Robert B. Bruce, *A Fraternity of Arms: America & France in the Great War* (2003); John W. Chambers, *To Raise an Army* (1987); J. Garry Clifford, *The Citizen Soldiers* (1972); Edward M. Coffman, *The War to End All Wars* (1968); Byron Farrell, *Over There* (1999); Kenneth J. Hagan, *This People's Navy* (1991); Jennifer D. Keene, *The Doughboys, the Great War, and the Remaking of America* (2002); Thomas C. Leonard, *Above the Battle* (1978); Bullitt Lowry, *Armistice, 1918* (1997); David F. Trask, *The AEF and Coalition Warmaking* (1993), *Captains & Cabinets: Anglo-American Naval Relations, 1917–1918* (1980), and *The United States in the Supreme War Council* (1961); David R. Woodward, *Trial by Friendship: Anglo-American Relations, 1917–1918* (1993); Susan Zeiger, *In Uncle Sam's Service* (1999) (women); and Robert H. Zieger, *America's Great War* (2001).

For the wartime home front, civil-liberties issues, and propaganda, see Allan M. Brandt, *No Magic Bullet* (1985) (venereal disease); Alfred W. Crosby, *America's Forgotten Pandemic* (1989); Leslie Midkiff De-

Bauche, *Reel Patriotism* (1997); Mark Ellis, *Race, War, and Surveillance* (2002); David M. Kennedy, *Over Here* (1980); Elizabeth McKillen, *Chicago Labor and the Quest for a Democratic Diplomacy* (1995); Joseph A. McCartin, *Labor's Great War* (1998); Paul L. Murphy, *World War I and the Origin of Civil Liberties* (1979); Richard Polenberg, *Fighting Faiths* (1987); Ronald Schaffer, *America in the Great War* (1991); John A. Thompson, *Reformers and War* (1986); and Stephen Vaughn, *Hold Fast the Inner Lines* (1980) (Committee on Public Information).

The Versailles peacemaking and League debate are discussed in Lloyd E. Ambrosius, *Wilsonian Statecraft* (1991) and *Woodrow Wilson and the American Diplomatic Tradition* (1987); Manfred F. Boeneke et al., eds., *The Treaty of Versailles* (1998); John M. Cooper, Jr., *Breaking the Heart of the World* (2002); Inga Floto, *Colonel House in Paris* (1973); Lawrence E. Gelfand, *The Inquiry* (1963); Derek Heater, *National Self-Determination* (1994); Warren F. Kuehl, *Seeking World Order* (1969); Warren F. Kuehl and Lynne K. Dunne, *Keeping the Covenant* (1997); Antony Lentin, *Lloyd George, Woodrow Wilson, and the Guilt of Germany* (1985); Margaret MacMillan, *Paris 1919* (2002); Herbert F. Margulies, *The Mild Reservationists* (1989); Stuart I. Rochester, *American Liberal Disillusionment in the Wake of World War I* (1977); Klaus Schwabe, *Woodrow Wilson, Revolutionary Germany, and Peacemaking* (1985); Alan Sharp, *The Versailles Settlement* (1991); Ralph A. Stone, *The Irreconcilables* (1970); Marc Trachenberg, *Reparations in World Politics* (1986); and Arthur Walworth, *America's Moment, 1918* (1977) and *Wilson and His Peacemakers* (1986).

The U.S. response to Bolshevism, intervention in Russia, and the Red Scare are investigated in Leo Bacino, *Reconstructing Russia* (1999); Donald E. Davis and Eugene P. Trani, *The First Cold War* (2000); Victor M. Fic, *The Collapse of American Policy in Russia and Siberia, 1918* (1995); David S. Foglesong, *America's Secret War Against Bolshevism* (1995); Lloyd Gardner, *Safe for Democracy* (1984); George F. Kennan, *Russia Leaves the War* (1956) and *The Decision to Intervene* (1958); Linda Killen, *The Russian Bureau* (1983); N. Gordon Levin, Jr., *Woodrow Wilson and World Politics* (1968); Arthur S. Link, ed., *Woodrow Wilson and a Revolutionary World, 1913–1921* (1982); Arno Mayer, *Politics and Diplomacy of Peacemaking* (1967); David W. McFadden, *Alternative Paths: Soviets and Americans, 1917–1920* (1993); William Pencak, *For God and Country* (1989) (American Legion); Benjamin D. Rhodes, *The Anglo-American Winter War with Russia, 1918–1919* (1988); Neil V. Salzman, *Reform and Revolution* (1991) (Robins); Norman Saul, *War and Revolution* (2001); Ilya Somin, *Stillborn Crusade: The Tragic Failure of Western Intervention in the Russian Civil War* (1996); John Thompson, *Russia, Bolshevism, and the Versailles Peace* (1966); and Betty Miller Unterberger, *America's Siberian Expedition* (1956) and *The United States, Revolutionary Russia, and the Rise of Czechoslovakia* (1989).

U.S. economic expansion abroad during the war is studied in Burton I. Kaufman, *Efficiency and Expansion* (1974); Emily S. Rosenberg, *World War I and the Growth of United States Predominance in Latin America* (1987); and Jeffrey J. Safford, *Wilsonian Maritime Diplomacy, 1913–1921* (1978).

Also see the General Bibliography, the following notes, and Robert L. Beisner, ed., *Guide to American Foreign Relations Since 1600* (2003).

For comprehensive coverage of foreign-relations topics, see the articles in the four-volume *Encyclopedia of U.S. Foreign Relations* (1997), edited by Bruce W. Jentleson and Thomas G. Paterson.

NOTES TO CHAPTER 3

1. Quoted in Thomas Bailey and Paul Ryan, *The* Lusitania *Disaster* (New York: Free Press, 1975), p. 81.
2. Quoted in Edward Ellis, *Echoes of Distant Thunder* (New York: Coward, McCann & Geoghegan, 1975), p. 195.
3. Quoted in Bailey and Ryan, Lusitania *Disaster*, p. 94.
4. Quoted *ibid.*, p. 82.
5. Quoted *ibid.*, p. 133.
6. Quoted in C. L. Droste and W. H. Tantum, eds., *The* Lusitania *Case* (Riverside, Conn.: 7 C's Press, 1972), p. 172.
7. Quoted in Burton J. Hendrick, *Life and Letters of Walter Hines Page* (Garden City, N.Y.: Doubleday, Page, 1922–1925; 3 vols.), II, 2.
8. William Jennings Bryan and Mary B. Bryan, *Memoirs* (Chicago: Winston, 1925), pp. 398–399.
9. Quoted in William Harbaugh, *The Life and Times of Theodore Roosevelt* (New York: Oxford University Press, 1975), p. 448.
10. John Milton Cooper, Jr., *The Warrior and the Priest* (Cambridge: Harvard University Press, 1983), p. 288.
11. R. S. Baker and W. E. Dodd, eds., *Public Papers of Woodrow Wilson* (New York: Harper & Brothers, 1926; 2 vols.), I, 321.
12. Quoted in Priscilla Roberts, "The Anglo-American Theme," *Diplomatic History*, XXI (Summer 1997), 340.
13. Quoted in August Heckscher, *Woodrow Wilson* (New York: Charles Scribner's Sons, 1991), p. 365.
14. *Foreign Relations, 1915, Supplement* (Washington, D.C.: Government Printing Office, 1928), p. 396.

15. Quoted in Richard R. Doerries, *Imperial Challenge* (Chapel Hill: University of North Carolina Press, 1989), p. 105.
16. David F. Houston, *Eight Years with Wilson's Cabinet* (Garden City, N.Y.: Doubleday, Page, 1926), 137.
17. Quoted in LeRoy Ashby, *William Jennings Bryan* (Boston: Twayne, 1987), p. 160.
18. Quoted *ibid.*, p. 161.
19. Quoted in Doerries, *Imperial Challenge*, p. 111.
20. Bailey and Ryan, *Lusitania Disaster*, p. 340.
21. Robert Lansing, *War Memoirs* (Indianapolis: Bobbs-Merrill, 1935), p. 128.
22. Ray S. Baker quoted in Arthur S. Link et al., eds., *The Papers of Woodrow Wilson* (Princeton: Princeton University Press, 1989), LXI, 383.
23. Quoted in Rohan Butler, "The Peace Settlement of Versailles, 1918–1933," in C. L. Mowat, ed., *The New Cambridge Modern History*, vol. *XII* (Cambridge, Eng.: Cambridge University Press, 1968), p. 214.
24. Quoted in Frank Ninkovich, *Modernity and Power* (Chicago: University of Chicago Press, 1994), p. 42.
25. Lansing quoted in Margaret MacMillan, *Paris 1919* (New York: Random House, 2002), p. 10.
26. Quoted in Robert E. Hannigan, *The New World Power* (Philadelphia: University of Pennsylvania Press, 2002), p. 228.
27. Quoted in Hendrick, *Life and Letters*, I, 310.
28. Baker and Dodd, *Public Papers*, I, 157–159.
29. Cecil Spring-Rice quoting Wilson in G. R. Conyne, *Woodrow Wilson* (New York: St. Martin's, 1992), p. 44.
30. Quoted in Alexander DeConde, *Ethnicity, Race, and American Foreign Policy* (Boston: Northeastern University Press, 1992), p. 86.
31. Quoted in Manfred F. Boeneke, "Woodrow Wilson's Image of Germany," in Manfred F. Boeneke, Gerald D. Feldman, and Elisabeth Glaser, eds., *The Treaty of Versailles* (New York: Cambridge University Press, 1998), p. 606.
32. Quoted in Barbara Tuchman, *The Guns of August* (New York: Dell [1962], 1963), p. 153.
33. *Life* quoted in Mark Sullivan, *Our Times* (New York: Charles Scribner's Sons, 1926–1937; 6 vols.), V, 59.
34. Quoted in Ray Stannard Baker, *Woodrow Wilson* (New York: Doubleday, Doran, 1927–1939; 8 vols.), V, 175.
35. Quoted in Elisabeth Glaser, "J. P. Morgan & Company and Aid for the Allies, 1914–1916," in Elisabeth Glaser and Hermann Wellenreuther, eds., *Bridging the Atlantic* (New York: Cambridge University Press, 2002), p. 230.
36. Quoted in Ross A. Kennedy, "Woodrow Wilson, World War I, and an American Conception of National Security," *Diplomatic History*, XXV (Winter 2001), 23.
37. Kathleen Burk, *Britain, America, and the Sinews of War, 1914–1918* (Boston: Allen & Unwin, 1985), p. 5.
38. Frederick Dixon quoting Wilson in Conyne, *Wilson*, p. 51.
39. Quoted in Frederick S. Calhoun, *Uses of Force and Wilsonian Foreign Policy* (Kent, Ohio: Kent State University Press, 1993), p. 100.
40. Quoted in Arthur S. Link, *Woodrow Wilson and the Progressive Era, 1910–1917* (New York: Harper and Row, 1954), p. 203.
41. French report quoted in Joyce G. Williams, *Colonel House and Sir Edward Grey* (Lanham, Md.: University Press of America, 1984), p. 83.
42. Quoted in Arthur S. Link, *Wilson: Confusions and Crises, 1915–1916* (Princeton: Princeton University Press, 1964), pp. 134–135.
43. Bryan and Bryan, *Memoirs*, p. 397.
44. *Foreign Relations, 1915, Supplement*, p. 461.
45. Link, *Papers of Wilson*, XXXVI (1981), 213–214.
46. Samuel Flagg Bemis, "A Worcester County Student in Wartime London and Paris (via Harvard): 1915–1916," *New England Galaxy*, XI (Spring 1970), 20.

47. Quoted in Patrick Devlin, *Too Proud to Fight* (New York: Oxford University Press, 1975), p. 517.
48. Quoted in Ninkovich, *Modernity and Power*, p. 50.
49. Quoted in Arthur S. Link, *Wilson: Campaigns for Progressivism and Peace, 1916–1917* (Princeton: Princeton University Press, 1965), p. 274.
50. Quoted *ibid.*, p. 289.
51. Lansing, *War Memoirs*, p. 212.
52. *Foreign Relations, 1917, Supplement 1* (Washington, D.C.: Government Printing Office, 1931), p. 147.
53. Quoted in Manfred F. Boeneke, "Woodrow Wilson's Image of Germany," in Boeneke, *Treaty of Versailles*, p. 610.
54. Quoted in John Milton Cooper, Jr., *Walter Hines Page* (Chapel Hill: University of North Carolina Press, 1977), p. 369.
55. Quoted in Thomas W. Ryley, *A Little Group of Willful Men* (Port Washington, N.Y.: Kennikat Press, 1975), p. 2.
56. Link, *Papers of Wilson*, XLI (1983), 519–527.
57. Quoted in Alan Dawley, *Changing the World* (Princeton: Princeton University Press, 2003), pp. 145–146.
58. Henry F. Ashurst quoted in Erika A. Kuhlman, *Petticoats and White Feathers* (Westport, Conn.: Greenwood, 1997), p. 90.
59. Quoted in Robert E. Osgood, *Ideals and Self-Interest in American Foreign Relations* (Chicago: University of Chicago Press, 1953), p. 177.
60. Quoted in Michael S. Sherry, *In the Shadow of War* (New Haven: Yale University Press, 1995), p. 8.
61. Susan Zeiger, "She Didn't Raise Her Boy to Be a Slacker," *Feminist Studies*, XXII (Spring 1996), 11–12.
62. Daniel J. Leab, "Movie Stereotypes, 1890–1918," in Glaser and Wellenreuther, *Bridging*, p. 190.
63. Bradley Fiske quoted in Jan S. Bremer, "Technological Change," in Peter Trubowitz, Emily O. Goldman, and Edward Rhodes, eds., *The Politics of Strategic Adjustment* (New York: Columbia University Press, 1999), p. 223.
64. Quoted in Kennedy, "Conception of National Security," p. 4.
65. Quoted in Kenneth J. Hagan, *The People's Navy* (New York: Free Press, 1991), p. 252.
66. Quoted in Dawley, *Changing the World*, p. 94.
67. Quoted in Barbara S. Kraft, *The Peace Ship* (New York: Macmillan, 1978), p. 1.
68. Quoted in Thomas J. Knock, *To End All Wars* (New York: Oxford University Press, 1992), p. 63.
69. Jane Addams, *Peace and Bread in Time of War* (New York: King's Crown Press, 1945), p. 58.
70. Quoted in Kuhlman, *Petticoats*, p. 56.
71. Quoted in J. Garry Clifford, *The Citizen Soldiers* (Lexington: University Press of Kentucky, 1972), p. 123.
72. Quoted in Clifford Putney, *Muscular Christianity* (Cambridge: Harvard University Press, 2001), p. 172.
73. General Tasker Bliss quoted in Calhoun, *Uses of Force*, p. 114.
74. Colonel Charles Stanton quoted in Robert B. Bruce, *A Fraternity of Arms* (Lawrence: University Press of Kansas, 2003), p. 94.
75. Quoted in Dawley, *Changing the World*, p. 153.
76. Quoted in Jorg Nagler, "German Imperial Propaganda," in Hans-Jürgen Schröder, *Confrontation and Cooperation* (Providence, R.I.: Berg, 1993), p. 172.
77. Quoted in Allen F. Davis, "Welfare, Reform, and World War I," *American Quarterly*, XIX (Fall 1967), 531.
78. Quoted in Ninkovich, *Modernity and Power*, p. 52.
79. Link, *Papers of Wilson*, XLVII (1984), 270.
80. Quoted in Donald Smythe, *Pershing* (Bloomington: Indiana University Press, 1986), p. 237.
81. Link, *Papers of Wilson*, XLV (1984), 529.
82. Addams, *Peace and Bread*, p. 58.

83. Quoted in Selig Adler, *The Isolationist Impulse* (New York: Collier Books, [1957], 1961), pp. 60–61.
84. H. G. Nicholas essay in *Wilson's Diplomacy* (Cambridge: Schenkman, 1973), p. 81.
85. Quoted in David F. Trask, *The United States in the Supreme War Council* (Middletown, Conn.: Wesleyan University Press, 1961), p. 155.
86. Quoted in Dawley, *Changing the World*, p. 242.
87. Quoted in James D. Startt, "American Propaganda in Britain During World War I," *Prologue*, XXVIII (Spring 1996), 20.
88. Knock, *To End All Wars*, p. 180.
89. Quoted in Inbal Rose, *Conservatism and Foreign Policy During the Lloyd George Coalition 1918–1922* (London: Frank Cass, 1999), p. 121.
90. Quoted in William C. Widenor, "The Structure of the American Interpretation: The Pro-Treaty Version," in Boeneke, *Treaty of Versailles*, p. 550.
91. Quoted in David W. McFadden, *Alternative Paths* (New York: Oxford University Press, 1993), p. 209.
92. Quoted in Herbert Hoover, *The Ordeal of Woodrow Wilson* (New York: McGraw-Hill, 1958), p. 254.
93. Quoted in Walter A. McDougall, *Promised Land, Crusader State* (Boston: Houghton Mifflin, 1997), p. 139.
94. Quoted in Neil Smith, *American Empire* (Berkeley: University of California Press, 2003), p. 169.
95. Quoted in John Milton Cooper, Jr., *Breaking the Heart of the World* (New York: Cambridge University Press, 2001), p. 85; quoted in Noriko Kawamura, *Turbulence in the Pacific* (Westport, Conn.: Praeger, 2000), p. 148.
96. Quoted in Mark Philip Bradley, *Imagining Vietnam and America* (Chapel Hill: University of North Carolina Press, 2000), p. 10.
97. Quoted in Lawrence E. Gelfand, "Where Ideals Confront Self-Interest," *Diplomatic History*, XVIII (Winter 1994), 133.
98. Billy Hughes quoted in David Reynolds, *Britannia Overruled* (New York: Longman, 2000), p. 110.
99. U.S. Congress, Senate, *Treaties*, Senate Doc. 348 (Washington, D.C.: Government Printing Office, 1923), pp. 3336–3345.
100. Link, *Papers of Wilson, LV* (1985), 177.
101. Antony Lentin, *Lloyd George, Woodrow Wilson, and the Guilt of Germany* (Baton Rouge: Louisiana State University Press, 1984), p. 132.
102. Wilson quoted in Cooper, *Breaking the Heart*, p. 62.
103. Quoted in D. F. Fleming, *The United States and the League of Nations, 1918–1920* (New York: Russell & Russell, 1968), p. 134.
104. Quoted in Beth McKillen, "The Corporatist Model, World War I, and the Debate over the League of Nations," *Diplomatic History*, XV (Spring 1991), 174.
105. Link, *Papers of Wilson, LXI* (1989), 436.
106. Quoted in Louis Auchincloss, *Woodrow Wilson* (New York: Viking, 2000), p. 112.
107. Quoted in Kennedy, "Conception of National Security," p. 30.
108. Robert David Johnson, *The Peace Progressives and American Foreign Relations* (Cambridge: Harvard University Press, 1995), p. 102.
109. Quoted in William C. Widenor, "The United States and the Versailles Peace Settlement," in John M. Carroll and George C. Herring, Jr., eds., *Modern American Diplomacy* (Wilmington, Del.: Scholarly Resources, 1986), p. 49.
110. Quoted in Lloyd E. Ambrosius, *Woodrow Wilson and the American Diplomatic Tradition* (New York: Cambridge University Press, 1987), p. 139.
111. Quoted in Osgood, *Ideals and Self-Interest*, p. 286.
112. Johnson, *Peace Progressives*, p. 96.
113. Wilson quoted in Frank Ninkovich, *The Wilsonian Century* (Chicago: University of Chicago Press, 1999), p. 74.
114. Quoted in *ibid.*, p. 74.
115. Link, *Papers of Wilson, LXIII* (1990), 35.
116. Quoted in DeConde, *Ethnicity*, p. 97.
117. Quoted in H. W. Brands, *Woodrow Wilson* (New York: Times Books, 2003), p. 121.
118. Quoted in Knock, *To End All Wars*, p. 263.
119. Quoted in Auchincloss, *Wilson*, p. 118.
120. Walter Lippmann quoted in Walter LaFeber, "Age of American Unilateralism," in R. Laurence Moore and Maurizio Vaudagna, eds., *The American Century in Europe* (Ithaca: Cornell University Press, 2003), p. 34.
121. Quoted in John M. Thompson, *Russia, Bolshevism, and the Versailles Peace* (Princeton: Princeton University Press, 1966), pp. 3–4.
122. Quoted in David S. Foglesong, *America's Secret War Against Bolshevism* (Chapel Hill: University of North Carolina Press, 1995), p. 25.
123. Quoted in Norman Saul, *War and Revolution* (Lawrence: University Press of Kansas, 2001), p. 219.
124. Quoted in McFadden, *Alternative Paths*, p. 247.
125. Winston Churchill quoting Wilson in Lloyd C. Gardner, *Safe for Democracy* (New York: Oxford University Press, 1984), p. 239.
126. Quoted in Foglesong, *Secret War*, p. 43.
127. Quoted in McFadden, *Alternative Paths*, p. 104.
128. Foglesong, *Secret War*, p. 77.
129. Quoted in Alexander DeConde, *Presidential Machismo* (Boston: Northeastern University Press, 2000), p. 106.
130. Quoted in Leo J. Bacino, *Reconstructing Russia* (Kent, Ohio: Kent State University Press, 1999), p. 76.
131. Betty Miller Unterberger, "Woodrow Wilson and the Russian Revolution," in Arthur S. Link, ed., *Woodrow Wilson and a Revolutionary World, 1913–1921* (Chapel Hill: University of North Carolina Press, 1982), p. 70.
132. Foglesong, *Secret War*, p. 190.
133. Verne Bright quoted in Saul, *War and Revolution*, p. 329.
134. Victor M. Fic, *The Collapse of American Policy in Russia and Siberia, 1918* (New York: Columbia University Press, 1995), p. 141.
135. Saul, *War and Revolution*, p. 362.
136. Quoted in McFadden, *Alternative Paths*, p. 154.
137. Quoted in Benjamin D. Rhodes, *The Anglo-American War with Russia, 1918–1919* (Westport, Conn.: Greenwood, 1988), p. 123.
138. Foglesong, *Secret War*, p. 296.
139. Quoted *ibid.*, p. 291.
140. McKillen, "Corporatist Model," p. 173.
141. Arthur S. Link, *The Higher Realism of Woodrow Wilson* (Nashville: Vanderbilt University Press, 1971), p. 83.
142. Quoted in Gordon A. Craig, "The Revolution in War and Diplomacy," in Jack J. Roth, ed., *World War I* (New York: Knopf, 1967), p. 12.
143. Quoted in Robert H. Ferrell, *Woodrow Wilson and World War I* (New York: Harper and Row, 1985), p. 180.
144. Ozora Davis quoted in Putney, *Muscular Christianity*, p. 192.
145. Quoted in Leslie Midkiff DeBauche, *Reel Patriotism* (Madison: University of Wisconsin Press, 1997), p. 174.
146. Quoted in Lloyd E. Ambrosius, *Wilsonianism* (New York: Palgrave, 2002), p. 6.
147. Quoted in Tony Smith, *America's Mission* (Princeton: Princeton University Press, 1994), p. 102.
148. Quoted in Hans Schmidt, "Democracy in China," *Diplomatic History*, XXII (Winter 1998), 28.
149. MacMillan, *Paris 1919*, p. 493.
150. Link, *Papers of Wilson, LXII* (1990), 47.
151. Quoted in Foglesong, *Secret War*, p. 1.
152. Quoted in Donald E. Davis and Eugene P. Trani, *The First Cold War* (Columbia: University of Missouri Press, 2002), p. 201.

CHAPTER 4

Descending into Europe's Maelstrom, 1920–1939

Trojan Horse? *Many observers thought that President Franklin D. Roosevelt concealed too much in his foreign policymaking—that he not only misled but also lied. Fred O. Seibel of the* Richmond Times Dispatch *(February 4, 1939) portrayed such thinking shortly after a "Boston" bomber with a French pilot aboard crashed in Los Angeles. The British diplomat Lord Halifax saw as much confusion as deviousness in the Roosevelt administration, which he likened to "a disorderly line of beaters out shooting; they do put the rabbits out of the bracken, but they don't come out where you expect." (Courtesy of* Richmond Times Dispatch/*Franklin D. Roosevelt Library)*

ᘒᘓ *Roosevelt's Attempt to Extend America's Frontier to the Rhine, 1939*

DAUBED WITH RED, white, and blue U.S. Army Air Corps paint, the new A-20 ("Boston") twin-engine light bomber performed high-speed acrobatics over Los Angeles's municipal airport on January 23, 1939. The sleek craft climbed to 3,000 feet at more than 300 miles per hour. Test pilot John Cable then apparently cut one motor to attempt a climb on half power. Suddenly the plane went into a spin and hurtled toward the ground. Cable bailed out at 400 feet but he pulled his parachute ripcord too late. He died on impact.

Employees from a nearby plant extricated a civilian-clad survivor from the crashed bomber before it burst into flames. Reporters soon learned that the man with the broken leg was thirty-three-year-old Captain Paul Chemidlin, incognito member of a secret French purchasing mission to buy American-made warplanes for the French air force. The French were getting ready for World War II, which finally began in September.

Controversy soon engulfed Washington. General Henry "Hap" Arnold of the U.S. Army Air Corps happened to be testifying before the Senate Military Affairs Committee. One senator asked how a French officer could be aboard the "secret" bomber that had just crashed. Arnold disingenuously replied that the Frenchman had gone "out there under the direction of the Treasury Department with a view of looking into possible purchase of airplanes by the French Mission."[1] Formal authorization, he added, had come from the War Department, and all secret equipment was removed from the plane before the French saw it.

Senator Gerald P. Nye of North Dakota then summoned Treasury Secretary Henry Morgenthau, Jr., and Secretary of War Harry Woodring for further grilling. Morgenthau acidly pointed out that the army had not yet placed orders for the plane, which remained the sole property of the Douglas Company and could hardly be termed "secret" if flown from a municipal airport where anyone could see it. Woodring, however, admitted that the air corps had originally opposed the French mission but that "everyone [was] . . . in accord before the French went to the West Coast."[2] President Franklin D. Roosevelt muddied matters further by denying to the press that "this Government [had] taken any steps to assist or facilitate France in buying planes in this country." But French plane purchases "would be an excellent idea" to help "in building up" U.S. foreign trade, he noted blandly.[3]

A devotee of poker, the president "wasn't ready publicly to show his hand."[4] In seeking to deter a major war through nonmilitary methods, he had talked publicly in recent years about quarantines against aggression, held secret naval talks with the British, and toyed with calling a conference in Washington of major world leaders. His invitation to the king and queen of England to visit America in June 1939 seemed "a safe but effective way of dramatizing Anglo-American amity for the benefit of the dictators and the American public."[5] Roosevelt had mentioned "methods short of war" to Congress in early January, but he gave no details of what would amount to a shift in foreign policy in the months prior to World War II.[6]

Ever since the disastrous Munich Conference of September 1938, when England and France had agreed to German territorial demands against Czechoslovakia, FDR had seized on air power as a possible deterrent against another European war. "Had we . . . 5,000 planes and the immediate capacity to produce 10,000 per year," he had mused, "[Adolf] Hitler would not have dared to take the stand he did."[7] When the French financier-diplomat Jean Monnet visited in October 1938, the president confided that "the Germans can produce 40,000 planes per year, Britain and Canada 25,000 and France 15,000. 20–30,000 more will be needed to achieve decisive superiority over Germany and Italy; and they'll have to be found here, in the United States."[8] He urged England and France to place orders, thereby stimulating the lagging U.S. aviation industry and jump-starting military rearmament. When War Department officials balked at showing top-secret prototypes to foreign buyers, Roosevelt argued that "the only check to a world war, which would be understood by Germany, would be the creation of a great [French] air force and a powerful force in this country."[9] Only after a direct presidential order did General Arnold permit the French to inspect the Douglas bomber.

FDR also wanted to revise America's neutrality laws to permit the sale of arms and munitions to belligerents on a cash-and-carry basis. France and Britain could buy weapons legally in peacetime, but the current law forbade such sales in wartime. The president had secretly promised British prime minister Neville Chamberlain "the industrial resources of the American nation . . . in the event of war with the dictatorships."[10] The crash of the plane with the French officer aboard put Roosevelt's plans in jeopardy and threatened to expose rifts in his administration. The designation of his close friend Morgenthau to oversee all foreign purchases had aroused criticism. The bespectacled Treasury secretary served as an "intellectual rough-neck" who "bulled things through" with little regard for bureaucratic sensitivity. In this instance, the chief obstruction proved to be Secretary of War Woodring, a "fourth-rate" former governor of Kansas, "who not only couldn't see that our frontier was the Rhine, but couldn't see across the Hudson River."[11]

Roosevelt invited the Senate Military Affairs Committee to the White House on January 31, 1939, a day after Hitler had told the German Reichstag that "international finance Jewry" was plotting a second "world war" that would result in the "annihilation of the Jewish race in Europe."[12] FDR asked for confidentiality so as not "to frighten the American people." During the meeting, he asserted that the growing menace from Germany, Italy, and Japan necessitated fundamental changes in U.S. policies. He denied that "we can draw a line of defense around this country and live completely and solely to ourselves." Americans might hope that "somebody would assassinate Hitler or that Germany will blow up from within." Or they could "try to prevent the domination of the world—prevent it by peaceful means."

Strengthening America's "first line of defense" offered the best approach. In the Pacific, that defense consisted of "a series of islands, with a hope that through the Army and Navy and the airplanes we can keep the Japanese" from dominating the Pacific and denying "us access to the west coast of South America." In Europe and the Atlantic, the line of defense rested on "the continued independence"

Franklin D. Roosevelt (1882–1945). Although stricken by polio in the 1920s, Roosevelt remained energetic and optimistic. A talented politician who won four presidential elections, he moved haltingly to shore up Britain and France as they faced an aggressive Germany. Here FDR relaxes with stamp collecting, his favorite hobby. During World War II the president once showed British prime minister Winston Churchill a favorite stamp "from one of your colonies." Churchill asked: "Which one?" Roosevelt replied: "One of your last. . . . You won't have them much longer, you know." (Franklin D. Roosevelt Library)

of countries from Finland to Turkey. If England and France fell, however, the others would "drop into the [German] basket." Colonial Africa would "automatically" capitulate. The president claimed that the Germans could dominate South and Central America through subversion and economic penetration. He warned: "The Germans have 1,500 bombing planes that can go from Germany to Colombia inside of forty-eight hours. We have, I think, about eighty that can go down there."

Roosevelt emphatically defended the sale of aircraft, saying that "it is to our interest . . . to help the British and French maintain their independence." The American aviation industry also needed foreign orders to expedite mass production and "turn out nine or ten thousand planes per year" without at the same time delaying the buildup of U.S. air forces. He vowed to send them "all they can pay for on the barrelhead. . . . Now, that is the foreign policy of the United States."

A bravura performance, to be sure. Yet when asked if he meant that the United States had the "duty" to "maintain the independence of these nations . . . by whatever efforts may be necessary," Roosevelt shot back: "No. No! Listen: I probably saw more of the war [World War I] in Europe than any other living person." Describing his three-month tour of the battle zones as assistant secretary of the navy in 1918, "I spent days on the Belgian front, on the British front, on the French front, and on the American front. . . . Therefore, you may be quite sure that about the last thing this country should do is ever to send an army to Europe again."[13] Senator Nye, listening intently, went back to his office and immediately wrote a nine-page memorandum. "Get the uniforms ready for the boys," he noted. "I saw troops moving even though the Pres[ident] had declared he had no intent to go to war."[14]

The next day word leaked to the press that FDR had proclaimed that "the frontiers of the United States are on the Rhine."[15] The president angrily called the leak "a deliberate lie" that "some boob got off." He accused isolationists of trying to "make political capital" out of words he never spoke. He specifically singled out Senator Nye as "an unscrupulous person."[16] As reverberations echoed in the press, Neville Chamberlain noted that "Roosevelt is saying Heaven knows what but anyhow something disagreeable to the dictators."[17]

Did FDR lie? According to a stenographic transcript of his meeting with the senators, he never said exactly that America's frontier extended to the Rhine, but his argument that the nation's first line of defense depended on the independence of England and France carried the same meaning. Several times, Morgenthau later recalled, the president did say privately: "Our frontier is on the Rhine."[18] Yet in all likelihood Roosevelt believed he spoke the truth. A deft "juggler" who always kept options open, the smiling squire of Hyde Park wanted above all else to deter a European war while at the same time to prepare for possible U.S. participation.[19] He sought "methods short of war" because "sending a large army abroad was . . . politically out of the question."[20] As the historian Michael Sherry has written, "repudiation of armed intervention did not exclude intervention by display of arms. Methods short of war could still embrace the capacity for deterrence that rearmament implied."[21] Roosevelt persisted in selling aircraft to the French and British, even threatening to exile General Arnold to Guam if he did not "play ball."[22] Although the 555 combat planes eventually delivered to France did not deter war, the French orders quadrupled airplane production and laid the foundation "for the gigantic later expansion of the U.S. aircraft industry."[23]

The bomber affair also caused FDR to abandon any sustained personal effort to educate Congress and public opinion about revising American neutrality laws before the outbreak of war in Europe. Only after the German invasion of Poland in September 1939 did the administration succeed in repealing the arms embargo, and even then the president remained conspicuously in the background. His encounter with the senators over the French air mission remained so disturbing that he hesitated to lead boldly: "Recall the colorful and untrue reports of over a year ago about our frontier being on the Rhine; . . . about the death of a French officer caused by the crash of an airplane in California," he told a prominent publisher in June 1940. "The government . . . cannot change its 'editorial' policy overnight. . . . Governments, such as ours, cannot swing so far or so quickly."[24] Of course, the French officer had not died, but Roosevelt sometimes exaggerated for effect.

Some six years and two months after FDR made his alleged remarks about America's frontier on the Rhine, U.S. soldiers seized the bridge at Remagen and crossed the Rhine into Germany. Another European war, which American diplomacy and arms sales to France had failed to prevent, then definitively extended the frontiers of the United States.

"Prize Fighters with a Very Long Reach": The Independent Internationalists

The French airplane incident of 1939 illustrates salient themes of interwar foreign relations. It demonstrates that even on the eve of World War II in Europe, the United States still sought methods short of war to deter potential aggressors in areas vital to the national interest. Because foreign airplane orders also meant "prosperity in this country and we can't elect a Democratic Party unless we get prosperity," as Roosevelt put it, the episode reveals the impact of the Great Depression on foreign trade, domestic politics, and international security.[25] Even in failure, it shows how an activist president can use subterfuge and surrogates to circumvent bureaucratic rivalries and congressional opposition. The episode underlines the lessons learned from American intervention in World War I and the determination to avoid the mistakes attributed to Woodrow Wilson. In view of FDR's claim that America's national security had become tied to the independence of France and England, it also proves that important U.S. leaders recognized global interdependence and rejected an ostrichlike, isolationist course during the interwar years.

The United States had emerged from World War I a recognized world power. Under the Versailles treaty, U.S. military forces even occupied the left bank of the Rhine near Coblenz until early 1923. Postwar diplomats, closer to a global perspective than ever before, knew that even if they wanted to, Americans could not be bystanders in world affairs. True, between World Wars I and II Americans hoped to avoid foreign entanglements and concentrate on domestic matters. But, within the limits of U.S. power, American leaders pursued an active foreign policy befitting their nation's high international status. They worked to create a community of peaceful nations characterized by legal and orderly processes, the Open Door, and economic and political stability. Washington emphasized nonmilitary means—treaties, conferences, disarmament, economic and financial agreements, banking reform—in its pursuit of world order. A British diplomat likened the United States to a "prize fighter with a very long reach. He stands with his left arm stretched out, and the opponent may dance round and round in the ring and never come to close quarters."[26] America between the wars wanted to isolate itself from war, to scale down foreign military interventions, and to preserve the freedom to make independent decisions in international affairs. "Independent internationalism," rather than "isolationism," best characterizes American practice—active on an international scale, but independent in action.[27]

Where the United States lacked viable power, such as in Asia, it moved haltingly. Where it possessed power, as in Latin America, it moved vigorously. As for Europe, "economic imperatives, humanitarian instincts, and ideological impulses compelled American officials to take an active interest."[28] Until 1933 the Republican administrations seriously worked to contain but rehabilitate Germany, relieve French strategic anxieties, tame Soviet radicalism while seeking to integrate Russia into the community of nations, advance disarmament, resolve controversies over war debts and reparations, stabilize European currencies, foster American exports, and systematize the flow of private American capital abroad. In seeking peace and prosperity, the U.S. government encouraged private experts in business, finance, labor, and agriculture to cooperate with public officials in a system of "corporatism." By the mid-1930s, with international stability shattered by the Great Depression and Europe torn by conflict, Americans tried to protect themselves from war through neutrality laws. Not until 1939 did policymakers again risk war to achieve world order.

In the 1920s especially, weak presidential leadership, congressional-executive competition, and increased professionalism in the Foreign Service characterized

Charles Evans Hughes (1862–1948) and Warren G. Harding (1865–1923). The secretary of state (left) and president were quite different in background and intellect, but as conservatives both sought a stable, nonrevolutionary world order. (Ohio Historical Society)

U.S. policymaking. Presidents Warren G. Harding and Calvin Coolidge gave minimal attention to foreign affairs, leaving that field to their secretaries of state. Harding's world was his hometown of Marion, Ohio. Wilson's League of Nations fiasco persuaded Harding to eschew a conspicuous role in foreign policy. On one occasion, when a European correspondent talked with Harding, the president cut him short: "I don't know anything about this European stuff."[29]

Calvin Coolidge managed in his autobiography to avoid mentioning foreign policy, although as a politician he often waxed noisy on the issue of Bolshevism. The taciturn president once shocked the British ambassador by saying he would "never visit Europe because he could learn everything he needed to know by remaining in America."[30] Coolidge's relaxed approach to problems, exemplified by long afternoon naps in the White House and by his fawning worship of American business, created a deceptively passive image. The simple man from Vermont, preaching self-reliance, grew impatient with Europeans—who, he believed, always looked to the United States to bail them out. "We couldn't help people very much until they showed a disposition to help themselves," he noted in 1926.[31]

Herbert Hoover held much the same philosophy, but he had considerable knowledge about foreign affairs and adopted an active presidential role. His distinguished career included experience in international business (mining), food relief (Belgium and Russia), and diplomacy (reparations adviser at Versailles). As secretary of commerce under Harding and Coolidge, he energetically expanded American economic interests abroad. Known as the "Great Engineer," Hoover had a telephone installed at his elbow in the White House, further enhancing his reputation for administrative efficiency. A plodding speaker with a shy personality, Hoover entered the presidency as the Great Depression struck, wrecking his political career. True to

Makers of American Foreign Relations, 1920–1939

Presidents	Secretaries of State
Woodrow Wilson, 1913–1921	Bainbridge Colby, 1920–1921
Warren G. Harding, 1921–1923	Charles E. Hughes, 1921–1925
Calvin Coolidge, 1923–1929	Frank B. Kellogg, 1925–1929
Herbert C. Hoover, 1929–1933	Henry L. Stimson, 1929–1933
Franklin D. Roosevelt, 1933–1945	Cordell Hull, 1933–1944

his Quaker background, he sought nonmilitary, noncoercive solutions to international crises and emphasized cooperative economic relations.

The secretaries of state in the 1920s often compensated for presidential shortcomings. Magisterial Charles Evans Hughes was a distinguished jurist (Supreme Court), an experienced politician (governor of New York and unsuccessful Republican candidate for president in 1916), and a confirmed nationalist and expansionist. Under Harding and Coolidge the patient, pragmatic Hughes enjoyed considerable freedom in diplomacy, receiving little presidential instruction. International law and the sanctity of treaties served as his primary guides to world order. Frank B. Kellogg succeeded Hughes. Ingloriously called "Nervous Nellie" because of one blind eye and a trembling hand, the former senator and ambassador to Britain moved cautiously, often consulting a major critic of interventionism, William Borah, chair of the Senate Foreign Relations Committee. Because of jurisdictional disputes with the Commerce Department, one of Kellogg's subordinates commented: "diplomatic functions today are mainly economic; this places the Department of Commerce in control of the substance of diplomacy, and leaves the State Department with social relationships."[32]

President Hoover named as secretary of state mustachioed Henry L. Stimson, one of America's most distinguished public servants. The strong-willed, confident, reserved, punctual, sexist, mannered, wealthy Stimson lived on his Long Island estate like an English squire. His resumé included Phillips Andover Academy, Yale University, Harvard Law School, and tutelage under the eminent Elihu Root. Before becoming secretary, Stimson headed the War Department under Taft. In 1927 he went as a diplomatic troubleshooter to Nicaragua, and during 1927–1929 he served as governor-general of the Philippines. He had been Colonel Stimson in World War I—and let few forget it. Hoover disliked Stimson's combative personality and his eagerness to "march toward the guns."[33]

Franklin D. Roosevelt came to office with some foreign-affairs experience, having served in the Navy Department under Woodrow Wilson. He admired both the big-sticking of his cousin Theodore and the liberal internationalism of Wilson. As a vice-presidential candidate in 1920, Roosevelt had defended the League and the Versailles treaty, but in the 1932 campaign he abandoned the League ("an emasculated constituency") to garner the endorsement of the influential newspaper

Herbert Hoover (1874–1964). The thirty-first president graduated from Stanford University. Cautious and stubborn, Hoover advocated healthy trade relations, military retrenchment, and foreign loans for "reproductive purposes" as routes to peace. Conversation with the president, increasingly frustrated by the Great Depression during his final two years, was "like sitting in a bath of ink," noted Secretary of State Henry L. Stimson. (Library of Congress)

Cordell Hull (1871–1955).
The historian Michael A. Butler
has characterized the long-
tenured secretary of state
(1933–1944) as a "cautious
visionary" whose free-trade
philosophy was "unfortunately ill
suited in dealing with a world in
which dictators and military power
predominated." Hull once
declared: "If the goods can't cross
borders, soldiers will." (National
Portrait Gallery, Smithsonian
Institution)

magnate William Randolph Hearst.[34] "I am not a Wilsonian idealist, I have problems to solve," he once said.[35] Fully conscious of the war clouds billowing in Europe and Asia, FDR nonetheless gave priority to his domestic New Deal recovery program. At least until 1937, one scholar argues, "Roosevelt offered no signs that American military power would be used abroad in a major war, for he had no intentions that it should be."[36]

With his "happy-go-lucky, snap-of-the-moment style," FDR relished personal diplomacy, often taking command of negotiations and more than once failing to tell the Department of State what he was doing.[37] He centralized decisionmaking in the White House; but dangers lurked in his methods because too often he possessed only a superficial understanding of other national cultures and histories. Sometimes he misled diplomats with his easy smile; sometimes his agreements lacked precision, depending for their authority on the honor of gentlemen's words; sometimes the formal diplomatic document did not properly capture the "spirit" of a meeting; sometimes U.S. diplomacy moved forward with the dizziness of a confused bureaucracy. A consummate politician, Roosevelt compromised frequently and resorted to deception if it served his goals. One historian has called Roosevelt "an intellectual jumping-jack . . . hopping helter-skelter in several directions at once"; another scholar has likened him to a college professor who prefers to teach without a syllabus.[38]

Roosevelt chose Tennessean Cordell Hull as his secretary of state. A powerful senator devoted to free trade, the chronically ill sexagenarian (he secretly suffered from diabetes, claustrophobia, and tuberculosis) reluctantly accepted. FDR picked Hull because the appointment would please old Democratic party members, southern conservatives, and unreconstructed Wilsonians. Roosevelt often undercut him, although Hull and the State Department remained dominant in formulating Asian and Latin American policy. Rexford Tugwell, a presidential aide, noted as early as 1933 that "Hull doesn't know half of what goes on."[39] Indeed, Roosevelt sent Hull to the World Economic Conference in London that June without consulting him on the makeup of the delegation, and then embarrassed him by rejecting a currency stabilization plan and effectively ending the conference. Once dubbed "Miss Cordelia Dull" for his "congenital procrastination," the secretary had contemplated resigning earlier that spring when the president delayed sending to Congress Hull's pet project, the reciprocal trade bill.[40] Hull's deliberate methods wearied the president, who preferred quickness and repartee. The secretary resented the president's practice of dispatching personal envoys overseas, of conspicuously excluding Hull from conferences, and of relying on friends such as Sumner Welles (after 1937 under secretary of state), Morgenthau, and Ambassador William C. Bullitt, instead of Hull himself. "They all come at me with knives and hatchets," Hull once complained.[41] But he stayed on until 1944, the longest tenure of any secretary of state, forever disliking the pomp of official dinners, always charming his listeners with his hill-country drawl and lisp, and impressing all with his personal dignity, hard work, and deep commitment to the premise that wars grew out of international economic competition.

The Foreign Service over which Hull presided improved during the interwar period. It certainly needed reform. Frequenting the dark corridors and Victorian furnishings of the old State, War, and Navy Building on Pennsylvania Avenue were

U.S. diplomats noted for their elite backgrounds (urban, wealthy, eastern, and Ivy League–educated). Some derided them as "cookie pushers" and "striped pants," as purveyors of "pink peppermint and protocol." Foreign Service Officers nonetheless believed that "they belonged to a pretty good club. That feeling has fostered a healthy *esprit de corps*."[42] Many diplomatic appointees could not speak the language of the country to which they were assigned. Under the spoils system, faithful politicians received top diplomatic posts.

The heavy work load imposed on Foreign Service personnel during World War I had exposed the shortcomings. The immigration laws of 1921 and 1924, establishing quotas, demanded a more efficient consular staff; the revolution in China required observers who could intelligently interpret that convulsion; and economic expansion depended on sound reporting about market conditions abroad. The Rogers Act of 1924 merged the previously unequal consular and diplomatic corps into the Foreign Service of the United States and provided for examinations, increased salaries, promotion by merit, and overseas living allowances. At about the same time, the State Department began training specialists in Soviet affairs, with George F. Kennan and Charles E. Bohlen (both later ambassadors to the Soviet Union) as initiates who mastered the language and culture of Russia. These trainees came to share hard-line attitudes toward the Soviet Union. Despite persistent cliques, political favoritism, snobbery, sexism, anti-Semitism, and lower salaries and staff cutbacks during the depression, the Foreign Service slowly became more efficient and professional.

Economic and Cultural Expansion in a Rickety World

The Foreign Service helped facilitate conspicuous American economic expansion abroad after World War I. Measured by statistics, the United States had become the most powerful nation in the world, accounting for 70 percent of the world's petroleum and 40 percent of its coal production. Most impressive, the United States produced 46 percent of total world industrial goods (1925–1929 figures). It also ranked first as an exporter, shipping more than 15 percent of total world exports in 1929, and it replaced Great Britain as the largest foreign investor and financier of world trade. Throughout the decade the United States enjoyed a favorable balance of trade, exporting more than it imported. In the period 1914–1929, the value of exports more than doubled, to $5.4 billion, and American private investments abroad grew from $3.5 billion in 1914 to $17.2 billion by 1930. "American money power," warned British prime minister Stanley Baldwin, "is trying to get hold of the natural resources of the empire."[43]

"The growth of U.S. stakes abroad during the 1920s represented not simply an increase in scale," the historian Mira Wilkins has noted. "Rather, U.S. companies were (1) going to *more countries,* (2) building *more plants* in a particular foreign country, (3) manufacturing or mining *more end products* in a particular foreign land, (4) investing in a single alien nation in a *greater degree* of integration, and (5) diversifying on a *worldwide* basis."[44] U.S. Rubber bought its first Malayan plantation; Anaconda moved into Chilean copper mining; General Electric joined international cartels and invested heavily in Germany; oil companies began to penetrate the Middle East; Americans controlled 83 percent of the automobile industry in Canada; General Motors purchased Opel, by 1929 the best-selling automobile in Germany; Henry Ford helped build an automobile plant in Soviet Russia; and American firms handled about one-third of oil sales in France.

American culture—including household appliances, foods, language, music, film, and appreciation for machines—also spread worldwide. "Today we go to America as the Japanese once came to Germany," an industrialist from Weimar Germany wrote after visiting Detroit to observe American mass-production techniques.[45] U.S. government support for the expansion of the communications industry helped International Telephone and Telegraph (ITT), Radio Corporation of America (RCA), Associated Press (AP), and United Press (UP) become international giants by 1930. American movies so dominated the global market that the "sun . . . never sets on the British Empire and the American motion picture." Indeed, "trade follows the film," and together they so advertised U.S. culture abroad that some foreigners feared that "Americanization" would engulf them.[46] As "the most pervasive and persuasive of American contributions to European culture," Hollywood movies "epitomized American culture in its mass orientation, tempo, monumentalism, sensationalism and profit urge."[47] Thus did street urchins in London adopt American slang: "O.K., kid" and "What are you doing tonight, babe?"[48] In 1929 alone, some 251,000 American tourists visited Europe, where they spent $323 million. F. W. Woolworth had opened 350 stores in England, with nothing priced above a sixpence. For German women "Americanization" produced, among other things, an advertisement from Siemens describing "How the Buschmüllers Got a Vacuum."[49] Despite elitist fears of being "swamped" by a vulgar *Unkultur,* American products from jazz to gym shoes claimed an eager international clientele.[50]

When the Rockefeller Foundation sponsored programs in preventive medicine, hygiene, public health, and nursing in Eastern and Central Europe in the 1920s, this philanthropic institution also introduced America to foreigners. Under Rockefeller auspices, for example, "Kentucky closets" (outdoor toilets) became ubiquitous in Croatian villages.[51] The foundation also battled yellow fever in Latin America and supported colleges to train doctors in Lebanon and China—all under the philosophy that culture adoption, economic expansion, and social and political stability went hand in hand.

This "making-getting-spending" faced obstacles.[52] Mexican nationalism, confiscation of property in Soviet Russia, European resentments, a wrecked German economy, wartime destruction in Europe, growing tariff walls, and the dislocation of international finance caused by World War I debts and reparations—all hindered enterprising Americans. U.S. government decisions offered welcome but limited help. The Webb-Pomerene Act (1918) permitted American companies to combine for purposes of foreign trade without prosecution under the antitrust laws; the Edge Act of 1919 legalized branch banks abroad; and the Merchant Marine Act of 1920 authorized the federal government to sell vessels to private companies and to make loans for the construction of new ships. New tax laws also permitted foreign tax credits for American investors abroad. The Department of Commerce provided businesses with research data and advice. To help financiers avoid unproductive for-

The Weight of the United States in the World Economy

Relative Value of Industrial Production, 1925–1929

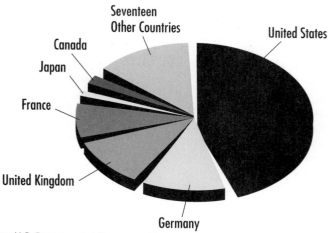

Source: U.S. Department of Commerce, *The United States in the World Economy* (Washington, D.C.: Government Printing Office, 1943), p. 28.

eign lending and risky foreign bonds, official Washington tried to oversee loans and bond sales, but the practice never became consistent or thorough. For example, the government discouraged the sale in the United States of the bonds of a Czech brewery because it would violate the "spirit" of prohibition laws, but tolerated an unproductive loan for a sports palace in Germany.

Believing trade essential to domestic prosperity, the United States continued to proclaim the Open Door policy but applied it selectively. U.S. officials usually invoked the policy where the United States faced vigorous competition, as in Asia and the Middle East. In Latin America and the Philippines, however, where American capital and trade dominated, something approximating a "closed door" developed. Europeans complained bitterly that the United States followed a double standard. They also resented American tariff policy, which made it difficult to sell to the United States—as they had to do in order to obtain the dollars necessary to buy American goods. The tariff acts of 1922 (Fordney-McCumber) and 1930 (Hawley-Smoot) raised duties to protect domestic producers and invited retaliation against American products. Economists lamented the irrationality of Washington's seeking, "on the one hand, to promote exports . . . , while on the other hand, by increasing tariffs it makes exportation ever more difficult." They predicted "a tariff war" that would disturb world peace.[53] Some twenty-five nations by 1932 had retaliated against American imports. Hoover held that high tariffs and overseas economic expansion could proceed hand in hand, and until the Great Depression struck in 1929 the seeming contradiction appeared to work.

The depression raised havoc with the international economy. Only two countries might have led the world out of depression, but the "British couldn't and the

Americans wouldn't."[54] Economic nationalism guided most countries as they tried to protect themselves from the cataclysm with higher tariffs and import quotas. World trade declined 40 percent in value and 25 percent in volume from 1929 to mid-1933. In 1933 the United States exported goods worth $2.1 billion, down from the 1929 figure of $5.4 billion. American capital stayed at home, and foreign holders of American loans defaulted. American private investments abroad slumped to $13.5 billion, down from the $17.2 billion figure of 1930. President Hoover flatly—and wrongly—called it a "patently European crisis."[55] His successor, Franklin D. Roosevelt, confronting 13 million unemployed Americans in 1933, also succumbed to economic nationalism as he created his New Deal recovery program. He abruptly sabotaged the London Economic Conference, indicating that the United States would henceforth "pursue domestic recovery by means of a policy of unilateralism."[56] But Hull gradually persuaded him that lowered tariffs would spur U.S. foreign trade and spark an economic upturn at home. Hull also preached that healthy world trade would contribute to stable politics and peace at a time when Japan, Germany, and Italy were turning to political extremes and threatening ag-

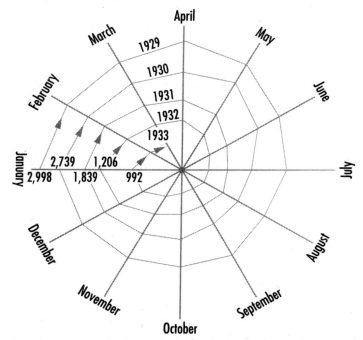

The Contracting Spiral of World Trade

January 1929 to March 1933
Total Imports of 75 Countries in Millions of Dollars

Source: Charles P. Kindleberger, *The World in Depression, 1929–1939* (Berkeley and Los Angeles: University of California Press,1973), p. 172. Copyright © 1973 by the Regents of the University of California; reprinted by permission of the University of California Press.

gression. It would also deter Bolshevism from exploiting Europe's economic and social turmoil. "International commerce," Hull avowed, "is not only calculated to aid materially in the restoration of prosperity everywhere, but it is the greatest civilizer and peacemaker in the experience of the human race."[57]

In 1934 Hull piloted through Congress the Reciprocal Trade Agreements Act, which empowered the president to reduce tariffs by as much as 50 percent after agreements with other nations under the doctrine of the most-favored nation. This principle, which had traditionally guided American trade, meant that the United States was entitled to the lowest tariffs imposed by a country (in short, the best favor that country granted any other nation) with which the United States had a reciprocal agreement, and vice versa. The reciprocal trade program did retard the deterioration of world trade, but, as President Roosevelt confessed, "those trade treaties are just too goddamned slow. The world is moving too fast."[58] Hull also created in 1934 the Export-Import Bank, a governmental agency designed to provide loans to expand foreign trade. Yet in 1937 FDR waxed skeptical in thinking that "an economic approach to peace is a weak reed."[59]

The reciprocal trade program and the bank came too late to help solve one of the major troubling legacies of World War I and Versailles—the debts-reparations tangle. Whereas before the war U.S. citizens owed some $3 billion to Europeans, after the war European citizens owed private Americans $3 billion and their governments owed another $10 billion, largely because of wartime loans. America had gone dramatically from a debtor to a creditor nation. But how would Europeans earn dollars to pay such a huge sum? American investments, sale of goods to the United States, U.S. tourist spending, and income from German reparations payments ranked as the most promising sources. But the Germans proved unwilling to meet the indemnity of $33 billion, so in the early 1920s the British began quoting Scripture: "Forgive us our debts," arguing that Americans should write them off a contribution to the Allied victory.[60] Europeans, then, looked on the war loans as essentially political in character, rather than as business transactions. Anyway, they pointed out, they had suffered huge losses of lives and property, while Americans, neutral until 1917, had enjoyed prosperity and profits from sales to the Allies. Washington indignantly rejected this argument, prompting one British leader to note that "even in its gifts and its goodness" the United States "has an attitude and a spirit that makes one's soul shrink up and shrivel."[61] The humorist Will Rogers joked that the only "way we could be worse with the Europeans" would be to "have helped them out of two wars instead of one."[62] Congress created the War Debt Commission in 1922 to negotiate full payment. The commission ultimately forgave or canceled about half of the Allied debts. From 1918 to 1931 the United States actually received only $2.6 billion in Allied debts payments.

By stabilizing European finances, restoring trade, and encouraging the flow of private capital to Germany, U.S. diplomats sought to "harness Germany's resources to the cause of European recovery without restoring its prewar hegemony or reinvigorating the economic nationalism and autarky" that could lead to war.[63] The debts-reparations imbroglio eventually undercut this strategy. Wild inflation, a crippled economy, inadequate exports, and anti-Versailles hostility prompted the Germans to default on reparations payments in 1922–1923. France and Belgium thereupon aggravated Germany's plight by seizing the rich Ruhr Valley. In 1924 the State Department encouraged the businessman Charles G. Dawes to negotiate the Dawes Plan, whereby American investors such as the J. P. Morgan Company loaned millions to Germany, and Berlin accepted a reparations payment schedule. But the European economy simply could not bear the heavy debts (Europeans also owed money to other Europeans) and the reparations. Nor could American capital keep Europe afloat. Under the Young Plan of 1929, another salvaging effort reduced German reparations to $9 billion. That year, too, Hoover informed the British that he would cancel their debt if they transferred Bermuda, British Honduras (Belize), and Trinidad to the United States. London refused. In 1931 he declared a one-year moratorium on debts payments. Thereafter only Finland met its debt obligations, forever winning a place in American hearts.

Debtors defaulted, Germany stopped paying reparations, and the world settled into the devastating depression of the 1930s. "It was hardly surprising," the historian Bruce Kent has written, "that this rickety financial structure, the maintenance of which depended on a vigorous expansion of world trade and a buoyant international credit system, should have been shaken to its foundations by the economic contractions" of the depression.[64]

Peace Seekers for a World Without War

"Come on in, I'll treat you right. I used to know your daddy."

"Come on in. I'll treat you right. I used to know your daddy." C. D. Batchelor's cartoon won a Pulitzer Prize in 1937. As the historian Michael Sherry has noted, the depiction of war as "a diseased whore luring men to their death" revealed the "strikingly—sometimes maliciously—gendered ways in which war was often portrayed in modern American culture." (Library of Congress)

If Europeans and Americans failed to resolve the mammoth problems plaguing the international economy, they also failed to curb a growing arms race, although the Washington treaties of 1922 held promise (see Chapter 5), and peace sentiment ran high in the United States. In 1923, when the publisher Edward Bok sponsored a contest for the best peace plan, he received more than 22,000 entries. Eleanor Roosevelt, Franklin's wife, helped organize the bipartisan peace prize. The winner of $100,000 was a member of the New York Peace Society who recommended joining the World Court and working with the League of Nations. Some peace advocates, such as the Carnegie Endowment for International Peace, placed their hopes in such global institutions. Pacifists in the Fellowship of Reconciliation, the War Resisters League, and the Women's Peace Union, in contrast, renounced individual participation in war. Religious groups pointed to the un-Christian character of war. Salmon Levinson, a Chicago lawyer who organized the American Committee for the Outlawry of War, argued that "war is an institution in the same sense as the church, the school or the home. It will never cease to be an institution until it becomes illegal."[65] Some business leaders, such as Thomas J. Watson of International Business Machines (IBM), endorsed the theme of "world peace through world trade."[66] Women gravitated to their own organizations, such as Carrie Chapman Catt's moderate Committee on the Cause and Cure of War and Jane Addams's and Emily Greene Balch's radical U.S. Section of the Women's International League for Peace and Freedom (WILPF), because they lacked influence in male-dominated groups and because of the popular assumption that women—as life givers and nurturing mothers—had a unique aversion to violence and war. Disarmament and anticolonialism became the missions of many peace-oriented people. Radical pacifists and antiwar advocates agitated for fundamental social and economic change in order to remove social injustice, which they saw as the capitalist wellsprings of impe-rialism and war. The National Council for the Prevention of War, founded in 1921, served as an organizational umbrella for the divergent peace groups.

Most peace activists believed that the United States, because of its basically democratic and pacific inclinations, could regenerate habitually war-prone Europe. In the 1920s, such reformist ideas did not seem farfetched: arms seemed controllable (technology had not yet produced global bombers or atomic weapons); domestic economies still did not rely heavily for their prosperity on defense production; the revulsion against World War I remained intense; and few warmongers had yet seized governments. Yet when Dorothy Detzer of WILPF threatened the loss of a million female votes if President Hoover did not name Mt. Holyoke College president Mary Wooley as a delegate to the Geneva Disarmament Conference, Secretary Stimson grumbled that Wooley "knows nothing about the subject. I presume, however, that she can read."[67] Notwithstanding Wooley's active participation, and a WILPF-sponsored Transcontinental Peace Caravan that forwarded several hundred thousand signatures to Geneva, the disarmament talks ran afoul of the Manchurian crisis (see Chapter 5) and accomplished little.

One of the peace movement's few achievements was the Kellogg-Briand Pact of 1928. France, prodded by James T. Shotwell, a Columbia University professor and trustee of the Carnegie Endowment for International Peace, asked the United States to sign a bilateral treaty renouncing war between the two nations. The security-conscious French, ever worried about a revived Germany, seemed to want an "American Locarno," in which Washington would support the European guar-antee of France's eastern boundary as stipulated in the Locarno Treaty of 1925.[68] Washington coolly received the request. But a publicity campaign for a multilateral treaty launched by Shotwell, Salmon Levinson, and Senator William Borah, as well as pressure from women's delegations ("a set of God-damned fools"), prodded Sec-retary Kellogg into action.[69] In February 1928 he sent a draft treaty to France and other powers. Foreign Minister Aristide Briand fumed; Kellogg and the peace ad-vocates had transformed his Franco-American security treaty into a universal dec-laration against war. That August in Paris, the signatories, eventually numbering sixty-two, agreed to "condemn recourse to war for the solution of international controversies, and renounce it as an instrument of national policy."[70]

The Kellogg-Briand Pact required no real sacrifices and established no precise responsibilities. On January 15, 1929, the Senate approved it 85 to 1, with John J. Blaine of Wisconsin opposing because it legalized British rule "over four hun-dred million people without their consent."[71] With one supporter dismissing the treaty as "the last stage of nervous and degenerate effeminacy," the Senate that same day approved funds for fifteen new cruisers.[72] Peace advocates did not naively be-lieve that Kellogg-Briand guaranteed a peaceful world. Because "many people . . . are unwilling to support the Secretary of State's proposals for outlawing big wars while he continues to wage little wars" in places such as Nicaragua (see Chapter 5), Dorothy Detzer regarded it as a first step in a long process and championed the pact as a way of alerting the American people to think once again of the costs of war.[73] Thus it held educational value. And the pact gave the Allies the legal grounds after World War II to punish Axis leaders for plotting aggressive war.

The League of Nations, itself designed to check wars, opened in Geneva without the United States. Washington at first ignored League communications. But by 1925 U.S. diplomats were discreetly participating in League functions. By 1930, unofficial American "observers" had attended more than forty League conferences on such questions as health, prostitution, obscene materials, codification of international law, and opium. In October 1931, U.S. envoy Prentiss B. Gilbert formally participated in League Council meetings on the Manchurian crisis, but Washington would only push the League to cite the Kellogg-Briand Pact and condemn Japan for aggression (see Chapter 5). The United States nearly did join the League-sponsored Permanent Court of International Justice (World Court), which sought to arbitrate international disputes when requested to do so. In 1926 the Senate approved U.S. membership but so qualified it that the court could not accept the American proposal. In 1935 a treaty of membership nearly gained the two-thirds vote, aided by FDR's claim that "the sovereignty of the United States [would] in no way be diminished or jeopardized."[74] That eminent jurists such as Charles Evans Hughes did sit as judges in the World Court offered internationalists some solace.

American participation in disarmament conferences in 1922 (Washington), 1927 (Geneva), 1930 (London), 1932–1933 (Geneva), and 1935–1936 (London) also demonstrated America's international but independent diplomatic course. At those conferences, the United States sought arms limitations, especially on navies, in part because it hoped to shackle others at a time when a parsimonious Congress restrained military U.S. growth. Except for some naval restrictions negotiated at the Washington and London conferences, little was accomplished. Without building to treaty limits, the United States sought to check the quantitative growth of other navies; France would not endorse disarmament until it received security guarantees; the British had a huge empire to protect and police by sea; Italy and Germany plotted military buildups; Japan eyed naval expansion in the Pacific. German rearmament under Adolf Hitler after 1933 and Japanese renunciation of Washington treaty provisions in 1934 signalled the failure of the peace seekers as the world lurched toward global war.

Cold as Steel: Soviet-American Encounters

Soviet Russia signed the Kellogg-Briand Pact and joined the League of Nations in 1934. Yet most European nations and the United States treated Bolshevik Russia as an outsider, a revolutionary disease to be isolated. It was like "having a wicked and disgraceful neighbor," Hoover wrote. "We did not attack him, but we did not give him a certificate of character by inviting him into our homes."[75] Only when Europe tottered on the brink of war in 1939 did Germany on the one hand and France and Britain on the other seriously woo Soviet Russia. Only grudgingly did the United States establish contacts with the Soviets during the interwar years.

Even though V. I. Lenin had said in 1918 that "with the United States we have friction, encounters, struggle, but there can also be agreement," Washington in the 1920s adhered to the nonrecognition policy set by Woodrow Wilson.[76] The Bolsheviks had confiscated American-owned property valued at $336 million, and Russia owed another $192 million to the U.S. government and still another $107 million to American nationals (Tsarist and Provisional government debts). Until Moscow paid, recognition would be denied. Antiradical opinion in the United States, more-over, saw the Bolsheviks as godless, uncivilized, anticapitalist, violent revolutionar-ies who chained their workers like slaves to an authoritarian system. The *New York Times,* American Legion, and American Federation of Labor, among others, bitterly castigated the Soviet experiment. Stimson, wary of the American Communist party, promised in 1930 to deny recognition until Russia "ceased to agitate for the over-throw of American institutions by revolution."[77] Some Americans, such as Senator Borah and the International Ladies Garment Workers Union, urged tolerance and recognition while they criticized the Soviet system.

If most Americans shunned the Bolsheviks, others edged closer. In 1921 Rus-sia suffered a devastating famine. Secretary of Commerce Hoover organized ship-ments of food and medicine to needy areas. Moved by humanitarianism, Hoover also believed that this aid would help implant American influence in Russia and serve as a counterrevolutionary force. From 1921 to 1924 the American Relief Ad-ministration collected $50 million from the federal government and private citizens for assistance to 10 million Russians.

American businesses seemed willing to "sell the misguided fanatics all they are willing to pay for."[78] The State Department separated its distaste for Bolshevism from its desire for economic expansion and permitted important commercial relations. In-ternational Harvester, General Electric, and Du Pont signed trade and technical assis-tance contracts with the Soviet government, often through its purchasing agency in New York, the Trading Corporation. By 1924 Soviet purchases of American products had jumped seven times over the 1923 figure. The entrepreneur W. Averell Harriman obtained monopolistic rights to rich manganese deposits in Soviet Georgia valued at $1 billion, from which Harriman eventually earned a "reasonable profit."[79] In 1928, Americans accounted for 24 percent of all foreign investment in Soviet Russia. Com-munist plans for industrialization and collectivization could not have advanced with-out American machinery, technology, and engineers (1,000 by 1931), although German trade and investments also figured heavily in Soviet economic growth.

For people who believed that capitalism and communism could never meld, Henry Ford's contract with the Soviet Union in 1929 seemed remarkable. Yet the auto mag-nate agreed to supply technical information needed for the large Nizhni-Novgorod au-tomobile factory, which would buy Ford parts and produce a car like the Model A and a truck like the Model AA. Ford eventually lost $578,000 on this multimillion-dollar venture, which terminated in 1934. Expecting a "market for Ford products which . . . may someday surpass in volume all the rest of Europe and Asia combined," the auto en-trepreneur did sell the Soviets on mass-production techniques (*Fordizatsia*).[80] By 1927, 85 percent of the Soviets' tractors were "Fordsons." Once Moscow acquired Western skills and technology, the Soviet leader Leon Trotsky predicted, "Americanized Bolshe-vism will defeat and crush imperialist Americanism."[81] Not so.

American-Russian economic ties began to loosen in the early 1930s. With the Great Depression causing widespread unemployment, government and business of-ficials resented Soviet announcements in the United States that jobs were available in Russia. Russia also began selling goods ("dumping") in the world market below American prices. The United States banned imports of Soviet paper pulp, claiming that convict labor produced it. In retaliation the Soviets reduced drastically their

SO YOU'RE THE BIG BAD BEAR!

"So You're the Big Bad Bear!"
Roosevelt and Soviet commissar for foreign affairs Maxim Litvinov met in Washington in 1933. The atmosphere was friendly and U.S. recognition of the Soviet Union followed. (*Washington Evening Star,* Library of Congress)

buying of American products. In another abortive venture, the famed Russian director Sergei Eisenstein came to Hollywood in 1930 to film Theodore Dreiser's *An American Tragedy,* only to have Paramount terminate his contract and U.S. authorities deport him to Mexico. Eisenstein thereafter always expressed contempt for capitalist "Californica."[82] By 1932 American exports to Russia had declined 90 percent from the 1931 trade. Business executives eager for markets began to argue that official diplomatic recognition might restart stalled commercial relations. The Reconstruction Finance Corporation, a U.S. government agency, helped by extending Russia a $4 million credit for the purchase of American cotton.

The Roosevelt administration, because it wanted to improve trade and deter further Japanese encroachment on China, and simply because nonrecognition served no useful purpose, formally recognized the Soviet Union in November 1933. Roosevelt himself conducted the negotiations. "We would recognize the Devil with a false face if he would contract for some pitchforks," Will Rogers quipped.[83] But the exchange of embassies did not smooth relations or halt Japan. American trade with Russia improved little, despite the signing of a trade treaty in 1935 and the establishment of the Export-Import Bank. The loan or credit that Roosevelt and Commissar for Foreign Affairs Maxim Litvinov had discussed at the time of recognition never materialized because of disagreement over compensation for debts. When American communists spoke critically of the United States at Moscow's Seventh International Communist

(Comintern) Congress in 1935, Secretary Hull charged a violation of Russia's no-propaganda pledge. The Kremlin expected governments to "fall like ripe fruit from their capitalist treetops," noted another U.S. diplomat.[84]

Other issues disrupted Soviet-American relations. Named the first ambassador to Moscow, William Bullitt left America in 1933 as a friend of Russia. Two years later he resigned, convinced that the Soviet government "is a conspiracy to commit murder and nothing else."[85] He had changed his mind because of difficult living conditions in Moscow, spies among his servants, indignities inflicted by rude Soviet bureaucrats, his own volatile prejudices (he called one Soviet commissar "a wretched little kike"), and the ubiquitous Soviet tyranny.[86] Bullitt soon "deviled the Russians. I did all I could to make things unpleasant."[87] He mocked the Comintern's call for a popular front against Germany as similar to the tiger's "historic ride with the young lady of Niger. The Communists feel sure they will come back from the ride with the Socialists and Democrats inside."[88]

The ghastly purges that began in 1935 also moved Bullitt and others to a hard line. "The last mass trials were a great success. There are going to be fewer but better Russians," quipped an unsmiling Greta Garbo in the movie *Ninotchka* (1939).[89] Bullitt's successor as ambassador, the wealthy Joseph E. Davies, thought Soviet Premier Joseph Stalin "cold as steel" and the trials "a nightmare."[90] George F. Kennan, a member of the embassy staff, endured a "liberal education in the horrors of Stalinism."[91] Kennan, who had much enjoyed the "fraternity-like atmosphere" and "homosocial bonding" of 1933–1934 ("the high point of [my] life . . . in comradeship, in gaiety, in intensity of experience"), attended the purge trials in person. So intense was the "eroticized discourse" of Kennan, Bullitt, and other diplomats, the historian Frank Costigliola has suggested, that their passionate outrage at official Soviet cruelties resembled that of spurned suitors thwarted in their wooing of the Russian people.[92] The journalist Eugene Lyons, a United Press correspondent in Russia from 1928 to 1934, also became sickened by the callousness of Stalin's regime: "The great tragic themes of peasant liquidation, persecution of intellectuals, tightening food shortage were bodied forth in hundreds of individual tragedies," he sadly wrote.[93]

If the purges stunned many Americans, the Nazi-Soviet Pact of August 1939 outraged them. Stalin believed that the Western European powers and the United States had let Hitler expand uninhibited to encourage the German's design to conquer Russia. And Stalin had so depleted the officer ranks of his army through the purges that he was in no position to stave off an expected German attack. In the United States, the nonaggression pact, which secretly divided Poland, reinforced charges that Stalin had become Hitler's friend. When World War II erupted in September 1939, many Americans blamed the Soviet Union.

Hitler's Germany, Appeasement, and the Outbreak of War

By exploiting the depression-afflicted economy and the vehement attitudes against the Versailles treaty in Germany, the Nazi leader Adolf Hitler came to power in January 1933. Racist toward Jews and emphatically anti-Bolshevik, Hitler quickly

Benito Mussolini (1883–1945). *Il Duce* excited a revival of Italian imperial grandeur by attacking Ethiopia in 1935. In the mistaken belief that Mussolini would help to stabilize Europe, President Roosevelt had earlier referred to *Il Duce* as "that admirable Italian gentleman." British foreign secretary Anthony Eden called him "the complete gangster [whose] pledged word means nothing." (National Archives)

alarmed diplomats with his "fanatic chauvinism coupled with his hatred of democratic government and the parliamentary system."[94] In October 1933, Hitler withdrew Germany from the faltering League of Nations and denounced disarmament talks. He told an associate that the European powers would "never act! They'll just protest. And they will always be too late."[95] Indeed, France and Britain settled on a timid policy of "appeasement," hoping to satisfy what they thought were Hitler's limited goals and to avert another European war. By 1935 Britain, France, Italy, and the League of Nations had censured Germany for building a huge army and air force. Yet at the same time, Britain agreed that Germany could rebuild its navy to 35 percent of the size of the British navy, another costly concession to German militarism.

Hardly adjusted to the rise of Nazi Germany, the world watched as Italy invaded the African state of Ethiopia in October 1935. The fascist Benito Mussolini had governed Italy since 1922, and he had long dreamed of creating an Italian empire. Already holding Somaliland and Eritrea as African colonies, Mussolini gradually pressed Ethiopian leader Haile Selassie until military skirmishes broke out. Then Mussolini invaded and annexed Ethiopia. The League imposed an embargo on the shipment of war-related goods (except oil) to Italy. But the French, with their own empire in Africa, and the British, fearful that Italy might disrupt their imperial lifeline in the Mediterranean, seemed willing to sacrifice Ethiopia, a mere "corridor for camels."[96] They also feared that further hostilities would "play into Germany's hands" and "might mean a general war in Europe."[97]

Apparently encouraged by Anglo-French docility over Ethiopia, Hitler in March 1936 ordered his goose-stepping troops into the Rhineland, the area bordering Belgium and France that the Versailles treaty had declared permanently demilitarized. After World War I, the French had erected the Maginot Line, a series of large guns and defensive bunkers along the German-French border. By seizing the Rhineland, Germany could outflank the line. The French, fearful of igniting another war, did

Adolf Hitler (1889–1945). When Hitler took power in 1933, some Americans likened his mustachioed face to that of the actor Charlie Chaplin. One political scientist described Hitler's oratory as a "combination of Ku Klux Klan, Negro revival meeting, and Billy Sunday harangue." In this propagandistic German painting, the anticommunist, anti-Semitic Nazi leader is surrounded by swastikas and saluting followers. Hitler called the United States a "mongrel society" that was "hopelessly weak," but he learned otherwise. (U.S. Army)

**Joachim von Ribbentrop (1893–1946) and
Joseph Stalin (1879–1953).** The German
foreign minister (left) and Soviet premier smile their
approval of the Nazi-Soviet nonaggression pact signed
in August 1939. The news angered but did not surprise
American officials, who monitored the secret
negotiations through reports from a cooperative
German diplomat in Moscow. (World War II Collection
of Seized Enemy Records, National Archives)

not resist the German advance. Meanwhile, in June, the League of Nations lifted the
economic sanctions against Italy. Victories by German athletes at the Berlin
Olympiad in summer 1936, moreover, proved "as conducive to [Hitler's] self-esteem
as a 98% plebiscite—and perhaps more convincing," observed U.S. ambassador
William E. Dodd.[98] That same fall, after Hitler signed the Rome–Berlin Axis agreement with Italy and the Anti-Comintern Pact with Japan, U.S. military attachés sent
ominous reports on German military maneuvers, including *Panzer* brigades, warning of "a revolution in military methods."[99]

Spain became contested ground, too. "Nationalist" soldiers under General
Francisco Franco started the Spanish civil war in July 1936 by attacking the "Loyalist" Republican government. Eager for a Franco government hostile to France,
Hitler and Mussolini poured military equipment and troops into the Nationalist effort. The tepid Anglo-French response produced an International Non-
Intervention Committee of twenty-seven nations, remarkably including Germany
and Italy. Although the signatories pledged to stay out of the Spanish conflict,
Hitler and Mussolini continued covert aid, and France and Britain lived with the
fiction that they had isolated the Spanish civil war. The Soviet Union and Mexico
sent help to the Republicans, and some 3,000 Americans fought alongside them in
the Abraham Lincoln Brigade. Franco and his brand of fascism nonetheless prevailed in early 1939.

The 1937 election of Neville Chamberlain as British prime minister enshrined
the appeasement policy. He believed that Germany had good reason to want to reject
the humiliating Versailles treaty and to claim status as a major power. Tolerant of
Hitler's demand for mastery over people of German descent living in Austria, Czechoslovakia, and Poland, Chamberlain also judged that "Germany lacked the economic
strength and political cohesion seriously to contemplate war and that she could be

weaned from aggression by his blend of conciliation and firmness, carrot and stick."[100] An appeased Germany could also serve as a useful restraint on Soviet Russia.

In March 1938, German troops crossed into Austria and annexed it to the German Reich. Months of terrorism against Jews and opponents of Nazism in Austria followed. Hitler next demanded the Sudeten region of Czechoslovakia, where 3 million ethnic Germans lived. Hitler assured Chamberlain that this marked Germany's last territorial demand. Britain and France (which had a defense treaty with Prague) granted the Nazi this additional prize. The end of Czechoslovakia's independence came at the Munich Conference of September 29–30, 1938, where Italy, Germany, France, and Britain agreed never to make war against one another and to sever the Sudetenland from Czechoslovakia. The Czechs were not consulted. Unwilling to wage "a war today in order to prevent a war hereafter," Chamberlain proclaimed "peace for our time."[101] His opponents gibed: "if at first you can't concede, fly, fly, fly again."[102] Hitler soon accelerated his persecution of German Jews and in March 1939 swallowed the rest of Czechoslovakia. The following month Italy absorbed Albania.

Poland came next. Refusing Hitler's demands for the city of Danzig, the Poles soon faced German pressure. But London and Paris announced in March 1939 that they would stand behind an independent Poland. A grim Chamberlain judged it "impossible to deal with Hitler after he had thrown all his own assurances to the wind."[103] The Soviet Union then emerged as a central actor in the European tumult. Germany, Britain, and France opened negotiations with Moscow in attempts to gain Soviet allegiance. Stalin chose Germany. "Britain and France wanted us to be their hired hand . . . and without pay," he remarked.[104] On August 23, Nazi Germany and Soviet Russia signed the nonaggression pact. Poland, the immediate victim, found itself divided between the two powers. As he watched Hitler cavort with the Bolshevik devil, one U.S. senator wrote privately: "If Germany can organize Russia and they make England give up her fleet, look out—we'll have a Nazi, or nasty, world."[105] On September 1, German soldiers invaded Poland. Two days later Britain and France declared war against Germany. On September 17, Soviet troops struck Poland, taking half the nation.

Throughout these years of descent into World War II, Hitler both admired and underrated the United States. Impressed by anti–Semite Henry Ford and his production techniques, he sent German car designers to Detroit before launching the *Volkswagen*. Nonetheless, he scorned U.S. influence in world affairs. Although his advisers told him that American isolationism might not last, he deemed the United States "incapable of conducting war"—a "Jewish rubbish heap," incapacitated by economic and racial crises, crime, and inept political leadership. "The inferiority and decadence of this allegedly new world is evident in its military inefficiency," he claimed.[106] Hitler's Nazis also viewed emancipated American women as "egoistic, manipulative, overly sexual, and unerotic," in stark contrast to "the Nazi ideal of a devoted Gretchen bearing future soldiers for the Third Reich's wars of conquest."[107] Despite the popularity of "swing" music and American films (especially those of Shirley Temple and "Micky Maus"), the Nazis outlawed "Nigger-Jew jazz" and soon banned Hollywood imports, even as Hitler enjoyed private screenings of *Gone with the Wind* (1939).[108] Although the *Fuehrer*'s long-range goals probably included aggressive war against the United States, his intial perceptions of America as a "half-Judaized, half negrified" country with a large navy and minuscule army caused him to discount growing U.S. support for England and France.[109]

American Isolationism and the Neutrality Acts

"This nation will remain a neutral nation," President Roosevelt announced on September 3, 1939, "but I cannot ask that every American remain neutral in thought as well."[110] Second thoughts about neutrality came only late in the decade. During the early 1930s the United States attempted to shield itself from conflict in Europe and remain rigidly neutral. Although most Americans, such as the novelist Thomas Wolfe, strongly disapproved of Hitler and his "brutal, beer swilling people," they tried to isolate themselves from a continent they thought prone to self-destruction.[111] If Britain and France could not handle German aggression in their own backyards, America could not do the job for them.

Americans also drew lessons from World War I. Disillusioned writers and "revisionist" historians argued that Germany had not solely precipitated war in 1914, that business leaders and propagandists had influenced a pro-British Wilson, and that the costs and results of war did not justify American participation. In 1934 the best-selling book *Merchants of Death* (by Helmuth Englebrecht and Frank Hanighen) argued that profiteering arms manufacturers had exploited the American economic and political system to compromise U.S. neutrality. Encouraged by President Roosevelt, Senator Gerald P. Nye held hearings during 1934–1936 to determine if munitions makers and bankers had lobbied Wilson into war. The committee never proved the allegation but did uncover substantial evidence that these entrepreneurs had exerted influence on behalf of the Allies. By identifying an "unhealthy alliance" among business, the military, and the government, the Nye Committee anticipated "with remarkable accuracy . . . the growth of the structure later called the military-industrial complex."[112] Popular sentiment held that World War I had been a tragic blunder and that Americans "must think of the next war as they would of suicide."[113]

Although they might disagree on particulars, peace groups, the scientist Albert Einstein, Herbert Hoover, the anti-Semite Father Charles E. Coughlin, the historian Charles Beard, and Senators William Borah, Hiram Johnson, and George Norris shared the traditional belief in political and military nonentanglement—"a north star, constant and steady, which will hold us true to our course."[114] The antiwar movement grew strong on college campuses and among women. Princeton University students organized the Veterans of Future Wars in 1936 and demanded $1,000 each as a bonus *before* going into battle, because few, they predicted, would live through the next war. The journalist William Allen White predicted that "the next war will see . . . the same bowwow of the big dogs to get the little dogs to go out and follow the blood scent and get their entrails tangled in the barbed wire."[115] In 1938, member of Congress Louis Ludlow introduced a constitutional amendment calling for a national referendum on decisions for war. Warned Ludlow: "It is impossible to imagine the next large-scale war being anything less than a vast carnival of death."[116] Roosevelt claimed that the amendment "would cripple any President in his conduct of our foreign relations," and even the isolationist Senator Arthur Vandenberg protested that it "would be as sensible to require a town meeting before permitting the fire department to put out the

Senator Hiram W. Johnson (1866–1945). The California progressive reformer, anti-imperialist, and firm isolationist served in the U.S. Senate for twenty-eight years. He opposed U.S. membership in the League of Nations and the World Court and called for strict U.S. neutrality toward Europe. The United States, Johnson insisted, "cannot strut as a knight-errant to reform the world." In 1941, however, he voted for U.S. entrance into World War II after the Japanese attack on Pearl Harbor. (Library of Congress)

blaze."[117] A motion to discharge Ludlow's resolution from the Rules Committee failed by only 209 to 188.

Many so-called progressive isolationists believed that American entry into a European war would undercut the New Deal's attempts to recover from the depression. They also remembered how the Wilson administration had savaged critics in World War I, how Wilson had cooperated with big business to win the war. Convinced that business expansionists helped create the conditions that spawned war, progressive isolationists sought to curb business adventures abroad that entangled the United States. The statistics were not as readily available to them as they are now to historians. By 1937, for example, twenty of the top one hundred American corporations had negotiated important agreements with Nazi Germany, some with the core of the German military machine, the I. G. Farben Company. Du Pont, Union Carbide, and Standard Oil signed contracts, with Standard Oil helping Germany develop synthetic rubber and aviation fuel. "American businessmen publicly opposed war as much as anyone else," one scholar has concluded, "but it would seem that the one price they would not pay for peace was private profit."[118]

Although sharply critical of fascism abroad, Dorothy Detzer, the dynamic executive secretary of the WILPF, also feared a "peculiar type of American Fascism" in which "women would be thrown back into the kitchen, as . . . in Germany."[119] Detzer and other peace progressives worked behind the scenes on behalf of the Nye Committee and neutrality legislation. Roosevelt wanted a neutrality law that would permit him to ban sales of arms to aggressors. Congress instead passed the Neutrality Act of 1935, requiring an American arms embargo against all belligerents after the president had officially proclaimed the existence of war. "Leave as little to the discretion of the President as possible," urged Detzer.[120] Subsequent legislation banned loans to belligerents (Act of 1936) and required belligerents wishing to trade with the United States to carry away U.S. goods in their own ships ("cash and carry"), after payment on delivery (Act of 1937). The latter also forbade U.S. citizens to travel on belligerent vessels. An amendment of 1937 made the United States neutral in the Spanish civil war.

The Neutrality Acts erred in providing for no discrimination among the belligerents, no punishment of the aggressor. They denied the United States any forceful word in the cascading events in Europe. They amounted to an abdication of power. Yet, at the same time, much of what the isolationists said about the fruits of war rang true. Their criticisms of imperialism and business expansion were honest and telling. They scorned the British Empire and U.S. intervention in Latin America. They compared Italy's subjugation of Ethiopia to Britain's supremacy in India. Many of them warned about increasing the power of the president in foreign affairs beyond congressional reach. Their noble commitment to peace and their rejection of war as a solution to human problems were compelling. Denounced by Neville Chamberlain as "those pig-headed and self-righteous nobodies," isolationists nonetheless comprised "a large, responsible, and respectable segment of the American people."[121] In condemning all imperialism—American, British, or German—the isolationists often refused to make the choice of the lesser of two or three evils. However praiseworthy their thought, their formulas for the 1930s proved as misguided as Britain's appeasement policy.

Roosevelt Shifts and Congress Balks on the Eve of War

President Roosevelt, sensitive to American sentiment against U.S. entanglement in Europe and sharing much of the pacifist loathing of war, responded haltingly to the events of the 1930s. His foreign policy fed appeasement. When Italy attacked Ethiopia, Roosevelt stated that the United States sought above all to avoid war. America would set a peaceful example for other nations to follow. He and Hull invoked the Neutrality Act, warned Americans not to travel on belligerent ships, and suggested a moral embargo against trade with the warring parties. Actually, American businesses ignored the moral embargo and increased commerce with Italy, especially in oil. At the same time, aggression in Africa sparked "the first great manifestation of Afro-American interest in foreign affairs."[122] In addition to anti-Italian boycotts and petitions by black churches to the pope, the African-American poet Langston Hughes composed a "Ballad of Ethiopia" in support of black solidarity.[123] In August 1936, the president gave a stirring speech at Chautauqua, New York, recalling World War I: "I have seen war. . . . I have seen blood running from the wounded. I have seen men coughing out their gassed lungs. . . . I hate war."[124]

In January 1937, Roosevelt asked Congress for an arms embargo against Spain. Congress obliged, but the decision sparked considerable debate. It produced "malevolent neutrality" that worked against the "Loyalist" Republican government and in favor of Franco.[125] In this case, many isolationists protested neutrality—the sacrifice of Spanish democracy. They agonized: How can one be commited to both peace and liberty? Roosevelt and Hull chose strict neutrality, in essence backing feeble British-French efforts to contain the civil war and aligning themselves with the pro-Franco views of the Catholic hierarchy at home. Yet Roosevelt privately pondered ways to curb the aggressors.

In July, when Japan plunged into undeclared war against China, Roosevelt favored China by not invoking the Neutrality Act, thereby permitting the Chinese government to buy and import American war goods (see Chapter 5). Then in October he delivered his famous "quarantine" speech, calling for the isolation of international lawbreakers. Hoping that "people realize that war will be a greater danger . . . if we close all the doors and windows than if we go in the street and use our influence to curb the riot," FDR approached the British ambassador about a joint cruiser blockade against Japan and sent a naval officer to London for secret staff talks.[126] Under Secretary of State Sumner Welles also proposed a world conference on disarmament and international law in Washington, at which Roosevelt might quietly stiffen British diplomacy. Chamberlain, however, blocked the meeting in early 1938 because it interfered with his efforts to negotiate with the aggressors. Convinced that he could "count on nothing from the Americans but words," Chamberlain continued to pursue appeasement.[127]

During the Czech crisis of 1938 the United States kept at a safe distance. The president appealed for negotiations to head off war, while telling Hitler that the United States had "no political involvements in Europe and will assume no obligations in the conduct of the present negotiations."[128] "Good man," Roosevelt cabled Chamberlain when he heard that the prime minister would go to Munich.[129]

"Uncomfortable Grandstand." The British cartoonist David Low obviously did not think that a neutral United States could remain safe after the outbreak of war in Europe. President Roosevelt turns a quizzical face to Secretary of State Hull as the bombs fly and burst. (*London Evening Standard*/ Solo)

Yet the dismemberment of Czechoslovakia, combined with the Japanese terror in China, soon prompted the president to confess privately that Munich had failed and that Hitler was "a pure unadulterated devil" who must be stopped.[130] Worried about the insidious effects of "too much Eton and Oxford," FDR thought the British needed "a good stiff grog, inducing not only the desire to save civilization but the continued belief that they can do it."[131]

In October 1938, Roosevelt asked Congress for $300 million for national defense. He encouraged the State Department and Senator Key Pittman, the hard-drinking, gun-packing, incompetent chair of the Foreign Relations Committee, to lobby for the repeal of the arms embargo law. In November, in protest against Hitler's vicious persecution of the Jews, he recalled Ambassador Hugh Wilson from Berlin and never let him return. That same month, FDR initiated a program to build more than 10,000 warplanes per year, in order "to have something to back up my words."[132] He also secretly arranged for the French government to place orders for planes. In December the administration rallied behind a declaration of joint defense against aggression in the Western Hemisphere and loaned $25 million to China.

In January 1939, Roosevelt again urged revision of the Neutrality Act so that it would not "actually give aid to an aggressor and deny it to the victim."[133] The crash of the A-20 bomber in Los Angeles and FDR's garbled statement about America's frontier on the Rhine stalled this initiative. The president thus delayed until March the introduction of a bill specifically repealing the arms embargo, and throughout the spring he allowed the erratic Pittman to direct legislative strategy. Reluctant to risk battle against sizable political odds, FDR failed to lead at a critical time. In April he asked Hitler and Mussolini to refrain from attacking countries named on a list, but his request met open derision, *Il Duce* saying that Italy would not respond to "Messiah-like messages."[134] The Senate Foreign Relations Committee, by a 12 to 11 vote, refused in July to report out a bill repealing the arms embargo. "I've fired my last shot," the president groaned.[135] Not until November 1939—after Germany's conquest of Poland—did Congress finally revise the Neutrality Act so that England and France, as belligerents, could purchase American arms on a cash-and-carry basis.

Even in fall 1939, however, most Americans joined their president in wanting to avoid participation in World War II. "We cannot expect . . . the United States to evolve quicker than we did," the British ambassador reported.[136] By sending Sumner Welles to Berlin, London, Paris, and Rome in the winter of 1940, FDR evidently thought he might "intervene as a kind of umpire."[137] Hitler's *blitzkrieg* in the west that spring killed any such possibility. The Democratic party platform of 1940, on which Roosevelt ran for a third term, reflected the American desire to avoid war but also to prepare for it: "We will not participate in foreign wars, and we will not send our army, naval or air forces to fight in foreign lands outside of the Americas except in case of attack." Still, it also promised "an invincible air force, a navy strong enough to protect all our seacoasts and our national interests, and a fully equipped and mechanized army."[138] As in World War I, because of their international interests, because U.S. power became intertwined in the war, and because they gradually abandoned neutrality to aid the Allies, Americans once again found themselves risking major war. The interwar quest for world order and peace had failed; the several Neutrality Acts had failed; independent internationalism had failed.

FURTHER READING FOR THE PERIOD 1920–1939

Overviews include Warren I. Cohen, *Empire Without Tears* (1987); Robert A. Divine, *The Reluctant Belligerent* (1979); Justus D. Doenecke and John E. Wilz, *From Isolation to War* (2003); Robert H. Ferrell, *American Diplomacy in the Great Depression* (1957) and *Peace in Their Time* (1952); Margaret Louria, *Triumph and Downfall* (2001); Sally Marks, *The Illusion of Peace* (1976); Arnold Offner, *The Origins of the Second World War* (1975); Brenda Gayle Plummer, *Rising Wind* (1996) (African Americans); Benjamin D. Rhodes, *United States Foreign Policy in the Interwar Period, 1918–1941* (2001); Robert Schulzinger, *The Making of the Diplomatic Mind* (1975); and Geoffrey S. Smith, *To Save a Nation* (1992).

The presidents and their presidencies are treated in David Burner, *Herbert Hoover* (1978); Martin Fausold, *The Presidency of Herbert C. Hoover* (1985); Robert H. Ferrell, *The Presidency of Calvin Coolidge* (1998); Alonzo L. Hamby, *For the Survival of Democracy: Franklin Roosevelt and the World Crisis of the 1930s* (2004) (Roosevelt); Ellis W. Hawley, ed., *Herbert Hoover: Secretary of Commerce* (1981); Donald R. McCoy, *Calvin Coolidge* (1967); Robert K. Murray, *The Harding Era* (1969); and Joan Hoff Wilson, *Herbert Hoover* (1975).

For Franklin D. Roosevelt, see James M. Burns, *The Lion and the Fox* (1956); Wayne S. Cole, *Roosevelt and the Isolationists* (1983); Robert Dallek, *Franklin D. Roosevelt and American Foreign Policy, 1933–1945* (1979); Kenneth R. Davis, *FDR* (1972–1993); Robert A. Divine, *Roosevelt and World War II* (1969); Frank Freidel, *Franklin D. Roosevelt* (1952–1973) and *Franklin D. Roosevelt* (1990); William E. Leuchtenburg, *Franklin D. Roosevelt and the New Deal* (1963); Frederick W. Marks III, *Wind over Sand*

(1988); George McJimsey, *The Presidency of Franklin Delano Roosevelt* (2000); Arthur M. Schlesinger, Jr., *The Age of Roosevelt* (1957–1960); and Cornelius A. van Minnen and John F. Sears, eds., *FDR and His Contemporaries* (1992).

For the secretaries of state, see McGeorge Bundy, *On Active Service in Peace and War* (1948) (Stimson); Michael Butler, *Cautious Visionary* (1998) (Hull); L. Ethan Ellis, *Frank B. Kellogg and American and Foreign Relations* (1961); Robert H. Ferrell, *Frank B. Kellogg* (1963) and *Henry L. Stimson* (1963); Betty Glad, *Charles Evans Hughes and the Illusions of Innocence* (1967) (Stimson); Elting E. Morison, *Turmoil and Tradition* (1960) (Stimson); Julius Pratt, *Cordell Hull* (1964); and David F. Schmitz, *Henry L. Stimson* (2001).

Other diplomats and politicians are studied in Leroy Ashby, *The Spearless Leader* (1972) (Borah); Fred A. Bailey, *William Edward Dodd* (1997); Will Brownell and Richard N. Billings, *So Close to Greatness* (1988) (Bullitt); Wayne S. Cole, *Senator Gerald P. Nye and American Foreign Relations* (1962); Ralph de Bedts, *Ambassador Joseph Kennedy* (1985); Irwin Gellman, *Secret Affairs* (1995) (Hull and Welles); Betty Glad, *Key Pittman* (1986); Frank W. Graff, *Strategy of Involvement* (1988) (Welles); Waldo Heinrichs, *American Ambassador* (1966) (Grew); Kenneth P. Jones, *Diplomats in Europe, 1919–1941* (1981); Richard C. Lower, *A Bloc of One* (1993) (Hiram Johnson); Richard Lowitt, *George W. Norris* (1963–1978); Elizabeth K. MacLean, *Joseph E. Davies* (1992); Peter Schlinger and Holman Hamilton, *Spokesman for Democracy: Claude G. Bowers* (2000); Jesse H. Stiller, *George S. Messersmith* (1987); Michael Weatherson and Hal W. Bochin, *Hiram Johnson* (1995); and Benjamin Welles, *Sumner Welles* (1997).

Economic foreign relations receive attention in Frederick Adams, *Economic Diplomacy* (1976); Derek H. Aldcroft, *From Versailles to Wall Street, 1919–1929* (1977); Joseph Brandes, *Herbert Hoover and Economic Diplomacy* (1962); Patricia Clavin, *The Failure of Economic Diplomacy* (1996); Lloyd C. Gardner, *Economic Aspects of New Deal Diplomacy* (1964); Michael J. Hogan, *Informal Entente* (1977); Burton I. Kaufman, *Efficiency and Expansion* (1974); Charles P. Kindleberger, *The World in Depression, 1929–1939* (1986); Carl Parrini, *Heir to Empire* (1969); Stephen J. Randall, *United States Foreign Oil Policy, 1919–1948* (1986); William Stivers, *Supremacy and Oil* (1982); Mira Wilkins, *The Maturing of Multinational Enterprise* (1974); Joan Hoff Wilson, *American Business and Foreign Policy, 1920–1933* (1971); and Gilbert Ziebura, *World Economy and World Politics, 1924–1931* (1990).

The German reparations issue is explored in Bruce Kent, *The Spoils of War* (1989); Stephen Schuker, *American "Reparations" to Germany* (1988); and Marc Trachtenberg, *Reparation in World Politics* (1980).

Cultural issues and industries are highlighted in Frank Costigliola, *Awkward Dominion* (1984) (Europe); David H. Culbert, *News for Everyman: Radio and Foreign Affairs in Thirties America* (1976); George Q. Flynn, *Roosevelt and Romanism: Catholics and American Diplomacy, 1937–1945* (1976); Emily S. Rosenberg, *Spreading the American Dream* (1982); Thomas J. Saunders, *Hollywood in Berlin* (1994); Lawrence Spinelli, *Dry Diplomacy* (1989) (Prohibition); Richard W. Steele, *Propaganda in an Open Society* (1985); Arnold H. Taylor, *American Diplomacy and the Narcotics Traffic, 1900–1931* (1969); and Robert C. Williams, *Russian Art and American Money* (1980).

Defense preparedness and arms-control questions are discussed in James L. Abrahamson, *America Arms for a New Century* (1981); Thomas Buckley, *The United States and the Washington Conference* (1970); Roger Dingman, *Power in the Pacific: The Origins of Naval Arms Limitation, 1914–1922* (1976); Richard W. Fanning, *Peace and Disarmament* (1995); Emily O. Goldman, *Sunken Treaties* (1994) (naval arms control); Robert Kaufman, *Arms Control During the Pre-Nuclear Age* (1990); Paul A. C. Koistinen, *Planning War, Pursuing Peace* (1998); Ernest R. May, *Knowing One's Enemy* (1984) (intelligence assessment); Stephen Pelz, *Race to Pearl Harbor* (1974) (Second London Naval Conference); and Michael S. Sherry, *The Rise of American Air Power* (1987).

For peace advocates and the League of Nations, see Harriet H. Alonso, *The Women's Peace Union and the Outlawry of War* (1989); Jason Berger, *A New Deal for the World* (1981) (Eleanor Roosevelt); Charles Chatfield, *For Peace and Justice* (1971); Blanche Wiesen Cook, *Eleanor Roosevelt* (1992, 1999); Merle Curti, *Peace or War* (1936); Charles DeBenedetti, *Origins of the Modern American Peace Movement, 1915–1929* (1978) and *The Peace Reform in American History* (1980); Michael Dunne, *The United States and the World Court* (1988); D. F. Fleming, *The United States and World Organization, 1920–1933* (1938); Carrie Foster, *The Women and the Warriors* (1995); Catherine Foster, *Women for All Seasons* (1989); Robert D. Johnson, *The Peace Progressives and American Foreign Relations* (1995); Harold Josephson, *James T. Shotwell and the Rise of*

Internationalism in America (1976); Warren F. Kuehl and Lynne K. Dunn, *Keeping the Covenant* (1997) (League); Cecilia Lynch, *Beyond Appeasement* (1999); Gary B. Ostrower, *Collective Insecurity* (1979) (League); Lois Scharf, *Eleanor Roosevelt* (1987); Linda K. Schott, *Reconstructing Women's Thoughts* (1997) (WILPF); Joan Hoff Wilson and Marjorie Lightman, eds., *Without Precedent* (1984) (Eleanor Roosevelt); and Lawrence S. Wittner, *Rebels Against War* (1984).

For American isolationism, see overviews cited in the first paragraph and Warren I. Cohen, *The American Revisionists* (1967); Thomas Guinsburg, *The Pursuit of Isolationism* (1981); Manfred Jonas, *Isolationism in America* (1966); Thomas C. Kennedy, *Charles A. Beard and American Foreign Policy* (1975); and John Wiltz, *In Search of Peace* (1963) (Nye Committee).

Relations with Europe and Germany and the coming of World War II are studied in many of the works cited above and in James J. and Patience P. Barnes, *Hitler's* Mein Kampf *in Britain and America* (1980); Edward W. Bennett, *German Rearmament and the West, 1932–1933* (1979); Peter H. Buckingham, *International Normalcy: The Open Door Peace with the Former Central Powers, 1921–29* (1983); Bernard Burke, *Ambassador Frederick Sackett and the Collapse of the Weimar Republic* (1995); James V. Compton, *The Swastika and the Eagle* (1967); Jean-Baptiste Duroselle, *France and the United States* (1978); Barbara R. Farnham, *Roosevelt and the Munich Crisis* (1997); John Haight, Jr., *American Aid to France, 1938–1940* (1970); Linda Killen, *Testing the Peripheries* (1994) (Yugoslavia); Melvyn Leffler, *The Elusive Quest* (1979) (France); Charles S. Maier, *Recasting Bourgeois Europe* (1975); Brian McKercher, ed., *Anglo-American Relations in the 1920s* (1991); and *Transition of Power* (1999) William C. McNeil, *American Money and the Weimer Republic* (1986); Wolfgang Mommsen and Lothar Kettenacker, eds., *The Fascist Challenge and the Policy of Appeasement* (1983); John E. Moser, *Twisting the Lion's Tail: American Anglophobia between the World Wars* (1999); Mary Nolan, *Visions of Modernity* (1994) (American business in Germany); Arnold Offner, *American Appeasement* (1969); R. A. C. Parker, *Chamberlain and Appeasement* (1993); Neal Pease, *Poland, the United States, and the Stabilization of Europe, 1919–1933* (1986); David Reynolds, *The Creation of the Anglo-American Alliance, 1937–41* (1982); David Reynolds and David Dimbleby, *An Ocean Apart* (1989); William R. Rock, *Chamberlain and Roosevelt* (1988); David F. Schmitz, *The United States and Fascist Italy* (1988); David F. Schmitz and Richard D. Challener, eds., *Appeasement in Europe* (1990); Dan P. Silverman, *Reconstructing Europe After the Great War* (1982); D. C. Watt, *How War Came* (1989); Gerhard Weinberg, *The Foreign Policy of Hitler's Germany* (1970, 1980); and Marvin Zahniser, *Then Came Disaster: France and the United States, 1918–1940* (2002).

Soviet-American relations and recognition are discussed in Edward Bennett, *Recognition of Russia* (1970) and *Franklin D. Roosevelt and the Search for Security* (1985); Peter G. Boyle, *American-Soviet Relations* (1995); Dennis Dunn, *Caught Between Roosevelt and Stalin* (1998); Keith D. Eagles, *Ambassador Joseph E. Davies and American-Soviet Relations, 1937–1941* (1985); Beatrice Farnsworth, *William C. Bullitt and the Soviet Union* (1967); Peter Filene, *Americans and the Soviet Experiment* (1967); John Lewis Gaddis, *Russia, the Soviet Union, and the United States* (1990); Jonathan Haslam, *The Soviet Union and the Struggle for Collective Security in Europe* (1984); George F. Kennan, *Russia and the West Under Lenin and Stalin* (1960); Melvyn Leffler, *The Specter* (1994); James K. Libbey, *Alexander Gumberg and Soviet-American Relations* (1977); Thomas R. Maddux, *Years of Estrangement* (1980); David Mayers, *The Ambassadors and America's Soviet Policy* (1995); Bertrand Patenaude, *The Big Show in Bololand* (2002) (Relief for Russia); Katherine Siegel, *Loans and Legitimacy* (1996); Anthony Sutton, *Western Technology and Soviet Economic Development* (1968); Christine A. White, *British and American Commercial Relations with Soviet Russia* (1993); and Joan Hoff Wilson, *Ideology and Economics* (1974).

For the Spanish civil war, see Michael Alpert, *A New International History of the Spanish Civil War* (1998); Peter N. Carroll, *The Odyssey of the Abraham Lincoln Brigade* (1994); Mark Falcoff and Fredrick B. Pike, *The Spanish Civil War, 1936–1939* (1982); Allen Guttman, *The Wound in the Heart* (1962); Douglas Little, *Malevolent Neutrality* (1985); R. Dan Richardson, *Comintern Army* (1982); and Richard Traina, *American Diplomacy and the Spanish Civil War* (1968).

See also "Further Reading" in Chapters 5 and 6, the General Bibliography, Robert L. Beisner, ed., *Guide to American Foreign Relations Since 1600* (2003), and the following notes.

For comprehensive coverage of foreign-relations topics, see the articles in the four-volume *Encylocpedia of U.S. Foreign Relations* (1997), edited by Bruce W. Jentleson and Thomas G. Paterson.

NOTES TO CHAPTER 4

1. Quoted in Kenneth S. Davis, *FDR: Into the Storm* (New York: Random House, 1993), p. 401.

2. Quoted *ibid.*, p. 402.

3. Quoted *ibid.*, p. 401.

4. Henry Morgenthau, Jr., quoted in conference transcript, March 21, 1946, Box 391, Henry Morgenthau, Jr., Papers, Franklin D. Roosevelt Library, Hyde Park, N.Y.

5. David Reynolds, *The Creation of the Anglo-American Alliance, 1937–1941* (Chapel Hill: University of North Carolina Press, 1982), p. 43.

6. Quoted in Wayne S. Cole, *Roosevelt and the Isolationists* (Lincoln: University of Nebraska Press, 1983), p. 297.

7. Quoted in Michael S. Sherry, *The Rise of American Air Power* (New Haven: Yale University Press, 1987), pp. 79–80.

8. Quoted in Jean Monnet, *Memoirs* (London: Collins, 1978), p. 119.

9. Quoted in Sherry, *Air Power*, p. 80.

10. Quoted in Cole, *Roosevelt and Isolationists*, p. 301.

11. Quoted in conference transcript, "The French Airplane Mission," April 25, 1946, Box 391, Morgenthau Papers.

12. Quoted in David Reynolds, "The Origins of Two 'World Wars,' " *Journal of Contemporary History*, XXXVIII (January 2003), 38.

13. Transcript of "Conference with Senate Military Affairs Committee, Executive Offices of the White House, January 31, 1939, 12:45 P.M.," Personal Files, PPF 1-P, Franklin D. Roosevelt Papers, Roosevelt Library.

14. Quoted in J. Garry Clifford, "A Note on the Break Between Senator Nye and President Roosevelt in 1939," *North Dakota History*, XLIX (Summer 1982), 17.

15. *New York Times*, February 1, 1939.

16. Quoted in Clifford, "A Note," p. 14.

17. Quoted in Reynolds, *Creation*, p. 37.

18. Transcript, "French Airplane Mission."

19. Warren F. Kimball, *The Juggler* (Princeton: Princeton University Press, 1991), p. 7.

20. Quoted in Sherry, *Air Power*, p. 79.

21. *Ibid.*, p. 82.

22. Henry Arnold quoted in John M. Haight, Jr., *American Aid to France, 1938–1940* (New York: Atheneum, 1970), p. 204.

23. Francois Duchêne, *Jean Monnet* (New York: Norton, 1994), p. 69.

24. Franklin D. Roosevelt to Helen Rogers Reid, June 6, 1940, Reid Papers, Library of Congress, Washington, D.C.

25. Quoted in John M. Blum, *From the Morgenthau Diaries* (Boston: Houghton Mifflin, 1959–1967; 3 vols.), I, 118.

26. Ambassador Ronald Lindsey quoted in Greg Kennedy, *Anglo-American Strategic Relations and the Far East, 1933–1939* (Portland, Ore.: Frank Cass, 2000), p. 229.

27. Joan Hoff Wilson, *American Business and Foreign Policy, 1920–1933* (Boston: Beacon Press, 1973 [c. 1971]), p. x.

28. Melvyn P. Leffler, *The Elusive Quest* (Chapel Hill: University of North Carolina Press, 1979), p. 362.

29. Quoted in L. Ethan Ellis, *Republican Foreign Policy, 1921–1933* (New Brunswick, N.J.: Rutgers University Press, 1968), p. 40.

30. Robert H. Ferrell, *The Presidency of Calvin Coolidge* (Lawrence: University Press of Kansas, 1998), p. 145.

31. Howard H. Quint and Robert H. Ferrell, eds., *The Talkative President* (Amherst: University of Massachusetts Press, 1964), p. 298.

32. Quoted in Frank Ninkovich, *Modernity and Power* (Chicago: University of Chicago Press, 1994), p. 80.

33. Stimson quoted in David F. Schmitz, *Henry L. Stimson* (Wilmington, Del.: Scholarly Resources, 2001), p. 79.

34. Warren F. Kuehl and Lynne K. Dunne, *Keeping the Covenant* (Kent, Ohio: Kent State University Press, 1997), p. 196.

35. Quoted in Warren F. Kimball, "The Second World War," in Dale Carter and Robin Clifton, eds., *War and Cold War in American Foreign Policy, 1942–62* (New York: Palgrave, 2002), p. 40.

36. Michael A. Sherry, *In The Shadow of War* (New Haven: Yale University Press, 1995), p. 28.

37. Stimson quoted in Justus D. Doenecke and John E. Wilz, *From Isolation to War, 1931–1941* (Wheeling, Ill.: Harlan Davidson, 2003; 3d ed.), p. 49.

38. Willard Range, *Franklin D. Roosevelt's World Order* (Athens: University of Georgia Press, 1959), p. xii.

39. Quoted in Frank Freidel, *Franklin D. Roosevelt: Launching the New Deal* (Boston: Little, Brown, 1973), p. 459.

40. Benjamin Welles, *Sumner Welles* (New York: St. Martin's, 1997), p. 199.

41. Quoted in Jordan A. Schwarz, *Liberal* (New York: The Free Press, 1987), p. 191.

42. Wilbur Carr quoted in Martin Weil, *A Pretty Good Club* (New York: Norton, 1978), p. 47.

43. Quoted in Gregory Johnson and David A. Lenarcic, "The Decade of Transition," in B. J. C. McKercher and Lawrence Aronson, eds., *The North Atlantic Triangle in a Changing World* (Toronto: University of Toronto Press, 1996), p. 99.

44. Mira Wilkins, *The Maturing of Multinational Enterprise* (Cambridge: Harvard University Press, 1974), p. 138.

45. Quoted in Mary Nolan, *Visions of Modernity* (New York: Oxford University Press, 1994), p. 24.

46. Edward G. Lowry, "Trade Follows the Film," *Saturday Evening Post*, CXCVIII (November 7, 1925), 12.

47. Thomas Saunders, *Hollywood in Berlin* (Berkeley: University of California Press, 1994), p. 11.

48. Quoted in David Reynolds and David Dimbleby, *An Ocean Apart* (New York: Vintage, 1989), p. 116.

49. Quoted in Nolan, *Visions*, p. 216.

50. Quoted in Volker R. Berghahn, "Elitism, Money, and Popular Culture," in R. Laurence Moore and Maurizio Vaudagna, eds., *The American Century in Europe* (Ithaca: Cornell University Press, 2003), p. 123.

51. Quoted in Paul Weindling, "Public Health and Political Stabilization: The Rockefeller Foundation in Central and Eastern Europe Between the Two World Wars," *Minerva*, XXXI (Autumn 1993), 261.

52. David W. Ellwood, "The Quest for a British Modernity," in Moore and Vaudagna, *American Century*, p. 137.

53. *New York Times*, May 5, 1930.

54. Charles Kindleberger, *The World in Depression, 1929–1939* (Berkeley: University of California Press, 1973), p. 222.

55. Quoted in Patricia Clavin, *The Failure of Economic Diplomacy* (New York: St. Martin's, 1996), p. 16.

56. Quoted in Robert A. Hathaway, "1933–1945: Economic Diplomacy in a Time of Crisis," in William H. Becker and Samuel F. Wells, Jr., eds., *Economics and World Power* (New York: Columbia University Press, 1984), p. 285.

57. Quoted in Julius W. Pratt, *Cordell Hull* (New York: Cooper Square, 1964; 2 vols.) I, 112.

58. Quoted in Blum, *Morgenthau Diaries, I*, 151.
59. Quoted in Richard A. Harrison, "The United States and Great Britain," in David F. Schmitz and Richard D. Challener, eds., *Appeasement in Europe* (Westport, Conn.: Greenwood, 1990), p. 116.
60. Ambassador Ronald Lindsay quoted in Doenecke and Wilz, *From Isolation*, p. 54.
61. Ramsay MacDonald quoted in B. J. C. McKercher, *Transition of Power* (New York: Cambridge University Press, 1999), p. 32.
62. Will Rogers, *Letters of a Self-Made Diplomat to His President* (New York: A. & C. Boni, 1926), p. xii.
63. Michael J. Hogan, "Revival and Reform," *Diplomatic History, VIII* (Fall 1984), 289.
64. Bruce Kent, *The Spoils of War* (New York: Oxford University Press, 1989), p. 10.
65. Quoted in Harold Josephson, *James T. Shotwell and the Rise of Internationalism in America* (Rutherford, N.J.: Fairleigh Dickinson University Press, 1975), p. 140.
66. Quoted in Charles DeBenedetti, "Peace Was His Profession," in Frank Merli and Theodore A. Wilson, eds., *Makers of American Diplomacy* (New York: Charles Scribner's Sons, 1974), p. 390.
67. Quoted in Rhodri Jefferys-Jones, *Changing Differences* (New Brunswick, N.J.: Rutgers University Press, 1995), p. 53.
68. James Shotwell quoted in Charles DeBenedetti, *Origins of the Modern American Peace Movement, 1915–1929* (Milwood, N.Y.: KTO Press, 1978), p. 187.
69. Kellogg quoted in Doenecke and Wilz, *From Isolation*, p. 14.
70. *The General Pact for the Renunciation of War* (Washington, D.C.: Government Printing Office, 1928).
71. Quoted in Robert David Johnson, *The Peace Progressives and American Foreign Relations* (Cambridge: Harvard University Press, 1995), p. 252.
72. James Cabell Bruce quoted *ibid.,* p. 178.
73. Quoted in Richard W. Fanning, *Peace and Disarmament* (Lexington: University Press of Kentucky, 1995), p. 85.
74. Quoted in Michael Dunne, *The United States and the World Court* (New York: St. Martin's, 1988), p. 264.
75. Quoted in Melvyn P. Leffler, *The Specter of Communism* (New York: Hill & Wang, 1994), p. 19.
76. Quoted in David McFadden, *Alternative Paths* (New York: Oxford University Press, 1993), p. 26.
77. Quoted in David J. Danelski and Joseph S. Tulchin, eds., *The Autobiographical Notes of Charles Evans Hughes* (Cambridge: Harvard University Press, 1973), p. 262.
78. Loy Henderson quoted in Peter G. Boyle, *American-Soviet Relations* (London: Routledge, 1995), p. 23.
79. Katherine A. S. Siegel, *Loans and Legitimacy* (Lexington: University Press of Kentucky, 1996), p. 126.
80. Quoted in Christine A. White, *British and American Commercial Relations with Soviet Russia, 1918–1924* (Chapel Hill: University of North Carolina Press, 1992), p. 223.
81. Quoted in Reynolds and Dimbleby, *Ocean Apart*, p. 118.
82. Quoted in David Bordwell, *The Cinema of Eisenstein* (Cambridge: Harvard University Press, 1993), p. 19.
83. Will Rogers, *How We Elect Our Presidents* (Boston: Little, Brown, 1952), p. 148.
84. John Wiley quoted in Thomas R. Maddux, *Years of Estrangement* (Tallahassee: University Presses of Florida, 1980), p. 21.
85. Quoted in Irwin Gellman, *Secret Affairs* (Baltimore: Johns Hopkins University Press, 1995), p. 141.
86. Quoted in David Mayers, *The Ambassadors and America's Soviet Policy* (New York: Oxford University Press, 1995), p. 113.
87. Quoted in Beatrice Farnsworth, *William C. Bullitt and the Soviet Union* (Bloomington: Indiana University Press, 1967), p. 153.
88. Quoted in Mayers, *Ambassadors,* p. 115.
89. Quoted in Melvin Small, "Buffoons and Brave Hearts: Hollywood Portrays the Russians, 1939–1944," *California Historical Quarterly, LII* (Winter 1973), 327.
90. Quoted in Elizabeth Kimball MacLean, *Joseph E. Davies* (Westport, Conn.: Praeger, 1992), pp. 50, 55.
91. George F. Kennan, *Memoirs, 1925–1950* (Boston: Little, Brown, 1967), p. 67.
92. Frank Costigliola, "'Unceasing Pressure for Penetration,' " *Journal of American History, LXXXIII* (March 1997), 1316, 1321, 1329.
93. Eugene Lyons, "To Tell or Not to Tell," *Harper's, CLXXI* (June 1935), 102.
94. Ambassador Frederick Sackett quoted in Margot Louria, *Triumph and Downfall* (Westport, Conn: Greenwood Press, 2001), p. 220.
95. Quoted in Arnold A. Offner, *American Appeasement* (New York: Norton, 1976 [c. 1969]), p. 50.
96. Quoted in Raymond J. Sontag, *A Broken World, 1919–1939* (New York: Harper and Row, 1971), p. 290.
97. Ambassador Robert Bingham quoted in David F. Schmitz, *The United States and Fascist Italy, 1922–1940* (Chapel Hill: University of North Carolina Press, 1988), pp. 161–162.
98. Quoted in George Eisen, "The Voices of Sanity: American Diplomatic Reports from the 1936 Berlin Olympiad," *Journal of Sports History, XI* (Winter 1984), 75.
99. Col. Truman Smith quoted in Thomas G. Mahnken, *Uncovering Ways of War* (Ithaca: Cornell University Press, 2002), p. 104.
100. Reynolds, *Creation*, p. 9.
101. Quoted in David Reynolds, *Britannia Overruled* (New York: Longman, 2000), p. 127.
102. Quoted *ibid.,* p. 129.
103. Quoted in Roy Douglas, "Chamberlain and Appeasement," in Wolfgang J. Mommsen and Lothar Kettenacker, eds., *The Fascist Challenge and the Policy of Appeasement* (London: Allen & Unwin, 1983), p. 87.
104. Quoted in Leffler, *Specter,* p. 26.
105. Harry S. Truman quoted in Robert H. Ferrell, ed., *Dear Bess* (New York: Norton, 1983), p. 419.
106. Quoted in James V. Compton, *The Swastika and the Eagle* (Boston: Houghton Mifflin, 1967), pp. 17, 25.
107. V. R. Bergahn, "Germany's America," *American Heritage, XLVI* (May/June 1995), 68; Uta G. Poiger, *Jazz, Rock, and Rebels* (Berkeley: University of California, Press, 2000), p. 15.
108. Quoted *ibid.,* p. 26; and movie poster quoted in Sabine Hake, *Popular Cinema of the Third Reich* (Austin: University of Texas Press, 2001), p. 133.
109. Quoted in Compton, *Swastika,* p. 33.
110. Samuel I. Rosenman, ed., *Public Papers . . . of Franklin D. Roosevelt, 1939* (New York: Macmillan, 1938–1950; 13 vols.), VIII, 463.
111. Quoted in Michaela Honicke Moore, "American Interpretations of National Socialism, 1939–1945," in Allen E. Steinweiss and Daniel E. Rogers, eds., *The Impact of Nazism* (Lincoln: University of Nebraska Press, 2003), p. 10.
112. Paul A. C. Koistinen, *Planning War, Pursuing Peace* (Lawrence: University Press of Kansas, 1998), p. 301.
113. Eleanor Roosevelt quoted in Blanche Wiesen Cook, "Eleanor Roosevelt and Human Rights," in Edward P. Crapol, ed., *Women and American Foreign Policy* (Wilmington, Del.: Scholarly Resources, 1992; 2nd ed.), p. 97.

114. Ernest Lundeen quoted in Thomas N. Guinsburg, "The Triumph of Isolationism," in Gordon Martel, ed., *American Foreign Relations Reconsidered, 1890–1993* (London: Routledge, 1994), p. 99.

115. Quoted in Sherry, *Shadow of War,* p. 26.

116. Quoted in Thomas G. Paterson, *Meeting the Communist Threat* (New York: Oxford University Press, 1988), p. 216.

117. Quoted in Robert A. Divine, *The Reluctant Belligerent* (New York: Wiley, 1979; 2nd ed.), p. 52; and in Justus D. Doenecke and John E. Wilz, *From Isolation to War* (Arlington Heights, Ill.: Harlan Davidson, 1991; 2nd ed.), p. 15.

118. Offner, *American Appeasement,* p. 103.

119. Quoted in Carrie Foster, *The Women and the Warriors* (Syracuse: Syracuse University Press, 1995), p. 190.

120. Quoted in Linda K. Schott, *Reconstructing Women's Thoughts* (Syracuse: Syracuse University Press, 1997), p. 115.

121. Chamberlain quoted in Thomas E. Mahl, *Desperate Deception* (New York: Brassey's, 1998), p. 5; Manfred Jonas, *Isolationism in America, 1935–1941* (Ithaca: Cornell University Press, 1966), p. viii.

122. Brenda Gayle Plummer, *Rising Wind* (Chapel Hill: University of North Carolina Press, 1996), p. 37.

123. Quoted in Alexander DeConde, *Ethnicity, Race, and American Foreign Policy* (Boston, Northeastern University Press, 1992), p. 107.

124. Rosenman, *Public Papers, 1936, V,* 289.

125. Douglas Little, *Malevolent Neutrality* (Ithaca: Cornell University Press, 1985), p. 265.

126. Roosevelt to Edward M. House, October 19, 1937, Edward M. House Papers, Sterling Library, Yale University, New Haven, Conn.

127. Quoted in Christopher Thorne, *Allies of a Kind* (New York: Oxford University Press, 1978), p. 38.

128. *Foreign Relations, 1938, I* (Washington, D.C.: Government Printing Office, 1955), 685.

129. *Ibid.,* p. 688.

130. Roosevelt quoted in David F. Schmitz, *Thank God They're on Our Side* (Chapel Hill: University of North Carolina Press, 1999), p. 122.

131. Quoted in Reynolds, *Creation,* p. 43.

132. Quoted in Blum, *Morgenthau Diaries, II,* 49.

133. Rosenman, *Public Papers, 1939, VIII,* 4.

134. Quoted in William L. Langer and S. Everett Gleason, *The Challenge to Isolation* (New York: Harper & Brothers, 1952), p. 87.

135. Quoted in Robert Dallek, *Franklin D. Roosevelt and American Foreign Policy, 1932–1945* (New York: Oxford University Press, 1979), p. 192.

136. Lord Lothian to Lord Halifax, September 27, 1939, vol. 24, Halifax Papers, Public Record Office, Kew, Eng.

137. FDR Quoted in David Reynolds, *From Munich to Pearl Harbor* (Chicago: Ivan R. Dee, 2001), p. 75.

138. Kirk H. Porter and Donald B. Johnson, eds., *National Party Platforms, 1840–1972* (Urbana: University of Illinois Press, 1973), p. 382.

CHAPTER ❦ 5

Asia, Latin America, and the Vagaries of Power, 1920–1939

William E. Borah (1865–1940) and Henry L. Stimson (1867–1950). *The Idaho senator (left) chaired the Foreign Relations Committee (1925–1933). An isolationist, he opposed U.S. membership in the League of Nations and promoted neutrality; an anti-imperialist, he condemned U.S. interventions in Latin America; a peace advocate, he saluted the Kellogg-Briand Pact. A noted orator, Borah said much on most issues. "Borah this and Borah that, Borah here and there, Borah does and Borah doesn't, until you wish that Borah wasn't," wrote a journalist. In a February 1932 letter to Borah, Secretary of State Stimson defended the Open Door policy during the Manchurian crisis. (Library of Congress)*

139

DIPLOMATIC CROSSROAD

➳ *The Manchurian Crisis, 1931–1932*

IT APPARENTLY STARTED with thirty-one inches of steel. At 10:20 P.M., just outside the Manchurian capital of Mukden on September 18, 1931, an explosion apparently blasted a short section from the South Manchurian Railway. Japanese soldiers apparently killed some Chinese attempting to escape from the area. Apparently? Yes, because Japanese army officers had a most difficult time explaining the events of that dark night. The Mukden Express somehow crossed over that very section of track *after* the alleged explosion. It appears that independent-minded young officers of the Guandong (Manchurian) army fabricated the "Mukden Incident" of September 18. They had plotted for months to seize Manchuria from China. Feverish in their quest for Japanese grandeur and Asian power, they or their followers had already, in 1930, assassinated the Japanese premier. So when the news from Mukden reached Tokyo, one civilian official remarked, "They've done it at last."[1]

For the Japanese—civilian or military—Manchuria ranked as a vital interest. As large as France and Germany with a population of 30 million (28 million Chinese), Manchuria served as a defensive buffer against the communists. More important, the territory teemed with the raw materials (coal, iron, timber, soybeans) so desperately needed by the import-hungry Japanese islands. Manchuria held more than half of Japan's foreign investments. The Japanese-run South Manchurian Railway interlaced these large economic holdings. Ever since their 1905 victory in the Russo-Japanese War, the Japanese had been driving in their imperial stakes. By treaty they had acquired the right to station troops along the railroad. The United States had recognized Japan's primacy in Manchuria through the Root-Takahira and Lansing-Ishii agreements (see Chapter 2).

Chinese nationalists throughout the 1920s had resisted Japanese intrusions. Nationalist leader Jiang Jieshi (Chiang Kai-shek) encouraged Chinese to move to Manchuria and sought to build a railroad to compete with the South Manchurian. The Chinese boycotted Japanese products, a particularly alarming practice during the Great Depression, when Japan's foreign trade slumped. Chinese and Japanese blood spilled in isolated incidents. Such cumulative provocations amounted to "a case where a thousand pinpricks equalled a slash of the saber."[2]

The Mukden news of September 18, 1931, reached an irritable Secretary of State Henry L. Stimson, worn low by Washington's hot, humid temperatures. The weather accentuated what President Herbert Hoover called Stimson's "combat psychology."[3] The forthright secretary shared prevalent American attitudes toward "inferior" races and the "Oriental mind."[4] He also embraced the Open Door policy and the sanctity of law. Japanese aggression in Manchuria violated treaties signed at the Washington Conference (1922), which endorsed the Open Door, and the Kellogg-Briand Pact (1928), which outlawed war. Stimson saw the Manchurian crisis as "an issue between the two great theories of civilization and economic methods."[5]

"The Open Door." The Japanese thrust into Manchuria in 1931 called into question the peace and disarmament agreements of the previous decade. A. U.S. diplomat described Japan in 1934 as "the combination of national centralization with feudal loyalty, of mysticism with technical efficiency, of medievalism with tanks and airplanes. . . . They dwell in a no-man's zone of time, their springs of action in the Middle Ages, their instruments of action out of the twentieth century." (*The Outlook,* 1931)

Stimson hoped at first that the "Mukden Incident" would remain a localized mutiny of the Japanese army. No American wanted the United States to become ensnarled "all by itself" in this imbroglio "full of hidden explosives, dense underbrush, [and] quicksand," noted State Department official Stanley K. Hornbeck.[6] The United States possessed little power in Asia. The British, interested in preserving their own Asian empire and hobbled by economic crisis at home, preferred to appease Japan. The French foundered in their frequent domestic political confusion. Soviet Russia, still not recognized by the United States, could hardly be called on for help. And the feeble League of Nations, the humorist Will Rogers astutely observed, could "make the little fellows behave" but had "no more power than a Senate investigating committee" to discipline "the big fellows."[7]

Stimson decided on a meek policy of letting "the Japanese know we are watching them."[8] On September 24, 1931, he urged the Chinese and Japanese to cease hostilities. A few days later the League began to discuss the Manchurian crisis, and a U.S. representative sat at the League table, if only as an "observer." Stimson and Hoover feared that the international organization would "dump" the "Manchurian baby" in Washington's lap, but the League passed mild peace resolutions and set up the Lytton Commission to investigate.[9] After Japanese forces occupied all of Manchuria by early December, Stimson thought Japan "in the hands of virtually mad dogs," with its army "running amok."[10]

The secretary of state had few options. He could not intervene militarily. Economic sanctions seemed a possibility. Stimson knew that the island empire depended on imports of American oil, that it was the third largest buyer of American exports, and that the United States took about 40 percent of Japan's exports. Maybe economic pressure would force Tokyo to disgorge Manchuria. Hoover, however, refused to stick "pins in tigers."[11]

Thus, nonrecognition. On January 7, 1932, Stimson issued what became known as the Stimson Doctrine. He threw tradition and law against Japan: The United States would not recognize any arrangements in China that might impair American treaty rights, violate the Open Door policy, or subvert the Kellogg-Briand Pact. Defiantly, on January 28, the Japanese marched into Shanghai, far to the south of Manchuria. A belligerent Stimson persuaded Hoover to reinforce the American military garrison in that city. Reminded of the German attack on Belgium in 1914, the secretary set his jaw against this new aggression.

Armed only with "spears of straw and swords of ice," Stimson tried to bluff.[12] He wanted to frighten Japan without revealing that it had no reason to be afraid. On February 23, 1932, Stimson sent a public letter to Senator William Borah, chair of the Senate Foreign Relations Committee—a letter the secretary hoped would "encourage China, enlighten the American public, exhort the League, stir up the British, and warn Japan."[13] Citing the Open Door policy, Stimson chastised Japan for violating the administrative and territorial integrity of China and the Kellogg-Briand agreement. He threatened to fortify Guam and build up the U.S. Navy in the Pacific if Japan did not halt its aggression. This protest made little impact, although Japan soon signed an armistice in Shanghai and the League endorsed nonrecognition. In February, Japan actually reconstituted Manchuria as the puppet state of Manchukuo. In October the Lytton Commission chided the Japanese for misconduct in Manchuria. Japan thereupon resigned from the League in early 1933. "In Japan," Stimson wrote, "the cause of Mr. Hyde against Mr. Jekyll has in large measure been victorious, and my efforts on behalf of the latter without much seeming result."[14]

A Question of Power

Stimson's diplomatic efforts raise questions about the choices, opportunities, and limitations facing U.S. leaders in the 1920–1939 period. Was it wise for Stimson to rail against Japanese machinations in Manchuria? Did it perhaps help the Japanese military gain support from other nationalists who also considered Manchuria vital? Did nonrecognition reveal just how weak the United States was in Asia? Did it not also expose China's abandonment by other nations? Yet, should and could Stimson have ignored treaty violations? Or should he have let the Asians settle their own differences? Did the Manchurian crisis threaten U.S. national interest?

Soon, Stimson admitted that nonrecognition had not worked. Moral exhortation may only have soothed the American conscience and stirred up the aggressor, to nobody's benefit. The diplomat Hugh Wilson reflected on Stimson's tactics: "If the nations of the world feel strongly enough to condemn, they should feel strongly

Makers of American Foreign Relations, 1920–1939

Presidents	Secretaries of State
Woodrow Wilson, 1913–1921	Bainbridge Colby, 1920–1921
Warren G. Harding, 1921–1923	Charles E. Hughes, 1921–1925
Calvin Coolidge, 1923–1929	Frank B. Kellogg, 1925–1929
Herbert C. Hoover, 1929–1933	Henry L. Stimson, 1929–1933
Franklin D. Roosevelt, 1933–1945	Cordell Hull, 1933–1944

enough to use force." More: "Condemnation creates a community of the damned who are forced outside the pale, who have nothing to lose by the violation of all laws of order and international good faith."[15] Still, despite minimal American economic interests in Manchuria, the principle of the Open Door, both as diplomatic tool and as ideology, stood at risk. If Tokyo could violate the Open Door in Manchuria, it could do so elsewhere, Stimson argued.

America's timid response to the Manchurian crisis demonstrated that the United States could not manage affairs in Asia. U.S. gunboats still chugged on Chinese rivers, American troops garrisoned on Chinese soil, American business interests formed the Shanghai Power Company in 1928 and thus "Americanized" the city, and the Philippines remained a colony, but in Asia the Japanese had hegemony. America could lecture but not enforce.

By contrast, the United States held considerable power—economic, cultural, naval, military, political—in Latin America. Central America and the Caribbean were to the United States what China, especially Manchuria, was to Japan. The Japanese, in fact, often commented that their actions in China simply resembled U.S. actions in Latin America. In Latin America the United States practiced the "closed door"; in Asia it appealed for the "Open Door."

The Manchurian crisis also revealed the ineffectiveness of the treaties of the 1920s and the reluctance of the European powers to check aggression in the 1930s, when appeasement became the policy of the day (see Chapter 4). What frightened Stimson and Hoover was "not so much China's fate as the specter of the great powers seizing new empires to rescue themselves from economic depression."[16] Japan's violation of the Nine Power Treaty eroded "the Washington Conference system," threatening international stability.[17] Given the timidity of the Europeans and the League, Americans recognized the limits of their own power and nurtured their independent internationalism. The United States worked to create with nonmilitary means a world characterized by legal, orderly processes, the Open Door, and economic and political stability. The Hoover-Stimson response to the Manchurian episode typified these goals and methods. America hoped to muzzle the dogs of war in order to stimulate domestic prosperity, expand foreign trade, and ensure national security. As in Europe, so in Asia would U.S. efforts fall short.

Facing Japan: The Washington Naval Disarmament Conference and China

The American pursuit of independent internationalism and a nonmilitary foreign policy began conspicuously at the Washington naval conference of November 12, 1921, through February 6, 1922. After World War I a naval arms race loomed among the United States, Britain, and Japan. All parties recoiled from the spiraling financial costs. Japan was pumping as much as one-third of its national budget into naval construction. The United States, possessing the second largest navy in the world, alarmed third-ranked Japan by stationing most of its heaviest battleships in the Pacific Fleet, by developing the base at Pearl Harbor, and by talking about fortifying the Philippines and Guam. First-ranked Britain already had Singapore, but lacked funds to engage in a naval arms race. The U.S. Congress might not appropriate funds either. Thus all three powers welcomed arms control to check one another. With prodding from Senator Borah, the Harding administration invited eight nations (Britain, France, Italy, Japan, China, Belgium, the Netherlands, and Portugal) to Washington to discuss naval arms limitations and competition in Asia.

The Washington conference opened with dramatic words from bewhiskered Secretary of State Charles Evans Hughes. The United States would scrap thirty ships. Then he turned to the British and sank twenty-three of their ships. British admiral Lord David Beatty, noted a reporter, leaned forward like a "bulldog, sleeping on a sunny doorstep, who has been poked in the stomach by the impudent foot of an itinerant soap canvasser."[18] The secretary next scuttled twenty-five Japanese vessels. One commentator wrote that "Hughes sank in thirty-five minutes more ships than all the admirals of the world have sunk in a cycle of centuries."[19]

Despite grumblings of doom from navy officers, the diplomats hammered out a naval limitations pact—the Five Power Treaty. It set a ten-year moratorium on the construction of capital vessels (defined as warships of more than 10,000 tons displacement or carrying guns larger than eight inches in bore diameter) and limited the tonnage for aircraft carriers. The treaty also established a tonnage ratio for capital ships of 5 : 5 : 3 : 1.75 : 1.75 (United States : Britain : Japan : France : Italy; 1 equaling approximately 100,000 tons displacement). The top three naval powers agreed to dismantle sixty-six capital ships, many of them battleships. They also pledged not to build new fortifications in their Pacific possessions, such as the Philippines and Hong Kong, thus reassuring the Japanese, who had sarcastically accepted naval inferiority by translating 5 : 5 : 3 as Rolls Royce : Rolls Royce : Ford.

Another treaty—the Four Power—abolished the Anglo-Japanese Alliance and simply obligated signatories to respect each other's Pacific territories. All delegations also signed the Nine Power Treaty, an endorsement of the Open Door for the preservation of China's administrative integrity and equal trade opportunity. In other agreements, Japan consented to evacuate troops from the Shandong Peninsula; the United States obtained cable rights to the Pacific island of Yap; and Japan withdrew its troops from Russian Siberia and the northern half of Sakhalin Island. Hughes's diplomatic success owed much to the State Department's "Black Chamber" code-breakers, who deciphered some 1,600 secret Japanese cables during the conference, proving that "stud poker is not a very difficult game after you've seen your opponent's hole card."[20]

The treaties signed in Washington essentially recognized the status quo in Asia. Japan had regional superiority, and the other powers could not challenge it without undertaking massive naval construction and expensive fortifications. Geography worked in Japan's favor in Asia, as it did for the United States in Latin America. The United States gave up only the *potential* of naval superiority—ships that Congress had no intention of funding ("phantom vessels sailing on seas of fancy," as one diplomat remarked).[21] The United States secured temporary protection of the vulnerable Philippines and abolition of the Anglo-Japanese Alliance.

Shortcomings emerged. The Five Power Treaty did not limit submarines, destroyers, or cruisers, thus sparking in those categories an arms race that agreements at the London conference of 1930 only partly curbed. Nor did the naval treaty provide means for verification. The Soviet Union, with major stakes in Asia, did not attend the Washington conference, since the major powers were still attempting to isolate the Bolsheviks. None of the pacts contained enforcement provisions. In time, the Washington treaties fell victim to what one historian has called the "Icarus Factor"—that is, the "waxwork of political webs" that sustained disarmament at the beginning and later "melted" before the "Rising Sun" of Japanese expansion.[22]

China lost the most. Not representing Sun Zhongshan's (Sun Yat-sen's) Guomindang government at Guangzhou (Canton), Chinese delegates spoke instead for the weak Beijing regime (the British cynically described it as "a group of persons who call themselves a government but who have long ceased to function as such").[23] Chinese pleas for tariff autonomy, withdrawal of foreign troops, and an end to extraterritoriality fell on stony ground. Washington helped by negotiating the Japanese out of Shandong, but the imperial powers rejected full sovereignty for China and continued to do so even as the Guomindang triumphed over its rivals later in the decade. The Washington conference took a worthy step toward disarmament, but the absence of enforcement provisions left China vulnerable.

U.S. relations with the anti-imperialist, nationalist Chinese proved nettlesome. In 1898 Americans had perceived the Philippines as stepping-stones to China; three decades later, in a historical flipflop, a strong, friendly China seemed necessary to protect the islands. China thus took on strategic importance for Americans in the 1920s and 1930s. Also, many Americans remained mesmerized by the mirage of the China market and the inviolability of the Open Door principle. Sentimental considerations partly accounted for the attachment to China. Pearl Buck's best-selling *The Good Earth* (1931), made into a powerful movie six years later, captured for Americans the romance of hard-working, persevering Chinese peasants. John Paton Davies, a young Foreign Service Officer in China, recalled America's "righteous infatuation" with China, stemming from years of religious missionary activity and a misguided and self-congratulatory belief that the United States had become China's special friend by virtue of the Open Door notes. In Asia, wrote Davies, "Washington preached to everyone, including the Chinese."[24]

Washington sermonized most fervently to the Japanese, Soviets, and Chinese Nationalists, all of whom strove to check the United States and the other Western imperialists in Asia. For the United States, peaceful change, the Open Door, protection

American Gunboat on the Yangtze River, China. The shallow-draft gunboat U.S.S. *Monocacy* served in the Yangtze Patrol, evacuating besieged Americans and protecting missionaries and commerce. After entanglement with Chinese civil disturbances and Japanese military thrusts, the *Monocacy* in 1939 was decommissioned, towed to sea, and sunk. (U.S. Navy)

of American property and citizens, and the treaty rights of trade and judicial extraterritoriality (criminal trials for its nationals in American rather than Chinese courts) seemed threatened. Sun Zhongshan, leader of the Chinese Revolution from its outbreak in 1911 until his death in 1925, bristled when U.S. gunboats visited Guangzhou in 1923 to halt a potential Chinese takeover of foreign-dominated customshouses. After declaring that the Chinese Revolution took its inspiration from America, the Christian, English-speaking Sun "might well have expected that an American Lafayette would fight on our side in this good cause. In the twelfth year of our struggle towards liberty there comes not a Lafayette but an American Admiral with more ships of war than any other nation in our waters."[25]

The United States did little to assist the two potential roadblocks to Japanese expansion—Soviet Russia and the Chinese Nationalists. Americans applauded the Chinese nationalistic spirit but insisted on U.S. treaty privileges. The Chinese turned to another possible means of support, the Soviet Union. Seeking to restrain Japan, spank imperialist capitalists, and implant communism, Moscow sent Michael Borodin to help the Nationalists centralize the structure of the Guomindang party. Americans understood neither the depth of Chinese nationalism nor Sun's use of Soviet agents for Chinese purposes; some Americans attributed China's intense antiforeign sentiment to Bolshevik agitation.

In 1925, Sun died and the Nationalist outpouring in the May 30th Movement of that year led to attacks on foreign nationals and missionaries. Lieutenant Colonel George C. Marshall summed up his experience with the Fifteenth Infantry in China over the next two years: "We are either just out of near trouble with the Chinese or trouble is just hovering near us."[26] Anti-imperialist opinion at home and Chinese pressure prompted Washington to reconsider treaty privileges. The outbreak of civil war within the Nationalist ranks also dictated a reevaluation. The ambitious Guomindang leader Jiang Jieshi turned fiercely on his communist allies in 1926–1927, booting Borodin back to Moscow and killing Chinese communists by the thousands. The communist leader Mao Zedong fled south to Kiangsi Province, where he set up a rebel government. Jiang told U.S. officials that only American assistance could buttress China in "holding off" Japan and Soviet Russia and averting "a great war in the Pacific."[27] With Senator Borah likening Jiang to a "Western frontier gambler—slick, suave, cunning, insincere," Washington signed a trade treaty in 1928 that restored tariff autonomy to China and granted most-favored-nation treatment.[28] By 1930 more than 500 American companies were operating in China, with investments amounting to $155 million, still only 1 percent of total American foreign investments. From 1923 to 1931 the United States sent only 3 percent of its exports to China. American trade with Japan totaled twice as much.

Although at least one U.S. sailor left China having "seen enough of this yeller race to suit me awhile," Washington waxed hopeful because American-trained Chinese "cosmopolitans" such as H. H. Kung, Hu Shi, and T. V. Soong were gaining influence in the Guomindang.[29] The Rockefeller Foundation was training an English-speaking elite through institutions such as the Peking Union Medical College, where American "modernizers" introduced "scientific medicine" and purported to "make over a medieval society in terms of modern knowledge."[30] Jiang had joined the crusade against communism. In 1930, furthermore, he converted to Christianity and married Meiling Soong, daughter of the American-educated, prominent Chinese businessman Charles Soong. "Part dreamy lotus flower, part sullen tiger lily, and part American rose," the Wellesley College honors graduate spoke impeccable English and soon established ties with prominent Americans, later called the China Lobby.[31] The beautiful, intelligent, and "Westernized" Madame Jiang became the perfect "damsel in distress" as she—and the new God-fearing China—appealed to American notions of "mission, chivalry, and machismo."[32]

Japan's Footsteps Toward a New Pacific Order

Zealous expansionists, the Japanese feared the future. As their population grew, land became scarce (in 1931, 65 million people lived in an area smaller than Texas), and they became dependent on outside sources for vital raw materials. The Japanese also complained that Western nations had for years intruded into their sphere of influence and controlled products central to their economy, such as oil. Japan sought self-sufficiency because "a tree must have its roots," citing U.S. "roots" in Latin America as an example.[33] Japan was only doing what the Western powers had done, Tokyo explained. The imperialists had taught Japan the game of poker but then, after winning most of the chips, pronounced the game immoral and took up contract bridge. As a Japanese diplomat noted during the Manchurian crisis: "Did not the United States send 6,000 troops into Nicaragua to protect only 600 Americans . . . for the same reason as the Japanese are acting?"[34] In August 1936 Tokyo secretly adopted the "Fundamental Principles of National Strategy," which called for both southern expansion by peaceful "footsteps" toward the British, Dutch, and French empires of Southeast Asia (favored by the navy) and a northern advance into China and Mongolia (favored by the army).[35] Three years later Japan announced its imperial ambitions by defining the "Greater East Asia Co-Prosperity Sphere."

Japan ranked the United States first on its list of potential enemies. A Japanese navy study of 1936 stated that "in case the enemy's [America's] main fleet is berthed at Pearl Harbor the idea should be to open hostilities by surprise attacks from the air."[36] American naval leaders used Japan as the enemy on the war-game board at the Naval War College. Naval competition intensified in 1935–1936 when the London conference broke up without agreement and Japan announced its abrogation of earlier treaties. The Immigration Act of 1924, blatantly discriminatory in excluding Japanese citizens from entering the United States, rankled Tokyo "right down to the bone."[37] Secretary Hughes lamented that the law had "undone the work of the Washington conference and implanted the seeds of an antagonism."[38] Trade disputes also intensified. Inexpensive Japanese goods, especially textiles, entered the American market, undercutting some domestic producers. "Buy America" campaigns and public boycotts of Japanese goods followed. Japan began to close the trade and investment door in China.

Japan and the United States did have two common interests: Their mutual trade continued at high levels, and both counted the Soviet Union as a threat (Japan joined the Anti-Comintern Pact with Germany in 1936).

When Franklin D. Roosevelt became president in early 1933, he continued Stimson's nonrecognition policy. This policy reflected American weakness in Asia. But at least until 1937, the long lull in fighting between China and Japan did not seem to require U.S. action. Roosevelt did move to bring the navy up to the strength permitted by the Washington and London conference treaties. Under New Deal programs in 1933, the president allocated funds for thirty-two new vessels, including two aircraft carriers, and by 1937 naval appropriations had doubled. Two years earlier the United States staged large-scale naval maneuvers near Midway Island in the Pacific to impress the Japanese. Instead of deterring Tokyo, these naval activities reinforced Japan's secret decision in May 1937 to outbuild the Americans and construct warships "above and beyond the quantitative and qualitative limits of the naval treaties"—including the huge 64,000-ton battleships *Yamato* and *Musashi*.[39] FDR's diplomatic recognition of the Soviet Union in 1933 aimed in part to cow Japan with the suspicion that Moscow and Washington had linked arms in Asia. Four years later, Captain Claire Chennault, retired from the U.S. Army Air Corps, joined the Chinese air force as chief adviser. By 1940 American volunteer pilots manned his "Flying Tigers" unit.

On July 7, 1937, Japanese and Chinese troops clashed at the Marco Polo Bridge near Beijing. This skirmish grew quickly into the "China Incident" (not a "war" because the Kellogg-Briand Pact outlawed wars). Fighting spread throughout China. Shanghai fell to Japan in November after a costly battle and the cruel bombing of civilians. The "rape" of Nanjing followed in December, an "orgy of violence more than a planned extermination."[40] Journalists reported "wholescale atrocities," as Japanese soldiers raped 80,000 women and massacred some 300,000 residents of China's then capital city.[41] A U.S. military observer recoiled at bloated corpses— "like grotesque inflated rubber figures which children sometimes play with . . . at seaside resorts. The stench was almost unbearable."[42]

To make matters worse, the civil war between Jiang's Guomindang forces and Mao Zedong's communists further sapped China. The communists had declared

Shanghai, China, 1937. This photograph of a baby amid the ruins of North Station after Japanese bombing galvanized American opinion. Senator George Norris, who gradually abandoned his isolationism because of scenes like this, denounced the Japanese as "disgraceful, ignoble, barbarous, and cruel, even beyond the power of language to describe." By 1938, the omniscient Japanese detective Mr. Moto disappeared from the Hollywood screen, while his Chinese counterpart, Charlie Chan, became more popular than ever. (United Press International)

war on Japan in 1932, charging Jiang with appeasing Tokyo. Until 1937 Jiang fought the communists more than he fought the Japanese. From 1935 to 1937, the communists took the dramatic "Long March" from their southern haven to Yan'an (Yenan) in the north—an expedition of 6,000 miles. In late 1936 dissident Chinese army forces in Manchuria kidnapped Jiang, hoping to end the civil war by creating a coalition government. Joseph Stalin and the Chinese communists soon secured his release and persuaded him to institute a tenuous united front against Japan in early 1937. Indeed, a Sino-Soviet nonaggression pact in August led to a "multifaceted alliance" wherein Moscow increased arms sales and technical assistance to Jiang and Soviet troops delivered a "firm rebuff" to the Japanese in border clashes along the Manchurian and Mongolian frontiers in 1938 and 1939.[43]

Having refused to invoke American neutrality after the Marco Polo Bridge incident, thereby permitting valuable trade to continue with China, Roosevelt addressed a Chicago audience on October 5, 1937. He called vaguely for a "quarantine" on aggressors to check the "epidemic of world lawlessness."[44] After the speech, FDR admitted that he evoked an attitude more than a "policy." He privately toyed with economic warfare—a naval blockade or embargo—but American isolationists responded to the speech by warning against trying "to police a world that chooses to follow insane leaders" and recalling "our plunge into the European war in 1917."[45] In November Roosevelt sent representatives to a conference in Brussels, but it disbanded without taking a stand—only the Soviet Union pushed for reprisals against Japan. In December the American gunboat *Panay*, escorting on the Yangtze River three Standard Oil Company tankers flying American flags, took destructive fire from zealous Japanese pilots. Two U.S. sailors died. With Secretary Hull blasting the perpetrators as "wild, runaway, half-insane men," Tokyo quickly apologized and paid an indemnity of $2,214,007.36.[46]

As Japan plunged deeper into China in 1938 and U.S. military observers reported that "the Japanese fly has at last got himself well entangled in the Chinese flypaper," the Roosevelt administration cautiously initiated new measures.[47] First, in purchasing Chinese silver, the United States gave China dollars with which to buy American military equipment. Second, Secretary Hull imposed a "moral embargo" on the sale of aircraft to Japan. Third, the United States extended technical assistance to improve the Chinese transportation system. Fourth, a naval bill authorized two new carriers and the doubling of naval airplanes. Fifth, the United States occupied several Pacific islands (Enderbury, for example) as potential naval bases. Sixth, Roosevelt sent a secret naval emissary to London to discuss contingency plans in case of war in the Pacific. These actions did not deter the Japanese, who by the end of 1938 controlled virtually all major Chinese seaports, had established exploitative development companies, and had begun to install a puppet Chinese regime. An American trade commissioner in Shanghai accurately noted that the "Open Door" was being "banged, barred, and bolted."[48]

With war clouds billowing in Europe in summer 1939 (see Chapter 4), Roosevelt abrogated the Japanese-American commercial treaty of 1911. He hoped the threat of economic pressure might temper Japan's onslaught in China. In 1938 the United States had supplied Japan with 44 percent of its imports, mostly automobiles, machinery, copper, oil, iron, and steel. The abrogation, effective January 1940, by no means ended trade, for Washington remained reluctant to impose a rigid economic embargo. Grew's talks with the Japanese foreign minister in the fall of 1939 failed to secure U.S. trading rights in China but did elicit a Japanese pledge to curtail brutalities against foreigners. In November 1939 another American naval bill authorized two more battleships. By then World War II had begun in Europe, and Japanese-American relations had stalemated. Unwilling to fight over China, Washington had to decide what to do if Japan expanded beyond China.

Making and Managing Good Neighbors in Latin America

In contrast with Asia, U.S. power in the Western Hemisphere remained unmatched and U.S. methods bold. Indeed, shortly after World War I, U.S. armed forces used the Caribbean for maneuvers—as preparation for a possible war with Japan in the Pacific. And when Germany and Japan marched aggressively in the 1930s, the United States brought most of the Latin American states into a virtual alliance to resist foreign intrusions in the U.S. sphere of influence. The imperial net in Latin America had been stitched before and during World War I, especially in Central America and the Caribbean, through military occupations, naval demonstrations, Panama Canal, management of national finances, threat of intervention, nonrecognition, and economic ties. A U.S. diplomat in Guatemala reported in 1921 that "the bacillus of revolution is in the blood of these people, and will never be eradicated until some strong hand is placed over them and the serum of hard work is injected into them by force."[49] The Roosevelt Corollary to the Monroe Doctrine provided the overriding justification for U.S. hegemony (see Chapter 2). Swaggering American marines in the streets of Havana, Managua, or Port-au-Prince represented only the most conspicuous evidence of North American imperial management.

The use of marines as instruments of policy, however, became unpopular and counterproductive, and nationalist sentiment, especially in Mexico and Argentina, placed limits on U.S. power. Anti-imperialists such as Senators George Norris and

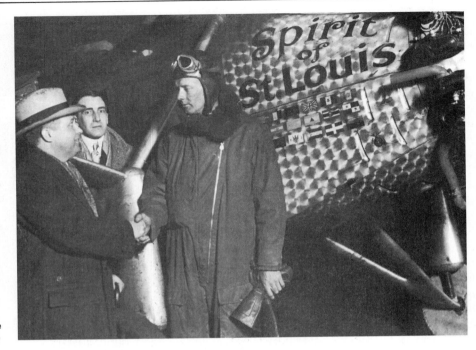

Charles A. Lindbergh (1902–1974) Returns from Latin America, 1928. Lindbergh made aviation history on May 20, 1927, when he flew nonstop from New York to Paris in the *Spirit of St. Louis.* To promote U.S. goodwill toward Latin America, the aviator began a tour in December 1927 that first took him to Mexico. There he met Anne Morrow, the daughter of Ambassador Dwight Morrow; later Lindbergh would marry her. After visiting Guatemala, Panama, Venezuela, and other countries, Lindbergh returned from Cuba in February 1928. In the late 1930s Lindbergh became an isolationist, and in his last years he earned yet another reputation as a conservationist. (Lindbergh Picture Collection, Yale University Library)

William Borah demanded self-determination for Latin Americans. Congress resented the costs of military interventions, as well as the president's usurpation of Congress's power to declare war when he unilaterally dispatched troops to the Caribbean. Business leaders came to believe that military expeditions, because they aroused anti-U.S. sentiment and violence, endangered rather than protected their properties. Referring to Japan's seizure of Manchuria, and alert to a double standard, Secretary Stimson commented in 1932: "If we landed a single soldier among those South Americans now . . . it would put me absolutely in the wrong in China, where Japan has done all this monstrous work under the guise of protecting her nationals with a landing force."[50]

Between the world wars, therefore, the United States increasingly sought nonmilitary methods to maintain its hegemony in Latin America. Washington forswore armed interference and employed economic penetration, political subversion, non-recognition, support for dictators who kept order, arbitration treaties, Pan Americanism, financial supervision, Export-Import Bank loans, and the training of national guards. At times U.S. officials pressed for negotiated settlements, as when, in 1929, Secretary Kellogg helped settle the Tacna-Arica dispute between Chile and Peru. These tactics translated into a catchy phrase popularized (but not invented) by Franklin D. Roosevelt—the Good Neighbor policy. FDR hailed in early 1933 "the policy of the good neighbor—the neighbor who resolutely respects himself and, because he does so, respects the rights of others—the neighbor who respects his obligations and respects the sanctity of his agreements in and with a world of neighbors."[51] Although Latin Americans welcomed the new spirit, the goal of U.S.

hegemony in the hemisphere had not changed, only the means for maintaining it. Roosevelt defined the "new approach" toward Latin America: "Give them a share. They think they are just as good as we are, and many of them are."[52] As the Axis specter loomed larger in the late 1930s, the Good Neighbor policy came to mean cooperation against the aggressors.

Economic decisions by U.S. leaders, private and governmental, held immense importance for Latin American nations. In the Dominican Republic, Cuba, and Haiti, for example, officials had to obtain U.S. consent before borrowing foreign capital. With its ambassador in Washington working to influence U.S. decisions on copper purchases and Chilean bonds, both vital to his nation's livelihood, Chile in the 1930s had never "felt so totally controlled by the unpredictable attitudes of a foreign power."[53] In Cuba, where North American interests accounted for about two-thirds of sugar production, U.S. investments helped lock the country into a risky one-crop economy subject to fluctuating world sugar prices. In Honduras, U.S. companies provided cannon and machine guns to one political group that conducted a successful coup in 1924. In 1929 U.S. firms produced more than half of Venezuela's oil. Their bribery of Venezuelan government officials, including the president, was not uncommon. In Guatemala, the arrogance of American shipping and rail magnates caused a State Department official in 1938 to question "the propriety of an American corporation, possessing a monopoly of essential transportation facilities in a foreign country, and operating in virtually complete independence of . . . either the American or Guatemalan governments."[54]

In a process sometimes called "colonialism by contract," professional economists such as Edward Kemmerer of Princeton University served as financial advisers (or "money doctors") to Colombia, Chile, Ecuador, and Peru during the 1920s, usually recommending gold-exchange currency reforms managed by a central bank, new taxes, revised tariffs, and private American loans for public-works projects tied to U.S. firms.[55] These icons of "progress who emblemized manly professionalism" devised systems to instill "duty, regularity, self-restraint, and responsibility," thus embodying the "spirit of (white) manhood and its destiny to supervise lesser beings."[56] Popular at first, such programs aroused nationalist backlashes in the 1930s when declining exports, excessive indebtedness, and contracting capital markets caused massive defaults throughout Latin America, where "money doctors" were again seen as Wall Street, Yankee imperialists.

The Argentine writer Manuel Ugarte bluntly identified a "new Rome" in the mid-1920s. The United States, he explained, annexed wealth rather than territory, thus enjoying the "essentials of domination" without the "dead-weight of areas to administrate and multitudes to govern." U.S. economic penetration always "invoked peace, progress, civilization and culture; but its motives, procedure, and results have frequently been a complete negation of these premises."[57] The journalist Walter Lippmann agreed, writing in 1927 that "we go on creating what mankind calls an empire while we continue to believe quite sincerely that it is not an empire because it does not feel to us in the way we imagine an empire ought to feel."[58] Nonetheless, President Roosevelt's smiling personification of the Good Neighbor seemed to make the Yankee presence more palatable. "Here was a gringo in the Latin mold, a man they could understand and empathize with as a projection of their own political

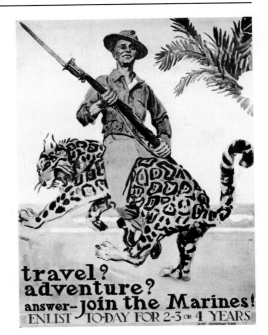

Marine Recruiting Poster. Marines saw many parts of Latin America, especially the Caribbean. But battle and occupation conditions were hardly as pleasant as depicted in James Montgomery Flagg's drawing. And, asked critics, once you are on the jaguar's back, how do you get off? (Library of Congress)

style," the scholar Fredrick B. Pike has written. "The man was so simpatico: and that papered over a multitude of sins."[59]

Although Latin American intellectuals often regarded North American "intruders as crass émigrés from a materialist culture," a U.S. consul in Brazil appreciated one of the ways the United States cultivated ruling elites.[60] He praised Rotary International, whose "meetings are attended by members of the Federal Cabinet, mayors of cities, and other officials who . . . welcome our support and cooperation."[61] Still, too many North Americans resembled the boorish member of Congress who insulted a Latin American diplomat's wife: "Señora, I regret that I know only two words of your beautiful language: mañana, which means tomorrow, and pyjama, which means tonight."[62] When a young Nelson Rockefeller visited Venezuela in the early 1930s to look after his oil investments, he noticed that U.S. citizens there seldom learned Spanish. "Why should I?" asked one American. "Who would I talk to in Spanish?"[63] Rockefeller thereupon hired twelve Berlitz instructors to begin Spanish classes for company employees. A decade earlier the Rockefeller Foundation had begun to spend millions to destroy the mosquito in Latin America to combat yellow fever and succeeded in "unhooking the hookworm" in Colombia.[64]

U.S. investments in and trade with Latin America reached a "boom" stage after World War I. The direct investments of U.S. citizens (excluding bonds and securities) jumped from $1.26 billion in 1914 to $3.52 billion in 1929, mostly in electric power, railroads, bananas, sugar, oil, and minerals. By 1936, because of the devastating impact of the global depression, the amount dropped to $2.77 billion. These figures represented about one-third of total U.S. investments abroad. One of the nation's largest corporations, Standard Oil of New Jersey, operated in eight countries,

Nelson A. Rockefeller (1908–1979) and Anastasio Somoza García (1896–1956). The grandson of Standard Oil millionaire John D. Rockefeller, Sr., Nelson (second from right) served as director of the family oil business in Venezuela during the 1930s. An advocate of improved U.S. cultural, scientific, and educational relations within the hemisphere, Rockefeller served as coordinator of the Office of Inter-American Affairs for the State Department during World War II. Elected governor of New York in 1958, Rockefeller became vice president in 1974 under President Gerald Ford following President Richard Nixon's resignation during the Watergate scandal. Rockefeller is dining here with Nicaraguan strongman Somoza, who ruled from 1937 to 1956, aligned himself with the United States, and created a corrupt family dynasty in his country. (National Archives)

and United Fruit Company held a large stake in the "banana republics" of Central America. International Telephone and Telegraph controlled communications in Cuba, where, between 1919 and 1933, overall U.S. investments increased 536 percent. Worried about diminishing domestic oil reserves after World War I, Washington urged "companies to acquire oil territory in South America and elsewhere before the European companies preempted all of it." Commerce Secretary Hoover described the result: "A conference of the leading oil producers was called and such action taken that most of the available oil lands in South America were acquired by Americans."[65] In the period 1925–1929 in Latin America, the average annual income outflow from U.S. investments totaled $100 million more than the U.S. capital inflow.

Confirming the axiom that "trade follows investments," U.S. exports to Latin America tripled in value from 1914 to 1929, reaching the billion-dollar figure, approximately 20 percent of total U.S. exports. Although this impressive trade slumped during the Great Depression, for many Latin American countries commercial relationships with the United States remained critical. Nicaragua, for example, shipped 96 percent of its exports to the United States by 1941. In 1920 the United States supplied Cuba with 73 percent of its imports; that trade shrank to 59 percent in 1929 because of the depressed Cuban sugar economy. Cuba's exports to the United States also dropped off, although they still comprised 68 percent of all the island's exports. American investments in and trade with Venezuela moved the British out and helped that country to become the world's leading exporter of oil. Trade with Chile in nitrates and copper jumped after U.S. investments there doubled from $200 million in 1920 to $400 million in 1928. Worried by declining world trade during the 1930s, Secretary Hull sought wider markets in Latin America when he launched the Export-Import Bank (directing loans to inter-American commerce) and the Reciprocal Trade Agreements Program. His efforts helped increase exports to Latin America from $244 million in 1933 to $642 million in 1938.

Creating Dictators in the Dominican Republic, Nicaragua, and Haiti

After Spain left the Dominican Republic in 1865 and until the U.S. military occupation in 1916, that impoverished Caribbean country knew little peace. Corrupt politics and mismanagement of national revenues produced economic stagnation, political factionalism, foreign indebtedness, and U.S. intervention (see Chapter 2). In May 1916, when a contest between the Dominican congress and president threatened to postpone U.S. demands for expanded authority, American marines went ashore. Although U.S. forces occupied the major cities and established martial law, the peasants and caudillos in the mountainous east waged bloody guerrilla war from 1917 to 1922. The marines retaliated in kind against rebels who "are almost all touched with the tarbrush," as Military Governor Harry Knapp crudely put it.[66] Marine atrocities against Dominican people of color usually went unpunished. Sumner Welles, the American commissioner to the Dominican Republic (1922–1924), later criticized the U.S. officers who ran the occupation—"none of whom had any knowledge or experience of Dominican affairs or problems, and the great majority of whom could not even speak the language of the country."[67]

The military intervention in the Dominican Republic became a hot political issue at home and abroad. Warren G. Harding accused Wilson of the "rape of Haiti" in the 1920 campaign but continued the Dominican and Haitian occupations as president.[68] *The Nation* (1920) demolished the argument that improved hospitals and schools justified imperialism by noting that the "Germans improved sanitation during their occupation of some of the villages of northern France, but no officer of the Marine Corps ever suggested that these reforms justified the German presence in France."[69] When Washington ended the occupation in 1924, after forcing on the Dominican government a stabilization loan to liquidate past debt, and when the new national guard consumed a quarter of the Dominican budget, Hughes ingeniously claimed that the departure proved that the United States was "anti-imperialistic."[70] Franklin D. Roosevelt agreed in a 1928 article in *Foreign Affairs*: "We accomplished an excellent piece of constructive work, and the world ought to thank us."[71] With Americans running the country's fiscal affairs until 1941, FDR ignored Welles's observation of "the lasting hostility towards the American people which the occupation created in the hearts of . . . the Dominican people."[72]

The U.S. occupation also begot Rafael Leonidas Trujillo. In early 1919 he received a commission as a second lieutenant in the U.S.-created national guard. The onetime thief, forger, and pimp earned high marks from U.S. military officers and became chief of staff of the army in 1928. Through the fraudulent election of 1930, Trujillo won the presidency. The State Department initially looked on Trujillo as "a kind of Frankenstein, brought to life by the marines" and likely to spawn new insurrections, but Washington gradually warmed to him when his strong-arm tactics created internal order and precluded U.S. military intervention.[73] Thanks to beneficent U.S. control of the customs, Trujillo could divert funds to his army for the suppression of internal dissent. Political corruption, military muscle, torture, murder, nepotism, commercial monopolies, and raids on the national treasury enabled Trujillo to quiet opponents and amass a fortune of $800 million.

From 1930 until his assassination in 1961, sometimes as president, sometimes through puppets, Trujillo became "the dictatingest dictator who ever dictated," as *Time* called him.[74] U.S. military arms filled Dominican arsenals. U.S. business leaders, who dominated sugar production, endorsed him. Most imports came from the United States. The National City Bank became the official depository for Dominican revenues. By World War II the Dominican Republic stood as a success story for the new Good Neighbor policy. But good neighbors with whom? Roosevelt reportedly gave an answer in reference to Trujillo: "He may be an S.O.B., but he is our S.O.B."[75]

Nicaragua, like the Dominican Republic, developed in the twentieth century under the weight of U.S. military occupation and the Good Neighbor policy. From 1912 to 1925 the United States ruled Nicaragua and kept in power the pliant Conservative party. Nicaragua by 1925 appeared to be solvent, secure, and stable. The marines departed, but in late 1926 they returned because, in President Coolidge's words, Nicaragua "went to hell in a hack."[76] The Coolidge administration explained—in an overstated report titled "Bolshevik Aims and Policies in Mexico and Latin America"—that communists were fomenting trouble in Nicaragua. The U.S. embassy in Mexico had greatly exaggerated the activities of American leftists in Mexico (including the Marxist writer Bertram Wolfe), and Washington found the anti-Bolshevik rationale irresistible. In fact, Nicaraguan Liberals had used Mexico as a sanctuary to challenge the Conservatives. "We are not making war on Nicaragua," Coolidge opined, with tones of the Roosevelt Corollary, "any more than a policeman on the street is making war on passersby."[77] Nicaraguans in the Coco River basin saw it differently: "The Machos are coming," they said of the marines. "They will burn our houses."[78]

The Nicaraguan intervention generated rancorous debate in the United States. The assertion of a communist plot persuaded few. Congress again resented presidential initiatives that ignored the legislature's power to declare war. Senator Burton K. Wheeler suggested that if U.S. soldiers intended to "stamp out banditry, let's send them to Chicago to stamp it out there. . . . I wouldn't sacrifice . . . one American boy for all the damn Nicaraguans."[79] Bloodshed and destruction in Nicaragua raised further outcries after Secretary of the Navy Curtis D. Wilbur matter-of-factly reported in 1928: "Several houses were destroyed in the village of Quilali in order to prepare a landing field for airplanes so that 19 wounded Marines could be evacuated to a hospital."[80] From 1927 to 1933 the Liberal insurgent César Augusto Sandino, who railed against the "dastardly invaders" who were "trampling Nicaragua's sovereignty underfoot," earned an international reputation as he waged guerrilla war against U.S. troops, which numbered 50,000 in early 1929.[81] Two Hollywood films in 1929, *Flight* and *Cock-eyed World,* turned Nicaragua into "Indian country" by casting burly Victor McLaglen as a virile U.S. marine who battled sinister and swarthy bandits, thereby visually reinforcing familiar images that "made U.S. dominance seem natural."[82]

Rafael Trujillo (1891–1961). The strongman of the Dominican Republic graduated from an American military training school and went on to rule his nation from 1930 to 1961, when he was assassinated. The historian Eric Paul Roorda explains that a "group of pro-Trujillo businessmen, legislators, and paid advocates constituted a kind of 'Dominican Lobby' in the United States with Joseph E. Davies at the center." In 1933 Davies became Trujillo's counsel—negotiating, lobbying, and propagandizing for the regime in the United States. Four years later President Roosevelt appointed his friend Davies U.S. ambassador to the Soviet Union. (*The Reporter,* 1961. Copyright 1961 by The Reporter Magazine Co.)

César Augusto Sandino (1895–1934). President Hoover called him a "cold-blooded bandit," but Nicaraguans have hailed Sandino as a hero. Determined that Nicaragua control its natural resources and help the poor, Sandino blasted the Monroe Doctrine as meaning "America for the Yankees." Accused of administering "machete justice" to members of the Guardia Nacional, Sandino explained that "liberty is not conquered with flowers." The revolutionaries who overthrew the Somoza dictatorship in 1979 called themselves "Sandinistas." (Library of Congress)

With critics urging Washington to trade the "big bully" for the "big brother" in Nicaragua, special emissary Henry L. Stimson brought Liberals and Conservatives together in the "Peace of Tipitapa" (1927) and provided for U.S. supervision of the election of 1928.[83] Most important, he and General Frank R. McCoy created an American-trained national guard to perpetuate the domestic order that the marines had imposed. Shortly after U.S. troops withdrew in 1933, Sandino signed a truce with the Nicaraguan government. But General Anastasio Somoza, who had studied at a business school in Philadelphia and knew colloquial English, gained command of the U.S.-trained Guardia Nacional. Somoza then captured and executed Sandino, notwithstanding his "word of honor" that no harm would come to him.[84] In 1936 Somoza seized power and established a self-enriching family dictatorship that lasted until 1979. A U.S. collector-general remained to handle customs collections until 1944, and the United States retained a naval base. The Roosevelt administration in 1939 constructed an interoceanic highway (the Rama Road) to spur economic development.

Few benefits accrued to the United States from its years of interference in Nicaragua. Trade never reached important levels, although the United States dominated the Central American nation's economy. From 1914 to 1930 U.S. investments grew from $4.5 million to $13 million. Although the stormy occupation of Nicaragua may have indirectly fostered the Good Neighbor policy, for Nicaraguans that policy meant continued foreign financial management and replacement of the U.S. Marine Corps by a home-grown dictator who did "preserve order" and was "insistently '*Americanista*'" in following Washington.[85]

Haiti, too, drew Washington's hegemonic attention. A marine officer depicted the Haitians as "real nigger and no mistake—there are some very fine looking, well educated polished men here but they are real nigs beneath the surface."[86] When U.S. soldiers went abroad, of course, they carried American prejudices as well as canteens. For nineteen years, from 1915 to 1934, marines governed the tiny black French-speaking nation of Haiti in the Caribbean. The venture only deepened Haiti's distress. The Wilson administration ordered U.S. marines into Haiti on July 28, 1915, because it feared German intrigue during World War I, sought to protect American financial interests, and insisted on order in the Caribbean.

The occupation built highways, technical schools, lighthouses, hospitals, and railroads. Americans improved public health and sanitation, but never eradicated Haiti's profound human squalor. By the mid-1960s Haiti had the lowest life expectancy (thirty-five years) and the lowest literacy rate (10 percent) in Latin America. Many of the roads had been built in 1916–1918 by forced labor—the *corvée* system under which Admiral William Caperton ordered workers into labor gangs. The NAACP official James Weldon Johnson, who toured Haiti, protested: "They were maltreated, beaten and terrorized . . . [like] the convicts in the Negro chain gangs that are used to build roads in many of our southern states."[87] Haitians rebelled against the *corvée;* in 1919 alone the marines killed 2,000 to quell the insurrection.

American racism reached into Haiti. U.S. personnel introduced to Haitians the words "nigger," "gook," and "coon" and enforced segregation between blacks and whites. When an aide objected to inviting Haitian diplomats to tea, Secretary Hull responded in both race and class terms: "When they [blacks] speak French, that's

Comic Strips in Nicaragua. In this 1927 photograph of the tranquil side of intervention, marines read newspaper comic strips to Nicaraguan children. Said Clifford Hamm, collector-general of customs in Nicaragua: "Three cheers for the American marine who is teaching baseball and sportsmanship! It is the best step towards order, peace, and stability." (Marine Corps, National Archives)

different."[88] Americans bestowed higher status on the mulattos (the "elites") than on the *authentiques* (blacks) but neither wooed nor fraternized with the Haitian bourgeoisie. They did not do so because of intense hostility to mixed bloods based on the belief "that such persons, as links between the races, endangered the established order in what should be a rigidly color-defined world."[89] Anthropological research in the 1930s by Franz Boaz and others that showed complex linkages among African, European, and indigenous cultures could not displace the prevailing Hollywood film stereotype of Haiti as "America's Africa"—the land of voodoo and zombies.[90]

Transportation improvements expanded commercial contacts between cities and rural farmers. Pan American Airways began flights between Miami and Port-au-Prince. Irrigation systems and a telephone network contributed to economic growth. Sugar and cotton exports increased, although the heavy dependence on one crop, coffee, left Haiti susceptible to fluctuations in world prices. The United States became Haiti's largest trading partner. American capital investments grew from $11.5 million in 1914 to $28.5 million in 1930. The National City Bank of New York owned the Banque Nacional. Under U.S. financial supervision, Haiti actually paid its foreign debts (largely French) ahead of schedule.

U.S. military authorities trained a national guard, the Garde d'Haiti. U.S. officers so dominated this *gendarmerie* that no Haitian had reached captain's rank by 1930. The first commandant, Major Smedley D. Butler of the marines, had experience in putting down "natives" in China, Honduras, Nicaragua, Panama, and Mexico. The brash Butler worked "hard with my little black Army" and began to "like the little fellows" who did well "as long as white men lead them."[91] The

"The Rights of Small Nations: Haiti." A harshly critical view of the marine occupation of Haiti, 1915–1934. Mary Renda, in *Taking Haiti* (2001), writes that paternalistic language became "the cultural flagship of the United States in Haiti." By referring to Haitians as wards, U.S. officials asserted their "authority, superiority, and control expressed in the metaphor of a father's relationship with his children. It was a form of dominance . . . masked as benevolent by its reference to paternal care and guidance." (*Good Morning,* 1921)

national guard served as judges, tax collectors, and paymasters for teachers, enforced martial law, and wielded deciding political force.

The United States failed to establish respect for honest government by law and neglected to train efficient civil servants. Washington officials drafted the 1918 constitution and forced it on Haitians; the press was censored and elections were rigged. U.S. authorities suspended the legislature for thirteen years. When President Philippe Sudre Dartiguenave's term ended in 1922, Americans jilted him in favor of Louis Borno, an acquiescent lawyer who collaborated with the American high commissioner, General John H. Russell of Georgia, to rule Haiti from 1922 to 1930. Borno "has never taken a step without first consulting me," Russell boasted.[92] The marines had made Haiti "safe for almost everybody but the Haitians," gibed *The Nation* in 1926.[93]

Haitians resented their colonial status. The peaking of discontent in 1929 came after a slump in coffee exports and exposure of Borno's political machinations. Protests and strikes spread across the country. President Hoover appointed an investigating commission chaired by W. Cameron Forbes, former governor-general of the Philippines. His report of 1930 noted "the failure of the Occupation to understand the social problems of Haiti."[94] The commission promoted "Haitianization" to ease Haitians into positions of responsibility. Hoover started the withdrawal; Roosevelt completed it in 1934.

After the marines departed, strong-arm presidents ruled with the help of Export-Import Bank loans and ties with Washington. During World War II the United States used Haitian bases, and until 1947 U.S. officials supervised Haitian national finances. A revolution in 1946 placed the government in the hands of the Garde, and the revolution of 1956–1957 produced the callous dictatorship of Dr. François ("Papa Doc") Duvalier. He ruled with the ruthless help of his secret police force, the Touton Macoutes, until his death in 1971, when his son "Baby Doc" assumed power. Driven out in 1986, he left behind abject poverty and rampant civil strife. In 1994 U.S. armed forces once again invaded Haiti to stabilize politics (see Chapter 12).

Subverting Nationalism in Cuba and Puerto Rico

Cubans bristled under the Platt Amendment and U.S. military interventions (see Chapter 2). Through the 1920s and into the 1930s the United States helped conduct elections, enlarged the national army, managed the national budget, and maintained economic control over the island. North American investment, particularly in sugar, soared to $1.5 billion in 1929. Approximately half a million fun-seeking Americans a year visited the capital city of Havana, where, as Irving Berlin's lyrics suggested, "dark-eyed Stellas/Light their fellers' panatelas."[95]

Gerardo Machado ruled from 1924 to 1933; he suppressed free speech, jailed or murdered leftists, journalists, labor leaders, and students, and used the army as a political weapon. Obtaining loans from U.S. bankers, he prohibited strikes and looked after North American business interests "as if they were my own."[96] Cuban resentment against Machado intensified in the late 1920s when sugar prices began to drop. Dependent on sugar and exports to the United States, Cuba sank further into economic crisis when the United States instituted the restrictive Smoot-Hawley Tariff of 1931. Unemployment rates shot up. Machado's army beat back protesters. Because armed intervention would violate the newly stated Good Neighbor policy, Roosevelt and his advisers chose to ease out the unpopular Machado.

Suave Sumner Welles, a Groton School friend of Roosevelt already experienced in the Dominican Republic, went as ambassador to Havana in 1933. While U.S. warships patrolled Cuban waters and a general strike rocked the country, Welles persuaded Machado to flee. But Welles lost control; his handpicked government lasted less than a month. Military dissidents, commanded by Sergeant Fulgencio Batista, staged the "Sergeants' Revolution" of September 1933 and installed Professor Ramón Grau San Martín as president.

An exile under Machado, critic of the Platt Amendment, and friend of the left, Grau stood as "the hope and the symbol of the forces of nationalism, patriotism, and reform."[97] Yet the U.S. ambassador refused recognition because "we owe it to the Cuban people not to assist in saddling upon them for an indefinite period a government which every responsible element in the country violently opposed."[98] Grau soon promulgated economic and social reforms, suspended payment on Chase National Bank loans, and seized some North American–owned sugar mills. Welles decried the "confiscatory" decrees of this "social revolution" and conspired with Batista, who feared that Grau's economic nationalism would spawn U.S. intervention.[99] Welles left Cuba in December 1933, and in January Batista toppled Grau, who fled to Mexico. A Batista-backed president took over, and the United States quickly granted recognition.

Batista ruled Cuba, sometimes as president, sometimes from the shadows, from 1934 to 1959. At the start of the Batista era, the United States abrogated the unpopular Platt Amendment (1934), lowered the sugar tariff, granted a favorable quota to Cuban sugar imports (1934), and issued Export-Import Bank loans ($8 million in 1934). In 1940, Cuba granted American armed forces the use of ports and airfields (besides Guantánamo) in exchange for military aid. Even popular Hollywood movies influenced Cuban politics, as *gangsterismo* passed into the vernacular to describe the

Fulgencio Batista (1901–1973). Born of farm folk in the United Fruit Company town of Banes, Batista joined the Cuban army at age twenty. A smiling, ruthless dictator, he became a staunch U.S. ally, bought real estate in Daytona Beach, Florida, and turned Havana into a playground of casinos and brothels for American tourists. Fidel Castro's 26th of July Movement overthrew the corrupt regime in 1959. Batista died in exile in Portugal. (National Archives)

come more and more provocative. If the Germans did not like it, they could attack American forces."[47] When a U-boat torpedoed the destroyer *Kearny* off Iceland on October 17, killing eleven men, the president seized the moment: "The shooting has started. And history has recorded who fired the first shot."[48] Roosevelt also warned of "secret landing fields in Colombia, within easy range of the Panama Canal."[49] The president hoped to persuade Congress to repeal the sections of the 1939 Neutrality Act that prohibited the arming of merchant ships and banned such vessels from war zones. After a U-boat sank the destroyer *Reuben James* on October 31, killing more than one hundred men, the isolationist America First Committee charged that the White House was "asking Congress to issue an engraved drowning license to American seamen."[50] Following bitter debate, repeal passed in November by narrow margins, 50 to 37 in the Senate and 212 to 194 in the House. For the first time since the outbreak of war in 1939, U.S. merchant vessels could legally carry munitions to England.

Roosevelt charted an oblique course toward war because he believed he had no other choice. "Haranguing the country doesn't help," he said. "It will take a 'shock' like 1932" to change isolationist attitudes.[51] In October 1941 he bluntly told the British ambassador that "if he asked for a declaration of war, he wouldn't get it, and opinion would swing against him."[52] FDR thus chose indirection over candor and relied on events and his own manipulative ability to inch ahead. Without decisive presidential leadership, the internationalist-isolationist debate thus hardened into stalemate by autumn 1941. Some 80 percent of the American people still opposed entering the war, while a higher percentage wanted an Axis defeat. In the Chicago area, for example, "at no time did more than a minority of the proponents of aid view the policy as a springboard to full U.S. entry into the war. Until Pearl Harbor, most Americans desired peace. But they wanted even more to see Hitler beaten."[53] So long as FDR touted aid to the Allies as the best way to avoid war, Americans could apparently fulfill both goals. The narrow vote over repeal of the Neutrality Act in November reinforced the president's reluctance to ask for outright intervention. "The day of the white rabbits has passed," Senator Josiah Bailey of North Carolina wrote, "and the great magician who could pull them out of any silk hat . . . cannot find the rabbit."[54]

Asian Collision Course: Japanese-American Relations, 1939–1941

Events in Asia, not Europe, plunged the United States into World War II. Ambassador Joseph C. Grew expressed surprise at increased anti-Japanese sentiment during a trip home in the summer of 1939, as his old Groton and Harvard friend Franklin Roosevelt talked truculently of intercepting the Japanese fleet if it moved against the Dutch East Indies. With the announcement in July that the 1911 commercial treaty with Japan would terminate in six months, Grew feared that economic sanctions and war might follow. "[It] is going to be up to me," he noted, "to let this American temper discreetly penetrate into Japanese consciousness. Sparks will fly before long."[55]

Ponce, Puerto Rico, 1938.
The U.S. Farm Security Administration photographer Edwin Rosskam captured class divisions in Puerto Rico, where U.S. neglect helped perpetuate the island's poverty. At the top of the hill sits the villa of the owner of a sugar plantation and refinery. The shacks of workers cling to the hillside. (Library of Congress)

"shoot-outs and gun battles among groups of opposing political persuasions" in the Batista era.[100]

Elsewhere in the Caribbean, Puerto Rico stagnated under American paternalism. Throughout the interwar years, mediocre and often crude U.S. governors who could not speak Spanish castigated Puerto Ricans as "unsteady, unprincipled children" unable to govern themselves.[101] Although the Jones Act of 1917 had granted Puerto Ricans U.S. citizenship, Washington stiff-armed requests for the colony's independence or statehood. Puerto Ricans did not gain the right to elect their own governor until 1947. Absentee American landowners and sugar barons ran the island's economy. Despite improved roads and new schools, Governor Theodore Roosevelt, Jr. (1929–1932) observed "farm after farm where lean underfed women and sickly men repeated again and again the same story—little food and no opportunity to get more."[102] Eighty percent of peasants remained landless and many crowded into urban slums.

Encouraged by New Deal reformers to act "as a cultural bridge between the Americas," faculty and alumni at the University of Puerto Rico actually became critical of U.S. hegemony.[103] The Harvard-educated lawyer Pedro Albizu Campos headed the Nationalist party, which advocated the violent overthrow of U.S. rule. On Palm Sunday, 1937, police fired on unarmed Nationalist marchers, killing nineteen in the "Ponce Massacre." Albizu went to federal prison until 1947. Other Puerto Ricans rallied behind the socialist Luis Muñoz Marín, whose Popular Democratic party ultimately advocated "commonwealth" status (attained in 1952). New Deal relief and public works projects brought in $1 million a month, along with funds to attract mainland tourists to Puerto Rico—to don a "coat of tan" and to mingle with "beautiful señoritas" on San Juan's beaches.[104] Yet when Governor Rexford Tugwell arrived in 1941, he found the island "still sunk in hopeless poverty."[105]

Compromising with Mexico: Oil and Nationalism

The ongoing Mexican Revolution, which began in 1910, presented the United States with a test of the nonmilitary emphasis of the Good Neighbor policy. Before the 1920s it had appeared that Mexico would be treated like other U.S. neighbors—invaded, occupied, and owned by Americans, who by 1910 controlled 43 percent of Mexican property and produced more than half of Mexico's oil. Hollywood films perpetuated stereotypes by portraying the Mexican as a bandit or villainous "greaser."[106] Scholars and artists promoted cultural interaction to counter such negative images. Professor Herbert E. Bolton of the University of California, Berkeley, emphasized a shared borderlands history, drawing large numbers of students to his course on "Greater America." In the 1930s at U.S. universities, the Mexican artist José Clemente Orozco painted colorful murals of revolutionary struggle. A decade earlier Mexico City had become a "Yankee Bohemia" where expatriot writers and artists sympathetically interpreted Mexican politics and culture.[107] These contacts did not diminish the nationalism of either nation, but they probably did encourage an environment of tolerance and understanding based on mutual experience that undercut war hawks bent on military confrontation.

The Mexican Constitution of 1917 alarmed capitalist Americans, because its Article 27 held that all "land and waters" and all subsoil raw materials belonged to the Mexican nation. Three hundred million dollars in American investments in oil and mines seemed jeopardized. Mexico also began to tax American oil producers heavily. Unwilling to see its resources "rapidly sucked away by international firms," Mexico proved that "it was not a Caribbean nation that the United States could push around at will."[108]

Washington continued to claim economic rights for its nationals in Mexico and refused to recognize the government of Alváro Obregón. In 1923, however, Mexico and the United States signed the Bucareli Agreements. In exchange for U.S. recognition, Mexico agreed that Americans who held subsoil rights before the 1917 Constitution could continue those concessions and that Americans whose agricultural lands were expropriated would receive Mexican bonds in compensation. Then Americans owned about 60 percent of Mexico's oil industry. But a new law passed by the Mexican congress in 1925 stated that oil lands secured before 1917 could be held for a maximum of only fifty years. In part because American oil companies had begun to exploit the oil fields of Venezuela, Washington rejected intervention and resorted to nonmilitary methods instead.

In early 1927, President Coolidge selected Dwight W. Morrow, an old college chum and a partner in the Wall Street firm of J. P. Morgan and Company, as the new ambassador to Mexico City. In the belief that "we can best defend the right of

Lázaro Cárdenas (1895–1970) and Josephus Daniels (1862–1949). A former newspaper publisher and secretary of the navy during the Wilson administration, Daniels (second from left) donned Mexican national costumes, adopted a warm, folksy style, and became a popular ambassador to Mexico (1933–1941) under his friend President Franklin D. Roosevelt. As president of Mexico (1934–1940), Cárdenas (center with mustache) attempted to regain control of his nation's oil resources from multinational corporations. In contrast to the frightened pro-business attitudes of professional diplomats in Mexico, and to FBI director J. Edgar Hoover's warning that Cárdenas was "anti-foreign due to his Indian antecedents," Daniels assured FDR that Cárdenas was simply another "New Dealer" trying to improve his country's living conditions. According to the historian Friedrich E. Schuler, Daniels, through his defense of Cárdenas's expropriation of U.S. oil companies in 1938, "represented the proverbial good neighbor in Mexico more than any other U.S. ambassador to Latin America during all of Roosevelt's administrations." (Library of Congress)

our own country when we understand the rights of other countries," he engaged in "ham-and-eggs diplomacy" by having breakfast with the Mexican president instead of sending formal notes.[109] Learning a little Spanish, having "Lone Eagle" Charles Lindbergh fly nonstop from Washington, D.C., and even bringing the humorist Will Rogers (that "most *simpatico* citizen") to the Mexican capital, Morrow ingratiated himself.[110] Morrow then negotiated an agreement that confirmed *pre-1917* ownership of petroleum lands. Thus in 1927–1928 the oil controversy seemed defused through compromise. The United States protected its citizens' oil investments and tacitly conceded that Mexico legally controlled its own raw materials. This arrangement lasted until 1938, when President Lázaro Cárdenas defiantly expropriated the property of all foreign oil companies, then attempting to thwart an oil workers' strike for higher wages. "An entire nation, accustomed for centuries to the perpetual humiliation of the underdog, reared its head proudly for the first time," wrote one Mexican journalist. "No more humble pie, no more kowtowing to arrogant foreign officials."[111]

Ambassador Josephus Daniels, who as secretary of the navy in 1914 had ordered the marines to Veracruz, dispelled early suspicions and persuaded Mexican leaders that he and Washington had changed. Daniels would not accept Hull's "get tough" policies, softening an intemperate State Department blast when he delivered it to the Mexican foreign minister. Refusing to see the Good Neighbor policy "drown in Mexican oil," Daniels opposed Washington's economic coercion through the reduction of U.S. purchases of Mexican silver.[112] For their part the American oil companies refused to sell petroleum equipment to Mexico, and they persuaded shipping firms not to carry Mexican oil. Standard Oil of New Jersey financed false propaganda in the United States with the message that Cárdenas plotted to turn Mexico communist. In 1938 Daniels cabled Hull that "some of the oil men are predicting revolution" so that they can "return to conditions here as existed under Díaz or Huerta."[113]

Viewing Cárdenas as "one of the few Latin leaders who was actually preaching and trying to practice democracy," FDR ruled out intervention and sought compensation.[114] Increased purchases of Mexican oil by Germany, Italy, and Japan underscored the urgent need for a diplomatic settlement. Indeed, once war broke out in Europe in September 1939, the "nervous Nelly of American intelligence," FBI director J. Edgar Hoover, reported false rumors about 250 Nazi pilots in Mexico, eight German submarines operating out of Veracruz, and Hitler's promise of British Honduras if Mexico agreed to supply Germany with petroleum.[115] Protracted Mexican-American talks finally produced an agreement in 1941. The United States conceded the principle that Mexico owned its own raw materials, and Mexico promised to pay for expropriated properties. The Export–Import Bank extended a $30 million loan. Because "an unfriendly Mexico, as it was from 1914 to 1918, could create manifold . . . problems," compromise with Mexican nationalism became a strategic necessity as the United States readied itself for World War II.[116]

Pan Americanism and the Approach of the Second World War

In 1889, Secretary of State James G. Blaine spurred formation of the International Bureau of American Republics, renamed in 1910 the Pan American Union. The U.S. secretary of state became its permanent chair. "Pan Americanism" at first focused on improvement of trade in the Western Hemisphere and symbolized a mythical inter-American "cooperative ideal."[117] The union's elegant quarters, financed by steel baron Andrew Carnegie, stood, significantly, near the Department of State building. One Argentine diplomat sneered that "there is no Pan Americanism in South America; it exists only in Washington."[118] The declarations of neutrality during World War I by seven Latin American governments suggested the hollowness of Pan American solidarity.

In 1923 the Fifth International Conference of American States met in Santiago, Chile. The United States controlled the agenda, and the delegates endorsed a Treaty to Avoid or Prevent Conflicts Between the American States (Gondra Treaty). The Havana conference of 1928 proved quite different, because it convened shortly after U.S. troops had landed in Nicaragua. Washington anticipated trouble and thus appointed former secretary of state Hughes to head its delegation. Even President Coolidge traveled to Cuba to address the conference with soothing banalities. The cooperative Machado dictatorship censored critical newspaper comments about the United States. At the conference, the delegate from El Salvador boldly moved that "no state has the right to intervene in the internal affairs of another."[119] Mexico and Argentina backed this challenge to the United States. Hughes defended the right of "interposition of a temporary character," and he manipulated the conference to table the resolution.[120]

The seventh Pan American conference, in Montevideo, Uruguay (1933), met under the aura of the Good Neighbor policy. The nonintervention resolution was once again introduced. Secretary Hull cast an affirmative vote but retained a U.S. right to intervene "by the law of nations as generally recognized and accepted."[121]

Further confusion about the meaning of the nonintervention pledge became evident at the 1936 Buenos Aires conference, where the United States seemingly endorsed an unequivocal statement. The U.S. definition, however, intended to outlaw *military* intervention, whereas many Latin American countries argued that Washington could not interfere through economic or political pressure when countries nationalized American-owned property.

Pan Americanism took a decided turn toward hemispheric security in the late 1930s, as Germany, Italy, and Japan attempted to improve their economic and political standing in Latin America. As Germany's trade with Latin America climbed, Hull thought the danger "not limited to the possibility of a military invasion. It was more acute in its indirect form of propaganda, penetration, organizing political parties, buying some adherents, and blackmailing others."[122] Adolf Hitler dreamed of creating "a new Germany" in Brazil and instigated subversive activities there and in Uruguay, Argentina, and Mexico, but the United States overreacted.[123] With such fears, Washington decided to form what Assistant Secretary of State Adolf Berle called "a north-south axis" at the Lima Pan American conference of 1938, where Argentina, Uruguay, and Chile fought Hull's proposal to knit the Latin American countries together in a quasi-alliance.[124] The anti-German sentiment of most delegates, aroused by the recent Munich crisis, helped Hull achieve solidarity. The conferees endorsed the Declaration of Lima, a pledge to resist foreign intervention in the Americas. A secret U.S. Army Air Corps study in early 1939 warned that "airdromes in the north-west part of Brazil . . . would place Nazi-Fascist bombers less than 1,000 miles from the Panama Canal, well within their operating radius of action with [a] heavy load of bombs."[125] That autumn the Declaration of Panama established a security belt around the Western Hemisphere to rebuff possible Axis intrusions. At the same time, the United States persuaded Latin American nations to reduce or cease trade with the Axis powers and to ship strategic raw materials to the United States. To advance hemispheric unity even more, Roosevelt in 1940 appointed Nelson Rockefeller coordinator of inter-American affairs. His office encouraged Hollywood to produce films, such as *The Road to Rio* (1941) and *Simon Bolivar* (1941), which "strengthened popular support for U.S. foreign policy."[126]

The post–World War I search for international order had broken down by 1939. In both Asia and Latin America, fervent nationalists challenged the United States. In both areas the viability of American diplomacy derived from the power the United States possessed and exercised. In Asia, after the Manchurian crisis of 1931–1932, the United States sought, without success, to build a counterforce to Japan. Even the Philippines became a virtual hostage that the U.S. military said it could not defend. By spring 1939 the possibility of simultaneous war with Germany, Italy, and Japan prompted the U.S. Joint Army-Navy Board to modify war plan ORANGE (which emphasized a naval offensive in the Pacific) in favor of RAINBOW plans for hemispheric defense based on the primacy of the Atlantic and Caribbean approaches.

The Great Depression prostrated international relations. World trade and investment collapsed; tariffs went up. The island-bound and trade-conscious Japanese accelerated efforts to build a "co-prosperity" sphere in Asia. In Latin America, where many countries depended on the exportation of one commodity, revolutions and coups erupted, feeding on incipient nationalism. Social unrest and political instability rocked the area from which the United States was withdrawing its marines. While U.S. culture was spreading, political upheavals in the Dominican Republic, Argentina, Brazil, and Chile in 1930, Peru in 1931, Cuba in 1933—all threatened U.S. hegemony. Devastated by the depression, Latin Americans gained a new awareness of the extent to which foreigners made their national choices and the degree to which foreign companies drained profits from them. By World War II, Latin Americans held a more favorable image of the United States, which seemed to have abandoned military intervention under the Good Neighbor policy. But they harbored fresh suspicions that invigorated inter-American economic relations would continue U.S. hegemony. Yankeephobia simmered even as Latin Americans joined the United States in the fight against the Axis.

FURTHER READING FOR THE PERIOD 1920–1939

For general studies and biographies for this period, see works cited in Chapter 4.

For Asia, see Tokomo Akami, *Internationalizing the Pacific* (2000); Irvine H. Anderson, *The Standard-Vacuum Oil Company and United States East Asia Policy* (1974); Richard D. Burns and Edward M. Bennett, eds., *Diplomats in Crisis* (1974); Roger Dingman, *Power in the Pacific* (1976); Akira Iriye, *Across the Pacific* (1967), *After Imperialism* (1969), and *The Origins of the Second World War in Asia and the Pacific* (1987); Greg Kennedy, *Anglo-American Strategic Relations and the Far East, 1933–1939* (2002); Brian M. Linn, *Guardians of Empire: The U.S. Army and the Pacific, 1902–1940* (1997); Jonathan Marshall, *To Have and Have Not: Southeast Asian Raw Materials and the Origins of the Pacific War* (1995); and William R. Nestor, *Power Across the Pacific* (1996).

For relations with Japan, consult Michael Barnhart, *Japan Prepares for Total War* (1987); Dorothy Borg and Shumpei Okamoto, eds., *Pearl Harbor as History* (1973); Justus D. Doenecke, *When the Wicked Rise* (1984) (Manchurian crisis); Peter Duus et al., eds., *The Japanese Wartime Empire, 1931–1945* (1996); Carol Gluck and Stephen Graubard, eds., *Showa: The Japan of Hirohito* (1992); Izumi Hirobe, *Japanese Pride, American Prejudice* (2001) (Exclusion Clause); Saburō Ienaga, *The Pacific War* (1978); Manny T. Koginos, *The Panay Incident* (1967); Walter LaFeber, *The Clash* (1997); Frank P. Mintz, *Revisionism and the Origins of Pearl Harbor* (1985); James W. Morley, ed., *Deterrent Diplomacy: Japan, Germany and the U.S.S.R., 1934–1940* (1977); Charles E. Neu, *The Troubled Encounter* (1975); Ian Nish, *Japanese Foreign Policy in the Interwar Period* (2002); Mark R. Peattie, *Sunburst: The Rise of Japanese Naval Power, 1909–1941* (2003); Nicholas Tarling, *A Sudden Rampage* (2001); Christopher Thorne, *The Limits of Foreign Policy* (1972); Jonathan G. Utley, *Going to War with Japan, 1937–1941* (1985); and Dandra Wilson, *The Manchurian Crisis and Japanese Society, 1931–1933* (2002).

China and the United States are explored in Russell D. Buhite, *Nelson T. Johnson and American Policy Toward China* (1968); Mary B. Bullock, *An American Transplant* (1980) (Rockefeller Foundation); Warren I. Cohen, *America's Response to China* (1990) and *The Chinese Connection* (1978); Bernard Cole, *Gunboats and Marines* (1983); John W. Garver, *Chinese-Soviet Relations, 1937–1945* (1988); David H. Grover, *American Merchant Ships on the Yangtze* (1992); Shizhang Hu, *Stanley K. Hornbeck and the Open Door Policy* (1995); T. Christopher Jespersen, *American Images of China* (1996); Fei Fei Li et al., *Nanking 1937* (2002); Xi Lian, *The Conversion of Missionaries* (1997); Kathleen Lodwink, *Educating the Women of Hainan* (1995); Patricia Neils, *China Images in the Life and Times of Henry Luce* (1990); Youli Sun, *China and the Origins of the Pacific War* (1993); Barbara Tuchman, *Stilwell and the American Experience in China* (1971); and Stephen J. Valone, "*A Policy Calculated to Benefit China*" (1991).

Inter-American relations and the Good Neighbor policy are treated in Cole Blasier, *The Hovering Giant* (1976); John A. Britton, *Carleton Beals* (1987); Marcos Cueto, ed., *Missionaries of Science* (1994) (Rockefeller Foundation); Alexander DeConde, *Herbert Hoover's Latin American Policy* (1951); Alton Frye, *Nazi Germany* and the American Hemisphere, 1933–1941 (1967); Irwin F. Gellman, *Good Neighbor Diplomacy* (1979); Mark T. Gilderhus, *The Second Century* (2000); David Green, *The Containment of Latin America* (1971); Kenneth J. Grieb, *The Latin American Policy of Warren G. Harding* (1976); David G. Haglund, *Latin America and the Trans-formation of U.S. Strategic Thought, 1936–1940* (1984); Gilbert M. Joseph et al., *Close Encounters of Empire* (1998); Thomas L. Karnes, *Tropical Enterprise: The Standard Fruit and Steamship Company in Latin America* (1978); Michael L. Krenn, *U.S. Policy Toward Economic Nationalism in Latin America* (1990); Lester D. Langley, *America and the Americas* (1989); Abraham F. Lowenthal, ed., *Exporting Democracy* (1991); John Major, *Prize Possession* (1993) (Panama Canal); Carlos Marichal, *A Century of Debt Crises in Latin America* (1989); Thomas O'Brien, *The Revolutionary Mission: American Enterprise in Latin America* (1996); Fredrick B. Pike, *FDR's Good Neighbor Policy* (1995); Emily S. Rosenberg, *Financial Missionaries to the World* (1999); Lars Schoultz, *Beneath the United States* (1998); David F. Schmitz, *Thank God They're on Our Side* (1999) (dictatorships); James Schwoch, *The American Radio Industry and Its Latin American Activities* (1990); Sarah E. Sharbach, *Stereotypes of Latin America* (1993); Peter H. Smith, *Talons of the Eagle* (1996); Joseph Tulchin, *The Aftermath of War: World War I and U.S. Policy Toward Latin America* (1971); and Bryce Wood, *The Making of the Good Neighbor Policy* (1961).

For the Caribbean and Central America, see G. Pope Atkins and Larman C. Wilson, *The United States and the Trujillo Regime* (1972) and *The Dominican Republic and the United States* (1998); Bruce Calder, *The Impact of Intervention* (1984) (Dominican Republic); Raymond Carr, *Puerto Rico* (1984); Arturo Morales Carrión, *Puerto Rico* (1983); Truman P. Clark, *Puerto Rico and the United States, 1917–23* (1975); Paul J. Dosal, *Doing Business with the Dictators* (1993) (United Fruit, Guatemala); Ronald Fernandez, *The Disenchanted Island* (1992) (Puerto Rico); Walter LaFeber, *Inevitable Revolutions* (1993); Lester D. Langley, *The United States and the Caribbean* (1980); A. W. Maldonado, *Teodoro Moscoso and Puerto Rico's Operation Bootstrap* (1997); Dana Munro, *The United States and the Caribbean Republics, 1921–1933* (1974); Brenda G. Plummer, *Haiti and the United States* (1992); Mary Renda, *Taking Haiti* (2001); Eric Paul Roorda, *The Dictator Next Door* (1998) (Trujillo); Robert I. Rotberg, *Haiti* (1971); Richard V. Salisbury, *Anti-Imperialism and International Competition in Central America* (1989); and Hans Schmidt, *The United States Occupation of Haiti* (1971) and *Maverick Marine* (1987) (Butler).

For Nicaragua and the U.S. intervention, see Paul C. Clark, Jr., *The United States and Somoza* (1992); Thomas J. Dodd, *Managing Democracy in Central America* (1992); William Kamman, *A Search for Stability* (1968); Neil Macaulay, *The Sandino Affair* (1967); Richard Millett, *Guardians of the Dynasty* (1977); Marco Aurelia Narro-Genie, *Augusto "Cesar" Sandino* (2002); and Knut Walter, *The Regime of Anastasio Somoza* (1993).

For South America, see Elizabeth A. Cobbs, *The Rich Neighbor Policy: Rockefeller and Kaiser in Brazil* (1992); Paul W. Drake, *The Money Doctor in the Andes* (1988); Stanley Hilton, *Brazil and the Great Powers* (1975); Michael Grow, *The Good Neighbor Policy and Authoritarianism in Paraguay* (1981); Frank McCann, *The Brazilian-American Alliance* (1973); Michael Montéon, *Chile in the Nitrate Era* (1982); Stephen G. Rabe, *The Road to OPEC* (1982) (Venezuela); and Stephen J. Randall, *The Diplomacy of Modernization* (1977) (Colombia).

Studies of U.S.-Mexican relations include Leslie Bethell, ed., *Mexico Since Independence* (1991); John A. Britton, *Revolution and Ideology: Images of the Mexican Revolution in the United States* (1995); E. David Cronon, *Josephus Daniels in Mexico* (1960); Helen Delpar, *The Enormous Vogue of Things Mexican* (1992) (culture); Linda B. Hall, *Oil, Banks, and Politics* (1995); Catherine E. Jayne, *Oil, War, and Anglo-American Relations* (2001); Dan LaBotz, *Edward L. Doheny* (1991) (oil); Lorenzo Meyer, *Mexico and the United States in the Oil Controversy* (1977); Stephen R. Niblo, *War, Diplomacy, and Development* (1995); W. Dirk Raat, *Mexico and the United States* (1996); Ramón Ruíz, *The Great Rebellion* (1980); Friedrich E. Schuler, *Mexico Between Hitler and Roosevelt* (1998); and Robert F. Smith, *The United States and Revolutionary Nationalism in Mexico* (1972); and Daniela Spencer, *The Impossible Triangle* (1999).

For Cuba, see Jules R. Benjamin, *The United States and Cuba* (1978); Irwin F. Gellman, *Roosevelt and Batista* (1973); Louis A. Pérez, Jr., *Cuba and the United States* (1997), *Cuba Under the Platt Amendment,* (1968) and *Becoming Cuban* (1999); and Ramón Ruíz, *Cuba* (1968).

See also the General Bibliography, Robert L. Beisner, ed., *Guide to American Foreign Relations Since 1600* (2003), and the following notes.

For comprehensive coverage of foreign-relations topics, see the articles in the four-volume *Encyclopedia of U.S. Foreign Relations* (1997), edited by Bruce W. Jentleson and Thomas G. Paterson.

NOTES TO CHAPTER 5

1. Quoted in Elting E. Morison, *Turmoil and Tradition* (New York: Atheneum, 1964), p. 312.
2. Robert H. Ferrell, "The Mukden Incident," *Journal of Modern History, XXVII* (March 1955), 67.
3. Quoted in Morison, *Turmoil and Tradition*, p. 308.
4. Quoted in Richard N. Current, "Henry L. Stimson," in Norman A. Graebner, ed., *An Uncertain Tradition* (New York: McGraw-Hill, 1961), pp. 169, 171.
5. Quoted in Frank Freidel, *Franklin D. Roosevelt: Launching the New Deal* (Boston: Little, Brown, 1973), p. 120.
6. Quoted in Richard Dean Burns, "Stanley K. Hornbeck," in Richard Dean Burns and Edward M. Bennett, eds., *Diplomats in Crisis* (Santa Barbara: ABC-CLIO Press, 1974), p. 103.
7. Quoted in Justus D. Doenecke, *When the Wicked Rise* (Lewisburg, Pa.: Bucknell University Press, 1984), p. 37.
8. Quoted in Christopher Thorne, *The Limits of Foreign Policy* (New York: Capricorn, 1973), p. 158.
9. Quoted in Morison, *Turmoil and Tradition*, p. 310.
10. Quoted in Walter LaFeber, *The Clash* (New York: Norton, 1997), p. 70.
11. Quoted in Justus D. Doenecke and John E. Wilz, *From Isolation to War, 1931–1941* (Wheeling, Ill.: Harlan Davidson, 2003; 3d ed.), p. 37.
12. Stimson quoted in David F. Schmitz, *Henry L. Stimson* (Wilmington, Del.: Scholarly Resources, 2001), p. 111.
13. Quoted in Norman A. Graebner, "Hoover, Roosevelt, and the Japanese," in Dorothy Borg and Shumpei Okamoto, eds., *Pearl Harbor as History* (New York: Columbia University Press, 1973), p. 30.
14. Quoted in LaFeber, *Clash*, p. 173.
15. Hugh R. Wilson, *Diplomat Between the Wars* (New York: Longmans, Green, 1941), p. 280.
16. Michael Schaller, *The U.S. Crusade in China, 1938–1945* (New York: Columbia University Press, 1979), p. 5.
17. Akira Iriye, *The Origins of the Second World War in Asia and the Pacific* (London: Longman, 1987), p. 16.
18. Quoted in Thomas H. Buckley, *The United States and the Washington Conference, 1921–1922* (Knoxville: University of Tennessee Press, 1970), p. 72.
19. *Ibid.*, p. 73.
20. Cryptographer Herbert Yardley quoted in LaFeber, *Clash*, p. 140.
21. Robert Vansittart quoted in Richard W. Fanning, *Peace and Disarmament* (Lexington: University Press of Kentucky, 1995), p. 153.
22. Thomas H. Buckley, "The Icarus Factor," *Diplomacy & Statecraft, IV* (November 1993), 125.
23. Quoted in David Armstrong, "China's Place in the New Pacific Order," *Diplomacy & Statecraft, IV* (November 1993), 263.
24. John Paton Davies, *Dragon by the Tail* (New York: Norton, 1972), p. 95.
25. Quoted in Akira Iriye, *Across the Pacific* (New York: Harcourt Brace & World, 1967), p. 148.
26. Quoted in Dennis L. Noble, *The Eagle and the Dragon* (Westport, Conn.: Greenwood, 1990), p. 192.
27. Quoted in Bernard D. Cole, *Gunboats and Marines* (Newark: University of Delaware Press, 1983), p. 145.
28. Quoted in Robert David Johnson, *The Peace Progressives and American Foreign Relations* (Cambridge: Harvard University Press, 1995), p. 148.
29. Ernie Place quoted in Noble, *Eagle*, p. 150; James L. Huskey, "The Cosmopolitan Connection," *Diplomatic History, XI* (Summer 1987), p. 228.
30. Mary B. Bullock, *An American Transplant* (Berkeley: University of California Press, 1980), pp. 44, 47; Raymond Fosdick quoted in Frank Ninkovich, *The Wilsonian Century* (Chicago: University of Chicago Press, 1999), p. 40.
31. Clare Boothe Luce quoted in T. Christopher Jesperson, *American Images of China, 1931–1949* (Stanford: Stanford University Press, 1996), p. 54.
32. *Ibid.*, p. 91.
33. Quoted in Justus D. Doenecke and John E. Wilz, *From Isolation to War, 1931–1941* (Arlington Heights, Ill.: Davidson, 1991; 2nd ed.), p. 23.
34. Consul Uchiyama quoted in Sandra Wilson, *The Manchurian Crisis and Japanese Society, 1931–1933* (New York: Routledge, 2002), p. 94.
35. Quoted in Nicholas Tarling, *A Sudden Rampage* (Honolulu: University of Hawai'i Press, 2001), p. 43.
36. Quoted in Asada Sadao, "The Japanese Navy and the United States," in Borg and Okamoto, *Pearl Harbor*, p. 238.
37. Eugene Dooman quoted in Izumi Hirobe, *Japanese Pride, American Prejudice* (Stanford: Stanford University Press, 2001), p. 35.
38. Quoted in William L. Neumann, *America Encounters Japan* (Baltimore: Johns Hopkins University Press, 1963), p. 176.
39. Robert G. Kaufman, *Arms Control During the Pre-Nuclear Era* (New York: Columbia University Press, 1990), p. 181.
40. Ian Baruna, *Inventing Japan* (New York: Modern Library, 2003), p. 102.
41. Archibald Steele and F. Tilman Durdin quoted in Daqing Yang, "The Nanjing Massacre in Postwar China and Japan," in T. Fujitani, Geoffrey M. White, and Lisa Yoneyama, eds., *Perilous Memories: The Asia Pacific War(s)* (Durham: Duke University Press, 2001), p. 51.
42. Roger B. Jeans, ed., *Good-Bye to Old Peking* (Athens: Ohio University Press, 1998), p. 11.
43. John W. Garver, *Chinese-Soviet Relations 1937–1945* (New York: Oxford University Press, 1988), p. 15; Soviet commander quoted in Albert L. Weeks, *Stalin's Other War* (Lanham, Md.: Rowman & Littlefield, 2002), p. 55.
44. Samuel I. Rosenman, ed., *Public Papers and Addresses of Franklin D. Roosevelt* (New York: Macmillan, 1938–1943; 13 vols.), *VI*, 406–411.
45. Senator Gerald P. Nye quoted in Wayne S. Cole, "Congress and Political Parties," in Borg and Okamoto, *Pearl Harbor*, p. 314.
46. Quoted in Benjamin D. Rhodes, *United States Foreign Policy in the Interwar Period, 1918–1941* (Westport, Conn.: Praeger, 2001), p. 150.
47. Major David Barrett quoted in Youli Sun, *China and the Origins of the Pacific War* (New York: St. Martin's, 1993), p. 134.
48. Quoted in Frederick C. Adams, *Economic Diplomacy* (Columbia: University of Missouri Press, 1976), p. 233.
49. Quoted in Stephen M. Streeter, "Waging the Counterrevolution: The United States and Guatemala, 1954–1961" (Ph.D. diss., University of Connecticut, 1994), p. 4.
50. Quoted in Arthur P. Whitaker, "From Dollar Diplomacy to the Good Neighbor Policy," *Inter-American Economic Affairs, IV* (Spring 1951), 18.

51. Rosenman, *Public Papers, II,* 14.

52. Quoted in Mark T. Gilderhus, *The Second Century* (Wilmington, Del.: Scholarly Resources, 2000), p. 89.

53. Fredrick B. Pike, *Chile and the United States* (South Bend, Ind.: University of Notre Dame Press, 1963), p. 236.

54. Sumner Welles quoted in Paul J. Dosal, *Doing Business with Dictators* (Wilmington, Del.: Scholarly Resources, 1993), p. 8.

55. Emily S. Rosenberg and Norman L. Rosenberg, "From Colonialism to Professionalism," *Journal of American History, LXXIV* (June 1987), 79; Paul W. Drake, *The Money Doctor in the Andes* (Durham: Duke University Press, 1989).

56. Emily S. Rosenberg, "Revisiting Dollar Diplomacy," *Diplomatic History, XXII* (Spring 1998), 173–174.

57. C. Neale Ronning, ed., *Intervention in Latin America* (New York: Knopf, 1970), pp. 42–49.

58. Quoted in David Ryan, "The United States, Decolonization and the World System," in David Ryan and Victor Pungong, eds., *The United States and Decolonization* (New York: St. Martin's, 2000), p. 19.

59. Fredrick B. Pike, *FDR's Good Neighbor Policy* (Austin: University of Texas Press, 1995), p. 137.

60. Lester D. Langley, *America and the Americas* (Athens: University of Georgia Press, 1989), p. 125.

61. Quoted in Emily Rosenberg, *Spreading the American Dream* (New York: Hill & Wang, 1982), p. 112.

62. Quoted in Benjamin Welles, *Sumner Welles* (New York: St. Martin's, 1997), p. 93.

63. Quoted in Elizabeth A. Cobbs, *The Rich Neighbor Policy* (New Haven: Yale University Press, 1992), p. 28.

64. Christopher Abel, "External Philanthropy and Domestic Change in Colombian Health Care," *Hispanic-American Historical Review, LXXV* (August 1995), 350.

65. Herbert Hoover, *Memoirs: The Cabinet and the Presidency, 1920–1933* (New York: Macmillan, 1952), p. 69.

66. Quoted in Bruce J. Calder, *The Impact of Intervention* (Austin: University of Texas Press, 1984), p. 124.

67. Sumner Welles, *Naboth's Vineyard* (New York: Payson and Clark, 1928; 2 vols.), *II,* 797–798.

68. Quoted in Magdaline W. Shannon, *Jean Price-Mars, the Haitian Elite, and the American Occupation, 1915–1935* (New York: St. Martin's, 1996), p. 166.

69. Quoted in Joseph R. Juárez, "United States Withdrawal from Santo Domingo," *Hispanic American Historical Review, XLII* (May 1962), 180.

70. Quoted *ibid.*

71. Franklin D. Roosevelt, "Our Foreign Policy," *Foreign Affairs, VI* (July 1928), 583.

72. Quoted in Calder, *Impact of Intervention,* p. 252.

73. Eric Paul Roorda, "The Cult of the Airplane," in Gilbert M. Joseph, Catherine C. LeGrand, and Ricardo D. Salvatore, eds., *Close Encounters of Empire* (Durham: Duke University Press, 1998), p. 286.

74. Quoted in Eric Paul Roorda, *The Dictator Next Door* (Durham: Duke University Press, 1998), p. 106.

75. Quoted in Robert F. Smith, *The United States and Cuba* (New York: Bookman, 1960), p. 184.

76. Quoted in Benjamin T. Harrison, *Dollar Diplomat* (Pullman: Washington State University Press, 1988), p. 91.

77. Quoted in Albert K. Weinberg, *Manifest Destiny* (Chicago: Quadrangle, 1963 [c. 1935]), p. 441.

78. Quoted in Carleton Beals, "This Is War, Gentlemen!" *The Nation, CXXVI* (April 11, 1928), 406.

79. Quoted in Ivan Musicant, *The Banana Wars* (New York: Macmillan, 1990), p. 328.

80. U.S. Navy, *Operation of Naval Service in Nicaragua* (Senate Doc. 86, 70 Cong., 1 Sess., 1928), pp. 5–6.

81. Quoted in Michael J. Schroeder, "The Sandino Rebellion Revisited," in Gilbert, *Close Encounters,* p. 210.

82. Emily S. Rosenberg, *Financial Missionaries to the World* (Cambridge: Harvard University Press, 1999), p. 209.

83. Senator Clarence C. Dill quoted in Johnson, *Peace Progressives,* p. 125.

84. Quoted in Walter LaFeber, *Inevitable Revolutions* (New York: Norton, 1993; 2nd ed.), p. 70.

85. Ambassador Capus Waynick quoted in David F. Schmitz, *Thank God They're on Our Side* (Chapel Hill: University of North Carolina Press, 1999), p. 156.

86. Colonel Littleton Waller quoted in Robert I. Rotberg, *Haiti* (Boston: Houghton Mifflin, 1971), pp. 137–138.

87. James Weldon Johnson, "The Truth About Haiti," *The Crisis, XX* (September 1920), 223.

88. Quoted in Brenda G. Plummer, *Rising Wind* (Chapel Hill: University of North Carolina Press, 1996), p. 100.

89. Brenda G. Plummer, *Haiti and the United States* (Athens: University of Georgia Press, 1992), p. 129.

90. William F. Jordan quoted in Mary Renda, *Taking Haiti* (Chapel Hill: University of North Carolina Press, 2001), p. 124.

91. Quoted in *ibid.,* p. 201.

92. Quoted in Donald B. Cooper, "The Withdrawal of the United States from Haiti, 1928–1934," *Journal of Inter-American Studies, V* (January 1963), 83.

93. Quoted in Johnson, *Peace Progressives,* p. 224.

94. Quoted in Dana G. Munro, *The United States and the Caribbean Republics, 1921–1933* (Princeton: Princeton University Press, 1974), pp. 314–315.

95. Quoted in Louis A. Pérez, Jr., *On Becoming Cuban* (Chapel Hill: University of North Carolina Press, 1999), p. 190.

96. Quoted in Thomas F. O'Brien, *The Revolutionary Mission* (New York: Cambridge University Press, 1996), p. 228.

97. Quoted in Luis E. Aguilar, *Cuba 1933* (New York: Norton, 1974), p. 167.

98. Sumner Welles quoted in Irwin F. Gellman, *Secret Affairs* (Baltimore: Johns Hopkins University Press, 1995), p. 80.

99. Quoted in Louis A. Pérez, Jr., *Cuba Under the Platt Amendment, 1902–1934* (Pittsburgh: University of Pittsburgh Press, 1986), pp. 323–324.

100. Pérez, *On Becoming Cuban,* p. 297.

101. Arturo Morales Carrión, *Puerto Rico* (New York: W. W. Norton, 1983), p. 206.

102. Quoted in Raymond Carr, *Puerto Rico* (New York: Vintage, 1984), p. 54.

103. Ernest Gruening quoted in Robert David Johnson, "Anti-Imperialism and the Good Neighbour Policy," *Journal of Latin American Studies, XXIX* (February 1997), 109.

104. Tourist brochures quoted in Dennis Merrill, "Negotiating Cold War Paradise," *Diplomatic History, XXV* (Spring 2001), 1.

105. Quoted in Carr, *Puerto Rico,* p. 61.

106. Quoted in Helen Delpar, *The Enormous Vogue of Things Mexican* (Tuscaloosa: University of Alabama Press, 1992), p. 5.

107. John A. Britton, *Revolution and Ideology* (Lexington: University Press of Kentucky, 1995), p. 52.

108. Linda B. Hall, *Oil, Banks, and Politics* (Austin: University of Texas Press, 1995), p. 179.

109. Morrow quoted in Daniela Spenser, *The Impossible Triangle: Mexico, Soviet Russia, and the United States in the 1920s* (Durham: Duke University Press, 1999), pp. 139–140.

110. Lars Schoultz, *Beneath the United States,* (Cambridge: Harvard University Press, 1998), p. 282.

111. Verna Carlton Millan quoted in Britton, *Revolution,* p. 130.

112. Quoted in W. Dirk Raat, *Mexico and the United States* (Athens: University of Georgia Press, 1996), p. 145.

113. Quoted in Stephen R. Niblo, *War, Diplomacy, and Development* (Wilmington, Del.: Scholarly Resources, 1995), p. 45.

114. Quoted in Pike, *FDR's Good Neighbor,* p. 192.

115. David A. Haglund, *Latin America and the Transformation of U.S. Strategic Thought, 1936–1940* (Albuquerque: University of New Mexico Press, 1984), p. 154.

116. Lawrence Duggan quoted in Catherine E. Jayne, *Oil, War, and Anglo-American Relations* (Westport, Conn.: Greenwood Press, 2001), p. 146.

117. David Sheinin, "Pan Americanism," in Bruce W. Jentleson and Thomas G. Paterson, eds., *Encyclopedia of U.S. Foreign Relations* (New York: Oxford University Press, 1997), *III,* 356.

118. Quoted in J. Lloyd Mecham, *A Survey of United States–Latin American Relations* (Boston: Houghton Mifflin, 1965), p. 100.

119. Quoted in Samuel Guy Inman, *Inter-American Conferences* (Washington, D.C.: University Press, 1965), p. 117.

120. Quoted in Richard V. Salisbury, *Anti-Imperialism and International Competition in Central America, 1920–1929* (Wilmington, Del.: Scholarly Resources, 1989), p. 121.

121. Quoted in Bryce Wood, *The Making of the Good Neighbor Policy* (New York: Columbia University Press, 1961), p. 119.

122. Cordell Hull, *Memoirs* (New York: Macmillan, 1948; 2 vols.), *I,* 602.

123. Quoted in Holger H. Herwig, *Politics of Frustration* (Boston: Little, Brown, 1976), p. 187.

124. Quoted in Jordan A. Schwarz, *Liberal* (New York: Free Press, 1987), p. 123.

125. Quoted in John Major, *Prize Possession* (New York: Cambridge University Press, 1993), p. 295.

126. Peter H. Smith, *Talons of the Eagle* (New York: Oxford University Press, 1996), p. 85.

CHAPTER 6

Survival and Spheres: The Allies and the Second World War, 1939–1945

***Church Service on the* Prince of Wales.**   *On August 10, 1941, President Franklin D. Roosevelt and Prime Minister Winston S. Churchill, with their staffs, attended a stirring service aboard the British warship during the Atlantic Charter Conference. (Franklin D. Roosevelt Library)*

DIPLOMATIC CROSSROAD

✧✧✧ *The Atlantic Charter Conference, 1941*

IN HIS LONGEST walk since contracting polio twenty years earlier, President Franklin D. Roosevelt slowly limped the entire length of the battleship H.M.S. *Prince of Wales.* More than 1,500 men, including British prime minister Winston S. Churchill, stood at rigid attention as the president took his tortured steps, "determined to walk along that deck even if it killed him."[1] Roosevelt finally reached his seat near the bow, next to Churchill. British and American chiefs of staff stood behind them. Roosevelt and Churchill were attending church services in Placentia Bay near the harbor of Argentia, Newfoundland, on August 10, 1941.

The Sunday services aboard the *Prince of Wales* marked the "keynote" of the four-day summit meeting between the two leaders (August 9–13, 1941), some four months before Pearl Harbor catapulted the United States into World War II as a formal belligerent.[2] The sermon, from Joshua 1:1–9, seemed directed at the president: "As I was with Moses, so I will be with thee: I will not fail thee, nor forsake thee." Suggesting the need for U.S. aid in the war against Hitler was the hortatory hymn, "Onward Christian Soldiers," with its call for "marching as to war." For Roosevelt, who had already supplied destroyers, Lend-Lease, and other aid short of war, the moment evoked a rush of emotion. "If nothing else had happened," he later told his son, "that would have cemented us. 'Onward Christian Soldiers.' We *are,* and we *will,* go on, with God's help."[3] Churchill found symbolic unity that morning—"the Union Jack and the Stars and Stripes draped side by side; . . . the highest naval, military, and air officers of Britain and the United States grouped together behind the President and me; the close-packed ranks of British and American sailors . . . joining fervently in the prayers and hymns familiar to both."[4] Nobody aboard the *Prince of Wales* could know that Japanese bombs would destroy the majestic battleship off the coast of Malaya on December 10, 1941.

The four-day meeting in Placentia Bay was the first of many between Roosevelt and Churchill during World War II; altogether, the two leaders would spend some 120 days in each other's company. Notwithstanding the fears that the meeting might spark a clash of "prima donnas," the personalities blended well.[5] Churchill's willingness to pay deference to a man he regarded "almost with religious awe" and his own pride in being half-American (his mother) made him an ardent advocate of Anglo-American solidarity.[6] Roosevelt, although he sometimes saw the prime minister as the last of the Victorians, reciprocated Churchill's friendship. Under their leadership the two countries became "mixed up together . . . for mutual and general advantage" to a degree unmatched in modern times.[7] Indeed, the cultural "invasion" of the British Isles over the next four years by nearly 3 million rowdy, "jitterbugging and gum-chewing" American military personnel accelerated a trend that "began during the Jazz Age" and "continued on via the gyrations of Elvis Presley" to the present day.[8] "No lover ever studied the whims of his mistress as I did those of President Roosevelt," Churchill later boasted.[9]

Aside from the personal equation and cultural symbolism, Argentia produced few decisive results. The British asked for men, ships, planes, and tanks. Churchill urged that the U.S. navy extend its convoying of British vessels farther into the German submarine-infested North Atlantic. The British military chiefs, remembering the frightful casualties of World War I, argued that bombing, blockades, and propaganda might so weaken the Germans that they would surrender without a full-scale invasion. The Americans favored a more direct strategy, insisting on large ground armies. Army chief of staff General George C. Marshall declared that a U.S. military buildup had to take priority over British requests for weapons and equipment; "we might have lost everything we owned, including our pants," noted another U.S. general.[10] In the one tangible commitment at Argentia, FDR promised to convoy British merchant ships as far as Iceland, but he delayed any public declaration until September, when a German submarine fired torpedoes at the U.S. destroyer *Greer* near Iceland. Neglecting to mention that the *Greer* had shadowed the U-boat for three hours prior to the attack, Roosevelt announced on September 11 that henceforth American naval vessels would shoot at German submarines. Undeclared naval action (or "war in masquerade") was as far as Roosevelt would go in the months before Pearl Harbor.[11] Hitler himself reacted to the Argentia meeting by ordering the deportation of German and Austrian Jews to the east, a "massive step" in his genocidal Final Solution.[12]

At Argentia, discussions about Japan exposed British and American differences. Foreign Office diplomats argued that Japan, which had recently occupied the southern half of French Indochina, should receive an explicit U.S. warning against further encroachments, and that the United States should commit itself to war if the Japanese attacked British or Dutch territory in Southeast Asia. U.S. officials avoided any definite commitment. Roosevelt did promise a "mighty swat" at Japan. But when the president returned to Washington, Secretary of State Cordell Hull watered down the proposed statement. Instead of announcing that continued Japanese aggression would cause the United States to take measures that "might result in war," the actual warning merely read that Washington would take steps necessary "toward insuring the safety and security of the United States."[13] Roosevelt preferred to delay a confrontation in the Pacific until he strengthened his army and navy and cultivated a more favorable public opinion. He also intended to beat Hitler first.

The most famous product of the summit came in the eight-point statement of war aims—the Atlantic Charter. Reminiscent of Woodrow Wilson's Fourteen Points, the charter reaffirmed the principles of collective security, national self-determination, freedom of the seas, and liberal trading practices (see Chapter 3). The signatories also disclaimed any territorial aggrandizement and pledged economic collaboration. Behind the vision of a postwar world, however, lay Anglo-American differences. The Americans, particularly Under Secretary of State Sumner Welles, pressed for a statement explicitly endorsing freer trade. The British wanted to protect their discriminatory system of imperial preferences. The compromise called for "access, on equal terms, to the trade and to the raw materials of the world," leaving the British an escape clause that promised "due respect for their existing obligations." When he read these vague words later, Hull felt "keenly disappointed."[14] Churchill failed to gain Roosevelt's backing for a new League. Roo-

Winston S. Churchill (1874–1965) at Placentia Bay, August 1941. Churchill claimed later that after he and Roosevelt signed the Atlantic Charter, "America could not honourably stay out" of the war. American support for Churchill and Britain, FDR said privately, rested on "a mathematical proposition. If Hitler organizes Europe and Africa with their 400 million people, plus Japan, we would stand no chance with our 175 million (Canada and Mexico included). Not only would we have to reduce our standard of living, but in the end we would be beaten because of the manpower superiority of the other side. Therefore we *cannot* let Britain be defeated." (Franklin D. Roosevelt Library)

sevelt endorsed only "the establishment of a wider and permanent system of general security."[15] As "both realist and idealist, both fixer and preacher, both a prince and a soldier," the president wanted to be as cautious as he was eloquent about postwar goals.[16]

The Atlantic Charter became a propaganda tool against the Axis. Soon Voice of America radio broadcasts hailed the charter's call to "fight on all the world's battle-fields for these essential liberties: liberty of expression, of religion, and the right to live protected from need and from fear."[17] In September 1941, representatives of the nations battling Hitler formally adhered to the "common principles" set forth in the Atlantic Charter.[18] The Soviet Union gave qualified approval. Twenty-six nations, on January 1, 1942, signed the Declaration of the United Nations, which pledged cooperation in achieving the aims of the Atlantic Charter. Churchill and Roosevelt, however, provided no procedures for enforcement or implementation. Indeed, the prime minister insisted that the charter applied only to "nations of Europe now un-der the Nazi yoke," not to "the regions and peoples which owe allegiance to the British Crown."[19] Roosevelt came to view the principles as a "beautiful idea" rather than as set rules.[20] However much the president believed in the Argentia ideals, he seemed willing to postpone their application to accommodate pressing military and diplomatic priorities. "I dream dreams but am, at the same time, an intensely prac-tical person," he once said.[21]

By meeting secretly with Churchill on a British battleship, Roosevelt demonstrated America's commitment to the defense of Britain by all means short of war. Whatever his hopes that the theatrics of Argentia would galvanize American opinion for a firmer stance, Roosevelt maintained a "policy of influence without belligerence."[22] Not "a single American officer has shown the slightest keenness to be in the war on our side," one British participant noted.[23] Yet the Atlantic Charter, the Churchill-Roosevelt friendship, the Anglo-American strategic conversations, even the divergent views on international organization and postwar economic policy—all struck chords that would echo through the next four years of war. That the Soviet Union, which Germany had invaded some six weeks earlier, had no representatives at Argentia did not mean that the conferees did not discuss Soviet cooperation against the Axis. Presidential aide Harry Hopkins had visited Moscow two weeks before the Argentia conference, and his assurances that the USSR would withstand the Nazi onslaught buoyed the two leaders. In a joint communication to Joseph Stalin from Argentia, Churchill and Roosevelt hailed "the splendid defense that you are making against the Nazi attack" and promised the "very maximum" of supplies.[24] This Anglo-American commitment to the Soviet Union also carried large implications for the future.

Juggling Between War and Peace, 1939–1941

The conversations at Placentia Bay exemplified Roosevelt's distinctly personal approach to diplomacy during World War II. A deft juggler who "could keep all his balls in the air without losing his own," as Vice President Henry Wallace quipped, FDR delighted in face-to-face confrontations, always confident in his ability to charm even those who accused him of "messianic" delusions.[25] It mattered little that Secretary Hull learned of the conference when he read about it in the newspapers. The president did not mind that his military and naval advisers often had short notice to prepare for meetings. With selfless subordinates such as Sumner Welles and Harry Hopkins to do his bidding, Roosevelt relished the spotlight on himself. British foreign secretary Anthony Eden once compared FDR to "a conjurer, skillfully juggling with balls of dynamite, whose nature he failed to understand."[26]

The juggling act had begun two years earlier, when Germany started World War II by attacking Poland. FDR had avowed on September 3, 1939, just two days after the German invasion, that "this nation will remain a neutral nation." Still, "I cannot ask that every American remain neutral in thought as well."[27] Thus, in words pointedly different from Wilson's in 1914, did Roosevelt project the next twenty-six months of U.S. policy toward the war in Europe. Roosevelt proceeded from neutrality to nonbelligerency to undeclared war in the Atlantic and finally, after Pearl Harbor, to full-scale war against the Axis. Hoping to avoid war while giving as much aid as possible to Hitler's opponents, FDR did not always speak candidly about the possible and ultimate contradiction between these two goals.

On September 21, 1939, Roosevelt asked Congress to repeal the arms embargo in the Neutrality Act as the best way to stay out of the war. He stressed this deceptive argument, knowing that his real purpose was to permit England and France, with their superior sea power, to purchase arms and munitions on a cash-and-carry basis. He persuaded William Allen White, the Republican sage from Kansas, to form a Non-

Makers of American Foreign Relations, 1939–1945

Presidents	Secretaries of State
Franklin D. Roosevelt, 1933–1945	Cordell Hull, 1933–1944
	Edward R. Stettinius, Jr., 1944–1945
Harry S. Truman, 1945–1953	James F. Byrnes, 1945–1947

Partisan Committee for Peace Through Revision of the Neutrality Act. Although isolationists such as Republican senator Charles Tobey of New Hampshire opposed "our changing the rules after the war has broken out," FDR's tactics worked.[28] By a vote of 63 to 30 in the Senate and 243 to 181 in the House, the revised Neutrality Act became law on November 4, thus permitting Britain and France to buy arms.

The Pan American Conference at Panama City (September 23–October 3, 1939) also signaled the pro-Allied emphasis of U.S. policy. The conferees proclaimed neutrality, established a committee for economic coordination, and created a neutral zone 300 miles wide along the entire coast of the Western Hemisphere (except Canada), in which belligerent naval operations were prohibited. Roosevelt had told his cabinet in April 1939 that the Atlantic fleet would patrol such areas and "if we fire and sink an Italian or German [submarine] . . . we will say it the way the Japs do, 'so sorry.' 'Never happen again.' Tomorrow we sink two."[29] These "neutrality patrols" actually became the first step toward Anglo-American naval cooperation. By late summer 1940, conversations between staff officers began in London, soon followed by exchanges of personnel and cryptographic intelligence, actual coordination against German naval operations (such as the sinking of the battleship *Bismarck* in May 1941), and, in autumn 1941, convoying merchant ships across the Atlantic. Justified in terms of contingency planning and aid short of war, such naval measures nonetheless led the chief of naval operations, Admiral Harold R. Stark, to conclude in early 1941: "We cannot avoid having it [war] thrust upon us or our deliberately going in."[30]

Germany's *blitzkrieg* humbled Poland in two weeks, and then in winter 1939–1940 came a "phony war," or *sitzkrieg*. Most battle news from November to March flowed from northern Europe, where the Soviet Union defeated Finland in the "Winter war." Roosevelt sent his sympathies but little else to Finland. The fall of France in June 1940 stung FDR into bold measures. In a speech on June 10, Roosevelt condemned Italy for holding the dagger that "struck . . . the back of its neighbor," and he pledged to England "the material resources of this nation."[31] A week later he named the prominent Republicans Henry L. Stimson and Frank Knox, both vocal advocates of aid to Britain, as secretary of war and secretary of the navy, respectively. Then, after intricate negotiations, the president announced on September 3, 1940, that he was transferring to England some fifty old destroyers in exchange for leases to eight British bases stretching from Newfoundland to British Guiana. Two weeks later, he signed into law the Selective Service Act of 1940, the first peacetime military draft in American history.

That Roosevelt could accomplish so much at a time when isolationist sentiment still prevailed and he was seeking a controversial third presidential term testifies to his political astuteness. As for both selective service and the destroyers-for-bases agreement, FDR learned that his Republican presidential opponent, Wendell L. Willkie, would not make them campaign issues. In both cases Roosevelt also encouraged influential private citizens (the Century Group for the destroyers deal and the Military Training Camps Association for selective service) to lobby for his objectives. The larger Committee to Defend America by Aiding the Allies, headed by William Allen White, soon rallied behind the president to counter the isolationist America First Committee set up in September 1940. FDR avoided congressional scrutiny of the destroyers deal by presenting it as an executive agreement rather than as a treaty, and he deflected political opposition to conscription by having men of integrity, such as Secretary Stimson and General Marshall, attest to the military's need for a draft. Further, Roosevelt continued to promise that he would keep America out of war. Although Germany could regard the destroyers deal as an act of war, FDR called it instead "the most important action in the reinforcement of our national defense . . . since the Louisiana Purchase."[32] When Willkie made last-minute charges during the fall campaign that Roosevelt secretly sought war, the White House struck back: "Your boys are not going to be sent into any foreign wars." Willkie exploded: "That hypocritical son of a bitch! This is going to beat me!"[33] It did.

After the election Churchill cabled: "The moment approaches when we shall no longer be able to pay cash for shipping and other supplies."[34] Roosevelt soon held one of his breezy, jaunty press conferences, saying that he favored lending or leasing supplies to Britain. He likened it to lending a garden hose to a neighbor whose house was burning. Once the fire is out, "he gives it back to me and thanks me very much."[35] In a fireside chat on December 29, FDR admitted that sending armaments to Britain risked war, but the "sole purpose is to keep war away from our country and our people." Then, in a ringing phrase, Roosevelt called on the United States to "become the great arsenal of democracy."[36]

Over the next two months, Americans debated the Lend-Lease bill "in every newspaper, on every wave length—over every cracker barrel in all the land."[37] Although the vote of 60 to 31 in the Senate and 317 to 71 in the House seemed substantial, the White House did not win easily. Senator Burton K. Wheeler, an isolationist Democrat from Montana, warned that aid short of war was a dangerous delusion—"You can't put your shirt tail into a clothes wringer and pull it out suddenly when the wringer keeps turning."[38] Right-wing women's groups accused interventionists of "'bundling,' 'balling,' and curtseying for Britain."[39] Senator Hiram Johnson grumbled: "Like the dog gone back to his vomit, the country has become English again."[40]

To overcome such opposition, some deception became necessary. The administration's floor manager, Representative John W. McCormack, worried because his Irish constituents in South Boston would surely protest any "McCormack Bill" designed to aid the British Empire, induced the House parliamentarian to tag the Lend-Lease bill H.R. 1776. When one irate constituent still berated him, the future Speaker of the House thought quickly: "Madam, do you realize that the Vatican is surrounded on all sides by totalitarianism? Madam, this is not a bill to save the English, this is a bill to save Catholicism."[41]

The German Onslaught
1939–1942

The Lend–Lease Act became law on March 11, 1941. Under its terms the president could "sell, transfer title to, exchange, lease, lend, or otherwise dispose of" defense articles to "any country whose defense the President deems vital to the defense of the United States."[42] Although the initial appropriation totaled $7 billion, by war's end the United States had expended more than $50 billion on Lend–Lease. England eventually received $31.6 billion of that amount.

With German U–boats sinking 500,000 tons of shipping a month, it seemed logical that the United States would use its navy to ensure that Lend–Lease supplies

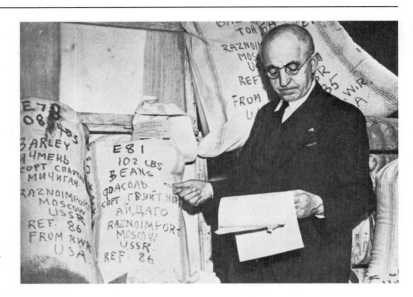

Lend-Lease to the USSR. A U.S. lend-lease official checks American food destined for the Soviet Union's hard-pressed people. The Soviets eventually lost nearly 27 million people in the war. (U.S. Information Agency, National Archives)

reached England safely. FDR hesitated, partly because of public opinion, but also because the Atlantic fleet lacked operational readiness. Instead, he extended naval "patrols" halfway across the Atlantic, announcing in April that U.S. vessels would monitor German warships. "We have got a tadpole that someday may be a frog," Secretary Hull told an aide.[43] U.S. troops also occupied Greenland the same month. Although interventionists urged U.S. Navy convoys for British ships, FDR declared a national emergency in late May but took no new action. He told the cabinet that "he expected a clash sooner or later but said the Germans would have to fire the first shots."[44]

When Hitler occupied the Balkans and invaded the Soviet Union in June 1941, the president announced the next month that 4,000 American marines would occupy Iceland for hemispheric defense. Roosevelt also began military Lend-Lease aid to the USSR in November, notwithstanding opinions from State Department and military advisers that the Soviet Union would quickly fall. (By the end of the war the USSR had received $11 billion in Lend-Lease.) "Now comes this Russian diversion," FDR wrote four days after the German assault. "If it is more than just that it will mean the liberation of Europe from Nazi domination."[45] When bureaucratic tangles inhibited the flow of goods to the USSR, Roosevelt insisted that supplies be sent "even if the Army and Navy authorities in America did not like it."[46] Then the president held his dramatic meeting with Churchill at Placentia Bay, and in early September, after German torpedoes just missed the *Greer,* he publicly ordered naval convoys as far as Iceland and issued a "shoot-on-sight" command to the navy.

By autumn 1941, Roosevelt probably anticipated an "incident" to induce U.S. entry into the war against Hitler. After the Placentia Bay conference, the president told Churchill that "he would wage war, but not declare it, and that he would be-

Grew had failed to grasp the Europe-first emphasis of Roosevelt's foreign policy. After 1937, when Japan marched deeper into China, Washington angrily reacted with protests but lacked the power to challenge Japanese predominance in East Asia. Even Roosevelt's much-heralded refusal to apply the Neutrality Act to the "incident" in China, thus making it legal to sell arms to Jiang Jieshi's government, could not obscure the preponderance of U.S. trade with Japan. As late as 1940, $78 million in American exports went to China, whereas $227 million were shipped to Japan. Ending the 1911 commercial treaty permitted economic sanctions against Japan, but oil, the most vital ingredient in Japan's war machine, flowed until July 1941. In keeping with Roosevelt's policy of all-out aid to England short of war, the navy revised its strategic thinking in November 1940. "Plan Dog" called for a defensive posture in the Pacific, depicted Germany as the country's primary enemy, and made preservation of England its principal goal. Roosevelt still hoped to avoid a confrontation, because "I simply have not got enough Navy to go around."[56] During 1941 he mentioned Hitler and the Nazis on more than 150 public occasions, but made only "four references" to Japan so as not to divert public attention from Europe.[57]

Japanese movement into Southeast Asia placed Washington and Tokyo on a collision course. With the Asian colonies of France and the Netherlands lying unprotected, Japanese expansionists demanded a thrust southward, thus completing the strangulation of China and transforming the whole region into the Greater East Asia Co-Prosperity Sphere. Japan pressed England and France to close down supply routes to the Guomindang through Burma and Indochina. Tokyo also demanded economic concessions from the petroleum-rich Dutch East Indies. Then, only four days after French representatives allowed Japanese troops to occupy northern Indochina, Japan signed the Tripartite Pact with Germany and Italy on September 27. The signatories pledged to aid one another if attacked by a nation not currently involved in the war. Because the pact explicitly exempted the Soviet Union, Washington had no doubt about being its target.

A new, more militant Japanese government, with Prince Fumimaro Konoe as prime minister and General Hideki Tojo as war minister, took the fateful steps. Foreign Minister Yosuke Matsuoka articulated the advantages of boldness—"one cannot obtain a tiger's cub unless he braves the tiger's den."[58] Matsuoka intended the Tripartite Pact to deter the United States from intervening in the Atlantic or the Pacific, and to facilitate a rapprochement between Japan and the Soviet Union, which remained aligned with Germany in the Nazi-Soviet Pact. Tokyo might then induce Jiang Jieshi to join the Co-Prosperity Sphere, after which Japanese troops would gradually withdraw from China and civilian authorities could reassert control over the army.

Washington flashed warnings. In July 1940, Roosevelt withheld aviation fuel and top-grade scrap iron from Japan. In September, after the Tripartite Pact, he extended the embargo to all scrap metals. Even Grew urged firmness, labeling Japan "one of the predatory powers," lacking "all moral and ethical sense."[59] Administration "hawks" pressed the president to end oil exports as well. Backed by Hull and the Joint Chiefs, however, Roosevelt kept the oil flowing to Japan. Recognizing the interconnectness of Asian and European events, FDR expedited aid to China to keep Japan's army "busy and more or less tied up" so it could not "move southward in full force."[60] The president hoped to aid England while avoiding a showdown in the Pacific, which an oil embargo would likely precipitate.

In February 1941, Admiral Kichisaburo Nomura became ambassador to Washington. A personal friend of President Roosevelt, Nomura accepted the appointment only when assured by Konoe and Matsuoka that peace with the United States took precedence over Japan's commitment to the Axis. Private citizens known as the "John Doe Associates" and led by two Catholic missionaries, Father James M. Drought and Bishop James E. Walsh, also tried to effect conciliation. They held interviews with Konoe, Hull, and Roosevelt. Drought forwarded his own "Draft Understanding" to Hull in April. It called for a Konoe-Roosevelt meeting and U.S. pressure on China to recognize Japanese domination of Manchuria in exchange for Japan's disavowal of the Tripartite Pact. Hull thought the "Understanding" a Japanese proposal and accepted it as a basis of discussion, noting, however, that any agreement had to satisfy four basic principles: respect for the territorial integrity and sovereignty of all nations; noninterference in the internal affairs of other nations; respect for equal trade opportunity; and support for peaceful change in the Pacific. Nomura failed to attach appropriate importance to Hull's four points when he reported to Tokyo. Not until September did Tokyo learn that Hull's four principles could block any settlement of the China war. The John Doe efforts also muddled a possible Roosevelt-Konoe summit, as Tokyo asked in August for a meeting they thought the Americans had proposed in April, but Washington then rejected any high-level meeting without assurances on outstanding problems. Both sides suspected the other of retreating from earlier positions.

Japan's determination to hold China and to expand farther doomed these diplomatic efforts. In early July 1941, Roosevelt thought the Japanese were about to decide "which way they are going to jump—attack Russia, attack the South Seas . . . or whether they will sit on the fence and be more friendly with us."[61] Just as FDR received intelligence reports indicating that in the event of war between the United States and Japan, "Germany would declare war on U.S.A.," he signed an order freezing all Japanese funds when Japan seized southern Indochina in late July.[62] Hard-line bureaucrats interpreted the order to mean stopping all trade with Japan—including oil. Thereafter, Washington and Tokyo steered "a collision course that even statesmen of great flexibility would find it difficult to avoid."[63]

Unless the sale of American oil resumed, Japan determined to seize Dutch and British petroleum fields. "If we are going to fight," the navy chief of staff told Emperor Hirohito, "then the sooner . . . the better because our supplies are dwindling anyway."[64] But the United States would not turn on the oil spigot until Tokyo agreed to Hull's four principles, especially the pledge to respect China's sovereignty and territorial integrity. Key American officials also knew from cracking the Japanese diplomatic code (Operation MAGIC) that Japan's forces were massing to strike southward after mid-November, although most officials did not think Japan would attack the United States. Hard-liner Henry L. Stimson viewed the Japanese as "notorious bluffers" who backed down when confronted firmly.[65] As late as November 27, when MAGIC intercepts revealed the imminence of a Japanese strike somewhere, State Department Asian expert Stanley K. Hornbeck challenged his colleagues: "Tell me of one case in history when a nation went to war out of desperation."[66] Amid this

The PURPLE Machine. In September 1940, U.S. cryptanalysts of the Signal Intelligence Service cracked Japan's most secret diplomatic code. The American code-breakers, under Operation MAGIC, not only deciphered thousands of intercepted messages sent by Japanese officials around the world, but also duplicated the machine, called PURPLE, that generated the codes. Although these dispatches revealed through 1941 that Japan expected all-out war with the United States, they did not reveal military plans or the planned attack on Pearl Harbor. The intelligence gathered from MAGIC and British ULTRA intercepts of German signals may have shortened the war by two or three years. (National Archives)

atmosphere, the urging of army and navy leaders to string out negotiations until the Philippines could be reinforced went unheeded. An eleventh-hour U.S. modus vivendi envisioned a trickle of oil to Japan and negotiations between Chongqing and Tokyo, while maintaining American aid to China; Japan would have to abrogate the Tripartite Pact and accept basic principles of international conduct. Exhausted from months of negotiations, Hull advised Roosevelt to shelve the proposal. The secretary of state told Stimson: "It is now in the hands of . . . the Army and Navy."[67]

After months of discussion, the Japanese Imperial Conference of September decided to fight the United States if Washington did not lift its embargo by October 15—a date later extended to November 25 and then to November 29. Tokyo's final decision to attack the United States did not stem from irrationality or suicidal tendencies. Japan required 12,000 tons of oil each day, and desperate moderates and militants alike read U.S. pressure as provocative and life-strangling. In a choice between fighting the United States or pulling out of China, no Japanese leader recommended the latter. They knew America's power and industrial potential well enough, but as Tojo (who replaced Konoe as prime minister) put it: "You have to plunge into war if there is some chance, however slight, of winning victory."[68] The Japanese did not expect America to surrender, but they hoped that a stalemated war of endurance might persuade tired Americans to negotiate a compromise peace. "We would become a third-class nation . . . if we just sat tight," asserted Tojo.[69]

On November 25, 1941, a huge task force that included six carriers bearing some 350 airplanes headed across 3,000 miles of the Pacific Ocean. The target: Pearl Harbor, Hawai'i. After receiving the message "Climb Mt. Niitake" on December 2, every ship maintained radio silence to avoid detection and ensure complete surprise. In the early morning of Sunday, December 7, the carriers launched their planes. After a flight of 220 miles, the aircraft swept down on the unsuspecting American naval base. Within a few hours eight U.S. battleships had been sunk or damaged and 2,403

Pearl Harbor. A Japanese pilot's perspective on Ford Island, Pearl Harbor, Hawai'i. The three Pacific U.S. aircraft carriers were not in port and escaped the attack. Of the eight battleships hit at Pearl Harbor, six were repaired and eventually participated in the war. The historian John Fousek writes that "Pearl Harbor would enter U.S. public discourse as one of the code words for the almost universally accepted 'lessons' of World War II—never appease aggressors and always remain militarily prepared." (Navy Department National Archives)

Americans had died. The stunning news shot around the world. In London, Churchill thought: "So we had won after all!" Indeed, "greater good fortune has rarely happened to the British Empire."[70] In Chongqing, Jiang Jieshi "sang an old opera air, and played the Ave Maria all that day," also rejoicing in his new ally.[71]

Critics have charged that Roosevelt and his top advisers deliberately sacrificed the Pacific fleet to get into the war with Hitler via the "back door."[72] Most scholars reject the conspiracy theory and explain Pearl Harbor as the consequence of mistakes, missed clues, overconfidence, and plain bad luck. Better intelligence in Washington might have alerted Hawai'i, but American errors weighed less than the enormous care and skill with which the Japanese planned the attack. MAGIC intercepts on November 30, for example, read that "war may suddenly break out between the Anglo-Saxon nations and Japan . . . ; this war may come quicker than anyone dreams."[73] Yet the intercepts never revealed military plans, and Washington thought Japan would strike Southeast Asia, where troop ships were spotted heading for Malaya; no one thought Tokyo could undertake two major operations at once. As to hints of major Japanese interest in Pearl Harbor, including Grew's warning in February 1941 of a possible sudden attack, one scholar has written: "After the event a signal is always crystal clear. . . . But before the event it is obscure and pregnant with conflicting meanings. . . . In short, we failed to anticipate Pearl Harbor not for want of the relevant materials, but because of a plethora of irrelevant ones."[74] Many "ifs" cloud the question. If the radar operator had been able to convince his superiors on Oahu that the blips really were planes, if General Marshall had sent his last-minute warning by navy cable instead of Western Union telegraph, if MAGIC could have read Japan's naval communications as well as its diplomatic cables, if . . .

"Jap . . . You're Next!"
James Montgomery Flagg, already famous for his "I Want You" poster of World War I, offered this version of Uncle Sam in 1942. After Pearl Harbor, posters such as Flagg's helped focus public resentment on Japan, rather than on Hitler. "I can see why we are fighting the Japanese," observed one Gallup Poll respondent, "but I can't see why we are fighting the Germans." Yet Roosevelt did not want to adopt a "Pacific First" strategy and kept his "Europe First" strategy alive by supporting British proposals to invade North Africa in November 1942. (National Archives)

For Japan, Pearl Harbor proved a tactical victory but a strategic disaster. When President Roosevelt, referring to the "date which will live in infamy," asked for a declaration of war, Congress responded on December 8 with a unanimous vote in the Senate and only one dissent in the House—that of Jeannette Rankin, who had also voted "no" in 1917.[75] For Senator Vandenberg, the Japanese attack on Hawai'i "ended isolationism for any realist."[76] The deadly event acted "like a reverse earthquake, that in one terrible jerk shook everything disjointed, distorted, askew back into place. Japanese bombs had finally brought national unity to the U.S."[77] In the mistaken belief that Japan "would keep the bulk of American power tied up" indefinitely, Hitler declared war on the United States on December 11.[78] Congress's immediate declaration of war on Germany confronted Americans with a daunting two-theater conflict.

The Big Three: Strategies and Fissures, 1941–1943

The Atlantic Charter Conference and the events of 1939–1941 foreshadowed well the themes of wartime diplomacy. Giving material aid to Hitler's opponents became the main U.S. contribution to victory in Europe. Washington's commitment to a "Europe First" strategy derived from Anglo-American staff discussions prior to Pearl Harbor, as did the different American and British conceptions of that strategy. Americans favored a "massive thrust at the enemy's heart," and the British preferred "successive stabs around the periphery . . . like jackals worrying a lion before springing at his throat."[79] During the war Americans also revived Wilsonianism but combined it with a pragmatic determination to avoid Wilson's mistakes. This time the United States would join an international organization to maintain peace, even if it meant adding blatant balance-of-power features to the institution under Roosevelt's concept of the "Four Policemen" (United States, USSR, Britain, and China), each of which would maintain peace in a sphere of influence. This time there would be no debts-reparations tangle because Lend-Lease would eliminate the dollar sign. This time the enemy must surrender unconditionally. This time tariff walls must fall and trade doors must open. This time there would be postwar cooperation with the Soviets. FDR encouraged Hollywood to produce such pro-Soviet films as *Mission to Moscow* (1943), which he sent to Stalin with the message that Washington was "on the level—no axes to grind."[80] *Life* magazine described Russians as "one hell of a people" who "look like Americans, dress like Americans, and think like Americans."[81]

Global war brought new power and confidence to U.S. diplomacy. The Atlantic Charter reflected a commitment to shaping the postwar world in an American image. As Henry Luce's best-selling *American Century* phrased it in 1941, the United States must "exert upon the world the full impact of our influence, for such purposes as we see fit and by such means as we see fit."[82] By rearming, acquiring new bases, raising an army of more than 2 million, welding hemispheric unity, and revving up its industries, the United States built the sinews of global power even before Pearl Harbor. Churchill told Roosevelt in 1944: "You have the greatest navy in the world . . . the greatest air force . . . the greatest trade. You have all the gold."

But Churchill hoped that the Americans will avoid "vainglorious ambitions, and that justice and fair-play will be the lights that guide them."[83] Stirred by a wartime visit to the poverty-stricken British West African colony of Gambia (where the natives were "treated worse than their livestock," which "lived longer"), FDR irritated his European allies by his anticolonial pronouncements.[84] He won Stalin's support for postwar trusteeships by claiming that "after 100 years of French rule in Indochina, the inhabitants were worse off than they were before."[85] Churchill retorted: "I have not become the King's First Minister in order to preside over the liquidation of the British Empire."[86]

American-British-Soviet diplomacy in the "Grand Alliance" centered on boundaries in Eastern Europe and the timing of an Anglo-American "second front" in Western Europe. Shortly after Pearl Harbor, Stalin said he had no objections to the Atlantic Charter, which he regarded as "algebra," but he preferred "practical arithmetic"—that is, an agreement guaranteeing Soviet boundaries with Eastern Europe as they stood prior to Hitler's attack in 1941.[87] The British seemed inclined to grant what Stalin wanted, but Roosevelt vetoed any secret or public treaty on boundaries "until the war had been won."[88] Content with "a free hand," Stalin noted that "our frontiers" would be "decided by force."[89]

FDR viewed the second front with great urgency. The Soviets, fighting some 200 German divisions and dying by the hundreds of thousands, pleaded for a cross-channel attack as quickly as possible. Assuring V. M. Molotov in May 1942 that Roosevelt wanted to help, Harry Hopkins urged the diplomat to paint a deliberately "gloomy picture of the Soviet position to make the American generals understand the gravity of the situation."[90] Reputed to know only four English words, "yes," "no," and "second front," Molotov was promised a second front that year.[91] Yet the Anglo-American invasion of France did not take place until June 6, 1944, and during the interim, as FDR acknowledged, "the Russian armies are killing more Axis personnel and destroying more Axis material than all other twenty-five United Nations put together."[92] The delay produced serious fissures in the Grand Alliance.

American military leaders urged a cross-channel attack by spring 1943 at the latest, but the British, with Roosevelt's reluctant compliance, decided otherwise. A new plan, Operation TORCH, called for the invasion of French North Africa in November 1942, a decision that led logically to operations against Sicily and Italy in summer 1943 and effectively postponed a cross-channel attack (later dubbed Operation OVERLORD) until 1944. When General Dwight D. Eisenhower learned that the second front had been postponed, he pronounced it the "blackest day."[93] At numerous military conferences in 1942–1943, the Americans always suspected that British fixation on the Mediterranean demonstrated a desire to shore up imperial lifelines and not, as the British claimed, a coherent strategy to bloody Germany on the periphery before launching a full-scale invasion of France. Churchill said he no longer needed to woo the United States; "now that she is in the harem, we talk to her quite differently."[94] British strategy predominated in the two years after Pearl Harbor because England had fully mobilized, whereas America had not, and any combined operation had to depend largely on British troops, shipping, and casualties. U.S. matériel and forces, moreover, were being diverted to the Pacific theater at the insistence of General Douglas MacArthur and Admiral Ernest King. Once

American production and manpower surged by 1943, combined strategy gradually shifted toward Operation OVERLORD. A symbolic clash between the two competing strategies occurred in early 1944. Churchill insisted on an invasion of Rhodes, off the Turkish coast. "No American soldier is going to die on that goddam beach," barked General Marshall.[95] None did.

Roosevelt and Churchill knew how intensely Stalin wanted a second front in France, not in North Africa or Italy. The Red Army had stopped the Germans short of Moscow in 1941, but in summer 1942 German *panzers* drove into the Caucasus oil fields and laid siege to Stalingrad. Churchill told Stalin in August 1942 that a cross-channel attack was planned for spring 1943. Not until June 1943 did the Soviets learn officially that a cross-channel assault would not happen at all that year. Kremlin officials suspected that "the military calculations of both powers are based on the striving for the maximum exhaustion and wearing down" of the USSR "in order to diminish its role in deciding postwar problems."[96]

Tensions increased that summer, when the Soviet Union broke off diplomatic relations with the Polish exile government in London after the Poles asked the International Red Cross to investigate charges that the Russians had murdered more than 10,000 Polish prisoners in the Katyn Forest in 1941. Stalin claimed the victims had escaped "to Manchuria," but Russian archives later revealed that he had ordered the murders.[97] The Soviets also protested when the Allies suspended convoys carrying vital Lend-Lease supplies to Murmansk because of shipping needs in the Mediterranean and Pacific. In August 1943, Stalin complained to Roosevelt about separate peace talks with Italy. The Italians formally surrendered in early September, then declared war against Germany, only to have German forces occupy most of the peninsula before Anglo-American troops could land in force. Britain and the United States, said Stalin, only "informed" the USSR, and "this situation cannot be tolerated any longer."[98]

Stalin had to be "courted, wooed, constantly chatted up," so Churchill urged the Poles not to protest because "nothing you can do will bring them [the dead POWs] back."[99] FDR expedited Lend-Lease supplies to Russia without the usual quid pro quo arrangements. At the Casablanca Conference in January 1943, he announced that "the elimination of German, Japanese, and Italian war power means the unconditional surrender by Germany, Italy, and Japan."[100] Coming shortly after the Anglo-Americans made an agreement with the Vichy French collaborator Admiral Jean-François Darlan to gain French cooperation in North Africa, Roosevelt's "unconditional surrender" announcement signaled to a suspicious Stalin that Britain and the United States would not make a separate German peace with one of Hitler's subordinates. The doctrine brought a modicum of Allied unity by concentrating on a total military victory over Hitler, deferring troublesome peace terms until afterward. "Roosevelt is more friendly to us than any other prominent American," the Soviet ambassador reported in 1943.[101] Nonetheless, one U.S. official compared dealing with the Russians to playing "golf—the more you try, the more you press, and the worse you score."[102]

The foreign ministers' meeting in Moscow (October 19–30) established an Advisory Council for Italy to coordinate Allied policy and a European Advisory Commission to make recommendations for a final peace settlement. The Soviets told Hull that the 200,000 American battle casualties did not amount to much—"we lose that many each day before lunch. You haven't got your teeth in the war yet."[103] Hull replied: "I knew a bully in Tennessee. He used to get a few things his way by being a bully and bluffing other fellows. But he ended up by not having a friend in the world."[104] Suffering from tuberculosis, the seventy-two-year-old Hull got what he wanted: a Declaration of Four Nations on General Security (China included), the first definite commitment to a postwar replacement for the defunct League of Nations.

The Moscow Conference seemed a mere appetizer for "the turning point" at Teheran, Iran, November 28–December 1, 1943.[105] Meeting the Soviet leader for the first time, FDR thought Stalin "very confident, very sure of himself."[106] As one U.S. general recorded, Stalin ("the man of steel, fearless, brilliant mind, quick of thought and repartee, ruthless") emphatically told Churchill and Roosevelt that he favored a firm commitment to OVERLORD as opposed to any Anglo-American operations in the Balkans.[107] When Churchill backed an Adriatic landing, Stalin asked: "Do the British really believe in OVERLORD or are they only saying so to reassure the Russians?" Churchill lamely replied that "it was the duty of the British Government to hurl every scrap of strength across the channel."[108] At a dinner party two nights later Stalin playfully advocated the summary execution of 50,000 German officers, whereupon the prime minister protested that the British would "never tolerate mass execution."[109] When Roosevelt joked that only 49,500 should be shot, Churchill walked out in a huff. The prime minister complained that the "great Russian bear" and the "great American buffalo" were squeezing the "poor little English donkey."[110]

At Teheran, FDR called for a new international organization dominated by the "Four Policemen," who would deal immediately with threats to peace. Stalin agreed but doubted that the new peacekeeping body alone could block future German and Japanese aggression. He suggested the creation of "strong physical points"—bases—near the two nations to deter them.[111] The president said that the United States would supply only air and naval support in the event of a crisis in postwar Europe; troops would have to come from Britain and the USSR.

The conferees also discussed the postwar status of Eastern Europe and Germany. Churchill had proposed moving Poland's boundaries a considerable distance to the west, incorporating German lands. Polish territory in the east would pass to the Soviets to secure their western frontier. Roosevelt acquiesced in these plans for Poland but said he could not "publicly take part in any such arrangement at the present time." The election of 1944 loomed, and "as a practical man," he would not risk the votes of millions of Polish-Americans. Roosevelt also mentioned self-determination for the Baltic states. Stalin bristled. Those states, he insisted, belonged to the Soviet Union. Roosevelt replied that the American people "neither knew nor understood." Stalin shot back that "some propaganda work should be done."[112] But FDR never did explain publicly the differences between the Atlantic Charter and Soviet demands for security in Eastern Europe. On Germany, the conferees debated ways to divide the nation, but they left specific plans for "retribution" against Germany to the future.[113]

Although inconclusive on many points, the Teheran discussions pleased the Americans, especially because Stalin had confirmed that, once Hitler was defeated, the USSR would fight against Japan. Roosevelt suggested that the Soviets obtain a Chinese "free port" at Dairen (Dalian) as a reward. Stalin's preference for OVERLORD

Major Wartime Conferences, 1941–1945

Conference	Date	Participants	Results
Argentia, Newfoundland	August 9–12, 1941	Roosevelt, Churchill	Atlantic Charter
Washington, D.C.	December 22, 1941–January 14, 1942	Roosevelt, Churchill	Combined Chiefs of Staff; priority in war effort against Germany; United Nations Declaration
Washington, D.C.	June 19–25, 1942	Roosevelt, Churchill	North African campaign strategy
Moscow, USSR	August 12–15, 1942	Churchill, Stalin, Harriman	Postponement of second front
Casablanca, Morocco	January 14–24, 1943	Roosevelt, Churchill	Unconditional surrender announcement; campaign against Sicily and Italy
Washington, D.C.	May 12–25, 1943	Roosevelt, Churchill	Scheduling of cross-channel landing for May 1, 1944
Quebec, Canada	August 14–24, 1943	Roosevelt, Churchill	Confirmation of cross-channel landing (OVERLORD)
Moscow, USSR	October 19–30, 1943	Hull, Eden, Molotov	Postwar international organization to be formed; Soviet promise to enter the war against Japan after Germany's defeat; establishment of European Advisory Commission
UNRRA, Washington, D.C.	November 9, 1943	44 nations	Creation of UNRRA
Cairo, Egypt	November 22–26, 1943	Roosevelt, Churchill, Jiang	Postwar Asia: China to recover lost lands; Korea to be independent; Japan to be stripped of Pacific islands
Teheran, Iran	November 27–December 1, 1943	Roosevelt, Churchill, Stalin	Agreement on cross-channel landing and international organization; Soviet reaffirmation of intent to enter the war against Japan
Bretton Woods, New Hampshire	July 1–22, 1944	44 nations	Creation of World Bank and International Monetary Fund
Dumbarton Oaks, Washington, D.C.	August 21–October 7, 1944	U.S., Britain, USSR, China	United Nations Organization
Quebec, Canada	September 11–16, 1944	Roosevelt, Churchill	"Morgenthau Plan" for Germany
Moscow, USSR	October 9–18, 1944	Churchill, Stalin	Spheres of influence in Balkans (percentage scheme)
Yalta, USSR	February 4–11, 1945	Roosevelt, Churchill, Stalin	Polish governmental structure, elections, and boundaries; United Nations; German reparations; USSR pledge to declare war against Japan and to recognize Jiang's government; some Japanese territories to USSR
San Francisco, California	April 25–June 26, 1945	50 nations	United Nations Organization Charter
Potsdam (Berlin), Germany	July 17–August 2, 1945	Truman, Churchill/Attlee, Stalin	German reconstruction and reparations; Potsdam Declaration to Japan; Council of Foreign Ministers established

instead of a Balkans operation also resolved the Anglo-American debate over strategy, thus making Britain a "junior partner" to "its increasingly unsympathetic senior colleague."[114] A peace dictated by the big powers, an international organization, and a weakened postwar Germany signified important Allied cohesion. Stalin also paid tribute to Lend-Lease: "Without these planes from America the war would have been lost."[115] After Teheran the president remarked: "We are going to get along very well with him [Stalin] and the Russian people—very well indeed."[116] The Grand Alliance had temporarily closed some fissures.

In Search of a China Policy

Visiting Washington in December 1941, Winston Churchill was astonished that his hosts "rated the Chinese armies as a factor to be mentioned in the same breath as the armies of Russia."[117] America's infatuation with China, the legacy of the Open Door, the false image of China as "one of the great democracies of the world"—all reinforced an American determination that China should not "take the wrong path, like the Japs," as a British diplomat put it.[118] Some Americans, President Roosevelt included, even envisioned a strong, united China as a postwar client of the United States and a bridge to Asian peoples freeing themselves from colonialism. China's military importance soon diminished, however, as Japanese victories in early 1942 sent the British and Americans reeling. The fall of Burma in May closed the last remaining land route to Chongqing. The Americans wanted to keep China in the war, yet Roosevelt could not send troops needed elsewhere. He sent General Stilwell instead.

Joseph W. Stilwell arrived in Chongqing with the impressive title of Commanding General of the United States Forces in India, Burma, and China. As a junior officer he had served two tours of duty in China, had become fluent in Chinese, and had developed great admiration for the Chinese people. But he thought Jiang an untrustworthy scoundrel. In his diary, the always blunt Stilwell called the British "pig fuckers" and Roosevelt "old Rubberlegs."[119] In Chongqing "Vinegar Joe" sought to train and equip Chinese divisions. With these modernized forces, plus British help from India, Stilwell planned to reopen Burma, increase supplies to China, and thus make the mainland the staging point for the final invasion of Japan.

Stilwell's plans for military reform cut at the heart of the Guomindang system, which one journalist described as combining the "worst features of Tammany Hall and the Spanish Inquisition."[120] The general sputtered in his diary: "Why doesn't the little dummy [Jiang] realize that his only hope is the 30-division plan, and the creation of a separate, efficient, well-equipped, and well-trained force?"[121] Most of Jiang's armies were actually controlled by twelve commanders, several of them virtually autonomous warlords. Before making a decision, the generalissimo always had to ask: "What orders will my generals accept from me?"[122] Jiang actually preferred a U.S. Navy program that trained the Guomindang's secret police in counterguerilla tactics—"a sinister precedent for similar secret service activities" under the Central Intelligence Agency during the Cold War.[123] Some 500,000 of Jiang's best troops were blockading the communists in Yan'an as he waited out the war and mustered his strength for a final showdown with Mao Zedong. Jiang refused to fight in Burma without more Allied support, and the British balked at a Burma campaign. "It is an affectation to pretend that China is a Great Power," said Churchill privately, as he pushed for higher Anglo-American priorities in the Mediterranean.[124] Shortly after the landings in North Africa, Stilwell described his strategic dilemma: "Peanut [Jiang] and I are on a raft, with one sandwich between us, and the rescue ship is heading away from the scene."[125]

The Cairo Conference.   Jiang Jieshi (1887–1975) and Madame Jiang (1897–2003) with Roosevelt and Churchill in November 1943. Although President Roosevelt publicly heaped praise on the Chinese leader, FDR privately told General Stilwell at the Cairo meeting: "If you can't get along with Chiang [Jiang], and can't replace him, get rid of him once and for all. You know what I mean, put someone in you can manage." (Franklin D. Roosevelt Library)

President Roosevelt sought conciliation. To Chongqing he sent personal emissaries to buoy Chinese morale. Jiang received a half-billion dollar loan in 1942, and in 1943 the State Department negotiated a treaty abolishing the U.S. right of extraterritoriality in China. Next Roosevelt hosted Madame Jiang at the White House. The Wellesley College alumna addressed Congress and garnered applause for speaking "not only the language of your hearts, but also your tongue. So coming here . . . I am also coming home."[126] At the Cairo Conference in November 1943, Churchill and Roosevelt met with Jiang and formally pledged the return, after the war, of Taiwan, Manchuria, and other areas "stolen by Japan."[127] In December Congress repealed the exclusion laws, which had prohibited Chinese immigration. FDR talked confidently of postwar China as one of his "Four Policemen" that would keep the peace.

FDR also endorsed a plan of General Claire Lee Chennault, whom the Office of Strategic Services (OSS) thought had "fought the Japs more successfully and dealt with the Chinese more successfully than any other American."[128] The famed "Flying Tiger" claimed that with "a very modest American air force equipped with modern airplanes" he could destroy Japanese air power in "six months."[129] When Chennault's bombers began to draw blood in spring 1944, Japanese armies launched a massive counterattack and nearly overran all U.S. air bases. Jiang then refused to fight. This time Roosevelt made the extraordinary proposal that Jiang give Stilwell unrestricted command of all forces, Chinese and foreign, in China. Roosevelt sent an ultimatum that Stilwell delivered in person. "I handed this bundle of paprika to the Peanut and then sank back with a sigh. The harpoon hit the little bugger right in the solar plexus, and went right through him," Stilwell wrote in September.[130]

Mao Zedong (1893–1976) and Patrick J. Hurley (1883–1963). The Chinese communist leader (second from left) seems less than moved by Ambassador Hurley's dramatic gesture of welcome at Chongqing in 1945. Mao thought Hurley a "clown" who favored Jiang. Hurley once bellowed that Mao was a "motherfucker." The U.S. embassy staff soon called the ambassador "Colonel Blimp" and accused him of "crass stupidity," of being a "stuffed shirt playing at being a great man." The Office of Strategic Services (OSS) in China gave Hurley the code name "Albatross." In November 1945, Hurley suddenly resigned and flung wild charges at Foreign Service Officers who had disagreed with him. (National Archives)

Jiang never forgave Stilwell for such a personal humiliation, and rather than antagonize Jiang further, FDR soon replaced Stilwell.

In November, General Patrick J. Hurley became ambassador to China. A blunt-talking sixty-one-year-old Oklahoma Republican, Hurley concentrated on forming a coalition between Jiang's nationalists and the communists. Even though the Soviets, like the Americans, sent military supplies to Jiang's forces and not to Mao Zedong's communists, the communist-led troops had waged successful guerrilla war against the Japanese. The Yan'an communists had an effective intelligence network that extended behind Japanese lines. Members of the U.S. "Observer Mission" to Yan'an found it easier to talk with Mao and Zhou Enlai "than with the Nationalists. You knew the Nationalists were lying most of the time. The communists never lied," one diplomat recalled.[131] The communist revolutionary leadership, according to Foreign Service Officer John S. Service, "has improved the political, economic and social status of the peasant [and] . . . the Communists are certain to play a large, if not dominant, part in China's future."[132] Because most Americans in China shared the belief that the communists might defeat Jiang in a postwar struggle for power, Hurley's initial efforts at coalition building received unified support.

Hurley's first visit to communist Yan'an, in November 1944, proved a grand spectacle. Hurley alighted from his plane "with enough ribbons on his chest to represent every war . . . in which the United States had ever engaged except possibly Shays's Rebellion."[133] Then he completely discombobulated Zhou Enlai by letting out Choctaw war whoops. Later, after the communists rejected Jiang's offer of a virtually worthless seat on the National Military Council in return for merging the Yan'an army under Nationalist control, Hurley first accepted and then rejected Mao's counterproposal for full coalition and communist sharing in Lend-Lease supplies. Mao concluded that U.S. policy had changed from "uniting with the CCP

[Communists] and pressuring Jiang" to "supporting Jiang, dragging the CCP along [in order to] beat the Japanese."[134]

At this point Hurley began to diverge markedly from the Foreign Service Officers. The ambassador decided on his own that his objective was not to mediate but rather to "sustain" Jiang Jieshi and "to prevent the collapse of the Nationalist government."[135] Hurley had formed these views during an earlier visit to Moscow in August 1944, when Molotov had told him that the Chinese communists "had no relation whatever to Communism" and the Soviets would support Jiang Jieshi.[136] Other American officials in China feared that if denied U.S. aid, Mao would obtain assistance from Moscow and thus create a postwar squabble between the United States and the USSR over China. Contrary to Hurley, these "China hands" believed that the rift between the communists and Guomindang ran deep, and that they could obtain Chinese unity only by dealing with Yan'an separately as a way of pressing Jiang. Preliminary talks had already begun in Yan'an, and in January 1945, the head of the American Military Observers Mission cabled that "Mao and Zhou will be immediately available . . . should President Roosevelt express desire to receive them at White House as leaders of a primary Chinese party."[137] The Soviet representative in Yan'an depicted Mao as "clearly offering himself" to the United States to counterbalance the Soviet Union.[138] Mao hoped that if American forces landed in China, Roosevelt would abandon the "militarily impotent Nationalists" and choose "military cooperation" with the communists.[139]

The predictable explosion occurred when Hurley returned to Washington in February 1945 after the Yalta Conference. In Hurley's absence, the embassy officers at Chongqing sent a telegram to Washington urging the president to inform Jiang "in definite terms that we are required by military necessity to cooperate with and supply the communists against Japan."[140] These young "China hands" did not know that Stalin had reaffirmed future Soviet entry into the Japanese war at Yalta and, accordingly, that the military rationale for a Guomindang-communist coalition now became less urgent. When Hurley read the telegram, he charged that his subordinates had betrayed him. He called on Roosevelt, then about to take his final journey to Warm Springs, and the weary president gave him what he wanted— unqualified backing for Jiang's regime. The embassy diplomats, including John S. Service and John Paton Davies, found themselves transferred out of China as a timid State Department bowed to the demands of the rambunctious ambassador. Mao's communists, increasingly the "most effective organized group in China," reacted to Hurley's "deceptive abandonment" by openly opposing "the mistaken U.S.-China policy."[141]

Roosevelt's wartime policy toward China exposed the disparity between his military strategy and postwar political goals. When it became obvious in 1944 that China would not play a major role in the Japanese war and hardly deserved rank as one of the "Four Policemen," Roosevelt faced a choice. He could accelerate American military activities in China, giving the United States more leverage, and press Jiang to undertake the reforms necessary to maintain him in power. Or he could scale down his political expectations for China and limit military operations there. In fact, Roosevelt "tried to do both and ran the risk of succeeding in neither. He kept talking to and about China as a great power even while he was giving higher and higher military priorities to other military theaters."[142] When the feud between Hurley and the "China hands" ignited, moreover, Roosevelt drifted with existing policy rather than take a hard look at Chinese politics. When FDR could not easily resolve dilemmas, he usually left them to the future.

Bystanders to the Holocaust: Americans and the Murder of the Jews

Another problem finessed for the future was that of the refugees, hundreds of thousands of them Jews from Nazi-occupied territories. Many sought asylum in the United States. Although most Americans denounced Hitler's crusade to preserve the purity of the "Aryan race" through the persecution and extermination of European Jews, translating moral revulsion into effective policy proved difficult. U.S. immigration laws, traditional anti-Semitism, the depression, bureaucratic procedures, wartime fear of spies, and domestic politics shaped the timid American response.

The dark story began in 1933 when Hitler initiated his attacks on "non-Aryans." Throughout the 1930s, the Nazis systematically eliminated Jews from the professions and denied them ownership of businesses. In 1935 the Nuremberg Laws stripped Jews of their civil and political rights, in essence making them stateless beings. Hatemongers plastered signs on buildings: "Whoever buys from a Jew is a traitor."[143] In November 1938 a distraught Jewish youth living in Paris entered the German embassy and killed a German official. Nazi thugs beat up Jews on the streets, sacked and burned synagogues, and destroyed Jewish shops. After this *Kristallnacht* the German government fined its Jewish subjects $400 million and sent 50,000 Jews to concentration camps at Dachau and Buchenwald, detention centers where tortures and executions became common. Roosevelt called the U.S. ambassador home in protest, remarking, "I myself could scarcely believe that such things could occur in a twentieth century civilization."[144]

Such brutal events occurred again in Austria, Czechoslovakia, Poland, Hungary, and elsewhere as the Third Reich overran Europe. Urgent requests for transit to the United States flooded U.S. embassies and consulates. American immigration law, however, prescribed a quota for each country. The National Origins Act of 1924 openly discriminated against immigrants from eastern and southern Europe. The annual quota for Great Britain and Ireland was 83,575, for Germany and Austria 27,370, for Poland 6,000, for Italy 5,500, and for Romania 300. American consular officers also inhibited immigration by strictly enforcing procedures. Potential immigrants had to present documents attesting to their birth, health, financial status, and crime-free background. Many of these papers had to be obtained from uncooperative Nazi officials. Americans also rigidly denied entry to people "likely to become a public charge," which meant that persons could gain a place on the quota list only if they proved that they could support themselves once in the United States. Yet under Nazi law Jews could not take their property or savings from Germany. These restrictions, combined with the evaporation of American jobs during the depression, created a revealing statistic for the period 1933–1938: 174,067 people entered the United States and 221,239 departed, or a net *loss* of 47,172. To have opened America's doors to refugees, in short, would not have inundated a nation of 130 million.

The American Federation of Labor lobbied against any revision in the quotas or visa requirements. Foreigners should not compete with U.S. citizens for scarce jobs—a telling argument during the depression. Longstanding anti–Semitism fed such nativist thought. Father Charles E. Coughlin, a fiery Catholic priest from Michigan, equated Judaism and communism in his radio broadcasts, which reached 3.5 million listeners a week. Even the anti-Nazi diplomat George Messersmith, known as the "Jews' man" in the State Department, opposed the creation of a University of Exile at the New School for Social Research in New York because Jews teaching there might undermine the basic Anglo-Saxon Protestant nature of American society.[145] Opinion polls revealed that more than 80 percent of Americans opposed revision of the quotas to admit European refugees. Congress stood firmly behind the quota system. Already blistered by charges that his domestic reform program was a "Jew Deal," a label attached because he appointed such Jews as Henry Morgenthau, Jr., and Felix Frankfurter to prominent positions, the president played it safe.

Roosevelt mostly left the refugee problem to the Department of State, which "clung to a policy that was timid, rigidly legal, and without innovation."[146] In 1934 the department lobbied successfully against a Senate resolution condemning Germany's treatment of the Jews, fearful that the resolution would spark German comment about the segregation of black Americans. Despite his own wife's Jewish heritage, Secretary Hull opposed boycotts organized by American Jews against German products because such behavior interrupted normal trade. FDR "did quietly manipulate at the margins" with executive orders that combined German and Austrian quotas in 1938–1939 and temporarily relaxed enforcement of the "likely to become a public charge" clause, but many Jews still could not obtain documents.[147] The result: the German-Austrian quota went unfilled in 1933–1938 and 1940–1945. Emanuel Celler, member of Congress from New York, thought the State Department a "heartbeat muffled in protocol."[148]

In 1938 Roosevelt did call for an international conference on refugees, which met in Evian, France, to establish an Intergovernmental Committee on Refugees (IGC). Plans for refugee havens in Latin America and central Africa faltered. Hitler sneered that "the entire democratic world dissolves in tears of pity, but then, in spite of its obvious duty to help, closes its heart to the poor, tortured people."[149] In early 1939 Senator Robert Wagner of New York introduced a bill to allow 20,000 German refugee children to enter above the quota. With revision of the Neutrality Act then pending, the president scratched "File No action FDR," and the bill died in committee.[150]

In mid-1939 the ship *St. Louis* steamed toward Cuba from Hamburg carrying 930 Jewish refugees. Havana officials, however, would not permit them to land without proper visas. The ship then headed for Miami, tailed by Coast Guard cutters. American immigration officials would not let the passengers disembark, so the *St. Louis* had to return to Europe. Its passengers ultimately scattered to Britain, the Netherlands, Belgium, and France after refugee societies pressed their governments.

The plight of Jewish refugees deepened after the outbreak of war. Right-wing newspapers misreported that "Soviets' Christian victims have far outnumbered the

Buchenwald Concentration Camp, Germany. This large Nazi concentration camp held Jews and others who served as slave labor for local factories during World War II. Although Buchenwald did not have death-dealing gas chambers, many prisoners died there from disease, malnutrition, beatings, medical experiments, and executions. Representative Henry M. Jackson (Democrat of Washington), visiting Buchenwald after its liberation, reported: "The atrocities are the most sordid I have ever imagined." Thereafter Jackson became a staunch supporter of Israel. Even General Dwight D. Eisenhower, himself of German descent, wrote to his wife: "The German is a beast. . . . God, I hate the Germans." (Library of Congress)

Nazis' Jewish victims."[151] State Department visa regulations actually tightened. Refugee questions came under the jurisdiction of Breckinridge Long, who feared a potential fifth column of refugees in the United States. He and other officials blocked private efforts to save them and later erected a "wall of silence" about Hitler's genocidal policies.[152] U.S. consuls increasingly rejected visa applications, and ships returned to America half empty. Of Latin American countries, only the Dominican Republic gave asylum to 235 Jewish refugees. When asked to approach Portugal about opening its African colony of Angola, British ambassador Lord Halifax snapped: "Let the Americans do it."[153] Resettlement proposals for British Guiana, French Madagascar, and the Philippines also fell through; Britain restricted the movement of Jews to Palestine.

Reliable reports reached Washington in August 1942 that Germany had begun to exterminate the entire Jewish population in Europe. What followed revealed a large "gap between information and knowledge, even after the information had been received," as one historian puts it.[154] When Jan Karski, a Pole who had witnessed mass executions at Belzec and Treblinka, briefed FDR and Hull, they could not grasp the enormity of the Holocaust. Even Justice Felix Frankfurter, a Zionist, confessed that "he didn't believe what he was being told."[155] Yet the evidence mounted. The Jewish ghetto in Warsaw became a target of German barbarity; by fall 1942 only 70,000 of its 380,000 residents remained, and they desperately rebelled in the spring of the next year. Using Zyklon B gas and large crematoria, German officials murdered a million victims in the most notorious extermination camp at Auschwitz, Poland. Scholars have debated the feasibility of bombing Auschwitz and surrounding rail lines. The U.S. Air Force probably could have destroyed these installations by August 1944, but FDR reportedly vetoed the proposal because it "wouldn't have done any good" and "we would have been accused of destroying Auschwitz [by] bombing these innocent people."[156] The War Department also rejected any "diversions" that would delay victory, seen as the best hope for the Jews. Perhaps only the assassination of Hitler in 1943 or 1944 could have saved hundreds of thousands of Jews—if not more, but the Allies never tried, and attempts by German dissidents failed. By war's end at least 5.5 million Jews in Nazi-occupied Europe had been murdered.

In early 1943 British and U.S. representatives met in Bermuda and concluded that they had done all they could to rescue refugees. As Hull informed FDR: "The unknown cost of moving an undetermined number of persons from an undisclosed place to an unknown destination . . . is . . . out of the question."[157]

Hull never sought to solve the unknowns. Secretary of the Treasury Henry Morgenthau, Jr., did. At his request, Treasury general counsel Randolph Paul submitted the *Report to the Secretary on the Acquiescence of This Government in the Murder of the Jews,* a frank critique of the State Department. "It takes months and months to grant the visa and then it usually applies to a corpse," Paul wrote. The rescue of Jews "is a trust too great to remain in the hands of men indifferent, callous and perhaps hostile," warned Morgenthau.[158] To stop a "boiling pot" from exploding into a nasty scandal, FDR created the War Refugee Board, outside the auspices of the State Department.[159] Using private and public funds, board operatives established refugee camps in Italy, Morocco, Hungary, Sweden, Palestine, and Switzerland. The board thus saved some 200,000 Jews and 20,000 non-Jews by war's end. "What we did was little enough. . . . Late and little," its director concluded.[160] Given the "yawning gap" between the "benevolent rhetoric" of the Roosevelt administration and its actual achievements, Jewish refugees themselves took command of their survival after the war by leading the "exodus" to Palestine and creating the new nation of Israel in 1948.[161] Nearly a half century later, in honor of the Jewish tradition that "to save one life is to save the whole world," the film director Steven Spielberg in *Schindler's List* (1993) underscored what a few heroic individuals might have done to save thousands more.[162]

Planning the Postwar Peace, 1943–1945

The great European military battles of 1944, wherein the Anglo-American D-Day invasion of France in June coincided with a massive Soviet offensive that reached the Vistula River by August, gave postwar planning higher priority. Taking advantage of a "second chance" to overcome isolationism, economic depression, and war, U.S. officials helped launch several international organizations to secure peace and prosperity. Indeed, when FDR saw the Hollywood film *Wilson* (1944), with vivid scenes of his predecessor losing his health and the League, he exclaimed, "By God, that's not going to happen to me."[163] He thus made the Atlantic Charter a more flexible guide than the Fourteen Points. During 1943–1945 the United Nations Relief and Rehabilitation Administration (UNRRA), World Bank, International Monetary Fund, and United Nations Organization took form. Unlike World War I, this time the establishment of postwar institutions would not await the grand deliberations of one conference. Nor would plans to reform Germany.

On November 9, 1943, at the White House, forty-four nations signed the UNRRA agreement for the "relief of victims of war . . . through the provision of food, fuel, clothing, shelter and other basic necessities, medical and other essential services."[164] Some leaders feared that hungry, displaced people might, in desperation, turn to political extremes like communism; food and medicine would help stem postwar political chaos. The Department of State insisted that an American head UNRRA. Operating until mid-1947, UNRRA had a budget of $4 billion, $2.7 billion of which the United States donated. UNRRA dispensed 9 million tons of food; built hundreds of hospitals; prevented epidemics of diphtheria, typhoid, cholera, and venereal disease; revived transportation systems; and cared for at least a million displaced persons. China, Italy, Greece, and Austria absorbed about half of UNRRA's assistance. The other half went to Poland, other Eastern European nations, and the Soviet Union. American critics protested that an international organization was spending taxpayers' dollars to shore up communist governments. In fact, UNRRA tried to avoid politics, refusing to apply political tests to the needy. But Americans expected food aid to bring political returns. When it did not, Washington killed UNRRA in 1947 by cutting off funds.

Two other organizations proved more permanent. From July 1 to 22, 1944, the delegates of forty-four nations negotiated at Bretton Woods in New Hampshire. Working from an Anglo-American proposal, the conferees created the International Bank for Reconstruction and Development (World Bank) and the International Monetary Fund (IMF). The World Bank could extend loans to "assist in the reconstruction and development" of members, to "promote private investment," and to "promote the long-range balanced growth of international trade."[165] The IMF was intended to facilitate world trade by stabilizing the international system of payments through currency loans. After much debate, with critics charging "the worst swindle . . . in the history of the nation," Congress passed the Bretton Woods Agreement Act by margins of 345 to 18 and 61 to 16 in July 1945.[166]

From the start, U.S. economic power dominated the two organizations. Located in Washington, D.C., the World Bank has always had an American as president. The United States also possessed one-third of the votes in the bank by committing $3.175 billion of the total of $9.100 billion initial subscriptions. The United States also held one-third of the votes in the fund. As payer of the "piper," the United States would "call the tune."[167] Britain begrudged U.S. control but joined. The USSR did not join the bank or fund because the Soviets practiced state-controlled trade and finance, feared having to divulge economic data, and could not accept the emphasis on "private" enterprise or U.S. domination. Moscow's absence augured poorly for postwar Allied cooperation.

From August to October 1944, representatives of the United States, Britain, the Soviet Union, and China met in the Dumbarton Oaks mansion in Washington, D.C., to shape the United Nations Organization (UN). Public opinion polls indicated

United Nations Symbol.
A sign of peace for the new
international organization.
(United Nations)

that Americans strongly endorsed a new collective-security organization, and Congress had passed favorable resolutions. The conferees hammered out the UN's charter, providing for a powerful Security Council dominated by the great powers and a weak General Assembly. The Security Council, empowered to use force to settle crises, had five permanent members. When the United States pushed China as a permanent member, Churchill proposed France, calling China a "faggot vote on the side of the United States."[168] All supported the veto because it gave "absolute assurance to each of the Big Five that they will not be asked to use their armed forces in some military enterprise in which they do not concur."[169]

Two other issues also proved contentious: voting procedures in the Security Council and membership in the Assembly. The Soviet Union advocated an absolute veto for permanent members, whereas the United States argued that parties to a conflict should not veto discussion or action. Not until the Yalta Conference in early 1945 did the Allies agree that the veto would apply only to substantive questions such as economic or military sanctions, not to procedural questions. As for membership in the Assembly, Moscow brazenly requested seats for all sixteen Soviet republics. That outlandish request derived from Soviet fears of being badly outnumbered in the Assembly by the British Commonwealth "bloc" and the U.S.–Latin America "bloc." As the historian Robert Hilderbrand has written: "The Big Three saw the defense of their own security, the protection of their own interests, and the enjoyment of the fruits of their victory in the world war as more important than the creation of an international organization to maintain world peace."[170] At Yalta the Soviets accepted a compromise of three votes in the Assembly (see page 205).

Although Republican support for Dumbarton Oaks seemed as likely as "the Sermon on the Mount . . . being endorsed by the Gestapo," Secretary Hull successfully appealed to GOP presidential candidate Thomas E. Dewey to keep international organization out of the political campaign.[171] The resulting nonpartisanship and the inclusion of senators in the Dumbarton Oaks delegation helped the Roosevelt administration build its case for the UN. On January 10, 1945, the influential Senator Arthur H. Vandenberg of Michigan, an arch prewar isolationist expected to insist on reservations much as Lodge had a generation earlier (see pages 94–95), delivered a stunning speech urging U.S. participation in collective security as a curb on aggression. He further advised the major Allies to sign a security treaty to keep the Axis nations permanently demilitarized; he hoped thereby to allay Soviet fears of a revived Germany and hence render Soviet expansion unnecessary. Vandenberg could accept membership in the United Nations because "this is anything but a wild-eyed internationalist dream of a world State."[172]

Roosevelt rewarded Vandenberg by naming him a delegate to the San Francisco Conference of April 25–June 26, 1945, convened to launch the United Nations. The new secretary of state, Edward R. Stettinius, Jr., managed the conference. The 282 delegates did not make decisions without prior approval of the representatives of the big powers, who met each evening in Stettinius's penthouse at the Fairmont Hotel. The United States refused to admit Poland, because its government had not reorganized as required by Yalta (see p. 205). But then the U.S. delegation shocked all by requesting participation for Argentina, which had only declared war against Germany in March. The United States, believing that the Latin American republics

"Uncle Sam Pulls the Lever at the UN." Many foreign commentators believed that the United States dominated the new United Nations Organization. (*Ta Kung Pao* of Shanghai–Hong Kong in *United Nations World*, 1951)

would not vote for three Soviet seats in the Assembly unless Argentina were in-cluded, would not relent. By the lopsided vote of 32 to 4, with 10 abstentions, Argentina won its seat. When African-American leader W. E. B. Du Bois complained that Dumbarton Oaks had disenfranchised 750 million "colored peoples" who could seek equality only "through the philanthropy of masters," Stettinius replied that his "job in San Francisco was to create a charter," not to solve "the negro's question."[173]

Journalists detected an American "steamroller" at San Francisco.[174] So did the Soviet Union, which objected in blunt language. And so did smaller states, which protested their exclusion from key decisions and their impotence in the new United Nations Organization. Fifteen nations abstained in the vote on the veto formula. The UN Charter, as finally adopted, included the Economic and Social Council and the Trusteeship Council. The latter looked to the eventual independence of colonial areas but left the British and French empires intact and permitted the United States to absorb former Japanese-dominated islands in the Pacific (Marianas, Carolines, and Marshalls). *Time* magazine aptly termed the United Nations "a char-ter for a world of power."[175] Indeed, that characterization applied also to Article 51, which permitted regional alliances such as that the United States and Latin Amer-ica outlined in the Act of Chapultepec in March. The United States would "have our cake and eat it too"—freedom of action in the Western Hemisphere and an in-ternational organization to curb aggression in Europe.[176] Amid memories of 1919, the Senate approved the UN Charter on July 28, 1945, by a vote of 89 to 2.

While these plans for the victors unfolded, the debate over the fate of a defeated Germany centered on a "constructive" policy (rehabilitation, economic unity, and in-tegration into the European economy) or a "corrective" policy (strict reduction of in-dustry, large reparations, and a decentralized economy).[177] At the center of the

Henry Morgenthau, Jr. (1891–1967). A long-time friend of Franklin D. Roosevelt, Morgenthau served as FDR's secretary of the treasury (1933–1945) but often participated in the making of foreign policy. A deft bureaucratic infighter, Morgenthau pressed during World War II for an active U.S. stance against the genocide in Europe and for harsh peace terms against the Nazis after the war. Although successful in creating the War Refugee Board, he failed to impose the Morgenthau Plan on defeated Germany. (Franklin D. Roosevelt Library)

controversy stood Treasury Secretary Morgenthau, who proposed a "corrective" plan designed to despoil Germany of industries having potential military value. In early September 1944 he had advised Roosevelt that the coal- and iron-rich Ruhr area should be stripped of industry. At the Quebec Conference in September 1944, the president gained Churchill's reluctant signature to a memorandum "eliminating the war-making industries in the Ruhr and in the Saar" and "converting Germany into a country primarily agricultural and pastoral in its character."[178] Churchill apparently had approved the Morgenthau scheme in exchange for the promise of a postwar American loan.

Leaked to the press, the Morgenthau Plan caused "a hell of a hubbub" because Secretaries Hull and Stimson both opposed a harsh economic peace.[179] "Prosperity in one part of the world helps to create prosperity in other parts of the world," Stimson advised. "Poverty in one part of the world induces poverty in other parts."[180] Germany had to revive to spur postwar prosperity in Western Europe. Using his special access to the president, Morgenthau persuaded Roosevelt in September to approve an interim Joint Chiefs of Staff directive (JSC/1067), which ordered denazification and demilitarization, the dismantling of iron, steel, and chemical industries, a controlled economy, and limited rehabilitation. The new president, Harry S. Truman, however, thought "Morgenthau didn't know sh— from apple butter" and began a gradual retreat from the Morgenthau Plan and JCS/1067, especially after he eased Morgenthau out of office in July 1945.[181] By the end of the war, then, U.S. plans for postwar Germany remained unsettled.

Compromises at the Yalta Conference

Near the end of the European war Churchill, Roosevelt, and Stalin met once again, at the Livadia Palace near Yalta in the Crimea. Meeting from February 4 to 11, 1945, the Big Three, after considerable compromise, made important decisions for the war against the Axis and for the postwar configuration of international affairs, the Yalta "system." After the conclave, Yalta aroused heated controversy akin to the Munich Conference. To some critics, Yalta symbolized a "sell-out" to the Soviets, an example of Roosevelt's coddling of the communist menace. Worn low by the illness that would take his life two months later, critics have claimed, Roosevelt gave in to a guileful Stalin and failed to use superior U.S. economic power to force concessions. The president's detractors also pointed an accusing finger at Alger Hiss, a U.S. official at Yalta who later went to jail on a perjury charge for testifying that he had not served Moscow as a spy. Although one among hundreds of decrypted Soviet cables from World War II now available suggests that Hiss was "probably" an agent named "Ales," no definitive evidence has yet turned up in former Soviet (now Russian) archives.[182]

The Big Three entered the conference with different goals. Britain sought a zone in Germany for France, a curb on Soviet expansion into Poland, and protection of the British Empire. The Soviet Union wanted reparations to rebuild its devastated economy, possessions in Asia, influence over Poland, and a Germany so weakened that it could never again march eastward. The United States wanted a U.S.-managed United Nations, a Soviet declaration of war against Japan, a reduction of communist political power in Poland, and elevation of China to big-power

"The Two Thousand Yard Stare."
Combat artist Tom Lea captures the zombie-like demeanor of a young marine who has endured too much. Lea painted this portrait during the battle for Peleliu in the Palau Islands (September–November 1944), in which 2,000 Americans were killed and more than 8,500 were wounded. Some 11,000 Japanese also died. The journalist Ernie Pyle also described the same "look of dullness, eyes that look without seeing, eyes that see without conveying any image to the mind. It's a look that is the display room for what lies behind it—exhaustion, lack of sleep, tension for too long, weariness that is too great, fear beyond fear, misery to the point of numbness, a look of surpassing indifference to anything anybody can do." (U.S. Army, Center of Military History)

status. Although each participant suspected the others' motives, "a high incidence of consensus was reached at the Conference."[183]

The "consensus" at Yalta reflected the military and diplomatic realities of the moment. Britain and the United States had delayed the opening of the second front until June 6, 1944, and then, from mid-December to mid-January 1945—just before Yalta—Anglo-American troops bogged down in the Battle of the Bulge in Belgium. Asked to take pressure off the western front by stepping up the Soviet winter offensive in the east, Stalin obliged on January 12. "I am most grateful to you for your thrilling message," a relieved Churchill replied.[184] Throughout 1944 the Red Army had cut deeply into German lines on the eastern front. Indeed, by the time of the Yalta Conference, Russian soldiers were sweeping westward along a wide front through Poland, Czechoslovakia, and Hungary, with Romania already freed from German clutches. The Red Army, not Roosevelt, gave the Soviet Union influence in Eastern Europe.

Asian military realities also shaped diplomatic decisions. Japan was fiercely battling American forces in Luzon and the Marianas, and still had 1 million soldiers in China, 2 million in the home islands, and another 1 million in Manchuria and Korea. With some 54 percent of American battle deaths in the Pacific occurring in the last year of the war, both sides fought with increasing savagery. Japanese authorities depicted Americans as "albino apes" and "carnivorous beasts," and film audiences cheered when Popeye the Sailor punched out the "Jap-pansy" navy in *You're a Sap, Mr. Jap* (1942).[185] "We shot prisoners in cold blood, wiped out hospitals, strafed

The Yalta Conference. In this meeting with Churchill, a haggard Roosevelt betrayed symptoms of the cardiovascular disease that would kill him in April 1945. Robert H. Ferrell's *The Dying President* (1998), utilizing the records and diaries of FDR's heart doctor, concludes that the president was "arguably as incapacitated as President Wilson had been, a shell of his former self, unable to keep abreast of the great decisions he had left to the end of the war, too ill or too arrogant to inform his successor about them." (Franklin D. Roosevelt Library)

lifeboats," one U.S. war correspondent admitted, and "boiled the flesh off enemy skulls to make table ornaments for sweethearts, or carved their bones into letter openers."[186] One U.S. lieutenant in the Philippines campaign told his men: "Shoot them first, and then question them later."[187] Japan's suicidal *Kamikaze* resistance on Okinawa still lay in the future. In short, Roosevelt and Churchill still needed Soviet help to defeat Japan.

The Soviets strained to make their guests comfortable at Yalta, offering servants and lavish meals. The meetings proceeded amicably, although Stalin once became ruffled when he took Roosevelt's name for him—"Uncle Joe"—as ridicule rather than as a term of endearment, and Molotov wore his customary stone face. At the final dinner, Churchill informed Stalin that with general elections scheduled soon "I shall have to speak very harshly about the Communists. . . . You know we have two parties in England." "One party is much better," Stalin deadpanned.[188]

For Churchill, Poland counted as "the most urgent reason for the Yalta Conference."[189] The British and Americans recognized the conservative exiled government in London, led by Stanislas Mikolajczyk. Moscow recognized the communist-led provisional government in Lublin. Repeatedly reminding everyone that Germany had attacked the Soviet Union through the Polish corridor twice in the century, Stalin insisted not only on Allied support for the Lublin government but also "a mighty, free and independent Poland" that included part of Germany (with the Oder-Neisse line in the west) but gave Russia Polish territory in the east (the Curzon line).[190] Churchill and Roosevelt opposed a communist Poland but had little bargaining power because Soviet troops occupied much of the country. Roosevelt said he had several million Polish voters back home who demanded a more representative Polish government. Stalin remained adamant.

Compromises emerged. The Curzon line was temporarily set as the eastern boundary. The Yalta agreement stipulated also that the provisional government should be "reorganized on a broader democratic basis with the inclusion of democratic leaders from Poland itself and from Poles abroad," with "free and unfettered elections" held as soon as possible.[191] Roosevelt wanted the first election in Poland "to be like Caesar's wife. I did not know her but they said she was pure." "They said that about her," Stalin corrected, "but in fact she had her sins."[192] Until such an election the communist Lublin group would comprise the nucleus of the Polish government. When later asked about the Polish agreement by Assistant Secretary of State A. A. Berle, FDR replied: "I didn't say it was good, Adolf, I said it was the best I could do."[193] Churchill swallowed the bitter pill, in part because Stalin assured him that the Soviet Union would not intrude in British-dominated Greece, then rocked by civil war. Compromises on other issues also made the Polish settlement tolerable.

Britain reluctantly accepted Germany's dismemberment so long as France received a zone of occupation. Noting that Roosevelt had said that American troops would not long remain in Europe, Churchill cited France as a bulwark against Germany. Stalin grudgingly accepted a French zone. On reparations, which the Soviets vigorously demanded, Britain and America agreed on German reparations "in kind" and the creation of a Reparations Commission, but they refused to set a figure until they determined Germany's ability to pay.

The conferees reached compromises on Asia and the Pacific. By February 1945, the Japanese were reeling northward as General MacArthur's amphibious forces pressed them from the southwest Pacific and Admiral Chester Nimitz's carrier-backed amphibians forced them to retreat across the central Pacific. The home islands were under sustained attack by U.S. heavy bombers, but the Americans still feared very high casualties in the planned invasion of Japan. Soviet intervention and a Red Army thrust across Manchuria would draw off defenders and materially reduce American casualties during the landings in Kyushu and Honshu. A grateful FDR won Stalin's promise to declare war against Japan two or three months after Hitler's defeat, enough time to transfer his troops to Asia. Stalin also agreed to sign a pact of friendship and alliance with Jiang Jieshi's regime, not with Mao Zedong's rival communists. In return, the Soviet Union regained what Russia had lost in 1905: the southern part of Sakhalin, Dairen (Dalian) as a free port, Port Arthur as a naval base, and joint operation of Manchurian railroads. The Soviet Union also obtained the Kurile Islands. On these issues the Big Three never consulted China, a clear loser at Yalta.

The Allies reached agreement on the United Nations Organization. Dumbarton Oaks had added France and China as "permanent" members of the Security Council, possessing the veto. Although Churchill thought China would vote with the United States, FDR and Stalin expected France to support British positions. Thus outnumbered in the council, Stalin asked at Yalta for membership of all sixteen Soviet republics in the General Assembly. He also insisted on an absolute veto in the council on all issues, procedural and substantive. Roosevelt agreed to three Soviet seats in the General Assembly, and Stalin shelved the veto for procedural questions. The conference also reaffirmed national self-determination in the "Declaration of Liberated Europe," which Stalin signed because "we can fulfill it in our own way. What matters is the correlation of forces."[194]

Yalta marked the "dawn of the new day," said Harry Hopkins. "We were absolutely certain that we had won the first great victory of the peace."[195] "Poor

Neville Chamberlain believed he could trust Hitler," Churchill commented after Yalta. "He was wrong. But I don't think I'm wrong about Stalin."[196] Roosevelt, Churchill, and Stalin had deftly played the great-power game of building spheres of influence. Each went home with some major objectives satisfied. Although they had postponed some tough questions and written some vague language, they had faced military and political realities. None of the leaders, of course, had consulted weaker nations on whom the Yalta decisions weighed heavily.

Later, when the Yalta agreements collapsed, critics ignored U.S. gains from the conference—broadening of the Polish government, a UN voting formula, delay of the reparations question, the significant Soviet pledge to enter the Pacific war—and charged that FDR had conceded too much in "saying 'nice kitty' to Stalin."[197] The United States might have used reconstruction aid as a diplomatic weapon, but such tactics would have spoiled the spirit of compromise at Yalta, which served American interests. Churchill recognized the necessity of conciliation: "What would have happened if we had quarrelled with Russia while the Germans still had three or four hundred divisions on the fighting front?"[198] Indeed, "had the Grand Alliance fallen apart at Yalta or immediately after because Roosevelt refused to recognize Russia's security needs," the historian Lloyd C. Gardner has written, postwar Europe might have descended into "a series of civil wars or possibly an even darker Orwellian condition of localized wars along an uncertain border."[199] The spheres-of-influence agreement, the Yalta leaders believed, would serve as a transition to peace.

To Each Its Own: Allied Divergence and Spheres of Influence

Throughout World War II, the Allies attempted to protect and, if possible, extend their spheres of influence. Churchill's defense of the British Empire, from Argentia through Yalta, reflected this characteristic of wartime diplomacy. "If the Americans want to take Japanese islands," he remarked, "let them do so with our blessing. . . . But 'Hands Off the British Empire' is our maxim."[200] Some Americans suspected that Churchill's constant postponement of the second front and his strategies for North Africa and Italy aimed at preserving British interests. His advice to U.S. military leaders, near war's end, that they drive quickly to Berlin, and if possible even farther into Eastern Europe, to beat the Soviets there, also aroused suspicion.

The Churchill-Stalin percentage agreement of October 1944 was emblematic. In early 1944 Churchill concluded that "we are approaching a showdown with the Russians" in the Balkans, and he called for a frank settlement. Roosevelt agreed to a trial division of authority. Instability plagued Romania, where Soviet troops dominated; Yugoslavia, where independent communist Josip Tito and his Partisans were emerging; Bulgaria, where an indigenous communist movement grew with Soviet influence; and Greece, a British-dominated area plagued by civil war. At an October conference with Stalin in Moscow, Churchill scribbled some percentages on a piece of paper. In Romania, Russia would get 90 percent of the power and Britain 10 percent; in Greece, Britain would enjoy 90 percent and Russia 10 percent; in Yugoslavia

The Allies Push Japan Back, 1942–1945

NORTH POLE

UNION OF SOVIET SOCIALIST REPUBLICS

ALASKA

UNITED STATES

OUTER MONGOLIA

MANCHURIA

Attu *ALEUTIAN IS.*

Kiska

1943

C H I N A

Beijing

Yan'an

Chongqing

JAPAN

Tokyo

Nagasaki Hiroshima

Midway Is. *HAWAIIAN IS.* Oahu

1942

Ledo

Imphal

1944–45

Burma Rd.

Mandalay Lashio

BURMA

Kunming

(TAIWAN) FORMOSA

Okinawa

Iwo Jima

Marcus

Pearl Harbor

I N D I A

1945

1945

1945

Wake

Hong Kong

THAILAND

FR. INDO-CHINA

1944

Manila

PHILIPPINE ISLANDS

Leyte

MARIANAS IS.

Tinian I.

Guam

P A C I F I C   O C E A N

1944

Ceylon

MARSHALL IS.

EQUATOR

1944

MALAYA

Singapore

SUMATRA

BORNEO

CAROLINE   IS.

1944–1945

GILBERT IS.

1943

I N D I A N   O C E A N

NETHERLANDS EAST INDIES

CELEBES

JAVA

NEW GUINEA

1943

SOLOMON IS. Guadalcanal

1942

1942

NEW HEBRIDES

TIMOR

Coral Sea

1942

1942

AUSTRALIA

Norman Adams

Japanese-held areas

Limit of Japanese conquest

and Hungary, a 50–50 split; and in Bulgaria, 75 percent would go to Russia and 25 percent to "others." Churchill "pushed this across to Stalin," who "took his blue pencil and made a large tick upon it."[201] Stalin liked this arrangement that granted the Soviets predominant influence in Eastern Europe: "The United Kingdom had India and the Indian Ocean in her sphere of influence; the United States, China and Japan; the USSR had nothing."[202] Roosevelt did not protest.

Soviet support for the Lublin government, demands for Polish and Romanian territory, efforts to exclude the United States and Britain from the joint control commissions in Eastern Europe, and seizure of German-operated property underscored the growing power of the Soviet Union among its neighbors. Soviet handling of the Warsaw uprising of July 31, 1944, alarmed Western observers. With Soviet armies some twelve miles from Warsaw, the Polish underground gambled and attacked German forces, hoping that Soviet troops would dash to their aid. But the Red Army stopped. Over the next two months the Germans leveled half the city and killed 166,000 Poles, most of whom owed allegiance to the exiled government in London. "Confident that the alliance will not break up over Poland," Stalin dropped supplies to the besieged city in September but refused at first to let Allied planes land at Soviet airfields after carrying supplies to Warsaw.[203] He called the uprising a "reckless and fearful gamble" by "power-seeking criminals."[204] Whatever the military realities—Stalin claimed that his soldiers were meeting heavy German resistance—many charged that Stalin abetted the slaughter of the Warsaw Poles. Ambassador to the Soviet Union W. Averell Harriman called the Soviets a "world bully" who "misinterpreted our generous attitude toward them."[205] The liberation of Poland by Soviet forces in 1944 ultimately fixed a communist regime in Warsaw—one that Roosevelt's compromises at Yalta essentially recognized.

The United States itself was expanding and building spheres of influence during the war. Having drawn most of the Latin American states into a defense community at the Lima Conference (1938) and in the Declaration of Panama (1939), the United States moved to drive German investments and influence from the Western Hemisphere. The Export-Import Bank loaned $130 million to twelve Latin American nations in 1939–1941 to help them oust German businesses, cut trade with the Axis, stabilize their economies, and bring them into alignment with U.S. foreign policy. During the war, the United States increased its stake in Bolivian tin, helped build Brazilian warships, expanded holdings in Venezuelan oil, acquired bases in Panama and Guatemala, and nourished the Dominican dictatorship of Rafael Trujillo. Despite warnings that "lethal toys" might be used "for a very different purpose than they were intended," the U.S. military dispensed arms and training to Latin American forces.[206] During the war Latin America shipped 50 percent of its exports, largely much needed raw materials, to the United States. At the Rio de Janeiro Conference (January 15–28, 1942), all but Chile and Argentina voted to break diplomatic relations with the Axis nations. In March 1945, in the Act of Chapultepec, the United States and Latin America took another step toward a regional defense alliance. In early 1945 Secretary Stettinius unwittingly reminded many of Yankee dominance: "The United States looks upon Mexico as a good neighbor, a strong upholder of democratic traditions in this hemisphere, and a country we are proud to call our own."[207] Even Canadian prime minister W. L. Mackenzie King worried that Washington intended to take Canada "out of the orbit of the British Commonwealth and into their own orbit."[208]

U.S. leaders also sought to direct events in postwar Italy and Asia. They essentially excluded the Soviets from the Italian surrender agreement in 1943 and denied

Pacific Fleet Carriers. After Japan's attack on Pearl Harbor ended the U.S. Navy's addiction to the irresistible masculine sensuality of battleships, a major reason for U.S. victories in the Pacific and for a substantial American role in postwar Asia was the air superiority provided by aircraft carriers. The light aircraft carrier *Langley* and the heavy carrier *Ticonderoga* led this Pacific fleet task group. From 1940 to June 1945, the U.S. Navy grew from 1,099 to 50,759 vessels, including 8 new battleships, 92 new aircraft carriers, and 43,255 new landing craft. (Navy Department, National Archives)

them a role in the control commission. Some American officials recognized that Italy, where predominant power rested in their hands, set a precedent for later Soviet predominance in Romania and Hungary. U.S. officials also insisted on holding the conquered Japanese islands in the Pacific and in unilaterally governing postwar Japan. Hoping to "steer this great unwieldy barge . . . into the right harbor," the British Ministry of Information, in its propaganda efforts in the United States, emphasized the common theme of "white men in tough places" to encourage Americans to "see themselves as a global caretaker of many subject races."[209] With U.S. forces spearheading the counteroffensive in the southwest Pacific, Australian prime minister John Curtin acknowledged allegiance "to America, free of any pangs to our traditional links with the United Kingdom."[210] Thus did Washington envisage closer postwar ties with India, Australia, New Zealand, and Jiang's China.

In the Middle East the United States also expanded. In 1939 the Arabian-American Oil Company (Aramco) began to tap its 440,000-square-mile concession in Saudi Arabia's rich oil fields. By 1944 U.S. corporations controlled 42 percent of the proved oil reserves of the Middle East, a nineteenfold increase since 1936. In 1944, American companies, with Washington's encouragement, applied for an oil concession in Iran, then occupied by British and Soviet troops and used as a corridor for Lend-Lease shipments to the Soviet Union. This request touched off a three-cornered competition for influence in the heretofore British-dominated country. When Roosevelt promised in 1944 not to deprive the British of their traditional stakes in the Middle East, Churchill tartly thanked him "for your assurances about no sheeps' eyes at our oil fields in Iran and Iraq. Let me reciprocate by giving you fullest assurance that we have no thought of trying to horn in upon your interests or property in Saudi Arabia."[211]

Harry Hopkins (1890–1946).
A progressive reformer, the Iowa-born Hopkins became one of Franklin D. Roosevelt's most trusted New Deal administrators and advisers. During World War II, Roosevelt sent Hopkins on special missions and utilized his counsel at international conferences, including Yalta. When he traveled to Moscow for Truman in May 1945, Hopkins was suffering from the cancer that would cause his death within months. (Courtesy of FDR Library)

On a global scale, then, the Big Three jockeyed for power. "Spheres of influence do in fact exist," concluded Roosevelt's State Department in early 1945. "In view of the actual Eastern European sphere and the Western Hemispheric bloc (Act of Chapultepec), we are hardly in a position to frown upon . . . measures designed to strengthen the security of nations in other areas of the world."[212]

With Germany's surrender on May 8, 1945, the Third Reich collapsed in the rubble of bombed-out Berlin. President Harry S. Truman quickly ended Lend-Lease aid to the Soviet Union (he soon partially restarted it), thereby stirring up a hornet's nest in Moscow. With this issue and the Polish question troubling Soviet-American relations, the president sent Harry Hopkins to see Stalin in May, to "use diplomatic language or a baseball bat."[213] An irate Stalin warned Hopkins that the Americans had made "a fundamental mistake" in halting Lend-Lease "as pressure on the Russians in order to soften them up."[214] Hopkins expressed growing U.S. dismay about Stalin's obstruction of the Yalta agreement on elections in Poland—a symbol of Soviet-American trust. Stalin would not permit the anti-Soviet London Poles (the most likely winners of an election) to govern postwar Poland, because Poland had twice "served as a corridor for German attacks. . . . It is therefore in Russia's vital interest that Poland should be both strong and friendly."[215] Ambassador Harriman also reported to Truman that Stalin wondered "why we should want to interfere with Soviet policy in a country like Poland, which he considers so important to the USSR's security, unless we have some ulterior motive."[216] Stalin did agree that a few ministries should go to non-Lublin Poles. He also assured Hopkins, as promised at Yalta, that the Soviet Union would enter the war against Japan and respect Jiang's government. Truman then noted in his diary: "I'm not afraid of Russia. . . . They've always been our friends and I can't see any reason why they shouldn't always be."[217]

The Potsdam Conference and the Legacy of the Second World War

As the war in Asia wound down and the occupation of Germany commenced, the Big Three gathered near Berlin for the Potsdam Conference (July 16–August 2, 1945). Truman's first impression of his Soviet counterpart was favorable: "I can deal with Stalin. He is honest—but smart as hell."[218] That impression soon changed. Truman wrote his family that "you never saw such pigheaded people as are the Russians."[219] Harriman called the Russians "those barbarians."[220] Churchill took a liking to the new president, whom he described as a "man of exceptional character and ability with . . . simple and direct methods of speech, and a great deal of self-confidence and resolution."[221] Reports of the successful explosion of an atomic device in New Mexico had "tremendously pepped up" the president.[222]

By Potsdam, American intentions toward postwar Germany had moved a good distance from the Morgenthau Plan and JCS/1067. Reconstruction now became the watchword. U.S. officials saw Germany as a vital link in the economic recovery of Western Europe. When Germany came up for discussion, Truman thus resisted dismemberment and large reparations. The final Potsdam accord stated that Germany would be managed by military governors in four zones, treated as "a single economic unit," and permitted a standard of living higher than its low level of 1945.[223] Transportation, coal, agriculture, housing, and utilities industries were to be rehabilitated. As for reparations, desired by the Soviet Union for both revenge and the recovery of its hobbled economy, Stalin had to settle for an agreement that each occupying power would take reparations from its own zone and that the USSR would get some industrial equipment from the Western zones. In return, the Soviet Union would send food to the other three zones. The diplomat George F. Kennan described the reparations deal as "catch as catch can."[224]

When Churchill complained about no elections in Poland, Stalin mentioned the British domination of Greece. They did agree, however, to set the Oder–Neisse line as Poland's temporary western boundary, thereby granting Poland large chunks of German territory. The Soviet Union agreed to accept Italy as a member of the United Nations. The big powers also established the Council of Foreign Ministers to continue discussion on issues not resolved at Potsdam: peace treaties for the former German satellites; withdrawal of allied troops from Iran; postwar control of the Dardanelles; internationalization of inland waterways; and disposition of Italian colonies. Stalin promised again to enter the war against Japan, but U.S. officials also learned that they possessed a new atomic weapon that might force Japan's surrender. Britain and the United States issued the "Potsdam Declaration," demanding Japan's unconditional surrender and threatening it with destruction.

The seemingly minor issue of waterways became for Truman a test of Soviet intentions. At Potsdam he pushed for an international authority to govern the 800-mile-long Danube River, which wound its way through several countries, including the Soviet Union, to the Black Sea. Essentially combining two traditional American principles—free navigation and the Open Door—the proposal antagonized Moscow, which countered with a commission limited to those states through which the river flowed. Molotov pressed: "If it was such a good rule why not apply it to the Suez?"[225] The president simplistically concluded: Stalin's attitude on waterways showed "what he was after. . . . The Russians were planning world conquest."[226] For his part, Stalin interpreted London and Washington as wanting to "force us" to accept "their plans on questions affecting Europe and the world. Well, that's not going to happen."[227]

Potsdam left the world much as it had found it—divided and devastated. World War II ended on August 14, 1945, with Japan's surrender after Soviet intervention and two atomic bombs decimated Hiroshima and Nagasaki (see pages 222–227). But peace remained elusive because of the war's vast social, economic, and political dislocations in Europe and Asia. World War II claimed the lives of at least 55 million people—27 million in the USSR. Poland and Germany lost 6 million each; Yugoslavia suffered at least 1.6 million dead; Britain lost 400,000. The toll mounted in Asia, too: 15 million Chinese, 4 million Indonesians, 3 million Japanese, 1 million Vietnamese, 120,000 Filipinos, and more. A total of 405,395 Americans died fighting in the war—approximately one American death for every fifteen Germans and fifty-three Russians. Indeed, "more women lost their lives in the Soviet armed forces than men in the American military."[228] Millions of displaced persons became separated from their homelands. Transportation systems, communications networks, and factories shut down. Cities entered the postwar era as rubble heaps, including the German city of Dresden, which Allied planes had punished in February

Bombed-out French Town, 1944. Europe lay in ruins at the end of the war, and American help became essential to the reconstruction effort. (U.S. Office of War Information, National Archives)

1945 in a merciless attack of questionable necessity. The incendiary "area raid" on Tokyo in March killed at least 83,793 civilians and left more than one million homeless.[229] When General Dwight D. Eisenhower flew into the Soviet Union after V-E Day, he "did not see a house standing between the western borders of the country and the area around Moscow."[230] An unprecedented reconstruction task lay ahead.

With the imperial powers in disarray, their Asian colonies, encouraged by Japan during the waning days of the war, became rebellious. Without the necessary resources and manpower to curb the nationalist revolutions, the European empires began to crumble. The Dutch battled their Indonesian subjects; France fought the Vietnamese in Indochina; Britain reluctantly began its exit from Burma, India, and Ceylon (Sri Lanka).

The rise of the Soviet Union as a major international player counts as another legacy of World War II. Thanks to Hitler, said Truman at Potsdam, "we shall have a Slav Europe for a long time to come."[231] The Soviets resented any intimation that they should not have an influential voice in postwar questions. Reeling from heavy wartime losses, they asked for much—"like a greedy kid, never satisfied," noted one U.S. official.[232] "Whoever occupies a territory imposes on it his own social system," said Stalin. "It cannot be otherwise."[233]

The USSR rose, Britain declined, China floundered, and the United States galloped. "Unbombed, unoccupied, and relatively unbloodied," America had its economy moving in high gear at war's end.[234] The U.S. gross national product jumped from $90.5 billion in 1939 to $211.9 billion in 1945. Observers spoke of an American production miracle. By the end of the war the United States had become "the global workshop and banker, umpire and policeman, preacher and teacher."[235]

Alone in a position to provide the capital and goods for recovery abroad, Washington felt flushed with power. "Instead of being looked upon as . . . an ordinary, common, American official," a Foreign Service Officer recalled, "people just practically fawned in front of us."[236] Americans looked forward to creating the stable world order that had eluded them between the two world wars. State Department official Dean Acheson observed that the "great difference in our second attempt . . . is the wide recognition that peace is possible only if countries work together and prosper together. That is why the economic aspects are no less important than the political aspects of the peace."[237] Through the war years the United States had constructed institutions—UNRRA, World Bank, International Monetary Fund, United Nations—to ensure that peace.

The war also wrought changes in the decisionmaking process in the United States. Government agencies handling national security matters ballooned in size. The defense establishment became more active in making diplomatic choices. "Sabotage . . . obstruction, understaffing, and rival ambitions" distracted a State Department too often bypassed by FDR.[238] The war spawned a large espionage establishment, beginning with the Office of Strategic Services (OSS) in 1942 and culminating in the Central Intelligence Agency (CIA) five years later. The president centralized decisionmaking in the White House, while Congress neglected its foreign-affairs prerogatives in the constitutional system and applauded bipartisanship. Another consequence of the war was an enlarged "military-industrial complex," a partnership between business executives eager for lucrative defense contracts and military brass eager for increased budgets. The recruitment of universities bequeathed a long-term legacy. Science professors had developed the atomic bomb at the Universities of Chicago and California, Berkeley. Princeton received grants for ballistics research. Postwar federal subsidies flowed to colleges for arms development, research on Soviet studies, and intelligence gathering.

"The world was fluid and about to be remade" in 1945, the journalist Theodore White remembered.[239] After the setbacks of depression and war, the historian Allan Nevins wrote, "the old self-confident America is coming into its stride again."[240] But it did so now as the world's strongest power.

FURTHER READING FOR THE PERIOD 1939–1945

Biographical studies include Rudy Abrahamson, *Spanning the Century* (1992) (Harriman); Conrad Black, *Franklin Delano Roosevelt* (2003); James M. Burns, *Roosevelt: The Soldier of Freedom* (1970); Dik Alan Daso, *Hap Arnold and the Evolution of American Air Power* (2000); Kenneth R. Davis, *FDR* (1972–1993); Martin Gilbert, *Winston S. Churchill* (1983); Waldo H. Heinrichs, *American Ambassador* (1966) (Grew); John Huston, *American Air Power Comes of Age* (2002) (Hap Arnold); Warren F. Kimball, *The Juggler* (1991) (FDR); Joseph P. Lash, *Roosevelt and Churchill, 1939–1941* (1976); William Lasser, *Benjamin V. Cohen* (2002); John Lukacs, *Churchill* (2002); George McJimsey, *Harry Hopkins* (1987); Forrest C. Pogue, *George C. Marshall* (1963–1987); Edward J. Renehan, *The Kennedys at War* (2002); Neil Smith, *America's Empire* (2003) (Isaiah Bowman); Mark A. Stoler, *George Marshall* (1989); and works cited in Chapters 4 and 5.

FDR's health is the subject of Robert H. Ferrell, *The Dying President* (1998) and *Ill-Advised* (1992); and Bert E. Park, *The Impact of Illness on World Leaders* (1986).

For the United States and Europe, 1939–1941, and debates at home, see Mark Chadwin, *The Hawks of World War II* (1968); J. Garry Clifford and Samuel R. Spencer, Jr., *The First Peacetime Draft* (1986); Wayne S. Cole, *America First* (1953) and *Roosevelt and the Isolationists* (1983); James V. Compton, *The Swastika and the Eagle* (1967); Justus Doenecke, *The Battle Against Intervention* (1997) and *Storm on the Horizon* (2001); Max Paul Freidman, *Nazis and Good Neighbors* (2003); Richard F. Hill, *Hitler Attacks Pearl Harbor* (2002); Warren F. Kimball, *The Most Unsordid Act* (1969) (Lend-Lease); James R. Leutze, *Bargaining for Supremacy* (1977); Mark A. Lowenthal, *Leadership and Indecision* (1988); John Lukacs, *Five Days in London: May 1940* (2001); Thomas Mahl, *Desperate Deception* (1998); Thomas Mahnken, *Uncovering Ways of War* (2002); Norman Moss, *Nineteen Weeks* (2003); Arnold A. Offner, *The Origins of the Second World War* (1975); David L. Porter, *The Seventy-Sixth Congress and World War II, 1939–1940* (1979); Anthony Read and David Fisher, *The Deadly Embrace* (1989) (Nazi-Soviet Pact); David Reynolds, *The Creation of the Anglo-American Alliance, 1937–1941* (1982) and *From Munich to Pearl Harbor* (2001); James C. Schneider, *Should America Go to War?* (1989); Ivo Tasovac, *American Policy and Yugoslavia, 1939–1941* (1999); D. C. Watt, *How War Came* (1989); and Theodore A. Wilson, *The First Summit* (1991).

For the advent of war with Japan, see the books by Borg and Okamoto, Burns and Bennett, Feis, and Neu cited in Chapter 5; Michael A. Barnhart, *Japan Prepares for Total War* (1987); Robert J. C. Butow, *Tojo and the Coming of the War* (1961) and *The John Doe Associates* (1974); Hilary Conroy and Harry Wray, eds., *Pearl Harbor Reexamined* (1990); Henry G. Gole, *The Road to Rainbow* (2003); Akira Iriye, *The Origins of the Second World War in Asia and the Pacific* (1987); Walter LaFeber, *The Clash* (1997); Peter Lowe, *Great Britain and the Origins of the Pacific War* (1977); Martin V. Melosi, *The Shadow of Pearl Harbor* (1977); James Morley, ed., *The Fateful Choice: Japan's Advance into Southeast Asia, 1939–1941* (1980), ed., *The Final Confrontation* (1994), and, ed., *Japan's Road to the Pacific War: Japan's Negotiations with the United States, 1941* (1994); Gordon W. Prange, *At Dawn We Slept* (1981) and *Pearl Harbor* (1986); Emily Rosenberg, *A Date Which Will Live* (2003); Paul W. Schroeder, *The Axis Alliance and Japanese-American Relations, 1941* (1958); Youli Sun, *China and the Origins of the Pacific War* (1993); Nicholas Tarling, *A Sudden Rampage* (2001); Jonathan Utley, *Going to War with Japan* (1984); and Roberta Wohlstetter, *Pearl Harbor* (1962).

Allied relations and postwar planning are explored in David Alvarez, *Secret Messages* (2000) (codebreaking); Rick Atkinson, *An Army at Dawn* (2002); Alan H. Bath, *Tracking the Axis Enemy* (1998); Anthony Beevor, *The Fall of Berlin* (2002); Edward M. Bennett, *Franklin D. Roosevelt and the Search for Victory* (1990); Michael Beschloss, *The Conquerors* (2002); Douglas Brinkley and David Facey-Crowther, eds., *The Atlantic Charter* (1994); Susan A. Brewer, *To Win the Peace* (1997); Mark J. Conversino, *Fighting with the Soviets* (1997); R. D. Cuff and J. L. Granatstein, *Canadian-American Relations in Wartime* (1975); Robert Dallek, *Franklin D. Roosevelt and American Foreign Policy* (1979); Robert A. Divine, *Second Chance* (1967) and *Roosevelt and World War II* (1969); Alan P. Dobson, *U.S. Wartime Aid to Britain* (1986); Robin Edmonds, *The Big Three* (1991); Lloyd C. Gardner, *Spheres of Influence* (1993); Patrick Hearden, *Architects of Globalism* (2002); George C. Herring, Jr., *Aid to Russia, 1941–1946* (1973); Gary R. Hess, *The United States at War, 1941–1945* (1986); Gregory Hooks, *Forging the Military-Industrial Complex* (1990); Barry M. Katz, *Foreign Intelligence* (1989); Warren F. Kimball, ed., *America Unbound* (1992); Gabriel Kolko, *The Politics of War* (1968); Eric Larrabee, *Commander in Chief* (1987); Ralph Levering, *American Opinion and the Russian Alliance* (1976); Vojtech Mastny, *Russia's Road to the Cold War* (1979); Christopher Mauch, *The Shadow War Against Hitler* (2003); Steven M. Miner, *Between Churchill and Stalin* (1988) and *Stalin's Holy War* (2003); Samuel Eliot Morison, *Strategy and Compromise* (1958); Williamson Murray and Allen Millett, *A War to Be Won* (2000); Arnold A. Offner and Theodore A. Wilson, eds., *Victory in Europe 1945* (2000); William O'Neill, *A Democracy at War* (1993); Septimus Paul, *Nuclear Rivals* (2002); Robert Persico, *Roosevelt's Secret War* (2001); R. C. Raack, *Stalin's Drive to the West, 1938–1945* (1995); David Reynolds et al., eds., *Allies at War* (1994) and *Rich Relations: The American Occupation of Britain* (1995); Ronald Schaffer, *Wings of Judgment* (1985) (U.S. bombing); Stephen C. Schlesinger, *Act of Creation* (2003) (UN); Michael S. Sherry, *Preparing for the Next War* (1977); Bradley F. Smith, *Sharing Secrets with Stalin* (1996); Gaddis Smith, *American Diplomacy During the Second World War* (1985); Mark A. Stoler, *The Politics of the Second Front* (1977) and *Allies and Adversaries* (2000); Dwight W. Tuttle, *Harry L. Hopkins and Anglo-American-Soviet Relations, 1941–1945* (1983); Gerhard L. Weinberg, *A World at Arms* (1994); Steve Weiss, *Al-*

lies in Conflict (1996); Randall B. Woods, *A Changing of the Guard* (1990) (U.S.-Britain); and Llewellyn Woodward, *British Foreign Policy in the Second World War* (1970–1971).

For the Churchill-Roosevelt relationship and assessments of Churchill, see John Charmley, *Churchill's Grand Alliance* (1995); Martin Gilbert, *Winston S. Churchill* (1983–1986); Roy Jenkins, *Churchill* (2001); Warren F. Kimball, *Forged in War* (1997); and Keith Sainsbury, *Churchill and Roosevelt at War* (1994).

Big Three summit meetings are treated in Russell O. Buhite, *Decisions at Yalta* (1986); Diane Shaver Clemens, *Yalta* (1970); Keith Eubank, *Summit at Teheran* (1985); Keith Sainsbury, *The Turning Point* (1985) (Cairo and Teheran); and John L. Snell, ed., *The Meaning of Yalta* (1956).

For the creation of new international organizations, see Thomas Campbell, *Masquerade Peace* (1973) (UN); Robert C. Hilderbrand, *Dumbarton Oaks* (1990); Townsend Hoopes and Douglas Brinkley, *FDR and the Creation of the U.N.* (1997); and Greg Schild, *Bretton Woods and Dumbarton Oaks* (1995).

Propaganda and the mobilizing of public opinion in the era of World War II are studied in Steven Casey, *Cautious Crusade* (2001); Nicholas Cull, *Selling War* (1995) (British propaganda in the United States); Clayton Koppes and Gregory Black, *Hollywood Goes to War* (1987); Clayton Laurie, *The Propaganda Warriors* (1996); George H. Roeder, Jr., *The Censored War* (1993); Holly C. Shulman, *The Voice of America* (1991); Richard Steele, *Propaganda in an Open Society* (1985); and Michael S. Sweeney, *Secrets of Victory* (2000).

For the Pacific theater, China, and decolonization, see Wesley M. Bagby, *The Eagle-Dragon Alliance* (1992); David D. Barrett, *Dixie Mission* (1970); Günter Bischof and Robert Dupont, eds., *The Pacific War Revisited* (1997); Herbert P. Bix, *Emperor Hirohito and the Making of Modern Japan* (2001); Russell D. Buhite, *Patrick J. Hurley and American Foreign Policy* (1973); Francis B. Cogan, *Captured* (1999); John W. Dower, *War Without Mercy* (1986); T. Fujitani et al., *Perilous Memories: The Asia-Pacific War(s)* (2001); Akira Iriye, *Power and Culture* (1981); E. J. Kahn, Jr., *The China Hands* (1975); Xiaoyuan Liu, *A Partnership for Disorder* (1996) (China); William R. Louis, *Imperialism at Bay* (1978) (decolonization); Greg Robinson, *By Order of the President* (2001); Mark Roehrs and William Renzl, *World War II in the Pacific* (2003); Michael Schaller, *The U.S. Crusade in China, 1938–1945* (1978); John J. Sbrega, *Anglo-American Relations and Colonialism in East Asia* (1983); Peter Schrijvers, *The GI War Against Japan* (2002); Sterling Seagrave and Peggy Seagrave, *The Yamato Dynasty* (2001); Michael M. Sheng, *Battling Western Imperialism* (1997); Leon V. Sigal, *Fighting to the Finish: The Politics of War Termination in the United States and Japan, 1945* (1988); Ronald H. Spector, *Eagle Against the Sun* (1984); Christopher Thorne, *Allies of a Kind* (1977) and *The Issue of War* (1985); Barbara Tuchman, *Stilwell and the American Experience in China, 1911–1945* (1971); Frederick Wakeman, Jr., *Spymaster: Dai Li and the Chinese Secret Service* (2003); Odd Arne Westad, *Cold War and Revolution* (1993) (China); and Thomas Zeiler, *Unconditional Defeat* (2003).

For wartime relations with Latin America, see works cited in Chapter 5; Michael J. Francis, *The Limits of Hegemony* (1977) (Argentina and Chile); Michael Grow, *The Good Neighbor Policy and Authoritarianism in Paraguay* (1981); Frank D. McCann, Jr., *The Brazilian-American Alliance, 1937–1945* (1973); Stephen R. Niblo, *War, Diplomacy, and Development* (1995) (Mexico); María Emilia Paz, *Strategy, Security, and Spies* (1997) (Mexico); David Rock, ed., *Latin America in the 1940s* (1994); Charlie Witham, *Bitter Rehearsal* (2002) (British West Indies); and Randall B. Woods, *The Roosevelt Foreign Policy Establishment and the "Good Neighbor"* (1980) (Argentina).

For U.S. interest in the Middle East and oil, consult Irvine H. Anderson, *Aramco, the United States, and Saudi Arabia* (1981); Philip J. Baram, *The Department of State in the Middle East, 1919–1945* (1978); Aaron D. Miller, *Search for Security* (1980) (Saudi Arabia); and Michael B. Stoff, *Oil, War, and American Security* (1980).

The Holocaust and refugee problem are recounted in Robert H. Abzug, *Inside the Vicious Heart* (1985); Yehuda Bauer, *Jews for Sale?* (1994) and *Rethinking the Holocaust* (2001); Richard Breitman and Alan M. Kraut, *American Refugee Policy and European Jewry* (1987); Richard Breitman, *Official Secrets* (1998); Christopher Browning, *The Path to Genocide* (1992); Leonard Dinnerstein, *America and the Survivors of the Holocaust* (1982); Henry L. Feingold, *Bearing Witness* (1995) and *Politics of Rescue* (1970); Martin Gilbert, *Auschwitz and the Allies* (1981); Walter Laqueur, *The Terrible Secret* (1980); Deborah E. Lipstadt, *Beyond Belief* (1993); Louise London, *Whitehall and the Jews, 1933–1948* (2002); Arthur D. Morse, *While Six Million Died* (1968); William E. Nawyn, *American Protestantism's Response to Germany's Jews and Refugees* (1982); Verne Newton, ed., *FDR and the Holocaust* (1995); Arnold Offner, *American Appeasement* (1964); Monty N. Penkower, *The Jews Were Expendable* (1983); Brian M. Rigg, *Hitler's Jewish Soldiers* (2002); David Wyman, *The Abandonment of the Jews*

(1984), *Paper Walls* (1968), and ed., *The World Reacts to the Holocaust* (1996); and David S. Wyman and Rafael Medoff, *A Race Against Death* (2002).

See also the General Bibliography, the following notes, and Robert L. Beisner, ed., *Guide to American Foreign Relations Since 1600* (2003).

For comprehensive coverage of foreign-relations topics, see the articles in the four-volume *Encyclopedia of U.S. Foreign Relations* (1997), edited by Bruce W. Jentleson and Thomas G. Paterson.

NOTES TO CHAPTER 6

1. Quoted in Theodore A. Wilson, *The First Summit* (Lawrence: University Press of Kansas, 1991), p. 98.
2. FDR quoted in Warren F. Kimball, *Forged in War* (New York: Morrow, 1997), p. 98.
3. Elliott Roosevelt, *As He Saw It* (New York: Duell, Sloan, and Pearce, 1946), p. 33.
4. Winston S. Churchill, *The Grand Alliance* (Boston: Houghton Mifflin, 1950), p. 431.
5. Quoted in Robert E. Sherwood, *Roosevelt and Hopkins* (New York: Harper & Brothers, 1948), p. 236.
6. Harold Nicolson, *Diaries and Letters* (New York: Atheneum, 1966–1968; 3 vols.), II, 385.
7. Churchill quoted in David Reynolds, "Churchill, Roosevelt, and the Wartime Anglo-American Alliance, 1939–1945," in William Roger Louis and Hedley Bull, eds., *The "Special Relationship"* (New York: Oxford University Press, 1986), p. 40.
8. David Reynolds, *Rich Relations* (New York: Random House, 1995), p. 438
9. Quoted in "Briefly Noted," *New Yorker*, LXXIX (December 22 and 29, 2003), 157
10. Diary entry, August 14, 1941, in John W. Huston, ed., *American Air Power Comes of Age: General Henry H. "Hap" Arnold's World War II Diaries* (Maxwell Air Force Base: Air University Press, 2002, 2 vols.), I, 234.
11. David Reynolds, *The Creation of the Anglo-American Alliance, 1937–1941* (Chapel Hill: University of North Carolina Press, 1981), p. 195.
12. David Reynolds, "The Origins of the Two 'World Wars,' " *Journal of Contemporary History*, XXXVIII (January 2003), 40.
13. Quoted in Raymond Esthus, "President Roosevelt's Commitment to Britain to Intervene in a Pacific War," *Mississippi Valley Historical Review*, L (June 1963), 31.
14. Cordell Hull, *Memoirs* (New York: Macmillan, 1948; 2 vols.), II, 975–976.
15. *Foreign Relations, 1941* (Washington, D.C.: Government Printing Office, 1958), I, 368–369.
16. James MacGregor Burns, *Roosevelt: The Soldier of Freedom* (New York: Harcourt Brace Jovanovich, 1970), p. 550.
17. Quoted in Holly C. Shulman, *The Voice of America* (Madison: University of Wisconsin Press, 1990), p. 72.
18. *Foreign Relations, 1941*, I, 378.
19. Quoted in William H. McNeill, *America, Britain, & Russia* (London: Oxford University Press, 1953), p. 41.
20. Quoted in Lloyd C. Gardner, *Spheres of Influence* (Chicago: Ivan R. Dee, 1993), p. 241.
21. Quoted in Burns, *Soldier*, p. 609.
22. Mark A. Lowenthal, *Leadership and Indecision* (New York: Garland, 1988), p. 633.
23. Ian Jacob quoted in Martin Gilbert, *Winston S. Churchill* (Boston: Houghton Mifflin, 1983), p. 1161.
24. Quoted in Wilson, *First Summit*, p. 182.
25. Quoted in J. Garry Clifford, "Juggling Balls of Dynamite," *Diplomatic History*, XVII (Fall 1993), 636; Charles De Gaulle quoted in Deborah Kisatsky, "The United States, the French Right, and American Power in Europe, 1946–1958," *The Historian*, LX (Spring 2003), 627.
26. Anthony Eden, *The Reckoning* (Boston: Houghton Mifflin, 1965), p. 433.
27. Samuel I. Rosenman, ed., *Public Papers . . . of Franklin D. Roosevelt, 1939* (New York: Macmillan, 1938–1950; 13 vols.), VIII, 463.
28. Charles Tobey to James Richardson, September 28, 1939, Tobey Papers, Dartmouth College Library, Hanover, N.H.
29. Quoted in John M. Blum, *From the Morgenthau Diaries: Years of Urgency* (Boston: Houghton Mifflin, 1965), p. 91.
30. Quoted in B. Mitchell Simpson, *Admiral Harold R. Stark* (Columbia: University of South Carolina Press, 1989), p. 99.
31. Rosenman, *Public Papers, 1940*, IX, 263.
32. FDR and Willkie quoted in David Reynolds, *From Munich to Pearl Harbor* (Chicago: Ivan R. Dee, 2001), p. 101.
33. FDR quoted in Robert A. Divine, *Foreign Policy and U.S. Presidential Elections, 1940–1948* (New York: New Viewpoints, 1974), pp. 82–83.
34. Warren F. Kimball, ed., *Churchill & Roosevelt* (Princeton: Princeton University Press, 1984; 3 vols.), I, 108.
35. Rosenman, *Public Papers, 1940*, IX, 607.
36. *Ibid.*, pp. 640–643.
37. Quoted in George C. Herring, Jr., *Aid to Russia, 1941–1946* (New York: Columbia University Press, 1973), p. 4.
38. Quoted in Nicholas Cull, *Selling War* (New York: Oxford University Press, 1995), p. 75.
39. Elizabeth Dilling quoted in June Melby Benowitz, *Days of Discontent* (Dekalb: Northern Illinois University Press, 2002), p. 43.
40. Quoted John E. Moser, *Twisting the Lion's Tail* (New York University Press, 1999), p. 143.
41. Quoted in Warren F. Kimball, *The Most Unsordid Act* (Baltimore: Johns Hopkins University Press, 1969), p. 153.
42. *Congressional Record*, LXXVII (March 8, 1941), 2097.
43. Breckinridge Long Diary, May 12, 1941, Long Papers, Library of Congress, Washington, D.C.
44. Claude Wickard Diary, May 2, 1941, Wickard Papers, Franklin D. Roosevelt Library, Hyde Park, N.Y.
45. Quoted in Calvin L. Christman, "Franklin D. Roosevelt and the Craft of Strategic Assessment," in Williamson Murray and Allen R. Millett, eds., *Calculations* (New York: Free Press, 1992), p. 256.
46. Harry Hopkins quoted in Mark A. Stoler, *Allies and Adversaries* (Chapel Hill: University of North Carolina Press, 2000), p. 53.

47. August 19, 1941, CAB 65/19, War Cabinet Records 84, Public Record Office, London.

48. Rosenman, *Public Papers, 1941, X*, 438, 439.

49. Quoted in Max Paul Friedman, "United States-Colombian Relations, 1939–1945," *The Americas, LVI* (April 2000), 563.

50. Quoted in Wayne S. Cole, *America First* (Madison: University of Wisconsin Press, 1953), p. 163.

51. FDR quoted in Joseph Lash Diary, February 5, 1940, Joseph Lash Papers, Roosevelt Library.

52. Quoted in Steven Casey, *Cautious Crusade* (New York: Oxford University Press, 2001), p. 44.

53. James C. Schneider, *Should America Go to War?* (Chapel Hill: University of North Carolina Press, 1989), p. 219.

54. Josiah Bailey to I. M. Meekins, September 6, 1941, Bailey Papers, Duke University Library, Durham, N.C.

55. Quoted in Edward M. Bennett, "Joseph C. Grew," in Richard Dean Burns and Edward M. Bennett, eds., *Diplomats in Crisis* (Santa Barbara: ABC-CLIO, 1974), p. 78.

56. Harold L. Ickes, *The Secret Diary of Harold L. Ickes* (New York: Simon & Schuster, 1953; 3 vols.), *III*, 567.

57. Casey, *Cautious Crusade*, p. 39.

58. Quoted in Charles E. Neu, *The Troubled Encounter* (New York: Wiley, 1975), p. 168.

59. *Foreign Relations, 1940* (Washington, D.C.: Government Printing Office, 1955), *IV*, 602.

60. Quoted in Christopher Thorne, *The Issue of War* (New York: Oxford University Press, 1985), p. 22; Jonathan Marshall, *To Have and Have Not* (Berkeley: University of California Press, 1995), p. 251.

61. Quoted in Herbert Feis, *The Road to Pearl Harbor* (New York: Atheneum, 1967), p. 206.

62. *Magic* report quoted in Timothy Wilford, "British and Commonwealth Intelligence Before Pearl Harbor," *Intelligence and National Security, XVII* (Winter 2002), 137.

63. Jonathan Utley, *Going to War with Japan, 1937–1941* (Knoxville: University of Tennessee Press, 1984), p. 156.

64. Osami Nagano quoted in Herbert P. Bix, *Emperor Hirohito and the Making of Modern Japan* (New York: HarperCollins, 2000), p. 202.

65. Ickes, *Secret Diary, III*, 346.

66. Quoted in James C. Thomson, Jr., "The Role of the Department of State," in Dorothy Borg and Shumpei Okamoto, eds., *Pearl Harbor as History* (New York: Columbia University Press, 1973), p. 101.

67. Quoted in Kimball, *Forged in War*, p. 118.

68. Quoted in Walter LaFeber, *The Clash* (New York: Norton, 1997), p. 208.

69. Quoted in Nicholas Tarling, *A Sudden Rampage* (Honolulu: University of Hawai'i Press, 2001), p. 77.

70. Quoted in Thorne, *Issue of War*, p. 10.

71. Youli Sun, *China and the Origins of the Pacific War* (New York: St. Martin's, 1993), p. 155.

72. Charles Tansill, *Back Door to War* (Chicago: Regnery, 1952).

73. Quoted in Carl Boyd, *Hitler's Japanese Confidant* (Lawrence: University Press of Kansas, 1993), p. 36.

74. Roberta Wohlstetter, *Pearl Harbor* (Stanford: Stanford University Press, 1962), p. 387.

75. Rosenman, *Public Papers, 1941, X*, 514.

76. Arthur H. Vandenberg, Jr., ed., *The Private Papers of Senator Vandenberg* (Boston: Houghton Mifflin, 1952), p. 1.

77. *Time* quoted in George H. Roeder, Jr., *The Censored War* (New Haven: Yale University Press, 1993), p. 153.

78. Gerhard Weinberg, "Franklin Delano Roosevelt and Adolf Hitler," in Elizabeth Glaser and Hermann Wellenreuther, eds., *Bridging the Atlantic* (New York: Cambridge University Press, 2002), p. 215.

79. Samuel E. Morison, *Strategy and Compromise* (Boston: Little, Brown, 1958), p. 25.

80. Quoted in Todd Bennett, "Culture, Power, and *Mission to Moscow*," *Journal of American History, LXXXVIII* (September 2001), 504.

81. Quoted in Roeder, *Censored War*, p. 129.

82. Quoted in Geoffrey Perret, *Days of Sadness, Years of Triumph* (Baltimore: Penguin, 1973), p. 197.

83. Quoted in Warren F. Kimball, "Churchill and Roosevelt," *Prologue, VI* (Fall 1971), 181.

84. Quoted in Paul Orders, "Franklin Roosevelt and European Colonialism," in David Ryan and Victor Pungong, eds., *The United States and Decolonization* (New York: St. Martin's, 2000), p. 72.

85. Quoted in Mark Bradley, "Culture, Diplomacy, and the Origins of the Cold War in Vietnam," in Christian G. Appy, ed., *Cold War Constructions* (Amherst: University of Massachusetts Press, 2000), p. 21.

86. Quoted in Warren F. Kimball, *The Juggler* (Princeton: Princeton University Press, 1991), p. 136.

87. Eden, *Reckoning*, pp. 336–337.

88. Quoted in Stephen M. Miner, *Between Churchill and Stalin* (Chapel Hill: University of North Carolina Press, 1988), p. 217.

89. Quoted in David Reynolds, "The Wartime Alliance and Post-War Transitions, 1941–1947," *The Historical Journal, XLV* (Winter 2002), 217.

90. Quoted in Oleg Rzheshevsky, ed., *War and Diplomacy: Documents from Stalin's Archives* (Amsterdam, Neth.: Harwood, 1996), p. 120.

91. Quoted in Casey, *Cautious Crusade*, p. 88.

92. Quoted in Herbert Feis, *Churchill, Roosevelt, Stalin* (Princeton: Princeton University Press, 1957), p. 42.

93. Quoted in Rick Atkinson, *An Army at Dawn* (New York: Henry Holt, 2002), p. 18.

94. Quoted in Kimball, *Forged in War*, p. 130.

95. Quoted in Mark A. Stoler, *George Marshall* (Boston: Twayne, 1989), p. 106.

96. Maxim Litvinov quoted in Geoffrey Roberts, "Litvinov's Lost Peace, 1941–1946," *Journal of Cold War Studies, IV* (Spring 2002), 32.

97. Quoted in Steven Merritt Miner, *Stalin's Holy War* (Chapel Hill: University of North Carolina Press, 2003), p. 107.

98. Quoted in Robert Beitzell, *The Uneasy Alliance* (New York: Knopf, 1972), p. 159.

99. D. C. Watt, *Succeeding John Bull* (Cambridge: Cambridge University Press, 1984), p. 1; Winston S. Churchill, *The Hinge of Fate* (Boston: Houghton Mifflin, 1950), p. 759.

100. Quoted in Raymond G. O'Connor, *Diplomacy for Victory* (New York: Norton, 1971), p. 52.

101. Maxim Litvinov quoted in John Lewis Gaddis, *We Now Know* (New York: Oxford University Press, 1997), p. 15.

102. General John Dean quoted in Stoler, *Allies and Adversaries*, p. 187.

103. Memorandum of Conversation with Cordell Hull, November 30, 1943, "Black Notebooks," Box 1, Arthur Krock Papers, Princeton University Library, Princeton, N.J.

104. Hull, *Memoirs, II*, 1297.

105. Keith Sainsbury, *The Turning Point* (New York: Oxford University Press, 1985), p. 307.

106. Quoted in Keith Eubank, *Summit at Teheran* (New York: Morrow, 1985), p. 248.

107. Quoted in John W. Huston, ed., *American Air Power Comes of Age: General Henry H. "Hap" Arnold's World War II Diaries* (Maxwell Air Force Base, Alabama: Air University Press, 2002, 2 vols.), *II*, 90–91.

108. Quoted in Mark A. Stoler, *The Politics of the Second Front* (Westport, Conn.: Greenwood Press, 1977), p. 149.

109. Churchill, *Hinge of Fate*, p. 374.

110. Quoted in David Reynolds, "The Erosion of British Influence," in Charles Brower, ed., *World War II in Europe: The Final Year* (New York: St. Martin's, 1998), p. 40.

111. Quoted in Robert Dallek, *Franklin D. Roosevelt and American Foreign Policy* (New York: Oxford University Press, 1979), p. 435.

112. *Foreign Relations, Cairo and Teheran* (Washington, D.C.: Government Printing Office, 1961), pp. 594–595.

113. Churchill quoted in Sainsbury, *Turning Point*, p. 300.

114. Kevin Smith, *Conflict over Convoys* (Cambridge, Eng.: Cambridge University Press, 1996), p. 239.

115. Quoted in Burns, *Soldier*, p. 411.

116. Rosenman, *Public Papers, 1943, XII*, 558.

117. Churchill, *Hinge of Fate*, p. 133.

118. FDR quoted in George McJimsey, *The Presidency of Franklin D. Roosevelt* (Lawrence: University Press of Kansas, 2000), p. 225; Nevile Butler quoted in LaFeber, *The Clash*, p. 231.

119. Quoted in Jonathan Spence, *To Change China* (Boston: Little, Brown, 1969), p. 236; Christopher Thorne, "Indochina and Anglo-American Relations, 1942–1945," *Pacific Historical Review, XLIV* (February 1976), 76.

120. Theodore White quoted in LaFeber, *The Clash*, p. 232.

121. Theodore H. White, ed., *The Stilwell Papers* (New York: William Sloane Associates, 1948), p. 157.

122. Quoted in Robert P. Newman, *Owen Lattimore and the "Loss" of China* (Berkeley: University of California Press, 1992), p. 70.

123. Frederick Wakeman, Jr., *Spymaster: Dai Li and the Chinese Secret Service* (Berkeley: University of California Press, 2003), p. 307.

124. Quoted in Sainsbury, *Turning Point*, p. 156.

125. Quoted in Herbert Feis, *The China Tangle* (Princeton: Princeton University Press, 1953), p. 51.

126. Quoted in T. Christopher Jesperson, *American Images of China, 1931–1949* (Stanford: Stanford University Press, 1996), p. 94.

127. Quoted in Akira Iriye, "Japan Against the ABCD Powers," in Akira Iriye and Warren Cohen, eds., *American, Chinese, and Japanese Perspectives on Wartime Asia, 1931–1949* (Wilmington, Del.: Scholarly Resources, 1989), p. 233.

128. Quoted in Maochun Yu, *OSS in China* (New Haven: Yale University Press, 1996), p. 66.

129. Quoted in Martha Byrd, *Chennault* (Tuscaloosa: University of Alabama Press, 1987), p. 174.

130. White, *Stilwell Papers*, p. 333.

131. John Melby quoted in Nancy Bernkopf Tucker, ed., *China Confidential* (New York: Columbia University Press, 2001), p. 27.

132. *Foreign Relations, 1944* (Washington, D.C.: Government Printing Office, 1967), *VI*, 631–632.

133. David D. Barrett, *Dixie Mission* (Berkeley: University of California, 1970), p. 56.

134. Quoted in Michael M. Sheng, *Battling Western Imperialism* (Princeton: Princeton University Press, 1997), p. 94.

135. Quoted in Feis, *China Tangle*, p. 213.

136. Quoted in Russell D. Buhite, *Patrick J. Hurley and American Foreign Policy* (Ithaca: Cornell University Press, 1973), p. 152.

137. Quoted in Carolle J. Carter, *Mission to Yenan* (Lexington: University Press of Kentucky), p. 147.

138. Pyotr Vladimirov quoted in Wesley M. Bagby, *The Eagle-Dragon Alliance* (Newark: University of Delaware Press, 1992), p. 122.

139. Michael H. Hunt, *The Genesis of Chinese Communist Foreign Policy* (New York: Columbia University Press, 1996), p. 156.

140. Quoted in Feis, *China Tangle,* p. 269.

141. War Department report quoted in Kathleen Hartford and Stephen M. Goldstein, "Perspectives on the Chinese Communist Revolution," in Jeffrey M. Wasserstrom, ed., *Twentieth-Century China: New Approaches* (New York: Routledge, 2003), p. 141; Mao quoted in Chen Jian, *Mao's China and the Cold War* (Chapel Hill: University of North Carolina Press, 2001), p. 24.

142. Burns, *Soldier*, p. 545.

143. Quoted in Moshe Gottlieb, "The Berlin Riots and Their Repercussions in America," *American Jewish Historical Quarterly, LIX* (March 1970), 306.

144. Quoted in Cyrus Adler and Aaron M. Margalith, *With Firmness in the Right* (New York: American Jewish Committee, 1946), p. 381.

145. Quoted in Jesse H. Stiller, *George S. Messersmith* (Chapel Hill: University of North Carolina Press, 1987), p. 123.

146. Arnold A. Offner, *American Appeasement* (New York: Norton, 1976 [c. 1969]), p. 92.

147. Richard Breitman quoted in Verne Newton, ed., *FDR and the Holocaust* (New York: St. Martin's, 1996), p. 14.

148. Quoted in Henry L. Feingold, *Politics of Rescue* (New Brunswick, N.J.: Rutgers University Press, 1970), p. 19.

149. Quoted in Friedman, *No Haven*, p. 83.

150. Quoted in David Wyman, *Paper Walls* (Amherst: University of Massachusetts Press, 1968), p. 97.

151. *New York Daily News* quoted in Justus D. Doenecke, *Storm on the Horizon* (New York: Rowman & Littlefield, 2000), p. 212.

152. Quoted in Henry L. Feingold, *Bearing Witness* (Syracuse University Press, 1995), p. 173.

153. Quoted in A. J. Sherman, *Island Refuge* (Berkeley: University of California Press, 1973), p. 207.

154. Yehuda Bauer, *Rethinking the Holocaust* (New Haven: Yale University Press, 2001), p. 221.

155. Quoted in Henry L. Feingold, "Courage First and Intelligence Second: The American Secular Jewish Elite, Roosevelt, and the Failure to Rescue," in Michael Marrus, ed., *The Nazi Holocaust: Bystanders to the Holocaust* (Westport, Conn.: Meckler, 1989; 9 vols.) *II*, 781.

156. John J. McCloy quoting FDR in Michael Beschloss, *The Conquerors* (New York: Simon & Schuster, 2002), p. 66.

157. Quoted in Arthur D. Morse, *While Six Million Died* (New York: Random House, 1968), p. 63.

158. Quoted *ibid.,* pp. 93, 95.

159. Morgenthau quoted in David S. Wyman and Rafael Medoff, *A Race Against Death* (New York: The New Press, 2002), p. 48.

160. Quoted in David Wyman, "The United States," in Wyman, ed., *The World Reacts to the Holocaust* (Baltimore: Johns Hopkins University Press, 1996), p. 707.

161. Feingold, *Bearing*, p. 8.

162. Bauer, *Rethinking*, p. 222.

163. Quoted in Keith W. Olson, "Franklin D. Roosevelt, the Ghost of Woodrow Wilson, and World War II," in Silvo Hietanen, ed., *The Road to War* (Tampere, Finland: University of Tampere, 1993), p. 62.

164. Quoted in George Woodbridge et al., *The History of the United Nations Relief and Rehabilitation Administration* (New York: Columbia University Press, 1950), *I*, 4.

165. *Treaties and Other International Acts* (Washington, D.C.: Government Printing Office, 1946), series 1501–1502.

166. Congresswoman Jesse Sumner quoted in Randall B. Woods, *A Changing of the Guard* (Chapel Hill: University of North Carolina Press, 1990), pp. 236–237.

167. *Manchester Guardian* quoted in Richard N. Gardner, *Sterling-Dollar Diplomacy* (New York: McGraw-Hill, 1969; rev. ed.), p. 267.

168. Quoted in Diane Shaver Clemens, *Yalta* (New York: Oxford University Press, 1970), p. 48.

169. Senator Tom Connally quoted in Edward C. Luck, *Mixed Messages* (Washington, D.C.: Brookings, 1999), p. 154.

170. Robert C. Hilderbrand, *Dumbarton Oaks* (Chapel Hill: University of North Carolina Press, 1990), p. 246.

171. *New Republic* quoted in Townsend Hoopes and Douglas Brinkley, *FDR and the Creation of the U.N.* (New Haven: Yale University Press, 1997), p. 161.

172. Quoted in Gabriel Kolko, *The Politics of War* (New York: Random House, 1968), pp. 270–271.

173. Quoted in Carol Anderson, "From Hope to Disillusion," *Diplomatic History, XX* (Fall 1996), 535, 536.

174. Walter Lippmann quoted in Robert A. Divine, *Second Chance* (New York: Atheneum, 1967), p. 291.

175. Quoted *ibid.*, p. 297.

176. John J. McCloy quoted in Kolko, *Politics of War*, p. 470.

177. Arnold Wolfers, *United States Policy Toward Germany* (New Haven: Yale Institute of International Studies, 1947), p. 3.

178. *Foreign Relations, Conference at Quebec, 1944* (Washington, D.C.: Government Printing Office, 1972), p. 467.

179. John J. McCloy quoted in Beschloss, *Conquerors*, p. 144.

180. Henry L. Stimson to the president, September 15, 1944, Box 100, James Forrestal Papers, Princeton University Library.

181. Notebooks, Interview with Harry S. Truman, November 12, 1949, Box 85, Jonathan Daniels Papers, University of North Carolina Library, Chapel Hill.

182. Quoted in John Earl Haynes and Harvey Klehr, *Venona* (New Haven: Yale University Press, 1999), p. 171.

183. Clemens, *Yalta*, p. 287.

184. *Correspondence Between the Chairman, I*, 295.

185. Quoted in Alexander, *Ethnicity, Race, and American Foreign Policy* (Boston: Northeastern University Press, 1992), p. 123; *You're a Sap, Mr. Jap* (New York: King Features, 1942).

186. Edgar Jones quoted in John W. Dower, *War Without Mercy* (New York: Pantheon, 1986), p. 64.

187. Lt. Emil Matula quoted in Peter S. Kindsvatter, *American Soldiers* (Lawrence: University Press of Kansas, 2003), p. 215.

188. Quoted in Martin Gilbert, *Winston S. Churchill: Road to Victory, 1941–1945* (Boston: Houghton Mifflin, 1986), p. 1208.

189. Churchill, *Triumph and Tragedy*, p. 366.

190. Stalin quoted in Anthony Beevor, *The Fall of Berlin 1945* (New York: Viking, 2002), p. 81.

191. *Foreign Relations, Yalta* (Washington, D.C.: Government Printing Office, 1955), p. 973.

192. Quoted in Gardner, *Spheres*, p. 236.

193. Quoted in William L. O'Neill, *A Democracy at War* (New York: Free Press, 1993), p. 196.

194. Quoted in Vojtech Mastny, "Soviet Plans for Postwar Europe," in Antonio Varsari and Elena Calandri, eds., *The Failure of Peace in Europe, 1943–1948* (New York: Palgrave, 2002), p. 70.

195. Quoted in Sherwood, *Roosevelt and Hopkins*, p. 870.

196. Quoted in Reynolds, "Erosion," p. 51.

197. Isaiah Bowman quoted in Neil Smith, *American Empire* (Berkeley: University of California Press, 2003), p. 379.

198. Churchill, *Triumph and Tragedy*, p. 402.

199. Gardner, *Spheres*, p. xiii.

200. Quoted in Kolko, *Politics of War*, p. 465.

201. Churchill, *Triumph and Tragedy*, pp. 227–228.

202. Quoted in Robin Edmonds, *The Big Three* (New York: Norton, 1991), p. 419.

203. Stalin quoted in Vojtech Mastny, *The Cold War and Soviet Insecurity* (New York: Oxford University Press, 1996), p. 20.

204. Quoted in Mark J. Conversino, *Fighting with the Soviets* (Lawrence: University Press of Kansas, 1997), pp. 136–137.

205. Quoted in Rudy Abrahamson, *Spanning the Century* (New York: Morrow, 1992), p. 383.

206. John M. Cabot quoted in Thomas M. Leonard, "The New Pan Americanism in U.S. Central American Relations, 1933–1954," in David Sheinin, ed., *Beyond the Ideal* (Westport, Conn.: Praeger, 2000), p. 103.

207. Quoted in Richard L. Walker, *E. R. Stettinius, Jr.* (New York: Cooper Square Publishers, 1965), p. 333.

208. Quoted in John A. English, "Not an Equal Triangle," in B. J. C. McKercher and Lawrence Aronson, eds., *The North Atlantic Triangle in a Changing World* (Toronto: University of Toronto Press, 1996), p. 174.

209. Quoted in Mark A. Stoler, "Strategy, Grand and Otherwise," in Brower, *World War II*, pp. 58–59; Susan A. Brewer, *To Win the Peace* (Ithaca: Cornell University Press, 1997), pp. 170, 198.

210. Quoted in Kimball, *Forged in War*, p. 134.

211. *Foreign Relations, 1944* (Washington, D.C.: Government Printing Office, 1965), *III*, 103.

212. Quoted in Kolko, *Politics of War*, p. 482.

213. Harry S. Truman, *Memoirs* (Garden City, N.Y.: Doubleday, 1955–1956; 2 vols.), *I*, 258.

214. *Foreign Relations, Berlin* (Washington, D.C.: Government Printing Office, 1960; 2 vols.), *I*, 33.

215. *Ibid., I*, 39.

216. *Ibid., I*, 61.

217. Quoted in James L. Gormly, *From Potsdam to the Cold War* (Wilmington, Del.: Scholarly Resources, 1990), p. 21.

218. Quoted in Robert H. Ferrell, ed., *Off the Record* (New York: Harper and Row, 1980), p. 53.

219. Truman, *Memoirs, I*, 402.

220. Journal, August 1, 1945, Box 19, and Memorandum of Conversation with Harriman, July 17, 1945, Box 18, Joseph Davies Papers, Library of Congress.

221. "Note of the Prime Minister's Conversation with President Truman at Luncheon, July 18, 1945," Prem. 3, Prime Minister's Office Records, Public Record Office.

222. Quoted in Robert L. Messer, "World War II and the Coming of the Cold War," in John M. Carroll and George C. Herring, eds., *Modern American Diplomacy* (Wilmington, Del.: Scholarly Resources, 1986), p. 121.

223. *The Tehran, Yalta & Potsdam Conferences: Documents* (Moscow: Progress Publishers, 1969), p. 323.

224. George F. Kennan, *Memoirs, 1925–1950* (Boston: Little, Brown, 1967), p. 260.

225. *Foreign Relations, Berlin, II*, 365.

226. Truman, *Memoirs, I*, 412.

227. Stalin quoted in Andrei Gromyko, *Memoirs* (New York: Doubleday, 1989), p. 110.

228. Gerhard L. Weinberg, "World War II: Comments on the Roundtable," *Diplomatic History, XXV* (Summer 2001), 498.

229. Thomas R. Searle, "The Firebombing of Tokyo in March 1945," *Journal of Military History, LXVI* (January 2000), 103.

230. Quoted in Donald W. White, *The American Century* (New Haven: Yale University Press, 1996), p. 43.

231. Quoted in Marc Trachtenberg, "New Light on the Cold War?" *Diplomacy & Statecraft, XII* (December 2001), 12.

232. James F. Byrnes quoted in Huston, ed., *American Air Power II*, 378.

233. Quoted in Peter G. Boyle, *American-Soviet Relations* (New York: Routledge, 1993), p. 45.

234. David Reynolds, "World War II and Modern Meanings," *Diplomatic History, XXV* (Summer 2001), 470.

235. Thomas J. McCormick, *America's Half-Century* (Baltimore: Johns Hopkins University Press, 1989), p. 33.

236. Constance Ray Harvey quoted in Ann Miller Morin, *Her Excellency* (New York: Twayne, 1994), p. 27.

237. *Department of State Bulletin, XXII* (April 22, 1945), 738.

238. Isaiah Bowman quoted in Smith, *American Empire*, p. 385.

239. Theodore H. White, *In Search of History* (New York: Warner, 1979), p. 224.

240. Allan Nevins, "How We Felt About the War," in Jack Goodman, ed., *While You Were Gone* (New York: Simon & Schuster, 1946), p. 23.

CHAPTER ✺ 7

All-Embracing Struggle: The Cold War Begins, 1945–1950

Atomic Blast. *The second atomic bomb fell on Nagasaki August 9, 1945, killing at least 60,000. When the renowned scientist Albert Einstein heard that Japan had been blasted with an atomic bomb, he said: "Ach! The world is not ready for it." (U.S. Air Force)*

221

DIPLOMATIC CROSSROAD

✖ *The Atomic Bomb at Hiroshima, 1945*

THE CREW OF the B-29 group scrawled rude anti-Japanese graffiti on the "Little Boy." A major, thinking about his son and a quick end to the war, scratched "No white cross for Stevie" on the 10,000-pound orange and black bomb.[1] The 509th Bombardment Group had been training on the Mariana Island of Tinian since May. At last, the United States's secret atomic development program (Manhattan Project) neared fruition. In the evening of August 5, 1945, Colonel Paul Tibbets informed his crew that their rare cargo was "atomic." He did not explain the scientific process in which two pieces of uranium (U-235), placed at opposite ends of a cylinder, smashed into one another to create tremendous energy. Yet they knew what the equivalent of 20,000 tons of TNT meant.

At 1:37 A.M. on August 6 three weather planes took off for the urban targets of Hiroshima, Kokura, and Niigata. At 2:45, Tibbets's heavily laden B-29, the *Enola Gay,* named after his mother, lifted ponderously off the Tinian runway. The six-hour flight was uneventful except for the nerve-wracking final assembly of the bomb's inner components. Followed by two observation planes stocked with cameras and scientists, the *Enola Gay* spotted the Japanese coast at 7:30 A.M. The weather plane assigned to Hiroshima, the primary target, reported that "everything was peachy keen."[2] Tibbets headed for that city.

"This is history," he intoned over the intercom, "so watch your language."[3] At 31,600 feet and 328 miles per hour the *Enola Gay* began its run on Hiroshima. Bombardier Thomas Ferebee prepared to cross the hairs in his bombsight. At 8:15 A.M. he shouted "bombs away." The *Enola Gay* swerved quickly to escape. "Little Boy" fell for fifty seconds and then exploded about 2,000 feet above ground, a near perfect hit at hypocenter. A brilliant flash temporarily blinded the fliers. The aircraft trembled. "It looked like a pot of black, boiling tar," thought navigator Theodore Van Kirk, as he watched the huge cloud of smoke, dust, and debris rise 40,000 feet.[4] "What we saw made us feel that we were Buck Rogers twenty-fifth century warriors," co-pilot Robert Lewis remembered.[5]

Hiroshima ranked as Japan's eighth largest city, with 250,000 people. Manhattan Project director Lieutenant General Leslie Groves, with the president's approval, had put it first on the target list because it housed regional military headquarters, even though largely a residential and commercial city. On the cloudless, warm morning of August 6, 1945, Hiroshima's inhabitants heard the bombing alert siren. An "all clear" sounded when only a weather plane passed over. Everything seemed routine, for Hiroshima had largely escaped American bombs during the war. Few heard the *Enola Gay* overhead. Suddenly a streak of light raced through the sky. A blast of lacerating heat traveling near the speed of light rocked the city. The temperature soared to suffocating levels. Trees were stripped of their leaves. Buildings blew apart like firecrackers. Debris shot through the air like bullets. Permanent shadows etched themselves into concrete. The sky grew dark, lighted only by the

Enola Gay. On August 6, 1945, just before takeoff, Colonel Paul Tibbets waved from the cockpit of his aircraft *Enola Gay*. Tibbets hailed from Miami and had served in the European theater. For commanding the atomic mission, Tibbets received the Distinguished Service Cross. (U.S. Air Force)

"Little Boy." The nuclear weapon detonated over Hiroshima was 120 inches long and 28 inches in diameter and weighed about 10,000 pounds. (Los Alamos Scientific Laboratory, courtesy of the Harry S. Truman Library)

choking fires that erupted everywhere. In an example of "psychic numbing," one survivor recalled that the agony around him "no longer moved me in the slightest. At that time human beings on the point of death were no longer human: they became mere substance."[6]

As the giant mushroom cloud churned above, a Japanese child "clearly saw the demonic faces of our enemies, Roosevelt and Churchill, looking down on me."[7] Other victims remembered skin peeling off like ribbons, gaping wounds, vomiting and diarrhea, intense thirst. A badly wounded Dr. Michihiko Machiya said that "no one talked, and the ominous silence was relieved only by a subdued rustle among so many people, restless, in pain, anxious, and afraid, waiting for something else to happen."[8] The nightmare registered in statistics: about 130,000 dead, as many wounded, and 81 percent of the city's buildings destroyed. Some twenty-three U.S. prisoners of war also perished there. Nine days later in Fukuoka, Japan, seventeen captured American airmen were beheaded by Japanese soldiers, allegedly in retaliation for the "indiscriminate bombing" of civilians.[9]

Victims at Hiroshima. The total of immediate and longer-term deaths caused by the two bombings may be as high as 300,000. Official Japanese registries in the 1980s recognized 368,259 *hibakusha* (survivors). Of these, the vast majority— 71 percent in Hiroshima and 69 percent in Nagasaki—suffered acute radiation sickness immediately after the explosions. In the conventional bombing of Tokyo and other Japanese cities in 1945, as many as 600,000 Japanese were killed and more than 1 million wounded. The battle for Okinawa, which ended in June 1945, saw 12,000 American deaths and 60,000 wounded; 70,000 Japanese soldiers died, along with 150,000 Okinawan noncombatants killed. (Photograph courtesy of Dr. A. A. Liebow, Army Institute of Pathology)

American aircraft continued their destructive conventional bombing of other Japanese cities. On August 9, a second atomic bomb smashed Nagasaki, killing at least 60,000. The next day, shaken after "killing all those kids," President Harry S. Truman decided not to unleash a third atomic bomb.[10] The Japanese surrendered four days later. "We cried with relief and joy," a young American lieutenant recalled. "We were going to grow up to adulthood after all."[11] Presidential aide Admiral William D. Leahy later regretted that "in being the first to use it, we had adopted the ethical standard common to the barbarians of the Dark Ages."[12] No military or naval adviser, however, told Truman before Hiroshima that "the use of the A-bomb was unnecessary, or that the weapon should not be used, or both."[13]

Two flashes producing "the highest instant body count in the history of warfare" did elicit criticism within the small circle of government officials and scientists privy to the Manhattan Project.[14] Although Truman claimed that his atomic bomb decision became necessary to end the war and thus save American lives, some advisers and scientists disagreed. They presented what they considered viable alternatives to dropping the bomb on a civilian population: (1) follow up Japanese peace feelers; (2) blockade and bomb Japan conventionally; (3) have the USSR declare war on Japan; (4) warn Tokyo about the bomb and threaten its use; (5) demonstrate the bomb on an unpopulated island or area with international observers, including Japanese; (6) conduct a military landing on the outlying Japanese island of Kyushu. Many scientists believed that use of the bomb would constitute a moral blot on the American record, that it would jeopardize chances of postwar international control of the awesome weapon, and that it was unnecessary because Japan tottered on the verge of surrender.

Those who approved the use of the bomb stressed the need to save U.S. lives, "to prevent an Okinawa from one end of Japan to the other," in Truman's words.[15] Told that an invasion might cost "500,000 to 1,000,000 American lives," the president thought first "of the kids who won't be killed."[16] That simple reason helps to explain the decision, but decisions seldom derive from single factors and this one is no exception. Three primary and intertwined motives induced policymakers to inflict atomic horror on the citizens of Japan. Together, the three suggest that Truman

Office of War Information Bombing Leaflet. This photo of five airborne B-29 bombers appeared on approximately 1 million leaflets prepared by the Office of War Information (OWI) and dropped on Hiroshima, Nagasaki, and thirty-three other Japanese cities on August 1, 1945. The reverse side of the leaflet printed the following Japanese text: "Read this carefully as it may save your life. . . . In the next few days some or all of the cities named on the reverse side will be destroyed by American bombs. . . . Heed this warning and evacuate these cities immediately." After August 6, OWI dropped 5 million more leaflets describing the atomic bomb that incinerated Hiroshima and warning of more destroyed cities unless Japan surrendered. (Official Report to U.S. Information Service)

found no compelling reasons against dropping atom bombs on Hiroshima and Nagasaki and important advantages in doing so.

The first motive—emotion—dated from December 7, 1941, when the Japanese bombed Pearl Harbor without warning. Vengeful Americans never forgot or forgave that disaster. Nor did they forget Japanese atrocities. Revenge became the order of the day. Racialized American images of the Japanese as treacherous agents of a "Yellow Peril" strengthened this popular wartime attitude. Comics and movies crudely disparaged this people of color as "yellowbellies" and "yellow monkeys." *Kamikaze* air attacks in 1945 persuaded many that the Japanese, suicidal and bloodthirsty, deserved the worst of punishments. Americans hated the Japanese—the "slant-eyes"—more than they hated the Germans, and 13 percent in a Gallup Poll of December 1944 recommended the extermination of all Japanese. Others advised sterilization. A post-Hiroshima cartoon in the *Atlanta Constitution,* titled "Land of the Rising Sons," depicted apelike figures being propelled skyward by the atomic blast. This angry emotion carried influence. Truman himself said on August 11, 1945: "When you have to deal with a beast you have to treat him as a beast."[17]

The second motive—military momentum—merged with the first and dated from the establishment of the Manhattan Project in August 1942. This program began after European scientists, through a letter from Albert Einstein to President Franklin D. Roosevelt, warned that Germany might develop a nuclear device for military purposes. Officials in charge of the $2 billion project always assumed that once they developed a bomb they would use it to end the war. Truman inherited this assumption from the Roosevelt administration. Put another way, Truman really did not *decide* to drop the bomb. Rather, as General Leslie Groves remarked, the president practiced "noninterference—basically a decision not to upset the existing plans."[18] By 1945, too, the large-scale bombing of civilians, as in Dresden and Tokyo, had become accepted conduct. By August 1945, however, compelling momentum had taken on an irrational quality, for the Germans had surrendered and Japan faced certain defeat.

Hiroshima. The ruins of Japan's eighth largest city bespoke the birth of the atomic age. Regarding the reasons for Japan's surrender, the historian Herbert Bix writes: "The twin psychological shocks of the first atomic bomb and the Soviet entry into the war, coupled with . . . concern over the growing popular criticism of the throne and its occupant, and the possibility that, sooner or later, the people would react violently against their leaders if they allowed the war to go on much longer—these factors finally caused Hirohito to accept, in principle, the terms of the Potsdam Declaration." (U.S. Air Force)

The third factor that helped unleash the atomic bomb was the diplomatic "bonus" that might accrue to the United States.[19] This opportunity materialized when American leaders, while at Potsdam, learned about the successful test explosion at Alamogordo, New Mexico, on July 16, 1945. "Japs will fold up before Russia comes in," Truman wrote on learning the details. "I am sure they will when Manhattan appears over their homeland."[20] Throughout the war, Churchill and Roosevelt tried to keep the bomb a secret from the Soviet Union, in part to use it for diplomatic leverage in the postwar period. Some scientists and advisers protested that excluding the Soviet Union, an ally, from any knowledge, would jeopardize postwar negotiations. At Potsdam, Truman did cryptically inform Stalin that the United States had "a new weapon of unusual destructive force."[21] In fact, despite Soviet penetration of the Manhattan Project through espionage, Stalin "had no conception of the impact" of atomic weapons until after Hiroshima and Nagasaki.[22] Suddenly aware that the bomb had "shaken the whole world," Stalin soon authorized an accelerated program to catch up.[23] A nuclear arms race ensued.

Churchill learned about the Alamogordo test directly from the American delegation at Potsdam. "When he [Truman] got to the meeting after having read this report [from New Mexico] he was a changed man," the prime minister noted. "He told the Russians just where they got on and off."[24] Two diplomatic advantages suggested themselves. First, the bomb might strengthen the U.S.'s negotiating position vis-à-vis the Soviets. An intimidated U.S.S.R. might offer concessions on Eastern Europe if the

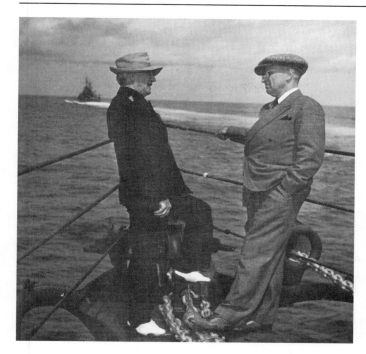

James F. Byrnes (1879–1972) and Harry S. Truman (1884–1972). Both the secretary of state and the president, here on their way back from the Potsdam Conference, welcomed the atomic bomb as a diplomatic bargaining weapon in the postwar period. "The only way to negotiate with the Russians," said Byrnes after Potsdam, "is to hit them hard, and then negotiate." Although Truman looks nonchalant in this photograph, Winston Churchill noted at Potsdam that the president was burdened by the "terrible responsibilities that rested upon him in regard to the unlimited effusion of American blood." (U.S. Navy, courtesy of the Harry S. Truman Library)

bomb revealed its destructive power on a Japanese city. Second, the bomb might end the war in the Pacific before the Soviets could declare war. Even though Washington had sought Soviet intervention against Japan prior to Alamogordo, quick use of the bomb might forestall Soviet military entry into Manchuria and deny the USSR any part of the postwar control of Japan. As it turned out, Moscow's declaration of war against Japan on August 8 caused greater alarm in Tokyo than did news of Hiroshima. "Now the jig is up," said Prime Minister Kantaro Suzuki as he and Emperor Hirohito maneuvered the deadlocked Supreme War Council into accepting surrender.[25]

All three factors—emotion, military momentum, and diplomatic advantage—explain the tragedies at Hiroshima and Nagasaki. The diplomatic aspect emerged as a late bonus; Truman would have dropped the bomb whether such a consideration existed or not. To have decided against dropping the atomic bomb, Truman would have had to deny the passion and momentum that had built up by mid-summer 1945. He could avenge Pearl Harbor, end the war quickly, save American lives, and shore up the U.S. diplomatic position—the advantages far outweighed the disadvantages in his mind. Still, the costs were not inconsequential. Some of the alternatives, or a combination of them, might have terminated the war without the heavy death toll and the grotesque suffering of the survivors. The failure to discuss atomic issues with the Soviets during the war bequeathed to the postwar generation both division and fear. "Seldom, if ever," the CBS radio commentator Edward R. Murrow stated, "has a war ended leaving the victors with such . . . a realization that the future is obscure and survival is not assured."[26]

The Big Two and the International System: Sources of the Long War

Because World War II left the international system in disarray, the transition to peace proved rough and contentious. Broken societies and economies needed repair, and competing models for a new future produced wrenching political turmoil. Some 35 million people died in Europe during the war, and homeless survivors struggled to live in the rubble. The contrast with prosperous America, untouched by enemy bombers or soldiers, became stark. "Like mice in the cage of the elephant," noted the British magazine *The Economist* in comparing the rest of the world to the United States, "they follow with apprehension the movements of the mammoth."[27] The war so weakened the French, British, and Dutch, moreover, that they began to retreat from empire. Britain granted independence to India in 1947 and Burma in 1948, and the Dutch left Indonesia a year later. The French clung precariously to Indochina in the face of nationalist rebellion (see Chapter 9). The decolonization process accelerated in what became known as the Third World.

As Washington moved to fill the power vacuums left by the defeated Axis and retreating colonial powers, it encountered an obstreperous competitor in Joseph Stalin's Soviet Union. Soon a bipolar international structure emerged from the Soviet-American rivalry—the Cold War. The Soviets' pushy behavior, suspiciousness, and blunt language rankled Americans. Even the stoic George Marshall complained that Stalin's brusque style was "not merely discourteous" but bordered on "contemptuousness," and if the Soviets wanted "to earn our ill will they were going about it most successfully."[28] Stalin told Americans: "To cooperate, it isn't necessary that nations have the same system."[29] At the end of the war, the Soviet Union had troops in several Eastern European countries and part of Germany. It lacked an effective navy or air force and had no atomic bomb, but it possessed strong regional power by virtue of its military exploits. Motivated by traditional Russian nationalism and communist ideology, craving security against a revived Germany and facing a major task of reconstruction, the Kremlin determined to make the most of its limited power. Still, compared with the United States, as chargé d'affaires George F. Kennan reported from Moscow, the Soviet Union stood as the "weaker force."[30]

The United States emerged from World War II a full-fledged global power for the first time in its history. An asymmetry—not a balance—of power existed. Washington flexed its multidimensional muscle to build even more power. Because of domestic public pressure, Washington may have demobilized its troops faster than Truman wished, but the Soviet Union also demobilized millions of soldiers. With troops in Asia and Europe, the world's largest navy and air force, a monopoly of the atomic bomb, and a high-gear economy, the United States claimed first rank in world affairs. "As long as we can outproduce the world, can control the seas and can strike inland with the atomic bomb," noted one official in 1948, "we can assume certain risks otherwise unacceptable."[31] In contrast, a Moscow study estimated that total Soviet war damages surpassed "the national wealth of England or Germany" and constituted "one-third of the overall national wealth of the United States."[32] So devastated, "Russia couldn't turn a wheel in the next ten years without our aid," bragged Truman.[33]

Joseph Stalin (1879–1953). General secretary of the Soviet Communist party since 1922, he ran an authoritarian state and conducted a foreign policy of suspiciousness. Because Stalin often played "good cop" to Molotov's "bad cop," President Truman once called the Soviet dictator a "prisoner of the Politburo," and Ambassador Averell Harriman wrote that if "it were possible to see [Stalin] more frequently . . . many of our difficulties would be overcome." (*The Reporter*, 1952. Copyright 1952 by Fortnightly Publishing Co., Inc.)

Makers of American Foreign Relations, 1945–1950

President	Secretaries of State
Harry S. Truman, 1945–1953	Edward R. Stettinius, Jr., 1944–1945
	James F. Byrnes, 1945–1947
	George C. Marshall, 1947–1949
	Dean G. Acheson, 1949–1953

American ideology held that world peace and order depended on the existence of prosperity and political democracy. Poverty and economic depression bred totalitarianism, revolution, communism, the disruption of world trade, and war. Prosperity became the handmaiden of stability, political freedom, unrestricted trade, and peaceful international relations. Americans had long believed that they were prosperous because they were democratic and democratic because they were prosperous.

American leaders determined that *this time,* unlike after World War I, the United States would seize the opportunity to fulfill its ideological premises. As one historian has described the diplomat Dean Acheson's historical understanding, "only the United States had the power to grab hold of history and make it conform."[34] The lessons of the 1920s and 1930s admonished the leaders of the 1940s to throw off the mistakes of the past, to make the most of the "second chance," and to install America's concept of "peace and prosperity" as the world's way.

The vital needs of the U.S. economy also influenced postwar expansionism. Truman and other leaders frankly stated that the United States *had* to export American goods and *had* to import strategic raw materials. By 1947 U.S. exports accounted for one-third of total world exports and were valued at $14 billion a year. Pivotal industries, such as automobiles, trucks, machine tools, steel, and farm machinery, relied heavily on foreign trade for their well-being. Farmers exported about half of their wheat. Many Americans, remembering the Great Depression, predicted economic catastrophe unless foreign trade continued and expanded. Although less than 10 percent of the GNP, exports exceeded in volume such elements of the GNP as consumers' expenditures on durable goods, total expenditures by state and local governments, and private construction. Further, imports of manganese, tungsten, and chromite had become essential to America's industrial system. Foreign trade, however, was threatened by the sickness of America's best customer, Europe, which lacked the resources to purchase American products, and also by nationalists in former colonial areas, who controlled raw materials sources for both Europe and America. To protect its interests and to fulfill its ideology the United States undertook foreign-aid programs.

President Truman felt the flush of American power, shared the ideology, and knew well the economic needs of the country. A Democratic party regular from the Pendergast machine in Kansas City, Missouri, Truman had long experienced rough-and-tumble politics. "The buck stops here" read a sign on his desk. He prided himself on blunt language and quick decisions. The British ambassador

"What Next?" Jack Lambert's 1946 cartoon of Harry S. Truman captured the feeling of many Americans that the president, new at his job, was overwhelmed by postwar problems. FDR had kept Truman in the dark on foreign affairs. Recalling their first contentious meeting in April 1945, Molotov thought Truman "half-witted" and "far behind Roosevelt in intellect." Stalin called the president a "gentleman shopkeeper." (Jack Lambert, *Chicago Sun Times*)

once dismissed Truman as "an honest and intelligent mediocrity"—"a bungling if well-meaning amateur."[35] With intense eyes peering through thick lenses, Truman relished the verbal brawl. His hurried simplification of issues, superficial application of lessons from the past, and quick-tempered style spawned jokes that often fit the truth. Somebody rewrote a proverb: "To err is Truman." Although intelligent and energetic, Truman was a provincial nationalist of narrow vision who believed he could win the Cold War through the projection of U.S. power, and he expected the world to go America's way. When it did not, he sometimes lost his temper and spoke carelessly. Commerce Secretary Henry Wallace thought Truman "was looking one way and rowing another," but no one knew "which way he was looking or which way he was rowing."[36]

In April 1945, Soviet foreign minister V. M. Molotov visited the White House. President Truman gave him a vigorous tongue-lashing, charging that Moscow had not honored the Yalta accords. After the encounter, the first meeting between the new president and a high-ranking Soviet official, Truman gloated to a friend: "I gave it to him straight 'one-two to the jaw.' I let him have it straight."[37] Truman's assertive, "get tough" style drew strength from actual American power. Truman told Ambassador W. Averell Harriman that he did not fear the Soviets, because they "needed us more than we needed them." He did not expect to win 100 percent of the American case, but "we should be able to get 85 percent."[38]

The confrontation between the United States and the Soviet Union derived from the different postwar needs, ideology, style, and power of the two rivals and drew on a history of frosty relations. Each saw the other, in mirror image, as the world's bully. Each charged the other with assuming Hitler's aggressive mantle. Americans compared Nazism and communism, Hitler and Stalin, and coined the phrase "Red Fascism." Moscow and Washington became trapped in a "security dilemma": Every step taken by one side to ensure its security appeared to the other to be provocative. Still, one historian has argued, "in view of the overwhelming power of the United States and in view of the relative restraint exhibited by the Kremlin *outside its immediate periphery,* U.S. officials might have displayed more tolerance for risk."[39]

The advent of the air and nuclear ages made all nations vulnerable to surprise attack. "We are for all time de-isolated," wrote one observer.[40] And the Soviet and American quests for spheres of influence kindled a global contest for advantage—an "all embracing struggle" with an expensive arms race, military alliances, trade restrictions, and repeated interventions and client-state wars.[41] The Cold War era lasted more than forty years, claimed the lives of millions of victims, and nearly bankrupted the main protagonists because they eventually suffered decline from "imperial overstretch."[42]

Challenging the Soviet Sphere in Eastern Europe

The Soviet presence in Eastern Europe before 1947–1948 was neither uniform nor consistent. Soviet documents from 1945–1946 suggest that Stalin acted as "a cynical and ruthless opportunist rather than a revolutionary ideologue."[43] He had stated bluntly at Potsdam that "a freely elected government in any of these countries would be anti-Soviet, and that we cannot allow."[44] Yet he also encouraged local communists to "capitalize on circumstances, form coalition governments, and maneuver to gain power," but not to "precipitate conflict, alienate the Americans, or challenge the British" so long as "time was on his side."[45] Poland, with the Lublin communists in control, fell firmly within the Soviet grasp, as did Romania, where the Red Army imposed communist rule. In Bulgaria, indigenous communists won elections without much help from Moscow.

Hungary and other nations developed differently. The conservative Hungarian Smallholders' party of Ferenc Nagy won national elections in November 1945 by routing the communists, who gained only 17 percent of the vote. Although the communists ousted Nagy in spring 1947, a year later the U.S. minister still believed that "the Soviets and their Hungarian Communist allies are far too clever at this stage . . . to bring Hungary under complete domination."[46] Toward Finland, Stalin practiced "generosity by calculation," telling Finnish leaders "when we treat our neighboring countries well, they respond in kind."[47] So long as Helsinki remained neutral vis-à-vis the Soviet-American confrontation, the Finns retained their independence and in 1948 even ousted the lone communist from their cabinet. In Czechoslovakia, a democratic socialist country with political ties to the West, officials sought to steer a middle course

Changes in Europe After World War II

Territorial Changes After World War II

Notes: -The United States, British, and French Zones of Germany merged in 1949 as the Federal Republic of Germany.

-The Russian Zone of Germany became the German Democratic Republic in 1949.

-The four zones of Austria merged in 1955 to become the Federal Republic of Austria.

NORWAY

SWEDEN

FINLAND

To Russia

Leased to Russia until 1955

L. Ladoga

Leningrad

Gulf of Finland

ESTONIA *to Russia*

L. Pskov

NORTH SEA

DENMARK

BALTIC SEA

To Russia LATVIA

SOVIET RUSSIA

LITHUANIA *To Russia*

Niemen R.

To Russia

EAST PRUSSIA *To Poland*

Danzig

To Poland

Oder R. *Niesse R.*

Vistula R.

U.S. ZONE

NETH.

BRITISH ZONE

Berlin

GERMANY

W.

E.

RUSSIAN ZONE

BEL.

Rhine R.

FRENCH ZONE

POLAND

To Russia

Don R.

LUX.

UNITED STATES ZONE

CZECHOSLOVAKIA

NORTHERN BUKOVINA

FRANCE

SWITZ.

U.S.

FRENCH

Vienna

RUSSIAN

AUSTRIA

BRITISH

BRATISLAVA BRIDGEHEAD *To Czech.*

HUNGARY

SUBCARPATHIAN RUTHENIA

BESSARABIA *To Russia*

Dniester R.

Prut R.

VENEZIA-GIULIA *To Yugoslavia*

To France

Po R.

Trieste

Drava R.

ROMANIA

BLACK SEA

ITALY

ADRIATIC SEA

YUGOSLAVIA

Danube R.

DOBRUJA *To Bulgaria*

CORSICA

Rome

BULGARIA

SARDINIA

ALBANIA

GREECE

TURKEY

AEGEAN SEA

SICILY

DODECANESE IS. (To Greece from Italy)

MALTA (Br.)

CRETE

MEDITERRANEAN SEA

in the developing Cold War. A coalition government under noncommunist president Eduard Benes and Foreign Minister Jan Masaryk assumed office after free elections in May 1946. With Czech communists holding a minority position in the Prague government, the Soviet Union refrained from meddling directly in Czech affairs until a communist coup in February 1948 sharply intensified the Cold War. "Physical control of the Eurasian land mass and eventual control of the whole World Island is what the Politburo is aiming at—no less," an alarmed British Foreign Office concluded.[48] Yugoslavia, although a communist state, established its independence from Moscow under the leadership of Josip Broz Tito. When Belgrade and Moscow bitterly split in 1948, Washington at first considered the schism "a rathole to be watched, not an opportunity for decisive exploitation."[49] Within months, however, U.S. officials noted that the "germ of Titoism is growing" and began to consider "the judicious use of covert operations applied at the appropriate time" to roll back Soviet influence in the region.[50]

The Soviet presence in Eastern Europe before 1948, then, became conspicuous and often repressive, but not absolute. Stalin told French communists in 1947 that "cooperation between different systems . . . is completely possible."[51] Staggering from the loss of 27 million dead during the recent war, Soviet leaders above all else demanded security. "Give them twelve to fifteen years and they'll be on their feet again," Stalin said of the Germans.[52] He said repeatedly that Poland had been a corridor for attack and that a secure Poland meant life or death for the Soviets. Moscow also believed that the Yalta accords acknowledged its primary position in Eastern Europe. Thus the Soviet sphere expanded and tightened "by taking advantage of opportunities rather than implementing a design," as the scholar Vojtech Mastny has put it.[53]

Washington sought "free elections" and the "Open Door" for trade, both traditional principles calculated in part to reduce Soviet influence. The Soviets signed bilateral trade treaties with many Eastern European states, which established favors anathema to America's multilateral approach to trade. Despite minimal commercial ties with Eastern Europe, U.S. diplomats preached the Open Door as a way of driving a wedge into the area. "Free elections" proved difficult in Eastern Europe. First, except for Czechoslovakia, the region lacked democratic traditions. Second, free elections in most of those nations would have produced strongly anti-Soviet governments threatening Soviet security. The question of elections in Hungary demonstrates the complexity of the question. During late 1946 it was the *noncommunist* Nagy who delayed elections, because he knew that the communists would lose badly, alarming Moscow and perhaps triggering Soviet intervention.

The Soviets charged the United States with a double standard. "Poland—a big deal!" Molotov complained after Yalta. "But how governments are being organized in Belgium, France, Germany, etc., we do not know. We have not been asked, . . . We have not interfered."[54] Secretary of War Henry L. Stimson remarked: "Some Americans are anxious to hang on to exaggerated views of the Monroe Doctrine and at the same time butt into every question that comes up in Central Europe."[55] Molotov contended that an Open Door in Eastern Europe would mean ultimate American economic domination of war-weakened nations.

At the Yalta and Potsdam conferences, at the foreign ministers' conferences in London (September–October 1945) and Moscow (December 1945), at the Paris

"Red Fascism." This popular notion among Americans suggested that German Nazism and Soviet communism were really one and the same and that the 1940s would suffer totalitarian aggression like that of the 1930s. Such thinking aroused fears of another "Munich" or "appeasement" and thereby hindered negotiations. (*The Reporter,* 1950. Copyright 1950 by Fortnightly Publishing Co., Inc.)

Peace Conference (April–October 1946), and in numerous diplomatic notes, the United States sought influence in Eastern Europe to counter the Soviets. Washington tried nonrecognition of the pro-Soviet governments but abandoned that tactic when Stalin agreed to allocate a few "insignificant ministries" to noncommunists.[56] Some American leaders thought the atomic bomb would act as a compellant. Stimson recorded in his diary that Byrnes "looks to having the presence of the bomb in his pocket" at the London Conference.[57] At that conference, Molotov actually asked Byrnes if he had "an atomic bomb in his side pocket." "You don't know Southerners," Byrnes parried. "We carry our artillery in our pocket. If you don't cut out all this stalling and let us get down to work, I am going to pull an atomic bomb out of my hip pocket and let you have it."[58] Still, this jocular reference to the bomb did not budge the Soviets from Eastern Europe, and the United States never practiced a blatant "atomic diplomacy" of direct threat.

Stimson rejected the bomb as a diplomatic weapon when he told Truman in September 1945 that the United States should share atomic data to spur postwar cooperation. "For if we fail to approach them now and merely continue to negotiate with them, having this weapon rather ostentatiously on our hip, their suspicions and their distrust of our purposes and motives will increase." Stimson, then seventy-eight, offered sage advice: "The only way you can make a man trustworthy is to trust him; and the surest way you can make a man untrustworthy is to distrust him and show your distrust."[59] Stimson gained the support of Henry Wallace, but Secretary of the

"I Can't Give You All Up for One Angel of Peace." The burly Soviet savors the attention of the Eastern Europeans in this critical Turkish cartoon. The brutish caricature suggests a certain truth. According to the historian Norman Naimark, "women in the Eastern zone" of Germany "shared an experience for the most part unknown in the West, the ubiquitous threat and reality of rape, over a prolonged period of time." The raping by Soviet troops of an estimated 2 million German women prompted the U.S. military governor Lucius Clay to write: "We began to look like angels, not because we were angels, but we looked [like] that in comparison to what was going on in Eastern Europe." (*ULUS*, Ankara, in *United Nations World,* 1947)

Navy James V. Forrestal argued against any effort to "buy [Soviet] understanding and sympathy. We tried that once with Hitler."[60] Truman sided with Forrestal.

The United States also used foreign aid as a diplomatic weapon in Eastern Europe. Byrnes stated the policy in 1946:"We must help our friends in every way and refrain from assisting those who either through helplessness or for other reasons are opposing the principles for which we stand."[61] In short, no loans or aid for Eastern Europe. This policy backfired, for it left those countries dependent on Soviet aid and drove them deeper into the Soviet orbit. In Czechoslovakia, for example, the United States abruptly severed an Export-Import Bank loan. Noncommunist foreign trade minister Hubert Ripka complained bitterly in late 1947: "These idiots started the usual blackmail: 'Okay, you can have 200,000 or 300,000 or even 500,000 tons of wheat, but on one condition only—that you throw the Communists out of the Czechoslovak Government.'" The result:"And now these idiots in Washington have driven us straight into the Stalinist camp."[62]

Washington exaggerated the extent of Soviet control in Eastern Europe, and pressure tactics helped intensify the Cold War—that is, Moscow leaders read American policies as threats to their security and so tightened their grip. George F. Kennan has suggested that the Czech coup of 1948 represented the Soviet response to the Marshall Plan, a major American aid program that the Soviets considered a challenge to their tenuous position in Eastern Europe (see pages 243–245).

Stiffening Up: Early Cold War Crises

The question of Eastern Europe broke up the London Conference of Foreign Ministers (September–October 1945). Byrnes demanded representative governments in Bulgaria and Romania before he would sign any peace treaties with the former German satellites. Molotov countered with questions about British-dominated Greece and American-dominated Japan. At the Moscow Conference in December 1945, the secretary of state tempered his tough stand, and Stalin permitted a token broadening of the Romanian and Bulgarian regimes. The Soviets also accepted Byrnes's ideas for a general peace conference to be held in Paris and a United Nations Atomic Energy Commission to prepare plans for international control.

Truman grew impatient. In early 1946 he said "stop babying the Russians" and instructed Byrnes to "stiffen up," to make no compromises with the Soviets.[63] News of a Canadian spy ring that had sent atomic secrets to Moscow broke in February, about the time that Stalin gave a speech that persuaded some Americans that the Soviets had become intractable. From Moscow, on February 22, chargé d'affaires George F. Kennan wrote an alarmist and influential cable that declared that "we have here a political force committed fanatically to the belief that with [the] US there can be no permanent modus vivendi." Widely read in Washington, this "long telegram" depicted, in gendered terms, a rapacious, aggressive, hypermasculine Soviet Union, guided by an implacable communist ideology and a "neurotic view of world affairs."[64] Kennan, as one scholar has noted, repeated the word "penetration" five times in "reference to the Soviets' insistent, unwanted intrusion" into central Europe. To reassure the "tired and frightened" Europeans, Kennan urged the United States to "tighten" up, assert greater "cohesion, firmness and vigor," and rely on the

Winston S. Churchill (1874–1965) in Fulton.
Churchill (far left) received applause from President Harry
S. Truman (far right) during the former British prime minister's
visit to Westminster College in Fulton, Missouri. There
Churchill delivered his provocative oration against the "iron
curtain." (Truman Library and Westminster College)

manly virtues of "courage, detachment, objectivity, and . . . determination not to
be provoked" in dealing with Moscow.[65]

On March 5, Winston Churchill, no longer prime minister, spoke in Fulton,
Missouri. President Truman heard the eloquent orator lash out at the Soviets: "From
Stettin in the Baltic to Trieste in the Adriatic, an iron curtain has descended across
the Continent."[66] Most Americans liked his stern anti-Soviet tone, but they warmed
much less to his call for an Anglo–American alliance outside the fledgling United
Nations Organization. The reporter David Brinkley recalled that Churchill "threw
his whole body" into the speech but "managed to do so without excessive gestures
or histrionics," his speaking style "the highly distilled product of a thousand years of
upper-class English language and rhetoric."[67] The British ambassador saw the Fulton speech as the "sharpest jolt to American thinking of any utterance since the end
of the war."[68]

The Iranian crisis disturbed Soviet–American relations at the same time. The
crisis began quietly in 1944 when British and American oil companies applied for
Iranian concessions. In a classic example of competition for spheres of influence, the
Soviet Union soon applied for an oil concession too. By 1944 U.S. corporations
controlled 42 percent of the "proved" oil reserves of the Middle East, a nineteenfold
increase since 1936. Both the British and the Soviets grew alarmed by U.S. oil expansion, but the declining British saw the United States as a counterweight to the
Soviets in the region.

A 1942 treaty with Iran allowed the British and Soviets to occupy the country
and required them to leave six months after the end of the war. U.S. soldiers and
supply units also went to Iran, primarily to facilitate Lend-Lease shipments to the
Soviet Union. In mid-1945 the Soviets backed an indigenous rebellion in northern
Iran (Azerbaijan) against the central government in Teheran. In January 1946, working with U.S. officials, Iran took the question to the new United Nations Organi-

zation. Teheran and Moscow could not reach an accord by March 2, when all foreign troops, by treaty, had to depart. With U.S. and British troops already gone, Secretary Byrnes blustered that "we'll give it to them with both barrels."[69] The Soviets thus stood alone in defiance of the treaty and, in Truman's exaggerated view, threatened a "giant pincers movement" toward the Mediterranean and the Near East.[70] In April, however, Moscow and Teheran concluded an agreement and Soviet forces withdrew. In exchange, Iran agreed to establish a joint Iranian-Soviet oil company, subject to approval by its parliament. Stalin abandoned his Azerbaijani clients. In late 1946, Iranian armed forces, advised by Major General Robert W. Grow of the U.S. Army, crushed the insurrection in northern Iran. Not until October 1947 did Iran's legislature consider the joint oil company, rejecting it by a vote of 102 to 2.

The Soviets exploded in anger. They had departed Iran while Britain and the United States had driven in stakes. Arthur C. Millspaugh, former U.S. financial adviser to the Iranian government, pinpointed the security issue: "Iran's geographic relation to the Soviet Union is roughly comparable to the relation of Mexico or Canada to the United States."[71] The Soviets wanted what the British and Americans already had—oil and influence—and feared the foreign penetration of a neighboring state. Years later, Truman embellished the Iranian story by claiming that he had sent the Soviets an ultimatum to get out of Iran or face U.S. troops, but the State Department has denied the existence of such a message. Yet this myth suggests the simple lesson Americans drew from the conflict: "Get tough" and the Soviets will give way. Secretary Wallace, however, told a Madison Square Garden audience in September 1946: "'Getting tough' never brought anything real and lasting— whether for schoolyard bullies or businessmen or world powers. The tougher we get, the tougher the Russians will get."[72] Truman fired Wallace, lumping the "cat bastard" with "parlor pinks and soprano-voiced men" as a "national danger" and "a sabotage front for Uncle Joe Stalin."[73]

Other issues heightened friction in 1946 and illustrated Truman's "get tough" policy. During the war, Moscow asked Washington for a major postwar reconstruction loan. Seeing U.S. aid as one of America's cards in the Cold War game, Truman decided to treat assistance for the USSR's massive reconstruction task as a weapon rather than as a tool. But as Ambassador Harriman admitted, U.S. rejection of the Soviet loan request in early 1946 actually "may have contributed to their avaricious policies" in Eastern Europe.[74] In contrast, Washington granted Britain a $3.75 billion loan in mid-1946 in return for British promises to open trade in their Sterling Bloc.

The Baruch Plan of July 1946 also divided Washington and Moscow. The plan emerged from months of intra-administration talks, but its final touches belonged to Bernard Baruch, the uncompromising American negotiator. He outlined the proposal for control of atomic weapons: (1) creation of an international authority; (2) international control of fissionable raw materials by this authority; (3) inspections to prevent violations; (4) no Security Council vetoes of control or inspections; (5) global distribution of atomic plants for peaceful purposes; (6) cessation of the manufacture of atomic bombs; (7) destruction of existing bombs; (8) these procedures to occur in stages, with abandonment of the U.S. atomic bomb monopoly coming last.

Not until after the Soviets had given up atomic bomb development and fissionable materials, and submitted to inspections, would the United States relinquish

W. Averell Harriman (1891–1986). Graduate of Yale, heir to the Harriman railroad empire, investment banker of Brown Brothers, and diplomat, Harriman was one of America's great public servants in the twentieth century. He served as ambassador to Russia (1943–1946), ambassador to Great Britain (1946), secretary of commerce (1946–1948), and U.S. representative in Europe for the Marshall Plan. Later he advised Presidents John F. Kennedy and Lyndon B. Johnson. Maxim Litvinov once asked: "How can a man with a hundred million dollars look so sad?" (*The Reporter*, 1950. Copyright 1950 by Fortnightly Publishing Co., Inc.)

its "winning weapon."[75] Washington would also control a majority of the members of any authority. "We are telling the Russians that if they are 'good boys' we may eventually turn over our knowledge of atomic energy to them," Wallace wrote to the president.[76] About the same time, the Soviet ambassador in Washington, Nikolai Novikov, warned his superiors that the United States was "striving for world supremacy."[77] Moscow rejected the Baruch Plan, and the stalemate persisted until 1949, when the Soviets successfully exploded their first atomic device.

The issue of Germany—zones, reparations, central administration, demilitarization, and the dismantling of war-oriented factories—deepened the schism. *"Deutschland unter Allies"* consisted of British, French, American, and Soviet zones, wherein each occupying power did what it liked.[78] The vengeful French proved the most obstructionist, refusing to permit any centralized German agencies and pushing for permanent dismemberment. The Soviets tried with mixed success to grab reparations, thereby weakening the entire German economy. The British tried to bestow socialism on their district but generally wanted a strong Germany to which they could sell goods and from which they could receive coal. The United States sought, according to the Potsdam accords, to treat Germany as one economic unit to speed reconstruction. Never again, vowed Truman, would America "pay reparations, feed the world, and get nothing for it but a nose thumbing."[79] With the Morgenthau Plan shelved, new plans evolved to reconstruct steel- and coal-rich Germany as the vital center of a revived European economy. Thousands of GIs, meanwhile, "fraternized" or "went frattin" with German *frauleins* in the U.S. zone, while Project Paperclip recruited ex-Nazi scientists to assist in the "development of new types of weapons."[80]

The dismantling of industrial plants slowed, and in May 1946 U.S. military governor Lucius Clay halted all reparations shipments from the American zone. No more reparations, he told the Soviets, until they contributed to German economic unity. As ex-president Herbert Hoover concluded after a fact-finding mission: "We can keep Germany in these economic chains but it will also keep Europe in rags."[81] In December 1946, the British and Americans combined their zones into "Bizonia." "We really do not intend to accept German unification in any terms that the Russians might agree to," one U.S. diplomat wrote privately.[82] The Federal Republic of Germany (West Germany), a consolidation of "Bizonia" and the French zone, was formed in May 1949. The Soviets, after looting their zone, created their own client, the German Democratic Republic (East Germany), in October 1949. The U.S.S.R. "bolshevised" its zone, in one historian's words, "not because there was a plan to do so, but because that was the only way they knew how to organize society."[83]

Perhaps we can kick them out, Stalin told a German communist as he initiated the Berlin blockade (June 1948–May 1949) to impede unification of the western zones. Fearful of a Germany linked to the West, the Soviets sealed off land, rail, and water access to Berlin (inside the Soviet zone). Truman answered with an airlift. U.S. planes soon swept into the western part of the city with food, fuel, and other supplies. He also ordered B-29 bombers to England, concealing the fact that they went without any of the fifty atomic bombs then in the U.S. arsenal. The Soviet ambassador reported a "war psychosis" rampant in Washington, while the French foreign minister worried that "France and Western Europe will be occupied and devastated

Berlin Airlift. In May 1949, at the close of the crisis over the Berlin blockade, American military personnel celebrate victory for "Operation Vittles." Unlike 1944 and 1945, when Berliners rushed to air raid shelters at the sound of approaching Allied aircraft, German children during the airlift ran to catch candy dropped from U.S. transport planes, which they affectionately dubbed *Rosinenbomber* (raisin bombers). The historian Petra Goedde has written that the Germany encountered by American GIs after the war was "weak, submissive, and disproportionately female," and the ensuing interactions with German women and children helped the United States "create a new monolithic image of Germany: feminine victim of war and the Soviet menace." (U.S. Air Force)

by the Soviet hordes and [then] atomized by the United States."[84] One diplomat warned that any retreat from Berlin would be "the Munich of 1948," leaving Washington "gravely weakened, like a cat on a sloping tin roof."[85] Yet Stalin never interfered with the airlift and even permitted a half-million tons of supplies to reach Berlin from the Soviet zone.[86] Moscow lifted the blockade, but only after suffering worldwide reproach and the creation of the West Germany it had so wanted to prevent. Americans drew another Cold War lesson: To win, never flinch in the face of communist aggression.

The Truman Doctrine, Israel, and Containment

On March 12, 1947, President Harry S. Truman spoke dramatically to a joint session of Congress. Greece and Turkey, he said, faced grave threats. Unless the United States offered help, "we may endanger the peace of the world—and we shall surely endanger the welfare of this Nation." His most famous words became known as the Truman Doctrine: "It must be the policy of the United States to support free peoples who are resisting attempted subjugation by armed minorities or by outside pressures."[87] Truman asked for $400 million to ensure this policy's success. The president's address was short on analysis of the civil war in Greece and the Soviet-Turkish controversy over the strategic Dardanelles, but long on clichés and alarmist language. He played on the words *free* and *democratic,* implying that they fit the Greek and Turkish governments. Presidential aide Clark Clifford called it "the opening gun in a campaign to bring the people up to [the] realization that the war isn't over by any means."[88]

A British request for help in Greece and a lingering squabble over the Dardanelles served as immediate catalysts for the Truman Doctrine. When the Germans withdrew from Greece in 1944, much of the countryside had come under the control of communist and other leftist Greek nationalist resistance fighters—the ELAS (National Popular Liberation Army) and their political arm, the EAM (National Liberation Front). Intent on preserving their influence in the eastern Mediterranean, the British soon reinstated the Greek government-in-exile. Violence erupted in December 1944. British troops, transported to Greece on U.S. ships, joined by rightist sympathizers, and spurred by Churchill's pledge of "no peace without victory," engaged the leftists in vicious warfare.[89] The rebels, hoping to gain political power through elections, signed a peace treaty in February 1945.

From then until March 1946, when civil war flared again, the British-sponsored Athens regime set about to eliminate its political foes. The United States sent warships to Greek ports and offered aid through the Export-Import Bank. In September, Navy Secretary Forrestal announced a permanent U.S. fleet in the Mediterranean. Although wary about a Greek government that one American official described as "completely reactionary, . . . incredibly weak, stupid, and venal," Washington still considered a friendly regime better than a leftist or communist one.[90] Greece limped along, staggered by war-wrought devastation and civil turmoil. Britain, suffering its imperial death throes, could no longer pay the Greek bill. On February 21, 1947, the British informed Washington that they were pulling out. Truman's special message to Congress answered the British appeal with uncommon alacrity.

Critics charged that Truman backed a ruthless Greek regime. Others worried about the cost, preferred economic over military aid, recommended UN action, and feared that the Soviets would interpret the Truman Doctrine as threatening a world crusade. Critics also challenged the contention that Soviet aggression threatened Greece and Turkey. The EAM, although communist-led, had minimal ties with the Soviet Union. Despite Stalin's apparent desire for a "soft" Greece with "pro-Soviet elements powerful enough to veto any anti-Soviet initiatives," Churchill always credited Stalin for keeping the bargain he made at their 1944 Moscow conference to stay out of the Greek imbroglio.[91] In fact, Stalin disliked the nationalist Greek communists because the independent-minded Yugoslav leader Tito gave them aid. Yet Truman claimed that all communists took their orders from Moscow.

The Truman administration enlisted the support of Senator Arthur M. Vandenberg in a prime example of bipartisan foreign policy. The Michigan Republican predicted a "Communist chain reaction from the Dardanelles to the China Sea and westward to the rim of the Atlantic."[92] Most leaders accepted what would later be called the "domino theory." On April 22 the Senate passed the act for aid to Greece and Turkey, 67 to 23; the House followed on May 15 with a positive voice vote.

The Dardanelles question also had more complexity than Truman acknowledged. The United States urged international control over the straits. But the Soviets complained that the Turks had permitted German warships to pass through the straits into the Black Sea during World War II. As Stalin insisted at Yalta, he could not "accept a situation in which Turkey had a hand on Russia's throat."[93] When Turkey refused joint control with the Soviets, Moscow threatened to take action. The presence of Soviet troops near the Turkish border in August 1946 prompted the State-War-Navy Coordinating Committee to assert that "the only thing which will deter the Russians will be the conviction that the United States is prepared . . . to meet aggression with the force of arms."[94] Truman's ostentatious dispatch of a U.S. carrier task force to Istanbul may have caused the Soviets to moderate their demands. "We of course overdid it a bit," Molotov later recalled, but "backed down in time."[95] Ignoring legitimate Soviet concerns about the Dardanelles, Truman drew the simplistic conclusion that Stalin sought to subjugate Turkey. U.S. aid to Turkey under the Truman Doctrine pulled that Soviet neighbor into the U.S. orbit.

American aid and advisers flowed to Greece after 1947, with U.S. officials taking charge of the Greek government. More than 350 American officers accompanied the Greek army in its campaign against the EAM. Dependent on American assistance, Greece also entered the U.S. sphere of influence. Truman claimed another Cold War victory, but the Greek insurgents lost in October 1949 not only because of U.S. intervention but because the Soviet Union refused to help them and Tito sealed off the Yugoslav border to deny Greek leftists a sanctuary.

U.S. interest in the Mediterranean region also entangled the United States in the Palestine question, "an open sore, the infection from which tends to spread rather than to become localized."[96] Zionists had long sought a Jewish homeland, and at the end of World War II they pressed London and Washington to open British-mandated Palestine to Holocaust survivors. As Britain stalled, blocking immigration and turning back ships such as the *Exodus* loaded with Jewish refugees, extremist Zionists vowed to take up arms. At first, U.S. Mideast policy sought to satisfy the Arabs, who opposed increased Jewish immigration and a new Jewish state, because Washington valued Mideast oil and Arab anticommunism. At the same time, many Americans, including President Truman, welcomed the humanitarian opportunity to assist displaced persons once terrorized by Nazism. The astute politician in Truman also spoke: "I have to answer to hundreds of thousands who are anxious for the success of Zionism," he told U.S. diplomats posted in the Middle East. "I do not have hundreds of thousands of Arabs among my constituents."[97]

The beleaguered British decided to abandon the Palestine question to the United Nations, whose special commission recommended partition into Jewish and Arab states, with 56 percent of the mandate area assigned to the Zionists. America's UN ambassador embarrassingly exhorted Arabs and Jews to "settle this problem in a true Christian spirit."[98] Truman groped for a policy while he exploded against Zionists who castigated him for not backing an independent Jewish nation: "Neither Hitler nor Stalin has anything on them for cruelty or maltreatment of the underdog."[99] Although such statements smacked of anti-Semitism, the president hoped to win the large Jewish vote in the forthcoming presidential election, and he resented unyielding State Department officials who kept predicting that partition

Founders of the New Israel, 1948. Formerly the High Commissioner for Refugees under the League of Nations, America's first ambassador to Israel James G. MacDonald (1886–1964; on left) enjoys tea after presenting his credentials to Israel's President Chaim Weizmann (1874–1952) and Prime Minister David Ben-Gurion (1886–1973; on right). The historian Michelle Mart has observed that "Jews in the postwar period first symbolized a complete lack of masculinity for their role as victims and then masculine resurgence in their survival and construction of a new state," an image that commanded respect from Americans. (National Archives)

would alienate Arabs. In fall 1947 Truman chose partition. Fighting between Arabs and Jews escalated, and millions of private dollars from Jewish Americans flowed to co-religionists in Palestine to buy weapons.

Truman tilted further toward the Zionists after his old business partner Eddie Jacobson arranged a visit from Chaim Weizmann in March 1948. This Zionist leader (soon to be the first president of Israel) had once thought Truman "will never jeopardize his oil concessions for the sake of the Jews, although he may need them when the time of election arrives."[100] For reasons of politics and Cold War strategy, Truman formally extended diplomatic recognition to the new Jewish state on May 14, 1948. Two presidential aides and Zionist sympathizers, David Niles and Max Lowenthal, had persuaded Truman that Israel would "line up on the side of the United States a far abler force" than the Arabs, thereby bolstering the American position vis-à-vis the Soviet Union in the Middle East.[101] And Clark Clifford, another pro-Zionist assistant, advised that "shilly-shallying appeasement" of the Arabs would cause "contempt" for the United States around the world, thus serving Soviet ambitions.[102] Despite Secretary of State George Marshall's blunt comment that he "would vote against you" in the election if Truman recognized Israel for political expediency, subsequent Israeli military victories over the armies of five Arab states prompted even the State Department to reassess Israel's importance as a potential ally in the containment of the Soviet Union.[103] Moscow itself recognized Israel, reducing the risk that U.S. recognition would drive angry Arabs into the Soviet camp. (By war's end in early 1949, some 780,000 of 1,300,000 Arab residents had been displaced; many of these Palestinians became refugees in Lebanon and Jordan. Having jettisoned the partition plan, Jews came to occupy 77 percent of Palestine.)

Containment became the byword of the time, and George F. Kennan, director of the State Department's Policy Planning Staff, wrote the definitive statement. The July 1947 issue of the prestigious journal *Foreign Affairs* carried "The Sources of Soviet Conduct," written by a mysterious Mr. "X," soon revealed as Kennan. The United States must adopt a "policy of firm containment," he wrote, "designed to confront the Russians with unalterable counterforce, at every point where they show signs of encroaching upon the interests of a peaceful and stable world." Such pressure might force the "mellowing" of Soviet policy. Kennan sketched a picture of an aggressive, uncompromising Soviet Union driven by ideology. Mechanistic Soviet power, he wrote, "moves inexorably along a prescribed path, like a persistent toy automobile wound up and headed in a given direction, stopping only when it meets some unanswerable force."[104] Even though Kennan actually preferred "political, rather than military, means" to implement containment, his muscular language suggested otherwise.[105]

One of the most vocal critics of containment, the journalist Walter Lippmann, predicted trouble. Lippmann called containment a "strategic monstrosity" because it did not distinguish vital from peripheral areas. Containment would test American resources and patience without limit. Lippmann also prophetically observed that the "policy can be implemented only by recruiting, subsidizing and supporting a heterogeneous array of satellites, clients, dependents and puppets." Instead, he proposed the removal of all foreign troops from Europe to ease tension. He denied that Soviet forces stood poised to attack Western Europe, a point on which he and Kennan actually agreed. Finally, Lippmann sadly concluded that Truman and Mr. "X" in their major statements had abandoned their essential responsibility—diplomacy. "For a diplomat to think that rival and unfriendly powers cannot be brought to a settlement is to forget what diplomacy is about."[106]

George F. Kennan (b. 1904).
Graduate of Princeton, Pulitzer Prize–winning historian, career diplomat, and recognized expert on Soviet affairs, Kennan was Mr. "X" in 1947 when he articulated the containment doctrine. This brilliant man served Ambassador Harriman in Moscow and then headed the State Department's Policy Planning Staff (1947–1949). Later he became ambassador to Russia (1952) and Yugoslavia (1961–1963). In the 1970s and 1980s he emerged as a leading critic of the nuclear arms race. In 1946, Kennan wrote that "the greatest danger . . . is that we shall allow ourselves to become like those with whom we are coping." (The Institute for Advanced Study, Princeton, New Jersey)

On Its Feet and Off Our Backs: The Marshall Plan, NATO, and the Division of Europe

In 1947–1948, under the banner of containment, U.S. goals for Western Europe crystallized: economic reconstruction and hunger relief, linkage of Germany's western zones with a Western European economic system, reinvigorated trade with the United States, prevention of leftist political gains, ouster of communists from governments (especially in Italy and France), settlement of colonial disputes (as in Indochina and Indonesia) that were draining funds, blockage of neutralist tendencies, and building military allies. By 1947 the United States had already spent $9 billion in the region. Despite assistance through the United Nations Relief and Rehabilitation Administration (UNRRA), the World Bank, and the International Monetary Fund, plus the loan to Britain and expenditures for the military occupation of Germany, Europe remained economically hobbled and communists might exploit the economic chaos. Europe's multibillion-dollar deficit also meant that Europeans could not buy American products unless they received dollars from the United States.

V. M. Molotov (1890–1986).
Popularly known as "stone ass," the Soviet foreign minister (1939–1949; 1952–1956), a tough-minded negotiator, cleared most decisions with Stalin. When he became angry, a bump appeared on his forehead, alerting adversaries of trouble. In his memoirs Molotov stressed *realpolitik:* "What we did . . . we did superbly, we strengthened the Soviet state. That was my chief task. My task as minister of foreign affairs was to see to it that we weren't cheated." (*The Reporter,* 1956. Copyright 1956 by The Reporter Magazine Co.)

On June 5, 1947, at Harvard University, Secretary of State George C. Marshall called for a comprehensive, coordinated program to put Europe back on its feet. A halting, quiet orator, Marshall delivered a monumental message in only 1,500 words. A distraught Europe needed help to face "economic, social and political deterioration of a very grave character."[107] He vaguely called on the European nations to initiate a collective plan. Recognizing that "if we want to act singlehandedly, we lose everything," British foreign secretary Ernest Bevin and French foreign minister Georges Bidault conferred and soon accepted Marshall's proposal, ultimately shaping it according to American specifications.[108] They reluctantly invited Soviet foreign minister V. M. Molotov to join them for a meeting in Paris in June.

Kremlin leaders sniffed a capitalist trap. Opposed to any program dominated by the United States, Molotov suggested loosely structured arrangements designed to protect national sovereignties. Bevin and Bidault, knowing that Washington insisted on an integrated effort, rejected national shopping lists. Molotov abruptly left Paris, and he recalled in his unrepentant memoirs that "if *they* think we made a mistake in rejecting the Marshall Plan, that means we acted correctly."[109] Hoping that aid would "raise the Iron Curtain," Truman had never wanted Soviet participation in the European Recovery Program (ERP), as the Marshall Plan became known.[110] "At best," the historian Michael J. Hogan has written, "American officials saw Marshall's plan as a way to break Soviet influence in Eastern Europe; at worst, they were counting on Soviet opposition to galvanize support for the plan in Congress."[111] Moscow rejected the Marshall Plan because Eastern Europe was expected to ship raw materials to industrial Western Europe, thereby becoming "a tool against the USSR," because a large influx of dollars into the Soviet sphere of influence would directly challenge Soviet interests; and because the plan sought to revive West Germany.[112] In any case, Congress would probably have shunned funding a recovery program that included the Soviet Union and its neighbors. Finally demanding "total conformity and obedience" from his allies, Stalin announced the division of the world into "two camps" and instituted a feeble Molotov Plan for Eastern Europe.[113]

Congress in March 1948 passed the Economic Cooperation Act. The coup in Czechoslovakia, elections in Italy (would they go communist?), and the growing crisis over Germany, together with a March 17 Truman war-scare speech to a joint session of Congress, garnered the Marshall Plan a vote of 69 to 17 in the Senate and 329 to 74 in the House. Congress approved $4 billion for the program's first year. Before ending in December 1951, the Economic Cooperation Administration had sent $12.4 billion into the needy European economy.

The Marshall Plan proved a mixed success. In Europe it caused inflation, failed to solve a serious balance-of-payments problem, and took only tentative steps toward economic integration. But it sparked impressive Western European industrial production and investment and started the region toward self-sustaining economic growth. The ERP, noted the administrator Paul Hoffman, "got Europe on its feet and off our backs."[114] The Marshall Plan stimulated the U.S. economy by requiring recipients to spend some aid in the United States on American goods; in this way, the profitable flow of American exports to traditional European markets continued. The program "aided and accelerated . . . the anti-Communist shift of the European

Essen, Germany. In the rubble of this German city rested a new citizen, who because of American reconstruction aid could expect to have a full stomach. According to the historian Thomas A. Schwartz, "the United States pursued a 'dual containment' policy in Europe, designed to keep both the Soviet Union and Germany from dominating the Continent. . . . The two policies, which were inextricably linked, were always in a delicate balance; the United States could not contain the Soviet Union in Europe without German strength, and it could not maintain its hold over the German Federal Republic without the Soviet threat." (Harry S. Truman Library)

trade union movement," and it won votes for political parties that backed the generous U.S. project.[115]

The Marshall Plan had shortcomings, too. Europe became dependent on American aid, less able to make its own choices. The French complained about "Coca-colonization."[116] The publisher of *Le Monde* hyperbolically remarked that "France under the Marshall Plan . . . was becoming a sort of Philippines."[117] Some American money funded European resistance to colonial wars. The program bypassed the United Nations and the Economic Commission for Europe, where it might have operated with less divisiveness. The ERP encouraged restrictions on East-West trade and helped revive West Germany, thereby arousing Moscow's fears of its nemesis. In 1951 the Economic Cooperation Administration merged into the Mutual Security Administration, with 80 percent of American aid to Western Europe becoming military in nature.

Believing the Soviets capable of overrunning Western Europe in six months, bombing Alaska and Puget Sound, and even causing "serious internal disorders by subversion," the Pentagon sought greater rearmament without knowing that "the Soviet army in Germany was configured for defensive operations, rather than the quick march to the English Channel that formed the basis of U.S. military planning."[118] In July 1947, Congress passed the National Security Act, which streamlined the military

**Dollar and Atomic
Diplomacy.** In this Soviet view
of U.S. foreign policy, Truman
wields the atomic bomb and the
money bag. Note Winston
S. Churchill on the right. (*Krokodil,
USSR*)

establishment. The act created the Department of Defense, the National Security Council (NSC) to advise the president, and the Central Intelligence Agency (CIA) to gather and collate information. In "the visceral business of using any bastard as long as he was anti-communist," the CIA's Office of Policy Coordination soon recruited ex-Nazis and other agents for subversive activities in Eastern Europe.[119] In Europe in March 1948, Britain, France, and the three Benelux nations, with U.S. encouragement, signed the Brussels Treaty for collective defense. In June the Senate passed (64 to 4) Vandenberg's resolution applauding that effort and suggesting American participation.

The United States also implemented the Fulbright Program in 1948, "the most significant movement of scholars across the earth since the fall of Constantinople in 1453," as an Oxford don remarked.[120] The brainchild two years earlier of Senator J. William Fulbright, Democrat of Arkansas and a former Rhodes scholar and university president, this example of "public diplomacy" sought to breach cultural barriers and inculcate a favorable image of the United States among foreign peoples. The Fulbright Program sponsored educational exchanges; faculty and students went abroad to teach and study, and their counterparts from other countries came to the United States. By 1953 elites in twenty-eight nations participated in the program in Europe, Asia, and the Middle East. In some countries, former Fulbrighters achieved political prominence and helped keep their governments friendly to Washington. To combat anti-American propaganda in what President Truman described as a "great campaign of truth," some American and European intellectuals organized the Congress of Cultural Freedom in 1950; the CIA secretly subsidized this effort to promote America in Europe.[121]

The United States also endorsed in 1948 the World Health Organization (WHO), a specialized United Nations agency that fulfilled a "two-pronged strategy of education and disease-fighting." Targeting borderless epidemic diseases such as malaria, tuberculosis, and syphilis, with a "sense of international fellowship," WHO physicians blanketed the earth to promote prevention and administer vaccines.[122] Washington has traditionally supplied the largest share of WHO's budget.

Truman summarized American foreign policy in his inaugural address of January 20, 1949. Articulating simple juxtapositions of "communism" and "democracy," the president listed four central points. First, he endorsed the United Nations. Second, he applauded the European Recovery Program. Third, he announced that the United States was planning a North Atlantic defense pact. And fourth, "we must embark on a bold new program" of technical assistance for "underdeveloped areas," a reference to the Point Four Program, launched in 1950.[123] Under Point Four, countries such as Afghanistan received millions in Export-Import Bank loans for hydroelectric dams and other modernization projects to create "an environment in which societies which directly or indirectly menace ours will not evolve."[124]

On April 4, 1949, the United States, Canada, and ten European countries signed the North Atlantic Treaty in Washington. Article 5 provided "that an armed attack against one or more . . . shall be considered an attack against them all."[125] This article, said critics, would draw America into a war even if it did not want to go. Senator Robert Taft of Ohio saw NATO as a threat to the Soviet Union that would eventually force the United States to send military aid to Europe and spur an arms race. Taft also noted that the president could commit American troops almost at will without constitutional restraint. Some dissenters questioned the precise nature of the Soviet threat: Was it military, political, or ideological? After all, no Soviet military attack seemed imminent. Other critics from both left and right thought that the United States was overextending itself. George F. Kennan, increasingly disaffected from the American militarization and nuclearization of the Cold War, argued that, because few U.S. leaders anticipated a Soviet military thrust, NATO served no military need.

The United States welcomed NATO as much for political as for military purposes. A popular saying explained that NATO kept the Soviets out, the Americans in, and the Germans down. In other words, NATO gave the United States influence in Europe. Through NATO Washington could blunt neutralist tendencies or revival of an "appeasement psychology."[126] The alliance also permitted the United States to rearm West Germany while reassuring Europeans that Germany would be controlled by a multinational organization. U.S. officials also believed that Western Europe needed a "general stiffening of morale" through the creation of NATO, to stimulate capital investment and encourage an energetic reconstruction effort.[127] Depicting new allies as insecure members of the same family who "sublimated fear" of their "own inadequacy," Kennan recommended that "we must exhibit more confidence in them than we may actually feel—string them along a little."[128] "Europe under American water cans handled by British gardeners blossoms into a happy Garden of Eden," as one diplomat phrased it.[129]

On July 21, 1949, the Senate approved the NATO Treaty by an 82 to 13 margin. Two days later, Truman also sent the Mutual Defense Assistance Bill to Congress requesting more than a billion dollars for European military aid. Containment had taken a distinct turn to military means, and the stakes became bigger. After the Soviets exploded an atomic device in August 1949, Truman ordered development of a thermonuclear or hydrogen "superbomb," saying that "since we can't obtain international control we must be strongest in atomic weapons."[130] By mid-1950 the U.S. arsenal already included some 300 atomic bombs and more than 260 aircraft that could drop them on Soviet targets. The Soviets responded to NATO with the Warsaw Pact in 1955, the same year that they detonated their first hydrogen bomb, three years after the U.S. H-bomb.

In January 1950, Truman ordered a comprehensive review of U.S. military and foreign policy. Eventually tagged National Security Council Paper Number 68 (NSC-68), the April report predicted prolonged global tension, Soviet military expansion, and relentless communist aggression (some officials regarded Mao's recent triumph in China as an example of an international conspiracy). According to one scholar, "conventional rearmament and strategic superiority were now deemed indispensable for the risk-taking necessary to co-opt the industrial core of Eurasia, integrate it with the Third World periphery, and maintain America's preponderant position in the international system."[131] Washington had to persuade the public to support larger defense budgets and higher taxes. Paul Nitze, who replaced Kennan as head of the Policy Planning Staff, wrote most of NSC-68, and he glossed over complexities. The document treated communism as a monolith, ignoring differences within the communist community. It spoke of the "free world," overlooking

Dean Acheson (1893–1971). A graduate of Yale and Harvard and a wealthy lawyer, Acheson became secretary of state in 1949. Polished and arrogant, he served as secretary of state until 1953. In the Cold War with the Soviets, he once told President Truman, "We are playing for keeps," there were no "rules, no umpire, no prizes for good boys, no dunce caps for bad boys . . . good intentions are not worth a damn; moral principles are traps; weakness and indecision are fatal." (Portrait by Gardner Cox, National Portrait Gallery, Smithsonian Institution, Gift of Covington and Burling)

the many undemocratic nations allied with the United States. It postulated that communism orchestrated the world's troubles, neglecting the indigenous character of nationalist movements that challenged the colonial powers. It made sweeping assumptions about Soviet motives and capabilities without evidence. The report, in short, exaggerated the "threat." Lippmann's counsel against indiscriminate globalism went unheeded; the United States prepared to become the world's policeman. But how to convince Americans to support the report's prescriptions? "We were sweating over it, and then—with regard to NSC-68—thank God Korea came along," recalled an Acheson aide.[132] In September 1950, a few months after the outbreak of the Korean War, Truman ordered NSC-68's implementation.

Stalin initially responded to NATO and American rearmament with disdain. "America, though it screams war, is actually afraid of war," he told Mao Zedong in December 1949.[133] Yet, as the two sides consolidated their respective spheres, Moscow appealed in spring 1950 for a Soviet-American dialogue to reduce tensions. Secretary Dean Acheson ridiculed the Soviet "Trojan dove," vowing to contest the Soviets by building U.S. "situations of strength" throughout the world.[134] As Lippmann had predicted, diplomacy became a victim of the Cold War.

Asian Allies: Restoring Japan and Backing Jiang in China

Asia experienced a major reconfiguration after World War II. In Indochina, Burma, and Indonesia the old imperial system crumbled. The colonial powers looked to the United States to help them salvage what they could. Japan suffered defeat and occupation. Korea, formerly dominated by Japan, was divided along the thirty-eighth parallel by the Soviet Union and the United States. Civil war loomed in China.

The Pacific Ocean was becoming an American sphere of influence. If the Soviets ran some of the Eastern European countries, the Supreme Commander for the Allied Powers, General Douglas MacArthur, ran Japan. Unlike Germany, Japan had no zones. Despite a Far Eastern Advisory Commission with Soviet membership, the United States rejected Soviet requests for shared power, and MacArthur treated Stalin's representative like "a mere piece of furniture."[135] The United States also assumed control over Micronesia (the Marianas, Marshalls, and Carolines), Okinawa, Iwo Jima, and more than a hundred other Pacific outposts. As if to demonstrate the point, on July 7, 1946, the United States tested an atomic bomb on the Marshall Island of Bikini. To avoid the charge of imperial land grabbing, Washington had the United Nations place Micronesia under U.S. trusteeship. In 1949 MacArthur declared that "the Pacific had become an Anglo-Saxon lake."[136]

The first two years of occupation brought *demokurashii* to Japan: a new constitution, war crimes trials, women's rights, dismantling of feudal landownership, even American censorship of Japanese films so as to depict Emperor Hirohito not as a god but as a constitutional monarch and "symbol of the people's unity."[137] Postwar Japanese movies soon filled with "American icons, such as chewing gum and jazz—and a changing image of women."[138] Millions learned conversational English from the radio program "Come, Come English," and "Tokyo Boogie-

Woogie" became the hit song of 1948.[139] Japan seemed to bury its militarism as a more pacifist culture emerged. Then U.S. officials reversed course as the Cold War progressed and it appeared that communist Mao Zedong would win in China. Americans now needed a "stable Japan, integrated into the Pacific, friendly to the U.S."[140] During 1947–1950, labor unions were restricted, the reparations program curtailed, production controls in war-related industries relaxed, the antitrust program suspended, communists barred from government and university positions, and former Japanese leaders reinstated. In the end, as the historian John W. Dower has noted, "the ideals of peace and democracy took root in Japan—not as a borrowed ideology or imposed vision, but as a lived experience and a seized opportunity."[141]

General Douglas MacArthur (1880–1964) and Emperor Hirohito (1901–1989). This famous photograph of the first meeting of the Japanese emperor and the American supreme commander on September 27, 1945, has been called the "wedding photo" because, as Yoshikuni Igarashi points out in *Bodies of Memory* (2000), it suggests the "sexualized power relations" between a conquering United States and a submissive Japan. The meeting provided "the necessary ingredients for a melodrama—humiliation and the heroic acceptance of humiliation" by Hirohito. For many Japanese, "this photograph was material evidence that the authority of the U.S. occupation forces had displaced that of imperial Japan." (Courtesy of the General Douglas MacArthur Foundation)

The restoration of Japan carried international ramifications. The Chinese communists feared a devilish scheme to rebuild Japan as a base for aggression against China. Japanese recovery, U.S. officials argued in early 1950, also required the development of markets for Japanese products in Southeast Asia, Indonesia, the Philippines, southern Korea, and India, and hence, application of the containment doctrine to undercut communists. The Soviet Union suspiciously eyed U.S. expansion in Asia and protested America's peace treaty negotiations with Japan. In September 1951, the United States and fifty other nations signed a peace treaty that restored Japanese sovereignty, gave the United States a base on Okinawa, and permitted the retention of foreign troops in Japan. Moscow refused to sign. A separate Japanese-American security pact also permitted U.S. troops and planes on Japanese soil. From Pearl Harbor, a merciless war, and the atomic blasts to a peaceful occupation and Japanese-American cooperation—how to explain the dramatic shift? Continued demonic images and punishment no longer served the interests of either party. Americans sought a Cold War ally, and the Japanese sought a helping hand. "The same stereotypes that fed superpatriotism and outright race hate were adaptable to cooperation." For example, Americans considered the Japanese, in MacArthur's words, "like a boy of twelve" and able to become "good pupils" under U.S. tutelage. And the Japanese philosophy of "proper place" meant that the Japanese could become "good losers" who, as Prime Minister Shigeru Yoshida put it, end up "winning by diplomacy after losing in war."[142]

Americans wanted a peaceful China within their sphere of influence too. For decades they had preached the Open Door, dreamed of vast Chinese markets and Christian converts, and considered China a special friend, if not client. A recovering Japan also needed Asian markets. "Whether China is red or green," said Yoshida, "China is a natural market."[143] The Chinese communists had other ideas, challenging the American-backed regime of Jiang Jieshi. During 1945–1949, the United States became a counterrevolutionary force in a revolutionary country.

American postwar goals sought a united noncommunist country under Jiang, trade with the United States and China as a U.S. ally. At the end of the war, American troops took positions in northern China, including Beijing and Tianjin. They transported Jiang's soldiers to Manchuria in a race to beat Mao Zedong's communists there. As he promised at Yalta, Stalin signed a treaty of friendship with Jiang's regime in August 1945, telling Nationalist diplomats that "Japan will restore her might in 20, 30 years . . . our relations with China is [*sic*] based on this."[144] When pressed by Stalin to cooperate with Jiang, Mao grumbled that "the Soviet Union cannot help us."[145] Perhaps hoping that a "cooperative Nationalist China" might act as "a buffer" against a revived Japan, Stalin preferred a China that would pose no threat along the 4,150 miles of the Sino-Soviet border.[146] Stalin thought Mao too independent, too "Titoist," even calling him a "cave-dweller-like Marxist."[147] U.S. Foreign Service Officers such as John Paton Davies and John S. Service reported from China that relations between Moscow and Mao remained fractious and that the communists would probably defeat Jiang without much help from Moscow, despite the presence of Soviet troops in Manchuria.

Swashbuckling Ambassador Patrick J. Hurley managed to bring Mao and Jiang together for talks in fall 1945, but Jiang refused to make concessions, confident that "the evolution of the international situation" would bring him American backing.[148] The talks failed. In November, Hurley, with his typical blast-furnace approach, resigned and charged that "a considerable section of our State Department is endeavoring to support communism in . . . China," in favor of "Mouse Dung" and "Joe N. Lie" (as he called Mao and Zhou Enlai).[149] Hurley's attack on the professional diplomats fed the conspiracy-minded who needed scapegoats for the American frustration over China. The "China experts" had not preferred Mao; they had simply reported that Jiang was corrupt, reactionary, and unlikely to gain the allegiance of the Chinese people, and that the communists would thus gain support. Paying for their accuracy, the China hands were criticized for having "warm hearts, but thick heads" and eventually were forced from the State Department under pressure from red-baiting Senator Joseph McCarthy.[150]

After the Hurley debacle, in December 1945, Truman sent the "Marshall Mission" to China. Headed by the highly respected General George C. Marshall, it sought to unite the factions under a noncommunist government. The communists, not wanting a bloody civil war and seeing coalition government as a nonviolent route to power, accepted Marshall's cease-fire in January 1946. About the same time, the Soviets pulled out of Manchuria, after having seized equipment as war booty, leaving the area to superior communist forces. By May 1946, 90 percent of Manchuria rested in communist hands. Jiang's decision to storm into Manchuria to challenge Mao doomed the cease-fire. Marshall and the 1,000 U.S. military and naval personnel who advised Jiang's forces could not restrain the overconfident generalissimo. "We were taken in," said Mao of U.S. mediation efforts; "we won't be cheated again."[151] For the next two years the communists adopted a "talking but not doing" approach—namely, castigating the United States but avoiding direct conflict.[152] A chagrined Marshall returned to Washington in January 1947 to become secretary of state.

Still hopeful of preventing a communist victory, Truman dispatched the "Wedemeyer Mission" to China in July 1947. General Albert C. Wedemeyer criticized the disarray of the Nationalists but concluded that China, like Greece, needed an aid program to curb the communist menace. He also suggested that a UN commission govern Manchuria. Secretary Marshall vetoed both proposals as impractical, although he did release undelivered Lend-Lease goods to Jiang. In autumn 1947 Marshall offered more arms and ammunition and authorized the Army Advisory Group to train Chinese combat troops on Formosa. In part to answer critics who asked why Greece but not China should be saved from communism, the White

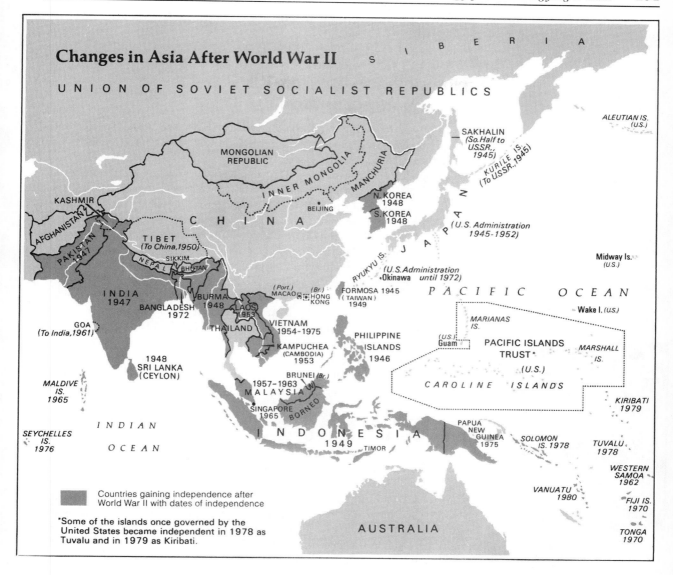

Changes in Asia After World War II

Countries gaining independence after World War II with dates of independence

*Some of the islands once governed by the United States became independent in 1978 as Tuvalu and in 1979 as Kiribati.

House asked Congress in early 1948 for $570 million in China aid. Under the China Aid Act of April, China obtained $400 million.

Despite $3 billion in aid to Jiang since V-J Day, Washington failed to stop Mao's ascent. Jiang let inflation run rampant, neglected tax and land reforms, launched risky military expeditions, tolerated corruption, and rejected negotiations. Dispirited soldiers defected from his army. U.S. military equipment fell into communist hands; ironically, in this roundabout way, Mao's troops got more aid from America than from the Soviet Union. "We picked a bad horse," the president lamented.[153]

Life magazine called Mao's triumph "a victory for the Soviet Union and a moral disaster for the U.S."[154]

The People's Republic of China and U.S. Nonrecognition

In June 1949, Mao Zedong stated that he was leaning to the side of socialism (the Soviet Union) against that "one great imperialist power" (the United States).[155] For many Americans, Mao's strident address simply confirmed Moscow's creation of another puppet state. Even though Stalin had given the Chinese communists only "limited" military aid ("not even a fart," as Mao complained), Americans preferred Acheson's words, in the *China White Paper* of August 1949, that "the Communist regime serves not [Chinese] interests but those of Soviet Russia."[156] The *White Paper* documents showed little the United States could have done because Jiang himself would do so little. In January 1949 he sent China's gold supplies to the island of Formosa (Taiwan); in December, his Nationalist government followed. Mao's People's Republic, established on October 1, assumed power.

Critics such as the publisher Henry R. Luce of *Time* magazine, Republican members of Congress, and missionaries trumpeted that "China had been sold down the Yangtze" by the Democrats.[157] Senator Styles Bridges and Representative Walter Judd headed an informal and influential "China Lobby," which for years had advocated a major U.S. intervention in the Chinese civil war. They asked: If American foreign policy sought the containment of communism without geographical limit, as stated in the Truman Doctrine, why did not the United States intervene in China? Truman officials answered that China was too large, a land war in Asia unthinkable, Jiang unmanageable, and the monetary costs prohibitive. "Unable to do anything positive themselves," a U.S. diplomat reported, the Chinese "always want the United States to do it first and for them."[158] Jiang's mishandling of U.S. funds confirmed Truman's private view of the Guomindong as "grafters and crooks."[159]

After Mao's victory, the United States refused to recognize the People's Republic of China. Behind the nonrecognition policy lay mounting Sino–American animosities. In June 1949 communist leaders asked American ambassador J. Leighton Stuart to meet with them. The Truman administration vetoed contact. Not only did Truman fear howling protest from the "China Lobby," but he also resented Chinese communist behavior. In bombastic speeches, they reminded Americans of their imperialist past, including military participation in the Boxer Rebellion, support for Japan's seizure of Shandong in 1919, and naval gunboat patrols on Chinese rivers in the 1920s and 1930s (see Chapter 5). They confiscated American property and used calculated harassment to "squeeze out" Western diplomatic personnel in Manchuria.[160] They kept the U.S. consul general at Mukden under house arrest for two years before expelling him as a spy in October 1949.

From December 1949 through February 1950, in Moscow, Mao negotiated a treaty of friendship and alliance. Fearful of a revived Japan and of the expanded U.S. presence in Asia, Mao needed an ally. Stalin treated Mao like an inferior "younger brother" until the latter blurted: "I only have had three tasks here: the first was to

"The Open Door." The communists, led by Mao Zedong, defeated the crumbling forces of Jiang Jieshi in 1949, opening a door that the United States had tried to keep closed. "In the blinking of a historical eye," the author Tom Englehardt writes, "the vast land of oppressed peasant individualists, immortalized in Pearl Buck's 1931 novel *The Good Earth,* had been transformed into a terrifying red blot on the map." *(The Reporter,* 1950. Copyright 1950 by Fortnightly Publishing Co., Inc.)

eat, the second was to sleep, and the third was to shit."[161] Mao eventually obtained an alliance obligating both parties to come to each other's assistance if attacked by a third party—"a big political asset to deal with the imperialist countries of the world."[162] U.S. observers played down both the meager foreign aid that Moscow promised and Sino-Soviet differences over Mongolia and Manchuria. Despite Acheson's changed view that "the very basic objectives of Moscow are very hostile to the basic objectives of China," Truman publicly stressed Sino-Soviet ideological affinity and denounced the treaty as the Soviet conquest of China.[163] The "Chi Commies," as official U.S. cables tagged the new Chinese leaders, would not receive U.S. diplomatic recognition. Born in failure and exaggeration, the non-recognition policy set the United States firmly against the largest (650 million people) and potentially most influential nation in Asia. Hoping eventually to drive a wedge between the two communist powers, Assistant Secretary of State Dean Rusk in early 1951 taunted the Chinese: "The Peiping regime may be a colonial Russian government—a Slavic Manchukuo on a larger scale. It is not the Government of China. It does not pass the first test. It is not Chinese."[164]

A Cold War Culture Emerges

"We thought we could do anything," noted a U.S. writer who recalled the end of World War II. "We were heirs to a smiling and victorious confidence."[165] Although Western Europeans sometimes complained about the "ham-fisted" style, they usually welcomed the American presence.[166] In addition to soldiers and dollars, Washington exported jazz and baseball, "blue jeans and T-shirts, Coca-Cola and chewing gum, U.S. comics and movie stars."[167] As early as August 1945, an occupation official in Austria cabled Washington: "They're killing me with inquiries about Walt Disney films. . . . The American occupation cannot be complete without Mickey Mouse and Donald Duck."[168] Although Japanese radio called a child fathered in 1946 by a U.S. serviceman a "rainbow across the Pacific," this first of some 200,000 Japanese-American children born during the occupation was destined to endure racial discrimination from both cultures.[169] The roughly 94,000 offspring of GIs in Germany by 1949 (including 3,000 "brown babies" begotten by African-American soldiers) prompted a German joke that "if America ever got into another war in Europe, it would not be necessary to send any troops—just the uniforms."[170] Because Western Europeans had "invited" the United States to create an empire and include them within it, some scholars have argued, Washington pursued its economic, ideological, and strategic goals all the more zealously.[171] Confident in the superiority of their culture and values, U.S. officials relished the chance to provide "leadership in restoring principles as a guide to conduct. If we do not do that, the world will not be worth living in," proclaimed John Foster Dulles.[172]

"After World War II," Senator J. William Fulbright remembered, "we were sold on the idea that Stalin was out to dominate the world. . . . Henry Wallace sensed it [differently], he had a feeling about it, but he was ridiculed for being a visionary, an appeaser, unrealistic."[173] As Fulbright suggested, Americans came to believe that the Soviet Union had launched a crusade to communize the world. Appearances fed such a notion. Austere, intransigent, and ruthless, Stalin became in American eyes

"Uncle Sam's World Wide Umbrella."   As the donor of large amounts of foreign aid, as the chief partner in military alliances, and as the professor of the containment doctrine, the United States undertook new global responsibilities after World War II. The depiction of smaller countries as children and Uncle Sam as the adult protector suggests a favorite American image/metaphor of family in which difficult allies were seen as naive children in need of tutelage and nurturing from the altruistic United States. *(The Reporter, 1950. Copyright 1950 by Fortnightly Publishing Co., Inc.)*

an obstructionist. Soviet diplomatic machinations and strong-arm rule in Eastern Europe alarmed Washington, and simple-minded communist propaganda offended. With threats more common than compromises, the rude Soviet diplomatic style caused Western diplomats to respond in the same "crabbed and rancorous" manner.[174]

In the turmoil of the immediate postwar years, Americans exaggerated the Soviet/ communist threat, imagining an omnipresent force. Americans made the communist adversary into something it was not, claiming for it a strength it did not possess, blaming it for trouble it did not start, identifying a monolith it did not resemble, and attributing to it accomplishments it did not achieve. True, the tough-talking Soviets eventually turned Eastern Europe into client states and probed in Berlin, but right after World War II the Soviets acted cautiously because they lacked a long-range air force, air defenses, the atomic bomb, and a surface fleet. Moscow actually snubbed independent communists such as Tito and Mao and could not control communists in Western Europe. "The most important thing," Stalin told an Albanian communist in January 1948, "is not to provoke our former allies."[175]

Americans nonetheless came to believe that Moscow ignited, fueled, and exploited unrest around the world, including revolutions. Most upheaval actually sprang from indigenous sources—colonial, tribal, ethnic, religious, cultural, economic. Yet Americans posited a mechanistic "domino theory." Erecting a global wall against communism, the United States supported imperialist allies such as France, which attempted to restore its colonial power in Vietnam against a popular nationalist movement (see pp. 321–323). Believing that the Soviet Union masterminded revolutions directed specifically against U.S. interests, Washington sniffed international conspiracy and refused to recognize the People's Republic of China, hardly a Soviet puppet. Only with respect to Finland ("the only [U.S.] penetration yet achieved in any part of the [Iron] Curtain") did the United States refrain "from acts . . . which might reasonably be regarded by the Soviet Union as a challenge to its essential interests."[176] Dependent on imports of uranium and other strategic minerals from South Africa to sustain a Cold War nuclear strategy and economy, the Truman administration backed white, anticommunist regimes that suppressed black nationalism, acting "as a reluctant uncle—or godparent—at the baptism of apartheid."[177]

Even in Latin America, indirect U.S. intervention to oust communists from the Costa Rican government in 1948 "mirrored the hardening of Washington's policies toward worldwide communism."[178] In 1945–1946 Washington had given tacit support for democratic interventions by exile groups against Caribbean dictatorships, but by the end of the decade it "placed a premium on stability out of concern that Communists might exploit situations of unrest."[179] Thus did Panama receive Point Four assistance in 1950 to combat "Communist-influenced subversive elements," and military aid flowed to the Péron regime in Argentina after 1947 because of Cold War fears.[180]

The Cold War mentality framed discourse in a "system of symbolic representation that defined America's national identity by reference to the un-American 'other,' usually the Soviet Union."[181] Federally funded behavioral scientists used statistical models that always posited the Soviets as a "predatory expansionist power" and the United States always as a "defensive status quo power."[182] Hollywood still featured films about World War II, but "the real unseen enemy was Communism," and postwar movies such as *Sands of Iwo Jima* (1949) and *Twelve O'Clock High* (1949) stressed the "psychological conditioning necessary for a new kind of 'war.' "[183] The expansive term "national security" took on an almost sacred aura, justifying huge military budgets that starved the infrastructure, the suspension of diplomacy in favor of confrontation, interventions far distant from the United States, a secrecy that undermined constitutional procedures, and actions Americans condemned others for—manipulating foreign governments, assassinating political foes abroad, and disseminating false information ("disinformation"). Because the Soviets acted similarly, they share responsibility for the extremes of the long Cold War.

To meet the communist threat and to protect and extend traditional overseas interests through preponderant power, American diplomats in the early Cold War pursued a self-conscious, expansionist, often unilateral foreign policy. In a world ravaged by war, American business and government officials cooperated to expand U.S. foreign trade. By 1947 the United States accounted for one-third of the world's exports. Americans exploited Middle Eastern oil and tapped the raw materials of the Third World, importing manganese ore from Brazil and India, for example. Open Door pronouncements helped spur this trade and facilitate the investment of $12 billion abroad by 1950. Stalin thought the "Open Door policy as dangerous to a nation as foreign military invasion."[184] Further, the expenditure of $1.314 billion in arms aid to NATO in 1949 marked "the beginning of an enormously costly program that," as one official feared, "will go first to Europe and then perhaps to Asia and then to South America and where does it stop?"[185]

The containment doctrine became commanding dogma. When Americans had doubts, the containment doctrine told them what to do. "Like medieval theologians," Fulbright noted, "we had a philosophy that explained everything to us in advance, and everything that did not fit could be readily identified as a fraud or a lie or an illusion."[186] Americans henceforth applied the historical lessons of the 1940s, failing to define precisely the "threat," placing few geographical limits on containment, and increasingly adopting military methods. Whereas Washington explained its mission as containment, Moscow charged "strangulation."[187]

Cold War competition also reshaped political priorities at home. The rhetoric of defending freedom abroad exposed America's "Achilles heel" of institutionalized racism.[188] With the United Nations calling racial discrimination a "burning question" of "immense importance," the President's Committee on Civil Rights warned that "the treatment which our Negroes receive" plays "into the hands of the Communist propagandists."[189] Truman himself acknowledged that "the top dog in a world . . . half colored ought to clean its own house" and took modest steps to desegregate the armed forces and back civil rights reforms.[190] In a brilliant stroke, he appointed Eleanor Roosevelt to the United Nations, where she exhibited "the will, the clout, and the skill" to push through the UN Declaration on Human Rights, adopted in 1948.[191] Yet too often Truman's administration used scare tactics ("clearer than truth," as Acheson put it) to get its way.[192] Most foreign policy debates centered on how much to spend, not whether to spend. Presidential authority expanded accordingly. One member of Congress even asserted that the president "ought to have the same powers as the executives or dictators representing the enslaved peoples in the totalitarian governments."[193] Bipartisanship also allowed

Truman to depict any critic as "a son-of-a-bitch and not a true patriot." If people "will swallow that," Acheson observed, "then you're off to the races."[194]

People swallowed it. Debate—testing assumptions and holding government leaders accountable—became shallow. Tolerance of dissenting views and the fearless inquiry so essential to democracy deteriorated during the early Cold War. Unprincipled demagogues exploited public anxiety about national security, charging that communist conspiracies wormed through official Washington. During the 1948 campaign, the president himself practiced the "red-baiting" so common to Cold War politics when he deliberately linked Progressive party candidate Henry A. Wallace, dissenter from the "get-tough" policy, to the communists. Three years before demagogic Senator Joseph McCarthy charged government officials with treason (see pages 279–280), the Truman administration itself instituted a federal employee loyalty program to identify and ferret out suspected subversives. By not clearly distinguishing dissent from subversion, Truman "helped produce the acids eroding the walls of domestic civility" that McCarthyism later exploited.[195]

As the Cold War grew more perilous, so too did the ominous presence of the atomic bomb. As much as Truman said he "disliked relying on nuclear weapons, he disliked deficits and taxes [from the costs of conventional forces] even more."[196] Military estimates projected that growing Soviet stockpiles of "10, 50, 100" atomic bombs could devastate American cities and kill tens of millions by 1953.[197] Government officials, magazine editors, strategic analysts, scientists, and fiction writers alike, again and again, issued doomsday forecasts, sketching pictures of a radioactive global wasteland if nuclear weapons were not controlled. "The best way to be alive when an atomic bomb goes off in your neighborhood is not to be there," a civil defense official disingenuously suggested.[198] In 1949, in the apocalyptic Cold War film *White Heat,* James Cagney played a gangster who makes it to the "top of the world" perched on a globe-shaped chemical tank that explodes in a mushrooming fireball.[199] Late that year, after the Soviet atomic success, the *Bulletin of the Atomic Scientists* moved the hands of its "doomsday clock" to three minutes before midnight. A few months after the United States exploded the first hydrogen bomb in 1953, the hands moved to two minutes before midnight. America, the poet Robert Frost wrote, had "invented a new Holocaust."[200]

FURTHER READING FOR THE PERIOD 1945–1950

Some works cited in Chapter 6 cover particular leaders and the transition from war to peace.

For general studies of the Cold War era relevant to this chapter and others that follow, see Stephen Ambrose and Douglas Brinkley, *Rise to Globalism* (1997); S. J. Ball, *The Cold War* (1998); H. W. Brands, *The Devil We Knew* (1993); Warren Cohen, *America in the Age of Soviet Power* (1993); Philip J. Funigiello, *American-Soviet Trade in the Cold War* (1988); John Lewis Gaddis, *The Long Peace* (1987), *Russia, the Soviet Union, and the United States* (1990), and *We Now Know* (1997); Alexander L. George et al., eds., *U.S.-Soviet Security Cooperation* (1988); Allen Hunter, ed., *Rethinking the Cold War* (1998); Robert H. Johnson, *Improbable Dangers: Conceptions of Threat in the Cold War and After* (1994); Charles W. Kegley, ed., *The Long Postwar Peace* (1991); Gabriel and Joyce Kolko, *The Limits of Power* (1972); Walter LaFeber, *America, Russia, and the Cold War* (2001); Klaus Lares and Ann Lane, eds., *The Cold War* (2001); Deborah W. Larson, *Anatomy of Mistrust* (1997); David Leebaert, *The Fifty-Year Wound* (2002); Stuart W. Leslie, *The Cold War and American Science* (1994); Ralph Levering, *The Cold War* (1994); Geir Lundestad, *The American "Empire"* (1990); Martin Medhurst and H. W. Brands, eds.,

Critical Reflections on the Cold War (2001); Robert J. McMahon, *The Cold War* (2003); Thomas J. McCormick, *America's Half Century* (1994); David S. Painter, *The Cold War* (1999); Thomas G. Paterson, *Meeting the Communist Threat* (1988) and *On Every Front* (1992); James T. Patterson, *Grand Expectations* (1996); David Reynolds, *One World Divisible* (2000); Michael S. Sherry, *In the Shadow of War* (1995); Hugh Thomas, *Armed Truce* (1987); and Marc Trachtenberg, ed., *Between Empire and Alliance* (2003).

U.S. leaders in the early Cold War period are studied in Rudy Abrahamson, *Spanning the Century* (1992) (Harriman); Allida Black, *Casting Her Own Shadow* (1995) (Eleanor Roosevelt); H. W. Brands, *Inside the Cold War* (1991) (Henderson); Douglas Brinkley, ed., *Dean Acheson and the Making of U.S. Foreign Policy* (1993); David Callahan, *Dangerous Capabilities* (1990) (Nitze); James Chace, *Acheson* (1998); John C. Culver and John Hyde, *American Dreamer* (2000) (Henry Wallace); Irwin F. Gellman, *The Contender* (1999) (Nixon); Mary Ann Glendon, *A World Made New* (2001) (Eleanor Roosevelt); Alonzo Hamby, *Man of the People* (1995) (Truman); James G. Hershberg, *James B. Conant and the Birth of the Nuclear Age* (1993); Townsend Hoopes and Douglas Brinkley, *Driven Patriot* (1992) (Forrestal); Walter Isaacson and Evan Thomas, *The Wise Men* (1986); Peter C. Kent, *The Lonely Cold War of Pope Pius XII* (2002); Nelson D. Lenkford, *The Last American Aristocrat* (1996) (David Bruce); David McCullough, *Truman* (1992); John T. McNary, *Acheson and Empire* (2001); Arnold Offner, *Another Such Victory* (2002) (Truman); William E. Pemberton, *Harry S. Truman* (1989); Forrest C. Pogue, *George C. Marshall* (1963–1987); Alan R. Raucher, *Paul G. Hoffman* (1986); Darlene Rivas, *Missionary Capitalist* (2002) (Nelson Rockefeller); David Robertson, *Sly and Able* (1994) (Byrnes); T. Michael Ruddy, *The Cautious Diplomat* (1986) (Bohlen); Jordan A. Schwarz, *The Speculator* (1981) (Baruch); Ronald Steel, *Walter Lippmann and the American Century* (1980); Mark A. Stoler, *George C. Marshall* (1989); J. Samuel Walker, *Henry A. Wallace and American Foreign Policy* (1976).

Many books, all with the main title *Stalin,* include and critique the Soviet leader's foreign policy: Robert Conquest (1991); Isaac Deutscher (1967); Walter Laqueur (1990); Robert H. McNeal (1988); Edward Radzinsky (1996); and Dmitri Volkogonov (1991).

The ideas and career of George F. Kennan are explored in Barton Gellman, *Contending with Kennan* (1984); Walter Hixson, *George F. Kennan* (1990); David Mayers, *George Kennan and the Dilemmas of U.S. Foreign Policy* (1988); Wilson D. Miscamble, *George F. Kennan and the Making of American Foreign Policy* (1992); and Anders Stephanson, *George Kennan and the Art of Foreign Policy* (1989).

For the origins of the Cold War, see works cited in the paragraphs above and Barton J. Bernstein, ed., *Politics and Policies of the Truman Administration* (1970); Kendrick A. Clements, ed., *James F. Byrnes and the Origins of the Cold War* (1982); Robert J. Donovan, *Conflict and Crisis* (1977); John Lewis Gaddis, *The United States and the Origins of the Cold War* (1972); Lloyd Gardner, *Architects of Illusion* (1970); Francesca Gori and Silvio Pons, *The Soviet Union and Europe in the Cold War* (1996); James L. Gormly, *The Collapse of the Grand Alliance* (1987); George Herring, *Aid to Russia, 1941–1946* (1973); Lynn B. Hinds and Theodore O. Windt, Jr., *The Cold War as Rhetoric* (1991); Michael J. Hogan, *A Cross of Iron: Harry S. Truman and the Origins of the National Security State* (1998); John Ikenberry, *After Victory* (2001); Frank Kofsky, *Harry S. Truman and the War Scare of 1948* (1993); Gabriel Kolko, *The Politics of War* (1968); Deborah W. Larson, *Origins of Containment* (1985); Melvyn P. Leffler, *A Preponderance of Power* (1992) and *The Specter of Communism* (1994); Ralph B. Levering et al., *Debating the Origins of the Cold War* (2002); Donald R. McCoy, *The Presidency of Harry S. Truman* (1984); Vojtech Mastny, *The Cold War and Soviet Insecurity* (1996); Robert Messer, *The End of an Alliance* (1982); Chester J. Pach, *Arming the Free World* (1991); Thomas G. Paterson, ed., *Cold War Critics* (1971); David Reynolds, ed., *The Origins of the Cold War in Europe* (1994); William Taubman, *Stalin's American Policy* (1982); Daniel Yergin, *Shattered Peace* (1977); and Vladislav Zubok and Constantine Pleshakov, *Inside the Kremlin's Cold War* (1996).

For the early years of the United Nations Organization, see James Barros, *Trygvie Lie and the Cold War* (1989); Thomas Campbell, *Masquerade Peace* (1973); Robert A. Divine, *Second Chance* (1967); Robert C. Hilderbrand, *Dumbarton Oaks* (1990); Townsend Hoopes and Douglas Brinkley, *FDR and the Creation of the U.N.* (1997); Evan Luard and Derek Herter, *The United Nations* (1993); and George Mazuzan, *Warren R. Austin at the U.N., 1946–1953* (1977).

The atomic bomb, nuclear questions, and their cultural impact are discussed in Gar Alperovitz, *Atomic Diplomacy* (1985) and *The Decision to Use the Atomic Bomb* (1995); Barton J. Bernstein, ed., *The Atomic Bomb*

(1975); Kai Bird and Lawrence Lifschultz, eds., *Hiroshima Shadows* (1998); Paul Boyer, *By the Bomb's Early Light* (1986) and *Fallout* (1998); McGeorge Bundy, *Danger and Survival* (1990); Robert J. C. Butow, *Japan's Decision to Surrender* (1954); Herbert Feis, *The Atomic Bomb and the End of World War II* (1966); Jonathan E. Helmreich, *Gathering Rare Ores: The Diplomacy of Uranium Acquisition* (1986); Margot A. Henriksen, *Dr. Strangelove's America* (1997); Gregg Herken, *The Winning Weapon* (1981); Richard Hewlett and Oscar Anderson, *The New World* (1962); Michael J. Hogan, ed., *Hiroshima in History and Memory* (1996); David Holloway, *The Soviet Union and the Arms Race* (1984) and *Stalin and the Bomb* (1994); Robert Jay Lifton and Greg Mitchell, *Hiroshima in America* (1995); M. Susan Lindee, *Suffering Made Real: American Science and the Survivors at Hiroshima* (1994); Robert J. Maddox, *Weapons for Victory* (1995); Robert P. Neuman, *Truman and the Hiroshima Cult* (1995); Robert S. Norris, *Racing for the Bomb* (2002) (Leslie Groves); Martin Sherwin, *A World Destroyed* (1975); Ronald Takaki, *Hiroshima* (1995); J. Samuel Walker, *Prompt and Utter Destruction* (1997); Samuel R. Williamson and Steven L. Rearden, *The Origins of U.S. Nuclear Strategy* (1993); Allan M. Winkler, *Life Under a Cloud* (1993); and Lawrence S. Wittner, *The Struggle Against the Bomb* (1993) (disarmament movement). The H-bomb is treated in Richard Rhodes, *Dark Sun* (1987), and Herbert F. York, *The Advisors* (1975).

Studies that focus on Eastern Europe and Finland include Debra J. Allen, *The Oder-Neisse Line* (2003); Phyllis Auty, *Tito* (1970); Michael M. Boll, *Cold War in the Balkans* (1984); James Jay Carafano, *Waltzing into the Cold War* (2002) (Austria); Charles Gati, *Hungary and the Soviet Bloc* (1983); Jussi M. Hanhimäki, *Containing Coexistence* (1997) (Finland); Lorraine M. Lees, *Keeping Tito Afloat* (1997); Richard Lukacs, *Bitter Legacy* (1982) (Poland); Geir Lundestad, *The American Non-Policy Towards Eastern Europe* (1975) and *America, Scandinavia, and the Cold War* (1980); Eric Roman, *Hungary and the Victor Powers* (1996); Walter Ullman, *The United States in Prague* (1978); Piotr Wandycz, *The United States and Poland* (1980); and Patricia Ward, *The Threat of Peace* (1979).

Anglo-American relations are discussed in Terry H. Anderson, *The United States, Great Britain, and the Cold War* (1981); Richard A. Best, Jr., *"Co-operation with Like-Minded Peoples"* (1986); Robin Edmonds, *Setting the Mould* (1987); Fraser J. Harbutt, *The Iron Curtain* (1986); Robert M. Hathaway, *Ambiguous Partnership* (1981); John Kent, *British Imperial Strategy and the Origins of the Cold War* (1993); Arieh Kochavi, *Post-Holocaust Politics* (2002) (Britain and U.S.); Klaus Larres, *Churchill's Cold War* (2002); W. Roger Louis and Hedley Bull, eds., *The Special Relationship* (1986); Ritchie Overdale, *The English Speaking Alliance* (1985); Kenneth W. Thompson, *Winston Churchill's World View* (1983); and Randall B. Woods, *A Changing of the Guard* (1990).

The United States in the world economy and economic expansion are treated in Irvine H. Anderson, *Aramco, the United States, and Saudi Arabia* (1981); Fred L. Block, *The Origins of International Economic Disorder* (1977); Alfred E. Eckes, Jr., *A Search for Solvency* (1975) (Bretton Woods) and *The United States and the Global Struggle for Minerals* (1979); Diane Kunz, *Butter and Guns* (1997); Aaron D. Miller, *Search for Security* (1980) (Saudi Arabia's oil); David S. Painter, *Oil and the American Century* (1986); Stephen J. Randall, *United States Foreign Oil Policy, 1919–1984* (1985); Michael B. Stoff, *Oil, War, and American Security* (1980); and Thomas Zeiler, *Free Trade, Free World* (1999).

Cultural relations are specifically explored in Christian G. Appy, *Cold War Constructions* (2000); Tom Engelhardt, *The End of Victory Culture* (1995); Benjamin O. Fordham, *Building the Cold War Consensus* (1998); John Fousek, *To Lead the Free World* (2000); Jessica C. E. Gienow-Hecht, *Transmission Impossible* (1999); Kyoko Hirano, *Mr. Smith Goes to Tokyo* (1992) (cinema in Japan); Christina Klein, *Cold War Orientalism* (2003); Peter J. Kuznick and James Gilbert, eds., *Rethinking Cold War Culture* (2001); Lary May, ed., *Recasting America* (1989); Frank A. Ninkovich, *The Diplomacy of Ideas* (1981); Richard Pells, *Not like Us* (1997); Uta G. Poiger, *Jazz, Rock, and Rebels* (2000); Frances Stoner Saunders, *The Cultural Cold War* (1999); William W. Savage, Jr., *Commies, Cowboys, and Jungle Queens* (1998); and Reinhold Wagnleitner, *Coca-Colonization and the Cold War* (1994) (Austria).

For Western European issues, including economic reconstruction, Austria, and the Marshall Plan, see John Bledsoe Bonds, *Bipartisan Strategy* (2002); Anthony Carew, *Labour Under the Marshall Plan* (1987); Audrey K. Cronin, *Great Power Politics and the Struggle over Austria* (1986); Jill Edwards, *Anglo-American Relations and the Franco Question, 1945–1955* (1999); David W. Ellwood, *Rebuilding Europe* (1992); Chiarello Esposito, *America's Feeble Weapon* (1994) (Marshall Plan); Richard Gardner, *Sterling-Dollar Diplomacy* (1969); Haim Genizi, *America's Fair Share* (1993) (displaced persons); John L. Harper, *America and the Reconstruction of Italy* (1986) and *American Visions of Europe* (1994); William I. Hitchcock, *France Restored* (2001); Michael J. Hogan, *The Marshall Plan* (1987); John Killick, *The United States and European Integration, 1945–1960* (1998); Boris N. Liedtke, *Embracing a Dictatorship* (1998) (Spain); James E. Miller, *The United States and Italy* (1986); Alan S. Milward, *The Reconstruction of Western Europe, 1945–51* (1984); Thomas G. Paterson, *Soviet-American Confrontation* (1973); Sallie Pisani, *The CIA and the Marshall Plan* (1991); Robert A. Pollard, *Economic Security and the Origins of the Cold War* (1985); Mark Trachtenberg, *A Constructed Peace* (1999); Irwin M. Wall, *The United States and the Making of Postwar France* (1991); Donald R. Whiting and Edgar Erickson, *The American Occupation of Austria* (1985); Imanuel Wexler, *The Marshall Plan Revisited* (1983); and John W. Young, *Britain, France, and the Unity of Europe* (1984).

For Germany, see John H. Backer, *Winds of History* (1984); Tom Bower, *The Paperclip Conspiracy* (1988); Jeffrey M. Diefendorf et al., eds., *American Policy and the Reconstruction of West Germany* (1993); Carolyn Eisenberg, *Drawing the Line* (1996); John Gimbel, *The American Occupation of Germany* (1968), *The Origins of the Marshall Plan* (1976), and *Science, Technology, and Reparations* (1990); Petra Goedda, *GIs and Germans* (2003); Maria Hohn, *GIs and Frauleins* (2002); Bruce Kuklick, *American Policy and the Division of Germany* (1972); James McAllister, *No Exit: America and the German Problem, 1943–1954* (2002); Norman Naimark, *The Russians in Germany* (1995); Thomas Parrish, *Berlin in the Balance, 1945–1949* (1998); Edward N. Peterson, *The American Occupation of Germany* (1978); Thomas A. Schwartz, *America's Germany* (1991); Avi Shlaim, *The United States and the Berlin Blockade, 1948–1949* (1983); Christopher Simpson, *Blowback* (1988) (recruitment of Nazis); and John Willoughby, *Remaking the Conquering Heroes* (2001).

For the Truman Doctrine and containment, consult G. M. Alexander, *The Prelude to the Truman Doctrine* (1984); David J. Alvarez, *Bureaucracy and Cold War Ideology* (1980) (Turkey); Richard Barnet, *Intervention and Revolution* (1972); Richard Freeland, *The Truman Doctrine and the Origins of McCarthyism* (1971); John Lewis Gaddis, *Strategies of Containment* (1981); Charles Gati, ed., *Caging the Bear* (1977); John O. Iatrides, *Revolt in Athens* (1972), ed., *Greece in the 1940s* (1981), and ed., *Greece at the Crossroads* (1995); Judith S. Jeffery, *Ambiguous Commitments and Uncertain Policies* (1999); Howard Jones, *"A New Kind of War"* (1989); Jon V. Kofas, *Intervention and Underdevelopment* (1989) (Greece); Bruce R. Kuniholm, *The Origins of the Cold War in the Near East* (1980); and Lawrence S. Wittner, *American Intervention in Greece, 1943–1949* (1982).

NATO and military questions are studied in John Baylis, *The Diplomacy of Pragmatism* (1993) (Britain); Timothy P. Ireland, *Creating the Entangling Alliance* (1981); Lawrence S. Kaplan, *The United States and NATO* (1984), *NATO and the United States* (1988), and *The Long Entanglement: NATO's First Fifty Years* (1999); S. V. Papacosma et al., *NATO After Fifty Years* (2001); Steven L. Rearden, *History of the Office of the Secretary of Defense* (1984); Olav Riste, ed., *Western Security* (1985); Gustav Schmidt, *A History of NATO* (2001); Edward J. Sheehy, *The U.S. Navy, the Mediterranean, and the Cold War* (1992); Michael S. Sherry, *The Rise of American Air Power* (1987); Nicholas Sherwen, ed., *NATO's Anxious Birth* (1985); E. Timothy Smith, *The United States, Italy, and NATO* (1991); and Joseph Smith, ed., *The Origins of NATO* (1990).

U.S. relations with Asia, including decolonization, are discussed in Robert Blum, *Drawing the Line* (1982); Russell Buhite, *Soviet-American Relations in Asia, 1945–1954* (1982); Kenton J. Clymer, *Quest for Freedom* (1995) (India); Nick Cullather, *Illusions of Influence* (1994) (Philippines); Hal M. Friedman, *Creating an American Lake* (2000); Marc S. Gallicchio, *The Cold War Begins in Asia* (1988); Gary Hess *The United States' Emergence as a Southeast Asian Power, 1940–1950* (1987); Akira Iriye and Warren Cohen, eds., *American, Chinese, and Japanese Perspectives on Wartime Asia, 1931–1949* (1990); James I. Matray, *The Reluctant Crusade* (1985) (Korea); Robert J. McMahon, *Colonialism and Cold War* (1981) (Indonesia), *The Cold War on the Periphery* (1994) (India and Pakistan), and *The Limits of Empire* (1999) (Southeast Asia); Yōnosuke Nagai and Akira Iriye, eds., *The Origins of the Cold War in Asia* (1977); Bonnie B. C. Oh, ed., *Korea Under the American Military Government, 1945–1948* (2002); Andrew Roadnight, *United States Policy Toward Indonesia in the Truman and Eisenhower Years* (2002); Andrew J. Rotter, *Comrades at Odds* (2000) (India); Anita I. Singh, *The Limits of British Influence* (1994) (South Asia); William Stueck, *The Road to Confrontation* (1981); and Nicholas Tarling, *Britain, Southeast Asia and the Onset of the Cold War, 1945–1950* (1998). For works on Vietnam and Indochina, see Chapter 9.

For Japan and the American occupation, see Ian Barnna, *Investigating Japan* (2003); William S. Borden, *The Pacific Alliance* (1984); Roger Buckley, *Occupation Diplomacy* (1982); John W. Dower, *Empire and Aftermath* (1979), *War Without Mercy* (1986), and *Embracing Defeat* (1999); Robert D. Eldridge, *The Origins of the Bilateral Okinawa Problem* (2001); Richard B. Finn, *Winners in Peace* (1992); D. Clayton James, *The Years of MacArthur* (1985); Yukiko Koshiro, *Trans-Pacific Racisms and the U.S. Occupation of Japan* (1999); Walter LaFeber, *The Clash* (1997); Tim Maga,

Judgment at Tokyo (1999); Michael S. Molasky, *The American Occupation of Japan and Okinawa* (1999); Nicholas E. Sarantakes, *Keystone* (2000) (Okinawa); Michael Schaller, *The American Occupation of Japan* (1985), *Douglas MacArthur* (1989), and *Altered States* (1997); and Gary H. Tsuchimochi, *Education Reform in Postwar Japan* (1993).

For China and the recognition question, see Dorothy Borg and Waldo Heinrichs, eds., *Uncertain Years* (1980); Russell Buhite, *Patrick J. Hurley and American Foreign Policy* (1973); Carolle J. Carter, *Mission to Yenan* (1997); Gordon Chang, *Friends and Enemies* (1990); Thomas J. Christensen, *Useful Adversaries* (1996); Warren Cohen, *America's Response to China* (2000); Sergei Goncharov, John Lewis, and Xue Litai, *Uncertain Partners* (1993); Harry Harding and Yuan Ming, eds., *Sino-American Relations, 1945–55* (1989); Michael H. Hunt, *The Genesis of Chinese Communist Foreign Policy* (1996); T. Christoper Jesperson, *American Images of China* (1996); Chen Jian, *Mao's China and the Cold War* (2001); E. J. Kahn, Jr., *The China Hands* (1975); Ronald C. Keith, *The Diplomacy of Zhou Enlai* (1989); Ross Koen, *The China Lobby in American Politics* (1974); Paul G. Lauren, ed., *The China Hands' Legacy* (1987); Gary May, *China Scapegoat* (1979); Robert P. Newman, *Owen Lattimore and the "Loss" of China* (1992); James Reardon-Anderson, *Yenan and the Great Powers* (1979); Michael M. Sheng, *Battling Western Imperialism* (1998); William Stueck, *The Wedemeyer Mission* (1984); Nancy B. Tucker, *Patterns in the Dust* (1983) and *Taiwan, Hong Kong, and the United States* (1994); Odd Arne Westad, *Cold War and Revolution* (1993); and *Decisive Encounters: The Chinese Civil War* (2003); Shaw Yu-Ming, *John Leighton Stuart and Twentieth-Century Chinese-American Relations* (1992); and Shu Guang Zhang, *Deterrence and Strategic Culture* (1992).

For the Middle East, Iran, and the new state of Israel, see books on oil cited above and Michael J. Cohen, *Palestine and the Great Powers* (1983) and *Truman and Israel* (1990); Leonard Dinnerstein, *America and the Survivors of the Holocaust* (1982); Bruce J. Evensen, *Truman, Palestine, and the Press* (1992); Louise L. Fawcett, *Iran and the Cold War* (1992) (1946 crisis); Zvi Ganin, *Truman, American Jewry, and Israel, 1945–1948* (1979); James F. Goode, *The United States and Iran, 1946–51* (1989); Peter L. Hahn, *The United States, Great Britain, and Egypt* (1991); Burton I. Kaufman, *The Arab Middle East and the United States* (1996); George Lenczowski, *American Presidents and the Middle East* (1989); Douglas Little, *American Orientalism* (2002); William Roger Louis, *The British Empire in the Middle East, 1945–1951* (1984); William Roger Louis and Robert W. Stookey, eds., *The End of the Palestine Mandate* (1986); Mark H. Lytle, *The Origins of Iranian-American Alliance, 1941–1953* (1987); John Quigley, *Palestine and Israel* (1990); Barry Rubin, *The Great Powers in the Middle East, 1941–1947* (1980); David Schoenbaum, *The United States and the State of Israel* (1993); John Snetsinger, *Truman, the Jewish Vote, and the Creation of Israel* (1974); and Robert W. Stookey, *America and the Arab States* (1975). See also works on the Middle East cited in following chapters.

Relations with other Third World nations, including Latin America, are explored in Charles D. Ameringer, *The Caribbean Legion* (1996); Scott L. Bills, *Empire and Cold War* (1990) and *The Libyan Arena* (1995); Thomas Borstelmann, *Apartheid's Reluctant Uncle* (1993) (South Africa); Mary Ann Heiss and Peter L. Hahn, eds., *Empire and Revolution* (2001); Zachary Karabell, *Architects of Intervention* (1999); Michael L. Krenn, *The Chains of Interdependence* (1996) (Central America); Walter LaFeber, *Inevitable Revolutions* (1993); Thomas M. Leonard, *The United States and Central America, 1944–1949* (1984); Kyle Longley, *The Sparrow and the Hawk* (1997) (Costa Rica); and Gaddis Smith, *The Last Years of the Monroe Doctrine* (1994).

For Canada-U.S. relations, see Robert Bothwell, *Canada and the United States* (1992); Greg Donaghy, ed., *Canada and the Early Cold War, 1943–1957* (1998); Joseph Jockel, *No Boundaries Upstairs* (1989); Denis Smith, *Diplomacy of Fear* (1988); and John H. Thompson and Stephen J. Randall, *Canada and the United States* (1998).

For espionage and the origins of the Central Intelligence Agency, see Richard Aldrich, *The Hidden Hand* (2001); Obert Benson and Michael Warner, eds., *Venona* (1996); Arthur B. Darling, *The Central Intelligence Agency* (1990); Peter Grose, *Operation Rollback* (2000); John Earl Haynes and Harvey Klehr, *Venona* (1999); Gregory Mitrovich, *Undermining the Kremlin* (2000); Katherine S. Olmsted, *Red Spy Queen* (2002) (Elizabeth Bentley); David F. Rudgers, *Creating the Secret State* (2000); Athan Theoharis, *Chasing Spies* (2002); Evan Thomas, *The Very Best Men* (1995); Thomas F. Troy, *Wild Bill and Intrepid* (1996); and Hugh Wilford, *The CIA, the British Left, and the Cold War* (2003).

For domestic politics, anticommunism, interest groups, and public opinion in the early Cold War period, see Carol Anderson, *Eyes off the Prize* (2003); Justus Doenecke, *Not to the Swift: The Old Isolationists in the Cold War Era* (1979); Bruce E. Field, *Harvest of Dissent: The National Farmers Union and the Early Cold War* (1998);

Richard M. Fried, *Nightmare in Red* (1990) and *The Russians Are Coming! The Russians Are Coming!* (1998); Aaron L. Friedberg, *In The Shadow of the Garrison State* (2003); Robert Griffith and Athan Theoharis, eds., *The Specter* (1974); John E. Haynes, *Red Scare or Red Menace?* (1996); William Keller, *The Liberals and J. Edgar Hoover* (1989); Harvey Klehr and Ronald Radosh, *The Amerasia Spy Case* (1996); David F. Krugler, *The Voice of America and the Domestic Propaganda Battles, 1945–1953* (2000); Azza Salama Layton, *International Politics and Civil Rights in the United States, 1941–1960* (1999); Scott Lucas, *Freedom's War* (1999); William L. O'Neill, *A Better World: Stalinism and the American Intellectuals* (1983); Brenda G. Plummer, *Rising Wind* (1996) (African Americans) and *Windows on Freedom* (2003); Ron Robin, *The Making of a Cold War Enemy* (2001); Timothy E. Smith, *Opposition Beyond the Water's Edge* (1999); Peter L. Steinberg, *The Great "Red" Menace* (1984); Athan Theoharis, *The Yalta Myths* (1970), *Seeds of Repression* (1971), and ed., *Beyond the Hiss Case: The FBI, Congress, and the Cold War* (1982); Penny von Eschen, *Race Against Empire* (1997) (African Americans); and Lawrence Wittner, *Rebels Against War.* For works on McCarthyism, see Chapter 8.

See also the General Bibliography and the following notes.

For comprehensive coverage of foreign-relations topics, see the articles in the four-volume *Encyclopedia of U.S. Foreign Relations* (1997), edited by Bruce W. Jentleson and Thomas G. Paterson.

NOTES TO CHAPTER 7

1. Quoted in Hanson W. Baldwin, "Hiroshima Decision," in *Hiroshima Plus 20* (New York: Delacorte, 1965), p. 41.
2. Harold M. Agnew quoted in *Time, CXXVI* (July 29, 1985), 46.
3. Quoted in John Toland, *The Rising Sun* (New York: Random House, 1970), p. 780.
4. Quoted in *New York Times*, August 6, 1995.
5. Quoted in William L. Laurence, *Dawn over Zero* (New York: Knopf, 1946), pp. 219, 221.
6. Wakashi Shigetosi quoted in M. Susan Lindee, *American Science and the Survivors at Hiroshima* (Chicago: University of Chicago Press, 1994), p. 4.
7. Toyonaga Keisaburo, "Colonialism and Atom Bombs," in T. Fujitani, Geoffrey M. White, and Lisa Yoneyama, eds., *Perilous Memories* (Durham: Duke University Press, 2001), p. 380.
8. Michihiko Hachiya, *Hiroshima Diary* (Chapel Hill: University of North Carolina Press, 1955), p. 6.
9. Quoted in Timothy L. Francis, "The Japanese Execution of American Aircrew at Fukuoka, Japan, During 1945," *Pacific Historical Review, LXVI* (November 1997), 481.
10. Quoted in John M. Blum, ed., *The Price of Vision* (Boston: Houghton Mifflin, 1973), p. 474.
11. Paul Fussell, "Hiroshima," in Michael B. Stoff, ed., *The Manhattan Project* (New York: McGraw-Hill, 1991), p. 276.
12. William D. Leahy, *I Was There* (New York: Whittlesey, 1950), p. 441.
13. Barton J. Bernstein, "Understanding the Atomic Bomb," *Diplomatic History, XIX* (Spring 1995), 267.
14. Tom Englehardt, *The End of Victory Culture* (New York: Basic Books, 1995), p. 55.
15. Quoted in Alvin D. Coox, "The Compromise of U.S. Plans to Invade Japan in 1945," *Journal of Military History, LXIV* (April 2000), 416.
16. Herbert Hoover quoted in D. M. Giangreco, "President Truman and Casualty Estimates for the Invasion of Japan," *Pacific Historical Review, LXXII* (February 2003), 95; quoted in Robert Messer, "American Perspectives on the Origins of the Cold War in Asia," in Akira Iriye and Warren Cohen, eds., *American, Chinese, and Japanese Perspectives on Wartime Asia, 1931–1949* (Wilmington, Del.: Scholarly Resources, 1990), p. 251.

17. Quoted in Barton J. Bernstein, "Roosevelt, Truman and the Atomic Bomb, 1941–1945," *Political Science Quarterly, XC* (Spring 1975), 61.
18. Quoted in Michael S. Sherry, *The Rise of American Air Power* (New Haven: Yale University Press, 1987), p. 341.
19. Barton J. Bernstein, "Japanese Buildup on Southern Kyushu," *Pacific Historical Review, LXVIII* (December, 1999), 903.
20. Quoted in Lloyd C. Gardner, "Unconditional Surrender: The Dawn of the Atomic Age," in Dale Carter and Robin Clifton, eds., *War and Cold War in American Foreign Policy, 1942–62* (New York: Palgrave, 2002), p. 71.
21. Harry S. Truman, *Memoirs* (Garden City N.Y.: Doubleday 1955–56; 2 vols.), I, 416.
22. David Holloway, *Stalin and the Bomb* (Stanford: Stanford University Press, 1994), p. 115.
23. Quoted *ibid.*, p. 132.
24. Quoted in Martin J. Sherwin, *A World Destroyed* (New York: Knopf, 1975), p. 224.
25. Quoted in Alvin D. Coox, "The *Enola Gay* and Japan's Struggle to Surrender," *Journal of American-East Asian Relations, IV* (Summer 1995), 165.
26. Quoted in Peter J. Kuznick and James Gilbert, "The Culture of the Cold War," in Peter J. Kuznick and James Gilbert, eds., *Rethinking Cold War Culture* (Washington, D.C.: Smithsonian Institution Press, 2001), p. 2.
27. Quoted in Donald W. White, *The American Century* (New Haven: Yale University Press, 1996), pp. 81–82.
28. Quoted in Marc Trachtenberg, *A Constructed Peace* (Princeton: Princeton University Press, 1999), p. 63.
29. Quoted in Melvyn Leffler, "The Beginning and the End: Time, Context, and the Cold War," unpublished paper, 2002, p. 3.
30. *Foreign Relations, 1946* (Washington, D.C.: Government Printing Office, 1969), VI, 707.
31. James A. Forrestal quoted in Gregory Mitrovich, *Undermining the Kremlin* (Ithaca: Cornell University Press, 2000), p. 12.
32. Quoted in Vladislav Zubok and Constantine Pleshakov, *Inside the Kremlin's Cold War* (Cambridge: Harvard University Press, 1996), p. 31.

33. Quoted in Arnold A. Offner, *Another Such Victory* (Stanford: Stanford University Press, 2002), p. 129.

34. Gaddis Smith, *Dean Acheson* (New York: Cooper Square, 1972), p. 416.

35. Lord Inverchapel quoted in Peter Boyle, "America's Hesitant Road to NATO, 1945–1949," in Joseph Smith, ed., *The Origins of NATO* (Exeter, Eng.: University of Exeter Press, 1990), p. 76.

36. Quoted in John C. Culver and John Hyde, *American Dreamer* (New York: Norton, 2000), p. 405.

37. Quoted in John Lewis Gaddis, *The United States and the Origins of the Cold War* (New York: Columbia University Press, 1972), p. 205.

38. Quoted in John Lewis Gaddis, "Harry S. Truman and the Origins of Containment," in Frank Merli and Theodore Wilson, eds., *Makers of American Diplomacy* (New York: Charles Scribner's Sons, 1974), p. 500.

39. Quoted in Melvyn P. Leffler, *A Preponderance of Power* (Stanford: Stanford University Press, 1992), p. 99.

40. Lester Markel, "Opinion—A Neglected Instrument," in Lester Markel et al., *Public Opinion and Foreign Policy* (New York: Harper, 1949), p. 4.

41. *Public Papers, Truman, 1952–53* (Washington, D.C.: Government Printing Office, 1966), p. 1199.

42. Paul Kennedy, *The Rise and Fall of the Great Powers* (New York: Random House, 1987), p. 515.

43. Vladimir O. Pechatnov, "Foreign Policy Correspondence Between Stalin and Molotov and Other Politiburo Members, September 1945–December 1946," Working Paper no. 26, *Cold War International History Project* (Washington, D.C., September 1999), p. 25.

44. Quoted in Edward Pessen, *Losing Our Souls* (Chicago: Ivan R. Dee, 1993), p. 62.

45. Leffler, "Beginning and End," p. 9.

46. U.S. Minister Selden Sapin quoted in Eric Roman, *Hungary and the Victor Powers, 1945–1950* (New York: St. Martin's, 1996), p. 189.

47. Quoted in Ralph B. Levering et al., *Debating the Origins of the Cold War* (New York: Rowman and Littlefield, 2002), p. 121.

48. Quoted in David Reynolds, *Britannia Overruled* (New York: Longman, 2000), p. 165.

49. CIA estimate quoted in Jussi Hanhimaki, *Containing Coexistence* (Kent, Ohio: Kent State University Press, 1997), p. 52.

50. Kennan quoted in Mitrovich, *Undermining*, p. 39.

51. Quoted in Melvyn P. Leffler, *The Specter of Communism* (New York: Hill & Wang, 1994), p. 43.

52. Quoted in Vladislav Zubok and Constantine Pleshakov, "The Soviet Union," in David Reynolds, ed., *The Origins of the Cold War in Europe* (New Haven: Yale University Press, 1994), p. 62.

53. Vojtech Mastny, "Soviet Plans for Postwar Europe," in Antonio Varsori and Elena Calandri, eds., *The Failure of Peace in Europe, 1943–48* (New York: Palgrave, 2002), p. 69.

54. Quoted in Trachtenberg, *Constructed Peace*, p. 36.

55. Quoted in Lloyd C. Gardner, *Economic Aspects of New Deal Diplomacy* (Madison: University of Wisconsin Press, 1964), p. 308.

56. Quoted in Levering, *Debating the Origins*, p. 113.

57. Quoted in Barton J. Bernstein, "American Foreign Policy and the Origins of the Cold War," in Barton J. Bernstein, ed., *Politics and Policies of the Truman Administration* (Chicago: Quadrangle, 1970), p. 36.

58. Quoted in Gregg Herken, *The Winning Weapon* (New York: Knopf, 1980), p. 48.

59. Henry L. Stimson and McGeorge Bundy, *On Active Service in Peace and War* (New York: Harper & Brothers, 1948), p. 644.

60. Walter Millis, ed., *The Forrestal Diaries* (New York: Viking, 1951), p. 96.

61. *Foreign Relations 1946, VII* (Washington, D.C.: Government Printing Office, 1969), 223.

62. Quoted in Alexander Werth, *Russia: The Post-War Years* (New York: Taplinger, 1971), pp. 328, 329.

63. Quoted in James L. Gormly, *The Collapse of the Grand Alliance, 1945–1948* (Baton Rouge: Louisiana State University Press, 1987), p. 147.

64. Quoted in Thomas G. Paterson, *Meeting the Communist Threat* (New York: Oxford University Press, 1988), pp. 114, 115.

65. Frank Costigliola, "'Unceasing Pressure for Penetration,'" *Journal of American History, LXXXIV* (March 1997), 1333.

66. Quoted in Fraser J. Harbutt, *The Iron Curtain* (New York: Oxford Univerity Press, 1986), p. 186.

67. David Brinkley, *David Brinkley* (New York: Knopf, 1995), p. 74.

68. Lord Halifax quoted in Klaus Larres, *Churchill's Cold War* (New Haven: Yale University Press, 2002), p. 109.

69. Quoted in Douglas Little, *American Orientalism* (Chapel Hill: University of North Carolina Press, 2002), p. 121.

70. Quoted in Louise L. Fawcett, *Iran and the Cold War* (Cambridge, Eng.: Cambridge University Press, 1992), p. 125.

71. Arthur C. Millspaugh, "Memorandum on . . . Iran," September 8, 1948, Box 20, John W. Snyder Papers, Harry S. Truman Library, Independence, Mo.

72. *Vital Speeches, XII* (October 1, 1946), 738–741.

73. Quoted in Arnold A. Offner, "Another Such Victory," *Diplomatic History, XXIII* (Spring 1999), 138.

74. W. Averell Harriman, "Certain Factors Underlying Our Relations with the Soviet Union," November 14, 1945, Harriman Papers, Library of Congress, Washington, D.C.

75. Baruch quoted in Shane J. Maddock, "The Nth Country Conundrum" (Ph.D. diss., University of Connecticut, 1997), p. 123.

76. Henry A. Wallace, "The Path to Peace with Russia," *The New Republic, CXV* (September 30, 1946), 401–406.

77. "The Novikov Telegram, Washington, September 27, 1946," *Diplomatic History, XV* (Fall 1991), 527.

78. Bob Hope, *So This Is Peace* (New York: Simon & Schuster, 1946), p. 167.

79. Quoted in Arnold A. Offner, "Harry S. Truman as Parochial Nationalist," in Thomas G. Paterson and Robert J. McMahon, eds., *The Origins of the Cold War*, 3rd ed. (Lexington, Mass.: Heath, 1991), p. 56.

80. Quoted in John Willoughby, *Remaking the Conquering Heroes* (New York: Palgrave, 2001), p. 33; quoted in John Gimbel, "Project Paperclip," *Diplomatic History, XIV* (Summer 1990), 351.

81. Quoted in Thomas A. Schwartz, *America's Germany* (Cambridge: Harvard University Press, 1991), p. 31.

82. Walter Bedell Smith quoted in Carolyn Eisenberg, *Drawing the Line* (New York: Cambridge University Press, 1996), p. 488.

83. Norman Naimark, *The Russians in Germany* (Cambridge: Harvard University Press, 1995), p. 467.

84. Alexander Paniushkin quoted in Vojtech Mastny, *The Cold War and Soviet Insecurity* (New York: Oxford University Press, 1996), p. 59; Georges Bidault quoted in James McAllister, *No Exit: America and the German Problem, 1943–1954* (Ithaca: Cornell University Press, 2002), p. 147.

85. Robert Murphy quoted in Offner, *Another Such Victory*, p. 256.

86. Andrei Gromyko quoted in Holloway, *Stalin and the Bomb*, p. 260.

87. *Public Papers, Truman, 1947* (Washington, D.C.: Government Printing Office, 1963), pp. 176–180.

88. Quoted in David W. Ellwood, *Rebuilding Europe* (London: Longman, 1992), p. 69.

89. Quoted in John O. Iatrides, *Revolt in Athens* (Princeton: Princeton University Press, 1972), p. 208.

90. Paul Porter quoted in Howard Jones, *"A New Kind of War"* (New York: Oxford University Press, 1989), p. 30.

91. Peter J. Stavrakis, "Soviet Policy in Greece," in John O. Iatrides and Linda Wrigley, eds., *Greece at the Crossroads* (University Park: Penn State University Press, 1995), p. 228.

92. *Congressional Record, XCIII* (April 22, 1947), 3772–3773.

93. *Foreign Relations, Yalta*, p. 903.

94. Quoted in Eduard Mark, "The War Scare of 1946," *Diplomatic History, XXI* (Summer 1997), 383.

95. Quoted *ibid.*, p. 414.

96. Loy Henderson quoted in H. W. Brands, *Inside the Cold War* (New York: Oxford University Press, 1991), p. 177.

97. Quoted in George Lenczowski, *American Presidents and the Middle East* (Durham: Duke University Press, 1990), p. 30.

98. Warren Austin quoted in Mark A. Stoler, *George C. Marshall* (Boston: Twayne, 1989), p. 172.

99. Truman Diary, July 21, 1947, Harry S. Truman Library, Independence, MO.

100. Quoted in Michael J. Cohen, *Truman and Israel* (Berkeley: University of California Press, 1990), p. 122.

101. Quoted *ibid.*, p. 193.

102. Quoted in Bruce J. Evensen, *Truman, Palestine, and the Press* (New York: Greenwood, 1992), p. 180.

103. Quoted in Warren Bass, *Support Any Friend* (New York: Oxford University Press, 2003), p. 31.

104. "X," "The Sources of Soviet Conduct," *Foreign Affairs, XXV* (July 1947), 566–582.

105. Kennan quoted in Wilson D. Miscamble, *George F. Kennan and the Making of American Foreign Policy, 1947–1950* (Princeton: Princeton University Press, 1992), p. 67.

106. Walter Lippmann, *The Cold War* (New York: Harper & Brothers, 1947), pp. 18, 21, 60.

107. *Department of State Bulletin, XVI* (July 15, 1947), 1159–1160.

108. Bidault quoted in René Girault, "The French Decision-Makers and Their Perception of French Power in 1948," in Josef Becker and Franz Knipping, eds., *Power in Europe?* (Berlin: Walter de Gruyter, 1986), p. 61.

109. Quoted in Woodford McClellan, "Molotov Remembers," *Cold War International History Project Bulletin*, no. 1 (Spring 1992), 18.

110. Quoted in Offner, *Another Such Victory*, p. 213.

111. Quoted in Michael J. Hogan, *The Marshall Plan* (New York: Cambridge University Press, 1987), p. 52.

112. Stalin quoted in Mikhail Narinskii, "The Soviet Union and the Marshall Plan," in Varsori and Calandri, *Failure of Peace*, p. 285.

113. Quoted in Vladislav Zubok, "Stalin's Plans and Russian Archives," *Diplomatic History, XXI* (Spring 1997), 299.

114. Quoted in John Ikenberry, *After Victory* (Princeton: Princeton University Press, 2001), p. 201.

115. Frederico Romero, *The United States and the European Trade Union Movement, 1944–1951* (Chapel Hill: University of North Carolina Press, 1992), p. 216.

116. Quoted in Irwin M. Wall, *The United States and the Making of Postwar France, 1945–1954* (Cambridge, Eng.: Cambridge University Press, 1991), p. 122.

117. Diary, November 23, 1948, Walter Lippmann Papers, Yale University Library, New Haven, Conn.

118. Joint Chiefs quoted in Mastny, *Soviet Insecurity*, p. 58; Matthew Evangelista, "The 'Soviet Threat,'" *Diplomatic History, XXII* (Summer 1998), 444.

119. Harry Rositzke quoted in Evan Thomas, *The Very Best Men* (New York: Simon & Schuster, 1995), p. 35.

120. Quoted in Randall B. Woods, *Fulbright* (New York: Cambridge University Press, 1994), p. 136.

121. Quoted in Frances Stoner Saunders, *The Cultural Cold War* (New York: New Press, 1999), p. 85.

122. Amy L. S. Staples, "Constructing International Identity" (Ph.D. diss., Ohio State University, 1998), pp. 361, 373.

123. *Public Papers, Truman, 1949* (Washington, D.C.: Government Printing Office, 1964), p. 114.

124. Quoted in Nick Cullather, "Damming Afghanistan," *Journal of American History, LXXXIX* (September 2002), 527.

125. *Department of State Bulletin, XX* (March 20, 1949), 340.

126. Quoted in Thomas G. Paterson, *On Every Front* (New York: Norton, 1992; rev. ed.), p. 87.

127. John Hickerson in *Foreign Relations, 1948* (Washington, D.C.: Government Printing Office, 1974), *III*, 183.

128. Quoted in Frank Costigliola, "The Nuclear Family," *Diplomatic History, XXI* (Spring 1997), 165, 166.

129. Pierson Dixon quoted in Anne Deighton, *The Impossible Peace* (New York: Oxford University Press, 1990), p. 190.

130. Quoted in Samuel R. Williamson and Steven L. Reardon, *The Origins of U.S. Nuclear Strategy, 1945–1953* (New York: St. Martin's, 1993), p. 109.

131. Leffler, *Preponderance of Power*, p. 314.

132. Edward W. Barrett in "Princeton Seminar," October 10–11, 1953, Box 65, Dean Acheson Papers, Truman Library.

133. Conversation between Stalin and Mao, December 16, 1949, in *Cold War International History Project Bulletin*, nos. 6–7 (Winter 1995/1996), 5.

134. Dean Acheson, *Present at the Creation* (New York: Norton, 1969), p. 379; *Department of State Bulletin, XXII* (March 20, 1950), 1037.

135. Stalin quoted in D. Clayton James, *The Years of MacArthur: Triumph and Disaster, 1945–1964* (Boston: Houghton Mifflin, 1985), pp. 26–27.

136. Quoted in John W. Dower, "Occupied Japan and the American Lake, 1945–1950," in Edward Friedman and Mark Selden, eds., *America's Asia* (New York: Vintage, 1971), p. 170.

137. Quoted in Kyoko Hirano, *Mr. Smith Goes to Tokyo* (Washington, D.C.: Smithsonian Institution Press, 1992), p. 113.

138. Warren I. Cohen, *The Asian-American Century* (Cambridge: Harvard University Press, 2002), p. 71.

139. Michael S. Molasky, *The American Occupation of Japan and Okinawa* (New York: Routledge, 1999), p. 10; Ian Baruna, *Inventing Japan* (New York: Modern Library, 2003), p. 137.

140. John Paton Davies quoted in Michael Schaller, "Securing the Great Crescent," *Journal of American History, LXXIX* (September 1982), 395.

141. John W. Dower, *Embracing Defeat* (New York: Norton, 1999), p. 23.

142. MacArthur and Yoshida quoted in Michael A. Schaller, *Altered States* (New York: Oxford University Press, 1997), pp. 7, 9.

143. John W. Dower, *War Without Mercy* (New York: Pantheon, 1986), pp. 302, 305.

144. Quoted in Sergei Goncharov, John Lewis, and Xue Litai, *Uncertain Partners* (Stanford: Stanford University Press, 1993), p. 10.

145. Quoted in Michael M. Sheng, *Battling Western Imperialism* (Princeton: Princeton University Press, 1997), p. 104.

146. John Lewis Gaddis, *We Now Know* (New York: Oxford University Press, 1997), p. 60.

147. Quoted in Ilya V. Gaiduk, *Confronting Vietnam* (Stanford: Stanford University Press, 2003), p. 4.

148. Jiang quoted in Edmund S. Wehrle, "Marshall, the Moscow Conference, and Harriman," in Larry I. Bland, ed., *George C. Marshall's Mediation Mission to China* (Lexington, Va.: George C. Marshall Foundation, 1998), p. 89.

149. Quoted in John Maxwell Hamilton, *Edgar Snow* (Bloomington: Indiana University Press, 1988), p. 171; Robert A. Hart, *The Eccentric Tradition* (New York: Charles Scribner's Sons, 1976), p. 156.

150. Clare Booth Luce quoted in T. Christopher Jesperson, *American Images of China* (Stanford: Stanford University Press, 1996), p. 181.

151. Quoted in He Di, "The Evoluton of the Chinese Communist Party's Policy Toward the United States," in Harry Harding and Yuan Ming, eds., *Sino-American Relations, 1945–1955* (Wilmington, Del.: Scholarly Resources, 1989), p. 40.

152. Quoted in Zhang Baijia, "The Shaping of New China's Diplomacy," *Chinese Historians, VII* (Spring and Fall 1994), 58.

153. Quoted in Thomas G. Paterson, "If Europe, Why Not China?" *Prologue, XIII* (Spring 1981), 37.

154. Quoted in Michael H. Hunt, "East Asia in Henry Luce's 'American Century,' " *Diplomatic History, XXIII* (Spring 1999), 328.

155. Quoted in William Stueck, *The Road to Confrontation* (Chapel Hill: University of North Carolina Press, 1981), p. 124.

156. Odd Arne Westad, "Losses, Chances, and Myths," *Diplomatic History, XXI* (Winter 1997), 108; Mao quoted in Li Zhisui, *The Private Life of Chairman Mao* (New York: Random House, 1994), p. 117; *United States Relations with China* (Washington, D.C.: Department of State, 1949), p. xvii.

157. Geraldine Fitch quoted in Jesperson, *American Images*, p. 179.

158. Lewis Clark quoted in Nancy Bernkopf Tucker, *Taiwan, Hong Kong, and the United States, 1945–1992* (New York: Twayne, 1994), p. 21.

159. Quoted in Gordon H. Chang, *Friends and Enemies* (Stanford: Stanford University Press, 1990), p. 13.

160. Quoted in Michael Sheng, "The United States, the Chinese Communists, and the Soviet Union, 1948–1950," *Pacific Historical Review, LXIII* (November 1994), 529.

161. Mao quoted in Chen Jian, *Mao's China and the Cold War* (Chapel Hill: University of North Carolina Press, 2001), p. 53; memorandum of Mao conversation, July 22, 1958, in *Cold War International History Project Bulletin*, nos. 6–7 (Winter 1995/1996), 156.

162. Quoted in Shu Guang Zhan, "In the Shadow of Mao," in Gordon A. Craig and Francis L. Loewenheim, eds., *The Diplomats* (Princeton: Princeton University Press, 1994), p. 349.

163. Quoted in Gaddis, *We Now Know*, p. 62.

164. *Department of State Bulletin, XXIV* (May 28, 1951), 847.

165. L. E. Sissman, "Missing the Forties," *Atlantic Monthly, CCXXXII* (October 1973), 35.

166. M. E. Dening quoted in William Roger Louis, *Imperialism at Bay* (New York: Oxford University Press, 1978), p. 550.

167. Reinhold Wagnleitner, "The Irony of American Culture Abroad," in Lary May, ed., *Recasting America* (Chicago: University of Chicago Press, 1989), p. 295.

168. Eugen Sharin quoted *ibid.*, p. 285.

169. Quoted in Yukiko Koshiro, *Trans-Pacific Racisms and the U.S. Occupation of Japan* (New York: Columbia University Press, 1999), p. 159.

170. Brenda Gayle Plummer, "Brown Babies," in Plummer, ed., *Window on Freedom* (Chapel Hill: University of North Carolina Press, 2003), p. 67; Petra Goedde, *GIs and Germans* (New Haven: Yale University Press, 2003), p. 94.

171. Geir Lundestad, " 'Empire by Invitation' in the American Century," *Diplomatic History, XXIII* (Spring 1999), 189–217.

172. Quoted in Fousek, *To Lead the Free World*, p. 76.

173. Quoted in Daniel Yergin, "Fulbright's Last Frustration," *New York Times Magazine*, November 24, 1974, p. 87.

174. British Ambassador Clark Kerr quoted in Frank Costigliola, "'Mixed Up' and 'Contact': Culture and Emotion in the Second World War," *International History Review, XX* (December 1998), 803.

175. Quoted in Mastny, *Soviet Insecurity*, p. 38.

176. H. Freeman Matthews quoted in Hanhimäki, *Containing Coexistence*, p. 17.

177. Thomas Borstelmann, *Apartheid's Reluctant Uncle* (New York: Oxford University Press, 1993), p. 197.

178. Kyle Longley, *The Sparrow and the Hawk* (Wilmington, Del.: Scholarly Resources, 1997), p. 159.

179. Charles D. Ameringer, *The Caribbean Legion* (University Park: Penn State University Press, 1996), p. 10.

180. Ambassador Monnet Davis quoted in John Major, *Prized Possession* (New York: Cambridge University Press, 1993), p. 273.

181. Michael J. Hogan, *A Cross of Iron* (New York: Cambridge University Press, 1998), p. 17.

182. Ron Robin, *The Making of a Cold War Enemy* (Princeton: Princeton University Press, 2001), p. 71

183. Garry Wills, *John Wayne's America* (New York: Simon & Schuster, 1997), p. 154.

184. Quoted in W. Averell Harriman and Elie Abel, *Special Envoy to Churchill and Stalin* (New York: Random House, 1975), p. 528.

185. Paul Hoffman quoted in Chester J. Pach, *Arming the Free World* (Chapel Hill: University of North Carolina Press, 1991), p. 231.

186. Fulbright quoted in Saunders, *Cultural Cold War*, p. 212.

187. Quoted in Levering, *Debating the Origins*, p. 130.

188. Azza Salama Layton, *International Politics and Civil Rights in the United States, 1941–1960* (New York: Cambridge University Press, 2000), p. 141.

189. Quoted in Paul Gordon Lauren, "The International Perspective," in Plummer, *Window on Freedom*, pp. 29, 31.

190. Quoted *ibid,* 23.

191. Carol Anderson, *Eyes off the Prize* (New York: Cambridge University Press, 2003), p. 133.

192. Quoted in Walter Russell Mead, *Special Providence* (New York: Routledge, 2002), p. 61.

193. Eldon Spence quoted in Robert David Johnson, "Congress and the Cold War," *Journal of Cold War Studies, III* (Spring 2001), 87–88.

194. Dean Acheson Oral History Interview, Truman Library.

195. Robert Beisner, "The Secretary, the Spy, and the Sage," *Diplomatic History, XXVII* (January 2003), 7.

196. Williamson and Reardon, *U.S. Nuclear Strategy*, p. 191.

197. George Kennan quoted in Mitrovich, *Undermining*, p. 50.

198. Val Peterson quoted in Kenneth D. Rose, *One Nation Underground* (New York: New York University Press, 2001), p. 4.

199. Quoted in Margot A. Henriksen, *Dr. Strangelove's America* (Berkeley: University of California Press, 1997), p. 23.

200. Quoted in Allan M. Winkler, *Life Under a Cloud* (New York: Oxford University Press, 1993), p. 50.

CHAPTER 8

Global Watch: The Korean War and Eisenhower Foreign Relations, 1950–1961

United Nations Leaflet in Korean War. *This leaflet, dropped by UN forces over North Korea, aimed to incite hostility in the Korean War among Chinese "volunteer" forces against their nation's leaders. The flyer shows a "Soviet advisor" manipulating the "Chinese Puppet" marionettes Liu Shaoqi, Mao Zedong, and Zhou Enlai. Such "psychological warfare," according to the scholar Ron Robin, was a "futuristic strategy for defeating the enemy by words" and images "rather than bullets." This propaganda piece reflected the widespread U.S. assumption that Joseph Stalin and his cohorts pulled the strings in China, North Korea, and other communist regimes. During the first eighteen months of the Korean War, U.S. aircraft dropped a billion leaflets on North Korean and Chinese forces. (Courtesy General Douglas MacArthur Foundation)*

DIPLOMATIC CROSSROAD

✎✐ *The Decision to Intervene in the Korean War, 1950*

AMERICAN AMBASSADOR TO South Korea John J. Muccio picked up the phone at 8:00 A.M. "Brace yourself for a shock," his chief deputy said, "the Communists are hitting all along the front!"[1] Muccio rushed out to check the alarming reports. United Press correspondent Jack James, also in Seoul, did the same and earned himself a rare scoop. At 9:50 A.M. he cabled UP in the United States that North Korean troops had crossed into South Korea. Muccio also cabled Washington about "an all-out offensive."[2]

At 4:00 A.M. that rainy Sunday morning of June 25, 1950, some 75,000 troops of the Democratic People's Republic of Korea (North Korea) bolted across the thirty-eighth parallel, the boundary drawn after World War II by the United States and the Soviet Union, cutting Korea into North and South. North Korean units attacked along a 150-mile front with armor and heavy artillary. As Soviet-made tanks rumbled forward, South Korean forces collapsed in a rout. General Douglas MacArthur remembered that the North Korean army "struck like a cobra."[3]

James's cable beat Muccio's to the United States, more than 7,000 miles away, by a few minutes. It was a hot, humid Saturday evening (June 24) in Washington, D.C., thirteen hours behind Seoul time. UP called the Department of State to verify James's report. Dumbfounded officers had no information. The "volcano" of civil strife had so long smoldered in Korea that its eruption caught the United States off guard.[4] Around 10:00 P.M. the bad news reached Secretary of State Dean Acheson, resting at his Maryland farm. When General MacArthur received word at his Tokyo post, he told visiting envoy John Foster Dulles: "This is probably only a reconnaissance in force. . . . I can handle it with one hand tied behind my back."[5] Dulles expected worse: "To sit by while Korea is overrun," he cabled, "would start a disastrous chain of events leading most probably to world war."[6]

Acheson convened an emergency session of the United Nations Security Council. The United States dominated that body, and the principle of collective security in the face of aggression seemed at issue. At 11:20 P.M. Acheson rang up President Harry S. Truman, at home in Independence, Missouri, with his family, saying that the president could do little at that point, so he should remain in Missouri and come to Washington the next day, June 25. State Department personnel worked through the night drafting a Security Council resolution that charged North Korea with a "breach of the peace."[7] The Pentagon and State Department debated courses of action. Orders went out to evacuate Americans from Seoul. World War III, thought some officials, had started.

President Truman possessed "an appetite, too much of one, really, for unhesitating decision."[8] He stood low in the public opinion polls at the time, in large part because Senator Joseph McCarthy of Wisconsin charged Truman with "softness toward communism."[9] Former State Department official Alger Hiss, to right-wing critics the ultimate "sell-out" spy, had been convicted of perjury in January, and China had "fallen" a few months before. Bold action now would disarm the president's critics. Truman pondered history. He frequently drew facile lessons from the past. The 1930s all over again: "Communism was acting in Korea just as Hitler, Mussolini, and the Japanese had acted ten, fifteen, and twenty years earlier."[10] No appeasement this time! Meanwhile, the Security Council passed the U.S. resolution condemning North Korea. Except for Yugoslavia's abstention, all members present voted "yes." The Soviet delegation, which could have vetoed the measure, remained surprisingly absent, boycotting the U.N. over its refusal to seat China's new communist government.

A stern, short-tempered Truman deplaned in Washington and headed for a meeting with top officials. Nobody present doubted that the Soviet Union had engineered the attack, using its North Korean allies to probe for a soft spot in the American containment shield. The relationship between the Soviet Union and North Korea, one official remarked, was like "Walt Disney and Donald Duck."[11] Worse still, the thrust into South Korea might be only one component of a worldwide communist assault. "If we let Korea down," Truman predicted, "the Soviet [*sic*] will keep right on going and swallow up one piece of Asia after another. . . . [Then] the Near East would collapse and no telling what would happen in Europe."[12] Truman ordered General MacArthur in Japan to send arms and equipment to the South Koreans and to use U.S. war planes to attack the North Korean spearhead. Further, he sent the Seventh Fleet into the waters between the Chinese mainland and Formosa to forestall conflict between the two Chinas.

Despite strong bipartisan support for Truman's decisions, some conservative Republicans indulged in McCarthyite recriminations. Senator William E. Jenner of Indiana waxed splenetic: "The Russian bear is sprawled across the Eurasian continent, biding its time, digesting its prey, and digging itself in for a long and cruel international winter. The Korean debacle also reminds us that the same sell-out-to-Stalin statesmen . . . are still in the saddle, riding herd on the American people."[13]

By Monday evening, North Korean forces neared Seoul. Truman learned about a downed North Korean plane, which he hoped "was not the last."[14] Diplomats and military leaders believed that the reputation of the United States stood at risk. If America did not defend containment, its image would tarnish and its power erode. Korea became a supreme Cold War test, a symbol, a link in a Cold War chain of events. To falter would forfeit world leadership, Truman officials claimed.

Truman ordered U.S. aircraft and warships into full-scale action below the thirty-eighth parallel; he declared Formosa (Taiwan) off limits to the mainland Chinese; and he dispatched military aid to Indochina and the Philippines. The president did not request a congressional declaration of war. Senator Tom Connally of Texas, chair of the Foreign Relations Committee, assured Truman of his right not to do so as commander in chief: "If a burglar breaks into your house, you can shoot him without going down to the police station and getting permission."[15] Truman simply informed key legislators about his decisions. While Senator Robert A. Taft complained that the president had done "the right thing the wrong way," most Americans applauded Truman's response.[16] "Never . . . have I felt such a sense of relief and unity pass through the city," wrote one veteran reporter.[17] The United Nations passed another U.S.-sponsored resolution urging members to aid South Korea, in essence endorsing actions the United States had already taken. Seoul nonetheless fell.

Dean Acheson (1893–1971). He, like the president, assumed that Moscow had initiated the Korean War and urged resolute American reaction. The new crisis, coming after Acheson's National Press Club speech of January 12, 1950, and other foreign-policy woes such as the communist victory in China, emboldened some of his critics to ask once again for his resignation. (*The Reporter*, 1952. Copyright 1952 by Fortnightly Publishing Co., Inc.)

The continued North Korean push into the South sparked talk on June 28 and 29 of sending U.S. troops. Presidential supporters cited historical precedent: Jefferson had ordered action against the Barbary pirates and McKinley had sent troops into China during the Boxer Rebellion without prior congressional sanction. On the twenty-ninth, Truman ordered U.S. pilots to attack above the thirty-eighth parallel. On Friday, June 30, after visiting the war front, MacArthur asked Truman to send U.S. soldiers to Korea. The president gave the order amid reports of a North Korean surge southward into the Pusan perimeter. "We will hurl back the North Koreans, and if the Russkies intervene we will hurl them back, too!" declared one general.[18] The nation mobilized for an undeclared but initially popular war against communism. Truman tagged it a "police action."[19]

Korea, the Cold War, and the "Trojan Horse" of National Security

At first the war went badly for the United States, South Korea, and the small number of troops offered by allies, all nominally under U.N. auspices. America's combat units took heavy losses, buying time to equip and transport a substantial force for offensive operations in Korea. Discussions began on whether U.S. troops should cross the thirty-eighth parallel and attempt to liberate the North from communism. In August the president decided in favor of this drastic change in U.S. war aims.

Meanwhile, MacArthur persuaded a reluctant Joint Chiefs of Staff to approve a difficult amphibious assault at Inchon, hundreds of miles behind North Korean lines. On September 15, U.S. marines landed at Inchon, pushed the North Koreans back, and quickly cut to Seoul. North Korean troops retreated north. "We want you to feel unhampered tactically and strategically to proceed north of the 38th Parallel," Secretary of Defense George C. Marshall told MacArthur.[20]

The Chinese warily watched these events. When Truman sent the Seventh Fleet to neutralize Formosa on June 27, Beijing called the decision "armed aggression against Chinese territory," revealing the "true imperialist face" of the United States.[21] Shortly after the Inchon landing, Mao Zedong, vowing not to wait "year after year unsure of when the enemy will attack us," began preparations to send "volunteers" into Korea.[22] Mao and Zhou Enlai also warned the United States to keep its troops away from the Yalu River boundary. MacArthur was certain the Chinese were bluffing. Even British intelligence dismissed reports of Chinese intervention as "based upon a single unconfirmed statement made by a single enemy prisoner of war who does not know what he is talking about."[23]

Stalin cabled Mao on October 1, urging the Chinese to "move at least five or six divisions toward the 38th parallel at once."[24] Mao cabled back the next day, ruling out intervention because it would provoke "open conflict" with the United States. "The wounds inflicted on the people by the [Chinese Civil] war have not healed, we need peace." Stalin then promised Soviet air support: "If war is inevitable, then let it be waged now, and not in a few years, when Japanese militarism will be restored as an ally of the USA."[25] After intense debate in Beijing, Mao reversed course because the "Americans would run more rampant" unless stopped.[26]

On October 8, United Nations forces under U.S. command trooped across the thirty-eighth parallel and marched deep into North Korea. Some 250,000 Chinese troops quietly crossed the Yalu on October 19, even after Stalin reneged on his promise of air support. On October 26, Chinese forces attacked. After fierce fighting, however, they retreated—"purposely showing ourselves to be weak," as their commander put it, "increasing the arrogance of the enemy, letting him run amuck, and luring them deep into our area."[27] U.S. officials abandoned caution. On November 8, for the first time, B-29 bombers struck bridges across the Yalu—bridges that linked North Korea and China. Then, on November 24, MacArthur launched

Douglas MacArthur (1880–1964). The West Point graduate commanded U.S. troops in Asia during World War II, directed the postwar occupation of Japan, and headed forces in Korea until relieved of duty by the president in April 1951. MacArthur later said he could have ended the Korean War in ten days: "I would have dropped between 30 and 50 atomic bombs" on China. (Library of Congress)

a major offensive that he predicted would "have the boys home by Christmas."[28] Two days later, what one U.S. general called "a glut of Chinamen" swept down on MacArthur's unsuspecting armies.[29] Within weeks Chinese engulfed the North, propelling UN forces southward. "We are not retreating," one harried commander told a reporter. "We are merely attacking in another direction."[30] MacArthur unsuccessfully requested Washington's approval of air strikes against China, now branded an "aggressor" by the United Nations. Truman hinted publicly that using nuclear weapons was under "active consideration."[31] "You can use the atomic bomb," Mao reportedly boasted. "I will respond with my hand grenade. I will catch the weak point on your part and defeat you."[32] British prime minister Clement Attlee hastened to Washington to protest that the United States should seek negotiations, not a dangerously expanded war. To Truman's assertion that the Chinese communists were "complete satellites" of Moscow, the British ambassador argued that war with China would tighten a Sino-Soviet alliance based "on a coincidence of Chinese and Russian views, not Chinese subservience to Russian views."[33] In fact, Truman and his advisers rejected a wider war because they deemed the nuclear arsenal too small and feared Soviet retaliation in Europe.

By March 1951, MacArthur had shoved communist forces back across the thirty-eighth parallel. With fighting stabilized at roughly the prewar boundary, Truman contemplated negotiations, but the "obstreperous," "vain," and, "egotistical" general was hell-bent on reversing earlier defeats and slashing China on behalf of the crusade against international communism.[34] MacArthur began publicly suggesting that his commander in chief preferred appeasement. To Representative Joseph Martin, he wrote, in a letter made public in April: "There is no substitute for victory."[35] On April 11 Truman, backed strongly by the Joint Chiefs of Staff, fired the seventy-one-year-old MacArthur for insubordination.

The general, who had so badly miscalculated Chinese reactions, returned home to ticker-tape parades. In a televised address he told Congress on April 19 that the war must be expanded. He closed with now-famous words: "Old soldiers never die; they just fade away."[36] Congressional hearings soon revealed that many Americans shared MacArthur's frustrations over military restraint. Americans were used to winning wars; Truman now conducted something alien—a "limited war," localized and without atomic weapons. Senator McCarthy spewed his venom, too, calling Truman a "sinister monster of many heads and many tentacles, a monster conceived in the Kremlin, and then given birth to by Acheson . . . , and then nurtured into Frankenstein proportions by the Hiss crowd, who still run the State Department."[37] The debate focused on different strategies for rolling back communism. "There was MacArthur's, which resembled a locomotive with no brakes. And there was Acheson's, a controlled rollback limited to Korea."[38]

Truman and Acheson pointed to the risk of world war. The chair of the Joint Chiefs of Staff, General Omar Bradley, argued that escalating the war would by no means guarantee victory, that it might bring the Soviets in, and that the United States would lose angry allies. A showdown with Soviet communism in Korea, he said, would be "the wrong war, at the wrong place, at the wrong time, and with the wrong enemy."[39] As one scholar points out, Bradley implied that the *right war* should be against the Soviet Union, "and the *right place* to fight it was not at the periphery, but at the heart of Soviet power," and the *right time* was only after the buildup of American power under NSC-68.[40]

Peace talks began at Panmunjom in July 1951 but made little headway. The fighting continued. Americans "want to subjugate the world," Stalin scoffed, "yet they cannot subdue little Korea."[41] During the 1952 presidential campaign, Republican candidate Dwight D. Eisenhower pledged, if elected, to go to Korea and seek an end to the conflict. Ike won, in part due to American frustration with limited war. He went to Korea, but found no easy solution. The most serious obstacle centered on prisoners of war (POWs). Thousands of Chinese and North Korean soldiers, encouraged by a "re-education" program in the South, refused repatriation. A few hundred captives in the North, having undergone communist "brainwashing," elected to remain above the thirty-eighth parallel. Despite the usual diplomatic practice of returning all prisoners, "the allure of many Chinese voting with their feet for Chiang [Jiang] rather than Mao validated" a U.S. policy toward Nationalist China that was "unpopular internationally."[42]

By 1953 the military buildup under NSC-68 had erased doubts about U.S. capabilities that had precluded escalation earlier in the war. Announcing that the United States considered "the atomic bomb as simply another weapon in our arsenal," Eisenhower tried to intimidate the Chinese.[43] Eisenhower's threat "pleased the public" but did little to resolve the standoff.[44] Jiang Jieshi's forces attacked the mainland, with Washington's approval. The March death of Stalin, combined with these actions, probably helped bring the peace talks to a conclusion. A more flexible Moscow urged Beijing to settle the prisoner question. When South Korean president Syngman Rhee tried to sabotage the talks by releasing thousands of North Korean POWs, the Chinese launched a final offensive against South Korean positions.

On July 27, 1953, the adversaries signed an armistice. They agreed to turn over the POW issue to a committee of neutral nations (ultimately the POWs stayed where they chose—including twenty-one Americans in North Korea). The conferees drew a new boundary line close to the thirty-eighth parallel, which gained South Korea 1,500 square miles of territory. The agreement also provided for a demilitarized zone between the two Koreas.

The Korean War ranks as one of the costliest in twentieth-century history. More than 4 million died: 2 million North Korean civilians and 500,000 North Korean soldiers; 1 million South Korean civilians and some 47,000 South Korean soldiers; and official Chinese statistics list 148,000 dead. The United States lost 54,246 dead and 105,000 wounded and spent some $20 billion. The United States supplied 80 percent of the naval power and 90 percent of the air support, as well as 90 percent of foreign combat troops, in this "United Nations" effort.

The Korean War has left many questions, some of which the partial opening of Chinese and Russian archives are helping to answer. Did Moscow start the Korean War? Truman officials claimed that the Soviet Union induced its North Korean client to attack. Perhaps Moscow sensed an opportunity, because Acheson had indicated in his speech on January 12, 1950, that South Korea lay outside the American defense perimeter. Acheson's remarks "produced a certain influence" on the North Korean leader Kim Il Sung, who visited Moscow in April and promised a surprise attack that would win the war in three days.[45] A cautious Stalin told Kim

MiG-15 Fighter and F-86 Sabre Jet.
The Soviets furnished the Chinese with aircraft, including Mikoyan and Guervich MiG-15 fighter jets, and trained Chinese and North Korean forces for combat against such American fighter-bombers as the F-86 Sabre jet. Recently declassified Russian sources show that some 72,000 Soviet air personnel participated covertly in air combat. Soviet pilots wore Chinese uniforms and were ordered not to send radio transmissions in Russian to evade detection. If captured, they were to say that they were "Chinese of Russian extraction." (National Archives, RG 342 NA II)

to check with Mao, who cited possible American intervention but endorsed Kim's plans. Stalin then backed Kim's scheme, probably gambling that North Korea could score a quick victory.

The "gamble thesis" raises difficult questions. Moscow did provide secret air cover, supplies, and training to North Korean and Chinese forces, but only after

China's intervention on October 19. If Stalin engineered the initial attack, why did the Soviets not veto the Security Council's June condemnation of North Korea, which paved the way for a UN-sponsored intervention? Why did Stalin delay aiding communist forces, and why was all such assistance kept covert? Why would Moscow launch a European movement for peaceful coexistence and then torpedo that effort by provoking war in Asia? "We are thus left to reconcile the ubiquitous American assumption that Stalin started the war," one scholar notes, "with the unambiguous evidence that he distanced Soviet interests, prestige, and armed might from the conflict, allowing the United States ultimately to pulverize North Korea."[46]

Soviet relations with China influenced Stalin's decisions on Korea. If he refused to support Korean unification, Stalin invited charges that he hindered revolution in Asia and potentially boosted Mao's China as a Soviet rival. Stalin may further have calculated that, even if the United States did not defend South Korea, Washington would never permit the additional loss of Taiwan. American efforts to protect Jiang Jieshi's government on Formosa would prevent rapprochement between Washington and Beijing and ensure China's continued reliance on Soviet economic and military aid. Whatever Stalin's motives, he knew that war in Korea risked Soviet economic and strategic interests in northeast Asia. As for Mao, who expected imminent U.S. aggression against China, he leaned toward intervention *after* Truman sent the Seventh Fleet into the Taiwan Strait and "exposed its [America's] imperialist face."[47] The initiative, and probably the timing, for the war came from Pyongyang, not from Moscow or Beijing.

This interpretation seems plausible because since 1945 a two-part civil war had wracked Korea: the conflict in the South and the conflict between South and North. In the South, "people's committees" resisted the rightist state backed by the United States. Peasant uprisings, leftist-initiated labor strife, and guerrilla warfare claimed tens of thousands of lives. The North encouraged the rebellions in the South, and skirmishes between northern and southern soldiers intensified in 1949 along the dividing parallel. Both Kim's North Korean communist government and Rhee's Republic of Korea in the South craved national unification. Both tapped foreign sources for material aid. Rhee, who had lived in the United States for almost four decades, used his American political connections well. In February 1950, Congress authorized $60 million in economic aid for South Korea; in March it voted almost $11 million in military assistance; and on June 5 it added another $100 million in military aid. Although U.S. occupation troops had departed in mid-1949, a U.S. Military Advisory Group remained to train Rhee's forces. In May elections, Rhee lost control of the South Korean National Assembly. All the while, Rhee "seemed like a tethered hound, constantly pulling at the [U.S.] leash."[48]

With a 150,000-soldier army well supplied with Soviet arms, including 150 T-34 tanks, Kim's authoritarian regime probably decided to strike before Rhee could utilize U.S. aid and stabilize his precarious political position. In any case, scholars interpret the major war that exploded in June 1950 as an extension of the ongoing civil war waged by North and South Korea, not simply as a conflagration ignited by the two Cold War superpowers.

Despite uncertainty over the war's origins, we *can* measure its consequences. "Like the Trojan horse sent into Troy," writes one historian, "President Harry

S. Truman's June 1950 decision to intervene" in Korea "laid the nation bare to a bombardment of economic, political, military, and social changes."[49] In the United States, the war "put an end to Truman's 'Fair Deal' [domestic reform program] and to a Democrat[ic] political hegemony that extended back two decades."[50] Public exasperation with the Korean stalemate led to the repudiation of the Democrats and the election of the Republican Eisenhower in 1952. The war wounded bipartisanship and fueled McCarthyism. It helped set off a "great debate" in the early 1950s over whether Europe or Asia ranked higher in the campaign against communism and whether the United States had overcommitted itself around the globe. Truman's handling of the Korean War also confirmed presidential supremacy in foreign policy; he neither consulted Congress nor asked for a declaration of war. Acheson did not wish to answer "ponderous questions" in drawn-out hearings that might have "muddled up" Truman's policy.[51]

The Korean War poisoned Sino-American relations while it strengthened Japanese-American ties. The Taiwan question became "locked in place" as the United States continued to intervene in China's civil war by aiding Jiang and adamantly refusing to recognize Mao's government, which now had shed American blood.[52] The war enabled the Chinese communists to consolidate their revolution at home and gain international prestige by battling the "American imperialists" to a draw.[53] The conflict also bolstered Japan and its alliance with the United States. Some $3 billion in U.S. procurement orders during the war revived Japanese industry. The "seedbed" for the Japanese economic "miracle" of the 1960s and 1970s was "planted."[54]

The Korean War further divided the world into two competing camps and drew Third World nations into its destructive wake as the domino theory took on new vigor. "We are fighting in Korea," Truman proclaimed, "so we won't have to fight in Wichita, or in Chicago, or in New Orleans, or on San Francisco Bay."[55] South Korea became a staunch ally, receiving, in 1953–1972, $5.5 billion in foreign aid. Viewing nationalist movements as potential Soviet allies, and determined to back allies in the aggravated Cold War, Washington increased aid to the French in their battle against Vietnamese nationalists (see Chapter 9).

The Korean War also "gave teeth to the mobilization planning process" already begun during Truman's presidency.[56] As Acheson noted, the dispatch of troops to Korea "removed the recommendations of NSC-68 from the realm of theory and made them immediate budget issues."[57] The Defense Department budget for fiscal year 1953 reached $52.6 billion, up from $17.7 billion in 1950. U.S. military expansion included a much enlarged army; development of tactical nuclear weapons; four more army divisions for Europe, making a total of six there; the 1952 maiden flight of a new jet bomber, the B-52; the explosion of a thermonuclear device in November 1952; and expansion of the Strategic Air Command (SAC) to 1,600 aircraft (nearly all atomic capable). The United States also acquired bases in Saudi Arabia and Morocco, began successful talks with fascist Spain for an air base, and initiated plans for the rearmament of West Germany. In 1951 the United States, Australia, and New Zealand formed the ANZUS Pact. The United States created a military alliance with Pakistan in 1954. Strategies for psychological warfare and propaganda culminated in the creation of the United States Information Agency (USIA) in 1953. The Korean War's most lasting legacy was the quickened militarization of the Cold War.

Makers of American Foreign Relations, 1950–1961

Presidents	Secretaries of State
Harry S. Truman, 1945–1953	Dean G. Acheson, 1949–1953
Dwight D. Eisenhower, 1953–1961	John Foster Dulles, 1953–1959
	Christian A. Herter, 1959–1961

Ambivalent Cold Warrior: Dwight D. Eisenhower

The stalemated Korean War and the "loss" of China provided Republicans with political ammunition in the 1952 presidential campaign. Although their candidate, General Dwight D. Eisenhower, conducted a smiling, moderate campaign, his party's right wing attacked vehemently. The Truman administration, which had launched containment, gotten "tough" with the Soviets, and established an internal security system, had somehow grown soft on communism. Vice-presidential candidate Richard M. Nixon ridiculed Democratic candidate Adlai E. Stevenson as "Adlai the Appeaser," a graduate of "Acheson's Cowardly College of Communist Containment."[58] John Foster Dulles, who authored the Republican party platform condemning Truman's leadership, mocked the administration's "treadmill policies," which threatened to "keep us in the same place until we dropped."[59]

Republicans called containment "futile and immoral."[60] Dulles proposed "liberation" as a replacement. By that he meant freeing "those captive peoples" in Eastern Europe from "communist enslavement."[61] He never explained precisely how to do so.

"Liberation" did not decide the 1952 election, but the rhyme "I like Ike" may have. Eisenhower appeared modest and sincere, with his homespun rhetoric and wholesome Midwestern image. Because the Cold War seemed more than ever a military matter, this professional soldier and war hero outshone the comparatively bland Stevenson, who later wondered, "Who did I think I was, running against George Washington?"[62] Eisenhower's promise to go to Korea certainly helped him win 55 percent of the popular vote.

The first Republican president since Hoover, Eisenhower appeared, but was not, simple-minded. He lacked a surefootedness for grammar. His utterances often displayed mangled syntax and colloquialisms that dizzied his listeners. "His ad-libbed sentences bounced around like dodgem cars at a carnival . . . with nobody quite sure what he said," remembered the journalist David Brinkley.[63] This idiosyncratic style masked a skillful politician whose "hidden hand" leadership dominated the policy process.[64] But the president's meandering remarks, platitudes, and apparent moments of confusion led critics to dismiss Eisenhower as a "lazy, passive, inarticulate, golf-playing, grinning mediocrity," out of touch with details, and vulnerable to right-wing demagoguery in his party.[65]

Richard M. Nixon (1913–1994). Before being elected vice president in 1952, Nixon graduated from Whittier College, earned a law degree from Duke University, and represented California in the U.S. House of Representatives (1947–1950) and Senate (1950–1953). An anticommunist alarmist who often used excessive language to score debating points, Nixon was, said Adlai Stevenson, "the kind of politician who would cut down a redwood tree, and then mount the stump and make a speech for conservation." (*The Reporter*, 1960. Copyright 1960 by The Reporter Magazine Co.)

Raised in Abilene, Kansas, Eisenhower graduated from West Point and led an obscure military life until appointed the supreme allied commander in Europe during World War II. After the war he served as army chief of staff, president of Columbia University, and NATO commander. Eisenhower admired business leaders and appointed many to high office in agencies shaping foreign policy. Representatives of business, finance, and law held 76 percent of such posts under Eisenhower, whereas the figure for Truman had been 43 percent. Conservative advocates of "private enterprise" in a world increasingly turning toward revolution and socialism, these "national security managers" sought to impose order on international relations.[66]

Believing in a "mutually cooperative, voluntarist society," Eisenhower and his advisers held that "only" through "free enterprise" could "democracy be preserved" and communism deterred.[67] Healthy world trade, they argued, stimulated cooperative capitalism. Eisenhower's Commission on Foreign Economic Policy, appointed in 1953, urged a more liberal trade policy through tariff reduction. The president extended the reciprocal trade agreements program, expanded the lending authority of the Export-Import Bank, and relaxed controls on trade with Eastern European nations. Total American exports expanded from $15 billion in 1952 to $30 billion in 1960. While initially favoring trade over aid, Eisenhower came to see foreign assistance "as the cheapest insurance in the world." He soon blended trade with extensive military aid, seeking to balance the budget and help developing nations.[68] During the 1950s, the United States spent more than $3 billion a year in foreign military assistance under the Mutual Security program. Eisenhower also added a new program in 1954, later called "Food for Peace," wherein the United States disposed of its agricultural surplus overseas. In ten years this program accounted for $12.2 billion in farm exports. And in 1959 the United States established the Inter-American Development Bank to spur hemispheric economic projects.

Eisenhower also waged "psychological warfare" in a "battle for men's minds" against the Soviets and their allies.[69] Voice of America, Radio Free Europe, and Radio Liberty beamed anticommunist propaganda abroad. The United States Information Agency disseminated American "life and culture" in order to "facilitate understanding" of U.S. foreign policy overseas.[70] Some historians argue that, although the Soviets jammed broadcasts and limited daily contact with the West, American "cultural diplomacy" "parted the curtain" (or at least "tore a big hole" in it) by eroding communist values and regimes.[71] Others question whether such efforts falsely promised East European dissidents that Washington would back its calls for "liberation" with military power.

The Eisenhower administration elevated the CIA as a major instrument of foreign policy. Under its director Allen W. Dulles, brother of the secretary of state, the CIA hired many Ivy League–educated lawyers and academicians to gather data on foreign countries and to prepare "estimates" about their policies, motives, and capabilities. But the agency also provided the president with the "quiet option" of "termination with extreme prejudice" or "health alteration"—that is, assassination.[72] Working under the assumption that the Cold War had "no rules" and that "longstanding American concepts of 'fair play' must be reconsidered," the CIA became empowered "to subvert, sabotage, and destroy our enemies."[73] Among those included on the CIA's assassination hit list were the Congo's Patrice Lumumba and

Titan II Missile. Ten stories high and packing in one nuclear warhead the explosive power of 9 million tons of TNT (equivalent to 700 Hiroshima bombs), this intercontinental ballistic missile (ICBM) was developed beginning in 1955 and successfully tested in 1959. The Titan II became part of the Strategic Air Command in 1963. Jay W. Kelley, lieutenant general of the U.S. Air Force (ret.), recalled "the tremendous, healthy rivalry that existed between the six Minuteman [missile] wings and the three Titan II wings. Inevitably, the argument would start with size and work its way to who had the biggest warhead." (U.S. Air Force)

Cuba's Fidel Castro. The agency hired mercenaries, conducted sabotage, co-opted labor unions, planted news stories, and covertly bribed foreign leaders such as King Hussein of Jordan. The CIA also successfully staged coups in Iran (1953) and Guatemala (1954) but failed to overthrow Indonesia's government in 1958. While operatives in 1959 spent a million pesos to influence the Philippines election, CIA efforts proved "long on ambition and short on results," especially in countering a growing "Filipino First" movement.[74]

At home, the CIA put American journalists and professors on its payroll, recruited business executives as "fronts," financed the National Student Association, funded research projects at universities, and used philanthropic foundations to pass money to organizations for anticommunist activities. By the mid-1960s, the CIA had clandestinely subsidized publication of some 1,000 books. In the name of Cold War research and without the knowledge of the victims, the agency used Americans as guinea pigs. Under a program called MKULTRA, researchers subjected unwitting Americans to the mind-altering drug LSD. Other projects exposed unsuspecting soldiers, prisoners, children, and sick people to radiation in secret experiments deemed by one writer an "unfortunate but unavoidable side effect" of America's anticommunist crusade.[75] Eisenhower remarked that he "knew so many things that I am almost afraid to speak to my wife."[76] He worked to keep his active

Dwight D. Eisenhower (1890–1969).
Well experienced in world affairs before becoming president, Eisenhower nurtured a "deeply rooted anti-Communism" and "an obsession with falling dominoes." He also "realized that unlimited war in the nuclear age was unimaginable, and limited war unwinnable," writes the biographer Stephen E. Ambrose. Eisenhower suffered a coronary thrombosis in September 1955 but went on to win reelection in 1956 against Democratic candidate Adlai Stevenson. (Dwight D. Eisenhower Library)

role secret "on the theory of why put burdens on people that they don't need to know about."[77] While sometimes portrayed as a "rogue elephant" acting on its own, the CIA's "mahout, the driver who sits on top and steers," as two scholars put it, "is always the president."[78]

Unlike Truman and Acheson, Eisenhower at least seemed willing to negotiate with the Soviets. Stalin's death in March 1953 removed one of the original Cold War architects, and in April the president's earnest "Chances for Peace" speech invited friendlier relations and revealed Ike's discomfort with militarism. "Every gun that is made, every warship launched, every rocket fired signifies, in the final sense, a theft from those who hunger and are not fed."[79] Soviet analysts deemed Eisenhower's remarks "irritating and provocative," unworthy of serious attention, while Secretary Dulles's tougher speech two days later confirmed Moscow's suspicion that the administration contained "resolute enemies" of peace.[80]

Fearing that "there aren't enough bulldozers to scrape the bodies off the street" following a nuclear war, especially once the Soviets exploded a thermonuclear device in August 1953, Eisenhower often recommended arms control measures.[81] But mere "denunciations" of nuclear "overkill" could not halt the dangerous momentum of the arms race.[82] Eisenhower's "Atoms for Peace" speech in December 1953 called for contributions of fissionable materials to an International Atomic Energy Agency that would then develop nonmilitary uses for atomic energy. Hardly slowing the arms race, the proposal did lead to America's signing agreements with thirty-nine nations to develop nuclear energy for peaceful purposes. In 1954 the president rejected advice to use nuclear weapons or send troops to Indochina to forestall a Vietnamese victory over France. In his "Farewell Address" of early 1961, Eisenhower warned against a "military-industrial complex" and a government-university scientific complex that threatened the "democratic process" and "possible domination of the nation's scholars by federal employment, project allocations, and the power of money."[83]

Ike's peace initiatives fizzled, and his antimilitarist sentiments seldom translated into effective policies. He unilaterally halted nuclear tests in 1958, but America's stockpile of nuclear weapons during his presidency rose from 1,200 to 22,229. He sent troops to Lebanon, and by 1959 a million Americans served overseas in forty-two countries. By 1960 the Defense Department controlled 35 million acres of land at home and abroad. Defense budgets averaged more than $40 billion a year, although Eisenhower, fearful of "busting ourselves" by overspending, angered generals who disputed his cuts in army personnel.[84]

John Foster Dulles, McCarthyism, and the New Look

Although Secretary of State John Foster Dulles (1953–1959) seemed a less flexible and more articulate Cold Warrior than Eisenhower, the two "held strikingly parallel views," and "the documents confirm that it was the president who made the decisions."[85] Tutelage from his Presbyterian minister father, education at Princeton and George Washington Law School, service as a negotiator on reparations at the Paris Peace Conference at Versailles, membership in the prestigious Wall Street firm of Sullivan and Cromwell, and worldwide activity on behalf of the Federal Council of Churches gave Dulles a varied, cosmopolitan experience before World War II. After the war he helped promote bipartisanship but in 1952 assailed the very policies of the Truman administration that he had helped to shape. He later admitted that his desire to elect Eisenhower had fueled this political gambit.

Forceful, ambitious, sharp, and self-righteous, Dulles blended moral "idealism" with hard-nosed political "pragmatism."[86] He told a journalist that the United States "is almost the only country strong enough and powerful enough to be moral."[87] One official mused that Dulles felt he had a "pipeline on high" and that he received "his instructions from a superior source."[88] A dull, flat speaker with a lecturing tone, Dulles favored face-to-face diplomacy, yet showed, according to Eisenhower, a "curious lack of understanding as to how his words and manner may affect another personality."[89] Dulles's calculated public reputation for being a "rigid thinker," one colleague remarked, "was absolutely just at odds with what one saw . . . around the table" during departmental meetings.[90] Still, influential foreign observers labeled Dulles a "fire-and-brimstone anti-Communist fanatic," an "awkward old buster" with "pachydermatous qualities," and a "bastard" who had a "terrible influence" on Eisenhower.[91]

John Foster Dulles (1888–1959). Watching Dulles "grapple with a problem," an aide recalled, "was like watching a bird dog sniffing for its prey. He got a little excited as he worked over a solution, breathed a little faster, and obviously enjoyed the thinking process." More biting, Soviet foreign minister V. M. Molotov described Dulles and his brother Allen, the CIA director, as "the sort who would pick your pockets and cut off your head in one stroke." (*The Reporter,* 1956. Copyright 1956 by the Reporter Magazine Co.)

Joseph McCarthy (1909–1957). Graduate of Marquette University, judge, and marine, the Republican senator from Wisconsin was once known as the "Pepsi-Cola Kid" for protecting the interests of that company. The scholar Ellen Schrecker, noting that anticommunist excesses were widespread, argues that the demagogic McCarthy was the "creature" not the "creator" of the 1950s Red Scare. But as the journalist Cabell Phillips wrote, McCarthy "spit in the eye of constituted authority, undermined public confidence in the government and its leaders, and tore at the nation's foreign policy with the indiscriminate ferocity of a bulldozer. He used lies, slander, and innuendo to smash his opponents and to build his own image of invincibility." The Senate formally condemned McCarthy in December 1954. (*The Reporter*, 1951. Copyright 1951 by Fortnightly Publishing Co., Inc.)

Stalin's death and growing Soviet nuclear capabilities prompted an early reassessment of defense strategy, code-named Solarium, which predicted as many as 12 million U.S. casualties if Moscow launched a surprise attack by 1955. The resulting Eisenhower-Dulles "New Look" coupled conventional military forces "adequate to deter" or to "counter aggression" with cost-saving "massive atomic capability" that permitted the United States to "respond vigorously" to threats "at places and with means of its own choosing."[92] What Dulles called "massive retaliation," the president tersely described as "blow hell out of them in a hurry if they start anything."[93] It was cheaper to rely on nuclear deterrence because "if we let defense spending run wild," the president reasoned, "you get inflation . . . then controls . . . then a garrison state . . . and *then* we've lost the very values we were trying to defend."[94] Later in the decade, Eisenhower and Dulles moved toward the idea of a "firebreak"—a delay between the onset of a crisis and a strategic nuclear strike.[95]

With its huge nuclear arsenal and strong armed forces, the United States practiced "brinkmanship": not backing down in a crisis, even if it meant going to the brink of war. "Victory goes to him who can keep his nerve to the last fifteen minutes," wrote Dulles.[96] "Three brinks and he's brunk," jibed critics.[97]

As for the Third World, Eisenhower in 1954 commented: "You have a row of dominoes set up, you knock over the first one, and . . . the last one . . . will go over very quickly."[98] Thus if one country in Asia fell to the communists, others supposedly would fall in rapid succession. The 1957 "Eisenhower Doctrine" stipulated that the United States would intervene in the Middle East if any government threatened by a communist takeover requested aid. Sold as dynamic departures from Truman policies, such slogans offered only tactical changes in a continuing containment strategy.

Eisenhower once said that "sometimes Foster is just too worried about being accused of sounding like Truman and Acheson."[99] Dulles had witnessed the harassment of Acheson by Senator Joseph McCarthy and his "small but strident band of political and religious zealots."[100] To avoid a similar fate, Dulles appointed an ex-FBI man and henchman of McCarthy, Scott McLeod, as the State Department's chief security officer. After seven months of tapping phones, McLeod's investigators fired 193 "security risks," only one of them a suspected subversive. The people "don't care whether they were drunks, perverts or communists," McLeod explained. "They just want us to get rid of them."[101] In early 1953, Dulles ordered books authored by "Communists, fellow travellers, et cetera" to be removed from the libraries of American overseas information centers.[102] Who was an "et cetera"? Bureaucrats gave the broadest interpretation and tossed out the books of such people as the historian Foster Rhea Dulles, the secretary of state's own cousin.

One prominent and tragic case centered on Foreign Service Officer John Carter Vincent, an independent-minded "China hand" who during World War II reported that Jiang Jieshi would probably lose. McCarthyites took this professional analysis to mean that Vincent plotted to defeat Jiang. A State Department Loyalty Board cleared Vincent, but the Civil Service Loyalty Review Board, by a vote of 3 to 2, doubted his loyalty to the United States. Dulles forced Vincent out. Dulles once asked Vincent if he had read Stalin's *Problems of Leninism*. Vincent said he had

"I Hear There's Something Wrong with Your Morale." Secretary Dulles launched a damaging purge of Foreign Service Officers. President Eisenhower, refusing to get into "a pissing contest with that skunk" McCarthy, whom he privately viewed as "a pimple on [the] path of progress," did nothing to halt the political onslaught against the State Department. (*Herblock's Here and Now,* Simon & Schuster, 1955)

not, and Dulles replied that Vincent would not have advocated the China policy he did if he had read it. One student of China affairs has commented that "since Stalin failed in China no less than Truman, one may wonder whether Stalin read his own book."[103] Another China specialist, John Paton Davies, also lost his job even though nine security reviews had cleared him. McCarthyism left deep wounds. "It's like a car that's been in an accident," one ambassador recalled. "You repair it, but somehow it's never quite the same."[104] "The wrong done," the journalist Theodore H. White has written, "was to poke out the eyes and ears of the State Department on Asian affairs, to blind American foreign policy."[105]

Nikita S. Khrushchev (1894–1971). "I made speeches to bolster the morale of my people," Premier Khrushchev recalled. "I wanted to give our enemy pause. . . . I exaggerated a little. I said that we had the capability of shooting a fly out of space with our missiles." He fell from power in 1964 and until his death aired his views through his memoirs. (*The Reporter*, 1956. Copyright 1956 by The Reporter Magazine Co.)

The Glacier Grinds On: Khrushchev, Eisenhower, and the Cold War

Like a huge glacier, the Cold War continued to move across the international landscape. After Stalin's death, Eisenhower asked, "what is the Soviet Union ready to do?"[106] The early signs for improved Soviet-American relations seemed auspicious. Moscow helped end the deadlock over Korea, opened diplomatic relations with Yugoslavia and Greece, abandoned territorial claims against Turkey, toned down its anti-American rhetoric, and launched a "peace offensive." Although the Soviet crushing of an East Berlin riot in June 1953 reminded Americans of the past, the freeing of victims from forced labor camps suggested that Stalin's heirs would not mimic their long-time autocrat.

Soviet leaders scrambled for position in the succession crisis. Nikita S. Khrushchev, for years the Communist party boss of the Ukraine, eventually climbed to the top of the Kremlin hierarchy. By September 1953, Khrushchev had become first secretary of the Central Committee of the party; five years later he became premier. Portly and amiable, Khrushchev impressed people as an impulsive, competitive person of coarse speech. Eisenhower found him "shrewd, tough, and coldly deliberate even when he was pretending to be consumed by anger."[107]

Eisenhower and Khrushchev continued their nations' military buildups. Although Soviet ground forces outnumbered the Americans by a 2 to 1 margin, the United States possessed many more strategic bombers and nuclear weapons. In an attempt to bolster Western defenses through greater integration, including West German units, Dulles sponsored the European Defense Community (EDC). When the French balked, he warned them that the United States would undertake an "agonizing reappraisal" of U.S. security commitments.[108] Paris called his bluff and rejected EDC, while one London magazine mocked Dulles's threat with a cartoon of a jewelry store sign reading: "Appraisals $2; Agonizing Reappraisals $5."[109] The secretary did gain West German membership in NATO in May 1955. That same year SEATO went into effect (see page 292), the American defense treaty with nationalist China became active, the Baghdad Pact formed, and West Germany joined NATO. In response, the Soviets formed their own military organization, the Warsaw Pact of Eastern European states.

On one issue, Austria, a "test case for détente," the two powers cooperated in a rare example of productive Cold War diplomacy.[110] They agreed in May 1955 to end their ten-year occupation and create an independent, neutral Austria. The agreement emerged not only because the Austrians adeptly pressed for it but because both the Soviets and the Americans found elements of "victory": Each side effectively denied Austria to the other's sphere; Moscow demonstrated a commitment to peaceful coexistence; Washington welcomed a possible model for Eastern European nations eager to roll back Soviet power. Perhaps the Red Army's withdrawal from Austria would become "contagious" in Eastern Europe.[111]

Also in May 1955, the Soviet Union and the United States, under UN-sponsored negotiations, seemed close to a treaty to prohibit the use and manufacture of nuclear weapons, reduce conventional forces, and create an inspection system to monitor compliance—all terms that the United States had insisted on for years. "The whole thing looks too good to be true," remarked one French official.[112] So

Preparation for the "Kitchen Debate." Khrushchev and Vice President Richard M. Nixon sip Pepsi-Cola at the American National Exhibition in Moscow in July 1959, just before their "kitchen debate" in which the Soviet leader admitted American superiority in consumer goods but boasted "when we catch you up, in passing you by, we will wave to you." (PepsiCo, Inc.)

it was. Within months, the United States backed away from the disarmament proposal. Why? Steeped in the Cold War mentality, U.S. officials, especially the Joint Chiefs of Staff, expected the Soviets to cheat. More important, Dulles and Eisenhower sought a "cold war victory," not merely a "thaw."[113]

Throughout 1954–1955 came calls for a summit meeting of the great powers. Winston Churchill made an eloquent plea, and Democrats in Congress urged negotiations. Dulles countered: A summit conference would permit the Soviets to use propaganda on a grand scale; it would let them appear equal to Americans; it might encourage neutralism, for other countries would fear less and align less; and the Soviets would not bargain seriously because totalitarianism depended on an outside enemy. "We have come such a long way by being firm," he said, "that I would hate to see the whole edifice undermined in response to a smile."[114] But while Eisenhower agreed that Moscow should not be permitted to "hit the free world in the face," he thought the "present" a "propitious time" to negotiate.[115]

The Soviet Union, the United States, Britain, and France met in Geneva, Switzerland, July 18–23, 1955. Eisenhower and Dulles assured Congress that "Geneva was not going to be another Yalta."[116] The reference was timely, for early in 1955 Dulles had engineered the publication of once-secret documents in the *Yalta Papers* in an abortive attempt to embarrass the Democrats. Geneva did not repeat Yalta because the Big Four struck no concrete agreements. In the end, a participant recalled, "not much was achieved at the meeting except that it had occurred."[117] Everybody tried to score points for prestige. East and West wanted to

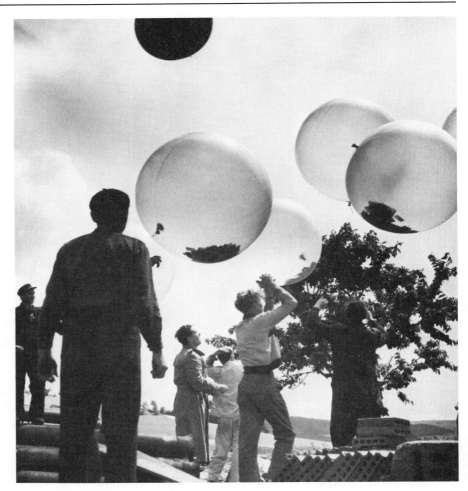

Propaganda Balloons for Eastern Europe. Although the United States did not send troops or military supplies to Hungary during the 1956 uprising, in the 1950s the Free Europe Committee floated message-filled balloons across the Iron Curtain from West Germany to stir up unrest. The CIA-front organization launched its first polyethylene balloons in 1951; its leaflets read: "Freedom will rise again." (Franklin D. Roosevelt Library)

unite Germany, but each on its own terms. Both sides favored arms control but parted over methods. Eisenhower's dramatic "Open Skies" proposal called for the Soviet Union and the United States to exchange maps and submit their military installations to aerial inspection.[118] About this U.S. propaganda ploy designed to counter Soviet appeals for disarmament, Eisenhower later remarked: "We knew the Soviets wouldn't accept it," but still "thought it was a good move."[119] "A bald espionage plot," sniffed Khrushchev.[120] Secrecy comprised one of the Soviets' deterrents, keeping Americans guessing on whether the inferior Soviets were catching up in airborne striking power. That secrecy ended in 1956 when the United States began covert reconnaisance flights by high-altitude U-2 planes over the Soviet Union.

Eisenhower nonetheless applauded a "new spirit of conciliation and cooperation" and assured Americans that he had not penned any secret agreements.[121] Soviets and Americans at Geneva drank "coexistence cocktails"—vodka and Coke.[122]

"I'll Be Glad to Restore Peace to the Middle East, Too." The ugly Soviet suppression of the Hungarian rebellion of 1956 prompted this telling cartoon by Herblock. (*Herblock's Special for Today,* Simon & Schuster, 1958)

After the largely ceremonial conference, Moscow recognized West Germany and Khrushchev endorsed "détente." Yet, he added, "if anybody thinks" that now "we shall forget about Marx, Engels, and Lenin, he is mistaken. This will happen when shrimps learn to whistle."[123]

The Geneva summit did initiate cultural exchanges, most notably Vice President Nixon's 1959 trip to the Soviet Union where, at a display of American products in a Moscow exhibition, he engaged Khrushchev in the "kitchen debate" on capitalism, communism, and the "commodity gap."[124] Even more impressive in spreading the U.S. message were goodwill jazz tours by American "jambassadors" such as Dizzy Gillespie, who reported to Eisenhower in 1956: "Our interracial group was powerfully effective against Red propaganda. Jazz . . . communicates with all people regardless of language or social barriers."[125] The Soviets responded with the Moscow Youth Festival of 1957, which one visitor likened to "a Cecil B. De-Mille production—and Nuremburg 1936."[126] Some 30,000 young people danced to U.S. musicians, picking up slang ("see ya later, alligator"), and calling themselves *bitniki* (beatniks).[127] As the "Cool War" gained converts, Voice of America's "Music USA" program attracted far more listeners than did its political broadcasts.[128] Washington's containment strategists never imagined "rollback as rock 'n' roll back."[129]

The Soviet-American confrontation in Europe nonetheless accelerated. Neither Moscow nor Washington had the power to force significant changes in European alignments, and neither side wanted to risk war to alter the status quo. The Soviets said they could wait for serious negotiations—"our asses aren't freezing in the wind," remarked Khrushchev.[130] Moscow still wanted Germany removed from NATO and NATO expunged from Europe. The United States still wanted the Soviets to leave Eastern Europe and the indefinite perpetuation of U.S. nuclear superiority.

In February 1956, Khrushchev, once the loyal supporter of Stalin's bloody purges of the 1930s, delivered a secret speech to the Twentieth Party Congress. He denounced Stalin as "monstrous" for his "grave abuse of power," initiated "de-Stalinization," embraced peaceful coexistence, and seemed to endorse different brands of communism.[131] After the CIA published the speech, Khrushchev's apparent acceptance of Titoism emboldened nationalists and victims of Stalinism to challenge autocratic leaders in Eastern Europe. The abolition of the Cominform in April seemed to demonstrate Moscow's new tolerance for diversity. Young people and intellectuals especially embraced self-determination. In Poland, a labor dispute in mid-1956 evolved into national resistance to Soviet tutelage. After using force to put down riots, Moscow compromised with Polish nationalism by reluctantly accepting Wladyslaw Gomulka as the Polish Communist party chairman, heretofore denied influence because Stalin thought him too "Titoist." The United States, which had been giving aid to Tito himself for years, soon offered Poland economic assistance.

Revolt erupted next in Hungary. A new government, backed by Budapest street demonstrators and countrywide local revolutionary councils, drastically announced Hungary's pullout from the Warsaw Pact and neutrality in the Cold War. An initially reluctant Khrushchev concluded that "we have no other course" but intervention.[132] A successful revolt would "give a great boost to Americans, English, and French" and weaken neighboring satellite states.[133] Soviet apparatchiks "would not understand a failure to respond with force in Hungary."[134] The Anglo-French-Israeli invasion of Egypt on October 31 (see page 301) offered a "favorable moment" for the Red Army to act.[135] Some 20,000 underarmed Hungarian students and workers and 3,000 Soviet troops died in hand-to-tank combat in the streets of Budapest in early November.

The Polish and Hungarian rebellions seemed to satisfy Dulles's dream of "liberation." In 1953, Congress had passed the first annual Captive Peoples' Resolution to spur self-determination in Eastern Europe. The Eisenhower administration had been encouraging discontent in Eastern Europe through Voice of America and CIA-financed Radio Free Europe. "Sure we never said rise up and revolt," one CIA agent recalled.[136] But in a 1955 Christmas message, Eisenhower declared that "any East European" displaying "visible opposition" to "Soviet oppression . . . can count on our help."[137] And the covert CIA program RED SOX/RED CAP trained East European émigrés for paramilitary action. Hungary nonetheless exposed "liberation" as a sham slogan "fashioned to appeal to domestic ethnic audiences."[138] To counter criticism of a "do nothing attitude," the administration permitted more than 20,000 Hungarian refugees to enter the United States and introduced a UN resolution condemning Soviet force.[139] Still, "the condemnations that rained down upon the administration for publicly advocating" but not supporting liberation "effectively discredited Eisenhower's policy throughout Eastern Europe."[140]

Missile Race, Berlin, and the U-2 Mess

In 1956–1957, the United States seemed on the defensive and the Soviets on the offensive. Washington hastened to patch up its crumbling European alliance, rocked by U.S. disapproval of British–French military actions in the Middle East. Washington reinvigorated NATO and deployed intermediate-range ballistic missiles in Britain and tactical nuclear weapons in Western Europe. Still, the French foundered amidst a colonial war in Algeria, where nationalists fighting to "restore" independence caused Paris to shift many French NATO contingents to Africa.[141] Many Western Europeans distrusted the U.S. push for German rearmament, worried about a resurgence of McCarthyism, and resented U.S. strictures on trade with communist countries. People in NATO nations also expressed doubt about America's credibility as an ally. Might not Americans fail to defend Western Europe against a Soviet attack lest U.S. countermeasures in Europe invite a Soviet nuclear onslaught against the United States itself? An American economic recession in 1957 further sapped Western vitality. John Foster Dulles's cancer surgery in November 1956 meant that President Eisenhower had to steer the United States through Eastern European and Mideast crises without his trusted adviser, who died in May 1959.

On October 4, 1957, the Soviets launched the world's first artificial space satellite, *Sputnik*. At twenty-two inches around and 184 pounds, this display of "Soviet scientific prowess" delivered "a severe blow" to American "pride."[142] It also offered "a noisy reminder" that "the Soviet missile program was proceeding just fine."[143] Two months earlier the Soviets had fired the first intercontinental ballistic missile. Critics lambasted Eisenhower for allowing American power to slip. Even though the USSR had test-fired only six ICBMs, Khrushchev bragged about turning out rockets "like sausages."[144] In fact, Khrushchev ran a "bluff"; he actually deployed only four unwieldy ICBMs by 1960, giving "the impression of Soviet strength . . . while actually playing from a position of inferiority."[145] A presidential commission study, the "Gaither Report," fed popular fears that the Soviets outstripped the United States militarily and economically. This bellicose report of November 1957 urged an expensive military buildup to improve U.S. "deterrent power."[146]

Despite Eisenhower's reluctance to expand the budget deficit, the committee's "impact" became "clear" in his costly decisions to build more missiles, disperse Strategic Air Command bombers, improve radar technology, beef up antimissile defense, and reorganize the Defense Department.[147] Ike nonetheless knew that *Sputnik* had not endangered U.S. security because highflying U-2 spy planes had been surveilling Soviet military capabilities since 1956. Privately fuming about "neurotic demagogues" who "leaked security information," the president tried to reassure Americans without releasing the intelligence data.[148] The public remained jittery.

In January 1958, rocket scientists successfully launched an American satellite named Explorer I. In July, Congress created the National Aeronautics and Space Administration (NASA), soon to be, with the Pentagon, the chief federal funding source for high-tech research in universities such as Stanford and Massachusetts Institute of Technology, where academic agendas came to follow "the requirements of the national security state."[149] *Sputnik* also boosted secondary education so that "Johnny" could keep up with "Ivan." The National Defense Education Act

"So Russia Launched a Satellite, But Has It Made Cars with Fins Yet?" Ross Lewis's cartoon suggested that Americans had become too fascinated by 1950s consumer products while the Soviets were advancing missile technology. It did not take long for the United States to establish superiority in the nuclear arms race through new intercontinental ballistic missiles. (Milwaukee Public Library)

(NDEA), passed in September 1958, provided federal aid to finance new educational programs in the sciences, mathematics, and foreign languages.

The continued militarization of the Cold War and new emphasis on missile development alarmed George F. Kennan, an earlier architect of containment. In 1957 Kennan delivered the "Reith Lectures" in London, calling for the "disengagement" of foreign troops from Eastern Europe and Germany, restrictions on nuclear weapons in that area, and a unified, nonaligned Germany. Earlier in the year, Polish foreign minister Adam Rapacki had advocated a "denuclearized zone" in Central and Eastern Europe.[150] The U.S. ambassador in Warsaw thought the Rapacki Plan would cause "trouble between the Poles and the U.S.S.R.," but Dulles and Eisenhower rejected the proposal as "highly dangerous."[151] Kennan tried to keep the idea alive through his eloquent lectures, widely broadcast over BBC radio. Also, in order to reduce Moscow's security fears, he sought to remove Germany from the Cold War and thereby permit a withdrawal of Soviet troops from Eastern Europe. Finally, Kennan urged the administration to "put our military fixations aside," to exercise diplomacy rather than to strengthen NATO.[152]

Kennan's suggestions sparked furious debate. Former secretary of state Dean Acheson joined the fray. Should Kennan's plan become reality, Acheson scolded, the Soviet Union might reintroduce troops into Eastern Europe, threaten Western Europe, and sign an anti-American military pact with the new united Germany. A rearmed West Germany must remain in the U.S. camp. The United States, Kennan

"Braggers." In this Japanese cartoon, Khrushchev and Eisenhower brag about their missiles. Despite his menacing public boasts, Khrushchev, like Eisenhower, dreaded the consequences of nuclear war. "We could never possibly use these weapons," he told an Egyptian journalist, "but all the same we must be prepared." (Nasu, courtesy of the State Historial Society of Missouri)

answered, would never know Moscow's intentions unless it negotiated. Walter Lippmann, who had criticized Kennan's containment in 1947, stood with him in 1957. Acheson and other hard-liners, Lippmann complained, resembled "old soldiers trying to relive the battles in which they won their fame and glory. . . . Their preoccupation with their own past history is preventing them from dealing with the new phase of the Cold War."[153]

A new crisis over Berlin demonstrated the importance of Kennan's call for defusing European issues. West Berlin, 110 miles inside communist East Germany, had become a "malignant tumor" that required "surgery," in Khrushchev's words.[154] Some 3 million East German defectors, many of them skilled workers, had used West Berlin as an escape route since 1949. For Americans and their allies, the city operated as an espionage and propaganda center. West Berlin's prosperity, induced by billions of dollars in U.S. aid, glittered next to drab East Berlin. Washington heated Soviet tempers by crowing about West Berlin's economic success and applauding the East German exodus. The United States also insisted that the two Germanies unite under free elections and refused to recognize the East German government. Finally, the continued rearmament of West Germany, including U.S. planes capable of dropping nuclear bombs, alarmed Moscow, which had endorsed the Rapacki Plan.

In November 1958 the Soviet Union boldly issued an ultimatum. Within six months, warned Khrushchev, unless East-West talks on Germany had begun, Moscow would sign a peace treaty with East Germany, thereby ending occupation agreements still in effect from World War II and turning East Berlin over to the East German regime. He recommended that Berlin become a "free city" without foreign troops. Washington knew that to deal with East Germany would confirm the Soviet claim of two Germanies. Such a confirmation would surrender occupation rights and hence the U.S. presence within West Berlin itself. Eisenhower feared that

U-2. The United States began work on this high-altitude reconnaissance aircraft in 1954. In 1956, the Lockheed-built 49-foot-long spy plane began overflights of the Soviet Union to gather intelligence on Soviet missile development, despite Khrushchev's warning that "we will shoot down all uninvited guests." With a range of 2,200 miles and a cruising speed of 460 miles per hour, the U-2 also conducted surveillance during the Suez crisis. On May 1, 1960, a U-2 crashed well inside the Soviet Union. (National Air and Space Museum, Smithsonian Institution, Photo No. 85-7309)

"if we let the Germans down they might shift their own position and even go neutralistic."[155] Urged to test Soviet intentions by sending U.S. military units through the corridors to West Berlin, the president stalled. He said privately that "in this gamble, we are not going to be betting white chips, building up the pot gradually and fearfully. Khrushchev should know that when we decide to act, our whole stack will be in the pot."[156] Khrushchev wanted to talk, not fight. "Do not hurry. . . . The conditions are not ripe as yet for a new scheme of things," he told militant East German leaders.[157] He agreed to a foreign ministers conference for May 1959, which proved inconclusive, a trip in September 1959 to the United States to speak directly with Eisenhower, and ultimately a Paris summit meeting in May 1960.

Warmly welcomed by Eisenhower, whom he grudgingly deemed "not without decency," Khrushchev began his U.S. visit of September 1959 with a dramatic speech at the United Nations, where he proposed "general and complete disarmament in three years."[158] More in the forefront of diplomacy following Dulles's death in May, the president hoped that firsthand exposure to America's vastness and variety would make a "favorable chip in the granite."[159] The premier, seeming altogether human, inspected an IBM plant, marveled at the fecundity of Midwest grain fields, and visited a Hollywood movie set where he took offense at the bare legs exposed in a cancan dance—a sign to him of the decadence of Western capitalism. Khrushchev plugged "peaceful coexistence" and said that no one should take his "we will bury capitalism" statement in a literal or military sense: "You may live under capitalism and we will live under socialism and build communism. The one whose system proves better will win."[160] After ten days on the road, the Soviet premier went to Camp David, that quiet, secluded presidential retreat near the Catoctin Mountains in Maryland. For two days the two leaders exchanged war stories and discussed Berlin.

Eisenhower would not agree to a new summit meeting until Khrushchev abandoned his Berlin ultimatum. The premier agreed to do so, evoking the "Spirit of Camp David"—a willingness on both sides to talk their way to détente. Eisenhower "sincerely wanted to liquidate the 'cold war' and improve relations," Khrushchev later told the Politburo, adding that the moderates who advised Eisenhower had gained the upper hand over the "madmen."[161]

In 1959–1960 Eisenhower himself took goodwill foreign trips in a deliberate effort to ease tensions. Just before Khrushchev's visit to the United States, the president flew to London, Paris, and Bonn for talks with European leaders. In December he traveled 22,000 miles to eleven nations in Europe, Asia, and North Africa. In February 1960, he toured Latin America for two weeks and encountered a mixed reception. And then he departed for the Paris summit meeting in May.

Two weeks before that summit meeting, on May 1, 1960, an American airplane carrying high-powered cameras and other reconnaissance instruments was shot down over Sverdlovsk in the Ural Mountains of northern Russia, 1,200 miles inside the Soviet Union. On a CIA mission, the U-2 intelligence plane was flying from a base in Pakistan to one in Norway. Although such flights had gone on for four years and the Soviets knew about them, this was the first time that Soviet firepower had reached the high-altitude craft. Pilot Francis Gary Powers's U-2 evidently had engine trouble and dropped several thousand feet before being shot down. He parachuted and was captured immediately, unable or unwilling to kill himself by taking his CIA-issued poison. NASA, used as "cover," announced routinely on May 3 that a "research airplane" studying weather patterns over Turkey had apparently crashed. When Khrushchev declared that the downed U.S. plane had violated Soviet air space, the State Department fabricated a claim that a civilian weather plane had simply flown off course. But on May 6, Khrushchev displayed photographs of the uninjured pilot, his spy equipment, and the crashed U-2. The president then defended the flights as necessary to prevent "another Pearl Harbor"—a "surprise attack" on "the United States and the Free World."[162] But for many the affair "reinforced the prevailing view that Eisenhower was not minding the store."[163]

The Berlin "can of worms" and nuclear-weapons testing controls stood high on the Paris summit meeting's agenda.[164] Apparently preferring to wait until a new president took office, perhaps seizing an opportunity to show domestic hard-liners and Chinese critics of peaceful coexistence that he could be tough, and certainly angry about U.S. violations of Soviet air space, Khrushchev denounced American aggression, demanded an apology for the U-2 flights, and stalked out. Thinking that a real opportunity to wind down the Cold War had been lost, Eisenhower bemoaned "the stupid U-2 mess" and looked forward to retirement on his Gettysburg farm.[165]

To the Brink with China; To the Market with Japan

The Chinese communists did not mourn this deterioration in Soviet-American relations. From the mid-1950s onward, Beijing castigated any sign of Soviet-American rapprochement. China repeatedly criticized Khrushchev for "yielding to evil" and "coddling wrong."[166]

As the Sino-Soviet schism widened, it became less tenable for U.S. officials to speak of a communist monolith, although many still did. But even John Foster Dulles admitted the split and seized the opportunity to drive a wedge between Moscow and Beijing by "exploiting potential jealousies, rivalries, and disaffection" and "placing additional stress on Russian-Chinese relations."[167] Many reasons other than U.S. pressure explain the Sino-Soviet split, including Moscow's refusal to help China develop nuclear capability. Scholars debate whether the "negative" U.S. approach toward China produced better results than a "positive" policy of trade and engagement might have achieved.[168] In any case, under Eisenhower-Dulles policies, the Sino-American chasm gaped ever wider.

In early 1953, to press the People's Republic of China to accept an armistice in the Korean War, President Eisenhower announced that the Seventh Fleet would no longer block Jiang Jieshi's attempts to attack the mainland. Jiang actually lacked the resources for a major fight, but the decision alarmed Beijing, especially after Nationalist bombing raids began to hit the coast. Throughout the 1950s, Jiang pledged a return to China and received an annual average of more than $250 million in U.S. economic and military aid. The Seventh Fleet remained in the Taiwan Strait to protect Formosa as a valued Asian military partner. In December 1954, Taiwan and the United States signed a mutual defense treaty. The following month, Congress, by a vote of 83 to 3 in the Senate and 410 to 3 in the House, authorized the president in the Formosa Resolution to "stand up to Communist aggression" by employing American troops as needed to defend Taiwan and the adjoining islands.[169]

In 1954 the United States created the Southeast Asia Treaty Organization (SEATO), which formally allied France, Britain, Australia, New Zealand, Thailand, Pakistan, and the Philippines against "Red China" and its support of revolution in Indochina. Mao later grumbled about "all the bases, like nails pounded in around us."[170] Washington also resisted cultural contacts with China, forbidding American journalists to accept Beijing's 1956 invitation to visit the mainland and banning the shipment of a panda to the United States from China. At the 1954 Geneva Conference on Indochina (see next chapter), Chinese and American diplomats barely mixed. At one point Foreign Minister Zhou Enlai approached Secretary Dulles intending to shake hands, but Dulles, afraid that photographers would record this contaminating event, brusquely shunned Zhou's outstretched hand. Washington also imposed a total trade embargo in order to increase China's "sense of ostracism" from the world.[171]

In a crisis that "illustrates the danger of mutual isolation," China and the United States lurched toward the brink in 1954–1955.[172] Jinmen (Quemoy) and Mazu (Matsu) lay just a few miles off southeastern China in the Taiwan Strait, two of some thirty small offshore islands that the Nationalists had managed to hold when they fled to Taiwan in 1949. Jiang had fortified the two islands with thousands of troops and used the outposts to raid the mainland. As the United States negotiated the defense treaty with Jiang in summer 1954, Beijing unfurled a "Liberate Taiwan" global propaganda campaign to counter the anticipated alliance. In response to the "plot of making a mutual security treaty" and to divert attention from preparations to invade another offshore island group called the Dachens, Chinese shore batteries began to bombard Jinmen early in September.[173] The Chinese did not intend to invade Jinmen, and they certainly did not anticipate the U.S. response.

Deeming the offshore islands militarily valuable to Taiwan (some 100 miles away), Washington had cautioned Jiang against escalating coastal warfare. "Quemoy is not our ship," Eisenhower said at first. People would ask, "What do we care what happens to those yellow people out there?"[174] But Senator William F. Knowland of California used a football analogy to explain. The defense, he said, "cannot wait until the team with the ball crosses the line of scrimmage before resisting."[175]

Despite British warnings that Jiang was a "palooka" who might ignite war "through impulsiveness," the United States signed the defense treaty with Taiwan, and Congress gave the president a blank check in the Formosa Resolution. Mao also practiced brinkmanship.[176] Claiming that "the U.S. cannot annihilate the Chinese nation with a small stack of atom bombs," Mao in mid-January 1955 sent his army to overrun the Dachens.[177] Heeding U.S. advice, Jiang pulled his troops out; then Washington took up Mao's challenge. Eisenhower brandished nuclear weapons, stating publicly that he would use them "just exactly as you would use a bullet or anything else."[178] The Joint Chiefs of Staff readied plans to drop several Hiroshima-size bombs on coastal cities with expected casualties in the millions.

Mao Zedong (1893–1976). Chief of the Communist party in "Red China," father of the successful Communist Revolution, and radical philosopher-poet, Mao said of the Taiwan Strait crisis: "I did not expect that the whole world would be so deeply shocked." (National Archives)

Lacking guaranteed support from the Soviet Union and reacting to alarms voiced by Asian nations attending the Bandung Conference (see page 299), China offered in April to discuss tensions with the United States. The crisis quickly quieted. In Geneva, and after 1958 in Warsaw, Chinese and American officials talked at the ambassadorial level about Taiwan, trade, and other topics. These limited discussions constituted the only positive element in Sino–American relations.

After the deployment of U.S. tactical nuclear weapons on Taiwan, and after Jiang had augmented his forces to more than 100,000 on the offshore islands, Mao answered in August 1958 by once again shelling Jinmen and Mazu. While perceiving a "long-range plan, 'with Soviet backing,' to retake Taiwan," Eisenhower resisted military advice to strike China with "low yield" nuclear weapons and possibly cause "millions of noncombatant casualties."[179] Khrushchev in fact leveled a "barrage of criticism" against Beijing, whose actions jeopardized Moscow's "peace offensive" with the West.[180] Soviet Foreign Minister Andrei Gromyko urged Mao to seek a peaceful settlement. America's European allies likewise counseled caution. Eisenhower instead ordered airlifts and Seventh Fleet escorts for Nationalist supply ships while Beijing vowed "resolute blows" against Jiang's "clique."[181] Mao told Gromyko that "it's getting so hot, and we want Eisenhower to take a shower."[182] "Those damned little offshore islands," the president griped. "I wish they'd sink."[183]

Eisenhower stepped back from the brink, as did Mao. After Dulles and Jiang agreed in October that Jiang would not use force against the mainland, the Nationalist leader withdrew some troops from Jinmen and Mazu, and Eisenhower suspended escorts of Nationalist vessels. Beijing relaxed its bombardment of the islands. But the People's Republic accelerated its efforts to acquire nuclear weapons "even if the Chinese people have to pawn their trousers for this purpose."[184] Alarm bells sounded in Washington and Moscow.

As it went to the brink with Beijing, the United States worked to "keep the Japanese on our side," all the while frightening China, the Soviet Union, the Koreas,

Neighborhood Street and Coca-Cola in Tokyo, Japan.   Although Japan developed a booming export economy in the 1950s, it also imported famous U.S. products. Wherever U.S. troops were stationed during the Cold War, Coca-Cola followed, as the Georgia-based company greatly expanded its global marketing. Despite complaints about "Coca-colonization," the beverage quickly became a popular soft drink abroad. "One could swallow it," one scholar notes, "without giving up one's cultural loyalties or sense of national identity." (Library of Congress)

and other past victims of Japan's aggression.[185] Two September 8, 1951, agreements guided Japanese-American relations for the decade. The first, a peace treaty signed by the United States and forty-seven other nations, provided for the ending of American occupation on April 28, 1952. The second, the Mutual Security Treaty signed by Washington and Tokyo, provided for U.S. defense of Japan and the stationing of American arms and forces on Japanese soil. Japan agreed to create a 110,000-strong military (Self-Defense Forces), which could not be used outside the nation. The military pact provoked considerable friction. Many Japanese resented the U.S. bases and the U.S. pressure to rearm, and throughout the 1950s, with popular opinion favoring "rice before guns," mass street demonstrations strained relations.[186] Meanwhile, American leaders who insisted that Japan pay for more of its own defense sharply criticized the Tokyo government for obstructing rearmament.

The plight of the *Fukuryu Maru* (*Lucky Dragon,*) a Japanese fishing boat, heightened the debate. On March 1, 1954, the United States tested its new hydrogen bomb in the Bikini Atoll (Marshall Islands), near where the boat fished for tuna. After a huge fireball erupted, shifting winds sprinkled radioactive fallout on the crew, causing severe nausea, fever, and blisters, and eventually killing one crew member. Disparaging Japan's "fancied martyrdom," Washington waited months to compensate the victims.[187] Widespread Japanese protests ensued. Two years later, the movie *Godzilla* offered an "eerie and realistic recalling" of the *Lucky Dragon* affair as a prehistoric monster, revived by atomic bomb tests, rampaged through Tokyo.[188]

After negotiators signed a renewed Japanese-American defense pact in January 1960, hundreds of thousands marched and rioted against the retention of U.S. bases.

The Japanese government pushed the new treaty through the Diet (parliament), but the prime minister was forced to resign, and President Eisenhower had to cancel his goodwill trip to Japan.

Even though huge U.S. military purchases in Japan during the Korean War—for Toyota trucks, for example—spurred economic recovery, Secretary Dulles still complained in 1954 that Japan "has been listless and drifting and apparently expecting merely to be taken care of by [the] U.S."[189] Eager to lower the costs of subsidizing Japanese reconstruction and to blunt possible communist exploitation of economic instability, U.S. officials encouraged Japan to develop a prosperous export-oriented economy. A bullish consumerism was inspired in part by the Japanese desire to adopt aspects of the American lifestyle after seeing Hollywood movies. By the mid-1950s, Japan experienced double-digit economic growth by using substantial U.S. aid to buy and adapt American technology (Motorola helped start the electronics industry), improving labor-management coordination to enhance efficiency and quality, and investing in research and development rather than in weapons. Americans "helped the Japanese reinvent themselves as 'people of plenty'—to use the historian David Potter's celebrated term."[190] With Japan's populace striving for the "three sacred treasures" (television, washing machine, and refrigerator), and with 2,500 Japanese intellectuals visiting the United States through academic exchange programs in the 1950s ("spreading favorable images of America as a model and . . . inspiration"), Japan became not only America's military ally but also eventually its economic competitor.[191]

The Third World Rises: Revolutionary Nationalism and Nonalignment

Between 1946 and 1960, thirty-seven new nations emerged from colonial status in Asia, Africa, and the Middle East. Eighteen countries gained independence in 1960 alone. In 1958, twenty-eight prolonged guerrilla insurgencies raged. Revolutions and the collapse of empires thus claimed a central place in global affairs. These great changes occurred in the "Third World"—a term for nations that belonged neither to the capitalist "West" nor to the communist "East." At first called "backward" and then "developing" countries, Third World nations generally consisted of nonwhite, agricultural peoples in the southern hemisphere. Such countries provided industrial nations with bountiful raw materials, military bases, intelligence facilities, and markets for manufactured goods. In 1959 more than one-third of American direct private investments abroad were in the Third World.

Volatile nationalist movements flourished in these "emerging" nations, often led by anticolonial revolutionaries who sought economic improvement without foreign ownership. Eisenhower claimed to "be on the side of the natives for once."[192] He wrote Churchill that "should we try to dam [nationalism] up completely it would, like a mighty river, burst through the barriers and could create havoc."[193] Yet many U.S. leaders "doubted the capacity of darker-skinned peoples to practice self-government."[194] Nixon in 1960 remarked that "some African peoples had only been out of the trees for fifty years."[195] Anticolonial revolutions often produced undemocratic regimes that

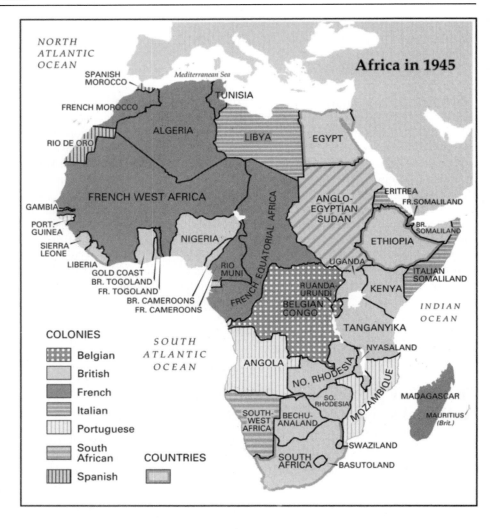

declared themselves "nonaligned" or "neutral" in the Cold War, a stance Washington condemned as helpful to communism. Convinced that Moscow caused much upheaval in the Third World and that "premature independence" would facilitate "Soviet colonialism," the administration endorsed a "middle path" of "acceding to continued colonial rule by anticommunist allies while verbally backing eventual self-determination" in Africa.[196] To blame communists for nationalist explosions, one scholar has written, "is like blaming the inherent danger in a huge mass of exposed combustible materials on the possible presence of arsonists."[197] The Eisenhower-Dulles team futilely applied containment to the Third World.

The nation's great wealth proved a mixed blessing. Americans found that foreigners both envied and resented America's unmatched abundance. The image of the "Ugly American" exacerbated foreign resentment. In 1958 William J. Lederer

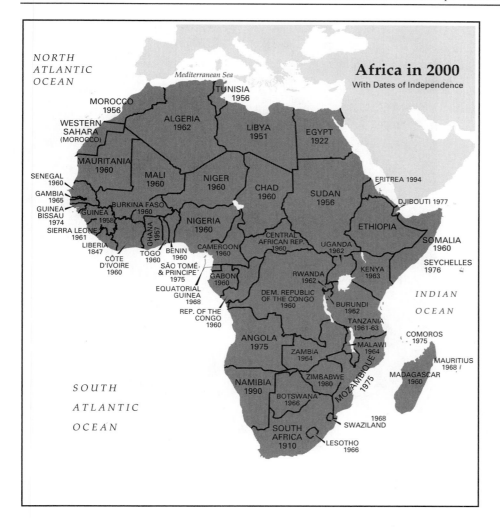

and Eugene Burdick wrote a novel with that title to satirize "fat," "ostentatious," "loud," and "stupid" American tourists abroad and U.S. diplomats who lived lavishly in a "Golden Ghetto."[198] The authors appealed for Foreign Service Officers who spoke the language of the host country. Unless U.S. officials moved more among "the people," they argued, Washington would lose the struggle against communism.

American racism, symbolized by Jim Crow practices, hovered like "the sword of Damocles . . . over American pretensions to world leadership after 1945."[199] In December 1952, the attorney general asked the Supreme Court to strike down segregation in public schools, arguing that "it is in the context of the present world struggle between freedom and tyranny that the problem of racial discrimination must be viewed."[200] So it was. In 1955 the dark-skinned Indian ambassador G. L. Mehta was "racially abused" at an airport restaurant in Texas.[201] In 1957 a Howard Johnson's in

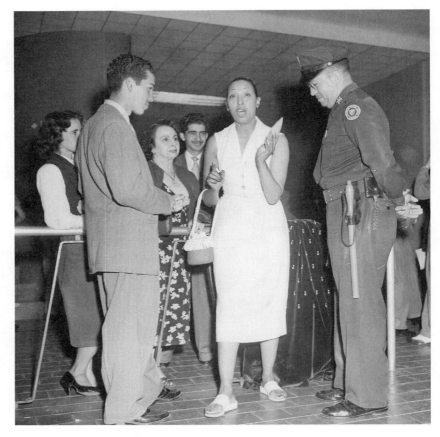

Josephine Baker in Cuba. The "saga" of jazz vocalist Josephine Baker, writes the historian Mary Dudziak, "underscores the importance to Cold War international politics of maintaining control over the narrative of race and American democracy." Outspoken at home and abroad on American racial inequality, Baker found herself surveilled and harassed by the FBI, the State Department, and the USIA, which together used disinformation falsely to discredit her as a communist in order to silence her allegedly "anti-American" views. She is shown protesting near a Havana, Cuba, radio station in February 1953 after the U.S. embassy successfully pressured her hosts to cancel Baker's scheduled performances on the island. (Corbis)

Dover, Delaware, denied food to Ghana's finance minister, K. A. Gbedemah, "even after he had identified himself to the manager."[202] Eisenhower invited Gbedemah to a White House breakfast to assuage the insult. That same year, the president sent federal troops to escort black children to school in Little Rock, Arkansas, amidst ugly white protests. Dulles bemoaned American racial strife as "worse for us than Hungary for the Russians."[203] Foreign observers concluded that "the United States has no moral claim to be leader of Western democracies," for "one can't be world champion of the colonial peoples while championing inequality in one's backyard."[204] At the Brussels World's Fair of 1958, the State Department, which itself remained largely "lily white," extolled "positive progress" on race with a controversial life-size photo of multiracial children playing ring-around-the-rosy.[205] Despite favorable European reaction, Eisenhower withdrew the display when segregationists in Congress protested the "unimaginable stupidity" of America's government "[apologizing] for racial segregation in the United States."[206]

Gender stereotypes joined racism and other cultural biases in shaping U.S. policies toward the Third World. In South Asia, for example, American officials thought that the "vigorous" and "virile" Pakistan, which had joined the Baghdad Pact and

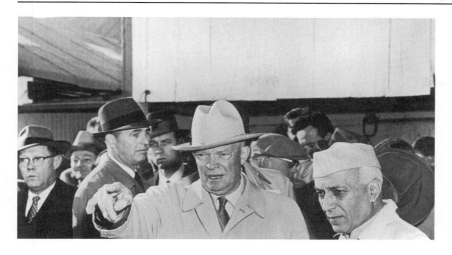

Eisenhower and Prime Minister Jawaharlal Nehru (1889–1964). The Indian prime minister and the American president are shown during Nehru's U.S. visit in 1956. The British-educated Brahmin enjoyed more cordial relations with Eisenhower than with either President Truman or John F. Kennedy. The two nonetheless remained far apart on such issues as Washington's military alliance with India's rival Pakistan (1954) and Nehru's leadership of the nonaligned movement in the Third World. As the historian Andrew Rotter has observed, Nehru's wearing of the traditional kurta, his preference for fruit juice instead of alcohol, and above all his refusal to ally with the West in the Cold War all invoked subliminal stereotypes of Indians as lacking decisiveness and male "potency." (Dwight D. Eisenhower Library, White House Album)

SEATO, showed "more masculinity" than the "mystics, dreamers, [and] hypocrites" of nonaligned India, which displayed an "almost feminine hypersensitiveness" regarding national prestige.[207] Israel, having shed the stereotype of passive victim of the Holocaust for that of the "tough Jew" or "virile, throbbing civilization" surrounded by "hostile enemies," likewise assumed the role of America's "democratic bulwark" in the Middle East.[208] Arab states, despite their valuable oil, were portrayed as cowardly "marauders," "devious" and undisciplined soldiers, or "problem [children]" in need of "an intelligent parent."[209]

When early-twentieth-century upheavals, as in Mexico, China, and Russia, rocked international equilibrium, the United States increasingly found itself a target rather than a model of revolution. As one postwar government report frankly stated: "The United States leans toward propertied classes who place a premium on order and trade."[210] Hence, in late 1960, when forty-three Afro-Asian states, led by India, sponsored a United Nations resolution championing liberation from colonialism, the United States abstained from voting, lest it offend such Cold War friends as Portugal.

The Soviets paid attention to the Third World, too. Both Marxism and the USSR's professed anticolonialism enjoyed wide appeal. In the mid-1950s Khrushchev toured India, Burma, and Afghanistan. Moscow granted some quarter billion dollars to Indonesia between 1954 and 1959 and funded an Indian steel plant and the Aswan Dam in Egypt. The Soviets also praised the Bandung Conference of April 1955, which convened twenty-nine "nonaligned" states (about one-quarter of the world's population) at the "first international conference of colored peoples in the history of mankind."[211] "While Washington and London fumble feebly, obsessed by visions of colored hordes clouding a lily-white horizon like locusts," the *Times of India* reported, "Moscow, Moses-like, beckons the dispossessed hosts onwards to the Promised Land."[212]

Yet the Soviet Union also bumped up against Third World nationalism. Egypt's Gamal Abdel Nasser and India's Jawaharlal Nehru would not become the "plaything" or "pawn" of either side.[213] When, during his 1955 trip to India, Khrushchev vehemently denounced the West, the neutralist Indians resented this blatant effort to bring the Cold War into their country. Arab nationalism, rather than Soviet communism, dominated the Middle East. And in Latin America, between 1945 and 1955, sixteen nations outlawed the Communist party. The Soviets, like the Americans, could not countenance independent nationalism. Nor could they explain away the contradiction between their own "promise" of self-determination and their hypocritical "performance" in suppressing independence in Eastern Europe.[214]

American officials remained fearful, however, that communists would exploit nationalistic sentiment and poverty in the Third World. Foreign aid became a primary U.S. tool. Whereas during the 1949–1952 period some three-quarters of total U.S. economic assistance went to Europe, in the years 1953–1957 three-quarters flowed to developing countries. By 1961 more than 90 percent of U.S. aid targeted the Third World. But to Washington's distress, many recipients refused to choose sides in the Cold War, thus drawing fire from Americans who demanded political returns from foreign aid. To Dulles, neutralism seemed but an "immoral and shortsighted" stage on the road to communism.[215]

Stormy Weather: Nationalism in the Middle East and Latin America

Crises in the Middle East and Latin America illustrated tense U.S.-Third World relations and elevated covert action and propaganda as major instruments of foreign policy. In 1952, Colonel Nasser led young Egyptian army officers against King Farouk, who fled to Europe with his harem and his wealth. Nasser initiated land reform and pledged to end British control of the Suez Canal. London reluctantly agreed in 1954 to a phased withdrawal. To prevent a defense "vacuum" in the Middle East, Washington in 1955 promoted the Baghdad Pact, a military alliance of Britain, Turkey, Iran, Iraq, and Pakistan.[216] An expansive "public diplomacy" campaign simultaneously used pamphlets, posters, media outlets, books, music, film, educational exchanges, and religion in order to guide "revolutionary and nationalistic pressures throughout the area into orderly channels not antagonistic to the West."[217] Iran was won over in 1953 when the CIA, jointly with British intelligence, overthrew the nationalist regime of Mohammed Mossedegh, an alleged "elderly lunatic" who unsettlingly fainted and wept, pajama-clad, during meetings with Westerners, and who crusaded to nationalize foreign oil interests.[218] U.S. companies produced about 50 percent of the Middle East's petroleum. Eighty-nine percent of Europe's crude oil imports came from that region.

Israel drew closer to the United States through foreign aid totaling $374 million from 1952 to 1961. Yet bitter Arab-Israeli conflict thwarted U.S. hopes for order in the Middle East. After the Israelis raided the Gaza Strip in 1955 and exposed Egypt's military weakness, Cairo signed an arms agreement with Czechoslovakia. Heretofore Western nations had monopolized arms sales in the Middle East. Meanwhile, Palestinian refugees languished in squalid camps, growing more militant each year. Persuaded that Israel was "over-aggressive," the State Department's Henry Byroade lectured Israelis to "drop the attitude of conqueror" toward their neighbors.[219] But he also implored Arabs to accept the "accomplished fact" of Israel's existence.[220]

Despite his dislike for Nasser's Pan Arabism and neutralism, Dulles tried to entice him toward the West with foreign aid. In December 1955 the secretary offered to fund Nasser's dream of the Aswan Dam on the Nile, a potential source of electricity and irrigation. During the next year the World Bank crafted a $1.3 billion project utilizing British, American, and World Bank monies. About the same time, Egypt joined an anti-Israeli military alliance with Saudi Arabia, Syria, and Yemen. Jewish Americans protested in Washington, while southern members of Congress balked at a project that would permit Egypt to produce competitive cotton. Eisenhower and Dulles worried that a Czech-Egyptian arms deal signified alignment with the Soviets. But Nasser always held that nationalism offered the best defense against communism and that Zionism and Western imperialism, not communism, ranked as Egypt's greatest enemies.

To no avail. On July 19, 1956, Dulles informed the Egyptian ambassador that the United States would not fund the Aswan Dam. The State Department publicly insulted the Egyptians by declaring their credit no good—despite the World Bank's decision that the dam represented a sound investment. "May you choke to death on your fury," Nasser fumed.[221] As a warning to Egypt and other neutrals to align with the United States, this hard-knuckled economic diplomacy failed miserably. Nasser quickly seized the Suez Canal, intent on using its $25 million annual profit to help build the Aswan Dam.

Gamal Abdul Nasser (1918–1970). The bold Egyptian leader once told John Foster Dulles that the Russians "have never occupied our territory . . . but the British have been here for seventy years." Nasser went on: "How can I go to my people and tell them I am disregarding a killer with a pistol sixty miles from me at the Suez Canal to worry about somebody who is holding a knife a thousand miles away?" (*The Reporter,* 1956. Copyright 1956 by The Reporter Magazine Co.)

Without consulting Washington, and defiant of U.S. advice to avoid violence, the British and French huddled with Israel to plan a military operation. In late October and early November 1956, British, French, and Israeli forces invaded Egypt and nearly captured the canal. "Nothing justifies double-crossing us," Eisenhower raged, complaining that the West had lost a "great chance to split the Arab world," which now rallied behind Nasser.[222] "We're going to do everything we can to stop this thing," the president vowed.[223] With Dulles in the hospital for cancer treatment, Eisenhower publicly upbraided the British and French for military action that invited Soviet interference in the Middle East and diverted attention from the simultaneous Soviet invasion of Hungary (see page 285). Moscow, preoccupied with Eastern Europe, actually did little during the Suez crisis except rail against the invaders.

U.S. officials introduced a UN resolution demanding withdrawal and refused Britain oil shipments to make up for losses due to the closing of the Suez Canal and the destruction of oil pipelines. Washington also refused to aid Britain financially when its currency (the pound) faltered and Bank of England reserves dwindled because of a dollar drain. Bowing to U.S. pressure, French and British troops pulled out by late December. Only after Washington threatened sanctions (economic aid had already been suspended) did Israel disengage its forces from the Sinai in March 1957. A UN peacekeeping force then took positions and returned the canal, now clogged with sunken ships, to Egypt.

After Suez, although the United States retained its oil interests, Washington failed to dissuade many Arabs from seeing the United States as anything more than another Western usurper. After all, the United States still stood at odds with the region's most popular figure, Nasser, whom Eisenhower labeled an "evil influence," but whom Arabs hailed as heroic for his daring confrontation with Western imperialism.[224] After withdrawing the High Dam offer and letting Moscow build the imposing structure, Eisenhower signalled his choice to assume the role of Middle East policeman—because "the Bear is still the central enemy."[225] Anti-imperialist and anti-Israeli Arabs bristled at the U.S. presumption that they needed a protective sheriff. Relations with Britain and France had fractured, but Eisenhower's ire soon subsided in favor of strengthening the NATO alliance. Suez nonetheless accelerated Britain's decline. As for Israel, Eisenhower coveted it as an anticommunist ally, and in August 1958 Washington made its first arms sale to the Jewish state.

Claiming that communists schemed to exploit the Mideast "vacuum" and that "it is 'curtains' for Israel" if the United States did not thwart Soviet-backed Arab radicals, the president and a recuperating Dulles revitalized containment in the Eisenhower Doctrine.[226] In a speech before Congress on January 5, 1957, Eisenhower requested authority to use U.S. armed forces, as well as military and economic aid, to help Middle East nations resist "overt armed aggression from any nation controlled by International Communism."[227] On January 30, both houses approved the request (72 to 19 in the Senate and 350 to 60 in the House). Although Iran and Lebanon endorsed the doctrine, Syria, Egypt, and Jordan soundly rejected it, while Iraq and Saudi Arabia seemed lukewarm. British Prime Minister Harold MacMillan called the policy a "gallant effort to shut the stable door after the horse had bolted."[228]

Tests soon came. In April 1957, when pro-Nasser Jordanians threatened to overthrow King Hussein, Eisenhower ordered the Sixth Fleet to patrol off the coast of Lebanon and suggested that he would send U.S. marines, too. Although the king had appealed for implementation of the Eisenhower Doctrine, this first application of the doctrine actually targeted Nasserite Arabs, not communists. In any case, the revolt failed. The second test came in Syria, where pro-Nasser radical military officers gained power and negotiated aid from the Soviet Union. Syrian officials exposed a CIA plot to oust them, and Dulles declared Syria a virtual Soviet satellite. In fact, the anticommunist Syrians looked mostly to Cairo, not Moscow. In February 1958, Syria and Egypt merged as the United Arab Republic; Nasser quickly banished the Communist party from Syria.

Iraq and Lebanon claimed attention next. In July 1958, Washington swallowed "a bitter pill" when Nasserites overthrew Iraq's government.[229] Fearing that Arab radicalism could spread, the United States acted to save the Christian-led, pro-American government in multireligious Lebanon, where since May a civil war had pitted Christians against pro-Nasser Muslims. On July 15, 14,000 U.S. marines waded ashore, "confronting ice-cream vendors, gawkers, and bikini-clad sunbathers, not hostile gunmen."[230] Lebanese politicians soon resolved the dispute, and U.S. forces departed in fall 1958. This first instance of the Eisenhower Doctrine at work offered "little more than ideological window dressing for American action" on behalf of status quo forces, because, as Dulles privately acknowledged, the country was never "under the control of international communism."[231] The incident thus set "dangerous precedents" by "misrepresenting the Third World nationalism as Soviet inspired, and by waging what amounted to a limited but undeclared presidential war."[232]

Nationalism also challenged in Latin America. Through the Rio Pact (a defensive military alliance formed in 1947), the Organization of American States (launched in 1948 but formally established in 1951 to help settle inter-American disputes), investments of $8.2 billion by 1959, economic assistance totaling $835 million for the period 1952–1961, and support for military dictators such as Fulgencio

Batista in Cuba, the United States perpetuated its hegemony over its neighbors. But many Latin Americans grew restless, and their nationalism became strident. Latin American poverty remained stark; illiteracy rates stood high; health care proved inadequate; a population explosion threatened scarce resources; productivity showed minuscule growth; profits from raw materials such as sugar and oil flowed through American companies to the United States. "To arrest the drift in the area toward radical and nationalistic regimes," Dulles said, the United States would intervene, the Good Neighbor policy notwithstanding.[233]

Guatemala became the United States's "prototype area for testing means and methods of combating Communism" in Latin America.[234] Jacobo Arbenz Guzmán won election as president by a wide margin, and after his inauguration in spring 1951, he set land reform as his central goal. Only 2 percent of the population owned 70 percent of the land. Under the agrarian reform law of mid-1952, Arbenz displayed vibrant "economic nationalism," expropriating about one-quarter of the nation's arable land and distributing it to some 500,000 peasants.[235] Food production increased. But Arbenz soon clashed with the United Fruit Company (UFCO), the U.S.-owned banana exporter and Guatemala's largest landholder. UFCO had to give up more than 400,000 acres of uncultivated land. When Arbenz offered compensation in government bonds, using the value of the land the company itself, for tax purposes, set at $1.2 million, UFCO claimed the expropriated properties represented $19 million. The State Department strongly backed UFCO: "If the Guatemalans want to handle a Guatemalan company roughly that is none of our business, but if they handle an American company roughly it is our business."[236] UFCO propagandists spread the false word: Communism had secured a beachhead in Central America.

The Soviet Union, prudently honoring the law of "geographical fatalism" in the face of superior U.S. regional power, actually showed little interest in Latin America in the 1950s.[237] Moscow looked skeptically at Arbenz and other anti-Yankee leftists who seemed more reformist than radical or communist. Still, indigenous communists backed Arbenz. He welcomed their help against entrenched interests, and he appointed some of them to administer land reform projects. Arbenz defended the communists as servants of Guatemalan nationalism who respected the electoral process. Given their Cold War mentality, however, U.S. diplomats thought the worst. As Ambassador John Peurifoy remarked, Arbenz "talked like a Communist, he thought like a Communist, he acted like a Communist, and if he is not one . . . , he will do until one comes along."[238]

The desire to save UFCO properties also motivated U.S. actions, but what worried Washington most was "the strong appeal" among Central American neighbors of Guatemala's "broad social program of aiding workers and peasants."[239] Simply put, Arbenz challenged U.S. hegemony in the region. "They would have overthrown us even if we had grown no bananas," Arbenz's friend José Manuel Fortuny recalled.[240]

Eisenhower approved the CIA plan PBSUCCESS to overthrow Arbenz. Using a base in Florida and $5–7 million, the CIA recruited Guatemalan exiles. Training camps in Nicaragua and Honduras prepared them for an invasion. Colonel Carlos Castillo Armas, a graduate of the army staff school at Fort Leavenworth, Kansas, won favor as the president-to-be. In early 1954 Washington prodded the Organization of American States to declare, by a 17 to 1 vote, that the domination of any

American state by the international communist movement would constitute a threat to the hemisphere. Washington also cut off technical assistance to Guatemala. Arbenz in turn accepted a large arms shipment from Czechoslovakia. "If Paul Revere were living today," U.S. House Representative Paul Lantaff declared, "he would view the landing of Red arms in Guatemala as a signal to ride."[241]

On June 18, after the CIA bribed Guatemalans, planted fictitious news stories about Arbenz's submission to the Soviets, and dropped supplies at United Fruit facilities, Castillo Armas's small force attacked from Honduras. U.S.-supplied rebel planes bombed Guatemala City. Abandoned by his military and fearful that Washington would order U.S. marines to Guatemala if Castillo Armas's invasion failed, an anguished Arbenz fled to Mexico, where he died in 1971.

Castillo Armas soon returned UFCO lands, jailed his detractors, and set Guatemala on a course of government-sponsored terror that by 1990 had left 100,000 Guatemalans dead. In 1957 he fell to assassination, but the new regime remained a staunch U.S. ally. When a cabinet member, following the Guatemala coup, urged that "we . . . stop talking so much about democracy" and say "we . . . support dictatorships of the right if their policies are pro-American," Eisenhower interjected: "you mean they're OK if their *our* s.o.b.s?"[242]

Vice President Richard Nixon felt Latin American resentment firsthand in April–May 1958 when he traveled south on a goodwill tour. In Montevideo, Uruguay, anti-Yankee pickets mingled with the cheering crowds when Nixon motored through the city. Determined to counter what he considered communist agitation, Nixon stopped at the University of the Republic and engaged students in debate on U.S. foreign policy. Nixon claimed a "victory" and went on to Peru. Anti-Yankee sentiment welled up at San Marcos University, but Nixon refused to cower before a "bunch of Communist thugs."[243] Stoned and spat on, he then headed for Caracas.

In Venezuela all hell broke loose. Earlier in 1958 a military junta had overthrown the dictatorship of Marcos Pérez Jiménez ("P.J."). A special friend of the United States during his seven-year rule, Jiménez "adopted the kind of policies which we think that other countries of South America should adopt," said Dulles. "Namely, they have adopted policies which provide in Venezuela a climate which is attractive to foreign capital to come in."[244] When Jiménez fled Caracas and the Eisenhower administration gave him asylum, Venezuelan bitterness toward the United States deepened.

Into this volatile environment stepped Nixon, emboldened by his earlier tangles with protesting students. "Communists, hoodlums, and thrill seekers" blocked Nixon's motorcade en route to a wreath-laying ceremony at Simón Bolívar's tomb.[245] Demonstrators spit, threw stones, shattered windows, smashed fenders, rocked the automobile, and threatened the vice president's life. Nixon's car somehow sped away. In Operation Poor Richard, Eisenhower dispatched two airborne infantry companies to the Caribbean in case Nixon had to be rescued. He did not, and his apparent toughness gained him admiration at home. But USIA Director George Allen worried that "we continue to act like adolescents. We boast about our richness, our bignesss, and our strength . . . Nations, like people, who boast can expect others to cheer when they fail."[246]

After Nixon's trip, Washington began to send more economic and military aid to the hemisphere. In 1959 the United States subscribed $500 million to the new

Inter-American Development Bank. To combat communist propaganda and dissuade opinion makers in Latin America from criticizing the United States, Nixon recommended that Washington distance itself from unpopular rulers: "a formal handshake for dictators; an *embraso* [*abrazo*] for leaders in freedom."[247] But in 1959, students and other nationalists in Panama rioted against U.S. control of the Canal Zone and tried to plant Panamanian flags there. Zone police and U.S. infantry beat them back. Recognizing that "one good missile with an atomic bomb could knock out one whole end of the Canal structure," Eisenhower eventually permitted the Panamanian flag to fly over the zone for the first time since the early twentieth century.[248] In Cuba, too, the United States met challenge. Nationalistic insurgents led by Fidel Castro overthrew Batista and launched a revolution to expel U.S. economic and military interests from the island (see pages 335–336). "Batten down the hatches," Assistant Secretary Thomas Mann told Latin American specialists in the State Department. "There's going to be some real stormy weather."[249]

Cultural Expansion and the Globalized Cold War

By decade's end, one of the most conspicuous signs of U.S. influence abroad came in the proliferation of American mass culture and the foreign adoption of American ways. As economic recovery occurred in Western Europe and Japan, people spent proportionally more of their incomes on luxuries such as electrical appliances, hi-fi phonographs, televisions, leisurewear, even glossy, befinned American cars. Although some foreign elites sneered at "fast-food emporiums, sugar-saturated soft drinks, . . . *Der Spiegel*-like imitations of *Time* and *Newsweek*," youth culture made clear choices—"worn-out jeans vs. neat trousers, 'Elvis-quiff' and ponytail vs. orderly . . . hairstyles, uninhibited rock'n'roll vs. civilized ballroom dancing, comic strips vs. Goethe."[250] At trade fairs, the USIA adopted the theme of "People's Capitalism" to tout middle-class consumerism.[251] At the Moscow exhibition of 1959, site of the Nixon-Khrushchev debate, the Miracle Kitchen of Today served up "17,500 dishes ranging from ready-to-bake biscuits and oven-ready vegetable pies to instant coffee and Jello."[252] The continued appeal of American films demonstrated what one Austrian scholar has called the "Marilyn Monroe Doctrine."[253] "Is the World 'Going American'?" *U.S. News & World Report* asked, as it described Hula-Hoops in France, canned beer in British pubs, traffic jams in Rome, Bonn, and Sydney.[254] Also suggested by the 1957 Hollywood musical *Silk Stockings,* in which even Soviet "apparatchiks swoon before the temptations of capitalist luxury," such "cultural infiltration" caused overseas peoples to identify Americans not only with nuclear superiority but with wealth and freedom.[255] In this sense, Americanization became a component of national security policy, equating consumerism with freedom. Yet cultural expansion generated both adoption *and* rejection, setting off cultural wars, as demonstrated by the "Ugly American" complaints of Europeans who detested the "intellectual fodder offered to the American masses, from scandal magazines to digests of books."[256]

The Eisenhower administration promoted the expansion of American culture and Americanization abroad as one of several means to contest and undermine the

Martha Graham in *Lamentation*. The famous modern dance choreographer Martha Graham, shown here in her solo piece *Lamentation* (1939), was among dozens of performing artists enlisted by the Eisenhower administration to help fight the Cold War. The President's Emergency Fund for International Affairs exported dance as a form of "cultural diplomacy," which, according to the scholar Naima Prevots, used "the arts—rather than bullets, occupying armies, or A-bombs—to win friends and influence policy" abroad. (© Barbara Morgan, Barbara Morgan Archive)

appeal of Arab nationalism, Latin American revolution, Third World neutralism, communism, the Soviet Union, and China. Despite the catchy phrases of the Eisenhower-Dulles years, however, no dramatic new departures occurred in foreign policy. "Liberation" and "rollback" had always been the ultimate goal of "containment." The "Eisenhower Doctrine" extended the "Truman Doctrine." Dulles's strictures against neutralism sounded very much like Truman's declaration that all nations must choose between two ways of life. The "domino theory" in Asia differed little from Truman's alarmist predictions that if Greece fell, the Middle East would fall and Europe would collapse. Eisenhower and Dulles reinforced the Truman-Acheson hostility to "Red China." Both administrations intervened, with different methods, in the Middle East. Both bolstered the nation's nuclear arsenal. Both nourished overseas economic interests as essential to U.S. and world stability. Both sought to draw West Germany into Western Europe. America's Cold War institutions, its high defense budgets, its large foreign-affairs bureaucracy, its assumptions from the past, its export of culture—all ground on.

But the world had changed. In 1945 the United States sat atop the international system. Few restraints obstructed its exercise of power. Americans confidently placed restraints on others. But as the Soviet Union and the United States built their economies and military forces toward a stalemate, particularly in Europe, the bonds of stability loosened elsewhere. Throughout the 1950s new nations claimed independence, threw off the shackles of colonialism, and charted an independent course in the Cold War. Troubles for the two major powers also erupted in their own spheres of influence, as client states and allies challenged great-power hegemony. Latin America increasingly resented U.S. tutelage, and political turmoil and anti-Yankeeism grew apace. The 1959 victory of nationalists in the Cuban Revolution symbolized the new challenge (see next chapter). Japanese rioters forced Eisenhower to cancel his trip to Japan, and Europeans such as Charles de Gaulle of France resisted U.S. influence. The Soviets faced growing discontent in Eastern Europe and the Sino-Soviet split. In short, Dulles and Eisenhower "overestimated the reach of communism" and "underestimated the power of nationalism."[257] Nuclear proliferation scared both sides. "Soon even little countries will have a stockpile of these bombs," Eisenhower worried in 1954, "and then we *will* be in a mess."[258] Britain (1952), France (1960), and China (1964) independently developed atomic bombs.

The world was becoming multipolar. Neither the Soviet Union nor the United States, tied to rigid policies and military programs, adjusted well to the more fluid international system. Although each professed sympathy with Third World needs and aspirations, both sought to curb national self-determination in decolonizing areas. U.S. antipathy toward revolutionary nationalism, socialism, and neutralism created an anti-American backlash among non-Western peoples. So did CIA activities in Iran and Guatemala, the training of counterrevolutionaries in South Vietnam (see next chapter), the sending of troops into Lebanon, and alliances such as SEATO and the Baghdad Pact. Both the United States and the Soviet Union, in their drive to win friends through foreign aid and subversion, saw Third World nations manipulate Cold-War rivalries to gain economic assistance and military hardware from both sides.

Unimaginative in dealing with the Third World, the Eisenhower administration also lacked innovation in its relations with the Soviet Union and China. The arms race evolved into a space race and missile race. Washington seemed only minimally interested in reducing tension in Central Europe and Germany, quickly rejecting the Rapacki Plan and "disengagement" proposals. The Soviet Union seemed serious about cooling the arms race, but Moscow, too, so distrusted the other side that negotiations produced little. Nonrecognition of China simply isolated the United States from one of the world's important nations. Standing firmly with Jiang on Formosa revealed obstinacy, not wisdom, when many other Western nations recognized Beijing and traded with the People's Republic.

McCarthyism inhibited movement toward détente, but it had waned by 1954. The president also deflected another challenge, a proposed amendment to the Constitution. The Bricker Amendment, first offered in 1951 by Republican senator John Bricker of Ohio, sought primarily to limit the effects in the United States of UN-sponsored agreements on human rights. But it also included restrictions on executive agreements to ensure that presidents did not skirt the treaty-making power of the Senate. Hoping to force the president to consult more with Congress on foreign-policy issues and to forestall another Yalta, the amendment's backers insisted that executive agreements be voted on like treaties. Vowing to "fight up and down the country" against this "stupid, blind violation of [the] Constitution by stupid, blind isolationists," Eisenhower, with help from liberal Democrats and moderate Republicans, beat back the amendment in a close Senate vote in February 1954.[259] Eisenhower thereafter consulted regularly with legislators on major foreign policies, with the conspicuous exception of covert operations. Congress usually granted his requests. The Cold War consensus shaped in the 1940s continued strong. The Eisenhower administration failed to devise new policies for new realities, then, not because of Joe McCarthy and the China Lobby but because of its own uncompromising assumptions.

In the election of 1960, the Democrats claimed that the Cold War could be won. They differed from Eisenhower over methods to continue the old fight and to reverse the declining position of the United States in the Third World. The Democratic party and its presidential candidate, Senator John F. Kennedy, embraced the anticommunist absolutes of the era as heartily as John Foster Dulles ever had. Eisenhower's political critics charged that he and his secretary of state had caused the United States to fall behind in the missile race and that they had squandered American power.

Historical assessments of the Eisenhower administration used to stress its rigid conservatism, passive style, limited achievements, and hesitancy to adjust to new circumstances. More recently, scholars have emphasized Eisenhower's "prudence and sober judgment"—his moderate approach to most problems, his command of policymaking, his political savvy, and his commitment to arms control.[260] Yet Eisenhower's loyalty program damaged the Foreign Service. His expansion of the CIA and covert operations proved dangerous and short-sighted. Whatever his doubts about the insanity of the nuclear arms race, he accelerated it and left a legacy of nuclear fear. Eisenhower distrusted Jiang's Nationalists and preferred a "two Chinas" policy, but a hard-line posture toward the People's Republic of China risked nuclear war more than once. Eisenhower revisionism has stimulated healthy reconsideration of the period. But while Ike did not go over the brink, he remained a zealous anticommunist of little flexibility and little innovation whose diplomatic record is at best mixed.

FURTHER READING FOR THE PERIOD 1950–1961

Some works cited in Chapter 7 also cover this period.

The Korean War is explored in Bruce Cumings, *The Origins of the Korean War* (1981 and 1990), *Korea's Place in the Sun* (1997), and ed., *Child of Conflict* (1983); Rosemary Foot, *The Wrong War* (1985) and *A Substitute for Victory* (1990); Sergei N. Goncharov, John W. Lewis, and Xue Litai, *Uncertain Partners: Stalin, Mao, and the Korean War* (1994); John Halliday and Bruce Cumings, *Korea* (1988); Jian Chen, *China's Road to the Korean War* (1994); Peter Lowe, *The Origins of the Korean War* (1997); Callum A. MacDonald, *Korea* (1987); John Merrill, *Korea* (1989); Bonnie B. C. Oh, ed., *Korea Under the American Military Government* (2002); Gordon L. Rottman, *The Korean War Order of Battle* (2002); Michael Schaller, *Douglas MacArthur* (1989); William Stueck, *Rethinking the Korean War* (2002); Richard C. Thornton, *Odd Man Out* (2000); John Toland, *In Mortal Combat* (1991); Richard Whelan, *Drawing the Line* (1990); and Shu Guang Zhang, *Mao's Military Romanticism* (1996).

For the 1950s and President Dwight D. Eisenhower, see Craig Allen, *Eisenhower and the Mass Media* (1993); Stephen E. Ambrose, *Eisenhower* (1983–1984) and *Nixon* (1987); Michael R. Beschloss, *MAYDAY* (1986) (U-2); Günter Bischof and Stephen E. Ambrose, eds., *Eisenhower* (1995); Meena Bose, *Shaping and Signaling Presidential Policy* (1998) (Eisenhower and Kennedy); H. W. Brands, Jr., *Cold Warriors* (1988); Jeff Broadwater, *Eisenhower and the Anti-Communist Crusade* (1992); Blanche W. Cook, *The Declassified Eisenhower* (1981); Mary L. Dudziak, *Cold War Civil Rights* (2002); Fred I. Greenstein, *The Hidden-Hand Presidency* (1982); Robert H. Johnson, *Improbable Dangers: U.S. Conceptions of Threat in the Cold War and After* (1994); Burton I. Kaufman, *Trade and Aid* (1982); Michael T. Klare, *American Arms Supermarket* (1985); Michael L. Krenn, *Black Diplomacy: African Americans and the State Department, 1945–1969* (1998); Elaine Tyler May, *Homeward Bound* (1988); Chester J. Pach, Jr., and Elmo Richardson, *The Presidency of Dwight D. Eisenhower* (1991); James T. Patterson, *Grand Expectations* (1996); William B. Pickett, *Dwight David Eisenhower and American Power* (1995); Brenda

G. Plummer, *Rising Wind* (1996) (African Americans); Caroline Pruden, *Conditional Partners* (1998) (United Nations); Michael S. Sherry, *In the Shadow of War* (1995); Duane Tananbaum, *The Bricker Amendment Controversy* (1988); and Tom Wicker, *Dwight D. Eisenhower* (2002).

John Foster Dulles is studied in Townsend Hoopes, *The Devil and John Foster Dulles* (1973); Richard H. Immerman, ed., *John Foster Dulles and the Diplomacy of the Cold War* (1990) and *John Foster Dulles* (1999); Frederick W. Marks, *Power and Peace* (1993); and Ronald W. Pruessen, *John Foster Dulles* (1982).

Other biographical studies include Jeff Broadwater, *Adlai Stevenson* (1994); Lee Feigon, *Mao* (2002); Jeffery C. Livingston, *Swallowed by Globalism* (2001) (John M. Vorys); G. Bernard Noble, *Christian A. Herter* (1970); James T. Patterson, *Mr. Republican* (1972) (Senator Robert Taft); and William Taubman, *Khrushchev* (2003).

For the Soviet Union and Europe, consult Volker R. Berghahn, *America and the Intellectual Cold Wars in Europe* (2001); Günter Bischof and Saki Dockrill, eds., *Cold War Respite: The Geneva Summit of July 1955* (1999); Frank Costigliola, *France and the United States* (1992); Audrey K. Cronin, *Great Power Politics and the Struggle over Austria* (1986); Ennio Di Nolfo, ed., *Power in Europe? II* (1992); Alexander L. George et al., eds., *U.S.-Soviet Security Cooperation* (1988); Jeffrey Glen Giauque, *Grand Designs and Visions of Unity* (2002) (European Union); Robert P. Grathwol and Donita M. Moorhus, *Berlin and the American Military* (1998); William Glenn Gray, *Germany's Cold War* (2003); Wolfram F. Hanrieder, *Germany, America, Europe* (1989); Hope M. Harrison, *Driving the Soviets up the Wall* (2003) (East Germany); Ted Hopf, *Social Constructions of International Politics* (2002) (Soviet Union); Klaus Larres, *Churchill's Cold War* (2002); William Roger Louis and Hedley Bull, eds., *The Special Relationship* (1986) (Britain); Thomas Risse-Kappen, *Cooperation Among Democracies: The European Influence on U.S. Foreign Policy* (1995); and Irwin M. Wall, *France, the United States, and the Algerian War* (2001).

The nuclear arms race, missile development, and antinuclear views are treated in Timothy Botti, *Ace in the Hole* (1996) (why nuclear weapons were not used); Campbell Craig, *Destroying the Village: Eisenhower and Thermonuclear War* (1998); Ian Clark, *Nuclear Diplomacy and the Special Relationship* (1994) (U.S.-Britain); Robert A. Divine, *Blowing on the Wind* (1978) and *The Sputnik Challenge* (1993); Stephen Endicott and Edward Hagerman, *The United States and Biological Warfare* (1999); Gregg F. Herken, *Counsels of War* (1985); Richard G. Hewlett and Jack M. Holl, *Atoms for Peace* (1989); Fred Kaplan, *The Wizards of Armageddon* (1983); Milton S. Katz, *Ban the Bomb* (1986); Dean W. Kohlhoff, *Amchitka and the Bomb: Nuclear Testing in Alaska* (2002); Walter A. McDougall, *The Heavens and the Earth* (1985); Peter Roman, *Eisenhower and the Missile Gap* (1995); David K. Stumpf and Jay W. Kelley, *Titan II* (2000); Marc Trachtenberg, *History and Strategy* (1991); Andreas Wenger, *Eisenhower, Kennedy, and Nuclear Weapons* (1997); and Lawrence S. Wittner, *The Struggle Against the Bomb* (1998).

For culture and cultural expansion, see works cited in Chapter 7 and Manuela Aguilar, *Cultural Diplomacy and Foreign Policy* (1996) (U.S.-Germany); Paul R. Edwards, *The Closed World* (1996) (computers); Robert H. Haddow, *Pavilions of Plenty* (1997); Margot A. Henriksen, *Dr. Strangelove's America* (1997); Walter L. Hixson, *Parting the Curtain: Propaganda, Culture, and the Cold War* (1997); Rob Kroes, *If You've Seen One, You've Seen the Mall* (1996); Laura McEnany, *Civil Defense Begins at Home* (2000); Yale Richmond, *Cultural Exchange and the Cold War* (2003); Ron Robin, *The Making of the Cold War Enemy* (2001) (military-industrial complex); and Kenneth D. Rose, *One Nation Underground* (2001) (fallout shelters).

Asian questions, including China, the offshore islands crises, and Japan, are studied in Robert Accinelli, *Crisis and Commitment* (1996) (Taiwan); S. Mahmud Ali, *Cold War in the High Himalayas* (1999); Stanley D. Bachrack, *The Committee of One Million* (1976) (China Lobby); Roger Buckley, *U.S.-Japan Alliance Diplomacy, 1945–1990* (1992); Gordon H. Chang, *Friends and Enemies: The United States, China, and the Soviet Union, 1948–1972* (1990); Thomas J. Christensen, *Useful Adversaries* (1996); Warren I. Cohen, *America's Response to China* (1990); Nick Cullather, *Illusions of Influence* (1994) (Philippines); Harry Harding and Yuan Ming, eds., *Sino-American Relations, 1945–1955* (1989); Audrey R. Kahin and George McT. Kahin, *Subversion as Foreign Policy* (1995) (Indonesia); Mercy A. Kuo, *Contending with Contradictions* (2001); Peter Lowe, *Containing the Cold War in East Asia* (1997); David A. Mayers, *Cracking the Monolith: U.S. Policy Against the Sino-Soviet Alliance* (1986); Nancy B. Tucker, *Taiwan, Hong Kong, and the United States* (1994); Odd Arne Wested, ed., *Brothers in Arms: The Rise and Fall of the Sino-Soviet Alliance, 1945–1963* (1999); Qiang Zhai, *The Dragon, the Lion, & the*

Eagle (1994); and Shu Guang Zhang, *Deterrence and Strategic Culture* (1992) (China). Studies of Indochina/Vietnam appear in Chapter 9.

For the Third World, see Richard J. Barnet, *Intervention and Revolution* (1972); H. W. Brands, *The Specter of Neutralism* (1989); Gabriel Kolko, *Confronting the Third World* (1988); Robert J. McMahon, *The Cold War on the Periphery* (1994) (India and Pakistan); Thomas J. Noer, *Cold War and Black Liberation* (1985) (Africa); Andrew J. Rotter, *Comrades at Odds* (2000) (India); Peter J. Schraeder, *United States Foreign Policy Toward Africa* (1994); and Stanley Wolpert, *Nehru* (1997). See also works cited in Chapters 7, 9–12.

For U.S. relations with the Middle East, especially with Egypt and Israel, see Isaac Alteras, *Eisenhower and Israel* (1993); Nigel J. Ashton, *Eisenhower, Macmillan, and the Problem of Nasser* (1996); George W. Ball and Douglas B. Ball, *The Passionate Attachment* (1992) (Israel); Abraham Ben-Zvi, *Decade of Transition* (1998) (Israel); William J. Burns, *Economic Aid and American Policy Toward Egypt* (1985); Irene Gendzier, *Notes from the Minefield* (1997) (Lebanon); Parker T. Hart, *Saudi Arabia and the United States* (1999); Zach Levey, *Israel and the Western Power, 1952–1960* (1998); Douglas Little, *American Orientalism* (2002); Gail E. Meyer, *Egypt and the United States* (1980); Michael Oren, *The Origins of the Second Arab-Israeli War* (1993); William R. Polk, *The Arab World Today* (1991); Cheryl Rubenberg, *Israel and the American National Interest* (1986); Barry Rubin, *The Arab States and the Palestine Conflict* (1981); Bonnie Saunders, *The United States and Arab Nationalism* (1996) (Syria); David Schoenbaum, *The United States and the State of Israel* (1993); and Steven L. Spiegel, *The Other Arab-Israeli Conflict* (1985).

The Suez crisis is included in many of the works above, but especially see Steven Freiberger, *Dawn over Suez* (1992); Diane B. Kunz, *The Economic Diplomacy of the Suez Crisis* (1991); William Roger Louis and Roger Owen, eds., *Suez 1956* (1989); and Selwyn Troen, ed., *The Sinai-Suez Crisis, 1956* (1990).

Latin American–U.S. relations and the intervention in Guatemala are treated in Elizabeth A. Cobbs, *The Rich Neighbor Policy* (1992); Nick Cullather, *Secret History* (1999) (CIA in Guatemala); Michael D. Gambone, *Eisenhower, Somoza, and the Cold War in Nicaragua* (1997); Piero Gleijeses, *Shattered Hope* (1991) (Guatemala); Michael R. Hall, *Sugar and Power in the Dominican Republic* (2000); Richard Immerman, *The CIA in Guatemala* (1982); Stephen Kinzer and Stephen Schlesinger, *Bitter Fruit* (1982) (Guatemala); John V. Kofas, *The Sword of Damocles* (2002) (Colombia, Chile); Walter LaFeber, *The Panama Canal* (1989) and *Inevitable Revolutions* (1993) (Central America); Abraham F. Lowenthal, ed., *Exporting Democracy* (1991); A. W. Maldonado, *Teodoro Moscoso and Puerto Rico's Operation Bootstrap* (1997); Nicola Miller, *Soviet Relations with Latin America, 1959–1987* (1989); Thomas G. Paterson, *Contesting Castro* (1994); Stephen G. Rabe, *Eisenhower and Latin America* (1988); Darlene Rivas, *Missionary Capitalist* (2002) (Venezuela); David F. Schmitz, *Thank God They're on Our Side* (1999) (right-wing dictatorships); Lars Schoultz, *Beneath the United States* (1998); Gaddis Smith, *The Last Years of the Monroe Doctrine* (1994); and Peter H. Smith, *Talons of the Eagle* (1996).

For the Central Intelligence Agency and its covert activities, see Stephen E. Ambrose, *Ike's Spies* (1981); Sigmund Diamond, *Compromised Campus: The Collaboration of Universities with the Intelligence Community* (1992); Peter Grose, *Gentleman Spy* (1994) (Allen Dulles); Loch K. Johnson, *America's Secret Power* (1989); Ludwell L. Montague, *General Walter Bedell Smith as Director of Central Intelligence* (1992); John Ranelagh, *The Agency* (1986); Frances Stoner Saunders, *The Cultural Cold War* (2000); Evan Thomas, *The Very Best Men* (1995); and Robin W. Winks, *Cloak & Gown* (1987).

For the impact of McCarthyism, consult works cited in Chapter 7 and Robert Griffith, *The Politics of Fear* (1987); M. J. Heale, *McCarthy's Americans* (1998); William W. Keller, *The Liberals and J. Edgar Hoover* (1989); Stanley I. Kutler, *The American Inquisition* (1982); Mary S. McAuliffe, *Crisis on the Left* (1978); Thomas C. Reeves, *The Life and Times of Joe McCarthy* (1982); Ellen W. Schrecker, *No Ivory Tower: McCarthyism and the Universities* (1986) and *Many Are the Crimes* (1998); Athan Theoharis and John S. Cox, *The Boss* (1988) (J. Edgar Hoover); Stephen Vaughn, *Ronald Reagan in Hollywood* (1994); and Stephen J. Whitfield, *The Culture of the Cold War* (1991).

See also the following notes, Robert L. Beisner, ed., *Guide to American Foreign Relations Since 1600* (2003), and the General Bibliography.

For comprehensive coverage of foreign-related topics, see the articles in the four-volume *Encyclopedia of U.S. Foreign Relations* (1997), edited by Bruce W. Jentleson and Thomas G. Paterson.

NOTES TO CHAPTER 8

1. Quoted in Glenn D. Paige, *The Korean Decision* (New York: Free Press, 1968), p. 82.
2. Glenn D. Paige, ed., *1950: Truman's Decision* (New York: Chelsea House, 1970), p. 49.
3. Quoted in David Rees, *Korea* (London: Macmillan, 1964), p. 36.
4. State Department officer Harold Joyce Noble quoted in William Stueck, *The Korean War* (Princeton: Princeton University Press, 1995), pp. 10–11.
5. Quoted in John Toland, *In Mortal Combat* (New York: Morrow, 1991), p. 34.
6. Quoted in Ronald W. Pruessen, *John Foster Dulles* (New York: Free Press, 1982), p. 454.
7. Paige, *1950*, p. 63.
8. Robert J. Donovan, *Tumultuous Years* (New York: Norton, 1982), p. 202.
9. Quoted in Athan Theoharis, *Chasing Spies* (Chicago: Ivan R. Dee, 2002), p. 35.
10. Harry S. Truman, *Memoirs* (Garden City, N.Y.: Doubleday, 1955–1956; 2 vols.), II, 333.
11. Quoted in *New York Times*, June 26, 1950.
12. Quoted in Melvyn P. Leffler, *A Preponderance of Power* (Stanford: Stanford University Press, 1992), p. 366.
13. *Congressional Record, XCVI* (June 26, 1950), 9188.
14. *Foreign Relations, 1950, VII* (Washington, D.C.: Government Printing Office, 1976), 179.
15. Quoted in Stanley Sandler, *The Korean War* (Lexington: University Press of Kentucky, 1999), p. 54.
16. Quoted in Gary R. Hess, *Presidential Decisions for War* (Baltimore: Johns Hopkins University Press, 2001), p. 26
17. Joseph C. Harsch quoted in Bruce Cumings, *The Origins of the Korean War* (Princeton: Princeton University Press, 1981, 1990; 2 vols.), II, 628.
18. John H. Church quoted in Stueck, *Korean War*, p. 47.
19. Quoted in Bruce Cumings, *Korea's Place in the Sun* (New York: Norton, 1997), p. 265.
20. Quoted in D. Clayton James, *Refighting the Last War* (New York: Free Press, 1993), p. 16.
21. Mao Zedong quoted in Hao Yufan and Zhai Zhihai, "China's Decision to Enter the Korean War," *China Quarterly*, no. 121 (May 1990), 101.
22. Quoted in Rosemary Foot, "Leadership, Perception, and Interest," *Diplomatic History, XX* (Summer 1996), 479.
23. Air Marshal Cecil Boucher quoted in Peter Lowe, *Containing the Cold War in East Asia* (New York: Manchester University Press, 1997), p. 206.
24. Quoted in Shen Zhihua, "The Discrepancy on Chinese Entry into the Korean War," *Cold War International History Project Bulletin*, nos. 8–9 (Winter 1996/1997), 237.
25. Quoted in Vladislav M. Zubok, "Stalin and the Nuclear Age," in John Lewis Gaddis et al., eds., *Cold War Statesmen Confront the Bomb* (New York: Oxford University Press, 1999), p. 57.
26. Quoted in Thomas G. Paterson, "The Korean War," in Bruce W. Jentleson and Thomas G. Paterson, eds., *Encyclopedia of U.S. Foreign Relations* (New York: Oxford University Press, 1997), III, 31.
27. Quoted in Melvyn P. Leffler, *The Specter of Communism* (New York: Hill & Wang, 1994), p. 107.
28. Quoted in Hess, *Presidential Decisions*, p. 59.
29. Edward Almond quoted in Cumings, *Origins, II*, 742.
30. O. P. Smith quoted in Stueck, *Korean War*, p. 128.
31. Quoted in Callum A. MacDonald, *Korea* (New York: Free Press, 1987), p. 71.
32. Quoted in Philip West, "Confronting the West," *Journal of American–East Asian Relations, II* (Spring 1993), 6–7.
33. Truman quoted in Arnold A. Offner, "Another Such Victory," *Diplomatic History, XXIII* (Spring 1999), 151; Oliver Franks quoted in Thomas J. Christensen, *Useful Adversaries* (Princeton: Princeton University Press, 1996), p. 184.
34. Sandler, *Korean War*, 137; Stueck, *Korean War*, p. 66.
35. Quoted in Michael Schaller, *Douglas MacArthur* (New York: Oxford University Press, 1989), p. 335.
36. *Congressional Record, XCVII* (April 19, 1951), 4125.
37. *Ibid.*, April 24, 1951, p. 4261.
38. Cumings, *Origins, II*, 713.
39. Quoted in Michael D. Pearlman, *Warmaking and American Democracy* (Lawrence: University Press of Kansas, 1999), p. 293.
40. Marc Trachtenberg, "A 'Wasting Asset': American Strategy and the Shifting Nuclear Balance," *International Security, XIII* (Winter 1988/1989), 27.
41. Quoted in Kathryn Weathersby, "Stalin, Mao, and the End of the Korean War," in Odd Arne Westad, ed., *Brothers in Arms* (Stanford: Stanford University Press, 1998), 105.
42. Rosemary Foot, *A Substitute for Victory* (Ithaca: Cornell University Press, 1990), p. 220.
43. Quoted in Thomas Risse-Kappen, *Cooperation Among Democracies* (Princeton: Princeton University Press, 1995), p. 62.
44. Alexander DeConde, *Presidential Machismo* (Boston: Northeastern University Press, 2000), p. 157.
45. General Chung Sang-chin of North Korea quoted in Kathryn Weathersby, "Soviet Aims in Korea and the Origins of the Korean War, 1945–1950," Working Paper no. 8, *Cold War International History Project* (Washington, D.C., November 1993), p. 26.
46. Cumings, *Origins, II*, 643.
47. Mao quoted in Christensen, *Useful Adversaries*, p. 162.
48. John Halliday and Bruce Cumings, *Korea* (New York: Pantheon, 1988), p. 34.
49. Paul G. Pierpaoli, *Truman and Korea* (Columbia: University of Missouri Press, 1999), p. 1.
50. Sandler, *Korean War*, p. 4.
51. "Princeton Seminar," February 13–14, 1954, Box 66, Dean Acheson Papers, Harry S. Truman Library, Independence, Mo.
52. Stueck, *Korean War*, p. 6.
53. Marshal Nie Rongzhen, "Beijing's Decision to Intervene," in Ziaobing Li et al., eds., *Mao's Generals Remember Korea* (Lawrence: University Press of Kansas, 2001), p. 40.
54. Quoted in Walter LaFeber, *The Clash* (New York: Norton, 1997), p. 294.
55. *Public Papers, Truman, 1952–1953* (Washington, D.C.: Government Printing Office, 1966), p. 708.
56. Aaron L. Friedberg, *In the Shadow of the Garrison State* (Princeton: Princeton University Press, 2000), p. 216.
57. Dean Acheson, *Present at the Creation* (New York: Norton, 1969), p. 420.
58. Quoted in Ronald R. Krebs, *Dueling Visions* (College Station: Texas A&M University Press, 2002), p. 20.
59. Quoted *ibid.*, p. 17.

60. Quoted *ibid.*, p. 17.

61. Quoted in Saki Dockrill, *Eisenhower's New-Look National Security Policy, 1953–61* (New York: St. Martin's, 1996), p. 18.

62. Quoted in Krebs, *Dueling Visions*, p. 16.

63. David Brinkley, *David Brinkley* (New York: Ballantine, 1995), p. 125.

64. Fred I. Greenstein, *The Hidden-Hand Presidency* (New York: BasicBooks, 1982).

65. Richard A. Melanson, "The Foundations of Eisenhower's Foreign Policy," in Richard A. Melanson and David Mayers, eds., *Reevaluating Eisenhower* (Urbana: University of Illinois Press, 1987), pp. 45–46.

66. Richard J. Barnet, *Intervention and Revolution* (New York: New American Library, 1972; rev. ed.), p. 36.

67. Eisenhower quoted in David L. Snead, *The Gaither Committee, Eisenhower, and the Cold War* (Columbus: Ohio State University Press, 1999), p. 15.

68. Quoted in Robert J. McMahon, "The Illusion of Vulnerability," *International History Review*, XVIII (August 1996), 617.

69. Kenneth A. Osgood, "Form Before Substance," *Diplomatic History*, XXIV (Summer 2000), 412; Frances Stonor Saunders, *The Cultural Cold War* (New York: New Press, 1999), p. 2.

70. National Security Council quoted in Manuela Aguilar, *Cultural Diplomacy and Foreign Policy* (New York: Peter Lang, 1996), pp. 59, 76, n. 28.

71. Naima Prevots, *Dance for Export* (Hanover, NH: University Press of New England, 1998); Walter L. Hixson, *Parting the Curtain* (New York: St. Martin's, 1997), pp. ix, xv; Harold Stassen quoted in Arch Puddington, *Broadcasting Freedom* (Lexington: University Press of Kentucky, 2000), p. 62.

72. Quoted in Loch K. Johnson, *America's Secret Power* (New York: Oxford University Press, 1989), pp. 17, 27.

73. Hoover Commission quoted *ibid.*, p. 10.

74. Nick Cullather, *Illusions of Influence* (Stanford: Stanford University Press, 1994), p. 176.

75. Eileen Welsome, *The Plutonium Files* (New York: Dial Press, 1999), p. 10.

76. Quoted in Stephen E. Ambrose, *Eisenhower, the President* (New York: Simon & Schuster, 1984), p. 226.

77. Quoted in DeConde, *Presidential Machismo*, p. 160.

78. Audrey R. Kahin and George McT. Kahin, *Subversion as Foreign Policy* (New York: New Press, 1995), p. 8.

79. *Public Papers, Eisenhower, 1953* (Washington, D.C.: Government Printing Office, 1960), pp. 182–183.

80. Quoted in Vojtech Mastny, "NATO in the Beholder's Eye," Working Paper no. 35, *Cold War International History Project* (March 2002), p. 6; Vladislav Zubok, "Soviet Intelligence and the Cold War," *Diplomatic History*, XIX (Summer 1995), 461.

81. Eisenhower quoted in Greg Herken, "Commentary: In the Service of the State," *Diplomatic History*, XXIV (Winter 2000), 112.

82. Michael Sherry, *In the Shadow of War* (New Haven: Yale University Press, 1995), p. 203.

83. *Public Papers, Eisenhower, 1960–61* (Washington, D.C.: Government Printing Office, 1961), pp. 1035–1040.

84. "Discussion at the 309th Meeting of the National Security Council, Friday, January 11, 1957," Box 7, NSC Summaries, NSC Series, Ann Whitman File, Dwight D. Eisenhower Papers, Dwight D. Eisenhower Library, Abilene, Kan.

85. Richard H. Immerman, "Conclusion," in Immerman, ed., *John Foster Dulles and the Diplomacy of the Cold War* (Princeton: Princeton University Press, 1990), p. 266.

86. Richard H. Immerman, *John Foster Dulles* (Wilmington, Del.: Scholarly Resources, 1999), pp. 2–3.

87. Quoted in Herbert S. Parmet, "Power and Reality," in Frank Merli and Theodore Wilson, eds., *Makers of American Diplomacy* (New York: Charles Scribners's Sons, 1974), p. 593.

88. Ambassador George V. Allen quoted in Andrew J. Rotter, "Christians, Muslims, and Hindus," *Diplomatic History*, XXIV (Fall 2000), 599.

89. Eisenhower quoted in Robert R. Bowie and Richard H. Immerman, *Waging Peace* (New York: Oxford University Press, 1998), p. 84.

90. Robert Bowie quoted in *John Foster Dulles* (Princeton: Woodrow Wilson School of Public and International Affairs, Princeton University, 1988), p. 10.

91. Immerman, *John Foster Dulles*, p. 44; British diplomat Roger Makins and Winston Churchill quoted in Kevin Ruane, *The Rise and Fall of the European Defence Community* (New York: St. Martin's, 2000), pp. 119, 136.

92. Quoted in Dockrill, *Eisenhower's New Look*, p. 4, and in William B. Pickett, *Dwight D. Eisenhower and American Power* (Arlington Heights, Ill.: Harlan Davidson, 1995), p. 104.

93. Quoted in Ronald E. Powaski, *The Cold War* (New York: Oxford University Press, 1998), p. 102.

94. Quoted in Shane J. Maddock, "The Fourth Country Problem," *Presidential Studies Quarterly*, XXVIII (Summer 1998), 554.

95. Wolfram F. Hanrieder, *Germany, America, Europe* (New Haven: Yale University Press, 1989), p. 70.

96. Quoted in Gordon H. Chang, *Friends and Enemies* (Stanford: Stanford University Press, 1989), p. 70.

97. Quoted in Nigel John Ashton, *Eisenhower, MacMillan, and the Problem of Nasser* (New York: St. Martin's, 1996), p. 5.

98. *Public Papers, Eisenhower, 1954* (Washington, D.C.: Government Printing Office, 1960), p. 383.

99. Quoted in Emmett John Hughes, *The Ordeal of Power* (New York: Dell, 1964 [c. 1962]), p. 98.

100. Lisle A. Rose, *The Cold War Comes to Main Street* (Lawrence: University Press of Kansas, 1999), p. 6.

101. Quoted in J. Garry Clifford, "McCarthyism," in Jentleson and Paterson, *Encyclopedia*, III, 120.

102. Quoted in Earl Latham, *The Communist Controversy in Washington* (New York: Atheneum, 1969), p. 338.

103. Ross Terrill, "When America 'Lost' China," *Atlantic Monthly*, CCXXIV (November 1969), 79.

104. Margaret Joy Tibbetts quoted in Ann Miller Morin, *Her Excellency* (New York: Twayne, 1994), p. 57.

105. Theodore H. White, *In Search of History* (New York: Warner, 1978), p. 395.

106. *Public Papers, Eisenhower, 1953*, p. 187.

107. Quoted in Steven I. Levine, "Soviet Asian Policy in the 1950s," in Warren I. Cohen and Akira Iriye, eds., *The Great Powers in East Asia, 1953–1960* (New York: Columbia University Press, 1990), p. 298.

108. Quoted in Allesandro Brogi, *A Question of Self-Esteem* (Westport, Conn.: Praeger, 2002), p. 151.

109. Quoted in Ashton, *Eisenhower, MacMillan*, p. 5.

110. Eisenhower quoted in Günter Bischof, "The Making of the Austrian Treaty and the Road to Geneva," in Bischof and Saki Dockrill, eds., *Cold War Respite* (Baton Rouge: Louisiana State University Press, 2000), p. 154.

111. Quoted in Kurt Steiner, "Negotiations for an Austrian State Treaty," in Alexander L. George et al., eds., *U.S.-Soviet Security Cooperation* (New York: Oxford University Press, 1988), p. 75.

112. Quoted in Matthew Evangelista, "Cooperation Theory and Disarmament Negotiations in the 1950s," *World Politics, XLII* (July 1990), 503.

113. Ronald W. Pruessen, "From Good Breakfast to Bad Supper: John Foster Dulles Between the Geneva Summit and the Geneva Foreign Minister's Conference," in Bischof and Dockrill, *Cold War Respite,* p. 268.

114. Quoted in Pruessen, "From Good Breakfast," p. 268.

115. Quoted in Richard H. Immerman, " 'Trust in the Lord but Keep Your Powder Dry,' " in Bischof and Dockrill, *Cold War Respite,* p. 41.

116. Sherman Adams, *Firsthand Report* (New York: Popular Library, 1962 [1961]), p. 177.

117. Raymond L. Garthoff, *A Journey Through the Cold War* (Washington, D.C.: Brookings Institution Press, 2000), p. 24.

118. Quoted in Richard G. Hewlett and Jack M. Holl, *Atoms for Peace and War* (Berkeley: University of California Press, 1989), p. 299.

119. Quoted in Herbert S. Parmet, *Eisenhower and the American Crusades* (New York: Macmillan, 1972), p. 406.

120. Quoted in Michael R. Beschloss, *MAYDAY* (New York: Harper and Row, 1986), p. 103.

121. *Public Papers, Eisenhower, 1955,* p. 730.

122. Quoted in James T. Patterson, *Grand Expectations* (New York: Oxford University Press, 1996), p. 302.

123. Quoted in Denis Healey, "When Shrimps Learn to Whistle," *International Affairs, XXXII* (January 1956), 2.

124. Elaine Tyler May, *Homeward Bound* (New York: BasicBooks, 1988), p. 164.

125. Quoted in Penny V. von Eschen, *Race Against Empire* (Ithaca: Cornell University Press, 1997), pp. 177–178.

126. Garthoff, *Journey,* p. 36.

127. Hixson, *Parting,* p. 159.

128. Reinhold Wagnleitner, "The Irony of American Culture Abroad," in Lary May, ed., *Recasting America* (Chicago: University of Chicago Press, 1989), p. 295.

129. Reinhold Wagnleitner, *Cocacolonization and the Cold War* (Chapel Hill: University of North Carolina Press, 1994), p. 4.

130. Quoted in Vladislav Zubok and Constantine Pleshakov, *Inside the Kremlin's Cold War* (Cambridge: Harvard University Press, 1996), p. 180.

131. Quoted in William Taubman, *Khrushchev* (New York: W. W. Norton, 2003), p. 397.

132. Quoted *ibid.,* p. 298.

133. Quoted in Mark Kramer, "New Evidence on Soviet Decision-Making and the 1956 Polish and Hungarian Crises," *Cold War International History Project Bulletin,* nos. 8–9 (Winter 1996/1997), 370.

134. Malcolm Byrne, "The 1956 Hungarian Revolution: A History in Documents," *National Security Archive Electronic Briefing Book* (November 4, 2002).

135. Quoted in Kramer, "New Evidence," p. 370.

136. Thomas Polgar quoted in Evan Thomas, *The Very Best Men* (New York: Simon & Schuster, 1995), p. 147.

137. Quoted in Puddington, *Broadcasting Freedom,* p. 113.

138. Krebs, *Dueling Visions,* p. xi.

139. Radio Free Europe survey quoted in László Borhi, "Rollback, Liberation, Containment, or Inaction?" *Journal of Cold War Studies, I* (Fall 1999), 67.

140. Gregory Mitrovich, *Undermining the Kremlin* (Ithaca: Cornell University Press, 2000), p. 189.

141. Matthew Connelly, *A Diplomatic Revolution* (New York: Oxford University Press, 2002), p. 73.

142. Campbell Craig, *Destroying the Village* (New York: Columbia University Press, 1998), p. 70.

143. Robert J. Watson, *History of the Office of the Secretary of Defense,* (Washington, D.C.: Office of the Secretary of Defense, 1997), *IV,* 124.

144. Quoted in Gregg Herken, *Counsels of War* (New York: Oxford University Press, 1987), p. 130.

145. Zubok and Pleshakov, *Kremlin's Cold War,* p. 172.

146. Quoted in Michael Mandelbaum, *The Nuclear Question* (New York: Cambridge University Press, 1979), p. 66.

147. Snead, *Gaither Committee,* p. 158.

148. Quoted in Peter Roman, *Eisenhower and the Missile Gap* (Ithaca: Cornell University Press, 1995), p. 139.

149. Stuart Leslie, *The Cold War and American Science* (New York: Columbia University Press, 1993), pp. 2, 43.

150. Noble Frankland, ed., *Documents on International Affairs, 1957* (London: Oxford University Press, 1960), p. 157.

151. Jacob Beam and Dulles quoted in Piotr Wandycz, "Adam Rapacki," in Gordon A. Craig and Francis L. Loewenheim, eds., *The Diplomats, 1939–1979* (Princeton: Princeton University Press, 1994), pp. 299–300.

152. George F. Kennan, *Russia, the Atom, and the West* (New York: Harper & Brothers, 1958), p. 92.

153. Quoted in Thomas G. Paterson, ed., *Containment and the Cold War* (Reading, Mass.: Addison-Wesley, 1973), p. 116.

154. Quoted in Taubman, *Khrushchev,* p. 397.

155. Quoted in William Burr, "New Sources on the Berlin Crisis, 1958–1962," *Cold War International History Bulletin,* no. 2 (Fall 1992), 22.

156. Quoted in Townsend Hoopes, *The Devil and John Foster Dulles* (Boston: Little, Brown, 1973), p. 470.

157. Quoted in Hope M. Harrison, "Ulbricht and the Concrete 'Rose,' " Working Paper no. 5, *Cold War International History Project* (Washington, D.C., May 1993), p. 21.

158. Quoted in David Wolff, " 'One Finger's Worth of Historical Events,'" Working Paper no. 5, *Cold War International History Project* (Washington, D.C.: August 2000), p. 12.

159. Dwight D. Eisenhower, *The White House Years: Waging Peace, 1956–1961* (Garden City, N.Y.: Doubleday, 1965), p. 432.

160. *Khrushchev in America* (New York: Crosscurrents, 1960), p. 120.

161. Quoted in Larson, *Anatomy,* p. 96.

162. Quoted in Philip Taubman, *Secret Empire* (New York: Simon & Schuster, 2003), p. 312.

163. *Ibid.,* p. 310.

164. Eisenhower quoted in Mark Trachtenberg, *A Constructed Peace* (Princeton: Princeton University Press, 1999), p. 260.

165. Quoted in Ambrose, *Eisenhower, President,* p. 580.

166. Quoted in Edward Crankshaw, *The New Cold War* (Baltimore: Penguin, 1965 [c. 1963]), p. 81.

167. Quoted in Shu Guang Zhang, *Economic Cold War* (Washington, D.C.: Woodrow Wilson Press, 2001), p. 115; and in John Lewis Gaddis, *The United States and the End of the Cold War* (New York: Oxford University Press, 1992), p. 75.

168. Diane Kunz, *Butter and Guns* (New York: Free Press, 1997), pp. 328–329.

169. Senator William F. Knowland quoted in Gayle B. Montgomery and James W. Johnson, *One Step from the White House* (Berkeley: University of California Press, 1998), p. 98.

170. Quoted in David Wolff, "'One Finger's Worth,'" p. 55.

171. Dulles quoted in Zhang, *Economic Cold War,* p. 123.

172. Gordon H. Chang and He Di, "The Absence of War in the U.S.-China Confrontation over Quemoy and Matsu in 1954–1955," *American Historical Review, XCVIII* (December 1993), 1523.

173. Military orders quoted in Xiaobing Li and Honshan Li, eds., *China and the United States* (Lanham, Md.: University Press of America, 1998), p. 55.

174. Quoted in Waldo Heinrichs, "Eisenhower and the Sino-American Confrontation," in Cohen and Iriye, *Great Powers,* p. 99.

175. Quoted in Montgomery and Johnson, *One Step,* p. 184.

176. Quoted in Qiang Zhai, *The Dragon, the Lion, & the Eagle* (Kent, Ohio: Kent State University Press, 1994), p. 161.

177. Quoted in Zhang, "Between 'Paper' and 'Real Tigers' " in Gaddis, *Cold War Statesmen,* p. 200.

178. Quoted in Shu Guang Zhang, *Deterrence and Strategic Culture* (Ithaca: Cornell University Press, 1992), p. 214.

179. Quoted in Dockrill, *Eisenhower's New Look,* p. 242; and in Melvin Gurtov, "The Taiwan Strait Crisis Revisited," *Modern China, II* (January 1976), 79.

180. Odd Arne Westad, "The Sino-Soviet Alliance and the United States," in Westad, *Brothers,* p. 176.

181. From Andrew J. Goodpaster's notes, quoted in Dockrill, *Eisenhower's New Look,* p. 242.

182. Quoted in Zhang, *Deterrence,* p. 255.

183. Quoted in Victor S. Kaufman, *Confronting Communism* (Columbia: University of Missouri Press, 2001), p. 92.

184. Chen Yi quoted in Zhang, "Between 'Paper' and 'Real Tigers,'" pp. 210–211.

185. Ambassador John M. Allison quoted in Aaron Forsberg, *America and the Japanese Miracle* (Chapel Hill: University of North Carolina Press, 2000), p. 30.

186. Quoted in Roger Buckley, *U.S.-Japan Alliance Diplomacy, 1945–1990* (Cambridge, Eng.: Cambridge University Press, 1992), p. 57.

187. Allison quoted in Lawrence S. Wittner, *Resisting the Bomb* (Stanford: Stanford University Press, 1997), p. 146.

188. Margot Henrikson, *Dr. Strangelove's America* (Berkeley: University of California Press, 1997), p. 58.

189. Quoted in Stuart Auerbach, "How the U.S. Built Japan, Inc.," *Washington Post National Weekly Edition,* July 26–August 1, 1993.

190. Sayuri Shimizu, *Creating People of Plenty* (Kent: Kent State University Press, 2001), p. 9.

191. Quoted in *Washington Post National Weekly Edition,* August 21–27, 1995; in Akira Iriye, "Japan Returns to the World," In Gordon Craig and Francis L. Loewenheim, eds., *The Diplomats, 1939–1979* (Princeton: Princeton University Press, 1994), p. 334.

192. Quoted in John Kent, "The United States and the Decolonization of Black Africa, 1945–1953," in David Ryan and Victor Pungong, eds., *The United States and Decolonization* (New York: St. Martin's, 2000), p. 177.

193. Quoted in Deborah Kisatsky, "Containment, Co-optation, Cooperation: The United States and the European Right, 1945–1955" (Ph.D. Diss., University of Connecticut, 2001), p. 274.

194. Dennis Merrill, "The Ironies of History," in Ryan and Pungong, *United States,* p. 102.

195. Quoted in Kent, "United States," p. 178.

196. Henry Byroade quoted in James H. Meriwether, *Proudly We Can Be Africans* (Chapel Hill: University of North Carolina Press, 2002), pp. 132, 166.

197. Robert L. Heilbroner, "Making a Rational Foreign Policy Now," *Harper's, CCXXXVII* (September 1968), 65.

198. Quoted in Hixson, *Parting,* p. 126; William J. Lederer and Eugene Burdick, *The Ugly American* (New York: Fawcett, 1958), p. 234.

199. Cary Fraser, "Crossing the Color Line in Little Rock," *Diplomatic History, XXIV* (Spring 2000), 235.

200. Quoted in Thomas Borstelmann, *The Cold War and the Color Line* (Cambridge: Harvard University Press, 2001), p. 93.

201. Andrew J. Rotter, *Comrades at Odds* (Ithaca: Cornell University Press, 2000), p. 166.

202. Azza Salama Layton, *International Politics and Civil Rights Policies in the United States, 1941–1960* (New York: Cambridge University Press, 2000), p. 100.

203. Quoted *ibid.,* p. 131.

204. Nigerian newspaper quoted in Fraser, "Crossing," p. 250.

205. Michael Krenn, *Black Diplomacy* (New York: Sharpe, 1999), p. 44; Cambridge Study Group quoted *ibid.,* p. 106.

206. Representative L. Mendel Rivers and Senator Herman Talmadge quoted *ibid,* p. 107.

207. Harold Isaacs quoted in Rotter, *Comrades,* p. 217; Elbert Matthews and Eustace Seligman quoted in Rotter, "Gender Relations, Foreign Relations," *Journal of American History, LXXXI* (September 1994), 525, 538.

208. Quoted in Michelle Mart, "Tough Guys and American Cold War Policy," *Diplomatic History, XX* (Summer 1996), 366, 371, 376.

209. Scott Lucas, "The Limits of Ideology," in Ryan and Pungong, *United States,* p. 141.

210. SWNCC, "Political and Military Problems in the Far East," November 29, 1945, James F. Byrnes Papers, Clemson University Library, Clemson, S.C.

211. Paul Robeson quoted in Layton, *International Politics,* p. 71.

212. Quoted *ibid.,* p. 70.

213. Quoted in Robert J. McMahon, *The Cold War on the Periphery* (New York: Columbia University Press, 1994), p. 38.

214. Michael H. Hunt, "Conclusions: The Decolonization Puzzle," in Ryan and Pungong, *United States,* p. 207.

215. *Department of State Bulletin, XXXIV* (June 18, 1956), 1000.

216. Quoted in Thomas G. Paterson, *Meeting the Communist Threat* (New York: Oxford University Press, 1988), p. 161.

217. State Department quoted in Joyce Battle, ed., "Documentation on Early Cold War U.S. Propaganda Activities in the Middle East," *National Security Archive Electronic Briefing Book,* no. 78 (December 13, 2002).

218. John Foster Dulles quoted in Immerman, *John Foster Dulles,* p. 67; Foreign Office quoted in Mary Ann Heiss, *Empire and Nationhood* (New York: Columbia University Press, 1997), p. 74.

219. Abraham Ben-Zvi, *Decade of Transition: Eisenhower, Kennedy, and the Origins of the American-Israeli Alliance* (New York: Columbia University Press, 1998), p. 39; Byroade quoted in William R. Polk, *The Arab World Today* (Cambridge: Harvard University Press, 1991), p. 388.

220. Byroade quoted in Polk, *ibid.,* p. 388.

221. Quoted in Gail E. Meyer, *Egypt and the United States* (Rutherford, N.J.: Fairleigh Dickinson University Press, 1980), p. 146.

222. Eisenhower quoted in Peter L. Hahn, *The United States, Great Britain, and Egypt, 1945–1956* (Chapel Hill: University of North Carolina Press, 1991), p. 230; and in Ray Takeyh, *The Origins of the Eisenhower Doctrine* (New York: St. Martin's, 2000), p. 139.

223. Eisenhower quoted in Hahn, *ibid.,* p. 230.

224. Quoted in Takeyh, *Origins,* p. 147.

225. Quoted in David Schoenbaum, *The United States and the State of Israel* (New York: Oxford University Press, 1993), p. 117.

226. John Foster Dulles quoted in Douglas Little, "The Making of a Special Relationship," *International Journal of Middle East Studies, XXV* (1993), 564.

227. Quoted in Takeyh, *Origins,* p. 152.
228. Ashton, *Eisenhower,* p. 109; Dulles quoted *ibid.,* p. 109.
229. Khrushchev quoted in Wolff, "'One Finger's Worth,'" p. 57.
230. Salim Yaqub, "Imperious Doctrines," *Diplomatic History, XXVI* (Fall 2002), 578.
231. Quoted in Ashton, *Eisenhower,* p. 110.
232. Douglas Little, "His Finest Hour?" *Diplomatic History, XX* (Winter 1996), 28.
233. Quoted in Thomas G. Paterson, *Contesting Castro* (New York: Oxford University Press, 1994), p. 10.
234. John M. Leddy quoted in Nick Cullather, *Secret History: The CIA's Classified Account of Its Operations in Guatemala, 1952–1954* (Stanford: Stanford University Press, 1999), p. 35.
235. James F. Siekmeier, *Aid, Nationalism, and Inter-American Relations—Guatemala, Bolivia, and the United States, 1945–1961* (Lewiston, N.Y.: Edwin Mellen, 1999), p. 17.
236. Quoted in Cullather, *Secret History,* p. 16.
237. Quoted in Nicola Miller, *Soviet Relations with Latin America, 1959–1987* (Cambridge, Eng.: Cambridge University Press, 1989), pp. 5–6, 10.
238. Quoted in Richard H. Immerman, *The CIA in Guatemala* (Austin: University of Texas Press, 1982), p. 181.
239. U.S. official Burrows quoted in Piero Gleijeses, *Shattered Hope* (Princeton: Princeton University Press, 1991), p. 365.
240. Quoted *ibid.,* p. 4.
241. Quoted in Cullather, *Secret History,* p. 79.
242. Stephen M. Streeter, *Managing the Counterrevolution* (Athens: Ohio University Press, 2000), p. 33.
243. Richard M. Nixon, *Six Crises* (Garden City, N.Y.: Doubleday, 1962), pp. 198–199.
244. U.S. Senate, Committee on Finance, *Trade Agreements Extension* (Hearings), 84 Cong., 1 Sess. (1955), Part 4, p. 2049.
245. White House statement quoted in Michael D. Gambone, *Eisenhower, Somoza, and the Cold War in Nicaragua, 1953–1961* (Westport, Conn.: Praeger, 1997), p. 141.
246. Quoted in Alan McPherson, *Yankee No!* (Cambridge: Harvard University Press, 2003), p. 35.
247. Quoted in Stephen G. Rabe, *Eisenhower and Latin America* (Chapel Hill: University of North Carolina Press, 1988), p. 104.
248. Quoted in John Major, *Prized Possession* (New York: Cambridge University Press, 1993), p. 334.
249. Quoted in Robert A. Stevenson Oral History, Foreign Affairs Oral History Program, Lauinger Library, Georgetown University, Washington, D.C., p. 29.
250. Richard Pells, "American Culture Abroad," in R. Kroes et al., *Cultural Transmissions and Receptions* (Amsterdam, Neth.: Vu University Press, 1993), p. 78; Kaspar Maase, "American Mass Culture in the Federal Republic of Germany," *ibid.,* p. 167.
251. Quoted in Hixson, *Parting,* p. 133.
252. Robert J. Haddow, *Pavilions of Plenty* (Washington, D.C.: Smithsonian Institution Press, 1997), pp. 212–213.
253. Wagnleitner, *Cocacolonization,* p. 4.
254. Quoted in Donald W. White, *The American Century* (New Haven: Yale University Press, 1996), p. 241.
255. Stephen J. Whitfield, *The Culture of the Cold War* (Baltimore: Johns Hopkins University Press, 1991), p. 72; Hixson, *Parting,* p. 179.
256. Franz Joseph and Raymond Aron quoted in Jessica C. E. Geinow-Hecht, "Shame on US?" *Diplomatic History, XXIV* (Summer 2000), 468.
257. Richard Immerman, *John Foster Dulles* (Wilmington, Del.: Scholarly Resources, 1999), p. 196.
258. Quoted in Shane J. Maddock, "The Nth Country Conundrum" (Ph.D. diss., University of Connecticut, 1997), p. 189.
259. Quoted in DeConde, *Presidential Machismo,* p. 158.
260. Bowie and Immerman, *Waging Peace,* p. 6.

CHAPTER 9

Passing the Torch: The Vietnam Years, 1961–1969

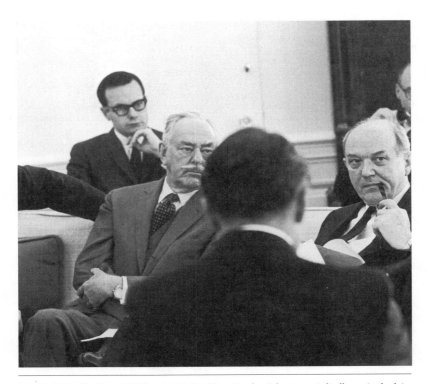

"Wise Men."   From 1965 to 1968, President Lyndon Johnson periodically received advice on Vietnam from experienced members of the foreign policy establishment (most were Truman-era diplomats and generals)—a group christened the "Wise Men." Dean Acheson (with mustache) and Secretary of State Dean Rusk (on the far right) are pictured here in a meeting with Johnson and aides. This group's consistent support for escalation led Assistant Secretary of Defense John McNaughton to remark that "a feeling is widely and strongly held" around the country that "the Establishment is out of its mind." After the Tet Offensive, when the Wise Men reversed course and urged LBJ to withdraw, the president grudgingly accepted their advice. (Lyndon Baines Johnson Library)

DIPLOMATIC CROSSROAD

⃟ *The Tet Offensive in Vietnam, 1968*

"THEY'RE COMING IN! They're coming in! VC in the compound," the young MP shouted into his radio.[1] Seconds later Vietcong (VC) commandos gunned him down. Moments before, about 3:00 A.M. that January 30, 1968, the U.S. Embassy in Saigon, South Vietnam, was quiet, the only noise coming from the whirring air conditioners and the fireworks exploding in celebration of Tet, the Lunar New Year. Completed in 1967 at a cost of $2.6 million, the six-story embassy building was protected by shatterproof Plexiglas windows, a concrete sun shield covering the entire structure, and a thick, eight-foot-high outer wall. Topped by a helicopter pad, the fortified building had become "the symbol of America's power" in Vietnam.[2]

At 2:45 A.M., a taxi cab and truck moved into the darkness from a repair shop near the embassy. About fifteen Vietcong leaped out after a huge explosion blew a three-foot hole in the wall. The VC scrambled through, firing automatic rifles at two embassy MPs (military police), who radioed for help before they died. The invaders then unleashed their antitank guns and rockets, transported into Saigon weeks before under shipments of tomatoes and firewood. The thick embassy doors took a direct hit, sending the U.S. seal crashing to the ground. Inside, a skeleton crew of Central Intelligence Agency and Foreign Service officials felt as if they were "in a telephone booth in the *Titanic*."[3] A few blocks away, aides roused Ambassador Ellsworth Bunker and whisked him away to a secret hiding place.

The news of the attack quickly reached the United States. Few U.S. leaders could believe that the enemy had breached "Bunker's bunker." On January 17, in his State of the Union message, President Lyndon B. Johnson himself had called most of South Vietnam secure, and the embassy seemed the most secure of all.

In Saigon's dim morning light, American soldiers counterattacked. Paratroopers landed by helicopter on the roof. By 9:15 A.M., with the compound secure, General William C. Westmoreland counted nineteen dead Vietnamese (four were friendly embassy employees), five dead Americans, and two Vietcong prisoners. He then declared an American victory. One reporter described the compound as a "butcher shop in Eden."[4]

The bold sally against the embassy comprised but one part of the massive, well-coordinated Tet offensive. The forays struck thirty-six of the forty-four provincial capitals, some one hundred other villages, the gigantic Tan Son Nhut air base, and numerous sites in Saigon (see map, page 352). The communist forces attacked after half of the South Vietnamese Army (ARVN) had gone on leave for the Tet holiday. The VC, or National Liberation Front (NLF), and North Vietnamese hoped to seize the cities, foment a general sympathetic uprising, force ARVN and U.S. troops to move to the cities—leaving a vacuum in the countryside—and disrupt the governmental bureaucracy. In the end, Washington would presumably negotiate American withdrawal.

"What the Hell's Ho Chi Minh Doing Answering Our Saigon Embassy Phone . . .?" Paul Conrad's cartoon of President Lyndon B. Johnson expressed well the startled American response to the attack on the U.S. Embassy in South Vietnam in January 1968. Johnson had earlier reported that most of South Vietnam had been secured against the Vietcong and North Vietnamese. But General Earl Wheeler explained that "in a city like Saigon people can infiltrate easily. . . . This is about as tough to stop as it is to protect against individual muggings in Washington, D.C." (© 1968, *Los Angeles Times*. Reprinted with permission Los Angeles Times Syndicate)

Yet the ARVN and U.S. armies struck back: "Forced to fight in the cities, they bombed, shelled, and strafed the most populous districts as if they saw no distinction between them and the jungle."[5] Americans at home watched on television, and many recoiled from the carnage. To fight enemy troops in Hue, South Vietnam's old imperial capital, U.S. and ARVN forces used everything from nausea gas to rockets. After three weeks of vicious warfare, the communists fled, 100,000 people had become refugees, thousands lay dead, and American bombings had reduced a once-beautiful city to rubble. The NLF executed hundreds, perhaps thousands, of civilians, most of them connected with the South Vietnamese government or Americans. The NLF commander at Hue later wrote: "There is never an easy 'political' victory . . . without first having to shed blood and scatter bones on the battlefield."[6]

In the northwest corner of South Vietnam, U.S. soldiers bravely resisted a siege of their two-square-mile hillside at Khe Sanh, which, according to Westmoreland, "served to lure North Vietnamese to their deaths."[7] North Vietnamese General Vo Nguyen Giap claimed in contrast that Khe Sanh was important "only to the extent" that America put its "prestige" at stake.[8] Hundreds of Americans died during the first months of 1968, as enemy rockets zeroed in on the strategic but vulnerable base. American B-52s countered by dropping tons of bombs on the surrounding area. By April, remembered a colonel, "the jungle had become literally a desert—vast stretches of scarred, bare earth. . . . a landscape of splinters and bomb craters."[9] Khe Sanh held, just barely.

The provincial capital of Ben Tre symbolized the costs of the Tet offensive. To ferret out the VC, American and ARVN forces leveled Ben Tre, killing a thousand civilians. In unforgettable words, a U.S. officer declared that "it became necessary to destroy the town to save it."[10] That statement joined a visual image to sear American memory. The NBC Huntley-Brinkley news program of February 2 showed a brief film clip of the national police chief of South Vietnam pointing a pistol at the head of a suspected VC. General Nguyen Ngoc pulled the trigger and blasted the young man. The fifty-two seconds of footage, said an NBC producer, broadcast the "rawest, roughest film anyone had ever seen."[11]

The Johnson administration, having claimed before Tet that South Vietnam had gained the upper hand in the war and having said that U.S. officials had expected a communist offensive, suffered an ever-growing "credibility gap" with the American people. January proved a bad month for Lyndon B. Johnson. On the twenty-third the North Koreans captured the American spy ship *Pueblo* and its entire crew off the Korean coast. The international balance of payments for the United States, Johnson learned, was running at an annual deficit of $7 billion. A B-52 with four H-bombs aboard crashed in Greenland. And Senator Eugene McCarthy, a "dove" on Vietnam, challenged Johnson's renomination to the presidency.

Critics probed the administration's assertion that Tet counted as a triumph. Senator Robert F. Kennedy, soon to become a candidate for the Democratic presidential nomination, said: "It is as if James Madison [had claimed] victory in 1812 because the British only burned Washington instead of annexing it to the British Empire."[12] After Secretary Robert S. McNamara recited enemy casualties, a reporter queried: "Isn't there something Orwellian about it, that the more we kill, the stronger they get?"[13] When the popular television newscaster Walter Cronkite of CBS judged the war a stalemate, LBJ moaned: "If I've lost Cronkite, I've lost middle America."[14]

Some 45,000 NLF, 2,000 ARVN, and 1,000 American soldiers died. Vietnamese civilians suffered a heavy toll, too. More than 14,000 died and 24,000 were wounded. One-eighth of the South Vietnamese people became homeless refugees in their own land. "Giap was callous," Westmoreland later charged. "Had any American general taken such losses he wouldn't have lasted three weeks."[15] Giap had actually opposed an ambitious offensive when NLF military leaders first proposed it in April 1967. Ho Chi Minh, the most eminent figure in the North Vietnamese government, sympathized with the Southern cadres' impatience with protracted war and overruled his chief general. But seeing the NLF devastated as a fighting force in the wake of Tet staggered Ho, who "silently regretted not having listened to Giap." Ho's health declined and "[u]nable even to sleep, he died the next year."[16]

Despite a brave front, the U.S. president also reeled from the impact of Tet. Johnson authorized 10,500 more troops for Vietnam, gave hawkish speeches against quitting under fire, and flamboyantly toured U.S. military bases.

"Give me the lesser of evils," said LBJ as he asked the new secretary of defense, Clark Clifford, a former Truman adviser, to undertake a major review of Vietnam policy.[17] In late February General Westmoreland had recommended that an additional 206,000 American troops join the more than 500,000 already there. The

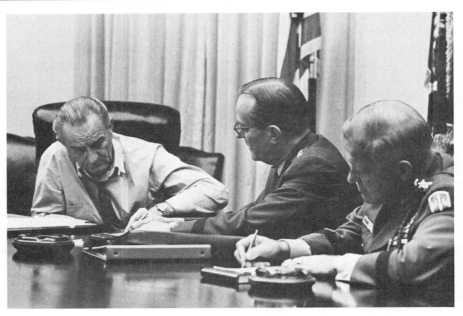

Lyndon Baines Johnson (1908–1973). A tired president confers with Generals Creighton Abrams and Earl Wheeler at the National Security Council Meeting of March 27, 1968. A few days later Johnson removed himself as a candidate in the presidential race. Johnson once told his vice president, Hubert Humphrey, "I'm not temperamentally equipped to be Commander in Chief. . . . I'm too sentimental to give the orders." (Courtesy of the Lyndon Baines Johnson Library)

generals planned a major new ARVN-U.S. offensive. Within the Pentagon, formerly timid dissenters pleaded for deescalation. "Let's go in and win or else get out," a group of U.S. governors recommended.[18] In early March, too, Secretary of State Dean Rusk suggested curtailing the bombing of North Vietnam to induce peace talks. In the New Hampshire Democratic primary on March 12, McCarthy made a strong showing by polling 42 percent of the vote to Johnson's 49 percent. Speaking for the Wise Men, former secretary of state Dean Acheson put it bluntly: "We can no longer do the job we ought to do in the time we have left and we must begin to take steps to disengage."[19]

Clifford came to the same conclusion. He grew appalled that the generals could not say for how long or how many more troops might be needed. "Nothing had prepared me for the weakness of the military's case," he recalled.[20] His Ad Hoc Task Force on Vietnam recommended in early March sending 20,000 additional American troops. But Clifford's group found "no reason to believe" that 206,000 more troops—"or double or triple that quantity"—could achieve victory. The strategy of attrition had created "a sinkhole," said the report. "We put in more—they match it. We put in more—they match it."[21] Johnson's advisers also expressed alarm that the Vietnam War had initiated a gold and dollar crisis that threatened the economic well-being of the United States. Nervous foreigners—especially Europeans—rushed to exchange their dollars for gold. On March 14 alone, foreigners redeemed $372 million for gold. A post-Tet military buildup would cost billions more, further bloat the deficit-burdened budget, and panic foreign owners of dollars even more. Clifford's friends in the business community found America "in a hopeless bog."[22] The "sheer accumulation" of negative views from advisers, opinion polls, the news media, and Congress turned Johnson toward deescalation. In a dream he also saw himself as Woodrow Wilson paralyzed from the neck down.

On March 31 LBJ spoke on television. "We are prepared to move immediately toward peace through negotiations," he announced. Although another 13,500 soldiers would go to South Vietnam, U.S. airplanes would halt their bombing of a major portion of North Vietnam. "Even this limited bombing of the North could come to an early end—if our restraint is matched in Hanoi [the North Vietnamese capital]."[23] To the amazement of viewers, Johnson also declared that he would not seek reelection. On April 3 the North Vietnamese agreed to go to the conference table. Discussions began on May 14. The fighting and talking—and dying—would go on for several years more. Many GIs no longer thought the war worth fighting, as they said in their familiar slogan: "It don't mean nothin'."[24]

Vietnamese Wars Before 1961

Why Vietnam? Why did this Southeast Asian land of peasant farmers become the site of America's longest war? The origins are found in the centuries-long story of Vietnamese resistance to foreigners—Chinese, French, Japanese, and American. In 1867 France colonized Vietnam and soon began to exploit the country's raw materials, as well as those of Laos and Cambodia, which became protectorates in 1883 and part of French Indochina in the 1890s. Rice, rubber, tin, and tungsten from the area flowed to European markets. France constructed a repressive imperial government and monopolized land holdings, while some 80 percent of the Vietnamese people subsisted as poor, rural peasants. From 1867 onward the embittered Vietnamese battled their French overlords.

Vietnam's most famous nationalist leader was Ho Chi Minh, born in 1890 to a low-level government employee. Described by a U.S. intelligence officer as a "wisp of a man . . . intelligent, well-versed in the problems of his country, rational, and dedicated," Ho traveled to Europe and at the time of World War I lobbied for independence.[25] In Paris, Ho's appeal to Wilson's principle of self-determination did not move the conferees. Because the Communist party seemed the only political force vigorously denouncing colonialism, Ho and other nationalists joined it. Throughout the twenties and thirties he lived and agitated in China and Russia. In 1930–1931 the French brutally suppressed a Vietnamese peasant rebellion.

During 1940–1941 the Japanese took over Vietnam but left collaborating French officials in charge. Vietnamese nationalists, including Ho's communists, went underground, used China as a base, and in 1941 organized the Vietminh, a coalition of nationalist groups led by the Communist party. In the final days of World War II, Vietminh guerrillas tangled with Japanese troops, liberated some northern provinces, and cooperated with the U.S. Office of Strategic Services (OSS). The agency later judged Ho "a convinced Democrat who has always rallied around himself all the revolutionary forces of the country for winning of independence under the aegis of democracy."[26] Ho sent formal messages to Washington, asked for recognition, and often spoke in understandable English about America— its history, its political ideals, its endorsement of self-determination, its support for "free, popular governments all over the world."[27] In late August 1945, Ho's Vietminh

Ho Chi Minh (1890–1969). His name meant "enlightened one" and was merely the most famous of more than fifty shifting aliases he used throughout his life. Described by the journalist David Halberstam as "part Gandhi, part Lenin, all Vietnamese," Ho often used the United States as an example of a successful anticolonial revolution. His chief biographer William Duiker, however, argues that Ho might not have been completely sincere in his overtures to Washington after World War II, contending that he "was quite willing to make tactical alliances with potential adversaries in the full understanding that such arrangements might only be temporary in character." After 1955, Ho delegated more and more authority to younger party members and took an increasingly ceremonial role in the affairs of North Vietnam. (© Picture Research Consultants)

organized the Democratic Republic of Vietnam (DRV) in Hanoi. On September 2, he proclaimed Vietnam's independence, borrowing phrases from America's document of July 4, 1776. Still, jilted in the past, Ho remained privately suspicious of Americans as "only interested in replacing the French. . . . They want to reorganize our country to control it. They are capitalists to the core."[28]

During World War II, President Franklin D. Roosevelt often remarked that France should relinquish Indochina. He toyed with the idea of a trusteeship. The Department of State valued the Southeast Asian countries as "potentially important markets for American exports. They . . . have important bearing on our security and the security of the Philippines."[29] Some American officials also worried that denying France its empire would alienate a potential European ally needed to stabilize the postwar world. Prime Minister Winston Churchill, moreover, informed

Roosevelt in no uncertain terms that Britain opposed the breakup of empires. Just before he died, Roosevelt retreated. He "did not want to get mixed up in any Indochina decision" with an agitated Churchill at Yalta, he said.[30] Roosevelt's anticolonial instincts never became policy.

The French, with British military help and American acquiescence, returned to Vietnam. Ignored by the United States, receiving no support from Moscow, and now facing French forces, the Vietminh accepted a compromise with France in March 1946: DRV status as a "free state" in the French Union and French military occupation of northern Vietnam. Vietminh and French soldiers clashed in December. One French bombardment of Haiphong killed several thousand civilians. The Vietminh responded with guerrilla terror. For the next eight years Vietnam endured bloody combat, with the French holding the cities and the Vietminh the countryside. One French military commander compared fighting the Vietminh "to ridding a dog of its fleas. We can pick them, drown them, and poison them, but they will be back in a few days."[31]

To win Paris's favor for its postwar policies in Europe, Washington tolerated the return of French colonialism to Vietnam. Conditioned by traditional notions of American cultural and racial superiority, U.S. diplomats dismissed the Vietnamese as not "particularly industrious"—lacking such traits as "honesty, loyalty, or veracity."[32] As the Cold War intensified in 1946–1947, Ho's Moscow "training" became a topic of American discussion. The Department of State designated him an agent of international communism, although some diplomats pointed out that Vietnamese leaders were nationalists, not servants of Moscow, and that Ho stood as an Asian Tito. Ho himself had earlier described himself to an OSS officer as a "progressive-socialist-nationalist"—that is, the leader of both a colonial rebellion against France and a social revolution for Vietnam.[33]

In 1948 the French installed Emperor Bao Dai, who had served the Japanese in World War II, as their Vietnamese leader. Paris actively lobbied for U.S. support of this puppet government, arguing that if the Vietnamese "believe we are supported by the United States," then "they will be more disposed to reach an agreement with France [and abandon the Vietminh]."[34] In February 1950, in a move inspired by fear of Communist Chinese expansion, Washington recognized the Bao Dai government. In May, moreover, the Truman administration extended aid to the French for their war in Vietnam.

The Korean War accentuated Washington's interest in the outcome of the Vietnamese rebellion. In 1950 Truman sent $150 million and a contingent of military advisers to Vietnam. For 1945–1954 the United States gave $2 billion of the $5 billion that Paris spent to keep Vietnam within the French empire. In 1954 U.S. aid covered 78 percent of the cost of the war, and some 300 Americans went to Vietnam as part of the Military Assistance Advisory Group—all to no avail.

In spring 1954, at Dienbienphu, a fortress where the besieged French had chosen to stand or fall, Vietminh forces moved toward a major, symbolic victory. To save the fortress, the French sought U.S. intervention. President Eisenhower received conflicting advice. The chair of the Joint Chiefs of Staff, Admiral Arthur Radford, urged massive night attacks on Vietminh positions by 300 U.S. carrier aircraft, possibly including tactical nuclear weapons. Army chief of staff Matthew Ridgeway, however, judged intervention a "hare-brained tactical scheme."[35] A Defense Department analyst agreed that "one cannot go over Niagara Falls in a barrel only slightly."[36]

Eisenhower cited the "falling domino" analogy to explain U.S. interests in Southeast Asia and then sounded out Congress, France, and Britain about internationalizing the war through "United Action." Members of Congress warned against an air strike that might lead next to ground troops and another Korea. London also balked. Without U.S. intervention, French forces at Dienbienphu surrendered on May 7.

A few days earlier, on April 26, 1954, representatives from France, the Soviet Union, Britain, China, the United States, Bao Dai's Vietnam, the DRV, Laos, and Cambodia met in Geneva to discuss Asian issues. The Eisenhower administration, fearing a French retreat, reluctantly agreed to discuss Vietnam at the conference. In fact, a new French government, headed by Pierre Mendès-France, came to power on June 12 and pledged to end the war. President Eisenhower expected to "gag" on any Geneva agreement but vowed to "salvage something" by organizing Southeast Asian states into a military pact and defending the southern half of Vietnam.[37] China's Zhou Enlai pressed Ho's Vietminh (now controlling two-thirds of Vietnam) to make peace so as to "consolidate and develop our forces in order to make further progress later on."[38]

On July 20 the DRV and France signed the Geneva agreements. The terms: temporary partition of Vietnam at the seventeenth parallel; French withdrawal to below that latitude; neither North nor South Vietnam to sign military alliances or permit foreign bases on Vietnamese soil; national elections to be held in 1956; unification of the country after elections; and elections also in neighboring strife-torn Laos and Cambodia, the other territories in French Indochina. Refusing to endorse the accords, the United States did state that it would "refrain from the threat or the use of force."[39] The National Security Council found the Geneva settlement a "disaster" that represented a "major forward stride of Communism which may lead to the loss of Southeast Asia."[40] The Bao Dai government in Saigon also blasted the agreements and declared that July 20 "would be observed as a day of shame."[41]

Because "we can't go on losing areas of the free world forever," Eisenhower established the Southeast Asia Treaty Organization in September 1954 to protect Cambodia, Laos, and South Vietnam from communist subversion and aggression.[42] SEATO violated the spirit of the Geneva Accords by specifying the defense of the southern half of Vietnam—now treated as a separate state. Although Great Britain, France, Pakistan, the Philippines, Thailand, Australia, and New Zealand joined the United States in the pact, only the last three later sent troops to fight in Vietnam. (SEATO disbanded in 1977.)

In the South, the United States backed the new government of Prime Minister Ngo Dinh Diem, a Vietnamese nationalist and Catholic who impressed U.S. diplomats as "a Messiah without a message."[43] A four-year residence in the United States gained him prominent friends such as Cardinal Francis Spellman, Supreme Court Justice William O. Douglas, and Senators Mike Mansfield and John F. Kennedy, who together constituted what might be called the Vietnam Lobby. An enlarged contingent of American advisers, in violation of Geneva, began to train a South Vietnamese army, and millions of dollars in U.S. military and economic aid flowed to Diem. He and U.S. officials cooperated to displace Bao Dai and the remnants of French influence. In mid-1955 the North proposed preliminary talks to

Eisenhower, Ngo Dinh Diem (1901–1963), and Dulles. The South Vietnamese nationalist Diem, from a mandarin and Catholic family, spent time in exile in the United States before returning to his country as premier (1954–1963). Dulles urged U.S. support of Diem when most people in the U.S. and West European foreign policy establishments dismissed him as "not overly intelligent" and "a fanatic." One American diplomat complained that Diem's "only present emotion, other than a lively appreciation of himself, is a blind hatred of the French." Although Diem claimed that many of the people imprisoned by his regime were communists, a large number had actually supported the French prior to 1954. (Dwight D. Eisenhower Library)

plan the national election scheduled by Geneva for 1956. Diem refused, and the Eisenhower administration, certain that Ho would win an election, endorsed cancellation of the electoral provisions of the Geneva Accords, thereby thwarting unification. In October 1955, Diem used blatant fraud to garner 98.2 percent of the vote in a referendum in the South.

The two Vietnams went their separate ways, with Ho's North receiving aid from both the Soviet Union and China, cautiously avoiding dependence on either. Ho launched land reform, ending a landlord system that had largely excluded peasants. Diem's Republic of Vietnam received U.S. aid of about $300 million a year (80 percent of it for the military). Working under CIA contract, Michigan State University police experts trained a "Civil Guard" to capture suspected Vietminh. Air Force colonel Edward Lansdale, on loan to the CIA, inaugurated a propaganda campaign. Slogans such as "Christ has gone to the South" along with disinformation about impending communist bloodbaths served to scare Catholics in the North into moving to the South.[44] Some 900,000 people, most of them Catholics, made the trek. Adopting the motto "To defeat the brigands, you must become brigands," Lansdale directed sabotage operations in the North and helped Diem defeat local rivals through bribes and threats, thus persuading skeptical U.S. officials that "proud, doughty little Ngo Dinh Diem" could bring "peace and stability" to his country.[45] In 1956 Diem jailed 20,000 to 30,000 suspected communists in "reeducation" camps. Torture became routine. In 1957 and 1958 southern rebels retaliated by killing village teachers, police officers, and government officials.

Capitalizing on general anti-Diem dissent, the Vietminh organized the National Liberation Front (NLF) in December 1960 as an umbrella organization. Hanoi encouraged this communist-dominated group. In the rural areas they controlled, NLF cadres won favor from peasants by distributing land and reducing rents. In contrast, Diem resisted land reform and placed family members in profitable positions. Ambassador Elbridge Dubrow criticized Diem and his brother Nhu for establishing a political party, the Can Lao, which "has created an authoritarian organization largely modeled on Communist lines."[46] The party also served as a means to line the Ngo Dinh family's pockets. But U.S. military advisers continued to defend Diem.

U.S. officials charged that North Vietnamese aggression initiated this new war in the South, but most scholars conclude that the NLF sprang from the peculiar, repressive environment of Diem's regime. Some analysts, in fact, have noted that the NLF, "with its appeal to Southern nationalism, actually represented a risk" for the North "in that it could become a breeding ground for separatist ideas."[47] Vietnam's history had thus evolved from a colonial rebellion to expel the French into several interacting wars and revolutions: post-Geneva social revolution in the North; civil war within Diem's South; civil war between North and South; and, finally, an anti-imperialist war to force the Americans out. Imbued with the Cold War mentality that shoehorned events into an East-West frame, however, Americans failed to understand the singularly *Vietnamese* character of these conflicts. Senator John F. Kennedy in 1956 called Diem's Vietnam the "cornerstone of the free world in Southeast Asia, the keystone of the arch, the finger in the dike."[48] In 1961, Kennedy became president.

John F. Kennedy and His "Action Intellectuals"

Vietnam figured little in the 1960 presidential contest between Richard M. Nixon and John F. Kennedy, both Cold Warriors who differed more in style than on policy. Kennedy, who won by a narrow margin, aroused support through the slogan "I think it's time America started moving again."[49] Both Nixon and Kennedy belonged to the "containment generation" that imbibed the popular lessons of World War II and the Cold War. Both had won seats in Congress in 1946 and endorsed the Truman Doctrine. In 1960, Kennedy charged that the Eisenhower-Nixon administration had neglected the Third World, losing it to communism. With the U-2 affair, the collapse of the Paris summit meeting, an adverse balance of payments, cancellation of a presidential visit to Japan, and crises in Cuba, the Congo, and Indochina as the immediate backdrop, Kennedy claimed that the United States was losing the Cold War. "History will make a judgment," JFK stated, "that these were the days when the tide began to run out"—"when the communist tide began to pour in."[50] Warning that the country had "gone soft—physically, mentally, spiritually soft," he ridiculed Nixon for saying in the "kitchen" debate with Khrushchev that, although behind in space, "we were ahead in color television." Asserted Kennedy: "I would rather take my television black and white and have the largest rockets in the world."[51]

Kennedy did not mind being called Truman with a Harvard accent. Born in 1917 to wealthy, Catholic, politically active parents, John Fitzgerald Kennedy graduated from Harvard College and served with honor in World War II. While his fa-

John F. Kennedy (1917–1963). Before becoming president, JFK represented Massachusetts in the House (1947–1953) and the Senate (1953–1961). His ghostwritten book *Profiles in Courage* (1957) won a Pulitzer Prize. One of the president's underpublicized achievements was the Trade Expansion Act of 1962 and the subsequent "Kennedy Round" of trade negotiations, which reduced tariffs. (*The Reporter,* 1962. Copyright 1962 by the Reporter Magazine Co.)

Kennedy and Kwame Nkrumah (1909–1972). Shown here greeting the president of Ghana in 1961, Kennedy won praise from African leaders because of his previous support of Algerian independence and for speeches advocating "a world safe for diversity." A student in the United States (1935–1945) before becoming his country's first president in 1957, Nkrumah welcomed American Peace Corps volunteers to train Ghana's educators and U.S. aid to build hydroelectric dams. While calling Kennedy "a real friend," Nkrumah also condemned Western imperialism and invited young Soviet "volunteers" to compete with the Peace Corps. On a visit to China in 1966 as a self-appointed mediator of the Vietnam War, Nkrumah was deposed by his own army. (John F. Kennedy Library)

ther served as ambassador to Great Britain, his senior thesis appeared as a book titled *Why England Slept* (1940), with the theme that England should have resisted Nazi aggression with force. For Kennedy's generation, the Munich agreement became the "Munich syndrome." As he once said: "The 1930s taught us a clear lesson: aggressive conduct, if allowed to go unchecked and unchallenged, ultimately leads to war."[52]

The new president exuded charisma. "All at once you had something exciting," recalled a student campaigner for Kennedy. "You had a young guy who had kids, and who liked to play football on his front lawn."[53] Call it psychology, charm, image, or mystique, Kennedy had it. Photogenic and quick-witted, he became a television star. Handsome, articulate, ingratiating, dynamic, competitive, athletic, cultured, bright, self-confident, cool, analytical, zealous—these were the traits universally ascribed to the president. People often listened not to what he said but to how he said it, and he usually said it with verve. Dean Rusk remembered him as an "incandescent man. He was on fire, and he set people around him on fire."[54] For the historian and presidential assistant Arthur M. Schlesinger, Jr., JFK had "enormous confidence in his own luck," and "everyone around him thought he had the Midas touch and could not lose."[55]

Style and personality influence diplomacy. Many of his friends have commented that a desire for power drove John F. Kennedy, because power ensured victory. His father, Joseph P. Kennedy, "pressed his children hard to compete, never to be satisfied with anything but first place. The point was not just to try; the point was to win."[56] Although Kennedy suffered from near-fatal Addison's disease and received regular injections of potent drugs, all of which he concealed through public disclaimers, JFK nonetheless projected the image of a healthy, vigorous man who played

Makers of American Foreign Relations, 1961–1969

Presidents	Secretary of State
John F. Kennedy, 1961–1963 Lyndon B. Johnson, 1963–1969	Dean Rusk, 1961–1969

Robert Strange McNamara (b. 1916). The mathematically minded secretary of defense graduated from the University of California, Berkeley. A former Ford Motor Company executive, McNamara applied efficiency methods to his department and served as war minister for Vietnam. In 1968 he became president of the World Bank. In the 1980s he criticized the nuclear arms race that he had accelerated in the 1960s. Senator Barry Goldwater called McNamara "an IBM machine with legs," and LBJ referred to "that man with the Stay-Comb in his hair." McNamara finally published a memoir, *In Retrospect* (1995), wherein he confessed that America's war in Vietnam had been "wrong, terribly wrong." (*The Reporter*, 1967. Copyright 1967 by The Reporter Magazine Co.)

to win. His appearances with Hollywood actresses such as Marilyn Monroe and his frequent extramarital sexual liaisons reflected his macho self-image. John F. Kennedy also saw foreign affairs as an arena for proving his toughness. "Who gives a shit about the minimum wage?" he once asked.[57] Kennedy soon gave Americans box scores on the missile race, the arms race, and the space race. He introduced new slogans: "The Grand Design" for Europe; the "New Africa" policy; "Flexible Response" for the military; and the "Alliance for Progress" for Latin America. Cocky, thinking themselves the "right" people, Kennedy and his advisers were, as one official complained, "sort of looking for a chance to prove their muscle."[58] Schlesinger captured the mood: "Euphoria reigned; we thought for a moment that the world was plastic and the future unlimited."[59] Kennedy's alarmist inaugural address pledged that "the torch has been passed to a new generation." He paid homage to historical memories when he noted that his generation had been "tempered by war" and "disciplined by a hard and bitter peace." Then came those moving, but in hindsight dangerously expansive, words: "We shall pay any price, bear any burden, meet any hardship, support any friend, oppose any foe to assure the survival and the success of liberty."[60]

The Kennedy people considered themselves "can-do" types who with careful calculation could manage crises and revive an ailing nation and world. Theodore H. White tagged them "the Action Intellectuals."[61] They had an inordinate faith in data. When a White House assistant attempted to persuade Secretary of Defense Robert McNamara, the "whiz kid" from Ford Motor Company, that the Vietnam venture would fail, McNamara shot back: "Where is your data? Give me something I can put in the computer. Don't give me your poetry."[62] Danger lurked in a heavy reliance on quantified information. "Ah, *les statistiques,*" said a Vietnamese general to a U.S. official. "If you want them to go up, they will go up. If you want them to go down, they will go down."[63] Despite McNamara's high standing with both JFK and LBJ, some experienced Washington hands were unimpressed. J. William Fulbright, chair of the Senate Foreign Relations Committee, recalled that McNamara "didn't know a thing" about international relations. "[H]e'd had a great success making cars" and then suddenly "he's running the whole military."[64]

Kennedy's secretary of state, Dean Rusk, worked uncomfortably with the crusading "action intellectuals" but remained a loyal member of the team. Rusk had served as a military intelligence officer in Asia during World War II, as an assistant secretary of state under Truman, and as president of the Rockefeller Foundation in the 1950s. A native of Georgia and son of a Presbyterian minister, Rusk agonized over Vietnam, opposing Americanization of the war but refusing to advise withdrawal until a noncommunist government stood secure. So he ended up backing military escalation. Lyndon Johnson appreciated his loyalty: "He has the compassion of a preacher and the courage of a Georgia cracker."[65]

Next to Attorney General Robert F. Kennedy, the president's brother who served as troubleshooter and confidant, McGeorge Bundy became Kennedy's chief foreign-relations counselor. The brilliant forty-one-year-old former Harvard dean had helped Henry L. Stimson write his memoirs and had worked for the Marshall Plan. As national security affairs adviser, Bundy centralized decisionmaking in the White House. Colleagues stood in awe of Bundy's "mathematical mind. . . . very clipped. Almost surgical," while others thought him "cold as ice and snippy about everything."[66] A self-professed member of the well-born elite, Bundy arrogantly asserted that "the United States is the engine of mankind, and the rest of the world is the caboose."[67]

Nation Building

The Kennedy administration emphasized military expansion. Kennedy had charged that the Eisenhower administration was losing the Cold War by tolerating a "missile gap" favorable to the Soviets. Eisenhower knew the politically motivated and unsubstantiated charge was nonsense. U–2 intelligence flights revealed a modest Soviet missile program. The United States had immense superiority. Kennedy and McNamara learned this, too, but, worried by Soviet boasting and Third World insurgencies, they began a mighty expansion of the military arsenal.

The administration called its defense strategy "flexible response," with a method for every kind of war.[68] The Special Forces, or Green Berets, would conduct counterinsurgency against wars of national liberation; conventional forces would handle limited wars; more and better missiles would deter war or serve as primary weapons in nuclear war; at home, fallout shelters would protect Americans under a civil defense plan. In 1961 Kennedy increased the defense budget by 15 percent. By 1963 the United States had 275 major bases in 31 nations, 65 countries hosted U.S. forces, and the U.S. military trained soldiers in 72 countries. Also, one and a quarter million military-related American personnel were stationed overseas. In 1961 the United States had 63 ICBMs; by 1963, 424. During 1961–1963, NATO's nuclear firing power increased 60 percent. Kennedy also created the U.S. Arms Control and Disarmament Agency, but his military buildup took priority.

The more missiles Americans acquired, the more vulnerable Americans seemed to become, because the Soviets tried to catch up by also building more. With Khrushchev about to test a fifty-megaton bomb "to hang over the heads of the capitalists," Kennedy sought to reassure Americans about nuclear supremacy as well as to warn Moscow not to miscalculate.[69] On October 21, 1961, Secretary McNamara's deputy, Roswell Gilpatric, announced that the United States had such a powerful nuclear retaliatory force that it could withstand a Soviet nuclear strike and still have enough missiles remaining to annihilate the Soviet Union. Moscow reacted to the speech by speeding up its ICBM program.

Kennedy met with Khrushchev at Vienna in June 1961 to discuss a test ban treaty, Berlin, and Laos. Aides warned that Khrushchev's moods ranged from "cherubic

U.S.S. *Sam Rayburn*.   Launched in 1962, this nuclear-powered submarine with sixteen Polaris ballistic missiles, each with a range of 2,875 miles, became part of a large Kennedy-inspired military buildup. The first Polaris submarine was commissioned in 1959. The deployment of Polaris submarines enabled the United States to withdraw from Italy and Turkey the land-based Jupiter missiles that so complicated the Cuban missile crisis in 1962. (U.S. Navy, Naval Photographic Center)

to choleric."[70] Kennedy went to Vienna to show the Soviets that they "must not crowd him too much."[71] With 30,000 refugees each month escaping from East Germany to West Berlin, Khrushchev speculated that "soon there will be nobody left in the GDR [East Germany] except for [Communist boss Walter] Ulbricht and his mistress."[72] Khrushchev told Kennedy that Berlin must become a "free city," thereby ending Western occupation. If the United States did not negotiate, Moscow would sign a separate treaty with East Germany, thus terminating the Soviet commitment to postwar occupation rights in Berlin. "Berlin is the testicles of the West," Khrushchev privately quipped. "Every time I want to make the West scream, I squeeze on Berlin."[73] Kennedy lamented: "What was I supposed to do to show how tough I was, take my shoe off and pound it on the table?"[74] Although the Kremlin leader may have left Vienna thinking that he had outdueled the young president, records of their meetings reveal that a tenacious Kennedy gave as good as he got. Still,

The Berlin Wall. This photograph, taken a decade after the concrete wall went up, shows a trench filled with oil and barbed-wire fencing, all designed to deter East Germans from scaling the Wall. From 1961 to 1989, East German guards killed eighty people trying to escape across the Wall. Mayor Willy Brandt, later West Germany's chancellor, grew disillusioned with the United States because it "merely frowned" when the Wall went up. "What was called my Ostpolitik was formed against this background. . . . Traditional formulas of Western policies had been shown to be ineffective and unrealistic." (National Archives)

because news accounts depicted Kennedy as "shaken and angry," the public perception developed that the Soviet leader had pushed Kennedy around.[75]

After Vienna the administration decided to force the Berlin question. On July 25, calling Berlin "the great testing place of Western courage and will," the president asked Congress for a $3.2 billion addition to the regular defense budget and authority to call up military reservists. He also requested $207 million to begin a civil defense, fallout shelter program—"in the event of an attack."[76] In a meeting with East German comrades, Khrushchev snorted that if Kennedy "starts a war then he would probably become the last president of the United States of America."[77]

On August 13 the East Germans, backed by Moscow, suddenly put up a barbed wire barricade, followed by an ugly concrete block barrier, between the two Berlins. Worried that his East German ally Walter Ulbricht might try to capture West Berlin, Khrushchev welcomed the wall solution to defuse the crisis. The wall did shut off the exodus of refugees. Kennedy remarked that "it seems particularly stupid to risk killing millions of Americans . . . because Germans want Germany to be reunified. . . . If I am going to threaten nuclear war it will have to be for much bigger . . . reasons than that."[78] So he begrudgingly accepted the Wall. Unbeknownst to the president, his special representative in Berlin, General Lucius Clay, had armed U.S. tanks with bulldozer attachments to knock down the wall. Soviet intelligence learned of these preparations. Ten American M-48 tanks suddenly found themselves facing ten Russian tanks on opposite sides of Checkpoint Charlie on October 27, nearly precipitating "a nuclear-age equivalent of the Wild West Showdown at the OK Corral."[79] With the NSC staff simulating war games in which European fatalities reached tens of millions, Kennedy used a secret channel to negotiate with

"Could You Point Out the Ground You've Taken? We're Here to Secure and Develop It Economically." A "nation-building" team cooperates with a counterinsurgency team in this parody of "modernization" efforts of Americans overseas. "The Americans always thought they discovered fire and . . . the wheel," jibed one veteran of a "modernization" project. (Editorial cartoon by Pat Oliphant, © 1976, *Los Angeles Times.* Reprinted with permission of Universal Press Syndicate)

Khrushchev. After sixteen tense hours, both Soviet and U.S. tanks withdrew and the crisis passed. Khrushchev later told a U.S. official that "it's been a long time since you could spank us like a little boy. Now we can swat your ass."[80] Kennedy visited West Berlin in 1963 to assuage bruised West German feelings.

Kennedy also attended to the Third World, the region he thought most vulnerable to revolution and communism and at the same time most susceptible to U.S. influence. "Nation building" became his watchword. Recognizing the force of nationalism in the Third World, the "action intellectuals" sought to use or channel it. They hoped that through modernization, or what the Kennedy team called middle-class revolution, Third World nations would grow from economic infancy to economic and political maturity, and that evolutionary economic development would ensure noncommunist political stability. The historian Michael E. Latham suggests that modernization theory, like the nineteenth-century ideology of Manifest Destiny, "defined the virtue of a benevolent United States in terms of its ability to assist peoples trapped in lower positions on a hierarchical, cultural, and developmental scale."[81] Kennedy targeted populous India because it followed a noncommunist model of economic development, bordered the People's Republic of China, and led the nonaligned movement. Although dollar assistance to India angered Pakistan, a U.S. ally, Washington nonetheless tilted toward New Delhi, especially during the Sino-Indian border war of fall 1962. In the early 1960s, India became the world's largest recipient of U.S. economic aid, for, if "we lose" the neutrals, "the balance of power could swing against us."[82]

Khrushchev's pledge of January 1961 to support wars of national liberation— such as that in Vietnam—seemed to raise the stakes in the Third World. To meet this test, U.S. counterinsurgency took several forms: the training of native police forces and bureaucrats, flood control, transportation and communications improvements, and community action projects. U.S. Special Forces units—Green Berets— received special attention. Kennedy personally elevated their status in the military and supervised their choice of equipment. Washington assumed it could apply America's finest technology in Vietnam to succeed where the French had failed.

Kennedy also created the Peace Corps. Established by executive order in 1961, this volunteer group of mostly young Americans numbered 6,646 by mid-1963 and 15,000 by mid-1966. Seeking "to live out the ideals of their culture," as one volunteer put it, they went into developing nations as teachers, agricultural advisers, and technicians.[83] Heeding Vice President Lyndon Johnson's admonition to reject any volunteers who matched the "three C's—the Communists, the consumptives, and the cocksuckers," Peace Corps officials won plaudits for their efforts to improve Third World living conditions.[84] Peace Corps monuments—irrigation systems, water pumps, larger crops—arose throughout Latin America and Africa, but the corps's humanitarian efforts fell far short of eradicating the Third World's profound squalor. In some cases, as in Ethiopia, Peace Corps volunteers went abroad with too little understanding of foreign languages and cultures.

The Kennedy administration also embarked on the Alliance for Progress in Latin America to head off Cuban-style revolution and communist subversion. Launched at the Punta del Este meeting of the Organization of American States in August 1961, the alliance envisioned spending $20 billion in funds from the United States and international organizations. In return, Latin Americans promised land and tax reform,

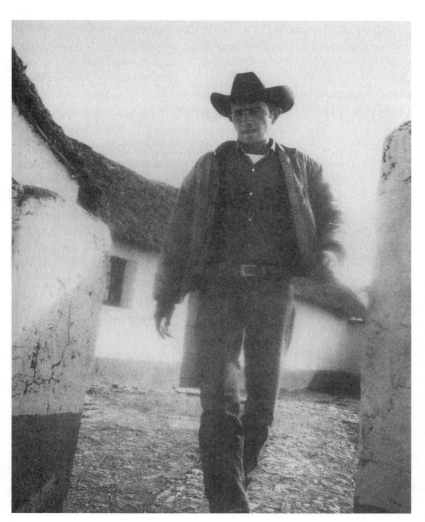

The New Frontier in the Third World. Tom Qualia, a Peace Corps volunteer in Bolivia, illustrates the belief, which the historian Fritz Fischer details in *Making Them Like Us* (1998), that the United States was "sending American youth into the new frontier of the third world." Not just a rhetorical device, "the volunteers were trained to expect conditions . . . similar to those of the mythic American West." The Peace Corps proved to be one of Kennedy's most popular programs and came to exemplify his reputed idealism. But he had little affection for the program, especially after the first director, his brother-in-law Sargent Shriver, persuaded Congress to make it independent of the State Department. After JFK lost that bureaucratic battle, Shriver complained that the president refused to give him any help, not even so much as a "light for a cigarette." (Courtesy of National Archives)

housing, and health improvements. Initiated with great fanfare, the alliance soon sputtered. American businesses did not invest as expected; the State Department dragged its feet; Latin American nationalists disliked U.S. control; elites resisted reforms and pocketed U.S. dollars; middle-class Latin Americans, whom Washington counted on, proved selfish. In the end, adult literacy and infant mortality rates improved, but Latin American economies registered unimpressive growth rates, class divisions widened, unemployment climbed, and agricultural production per person declined. U.S. interests also placed limits on how much Latin American economies could change and produced devastating environmental effects. A U.S. embargo shut off the flow of Cuban sugar to the United States (see page 161) and made increased imports from other countries a political priority to prevent the "damaging prospect of skyrocketing prices for the key commodity."[85] This demand for a single product "reduced biological diversity of wide reaches of land to little more than one species" and, along with the Alliance for Progress, helped cement U.S. "control of the Caribbean basin" and the rest of the hemisphere "during the later years of the Cold War."[86]

The difficulties of nation building appeared dramatically in the Congo, which obtained hurried independence from Belgium in mid-1960. Civil war quickly erupted. Backed by U.S. and European cobalt and copper interests, Moise Tshombe tried to detach Katanga Province from the new central government headed by Patrice Lumumba. The United States, fearing Soviet influence in "another Cuba,"

Where Are We?   The Alliance for Progress moved slowly and eventually abandoned its initial objective of reforming military dictatorships in Latin America. The diplomat Willard L. Beaulac concluded: "We told people whom we did not know how to solve problems that we did not understand." One architect of the alliance, Richard Goodwin, later admitted: "I had never set foot south of the border (aside from one orgiastic night just beyond the Texas border during the [1960] campaign which had little to do with high policy, but which an exceptionally imaginative psychiatrist might conclude had planted the seed of my love affair with Latin America)." (Edmund Valtman, *The Hartford Times*)

helped a UN mission quell the Katanga insurrection.[87] Although Lumumba was killed in 1961, by early 1963 the central Congolese government had defeated Tshombe. About a year later, however, a major leftist revolt supported by the Soviet Union, China, and Ghana broke out. With UN forces gone, the CIA soon bolstered former enemy Tshombe as the new leader of the central government, and with direct U.S. aid, including military advisers, he recruited white mercenaries. The rebels responded by terrorizing white foreigners. In November 1964 a small force of Belgian paratroopers dropped from U.S. aircraft into the Congo to rescue Belgian and U.S. citizens. The historian Thomas Borstelmann has noted that "the racial coding of the conflict in the Congo seemed brilliantly clear to most observers. Africans, African Americans, and antiracists around the world condemned Tshombe as a stooge of Belgian mining interests and were outraged by Lumumba's assassination, which they likened to an international lynching."[88] Nation building thus met resistance on both nationalist and racial grounds.

The Most Dangerous Area in the World: The Cuban Revolution and Latin America

In Latin America, events surrounding the Cuban Revolution claimed center stage. Because Cuba might export revolution to its neighbors, Kennedy considered Latin America "the most dangerous area in the world."[89] On July 26, 1953, a young lawyer and Cuban nationalist, Fidel Castro, attempted to overthrow the American-backed regime of Fulgencio Batista. Imprisoned and later released, Castro fled to Mexico. In late 1956, under the banner of the 26th of July Movement, he returned to Cuba. Almost captured, he escaped into the mountains, where for two years he augmented his guerrilla forces, gained popular support, and fought Batista's U.S.-supplied army. In January 1959, despite CIA plots to deny him power, the bearded rebel marched into Havana and initiated social and economic programs designed to reduce extensive U.S. interests that had developed since 1898 and had come to dominate Cuba's sugar, mining, and utilities industries.

Determined to dilute the North American cultural influence that they believed had undermined Cuba's national identity, the Castroites crippled the gangster-run gambling casinos and ousted from government the *batistianos* who had profited from close contact with U.S. investors. Castro avowed that "we no longer live in times when one had to worry when the American Ambassador visited the [Cuban] Prime Minister."[90] Indeed, "what happened in Guatemala will not happen here."[91]

Fearing that a successful Cuban revolution would cause the United States to "get kicked around in the hemisphere," but finding no evidence that Castro was a communist, Washington soon applied a series of tests: Cuba must respect North American–owned property, continue alignment with the United States on international questions, and adhere to a democratic politics that permitted pro-U.S. "moderates" to sustain ties with Washington.[92] Cuba failed the U.S. tests. Land reform struck at U.S. interests, the execution of Batista supporters reduced U.S. influence, and the moderates faltered in their competition with Castroite radicals. Castro postponed elections and evicted the U.S. military missions that had supported Batista.

In vehement anti–Yankee orations, Castro also called for revolutions throughout Latin America. Washington warned against his "Nasser-like ambition."[93] In late 1959 the CIA began to work with Castro's rivals to "replace" the revolutionary regime.[94] In January 1960, a furious Eisenhower labeled Castro a "mad man . . . who is going wild and harming the whole American structure."[95]

In March 1960, the president ordered the CIA to train Cuban exiles for an invasion of their homeland—this shortly after Cuba signed a trade treaty with the Soviet Union. In mid-1960, as the revolutionary government nationalized foreign properties, the United States suspended imports of Cuban sugar and then forbade U.S. exports to the island. These measures pushed Cuba toward a new economic lifeline—the Soviet Union. As Khrushchev later told Kennedy, Castro was no communist but "you are well on your way to making him a good one."[96] Embracing the thesis that Castro had moved from neutralism to communism, Washington broke diplomatic relations with Cuba in January 1961.

"The Castro regime is a thorn in the flesh," Senator J. William Fulbright argued, "but it is not a dagger in the heart."[97] Still, ignoring the U.S. contribution to Castro's anti-Americanism, President Kennedy defined Cuba as a test of will and gave the green light for a "covert" assault, dubbed "Operation Castration" by White House aide Arthur Schlesinger.[98] The CIA assured him that it could deliver another Guatemala, as in 1954. The agency predicted that the Cuban people would rise up against Castro and a CIA-hired assassin's bullet would kill him. The CIA pinpointed Bahía de Cochinos (Bay of Pigs) as the invasion site and organized a Cuban Revolutionary Council to take office. Kennedy, without consulting Congress, approved the invasion plan. He also prohibited U.S. military participation. The CIA did not protest this prohibition because "we felt that when the chips were down," Allen Dulles later wrote, "any action required for success would have been authorized [by the president] rather than permit the enterprise to fail."[99] Kennedy worried that the trained exiles would embarrass him politically if he scotched the expedition—the "disposal" problem.[100] Secretary Rusk dissented that "U.S. policy should not be driven" to drastic action "by the urgencies . . . of a single battalion of men."[101]

In mid-April 1961, 1,453 CIA-trained commandos departed from Nicaragua for Cuba (see map, page 419). They met early resistance from Castro's militia, no sympathetic insurrection occurred, and within two days the invasion had become a fiasco. One hundred fourteen commandos died, and more than 1,100 were captured. Some 150 Cuban defenders were killed. Four American pilots also died in the operation. Kennedy fumed: "I was assured by every son of a bitch I checked with . . . that the plan would succeed."[102] The adviser Walt Rostow, who pandered to Kennedy's machismo, reassured him that "we would have ample opportunity to prove we were not paper tigers in Berlin, Southeast Asia, and elsewhere."[103] After the disaster, President Kennedy, who had vetoed a desperate CIA request for U.S. air attacks during the last hours of the failing invasion, blamed the CIA and Joint Chiefs of Staff for faulty intelligence and sloppy execution. Cuban exiles cried betrayal, saying it was "like John Wayne backing down from a gunfight with an evil dwarf."[104] But even if the president had ordered more air strikes, then what? The brigade's meager forces would have had to face Castro's army of 25,000 and the nation's 200,000-strong militia.

Little sobered by the Bay of Pigs setback, the president issued secret orders making Cuba the "top priority . . . no time, money, effort, or manpower is to be spared."[105] Robert Kennedy, in Cassandra mode, warned, "If we don't want Russia to set up missile bases in Cuba, we had better decide now what we are willing to do to stop it."[106] Under Operations Mongoose and Northwoods, the Pentagon and CIA planned anti-Castro assassination plots and invasions while cooperating with anti-Castro exiles to stage hit-and-run sabotage raids against oil facilities and other island targets. Washington also tightened the economic embargo. This multitrack campaign did not knock Castro from his perch. What next? "If I had been in Moscow or Havana at that time," Secretary of Defense McNamara later remarked, "I would have believed the Americans were preparing for an invasion."[107] And rightly so, given that the Joint Chiefs of Staff in the spring of 1962 vigorously advocated "early military intervention in Cuba" even if the United States had to foment an incident to justify war.[108]

Spinning Out of Control: The Cuban Missile Crisis

Critical to understanding the missile crisis of fall 1962 is the relationship and timing between U.S. activities and Soviet/Cuban decisions to place on the island nuclear weapons that could strike areas of the United States where 92 million people

NOW IT'S OFFICIAL!

The Sun-Telegram, San Bernardino, Ca.

"Now It's Official." Jeff Yohn's anti-Castro, anti-Soviet cartoon appeared in the *San Bernadino Sun-Telegram* (California) newspaper in 1961. In July 1960, when the Soviet Union agreed to purchase Cuban sugar after the Eisenhower administration ended sugar imports from the island, Soviet premier Nikita Khrushchev declared the Monroe Doctrine dead and pledged military aid to Cuba—"if it became necessary." During the April 1961 Bay of Pigs crisis, Khrushchev told President Kennedy that the Soviets would give "to the Cuban government all the necessary assistance to repel aggression." In 1962 such aid included nuclear-tipped SS-4 missiles, setting off yet another crisis. (Library of Congress) lived. In May 1962, Soviets and Cubans first discussed the idea of such weapons; in July, during a trip by Raúl Castro to Moscow, representatives initialed a draft agreement; in late August/early September, during a trip by the Cuban leader Che Guevara to Moscow, an accord became final. These steps were taken while the United States was pressing Cuba on all fronts.

Not only did Castro learn about the assassination plots and witness the sabotage attacks, but his spies heard about possible U.S. military action against Cuba. The director of Operation Mongoose, Brigadier General Edward Lansdale, planned to ignite a revolt against Castro in October 1962 and recommended the use of U.S. forces to ensure success. American military maneuvers heightened Cuban fears. One well-publicized U.S. exercise, staged during April, included 40,000 troops and an amphibious landing on a small island near Puerto Rico. Some noisy American politicians, throughout 1962, called for the real thing: an invasion of Cuba. "Were we right or wrong to fear direct invasion?" Castro later asked.[109]

By midsummer, Cuban-Soviet plans for nuclear defense crystallized. After the Bay of Pigs invasion, Moscow had begun military shipments that included small arms, howitzers, armored personnel carriers, patrol boats, MiG jet fighters, and tanks. Under the Moscow-Havana agreement, the Soviets intended to send surface-to-air missiles (SAMs), 48 medium-range (SS-4) missiles, 32 intermediate-range (SS-5) missiles, 48 light IL-28 bombers, tactical nuclear weapons, and nuclear warheads. Kennedy rejected immediate action against the military buildup because the Soviets "may try to blockade Berlin and we would then try to blockade Cuba."[110] By mid-October only the intermediate-range missiles had not reached Cuba.

Had there been no Bay of Pigs invasion, no destructive covert activities, no assassination plots, no military maneuvers and plans, and no economic and diplomatic steps to harass, isolate, and destroy the Castro government, there might have been no Cuban missile crisis. The origins of the October 1962 crisis derived largely from the concerted U.S. campaign to quash the Cuban Revolution and from the Soviet-Cuban effort to deter the United States through missile deployment. Scholars have attributed other motives to the Soviets, such as their wanting to force negotiations on Berlin, to compel a trade for U.S. missiles stationed in Turkey, or to undermine Chinese criticism that Moscow had become too tolerant of the West. Perhaps because Pentagon officials had publicly announced decisive American nuclear superiority, Moscow also may have hoped to catch up in the nuclear arms race. But to stress only the global, Cold War dimension slights the local or regional sources of the conflict and misses the central point: Khrushchev would never have had the opportunity to install dangerous nuclear weapons in the Caribbean if the United States had not been attempting to overthrow the Cuban government. The United States helped precipitate what Dean Rusk called "an utterly crashing crisis."[111]

On October 14, a U-2 reconnaissance plane photographed medium-range (1,100-mile) missile sites under construction in Cuba. After gathering more data, American officials informed the president on October 16 that the Soviet Union had indeed placed missiles in Cuba. Kennedy created an Executive Committee of the National Security Council (Ex Comm), consisting of his "action intellectuals" and experienced diplomats from the Truman years. Joining McNamara, brother Robert, and McGeorge Bundy were Dean Acheson, Paul Nitze, and Robert Lovett, among others.

Soviet Missile Site at San Cristóbal, Cuba. This revealing U-2 photograph was taken in October 1962, when Soviet technicians were busily trying to assemble the various components of medium-range missiles. (U.S. Air Force)

Kennedy's immediate preference became clear: "We're certainly going . . . to take out these . . . missiles."[112] Ex Comm considered four options: "talk them out," "squeeze them out," "shoot them out," and "buy them out."[113] Ex Comm advisers initially gave only slight attention to negotiations and concentrated on military action. Acheson, among others, favored an air strike. Under Secretary of State George Ball countered that even a successful air strike would mean "carrying the mark of Cain on your brow for the rest of your life."[114] Air force officials reported they could not guarantee 100 percent success; some missiles might remain in place for firing against the United States. The Joint Chiefs of Staff recommended a full-scale military invasion. Although alluring, such a scheme could mean a prolonged war with Cuba, heavy U.S. casualties, and a Soviet retaliatory attack on Berlin. Ex Comm ruled out a private overture to Castro. Ambassador to the United Nations Adlai Stevenson's proposal that the United States publicly offer to trade the missiles in Turkey for those in Cuba met open derision. Ex Comm members, tired and irritable, finally settled on a naval blockade or quarantine of future arms shipments to Cuba. The quarantine, pushed ardently by McNamara as "a communications exercise, not a military operation," left open options for further escalation.[115]

Kennedy went on national television on October 22, announcing a blockade and insisting that Khrushchev "halt and eliminate this clandestine, reckless and provocative threat to world peace."[116] More than 180 warships patrolled the Caribbean, and marines reinforced the U.S. naval base at Guantánamo, on Cuba. A B-52 bomber force loaded with nuclear bombs took to the skies. On October 24, Soviet vessels approached the blockade, but the ships stopped. Assembly of the missiles already in Cuba continued. Secretary General of the United Nations U Thant urged talks; Khrushchev called for a summit meeting. Kennedy demanded removal of the missiles first. On October 26, in a confusing episode, ABC News correspondent John Scali heard a Soviet agent suggest one possible solution whereby Moscow would disengage its missiles if Washington publicly pledged not to invade Cuba. Scali reported the conversation to U.S. officials as a genuine Soviet proposal from "very high sources," but the KGB agent had not been authorized to make the offer.[117] Yet a long letter from Khrushchev soon arrived proposing much the same settlement.

The next day, October 27, the crisis intensified. A Soviet surface-to-air missile shot down a U-2 plane over Cuba. The Americans prepared to retaliate, not knowing that Soviet commanders had tactical nuclear weapons ready to use against an invasion. Later in the day, a U.S. spy aircraft strayed into Soviet air space, nearly sparking a dogfight with Soviet MiGs. More ominous, the commander of a Soviet submarine harassed by American warships prepared his nuclear torpedo, telling his crew "we will die but we will sink them all."[118] Another officer fortunately calmed him down and persuaded the commander to await further instructions from Moscow. By this time U.S. officials were analyzing another Khrushchev letter. The premier raised the stakes: He would withdraw the missiles from Cuba if the United States removed its missiles from Turkey. "We can't very well invade Cuba," JFK mused, "when we could have gotten them [Soviet ballistic missiles] out by making a deal on . . . Turkey."[119] Sidestepping this proposal, the president endorsed Khrushchev's first proposal: removal of the missiles in Cuba in exchange for a public U.S. pledge not to invade Cuba. Robert Kennedy assured the Soviets in private that the Jupiter missiles would be withdrawn from Turkey, but he warned that if Moscow divulged this secret deal, Washington would disavow it. A "very upset" Bobby said that "time is of the essence," that "many unreasonable heads" are "itching for a fight," that "a chain reaction will start that will be very hard to stop," and "millions of Americans and Russians will die."[120] If Khrushchev had balked, Rusk had secretly arranged for the United Nations to propose removing missiles from both Turkey and Cuba; "Kennedy would not let the Jupiters in Turkey become an obstacle," Rusk has insisted.[121] When Khrushchev agreed to withdraw the missiles because Soviet forces could not prevent an invasion, a livid Castro led crowds in chanting "*Nikita, mariquita, lo que se da no se quita!*" ("Nikita, you little homosexual, what is given should not be taken back!"), while the Chinese charged the Soviets with both "adventurism" and "capitulationism."[122] Having secured Cuba from invasion, Khrushchev said he was no "czarist officer who has to kill himself if I fart at a masked ball. It is better to back down than go to war."[123] Castro, moreover, believed Kennedy had halted invasion plans "to save Khrushchev, out of fear that any successor would be tougher."[124]

"We were in luck," John Kenneth Galbraith later commented, "but success in a lottery is no argument for lotteries."[125] As McGeorge Bundy remembered, the crisis came "so near to spinning out of control." Close calls (the U-2 incidents), flawed intelligence (Soviet troops in Cuba numbered 42,000, not the estimated 10,000), an inability to control local events (U.S. warships forced Soviet submarines to the surface without Kennedy's knowledge), inaccurate perceptions (the Soviet ambassador

Adlai Stevenson (1900–1965). Governor of Illinois and twice a Democratic presidential candidate, Stevenson became ambassador to the United Nations under Kennedy. During the missile crisis, Stevenson urged removal of Soviet missiles from Cuba and U.S. missiles from Turkey—advice that prompted President Kennedy to tell journalists that "Adlai wanted a Munich." Because Kennedy, in the final settlement, secretly promised the Soviets that the Jupiter missiles would be withdrawn from Turkey, the historian Mark White ranks Stevenson as "the unsung hero of the missile crisis." (National Portrait Gallery, Smithsonian Institution)

at first misreported Kennedy as a hot-tempered gambler already committed to invading Cuba)—all reveal something quite short of the artful crisis management often attributed to the president.[126] Declassified recordings of the Ex Comm meetings confirm that Washington never had a firm handle on the crisis. As the scholar James Nathan noted: "The voices are halting. The sentences are incomplete. Thoughts ramble. Memories slip and options ooze into the ether. At several points, Secretary of Defense Robert McNamara's distraction is abundantly clear." One senior aide remembers the defense secretary as "nearly hysterical," especially on the crucial day of October 27.[127] NATO allies, moreover, pointedly complained that they "can live with Soviet MRBMS, why can't [Americans]?"[128] Why not reduce tensions by publicly trading missiles in Turkey that U.S. officials privately considered "a pile of junk" and "worse than useless"?[129] Even the aftermath proved messy. Washington demanded that the IL-28 bombers that the Soviets had given to Cuba must be removed along with the missiles. Not until November 13 did Khrushchev agree to pull the IL-28s out. The three protagonists, moreover, never signed a formal agreement, leaving enough ambiguity to cause later crises in Cuban-Soviet-American relations (see pages 384, 427–428). A quarter-century later, McNamara offered a somber reassessment: "You *can't* manage" crises because of all the "misinformation, miscalculation, misjudgment, and human fallibility."[130]

The Cuban missile crisis both slowed and accelerated the Cold War. Having found communication difficult during the event, the antagonists installed a "hot line" or Teletype link between the White House and Kremlin. Both sides seemed frightened enough by nuclear danger to move toward a more accommodating relationship, producing the Limited Test Ban Treaty of July 1963, which prohibited atmospheric and underwater nuclear testing. In a speech at American University in June ("the best . . . by any president since Roosevelt," according to Khrushchev) Kennedy revealed uneasiness with large weapons spending, appealed for arms control, and asked Americans to reexamine Cold War attitudes.[131] Later Kennedy speeches, however, sounded hawkish once again.

The missile crisis carried long-term detrimental effects. The Soviet Union, revealed as a nuclear inferior, pledged to catch up in the arms race. That part of the Cold War contest was ratcheted up with new and more dangerous weapons systems. As for Cuba, despite a Castro initiative for rapprochement, U.S. officials vowed to intensify "our present nasty course."[132] The CIA quickly launched new dirty tricks and revitalized its assassination option by making contact with a cooperative Cuban official, Rolando Cubela Secades. Bearing the code name AM/LASH, he plotted with the CIA to kill Fidel Castro. On the very day that President Kennedy fell to assassination, AM/LASH rendezvoused with CIA agents in Paris, where he received a ballpoint pen rigged with a poisonous hypodermic needle. Like all other assassination plots against Castro, this one failed. The new Johnson administration put exploratory Cuban-American contacts at the United Nations on ice. From that time onward, U.S.-Cuba relations remained frozen.

In the afterglow of the missile crisis, Kennedy's civilian advisers ignored the close calls of October and rationalized their improvisations as "crisis management," especially Secretary McNamara, who believed that "carefully controlled and sharply limited military actions were reversible . . . at minimum risk and cost."[133] Proud of keeping their generals "on a short leash," they could confidently avoid nuclear holocaust, confine actual combat to Third World insurgencies, and win the Cold War through a calculated "display of superior American nerve and resolve."[134] Or so they thought, until Vietnam changed many of their minds.

Laos, Vietnam, and the Kennedy Legacy

As continued unrest destabilized Laos and Vietnam, they climbed higher on President Kennedy's agenda. Rostow saw an opportunity to use "our unexploited counterguerrilla assets"—helicopters and Special Forces units. "We are not saving them for the Junior Prom," he told Kennedy.[135] Landlocked Laos, wracked by civil war, became a testing ground. Granted independence at Geneva in 1954, Laos chose nonalignment in the Cold War when the nationalist leader Souvanna Phouma organized a coalition government of neutralists and the procommunist Pathet Lao in 1957. The Eisenhower administration opposed the government and built up the right-wing Laotian army. In 1958, CIA-backed rightists displaced Souvanna Phouma and shaped a pro-U.S. government without Pathet Lao participation. Washington dispatched military advisers to the new regime. Souvanna Phouma did return to power after a coup in 1960, but the United States again undermined him by equipping rightist forces. Souvanna soon took assistance from Moscow and North Vietnam. But in December he fled his country. For Eisenhower, "the fall of Laos to Communism" would initiate "a chain of events [that] would open the way to Communist seizure of all Southeast Asia."[136] Laos constituted the "cork in the bottle," claimed Ike.[137]

The Green Berets.   President Kennedy helped select equipment for the U.S. Army Special Forces units like this one at Fort Bragg, North Carolina. The Green Berets were trained in counterguerrilla methods and sent into the mountains and jungles of Vietnam and Laos. (U.S. Army)

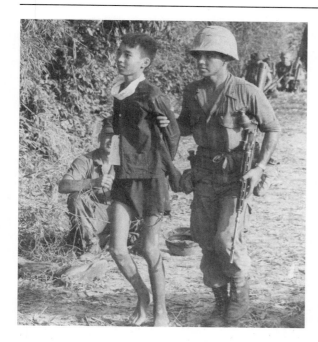

U.S. Marine and Vietcong Captive.
This photograph from 1966 underscores the
youthful innocence of two combatants in a
guerrilla war that lasted far too long.
(National Archives)

The incoming Kennedy administration did not perceive the Laotian problem much differently. As conspicuous Soviet aid flowed to the Pathet Lao, Kennedy ordered the Seventh Fleet into the South China Sea and moved marines with helicopters into Thailand. Then the Bay of Pigs disaster struck. Fearing to appear weak with one arm tied down in Cuba, Kennedy swung the other in Laos. The president instructed the several hundred U.S. military advisers in Laos, heretofore restricted to covert operations, to discard their civilian clothes and dress in more ostentatious military uniforms as a symbol of U.S. resolve. The Soviets wanted no fight in Laos. In April 1961 they endorsed Kennedy's appeal for a cease-fire. But the Pathet Lao battled on alone. The Joint Chiefs of Staff told Kennedy that they could win in Laos so long as they sent "120,000 to 140,000 men, with authority to use nuclear weapons if necessary."[138] Kennedy, however, listened more intently to retired General Douglas MacArthur, who argued that "it would be a mistake to fight in Laos" because the Chinese threat would be too great.[139]

After more than a year of continued bloodshed in Laos and hard bargaining in Geneva, W. Averell Harriman helped produce "a good, bad deal" among the major powers.[140] Laos, under a government led by Souvanna Phouma, would become neutral; it could not enter military alliances nor permit foreign military bases on its soil. Still, peace did not come. Both the United States and North Vietnam quickly violated the accords. Hanoi continued to supply the Pathet Lao and failed to remove all its troops from Laos. Washington secretly shipped arms to Souvanna's government, and the CIA also armed and trained Hmong mountain clans, an ethnic minority that gained little from the conflict while suffering "one of the highest

Strategic Hamlet, South Vietnam.
Introduced by the Diem regime in 1962 and funded by the United States, the strategic hamlet program sought to separate the NLF from its supporters among the people. The 6,000 hamlets, according to the historian David Trask, "isolated some Vietnamese from outside influences in ways reminiscent of reservations. . . . There was an effort to 'kill the Vietnamese' culturally that recalled earlier attitudes toward Native Americans." A Native American veteran agreed: "We were involved in the same kind of colonization process that was carried out by whites in this country." Many of the hamlets were poorly managed and defended, alienating the very people the Saigon government tried to win over. (Courtesy of M. W. Dow, from M. W. Dow, *Nation Building in Southeast Asia.* Boulder, Colo.: Pruett Press, 1966; rev. ed.)

mortality rates in modern war."[141] Without informing the American people, the United States began secret bombing raids against Pathet Lao forces in 1964. By then the problem of Laos derived from the country's proximity to Vietnam.

After the Bay of Pigs, the Berlin Wall, and the neutralization of Laos, Vietnam seemed to assume greater urgency. Rejecting Charles de Gaulle's warning that in Vietnam "we failed and you will fail," Kennedy advisers considered the corrupt Ngo Dinh Diem a liability, but as Vice President Lyndon B. Johnson put it, "Sh—, man, he's the only boy we got out there."[142] Kennedy said he did not want to launch a white man's war in Asia; Asians had to fight their own battles. But because he accepted the domino theory, thought that China fomented Vietnamese turmoil, and believed that nation building promised success, he expanded the U.S. presence. In January 1961, Kennedy authorized $28.4 million to enlarge the South Vietnamese army and another $12.7 million to improve the civil guard. In May he ordered 400 Special Forces soldiers and another 100 military "advisers" to South Vietnam. Meanwhile, the NLF captured more territory and accelerated the violence through assassinations of village chiefs. In October a U.S. intelligence study indicated that 80 to 90 percent of the 17,000 Vietcong in South Vietnam came from the South, not from North Vietnam, and that most of their supplies originated in the South. Although it contradicted official claims that the Vietnamese crisis started because of aggression by North Vietnam, the report apparently did not influence Kennedy.

The president in October dispatched two hawks, General Maxwell Taylor and Walt Rostow, to South Vietnam to study the war firsthand. Diem asked for more

A Suicide in Protest, Saigon. Quang Duc, a Buddhist monk aged seventy-three, set his gasoline-drenched yellow robes afire in June 1963 to protest Diem's restrictions on Buddhists. (Wide World Photos)

American military aid. The duo recommended sending 8,000 U.S. combat troops to avoid the "sickly pallor" of appeasement.[143] Rusk questioned such a "major additional commitment of American prestige to a losing horse."[144] Conscious that his decision violated the Geneva Accords but unwilling to say so publicly, Kennedy in November authorized an increase in U.S. forces or "advisers" in South Vietnam. By the end of 1961 they numbered 3,205. During the next year the figure jumped to 9,000, and at the time of Kennedy's death in November 1963 these forces had reached 16,700. American troops, helicopter units, minesweepers, and air reconnaissance aircraft went into action. In 1962, 109 Americans died and in 1963, 489. The strategic hamlet program fortified villages but proved disruptive and unpopular with villagers and permitted the NLF to appear as Robin Hoods. In February 1963, Rusk nonetheless announced that the "momentum of the Communist drive has been stopped."[145]

In May 1963 the difficulties of nation building became exposed when South Vietnamese troops opened fire on protesting and unarmed Buddhists in the city of Hue, massacring nine. The incident erupted after a Catholic provincial chief had enforced an old decree prohibiting the flying of Buddhist flags. A Catholic oligarchy governed the predominantly Buddhist population. The Buddhist demonstrations also expressed longstanding nationalist sentiment, an appeal for peace talks with the NLF, and resentment against U.S. interference in Vietnamese politics. In early June a Buddhist monk sat in a Saigon street, poured fuel over his body, and immolated himself. Appalled, Kennedy reportedly told a confidant that the Vietnamese "hate us. . . . they'll kick our asses out of there."[146] Madame Nhu chortled about Buddhist "barbecues" while her husband lamented his brother's "stupid order" about the flags.[147] During summer and fall the protest spread; so did Diem's suppression. Also, authorities arrested thousands of students. Kennedy publicly chastised Diem and reduced aid. Senior South Vietnamese generals, now aware that Diem no longer had American favor, asked U.S. officials how they would respond to a coup d'état. The new ambassador, Henry Cabot Lodge wanted to dump Diem, but officials in Washington hesitated.

Washington continued cool relations with Diem, who proved more and more resistant to U.S. advice. In early October 1963, as rumors swirled around Saigon "about secret contacts between Diem-Nhu and Ho Chi Minh," the Vietnamese generals prepared a coup.[148] Judging Diem's removal imperative to bring "this medieval country into the twentieth century," Lodge did not discourage them.[149] On November 1, as Diem "desperately radioed for assistance," he found no one listening except the "unsympathetic and the hostile."[150] The generals easily took Diem prisoner and murdered him. A few weeks later, on November 22, Kennedy himself was assassinated in Dallas. The day before his trip to Texas, Kennedy had told an aide that "we have got to review this whole thing [Vietnam] from the bottom to the top."[151] Scholars and former advisers have pointed to this and similar remarks to suggest that Kennedy would have withdrawn from Vietnam in 1965. Dean Rusk vigorously dissented, arguing that any president who left U.S. soldiers in danger merely to win reelection could not have lived "with himself or look[ed] his senior colleagues in the eye."[152] Other scholars similarly point to JFK's pledge as late as September 1963 that he was not in Vietnam "to see a war lost."[153] They argue that given Kennedy's Cold War mentality, his personal aversion to defeat, and his fear of right-wing charges that he was soft on communism, he would have pushed on in Vietnam, much as did his successor, Lyndon B. Johnson.

Nose to Nose: Lyndon B. Johnson and the World

Johnson kept on many of Kennedy's advisers. McNamara stayed until early 1968; Rusk until the end; replacing Bundy in 1966 was the zealous Walt Rostow, soon dubbed "the American Rasputin" by the veteran diplomat W. Averell Harriman.[154] Bundy called LBJ "a very majority leader president" who dealt with foreign leaders much as he had managed Senate committee chairmen from 1955 to 1961.[155] Alliance partners immediately sensed the change in presidential style. A British diplomat commented, "President Johnson is not at home in international affairs."[156] Less generous, French President Charles de Gaulle dismissed Johnson as "a cowboy radical" who "doesn't even take the trouble to pretend he's thinking"[157]

An experienced political operator, Johnson came from the poor hill territory of Texas between Fort Worth and San Antonio. He gulped his meals and talked incessantly. LBJ would thrust "his face close to the face of the person he was talking to, practically touching the other's nose," the Soviet ambassador wrote, "often pulling him closer by the lapel . . . in a heroic effort at persuasion."[158] It was "like being licked by a Great Dane," recalled one journalist.[159] Dean Acheson once called Johnson "a real centaur—part man, part horse's ass."[160] In his first year as president, LBJ helped prevent a Turkish-Greek war over Cyprus by telling the Greek ambassador: "America is an elephant. Cyprus is a flea. Greece is a flea. If these two fellows continue itching the elephant, they may just get whacked by the elephant's tail, whacked good."[161] A "credibility gap" dogged the administration, not so much because Johnson told barefaced lies, but because he consciously downplayed his commitment to "that bitch of a war" lest it divert attention from the "woman I really loved—the Great Society" domestic reform program.[162]

Abe Fortas Gets the Johnson Treatment. President Johnson used his formidable presence to cajole and persuade. Hubert Humphrey joked that LBJ at his most effective was like a "cowboy making love." Here the recipient of the famed treatment is Abe Fortas (1910–1982), Washington, D.C. lawyer, Supreme Court justice (1965–1969), and occasional presidential adviser on Vietnam. (Lyndon Baines Johnson Library)

Johnson left relations with the Soviet Union and China much as he had found them—calmer after the Cuban missile crisis but still strained and based on intense military competition. In 1967, LBJ attempted to slow the arms race when he met with Soviet premier Alexsei Kosygin in Glassboro, New Jersey. But the movement toward negotiations stalled in June 1968 when the Soviets invaded Czechoslovakia the day before a Johnson-Kosygin summit was to be announced. The coincidence of these events, said Rusk, "was like throwing a dead fish" in the president's face.[163] The United States, the Soviet Union, and more than fifty other nations signed a nuclear nonproliferation treaty in 1968 (ratified in 1969), a pledge not to spread nuclear weapons to other nations. But France and China, both members of the nuclear club, refused to sign. Nonsigner India joined the elite nuclear club in 1974, demonstrating again the diffusion of power in the international system.

In Latin America, smoldering nationalism, frequent military coups, and Castro's defiant survival defined Johnson's policies. Johnson put Assistant Secretary of State Thomas C. Mann in charge of the Alliance for Progress, and it soon withered away from neglect. Mann's declaration that the United States would support anticommunist military regimes received its first test in 1964, when the United States embraced a military coup in Brazil. That same year, Panamanians rioted against U.S. control of the Canal Zone. A macho-minded LBJ claimed that "I know these Latin Americans. . . . They'll come right into your yard and take it over if you let them. And the next day they'll be right up on your porch, barefoot, and weighing one hundred and thirty pounds and they'll take that too. But if you say to 'em right at the start 'hold on, just a minute,' they'll know they're dealing with somebody who'll stand up."[164]

Johnson had another opportunity to act on this self-proclaimed expertise when rebels launched a civil war in the Dominican Republic in 1965. Bragging that "he had just taken an action that will prove that Democratic presidents can deal with Communists as strongly as any Republican," he sent 24,000 soldiers to the Caribbean island.[165] He wanted to prevent the return of Juan Bosch as president. Bosch had initially won an election in 1962, but a coup ousted him in 1963. LBJ believed that a small number of communists controlled the rebels ("Our choice is . . . Castro or intervention") even though some of his advisers disagreed (McNamara scoffed, "I don't believe fifty-eight people" can control a rebellion).[166] As criticism mounted, Johnson accused Bosch's supporters of mutilating corpses, ordering his ambassador to "find some headless bodies."[167] In the end, a military regime quashed the democratic rebellion with U.S. support.

Congressional critics called for the resignations of Mann and U.S. ambassador to the Dominican Republic W. Tapley Bennett, but Johnson fumed, "I'm not going to let . . . a bunch of little yellow pinkos run them out of the government."[168] Proud of his actions, Johnson announced that the United States would henceforth prevent any communist government from taking office in the hemisphere. This frank statement of hegemony attempted to maintain the U.S. sphere in Latin America. (In 1968, the Soviets issued a similar statement after their invasion of Czechoslovakia, justifying their dominance of Warsaw Pact countries.)

"The Biggest Damned Mess": Johnson's Vietnam War

During Johnson's five years in office, Vietnam consumed his energies, his ambitions, his reputation. After Diem's death, "the NLF was ready and eager" to form a neutralist coalition government, according to a former North Vietnamese diplomat. He chided Americans: "There was an opportunity and you missed it."[169] Despite support for such a solution among American allies, the United Nations, and some U.S. officials, Johnson would have none of it. In December 1963, he insisted on "victory" to prevent "a communist takeover."[170] For Johnson and his advisers, Vietnam occupied only one front in the Cold War; to falter in Southeast Asia, they believed, would send a false signal that the United States would retreat elsewhere, too.

By early 1964, however, the war was going badly. "We ought [not] to take this government seriously," said Ambassador Lodge (who treated the South Vietnamese like an "emperor dealing with barbarian tribes"). "We have to do what we think we ought to do regardless of what the Saigon government does."[171] The Army of the Republic of Vietnam (ARVN) proved ineffective in the field, and desertions ran high. The strategic hamlet program collapsed. A coup by General Nguyen Khanh brought little progress, as Secretary McNamara reported that the Vietcong controlled 40 percent of the South Vietnamese countryside by March 1964. "We're getting into another Korea," LBJ grumbled in May. "I don't think it's worth fighting for and I don't think we can get out. It's just the biggest damned mess."[172] The president worried a great deal about a resurgent right wing, arguing that the loss of China and the stalemate in Korea may have sparked McCarthyism, but they "were chicken shit compared to what might happen if we lost Vietnam."[173]

Deterioration in Vietnam gave Johnson's political foes an issue in the 1964 presidential campaign. Conservative Republican candidate Barry Goldwater urged military action against Ho Chi Minh's North. The president publicly chided Goldwater as a dangerous warmonger. But in private his administration was already implementing plans and developing new contingencies to increase the U.S. presence in South Vietnam and U.S. pressure against North Vietnam. In early 1964, Washington dispatched more military advisers (reaching 23,000 by the end of the year). Air strikes hit Laos, through which supplies flowed south. In February a covert operation, tagged OPLAN 34-A, began to air-drop commandos into the North to conduct sabotage. To stiffen the Khanh government and to give Johnson flexibility to

NLF Tunnels. One writer described "a formless war against a formless enemy who evaporated into the morning jungle mists only to materialize in some unexpected place." When a Vietnamese communist was told that his side had never beaten U.S. troops in a major battle, he replied: "That is correct. It is also irrelevant." Guerrillas win as long as they do not lose. Well-hidden tunnels helped the NLF defy superior U.S. military power. The most famous tunnels, in the Cu Chi region near Saigon, served as a staging area for the Tet offensive. (U.S. Army)

reverse the negative trend in Vietnam, aides urged the president in June to ask Congress for a resolution "conveying our firmness of purpose in Southeast Asia."[174]

On August 2, 1964, North Vietnamese torpedo patrol boats opened fire on the American destroyer *Maddox* some ten miles offshore. American aircraft from the U.S.S. *Ticonderoga* entered the fray. U.S. forces drove off the attackers, sinking one boat and damaging others, with no American casualties. The *Maddox* was on an espionage mission, called a "DeSoto patrol," collecting intelligence on radar and coastal defenses. As the president admitted privately, "we were playing around up there" in support of an OPLAN 34-A operation against two islands, "and they came out, gave us a warning, and we knocked hell out of 'em."[175] After the incident, almost as if to bait North Vietnam, the *Maddox* and *C. Turner Joy* steered to within four miles of the islands. Rusk remarked: "If they [North Vietnamese] do it again, they'll get another sting."[176]

After dark on August 4, the captain of the *Maddox* interpreted his sonar data to mean that North Vietnamese gunboats had attacked the two ships. The *Maddox* and *C. Turner Joy* fired away wildly and American warplanes flew in to help. No evidence has ever confirmed a North Vietnamese attack. The ship's radar may have picked up a "'Tonkin Spook,' a radar anomaly found in the Gulf of Tonkin and . . . a few other limited areas."[177] The cause is unknown, but theories include weather patterns and seabirds. James B. Stockdale, who flew a Crusader jet from the *Ticonderoga* that night, saw "no boats, no wakes, no richochets off boats, no boat impacts, no torpedo wakes—nothing but black sea and American firepower."[178] Chinese intelligence correctly informed Hanoi that the second incident was "not an intentional act by the Americans" but caused by "mistaken judgment, based on wrong information."[179]

Despite the CIA's report that the North Vietnamese were simply defending their territory against commando raids, Johnson exploited the moment to punish North Vietnam and to seek passage of a congressional resolution. On August 4, the president announced air strikes against the North. Saying nothing about destroyer operations against the North, he charged the enemy with deliberate aggression in international waters. Johnson consciously misled the American people and the Congress. The "Tonkin Gulf Resolution" passed on August 7 by huge margins, 416 to 0 in the House and 88 to 2 in the Senate. Many voted "aye" unenthusiastically. Only Senators Ernest Gruening of Alaska and Wayne Morse of Oregon dissented. The resolution authorized the president to "take all necessary measures to repel armed attack against the forces of the United States and to prevent further aggression."[180] The resolution, said Johnson, was "like grandma's nightshirt—it covered everything."[181] In 1970, regretting this open-ended concession to the president, the Senate repealed it.

After LBJ safely won reelection in November 1964, the Pentagon expected him to escalate quickly in Vietnam. But the president hesitated, seeming a "querulous wall-flower, disappointingly reluctant to join the war dance in Southeast Asia."[182] On February 7, 1965, the NLF attacked an American airfield at Pleiku and killed eight Americans. McGeorge Bundy warned that a response should be couched in terms of defending the Vietnamese since the United States should not "get in a position that only white men get avenged."[183] By March, the United States had initiated a sustained bombing program—Operation Rolling Thunder—against the North. When the Joint Chiefs of Staff in April urged calling up the reserves to "show the American people we were serious," the president said: "You leave the American people to me. I know more about . . . [them] than anybody in this room."[184] With 80,000 U.S. troops in the South by July, the military asked for 100,000 more. On July 21 the president convened his high-level advisers. Only Under Secretary of State George W. Ball argued that the United States could not win a protracted war in an Asian jungle. Sending more troops would be "like giving cobalt treatment to a terminal cancer case," he warned. Johnson jumped in: "But, George, wouldn't all these countries say that Uncle Sam was a paper tiger," with America losing its credibility? Ball answered, "The worse blow would be that the mightiest power on earth is unable to defeat a handful of guerrillas."[185]

Friction between Johnson and his military advisers accompanied the decision to escalate. "Bomb, bomb, bomb. That's all you know," LBJ bellowed at one point. "You're not giving me . . . any solutions for this damn little pissant country."[186] Unwilling to let "some military idiots talk him into World War III," the president once told the Joint Chiefs to "get the hell out of my office."[187] Cowed by such tirades, the military professionals ("five silent men") never confronted Johnson with "the total forces they believed would ultimately be required in Vietnam."[188] The result was a McNamara-dominated strategy of graduated pressure, in which ground forces went to Vietnam in increments. The defense secretary contended: "It won't be that the South Vietnamese can win. But it will be clear to Hanoi that Hanoi can't win."[189] Incremental escalation also aimed at minimizing the chance of Chinese intervention. LBJ knew that all Pentagon war plans called for the use of nuclear weapons in such a contingency. In 1964, Rusk had warned the South Vietnamese government "that if escalation brought about a major Chinese attack, it would also involve use of nuclear arms."[190]

Caught in Battle. A Vietnamese peasant mother and her children emerge after battle between ARVN forces and Vietcong guerrillas near the village of Phung Hiep on July 23, 1965. Such a photograph is an exception to the caricatured images of the Vietnamese at war—"the shadowy foe darting through the underbrush or lying crumpled on the ground, the prostitute or crowd of children outside an American base camp, the venal official hobbling the Saigon government's war effort, the child in frightful flight from napalm," as the historian Michael H. Hunt has observed. (National Archives)

By the end of the year nearly 200,000 American troops were fighting in Vietnam; a year later the number reached 385,000. Not wanting to jeopardize Great Society reforms, Johnson built up forces without mobilizing the reserves or raising taxes. As Rusk later said: "In a nuclear world it is just too dangerous for an entire people to get too angry and we deliberately tried to do in cold blood what perhaps can only be done in hot blood."[191]

In 1966 American bombers hit oil depots in the North, and by midyear 70 percent of the North's storage capacity had been destroyed. With North Vietnamese and NLF forces increasing from 116,000 to 282,000 during the 1965–1967 period, the heavy bombing apparently had little impact on the enemy's ability to resist. During 1965–1968 the United States tried, in Air Force General Curtis Lemay's infamous phrase, "to bomb them back into the stone age" by dropping 400 tons of ordnance per day.[192] But the United States lost 918 aircraft valued at $6 billion. By war's end more than 7 million tons of U.S. bombs had battered Vietnam, the equivalent of 400 Hiroshima atomic blasts. General William Westmoreland kept asking for more troops, even though Secretary McNamara reported in October 1966 that "pacification has, if anything, gone backward."[193] The president nonetheless kept sending troops—peaking at 543,400 in early 1969.

At a "Wise Men's" meeting in November 1967, George Ball made "his usual plea for extrication to the usual deaf ears." Then he lost his temper: "You're like a flock of buzzards sitting on a fence, sending the young men off to be killed."[194] President Johnson took comfort in simplistic historical analogies: "Just like FDR and Hitler, just like Wilson and the Kaiser," Americans had to stop "aggression."[195]

In this period of escalation, 1965–1968, the bloodshed and dislocation staggered the Vietnamese people. Under General Westmoreland's ("Waste-more-men") questionable strategy of "attrition," U.S. and South Vietnamese forces bombed and destroyed villages that harbored suspected Vietcong, the "Charlie."[196] Hundreds of thousands of civilians died, many from fiery napalm attacks in areas called "free fire zones." "After . . . a while you forget that there are people down there," an American pilot explained.[197] Counting enemy bodies became "a macabre statistical competition" for Captain Colin Powell, who recalled the nightly ritual: " 'How many did your platoon get?' 'I don't know. We saw two for sure.' 'Well, if you saw two there were probably eight. So let's say ten.' "[198] To deny the enemy food and to expose hideouts, American defoliation teams sprayed chemicals such as Agent Orange on crops and forests, denuding the landscape and inadvertently exposing GIs to the dioxin-tainted herbicide. (After the war, some 39,000 veterans with cancer and nerve diseases filed claims with the U.S. government.) Beginning in 1967 the CIA supervised the Phoenix program, in which South Vietnamese operatives infiltrated rural areas and "neutralized" thousands of suspected Vietcong. "Infiltration of a couple of guys into our ranks created tremendous difficulties," a NLF leader later admitted.[199]

To many Americans, the My Lai massacre of March 16, 1968, where a U.S. Army platoon commanded by Lieutenant William Calley shot to death scores of helpless women and children, or "gooks," represented a depravity unbecoming a civilized nation. Because of official cover-ups, the My Lai story did not become public until twenty months later. Despite documented incidents of the deliberate shooting, raping, and torturing of civilians and prisoners, however, most U.S. soldiers were not committing atrocities. They were trying instead to save their young lives—the average age of the Vietnam GI was only nineteen—from snipers, booby traps, ambushes, mortar attacks, and firefights. Etched in their memories, too, was the inhospitable environment, "as if the sun and land were in league with the Vietcong," recalled the marine officer Philip Caputo in *A Rumor of War* (1977), "wearing us down, driving us mad, killing us."[200]

As the Doves Dissent, the Peace Efforts Fail

"Can the tortoise of progress in Vietnam stay ahead of the hare of dissent at home?" one official asked.[201] It could not. Students and faculties at universities began to hold "teach-ins" in 1965, first at the University of Michigan in March. Hundreds refused military draft calls and went to jail or fled to Canada. "By the early 1970s, there were more than 20,000 war resisters in Toronto" alone.[202] Others obtained deferments. Sit-ins greeted representatives of major corporations such as Dow Chemical, a maker of napalm, when they attempted to recruit on campus. In early 1967, 300,000 demonstrators marched in New York City; in November, 100,000 surrounded the Pentagon. Fed misleading information from the FBI and CIA, LBJ told sympathetic senators that communists "were going into colleges and the faculties and the student bodies" to stir up these protests.[203]

Prominent intellectuals, such as the linguist Noam Chomsky, the political scientist Hans Morgenthau, Jr., and the disaffected Arthur M. Schlesinger, Jr., called for withdrawal from Vietnam. Business executives, lawyers, and members of the

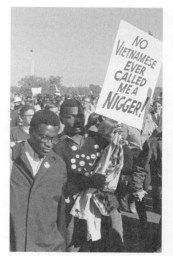

"Black Power" and the War. At the March on the Pentagon in 1967, a protester carries a sign symbolizing the coincidence of the civil rights and antiwar movements. Beginning in 1965, the slogan Black Power marked a more radical turn in the fight to end racial discrimination. New groups such as the Black Panther Party protested racism and the war, stating that "we will not fight and kill other people of color in the world, who like black people, are being victimized by the white racist government in America." (Frank Wolfe, LBJ Library Collection)

Vietnam War "Doves." Left to right, Senators J. William Fulbright, Mike Mansfield, Frank Church, and Wayne Morse—all members of the Foreign Relations Committee and critics of U.S. intervention in Vietnam. Church holds a portrait of Senator William E. Borah, who chaired the committee from 1925 to 1933. A cheerful maverick, Morse claimed that Vietnam "makes my blood boil. That purges me; it keeps me fit." Of Fulbright, Morse said: "Bill's a bleeder. He keeps agonizing over it." (Frank Church Collection, Boise State University Library)

clergy, too, joined antiwar groups. The pediatrician Benjamin Spock and Dr. Martin Luther King, Jr., the civil rights crusader, added their voices to the protest, as did the singers Pete Seeger and Joan Baez. The U.S. ambassador to India captured Third World peoples' hostility to U.S. military intervention when he commented that they saw a "powerful white Western nation attempting to clobber a small underdog brown-skinned Asian nation."[204] Radical pacifists, liberal reformers, conservative constitutionalists, strategic realists, religious moralists, hippies, trade unionists, and many others melded into a national, largely unstructured antiwar movement. Often stereotyped as the haven for long-haired, bearded college-age youth, the movement actually encompassed a wide spectrum of people. The strongest opposition to the war came from four groups: older, black, female, and lower-class Americans. Younger, white, male, and middle-class citizens tended to support escalation of the war and follow the president's lead—at least until 1968. In February of that year, after Tet, a majority of polled Americans for the first time said that the United States had made a "mistake" in sending troops to Vietnam.

The critics offered multifaceted arguments: the war cost too much and weakened needed reform at home; America's youth was dying—30,000 by 1968; inflation and a worsening balance of payments undermined the economy; the ghastly bloodshed and U.S. conduct of the war were immoral; the war damaged relations with allies and foes alike; Washington and Saigon could not win the war; the president was undermining the constitutional system of checks and balances; U.S. behavior in Vietnam debased the American principles of fair play and right to self-determination; and dissension was ripping domestic America apart. Above all else, the United States had succumbed to a debilitating globalism of anticommunism, overcommitment, and overextension. In short, some critics complained about how the war was being conducted, whereas others, more searching, criticized globalism and the containment doctrine itself.

The growing public disaffection encouraged dissent in Congress. Lingering doubts about the Tonkin Gulf Resolution prompted Senator Fulbright to hold publicly televised hearings before his committee. LBJ ridiculed him as Senator "Half Bright"—"a crybaby" because "I can't . . . kiss him every morning."[205] The president also used threats to quash questions from Congress, shouting at Senator Robert Kennedy, "I'll destroy you and every one of your dove friends. . . . You'll be dead politically in six months."[206] But dissenting senators kept asking the administration to explain exactly what in Vietnam the United States was trying to contain. The Soviet Union? China? North Vietnam? The Vietcong? Rusk settled on China as the main culprit, especially after the Chinese leader Lin Biao declared in 1965 that China would encourage wars of national liberation in the Third World. China did urge a protracted struggle in Vietnam. Mao thought guerrilla war might last a hundred years and promised metaphorically, "So long as the green mountain is there how can you lack for firewood."[207] But Hanoi and Beijing proved to be "both comrades and adversaries" in a contentious relationship.[208] Through 1966, China sent supplies along with 320,000 noncombat troops. Mao also assured Hanoi that more would be forthcoming if the U.S. forces crossed into North Vietnam: "The Chinese had legs . . . and if the United States could send troops to North Vietnam, why could not the Chinese?"[209] Hanoi's distrust of Beijing's intentions surfaced immediately, with a Chinese official sarcastically querying Hanoi, "Are you suspicious of us because we have so much enthusiasm? Do the Chinese want to take control over Vietnam?"[210] By 1966, North Vietnam tilted toward Moscow in the Sino-Soviet split and dubbed China "La Grand Impuissance" (Great Nonpower).[211] Moscow, Beijing, and Washington attempted to manipulate events in Vietnam to serve their national interests, but Hanoi acted as no one's puppet.

The administration's warning about Beijing carried little weight with Congress, especially after George F. Kennan, in his testimony at the Fulbright hearings, insisted that containment would not work in Asia and recommended gradual withdrawal. By early 1968, Senators Eugene McCarthy and Robert F. Kennedy mounted antiwar candidacies to displace LBJ as the Democratic nominee. As the United States continued to struggle to defeat what Johnson dismissed as a "raggedy-ass little fourth-rate country," doubters grew more numerous within administration ranks.[212] McNamara's increasing disenchantment and 1967 resignation angered the president, who blamed the defense secretary's departure on Robert Kennedy's telling McNamara he was "a murderer."[213] Yet Johnson resisted anything that would appear to be defeat in Vietnam.

Throughout the 1965–1968 escalation period, international groups suggested avenues for peace. "Everybody thinks Hanoi is ready; the Pope, the Poles, the Russians, but when you really get down to it," Johnson lamented. Hanoi would not "budge."[214] Moscow, for its part, pushed negotiations to eliminate the war as an obstacle to

Antiwar Buttons. Opponents of the Vietnam War demonstrated their protest in a panoply of buttons urging withdrawal and peace. (Division of Political History, Smithsonian Institution)

warmer ties with Washington and out of fear that China would not "show restraint if the war continued to escalate."[215] Although the United States and North Vietnam continued to make gestures toward negotiations, mistrust and fears about the domestic consequences of compromise hindered success. Johnson believed "you don't negotiate until the other side must want to negotiate. . . . That we know, from Munich on, that when you give, the dictators feed on raw meat."[216] Historical analogies also impeded compromise on the Vietnamese side. The NLF leadership felt "haunted" by the Geneva Conference, where they believed Ho Chi Minh had treated the South "as a sacrificial animal."[217] In 1966, General Giap warned a Polish diplomat that if North Vietnam opened talks with the United States, it could face NLF "accusations of 'selling' their interests in return for ending the bombing in the North."[218] Despite internal divisions among the Vietnamese, Washington appears to bear the greatest responsibility for squandering opportunities to end the war in 1966 and 1967. Two promising initiatives, MARIGOLD and SUNFLOWER, collapsed because Washington, especially National Security Adviser Walt Rostow, insisted on "capitulation by a Communist force that is far from beaten."[219] The bombing of the North and Hanoi's aid to the NLF proved to be key sticking points. MARIGOLD died when LBJ failed to call off a previously scheduled round of bombings, and SUNFLOWER withered when the United States insisted that Hanoi would have to prove it had stopped sending personnel and supplies down the jungle paths known as the Ho Chi Minh Trail (see map, page 352) before Washington would halt its aerial bombardment.

And then the Tet offensive of early 1968 wrought its havoc; military escalation and Johnson's political career derailed; the bombing scaled down; and the peace talks finally began in Paris. In November, Richard M. Nixon defeated Vice President Hubert Humphrey for the presidency. In 1961 John F. Kennedy had asked Americans to "pay any price" and "bear any burden." By 1969, many refused. The new Nixon administration faced the task of maintaining U.S. interests abroad while at the same time mollifying the evident discontent with globalism and the Vietnam War.

FURTHER READING FOR THE PERIOD 1961–1969

Several works cited in Chapters 7 and 8 on the Cold War and the Third World also survey this period, and not all are repeated here.

For John F. Kennedy and his foreign relations, see James D. Barber, *The Presidential Character* (1992); Irving Bernstein, *Promises Kept* (1991); Michael Beschloss, *The Crisis Years* (1991); Douglas Brinkley and Richard T. Griffiths, eds., *John F. Kennedy and Europe* (1999); Kenneth R. Crispell and Carlos F. Gomez, *Hidden Illness in the White House* (1989); Robert Dallek, *An Unfinished Life* (2003); Robert H. Ferrell, *Ill-Advised* (1992); Lawrence E. Freedman, *Kennedy's Wars* (2000); James N. Giglio, *The Presidency of John F. Kennedy* (1991); James N. Giglio and Stephen G. Rabe, *Debating the Kennedy Presidency* (2003); Seymour Hersh, *The Other Side of Camelot* (1997); Timothy P. Maga, *John F. Kennedy and New Frontier Diplomacy* (1994); Bert Park, *Ill-Fated History* (1993); Herbert S. Parmet, *JFK* (1983); Thomas G. Paterson, ed., *Kennedy's Quest for Victory* (1989); Richard Reeves, *President Kennedy* (1993); Thomas C. Reeves, *A Question of Character* (1991); W. J. Rorabaugh, *Kennedy and the Promise of the Sixties* (2002); J. Richard Snyder, ed., *John F. Kennedy* (1988); Mark J. White, *Kennedy* (1998); and Garry Wills, *The Kennedy Imprisonment* (1982). For Kennedy and specific countries and crises, see below.

For Lyndon B. Johnson and his administration (see Vietnam below), see Irving Bernstein, *Guns or Butter* (1996); Vaughn D. Bornet, *The Presidency of Lyndon B. Johnson* (1983); H. W. Brands, *The Wages of Globalism* (1995) and ed., *The Foreign Policies of Lyndon Johnson* (1999); David Burner, *Questioning History* (1996);

Warren I. Cohen and Nancy B. Tucker, eds., *Lyndon Johnson Confronts the World* (1995); Paul K. Conkin, *Big Daddy from the Pedernales* (1986); Robert Dallek, *Flawed Giant* (1998); Robert A. Divine, *Exploring the Johnson Years* (1981) and ed., *The Johnson Years* (1987–1994); Paul Y. Hammond, *LBJ and the Presidential Management of Foreign Relations* (1993); and Diane Kunz, ed., *The Diplomacy of the Crucial Decade* (1994).

For other prominent Americans, see Leroy Ashby and Rod Gramer, *Fighting the Odds* (1994) (Frank Church); William C. Berman, *William Fulbright and the Vietnam War* (1988); James A. Bill, *George Ball* (1997); Kai Bird, *The Color of Truth* (1998) (Bundy); Douglas Brinkley, *Dean Acheson* (1992); Jeff Broadwater, *Adlai Stevenson* (1994); David L. DiLeo, *George Ball, Vietnam, and the Rethinking of Containment* (1991); Gilbert C. Fite, *Richard B. Russell, Jr.* (1991); Dorothy Fosdick, ed., *Staying the Course* (1987) (Henry Jackson); Robert A. Goldberg, *Barry Goldwater* (1995); Walter Isaacson and Evan Thomas, *The Wise Men* (1986); Robert David Johnson, *Ernest Gruening and the American Dissenting Tradition* (1998); John B. Martin, *Adlai Stevenson and the World* (1977); John Prados, *Lost Crusader* (2003) (William Colby); Barry Riccio, *Walter Lippmann* (1989); Howard B. Schaffer, *Chester Bowles* (1993); Thomas J. Schoenbaum, *Waging Peace and War* (1988) (Rusk); Deborah Shapley, *Promise and Power* (1993) (McNamara); Carol Solberg, *Hubert Humphrey* (1984); Ronald Steel, *Walter Lippmann and the American Century* (1980); Evan Thomas, *Robert Kennedy* (2000); Randall B. Woods, *Fulbright* (1995); and Thomas W. Zeiler, *Dean Rusk* (1999).

Economic issues and trade policy are scrutinized in David P. Calleo, *The Imperious Economy* (1982); Frances J. Gavin, *Gold, Dollars, and Power* (2003); and Thomas Zeiler, *American Trade and Power in the 1960s* (1992).

Europe, the Berlin crisis, and the nuclear arms race are the subjects of Desmond Ball, *Politics and Force Levels* (1980); McGeorge Bundy, *Danger and Survival* (1988); Frank Costigliola, *France and the United States* (1992); Frank A. Mayer, *Adenauer and Kennedy* (1996); Kendrick Oliver, *Kennedy, Macmillan, and the Nuclear Test Ban Treaty* (1998); Thomas Risse-Kappen, *Cooperation Among Democracies* (1995); Thomas A. Schwartz, *Lyndon Johnson and Europe* (2003); Glenn T. Seaborg and Benjamin S. Loeb, *Kennedy, Khrushchev, and the Test Ban* (1981) and *Stemming the Tide* (1987) (arms control); Jeremi Suri, *Power and Protest* (2003); Andreas Wenger, *Living with Peril: Eisenhower, Kennedy, and Nuclear Weapons* (1997); and Peter Wyden, *The Wall* (1989).

Aspects of relations with the Third World in the 1960s include Warren Bass, *Support Any Friend* (2003) (Israel); Abraham Ben-Zvi, *Decade of Transition* (1998) (Israel); Gabriel Kolko, *Confronting the Third World* (1988); Michael F. Latham, *Modernization as Ideology* (2000); Timothy P. Maga, *John F. Kennedy and the New Pacific Community* (1990); Robert J. McMahon, *Cold War on the Periphery* (1994) (India and Pakistan) and *The Limits of Empire* (1999); Michael B. Oren, *Six Days of War* (2002) (Middle East); David L. Schalk, *War and the Ivory Tower* (1991) (Algeria); and Penny M. von Eschen, *Race Against Empire: Black Americans and Anticolonialism* (1998).

For the Cuban Revolution, Fidel Castro, Bay of Pigs, and missile crisis, see Jules Benjamin, *The United States and the Origins of the Cuban Revolution* (1990); James G. Blight, *The Shattered Crystal Ball* (1990); James G. Blight and Philip Brenner, *Sad and Luminous Days* (2002); James G. Blight and Peter Kornbluh, eds., *Politics of Illusion* (1998) (Bay of Pigs); James G. Blight and David A. Welch, *On the Brink* (1989); James G. Blight et al., *Cuba on the Brink* (1993); Jorge Domínguez, *To Make a World Safe for Revolution* (1989); Alexander Fursenko and Timothy Naftali, *"One Hell of a Gamble"* (1997); Raymond L. Garthoff, *Reflections on the Cuban Missile Crisis* (1989); Alexander L. George, ed., *Avoiding War* (1991); Alice L. George, *Awaiting Armageddon* (2003); Trumbull Higgins, *The Perfect Failure* (1987) (Bay of Pigs); Donna R. Kaplowitz, *Anatomy of a Failed Embargo: U.S. Sanctions Against Cuba* (1998); Richard Lebow and Janice G. Stein, *We All Lost the Cold War* (1994); Felix Masud-Piloto, *From Welcomed Exiles to Illegal Immigrants* (1995) (Cuban migration); Ernest R. May and Philip D. Zelikow, eds., *The Kennedy Tapes* (1997); Philip Nash, *The Other Missiles of October* (1997) (Jupiters); James A. Nathan, *Anatomy of the Cuban Missile Crisis* (2001); James A. Nathan, ed., *The Cuban Missile Crisis Revisited* (1992); Louis A. Pérez, Jr., *Cuba and the United States* (1997); Scott D. Sagan, *The Limits of Safety* (1993); Sheldon M. Stern, *Averting "The Final Failure"* (2003); Tad Szulc, *Fidel* (1986); Victor A. Triay, *Fleeing Castro* (1998); Lucien S. Vandenbroucke, *Perilous Options* (1993) (Bay of Pigs); Robert Weisbrot, *Maximum Danger* (2002); and Mark J. White, *The Cuban Missile Crisis* (1996) and *Missiles in Cuba* (1997).

U.S.–Latin America relations, including the Alliance for Progress, are explored in Eric Thomas Chester, *Rag-Tags, Scum, Riff-Raff, and Commies* (2001) (Dominican Republic); Piero Gleijeses, *The Dominican Crisis* (1978); Walter LaFeber, *Inevitable Revolutions* (1993); Lester D. Langley, *America and the Americas* (1989); Ruth

Leacock, *Requiem for Revolution* (1990) (Brazil); Abraham F. Lowenthal, *Exporting Democracy* (1991); John D. Martz, ed., *United States Policy in Latin America* (1988); Stephen G. Rabe, *The Most Dangerous Area in the World* (1999) (JFK); L. Ronald Scheman, ed., *The Alliance for Progress* (1988); Lars Schoultz, *Beneath the United States* (1998); and W. Michael Weis, *Cold Warriors & Coups D'État* (1993) (Brazil).

Studies of U.S. relations with Africa include David N. Gibbs, *The Political Economy of Third World Intervention* (1991) (Congo); Richard D. Mahoney, *JFK* (1983); Thomas J. Noer, *Cold War and Black Liberation* (1985); and Joseph E. Thompson, *American Policy and African Famine* (1990) (Nigeria).

For the Peace Corps, see Julius A. Amin, *The Peace Corps in Cameroon* (1992); Fritz Fischer, *Making Them Like Us* (1998); Elizabeth Cobbs Hoffman, *All You Need Is Love* (1998); and Gerald T. Rice, *The Bold Experiment* (1985).

For Vietnam, especially the experience of the 1960s, see David L. Anderson, ed., *Shadow on the White House* (1993); Loren Baritz, *Backfire* (1985); David M. Barrett, *Uncertain Warriors* (1993); Larry Berman, *Planning a Tragedy* (1982) and *Lyndon Johnson's War* (1989); Anne Blair, *Lodge in Vietnam* (1995); Robert K. Brigham, *Guerrilla Diplomacy: The NLF's Foreign Relations and the Viet Nam War* (1999); Robert Buzzanco, *Vietnam and the Transformation of American Life* (1999); Robert Buzzanco and Marilyn Young, eds., *Companion to the Vietnam War* (2002); Larry Cable, *Unholy Grail* (1991); Philip E. Catton, *Diem's Final Failure* (2002); Kenneth Conboy and Dale Andrade, *Spies and Commandos* (2000); Gerard DeGroot, *A Noble Cause?* (2000); William J. Duiker, *U.S. Containment Policy and the Conflict in Indochina* (1994); John Ernst, *Forging a Fateful Alliance* (1998) (Michigan State University contracts and Vietnam); Ilya V. Gaiduk, *The Soviet Union and the Vietnam War* (1996) and *Confronting Vietnam* (2003); Lloyd C. Gardner, *Pay Any Price* (1995); William C. Gibbons, *The U.S. Government and the Vietnam War* (1986–1994); Fred Greenstein et al., eds., *How Presidents Test Reality* (1989); Patrick L. Hatcher, *The Suicide of an Elite: American Internationalists and Vietnam* (1990); George C. Herring, *LBJ and Vietnam* (1994) and *America's Longest War* (1996); Paul Hendrickson, *The Living and the Dead* (1996); Gary R. Hess, *Vietnam and the United States* (1998); Michael H. Hunt, *Lyndon Johnson's War* (1996); Susan Jeffords, *The Remasculinization of America: Gender and the Vietnam War* (1989); Howard Jones, *Death of a Generation* (2003); George McT. Kahin, *Intervention* (1986); David Kaiser, *American Tragedy* (2000); Stanley Karnow, *Vietnam* (1991); Yuen Foong Khong, *Analogies of War* (1992); Gabriel Kolko, *Anatomy of a War* (1985); A. J. Langguth, *Our Vietnam* (2000); David W. Levy, *The Debate over Vietnam* (1991); Fredrik Logevall, *Choosing War* (1999); Robert Mann, *A Grand Delusion* (2001); H. R. McMaster, *Dereliction of Duty* (1997); Robert S. McNamara et al., *Argument Without End* (1999); Edwin F. Moïse, *Tonkin Gulf and the Escalation of the Vietnam War* (1996); Joseph G. Morgan, *The Vietnam Lobby* (1997); John M. Newman, *JFK and Vietnam* (1992); Caroline Page, *U.S. Official Propaganda During the Vietnam War* (1996); Douglas Pike, *Vietnam and the Soviet Union* (1987); William J. Rust, *Kennedy in Vietnam* (1985); Robert D. Schulzinger, *A Time for War* (1997); Orrin Schwab, *Defending the Free World* (1998); Neil Sheehan, *A Bright Shining Lie* (1988); Anthony Short, *The Origins of the Vietnam War* (1989); Ronald H. Spector, *After Tet* (1993); Sandra Taylor, *Vietnamese Women at War* (1999); William S. Turley, *The Second Indochina War* (1986); Brian VanDeMark, *Into the Quagmire* (1991) (Johnson); Frank E. Vandiver, *Shadows of Vietnam* (1997); Jayne S. Werner and Luu Doan Huynh, eds., *The Vietnam War* (1992); Marilyn Young, *The Vietnam Wars* (1991); James J. Wirtz, *The Tet Offensive* (1992); Randall B. Woods, ed., *Vietnam and the American Political Tradition* (2003); and Qiang Zhai, *China and the Vietnam Wars* (2000).

Laos and Cambodia are discussed in many of the studies above and in Timothy N. Castle, *At War in the Shadow of Vietnam* (1993) (Laos); David P. Chandler, *The Tragedy of Cambodian History* (1991); Michael Haas, *Cambodia, Pol Pot, and the United States* (1991); Jane Hamilton-Merritt, *Tragic Mountain* (1993) (Laos); Marie A. Martin, *Cambodia* (1994); William Shawcross, *Sideshow* (1979) (Cambodia); and Charles Stevenson, *The End of Nowhere* (1972) (Laos).

The colonial history of Vietnam, its wars against foreigners, and the development of its politics are examined in Mark Bradley, *Imagining Vietnam and America* (2000); Arthur J. Dommen, *The Indochinese Experience of the French and the Americans* (2001); William J. Duiker, *The Communist Road to Power in Vietnam* (1981) and *Ho Chi Minh* (2000); Bernard Fall, *The Two Viet-Nams* (1967); David Marr, *Vietnamese Anti-Colonialism, 1885–1925* (1971) and *Vietnamese Tradition on Trial, 1920–1945* (1981); and Douglas Pike, *History of Vietnamese Communism* (1978) and *Viet Cong* (1972).

Specific studies of the Truman and Eisenhower administrations and Vietnam are David L. Anderson, *Trapped by Success* (1991) (Eisenhower); Melanie Billings-Yun, *Decision Against War* (1988) (Dienbienphu); Lloyd C. Gardner, *Approaching Vietnam* (1988); Lloyd C. Gardner and Ted Gittinger, eds., *Vietnam: The Early Decisions* (1998); Lawrence S. Kaplan et al., eds., *Dien Bien Phu and the Crisis of Franco-American Relations* (1990); David G. Marr, *Vietnam 1945* (1995); Andrew J. Rotter, *The Path to Vietnam* (1987); Martin Shipway, *The Road to War* (1996) (French policy); and Stein Tönnesson, *The Vietnamese Revolution of 1945* (1991).

For the My Lai massacre, see David L. Anderson, *Facing My Lai* (1998); Seymour M. Hersh, *Cover-Up* (1972); James S. Olson and Randy Roberts, *My Lai* (1998); and Kevin Sim and Michael Bilton, *Four Hours in My Lai* (1992).

For province- and village-level studies that probe American interactions with a peasant society, see William Andrews, *The Village War* (1973); Eric M. Bergerud, *The Dynamics of Defeat* (1991); Jeffrey Race, *War Comes to Long An* (1972); and James W. Trullinger, Jr., *Village at War* (1980).

Military decisions and operations and the soldier's experience in Vietnam are studied in Christian G. Appy, *Working Class War* (1993) and *Patriots* (2003); Robert Buzzanco, *Masters of War: Military Dissent and Politics in the Vietnam Era* (1996); Jeffrey J. Clarke, *United States Army in Vietnam* (1988); Mark Clodfelter, *The Limits of Power* (1989) (bombing); Eric Dean, *Shook Over Hell* (1997) (post-traumatic stress disorder); Douglas Kinnard, *The Certain Trumpet* (1991) (Taylor); Andrew F. Krepinevich, Jr., *The Army and Vietnam* (1986); Otto J. Lehrack, *No Shining Armor* (1992) (marines); Donald J. Mrozek, *Air Power & the Ground War in Vietnam* (1989); Douglas Pike, *PAVN: People's Army of Vietnam* (1986); John Prados and Ray Stubbe, *Valley of Decision* (1991) (Khe Sanh); Jeffrey Record, *The Wrong War* (1998); Ronald H. Spector, *United States in Vietnam* (1983); Shelby Stanton, *The Rise and Fall of an American Army* (1985); and Harry G. Summers, *On Strategy* (1981).

American public opinion, media, and the antiwar movement are discussed in many of the works above and specifically in Milton J. Bates, *The Wars We Took to Vietnam* (1996); Charles DeBenedetti and Charles Chatfield, *An American Ordeal* (1990) (antiwar movement); Terry Dietz, *Republicans and Vietnam* (1986); Kenneth J. Heineman, *Campus Wars* (1993); Rhodri Jeffreys-Jones, *Peace Now!* (1999); Katherine Kinney, *Friendly Fire* (2000); Melvin Small, *Johnson, Nixon, and the Doves* (1988) and *Antiwarriors* (2002); Melvin Small and William D. Hoover, eds., *Give Peace a Chance* (1992); William Prochnau, *Once upon a Distant War* (1995) (journalists); Amy Swerdlow, *Women Strike for Peace* (1993); Robert R. Tomes, *Apocalypse Then: American Intellectuals and the Vietnam War, 1954–1975* (1998); Fred Turner, *Echoes of Combat* (1996); Kathleen J. Turner, *Lyndon Johnson's Dual War* (1985); Tom Wells, *The War Within* (1994); Philip West et al., *America's Wars in Asia* (1998); Lawrence S. Wittner, *Rebels Against War* (1984); Clarence R. Wyatt, *Paper Soldiers* (1993); and Nancy Zaroulis and Gerald Sullivan, *Who Spoke Up?* (1984).

See also the General Bibliography; Robert L. Beisner, ed., *Guide to American Foreign Relations Since 1600* (2003); and the following notes.

For comprehensive coverage of foreign-related topics, see the articles in the four-volume *Encyclopedia of U.S. Foreign Relations* (1997), edited by Bruce W. Jentleson and Thomas G. Paterson.

NOTES TO CHAPTER 9

1. Quoted in J. L. Dees, "The Viet Cong Attack That Failed," *Department of State News Letter*, no. 85 (May 1968), 22.
2. Tran-van Dinh, "Six Hours that Changed the Vietnam Situation," *Christian Century*, LXXXV (March 6, 1968), 289.
3. Don Oberdorfer, *Tet!* (Garden City, N.Y.: Doubleday, 1971), p. 25.
4. Quoted *ibid.*, p. 33.
5. Frances FitzGerald, *Fire in the Lake* (New York: Vintage, 1972), p. 524.
6. Tran Van Tra, "Tet," in Jayne Werner and Luu Doan Huynh, eds., *The Vietnam War* (Armonk, N.Y.: Sharpe, 1992), p. 58.
7. William C. Westmoreland, *A Soldier Reports* (Garden City, N.Y.: Doubleday, 1976), p. 348.
8. Quoted in Frank Vandiver, *Shadows of Vietnam* (College Station: Texas A&M University Press, 1997), p. 276.
9. Quoted in Townsend Hoopes, *The Limits of Intervention* (New York: McKay, 1969), p. 213.
10. Quoted in George Kahin and John Lewis, *The United States in Vietnam* (New York: Dell, 1969), p. 373.
11. Quoted in George A. Bailey and Lawrence W. Lichty, "Rough Justice on a Saigon Street," *Journalism Quarterly*, XLIX (Summer 1972), 222.
12. Quoted in *Newsweek*, LXXI (February 19, 1968), 24.
13. *Department of State Bulletin*, LVIII (February 26, 1968), 261.

14. Quoted in Philip B. Davidson, *Vietnam at War* (Novato, Calif.: Presidio Press, 1988), p. 486.

15. Quoted in David Lamb, *Vietnam, Now* (New York: Public Affairs, 2002), p. 148.

16. Gerard J. DeGroot, *A Noble Cause?* (New York: Longman, 2000), p. 182.

17. Quoted in George C. Herring, *LBJ and Vietnam* (Austin: University of Texas Press, 1994), p. 158.

18. Quoted in Robert Dallek, *Flawed Giant* (New York: Oxford University Press, 1998), p. 506.

19. Quoted in David M. Barrett, ed., *Lyndon B. Johnson's Vietnam Papers* (Austin: University of Texas Press, 1998), p. 713.

20. Clark Clifford, *Counsel to the President* (New York: Random House, 1991), p. 494.

21. Quoted in Robert Buzzanco, *Masters of War* (New York: Cambridge University Press, 1996), p. 333; in Herring, *LBJ and Vietnam*, p. 160.

22. David M. Barrett, *Uncertain Warriors* (Lawrence: University Press of Kansas, 1993), p. 111.

23. *Public Papers, Johnson, 1968* (Washington, D.C.: Government Printing Office, 1970), p. 470.

24. Quoted in Christian G. Appy, *Working-Class War* (Chapel Hill: University of North Carolina press, 1993), p. 208.

25. Archimedes Patti quoted in Stein Tönnesson, *The Vietnamese Revolution of 1945* (Newbury Park, Calif.: Sage, 1991), p. 311.

26. Quoted in Mark Philip Bradley, *Imagining Vietnam and America* (Chapel Hill: University of North Carolina Press, 2000), p. 139.

27. Quoted in David Marr, *Vietnam, 1945* (Berkeley: University of California Press, 1995), p. 289.

28. Quoted in Lloyd C. Gardner, *Approaching Vietnam* (New York: Norton, 1988), p. 65.

29. Quoted in Christopher Thorne, "Indochina and Anglo-American Relations, 1942–1945," *Pacific Historical Review, XLIV* (February 1976), 93.

30. Quoted in Richard H. Immerman, "Why and Why Not Vietnam," *New England Journal of History, LII* (April 1998), 25.

31. Quoted in Jeffrey Record, *The Wrong War* (Annapolis, Md.: Naval Institute Press, 1998), p. 60.

32. Quoted in George C. Herring, *America's Longest War* (New York: Knopf, 1996; 3rd ed.), p. 12.

33. Quoted in Archimedes L. A. Patti, *Why Vietnam?* (Berkeley: University of California Press, 1980), p. 203.

34. Quoted in Mark Atwood Lawrence, "Transnational Coalition-Building and the Making of the Cold War in Indochina, 1947–1949," *Diplomatic History, XXVI* (Summer 2002), 469.

35. Quoted in Robert Buzzanco, *Vietnam and the Transformation of American Life* (Malden, Mass.: Blackwell, 1999), p. 53.

36. Quoted in Herring, *America's Longest War*, p. 34.

37. Quoted *ibid.*, p. 41.

38. Quoted in Qiang Zhai, *China and the Vietnam Wars, 1950–1975* (Chapel Hill: University of North Carolina Press, 2000), p. 61.

39. Quoted in Marilyn Young, *The Vietnam Wars* (New York: HarperCollins, 1991), p. 42.

40. Quoted in *New York Times, The Pentagon Papers* (New York: Bantam, 1971), p. 14.

41. Arthur J. Dommen, *The Indochinese Experience of the French and the Americans* (Bloomington: Indiana University Press, 2001), p. 253.

42. Quoted in Robert J. McMahon, *The Limits of Empire* (New York: Columbia University Press, 1999), p. 67.

43. Chargé Robert McClintock in David Anderson, *Trapped by Success* (Columbia: University of Missouri Press, 1991), pp. 60–61.

44. Quoted in Robert D. Schulzinger, *A Time for War* (New York: Oxford University Press, 1997), p. 81.

45. Lansdale quoted in Anderson, *Trapped by Success*, p. 76; *Time* quoted in Michael H. Hunt, "East Asia and The American Century," *Diplomatic History, XXIII* (Spring 1999), 329.

46. Quoted in David Kaiser, *American Tragedy* (Cambridge: Harvard University Press, 2000), p. 61.

47. Dommen, *Indochinese Experience*, p. 423.

48. Quoted in George W. Ball, *The Past Has Another Pattern* (New York: Norton, 1982), p. 364.

49. Quoted in Theodore C. Sorensen, *Kennedy* (New York: Harper and Row, 1965), p. 199.

50. *New York Times*, August 25, 1960.

51. Quoted in Robert D. Dean, *Imperial Brotherhood* (Amherst: University of Massachusetts Press, 2001), p. 181.

52. *Public Papers, Kennedy, 1962* (Washington, D.C.: Government Printing Office, 1963), p. 807.

53. Don Ferguson in Peter Joseph, *Good Times* (New York: Morrow, 1974), p. 4.

54. Quoted in Thomas G. Paterson, "Introduction," in Thomas G. Paterson, ed., *Kennedy's Quest for Victory* (New York: Oxford University Press, 1989), p. 14.

55. Arthur M. Schlesinger, Jr., *A Thousand Days* (Boston: Houghton Mifflin, 1965), p. 259.

56. James Barber, *The Presidential Character* (Englewood Cliffs, N.J.: Prentice-Hall, 1992; 4th ed.), p. 345.

57. Quoted in Michael Beschloss, *The Crisis Years* (New York: HarperCollins, 1991), p. 48.

58. Oral History Interview by Chester Bowles, pp. 49, 90, John F. Kennedy Library, Boston.

59. Schlesinger, *Thousand Days*, p. 217.

60. *Public Papers, Kennedy, 1961* (Washington, D.C.: Government Printing Office, 1962), pp. 1–3.

61. Theodore H. White, "The Action Intellectuals," *Life, LXII* (June 1967), 43.

62. Quoted in David Halberstam, "The Programming of Robert McNamara," *Harper's, CCXLII* (February 1971), 62.

63. Quoted in Roger Hilsman, *To Move a Nation* (Garden City, N.Y.: Doubleday, 1967), p. 523.

64. Quoted in Paul Hendrickson, *The Living and the Dead* (New York: Vintage, 1996), p. 167.

65. "Memorandum of Conversation with President Johnson," by Max Frankel, July 8, 1965, Box 1, Arthur Krock Papers, Princeton University Library, Princeton, N.J.

66. Harvard Professor and Chester Cooper quoted in Kai Bird, *The Color of Truth* (New York: Simon and Schuster, 1998), pp. 190–191.

67. Quoted in Michael H. Hunt, *Lyndon Johnson's War* (New York: Hill & Wang, 1996), p. 48.

68. Quoted in Michael Mandelbaum, *The Nuclear Question* (New York: Cambridge University Press, 1979), p. 90.

69. Khrushchev quoted in Viktor Adamsky and Yuri Smirnov, "Moscow's Biggest Bomb," *Cold War International History Project Bulletin*, no. 4 (Fall 1994), p. 120.

70. Briefing Book, June 1961, Box 126, President's Office File, John F. Kennedy Papers, Kennedy Library.

71. Schlesinger, *Thousand Days*, p. 348.

72. Vladislav M. Zubok, "Khrushchev and the Berlin Crisis," Working Paper no. 6 *Cold War International History Project*, (May 1993), p. 20.

73. Quoted in Dean Rusk, *As I Saw It* (New York: Penguin, 1991), p. 227.

74. Quoted in W. J. Rorabaugh, *Kennedy and the Promise of the Sixties* (New York: Cambridge University Press, 2002), p. 34.

75. James Reston quoted in James N. Giglio, *The Presidency of John F. Kennedy* (Lawrence: University Press of Kansas, 1991), p. 78.

76. *Public Papers, Kennedy, 1961,* pp. 534, 536.

77. "Khrushchev's Secret Speech on the Berlin Crisis," *Cold War International History Project Bulletin,* no. 2 (Fall 1993), 59.

78. Quoted in James Nathan, *Anatomy of the Cuban Missile Crisis* (Westport, Conn.: Greenwood, 2001), p. 59.

79. Raymond L. Garthoff, "Berlin 1961," *Foreign Policy,* no. 84 (Fall 1991), 142.

80. Quoted in William Taubman, *Khrushchev* (New York: Norton, 2003), p. 539.

81. Michael E. Latham, *Modernization as Ideology* (Chapel Hill: University of North Carolina Press, 2000), p. 91.

82. John F. Kennedy quoted in Robert J. McMahon, *The Cold War on the Periphery* (New York: Columbia University Press, 1994), p. 273.

83. Lawrence Fuchs quoted in Elizabeth A. Cobbs, "The Foreign Policy of the Peace Corps," *Diplomatic History, XX* (Winter 1996), 104.

84. Johnson quoted in Elizabeth Cobbs Hoffman, *All You Need Is Love* (Cambridge: Harvard University Press, 1998), p. 70.

85. Richard P. Tucker, *Insatiable Appetite* (Berkeley: University of California Press, 2000), p. 51.

86. *Ibid.,* p. 55.

87. Quoted in Thomas Noer, "New Frontiers and Old Priorities in Africa," in Paterson, *Kennedy's Quest,* p. 262.

88. Thomas Borstelmann, "John Kennedy and Racial Revolutions in the American South and Southern Africa," *Diplomatic History, XXIV* (Summer 2000), 453.

89. Quoted in Stephen G. Rabe, *The Most Dangerous Area in the World* (Chapel Hill: University of North Carolina Press, 1999), p. 19.

90. Quoted in Jules Benjamin, *The United States and the Origins of the Cuban Revolution* (Princeton: Princeton University Press, 1990), p. 182.

91. Quoted in Thomas G. Paterson, *Contesting Castro* (New York: Oxford University Press, 1994), p. 242.

92. Roy R. Rubottom, Jr., in *Foreign Relations, 1958–1960, VI,* 656.

93. Quoted in Paterson, *Contesting,* p. 257.

94. Quoted in Piero Gleijeses, "Ships in the Night," *Journal of Latin American Studies, XXVII* (February 1995), 3.

95. Quoted in Stephen G. Rabe, *Eisenhower and Latin America* (Chapel Hill: University of North Carolina Press, 1988), p. 128.

96. Quoted in Anatoli I. Gribkov and William Y. Smith, *Operation Anadyr* (Chicago: Edition Q, 1994), p. 12.

97. Quoted in Schlesinger, *Thousand Days,* p. 251.

98. Quoted in Robert D. Dean, "Masculinity as Ideology," *Diplomatic History, XXII* (Winter 1998), 48.

99. Quoted in Lucien S. Vandenbroucke, "The 'Confessions' of Allen Dulles," *Diplomatic History, VIII* (Fall 1984), 369.

100. Allen Dulles quoted in Lucien S. Vandenbroucke, *Perilous Options* (New York: Oxford University Press, 1993), p. 22.

101. Quoted in Mark J. White, ed., *The Kennedys and Cuba* (Chicago: Ivan R. Dee, 1999), p. 19.

102. Quoted in Alexander DeConde, *Presidential Machismo* (Boston: Northeastern University Press, 2000), p. 174.

103. Walt W. Rostow, *The Diffusion of Power* (New York: Macmillan, 1972), pp. 210–211.

104. Quoted in James G. Blight and Peter Kornbluh, eds., *Politics of Illusion* (Boulder, Colo.: Lynne Rienner, 1998), p. 150.

105. Richard Helms memorandum, January 30, 1962, *ibid.,* p. 247.

106. Quoted in Donna Rich Kaplowitz, *Anatomy of a Failed Embargo* (Boulder, Colo.: Lynne Rienner, 1998), p. 47.

107. Quoted in *New York Times,* February 5, 1989.

108. Lyman Lemnitzer quoted in White, *Kennedys and Cuba,* p. 119.

109. Quoted in Frank Mankiewicz and Kirby Jones, *With Fidel* (New York: Ballantine, 1975), p. 130.

110. Quoted in Timothy Naftali, ed., *John F. Kennedy: The Great Crises* (New York: Norton, 2001), *II,* 22.

111. Quoted in Ernest R. May and Philip D. Zelikow, eds., *The Kennedy Tapes* (Cambridge: Harvard University Press, 1997), p. 258.

112. Transcript, "Off-the-Record Meeting on Cuba," 11:50 A.M.–12:57 P.M., October 16, 1962, Presidential Recordings, Kennedy Library.

113. Maxwell Taylor quoted in J. Anthony Lukacs, "Class Reunion," *New York Times Magazine,* August 30, 1987, p. 58; Abram Chayes quoted in James A. Nathan, "The Heyday of the New Strategy," in Nathan, ed., *The Cuban Missile Crisis Revisited* (New York: St. Martin's, 1992), p. 24.

114. Quoted in May and Zelikow, *Kennedy Tapes,* p. 149.

115. Quoted in H. R. McMaster, *Dereliction of Duty* (New York: HarperCollins, 1997), p. 30.

116. *Public Papers, Kennedy, 1962,* p. 808.

117. Quoted in James T. Graham, "Kennedy, Cuba, and the Press," *Journalism History, XXIV* (Summer 1998), 64.

118. Quoted in William Burr and Thomas S. Blanton, eds., "The Submarines of October," *National Security Archive Electronic Briefing Book No. 75* (October 31, 2002).

119. Transcript, "Cuban Missile Crisis meetings," October 27, 1962, Presidential Recordings, Kennedy Library.

120. Anatoly Dobrynin cable to Soviet Foreign Ministry, October 27, 1962, *Cold War International History Project Bulletin,* no. 5 (Spring 1995), p. 79.

121. Quoted in Barton J. Bernstein, "Reconsidering the Missile Crisis," in Nathan, *Cuban Missile Crisis,* p. 100.

122. Quoted in James G. Blight and Philip Brenner, *Sad and Luminous Days* (Lanham, Md.: Rowman & Littlefield, 2002), p. 25; quoted in Odd Arne Westad, "The Sino-Soviet Alliance and the United States," in Odd Arne Westad, ed., *Brothers in Arms: The Rise and Fall of the Sino-Soviet Alliance, 1945–1963* (Stanford: Stanford University Press, 1998), p. 179.

123. Quoted in Richard Ned Lebow and Janice Gross Stein, *We All Lost the Cold War* (Princeton: Princeton University Press, 1994), p. 110.

124. Quoted in Robert Weisbrot, *Maximum Danger* (Chicago: Ivan R. Dee, 2001), p. 212.

125. John Kenneth Galbraith, "The Plain Lessons of a Bad Decade," *Foreign Policy,* no. 1 (Winter 1970–1971), 32.

126. Quoted in McGeorge Bundy, *Danger and Survival* (New York: Random House, 1988), p. 426.

127. Nathan, *Anatomy,* p. 96.

128. McGeorge Bundy quoted in Thomas Risse-Kappen, *Cooperation Among Democracies* (Princeton: Princeton University Press, 1995), p. 148.

129. McNamara and Bundy quoted in Philip Nash, *The Other Missiles of October* (Chapel Hill: University of North Carolina Press, 1997), p. 3.

130. Quoted in James Blight and David Welch, *On the Brink* (New York: Hill & Wang, 1989), p. 100; Marc Trachtenberg, "Commentary," *Diplomatic History, XIV* (Spring 1990), 242.

131. Quoted in Raymond L. Garthoff, *A Journey Through the Cold War* (Washington, D.C.: Brookings Institution Press, 2001), p. 165.

132. McGeorge Bundy quoted in Stephen G. Rabe, "The Caribbean Triangle," *Diplomatic History, XX* (Winter 1996), 77.

133. McMaster, *Dereliction,* p. 326.

134. Michael S. Sherry, *In the Shadow of War* (New Haven: Yale University Press, 1995), p. 243.

135. Walt W. Rostow, Memorandum, March 29, 1961, Box 193, National Security File, Kennedy Papers.

136. Dwight D. Eisenhower, *Waging Peace* (Garden City, NY: Doubleday, 1965), p. 607.

137. Quoted in Edmund F. Wehrle, " 'A Good, Bad Deal,' " *Pacific Historical Review*, LXVII (April 1998), 353.

138. Quoted in Timothy N. Castle, *At War in the Shadow of Vietnam* (New York: Columbia University Press, 1993), p. 41.

139. Quoted in Noam Kochavi, "Kennedy, China, and the Laos Crisis, 1961–1963," *Diplomatic History*, XXVI (Winter 2002), 109.

140. Quoted in Wehrle, "Good, Bad Deal," p. 349.

141. Alfred W. McCoy, "America's Secret Wars in Laos, 1955–1975," in Marilyn B. Young and Robert Buzzanco, eds., *A Companion to the Vietnam War* (Malden, Mass.: Blackwell, 2002), p. 284.

142. Quoted in Frank Costigliola, *France and the United States* (Boston: Twayne, 1992), p. 140; in David Halberstam, *The Best and the Brightest* (Greenwich, Conn.: Fawcett, 1973), p. 77.

143. Walt Rostow quoted in Hunt, *Johnson's War*, p. 58.

144. Quoted in Howard Jones, *Death of a Generation* (New York: Oxford University Press, 2003), p. 113.

145. U.S. Senate, Foreign Relations Committee, *Foreign Assistance Act of 1968*, Part 1: *Vietnam* (Washington, D.C.: Government Printing Office, 1968), p. 218.

146. Charles Bartlett quoting Kennedy in Seymour Hersh, *The Dark Side of Camelot* (Boston: Little, Brown, 1997), p. 418.

147. Quoted in Beschloss, *Crisis Years*, p. 651; quoted in Jones, *Death*, p. 247.

148. Polish diplomat Mieczyslaw Maneli quoted in Fredrik Logevall, *Choosing War* (Berkeley: University of California Press, 1999), p. 7.

149. Quoted in McMahon, *Limits of Empire*, p. 111.

150. Philip E. Catton, *Diem's Final Failure* (Lawrence: University Press of Kansas), p. 202.

151. Quoted in Robert Dallek, *An Unfinished Life* (Boston: Little, Brown, 2003), pp. 685–686.

152. Quoted in Lloyd C. Gardner, "Introduction," in Lloyd C. Gardner and Ted Gittinger, eds., *Vietnam: The Early Decisions* (Austin: University of Texas Press, 1997), p. 3.

153. Quoted in Thomas W. Zeiler, *Dean Rusk* (Wilmington, Del.: SR Books, 2000), p. 131.

154. Quoted in Anatoly Dobrynin, *In Confidence* (New York: Random House, 1995), p. 174.

155. Quoted in Thomas A. Schwartz, *Lyndon Johnson and Europe* (Cambridge: Harvard University Press, 2003), p. 28.

156. Matthew Jones, *Conflict and Confrontation in South East Asia, 1961–1965* (New York: Cambridge University Press, 2002), p. 262.

157. Quoted in Schwartz, *Johnson and Europe*, pp. 28–29.

158. Dobrynin, *In Confidence*, p. 120.

159. Ben Bradlee, *A Good Life* (New York: Simon & Schuster, 1995), p. 263.

160. Quoted in Douglas Little, "Crackpot Realists and Other Heroes," *Diplomatic History*, XIII (Winter 1989), 103.

161. Quoted in H. W. Brands, *The Wages of Globalism* (New York: Oxford University Press, 1995), p. 80.

162. Quoted in Hunt, *Johnson's War*, p. 72.

163. Quoted in John Prados, "Arms Limitations Setbacks in 1968," in H. W. Brands, ed., *The Foreign Policies of Lyndon Johnson* (College Station: Texas A&M University Press, 1999), p. 32.

164. Quoted in Alan McPherson, *Yankee No! Anti-Americanism in U.S.-Latin American Relations* (Cambridge: Harvard University Press, 2003), p. 102.

165. Quoted in Eric Thomas Chester, *Rag-Tags, Scum, Riff-Raff, and Commies* (New York: Monthly Review Press, 2001), p. 80.

166. Quoted in Michael Beschloss, ed., *Reaching for Glory* (New York: Simon & Schuster, 2001), pp. 301, 317.

167. Quoted in Vandiver, *Shadows*, p. 76.

168. Quoted in Beschloss, *Reaching*, p. 327.

169. Luu Van Loi quoted in Robert S. McNamara, James G. Blight, and Robert K. Brigham, *Argument Without End* (New York: Public Affairs, 1999), p. 202.

170. Quoted in Kahin and Lewis, *U.S. and Vietnam*, p. 152.

171. Senator Richard Russell quoted in Michael D. Pearlman, *Warfighting and American Democracy* (Lawrence: University Press of Kansas, 1999), p. 357; Lodge quoted in Gardner, *Pay Any Price*, p. 232.

172. Quoted in Michael Beschloss, *Taking Charge* (New York: Simon & Schuster, 1997), p. 370.

173. Quoted in Logevall, *Choosing*, pp. 76–77.

174. McGeorge Bundy in Summary Record of Meeting, June 10, 1964, in Barrett, *LBJ's Vietnam Papers*, p. 54.

175. Quoted in Beschloss, *Taking Charge*, p. 493.

176. Quoted in Herring, *America's Longest War*, p. 134.

177. Edwin E. Moïse, *Tonkin Gulf and the Escalation of the Vietnam War* (Chapel Hill: University of North Carolina Press, 1996), p. 107.

178. Quoted in George Kahin, *Intervention* (New York: Knopf, 1986), p. 223.

179. Quoted in Zhai, *China and the Vietnam Wars*, p. 132.

180. *Congressional Record, CX* (August 7, 1964), 18471.

181. Quoted in Stanley Karnow, *Vietnam* (New York: Viking, 1991; rev. ed.), p. 374.

182. Joseph Califano quoted in Edwin E. Moïse, "JFK and the Myth of Withdrawal," in Young and Buzzanco, *Companion*, p. 165.

183. Quoted in Beschloss, *Reaching*, p. 176.

184. Quoted in Lewis Sorley, *Honorable Warrior: General Harold K. Johnson* (Lawrence: University Press of Kansas, 1998), p. 202.

185. Quoted in Jack Valenti, *A Very Human President* (New York: Norton, 1975), pp. 334, 335.

186. Quoted in Herring, *LBJ and Vietnam*, p. 31.

187. Quoted in Dallek, *Flawed Giant*, p. 342.

188. McMaster, *Dereliction*, pp. 328, 330.

189. Quoted in Beschloss, *Reaching*, p. 282.

190. Quoted in Daniel Ellsberg, *Secrets* (New York: Viking, 2002), p. 64.

191. Quoted in George C. Herring, "The Reluctant Warrior," in David L. Anderson, ed., *Shadow on the White House* (Lawrence: University Press of Kansas, 1993), p. 93.

192. Quoted in James P. Harrison, "History's Heaviest Bombing," in Werner and Huynh, *Vietnam War*, p. 135.

193. Quoted in Eric M. Bergerud, *The Dynamics of Defeat* (Boulder, Colo.: Westview Press, 1991), p. 163.

194. Quoted in David L. DiLeo, *George Ball, Vietnam, and the Rethinking of Containment* (Chapel Hill: University of North Carolina Press, 1991), p. 170.

195. Quoted in Doris Kearns, *Lyndon Johnson and the American Dream* (New York: Harper and Row, 1976), p. 329.

196. Quoted in Buzzanco, *Masters*, p. 350.

197. Quoted in Jonathan Mirsky, "The Root of Resistance," *The Nation, CCVII* (August 5, 1968), 90.

198. Colin L. Powell, *My American Journey* (New York: Random House, 1995), p. 146.

199. Quoted in Karnow, *Vietnam*, p. 617.

200. Philip Caputo, *A Rumor of War* (New York: Ballantine, 1977), p. 100.

201. Nicholas Katzenbach quoted in Melvin Small, *Antiwarriors* (Wilmington, Del.: Scholarly Resources, 2002), p. 67.

202. John Hagan, *Northern Passage: American Vietnam War Resisters in Canada* (Cambridge: Harvard University Press, 2001), p. 66.

203. Quoted in Beschloss, *Reaching,* p. 295.
204. Chester Bowles quoted in Richard Dauer, "Great Expectations Un-realized: Chester Bowles and U.S. Cold War Policy, 1951–1969" (Ph.D. diss., University of Connecticut, 1998), p. 343.
205. Johnson telephone conversation, March 27, 1964, in Beschloss, *Taking Charge,* p. 298; quoted in Walter LaFeber, "Johnson, Vietnam, and Tocqueville" in Nancy Bernkopf Tucker and Warren I. Cohen, eds., *Lyndon Johnson Confronts the World* (New York: Cambridge University Press, 1994), p. 45.
206. Quoted in Kevin Boyle, "The Price of Peace," *Diplomatic History XXVII* (January 2003), 61.
207. Quoted in William J. Duiker, *Ho Chi Minh* (New York: Hyperion, 2000), p. 541.
208. Zhai, *China and the Vietnam Wars,* p. 218.
209. Quoted in Yang Kuisong, "Changes in Mao Zedong's Attitude Toward the Indochina War, 1949–1973," Working Paper no. 34, *Cold War International History Project* (February 2002), p. 29.
210. Deng Xiaoping quoted in Zhai, *China and the Vietnam Wars,* p. 153.
211. Quoted in Ivan V. Gaiduk, *The Soviet Union and the Vietnam War* (Chicago: Ivan R. Dee, 1996), p. 150.
212. Quoted in Herring, *LBJ and Vietnam,* p. 37.
213. Quoted in Evan Thomas, *Robert Kennedy* (New York: Simon & Schuster, 2000), p. 350.
214. Quoted in James G. Hershberg, "Who Murdered 'Marigold,'" Working Paper no. 27, *Cold War International History Project* (April 2000), p. 74.
215. Boyle, "Price of Peace," p. 47.
216. Quoted in Beschloss, *Reaching,* p. 181.
217. Quoted in Robert K. Brigham, *Guerrilla Diplomacy* (Ithaca: Cornell University Press, 1998), p. 48.
218. Polish diplomat Jerzy Michalowski quoting Giap in Hershberg, "Who Murdered 'Marigold,'" p. 11.
219. Assistant Secretary of Defense John McNaughton quoted in Donald F. Lach and Edmund S. Wehrle, *International Politics in East Asia* (New York: Praeger, 1975), p. 338.

CHAPTER ⚜ 10

Détente and Disequilibrium, 1969–1977

Richard M. Nixon (1913–1994) and Zhou Enlai (1898–1976), 1972. *During his historic trip to China in February 1972, President Nixon met with the Chinese premier. Zhou asked at one point: "Can [the] U.S. control the 'wild horse' of Japan?" Nixon replied: "The United States can get out of Japanese waters, but others will still fish there"—a veiled reference to the Soviet Union. (Nixon Presidential Materials Project/National Archives)*

๛ *Richard M. Nixon's Trip to China, 1972*

THE PRESIDENT'S CHIEF security officer aboard the aircraft radioed to the Beijing airport: "What about the crowd?" The answer came back: "There is no crowd." The disbelieving officer asked: "Did you say, 'No crowd'?"[1] Indeed, when President Richard M. Nixon's jet, the *Spirit of '76,* touched down that wintry morning of February 21, 1972, the reception was decidedly restrained. Apparently the Chinese wanted to suggest that the United States desired this dramatic meeting more eagerly than did the People's Republic of China (PRC). Instead of cheering schoolchildren, only "a vast silence" welcomed Nixon.[2]

Greeting Nixon was trim seventy-three-year-old Premier Zhou Enlai, a veteran communist who had served Chairman Mao Zedong as key administrator since the success of the Chinese Revolution in 1949. Nixon and Zhou formally shook hands—the very gesture that Secretary John Foster Dulles had spurned at Geneva in 1954. The television cameras whirred, sending back to the United States, via satellite, picture postcards of the historic encounter. Zhou and Nixon sped toward Beijing in old Russian Zil limousines. Portraits of Mao and political signs hung everywhere. The Chinese had painted over one poster that read: "We Must Defeat the U.S. Aggressors and All Their Running Dogs."[3]

Nixon's "journey for peace" contrasted sharply with the previous quarter-century of no formal diplomatic relations between the two countries.[4] They had harangued each other as warmongers and had fought one another in Korea. The United States maintained close ties with the PRC's archenemy Jiang Jieshi in Taiwan, while China aided America's foe in Vietnam. Nixon and Zhou knew this history of hostility, but each now recognized that cooperation best served his own country's interests.

In 1969, newly inaugurated President Nixon had asked his assistant for national security affairs, Henry A. Kissinger, to review relations with China. When "tit-for-tat" border fighting between the Soviet Union and China broke out that year, Nixon told his cabinet: "The worst thing that could happen to us would be for the Soviet Union to gobble up Red China."[5] He soon sent signals to Beijing by scaling back U.S. Seventh Fleet operations in the Taiwan Strait and relaxing trade restrictions with China. The Chinese picked up the signals. Early in 1970 PRC diplomats once again began meeting with U.S. officials in Warsaw—talks that China had suspended two years earlier as a protest against American warfare in Vietnam. In December, Mao told the visiting American journalist Edgar Snow that he would welcome Nixon to China, "either as a tourist or as President."[6] Nixon responded by lifting restrictions against Americans wanting to travel to the People's Republic. In April 1971 a U.S. table tennis team competing in Japan accepted an invitation to visit China. Quips about "Ping-Pong diplomacy" and "the Ping heard round the world" did not detract from the symbolic significance of the team's trip.[7]

Using U.S. ally Pakistan as an intermediary, Kissinger made plans to go to China himself. In Islamabad (the Pakistani capital) in early July, he secretly boarded

Marco Polo. The political cartoonist Ray Osrin portrayed two reasons for the Nixon journey to China, 1972. Kissinger's secret 1971 trip to China was code-named "Polo." (Ray Osrin in *The Cleveland Plain Dealer*)

a plane for Beijing. Kissinger soon reported that "the process we have now started will send enormous shock waves around the world."[8] On July 15, President Nixon made the startling announcement that he would go to China to "seek the normalization of relations."[9]

Renewed Sino-American relations seemed to promise advantages. Because the Soviets had become China's "most dangerous and most important enemy," U.S. ties with Beijing might keep Moscow off balance.[10] "We're using the Chinese thaw to get the Russians shook," Nixon told an aide.[11] With the U.S. economy sagging, moreover, the legendary China market once again loomed large in American imaginations. Nuclear arms race questions also shaped U.S. motives. Having joined the nuclear club in 1964, China had rejected the 1968 Treaty on the Nonproliferation of Nuclear Weapons, and Washington sought Beijing's adherence. Then, too, U.S. recognition of China might influence Beijing to press North Vietnam to accept a political settlement of the Vietnam War.

The China trip also promised Nixon political profits at home. An antiwar Democrat, Senator George McGovern, had launched a campaign against Nixon's continued intervention in Vietnam, and in March, New Hampshire would hold the first presidential primary of 1972. Even though "the libs [liberals] will try to piss on it as an election year gimmick," Kissinger frankly remarked that Nixon's "political ass was on the line."[12] Liberal-left Americans had advocated relations with China for years, and Democrats soon applauded the China trip. At the same time, the right wing of the Republican party could hardly charge that Nixon, a proven anticommunist, had turned soft on communism. Finally, the China journey was central to the general Nixon-Kissinger policy of "détente"—the relaxation of international tensions with communist nations to protect U.S. interests. "We needed China to enhance the flexibility of our diplomacy," said Kissinger.[13]

The Chinese, still reeling from their destructive internal Cultural Revolution, now perceived the Americans as changing from a "monkey" to a "human being."[14] Military skirmishes in 1969 on the shared 4,150-mile border caused many Chinese, recalling the Soviet invasion of Czechoslovakia in 1968, to fear a Soviet attack. The Soviet Union constructed an air base in Mongolia; the Chinese dug bomb shelters and tunnel networks. Resuming Sino-American ties, then, might deter the "polar bear" to the north.[15] "We can work together to commonly deal with a bastard," Mao told Kissinger.[16] China also feared a revived Japan, and a Sino-American rapprochement might keep Tokyo off guard and cautious. Or it might, as actually happened, lead to the opening of Sino-Japanese relations, thereby strengthening China against the Soviet Union. Finally, China wanted trade and a reduced U.S. commitment to Taiwan.

On the flight to China, Nixon studied notebooks about Chinese politics, culture, and diplomacy. Included were CIA analyses of Mao and Zhou and "talking points" that Nixon committed to memory. Joining the presidential party of thirty-seven—which included Secretary of State William Rogers, upstaged as always by Kissinger—was a press corps of eighty-seven, heavy with television news personalities. Telling CBS reporter Dan Rather that there would be "tough, hard bargaining between people who have very great differences," the president carefully staged his pageant for prime-time screens back home.[17]

Nixon soon met Chairman Mao. Seated in overstuffed chairs, Nixon, Kissinger, Mao, and Zhou talked warmly for about an hour. Tang Wensheng, a Brooklyn-born Radcliffe graduate who had become a Chinese citizen, served as interpreter. Seventy-eight-year-old Mao, although suffering from congestive heart disease, remained an imposing figure, esteemed by the Chinese as the leader of the Long March and father of the People's Republic. Mao smiled and bantered. "Your book, *Six Crises,* is not a bad book," Mao commented. After the translation of that lukewarm review of his prepresidential memoirs, Nixon looked at Zhou and said: "He reads too much."[18] Born into a well-to-do mandarin family, Zhou spoke English, Russian, French, and Japanese as well as his native Chinese. A skillful negotiator with a sharp memory, Zhou shunned the limelight. U.S. diplomats contrasted his quiet, patient style with the blunt, haggling manner of Soviet diplomats.

That evening, in the Great Hall of the People, Zhou hosted a banquet for 800 guests. Sipping glasses of *mao tai,* a 150-proof rice liquor "roughly equivalent to lawn mower fuel," Americans and their hosts toasted each other in the traditional *"gan bei"* ("dry glass") fashion.[19] The Chinese military band played "America the Beautiful"—as "a toast to your next Inaugural," Zhou whispered to Nixon.[20] Then, tearing a page from Chinese communist history, Nixon called for a "long march together." And he even quoted Mao himself: "Seize the day, seize the hour. This is the hour."[21] "I like to deal with rightists," said Mao privately of Nixon. "They say what they really think—not like the leftists, who say one thing and mean another."[22]

While Nixon privately assured Zhou on February 22 that "I am removing this irritant [Vietnam] as fast as anyone in my position could," journalists filed reports on the Chinese lifestyle—clean streets, gauze masks to prevent infectious diseases, acupuncture techniques, anti-imperialist banners, expertise in table tennis, regimented schools, puritanical social habits, bicycles, the monotony of blue dress.[23] After years of thinking the Chinese a bestial enemy, Americans now found them loving and suffering like the rest of humanity. Whereas in the 1960s Americans used words such as "ignorant, warlike, treacherous, and sly" to describe the "Red Chinese," after the 1972 trip they described them as "hard-working, intelligent, progressive, artistic, and practical."[24] U.S. conservatives found themselves fascinated by Chinese students who "sat straight upright in their chairs and had short hair and respected their elders and adhered to family values" that were already "a matter of nostalgia in the United States," so one diplomat recalled.[25]

After late-night social events, an exhausted Kissinger helped fashion language for a joint communiqué. Issued on February 27, the document followed Zhou's formula of "seeking common ground while reserving differences."[26] Affirming existing ties with South Korea and Japan, Nixon assured his hosts that a continued U.S. military presence in Asia was "China's [best] hope for Jap restraint."[27] The Americans then stated their opposition to "outside pressure or intervention" in Asia—meaning Vietnam. The Chinese declared that they would continue to support "the struggles of all oppressed people" against large nations that attempt to "bully" the small. All foreign troops should withdraw from Asia, especially Vietnam. As for Taiwan, which the United States still recognized as the official government of China, the Chinese part of the communiqué admonished the United States to remove its military forces from the island. There was only one China. Pledging not to "sell Taiwan down the river," Nixon urged "language which will meet your [Beijing's] need yet does not stir up the animals," namely, a "peaceful settlement of the Taiwan question by the Chinese themselves."[28] Both parties agreed, however, that "neither should seek hegemony in the Asia-Pacific region and each is opposed to efforts by any other country or group of countries to establish such hegemony"—a slap at the Soviet Union. Finally, both sides appealed for increased cultural and commercial contacts.[29]

Diplomacy done, on the seventh day of his trip, February 28, the president bade farewell at Shanghai and proclaimed that "this was the week that changed the world."[30] Kissinger privately boasted that Washington and China had become "in plain words . . . tacit allies."[31] One negative headline proclaimed: "They Got Taiwan, We Got Eggroll."[32] The China trip seemed "comparable to conceding the existence of the Pacific Ocean," sniffed a critic.[33]

Nixon, Kissinger, and Their Critics

Nixon and Kissinger, quite different individuals who shared basic assumptions about U.S. foreign relations, orchestrated this surprising turnabout in Sino-American relations. Richard Milhous Nixon, the grocer's son from Whittier, California, relished the big play in politics; his "biggest asset," one scholar notes, was "his appreciation, abstract but keen, of the need and means to change course."[34] Nixon also wanted the Soviets and North Vietnamese to think him irrational and unpredictable. This self-professed "madman theory" would supposedly deter adversaries or cause them to settle on American terms.[35] A secretive, suspicious man, Nixon raged at his many "enemies." "One day we will get them," he told an aide, "get them on the floor and step on them, crush them, show no mercy . . . stick our heels in . . . and twist."[36]

Pinocchio and Jiminy Cricket. "A two-fisted, bare-faced liar"—so Republican Senator Barry Goldwater described Nixon before the Watergate crisis forced him from office. Using characters from the popular story of Pinocchio, the cartoonist Robert Grossman depicts Nixon as the untruthful youngster and Henry A. Kissinger as his faithful adviser. Nixon's biographer Richard Reeves writes: "So many layers of lies were needed to protect the layers of secrecy that no one, including the President himself, knew what the truth was anymore. . . . It was hard to keep track of the deceptions, even for the deceivers." (© Robert Grossman)

He had such scorn for the State Department that he offered ambassadorships to campaign contributors willing to pay "at least $250,000."[37]

His administration guarded itself against its critics through secrecy and executive crimes and corrupt political practices later known collectively as Watergate. Because he wanted documentation for his memoirs and to protect himself against misinformation, Nixon secretly recorded conversations in the White House. When made public by court order, the tapes inspired an impeachment process that Nixon himself, caught in lies, terminated by resigning from the presidency on August 8, 1974, thereby elevating Vice President Gerald Ford to the White House. Exposure of criminality such as the burglary of Democratic party headquarters and the payment of hush money weakened the executive branch in its ongoing struggle with Congress over foreign policy. Watergate also caused bewilderment abroad, as Moscow "did not (or would not) understand how the president of the United States could be prosecuted for what it viewed as a 'small matter.'" Not until the "last moment" did the Kremlin grasp that "Nixon could be forced to resign."[38]

After Nixon's ignoble departure, Henry A. Kissinger stayed on. Presidential assistant for national security affairs (1969–1976) and secretary of state (1973–1977), Kissinger thought Nixon an "egomaniac" apparently "obsessed by the fear that he was not receiving adequate credit" for foreign-policy triumphs such as the change in China policy.[39] Having escaped from Nazism in 1938, this ambitious political scientist had maneuvered successfully "through the polite, pervasively anti-Semitic world of the eastern foreign policy establishment."[40] Reflective, witty, energetic, persistent, and vain, "Henry the Navigator" became one of the most traveled diplomats in history. He reveled in personal diplomacy, in the give-and-take, the manipulation of power and people. His "devilish nimbleness" and evident rapport with people of different cultures brought him negotiating successes.[41] Kissinger managed an impressive number of roles: theorist, policymaker, negotiator, presidential adviser, bureaucratic infighter, and public spokesperson. He and Nixon agreed early that they would make policy in the White House, often sidestepping the foreign-affairs bureaucracy. When Kissinger used secret "back channels" to

Makers of American Foreign Relations, 1969–1977

Presidents	Secretaries of State
Richard M. Nixon, 1969–1974	William P. Rogers, 1969–1973
Gerald Ford, 1974–1977	Henry A. Kissinger, 1973–1977

communicate with foreign governments, "we had no record, except what Henry chose to recall, and what he then chose to tell us he recalled," one diplomat complained.[42] William P. Rogers served as a loyal secretary of state until 1973, but Nixon granted him little authority. Resenting its exclusion from policymaking, Congress reasserted its prerogatives by passing, over Nixon's veto, the War Powers Resolution (1973): The president could commit U.S. troops abroad for no more than sixty days, after which he had to obtain congressional approval. Congress also vexed Kissinger by cutting foreign aid to Turkey, Cambodia, South Vietnam, and Angola. Without Watergate and without congressional meddling, Kissinger lamented, he could have accomplished so much more. He nonetheless shared with North Vietnamese negotiator Le Duc Tho the Nobel Peace Prize in 1973.

Even though the UN ambassador and future president George H. W. Bush considered him "paranoid," "brutal," and "arrogant," Kissinger nonetheless remained a

"Some Chicken, Some Egg."   Henry A. Kissinger (b.1923) received his doctorate in 1954 from Harvard, where he taught until Nixon appointed him national security affairs adviser in 1969. An architect of détente, Kissinger also undertook extensive travel to trouble spots such as the Middle East and Africa to conduct personal negotiations. Critics on the left compared him to "Dr. Strangelove," the fictional Germanic presidential adviser, played by Peter Sellers in the movie of that name, who was so deranged that he welcomed a nuclear holocaust. Critics on the right thought Kissinger too conciliatory to the communists. (*The Economist,* London, 1975)

popular figure.[43] He charmed journalists and leaked secret information to generate favorable newspaper stories. A self-proclaimed "swinger" prior to his 1974 marriage, Kissinger once accused Anne Armstrong, the first U.S. woman ambassador to Britain, of crying when he excluded her from negotiations. "I might have bitten him," recalled Armstrong, "but I wasn't going to cry."[44] A Soviet official admitted: "I don't trust Nixon or his little professor."[45]

Kissinger's critics questioned the secrecy that surrounded foreign relations. When academicians, business executives, and lawyers, many of whom wrote for the prestigious journal *Foreign Affairs,* became disenchanted, Kissinger exploded: "What the hell is an Establishment for, if it's not to support the President?"[46] Critics argued that Kissinger followed the ruthless maxim that the ends justify the means: He wiretapped aides and journalists; he defended the president in the lowest days of Watergate; he relied recklessly on huge arms sales; he sponsored CIA plots abroad that held America up to ridicule for advocating democracy but undermining it; and he approved the deadly bombing of the peoples of Southeast Asia. Accused of first aiding and then abandoning Kurdish rebels in Iraq (thousands of whom later died at the hands of Iraqi dictator Saddam Hussein), Kissinger coldly replied that "one must not confuse the intelligence business with missionary work."[47] He similarly urged the military leaders of Argentina to get the "terrorist problem under control as quickly as possible"; his main concern was not human rights but that they "get it over quickly."[48]

Kissinger and Nixon considered themselves pragmatists, not ideologues. "[Woodrow] Wilson had the greatest vision of America's world role," the president once remarked. "But he wasn't practical enough."[49] Kissinger sought to purge "sentimentality" from U.S. foreign relations.[50] The term that most generally described the thrust of the Nixon-Kissinger diplomacy was "détente": limited cooperation with the Soviet Union and the People's Republic of China within a general environment of rivalry. Détente became a means, a process, a climate in which to reduce international tensions and sustain U.S. leadership in world politics. Détente was supposed to produce a geopolitical balance of power, or "equilibrium," by containing the Soviet Union and China and curbing radical revolution.[51] To Nixon, the world divided into roughly five power centers (including Japan and Western Europe) with each keeping order among smaller states and clients in its region and each respecting one another's sphere. Indeed, the historian Jeremi Suri has argued that détente marked a first step "toward a conservative world order after the global disruption" of the 1960s, as Nixon, USSR leader Leonid Brezhnev, and even Mao recoiled from nuclear threats and revolutionary upheavals.[52]

Nixon and Kissinger saw Soviet-American competition as the primary element in world affairs. They understood that by 1970 the Soviet Union had achieved nuclear parity or equality with the United States, that the Soviets suffered severe internal economic problems and needed outside help, that the Sino-Soviet split had widened, and that world power (capital and weaponry) had become diffused as nations had recovered from World War II and colonies had broken away from empires. Recognizing that Washington could not "conceive *all* the plans, design *all* the programs, execute *all* the decisions," the duo sought to move the United States from containment through confrontation to containment through negotiation.[53]

Détente, SALT, and the Nuclear Arms Race

The Nixon administration emphasized the triangular relationship formed by the Soviet Union, China, and the United States and attempted to play the two communist states against one another, to keep one worrying about what the United States was doing with the other. For the Soviets there would be both incentives (capital and trade) to encourage restraint, and penalties (large arms sales to Soviet adversaries and closer ties to China) to punish unacceptable behavior.

What one historian has called "drinking your Mao Tai and having your Vodka too" made sense to European allies who abhorred the U.S. "obsession with Southeast Asia."[54] Moscow and Beijing might help the United States extricate itself from war in Vietnam. The Cold War was also costing too much; détente supposedly offered a cheaper way of pursuing containment by reducing the necessity for interventions, spiraling military expenditures, and new nuclear weapons systems. The Nixon administration cut the armed forces from 3.5 million in 1968 to 2.3 million in 1973, ended the draft, and in 1972 negotiated a strategic arms limitation treaty. At a time when U.S. foreign trade needed a boost to eliminate a billion-dollar deficit in the balance of payments, détente conjured up images of expanded markets. Massive grain shipments flowed to the Soviet Union—in 1972, 25 percent of the American wheat crop—and corporations such as Pepsi-Cola and Chase Manhattan Bank started operations in the USSR. U.S. exports to the Soviet Union reached $2.3 billion in 1976. "They want credits, they want trade, and we'll give it all to 'em," said Nixon. "But for a price. We don't give it away cheap."[55]

Nixon-Kissinger grand strategy rested on some questionable assumptions. It overestimated the usefulness of China as a check on Moscow. It assumed wrongly that the Soviets could manage their "friends" in North Vietnam or India or the Middle East and that great-power cooperation could calm Third World problems. Still viewing small states as proxies of the great powers, Nixon paid too little attention to the local sources of disputes and the fierce independence of nationalist and neutralist governments. Kissinger spent much of his time trying to keep détente glued together in the face of conflicts in Asia, Africa, and the Middle East, and economic challenges from the Organization of Petroleum Exporting Countries (OPEC). Even America's friends caused difficulty: Iran insisted on huge arms shipments but raised oil prices, threatening the U.S. economy; Saudi Arabia demanded sophisticated weaponry but refused to help resolve the Arab-Israeli conflict.

Détente also ran afoul of domestic dissenters. In 1974 conservatives and liberals in Congress cooperated to deny most-favored-nation trade status to the Soviet Union until it permitted Jewish emigration. Americans of Eastern European descent berated détente as sellout—an abandonment of their homelands to Soviet domination. Liberals criticized Kissinger's arrogant presumption of superpower domination and his tolerance of authoritarian regimes that trampled on human rights. The Nixon and Ford administrations contradicted themselves by appealing for arms control while they broke records for arms sales abroad ($10 billion in 1976 alone). Hard-line anticommunists labeled Kissinger an appeaser who conceded the communists too much and who squandered U.S. supremacy in the international system. By 1976 the secretary of state bemoaned that "the principal danger we face is our own domestic divisions."[56]

Beijing Ball Park. This American magazine advertisement, titled "Yankees come here," appeared after Nixon's trip. It read: "The way things are going in China, hot dogs will be sold right along with egg rolls." Mao, of course, never donned a baseball uniform or blasted a home run over the Great Wall, but Sino-American détente inspired exaggerations like this. (Lucy Gould, *Parade*. Courtesy of Frankfurt Communications, Inc., New York)

The Nixon administration nonetheless claimed diplomatic triumphs. The opening to China ranked highest. The turnaround helped thwart reconciliation between the two communist giants. "Absolutely convinced that the Chinese want war" because "they have too many people," Moscow deployed more divisions in Asia—away from NATO.[57] China received top-grade intelligence on the Soviets. "You don't need a master spy. We give you everything," said Kissinger.[58] New ties between China and Japan contributed to Asian stability. Sino-American trade flourished, reaching $700 million in 1973. Also, cultural exchanges and travel between the once-distant nations reduced mutual ignorance. In 1973 Washington and Beijing exchanged "Liaison Offices" or mini-embassies. Formal diplomatic relations had to wait until 1979, after Watergate, Nixon's resignation, the 1976 presidential election, the deaths of Mao and Zhou, and new political alignments within China.

The Sino-American rapprochement did have some tragic side effects. In 1971 the Bengalis of East Pakistan rebelled against the military dictatorship of (West)

Pakistan and declared the independent nation of Bangladesh. The Pakistani government attempted to crush the revolution and carried out a slaughter that U.S. officials at the scene called "selective genocide."[59] India, which had just signed a treaty of friendship with the Soviet Union, intervened on behalf of the rebels. The White House, against considerable State Department objection, ordered a "tilt" in favor of Pakistan.[60] As an ally, Pakistan had granted the United States bases for U-2 flights over the Soviet Union and intelligence-gathering posts to monitor Soviet nuclear testing. American weapons soon flowed to Pakistan, foreign aid to India stopped, and a naval task force steamed into the Bay of Bengal. "A victory of India over Pakistan [would be] the same as a victory of the Soviet Union over China," Nixon told French President Georges Pompidou.[61] Indeed, the White House took a global rather than regional view of the crisis and saw India acting as Moscow's pawn trying to "goat" Pakistan into full-scale war.[62] But India never attacked West Pakistan, and the Soviet Union never encouraged it to attack. Pakistan, India, China, and the Soviet Union—*before* Kissinger's "frenetic crisis fever, histrionic signals, . . . and the meanderings of the American fleet"—all had indicated support for an agreement that matched the outcome: an end to hostilities and independence for Bangladesh.[63]

Despite blunt exchanges over the hot line during the Indo-Pakistani conflict, détente remained U.S. policy. The president and his national security affairs adviser traveled to the Soviet capital in May 1972 for a summit meeting. "My reputation is one of being a very hard-line, cold-war-oriented, anti-communist," Nixon told president Brezhnev, but Nixon now believed that capitalism and communism could "live together and work together."[64] They struck agreements on cooperation in space exploration (culminating in a joint space venture in 1975) and trade (large grain sales soon followed). They also discussed Vietnam and concluded that small nations should not disrupt détente. Only a few weeks earlier, when Nixon had escalated the bombing of North Vietnam, he feared that an angry Moscow might cancel the summit. The Soviets did not; to them détente came first.

The summit conferees concentrated on the Strategic Arms Limitation Talks (SALT) agreements. When the Nixon administration entered office, it inherited a legacy of doctrines and missiles that defined U.S. nuclear strategy. (See Glossary, p. 376.) In the 1960s, the doctrine of "massive retaliation" evolved into the concept of "mutual assured destruction," or MAD. MAD's viability depended on each side's "second-strike capability": the capacity to absorb a first strike and still destroy the attacker with a retaliatory or second strike. By 1969 American strategists sought a superiority of forces through the triad: land-based intercontinental ballistic missiles (ICBMs), long-range B-52 bombers, and submarine-launched ballistic missiles (SLBMs), all armed with nuclear weapons. To help guarantee superiority, the United States had also begun to flight-test the "multiple independently targetable reentry vehicle" (MIRV). Finally, Nixon inherited initial planning for an "antiballistic missile" (ABM) system to defend cities and ICBMs vulnerable to Soviet attack. Because ABMs theoretically protected offensive weapons from attack, critics feared that the ABM would stimulate the Soviets to build more missiles to overwhelm the ABM protection, thus further accelerating the nuclear arms race.

By 1968 Washington had deployed 1,054 ICBMs to the Soviets' 858; the United States also led in SLBMs 656 to 121, and in long-range bombers 545 to 155. The

United States ranked first in total nuclear warheads, about 4,200 to 1,100, and in the accuracy of its weapons systems. Yet U.S. officials knew that the Soviets were constructing new missiles, submarines, and bombers at a pace that would soon give the Soviets nuclear parity with the United States. The two great nuclear powers had become "fencers on a tightrope: each facing the other, weapon in hand, balancing precariously, neither willing . . . to thrust decisively because such a thrust would topple them both, attacker and victim, to mutual disaster."[65]

President Nixon soon abandoned the untenable doctrine of superiority and accepted parity of forces with the Soviet Union. Still, he decided to phase in the ABM system. Nixon also ordered the installation of MIRVs. Thus the United States could enter the SALT talks, he said, from a position of strength.

The first SALT talks began in Helsinki in November 1969 and alternated between that city and Vienna until 1972. SALT-I culminated on May 26, 1972, at the Moscow summit with two agreements. The first, a treaty, limited the deployment of ABMs for each nation to two sites. In essence the accord sustained the MAD doctrine, because it left urban centers in both countries vulnerable. The other accord, an interim agreement on strategic offensive arms, froze the existing number of ICBMs already deployed or in construction. At the time, the Soviet Union led 1,607 to 1,054. The interim agreements also froze SLBMs at 740 for the USSR and 656 for the United States. SALT-I did not limit the hydra-headed MIRVs, thus leaving the United States superior in deliverable warheads, 5,700 to 2,500. Nixon and Kissinger underestimated the speed with which the Soviets would deploy their own MIRVs on heavier missiles, and by not seeking a ban on MIRVs, which the Pentagon regarded as America's technological "trump card," they rendered American ICBMs theoretically vulnerable to a first strike.[66] After joking, "What are 3,000 MIRVs among friends," Kissinger later regretted that he had not "thought through the implications of a MIRVed world more thoughtfully."[67] Nor did the agreement restrict long-range bombers, in which the United States held a 450 to 200 advantage. Finally, SALT-I did not prohibit the development of new weapons. The United States, for example, moved ahead on the Trident submarine (to replace the Polaris–Poseidon fleet), the B-1 bomber (to replace the B-52), and the cruise missile. Indeed, as Kissinger remarked: "The way to use this freeze is for us to catch up."[68]

Still, SALT-I did begin frank strategic arms talks to place limits on nuclear weapons. In August 1972, the Senate passed the ABM treaty by an 88 to 2 vote; a joint congressional resolution later endorsed the interim agreement. Détente's reputation soared. Conservative critics charged, however, that despite possessing more nuclear warheads, the United States still lagged behind the Soviet Union in delivery vehicles (ICBMs, SLBMs, and strategic bombers). "What in the name of God is strategic superiority?" Kissinger challenged his detractors. "What do you do with it?"[69]

Negotiations on SALT-II opened in late 1972, but progress came slowly. At Vladivostok, in November 1974, Presidents Ford and Brezhnev initialed a set of principles to guide the talks. They agreed, first, to place a ceiling of 2,400 on the total number of delivery vehicles permitted each side. They agreed, second, that each side could equip no more than 1,320 missiles with MIRVs. Critics noted that the numerical ceilings actually projected higher levels than either side had reached.

The Nuclear Arms Race: A Glossary

Anti-ballistic missile (ABM): A defensive missile designed to destroy an incoming enemy ballistic missile before its warhead reaches its target.

Ballistic missile: A rocket-propelled missile that leaves the atmosphere and returns to earth in a free fall.

Cruise missile: A guided missile that flies to its target within the earth's atmosphere, close to the surface. The cruise missile can carry a nuclear warhead and can be launched from the air, land, or sea.

Delivery vehicle: A missile or strategic bomber that delivers a warhead to its target.

Deployment: Installing weapons, making them ready for action.

First strike: An initial nuclear attack by one country intended to destroy an adversary's strategic nuclear forces.

Intercontinental ballistic missile (ICBM): A land-based missile capable of traveling more than 3,000 nautical miles to deliver one or more warheads.

Intermediate-range nuclear forces (INF): Sometimes called theater nuclear forces, these weapons have a range of about 3,000 miles.

Missile experimental (MX): An American ICBM capable of carrying as many as ten MIRVs.

Multiple independently targetable reentry vehicle (MIRV): A vehicle loaded with a warhead and mounted, along with similar vehicles, on one ballistic missile. Once separated from the missile, each MIRV can be directed against a different target.

Mutual assured destruction (MAD): The ability of both the United States and the Soviet Union to inflict damage so severe that neither is willing to initiate a nuclear attack.

Neutron bomb: An "enhanced radiation weapon," this nuclear bomb is designed primarily to kill people and to inflict less damage on buildings than other bombs.

Nuclear freeze: The immediate halt to the development, production, transfer, and deployment of nuclear weapons.

Second strike: A retaliatory nuclear attack launched after being hit by an opponent's first strike.

Strategic Defense Initiative (SDI): Popularly known as "Star Wars," SDI was President Ronald Reagan's 1983 proposal to build a space-based, defensive system that could establish a protective shield over the United States and its allies with the capability to shoot down incoming ballistic missiles.

Strategic weapons or arms: Long-range weapons capable of hitting an adversary's territory. ICBMs, SLBMs, and strategic bombers are so classified.

Submarine-launched ballistic missile (SLBM): A ballistic missile carried in and launched from a submarine.

Surface-to-air missile (SAM): A missile launched from the earth's surface for the purpose of knocking down an adversary's airplanes.

Tactical nuclear weapons: Low-yield nuclear weapons for battlefield use.

Triad: The three-part structure of American strategic forces (ICBMs, SLBMs, and strategic bombers).

Warhead: The part of a missile that contains the nuclear explosive intended to inflict damage.

After 1974 the SALT-II talks bogged down over which types of weapons should count in the 2,400 ceiling. The United States insisted that the new Soviet bomber, the Backfire, be included, and the Soviet Union demanded inclusion of the U.S. cruise missile. Neither Moscow nor Washington yielded before 1977, the year the SALT-I agreements expired. By then the United States wielded 8,500 warheads, compared with 5,700 in 1972; comparable Soviet figures equaled 4,000 and 2,500. Total strategic delivery vehicles by 1978 numbered 2,059 for the United States and 2,440 for the Soviet Union. Détente had not checked the nuclear arms race.

In Europe, however, détente worked to ease tensions. Willy Brandt, the West German chancellor, pursued a policy of *Ostpolitik* to remove the two Germanies from great-power competition. A West German–Soviet treaty of August 1970 identified détente as the goal of both countries and recognized the existence of two Germanies. A few months later Brandt signed an agreement with Poland that confirmed the latter's postwar absorption of German territory to the Oder-Neisse line. Then, in June 1972, the four powers occupying Berlin signed an agreement wherein the Soviet Union guaranteed Western access to the city and relaxed restrictions on travel between the two Berlins. Finally, in December 1972, the two Germanies themselves initialed a treaty that provided for the exchange of diplomatic representatives and membership in the United Nations for both (effected in 1973). European East-West trade boomed, with the West German economy the chief beneficiary.

At the Conference on Security and Cooperation in Helsinki, Finland, in summer 1975, thirty-five nations assembled in what some observers called the peace conference that officially ended World War II. The delegates accepted the permanence of existing European boundaries, including adjustments made in Germany and Eastern Europe three decades earlier. The conferees pledged themselves to détente and endorsed human rights for all Europeans. While right-wing critics were "bitching about the borders we had done nothing to change when we had a nuclear monopoly," so-called Helsinki groups pressed communist governments to honor their pledge about human rights.[70] Such groups included Charter 77, headed by Václav Havel in Czechoslovakia, and Solidarity, led by Lech Walesa in Poland. Instead of the "consolidation of the postwar order that Moscow had so long desired," a Kissinger aide later noted, "the political status quo in Eastern Europe began to unravel."[71] In the short run, as "masters of our own house," the Kremlin arrested Soviet intellectuals who demanded freedom of speech.[72] When the dissident writer Aleksandr Solzhenitsyn, whose *Gulag Archipelago* (1974) described and condemned Soviet oppression, asked to visit the White House, President Ford turned down the "goddamned horse's ass" because he did not want to jeopardize progress toward SALT-II.[73]

Regional Tails Wagging the Superpower Dogs: The Middle East

The Nixon Doctrine, announced in July 1969, declared that henceforth the United States would supply military and economic assistance but not soldiers to help nations defend themselves. "We must avoid that kind of policy that will make countries in Asia so dependent upon us that we are dragged into conflicts such as the one that we have in Vietnam."[74] Washington sought to build up regional surrogate powers, such as Iran and Israel, thus apparently retiring its badge as the world's policeman. Nonetheless, Third World countries held a place in the Nixon-Kissinger scheme for equilibrium because of their vulnerability to destabilizing radicalism and hence to pernicious Soviet influence. Kissinger cited Moscow's endorsement of national liberation movements to argue, therefore, that the internal politics of developing nations intertwined with the "international struggle."[75] When troubles arose in the Third World, Nixon, Ford, and Kissinger reflexively interpreted them as moves in the game of great-power politics.

Problems in the Middle East sorely tested détente. Basic U.S. goals since World War II had been consistent for the region: ensure oil supplies; contain the Soviet Union; protect Israel; challenge neutralism; and blunt the appeal of Arab nationalism. After the 1956 Suez crisis, the Soviet Union and the United States armed Egypt

Golda Meir (1898–1978), Nixon, and Kissinger. In early 1973, the prime minister of Israel met with the president, who promised more U.S. airplanes. On the Nixon-Meir relationship, White House counsel Leonard Garment later wrote: "How could Nixon resist this mother of all mothers, Hannah Nixon squared—smart, spiky, and resolute in her simple schoolteacher frock?" (Department of State *Newsletter*)

and Israel respectively. In June 1967, after years of threats and counterthreats, Israel attacked Egypt and Syria. In the Six-Day War, the Israelis, using American-supplied weapons, captured the West Bank, including the ancient city of Jerusalem, from Jordan, the Golan Heights from Syria, and the entire Sinai Peninsula, including the eastern bank of the Suez Canal, from Egypt. Half of the Arab states broke diplomatic relations with Washington. Soviet vessels obtained access to Arab ports. Washington, in turn, sold fifty F-4 Phantom jets to Israel in December 1968 and winked at Israel's "rudimentary, but operational, nuclear weapons capability."[76]

The Middle East, said Nixon, had become a "powder keg."[77] His administration worried that the persistent Arab-Israeli conflict would open a Soviet avenue into the Middle East. As U.S. Phantom jets began to arrive in Israel, and as the Israelis conducted bombing raids deep into Egypt in January 1970, the Soviets shipped surface-to-air missiles (SAMs) to Egypt to defend against the Phantoms. Thousands of Soviet troops, advisers, and pilots answered Egypt's call for assistance. Washington gave Israel more F-4s and electronic equipment to improve Israeli accuracy. U.S. military credits for Israel totaled $1.2 billion from 1971 to 1973.

Meanwhile, Palestinian Arabs, many of them refugees ousted from their homes in 1948 when Israel won nationhood, grew more frustrated. The Palestine Liberation Organizaion (PLO), formed in 1964 by several guerrilla groups, came under the aggressive leadership of Yasir Arafat four years later. Many Arab leaders backed the organization in its demand for the elimination of the Jewish state and for the creation of a Palestinian homeland. In 1970 a radical wing of the PLO hijacked airliners and temporarily seized passengers, including Americans, as hostages. That same year, PLO troops with Syrian help battled King Hussein's armies in Jordan. Palestinian terrorists murdered Israeli athletes at the 1972 Olympic Games in Munich. The Israelis retaliated, assassinating PLO figures abroad.

Soviet relations with the PLO and Egypt grew frosty in the early 1970s, as Moscow tried to restrain both out of fear that Washington would scuttle détente if Mideast tensions continued. For its part, the Nixon administration, from 1970 to 1973, followed a "standstill diplomacy."[78] Israel possessed military superiority, Moscow displayed restraint, and a new, seemingly more moderate Egyptian government under the leadership of Anwar el-Sadat came to power after Nasser's death in September 1970. Fearful that détente would condemn Egypt to a "no war, no peace" paralysis, Sadat plotted a new strike against Isreal.[79] He withstood a Soviet-supported coup d'état attempt, and in summer 1972 he abruptly expelled several thousand Soviet technicians and military advisers. The United States continued to arm Israel; in early 1973 Washington promised planes. On October 6, 1973 (Yom Kippur, the holiest day on the Jewish calendar), Egyptian forces struck across the canal into Sinai while Syrian troops attacked Israel's northern border. The attack took Israel and the United States by surprise. At first the Israelis suffered heavy losses, and the Arabs regained land lost in 1967. Nixon promised Tel Aviv more Phantoms. "The best result," a cold-blooded Kissinger predicted, "would be if Israel comes out a little ahead but got bloodied in the process, and if the U.S. stayed clean."[80] As Moscow rushed arms to Syria, one senator asked: "Where in all this lies détente?"[81]

In the midst of the crisis, the shadow of Watergate lengthened over the Nixon administration. On October 10, Vice President Spiro Agnew resigned after evidence surfaced that he had accepted payoffs as governor of Maryland years before. Ten days later Nixon fired the special Watergate prosecutor for getting too close to damaging evidence. The concatenation of domestic and foreign crises frayed nerves. The White House staff feared that Moscow might think the U.S. government weak or incapacitated.

In a massive airlift of supplies, Nixon ordered "everything that will fly" to Israel on October 14.[82] Soviet premier Aleksei Kosygin flew to Cairo to persuade Sadat to accept a cease-fire. Kissinger flew to Moscow on October 20, learning en route that the Saudis had embargoed oil to the United States. By October 21 most Arab members of the Organization of Petroleum Exporting Countries had joined the embargo. Kissinger and the Soviets finally arranged a cease-fire on October 22. But the Israelis ignored the truce and surrounded the Egyptian Third Army. When Moscow pressed for Soviet and U.S. troops to enforce the truce jointly, Washington overreacted. An inebriated Nixon called it "the most serious thing since the Cuban Missile Crisis. Words won't do the job. We've got to act."[83] Kissinger thereupon ordered all U.S. forces on nuclear alert, a calculated ploy to shock Soviet decision-makers. Amid charges that Kissinger "lied to us" and sought to "unleash World War III," the Kremlin chose not to intervene unilaterally.[84] Kissinger pressed the Israelis to honor the truce. A new cease-fire held.

The Arab-Israeli contest threatened the American economy as well as the economies of U.S. allies. Arab states such as Saudi Arabia, which for years had supplied Western nations with inexpensive petroleum, now used their black riches as a weapon: They embargoed petroleum shipments to the United States and quadrupled the price of crude oil for Western Europe and Japan. "We are masters of our own commodity," the Saudi oil minister announced.[85] The United States, importing between 10 and 15 percent of its oil from the Middle East, suffered an energy

"You're Like a Bunch of . . . of . . . of . . . CAPITALISTS!!" The oil embargo by the OPEC nations in 1974 produced anger among Americans who found that gasoline stations ran out of fuel or that what they could buy had drastically risen in price. Venezuela and the Arab nations replied that they were only doing what the developed nations had done to them for decades. (Dennis Renault, *Sacramento Bee*)

crisis. Gasoline prices spun upward, and anxious drivers lined up, sometimes for hours, hoping to fuel their automobiles. The embargo ended in March 1974, but prices remained high and U.S. vulnerability had been exposed.

Kissinger launched "shuttle diplomacy" to prevent another Mideast blowup. With impressive stamina and patience, he bargained in Cairo and Tel Aviv and other capitals intermittently for two years. "Dr. Henry, you are my favorite magician," said Sadat.[86] Finally, on September 1, 1975, Egypt and Israel initialed a historic agreement that provided for an eventual Israeli pullback from part of the Sinai, created a United Nations–patrolled buffer zone, and placed U.S. technicians in "early warning" stations to detect military activities. Washington also promised substantial aid to both Egypt and Israel.

Thorny problems remained. The Palestinian Arabs still lived in refugee camps and demanded a homeland, while Israelis entrenched themselves in occupied territories, building industries, farms, and houses. Jordan still demanded the return of the West Bank, and Syrian-Israeli hostility persisted with the Golan Heights in Israel's hands. A bloody civil war broke out in Lebanon, which prompted Syria to send in troops in 1976. Washington continued to ship weapons to both Arabs and Israelis after the October war. In 1976, Sadat, who wanted U.S. technology and mediation, denounced the Soviet Union, saying that "99 percent of the cards in the game are in America's hands whether the Soviet Union likes it or not."[87] Once Cairo turned emphatically toward Washington, U.S. Mideast policy looked more like old-fashioned containment than détente. Kissinger's refusal to include the Soviets and Palestinians in Mideast diplomacy precluded a full Arab-Israeli settlement. The spectacular rescue by Israeli commandos of 259 hostages held captive by Palestinian terrorists in Entebbe, Uganda, on July 4, 1976, also galvanized U.S. public support for Israel. Especially for conservatives who deplored America's failure in Vietnam, this "very special birthday present" on the U.S. bicentennial seemed to prove that "*will* is the decisive factor" in military affairs.[88] After Entebbe, it became axiomatic that "the United States should not only act *with* Israel on foreign policy but *like* Israel in matters of unconventional warfare."[89] Moscow, in turn, gave more support to Libya's president Moammar Gadhafi, a radical Pan Arabist who came to power in 1969 and denounced all Mideast peace efforts.

As a counterweight to the Soviets and radical Arabs, the Nixon and Ford administrations fashioned a closer alliance with the Shah of Iran. In 1972 Washington promised the Shah non-nuclear weapons and U.S. technicians. The Shah's military gorged itself on modern American arms, paid for by galloping oil revenues ("petrodollars"). American corporate executives rushed to Iran to display their submarines, fighter aircraft, assault helicopters, and missiles. In 1977 his nation ranked as the largest foreign buyer of American-made arms, spending $5.7 billion that year alone. His armed forces became the most powerful in the region. But doubters thought such excessive military spending foolhardy when the Iranian per capita income stood at only $350 and such funds could have helped alleviate the nation's economic woes. Ruthlessly suppressing all dissent, the Shah said that "if there was any rough stuff it was necessary and that was the end of that."[90] To improve his image in the United States, the Shah hired a New York advertising agency and lavishly bestowed gifts on prominent Americans. U.S. officials remained committed to the Shah as their "unconditional ally" in the turbulent Middle East.[91] They did not see that "Iran was the regional tail wagging the superpower dog."[92]

Covert Action and Economic Relations in Latin America and Africa

Latin America remained an area of intense interest to the United States. Thousands of Latin American military officers still trained in the United States, some at the Inter-American Defense College in Washington, D.C., where they learned urban counterinsurgency and jungle warfare techniques. U.S. trade with the Western Hemisphere continued large. In the early 1970s one-third of Latin American exports went to the United States and two-fifths of the region's imports came from the United States. In 1976, Latin American countries supplied 34 percent of U.S. petroleum imports, 68 percent of its coffee, 57 percent of its sugar, 47 percent of its copper, and 98 percent of its bauxite. In that year U.S. direct investments in its southern neighbors totaled $17 billion. Latin American governments nonetheless increasingly challenged Washington. Soon after taking office, Nixon sent Governor Nelson Rockefeller on a fact-finding mission to Latin America. Demonstrations erupted, and parts of his trip had to be canceled. The governor reported in August 1969 that the United States caused deep resentment through its "paternalistic attitude" and attempts to "direct the internal affairs of other nations to an unseemly degree."[93]

Mexico refused to honor the economic blockade of Cuba, strongly criticized the 1965 Dominican intervention, boldly proclaimed the economic independence of small states and their right to expropriate foreign enterprises, and urged that developed nations share their wealth with poorer countries. In 1974 the United Nations approved these views by a 120 to 6 vote, with the United States voting no. The United States also engaged Peru and Ecuador in a "tuna war," after those nations declared a 200-mile territorial limit and began seizing American fishing vessels in coastal waters. After 1968, a new, radical (noncommunist) military government in Peru deliberately set out to break the country's economic dependence on the United States by nationalizing an Exxon oil subsidiary and other American-owned properties. Lima also defiantly purchased Soviet MiGs. Venezuela, too, searched for ways to reduce its economic reliance on the United States. A founding member of OPEC in 1960, Caracas joined the Arabs in drastically raising petroleum prices in the 1970s, and in 1976 it too nationalized American-owned oil companies.

Frank Church (1924–1984). Democratic senator from Idaho (1957–1981), Church became a major figure on the Foreign Relations Committee, serving as its chair (1979–1981). A critic of the Vietnam War and a great orator, Church chaired Senate investigations that revealed U.S. complicity in the overthrow of Chile's Salvador Allende and exposed CIA abuses such as assassination attempts on foreign leaders. One staff member quipped that Church's report should be titled "Bugs, Drugs, and Thugs." (Frank Church Collection, Boise State University Library)

Chile attracted Washington's rapt attention as a threat to U.S. hegemony in September 1970. That month Chileans elected as their president Salvador Allende, a physician by profession and a founder of Chile's Socialist party. The CIA had sent hundreds of thousands of dollars in bribe and propaganda money to Chile to thwart his electoral victory. The CIA also cooperated with the International Telephone and Telegraph Company's covert effort to back a right-wing candidate. Fearing a "democratically elected version of Fidel Castro," Nixon personally gave CIA official Richard Helms full authority ("a marshal's baton") to undermine the Allende government.[94] Following presidential instructions to "make the economy scream" in Chile in order to block the nationalization of American-owned copper corporations (Kennecott and Anaconda), the CIA worked with U.S. companies to stop the shipment of spare parts.[95] Washington also cut off economic aid and denied Export-Import Bank loans to Chile. Military assistance continued as the CIA conspired with Chilean army officers and spent $6 million to subsidize newspapers and political parties opposed to Allende. Allende criticized Washington's "oblique attack, covert, sinuous, but nonetheless harmful for Chile."[96]

In 1973 a military junta overthrew Allende. In the chaos, military officers murdered him, or he committed suicide. U.S. complicity probably stopped short of direct participation in the coup. Declassified documents indicate, however, that "sectors of the U.S. government" were directly involved in operations designed to create a "coup climate" in which the overthrow of Chilean democracy "would and could take place."[97] Vivid images of Allende's ouster recurred in the 1982 film *Missing,* starring Jack Lemmon and Sissy Spacek, a taut thriller in which Chilean authorities kill an American journalist fingered by the U.S. Embassy because he detected U.S. machinations. The new junta returned companies to private hands, suspended freedom of speech and press, and tortured and killed political opponents.

When Congress threatened to cut off arms sales to human rights violators in 1976, Kissinger assured Chilean dictator Augusto Pinochet that "you are a victim of left-wing groups around the world and that your greatest sin was to overthrow a government that was going Communist."[98]

The Nixon and Ford administrations also sought to keep Cuba isolated. Despite CIA reports that "Brezhnev thinks Castro is some sort of idiot, and Castro probably isn't too fond of Brezhnev either," Nixon still perceived Cuba as a Soviet puppet.[99] In fall 1970, Nixon concluded from sketchy U-2 evidence that the Soviets were building a nuclear submarine base at Cienfuegos, Cuba, in violation of their understanding after the 1962 missile crisis to refrain from placing offensive weapons on the island. When Nixon and Kissinger threatened "to face the Soviets down," Moscow denied building a submarine facility.[100] The crisis quickly passed, but the Nixon administration claimed a victory that "reaffirmed," "clarified," and "amplified" the 1962 understanding by prohibiting Soviet nuclear submarine facilities in Cuba.[101] In mid-1971, swine fever swept Cuba, causing health authorities to slaughter half a million pigs to prevent further spread of the disease. Not until 1977 did U.S. investigative journalists reveal that the CIA and an exile group had introduced the deadly virus into Cuba—another CIA dirty trick. Still seeking some accommodation with North America in the early 1970s, Castro deemphasized the export of revolution and aid to insurgencies, and in 1973 he signed an antihijacking treaty with Washington to discourage terrorism in the airways. Two years later the Organization of American States lifted its economic blockade of Cuba. During 1974–1975, U.S. officials met secretly with Cuban diplomats to explore possibilities for détente. In mid-1975 Kissinger rejected baseball commissioner Bowie Kuhn's efforts to arrange games between the United States and Cuba. When Cuban troops in Africa helped Angolan radicals come to power, hopes for a Cuban-American normalization faded.

Until the mid-1970s, Africa stood low on the Nixon-Ford-Kissinger list of diplomatic priorities. As Nixon wooed disenchanted white Democratic voters in a "Southern strategy" at home, so did he pursue a "Southern Africa" strategy by cozying up to white minority regimes in Portuguese Angola, Rhodesia, and South Africa.[102] The National Security Council explained in a memorandum (NSSM 39) that the entrenched whites would approve only moderate change. Washington calculated that the black majorities feared white military superiority and would therefore refrain from major violent confrontation. Nixon once told U.N. Ambassador Daniel P. Moynihan that he "loved" African diplomats—"they're so *kind* and so *nice* . . . and they're children!"[103] This crude, condescending remark about black Africans reflected the cynicism underlying U.S. policy. Washington relaxed the arms embargo to white South Africa; Congress in 1971 passed the Byrd Amendment permitting the United States to buy chromium from Rhodesia despite a United Nations–declared economic boycott of Ian Smith's white minority government. With Southern conservatives hailing Rhodesia as a "latter-day version of their own attempt to secure independence a century earlier," the Black Congressional Caucus blasted the "stifling hypocrisy" of Nixon's policies toward Africa.[104] In contrast to segregationist caricatures of African leaders as "boys in funny hats and monkey-skin coats" from "left-leaning hog-wallow and mangrove-swamp nations" only "slightly removed from cannibalism," dollar-conscious observers cited the more than $2 billion invested in black Africa and U.S. purchases of cobalt, oil, manganese, and platinum.[105]

Events in Angola eventually shattered American complacency. Since the early 1960s, black rebel groups had battled the Portuguese in Angola. Playing a double game in that decade, the CIA channeled funds to a faction of independence fighters while Washington officially backed Portugal and sold it military equipment to quell the nationalist rebellion. The Soviets began to support one of the guerrilla groups, the Popular Movement for the Liberation of Angola (MPLA). In 1975 the CIA spent $32 million on covert operations for propaganda, arms, communications gear, the hiring of white mercenaries, and payments to anti–MPLA political figures. The State Department official in charge of African affairs, Nathaniel Davis, argued that U.S. resources simply could not control the revolution or local events in Africa, but would stimulate increased Soviet activity. Davis urged that the United States appeal to African leaders in Tanzania and Zambia to negotiate a diplomatic solution. For "a test of strength with the Soviets," he advised Kissinger, "we should find a more advantageous place."[106] When President Ford nevertheless decided on covert intervention, Davis resigned.

In November 1975, Portugal granted independence to Angola. The insurgent factions then fought one another in a civil war, with the U.S. clients doing poorly. South Africa and Zaire also dispatched troops to support an American-backed group. "On their own and without consulting us," as one Soviet diplomat put it, the Cubans dispatched 12,000 troops and substantially increased their aid to the MPLA that fall; Moscow hesitated (lest it scuttle détente) but also sent arms and advisers when South African forces intervened.[107] Davis's resignation and leaks about the secret intervention stirred Congress. Another Vietnam? The administration asked for $25 million for arms. "That's when Congress pulled the plug," President Ford later wrote.[108] In December the Senate voted to stop military expenditures for Angola; the House followed suit in January 1976.

Kissinger raged at the failure "to preempt the probable loss to communism of a key developing country at a time of great uncertainty over our will and determination."[109] Yet critics thought it misleading to view an African civil war through a Cold War prism. The MPLA, after all, did not molest American oil companies and never ranked as a Soviet puppet. Given the MPLA's success, the United States hurt itself by choosing the losing side. Discussions with the MPLA—preventive diplomacy—might have reduced the violence. "You may be right in African terms, but I'm thinking globally," Kissinger retorted.[110] The conspicuous example of "Cubans running around" Angola actually encouraged Moscow, heretofore very cautious about backing revolutionary movements "outside its neighboring countries," to defend "African liberation and global anti-imperialism" in far-off Angola. This success fueled further "limited interventions" in Africa and Asia, ultimately leading to the Soviet disaster in Afghanistan in the 1980s.[111]

Ford's ban on using the word *détente* after Angola pointedly exposed the differing Soviet and American interpretations of that concept. What Nixon-Kissinger-Ford had intended as arms agreements and codes of conduct that would restrain Soviet expansion, Moscow saw as "the natural result of the correlation of forces in the world arena," a peaceful coexistence that "cannot in the slightest abolish or

Gerald R. Ford (b. 1913). In October 1973 Vice President Spiro Agnew pleaded no contest to charges of income-tax evasion and acceptance of bribes and resigned. Ford then assumed the office of vice president. A long-time conservative member of Congress from Michigan, Ford aroused controversy when, as president, he pardoned Richard M. Nixon. Ford tried to maintain a U.S. presence in Vietnam and Angola, but Congress rejected funding. (The White House)

change the laws of the class struggle."[112] Thus, as Washington sustained its regional clients and kept the Soviets out of the Mideast peace process, for example, the Brezhnev regime sought "to perform our international duty to other peoples" by assisting national liberation movements.[113]

The Angolan experience prompted reconsideration of U.S. policy toward Africa. So did the outbreak of racial violence in South Africa, where the white government in 1976 crushed a black rebellion in the township of Soweto. America's desire for bountiful Nigerian oil also suggested a change of course. The United States, reasoned Kissinger, "must grab the initiative" or "we will be faced with the Soviets, and Cuban troops," even race wars and African radicalism.[114] Arms shipments went to Kenya and Zaire. Economic ties were strengthened through investments by companies such as Bethlehem Steel and Kaiser Aluminum, in pursuit of titanium and bauxite, respectively. The secretary of state began to disengage the United States from white minority regimes in Rhodesia and South Africa, urging the latter to abandon its segregationist policy of apartheid. Such changes underscored the fact that Africa had become a Cold War arena.

Economic Competition, Environmental Distress, and the North-South Debate

"It's terribly important we be number one economically," said Nixon, "because otherwise we can't be number one diplomatically or militarily."[115] In the 1970s the international economic order created after World War II foundered. The Bretton Woods monetary mechanism (see page 199) faltered; the dollar skidded; famines starved millions at a time when grain stocks fell to record postwar lows; dwindling natural resources spawned political tensions; and the former colonies of the Third World challenged the industrial nations to share power. The global recession of the early 1970s became the worst since the 1930s. Inflation raised the cost of industrial goods for developing countries. Protectionist barriers rose, impeding world trade. Dramatically climbing OPEC oil prices hit poor and rich nations alike, while the price of other commodities, such as copper, slumped, causing economic downturns in nations dependent on the export of one product. Economists coined the term "Fourth World"—poor, less developed countries (LDCs) that lacked profitmaking raw materials, relied heavily on food imports, and built up large foreign debts.

The Soviet Union and the People's Republic of China engaged in world trade as never before, in quest of agricultural products and high technology, and enlarged East-West trade became a headline issue. So did the questions of how to regulate ocean-bed mineral resources and how to deal with powerful multinational corporations.

In this chaotic economy, the United States produced about one-third of all the world's goods and services and remained the world's largest trading nation. In 1970 U.S. exports stood at $27.5 billion; by 1977 they had climbed to $121.2 billion. Coca-Cola, Gillette, and IBM earned more than half of their profits abroad. Many American jobs depended on healthy foreign trade. In 1976, for example, one out of every nine manufacturing workers produced goods for export. Exports accounted for one out of every four dollars of agricultural sales in 1977.

American industry also relied on imports of raw materials: 75 percent of the tin, 91 percent of the chrome, 99 percent of the manganese, and 64 percent of the zinc consumed by Americans in 1975 came from foreign sources. In 1977 the nation imported more than 40 percent of the petroleum it used. These import needs had become conspicuous in 1971 when, for the first time since the depression decade of the 1930s, the United States suffered a trade deficit, importing more than it exported. Six years later, the trade imbalance reached $26.5 billion, due in large part to imported energy sources.

U.S. direct investments abroad—about half of the world's total of foreign direct investments—equaled $75.5 billion in 1970 and $149.8 billion in 1977, thus further defining the United States as a fulcrum of the international economy. The greatest part of these investments remained in developed countries (73 percent in 1975). Some investments faced political unrest, terrorist acts, and nationalization.

Despite its commanding status, the United States seemed to be losing its competitive edge. In the 1970s, ninety-eight nations had higher rates of economic growth than the United States. Japan and West Germany, strategic allies but commerical rivals, challenged America in the international marketplace. In fact, Japanese automobiles, televisions, and electronic equipment seized a large share of markets within the United States. Once dominant, American producers of computers, high technology, and aerospace machinery now struggled to retain high rank. Then, too, Americans worried that wealthy Arabs were buying up American banks, companies, and real estate.

The descent of the once mighty dollar further demonstrated the declining U.S. position. A "dollar glut" developed abroad, induced by U.S. foreign-aid programs, military expenditures ($90 billion in 1970 alone), private investments, inflation, and purchases of higher-priced oil. Foreigners held $78 billion in 1969; by 1977 the figure had jumped to $373 billion. Foreign holders of dollars wanted to exchange them for gold, thus putting pressure on America's diminishing gold stock. The dollar declined in value against currencies such as the German mark and Swiss franc. The United States faced a serious balance-of-payments crisis.

The Nixon administration adopted unilateral policies that shocked foreign capitals and upset the Bretton Woods system of cooperation. In August 1971, after the dollar had fallen to its lowest point against the mark since World War II, Nixon devalued the dollar (by increasing the dollar price of an ounce of gold) and suspended its convertibility into gold. The president also cut foreign aid by 10 percent and imposed a 10 percent surtax on all imports, seeking thereby to reduce the influx of Japanese and European goods and to put diplomatic pressure on other nations to revalue their currencies to make them less competitive with the dollar. "We'll fix those bastards," said Nixon when Treasury Secretary John Connally claimed that "foreigners are out to screw us. Our job is to screw them first."[116]

In December, representatives of ten leading trading nations gathered at the Smithsonian Institution in Washington to try to stabilize the international monetary system. After stormy sessions, America's economic competitors agreed to revalue their currencies to bring them more into line with the dollar. The United States then lifted its import surcharge and once more made the dollar exchangeable for gold. But the Smithsonian agreement did not work for long; in early 1973 the

United States again devalued the dollar, this time letting it "float," its value determined no longer by agreement but by supply and demand in the monetary marketplace. Efforts by the International Monetary Fund to restore an orderly system fell short.

International money problems intersected with foreign trade problems. Higher priced American goods could not easily compete with Japanese or European products, and the European Common Market engaged in preferential trade arrangements and export subsidies that hurt U.S. sales abroad. Highly protectionist at home yet aggressively penetrating global markets, Japan was "like the golfer who is shooting in the 80s with the same 25 handicap he used when he was shooting in the 100s."[117] When Nixon in 1971 threatened to "stick it to Japan" with quotas, Tokyo averted a trade war by voluntarily limiting textile exports to America.[118] Multilateral trade negotiations, under the auspices of the long-working General Agreement on Tariffs and Trade (1947), began in Tokyo in 1974. Five years later the "Tokyo Round" of negotiations finally produced accords that shrank tariffs about 30 percent. The signatories, including the United States, also wrote codes to regulate subsidies and dumping. Yet they failed to liberalize trade in agriculture. Many protectionist practices continued: "The free flow of world trade remains largely an ideal."[119]

In 1972, although the developing world had 74 percent of the world's population, it represented only 17 percent of the world's combined gross national product (GNP). From the perspective of the developing nations (the "South"), it seemed imperative that wealthier industrial nations (the "North") charge less for manufactured goods and technology, offer foreign assistance and loans at low rates, reduce tariffs, pay more for raw materials through commodity price agreements, and allow Third World nations to restrict foreign-owned corporations. Developing countries also insisted on a greater voice in international institutions such as the World Bank. "The object is to complete the liberation of the Third World countries from external domination" by changing the "structure of power," explained Tanzania's Julius K. Nyerere.[120]

The Group of 77, a coalition of developing nations organized in 1964, articulated the Third World's economic demands. More than one hundred countries by the 1970s, this consortium dominated the UN General Assembly, and in 1974 that body endorsed a New International Economic Order. The United States, Japan, and Western European nations agreed to talk and struck some compromises, but by the early 1980s a stalemate existed. U.S. officials did not take kindly to charges of American greed when many Third World nations themselves indulged in financial corruption and wasted resources on weaponry. India, fearing Chinese and Pakistani nuclear capabilities, allotted billions to produce a nuclear bomb in 1974 instead of devoting those funds to alleviating severe food shortages.

Famine intensified. Insufficient fertilizer, inadequate farm acreage, pollution, droughts, and shrinking fish supplies due to overharvesting condemned one-quarter of humankind to hunger. The drought that swept Africa in the early 1970s caused at least 10,000 deaths a day. A high birth rate and falling death rate put severe pressure on available food supplies. In 1975 the world's population passed 4 billion. Nutritionists estimated that between a half-billion and one billion people ate less than the calories required to sustain ordinary physical activity.

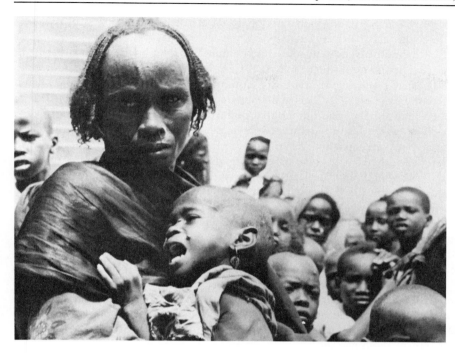

Famine in Chad, Africa. Drought-stricken Chad was only one of many poor nations that suffered in the world hunger crisis of the 1970s. Millions died. (CARE, New York)

At the 1974 World Food Conference in Rome, the United States voted to help finance an International Fund for Agricultural Development to expand food production in developing countries. But the United States continued to market surplus food for profit, most notably in large grain sales (dubbed "the great grain robbery") to the dollar-paying Soviet Union.[121] And food aid, always political, became more so; in 1973–1974 more than half of U.S. food assistance went to clients South Vietnam, Cambodia, and South Korea. At the same time, because of rising petroleum costs, the United States reduced its exports of petroleum-derived fertilizers, thus contributing to a worldwide decline in grain production of 15 million tons in 1974. As the CIA noted, "in bad years . . . Washington would acquire virtual life-and-death power over the fate of the multitudes of the needy."[122] The 1970s ranked as bad years.

U.S. foreign-aid strategy in the early 1970s aimed to assist especially the most impoverished people through projects to improve nutrition, family planning, health, education, and food production. But developing nations complained that the United States was cutting back when the need was greatest. Although total foreign aid (economic and military) had increased from $6.6 billion in 1970 to $7.8 billion in 1977, the proportion of GNP devoted to development assistance actually decreased. In 1977 Americans spent about four times as much on tobacco products as their government expended on development aid. Kissinger attempted to meet some of the developing nations' demands; he nonetheless voiced a growing American impatience with their "confrontational" manner and their assumption that growth was "a quick fix requiring only that the world's wealth be properly redistributed through tests of strength instead of a process of self-help over generations."[123]

North-South relations also became contentious over environmental issues. In the United States, books such as Rachel Carson's *Silent Spring* (1962), Paul Erlich's *The Population Bomb* (1968), and Barry Commoner's *The Closing Circle* (1971) raised public consciousness about environmental degradation and the growing imbalance between food supplies and burgeoning populations. Grassroots organizations such as the Worldwatch Institute reiterated the message that "the earth is in danger, that everything is connected to everything else, that too many people live here, that smaller is better."[124] In 1969 Greenpeace organized to protest nuclear-weapons tests, and the following year Americans celebrated the first Earth Day. Nixon bowed to congressional pressure to create the Environmental Protection Agency (EPA). Oil spills from oceangoing tankers, unsafe disposal of hazardous wastes, and the contamination of water sources revealed environmental questions as borderless, transnational issues requiring international attention. Environmental groups around the world pressed for action. But countervoices challenged the doomsday forecasts and "eco-hysterics" of "econuts."[125]

Alarmed by increasing air pollution and the resultant acid rain, the United Nations sponsored the Conference on the Human Environment in Stockholm in 1972. More than one hundred nations, 19 intergovernmental organizations (IGOs), and 400 nongovernmental organizations (NGOs) attended. North-South differences surfaced. Third World nations feared that measures to protect the environment would slow their economic development. Might not they be told to remain "green areas so that the constructed areas could continue to develop without being disturbed?" asked the Brazilian foreign minister.[126] The South demanded compensation for stricter environmental controls. The South also asked for the North's commitment to additional aid earmarked for environmental projects. Developed nations in turn worried that Third World industrialization would overwhelm the biosphere.

"People don't give a shit about the environment," said Nixon privately as he endorsed the global conference, pledged U.S. monies to the new environmental fund, and backed a moratorium on commercial whaling.[127] But he balked at more financial assistance to Third World countries and bristled at complaints that Washington had degraded the natural environment in Indochina. Still, the global conference spurred national environmental reforms, set up Earthwatch to monitor environmental conditions, and spotlighted transboundary pollution.

Water covers 70 percent of the earth's surface. In the 1960s a new question became urgent: Who owned the rights to the gas, petroleum, and minerals such as manganese and nickel that rested in the deep seabed? Offshore oil drilling was well advanced, but the exploitation of the ocean's mineral riches was just beginning. American companies invested large sums in new technology to explore the ocean floor. From the perspective of Third World nations, seabed resources were a "common heritage of mankind."[128] The United States endorsed this principle in 1970, but at the UN-sponsored Law of the Sea Conference, which opened in 1973 and continued into the early 1980s, U.S. officials rejected the South's call for a powerful international seabed agency with exclusive rights over the mining of ocean resources. Because the new authority would operate on a one-nation, one-vote basis, the United States and other industrial nations would lose their competitive advantage. Washington insisted on private commercial exploitation, with no limits on profits or access to sites. But in 1976–1977 the United States compromised, now recommending a dual system: private development and an international authority, the latter to be assigned exclusive exploitation of certain mining sites. Until such an agreement, Kissinger insisted, the United States would explore and mine on its own.

The South and North also debated multinational corporations, the South seeking tighter controls and a larger proportion of the giant companies' profits earned from operations in developing nations. Ten of the top twelve multinationals in the mid-1970s were U.S.-based, including General Motors, Exxon, and Ford Motor. They intervened in the politics of other nations or bribed foreign leaders to gain contracts. Lockheed Aircraft and Exxon, among others, spent millions to bribe overseas politicians—a practice Congress tried to halt through the 1977 Foreign Corrupt Practices Act. The multinationals' economic decisions—where to locate a plant, for example—held real importance for developing nations that welcomed multinational investments but resented outside control. The South also protested that the multinationals employed too few "locals" in high positions and exploited natural resources without adequate compensation. The multinationals, some charged, had become global mini-empires, beyond the reach of national laws. Defenders replied that multinational enterprises brought benefits to developing nations in higher wages, tax revenues, and technology transfers. Whether beneficial or detrimental, multinational corporations by the early 1970s had become major actors in the international system. Washington balked at restraining them because they brought profits home, but the South vowed to restrict them—one of the many economic issues that challenged the Nixon-Kissinger quest for a stable world order.

Vietnamization, Cambodia, and a Wider War

"What we are doing now with China is so great, so historic, the word 'Vietnam' will be only a footnote when it is written in history," Kissinger boasted in 1971.[129] With superpower relations paramount in Nixon-Kissinger foreign relations, Vietnam became simply a "cruel side show."[130] Cruel but no side show, America's longest war continued to claim rapt attention until 1975. The Nixon administration constantly worried that the persistent war could damage the president at home and spoil détente. "I'm not going to end up like LBJ," Nixon assured his advisers. "I'm going to stop that war. Fast."[131] But under what terms would the United States withdraw?

At the outset, Nixon weighed his options. He could simply pull out of the war, "lock, stock and barrel," as one senator advised.[132] Nixon vetoed that suggestion. He would not sacrifice an ally. Nixon vowed to end the war but not lose it—his purpose was not to defeat North Vietnam but "to avoid [the] defeat of America."[133] His strategy had several components. Washington capitalized on détente, trying to persuade China and the Soviet Union to force Hanoi to compromise. The United States itself, through military escalation, signaled Ho Chi Minh that Nixon intended to punish the enemy harshly where Johnson had not. By ordering a secret nuclear alert "to jar Soviets + NVN [North Vietnam]," Nixon's "madman" strategy sought concessions from Hanoi through hints of atomic blackmail.[134] The president would strengthen South Vietnam through huge infusions of foreign aid and the training of a larger South Vietnamese army (ARVN). Underscoring the Nixon Doctrine's emphasis on self-help, Vietnamization meant, said one critic, "only that the color of the bodies is now different."[135] Nixon gradually withdrew U.S. troops from Vietnam and gave flag-waving speeches to counteract growing public disapproval of the war. In the cynical belief that most antiwar protesters simply feared "getting their asses shot off," he cut back draft calls, announced a draft lottery in May 1969, and promised to end the draft because it "gives us breathing space on Vietnam."[136]

The multifaceted scheme did not work. Ho Chi Minh and the NLF leaders did not bow to foreign wishes, whether from Washington, Moscow, or Beijing. Having outlasted the Japanese and the French, Ho's legions had no intention of surrendering to the Americans. As for dissent at home, every new escalation swelled the ranks of the critics and finally prompted Congress to limit the president's ability to enlarge the war. By summer 1971, about one third of the American people approved Nixon's Vietnam policies. Nor did Vietnamization convert South Vietnam into a secure military state. Although U.S. ships, planes, helicopters, rifles, and millions of dollars poured in, South Vietnam became dependent on U.S. aid to keep its army in the field, thus undermining the ultimate objective of standing on its own feet. Aid sustained the corrupt regime of General Nguyen Van Thieu, a government of self-serving officials—"a network of cliques held together by American subsidies," unpopular and ultimately incapable of conducting a winning effort.[137] Finally, Vietnamization diminished *American* military effectiveness. "Why get killed now?" a U.S. marine recalled. "You didn't have that 'let's go out and find them' attitude anymore."[138]

In early 1969 the Paris peace negotiations stalled over Nixon's demand for North Vietnam to pull its forces out of the South and for the survival of the Thieu government. The communists continued to advance on the ground. Nixon decided to bomb communist sanctuaries in Cambodia—but secretly, so that neither Congress nor the American people knew about it. The bombing of Cambodia began in March 1969 with punishing B-52 sorties. But leaks soon brought the story out. A self-proclaimed "paranoiac . . . with regard to secrecy," Nixon ordered the FBI to wiretap several journalists and government officials in a futile attempt to catch the leakers.[139]

Kissinger, in August 1969, began a series of secret meetings with North Vietnamese representatives that lasted into 1973. Both sides repeatedly accused the other of negotiating in bad faith, each quoting a Vietnamese maxim: "*You cannot hide an elephant in a basket.*"[140] Meanwhile, U.S. soldiers were coming home, so that by the end of 1971 the troop level had dropped to 139,000. Protest against the war continued nonetheless. On October 15, 1969, a quarter-million people peacefully marched in Washington, calling for a moratorium on the war. The president asked the "great silent majority of my fellow Americans" to back him, and he urged Vice President Spiro Agnew to attack the news media.[141]

Events in Cambodia actually prompted Nixon to expand the war. In March 1970, a pro-American general, Lon Nol, overthrew the neutralist government. Nixon saw new opportunities: Aid Lon Nol against the Khmer Rouge (Cambodian communists) and the North Vietnamese, who used Cambodian territory as a staging area to attack South Vietnam; step up the attack on the North Vietnamese in Cambodia, already targets of American bombing raids; send unmistakable signals to Hanoi that it had better relent; and show his critics "who's tough."[142] Despite considerable opposition from the State and Defense departments, the president ordered U.S. troops to invade Cambodia in late April.

A cascade of protest rolled across America. Antiwar demonstrations rocked college campuses, as inexperienced national guard troops shot and killed four students at Kent State University in Ohio. Two students at all-black Jackson State College in Mississippi died when state police fired on a women's dormitory. Within the administration, three Kissinger aides, including Anthony Lake, resigned in protest against the thrust into Cambodia. In June the Senate terminated the Tonkin Gulf Resolution of 1964 and passed the Cooper-Church Amendment cutting off funds for military operations in Cambodia. Although the House failed to pass this measure, a "siege mentality" gripped the White House.[143]

Nixon declared the Cambodian operation a success. Communist arms, equipment, and food had been captured and enemy troops killed. Although the invasion probably slowed the communist momentum and bought time for Vietnamization, the venture also widened the war, caused the sanctuaries to spread out, and further bloodied Cambodia. North Vietnam substantially increased its aid to the Khmer Rouge insurgents, who gained new recruits radicalized by the U.S. invasion. Lon Nol became another besieged Asian leader dependent on U.S. assistance.

As the Paris negotiations ground on, the war in Vietnam dragged on. Nixon ordered "protective reaction strikes" against North Vietnam after U.S. reconnaissance planes were shot down. In early 1971, he approved a South Vietnamese invasion of Laos, where in six weeks of heavy fighting ARVN forces "got their tail beat off," thus turning Vietnamization's "first test" into its "biggest failure."[144]

At home the wider war wrought more turmoil. After a court-martial in March 1971 found First Lieutenant William Calley guilty of murdering unresisting children, women, and old men at My Lai in 1968 (see page 353), Nixon ordered him released from jail (Calley won parole in November 1974). Army juries acquitted and army officials dismissed murder and cover-up charges against all other personnel connected with the massacre. The uproar over the Calley case had hardly subsided when, in June 1971, the *New York Times* began to print the *Pentagon Papers,* a long, secret Defense Department history of U.S. intervention in Vietnam. Leaked by a former Pentagon official, Daniel Ellsberg, the papers fortified critics in their argument that U.S. presidents consistently had tried to win a military victory and frequently had withheld facts from the American public. "Hell, I wouldn't prosecute the *Times,*" exclaimed Nixon, "prosecute the Goddamn pricks that gave it to 'em."[145] After the Supreme Court refused to halt publication of the *Pentagon Papers,* Nixon set up a "plumbers" group to stop leaks and to find ways to discredit Ellsberg. Watergate soon followed.

The year 1972 saw the presidential trip to China and SALT-I—and even greater escalation in Vietnam. In Paris, Kissinger continued to meet with North Vietnamese representatives, always rejecting the communist demand that the United States abandon Thieu. After "Nixon gets his 21-gun salute in Peking, we'll be giving him a different kind of salute in South Vietnam," said Hanoi as it launched a full-scale offensive in March that threw the Saigon government into disarray.[146]

Although Nixon said he would "rather use the nuclear bomb," he ordered American B-52 bombers to pummel fuel depots around Hanoi and Haiphong, where four Soviet merchant ships were sunk.[147] "Why are you turning against *us* when it is Hanoi that has challenged you?" asked Ambassador Anatoly Dobrynin.[148] In May the president announced the mining of Haiphong harbor, a naval blockade of the North, and more massive bombing raids code-named LINEBACKER-I. "We've got to use the maximum power of this country against a shit-asshole country [North Vietnam] to win the war," he growled.[149] During the seven months of LINEBACKER-I, U.S. aircraft dropped 155,000 tons of bombs on North Vietnamese storage facilities, air bases, power plants, bridges, and by mistake, hospitals. Supplies to the South slowed but did not stop.

The Jabberwocky Peace Agreement, Withdrawal, and Defeat

In early October 1972, Kissinger and the North Vietnamese negotiator Le Duc Tho finally reached an agreement that provided for U.S. withdrawal sixty days after a cease-fire, the return of U.S. prisoners of war, and a political arrangement in the South that ultimately included elections. In short, both sides made concessions—North Vietnam gave up its demand that Thieu resign, and the United States dropped its insistence that North Vietnamese troops pull out of the South. When Kissinger traveled to Saigon, however, Thieu balked. Resentful at not having been consulted and opposed to North Vietnamese troops in the South, the South Vietnamese president said "we have been

"Une Grande, une Immense Majorité Silencieuse." President Nixon claimed support for his policies from the majority of Americans who remained silent during the vocal protests of the 1960s and 1970s. In this harsh sketch, Vazquez de Sola portrays Nixon's "silent majority" as war dead who cannot protest. (Swann Collection of Caricature and Cartoon)

sold out by the U.S." and "if we accept the document as it stands, we will be committing suicide."[150] Fearing that Thieu might cry betrayal just before the U.S. presidential election, Nixon told Kissinger to try again. The communists, suspecting trickery, published the agreement that they had crafted with Kissinger. Still, on October 31, Kissinger told the press "peace is at hand."[151] Not quite.

Back in Paris, on November 20, Kissinger and Le Duc Tho resumed their meetings. In early December they reached terms very much like those Thieu and Nixon had torpedoed in October. But a final agreement faltered over the status of the Demilitarized Zone (DMZ). Kissinger thought the communists were stalling and counting on military victory. So he broke off the talks.

The carrot for Saigon (more arms), the stick for Hanoi. Nixon ordered the bombing of North Vietnam above the twentieth parallel. From December 18 to 28, LINEBACKER-II planes pounded North Vietnam hour upon hour in what Nixon told the Joint Chiefs was "your last chance to use military power to win this war."[152] Everything from factories to water supplies took hits in the "Christmas bombing." Fifty-foot bomb craters gaped in Hanoi and Haiphong. At least 2,000 civilians perished. Swedish prime minister Olof Palme cited such atrocities as "Guernica, Oradour, Katyn, Lidice, Sharpville, Treblinka. Now there is another name to add to the list—Hanoi, Christmas 1972."[153]

On December 22, Washington offered to stop the bombing if Hanoi agreed to reopen negotiations. Prodded by Zhou Enlai to "let the Americans leave," Le Duc Tho resumed talks with Kissinger, and on January 27, 1973, the two men signed what has been termed a "Jabberwocky" peace accord.[154] The United States promised to withdraw its remaining troops within sixty days; both sides would exchange prisoners; an international commission would oversee the cease-fire; and a coalition would conduct elections in the South. New language settled the DMZ issue. Although the NLF accepted the terms, Thieu as before stood aloof. If Thieu "bucks more," advised Senator Barry Goldwater, "to hell with him."[155] Nixon gave his secret promise that "we will respond with full force" if Hanoi violated the agreement. This promise, combined with the bombing of the North, persuaded Thieu to capitulate, albeit bitterly.[156] "Ah, these great powers who divide the world among themselves!" he remarked.[157] In the four years of the Nixon-Kissinger war, 20,553 Americans and half a million Vietnamese had died when "we could have gotten essentially the same deal anytime after the 1968 bombing halt," as one diplomat put it.[158]

Nixon claimed that the bombings had forced the enemy to accept U.S. terms. A Kissinger aide stated more accurately: "We bombed the North Vietnamese into accepting our concessions."[159] In the twelve days of bombing, the United States lost twenty-six planes over North Vietnam, fifteen of them expensive B-52s. In private, Nixon "kept coming back to the B-52 loss problem, saying we can't back off, but will we get three losses every time [we raid]?"[160] The final agreement, moreover, resembled the one reached in October, before the bombing. Finally, the popular outcry in the United States against Nixon's "war by tantrum" grew so loud that the president could not ignore it.[161] With the "new Congress still more anxious than its predecessor to end American involvement in the war," Nixon "had to act quickly or not at all."[162]

Vietnam Refrain. Presidents Eisenhower through Ford kept predicting victory in Vietnam but kept losing the war. As the historian T. Christopher Jespersen has argued, even Gerald Ford "refused to acknowledge" the rapid disintegration of South Vietnam in April 1975 and "attempted to saddle Congress with the ultimate burden of having lost Southeast Asia." (Mike Peters, *Dayton Daily News,* 1975)

The cease-fire broke down quickly as each side moved to strengthen itself militarily. The United States maintained military and CIA "advisers" in Vietnam and transferred equipment and bases to the Saigon regime. One peace provision called for the United States to provide Hanoi with reconstruction funds. But when the cease-fire collapsed, that promise died. U.S. warships still cruised off the coast, and the bombing of Cambodia continued. Congress acted again, this time against a president weakened by Watergate, voting in June 1973 to require the president to cease military actions in all parts of Indochina. Nixon vetoed the measure but accepted a compromise deadline of August 15. In November came the War Powers Resolution. In 1974 Congress rejected Kissinger's appeal for $1.5 billion in military aid for Thieu's collapsing government, voting $700 million instead.

Pressed by North Vietnamese and Vietcong advances, Thieu and his coterie seemed paralyzed by early 1975. Then the communists launched an offensive whose swift success surprised even themselves. The Army of the Republic of Vietnam disintegrated as a fighting force. Many ARVN troops deserted, were captured, or were killed. Refugees clogged highways; the turmoil in the countryside and cities left some civilians near starvation. "What's the point of supporting a government that has no will to fight?" asked one Republican senator.[163]

On April 30, 1975, the victorious Vietcong and North Vietnamese streamed into Saigon. For days, frantic Vietnamese had surged toward the Tan Son Nhut air base near Saigon, where U.S. planes loaded evacuees. But there were not enough planes, people blocked runways, and enemy rockets smashed into frightened crowds. Thousands of scrambling, crying Vietnamese engulfed the U.S. Embassy, whose roof served as a landing pad for helicopters from offshore ships. Thieu, the generals, other high-ranking officials, and those who had the money to bribe their passage, had managed to escape earlier, but they abandoned thousands of Vietnamese compromised by their years of cooperation with the United States. Some were later sent to communist "reeducation camps." Approximately one million Vietnamese escaped as "boat people" and sailed away in unseaworthy craft with inadequate water and food. Human tragedy also struck Cambodia and Laos, where, in 1975, the communist insurgents also triumphed. In Cambodia the Khmer Rouge imposed a genocidal regime that killed millions.

The Americans exited from their longest war without victory. Some 58,219 Americans died in Vietnam. At least 3 million Vietnamese died. Hundreds of thousands of people were maimed, and millions became refugees. Civilian deaths in Cambodia and Laos, before and after 1975, also numbered in the millions. The United States spent at least $170 billion in Southeast Asia. Perhaps $200 billion more would be paid to veterans of the war until "the middle of the next century," estimated one senator, "and for what?"[164] The prolonged Vietnam War alienated U.S. allies, undercut détente, and spoiled relations with the Third World. At home the war fueled inflation and political instability. Nixon's Watergate abuses stemmed in large part from the strains the war placed on the White House and from frustrations over leaks. The war wrecked two presidencies—Johnson's and Nixon's. Believing that their highest officials had too often lied and deceived, Americans' trust in their government plummeted. Blaming others rather than his own flawed policies for failure in Vietnam, the historian Jeffrey Kimball has noted, Nixon "contributed to the bitterness that haunted American politics and the confusion of purpose and meaning that plagued American foreign policy in the years ahead."[165]

The Many Lessons and Questions of Vietnam

Americans only reluctantly searched for lessons after the Vietnam debacle, and most discussion took place among the intellectual and governmental elite. Most citizens seemed more relieved that it had ended than inquisitive about consequences. They switched it off like a TV set. The 1976 presidential campaign passed with barely a word uttered about Vietnam.

Hawkish leaders feared that defeat in Vietnam had weakened U.S. credibility, inviting the nation's adversaries to exploit Washington's setback. They decried a "Vietnam syndrome" that allegedly prevented America from sustaining its role as world leader. "Sir, do we get to win this time?" asked the fictional John Rambo as he returned to Vietnam in the popular film *Rambo II* (1985).[166] Generals Maxwell Taylor and William Westmoreland lamented that they could have gained victory if only the American people had not suffered a failure of will during the Tet offensive: Just let the military do its job next time, unencumbered by fickle public opinion, inquisitive journalists, and congressional watchdogs. "We didn't know our ally [South Vietnam]," Taylor later admitted, but "we knew even less about the enemy. And, the last, most inexcusable of our mistakes, was not knowing our own people."[167] A recent scholar has called Vietnam a disastrous but "necessary war" that "cannot be understood except as a failed campaign in a successful war against imperial [communist] tyrannies that slaughtered and starved more of their own subjects than any regimes in history."[168]

Some political scientists, such as Graham Allison in *Essence of Decision* (1971), emphasized a bureaucratic politics model to interpret events. They suggested that it is difficult to hold individuals accountable for decisions and "outcomes," because of the way the impersonal, oversized bureaucracy resists change, follows standard operating procedures, and becomes rutted in traditional channels.[169] This bureaucracy had to be reformed to encourage more intragovernment dissent and debate, eschew fixed doctrines and kneejerk anticommunism, and "think in time"—that is, become alert to the historical record to avoid making the same mistakes again and again.[170] Critics of this analysis, however, blamed Vietnam on strong presidents such as Johnson, who actually controlled the bureaucracy through appointments, an overpowering personality, and a pervasive ideology. This viewpoint implied that a future change in presidents would bring about diplomatic reformation. A more assertive Congress, some argued, could rein in the "imperial presidency," as exposed by Senator Frank Church's 1975 intelligence committee revelations about CIA "abuses and aberrations," including attempted assassinations of Fidel Castro and other foreign leaders.[171]

Other opinions differed radically: Vietnam was a prime example of American global expansionism and arrogance, encouraged by a zealous belief that the United States, through superior power and ideals, could and should manage events almost everywhere. Richard J. Barnet of the Institute for Policy Studies in Washington, D.C., in his *Roots of War* (1972), wrote that the nation had to examine "those drives . . . that impel us toward destruction," among them a capitalist economy and business creed that required intervention abroad.[172]

Two post–Vietnam incidents in 1975 seemed to suggest as much. With polls in Europe indicating major declines in U.S. standing after the fall of Saigon, Cambodian patrol boats seized the U.S. merchant ship *Mayaguez* in May. "Let's look ferocious," said Kissinger, so as to refute charges that Washington had become a helpless giant after Vietnam.[173] U.S. marines assaulted Koh Tang Island off the Cambodian coast, and U.S. warships and planes attacked Cambodian targets, nearly killing the *Mayaguez* crew in the process. Cambodians released the *Mayaguez* and its crew, but forty-one Americans died. Similarly, when the inhabitants of Portuguese East Timor tried to assert their independence in December 1975, Ford and Kissinger flashed a green light for the Indonesian military regime to annex the island, telling President Kemusu Suharto that "it is important that whatever you do succeeds quickly."[174] A bloody invasion and civil war followed, leaving some 200,000 Timorese dead.

The Vietnam War, said other critics, revealed the shortcomings of the containment doctrine, which had failed to make distinctions between peripheral and vital areas and which applied military force to political problems. The analyst Edmund Stillman wrote: "Freedom *is* divisible. Some places are worthy of defense. Some are not. Some are capable of being defended. Some are not."[175] Ronald Steel, an eloquent critic of *Pax Americana,* likewise concluded: "Never confuse knights and bishops with pawns."[176]

The historian Henry Steele Commager concluded that "some wars are so deeply immoral that they must be lost, that the war in Vietnam was one of these wars, and that those who resist it are the truest patriots."[177] To some, then, defeat became a victory for humane values. In contrast to those who blamed the antiwar activists for encouraging the enemy and weakening congressional resolve, historians of the peace movement have offered a more modest judgment. Antiwar opponents "produced an awareness of an alternative America that stripped away through dissent and resistance the rational, moral, and political legitimacy of Washington's war in Indochina."[178] Thus: "The dissidents did not stop the war. But they made it stoppable."[179] Some commentators urged "neo-isolationism" after Vietnam. "Compared to people who thought they could run the universe," remarked the famed journalist Walter Lippmann, "I *am* a neo-isolationist and proud of it."[180] Never again should the United States practice unrestrained global interventionism.

By the late 1970s public discussion of the Vietnam experience and its consequences increased. Films such as *Coming Home* (1978), *The Deer Hunter* (1978), and *Apocalypse Now* (1979) heightened public attention. Depicting the soldiers' Vietnam were memoirs such as C. D. B. Bryan's *Friendly Fire* (1976), Ron Kovic's *Born on the Fourth of July* (1976), Philip Caputo's *A Rumor of War* (1977), and Michael Herr's *Dispatches* (1977); oral histories such as Al Santoli's *Everything We Had* (1981) and Mark Baker's *Nam* (1981); and novels such as James Webb's *Fields of Fire* (1978).

The dedication of the Vietnam Veterans Memorial in Washington in November 1982 gave the 2.8 million survivors of service in the war "a wailing wall. We came to find the names of those we lost in the war, as if by tracing the letters cut into the granite we could find what was left of ourselves."[181] Early stereotypes of Vietnam veterans as "walking time bombs" and emotional cripples unable to adjust to civilian life were replaced by "survivor-heroes," gritty, can-do, take-charge supermen, as portrayed by Sylvester Stallone and Chuck Norris in the back-to-Vietnam films of the Reagan era. Despite all the "psychobabble" about tormented misfits, studies indicate that only 2 percent of 2.8 million Vietnam veterans suffered from posttraumatic stress disorder and that the reported high rates of suicides were comparable to those of the civilian population.[182]

Post-Vietnam writings, television documentaries, and college courses on the war have emphasized the *American* experience in Vietnam, even as hundreds of thousands of Vietnamese, Cambodian, and Laotian refugees came to the United States and gained citizenship over the next two decades. When one professor asked his students to consider the Vietnamese and their response to the war, he found that most "cannot grasp that the war had something to do with other people." Instead of a real country on the far side of the Pacific with its own history and culture, Vietnam had become, as one writer put it, "another word for mistakes or dishonesty or whatever."[183] The only "Vietnamese words we learned were the cusswords," recalled one veteran.[184]

Debate on the war came to center on whether the United States could have won. Many conservatives articulated a "stab-in-the-back" theory, namely, that the United States could have won had protesters not impeded the war effort and had civilian officials not restrained the military.[185] President Ronald Reagan declared that American troops "were denied permission to win."[186] "It takes the full strength of a tiger to kill a rabbit," argued General William C. Westmoreland.[187]

Doubters have raised imposing questions about such thinking. Because the bombing of North Vietnam did not significantly impede the flow of matériel and soldiers to the South, perhaps only a U.S. invasion of the North would have sufficed to defeat the enemy. This strategy would have entailed heavy American casualties and a long occupation of a hostile population that had demonstrated its tenacity

Vietnam Memorials.   These statues, part of the memorial site in Washington, D.C., honor the men and women who served in the Vietnam War. On the left is the Vietnam Veterans Memorial by Frederick Hart, and on the right is the Vietnam Women's Memorial by Glenna Goodacre. Both stand near the long wall on which the names of Americans who died in Vietnam are etched. (National Park Service)

against foreigners for decades. Would Americans accept the killing of tens of thousands of people by bombing the irrigation dikes of the North? Would Americans volunteer for a cause with such an uncertain end? Would they tolerate huge draft calls? An invasion of the North, moreover, would have risked war with both the Soviet Union and China. Détente might have restrained the Soviets from rescuing the North, but China sent substantial forces to North Vietnam between 1965 and 1969, credibly threatening intervention if the United States moved north with "dire consequences for the world."[188] To say that the United States lacked the "will" to win misses the real limits on U.S. power. "What distinguishes me from [Lyndon] Johnson," Nixon once said, "is that I have the *will* in spades."[189] Yet Nixon wisely rejected tactical nuclear weapons or an invasion of the North because he recoiled from the domestic and international consequences.

To have won, suggested some, the United States would also have had to destroy what it was trying to save—that is, using more military power would have produced more deaths and more refugees. What would remain after "victory"? Perhaps at best an internally divided, economically feeble nation needing huge infusions of U.S. aid but still vulnerable to collapse. Even with the military unleashed—and dropping on Indochina three times the tonnage of bombs used in all theaters during World War II hardly suggests restraint—it would still have faced intractable problems: an inhospitable terrain and climate; an elusive adversary deeply committed to its cause, battle-tested, and able to live off the land (*its* land); and a South Vietnamese people who often sheltered communist soldiers. Doubters of the "win" thesis also note that the United States received very little help from its allies. Most European partners urged Washington to stop wasting its resources on a fruitless venture. Of America's forty allies by treaty, only Australia, New Zealand, South Korea, and Thailand sent combat troops.

The United States could not have won, others have argued, because it lacked a political base on which to build. Coups and attempted coups too often rocked the unpopular Saigon governments. The South Vietnamese desertion rate ran high. ARVN troops were "armed farces," said one U.S. adviser, "very poor fighters" whose "timidity endangered American lives."[190] ARVN forces suffered the same problems that afflicted their government: poor morale, corruption, and nepotism. The "war of attrition" alienated many South Vietnamese, as did the unsettling strategic hamlet program, disruptive "search and destroy" missions, leveling of villages, requiring of identity cards, bombings of innocents, and spraying of Agent Orange. Cultural differences also separated Americans from Vietnamese. Bars and prostitution flourished in a rural Buddhist society made rapidly urban by fleeing refugees. High-tech computers hummed and giant war machines rumbled in a land of water buffalo, rice paddies, and traditional peasant folk.

Problems in the U.S. military itself reduced the chances for victory. Because officers wanted to reassure superiors that they were turning back the enemy, some suppressed intelligence information and submitted false reports on the numbers killed. "If he's dead and Vietnamese, he's VC [Vietcong]" became the prevailing assumption in the field.[191] Decisionmakers in Washington did not fully know how badly the war was going. The military also suffered from corruption and mismanagement—even a black market for equipment developed. By early 1971 some 40,000 GIs had become heroin addicts. Racial tension between "bloods" (blacks) and "honkies" (whites) and "fragging"—the murder of officers by enlisted soldiers by means of a hand grenade or other weapon—further reduced combat effectiveness. Educational deferments under the draft system meant that "high school dropouts were three times more likely to experience heavy combat than were college graduates."[192] The rotation system for officers—one year in Vietnam to "punch your ticket"—undermined military cohesion and the benefits of experience. "About the time they [officers] gain the experience and not get your butt killed," one enlisted man remembered, "they get sucked back in the rear with the gear, and you get a brand-new butter bar and . . . go through the whole process again."[193] Disgusted with the "groupthink pressure" and "pretense," General Colin Powell later wrote that many of "my generation . . . vowed that when our turn came to call the shots, we would not quietly acquiesce in half-hearted warfare for half-baked reasons that the American people could not understand or support."[194]

The United States also faced tenacious adversaries who suffered remarkable losses but kept coming. "I know Americans," Ho had said. "They are an impatient people. They will leave."[195] Defending their nation against outsiders, the Vietnamese enemy seemed indomitable. "Everything we knew commanded us to fight," a Vietcong veteran remembered. "Our ancestors called us to war. Our myths and legends called us to war."[196] The Vietnamese had always fought those who brought "elephants home to trample the graveyards of their ancestors."[197] Such elephants "could make the earth tremble" but "couldn't conquer the ants that lived on it."[198]

Whatever the answer to the Vietnam tragedy, succeeding administrations would have to operate in a domestic political setting of uncertainty about the direction of American foreign relations. Conservative defenders of the war stood ready to criticize any policy that smacked of retrenchment or "another Munich." Liberals and radicals stood alert to dispute any policy that seemed to offer "another Vietnam."

FURTHER READING FOR THE PERIOD 1969–1977

See works on the Cold War, the Third World, and other topics cited in earlier chapters.

For foreign relations during the Nixon and Ford presidencies, and for Richard M. Nixon the person, see Stephen E. Ambrose, *Nixon* (1989, 1991); James Cannon, *Time and Chance* (1994) (Ford); Terry L. Deibel, *Presidents, Public Opinion, and Power* (1987); Jean A. Garrison, *Games Advisers Play: Foreign Policy in the Nixon and Carter Administrations* (1999); Michael Genovese, *The Nixon Presidency* (1990); John R. Greene, *The Limits of Power* (1992) and *The Presidency of Gerald R. Ford* (1994); Jussi Hanhimaki, *Flawed Architect* (2004); Joan Hoff, *Nixon Reconsidered* (1994); Ole Holsti and James R. Roseneau, *American Leadership in World Affairs: Vietnam and the Breakdown of Consensus* (1984); Richard A. Melanson, *American Foreign Policy Since the Vietnam War* (1996); Roger Morris, *Richard Milhous Nixon* (1989); Richard Reeves, *President Nixon* (2001); Franz Schurmann, *The Foreign Politics of Richard Nixon* (1987); Melvin Small, *The Presidency of Richard Nixon* (1999); Lewis Sorley, *Arms Transfers Under Nixon* (1983) and *A Better War* (1999); and Garry Wills, *Nixon Agonistes* (1970).

For Henry A. Kissinger, see Dan Caldwell, ed., *Henry Kissinger* (1983); Gregory D. Cleva, *Henry Kissinger and the American Approach to Foreign Policy* (1989); Gordon A. Craig and Francis L. Lowenheim, eds., *The Diplomats* (1994); Christopher Hitchens, *The Trial of Henry Kissinger* (2001); Walter Isaacson, *Kissinger* (1992); Bernard and Marvin Kalb, *Kissinger* (1974); Roger Morris, *Uncertain Greatness* (1977); Robert D. Schulzinger, *Henry Kissinger* (1989); Harvey Starr, *Henry Kissinger* (1984); and John Stoessinger, *Henry Kissinger* (1976).

For Congress, including the Church committee's investigations, see Thomas Franck and Edward Weisband, *Foreign Policy by Congress* (1979); Loch K. Johnson, *A Season of Inquiry* (1985) and *Bombs, Bugs, Drugs, and Thugs* (2000); Robert G. Kaufman, *Henry M. Jackson* (2000); Kathryn S. Olmsted, *Challenging the Secret Government* (1997); Keith W. Olson, *Watergate* (2003); and John Prados, *Lost Crusader* (2003) (William Colby).

For Soviet-American relations, détente, and SALT, see Richard J. Barnet, *The Giants* (1977); Robin Edmonds, *Soviet Foreign Policy* (1983); Michael B. Froman, *The Development of the Idea of Détente* (1992); Raymond L. Garthoff, *Détente and Confrontation* (1995); Alexander L. George et al., eds., *Managing U.S.-Soviet Rivalry* (1982); Marshall I. Goldman, *Détente and Dollars* (1975); Jonathan Haslam, *The Soviet Union and the Politics of Nuclear Weapons in Europe* (1990); David Holloway, *The Soviet Union and the Arms Race* (1983); Robert S. Litwak, *Détente and the Nixon Doctrine* (1984); Wilfred Loth, *Overcoming the Cold War* (2002); Michael Mandelbaum, *The Nuclear Question* (1979); Keith L. Nelson, *The Making of Détente* (1995); John Newhouse, *Cold Dawn* (1973); Matthew J. Ouimet, *The Rise and Fall of the Brezhnev Doctrine in Soviet Foreign Policy* (2002); M. E. Sarotte, *Dealing with the Devil* (2001) (Ostpolitik); Morton Schwartz, *Soviet Perceptions of the United States* (1978); Gordon B. Smith, ed., *The Politics of East-West Trade* (1984); Richard W. Stevenson, *The Rise and Fall of Détente* (1985); Jeremi Suri, *Power and Protest* (2003); Terry Terriff, *The Nixon Administration and the Making of U.S. Nuclear Strategy* (1995); and Adam B. Ulam, *Dangerous Relations* (1983).

For China and Japan, see Rosemary Foot, *The Practice of Power* (1995); Gene T. Hsiao, ed., *Sino-American Détente and Its Policy Implications* (1974); Arnold Xiangze Jiang, *The United States and China* (1988); Ronald C. Keith, *The Diplomacy of Zhou Enlai* (1989); Walter LaFeber, *The Clash* (1997) (Japan); James Mann, *About Face* (1999) (China); Robert S. Ross, *Negotiating Cooperation* (1995); Robert S. Ross and Jiang Changbin, eds.,

Re-Examining the Cold War (2001); Michael Schaller, *The United States and China* (1990) and *Altered States* (1997) (Japan); David Shambaugh, *Beautiful Imperialist* (1991); Robert G. Sutter, *The China Quandary* (1983); Ross Terrill, *Mao* (1993); Nancy B. Tucker, *Taiwan, Hong Kong, and the United States* (1994) and *China Confidential* (2001); Patrick Tyler, *A Great Wall: Six Presidents and China* (2000).

The end and lessons of the Vietnam War are explored in Dale Andrade, *America's Last Vietnam Battle* (2001); Pierre Asselin, *A Bitter Peace* (2002); Michael R. Belknap, *The Vietnam War on Trial* (2003); Larry Berman, *No Peace, No Honor* (2001); Anthony S. Campagna, *The Economic Consequences of the Vietnam War* (1991); Walter H. Capps, *The Unfinished War* (1982); David A. Cook, *Lost Illusions: American Cinema in the Shadow of Watergate and Vietnam, 1970–1979* (2000); Eric Dean, Jr., *Shook Over Hell* (1997); John H. Ely, *War and Responsibility* (1993); Leslie H. Gelb and Richard K. Betts, *The Irony of Vietnam* (1979); Allan E. Goodman, *The Lost Peace* (1978); John Hellmann, *American Myth and the Legacy of Vietnam* (1986); Susan Jeffords, *The Remasculinization of America* (1989); Rhodri Jeffreys-Jones, *Peace Now! American Society and the Ending of the Vietnam War* (1999); Ben Kiernan, *The Pol Pot Regime* (2002); Jeffrey Kimball, *Nixon's Vietnam War* (1998); Michael Lind, *Vietnam: The Necessary War* (1999); Timothy J. Lomperis, *The War Everyone Lost—and Won* (1984); Myra MacPherson, *Long Time Passing* (1984); Richard A. Melanson, *Writing History and Making Policy* (1983) and *Reconstructing Consensus* (1990); Gareth Porter, *A Peace Denied* (1975); Earl C. Ravenal, *Never Again* (1978); William Shawcross, *Sideshow* (1979) (Cambodia); Wayne Thompson, *To Hanoi and Back* (2000); and Randall B. Woods, ed., *Vietnam and the American Political Tradition* (2003). See also works listed in Chapter 9.

International economic questions, including the North-South debate, are covered in Richard J. Barnet, *The Lean Years* (1980); Richard J. Barnet and Ronald Müller, *Global Reach* (1974); David P. Calleo, *The Imperious Economy* (1982); Albert L. Danielson, *The Evolution of OPEC* (1982); I. M. Destler, *Making Foreign Economic Policy* (1980); I. M. Destler, Haruhiro Fukui, and Hideo Sato, *The Textile Wrangle* (1979); Jeffrey A. Hart, *The New International Economic Order* (1983); Stephen Krasner, *Defending the National Interest* (1978); Diane B. Kunz, *Butter and Guns* (1997); Allen J. Matusow, *Nixon's Economy* (1998); David Morawetz, *Twenty-five Years of Economic Development* (1977); Robert K. Olson, *U.S. Foreign Policy and the New International Economic Order* (1981); Robert A. Pastor, *Congress and the Politics of U.S. Foreign Economic Policy* (1980); and Brian Tew, *The Evolution of the International Monetary System* (1982).

Environmental issues, population, food, and their intersection with the international economy and world politics are examined in Scott Barrett, *Environment and Statecraft* (2003); Robert Boardman, *International Organization and the Conservation of Nature* (1981); Lynton K. Caldwell, *International Environmental Policy* (1984); Alfred E. Eckes, Jr., *The United States and the Global Struggle for Minerals* (1977); Ann L. Hollick, *U.S. Foreign Policy and the Law of the Sea* (1981); Raymond F. Hopkins and Donald J. Puchala, *Global Food Interdependence* (1980); John McCormick, *Reclaiming Paradise: The Global Environmental Movement* (1989); William Murdoch, *The Poverty of Nations* (1980); William and Paul Paddock, *Time of Famines* (1976); Clyde Sanger, *Ordering the Oceans* (1987); Ross B. Talbott, *The Four World Food Agencies in Rome* (1990); Mitchel B. Wallerstein, *Food for War–Food for Peace* (1980).

For Africa and some Third World issues, see Andrew DeRoche, *Black, White, and Chrome* (2001) (Zimbabwe); Piero Gleijeses, *Conflicting Missions* (2001); Fernando A. Guimarães, *The Origins of the Angolan Civil War* (1998); Gerald Horne, *From the Barrel of a Gun* (2001) (Zimbabwe); Charles A. Jones, *The North-South Dialogue* (1983); Anthony Lake, *The "Tar Baby" Option* (1976) (Southern Rhodesia); Robert J. McMahon, *The Limits of Empire* (1999); and P. David Searles, *The Peace Corps Experience: Challenge and Change, 1969–1976* (1997).

For the Middle East, oil, and the Arab-Israeli conflict, see Warren Bass, *Support Any Friend* (2003); James A. Bill, *The Eagle and the Lion* (1988) (Iran); George W. Breslauer, *Soviet Strategy in the Middle East* (1990); Avner Cohen, *Israel and the Bomb* (1998); Trevor N. Dupuy, *Elusive Victory* (1978); James F. Goode, *The United States and Iran* (1997); Robert D. Kaplan, *The Arabists* (1993); George Lenczowski, *The Middle East in World Affairs* (1980); Douglas Little, *American Orientalism* (2002); Melani McAlister, *Epic Encounters* (2001); Donald Neff, *Warriors Against Israel* (1988); William R. Polk, *The Arab World Today* (1991); William B. Quandt, *Decade of Decisions* (1977); Bernard Reich, *Quest for Peace* (1977); Cheryl A. Rubenberg, *Israel and the American National Interest* (1986); Barry Rubin, *Paved with Good Intentions* (1977) (Iran); Yezid Sayigh, *Armed Struggle and the Search for State* (1998) (Palestinians); David Schoenbaum, *The United States and the State of Israel* (1993); Mohammed K. Shadid, *The United*

States and the Palestinians (1981); Benjamin Shwadran, *Middle East Oil* (1977); Steven L. Spiegel, *The Other Arab-Israeli Conflict* (1985); Kenneth W. Stein, *Heroic Diplomacy* (1999); and Daniel Yergin, *The Prize* (1991) (oil).

Latin America–U.S. relations, including Chile, are treated in Robert J. Alexander, *The Tragedy of Chile* (1978); Richard R. Fagen, ed., *Capitalism and the State in U.S.–Latin American Relations* (1979); Peter Kornbluh, *The Pinochet File* (2003); T. H. Moran, *Multinational Corporations and the Politics of Dependence: Copper in Chile* (1974); Morris H. Morley, *Washington, Somoza, and the Sandinistas* (1994); James Petras and Morris Morley, *The United States and Chile* (1975); Stephen G. Rabe, *The Road to OPEC* (1982) (Venezuela); Lars Schoultz, *Beneath the United States* (1998); Paul E. Sigmund, *The United States and Democracy in Chile* (1993); Peter H. Smith, *Talons of the Eagle* (1996); and Arthur P. Whitaker, *The United States and the Southern Cone* (1976).

See also the General Bibliography; Robert L. Beisner, ed., *Guide to American Foreign Relations Since 1600* (2003); and the following notes.

For comprehensive coverage of foreign-relations topics, see the articles in the four-volume *Encyclopedia of U.S. Foreign Relations* (1997), edited by Bruce W. Jentleson and Thomas G. Paterson.

NOTES TO CHAPTER 10

1. Quoted in Bernard Kalb and Marvin Kalb, *Kissinger* (Boston: Little, Brown, 1974), p. 266.
2. Hugh Sidey in *Life, LXXII* (March 3, 1972), 12.
3. *Newsweek, LXXIX* (February 28, 1972), 13.
4. *Department of State Bulletin, LXVI* (March 6, 1972), 290.
5. People's Liberation Army quoted in Allen S. Whiting, "China's Use of Force, 1950–1996," *International Security, XXVI* (Fall 2001), 117; quoted in John Lewis Gaddis, *Strategies of Containment* (New York: Oxford University Press, 1982), 296.
6. Quoted in John Maxwell Hamilton, *Edgar Snow* (Bloomington: Indiana University Press, 1988), p. 269.
7. Quoted in Chen Jian, *Mao's China & the Cold War* (Chapel Hill: University of North Carolina Press, 2001), p. 256.
8. Henry Kissinger, *White House Years* (Boston: Little, Brown, 1979), p. 754.
9. *Public Papers, Nixon, 1971* (Washington, D.C.: Government Printing Office, 1972), p. 819.
10. Mao quoted in Joseph Y. S. Cheng, "Mao Zedong's Perception of the World in 1968–1972," *Journal of American–East Asian Relations, VII* (Fall–Winter 1998), 254.
11. Entry of April 20, 1971, in H. R. Haldeman, *The Haldeman Diaries* (New York: Putnam, 1994), p. 275.
12. Quoted in Joan Hoff, "A Revisionist View of Nixon's Foreign Policy," *Presidential Studies Quarterly, XXVI* (Winter 1996), 117.
13. Kissinger, *White House Years,* p. 1049.
14. Mao quoted in Jian, *Mao's China,* p. 267.
15. Mao quoted in Li Zhisui, *The Private Life of Chairman Mao* (New York: Random House, 1994), p. 565.
16. Quoted in Rosemary Foot, *The Practice of Power* (New York: Oxford University Press, 1995), p. 137.
17. Quoted in Robert S. Ross, *Negotiating Cooperation* (Stanford: Stanford University Press, 1995), p. 45.
18. Richard Nixon, *RN* (New York: Grosset & Dunlap, 1978), p. 564.
19. Walter Isaacson, *Kissinger* (New York: Simon & Schuster, 1992), p. 402; John H. Holdridge, *Crossing the Divide* (Lanham Md.: Rowman & Littlefield, 1997), p. 87.
20. Entry of February 22, 1972, *Haldeman Diaries,* p. 416.
21. Kissinger memorandum of conversation, February 21, 1972 in William Burr, ed., *The Kissinger Transcripts* (New York: New Press, 1998), p. 64.

22. Quoted in Li, *Chairman Mao,* p. 514.
23. Quoted in Jussi Hanhimaki, "Kissinger, Triangular Diplomacy, and the End of the Vietnam War, 1971–73," *Diplomacy and Statecraft, XIV* (March 2003), 170.
24. George Gallup in *Hartford Courant,* March 12, 1972.
25. Charles Freeman quoted in Nancy Bernkopf Tucker, ed., *China Confidential* (New York: Columbia University Press, 2001), p. 280.
26. Quoted in Ronald C. Keith, *The Diplomacy of Zhou Enlai* (New York: St. Martin's, 1989), p. 199.
27. Quoted in Michael A. Schaller, *Altered States* (New York: Oxford University Press, 1997), p. 227.
28. Quoted in Richard Reeves, *Richard Nixon* (New York: Simon & Schuster, 2001), p. 445; quoted in Nancy Bernkopf Tucker, *Taiwan, Hong Kong, and the United States* (New York: Twayne, 1994), p. 104.
29. *Department of State Bulletin, LXVI* (March 20, 1972), 435–438.
30. Nixon, *RN,* p. 580.
31. Quoted in Michael Schaller, "Détente and the Strategic Triangle," in Robert S. Ross and Jiang Changbin, eds., *Re-examining the Cold War: U.S.-China Diplomacy, 1954–1973* (Cambridge: Harvard University Press, 2001), p. 358.
32. *Philadelphia Inquirer* quoted in Melvin Small, *The Presidency of Richard Nixon* (Lawrence: University Press of Kansas, 1999), p. 124.
33. Lewis Lapham, *The Theater of War* (New York: New Press, 2002), p. 16.
34. Michael S. Sherry, *In the Shadow of War* (New Haven: Yale University Press, 1995), p. 310.
35. H. R. Haldeman, *The Ends of Power* (New York: Times Books, 1978), p. 98.
36. Quoted in Lapham, *Theater,* p. 18.
37. Tape recording, June 23, 1971, in Stanley I. Kutler, ed., *Abuse of Power* (New York: Free Press, 1997), p. 4.
38. Anatoly Dobrynin, *In Confidence* (New York: Random House, 1995), p. 310.
39. Quoted in Richard Valeriani, *Travels with Henry* (New York: Berkeley, 1980), p. 123; Kissinger, *White House Years,* p. 1094.
40. Leonard Garment, *Crazy Rhythm* (New York: Times Books, 1997), p. 186.
41. Stanley Hoffmann, *Primacy or World Order* (New York: McGraw-Hill, 1978), p. 33.
42. Marshall Green quoted in Tucker, *China Confidential,* p. 233.

43. George H. W. Bush, December 10, 1971, in Sajit Gandhi, ed., "The Tilt: The U.S. and the South Asian Crisis of 1971," *National Security Archive Electronic Briefing Book No. 79* (December 16, 2002).

44. Quoted in Ann Miller Morin, *Her Excellency* (New York: Twayne, 1994), p. 110.

45. Arkady Sevchenko quoted in Small, *Nixon*, p. 111.

46. Quoted in J. Garry Clifford, "Change and Continuity," in James Patterson, ed., *Paths to the Present* (Minneapolis: Burgess, 1975), p. 137.

47. Quoted in Thomas G. Paterson, "Oversight or Afterview?" in Michael Barnhart, ed., *Congress and United States Foreign Policy* (Albany: State University of New York Press, 1987), p. 155.

48. Quoted in Carlos Osorio, ed., "Argentine Military Believed U.S. Gave Go-Ahead for Dirty War," *National Security Archive Briefing Book No. 73* (August 21, 2002).

49. Quoted in Garry Wills, *Nixon Agonistes* (Boston: Houghton Mifflin, 1970), p. 20.

50. Kissinger, *White House Years*, p. 191.

51. *Ibid.*, p. 55.

52. Jeremi Suri, *Power and Protest: Global Revolution and the Rise of Détente* (Cambridge: Harvard University Press, 2003), p. 258.

53. Kissinger quoted in Robert J. McMahon, *The Limits of Empire* (New York: Columbia University Press, 1999), p. 157.

54. Schaller, "Détente," in Ross and Changbin, *Re-examining the Cold War*, p. 361; memorandum of White House meeting, December 7, 1970, Box 68, Dean Acheson Papers, Yale University, New Haven, Conn.

55. Quoted in Jeffrey Kimball, *The Vietnam War Files* (Lawrence: University Press of Kansas, 2003), p. 15.

56. Elaine P. Adam and Richard P. Stebbins, eds., *American Foreign Relations, 1976* (New York: New York University Press, 1978), p. 13.

57. Egon Bahr quoted in M. E. Sarotte, *Dealing with the Devil* (Chapel Hill: University of North Carolina Press, 2001), p. 41.

58. Quoted in David M. Lampton, *Same Bed, Different Dreams* (Berkeley: University of California Press, 2001), p. 223.

59. Archer Blood quoted in Gandhi, "The Tilt."

60. Quoted in Robert J. McMahon, *The Cold War on the Periphery* (New York: Columbia University Press, 1994), p. 346.

61. Quoted in Dennis Kux, *Disenchanted Allies* (Baltimore: Johns Hopkins University Press, 2001), p. 203.

62. President's Briefing, November 16 and 17, 1971 in Gandhi, "The Tilt."

63. Raymond G. Garthoff, *Détente and Confrontation* (Washington, D.C.: Brookings Institution, 1995; rev. ed.), p. 311.

64. Nixon, *RN*, p. 527.

65. Michael Mandelbaum, *The Nuclear Question* (Cambridge, Eng.: Cambridge University Press, 1979), p. 218.

66. Gerard C. Smith, *Disarming Diplomat* (New York: Madison Books, 1996), p. 167.

67. Quoted in Burr, *Kissinger Transcripts*, p. 258; quoted in Gregg Herken, *Counsels of War* (New York: Oxford University Press, 1987), p. 255.

68. Kissinger, *White House Years*, p. 1245n.

69. Quoted in Donald R. Baucom, *The Origins of SDI* (Lawrence: University Press of Kansas, 1992), p. 75.

70. Kissinger quoted in Piero Gleijeses, *Conflicting Missions* (Chapel Hill: University of North Carolina Press, 2002), p. 388.

71. William Hyland quoted in Isaacson, *Kissinger*, p. 663.

72. Andrei Gromyko quoted in Matthew J. Ouimet, *The Rise and Fall of the Brezhnev Doctrine in Soviet Foreign Policy* (Chapel Hill: University of North Carolina Press, 2003), p. 87.

73. Ford quoted in John Robert Greene, *The Presidency of Gerald R. Ford* (Lawrence: University Press of Kansas, 1995), p. 151.

74. *Public Papers, Nixon, 1969*, p. 548.

75. Kissinger, *White House Years*, p. 117.

76. Avner Cohen, *Israel and the Bomb* (New York: Columbia University Press, 1998), p. 1.

77. Quoted in David Schoenbaum, *The United States and the State of Israel* (New York: Oxford University Press, 1993), p. 171.

78. William B. Quandt, *Decade of Decisions* (Berkeley: University of California Press, 1977), p. 127.

79. Sadat quoted in Yazid Sayigh, *Armed Struggle and the Search for State* (New York: Oxford University Press, 1997), p. 152.

80. Quoted in Richard Ned Lebow and Janice Gross Stein, *We All Lost the Cold War* (Princeton: Princeton University Press, 1994), p. 189.

81. Henry M. Jackson quoted in Robert G. Kaufman, *Henry M. Jackson* (Seattle: University of Washington Press, 2000), p. 277.

82. Quoted in Douglas Little, *American Orientalism* (Chapel Hill: University of North Carolina Press, 2002), p. 106.

83. Alexander Haig quoting Nixon in Garthoff, *Détente and Confrontation*, p. 426.

84. Aleksei Kosygin and Yuri Andropov quoted in Victor Israelyan, *Inside the Kremlin During the Yom Kippur War* (University Park: Penn State University Press, 1995), p. 180.

85. Ahmed Zakhi Yamani quoted in Daniel Yergin, *The Prize* (New York: Simon & Schuster, 1991), p. 606.

86. Quoted in Edward R. F. Sheehan, "How Kissinger Did It," *Foreign Policy*, no. 22 (Spring 1976), 48.

87. Quoted in *New York Times*, March 15, 1976.

88. State Department and *National Review* quoted in Melani McAlister, *Epic Encounters* (Berkeley: University of California Press, 2001), pp. 184–185.

89. Melani McAlister, "A Cultural History of the War without End," *Journal of American History, LXXXIX* (September 2002), 445.

90. Richard Helms quoting the Shah in James F. Goode, *The United States and Iran* (New York: St. Martin's, 1997), p. 186.

91. Kissinger quoted in James A. Bill, *The Eagle and the Lion* (New Haven: Yale University Press, 1988), p. 203.

92. Gary Sick quoted in Little, *American Orientalism*, p. 148.

93. Quoted in Samuel Baily, *The United States and the Development of South America* (New York: New Viewpoints, 1976), p. 118.

94. Walter LaFeber, "The Tension between Democracy and Capitalism," *Diplomatic History, XXIII* (Spring 1999), 178; Helms quoted in William Bundy, *A Tangled Web* (New York: Hill & Wang, 1998), p. 201.

95. Quoted in Richard Helms, *A Look over My Shoulder* (New York: Random House, 2003), p. 404.

96. Quoted in William F. Sater, *Chile and the United States* (Athens: University of Georgia Press, 1990), p. 184.

97. Peter Kornbluh, *The Pinochet File* (New York: New Press, 2003), p. 114.

98. Quoted in Christopher Hitchens, *The Trial of Henry Kissinger* (New York: Verso, 2001), p. 70.

99. Quoted in Peter Kornbluh, ed., "Conflicting Missions: Secret Cuban Documents on History of Africa Involvement," *National Security Archive Electronic Briefing Book No. 67* (April 1, 2002).

100. Kissinger, *White House Years*, p. 645.

101. Quoted in Garthoff, *Détente and Confrontation*, p. 92.

102. Quoted in Thomas Borstelman, "The United States and the Final Years of White Rule in Zimbabwe," *Reviews in American History, XVII* (January 2003), 159.

103. Quoted in Kate Doyle, ed., "The Nixon Tapes," *National Security Archive Electronic Briefing Book* (August 18, 2003).

104. Gerald Horne, *From the Barrel of a Gun* (Chapel Hill: University of North Carolina Press, 2001), p. 71; quoted in Steven Metz, "Congress,

the Anti-Apartheid Movement, and Nixon," *Diplomatic History, XII* (Spring 1988), 177.

105. Quoted in Thomas Noer, "Segregationists and the World," in Brenda Gayle Plummer, ed., *Window on Freedom* (Chapel Hill: University of North Carolina Press, 2003), pp. 143, 148.

106. Quoted in Gleijeses, *Conflicting Missions*, p. 291.

107. Anatoly Dobrynin quoted in Piero Gleijeses, "Havana's Policy in Africa," *Cold War International History Project Bulletin*, nos. 8–9 (Winter 1996/1997), p. 13.

108. Gerald R. Ford, *A Time to Heal* (New York: Harper and Row, 1979), p. 345.

109. Quoted in John Prados, *Lost Crusader* (New York: Oxford University Press, 2003), p. 317.

110. Quoted in Thomas W. McCormick, *America's Half Century* (Baltimore: Johns Hopkins University Press, 1996; rev. ed.), p. 189.

111. Kissinger quoted in Burr, *Kissinger Transcripts*, p. 445; Soviet Foreign Office quoted in Odd Arne Westad, "Moscow and the Angolan Crisis," *Cold War International History Project Bulletin*, nos. 8–9 (Winter 1996/1997), pp. 27, 29.

112. Leonid Brezhnev quoted in Wilfred Loth, *Overcoming the Cold War* (New York: Palgrave, 2002), p. 133.

113. Dobrynin, *In Confidence*, p. 472.

114. Quoted in Gleijeses, *Conflicting Missions*, p. 390.

115. Quoted in Reeves, *President Nixon*, p. 343.

116. Quoted in Reeves, *President Nixon*, p. 341; quoted in Diane B. Kunz, *Butter and Guns* (New York: Free Press, 1997), 218.

117. U.S. business executive quoted in Walter LaFeber, *The Clash* (New York: Norton, 1997), p. 353.

118. Quoted in Small, *Presidency*, p. 146.

119. Reuben Askew quoted in Charles W. Kegley, Jr., and Eugene R. Wittkopf, *World Politics* (New York: St. Martin's, 1981), p. 181.

120. Quoted in Thomas G. Paterson, *On Every Front* (New York: Norton, 1992; 2nd ed.), p. 217.

121. Quoted in Fraser Harbutt, *The Cold War Era* (Malden, Mass.: Blackwell, 2002), p. 231.

122. Quoted in Robert C. Johansen, *The National Interest and the Human Interest* (Princeton: Princeton University Press, 1980), p. 13.

123. Quoted in Adam and Stebbins, *American Foreign Relations, 1976*, p. 478.

124. Quoted in Mark H. Lytle, "An Environmental Approach to American Diplomatic History," *Diplomatic History, XX* (Spring 1996), 287.

125. Petr Beckmann quoted in John McCormick, *Reclaiming Paradise* (Bloomington: Indiana University Press, 1989), p. 85.

126. Mario Gibson Barbaroza quoted in Charles McGraw, "Removed from Planet Earth" (Unpub. paper, 1994), p. 7.

127. Quoted in Small, *Presidency*, p. 163.

128. United Nations, General Assembly, *Official Records*, 22nd Session, August 18, 1967, Document A/6695, p. 1.

129. Quoted in Michael Roskin, "An American Metternich," in Frank J. Merli and Theodore A. Wilson, eds., *Makers of American Diplomacy* (New York: Charles Scribner's Sons, 1974), p. 698.

130. White House official quoted in Tad Szulc, "How Kissinger Did It," *Foreign Policy*, no. 15 (Summer 1974), 35.

131. Quoted in McMahon, *Limits of Empire*, p. 255.

132. Mike Mansfield quoted in Stanley Millet, ed., *South Vietnam* (New York: Facts on File, 1973–1974; 7 vols.), IV, 64.

133. H. R. Haldeman notes quoted in Michael A. Genovese, *The Nixon Presidency* (Westport, Conn.: Greenwood, 1990), p. 134.

134. Quoted in William Burr and Jeffrey Kimball, eds., "Nixon's Nuclear Ploy," *National Security Archive Briefing Book No. 81* (December 23, 2002).

135. Quoted in Clarence R. Wyatt, *Paper Soldiers* (New York: Norton, 1993), p. 193.

136. Quoted in Melvin Small, "Containing Domestic Enemies," in David L. Anderson, ed., *Shadow on the White House* (Lawrence: University Press of Kansas, 1993), p. 137; Nixon tape quoted in *Washington Post National Weekly Edition*, January 4, 1999.

137. Frances FitzGerald, *Fire in the Lake* (New York: Vintage, 1972), p. 544.

138. Ken George quoted in Otto J. Lehrack, *No Shining Armor* (Lawrence: University Press of Kansas, 1992), pp. 337–338.

139. Quoted in *Time, CXXIII* (April 16, 1984), 24.

140. Quoted in Larry Berman, *No Peace, No Honor* (New York: Free Press, 2001), p. 73.

141. *Public Papers, Nixon, 1969*, p. 909.

142. Morris, *Uncertain Greatness*, p. 175.

143. Charles Colson quoted in George C. Herring, *America's Longest War* (New York: Knopf, 1986), p. 239.

144. Ambassador William Sullivan and Foreign Minister Nguyen Co Thach quoted in McMahon, *Limits of Empire*, p. 264.

145. Quoted in Thomas S. Blanton, ed., "The Pentagon Papers," *National Security Archive Electronic Briefing Book No. 48* (June 5, 2001).

146. Quoted in Qiang Zhai, *China and the Vietnam Wars, 1950–1975* (Chapel Hill: University of North Carolina Press, 2000), p. 201.

147. Quoted in *Hartford Courant*, March 1, 2002.

148. Quoted in Nixon, *RN*, p. 605.

149. Quoted in Jeffrey Kimball, *The Vietnam War Files*, (Lawrence: University Press of Kansas, 2004), p. 221.

150. Quoted in Hanhimaki, "Kissinger," p. 180.

151. Kissinger, *White House Years*, p. 1399.

152. Quoted in Dale Andrade, *America's Last Vietnam Battle* (Lawrence: University Press of Kansas, 2001), p. 480.

153. Quoted in Fredrik Logevall, "The Swedish-American Conflict over Vietnam," *Diplomatic History, XVII* (Summer 1993), 441.

154. Zhou quoted in Hanhimaki, "Kissinger," p. 185; Larry Berman, *No Peace, No Honor*, p. 241.

155. Quoted in Robert Alan Goldberg, *Barry Goldwater* (New Haven: Yale University Press, 1995), p. 269.

156. Quoted in Bundy, *Tangled Web*, p. 362.

157. Quoted in Oriana Fallaci, *Interview with History* (Boston: Houghton Mifflin, 1976), p. 56.

158. Richard Holbrooke quoted in Isaacson, *Kissinger*, p. 483.

159. John Negroponte quoted in Marilyn B. Young, *The Vietnam Wars* (New York: HarperCollins, 1991), p. 279.

160. Entry of December 20, 1972, *Haldeman Diaries*, p. 558.

161. James Reston, *Deadline* (New York: Random House, 1991), p. 408.

162. Wayne Thompson, *To Hanoi and Back: The U.S. Air Force and North Vietnam, 1966–1973* (Washington, D.C.: Smithsonian Institution Press, 2000), p. 258.

163. Milton Young quoted in Robert D. Schulzinger, "Nixon, Congress, and the War in Vietnam," in Randall B. Woods, ed., *Vietnam and the American Political Tradition: The Politics of Dissent* (New York: Cambridge University Press, 2003), p. 298.

164. Mike Mansfield quoted in Donald A. Ritchie, "Mike Mansfield and the Vietnam War," in Woods, *Vietnam*, p. 201.

165. Jeffrey Kimball, *Nixon's Vietnam War* (Lawrence: University Press of Kansas, 1998), p. 371.

166. Quoted in George C. Herring, "Vietnam: The War That Never Seems to Go Away," *New England Journal of History, LIV* (Spring 1998), 8.

167. Quoted in Thomas G. Paterson, "Historical Memory and Illusive Victories," *Diplomatic History, XII* (Winter 1988), 14.

168. Michael Lind, *Vietnam: The Necessary War* (New York: Free Press, 1999), p. 282.

169. Quoted in J. Garry Clifford, "Bureaucratic Politics," in Michael J. Hogan and Thomas G. Paterson, eds., *Explaining the History of American Foreign Relations* (New York: Cambridge University Press, 2004; 2d ed.), p. 91.

170. Richard E. Neustadt and Ernest R. May, *Thinking in Time* (New York: Free Press, 1986).

171. Church quoted in Kathryn S. Olmstead, *Challenging the Secret Government* (Chapel Hill: University of North Carolina Press, 1996), p. 81.

172. Richard J. Barnet, *Roots of War* (Baltimore: Penguin, 1972), p. 9.

173. Quoted in Greene, *Ford*, p. 150.

174. Kissinger quoted in William Burr and Michael L. Evans, eds., "Ford, Kissinger, and the Indonesian Invasion, 1975–76," *National Security Archive Electronic Briefing Book No. 62* (December 6, 2001).

175. Edmund Stillman, in "America Now: A Failure of Nerve?" *Commentary, LX* (July 1975), 83.

176. Ronald Steel, *ibid.*, p. 79.

177. Henry Steele Commager, "The Defeat of America," *New York Review of Books*, October 5, 1972, p. 13.

178. Charles DeBenedetti, *The Peace Reform in American History* (Bloomington: Indiana University Press, 1980), p. 174.

179. Charles DeBenedetti, "On the Significance of Peace Activism," *Peace and Change, IX* (Summer 1983), 14.

180. Quoted in Ronald Steel, *Walter Lippmann and the American Century* (Boston: Little, Brown, 1980), p. 586.

181. Bruce Weigl quoted in Young, *Vietnam Wars*, p. 328.

182. Eric T. Dean, Jr., *Shook Over Hell* (Cambridge: Harvard University Press, 1997), pp. 21, 211.

183. William Duiker and Kevin Farrell quoted in Arnold R. Isaacs. *Vietnam Shadows* (Baltimore: John Hopkins University Press, 1997), p. 147.

184. C. W. Bowman quoted in Eric Bergerud, *Red Thunder, Tropic Lightning* (New York: Penguin, 1994), p. 224.

185. Jeffrey P. Kimball, "The Stab-in-the-Back Legend and the Vietnam War," *Armed Forces and Society, XIV* (Spring 1988), 433.

186. Quoted in George C. Herring, "The 'Vietnam Syndrome,' " *Virginia Quarterly Review, LVII* (Fall 1981), 595.

187. Quoted in Thomas G. Paterson, *Meeting the Communist Threat* (New York: Oxford University Press, 1988), p. 259.

188. Qiang Zhai, "Reassessing China's Role in the Vietnam War," in Xiaobing Li and Hongshan Li, eds., *China and the United States* (Lanham, Md.: University Press of America, 1998), p. 111.

189. Quoted in Andrade, *America's Last*, p. 475.

190. John Pancrazio quoted in Bergerud, *Red Thunder*, p. 246.

191. Quoted in Philip Caputo, *A Rumor of War* (New York: Ballantine, 1977), p. 69.

192. Christian G. Appy, *Working Class War* (Chapel Hill: University of North Carolina Press, 1993), p. 26.

193. John Kniffen quoted in Richard Stacewicz, *Winter Soldiers* (New York: Twayne, 1997), p. 107.

194. Colin L. Powell, *My American Journey* (New York: Random House, 1995), p. 149.

195. Quoted in McMahon, *Limits of Empire*, p. 132.

196. Le Ly Hayslip, *When Heaven and Earth Changed Places* (Garden City, N.Y.: Doubleday, 1989), p. xiv.

197. Quoted in Ngo Vinh Long, "Vietnamese Perspectives," in Stanley I. Kutler, ed., *Encyclopedia of the Vietnam War* (New York: Scribner, 1996), p. 608.

198. Alistair Cooke quoted in Donald W. White, *The American Century* (New Haven: Yale University Press, p. 378.

CHAPTER 11

To Begin the World Over Again: Carter, Reagan, and Revivalism, 1977–1989

American Hostage in Iran. *On November 8, 1979, this blindfolded, hand-tied American captive was paraded on the grounds of the U.S. Embassy in Teheran. A jeering crowd taunted the frightened American early in the Iranian hostage crisis. (AP/Wide World Photos)*

DIPLOMATIC CROSSROAD

༄ *The Iranian Hostage Crisis, 1979–1981*

"DEATH TO THE Shah! Death to Carter! Death to America!" chanted the radical Islamic student demonstrators outside the U.S. Embassy in Teheran, Iran, on November 4, 1979.[1] Suddenly, they stormed the embassy that their religious leader Ayatollah Ruhollah Khomeini had branded a "nest of spies."[2] Hundreds spread over the twenty-seven-acre compound. In the chancery, CIA officers operating undercover as Foreign Service personnel shredded classified documents. "Man, we're gonna have an Alamo," said one U.S. marine as the armed militants broke into rooms and seized frightened Americans, including Ann Swift, a political officer who maintained contact with Washington until she put down the telephone and surrendered.[3] "We're paying you back for Vietnam," snarled one attacker.[4]

All told, sixty-six Americans were captured. Three were visiting the Iranian Foreign Ministry at the time; they remained there throughout the crisis. A few U.S. officials escaped, and Canadian diplomats later spirited them out of Iran. According to the jubilant students, the kidnapped Americans would go free only after Shah Mohammad Reza Pahlavi returned to Iran for trial.

The admission of the exiled Shah to a New York hospital two weeks earlier had provided the immediate catalyst for seizing the embassy. But Iranian hostility had been smoldering since the 1950s. The Shah had risen to power in 1941, replacing his father, who had claimed the Peacock Throne by force in the 1920s. The young Shah increasingly relied on U.S. advice and assistance—a dependence demonstrated most emphatically in 1953 after he left Iran, when nationalists, led by Prime Minister Mohammad Mossadegh, nationalized the Anglo-Iranian Oil Company. In Operation AJAX, the CIA plotted with royalist Iranians and British officials, restored the Shah to the throne, and drove Mossadegh from the country. The Shah soon became a staunch anticommunist ally of the United States. In 1957, with CIA assistance, he organized SAVAK, a secret police organization that suppressed dissent and terrorized the people. "We will teach the CIA not to do these things in our country," said a militant student to one hostage.[5]

In the 1970s popular discontent with the Shah swelled. Muslim clergy resented Western influences, including Hollywood movies and rights for women. Intellectuals and students protested the suppression of civil liberties. Social democrats who had fled with Mossadegh in the 1950s demanded a constitutional government. For different reasons, merchants, young workers, and feudal landholders felt aggrieved by the Shah's modernization of the economy. Inflation, unemployment, inadequate housing, and preferential jobs for skilled foreigners also created unrest. Ethnic separatists in Kurdistan fought for autonomy. SAVAK, symbol of the Shah's police state, committed untold brutalities that helped to unite disparate groups against the monarch and his sponsor, the United States.

Some Iranians also objected to massive purchases of arms from the United States. In the period 1973–1978, the Shah spent $19 billion of the nation's oil wealth

Jimmy Carter's World. The Iranian crisis joined domestic economic turmoil to trouble President Carter. A White House aide remembered that "before conferring with a foreign leader, Carter would often sit by his globe . . . trying to imagine the political, economic, and military pressures experienced by the leader." (Cartoon by Tony Auth. Reprinted with permission from *Foreign Policy,* no. 31, Summer 1978. Copyright 1978 by the Carnegie Endowment for International Peace)

on American weapons. He bought helicopters, fighter aircraft, destroyers, and missiles, because, he argued, Iran had to fend off numerous enemies—the Soviet Union, Iraq, radical Arabs, domestic radicals—and had to police the Persian Gulf. Iran possessed the mightiest military in the Middle East, but many Iranians thought that the Shah squandered the nation's resources as a stooge of the United States.

President Jimmy Carter, visiting Teheran in late 1977, praised the Shah for making Iran "an island of stability in one of the more troubled areas of the world."[6] U.S. diplomats were "dumbfounded" by Carter's remarks, for the president had identified human rights (hardly the Shah's strongest point) as a major U.S. foreign-policy goal.[7] The president, of course, was paying polite deference to an ally, and after Vietnam, American leaders looked to regional powers such as Iran to assist the United States in preserving its global interests. Reports of unrest in Iran elicited a standard Washington response: "It's not our country; the Shah is in control; we don't know enough about what could happen if he lost control—the communists might take over."[8] Carter did not know that the Shah was dying of cancer—a condition perhaps making the monarch fatalistic and lethargic.

In 1978, demonstrations, riots, and strikes shook Iran. The Shah declared martial law, and the United States equipped his forces with riot-control equipment. "Hang firm and . . . count on our backing," Carter told him.[9] National Security Affairs Adviser Zbigniew Brzezinski urged that the Iranian army smash the opposition and stage a coup. Secretary of State Cyrus Vance rebutted that the "iron fist" denied the central thrust of Carter's foreign policy and would not work because the largely conscript Iranian army would disintegrate.[10] From Teheran, U.S. ambassador William Sullivan sided with Vance. Officials in Washington had rejected Sullivan's advice to open direct communication with Khomeini, the evident leader of the revolution, then in exile in Paris. Not until senior "Wise Man" George Ball visited Iran in November did Washington fully understand "that the Shah was on the way to a great fall" and "like Humpty Dumpty, his regime could not be put together again."[11]

The Shah appointed a civilian government acceptable to his generals and flew to Egypt on January 16, 1979. Making it clear that Islamic clerics intended to govern Iran, the Ayatollah rejected the new regime and soon installed his own. When he fueled rampant anti-Americanism in angry speeches, American citizens began to depart. On February 14 a revolutionary group seized the U.S. Embassy, but the Iranian government forced the intruders to abandon the compound.

After leaving Teheran, the Shah moved from Egypt to Morocco to the Bahamas to Mexico. Few nations wanted to give sanctuary to a repudiated despot. Even Carter rescinded an American offer of welcome to the Shah. Former secretary of state Henry A. Kissinger and David Rockefeller, whose Chase Manhattan Bank had substantial financial ties to Iran, petitioned the White House to cease treating the Shah like "a flying Dutchman" in search of a safe place to land.[12] In October the president learned that the Shah would die of a malignant lymphoma unless a New York hospital admitted him. Despite warnings that such a move could ignite protest against Americans in Iran, Carter invited him to the United States. The Shah arrived in New York on October 22; on November 4 militant students seized the embassy.

As stunned Americans watched "America Held Hostage" each night on television, it became clear that the hostage-takers wanted more than the Shah.[13] First,

the hostage-grabbing was Iran's way of preventing the Shah from launching a counterrevolution from the United States in a replay of 1953. Second, the hostage-taking
helped Iran break diplomatic relations with the United States, which Khomeini
called a "global Shah" never to be trusted.[14] Finally, the hostage drama permitted
the eighty-one-year-old Khomeini—whose dark, piercing eyes glared from posters
throughout the country—to use anti-Americanism to overwhelm civilian moderates who competed with his clerics for control of the revolution.

Spending sleepless nights, President Carter felt "the same kind of impotence
that a powerful person feels when his child is kidnapped."[15] Within the administration, Vance and Brzezinski differed bitterly. Recalling the successful Israeli commando raid to rescue hostages from Entebbe airport in Uganda in 1976, the latter
advocated retaliatory action to preserve U.S. honor, even at the cost of lives. Citing
the U.S.S. *Pueblo* affair of 1968, in which he had helped to secure the release of U.S.
sailors held captive by North Korea after months of negotiations, Vance urged "care
and caution in trying to achieve a solution . . . without spilling blood."[16] On November 14 the president froze Iranian assets in the United States valued at about $8
billion. U.S. officials secretly asked Palestine Liberation Organization leader Yasir
Arafat to help. He did, persuading the revolutionary government to release thirteen
hostages (most of those released were women and African Americans). All other efforts through intermediaries came to naught.

As the diplomats struggled to negotiate with an Iranian government that often
seemed incapable of functioning, the hostages languished in captivity. Although never
mutilated or sexually abused, the hostages suffered through an ordeal lasting 444 days.
At first blindfolded with their hands and feet tied, they thought that they would be
either released quickly or killed. For a long time they could not speak or read newspapers. The hostages lost weight and became sick. They received books and games
later, but they constantly fought boredom, melancholy, and fear. The worst terror they
endured was a mock execution, preceded by abusive interrogation. Asked later if he
would ever return to Iran, one freed hostage shot back: "Yeah, in a B-52."[17]

On April 7, 1980, after Teheran jettisoned another secret diplomatic overture,
the United States broke relations with Iran. With the CIA saying that "pulling a
Mussadiq [toppling the regime] was beyond our reach" and political advisers warning that "you can forget about a second term" if he did nothing, Carter ordered the
Joint Chiefs of Staff to launch a rescue mission.[18] "Stunned and angry that such a
momentous decision had been made in my absence," Vance asked for reconsideration when he returned from a trip.[19] Carter called a meeting of the National Security Council to hear Vance's "volcanic" objections.[20] First, the secretary said, the
United States had just pressed its allies to impose economic sanctions on Iran; a military maneuver, without prior warning, would make them feel deceived. Second,
the Iranian parliament, about to meet, might provide a solution. Third, the hostages
faced no immediate physical danger. Even if the raid succeeded, numerous hostages
would die. Fourth, the Iranians might retaliate by seizing U.S. journalists and other
Americans in Teheran, creating another hostage crisis. Fifth, the whole Middle East
might become inflamed. And last, such a military venture might push the Iranians
into the arms of the Soviets. No one at the meeting agreed with Vance. Angry that
Vance had put "a knife in my back," Carter vowed to "stick with the decision I

made."[21] "Lance the boil" of U.S. frustration, urged Brzezinski.[22] "America needs a win . . . real, real bad," remarked "Chargin' Charlie" Beckwith, the rescue mission's ground commander.[23] Later he admitted that "the probability of success was about 50 percent."[24]

On April 24, eight helicopters lifted off the supercarrier *Nimitz* in the Arabian Sea. At the same time, six C-130 Hercules transports took to the skies from Egypt. All the aircraft headed for a rendezvous in the Iranian desert; from there rescue teams of Green Berets and Rangers planned to infiltrate Teheran and assault the U.S. Embassy to free the hostages. But the helicopters ran into dust storms, or "*haboobs*" ("flying in a bowl of milk"); two malfunctioned before reaching Iran, and another lost a hydraulic line at the rendezvous point.[25] The president accepted Colonel Beckwith's recommendation to abort the mission. In the hasty and dusty exit, a helicopter and a C-130 collided, killing eight crew members. The saddened president asked for a copy of the speech that John F. Kennedy had made after the disastrous 1961 Bay of Pigs invasion; then he told the nation the news. Vance, who said that he would resign whether or not the rescue attempt succeeded, quietly left the administration. Critics pounded Carter for undertaking a project sure to cause the deaths of many hostages. "Thank God for the sandstorm," later remarked one hostage.[26] While some speculated that Carter may have ordered Operation Eagle Claw to bolster his sagging political fortunes, others asked if "the Three Stooges now directed foreign policy."[27]

After the rescue attempt, Americans seemed resigned to a prolonged crisis. Many citizens displayed yellow ribbons to symbolize their prayers, while radio stations belted out "Bomb Iran" to the tune of the Beach Boys' hit song "Barbara Ann."[28] "People who ran around in robes and looked funny could do all this to us and we couldn't do anything about it," lamented Carter's press secretary.[29]

Four events finally facilitated a resolution. First, the Shah died in Egypt in July 1980. So suspicious were the Iranian militants, one hostage recalled, that many would not believe the Shah was sick "until he actually died, and even then [they doubted it]."[30] Second, Khomeini's Islamic clerics won control of the parliament and thus no longer needed the hostages for their political purposes. Third, in September, Iraq and Iran went to war, and Iran found that it had few friends or funds. Iran's oil exports had slowed because of equipment breakdowns and war-related destruction of petroleum facilities and pipelines. And fourth, Ronald Reagan, who promised a tougher posture, was elected president.

As these events unfolded, American and Iranian diplomats met with Algerian mediators. On the day before Reagan took office, an agreement was struck: release of the hostages in exchange for unfreezing Iranian assets in the United States. On January 20, 1981—shortly after Ronald Reagan's inauguration—the hostages gained their freedom. After 444 days they returned home to a relieved nation that celebrated briefly and then tried to forget.

"*No one* spoke to any of the Persian-speaking political officers among the hostages to find out what happened" until months later, because U.S. officials "just didn't care," one hostage recalled.[31] Some second-guessing did occur. Should Carter have played up the hostage issue so much, thereby signaling to the Iranians that they had in fact stung and would continue to sting Americans? But with the Iranians jeer-

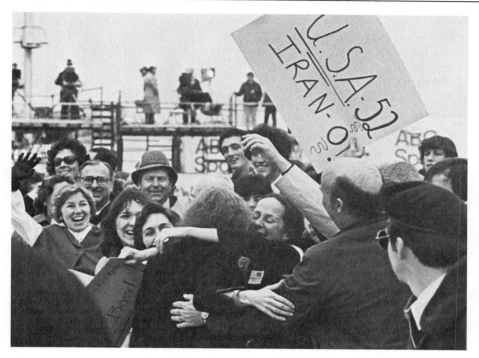

The Hostages Return. After 444 days in captivity, the fifty-two Americans held prisoner in Iran came home to celebrations. At the start, sixty-six had been seized. Fourteen had been released from bondage earlier. This placard awarded victory to the United States. Some twenty years later, eight of the hostages and their families won federal lawsuits of more than $213 million, to be paid out of Iran's frozen assets. (U.S. Department of State. Photograph by Rover Kalser)

ing Washington day after day, with television cameras daily chronicling this gross violation of diplomatic immunity, with Carter's vaunted compassion for other human beings—could the president have done otherwise?

The United States had lost an ally with a large army, huge quantities of oil, intelligence posts that yielded critical data on Soviet missile tests, and billions of dollars to spend on American-made weapons. The long crisis had wounded American pride, raising questions in the post-Vietnam era about the ability of the United States to lead. The hostage ordeal helped bring down the Carter presidency. President Reagan drew a simple lesson: America had to build up its military to deter enemies. Other Americans urged separation from right-wing regimes and clients so that the United States could avoid becoming the target of revolutionary ire. Perhaps the hostage travail reinforced a lesson of Vietnam: American aid and weaponry, such as had flowed to the Shah, cannot guarantee the survival of an unpopular regime. As the Iranian revolution descended into tyranny, executions of Khomeini foes, and disputes with other Muslims in the Middle East, some Americans prided themselves on once having supported the Shah. Despite Khomeini's charge that "America is the number-one enemy of the deprived and oppressed people of the world," some officials found solace because Iran remained ardently anti-Soviet.[32] Very quickly Washington sought new security ties with other "regional influentials"—Pakistan, Turkey, Saudi Arabia, and even Iraq.[33]

The outpouring of emotional patriotism that greeted the returning hostages suggested another conclusion: The nation hungered for heroes who could rekindle American pride. "If television coverage of Vietnam had converted the American people into temporary pacifists," wrote one analyst, "the video images from Iran turned them into a pack of snarling wolves."[34] An Oklahoma man who judged Carter too timid looked to the imperial past for inspiration: "I agree with Teddy Roosevelt. Walk softly and carry a big stick," the Oklahoman said. "And club the hell out of them if you need to."[35]

Zbigs and Zags: Carter's Divided Administration

Teddy Roosevelt's "big stick" was exactly what Jimmy Carter had found wrong with American foreign policy when he came to office in 1977—too much bluster, too much military, and too much insensitivity toward Third World peoples. During the 1976 campaign, Carter promised "no more immoral *realpolitik,* no more Watergate-type secrecy, no more destabilizing CIA interventions."[36] He promised to reduce military budgets, bring some of America's overseas forces home, trim arms sales abroad, and slow nuclear proliferation. He berated the Republicans for supporting dictatorial regimes. Yet at times Carter sounded like an inveterate Cold Warrior. He claimed that the Republicans had permitted a decline of U.S. power. He mocked détente: "We've been outtraded in almost every instance."[37] He criticized the White House for accepting Soviet domination of Eastern Europe and authorizing huge grain sales to the Soviet Union. President Gerald Ford thought that Carter was cynically attracting the hawks by bemoaning the descent of American power and wooing the doves by advocating cuts in defense spending. "He wavers, he wanders, he wiggles, and he waffles," Ford complained.[38]

After the downbeat years of Watergate, Vietnam, CIA abuses, and soaring OPEC oil prices, the election of the wealthy peanut farmer with a toothy smile inspired hope. After graduating from the Naval Academy and serving on a nuclear submarine, Carter entered politics as a Georgia state senator in the 1960s and, in 1970, became governor. After a four-year gubernatorial term, this relatively obscure Democrat set out to win the presidency and astounded the professionals by doing so. Carter cherished hard work, family responsibility, and religion. A devout Baptist, he became a "born again" Christian, awakened to a religious revival by his evangelical sister Ruth, a faith-healer. Energetic, ambitious, and self-confident, Carter seemed to some people sanctimonious and arrogant. A quick learner, he paid meticulous attention to details. Carter ran the presidency like a "family farmer: Plow the field, plant the seeds, fertilize the crop, . . . overseeing every last detail."[39] Unwilling to prioritize, he tried to be "desk officer for everything."[40]

An "outsider" to Washington politics, Carter had little experience in foreign affairs. He did hold membership in the Trilateral Commission, organized by the Columbia University political scientist Zbigniew Brzezinski and the banker David Rockefeller to bring together business, political, and academic notables for discussions of global problems bedeviling industrial nations. And Carter had followed the fractious debate over Vietnam and knew that a new national foreign-policy consensus had not yet taken form. "Deeply troubled by the lies our people had been told," he sensed a need for national redemption.[41]

Cyrus R. Vance (1917–2002). "Cy" Vance brought extensive diplomatic experience to his post as secretary of state. Vance won plaudits for negotiating the Panama Canal treaties and SALT-II. His resignation in 1980 was the first such act made in protest by a secretary of state since that of William Jennings Bryan in 1915. (National Archives)

Makers of American Foreign Relations, 1977–1989

Presidents	Secretaries of State
Jimmy Carter, 1977–1981	Cyrus R. Vance, 1977–1980
	Edmund Muskie, 1980–1981
Ronald Reagan, 1981–1989	Alexander M. Haig, Jr., 1981–1982
	George P. Shultz, 1982–1989

Carter selected Cyrus Vance as his secretary of state. A wealthy, West Virginia–born, Yale-educated lawyer, Vance held top posts in the Department of Defense in the 1960s. He doubted the efficacy of military intervention, having learned from Vietnam that the United States could not "prop up a series of regimes that lacked popular support."[42] He did not believe that the Soviets fomented most local conflicts, and he advised quiet diplomacy to improve Soviet-American relations. When Vance resigned in April 1980, he did so not only to protest the hostage rescue mission, but also to register his disenchantment with Carter for embracing the "visceral anti-Sovietism" of Zbigniew Brzezinski, the national security affairs adviser.[43]

Outspoken and tenacious, arrogant and aggressive, Brzezinski blamed most of the world's troubles on the Soviets. He sought military superiority and worked to play China off against the Soviet Union. To counter Vance's argument that a military coup in Iran would produce bloodshed, Brzezinski coldly lectured President

Carter (b. 1924) and Zbigniew Brzezinski (b. 1928). A Warsaw-born son of a Polish diplomat, Brzezinski emigrated to the United States in 1953. A long-time professor of political science at Columbia University, he became noted for his Cold War views before serving as Carter's adviser. Asked if he regretted that U.S. aid to anti-Soviet Muslims in Afghanistan helped to install a hostile Taliban regime that sponsored terrorism against the West, Brzezinski replied in 1998: "What is more important in world history? The Taliban or the collapse of the Soviet empire? Some agitated [Muslims] or the liberation of Central Europe and the end of the Cold War?"

Andrew Young (b. 1932). A graduate of Howard University and the Hartford Theological Seminary, the Reverend Young had been Dr. Martin Luther King's right-hand man in the civil rights movement of the 1950s–1960s and a member of Congress from Georgia before Carter named him ambassador to the United Nations. Young was forced to resign in 1979 when he admitted meeting with representatives of the Palestine Liberation Organization, whose participation in negotiations he deemed essential to Middle East peace. (United Nations. Photograph by Y. Nagata)

Carter that "world politics was not a kindergarten."[44] State Department officers often bristled over Brzezinski's strong-arm bureaucratic methods, his attempts to become a public spokesperson for policy, and his back-channel contacts with foreign leaders. "While Mr. Vance played by the Marquis of Queensberry rules," remarked one official, "Mr. Brzezinski was more of a street fighter."[45]

The president believed that Vance and Brzezinski would balance one another in both style and substance, and that he could manage any conflict: "Zbig would be the thinker, Cy would be the doer, and Jimmy Carter would be the decider."[46] But acrimonious infighting soon made the administration's foreign policy appear inconsistent, marked by zigs and zags.

The Carter administration pursued basically traditional goals. "U.S. foreign policy is like an aircraft carrier," remarked Brzezinski. "You simply don't send it into a 180-degree turn; at most you move a few degrees to port or starboard."[47] At the start Carter officials rejected the extreme options of Fortress America (isolationism) and Atlas America (global policeman) in favor of Participant America. That meant emphasizing worldwide preventive diplomacy: advancing the peace process in the Middle East; reducing nuclear arms; normalizing relations with China; mediating conflict in the Third World; stimulating improvements in human rights; and creating economic stability through talks on the law of the sea, energy, and clean air and water. The president wanted to avoid a reactive foreign policy enmeshed in short-term, day-to-day crises. With reformist zeal, Carter set out to apply "morality, reason, and power" to American diplomacy.[48]

Carter especially sought to restore U.S. power and influence in the Third World. He preferred to emphasize North–South rather than East–West issues and to make concessions to nationalism, even to leftist regimes. Third World problems, he argued, sprang not from communist plots but from deep-seated, indigenous economic, social, racial, and political problems. The appointment of Andrew Young as ambassador to the United Nations symbolized Carter's sympathetic approach. An African American once active in the civil rights movement, Young gradually improved the U.S. dialogue with suspicious Third World diplomats. But in 1979 Carter had to fire Young after the ambassador made unauthorized contact with representatives of the Palestine Liberation Organization, a group that the United States refused to recognize. It later became known that the U.S. ambassador to Lebanon also held thirty-five secret yet officially sanctioned meetings with PLO representatives during the same period.

The soul of American foreign policy, Carter insisted, should be the defense and expansion of human rights for foreign peoples. By internationalizing the Bill of Rights, America could recover its prestige and pride and add moral force to the nation's arsenal. Drawing on his own religious commitment, Carter vowed to win for all peoples the freedom to work, vote, worship, travel, speak, assemble, and receive a fair trial. Slavery, genocide, torture, forced labor, arbitrary arrest, rigged elections, and suspensions of civil liberties all became anathema. Dictators must respect human rights or face cutbacks in American foreign aid.

Although Carter emphasized that Americans should put their "inordinate fear of communism" behind them, he actually reinvigorated the containment doctrine by initiating new weapons systems and streamlining conventional forces, by encouraging nationalism in Eastern Europe, and by cultivating Third World governments.[49] Improved Sino-American ties (the "China card"), continued strategic arms limitations talks, and public denunciations of Soviet violations of human rights also might check Moscow. By 1979 Carter, having moved closer to Brzezinski's views, sounded the familiar Cold War calls for "a more muscular foreign policy."[50] The following year he proclaimed the Carter Doctrine, or containment in the Middle East. Confrontation more than cooperation came to mark Soviet-American relations under Carter.

The Panama Canal and High Voltage Nationalism in Latin America

Although the Iranian hostage crisis and the rivalry with the Soviet Union came to dominate the president's foreign policy, at the outset Carter launched an active diplomacy toward Latin America, the Middle East, and Africa. In Latin America, Carter championed human rights and democratization and worked to accommodate nationalism. More than ever before, the Latin American governments claimed an independent role in world politics and shunned U.S. advice. They petitioned Washington for lower tariffs, higher commodity prices, less diplomatic backing of North American corporations locked in disputes with their governments, and the transfer of technology on convenient terms. The Carter administration saw high stakes: $59 billion in trade (1979); investments of $24.4 billion (1979); vital imports of petroleum, copper, and tin; and Latin America's thirty votes in the United Nations. Foreign aid ($726 million in 1977–1978) continued as one means of exerting influence, but Carter also sought negotiations.

Panama became the first testing ground. Panamanians had long resented the 1903 treaty granting the United States the Canal Zone, a ten-mile-wide, 500-square-mile slice of territory that cut their nation in half—"a foreign flag piercing its own heart," according to Panamanian General Omar Torrijos.[51] After bloody anti-American riots in 1964, President Lyndon B. Johnson had started talks, but they barely crawled forward.

Carter brought the negotiations to fruition. Two treaties were signed in 1977 and ratified the following year. One treaty, abrogating the 1903 document, provided for the integration of the Canal Zone into Panama and increased Panama's percentage of the canal's revenues to boost the small nation's ailing economy. The other treaty stated that the United States had the right to defend the "neutrality" of the canal forever. In a national vote, Panamanians approved the treaties by a 2 to 1 margin, but nationalistic sentiment against a continued U.S. role in Panamanian affairs ran high. When Torrijos identified "lots of electric currents" in his country, the U.S. negotiator Ellsworth Bunker thanked him for "keeping the voltage down."[52]

Conservative critics in the United States soon denounced the treaties as diabolical instruments of appeasement and retreat. After Vietnam, Americans had to draw the line somewhere: "Panama is the place and now is the time."[53] Many Americans thought that the United States owned the canal. Ronald Reagan mangled the historical record: "We bought it, we paid for it, it's ours, and we're going to keep it."[54] Giving up a key waterway would supposedly weaken U.S. defense and leave

Panama vulnerable to Soviet or Cuban subversion. Veterans' groups lined up against the treaties, and the Conservative Caucus flooded senatorial offices with claims that the treaty would turn the Caribbean into a "Red Lake."[55]

The Carter administration countered with a full-court press. The Committee of Americans for the Canal Treaties enlisted veteran diplomat W. Averell Harriman, labor leader George Meany, and army general Maxwell Taylor, among others. Gerald Ford and Henry Kissinger also worked for approval. The National Association of Manufacturers and multinational corporations holding large investments in Latin America endorsed the agreements. Treaty advocates stressed the goodwill that Washington would gain after terminating the imperialistic document of 1903. Non-ratification could "poison" trade with Latin America and invite terrorist attacks on the canal.[56] "A single Panamanian" with a bazooka "could put the great locks out of commisson for months."[57] The canal's value had diminished because modern aircraft carriers had too much beam to pass through the waterway. Moreover, less than 10 percent of U.S. foreign trade went through it, and the new, large cargo ships and supertankers could not squeeze through the locks. The actor John Wayne, a personal friend of General Torrijos, publicly rebuked Governor Reagan "point by God damn point in the Treaty where you are misinforming people."[58]

As the debate peaked in early 1978, the administration used arguments that alarmed Panamanians. A "memorandum of understanding," signed by Torrijos and Carter and later added to the treaty by the Senate, provided for U.S. intervention after the year 2000 to thwart "any aggression or threat directed against the Canal or against the peaceful transit of vessels through the Canal."[59] When asked what the United States would do after 2000 if the Panamanians closed the canal for repairs, Brzezinski answered: "Close down the Panamanian government for repairs."[60] A "condition," which Torrijos accepted only after Carter's personal plea, stated that if canal operations ever stopped, the United States had the right to intervene, "including the use of military force in the Republic of Panama."[61] On March 16, 1978, the Senate approved the neutrality treaty 68 to 32; the other treaty passed on April 18 by a similar count—in both cases with only one vote more than the two-thirds tally needed. Carter later acknowledged that "some fine members of Congress had to pay with their political careers for their votes."[62]

The Carter administration also contended with nationalist stirrings in Nicaragua. Since 1936 the Somoza family had ruled that Central American state (see page 158). Dictatorial, brutal, and corrupt, the Somoza dynasty nevertheless had gained grudging U.S. support as a reliable anticommunist ally and had received military aid, which it often used to suppress critics. Nicaragua had served as a staging area for CIA operations against Guatemala (1954) and Cuba (1961). All the while, Nicaraguans suffered high rates of poverty, malnutrition, and illiteracy, and the Somozas amassed great wealth, coming to own much of the country's land and industry. After a devastating 1972 earthquake, the Somoza family callously drained off international relief aid. A long-smoldering popular rebellion exploded in 1978, led by the leftist Sandinista National Liberation Front (FSLN). Founded in 1962, the FSLN took its name from the insurgent César Augusto Sandino, who had fought U.S. occupation in the 1920s and 1930s (see pages 157–158). Business executives, Catholic clergy, and intellectuals joined the crusade to unseat the Somozas

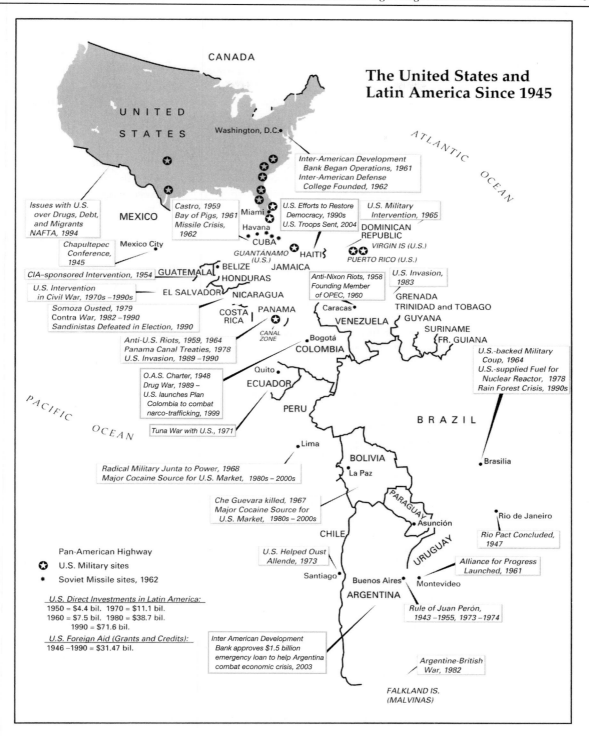

The United States and Latin America Since 1945

CANADA

UNITED STATES

Washington, D.C.

ATLANTIC OCEAN

Inter-American Development Bank Began Operations, 1961
Inter-American Defense College Founded, 1962

Issues with U.S. over Drugs, Debt, and Migrants NAFTA, 1994

MEXICO

Castro, 1959
Bay of Pigs, 1961
Missile Crisis, 1962

Miami

Havana

U.S. Efforts to Restore Democracy, 1990s
U.S. Troops Sent, 2004

U.S. Military Intervention, 1965

DOMINICAN REPUBLIC

VIRGIN IS (U.S.)

PUERTO RICO (U.S.)

Chapultepec Conference, 1945

Mexico City

CUBA

GUANTÁNAMO (U.S.)

HAITI

JAMAICA

CIA–sponsored Intervention, 1954

GUATEMALA

BELIZE

HONDURAS

U.S. Intervention in Civil War, 1970s –1990s

EL SALVADOR

NICARAGUA

Somoza Ousted, 1979
Contra War, 1982 –1990
Sandinistas Defeated in Election, 1990

COSTA RICA

PANAMA

CANAL ZONE

Anti-Nixon Riots, 1958
Founding Member of OPEC, 1960

Caracas

VENEZUELA

U.S. Invasion, 1983

GRENADA

TRINIDAD and TOBAGO

GUYANA

SURINAME

FR. GUIANA

Anti-U.S. Riots, 1959, 1964
Panama Canal Treaties, 1978
U.S. Invasion, 1989 –1990

Bogotá

COLOMBIA

U.S.-backed Military Coup, 1964
U.S.-supplied Fuel for Nuclear Reactor, 1978
Rain Forest Crisis, 1990s

O.A.S. Charter, 1948
Drug War, 1989 –
U.S. launches Plan Colombia to combat narco-trafficking, 1999

Quito

ECUADOR

PERU

BRAZIL

PACIFIC OCEAN

Tuna War with U.S., 1971

Lima

Brasília

BOLIVIA

La Paz

Radical Military Junta to Power, 1968
Major Cocaine Source for U.S. Market, 1980s – 2000s

Che Guevara killed, 1967
Major Cocaine Source for U.S. Market, 1980s – 2000s

PARAGUAY

Asunción

Rio de Janeiro

Rio Pact Concluded, 1947

CHILE

URUGUAY

Alliance for Progress Launched, 1961

U.S. Helped Oust Allende, 1973

Santiago

Buenos Aires

Montevideo

ARGENTINA

Rule of Juan Perón, 1943 –1955, 1973 –1974

Legend

⬟ Pan-American Highway
✪ U.S. Military sites
• Soviet Missile sites, 1962

U.S. Direct Investments in Latin America:
1950 = $4.4 bil. 1970 = $11.1 bil.
1960 = $7.5 bil. 1980 = $38.7 bil.
       1990 = $71.6 bil.

U.S. Foreign Aid (Grants and Credits):
1946 –1990 = $31.47 bil.

Inter American Development Bank approves $1.5 billion emergency loan to help Argentina combat economic crisis, 2003

Argentine-British War, 1982

FALKLAND IS. (MALVINAS)

and reduce U.S. influence. General Anastasio Somoza Debayle, a graduate of West Point (1946), answered with torture, executions, and bombings of civilians.

Carter tried to shape a new government that would ensure Somoza's departure and restrict the radical Sandinistas. Somoza balked and the effort failed. After the FSLN opened its final offensive in mid-1979, Washington encouraged the national guard—Somoza's hated personal army—to preserve order. When this tactic also misfired, diplomats pressed the new, broadly based provisional government to share power with more nonradicals or else forfeit reconstruction assistance. On July 17, 1979, Somoza fled the battle-scarred country; he was later assassinated in Paraguay.

The new Nicaraguan government promised a mixed economy and pluralistic politics. But only after Mexico, Venezuela, and others offered loans did Carter ask Congress to appropriate $75 million in economic assistance. Not until July 1980 did Congress allocate funds, with conservatives calling the Sandinistas communists because they welcomed Cuban advisers and issued caustic anti-Yankee propaganda. Many Nicaraguans resented Washington's long-time ties with Somoza, which Nicaraguans saw as "a needle in the spine."[63] Tension soon ran high, especially when Carter suspended economic aid in early 1981 after the Sandinistas aided rebels who were challenging the U.S.-backed government of El Salvador.

Mexico's announcement in 1981 that it was "tightening the links of friendship that bind us with the revolutions of Cuba and Nicaragua" suggested diplomatic troubles even closer to home.[64] By 1980 Mexico ranked as the United States's third most important trading partner, after Japan and Canada, yet the two neighbors squabbled over oil and natural gas prices. Crossing the shared 2,000-mile border in the 1970s, at least 2 million Mexicans, most of them young males, entered the United States without immigration papers. "It is not a crime to look for work," remarked President José López Portillo, especially when U.S. employers offered jobs.[65] U.S. critics contended that these illegal laborers displaced American workers, drove down wages, and burdened taxpayers by ending up on the welfare rolls. U.S. law seemed contradictory: It was illegal for undocumented migrants to take jobs but legal for employers to hire them. In August 1977, Carter asked for new legislation, but not until 1986 did Congress pass the Immigration Reform and Control Act, which provided amnesty and legal residence for illegal migrants already in the United States, fines for employers who hired undocumented workers, and stricter border controls.

Elsewhere in Latin America, Cuba remained high on the hemisphere's agenda. Carter initially sought to reduce tensions with Fidel Castro. In March 1977, U.S. and Cuban negotiators began to discuss normalization of relations. In September, Cuba and the United States established "interests sections" in each other's country (essentially embassies without full diplomatic recognition). Carter also lifted the ban on travel to Cuba. Castro in 1978 made gestures toward improved relations by releasing 3,600 political prisoners. Several irritants diminished these positive steps. The Soviet Union was pouring about $3 million a day into Cuba to sustain the island's fragile economy, weakened by the longstanding U.S. trade embargo and Castro's mismanagement. Washington argued that Cuba had become a Soviet puppet and charged that Cuban troops in Angola and Ethiopia acted as Soviet surrogates. Castro retorted that he was pursuing Cuba's commitment to revolutions in the

Third World. The Cubans had entered Angola as early as the 1960s, independently of the Soviets. Secret, high-level U.S.-Cuba talks in 1978–1980 failed to normalize relations or relax the trade embargo. And the question of a Soviet brigade in Cuba poisoned chances for rapprochement with Havana (see page 428).

In spring 1980, Castro suddenly announced that Cubans wishing to leave the country could use Peruvian visas if they could get them. Thousands jammed into the Peruvian Embassy grounds in Havana. Carter thereupon announced that Cubans who wanted to join their families already in the United States would be welcome. Castro soon declared that any Cuban who wanted to emigrate could do so by boat from the port of Mariel. Watercraft began to shuttle between Cuba and Florida in a "freedom flotilla"; about 100,000 Cubans entered U.S. processing centers. Castro emptied his jails of "undesirables" and cynically put them on boats to the United States. "Fidel has flushed his toilet on us," the mayor of Miami bitterly charged.[66] Many new arrivals languished in detention centers in the United States; others rioted. Americans felt tricked, especially as evidence mounted that many *Marielitos* had criminal records.

Elsewhere in Latin America, right-wing governments resisted Carter's efforts to improve human rights, although Haiti, Argentina, and the Dominican Republic did release hundreds of political prisoners. In 1977 Carter suspended military aid to Guatemala when its regime sanctioned the murder and torture of political opponents; two years later he froze U.S. aid to Bolivia after that nation's military seized power. Military assistance to Latin America dropped from $210 million in 1977 to only $54 million in 1979, as Carter kept dictators at arm's length. Henry Forde, prime minister of Barbados, remarked that Carter had done much "to correct the image of the United States as an unfeeling giant."[67]

Carter's Activism in the Middle East and Africa

The Iranian revolution and hostage crisis, civil war in Lebanon, Arab-Israeli conflict, Iran-Iraq War, Soviet thrust into Afghanistan (see page 428), and Western reliance on Persian Gulf oil put the Middle East in the headlines. The United States had significant economic, military, and diplomatic interests there. Saudi Arabia served as America's largest supplier of imported oil. In 1980 Israel and Egypt together received about one-third of all U.S. foreign aid. During the period 1971–1981, the United States sold $47.7 billion worth of arms to Mideast countries. U.S. weapons became the instruments of war in the region: Israel used U.S. warplanes to attack Palestinian communities in Lebanon and Iran used American arms to battle Iraq. Syrians and Iraqis, on the other hand, brandished Soviet armaments.

Building on Kissinger's efforts, Carter concentrated on bringing Egypt and Israel to the peace table. Israeli leaders encouraged the president, because "if you take one wheel off a car, it won't drive. If Egypt is out of the conflict, there will be no more war."[68] President Anwar el-Sadat of Egypt personally advanced the peace process. In November 1977 he astonished the world by journeying to Jerusalem to offer peace and security to Israel in exchange for an Israeli withdrawal from lands occupied since 1967. When the Sadat initiative faltered, Carter interceded, inviting Sadat and Israeli prime minister Menachem Begin to Camp David. Brzezinski

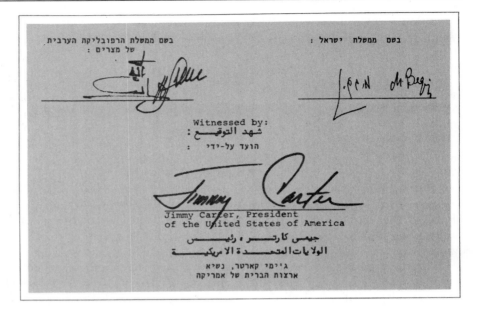

בשם ממשלת הרפובליקה הערבית
של מצרים :   בשם ממשלת ישראל :

Witnessed by:
شهد التوقيـــع :
הועד על-ידי :

Jimmy Carter, President
of the United States of America
جيمس كارتــــــر، رئيــــــس
الولايات المتحـــــدة الامريكيـــــة
ג'ימי קארטר, נשיא
ארצות הברית של אמריקה

Signatures on the Egyptian-Israeli Peace Treaty of March 26, 1979. The historic document, hammered out under the patient guidance of the American president, was signed by Egypt's president Anwar el-Sadat, Israeli prime minister Menachem Begin, and President Jimmy Carter. (U.S. Department of State)

wanted to bug the Egyptian and Israeli cabins so "we all knew what they were saying," but Carter and Vance overruled him.[69] From September 5 to 17, 1978, the three leaders and their aides engaged in often heated discussion. Saying that "Sadat was right—what you [Begin] want is land," Carter pressed Begin to withdraw to Israel's 1967 border so that the restored territories might provide a homeland for Palestinians.[70] Israel could not have both peace and captured territories, Carter reasoned. Carter favored an agreement based on the 1967 United Nations Resolution 242, by which Arabs would recognize Israel's right to live in peace and security in exchange for Israeli withdrawal from seized territories. Playing "the role of draftsman, strategist, therapist, friend, adversary, and mediator," Carter wooed and cajoled.[71] Worried about the Jewish vote in the United States and confronted with Begin's intransigence, Carter persuaded Sadat to accept compromises since the Egyptian leader seemed to want an agreement more than did Begin. Carter promised both sides huge amounts of aid if they would settle their differences.

Egypt and Israel signed two Camp David Accords. The first stated goals: negotiations leading to self-government for the West Bank and Gaza and subsequent participation of Jordanians and Palestinians in the peace process. The second, a "framework" for peace, provided for Israeli withdrawal from the Sinai in exchange for Egyptian diplomatic recognition. Once resumed, the Egyptian-Israeli negotiations stumbled again. Carter pressed for compromise. In March 1979, he flew to the Middle East to meet separately with Begin and Sadat.

The presidential presence worked again. Signed on March 26, 1979, the Egyptian-Israeli Peace Treaty provided for the phased withdrawal of Israel from the Sinai, to be completed in 1982; the stationing of UN forces along the Egyptian-Israeli boundary; full economic and diplomatic relations between Cairo and Tel Aviv; and

U.S. Dependence on Imports of Raw Materials, 1980

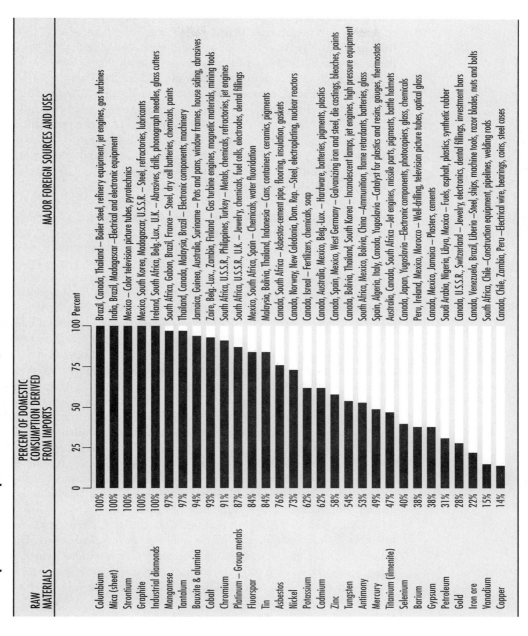

RAW MATERIALS	PERCENT OF DOMESTIC CONSUMPTION DERIVED FROM IMPORTS	MAJOR FOREIGN SOURCES AND USES
Columbium	100%	Brazil, Canada, Thailand — Boiler steel, refinery equipment, jet engines, gas turbines
Mica (sheet)	100%	India, Brazil, Madagascar — Electrical and electronic equipment
Strontium	100%	Mexico — Color television picture tubes, pyrotechnics
Graphite	100%	Mexico, South Korea, Madagascar, U.S.S.R. — Steel, refractories, lubricants
Industrial diamonds	100%	Ireland, South Africa, Belg.-Lux., U.K. — Abrasives, drills, phonograph needles, glass cutters
Manganese	97%	South Africa, Gabon, Brazil, France — Steel, dry cell batteries, chemicals, paints
Tantalum	97%	Thailand, Canada, Malaysia, Brazil — Electronic components, machinery
Bauxite & alumina	94%	Jamaica, Guinea, Australia, Suriname — Pots and pans, window frames, house siding, abrasives
Cobalt	93%	Zaire, Belg.-Lux., Zambia, Finland — Gas turbine engines, magnetic materials, mining tools
Chromium	91%	South Africa, U.S.S.R., Philippines, Turkey — Metals, chemicals, refractories, jet engines
Platinum — Group metals	87%	South Africa, U.S.S.R., U.K. — Jewelry, chemicals, fuel cells, electrodes, dental fillings
Fluorspar	84%	Mexico, South Africa, Spain — Chemicals, water fluoridation
Tin	84%	Malaysia, Bolivia, Thailand, Indonesia — Cans, containers, ceramics, pigments
Asbestos	76%	Canada, South Africa — Asbestos-cement pipe, flooring, insulation, gaskets
Nickel	73%	Canada, Norway, New Caledonia, Dom. Rep. — Steel, electroplating, nuclear reactors
Potassium	62%	Canada, Israel — Fertilizers, chemicals, soap
Cadmium	62%	Canada, Australia, Mexico, Belg.-Lux. — Hardware, batteries, pigments, plastics
Zinc	58%	Canada, Spain, Mexico, West Germany — Galvanizing iron and steel, die castings, bleaches, paints
Tungsten	54%	Canada, Bolivia, Thailand, South Korea — Incandescent lamps, jet engines, high pressure equipment
Antimony	53%	South Africa, Mexico, Bolivia, China — Ammunition, flame retardants, batteries, glass
Mercury	49%	Spain, Algeria, Italy, Canada, Yugoslavia — Catalyst for plastics and resins, gauges, thermostats
Titanium (ilmenite)	47%	Australia, Canada, South Africa — Jet engines, missile parts, pigments, battle helmets
Selenium	40%	Canada, Japan, Yugoslavia — Electronic components, photocopiers, glass, chemicals
Barium	38%	Peru, Ireland, Mexico, Morocco — Well-drilling, television picture tubes, optical glass
Gypsum	38%	Canada, Mexico, Jamaica — Plasters, cements
Petroleum	31%	Saudi Arabia, Nigeria, Libya, Mexico — Fuels, asphalt, plastics, synthetic rubber
Gold	28%	Canada, U.S.S.R., Switzerland — Jewelry, electronics, dental fillings, investment bars
Iron ore	22%	Canada, Venezuela, Brazil, Liberia — Steel, ships, machine tools, razor blades, nuts and bolts
Vanadium	15%	South Africa, Chile — Construction equipment, pipelines, welding rods
Copper	14%	Canada, Chile, Zambia, Peru — Electrical wire, bearings, coins, steel cases

the opening of negotiations on Palestinian rights in the occupied West Bank and Gaza (see map, page 378). After thirty years of war, peace formally came to part of the Middle East. Other Arabs, especially the PLO, denounced the treaty for not recognizing the right of Palestinians to a homeland. Even Jordan's King Hussein, long considered an Arab moderate, blasted the peace as a "dead horse" because it ignored the homeland question.[72] By the end of Carter's administration, the troops of Israel and the PLO, the latter with Syrian help, were shooting at one another in Lebanon (see page 448).

Although sub-Saharan African issues lacked the urgency of Middle Eastern problems, the Carter administration strove to identify the United States with black African nationalism and to end the "last vestiges of colonialism" in Zimbabwe/ Rhodesia and Namibia.[73] Ambassador Young became the president's chief adviser, with "African solutions for African problems" as his motto. He believed that support for a strong and stable black Africa, through aid and trade, would reduce Soviet influence on the continent. African nationalism, not U.S. intervention, would contain the USSR and protect U.S. interests.

Much seemed at stake in Africa. The continent had political clout—a third of the membership in the United Nations. Africa possessed a bulging storehouse of raw materials. For example, Zaire ranked as the United States's largest supplier of cobalt; Nigeria ranked as the second largest source of imported oil; Gabon supplied manganese; Namibia had the world's largest uranium mine; and South Africa shipped manganese, platinum, chromium, and antimony. Fifty nations hungered for development capital and modern technology. By 1979 Americans had invested some $4 billion in black Africa and about $2 billion in South Africa. Total annual trade with Africa passed the $30 billion figure. Africa's ports and airfields also lay along major sea lanes through the Persian Gulf, Indian Ocean, and Atlantic Ocean. The region's political instability invited great-power competition. Because American blacks had descended from Africans, they kept national leaders alert to African issues and politically accountable for their decisions.

The Carter administration worked especially hard to cultivate Nigerian friendship. Africa's most populous nation, Nigeria ranked seventh in world oil production and carried weight in African politics. Nigeria became independent in 1960 and in 1967 suffered a civil war in which victory over Biafran separatists cost half a million lives. World opinion, including that of the United States, grew hostile toward the military regime that had perpetrated this tragedy. But in the 1970s, when America suffered its energy crisis and Nigeria expanded its oil production, relations improved. Both Carter and Young visited Nigeria.

South Africa's riches, traditional ties to the United States, occupation of Namibia, blatant racism, and white minority government ensured its continuing prominence on the U.S. diplomatic agenda. Carter chided white South African rulers for apartheid—an official system of segregating nonwhites and whites that included removals of blacks to designated homelands, discriminatory wages based on race, and denial of voting rights and civil liberties for blacks. Visiting South Africa, Vice President Walter Mondale angered whites by calling for a one-person, one-vote policy (85 percent of South Africa was nonwhite), because "perpetuating an unjust system is the surest incentive to increase Soviet influence and even racial war."[74] Carter rejected economic sanctions as a means to foster change, because trade stood at $4 billion in 1979 and the largest concentration of American investment in the continent rested in South Africa. In the mid-1970s, America's top corporations operated there, including General Motors, Mobil, Exxon, Ford, General Electric, and Firestone. Although critics argued for disinvestment, the most some American companies would do was to accept the Sullivan Principles. Devised by the black Philadelphia minister Leon H. Sullivan, also a member of the General Motors board of directors, the guidelines amounted to a voluntary pledge to follow nondiscriminatory employment practices in South Africa. By 1979 only 116 of the 300 American firms active there had endorsed the principles.

Many black African leaders favored a U.S. economic boycott and protested the sale of American aircraft to the regime. They criticized Carter's approval of Export-Import Bank loans (subsequently stopped by Congress). One Nigerian official condemned America's "outright collaboration with South Africa" and pressed Washington to honor its rhetoric of human rights.[75] The Carter administration defended its policies: The United States needed strategic minerals from South Africa; disinvestment would hurt native blacks by causing unemployment; if American investors pulled out, competitors would simply move in, and economic warfare would have limited impact, given South Africa's unusual self-sufficiency. Carter officials believed that steady pressure, short of economic sanctions, would move South Africa to reform. The white regime's changes, however, amounted to little more than the "desegregation of the deck chairs on the *Titanic*."[76]

In Zimbabwe/Rhodesia, the civil war between whites and insurgent blacks finally ended. Ian Smith's white government, formed in 1965, had made token gestures to black majority rule, but Carter insisted on real change. The president persuaded Congress in 1977 to repeal the Byrd Amendment (1971), which had permitted the United States to trade with Zimbabwe/Rhodesia in chromium, despite the UN-declared economic boycott of Smith's regime. Carter in 1979 refused to endorse white-manipulated elections. Finally, in a rare example of a civil war resolved by diplomacy, British-led negotiations culminated in an all-races, nationwide election held in April 1980, which produced a new government for Zimbabwe led by the former black rebel Robert Mugabe.

By the end of Carter's term, U.S. influence in Africa stood higher than ever, and trade was improving. The United States gained access to military facilities in Somalia after that nation expelled the Soviets in 1977. Soviet and Cuban influence in Africa confined itself mainly to Ethiopia and Angola. Nigeria's President Obasanjo reflected widespread opinion when he warned Moscow and Havana that Africa would not welcome a "new imperial power."[77] Zambia's President Kenneth Kaunda hailed Carter for bringing "fresh air to our troubled world."[78]

The Red Thread: SALT-II, Afghanistan, and the Carter Record

Carter's efforts in the Third World ultimately became overshadowed by the old question of containing the Soviet Union. From the outset, conflicting interpretations of Soviet behavior beset the Carter administration. Some officials believed that global problems did not always stem from Soviet intrigue and that the Soviet Union suffered domestic troubles, an unimaginative and aged leadership, and nationalist stirrings in Eastern Europe. Carter himself wanted to "put our relations with the Soviet Union on the same basis as they are with England," but Brzezinski and his NSC staff countered that Soviet expansionism in the Middle East and Africa had to be faced down, not negotiated away.[79]

Buffeted by these competing views, Carter once asked Vance and Brzezinski to submit separate memoranda for a major 1978 speech on Soviet-American relations. Predictably, two contrasting statements reached the Oval Office. In essence stapling the different papers together, the president gave an address marked by a glaring contradiction between toughness and conciliation, between the "mailed fist and the dove's coo."[80] Still, the president eventually leaned toward the hard-line Brzezinski.

Barely a month in office, the administration exhorted Moscow to permit Dr. Andrei Sakharov, a leading dissident, to speak freely against the Soviet government. The Kremlin testily warned Americans to stop meddling in Soviet domestic affairs. "For the sake of arms control," Soviet ambassador Anatoly Dobrynin recalled, "we were prepared to consider some concessions," but "President Carter continued to attack us in public, in public, in public. Always in public."[81] The Soviets defied Carter's sermons by harassing Jews who applied to emigrate from the Soviet Union to Israel and dissident intellectuals who criticized the communist regime. From the American perspective, too, the Soviets seemed bent on a military buildup: Cuban troops and Soviet advisers stayed in Angola; the Soviet navy and Warsaw Pact forces modernized; and greater numbers of missiles pointed at NATO countries. "We were enthusiastically arming ourselves, like binging drunks, without any apparent political need," one Soviet official later admitted.[82] In this environment laced with suspicion and hostility, Secretary Vance journeyed to Moscow in March 1977 to reenergize SALT (Strategic Arms Limitation Talks) with a sudden, publicized proposal for deep cuts in ICBMs—precisely the category in which the Soviets were strongest. The Soviets thought Carter was saying: "Either you accept our position or we start an arms race and the Cold War again." Washington "was weaseling out of the SALT process," a Soviet official remarked.[83] Vance made no headway: "We got a wet rug in the face and were told to go home."[84]

In March 1978 Carter denounced the Kremlin for conducting a proxy war in Ethiopia by using Cubans to battle Somalia, a newfound American friend that had futilely invaded Ethiopia to seize disputed land. The president's blunt speech, boasted Brzezinski, meant "we weren't soft."[85] In May, Brzezinski traveled to China to remind the Soviets that they should worry about Sino-American "parallel interests."[86] After the NSC adviser challenged his hosts to a footrace at the Great Wall, saying the "last one to the top fights the Russians in Ethiopia," the Chinese dubbed him "the polar bear tamer."[87] Hints of American arms sales to the People's Republic prompted one Soviet official to complain that the United States was "smuggling" weapons aimed against the USSR through the "back door" in Asia.[88] As Soviet-American trade increased, Moscow understandably expressed puzzlement over "constant zigzags" in U.S. behavior.[89]

The two superpowers gradually moved toward a new strategic arms limitation agreement. In the SALT-II talks of 1977–1979, the Soviets tried but failed to block

We have 10,000 tanks.
He has 45,000.

Honeywell technology helps
even the odds.   Being outnumbered is nothing new.
Being outsmarted is unacceptable.
Honeywell's technology base and systems
experience are committed to finding

14

NATIONAL DEFENSE

Honeywell Corporation Exploits the Cold War Rivalry. Defense firms such as Honeywell, as this magazine advertisement of 1978 illustrates, frankly played on Cold War tensions and the arms race. In this case, Honeywell pictures a menacing Soviet officer and claims that the United States lagged far behind the Soviet Union in tanks. Although President Eisenhower had warned against a "military-industrial complex," Honeywell and other companies championed themselves as necessary elements of national defense in order for the United States to compete with the Soviet Union. In the 1980s, the Pentagon spent vast sums and defense contractors earned impressive incomes by building armaments, but American business lost its global reputation for Yankee know-how in automobiles and machine tools. (Honeywell)

American development of the new MX (missile experimental), an improved ICBM designed to carry ten MIRVs; the Trident-II submarine-launched ballistic missile, capable of carrying fourteen warheads; and the cruise missile (see Glossary, page 376). The Americans sought but failed to restrict the new Soviet supersonic "Backfire" bomber. Its range of 5,500 miles threatened Western Europe and China, and in a desperate one-way mission it could also strike the United States. Prolonged negotiations nonetheless culminated in the SALT-II treaty, signed at the Vienna summit in June 1979.

The agreement for the first time established numerical equality between the United States and the Soviet Union in total strategic nuclear delivery vehicles, each limited to 2,400 (reduced to 2,250 in 1982). The treaty capped MIRVed launchers at 1,200 and limited the number of warheads per delivery vehicle. Whereas the treaty required the Soviets to dismantle more than 250 existing delivery vehicles, the Americans could expand from their current 2,060 to the ceiling of 2,250. Each nation could conduct technical verification of the other's compliance without interference.

SALT-II soon fell victim to the deteriorating Soviet-American relationship. The influential Paul Nitze, who had composed NSC-68 in 1950, opposed the accord because "it is time for the United States to stand up and not be a patsy."[90] In the Senate, opponents argued that progress on nuclear-arms control should be linked to Soviet behavior on other issues, such as human rights and Africa. Democratic

MX Launch Test. The "missile experimental" carried ten warheads and was first deployed in 1986. President Reagan decided to place MX missiles in fixed ICBM silos, reversing President Carter's decision to deploy the missiles in a network of tracks and underground shelters, shuttling the MXs so that the Soviets could not target them. (U.S. Air Force)

senator Henry Jackson of Washington and other hawks also claimed that the Soviets, by the mid-1980s, could exploit a "window of vulnerability" and destroy America's land-based missiles in a first strike.[91] SALT-II therefore endangered American security. Conservatives asserted, too, that accurate verification could not be guaranteed. Dovish critics, however, found SALT-II limitations too meager, permitting continued nuclear-weapons growth.

Admitting that SALT-II was but a small step toward deep-cut agreements, the Carter administration concentrated on rebutting conservative critics. Without SALT-II, the State Department explained, the Soviets would enlarge their nuclear forces at a brisker pace. Compelled to keep up, the United States would fuel an expensive arms race. As for the alleged vulnerability of American ICBMs, Carter officials explained that the Soviets would have to deposit two warheads squarely on every ICBM silo to ensure destruction—an unlikely scenario: The timing would have to be near-perfect so that one incoming warhead would not explode and destroy other warheads before they reached their targets ("fratricide"). The Soviets would have to assume that the president would stand by—even with twenty to thirty minutes' warning—and let American ICBMs be destroyed in their silos. Even if a Soviet first strike somehow destroyed the land-based ICBMs (only 30 percent of U.S. nuclear forces), the rest of the triad—SLBMs and strategic bombers—would remain to annihilate tens of millions of Soviet people. "They [Soviets] are not supermen; they are not fools either," remarked one official.[92]

Carter jeopardized ratification by mishandling a "pseudo-crisis" in fall 1979.[93] He accused the Soviets of sneaking a combat brigade of 2,600 troops into Cuba to threaten other Caribbean islands. When the surprised yet conciliatory Soviets replied that the unit had been stationed there for many years, Carter retreated from the storm he had stirred up. The episode further poisoned the atmosphere for SALT-II by suggesting that the Soviets were once again up to no good and that Carter was inept. Senator Frank Church of Idaho, chair of the Foreign Relations Committee, temporarily postponed hearings on SALT-II and exploited the brigade issue in order to improve his own chances in a tough reelection campaign.

With senatorial approval of the treaty in doubt, Carter tried to win votes from hawks by announcing an expensive five-year military expansion program and a plan to deploy 572 Pershing-II ballistic missiles and ground-launched cruise missiles in Western Europe to counter the Soviet medium-range SS-20 missiles aimed at America's allies.

The Soviet invasion of Afghanistan in late December 1979 killed the SALT-II treaty and elevated to orthodoxy Brzezinski's hard-line views about a malevolent Soviet Union. Some 50,000 Red Army troops marched into neighboring Afghanistan to sustain a Soviet client challenged by Islamic rebels. The Soviets also intervened because they wanted to maintain Afghanistan as a "buffer" against the spread of Islamic fundamentalism in central Asia.[94] Fearful that covert CIA assistance to the insurgents since July might cause the Afghans to "do a Sadat on us" by aligning with the United States, Moscow also worried that U.S. invasion of Iran would "seriously alter the military-strategic situation in the region."[95] Was Afghanistan the first step in a Soviet master plan to take over the oil-rich Persian Gulf region? With an eye on domestic opinion, Carter hyperbolically proclaimed "the greatest threat to peace since the Second World War."[96] "Putting 'a Red thread' through the complexities of the Gulf area seemed to us to be a desirable and justified simplification" to arouse the American people, Brzezinski later admitted.[97]

In early 1980 Carter tried to punish the Soviet Union. He withdrew the SALT-II treaty from the Senate. He stopped high-technology sales and grain shipments to the USSR. He pulled the United States out of the Summer Olympic Games scheduled for Moscow and urged other nations to boycott the event. Carter also outlined military measures: arms assistance for Pakistan, a state bordering the Soviet Union; creation of U.S. naval facilities in Oman, Kenya, Somalia, and Egypt; formation of a rapid deployment force for use in the Middle East; positioning of two aircraft carrier groups in the region; and a much increased defense budget. Further, the president asked an obliging Congress to require young men to register for the draft so as to mobilize forces quickly in the event of war. And last, CIA assistance began to sustain Afghan resistance in a ten-year struggle that would become, as Brzezinski told Carter, the Soviet Union's "Vietnam War."[98]

On January 24, 1980, the president proclaimed the Carter Doctrine: "An attempt by any outside force to gain control of the Persian Gulf region will be regarded as an assault on the vital interests of the United States of America, and such an assault will be repelled by use of any means necessary, including military force."[99] As a statement of containment, it sounded familiar themes. But serious problems impeded implementation. When Washington offered $400 million to Pakistan, its prime minister said "peanuts" and demanded more.[100] The Saudis refused to let the U.S. military use their facilities. When Carter admitted the Soviets would not evacuate Afghanistan, West German chancellor Helmut Schmidt concluded that "what he [Carter] was after was domestic prestige" and thus refused to stop German trade with the USSR and Eastern Europe.[101] Most nations rejected the Olympics boycott.

The Carter Doctrine also sparked debate at home. George F. Kennan denied that the Soviet attack on Afghanistan signaled further aggression. Carter also had played all of his cards at the outset, and the Soviets remained in Afghanistan. Other critics thought that Carter had capitulated fully to Cold Warriors such as Brzezinski in another diplomatic lurch, going too far too fast, and that he had exaggerated the issue to boost his low political standing. A State Department official later revealed that the Carter Doctrine "grew out of last-minute pressures for a presidential speech" rather than from a cool calculation of policy.[102]

As Soviet-American relations deteriorated, Sino-American ties improved. Both Beijing and Washington sought to use each other to contain the Soviet Union. Following U.S. diplomatic recognition in early 1979, China embarked on a three-week incursion against Vietnam to show it "had no fear of the Soviet Union."[103] A U.S.-China trade agreement in 1980 enabled the Export-Import Bank to extend credits to the People's Republic. American companies signed contracts to tap China's oil. Chinese markets beckoned American farmers. In 1977–1980 China ranked fourth in the world as a buyer of U.S. agricultural exports, taking about half of the nation's cotton exports in 1979 alone. Mineral-short America eyed China's large deposits of tin, chrome, and tungsten. In 1980 American exports to China totaled $4 billion, up from $807 million in 1974. China replaced the Soviet Union as the United States's largest communist trading partner; in 1980 U.S. exports to the Soviet Union stood at a comparatively low $1.5 billion.

Taiwan's status, however, remained contentious. The United States severed formal diplomatic relations with the Republic of China on Taiwan, unilaterally terminated the 1954 mutual defense treaty, and withdrew all U.S. forces and military installations from the island. But private Americans maintained strong economic links, and the U.S. government continued low-level official ties through an "Institute." Washington also kept up the flow of military aid. The People's Republic insisted on ultimately repossessing Taiwan, but threats of force subsided. U.S. cultural interactions with Taiwan remained strong, especially so when Taiwanese teams won a "series of world championships" in Little League baseball during the 1970s.[104]

During the Carter presidency, many Americans sensed that the nation's power had slipped, that its role as the world's sheriff, banker, business manager, and teacher had eroded. High OPEC prices, huge deficits in the balance of payments, haunting memories of Vietnam, revolution in Nicaragua, return of the Canal Zone to Panama, Castro's defiance, Soviet nuclear equivalence and the jilted SALT-II, the Iranian hostage crisis, and Afghanistan—all seemed to project an image of American weakness. (See graph on p. 426 for growing dependence on imports.) Carter did not persuade Americans that a decline in U.S. power was inevitable in an interdependent, multipolar world of some 150 nations. He talked bluntly of the 1970s and 1980s as decades of limits and scarcity. Yet when he urged energy conservation as "the moral equivalent of war," wags spelled out the acronym MEOW.[105] Carter failed in "not communicating the substance of his policies to the public and making the public appreciate how much is being done," Brzezinski acknowledged.[106] Indeed, the American people suffered "a serious case of empire shock for the first time in their cultural history."[107]

Carter left a mixed record. Too often, administration policy appeared erratic because of the constant feuding between the State Department and Brzezinski's National Security Council. Carter also seldom gave a rousing speech or pounded the bully pulpit—too "de-pomped," wrote one specialist on presidential power.[108] Carter lacked FDR's charm, Eisenhower's popularity, JFK's television presence, LBJ's ability to handle Congress, and Nixon's talent for exploiting the spectacular. Carter also violated some of his stated goals. Despite his pledge to reduce the American military presence abroad, more military personnel served overseas in 1980 (489,000) than in 1976 (460,000). He promised to withdraw U.S. forces from South Korea but then reversed himself. Strongly advocating nuclear nonproliferation, he nonetheless agreed in 1980 to ship 38 metric tons of enriched uranium fuel to India, even though New Delhi had snubbed the nonproliferation treaty. He promised to reduce defense spending but actually increased the Pentagon's budget by 14.5 percent in his last year. Although the president vowed to trim arms sales abroad, they climbed from $12.8 billion in 1977 to $17.1 billion in 1980.

Carter's human-rights policy also seemed selective. Despite his emphatic repudiation of past "mixed signals on human rights from us" in countries such as Argentina, Carter chose *realpolitik* when Vietnamese armies overthrew the genocidal Pol Pot regime in Cambodia in late 1978. U.S. aid went to Khmer Rouge guerrillas to contain the perceived expansion of Soviet influence through the Vietnamese attack at the expense of America's new friend, China, even though Carter had called the Khmer Rouge "the worst violators of human rights in the world today."[109] Amnesty International, founded in 1961 to monitor the worldwide status of human rights, cited the governments of Argentina, Brazil, Guatemala, Indonesia, Iran, Morocco, the Philippines, South Korea, Taiwan, and Thailand for condoning or practicing torture, political terrorism, or arbitrary arrest. In 1976–1980 the United States delivered $2.3 billion in military aid to those ten nations and sold them weapons worth $13.7 billion. Thousands of foreign officers and police also trained at U.S. military schools. Conservative critics, in contrast, complained that Carter was behaving like an evangelical preacher in a world of sinners, that he invited revolutions such as the one in Iran by weakening leaders whom America needed as strategic partners. Carter's human-rights efforts led to the freeing of hundreds of political prisoners abroad, but the president's detractors faulted his effort as either too little or too meddlesome.

The president's defenders attributed his uneven record to domestic politics. Carter may have played politics with the Cuban brigade issue, the rescue attempt in Iran, and the Afghan crisis, they admitted, but vigorous right-wing pressure made him do so. They blamed noisy Cold Warriors in the Committee on the Present Danger. Founded in 1976, this pressure group included hawks such as former secretary of state Dean Rusk and the veteran policymaker Paul Nitze. The organization advocated scrapping SALT-II and enlarging the military. Carter's bow to the conservatives epitomized the dictum that "smart politics produce bad policies."[110]

Carter officials believed that the administration pursued noble goals, achieved diplomatic successes, and infused morality into American foreign policy to prove that U.S. power lay not simply in military capabilities but also in the nation's values. The administration candidly explained the limits of U.S. influence in a world of diffused power and stressed the need to deal with long-range issues, not just immediate crises. Pointing to the Egyptian-Israeli peace, Panama Canal treaties, normalization of relations with China, progress on the law of the sea, North-South dialogue, end to civil war in Zimbabwe, nuclear modernization of NATO, and an improved American status in Africa, Professor Brzezinski proudly filled out the administration's report card: A−/B+.

The 1980 Republican presidential candidate, Ronald Reagan, disputed that high grade. The former Hollywood actor and California governor slammed Carter for leading America into decline. In a display of raw anticommunism, Reagan declared that an expansionist Soviet Union "underlies all the unrest that is going on. If they weren't engaged in this game of dominoes, there wouldn't be any hot spots in the world."[111] Confounded by domestic economic troubles, the unresolved Iranian hostage crisis, and Carter's unsteady leadership, and rallying to Reagan's promise to "make America great again," the electorate turned Carter out by giving him only 41 percent of the popular vote.[112] The Republicans also gained control of the Senate; liberal, dovish senators Birch Bayh of Indiana, Frank Church of Idaho, John Culver of Iowa, and George McGovern of South Dakota joined Carter in defeat.

Coke in China. In 1981 the Coca-Cola Company opened a plant in China, where the famous soft drink is known as "tasty happiness." The humorist Art Buchwald commented: "I don't mind 800 million Chinese drinking a bottle a day, but I don't want them to bring back the empties." (Courtesy The Coca-Cola Company, 1979)

Ronald Reagan's Mission to Revive Hegemony

Ronald Reagan had no experience in national government or foreign affairs before he became president. He preferred movies and television to reading books, riding horses to roundtable discussions. Time and time again, he revealed an ignorance of fundamental information. After returning from his first trip to South America, he announced: "Well, I learned a lot. You'd be surprised. They're all individual countries."[113]

Ronald Reagan (1911–2004).
Born in Illinois, a graduate of
Eureka College, a long-time
professional actor, and governor
of California (1967–1975), Reagan
displayed a sunny disposition that
helped return optimism, even
chauvinism, to the national mood.
As the vaunted "Great
Communicator," Reagan proved
adept at "using every
communcations medium save
Morse Code and smoke signals,"
according to one journalist.
Although opponents called him "an
amiable dunce" and "George
Wallace sprinkled with eau de
cologne," his wife Nancy
remarked: "He is more complex
then people think." (Peter Souza
Photo, The White House)

When Reagan told French president François Mitterrand, a Socialist, that he thought communism and socialism were the same thing, Mitterrand wondered: "What planet is that man living on?"[114] Reagan also became noted for reckless and exaggerated statements, factual inaccuracies, and right-wing sloganeering. He acted more on his instincts than on patient reasoning. His staff, fearing ill-thought utterances, carefully managed his public performances. Surrounded by pollsters and communications specialists who tapped his natural talent, Reagan proved an effective communicator. With "a smile that could melt glaciers," he camouflaged his shallow grasp of many issues.[115] "Being a good actor pays off," he told students at China's Fudan University.[116]

Reagan became a very popular president, winning a landslide reelection in 1984 against former vice president Walter Mondale. Even when Reagan suffered setbacks, he retained "an almost mesmeric" hold on public affection.[117] Americans applauded his poised, amiable, down-to-earth, speak-from-the-heart manner, his self-deprecating humor (especially about his age), and his dogged consistency in his convictions. This "warmly ruthless man," one aide wrote, made decisions like "a Turkish pasha, passively letting his subjects serve him, selecting only those morsels of public policy that were especially tasty."[118]

Several beliefs rooted in the American past guided the Reagan administration. First, Reagan and his conservative allies believed in a devil theory: A malevolent Soviet Union instigated international insecurity—the bully on the block who ignited civil wars, promoted terrorism, and built an "evil empire."[119] Soviet leaders, the president avowed, stood poised "to commit any crime, to lie, to cheat" to achieve a communist world.[120] Such rhetoric poisoned the diplomatic environment. Reagan's dark view of the Soviets overlooked the many successful Soviet-American agreements of the recent past. He also left the United States open to charges of a double standard, because Washington itself sponsored "disinformation" programs and engaged in covert skullduggery. Reagan officials thought in terms of bipolarism, global containment, and confrontation—with one exception: They lifted the grain embargo so that U.S. farmers could sell billions of dollars of wheat and corn to the Soviet Union.

Second, because the Soviets had allegedly "engaged in the biggest military buildup in the history of man" and had achieved "a definite margin of superiority," Reagan vowed to surpass them.[121] "Defense is not a budget item," he told the Pentagon. "Spend what you need."[122] They did—and more. Running up huge federal deficits, he launched the largest peacetime arms buildup in American history, spending $2 trillion. Reagan pushed plans for the B-1 bomber (Carter had refused to fund it); ordered the stockpiling of the neutron bomb (Carter had vetoed this weapon); and resumed production of poison gas for chemical warfare. The administration, moreover, expanded the navy, beefed up special forces units for counterinsurgency warfare, and continued the Trident-II submarine, MX, cruise missile, Stealth bomber, and mobile Midgetman missile programs. To outspend the Soviets into economic collapse, as one Reagan aide later boasted, "the screws were tightened, one turn at a time."[123] Military appropriations increased by 50 percent, growing from $143.9 billion in 1980 to $294.7 billion in 1985. In 1985 the Pentagon was spending $28 million an hour, twenty-four hours a day, seven days a week. Reagan also embraced a nuclear abolitionist's faith that American technology could devise an invulnerable space shield that would protect civilian populations from nuclear annihilation. The former actor likened the arms race to "two Westerners standing in a saloon aiming their guns at each other's heads—permanently. There had to be a better way."[124]

Third, Reagan believed it important to change America's mood to gain public support for a more militarized, interventionist foreign policy. He implored the American people to abandon their post-Vietnam "self-doubt" in favor of a "national reawakening."[125] Whipping up emotional patriotism, Reagan reassured Americans that "we've closed the door on a long, dark period of failure."[126]

The fourth driving force became known as the Reagan Doctrine. The president in 1985 pledged support for anticommunist "freedom fighters" who battled the Soviets or Soviet-backed governments. The CIA, with congressional approval, funneled aid to insurgents in Afghanistan, Nicaragua, Angola, Cambodia, and Ethiopia. Reagan made overt what had been covert: the attempted overthrow of governments deemed inimical to U.S. interests. The Reagan Doctrine emphasized a commitment to low-intensity conflict: military action through allies, proxies, and paramilitary assets so that fewer American soldiers would fight and die in foreign lands as elite forces organized others to do the dirty work of shadow wars.

Fifth, Reagan and his advisers believed that nations must embrace private capitalism and privatize managed economies. American leaders frequently lectured Third World nations on the "magic of the marketplace."[127] The United States even cast the only "no" vote against a UN resolution to restrict the sale of baby formula in developing nations. Medical authorities had reported that companies marketed their infant products so aggressively that many mothers were forgoing healthy breastfeeding in favor of the artificial liquid, which they then mixed with polluted water. The Reagan administration also refused to sign the long-awaited Law of the Sea Treaty, protesting that the agreement did not adequately protect American deep-sea mining companies.

Sixth, drawing lessons from the failure of the Carter administration to support friendly dictators in Iran and Nicaragua, the Reaganites accepted Ambassador to the United Nations Jeane Kirkpatrick's distinction between "authoritarian" and "totalitarian" regimes.[128] Authoritarian regimes in countries such as the Philippines,

"Give War a Chance."   During his confirmation hearings in January 1981, Secretary of State–designate Alexander M. Haig, Jr., said: "There are more important things than peace—there are things which we Americans must be willing to fight for." Some people thought him too eager to apply military solutions to political problems and too inclined toward confrontation with the Soviet Union and leftist Third World nations. As for El Salvador, where Haig and Reagan thrust the United States into a civil war, the secretary declared: "We are going to succeed and not flounder as we did in Vietnam." (Bob Englehart, *Hartford Courant*)

Chile, South Korea, and South Africa sustained capitalist economies and would supposedly respond to U.S. suggestions for reform. Communist totalitarian regimes imposed managed economies and resisted change. Given such thinking, Reagan officials downgraded human-rights tests for friendly authoritarian governments.

Finally, another central belief of the Reagan team was that the United States must serve as a model for other nations. "The United States is the economic miracle," bragged the president. "The world's hopes rest with America's future."[129] This reformist zealotry found expression through institutions such as the National Endowment for Democracy, created in 1983 as a propaganda agency using federal and private funds to promote free enterprise and democratic politics. The endowment gave millions of dollars to foreign political parties, labor unions, and publishers, many with an antileft bias. Reagan could even quote Tom Paine and Thomas Jefferson: "we have it in our power to begin the world over again" and "to spread the sacred fire of liberty" everywhere.[130]

Reagan named General Alexander M. Haig, Jr., secretary of state. A steely-eyed military professional who became famous for his mixed metaphors and his ambition, Haig feuded with just about everybody. "Sometimes our right hand doesn't know what our far-right hand is doing," Reagan once joked.[131] The volatile secretary abruptly resigned in June 1982. Haig found the White House "as mysterious as a ghost ship; you heard the creak of the rigging and the groan of the timbers and even glimpsed the crew on deck. But which one of the crew was at the helm?"[132] George P. Shultz followed Haig. A founding member of the Committee on the Present Danger, Shultz was an economist and business executive. He often clashed with Secretary of Defense Caspar W. ("Cap") Weinberger, especially after Weinberger announced in 1984 that the United States should use military force only under certain conditions: with long-term public and congressional support; for "clearly defined political and military objectives"; and with "the clear intention of winning."[133] Shultz chastised Weinberger as a big spender who refused to use newly augmented U.S. forces. "A somewhat stolid, serious, and utterly dependable conversational partner," according to one diplomat, Shultz also battled hawkish CIA director William J. Casey, who once asserted that "the business of Congress is to stay out of my business."[134]

July 4, 1986. Here, with Nancy Reagan, the president stands before a ship's gun on Independence Day. Mrs. Reagan encouraged her husband to negotiate with the Soviets. After a private White House dinner, she whispered the word "peace" when saying good-bye to Soviet foreign minister Andrei Gromyko. "Tell that to your husband tonight in your bedroom," Gromyko replied. (Terry Arthur Photo, The White House)

Richard V. Allen, a business consultant noted for his anticommunist zeal, became Reagan's assistant for national security affairs. After Allen departed in 1982 under suspicion of scandal, the office of national security adviser suffered instability, further undistinguished leadership, and more scandal. Under William Clark, Reagan's political crony from California, NSC staffwork became so cumbersome that Shultz thought it "worse than a university."[135] Then came Robert C. McFarlane, a former marine who never argued against misguided policies because "if I'd done that, Bill Casey, Jeane Kirkpatrick, and Cap Weinberger would have said I was some kind of commie."[136] John M. Poindexter, an active-duty admiral with a Ph.D. in nuclear physics, succeeded McFarlane, but he had to resign in late 1986 when the Iran-contra affair erupted.

Despite strong opposition from Weinberger and Shultz, Reagan ordered the National Security Council to carry out a covert project to trade arms to Iran in return for the release of U.S. hostages held in Lebanon. Because he also empowered

" WHAT DO I KNOW ...AND WHEN WILL I KNOW IT ?"

Reagan in Doubt. When the crisis over the arms sale to Iran and aid to the *contras* erupted in 1986–1987, Reagan could not remember the details of his decisions. Diagnosis of Alzheimer's disease in 1994 raised the question of whether Reagan had suffered any mental impairment during his presidency. His official biographer, Edmund Morris, writes that after Reagan's near assassination in March 1981 "he lost his quickness. And for the rest of his presidency it was a very, very slow and steady mental and physical decline." Because doctors had apparently not tested him for Alzheimer's disease while president, it seemed impossible to judge whether Reagan's mental lapses were the result of dementia or simply the normal failings of an elderly president who remembered only the details that interested him. (Bill Schorr © 1987, The Los Angeles Times Syndicate)

the NSC secretly to aid the Nicaraguan *contras* (see pages 445–446), the two operations eventually commingled. To ensure secrecy, McFarlane and Poindexter ran both schemes in total disregard of Congress and almost completely outside the purview of the Defense and State Departments. Relying on CIA connections, the action officer in charge of both operations, marine lieutenant colonel Oliver North, flaunted his contempt for Congress, professional diplomats, and traditional bureaucrats. "Colonel North was given a very broad charter," Poindexter later testified, "and I did not micromanage him."[137] When North diverted profits from the Iranian arms sales to the *contras,* Poindexter approved but said he did not tell Reagan because he wanted the president "to have some deniability so that he would be protected."[138] Shultz later portrayed Reagan as an innocent dupe misled by his inner circle. Yet the record shows that at top-level meetings on Iran-Contra, President Reagan made the basic decisions, without monitoring every operational detail. "The old man loves my ass," North boasted, but White House logs show that Reagan met North only four times and never saw him alone.[139]

Reagan's appointment of Frank C. Carlucci, a seasoned diplomat and administrator, and then General Colin Powell, as his next NSC advisers did not quiet a national crisis that badly besmirched the Reagan presidency. In 1989 North was found guilty of three felonies (obstructing Congress, destroying documents, and receiving illegal gratuities), and in early 1990 Poindexter was convicted of five felony charges, including lying to Congress. A federal appeals court later overturned both convictions because Congress had granted immunity to the two men for testimony given to congressional committees. President George H. W. Bush later pardoned CIA officers guilty of a cover-up, and when Secretary of Defense Caspar Weinberger was indicted, Bush also pardoned him before a trial could take place. All told, some 190 Reagan officials were indicted or convicted of illegal activities.

Soviet-American Crises and Antinuclearism

Reagan assumed that the Soviet Union outspent the United States on armaments and outdistanced it in nuclear weapons. He had campaigned on an anti–SALT-II platform and displayed undisguised distaste for nuclear-arms control talks. The United States had to close the "window of vulnerability"—the theoretical vulnerability of American land-based ICBMs to a Soviet first strike—by enlarging the American nuclear arsenal.[140] The Soviets outranked the United States in ICBMs and SLBMs but lagged behind in strategic bombers and nuclear warheads. And at least two-thirds of Soviet nuclear arms consisted of vulnerable ICBMs in fixed silos. The president failed to count on the American side the defense spending of NATO allies. As for the "window of vulnerability," in 1983 the president's own Commission on Strategic Forces reported that the window did not exist and that America's triad of air-, sea-, and land-based nuclear weapons provided sufficient deterrence.

Statements by Reagan officials about winning a nuclear war stimulated a transatlantic debate. The evangelist Billy Graham, World Council of Churches, and Union of Concerned Scientists urged restraint in the nuclear arms race. The American Medical Association declared that "there is no adequate medical response to a nuclear holocaust," and one doctor called nuclear war the "final epidemic."[141] George F. Kennan added his voice to the antinuclear movement. "Cease this madness," he implored.[142] Calling Reagan's views on the USSR "an intellectual primitivism," Kennan recommended an immediate 50 percent cut in nuclear arsenals on both sides, the denuclearization of much of Europe, a complete ban on nuclear testing, and a freeze on new weapons.[143] The House of Representatives in 1983 also passed a freeze resolution. Proponents argued that America's infrared satellites could verify a freeze on the testing and deployment of ballistic missiles.

In May 1983 the Roman Catholic Bishops of the United States issued a pastoral letter that called "the arms race one of the greatest curses on the human race. . . . We are the first generation since Genesis with the power to virtually destroy God's creation."[144] Feminists ridiculed the sexual nature of the discourse on nuclear strategy wherein "white men in ties" talked about "missile size, . . . vertical erector launchers, thrust-to-weight ratios, soft lay downs, deep penetrations," and what one Reagan adviser called "releasing 70 to 80 percent of our megatonnnage in one orgasmic whump."[145] In November 1983 an ABC television dramatization titled *The Day After* left President Reagan and the American people "greatly depressed" by its vivid depiction of the human costs of a nuclear war.[146] Scientists postulated that even people who survived a nuclear exchange would face a devastating "nuclear winter": Clouds of debris, dust, and smoke from mass fires would block the sun's rays, cooling the earth's temperatures and killing plant and animal life.

Europeans also criticized "America the violent, America the crass, America the inept."[147] In 1981, huge crowds in Bonn, London, Rome, and Amsterdam called

George Shultz (b. 1920). A graduate of Princeton University (he had a tiger tattoo on his buttocks) and the Massachusetts Institute of Technology (Ph.D., 1949), Shultz served as secretary of labor, director of the Office of Management and Budget, and secretary of the treasury in the Nixon administration. In 1982 he joined the Reagan cabinet as secretary of state. One pundit said Shultz had "the charisma of a drowsy clam." (Department of State)

for a ban on the installation of Pershing and cruise missiles. "The most important mass-based challenge to NATO in its entire history" demanded that both Washington and Moscow sit down to talk.[148] Statements by U.S. officials evoked alarm. Reagan mentioned the possibility of a limited nuclear war in Europe, thus sparing the two great powers. On other occasions he revealed his "stunning ignorance about the capabilities of the weapons over which he had authority."[149] He once stated that cruise missiles were defensive weapons—in fact, they were designed to overcome Soviet defenses and to strike deep in the USSR. He even said that SLBMs could be recalled after firing.

To satisfy Western European leaders who welcomed U.S. missiles but wanted less domestic protest, and to quiet the American antinuclear movement, Reagan reluctantly agreed to begin talks in Geneva on intermediate-range nuclear forces (INF) in Europe. For these negotiations, which opened in November 1981, the United States proposed to stop planned deployment of the new Pershings and cruise missiles in NATO nations if the Soviet Union would dismantle its growing arsenal of SS-20, SS-4, and SS-5 missiles pointed at Western Europe. The Soviets initially

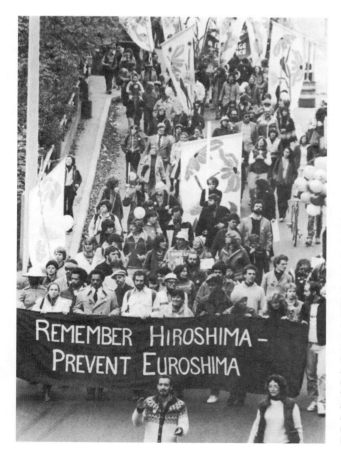

Antinuclear March. In October 1983, the civil rights leader Jesse Jackson (front, left) led a march in Cambridge, Massachusetts, against nuclear weapons, especially the Pershing-II missiles scheduled for deployment in Europe. This protest was part of an international weekend campaign. According to the Pentagon official Thomas K. Jones, Americans could easily survive nuclear war: "Dig a hole, cover it up with a couple of doors and then throw three feet of dirt on top. . . . If there are enough shovels to go around, everybody's going to make it." (AP/Wide World Photos)

rejected this "zero option," because it excluded British and French nuclear forces and U.S. weapons on submarines and aircraft. Also, argued Moscow, the new NATO missiles could reach the USSR, but the SS-20s could not hit the United States. The Soviets deployed more triple-warhead SS-20s, and the United States began in 1983 to put Pershing-IIs into NATO countries, first Great Britain and then West Germany. In November 1983, to express their displeasure over these new missiles, the Soviets suspended the INF talks. Meetings did not resume until early 1985, only to falter again. Moscow hard-liners nearly responded to the Pershings by repeating the "Cuban scenario" of 1962 by an equally provocative deployment of missiles in the immediate vicinity of the United States.[150]

Negotiations on strategic nuclear weapons did not fare much better. Reagan replaced SALT with START—Strategic Arms Reduction Talks. ("How about 'Faster Arms Reduction Talks'?" one White House aide quipped.)[151] Negotiations began in Geneva in 1982, but the U.S. proposal for deep cuts stalled. The reason became obvious: The American plan sought drastic reductions in those very weapons that constituted the bulk of Soviet deterrent power.

Chances for a START agreement also became complicated because of President Reagan's announcement of the Strategic Defense Initiative in March 1983. Soon dubbed "Star Wars," SDI envisioned an anti-ballistic missile defense system in space—a laser or particle beam shield over the United States that could intercept Soviet ballistic missiles and destroy them in space. Jerome B. Wiesner, former scientific adviser to the White House, skeptically cited "10,000 or more nuclear weapons on each side. A defense system that would knock out 90 or 95 percent would be a miracle—and the remaining 5 or 10 percent would be enough to totally destroy civilization."[152] Others argued that if SDI ever did work, it would undermine deterrence itself by eliminating the danger of Soviet attack, thus freeing the United States to use nuclear weapons without fear of retaliation. Although some saw SDI as a multibillion-dollar "turkey," it acted as a "secret weapon . . . to undercut the freeze crusade."[153] The president optimistically viewed it as the perfect defense, a way to "get rid of those atomic weapons. Every one," he said privately.[154] As SDI research advanced, with some test results actually faked to keep congressional funds flowing, START sputtered.

Other events spoiled the negotiating environment. As the Reagan administration closed out its first year, the Solidarity labor movement in Poland, having earned concessions from the communist government through strikes and protests, called for a national referendum on the future of that government and for a reexamination of Poland's military alliance with the Soviet Union. For months Moscow had warned the Poles against weakening the communist regime. In December the Polish military cracked down, imposing martial law and arresting Solidarity leaders. Washington reacted quickly. It suspended economic agreements with Poland. Reagan cut back Soviet-American trade and banned Soviet airline flights to the United States. NATO countries reacted cautiously, in part because they possessed little leverage in Polish affairs and because they wanted to continue their lucrative trade with the Soviets and Soviet clients.

On September 1, 1983, Korean Air Lines Flight 007, en route from Anchorage, Alaska, to Seoul, South Korea, strayed some 300 miles off course and for a time

"Star Wars" in 1984. President Reagan made a passionate case for the Strategic Defense Initiative to prevent a "madman" with missiles from blackmailing "all of us." Some scientists assured him that they could create his "dream"—an effective ballistic missile defense system. In this artist's sketch, a space-based electromagnetic ray gun destroys a nuclear-armed reentry vehicle presumably launched from the Soviet Union. SDI development still limped along in the new century. (U.S. Army/Department of Defense, Still Media Records Center)

cruised in Soviet airspace near a strategic nuclear base. Soviet planes scrambled. When the Korean pilot did not acknowledge warning signals and shots, a Soviet jet blasted the Boeing 747 with one missile, killing all 269 passengers aboard. Reagan branded the shootdown "an act of barbarism."[155] Even though jet pilot Gennadi Osipovich identified KAL 007 as "a civilian plane," Soviet officials claimed it was on a spy mission for the United States.[156] Moscow later revealed that the shootdown had occurred in international airspace and that Soviet authorities had crudely covered up their error. Yet the "simplistic overreaction" to the shootdown in the United States so exacerbated tensions that NATO military exercises in November caused the frightened Kremlin leadership to fear a nuclear first strike.[157] Informed about this nuclear "near-miss," Reagan recited to aides the biblical story of Armageddon and made his first public plea to banish nuclear weapons "from the face of the earth."[158] Until tempers cooled, we "can't cook porridge together," Ambassador Dobrynin told U.S. officials.[159]

Another obstacle to an arms-control agreement was the instability and incapacity of Soviet leadership—until the arrival of Mikhail S. Gorbachev in 1985. Leonid Brezhnev died in 1982; his first successor, Yuri Andropov, died in 1984; and his second successor, Konstantin Chernenko, died the following year after a prolonged illness. Gorbachev became the new general secretary of the Communist party, at age fifty-four one of the Soviet Union's youngest leaders, with a personality quite "different from the wooden ventriloquism of the average Soviet apparatchik," as British

Mikhail Gorbachev (b. 1932) and Reagan. In May 1988, at the Moscow summit meeting, the two leaders continued the warm personal relationship that helped end the Cold War. When asked if he minded the U.S. public's growing adulation for Gorbachev, Reagan replied: "I don't resent his popularity. Good Lord, I costarred with Errol Flynn once." (Photo by Bill Fitz-Patrick, The White House, Courtesy Ronald Reagan Library)

prime minister Margaret Thatcher put it.[160] Determined to reform the sluggish Soviet economy through restructuring (*perestroika*) and to open the suffocating authoritarian political system through liberalization (*glasnost*), Gorbachev initiated stunning changes in his own nation and across the globe (see Chapter 12).

"Deeply affected" by the disastrous accident at the Chernobyl nuclear power station in 1986, the new secretary general altered the Soviet position on nuclear weapons.[161] He unilaterally stopped further deployment of intermediate-range missiles. He halted nuclear-weapons tests. In November 1985 Gorbachev and Reagan met in Geneva. Although they could not agree on SDI or an extension of SALT-II, they established warm personal relations during their talks. "I bet the hard-liners in both our countries are bleeding," whispered Reagan as he shook Gorbachev's hand.[162] Then in early 1986 Gorbachev called for an end to all nuclear weapons by the year 2000. Another summit meeting in Reykjavík, Iceland, in October 1986, seemed close to producing a substantial treaty. The conferees made tremendous progress by agreeing to reduce warheads, missiles, and bombers and to remove all American and Soviet intermediate missiles from Europe. Reagan found the results "breathtaking." But when Gorbachev said that "this all depends, of course, on your giving up SDI," Reagan "reacted as if he had been asked to toss his favorite child into an erupting volcano."[163] The meeting quickly ended. Yet the atmosphere had clearly changed for the better.

The Washington summit meeting in December 1987 finally saw the signing of the Intermediate-Range Nuclear Forces (INF) Treaty, which provided for the elimination of all U.S. and Soviet INF missiles anywhere and verification of their de-

Destruction of a Cruise Missile under the INF Treaty. Under the terms of the Intermediate-Range Nuclear Forces Treaty, signed in late 1987 and effective in mid-1988, both the United States and the Soviet Union (and its successor states) eliminated INF missiles in Europe, including Soviet SS-20s and U.S. Pershing-II and cruise missiles. To destroy this cruise missile, a demolition crew cut it in half. (U.S. Arms Control and Disarmament Agency)

struction through on-site inspections. What had changed? Gorbachev had taken the initiative by accepting the "zero option" and giving Washington "120 percent of what it wanted" in negotiations.[164] The warmth between Reagan and Gorbachev facilitated negotiations. "When I told him [Gorbachev] we should put our cards on the table, he took out his Visa and Mastercard," Reagan later joked.[165] "We will leave Afghanistan," promised foreign minister Eduard Sheverdnadze, a welcome change from the dour Andrei Gromyko.[166] "I, too, have problems with my bureaucracy," Shultz told the Soviets, before the resignations of Weinberger and other hard-liners.[167] The antinuclear movement had produced strong antinuclear public opinion in Europe and America. Most obvious, the two superpowers saw the treaty as beneficial to their quite different national interests. Both faced economic troubles spawned by the long Cold War. "Our economy," said one Soviet official, "has been literally eviscerated by military spending."[168] Despite right-wing protests that President "Reagachev" had become "nothing more than a useful idiot for Soviet propaganda," the Senate approved the INF Treaty by a 95 to 5 vote in May 1988, and the dismantling of missiles began that summer.[169]

Gorbachev also boldly advanced other issues. In April 1988 he signed a UN-mediated accord providing for the withdrawal of all Soviet forces from Afghanistan. They departed early the next year, acknowledging a conspicuous defeat for the Soviet military, caused in part by the "Stinger" antiaircraft weapons that the United States had shipped to the Afghan *mujahedeen* ("holy warriors"). In December 1988 the Soviet leader announced a unilateral Soviet cut of 500,000 ground troops. Moscow reduced its support for the Sandinistas in Nicaragua and negotiated for the removal of Cuban troops from Angola. The Soviets also stopped jamming Voice of America broadcasts.

The "Backyard": Central America and the Caribbean

The Reagan administration read events in the Third World as related chapters in an East-West, Cold War book written by the two superpowers, not as independent short stories composed by distinct, indigenous sources. In the Third World, argued Reagan officials, U.S. influence had to be restored to repel "beachheads of tyranny, subversion, and terror."[170] Hegemony was at stake. Reagan quoted the Truman Doctrine, resuscitated the domino theory, and stressed military and covert means over negotiations. Central America, long in the United States's grip but restless under the burden of profound economic, political, and social divisions, figured prominently in Reagan's counterrevolutionary crusade.

The State Department claimed that Moscow used Cuba to propagandize revolution, train insurgents, and promote "Cuba-model states" that would "provide platforms for subversion, compromise vital sea lanes, and pose a direct military threat at or near our borders."[171] At times President Reagan imagined radicals crossing the border from Mexico into Texas, but increasingly he made a strategic case: As a major trade route, the Caribbean provided "our lifeline to the outside world," and "Soviet military theorists want to destroy our capacity to resupply Western Europe in case of an emergency. They want to tie down our attention and forces on our own southern border and so limit our capacity to act in more distant places such as Europe, the Persian Gulf, the Indian Ocean, the Sea of Japan."[172] Fearing "another Cuba," Reagan officials determined to defeat leftist insurgents in El Salvador, to topple the Sandinista government in Nicaragua, and to draw Guatemala and Honduras into a tighter U.S. military network. Through billions of dollars in aid (including the Caribbean Basin Initiative announced in 1982), CIA operations, weapons and advisers, splashy military maneuvers, and support for the anti-Sandinista army known as the *contras*, Washington plunged more deeply into Central America—an area "colossally important to the U.S. national interest," Ambassador Kirkpatrick solemnly avowed (see map, page 419).[173]

Critics charged that Reagan exaggerated the Soviet-Cuban threat, underplayed the local causes of disorder, bypassed opportunities for negotiations, and shored up the right wing and military, thus spurring further political polarization. Such policies helped invite what Washington wanted most to prevent: Soviet influence in the area. Senator Christopher Dodd, a Democrat from Connecticut and former Peace

CENTRAL AMERICAN EYE CHART

P
OV
ERTY
HUNGER
INJUSTICE
CORRUPTION
REVOLUTION

DEMOCRATS

Sacramento Bee

'C - O - uh - M - M - uh - U - uh - N - uh - I - S - M!'

"Communism." Critics of Reagan's interventionism in Central America believed that the president misread the sources of instability in the region. (Dennis Renault, *Sacramento Bee*)

Corps volunteer in Latin America, decried the "ignorance" of the Reagan diplomats who "seem to know as little about Central America in 1983 as we knew about Indochina in 1963." Downplaying a Soviet threat and emphasizing Central America's economic underdevelopment, inadequate medical care, illiteracy, and class structure, Dodd declared that "if Central America were not racked with poverty, there would be no revolution."[174]

In El Salvador, the Reagan administration nevertheless found a textbook "case of armed aggression against a small country by Communist powers acting through Cuba."[175] A presidential assistant explained that "El Salvador itself doesn't matter—we have to establish credibility."[176] Reagan said it simply: "We are the last domino."[177] El Salvador was a poor country plagued by a high infant mortality rate, illiteracy, and violence. The army and a small landed elite had long ruled the nation. Two percent of the people owned half the land. In October 1979, however, reform-minded colonels seized power and organized a new government under José Napoleón Duarte, a Christian Democratic party leader. The elite responded by organizing "death squads" to assassinate moderates and radicals alike. Leftists formed the Farabundo Martí Front for National Liberation (FMLN). In 1980 national guard troops raped and killed four American churchwomen, but the Salvadoran government refused to prosecute the officers who ordered the murders. Ambassador Kirkpatrick seemed to excuse the slayings by saying "the nuns were not just nuns" but "political activists" for the FMLN.[178]

Determined to find a non-Marxist solution to the Salvadoran civil war through land reform, the Carter administration had extended economic aid to the Duarte government. But it had also dispatched military advisers and military aid. The Reagan administration dramatically increased the military assistance program and expanded economic aid. "They thought it was like rolling a drunk," former ambassador to El Salvador Robert E. White remarked.[179] "El Salvador is Spanish for Vietnam" became a popular bumper sticker.[180]

While reluctantly funding Reagan's Salvadoran programs, Congress insisted that the administration certify human-rights progress in the country. Every six months officials dutifully issued optimistic but disingenuous statements. "Everybody *knew*, Congress *knew*, what they [Salvadoran military forces] were doing," a U.S. embassy official recalled. "What's improvement, any way? You kill eight hundred and it goes down to two hundred, that's improvement."[181] The UN Truth Commission reported in 1993 that 85 percent of the 75,000 people killed in the Salvadoran civil war died at the hands of government forces and gun-for-hire death squads. U.S. military advisers trained some of the units responsible for murdering civilians. Although they wanted to curb death-squad killings, U.S. diplomats did not exert "high-level pressure for change on Salvadoran military leaders."[182]

The election of 1982, boycotted by the FMLN, installed a right-wing government. The Reagan administration improved the Salvadoran military's ability to stage air assaults and bombing raids, but the growing civilian death count from the air war actually may have facilitated the FMLN's recruitment of followers. Although Reagan spent $4.5 billion in El Salvador during the 1980s, victory in the bloody civil war still eluded him when he left office. Only after four more years of killing on both sides did the combatants finally negotiate a United Nations–sponsored peace in January 1992.

The Reagan administration blamed much of the Salvadoran trouble on Cuba and Nicaragua, which sent small supplies of arms to the insurgents. Secretary Haig announced that the Soviets had a "hit list" of Central American states, with Nicaragua first, El Salvador second.[183] The Sandinistas invited thousands of Cuban medical specialists and teachers into their poor country, used Cuban advisers and Soviet weapons to build a strong military, and limited free speech as they moved to a one-party government. "Our function [once] was to grow sugar, cocoa, and coffee for the United States; we served the dessert at the imperialist dinner table," remarked Minister of Agrarian Reform Jaime Wheelock. "We have to be against the United States in order to reaffirm ourselves as a nation."[184]

As the United States had long treated Cuba, so it treated Nicaragua in the 1980s: putting pressure on a small, proud, doggedly radical government to the point where it faced a choice between capitulation or seeking outside help for defense. Reagan first cut off all foreign aid. In November 1981, he ordered the CIA to train

The Vietnam Syndrome Cured by the Reagan Doctrine. President Reagan's interventionism in the Third World supposedly ended the Vietnam syndrome, but many critics, including a majority of the American people, feared another Vietnam. (Dan Wasserman for *The Boston Globe* © 1985, Los Angeles Times Syndicate. Reprinted with permission)

and arm the anti-Sandinista *contras* in a prime example of the low-intensity-conflict strategy. "Let's make the bastards sweat," CIA director William Casey told his covert operators.[185] A mercenary army of 15,000, including former supporters of Somoza, the *contras* were "a mixed bag," according to General Colin Powell. "We worked with what we had."[186] From bases in Honduras and Costa Rica the *contras* raided Nicaragua, sabotaging bridges, oil facilities, and crops, and using CIA "coercive techniques" (including "direct physical brutality") against civilians.[187]

Although in 1982 Congress had prohibited the use of funds to overthrow the Nicaraguan government, Reagan officials winked at the restriction. In early 1984 Congress discovered that the CIA had worked with *contra* commandos to mine three Nicaraguan ports. "I am pissed off," roared Senator Barry Goldwater at the CIA's Casey. "It is an act of war. . . . I don't see how we're going to explain it."[188] When Nicaragua went to the World Court to charge a breach of international law, Washington refused to recognize the court's jurisdiction. (In June 1986, the court decided that the United States had violated international law by funding the *contras* and ordered Washington to pay an indemnity to Nicaragua; Reagan ignored the ruling.) In mid-1984, Congress banned aid to the *contras*. Meanwhile, Nicaraguan-American talks in Mexico produced no agreement.

The congressional prohibition did not stop aid to the *contras*. Following Reagan's explicit instructions "to do whatever you have to do to help these people keep body and soul together," CIA, Pentagon, and NSC officials rerouted money from Defense appropriations and solicited funds from foreign countries and private donors to supply the *contras*.[189] In 1985–1986 Colonel North of Reagan's NSC shifted to the *contras* profits from secret arms sales to Iran by using Israeli intermediaries and a Swiss bank account. North also coordinated a network of planes and ships (without "USG fingerprints") and funded the building of a large airstrip in Costa Rica—all without informing Congress.[190] As an independent federal prosecutor later concluded, President Reagan "created the conditions which made possible the crimes committed by others" and "knowingly participated" in the illegal aid effort.[191] Reagan said that if the "story gets out, we'll all be hanging by our thumbs in front of the White House."[192] Defeating "Communism in Central America" took precedence over "obeying the law," one scholar has written, so Reagan officials "lied about what they were doing—publicly, privately, repeatedly, egregiously."[193]

In early 1985 Reagan admitted publicly what he had long denied: Washington sought to topple the Sandinista government—he wanted it to say "uncle."[194] In May he imposed an economic embargo and blocked loans to Nicaragua from the World Bank and the Inter-American Development Bank. Congress appropriated $27 million for "humanitarian" aid to the *contras*. Still, the *contra* war did not go well. The insurgents constantly feuded among themselves, generated little popular support, and could not seize and hold towns. But they forced the Sandinistas to shift funds from social programs to defense and to restrict civil liberties, thus slowing the revolution and arousing internal dissent. An opponent of *contra* aid, Republican Mark O. Hatfield of Oregon, remembered Vietnam: "Here we are again, old men creating a monster for young men to destroy."[195]

"Don't be a pilgrim," Casey once told George Shultz. "What's that?" "An early settler," said Casey.[196] Hence Reagan officials treated negotiations as "nothing more than a necessary smokescreen to quiet opposition to the paramilitary program."[197] Washington snubbed the Contadora group (Mexico, Venezuela, Panama, and Colombia), which in 1983 had persuaded the five Central American states to limit foreign advisers, reduce arms, and promote democracy. Reagan officials stiff-armed the 1987 peace plan by Costa Rican president Oscar Arias Sánchez but had to negotiate when Congress again banned military aid (which it had reinstated in 1986) and the *contras* agreed to a cease-fire in March 1988. Hobbled by the Iran-Contra scandal, Reagan resisted appeals for more aid to the *contras*. When Reagan left office, the Sandinistas still governed. Under arrangements brokered by the Central American presidents, the Washington-backed candidate Violetta Barrios de Chamorro soundly defeated Sandinista President Daniel Ortega Saavedra in elections finally held in 1990. After nearly a decade of civil war, 30,000 Nicaraguans had died and the ravaged economy had sunk to the second poorest in the hemisphere.

Haig claimed that Cuba was "exporting revolution and bloodshed" to El Salvador and Nicaragua.[198] He promised to "close Castro down" by going to the "source."[199] "I'll make that island a fucking parking lot," Haig thundered.[200] Reagan banned tourist and business visits to Cuba, denied Cuban officials visas for travel in the United States, and restricted importation of Cuban newspapers and magazines. Cuba actually endorsed the Contadora process and urged the Salvadoran rebels and Nicaraguans to negotiate in order to obviate U.S. intervention. In December 1984 Havana and Washington did sign an immigration agreement: The

United States would return to Cuba about 2,700 criminals who had come by boat in the 1980 Mariel exodus, and Cuba would let Cubans reunite with families in the United States. But when the United States, in mid-1985, started up Radio Martí to act as "an electronic Bay of Pigs" beaming propaganda into Cuba, Castro angrily abrogated the accord and "defiantly prepared to be the last adversary of the United States."[201] America's allies, such as Canada and Britain, undermined the U.S. economic embargo by expanding their trade with Cuba.

When U.S. troops invaded the tiny Caribbean island of Grenada on October 25, 1983, Washington wanted to "send shivers up Castro's spine about whether or not they [the Cubans] might be next."[202] In what one reporter called a "lovely little war," more than 6,000 Americans went ashore to oust a Marxist regime that Reagan termed "a Soviet-Cuban colony, being readied as a major military bastion to export terror."[203] More than 100 people died, including about 25 Cubans helping to build an airstrip. Reagan claimed that the airfield would serve the Cuban and Soviet militaries, but British engineers explained that its purpose was to boost Grenada's tourist trade. The administration also justified the invasion as the rescue of 1,000 Americans, many of them medical students. But critics argued that the Americans faced no immediate danger. By mid-December, having deported surviving Cubans from the island and closed the Soviet Embassy, U.S. forces evacuated Grenada. The mission had cost $75.5 million. World opinion disapproved this modern example of a "Gilbert-and-Sullivan war."[204] When the UN Security Council deplored the invasion, the United States vetoed the resolution. North Americans celebrated victory, only days after a bomb killed 241 American soldiers in Lebanon (see page 448).

Hornets' Nests in the Middle East, Africa, and Asia

The Reagan administration failed to sustain Carter's initiatives in the Middle East. A "Hollywood poolside Zionist" who had resigned from a country club in 1948 to protest the exclusion of Jews, Reagan sought to gain some sort of homeland for the Palestinians and to guarantee Israel's security through a new Arab-Israeli accord.[205] But Lebanon descended into savage civil war and suffered a punishing Israeli invasion and Syrian occupation; the Iran-Iraq War disrupted oil shipments; Libya and the United States skirmished; Israel and the United States bickered bitterly; and terrorists victimized the innocent, including many Americans. Saudi Arabia and Jordan refused to relax tensions with Israel yet kept placing large orders for arms. (For example, Reagan in 1981 approved the sale of high-tech military equipment valued at $8.5 billion to the Saudis.) Reaganites assumed that the Soviet Union coveted the region. But Israel considered the PLO and Arab nationalism the greater threats; and the Arabs designated Israel, not Moscow, as enemy number one.

In late 1981, in open defiance of Reagan's position, Israel suddenly announced its annexation of the Golan Heights. When Reagan suspended an Israeli-American military agreement, Prime Minister Menachem Begin exploded, "Are we a banana republic?" To American protests against Israeli bombing raids of PLO camps in

Lebanon, Begin cited U.S. bombing in Vietnam—"You don't have a right, from a moral perspective, to preach to us."[206] Then came the Egyptian radicals' assassination of President Sadat and Israel's invasion of Lebanon.

Lebanon had long suffered factionalism, especially between Muslims and Christians. For decades, displaced Palestinians had moved into the country, and in 1970–1971 PLO fighters driven from Jordan joined them. When civil war erupted in the mid-1970s, Lebanon invited Syria to restore order; Syrian troops arrived and stayed. From bases in Lebanon the PLO harassed and murdered Israelis. Israel invaded Lebanon in June 1982 in the hope of "cleansing" the nation of Palestinians.[207] Israeli forces drove to Beirut, helping to destroy much of the capital city. Reagan finally telephoned Begin. "Menachem, this is a holocaust," he said. "Mr. President," Begin replied, "I think I know what a holocaust is."[208] Nonetheless the Israeli bombing of Beirut stopped.

U.S. officials arranged the withdrawal of both the PLO and Israel from Beirut and created a peacekeeping force that included U.S. marines. Soon Muslims targeted Americans. In April 1983 bombs hit the U.S. Embassy in Beirut, killing 63 people. Then, in October, a terrorist drove a truck loaded with explosives into a building full of sleeping American troops, killing 241 of them. Weinberger's aide, General Colin Powell, thought the United States had "stuck its hand into a thousand-year-old hornet's nest with the expectation that our presence might pacify the hornets."[209] In February 1984, with public criticism rising, Reagan withdrew the marines.

After 533 days and scores of deaths, the marines could not quell Lebanon's multifaceted war. Critics chastised the administration for compliantly following Israel's lead into disaster and for not penalizing Israel for its use of U.S. weapons in violation of contractual restrictions. When the veteran diplomat George Ball claimed that Israel's "roving Air Force" and "rampaging Army" had "devastated a nation [Lebanon]," Cold War hawks accused him of anti-Semitism.[210] Washington soon patched up relations with Israel, which in 1985 received the largest U.S. foreign-aid package of any nation—$3 billion, or more than $700 per person.

Israeli-American relations soured again after the Palestinian uprising (in Arabic, the *intifada*) began in December 1987 in the West Bank and Gaza. The Israelis had been ruling the 1.5 million inhabitants since 1967. Like other Palestinians in the Middle East (some 5 million), the PLO-backed participants in the *intifada* wanted a homeland. As youthful demonstrators were shot down by Israeli troops, and as shopkeepers organized anti-Israeli boycotts, Shultz urged an international conference to work out a "land for peace" solution. Both Israel and the PLO adamantly rejected the idea. Jordan decided to relinquish the West Bank to the PLO, which then declared an independent Palestinian state and endorsed UN Resolution 242 (see page 422). PLO leader Yasir Arafat launched a peace initiative of his own, but when he asked to speak before the General Assembly, Shultz denied him a visa. UN members thereupon voted to hear Arafat in Geneva, Switzerland, where the PLO leader recognized Israel's right "to exist in peace and security" and renounced "all forms of terrorism."[211] Shultz accepted Arafat's pledge, and U.S. diplomats on December 16, 1988, opened talks in Tunisia with the PLO for the first time ever. The Israeli government denounced the negotiations.

The Muddle East. To many Americans, including the cartoonist Toles, the turbulent Middle East seemed a strange, even irrational region. (TOLES © 1986 The Buffalo News. Reprinted with permission of UNIVERSAL PRESS)

Reagan had announced in his first inaugural that "terrorism" would replace Carter's focus on "human rights" as the principal concern of foreign policy.[212] In 1985 alone, more than 800 terrorist incidents in the world claimed some 900 lives, 23 of them Americans. But Mideast terrorists drew the greatest attention. Passengers on American commercial jets became hijack and murder victims, and U.S. citizens were taken hostage. In one case in 1985, U.S. warplanes forced to the ground an Egyptian airliner known to be carrying four Palestinians who had earlier seized the Italian cruise ship *Achille Lauro* and murdered a wheelchair-bound American. "You can run but you can't hide," warned Reagan.[213]

The Reagan administration especially blamed Libyan radical Muslim ruler Moammar Gadhafi for much of the terrorism. Diplomatic relations between Libya and the United States were severed in early 1981; the following year Washington imposed an embargo on oil imports from Libya; and in early 1986 Reagan banned all trade. After a series of terrorist attacks at busy European airports, Reagan officials fingered Libyan responsibility, sent U.S. warships into the Gulf of Sidra, and attacked patrol boats, shore batteries, and radar sites. When a terrorist explosion killed a GI in West Berlin in April, Reagan launched Operation El Dorado Canyon, in which U.S. fighter-bombers demolished Gadhafi's Soviet-built air force and bombed his official residence, killing dozens, including the dictator's adopted

Shaking Hands with Saddam Hussein. Iraqi President Saddam Hussein (b. 1937) greets Donald Rumsfeld (b. 1932), then special envoy of President Ronald Reagan, in Baghdad on December 20, 1983. The Reagan administration pragmatically extended aid to Iraq in its war with Iran, even though Saddam Hussein had invaded his neighbor, harbored known terrorists, abused the human rights of Iraqi citizens, used chemical weapons against Iranians, and pursued long-range nuclear aspirations that included an eventual nuclear weapons capability. As secretary of defense twenty years later, Rumsfeld directed more bellicose policies toward Saddam Hussein and Iraq. (CNN TV photo from National Security Archive, © Getty Images)

daughter. "Nothing was heard from [Gadhafi] for months after the attack," boasted Weinberger in his memoirs.[214] That same year audiences cheered Hollywood heartthrob Tom Cruise as he went from "hot dog" to *Top Gun* (1986) in celluloid dogfights against Libyan MiGs.[215]

Reagan also tilted toward Iraq in the Iran-Iraq War. Iraq had begun the bloody conflict in 1980 to seize Iranian oil lands, control the Shatt al Arab waterway, and topple the Khomeini regime, which had incited Shiite Muslims in Iraq to rebel. While vowing to keep the Persian Gulf open to international commerce, Washington quietly supplied Iraq with military intelligence, a half-billion dollars in credits, and dual-use technology, even though "we knew [Iraqi dictator Saddam Hussein] was an S.O.B., but he was our S.O.B."[216] In May 1987 two sea-skimming missiles fired by an Iraqi aircraft hit the U.S. frigate *Stark,* killing 37 crewmen. Iraq apologized. Reagan soon beefed up the U.S. naval presence in the Gulf and "reflagged" Kuwaiti oil tankers as American vessels. In October, after Iranian missiles struck a reflagged Kuwaiti tanker, American aircraft attacked two Iranian oil platforms. The next year, in July, the U.S.S. *Vincennes,* thinking itself under attack despite sophisticated equipment that should have told its captain otherwise, shot down a civilian Iranian airliner, killing all 290 aboard. Washington admitted error while covering up the fact that the *Vincennes,* violating international law, was inside Iranian territorial waters at the time of the shootdown. At last, in August 1988, Iran and Iraq agreed to end a conflict that had killed hundreds of thousands.

In Africa, too, Reagan had to deal with knotty, long-term issues. Death-dealing famine, as in Sudan in the mid-1980s; civil wars in Angola and Ethiopia, where Soviet and Cuban troops assisted ruling regimes and covert CIA aid helped insurgents; the unresolved status of South Africa–dominated Namibia; and the dehumanizing policy of apartheid in South Africa—all demanded attention. Reagan again espied Soviet adventurism. Toward white-ruled South Africa he at first launched "constructive engagement."[217] An example of Ambassador Kirkpatrick's friendly authoritarian regimes ("a racist dictatorship is not as bad as a Marxist dictatorship"), South Africa endured Washington's official disapproval of apartheid and urgent requests for reforms, but no economic sanctions.[218] The policy amounted to a "kid-glove, all carrot-and-no-stick approach," said critics.[219]

Reagan soon abandoned constructive engagement. When the Pretoria government rejected serious reform, black South Africans marched, protested, and died, demanding that people around the world take sides. As violence spread across South Africa, Reagan worried that the opportunistic Soviets might exploit the turmoil. Protest in the United States, led by the Free South Africa Movement, a broad-based coalition, forced the issue onto the American political agenda. Claiming that "sanctions may hurt, but apartheid kills," members of Congress joined with church, labor, and intellectual leaders to picket the South African embassy in Washington, D.C.[220] South African bishop Desmond M. Tutu, the 1984 Nobel Peace Prize recipient, toured the United States appealing for economic pressure against his government. Cities and states passed divestiture laws requiring the sale of stock they owned in U.S. companies operating in South Africa. Such black entertainers as Ray Charles, the O'Jays, the Temptations, Roberta Flack, and Stephanie Mills also pressed U.S. corporations to begin divestment—the sale of their businesses in South Africa. Some companies pulled out; by 1986, U.S. investments had dropped to $1.3 billion from $2 billion in 1981.

To head off congressional action, Reagan, in September 1985, added a few sanctions to the earlier (1962) embargo on arms sales to South Africa. This time he restricted nuclear and computer sales and prohibited American bank loans to the South African government. But in October 1986, with an unusual bipartisan consensus and over Reagan's veto, Congress passed stiffer economic sanctions, including a ban on new American investments in and oil exports to South Africa and on imports of certain South African products.

Good news did come from Namibia. South Africa had governed this former German colony since World War I, even defying the United Nations when it revoked Pretoria's mandate in 1966 and demanded independence. Since the early 1970s the radical South West African People's Organization (SWAPO), with Cuban and Soviet support, had battled South African armies from bases in Angola and Zambia. After twelve years of sporadic negotiations, however, Angola, Cuba, and South Africa signed a U.S.-mediated agreement in December 1988 for a Cuban troop withdrawal from Angola and black majority rule in Namibia. Formal independence came in March 1990.

In Asia, Ferdinand Marcos's Philippines became a troublesome ally. Elected president in 1965, Marcos had created a dictatorship marked by corruption, martial law, and personal enrichment. By the early 1980s his country groaned under a huge foreign debt of more than $20 billion, high unemployment, and economic stagnation. He jailed critics, whom security forces tortured and murdered. Business, Roman Catholic Church, civil libertarian, and professional leaders demanded reform. Two insurgencies fed on Filipino discontent: the New People's Army led by communists and the Moro National Liberation Front of Muslims in the south. The accelerating discontent with Marcos came suddenly to a head in August 1983, after assassins gunned down the anti-Marcos leader Benigno S. Aquino. The evidence pointed to a successful military conspiracy.

American investments of $2 billion, trade sales of similar value, and outstanding debts owed to American banks seemed in jeopardy. So, too, did two major American bases: Subic Bay Naval Station and Clark Air Base. The Reagan administration distanced itself from Marcos and pressed for reforms. When Marcos stole an election from Benigno Aquino's widow, Corazon Aquino, turmoil tore across the Philippines. Besieged by his own people and abandoned by the United States, Marcos, on February 25, 1986, went into exile in Hawai'i. U.S. aid soon flowed to the Aquino government.

An altogether different kind of issue stood at the center of Japanese-American relations: a huge trade deficit. Although Japan remained a solid strategic partner, providing bases for the U.S. military and foreign aid to U.S. allies such as South Korea, Turkey, and Pakistan, it also grew dramatically as an economic competitor. "We send Japan low-value soybeans, wheat, coal and cotton," one business leader remarked. "They send us high-value autos, motorcycles, TV sets, and oil-well casings. It's 1776 and we're a colony again."[221] In 1985 the total U.S. trade deficit (more imports than exports) mounted to an all-time high of $148.5 billion—$50 billion of it with Japan. The overall deficit derived in large part from the strong dollar abroad (making American goods expensive in other countries and imports less expensive in the United States) and the indebtedness of Third World nations, which forced them to buy fewer U.S. products. Japan's tariff barriers, cartels, and government subsidies also made it difficult for American goods such as plywood, paper, and cosmetics to penetrate Japanese markets. Protectionists demanded retaliatory, higher tariffs on Japanese goods so that ailing American industry could better meet import competition and American workers could hold their jobs. In 1985 Japan voluntarily set quotas on automobile and carbon-steel shipments to the United States and promised trade liberalization at home, but Washington wanted more. In 1987 Reagan imposed restrictions on some Japanese imports. The 1988 Omnibus Trade and Competitiveness Act "had Japan in its sights" when it authorized U.S. retaliation against nations that refused to negotiate reductions in trade barriers.[222] As the Reagan era ended, Japan's foreign minister characterized the Japanese-American trade relationship as "at its worst since the war."[223]

Triumphs and Hazards: The Reagan Legacy

Reagan claimed foreign-policy successes, especially in the twilight of his presidency: Namibia, the INF Treaty, the departure of dictators in Haiti (Jean-Claude Duvalier) and the Philippines (Ferdinand Marcos), termination of the Iran-Iraq War, talks with the PLO, and Cuban withdrawal from Angola. At the end, Reagan seemed less ideological, more adaptable. Improved relations with the Soviet Union suggested that the Cold War was winding down (see Chapter 12). The Soviets pulled out of Afghanistan and loosened their grip on Eastern Europe. Some analysts argued that the huge Reagan military spending forced the economically hobbled Soviets to make concessions. Others noted that much of the money was misspent and wasted (especially on SDI), and that the remarkable changes initiated by Gorbachev sprang not from U.S. pressure but from a new generation of Soviet leaders and courageous Eastern European dissidents. The large U.S. defense buildup may actually have delayed the end of the Cold War by undermining Soviet moderates in their struggle against Kremlin hawks. Reagan very well may have undercut American power and prestige in the long run by spending the United States into tremendous debt and neglecting to repair the American economy or to improve American education to make the United States more competitive in the international marketplace. The conservative columnist George F. Will wrote that Reagan "has been a great reassurer, a steadying captain who calmed the passengers and, to some extent, the sea." But, Will added, Reagan's "cheerfulness" was "a narcotic, numbing the nation's senses about hazards just over the horizon."[224]

Reagan bequeathed to his successor, Republican Vice President George Bush, several failures and unresolved international issues. Reagan (and Bush) had paid little attention to global environmental questions. Soil erosion reduced food production at a time when the world's population was growing rapidly. Toxic wastes, acid rain, shortages of clean water, the overcutting of forests, and the overgrazing of fields hurried environmental decline, which in turn burdened governments. "Encroaching deserts now pose a greater threat to national security, and indeed national survival, than do invading armies," warned one specialist.[225] A warming of the earth's climate owing to the "greenhouse effect" of carbon dioxide and other gases building up in the atmosphere, scientists reported, might raise ocean levels, flooding farmlands and dislocating millions of people. Unless corrected, these problems would spawn political unrest. Some positive signs appeared: population-control programs in many Third World nations; public-health programs providing an effective vaccine against malaria; immunization programs against measles and polio; India's attainment of self-sufficiency in food production; and the conservation of minerals. But the Reagan administration barely noticed.

Environmental questions also figured in Canadian-American relations. Canadians grew alarmed that polluted American air in the form of acid rain was destroying their forests and contaminating their water. Tension between Ottawa and Washington reached an awkward high. Canadian prime minister Pierre Trudeau once mused: "Living next to you is in some ways like sleeping with an elephant. No matter how friendly and even-tempered is the beast, if I may call it that, one is affected by every twitch and grunt."[226] Although Reagan showed scant interest in acid rain, he did launch negotiations leading to the United States–Canada Free Trade Agreement of 1988. This accord created the world's largest free trade area. The two nations exchanged more goods and services each year, worth about $166 billion in 1989, than any other two countries.

Any accounting of the Reagan legacy includes the president's failure to energize the peace process in the Middle East. The Iran-Contra scandal and intervention in Lebanon rank as major foreign-policy blunders. In Central America, Reagan registered a large death count, continued civil wars, economic disarray, and a bankrupt attachment to the *contras*. On South Africa, Congress had to push Reagan to express serious disapproval of apartheid. The trade and budget deficits grew to huge proportions in the Reagan years (the national debt tripled to $2.8 trillion), and the United States became a debtor nation. Trade conflict with Japan intensified as the United States struggled to compete with the trans-Pacific power. The Third World "debt bomb" also jeopardized a stable economic future.

In the 1980s, after Vietnam and the Iranian hostage crisis, Americans worked to reassert their international supremacy. They built up massive military and nuclear forces; they financed insurgencies; they defended their global interests; they continued to assume that they had answers to others' problems; they reaffirmed their self-appointed mission to purify an imperfect world; they restated their belief in American exceptionalism. In his upbeat farewell address, Ronald Reagan declared that "America is respected again in the world, and looked to for leadership."[227] Other voices suggested that he "may have left time bombs ticking away for the future."[228]

FURTHER READING FOR THE PERIOD 1977–1989

For overviews and various topics, see William C. Berman, *America's Right Turn* (1994); John Ehrman, *The Rise of Neoconservatism: Intellectuals and Foreign Affairs, 1945–1994* (1995); Tom J. Farer, *The Lost Consensus* (1987); Raymond L. Garthoff, *Détente and Confrontation* (1985) and *The Great Transition* (1994); Robert C. Gray and Stanley J. Michalak, Jr., eds., *American Foreign Policy Since Détente* (1984); Ole R. Holsti and James N. Rosenau, *American Leadership in World Affairs* (1984); Robert C. Johansen, *The National Interest and the Human Interest* (1980); Paul Kennedy, *The Rise and Fall of the Great Powers* (1987); Wilfred Loth, *Overcoming the Cold War* (2002); Don Oberdorfer, *From the Cold War to a New Era* (1998); Odd Arne Westad, ed., *The Fall of Détente* (1995); and William C. Wohlforth, *Cold War Endgame* (2003). See also books listed in Chapters 7, 10, and 12.

For Jimmy Carter and his foreign relations (specific policies and regions are listed later), see Douglas Brinkley, *The Unfinished Presidency* (1998); John Drumbell, *The Carter Presidency* (1993); Gary M. Fink and Hugh Davis Graham, eds., *The Carter Presidency* (1998); Betty Glad, *Jimmy Carter* (1980); Erwin C. Hargrove, *Jimmy Carter as President* (1988); Burton I. Kaufman, *The Presidency of James Earl Carter, Jr.* (1993); David S. McLellan, *Cyrus Vance* (1985); Kenneth E. Morris, *Jimmy Carter, American Moralist* (1996); A. Glenn Mower, *The United States, the United Nations, and Human Rights* (1979) and *Human Rights and American Foreign Policy* (1987); Nancy P. Newell and Richard S. Newell, *The Struggle for Afghanistan* (1981); Kenneth A. Oye et al., eds., *Eagle Entangled* (1979); Jerel A. Rosati, *The Carter Administration's Quest for Global Community* (1987); Herbert O. Rosenbaum and Alexej Ugrinsky, eds., *Jimmy Carter* (1993); David Skidmore, *Reversing Course* (1996); Gaddis Smith, *Morality, Reason, & Power* (1986); Robert A. Strong, *Working in the World* (2000); and Sandy Vogelsang, *American Dream, Global Nightmare* (1980) (human rights).

Reagan policies are studied in Coral Bell, *The Reagan Paradox* (1989); Larry Berman, ed., *Looking Back on the Reagan Presidency* (1990); Sidney Blumenthal and Thomas B. Edsall, eds., *The Reagan Legacy* (1988); Paul Boyer, ed., *Reagan as President* (1990); Lou Cannon, *President Reagan* (1991); Robert Dallek, *Ronald Reagan* (1984); Theodore Draper, *A Very Thin Line* (1991) (Iran-Contra); Beth A. Fischer, *The Reagan Reversal* (1997); Frances FitzGerald, *Way Out There in the Blue* (2000); Allan Gerson, *The Kirkpatrick Mission* (1991) (UN); Haynes Johnson, *Sleepwalking Through History* (1991); Susan Jeffords, *Hard Bodies* (1993); Peter Kornbluh and Malcolm Byrne, eds., *The Iran-Contra Scandal* (1993); David E. Kyvig, ed., *Reagan and the World* (1990); Mark P. Lagon, *The Reagan Doctrine* (1994); Alexandre Laurien, *The Voice of America* (1988); Thomas E. Mann, *A Question of Balance* (1990) (Congress); Jeff McMahan, *Reagan and the World* (1986); Morris Morley, *Crisis and Confrontation* (1988); Edmund Morris, *Dutch* (1999); Kenneth A. Oye et al., eds., *Eagle Defiant* (1983) and *Eagle Resurgent?* (1987); William E. Pemberton, *Exit with Honor* (1997); Michael Rogin, *Ronald Reagan* (1987); Michael Schaller, *Reckoning with Reagan* (1992); Peter Schweizer, *Reagan's War* (2002); James M. Scott, *Deciding to Intervene* (1996) (Reagan Doctrine); and Garry Wills, *Reagan's America* (1987). Specific topics and regions are listed below.

Economic and environmental issues can be explored in C. Fred Bergsten and William R. Cline, *The United States–Japan Economic Problem* (1987); Margaret P. Doxey, *Economic Sanctions and International Enforcement* (1980); Robert Gilpin, *The Political Economy of International Relations* (1987); Edward Goldsmith and Nicolas Hildyard, eds., *The Earth Report* (1988); Edward M. Graham and Paul R. Klugman, *Foreign Direct Investment in the United States* (1995); Gary C. Hufbauer et al., *Economic Sanctions Reconsidered* (1985); Anne G. Keatley, ed., *Technological Frontiers and Foreign Relations* (1985); John H. Makin, *The Global Debt Crisis* (1984); John McCormick, *Reclaiming Paradise* (1989); Jürgen Schmandt et al., eds., *Acid Rain and Friendly Neighbors* (1988); Jeffrey J. Schott, *The Uruguay Round* (1994); Gilbert R. Winham, *International Trade and the Tokyo Round Negotiations* (1986); and Donald Worster, ed., *The Ends of the Earth* (1988).

For relations with the Soviet Union (except for the nuclear arms race, listed below), see Garthoff above; Dana H. Allin, *Cold War Illusions: America, Europe, and Soviet Power* (1995); Seweryn Bialer, *The Soviet Paradox* (1986); Seweryn Bialer and Michael Mandelbaum, eds., *Gorbachev's Russia and American Foreign Policy* (1988); Archie Brown, *The Gorbachev Factor* (1996); Alexander Dallin, *Black Box* (1985) (KAL 007); Seymour M. Hersh, *"The Target Is Destroyed"* (1986); Jerry Hough, *Russia and the West* (1988); Bruce Jentleson, *Pipeline Politics* (1986) (East-West energy trade); Robert G. Kaiser, *How Gorbachev Happened* (1991); Michael MccGwire, *Perestroika and Soviet National Security* (1991); Michael Mandelbaum and Strobe Talbott, *Reagan and Gorbachev* (1987); Matthew Ouimet, *The Rise and Fall of the Brezhnev Doctrine in Soviet Foreign Policy* (2003); Leon V. Sigal, *Hang Separately* (2000); Helene Sjursen, *The United States, Western Europe and the Polish Crisis* (2003); and Strobe Talbott, *The Russians and Reagan* (1984).

For the nuclear arms race, SALT-II, SDI, and the antinuclear movement, see Ruth Adams and Susan Cullen, eds., *The Final Epidemic* (1981); William Arkin and Richard Fieldhouse, *Nuclear Battlefields* (1985); Donald C. Baucom, *The Origins of SDI* (1992); Dan Caldwell, *The Dynamics of Domestic Politics and Arms Control* (1991) (SALT-II); David Callahan, *Dangerous Capabilities* (1990) (Nitze); Lynn Eden and Steven E. Miller, eds., *Nuclear Arguments* (1989); Matthew Evangelista, *Innovation and the Arms Race* (1988); Jonathan Haslam, *The Soviet Union and the Politics of Nuclear Weapons in Europe* (1990); Robert Jervis, *The Meaning of the Nuclear Revolution* (1989); William W. Kaufmann, *A Reasonable Defense* (1986); Michael T. Klare, *American Arms Supermarket* (1984); Edward T. Linenthal, *Symbolic Defense* (1989) (SDI); David S. Meyer, *A Winter of Discontent* (1990) (freeze); John Mueller, *Retreat from Doomsday* (1989); John Newhouse, *War and Peace in the Nuclear Age* (1989); Janne E. Nolan, *Guardians of the Arsenal* (1989); Jerome Price, *The Antinuclear Movement* (1989); Thomas R. Rochon, *Mobilizing for Peace* (1988); Scott D. Sagan, *Moving Targets* (1989); Steven K. Smith and Douglas A. Wertman, *U.S.–Western European Relations During the Reagan Years* (1992); Strobe Talbott, *Endgame* (1979) (SALT-II), *Deadly Gambits* (1984), and *The Master of the Game* (1988) (Nitze); Douglas C. Waller, *Congress and the Nuclear Freeze* (1987); Daniel Wirls, *Buildup* (1992); and Thomas W. Wolfe, *The SALT Experience* (1979).

The CIA, U.S. covert operations, counterinsurgency, and counterrevolution are explored in Daniel P. Bolger, *Americans at War, 1975–1986* (1988); Anne H. Cahn, *Killing Détente: The Right Attacks the CIA* (1998); Loch Johnson, *America's Secret Power* (1989); Michael T. Klare and Cynthia Arnson, *Supplying Repression* (1981); Michael T. Klare and Peter Kornbluh, eds., *Low-Intensity Warfare* (1988); David C. Martin and John Wolcott, *Best Laid Plans* (1988); Michael McClintock, *Instruments of Statecraft* (1992); Kathryn S. Olmsted, *Challenging the Secret Government* (1996) (investigations of CIA); Joseph E. Persico, *Casey* (1990); John Prados, *Presidents' Secret Wars* (1986); John Ranelagh, *The Agency* (1986); D. Michael Shafer, *Deadly Paradigms* (1988); and Gregory F. Treverton, *Covert Action* (1987).

For U.S. relations with the Third World, see Richard E. Feinberg, *The Intemperate Zone* (1983); John L. Girling, *America and the Third World* (1980); Melvin Gurtov and Ray Maghroori, *Roots of Failure* (1984); Gabriel Kolko, *Confronting the Third World* (1988); Stephen D. Krasner, *Structural Conflict* (1985); Barry Rubin, *Modern Dictators* (1987); Peter J. Schraeder, *Intervention in the 1980s* (1989); and Marshall D. Shulman, ed., *East-West Tensions in the Third World* (1986).

Middle East topics, Arab-Israeli conflict, and the peace process are examined in Fouad Ajami, *The Arab Predicament* (1981); George W. Ball, *Error and Betrayal in Lebanon* (1984); Mahmoud G. El-Warfally, *Imagery and Ideology in U.S. Policy Toward Libya* (1988); Nicholas Lahan, *Selling AWACS to Saudi Arabia* (2002); George Lenczowski, *American Presidents and the Middle East* (1989) and *The Middle East in World Affairs* (1980); Zachary

Lochman and Joel Beinin, eds., *Intifada* (1989); A. F. K. Organski, *The $36 Billion Bargain* (1990) (aid to Israel); Don Peretz, *Intifada* (1990); William R. Polk, *The Arab World Today* (1991); William B. Quandt, *Camp David* (1986), *The United States and Egypt* (1990), and *The Peace Process* (1993); Cheryl Rubenberg, *Israel and the American National Interest* (1986); Yezid Sayad, *Armed Struggle and the Search for State* (1997); David Schoenbaum, *The United States and the State of Israel* (1993); Steven L. Spiegel, *The Other Arab-Israeli Conflict* (1985); Joseph T. Stanik, *El Dorado Canyon: Reagan's Undeclared War with Qaddafi* (2002); and Daniel Yergin, *The Prize* (1991) (oil).

For U.S.-Iranian relations and the hostage crisis, see James A. Bill, *The Eagle and the Lion* (1988); Richard Cottam, *Iran and the United States* (1988); Charles-Phillippe David et al., *Foreign Policy in the White House* (1993); Mark J. Gasiorowski, *U.S. Foreign Policy and the Shah* (1991); James E. Goode, *The United States and Iran* (1997); Daniel Patrick Houghton, *U.S. Foreign Policy and the Iran Hostage Crisis* (2001); Nikki R. Keddie, *Iran, the United States, and the Soviet Union* (1990); Russell L. Moses, *Freeing the Hostages* (1996); R. K. Ramazani, *Revolutionary Iran* (1987); Barry Rubin, *Paved with Good Intentions* (1980); Paul Ryan, *The Iranian Rescue Mission* (1985); Ofira Seliktat, *Failing the Crystal Ball Test* (2000) (Carter and Iran); William Shawcross, *The Shah's Last Ride* (1988); Gary Sick, *All Fall Down* (1985) and *October Surprise* (1991) (hostages and Reagan election); and Marvin Zonis, *Majestic Failure* (1991).

For Asia, see David Bain, *Sitting in Darkness* (1984) (Philippines); C. Fred Bergsten and William R. Cline, *The United States–Japan Economic Problem* (1987); Raymond Bonner, *Waltzing with a Dictator* (1987) (Marcos); H. W. Brands, *Bound to Empire* (1992) (Philippines); Roger Buckley, *U.S.-Japan Alliance Diplomacy* (1992); Sandra Burton, *Impossible Dream* (1989); Lynn D. Feintech, *China's Four Modernizations and the United States* (1982); William H. Gleysteen, Jr., *Massive Entanglement, Marginal Influence* (1999) (South Korea); Yufan Hao and Guocang Huan, eds., *The Chinese View of the World* (1989); Harry Harding, *A Fragile Relationship* (1992) (China); Stanley Karnow, *In Our Image* (1989) (Philippines); Richard J. Kessler, *Rebellion and Repression in the Philippines* (1989); Walter LaFeber, *The Clash* (1997); Edith Terry, *How Asia Got Rich: Japan, China, and the Asian Miracle* (2002).

For Latin America and the Panama Canal treaties, see Paul Drake and Iván Jaksić, eds., *The Struggle for Democracy in Chile* (1991); David W. Engstrom, *Presidential Decision Making Adrift* (1997) (Mariel boatlift); J. Michael Hogan, *The Panama Canal in American Politics* (1986); Eldon Kenworthy, *America/Américas* (1995); Walter LaFeber, *The Panama Canal* (1989); Gordon K. Lewis, *Grenada* (1987); Abraham F. Lowenthal, ed., *Partners in Conflict* (1987) and *Exporting Democracy* (1991); John Major, *Prize Possession* (1993) (Panama); Christopher Mitchell, ed., *Western Hemisphere Immigration and United States Foreign Policy* (1992); Louis A. Pérez, Jr., *Cuba and the United States* (1997); and Lars Schoultz, *Human Rights and United States Policy Toward Latin America* (1981), *National Security and United States Policy Toward Latin America* (1987), and *Beneath the United States* (1998).

Mexican-American relations are the subject of Wayne Cornelius, *Building the Cactus Curtain* (1980); Paul R. Erlich et al., *The Golden Door* (1981); George W. Grayson, *The Politics of Mexican Oil* (1980) and *Oil and Mexican Foreign Policy* (1988); Jacqueline Mazza, *Don't Disturb the Neighbors* (2001); Robert A. Pastor and Jorge G. Castañeda, *Limits of Friendship* (1988); W. Dirk Raat, *Mexico and the United States* (1996); Peter H. Smith, *Mexico* (1980); and Stanley Weintraub, *Marriage of Convenience* (1989).

For Central America, especially Nicaragua and El Salvador, see Ariel C. Armony, *Argentina, the United States, and the Anti-Communist Crusade in Central America* (1997); Cynthia J. Arnson, *Crossroads* (1994); Bruce M. Bagley, ed., *Contadora and the Diplomacy of Peace in Central America* (1987); Leslie Bethell, ed., *Central America Since Independence* (1991); Morris J. Blachman et al., eds., *Confronting Revolution* (1986); Kenneth M. Coleman and George C. Herring, eds., *Understanding the Central American Crisis* (1991); Roy Gutman, *Banana Diplomacy* (1987) (Nicaragua); Martha Honey, *Hostile Acts* (1994) (Costa Rica); Stephen Kinzer, *Blood of Brothers* (1991) (Nicaragua); Peter Kornbluh, *Nicaragua* (1988); Clifford Krauss, *Inside Central America* (1991); Walter LaFeber, *Inevitable Revolutions* (1993); Anthony Lake, *Somoza Falling* (1989); William M. LeoGrande, *Our Own Backyard* (1998); Morris H. Morley, *Washington, Somoza, and the Sandinistas* (1994); Robert Pastor, *Condemned to Repetition* (1987) (Nicaragua); Holly Sklar, *Washington's War on Nicaragua* (1988); Christian Smith, *Resisting Reagan: The U.S. Central America Peace Movement* (1996); Gaddis Smith, *The Last Years of the Monroe*

Doctrine, 1945–1993 (1994); and Thomas W. Walker, *Reagan vs. the Sandinistas* (1987), and ed., *Revolution and Counterrevolution in Nicaragua* (1991).

South Africa and African questions are treated in Pauline H. Baker, *The United States and South Africa* (1989); James Barber and John Barratt, *South Africa's Foreign Policy* (1990); Gerald J. Bender et al., eds., *African Crisis Areas and U.S. Foreign Policy* (1985); Alexander deWaal, *Famine That Kills: Darfur, Sudan, 1984–1985* (1989); Peter Duignan and Lewis H. Gann, *The United States and Africa* (1987); Richard W. Hull, *American Enterprise in South Africa* (1990); Janice Love, *The U.S. Anti-Apartheid Movement* (1985); Robert K. Massie, *Loosing the Bonds* (1997) (South Africa); Martin Meredith, *In the Name of Apartheid* (1988); William Minter, *King Solomon's Mines Revisited* (1986); Robert I. Rotberg, *Suffer the Future* (1980); and Jennifer S. Whitaker, *How Can Africa Survive?* (1987).

See also the General Bibliography, Robert L. Beisner, ed., *Guide to American Foreign Relations Since 1600* (2003), and the following notes.

For comprehensive coverage of foreign-relations topics, see the articles in the four-volume *Encyclopedia of U.S. Foreign Relations* (1997), edited by Bruce W. Jentleson and Thomas G. Paterson.

NOTES TO CHAPTER 11

1. Quoted in Robert D. McFadden et al., *No Hiding Place* (New York: Times Books, 1981), p. 3.
2. Quoted in William B. Quandt, "The Middle East Crisis," *Foreign Affairs: America and the World, 1979, LVIII* (1980), 544.
3. Moorhead Kennedy quoting a marine in discussion of "Iran Hostage Mission," in Herbert B. Rosenbaum and Alexej Ugrinsky, eds., *Jimmy Carter* (Westport, Conn.: Greenwood, 1994), p. 232.
4. Quoted in Doyle McManus, *Free at Last!* (New York: New American, 1981), p. 16.
5. Quoted in Tim Wells, *444 Days* (San Diego: Harcourt Brace Jovanovich, 1985), p. 70.
6. Quoted in Ussama Mukdisi, "'Anti-Americanism' in the Arab World," *Journal of American History, LXXXIX* (September 2002), 548.
7. Pierre Salinger, *America Held Hostage* (Garden City, N.Y.: Doubleday, 1981), p. 5.
8. Quoted in James F. Goode, *The United States & Iran* (New York: St. Martin's, 1997), p. 186.
9. Jimmy Carter, *Keeping Faith* (New York: Bantam, 1982), p. 439.
10. Cyrus Vance, *Hard Choices* (New York: Simon & Schuster, 1983), p. 331.
11. Ball quoted in Douglas Little, *American Orientalism* (Chapel Hill: University of North Carolina Press, 2002), p. 225.
12. Quoted in *New York Times*, November 18, 1979.
13. Quoted in Daniel Yergin, *The Prize* (New York: Simon & Schuster, 1991), p. 701.
14. Quoted in Harold H. Saunders, "Diplomacy and Pressure," in Warren Christopher et al., *American Hostages in Iran* (New Haven: Yale University Press, 1982), p. 102.
15. Quoted in McFadden, *No Hiding Place,* p. 214.
16. Quoted in David Patrick Houghton, *US Foreign Policy and the Iran Hostage Crisis* (New York: Cambridge University Press, 2001), p. 95.
17. Quoted in Wells, *444 Days,* p. 439.
18. Stansfield Turner quoted in Russell L. Moses, *Freeing the Hostages* (Pittsburgh: University of Pittsburgh University Press, 1996), p. 186; Brzezinski quoting Hamilton Jordan in Houghton, *Iran Hostage Crisis,* p. 207.
19. Vance, *Hard Choices,* p. 409.
20. Warren Christopher, *Chance of a Lifetime* (New York: Scribner's, 2001), p. 100.
21. Carter quoted in Robert A. Strong, *Working in the World* (Baton Rouge: Louisiana State University Press, 2000), p. 247.
22. Zbigniew Brzezinski, "The Failed Mission," *New York Times Magazine,* April 18, 1982, p. 64.
23. Quoted in Phillip Keisling, "Desert One," *Washington Monthly, XV* (December 1983), 56.
24. Quoted in Lucien S. Vandenbroucke, *Perilous Options* (New York: Oxford University Press, 1993), p. 140.
25. Pilot quoted in Paul R. Ryan, *The Iranian Rescue Mission* (Annapolis, Md.: Naval Institute Press, 1985), p. 252.
26. Quoted in Ryan, *The Iranian Rescue Mission,* p. 127.
27. Michael Schaller, *Reckoning with Reagan* (New York: Oxford University Press, 1992), p. 21.
28. Quoted in Walter Russell Mead, *Special Providence* (New York: Routledge, 2002), p. 221.
29. Hodding Carter quoted in John Dumbrell, *The Carter Presidency* (New York: Manchester University Press, 1993), p. 169.
30. Michael Metrinko quoted in Houghton, *Iran Hostage Crisis,* p. 60.
31. John Limbert quoted in James A. Bill, *The Eagle and the Lion* (New Haven: Yale University Press, 1988), p. 303.
32. Quoted in Makdisi, " 'Anti-Americanism,'" p. 551.
33. Zbigniew Brzezinski quoted in Bruce R. Kuniholm, "9/11, the Great Game, and the Vision Thing," *Journal of American History, LXXXIX* (September 2002), 430.
34. Sanford J. Ungar, "The Roots of Estrangement," in Ungar, ed., *Estrangement* (New York: Oxford University Press, 1985), p. 7.
35. Quoted in Steven V. Roberts, "The Year of the Hostage," *New York Times Magazine,* November 2, 1980, p. 63.
36. Quoted in William Stueck, "Placing Jimmy Carter's Foreign Policy," in Gary M. Fink and Hugh Davis Graham, eds., *The Carter Presidency* (Lawrence: University Press of Kansas, 1998), p. 245.
37. Quoted in Jules Witcover, *Marathon* (New York: Viking, 1977), p. 596.
38. Quoted in Betty Glad, *Jimmy Carter* (New York: Norton, 1980), p. 391.
39. Douglas Brinkley, "The Rising Stock of Jimmy Carter," *Diplomatic History, XX* (Fall, 1996), 515.

40. William Quandt in discussion of "Negotiations at Home and Abroad" in Rosenbaum and Ugrinsky, *Carter,* p. 62.
41. Carter, *Keeping Faith,* p. 143.
42. Quoted in *Washington Post,* January 12, 1977; *New York Times,* May 2, 1979.
43. Vance, *Hard Choices,* p. 394.
44. Brzezinski, *Power and Principle,* p. 380.
45. Leslie H. Gelb in *New York Times,* April 29, 1980.
46. Hamilton Jordan, *Crisis* (New York: G. P. Putnam's Sons, 1982), p. 47.
47. Quoted in *Newsweek, LXXXVIII* (December 27, 1976), 19.
48. Gaddis Smith, *Morality, Reason, & Power* (New York: Hill & Wang, 1986).
49. Quoted in John Lewis Gaddis, *Strategies of Containment* (New York: Oxford University Press, 1982), p. 345.
50. Smith, *Morality, Reason, & Power,* p. 9.
51. Quoted in Richard Hudson, "Storm Over the Canal," *New York Times Magazine,* May 16, 1976, p. 24.
52. Quoted in William J. Jorden, *Panama Odyssey* (Austin: University of Texas Press, 1984), p. 436.
53. Quoted in William L. Furlong and Margaret E. Scranton, *The Dynamics of Foreign Policymaking* (Boulder, Colo.: Westview Press, 1984), p. 55.
54. Quoted in Lou Cannon, *President Reagan* (New York: Simon & Schuster, 1991), p. 342.
55. Quoted in Leroy Ashby and Rod Gramer, *Fighting the Odds* (Pullman: Washington State University Press, 1994), p. 543.
56. George Moffett Exit Interview, December 5, 1980, Jimmy Carter Presidential Library, Atlanta, Ga.
57. Sol Linowitz quoted in John Major, *Prize Possession* (New York: Cambridge University Press, 1993), p. 351.
58. Quoted in Ashby and Gramer, *Fighting,* p. 544.
59. *Department of State Bulletin, LXXVIII* (May 1978), 52.
60. Brzezinski, *Power and Principle,* p. 136.
61. *Department of State Bulletin, LXXVIII* (May 1978), 53.
62. Quoted in Charles O. Jones, *The Trusteeship Presidency* (Baton Rouge: Louisiana State University Press, 1988), p. 160.
63. Minister of Planning Henry Ruíz quoted in Morris H. Morley, *Washington, Somoza, and the Sandinistas* (New York: Cambridge University Press, 1994), p. 306.
64. López Portillo quoted in W. Dirk Raat, *Mexico and the United States* (Athens: University of Georgia Press, 1992), p. 161.
65. Quoted in Michael S. Teitelbaum, "Right Versus Right," *Foreign Affairs, LIX* (Fall 1980), 46.
66. Quoted in Saul Landau, "The Bay of Pigs," *Los Angeles Times,* April 19, 1981.
67. Quoted in *Hartford Courant,* November 20, 1980.
68. Moshe Dayan quoted in William B. Quandt, *Peace Process* (Washington, D.C.: Brookings, 1993), p. 268.
69. William Quandt in discussion of "The Camp David Accords," in Rosenbaum and Ugrinsky, *Carter,* p. 186.
70. Quoted in Little, *American Orientalism,* p. 290.
71. William B. Quandt, *Camp David* (Washington, D.C.: Brookings, 1986), p. 258.
72. Quoted in *Hartford Courant,* December 22, 1980.
73. Quoted in Elaine P. Adam and Richard P. Stebbins, eds., *American Foreign Relations, 1977* (New York: New York University Press, 1979), p. 301.
74. *Ibid.,* p. 309.
75. General Obasanjo quoted in Donald Rothchild, "U.S. Policy Styles in Africa," in Kenneth A. Oye et al., eds., *Eagle Entangled* (New York: Longman, 1979), p. 327.
76. Clyde Ferguson and William R. Cotter, "South Africa," *Foreign Affairs, LVI* (January 1978), 262.
77. Quoted in Foreign Policy Association, *Great Decisions, '79* (New York: Foreign Policy Association, 1979), p. 60.
78. Quoted in Kaufman, *Carter,* p. 91.
79. Quoted in Stueck, "Carter's Foreign Policy," p. 250.
80. Hodding Carter III, "Life Inside the Carter State Department," *Playboy, XXVIII* (February 1981), 215.
81. Quoted in Odd Arne Westad, "The Fall of Détente and the Turning Tides of History," in Westad, ed., *The Fall of Détente* (Boston: Scandinavian University Press, 1995), p. 17.
82. Georgi Arbatov quoted in Thomas M. Nichols, "Carter and the Soviets," *Diplomacy & Statecraft, XIII* (June 2002), 28.
83. Georgy Kornienko quoted in Vladislav Zubok, "An Offered Hand Rejected?" in Rosenbaum and Ugrinsky, *Carter,* p. 365.
84. Quoted in Westad, "Fall of Détente," p. 16.
85. Quoted in Lawrence Caldwell and Alexander Dallin, "U.S. Policy Toward the Soviet Union," in Oye, *Eagle Entangled,* p. 220.
86. Quoted in *New York Times,* May 29, 1978.
87. Quoted in Thomas J. McCormick, *America's Half-Century* (Baltimore: Johns Hopkins University Press, 1996, rev. ed.), p. 206.
88. Georgi Arbatov quoted in Joseph Kraft, "Letter from Moscow," *The New Yorker, LIV* (October 16, 1978), 122–124.
89. Quoted in George McGovern, "How to Avert a New 'Cold War,'" *Atlantic Monthly, CCXLV* (June 1980), 52.
90. Quoted in David Callahan, *Dangerous Capabilities* (New York: HarperCollins, 1990), p. 409.
91. Quoted in Frances FitzGerald, *Way Out There in the Blue* (New York: Simon & Schuster, 2000), p. 87.
92. Leslie H. Gelb, "The Facts of SALT II," April 1979, Department of State Current Policy No. 65.
93. Senator Robert Byrd quoted in *New York Times,* October 4, 1979.
94. Garthoff, *Détente and Confrontation,* p. 928.
95. Leonid Shebarshin quoted in Odd Arne Westad, "New Russian Evidence on the Soviet Intervention in Afghanistan," *Cold War International History Project,* nos. 8–9 (Winter 1996/1997), p. 130; General Dimitrii Ustinov quoted in Matthew J. Ouimet, *The Rise and Fall of the Brezhnev Doctrine in Soviet Foreign Policy* (Chapel Hill: University of North Carolina Press, 2003), p. 93.
96. Quoted in Wilfred Loth, *Overcoming the Cold War* (New York: Palgrave, 2002), p. 162.
97. George Urban, "A Long Conversation with Dr. Zbigniew Brzezinski," *Encounter, LVI* (May 1981), 18.
98. Quoted in Irene L. Gendzier, "Invisible by Design," *Diplomatic History, XXVI* (Fall 2002), 606.
99. *Department of State Bulletin, LXXX* (February 1980), Special B.
100. Quoted in Smith, *Morality, Reason, & Power,* p. 232.
101. Helmut Schmidt, *Men and Powers* (New York: Random House, 1989), p. 207.
102. David D. Newsom, "America Engulfed," *Foreign Policy,* no. 43 (Summer 1981), 17.
103. Deng Xiaoping quoted in Allen S. Whiting, "China's Use of Force," *International Security, XXVI* (Fall 2001), 120.
104. Nancy Bernkopf Tucker, *Taiwan, Hong Kong, and the United States* (New York: Twayne, 1994), p. 156.
105. Quoted in Michael S. Sherry, *In the Shadow of War* (New Haven: Yale University Press, 1995), p. 350.
106. Exit Interview with Zbigniew Brzezinski, February 18, 1980, Carter Library.
107. William A. Williams letter, *The Nation, CCXXXII* (February 14, 1981), 162.

108. Richard E. Neustadt, *Presidential Power and the Modern Presidents* (New York: Free Press, 1990), p. 261.
109. Patricia Derian quoted in "The Pentagon and the CIA Sent Mixed Message to the Argentine Military," *National Security Archive Electronic Briefing Book* (March 28, 2003); quoted in Kenton Clymer, "Jimmy Carter, Human Rights, and Cambodia," *Diplomatic History,* XXVII (April 2003), 246.
110. Cyrus Vance quoted in *New York Times,* June 6, 1980.
111. Quoted in Hedrick Smith, "Reagan," *New York Times Magazine,* November 16, 1980, p. 172.
112. Quoted in Cecil V. Crabb, Jr., "The Reagan Victory," in Ellis Sandoz and Cecil V. Crabb, Jr., eds., *A Tide of Discontent* (Washington, D.C.: Congressional Quarterly Press, 1981), p. 158.
113. Quoted in Robert G. Kaiser, "Your Host of Hosts," *New York Review of Books,* June 28, 1984, p. 38.
114. Quoted in Pierre E. Trudeau, *Memoirs* (Toronto: McClellan and Stewart, 1993), p. 332.
115. Little, *American Orientalism,* p. 245.
116. Quoted in Kaiser, "Your Host," p. 39.
117. Paul Boyer quoted in Fraser J. Harbutt, *The Cold War Era* (Malden, Mass.: Blackwell, 2002), p. 268.
118. Martin Anderson, *Revolution* (Stanford: Stanford University Press, 1990), pp. 288, 290.
119. Quoted in Strobe Talbott, *The Russians and Reagan* (New York: Vintage, 1984), p. 32.
120. *Public Papers, Reagan, 1981* (Washington, D.C.: Government Printing Office, 1982), p. 57.
121. Reagan quoted in David Wirls, *Buildup* (Ithaca: Cornell University Press, 1992), pp. 32–33.
122. Quoted in Schaller, *Reckoning,* p. 47.
123. Richard Allen quoted in FitzGerald, *Way Out,* p. 175.
124. Ronald Reagan, *An American Life* (New York: Simon & Schuster, 1990), p. 547.
125. *Public Papers, Reagan, 1981,* p. 464; *ibid., 1983* (Washington D.C.: Government Printing Office, 1984–1985, 2 vols.), I, 265.
126. *Public Papers, Reagan, 1983, II,* 1189.
127. *Department of State Bulletin, LXXXIV* (May 1984), 4.
128. Quoted in Walter LaFeber, *Inevitable Revolutions* (New York: Norton, 1993; 2nd ed.), p. 276.
129. *Weekly Compilation of Presidential Documents, XXII* (February 10, 1986), 136, 140.
130. *Department of State Bulletin, XXII* (November 1984), 7; quoted in Michael J. Mazarr, "George W. Bush, Idealist," *International Affairs, LXXIX* (June 2003), 515.
131. Quoted in Cannon, *President Reagan,* p. 160.
132. Alexander M. Haig, Jr., *Caveat* (New York: Macmillan, 1984), p. 85.
133. Quoted in Michael McClintock, *Instruments of Statecraft* (New York: Pantheon, 1992), p. 378.
134. Hans Dietrich Gentscher, *Rebuilding a House Divided* (New York: Broadway Books, 1998), p. 205; Casey quoted in Robert David Johnson, "Congress and the Cold War," *Journal of Cold War Studies, III* (Spring 2001), 96.
135. George P. Shultz, *Turmoil and Triumph* (New York: Charles Scribner's sons, 1992), p. 275.
136. Quoted in Robert A. Pastor, "The Centrality of Central America," in Larry Berman, ed., *Looking Back on the Reagan Presidency* (Baltimore: Johns Hopkins University Press, 1990), p. 40.
137. Quoted in Theodore S. Draper, *A Very Thin Line* (New York: Simon & Schuster, 1991), p. 565.
138. Quoted *ibid.,* p. 560.
139. North quoted in William E. Pemberton, *Exit with Honor* (Armonk, N.Y.: Sharpe, 1998), p. 173.
140. Quoted in Robert E. Osgood, "The Revitalization of Containment," *Foreign Affairs: America and the World, 1981, LX* (1982), 475.
141. Quoted in *New York Times,* December 10, 1981.
142. George F. Kennan, "Cease This Madness," *Atlantic Monthly, CCXLVII* (January 1981), 25–28.
143. George F. Kennan, "On Nuclear War," *New York Review of Books,* January 21, 1982, pp. 10, 12.
144. Quoted in Allen M. Winkler, *Life Under a Cloud: American Anxiety About the Atom* (New York: Oxford University Press, 1993), p. 200.
145. General William Odum quoted in Carol Cohn, "Sex and Death in the Rational World of Defense Intellectuals," *Signs, XII* (Autumn 1987), 692–693.
146. Reagan quoted in Beth A. Fischer, *The Reagan Reversal* (Columbia: Unviersity of Missouri Press, 1997), p. 120.
147. Ambassador Charles Price quoted in Daniel W. Ellwood, "Comparative Anti-Americanism in Western Europe," in Heide Fehrenbach and Uta G. Poiger, eds., *Transactions, Transgression, Transformations* (New York: Berghahn Books, 2000), p. 32.
148. Steven K. Smith and Douglas A. Wertman, *US–West European Relations During the Reagan Years* (New York: St. Martin's, 1992), p. 58.
149. Strobe Talbott, *The Master of the Game* (New York: Viking, 1989), p. 5.
150. Soviet official Oleg Grinevsky quoted in Vladislav M. Zubok, "Gorbachev and the End of the Cold War," in William C. Wohlforth, ed., *Cold War Endgame* (University Park: Pennsylvania State University Press, 2003), p. 209.
151. James Baker quoted in Strobe Talbott, *Deadly Gambits* (New York: Viking, 1984), p. 223.
152. Quoted in *New York Times,* March 27, 1983.
153. Gregory Fossedal of the Heritage Foundation quoted in Wirls, *Buildup,* p. 149.
154. Suzanne Massie quoting Reagan in Deborah H. Strober and Gerald S. Strober, eds., *Reagan* (Boston: Houghton Mifflin, 1998), p. 128.
155. Ronald Reagan, "Korean Airline Massacre," September 5, 1983, Department of State Current Policy no. 507.
156. Quoted in *New York Times,* December 9, 1996.
157. Geoffrey Howe, *Conflict of Loyalty* (London: Macmillan, 1994), p. 350.
158. Reagan quoted in Fischer, *Reagan Reversal,* p. 135.
159. Anatoly Dobrynin, *In Confidence* (New York: Random House, 1995), p. 538.
160. Margaret Thatcher, *The Downing Street Years* (New York: HarperCollins, 1993), p. 461.
161. George Shultz quoted in Archie Brown, *The Gorbachev Factor* (New York: Oxford University Press, 1996), p. 231.
162. Quoted in Robert G. Kaiser, *How Gorbachev Happened* (New York: Simon & Schuster, 1991), p. 119.
163. Reagan, *American Life,* p. 675; Jack F. Matlock, *Autopsy on an Empire* (New York: Random House, 1995), p. 97.
164. Ambassador Jack Matlock quoted in Carolyn M. Ekedal and Melvin A. Goodman, *The Wars of Eduard Shevardnadze* (University Park: Penn State University Press, 1997), p. xix.
165. Quoted in LaFeber, *America, Russia,* p. 325.
166. Quoted in Leon V. Sigal, *Hang Separately* (New York: Century Foundation Press, 2000), p. 91.
167. Quoted in Ekedahl and Goodman, *Shevardnadze,* p. 147.
168. Georgi Arbatov, *The System* (New York: Times Books, 1992), p. 350.

169. Quoted in FitzGerald, *Way Out*, p. 439.
170. Reagan quoted in Knud Krakau, "Policy as Myth and Myth as Policy," *Revue Française d'Études Américaines*, XVII (August 1994), 263.
171. Quoted in Harold Molineu, *U.S. Policy toward Latin America* (Boulder, Colo.: Westview Press, 1986), p. 176; NSC paper of April 1982 quoted in *New York Times*, April 7, 1983.
172. *Public Papers, Reagan, 1983*, I, 373, 601.
173. Quoted in Doug Stokes, "Countering the Soviet Threat?" *Cold War History*, III (April 2003), 82.
174. Quoted in *New York Times*, April 28, 1983.
175. White Paper quoted in Stokes, "Countering," p. 82.
176. Quoted in William M. LeoGrande, "A Splendid Little War," *International Security*, VI (Summer 1981), 27.
177. Quoted *ibid.*, p. 45.
178. Quoted in LaFeber, *Inevitable Revolutions*, p. 277.
179. Quoted in Marvin Gettleman et al., eds., *El Salvador* (New York: Grove, 1981), p. 355.
180. Robert Buzzanco, "'El Salvador is Spanish for Vietnam,'" *The Long Term View*, V (Summer 2000), 11.
181. Howard Lane quoted in Mark Danner, "The Truth of El Mozote," *The New Yorker*, LXIX (December 6, 1993), 118.
182. Thomas Carothers, "Reagan Years," in Abraham F. Lowenthal, ed., *Exporting Democracy* (Baltimore: Johns Hopkins University Press, 1991), p. 93.
183. Quoted in *New York Times*, March 19, 1981.
184. Quoted in Stephen Kinzer, "Nicaragua," *New York Times Magazine*, August 28, 1983, p. 24.
185. Quoted in Bob Woodward, *Veil* (New York: Simon & Schuster, 1987), p. 281.
186. Colin L. Powell, *My American Journey* (New York: Random House, 1995), p. 339.
187. CIA manual quoted in *New York Times*, January 29, 1997.
188. Quoted in Thomas G. Paterson, "Oversight or Afterview?" in Michael Barnhart, ed., *Congress and United States Foreign Policy* (Albany: State University of New York Press, 1987), p. 154.
189. Quoted in Pemberton, *Exit*, p. 173.
190. Oliver North to John Poindexter, September 25, 1986, in Tom Blanton, ed., *White House E-Mail* (New York: New Press, 1995), p. 99.
191. Lawrence Walsh quoted in Theodore Draper, "Walsh's Last Stand," *New York Review of Books*, March 3, 1994, p. 27.
192. Quoted in Joel Brinkley, "The Cover-Up That Worked," *New York Times*, January 23, 1994.
193. LeoGrande, *Backyard*, p. 587.
194. Quoted in *New York Times*, February 23, 1985.
195. Quoted *ibid.*, August 13, 1986.
196. Shultz, *Turmoil and Triumph*, p. 305.
197. Robert M. Gates, *From the Shadows* (New York: Simon & Schuster, 1996), p. 273.
198. Quoted in Peter Kornbluh, "The Haig-Rodríguez Secret Talks," *Cold War International History Project Bulletin*, nos. 8–9 (Winter 1996/1997), p. 219.
199. Quoted in Robert McFarlane, *Special Trust* (New York: Cadell & Davies, 1991), p. 177.
200. Michael Deaver quoting Haig in Schaller, *Reckoning*, p. 123.
201. Laurien Alexandre, *The Voice of America* (Norwood, N.J.: Ablex, 1988), p. 139; Kenneth N. Skoug, Jr., *The United States and Cuba Under Reagan and Shultz* (Westport, Conn.: Praeger, 1996), p. 207.
202. Robert McFarlane quoted in Strober and Strober, *Reagan*, p. 290.
203. Quoted in Michael D. Pearlman, *Warfighting and American Democracy* (Lawrence: University Press of Kansas, 1999), p. 397; quoted in Lars Schoutz, *Beneath the United States*, (Cambridge: Harvard University Press, 1998), p. 365.
204. Sherry, *Shadow*, p. 339.
205. Quoted in David Schoenbaum, *The United States and the State of Israel* (New York: Oxford University Press, 1993), p. 273.
206. Quoted in *New York Times*, December 21, 1981.
207. Ariel Sharon quoted in Quandt, *Peace Process*, p. 346.
208. Quoted in Schoenbaum, *U.S. and Israel*, p. 285.
209. Powell, *My American Journey*, p. 281.
210. Quoted in James A. Bill, *George Ball* (New Haven: Yale University Press, 1997), pp. 194–195.
211. Quoted in Yezid Sayid, *Armed Struggle and the Search for State* (New York: Oxford University Press, 1997), p. 624.
212. Quoted in Melani McAlister, "A Cultural History of the War Without End," *Journal of American History*, LXXXIX (September 2002), 448.
213. Quoted in *New York Times*, October 15, 1985.
214. Caspar Weinberger, *Fighting for Peace* (New York: Warner Books, 1990), p. 201.
215. Tom Engelhardt, *The End of Victory Culture* (New York: Basic Books, 1995), p. 269.
216. Geoffrey Kemp quoted in Little, *American Orientalism*, p. 227.
217. Chester A. Crocker, "South Africa: Strategy for Change," *Foreign Affairs*, LIX (Winter 1980/1981), 346.
218. Quoted in Donald Culverson, "Antiapartheid Activism," in Brenda Gayle Plummer, ed., *Window on Freedom* (Chapel Hill: University of North Carolina Press, 2003), p. 62.
219. Donald Rothchild and John Ravenhill, "From Carter to Reagan," in Kenneth Oye et al., eds., *Eagle Defiant* (Boston: Little, Brown, 1983), p. 349.
220. Member of Congress William Gray quoted in Stephen R. Weissman, *A Culture of Deference* (New York: BasicBooks, 1995), p. 171.
221. Lee Iacocca quoted in Donald W. White, *The American Century* (New Haven: Yale University Press, 1996), p. 395.
222. George Shultz quoted in Walter La Feber, *The Clash* (New York: Norton, 1997), p. 380.
223. Abe Shintaro quoted *ibid.*
224. George F. Will, "How Reagan Changed America," *Newsweek*, CXIII (January 9, 1989), 13, 17.
225. Lester R. Brown quoted in *World Development Forum*, IV (August 31, 1986), 1.
226. Quoted in Ivo D. Duchacek, *Nations and Men* (Hinsdale, Ill.: Dryden Press, 1975; 3rd ed.), p. 146.
227. Quoted in Foreign Policy Association, *Great Decisions 1990* (New York: Foreign Policy Association, 1990), p. 16.
228. Terry Deibel, "Reagan's Mixed Legacy," *Foreign Policy*, no. 75 (Summer 1989), 49.

CHAPTER 12

Imperial America: The United States and the World Since 1989

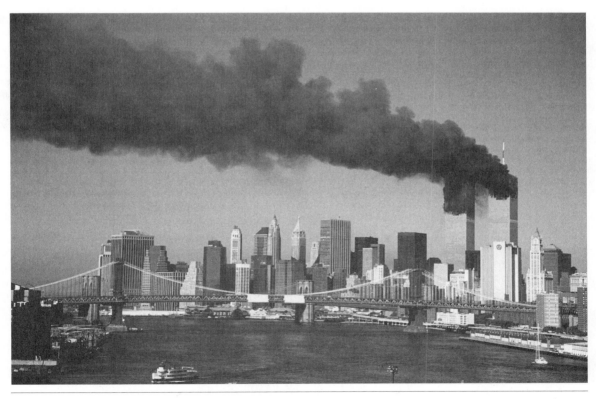

September 11, 2001. *Billowing smoke over the Manhattan skyline marked the first hostile attacks on the American mainland since British forces burned Washington in 1814. The United States found itself at war with international terrorists. (Reuters Corbis)*

9/11 and After

A PRESIDENTIAL SPEECHWRITER called it "the worst crime ever recorded on video-tape."[1] Early in the morning of September 11, 2001, fifteen Saudi Arabians and four Egyptians, secretly armed with box-cutters, boarded four commercial airliners. Two planes took off from Boston, the other two from Newark, New Jersey, and Washington, D.C. At 8:46 A.M. and 9:03 A.M., respectively, the two hijacked Boston aircraft exploded into the north and south towers of the World Trade Center in New York City. "Another plane hit! Another plane hit the building!" shouted an emergency dispatcher at the nearby Port Authority building.[2] At 9:39 A.M., the Washington jetliner struck and destroyed a portion of the Pentagon. At 10:10 A.M., the Newark aircraft, possibly intended for the White House or Capitol, plunged to a fiery demise in a field in western Pennsylvania after passengers overpowered the plane's hijackers. By midday both World Trade Center towers had collapsed and the death toll (including airline passengers) numbered 2,823 in New York City, 45 in Pennsylvania, and 189 in Washington, D.C. The victims came from more than eighty countries around the world.

Stunned Americans gaped in disbelief as television networks played and replayed the horrific montage. The novelist John Updike watched from a tenth-floor apartment in Brooklyn Heights as the south tower "fell straight down like an elevator, with a tinkling shiver and a groan of concussion distinct across the mile of air."[3] New York Mayor Rudy Guiliani, rushing to the World Trade Center, "looked up and saw a man jump out—above the fire, must have been at least hundred stories—and my eye followed him, almost transfixed, all the way down."[4] An anguished police officer reported "body parts . . . five blocks away."[5] For those conditioned by films such as *Black Sunday* (1977) or *Air Force One* (1997), the images seemed "right out of a big-budget Hollywood production," making the reality "almost impossible to believe."[6] In Florida at the time of the attacks, President George W. Bush viewed replays of the second New York explosion and commented tersely: "We're at war."[7] En route to Washington, the president learned of the assault on the Pentagon. "We're going to find out who did this," Bush vowed, "and we're going to kick their asses."[8] That evening, over national television, he announced what came to be known as the Bush Doctrine: "We will make no distinction between the terrorists who committed these acts and those who harbor them."[9] Before going to bed he noted in his diary: "The Pearl Harbor of the twenty-first century took place today."[10]

In the nation's capital, the intelligence community belatedly "connected the dots."[11] Only minutes before the attacks, CIA Director George L. Tenet told a member of Congress that the Saudi exile Osama bin Laden and his terrorist network Al-Qaeda (Arabic for "the Base"), operating out of Afghanistan, were "going to do something big."[12] Tenet proved prophetic. The passenger manifests of the plane that plowed into the Pentagon listed three known Al-Qaeda operatives. Federal investigators pieced together evidence that the nineteen hijackers—trained in Afghanistan,

George W. Bush (b. 1946). Looking pensive, the president viewed the damaged Pentagon from a helicopter on September 14, 2001. Prior to the terrorist attacks, the Bush administration had pursued a "go-it-alone" foreign policy—rejecting the Kyoto Protocol on global warming, withdrawing from the Anti-Ballistic Missile Treaty, refusing to back the International Criminal Court, and showing little interest in negotiations with North Korea or between Israel and the Palestinians. Characterizing himself as a person who did not "sit around trying to analyze myself a lot," Bush reportedly did not ask hard questions of his advisers. Asked if he consulted his father, the ex-president, Bush replied: "There is a higher father I appeal to." Treasury Secretary Paul O'Neill described the president in NSC meetings as "a blind man in a roomful of deaf people." In *Against All Enemies* (2004), the White House counter-terrorism expert Richard Clarke claimed that Bush had done a "terrible job" by ignoring the threat from Al-Qaeda prior to 9/11. (© AP Wide World Photos/White House/Eric Draper)

organized and financed in Germany, England, and Spain with money sent from around the world—had entered the United States on tourist or student visas. They adopted American lifestyles (including the consumption of alcohol, forbidden in the Muslim religion) to avoid suspicion, in some cases living in quiet, middle-class communities for several years prior to the attacks. Some took rudimentary flight training in California and Florida, which enabled them to operate the jetliners after they had killed or intimidated pilots and crews. The hijack leaders believed that they were participating in a "martyrdom operation."[13] Communicating primarily through the Internet, the terrorists exploited "the very global transportation, communication, and economic system they protested" by attacking Wall Street and the Pentagon, the symbols of America's global predominance.[14] Osama bin Laden himself, wearing a military fatigue jacket, soon appeared on videotape to praise the hijackers: "Here is America struck by God Almighty in one of its vital organs. . . . God has blessed a group of vanguard Muslims, the forefront of Islam, to destroy America!"[15]

As Bush's national security adviser, Condoleezza Rice, later put it, great earthquakes can "shift the tectonic plates of international politics."[16] Thus did 9/11 (soon a universally adopted shorthand) trigger what has been called "the most rapid and

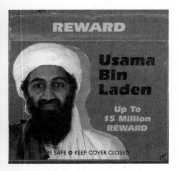

**WANTED DEAD OR ALIVE.
Osama bin Laden (b. 1957).**
The mastermind behind 9/11 and
Al-Qaeda's earlier attacks on the
U.S. embassies in Kenya and
Tanzania (1998) and the navy
destroyer *Cole* (2000), bin Laden
had declared a *jihad* (or holy war)
against Americans. Distributed by
the Rewards for Justice Program
through the State Department,
matchbook covers bearing the Al-
Qaeda leader's likeness offered
payments of up to $5 million for
information leading to his capture.
(Robert E. Goodrich)

dramatic change in the history of U.S. foreign policy."[17] Before the terrorist attacks, the Bush administration had espoused a realist foreign policy that designated China and Russia as Washington's competitors and rejected nation-building in the developing world. Less than a year after 9/11, the administration set forth a new national security strategy, acknowledging that "we are menaced less by fleets and armies than by catastrophic technologies falling into the hands of the embittered few." Instead of global rivalry, "today, the world's great powers find themselves on the same side—united by common dangers of terrorist violence and chaos."[18] The new approach also stressed the need to use force preemptively against the "unknown, the uncertain, the unseen, and the unexpected," as Defense Secretary Donald H. Rumsfeld phrased it.[19]

Even as most of the world after 9/11 rallied behind Washington's demand that the Islamic fundamentalist Taliban government of Afghanistan hand over bin Laden and his followers, President Bush declared a global war against terrorism "to rid the world of evil."[20] He did not want other countries dictating terms or conditions. "At some point," he told aides, "we may be the only ones left. That's okay with me. We are America."[21] Notwithstanding a successful autumn military campaign that ousted the Taliban from Kabul and bloodied Al-Qaeda (but failed to find bin Laden), Bush raised the stakes in his State of the Union address in January 2002. Modeled after FDR's "day of infamy" speech, Bush's rhetoric singled out Iraq, Iran, and North Korea "and their terrorist allies" as "an axis of evil, arming to threaten the peace of the world [with] weapons of mass destruction." Iraq especially posed a "grave and growing danger." Bush gave notice: "I will not stand by as peril grows closer and closer."[22]

Over the next fifteen months the Bush administration pushed relentlessly for preemptive war against Iraq. Linkages between Saddam Hussein's regime and 9/11 proved elusive, despite claims by Bush officials that they had "bulletproof" evidence of Hussein's ties to Al-Qaeda.[23] Some critics thought that the younger Bush sought to finish what his father had started in the first Gulf War of 1991 (see page 492). Administration hawks apparently saw an opportunity to build a new pillar of U.S. power in the Middle East, replacing Saudi Arabia with a democratic Iraq that was friendly to Israel, harbored no terrorists, and could pump oil for the world economy "at the right price."[24] Hard-liners led by Rumsfeld, Deputy Secretary of Defense Paul Wolfowitz, and Vice President Richard Cheney increasingly argued for "regime change" in Baghdad because Hussein allegedly threatened "America and the world with horrible poisons and diseases and gases and atomic weapons." "Imagine a September eleventh with weapons of mass destruction," warned Rumsfield. "It's not three thousand—it's tens of thousands of innocent men, women, and children." It was "a slam dunk" that Iraq had the weapons, Tenet assured Bush, and Condoleezza Rice warned that "we don't want the smoking gun to be a mushroom cloud."[25] Bush admonished the United Nations on the first anniversary of 9/11: "If [other governments] do not act, America will."[26] Backed by a congressional joint resolution authorizing military force against Iraq, the president in January 2003 uttered sixteen words that turned out to be false: "The British government has learned that Saddam Hussein has recently sought significant quantities of uranium from Africa."[27] Forged documents and faulty intelligence underlay that claim. When ten million people in six hundred cities around the world marched on February 15 against the impending invasion of Iraq, probably the largest one-day protest in history, President Bush claimed never to listen to "focus groups."[28] When the UN Se-

Why We Are in Iraq. Human Rights Watch estimated that 290,000 Iraqis went missing between 1979 and 2003, victims of state-sponsored murder. As this political cartoon from the *South Florida Sun-Sentinel* suggests, however, the George W. Bush administration gave shifting explanations for the war against Iraq and its turbulent aftermath. By spring 2004, Senator Edward M. Kennedy (Democrat-Massachusetts) was calling Iraq "Bush's Vietnam." (Chan Lowe, Copyright © 2004, Tribune Media Services. Reprinted with permission.)

curity Council debated a resolution for war against Iraq later that month, U.S. representatives told allies that the decision "is ours, and we have made it. The only question now is whether the Council will go along with it or not."[29] Calling Washington a "reckless," "naïve," "simplistic," and "unilateralist . . . cowboy," France, Germany, Russia, and China mustered a majority to defeat an explicit UN resolution.[30] Bush went ahead and attacked Iraq anyway.

Operation Iraqi Freedom began on March 20, 2003, with forty cruise missiles and several satellite-guided bombs striking a compound near Baghdad where Saddam Hussein and his sons were reportedly meeting. Even though this "decapitation" attempt failed to kill the Iraqi dictator, the ensuing twenty-six day campaign proved spectacularly successful. At a cost of only 161 dead, the U.S.- and British-led coalition, numbering some 250,000 troops, conquered Iraq in "almost half the time, with one-third the casualties, and at one-fourth the cost" of the first Gulf War of 1991 (see p. 493).[31] Despite initial delays because of the "mother of all [sand] storms" and gloomy prognostications that Baghdad would become another Stalingrad, superior weapons and tactics turned the war into a rout.[32] Iraqi civilian deaths were reportedly near 3,000. The toppling of Saddam Hussein's statue in the heart of Baghdad on April 9 signaled the end of his brutal regime. Coalition forces occupied the rest of battered Iraq within a week. On May 1, greeted by a huge banner spelling MISSION ACCOMPLISHED, Bush made a flashy tail-hook landing in a navy jet aboard the returning aircraft carrier *Abraham Lincoln* off the California coast and pronounced the official end of major combat operations.

UDAY SADDAM HUSAYN
National Assembly Member/
Olympic Chairman/
Saddam Feyadeen Chief

QUSAY SADDAM HUSAYN
AL-TIKRITI
Special Security Organization
(SSO) Supervisor/Baêth Party
Military Bureau Deputy Chairman

Uday Hussein (1964–2003) and Qusay Hussein (1966–2003). These Pentagon "playing cards" with photographs of Saddam Hussein's sons (the Ace of Hearts and the Ace of Clubs) were part of an effort to identify leading Iraqi officials as "high-value targets" during and after the invasion of Iraq. Identified by a neighbor (who reportedly collected $30 million in reward money), Uday and Qusay were killed during a firefight in Mosul by soldiers of the U.S. 101st Airborne's Second Combat Team in July 2003. (Liberty Playing Cards)

Military triumph brought gloating and grand expectations. "Not since Rome has one nation loomed so large over the others," wrote one scholar who called "American empire" the "dominant narrative of the twenty-first century."[33] Victory proved that virile Americans were "from Mars" and hesitant Europeans ("old Europe," in Rumsfeld's dismissive words) were "from Venus."[34] Bush officials likened the coming democratization of Iraq to that of Germany or Japan after World War II, "a shining example" and "demonstration effect" for the Arab world so that "it will no longer produce ideologies of hatred that lead men to fly airplanes into buildings in New York and Washington."[35]

Yet euphoria dissipated quickly. After months of futile searching, even after interviewing captured Iraqi scientists, the chief inspector of the 1,400-strong U.S. Iraq Survey Group admitted that "we were all wrong" about the weapons of mass destruction that had supposedly posed such an imminent threat; nor did the belated capture of Saddam Hussein ("We got him!") in December 2003 ease the increasingly dangerous tasks of military occupation.[36] From looting in the first weeks after the fall of Baghdad, to small hit-and-run attacks during June, to suicide truck bombings in

August, to more coordinated assaults well into 2004, American Occupation forces faced an escalating "guerrilla-type campaign"—a "long, hard slog," in Rumsfeld's phrase.[37] Displaying "spectacular incompetence in planning for the aftermath," the Pentagon and State Department struggled to devise a scheme to transfer sovereignty to a provisional government, to train a professional army and police forces, and to plan economic reconstruction in a country where the unemployment rate reached as high as sixty percent.[38] The Coalition Provisional Authority (dubbed "Condescending Patronizing Americans") relied on ill-trained interpreters who could barely "tell the difference between a burro and a burrito."[39] Instead of deterring terrorism, the chaos following victory seemed to attract extremists to Iraq, including members of Al-Qaeda, who "weren't there before."[40] The number of U.S. soldiers killed during the occupation soon surpassed the death toll (138) during the combat war, reaching more than 800 by summer 2004. Faced with mounting occupation costs of $4 billion per month, Bush asked Congress on the second anniversary of 9/11 for an additional $87 billion in reconstruction funds, thus increasing the federal deficit for 2004 to $562 billion. The president claimed that Iraq was the "central front" where "enemies of freedom are making a desperate stand," and he pledged to do "whatever is necessary" to achieve "this central victory in the war against terror."[41]

Thus did the United States persevere in what one Bush supporter called "a world war" against "Islamic fundamentalism."[42] This new Cold War for the "American Millennium" once again seemed to ensnare the nation in a protracted international conflict that invited possibly limitless commitments.[43] Vice President Cheney predicted after 9/11 that the crusade against terrorism might require military action against "forty or fifty countries" and last more than fifty years.[44] Unlike the collapsed Soviet empire, as one critic dryly noted, "Hell [Axis of Evil] could be relied upon never to go bankrupt or abandon the war for the soul of mankind."[45] This time the doctrine of preemptive war, rather than containment, propelled decision making. "A la carte multilateralism," as one State Department official called it, replaced collective security.[46] States of the former Soviet bloc became America's new allies, while many former Western partners distanced themselves from Washington's increasingly imperial preeminence. The world had been considerably reshuffled in little more than a decade since George W. Bush's father, George H. W. Bush, presided over the end of the first Cold War and hailed a "new world order" of peace and prosperity.

The Earthquakes of 1989–1991

The post–Cold War era had started promisingly enough with the fall of the Berlin Wall in 1989. When officials of the German Democratic Government (GDR) unexpectedly announced on November 9, 1989, that citizens could leave the country at any spot, including the crossing points along the infamous twenty-eight-mile-long Berlin Wall, a raucous, three-day celebration ensued. As West Berlin exploded with fireworks and dancing, thousands of Berliners cavorted atop the ten-foot Wall in front of the Brandenburg Gate. Down came sections of the concrete edifice, and workers dismantled the famous platform where distinguished visitors, including John F. Kennedy and Ronald Reagan, had hurled defiant speeches across the Wall.

West German chancellor Helmut Kohl told President George H. W. Bush by phone: "Without the United States this day would not have been possible."[47]

The foundations of the Wall had begun to crumble the previous May, when Hungary opened its border with Austria. In August tens of thousands of East Germans went on holiday to Hungary, then traveled across the Austro-Hungarian border and eventually to West Germany, where they could obtain automatic rights of citizenship. East Germany soon banned travel to Hungary, but this restriction only temporarily stemmed the flood, as more East Germans voted with their feet, some escaping through Czechoslovakia. By late October the number of refugees from the GDR had swelled to 200,000.

That same month, popular demonstrations in Leipzig and East Berlin led to the resignation of Erich Honecker's government. His successor, Egon Krenz, sensing that "no matter what we do . . . we'll be making the wrong move," opened the Wall on November 9 and promised free elections for 1990, a signal that East Germany would soon join Hungary and Poland in abandoning communism.[48] The day after the Wall came down, moreover, a bloodless coup in Sofia, Bulgaria, ousted Todor Zhivkov, the hard-line Communist party boss for the past thirty-five years. By the end of November, mass demonstrations were peacefully terminating communist rule in Czechoslovakia, and during Christmas week a bloody popular uprising toppled the tyrannical regime of Nicolae Ceaucescu in Romania.

The breaching of the Wall also raised the prospect of German reunification. Chancellor Kohl proclaimed: "We are and remain one nation. Long live a free German fatherland!"[49] The precise blueprints for reunification remained vague, but "it was one of those rare times," according to *Time* magazine, "when the tectonic plates of history shift beneath men's feet, and nothing after is quite the same."[50]

The seismic events of the *annus mirabilis* (year of miracles) 1989 would not have occurred without major impetus from Soviet president Mikhail S. Gorbachev. Since his accession to leadership in the Kremlin in March 1985, Gorbachev's bold effort at reforming the Soviet Union through political liberalization (*glasnost*) and economic restructuring (*perestroika*) had acquired a momentum of its own. To revive the sick Soviet economy, plagued by declining productivity and a demoralized work force, the Soviet leader warned that "everyone must change, from the worker to the minister to the secretary of the central committee."[51] A "revolution from above . . . [to] prevent a revolution from below" required changes in external policies.[52] What started out as a fairly limited foreign-policy agenda—ending the war in Afghanistan, improving relations with China, and negotiating arms-control agreements with the United States—quickly mushroomed.

Gorbachev identified the huge drain on Soviet resources caused by the superpower competition as one area of potential savings. He decided on military cuts *despite* the Reagan military buildup, "wasteful expenditures that we were not going to match," he later insisted.[53] Improving East-West trade and achieving serious arms reductions meant that Gorbachev could not simultaneously reform Soviet society and carry on the Cold War as usual. Thus, in his "Fulton in reverse" speech of December 1988, Gorbachev astounded the world by announcing that over the next two years his country would unilaterally cut its military forces by 500,000 men and 10,000 tanks, approximately 10 percent of the total Soviet manpower and 25 per-

Meeting at Camp David, 1990. Secretary of State James Baker (b. 1930), Barbara Bush (b. 1925), President George Bush (b. 1924), Raisa M. Gorbachev (1936–1999). President Mikhail S. Gorbachev (b. 1932), Foreign Minister Eduard Shevardnadze (b. 1928), Assistant for National Security Affairs Brent Scowcroft (b. 1925), and Marshal Sergei Akhromeyev (1923–1991), left to right, at an informal meeting on June 2, 1990, at the Maryland presidential retreat. According to the historian Vladislav Zubok, Gorbachev "remained an incorrigible optimist as much as [Joseph] Stalin was a dark pessimist." (Courtesy of the Bush Presidential Materials Project)

cent of the Red Army's tanks in Eastern Europe.[54] In visits to Western Europe in spring and summer 1989, the charismatic Soviet leader called for a "common European home" that would eliminate "the probability of an armed clash."[55] Gorbachev quietly passed the word to East European officials that Soviet troops would not intervene to put down uprisings—the Brezhnev Doctrine was dead.

All too aware that "ideology had stopped working long ago," the veteran communist oligarchs of Eastern Europe heard the message and lost their nerve.[56] At year's end in Prague, a large sign tallied up the results: "Poland—10 Years / Hungary—10 Months / East Germany—10 Weeks / Czechoslovakia—10 Days / Romania—10 Hours."[57]

Not expecting Eastern Europe to self-destruct "like a beheaded Hydra," Gorbachev encouraged the process.[58] "Life punishes harshly anyone who is left behind in politics," he told cheering crowds in Berlin on October 7, the fortieth anniversary of the founding of the GDR.[59] Gorbachev advised East Germans to open the Wall to "avoid an explosion."[60]

Just as *glasnost* and *perestroika* accelerated the liberation of Eastern Europe, so too did the toppling of communist regimes have repercussions inside the Soviet Union. During late August 1989, a million citizens of Estonia, Latvia, and Lithuania linked arms to form a human chain four hundred miles long in protest against the fiftieth anniversary of the Nazi-Soviet Pact that had led to Stalin's annexation of the Baltic states. In December Lithuanian communists broke with the party leadership in Moscow. In March 1990 the Lithuanian Parliament declared formal independence from the Soviet Union, and Estonia's governing body renounced Soviet law. In May Latvia declared independence, and in July Ukraine proclaimed itself sovereign. Gorbachev tried to slow the surging separatist tide, but he promised not to use force.

Facing down the Soviet hard-liners who accused him of "sell-outs," Gorbachev went from confident master of events to bewildered victim of forces he

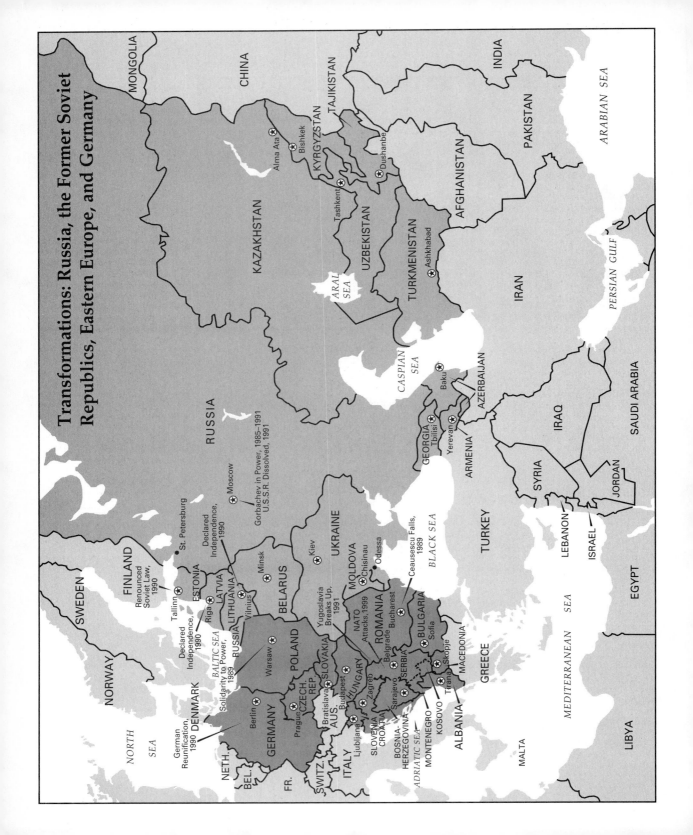

Transformations: Russia, the Former Soviet Republics, Eastern Europe, and Germany

MONGOLIA

CHINA

INDIA

ARABIAN SEA

PAKISTAN

TAJIKISTAN

KYRGYZSTAN

Bishkek

Alma Ata

Dushanbe

KAZAKHSTAN

Tashkent

UZBEKISTAN

AFGHANISTAN

TURKMENISTAN

Ashkhabad

IRAN

ARAL SEA

PERSIAN GULF

CASPIAN SEA

IRAQ

SAUDI ARABIA

Baku

AZERBAIJAN

GEORGIA

Tbilisi

Yerevan

ARMENIA

SYRIA

JORDAN

RUSSIA

Gorbachev in Power, 1985–1991
U.S.S.R. Dissolved, 1991

Moscow

St. Petersburg

Declared
Independence,
1990

LEBANON

ISRAEL

EGYPT

TURKEY

BLACK SEA

Ceausescu Falls,
1989

UKRAINE

Kiev

MOLDOVA

Chisinau

Odessa

FINLAND

Renounced
Soviet Law,
1990

SWEDEN

Tallinn

ESTONIA

Declared
Independence,
1990

Riga

LATVIA

BALTIC SEA

LITHUANIA

Vilnius

Minsk

BELARUS

RUSSIA

Solidarity to Power,
1989

NORWAY

Warsaw

POLAND

Yugoslavia
Breaks Up,
1991

NATO
Attacks, 1999

ROMANIA

Bucharest

Belgrade

BULGARIA

Sofia

Skopje

NORTH
SEA

DENMARK

German
Reunification,
1990

Berlin

GERMANY

Prague

CZECH.
REP.

Bratislava

SLOVAKIA

AUS.

Budapest

HUNGARY

Zagreb

SERBIA

Sarajevo

MACEDONIA

Tirana

GREECE

NETH.

BEL.

FR.

SWITZ.

ITALY

Ljubljana

SLOVENIA

CROATIA

BOSNIA-
HERZEGOVINA

MONTENEGRO

KOSOVO

ALBANIA

ADRIATIC SEA

MEDITERRANEAN
SEA

MALTA

LIBYA

had unleashed.[61] He won the Nobel Peace Prize but lost his country. By the end of 1991 the economically hobbled Soviet Union had disintegrated into sixteen squabbling independent nations. The Communist party disbanded, and the weakened central government recognized the independence of the three Baltic states. Russia declared its independence and with many of the republics formed the Commonwealth of Independent States in December. Boris Yeltsin's Russian government soon took over the Kremlin, the KGB, and the Soviet Foreign Ministry. Gorbachev stepped down. On Christmas day 1991, at 7:32 P.M. (Moscow time), the red hammer-and-sickle flag atop the Kremlin fluttered downward for the last time, soon replaced by the red, white, and blue Russian flag.

Indispensable Nation: Bush-Clinton-Bush and Post–Cold War Priorities

Studied nonchalance appeared to be the official U.S. reaction to the opening of the Berlin Wall. No special "Berlin task force" monitored events. President George Bush left "the impression that he didn't know quite what to do but was determined to do it prudently."[62] Appearances were partly deceiving. Although the process of reassessment took several months, by the time the Berlin Wall came down the Bush administration had made up its collective mind that Gorbachev was "for real" and that Washington would cooperate with Moscow in smoothing the transition to a post–Cold War world.[63] The quiescent response to events in Berlin was deliberate— a signal that the United States did not seek to exploit the upheavals in Eastern Europe.

Václav Havel (b. 1936) of Czechoslovakia. When this former Prague brewery worker, playwright, and political prisoner was sworn in as president of Czechoslovakia by communist officials who had jailed him twice, one observer said, "it was as though Kafka's Joseph K. had been retried and acquitted." Havel eloquently proclaimed that "all of us are responsible, each to a different degree, for keeping the totalitarian machine running. None of us is merely a victim, because all of us helped to create it together." When Czechoslovakia splintered in 1993, Havel became president of the Czech Republic. (Courtesy of the Bush Presidential Materials Project, photo by Carol T. Powers)

Prudence became the watchword. George Bush and his foreign-policy team were cautious about almost everything. Reactive, ad hoc, adaptable rather than ideologically zealous, conservative, fearful of doing the wrong thing, Bush prided himself on "my hyper-adrenalin, political instincts."[64] A former Yale University baseball captain, Bush could quote the famed Yankee catcher Yogi Berra: "I'll make plenty of mistakes, but I don't want to make the wrong mistakes."[65] Although many applauded the absence of Reaganite hyperbole and misstatement, others thought that Bush should do more to shape fast-moving events. Bush's conservatism had deep roots. Born in Massachusetts in 1924 to a wealthy, old Yankee family, Bush became a decorated navy pilot in World War II, attended Yale (B.A., 1948), and then moved to Texas, where he amassed greater wealth in the booming oil industry of the 1950s. After serving in Congress (1967–1971) and as ambassador to the United Nations (1971–1973), chair of the Republican National Committee (1973–1974), U.S. representative to China (1974–1975), and CIA director (1976–1977), he unsuccessfully challenged Ronald Reagan for the Republican presidential nomination in 1980 and then accepted second spot on the ticket. Always a loyalist, Bush supported Reagan's policies.

Bush selected a compatible secretary of state in James A. Baker III, a close friend from Texas who had skillfully managed his political campaigns. Like Bush, born (1930) to the elite, Baker had become a Texas corporate lawyer after graduation from Princeton University. The secretary's "pragmatic" problem-solving abilities lay in the art of "fixing," British prime minister Margaret Thatcher observed.[66] "This is a man I can accomplish things with," Soviet foreign minister Eduard Shevardnadze

McDonald's in Moscow. A worldwide symbol of capitalist bounty came to Moscow in early 1990 when McDonald's opened in Pushkin Square. McDonald's Canadian subsidiary had spent fourteen years negotiating a contract with Soviet authorities. Notwithstanding McDonald's outlets in Panama City and Belgrade, the journalist Thomas Friedman has posited the "Golden Arches Theory of Conflict Prevention" by claiming that no two countries with McDonald's restaurants have ever gone to war with one another. By 2003, 29,000 McDonald's in 120 countries were serving Big Macs to 16 billion customers per year. (McDonald's Corporation)

Nobel Peace Prize Winners, 1989–2003

1989	Dalai Lama, exiled leader of Tibet.
1990	Mikhail S. Gorbachev, Soviet leader who launched *glasnost and perestroika.*
1991	Dow Aung San Suu Kyi, Burmese woman who organized political opposition to the repressive military government in her country.
1992	Rigoberto Menchú, Guatemalan woman who struggled for the rights of indigenous peoples.
1993	Frederick W. de Klerk, president of South Africa, and Nelson Mandela, head of the African National Congress, who cooperated to end apartheid and initiate majority rule in South Africa.
1994	Yasir Arafat, Chair of the Palestine Liberation Organization, and Prime Minister Yitzhak Robin and Foreign Minister Shimon Peres of Israel, who negotiated a peace accord.
1995	Joseph Rotblat and the Pugwash Conferences on Science and World Affairs which Rotblat helped found in Great Britain, for their compaign against nuclear weapons.
1996	Carlos Filipe Ximenes Belo and José Ramos-Horta of East Timor, who worked for peace in East Timor.
1997	The International Campaign to Ban Landmines and its coordinator Jody Williams of the United States.
1998	John Hume, head of the Catholic Social Democrat and Labor Party, and David Trimble, leader of the Ulster Unionist Party, both of Northern Ireland, for their roles in reducing conflict in Northern Ireland.
1999	Doctors Without Borders for the organization's pioneering humanitarian work.
2000	Kim Dae Jung of South Korea who worked for democracy, human rights, and reconciliation with North Korea.
2001	The United Nations and Secretary General Kofi Annan for efforts at securing a more peaceful world.
2002	Jimmy Carter for efforts to find peaceful solutions to international conflicts.
2003	Shirin Ebadi, Iranian human rights activist and judge who worked to improve the rights of women and children.

Makers of American Foreign Relations Since 1989

Presidents	Secretaries of State
George H. W. Bush, 1989–1993	James A. Baker III, 1989–1992
	Lawrence Eagleburger, 1992–1993
William J. Clinton, 1993–2001	Warren M. Christopher, 1993–1997
	Madelaine K. Albright, 1997–2001
George W. Bush, 2001–	Colin L. Powell, 2001–

reported after their first meeting.[67] Reactive and conservative like Bush, Baker preferred to deal with the task at hand rather than with the opportunity ahead. National Security Adviser Brent Scowcroft worked easily with Baker and with Baker's successor, Lawrence Eagleburger, without the feuding of previous administrations. A former army general "with few edges and fewer enemies," Scowcroft acted as facilitator, broker, and coordinator, not as architect of policy.[68]

The election of former five-term Arkansas governor Willam J. Clinton in 1992 seemed to bring a different generational perspective to the White House. A graduate of Georgetown University and Yale Law School, Rhodes scholar, intern to Senator J. William Fulbright, Vietnam War protester and draft avoider, and at age forty-six the second youngest elected president, Clinton pledged during the campaign to maintain America's global leadership. Yet he came to Washington hoping to "keep foreign policy submerged" until he dealt with domestic priorities such as taxes, deficits, economic growth, health care, and welfare reform.[69] His campaign slogan, "It's the economy, stupid," might also have applied to Russian relations, for Clinton later regretted that "we should have done more—*much* more" to underwrite Russia's transition to a market economy.[70] Notwithstanding Clinton's election to a second term in 1996, Republican majorities in Congress after 1994 brought to the fore "a very strong element that is anti-internationalist, unilateralist, even isolationist—very xenophobic, extremely touchy," as one diplomat put it.[71] There followed cuts in foreign aid, delays in ambassadorial appointments, and the Senate's rejection of the Comprehensive Nuclear Test Ban Treaty in 1999. Also bedeviling the president in 1998–1999 were unsuccessful impeachment proceedings started by Congress after Clinton's apparent perjury over a sex scandal.

Sixty-seven-year-old Warren M. Christopher became Clinton's first secretary of state. An alumnus of the University of Southern California and Stanford Law School, this "lawyer's lawyer" had served as deputy secretary of state during the Carter years and had negotiated the release of American hostages from Iran in 1980–1981.[72] Disciplined, dignified, and dour ("Dean Rusk without the charisma"), Christopher proved an indefatigable negotiator.[73] Replacing Christopher for the second term was UN ambassador Madeleine Albright, a former assistant to Zbigniew Brzezinski and Georgetown University professor who resurrected Cold War certitudes. "My mindset is Munich," she proclaimed. "Most of my generation's is

Madeleine Korbel Albright (b. 1937).   Born in Prague, the daughter of a Czech diplomat who defected to the United States in 1948, Albright was raised as a Roman Catholic and apparently did not learn until she became secretary that her parents had been born Jewish and three of her grandparents had died in the Holocaust. The family experience of "being driven twice from our home in Czechoslovakia—first by Hitler and then by Stalin" greatly shaped her worldview. After attending Wellesley College (B.A. 1959) and earning a Ph.D. at Columbia University (1976), Albright served on the National Security Council staff during the Carter administration and later taught political science at Georgetown University. As Clinton's ambassador to the United Nations (1993–1996), she at first supported the UN's expanded role in international peacekeeping. Dubbed "Lady of Steel" by Russian diplomats, Secretary Albright was "willing to fire a missile at anybody," remarked one admirer. In her memoir *Madame Secretary* (2003), she summed up Clinton's foreign policy as "determined to do the right thing but in a tough-minded way." (Bureau of Public Affairs, U.S. Department of State)

Vietnam."[74] The blunt-speaking Albright quickly earned a hawkish reputation. "If we have to use force," she announced, "it is because we are America. We are the indispensable nation."[75]

Christopher maintained collegial relations with Clinton's national security affairs adviser, Anthony Lake. This Harvard and Princeton graduate had entered the Foreign Service in 1962 but resigned from Henry Kissinger's National Security Council staff in protest against the U.S. invasion of Cambodia in 1970. He served in the Carter State Department and later taught political science at Mount Holyoke College. Nicknamed "the submarine" for his aversion to publicity, Lake exhibited little of the egotism and manipulative qualities often found in White House advisers.[76] Asked to define a new grand strategy for the post–Cold War era, Lake in 1993 proposed the "enlargement" of free markets and democracies as a substitute for containment. Lake's equally self-effacing deputy and successor, Samuel R. "Sandy" Berger, a specialist in global monetary transactions, outlined more concrete goals for Clinton's second term—integrating Eastern and Western Europe without provoking Russia; liberal trade expansion; cooperation against "transnational threats" such as terrorism and drugs; and working toward a "strong, stable Asia Pacific Community."[77]

Clinton faced an increasingly disinterested public. As the U.S. economy improved in the 1990s, the president quickly recognized that the "new virility symbols are exports and productivity and growth rates" rather than nuclear missiles.[78] He skillfully lobbied through Congress the North American Free Trade Agreement

(NAFTA) (see page 487). In 1994, Washington signed the "Uruguay Round" of GATT accords liberalizing world trade. The agreement also created a new World Trade Organization, which Clinton hailed as promoting "a vision of economic renewal" for the United States and the world.[79] In pushing as well for U.S. participation in both a future Free Trade Area of the Americas and the Asia Pacific Economic Cooperation forum, the president preached the new "gospel of geoeconomics."[80] Clinton claimed credit for the economic upturn of the mid-1990s. "If you see a turtle sitting on top of a fence post," he would say, "it didn't get there by accident."[81] Worrisome, however, was the 1998 U.S. trade deficit of $233.4 billion—a record.

Nowhere was the primacy of geoeconomics more evident than in American initiatives, in conjunction with the International Monetary Fund (IMF), to act as the "drivewheel" of the international political economy.[82] When the Mexican peso collapsed in 1994, Washington fashioned an international financial bailout that included a $50 billion credit, with the United States ($20 billion) and the IMF ($18 billion) the chief backers. With the United States contributing 18 percent of the IMF's resources, the announcement of a $10.2 billion credit line to Russia during Boris Yeltsin's reelection campaign in 1996 clearly reflected Washington's policy preferences. The United States contributed $5 billion to an overall $41.5 billion loan to Brazil in fall 1998, provided that Brazil implement IMF-approved measures to balance its huge budget deficit.

During the Asian financial crisis of 1997–1998, U.S. Treasury officials, working through the IMF, orchestrated a financial package of $115 billion, in return for which Asian countries promised banking and budget reforms. With financial markets gyrating wildly in January 1998, Deputy Treasury Secretary Lawrence Summers jetted to China, Hong Kong, Thailand, Malaysia, Singapore, and South Korea to contain the "Asian economic flu."[83] Despite conservative criticism of IMF bailouts for encouraging irresponsible policies by governments and investors, and leftist complaints that IMF requirements undercut social welfare reforms and increased unemployment, Summers contrasted Clinton's successful rescue with the Coolidge-Hoover failure to assist the war-stricken European economies in the 1920s and 1930s. Clinton's successor reaffirmed the "Washington consensus" in support of free trade and globalization by pledging after the World Trade Center attacks that "we will defeat [the terrorists] by expanding and encouraging world trade."[84]

Fifty-four-year-old George W. Bush, eldest son of the ex-president, entered the White House in 2001. The younger Bush graduated from Yale University and Harvard Business School, drilled for oil in Texas, served as an Oval Office factotum to his father, and briefly owned the Texas Rangers baseball team. An excessive drinker in his youth, Bush embraced religion at age forty and modeled himself on Sam Houston, another famous Texan, whose victory over alcohol had been "transformative."[85] During the 2000 campaign, the self-described "gut player" and "clear-eyed realist" promised humility and "moral clarity."[86] "If we're a humble nation but strong, they'll welcome us," he said.[87]

Bush chose two African Americans, Colin Powell and Condoleezza Rice, as secretary of state and national security adviser, respectively. The "most politically adroit general since . . . Eisenhower," Powell had already served as national security adviser under Reagan and as chair of the Joint Chiefs of Staff under the elder Bush and

Clinton.[88] The Vietnam War veteran accepted Bush's appointment despite having castigated "the sons of the powerful" who had avoided service in Vietnam by wangling "slots in Reserves and National Guard units," as Bush had done.[89] A reluctant warrior, Powell often clashed with the hawkish defense secretary Rumsfeld, who once said that Powell's job "is to talk them to death, and mine is to hit them over the head."[90] Despite "all the Texas, Alamo macho that made Powell uncomfortable," his soldierly code of obedience kept him in "my own lane," as he put it.[91] Once, however, when told that his boss slept early and soundly, Powell retorted: "I sleep like a baby, too—every two hours I wake up screaming."[92] Rice, a former Stanford University political scientist, tried to coordinate between contending factions, leading Bush to compare her fondly to a "mother hen."[93] In her first year she regarded Iraq and terrorism as peripheral issues ("chump change") and wanted to "get on with the big issues: Russia, China, NATO expansion."[94] Priorities changed after 9/11.

Europe Transformed: Russian Disintegration, German Reunification, NATO Expansion, Balkan Hell

The senior Bush's initial response to Mikhail Gorbachev in early 1989 was to institute "the pause."[95] Hard-line "squeezers" who sought to harass the Kremlin into collapse still competed with "dealers" who thought the time ripe to negotiate with the Soviets on a whole spectrum of issues.[96] A national security review eventually endorsed the banal goal of "status quo plus."[97] "Our marching orders," noted the U.S. ambassador to Moscow: "Don't do something, *stand there!*"[98]

The turning point seems to have been Secretary Baker's visit to Moscow in early May 1989, when Gorbachev offered specific reductions for the Conventional Forces in Europe negotiations (CFE) that came close to NATO's proposals. A cordial meeting in September between Baker and Foreign Minister Shevardnadze in Jackson Hole, Wyoming, broke the impasse over Strategic Arms Reduction Talks (START) when the Soviets dropped their demand that the United States abandon its SDI research. Gorbachev prompted jubilation at the Malta summit in December by renouncing Soviet "bridgeheads in Cuba and Central America" and recognizing America's permanent role in Europe.[99] At the Washington summit of June 1990, Bush and Gorbachev signed agreements to improve trade, to reduce chemical weapons, to expand university undergraduate exchanges, and to negotiate deeper cuts in strategic arms.

Bush continued his special relationship with Gorbachev over the next two years. During Germany's rapid reunification Bush and Baker helped to ensure Soviet acquiescence by emphasizing that only Germany's membership in NATO could keep the new Germany from ever moving hostilely eastward. When Iraq invaded Kuwait in early August 1990, Washington and Moscow jointly called for an "international cutoff of all arms supplies" to Iraq.[100] Bush kept in telephone touch with Gorbachev throughout the Gulf crisis (see pages 491–494).

The relationship also paid off in the START-I accord signed in Moscow in July 1991. Bypassing hard-liners in their respective military bureaucracies, the two presidents ironed out the final compromises in personal correspondence. The treaty limited each nuclear superpower to 1,600 delivery vehicles and 6,000 strategic nuclear devices. Only 4,900 such devices could be carried by intercontinental ballistic missiles (ICBMs) or sea-launched missiles (SLBMs). The remaining 1,100 devices permitted under the treaty included warheads and bombs carried by cruise missiles and strategic bombers. The Americans and Soviets pledged to reduce their nuclear arsenals by half.

Then came the abortive coup against Gorbachev of August 18–21. The conspirators proved inept as they allowed Russian president Boris Yeltsin and his top aides to hole up in the Russian parliament building. With Gorbachev deprived of his "nuclear suitcase" for seventy-three hours, Bush ordered the National Security Agency to help Yeltsin make "secure calls" to Soviet military commanders.[101] By the fourth day the revolt had fizzled. Bush and his advisers understood that legitimate authority had shifted to Yeltsin and the Russian republic. Even though Bush saw a strong central government as essential for keeping control over the Soviet nuclear arsenal, he quickly adapted to a Yeltsin-led Russia, as evidenced by a $24-billion Western aid package to Russia. Just before Bush left office in January 1993, he and Yeltsin signed a START-II agreement in Moscow that provided for the cutting of nuclear warheads and bombs to 3,500 (U.S.) and 2,997 (Russia) and for eliminating all multiple warhead (MIRV) intercontinental missiles by the year 2003.

The Clinton administration also pursued a "Russia first" policy.[102] Viewing Yeltsin as "the personification of reform," Clinton's principal expert on Russian affairs, Strobe Talbott, urged "shock therapy" and tightfisted monetarism to create "the kind of Russia we want," despite high unemployment and the removal of safety nets for the Russian people.[103] Clinton regularly wrote Yeltsin detailed letters and gave Yeltsin unconditional support when he dissolved the Russian Duma (parliament) in October 1993 and then turned army guns on recalcitrant legislators.

Clinton's critics claimed that by sticking to Yeltsin "like Krazy Glue," he was repeating Bush's mistake with Gorbachev. Such criticism seemed valid, as Russia's gross national product fell by 20 percent during the first four years of reforms, as inflation ate up personal savings, as thousands of Russian troops failed to suppress a revolt in the breakaway republic of Chechnya in 1994–1996, as a Russian Mafia exploited a growing black market in Russia's cities, and as the economy became "dominated by seven banking houses in unholy collusion with remnants of the old state apparatus."[104] Notwithstanding several summit meetings with "my friend Bill," Yeltsin's failing health and inability to cope with Russia's economic crisis made him an unreliable partner.[105] Nor could more than $60 billion in Western loans since 1992 prevent the Russian economy from collapsing into a "Zaire with Permafrost."[106] Yeltsin's successor after 1999, former KGB officer Vladimir Putin, brought a modicum of stability to the Kremlin, and his immediate support for America's war against terrorism after 9/11 earned him the status of "soul brother" to President George W. Bush.[107] Despite Washington's unilateral withdrawal from the ABM Treaty in November 2001, Bush and Putin signed a treaty in May 2002 wherein each country promised to reduce its strategic nuclear warheads to between 1,700 and 2,200 by the year 2012. Given its own "terrorist" threat from Chechen separatists, Russia's continued alignment with the West under Putin seemed far

A United Germany in NATO.
Mikhail Gorbachev, remembering with many other Soviet citizens the German onslaught of World War II, at first resisted the U.S. push for a united Germany in the North Atlantic Treaty Organization (NATO). But Gorbachev recognized that he could not stop the realignment of European power. (By permission of Mike Luckovich and Creators Syndicate)

preferable to links "with the Iraqs and Irans, the North Koreas, and Cubas of the world," as a former Soviet diplomat put it.[108]

As for the new Germany, Chancellor Kohl put forward a plan for confederation between East and West Germany, thus making reunification "a matter for Germans to decide."[109] Although the elder Bush tried to influence the process by keeping an "arm around the shoulder" of the West Germans, the pell-mell rush of events upset predictions.[110] East Germany's citizens continued to migrate to the West at a high rate. Local government, public services, the economy, and civic morale in the GDR steadily eroded. In early 1990, West German politicians and parties built alliances in the East for an anticipated postelection unification. German reunification became "a kind of runaway freight train that nobody—East or West— seems able to contain."[111] The Kohl-supported center-conservative coalition won a landslide victory in the March GDR elections. Kohl initiated currency union and economic merger in July 1990. Then, in September, the four powers agreed to end their postwar occupation. In October the two Germanies formally reunited.

Washington backed Kohl's quest for rapid reunification because of the chancellor's continued commitment to NATO and European integration. Bush's advisers believed that "an unattached Germany on the loose in Central Europe" looked more threatening to Moscow "than one embedded in NATO."[112] In July 1990 Gorbachev dropped objections to a reunited Germany in NATO in exchange for a promise of Western economic aid and a smaller German army. Bush had "provided a skillful accompaniment" to European events, "but the main musicians were not in Washington; they were in Bonn and in Moscow."[113]

What Margaret Thatcher nervously called "the German juggernaut" stood in the center of Europe—nearly 80 million people between the Rhine and the Oder with a potential combined military force of 1.8 million and a strong export-driven economy.[114] Kohl moved quickly to dispel fears of "hob-nailed boots and spike helmets" by limiting future troop strength and pledging never to build nuclear, chemical, or biological weapons.[115] Germany became the dominant voice in the European Community (EC), pressed for aid to Eastern Europe and the former Soviet republics, and pledged billions of dollars (but not troops) to the Gulf War (see pages 491–493). Steadfast in their commitment to European integration and NATO, Germans chose the "European road" rather than "go their own special, isolated way," as Foreign Minister Hans-Dietrich Gentscher put it.[116] Bonn contributed to peacekeeping missions in the Persian Gulf, Somalia, Yugoslavia, and Afghanistan. Clinton established his friendliest European relationship with Chancellor Kohl, even kidding him about their sumo wrestler girths after one diplomatic banquet. Kohl's successor, Gerhard Schroeder, continued to cooperate by deploying troops and warplanes in the Kosovo conflict in 1999 (see page 481). Differences over Iraq in 2002–2003 temporarily "poisoned" relations, as Schroeder opposed Washington's unilateral "adventure" and his justice minister compared George W. Bush to the "Nazi Adolf."[117]

The conversion of the Economic Community into the European Union (EU) through ratification of the Maastricht Treaty in fall 1993 advanced integration in the west but ignored disintegration in the east, as European reluctance to intervene in Bosnia underscored the continent's continued disunity. In the Eastern European nations, Poland, Hungary, and Czechoslovakia (divided into Czech and Slovak republics in 1993) progressed most quickly in organizing market economies and democratic governments and looked to membership in the European Union. The other former Soviet republics and clients faced tremendous obstacles, not the least of which were smoldering ethnic and national rivalries long frozen by the Cold War. The European Union nonetheless established budgetary and financial criteria for entry that East European countries could not possibly meet. The EU Council decided in 1995 to establish a European Central Bank, issue a common currency (the "Euro"), and complete European Monetary Union by July 2002. In 2002 the EU did invite Estonia, Latvia, Lithuania, Cyprus, the Czech Republic, Hungary, Malta, Poland, Slovenia, and Slovakia to join, with full integration achieved in May 2004.

President Clinton announced in 1994 that the question of NATO expansion eastward was no longer "whether" but "when and how."[118] Despite Pentagon fears that expansion would "dilute" the alliance, National Security Affairs Adviser Lake and Assistant Secretary of State for European Affairs Richard Holbrooke "bludgeoned" the decision through.[119] Clinton publicly designated Poland, Hungary, and the Czech Republic as the first beneficiaries of NATO membership. European leaders proceeded to rubber-stamp Clinton's proposals, notwithstanding George F. Kennan's prediction that this "most fateful error" would "impel Russian foreign policy in directions decidedly not to our liking."[120] The three new members officially joined NATO in March 1999, and in March 2004 seven more countries joined the alliance: Estonia, Latvia, Lithuania, Slovenia, Slovakia, Romania, and Bulgaria. Russia accepted partnership status.

President William Jefferson Clinton (b. 1946) and Richard C. Holbrooke (b. 1941). Photographed in 1997, President Clinton (right) was using crutches because of a knee injury. Clinton's presidency subsequently suffered a serious blow when a sex scandal caused him to become only the second president to be impeached. A former aide to Henry Kissinger, Holbrooke served in Jimmy Carter's State Department and later as ambassador to Germany, assistant secretary of state for Europe, and chief diplomatic troubleshooter in the Balkans for the Clinton administration. After successfully negotiating the 1995 Dayton agreement, which ended the war in Bosnia, Holbrooke in 1998 helped to broker a temporary cease-fire in the southern Yugoslavian province of Kosovo, where Muslim ethnic Albanians battled against their Serbian overlords. A persistent negotiator, Holbrooke characterized diplomacy not as chess but "more like jazz—a constant improvisation on a theme." (White House Photo)

NATO had already demonstrated its ineffectiveness in dealing with the Balkan crisis. Despite CIA predictions that Yugoslavia would disintegrate into bloody ethnic violence, the Bush administration deferred to European allies when they recognized an independent Croatia and Slovenia in summer 1991. The United States "had no dog in that conflict," Secretary Baker famously remarked.[121] Serbia proclaimed a new Federal Republic of Yugoslavia (including Montenegro) and incited Serbs living in the other republics—especially in Bosnia—to take up arms. Croats and Muslims living in Bosnia declared an independent state. After Bosnia-Herzegovina became independent in April 1992, Serbs began to shell Sarajevo, the city where a 1914 assassination had triggered World War I. Bosnian Serbs grabbed territory and displaced Bosnian Muslims through the horrors of "ethnic cleansing," which included the mass rape of Muslim women by Serbian soldiers.[122]

The European Community imposed trade sanctions on Serbia-Montenegro and handed the issue over to the United Nations. Serbian militia seized approximately 70 percent of the Bosnian hinterland while systematically bombarding and starving the people of Sarajevo. France and Britain dispatched "Blue Helmets" (UN troops) to safeguard relief supplies but recoiled from military intervention. By 1993 perhaps as many as 150,000 people had perished.

Clinton inherited this "problem from hell."[123] Americans feared getting bogged down in age-old ethnic rivalries impervious to outside influence. When Clinton asked for military options, moreover, the Pentagon took note of the rugged terrain and reportedly told him: "We do deserts, we don't do mountains."[124] The pressure to act mounted during spring 1993. Ambassador Madeleine Albright asked: "What's the point of having this superb military . . . if we can't use it?" General Powell promised to "carry out any mission [he] was handed," but the "tough political goals had to be set first."[125] Although Clinton issued warnings to the Serbs and proclaimed America's humane concern, he lacked foreign support and a domestic consensus. "Getting creamed" in the media for doing too little, Clinton proposed lifting the arms embargo against Bosnia and launching air strikes against the Bosnian Serbs, but NATO balked because of its own peacekeeping forces on the ground.[126]

Starting in February 1994, NATO did carry out air strikes against Serbian planes in "no-fly" zones and against Serb artillery that was shelling Sarajevo. Bosnian Serbs nonetheless succeeded in displacing Muslims from much of Bosnia. When Bosnian Serbs in July seized the safe havens of Srebenica and Zepa and massacred thousands of Muslims within sight of UN peacekeepers, Washington flashed a green light, whereupon the Croatian army overran Serb-held territory in northwest Bosnia and NATO intensified its air attacks. Yugoslav president Slobodan Milosevic asserted his authority over the Bosnian Serbs and agreed to a cease-fire in October 1995.

A peace conference convened at Wright-Patterson Air Force Base in Ohio. Assistant Secretary Holbrooke "cajoled, harassed, and pressured" the presidents of Serbia, Bosnia, and Croatia into an agreement.[127] The Dayton Accords of December 14, 1995, retained a Croat-Muslim Federation and a Serb Republic within a single Bosnian state, with Sarajevo to remain as a multiethnic capital. The United States agreed to contribute 20,000 personnel as part of a 60,000-member NATO implementation force that would separate the parties and assist in reconstruction.

In 1999, Kosovo became the next Balkan crisis to spark international consequences. In this largely ethnic Albanian, Muslim province of Yugoslavia, President Milosevic ordered and his Serb forces implemented a brutal ethnic cleansing. When Milosovic rejected NATO's demands to halt the persecution and preserve Kosovo's autonomy, Clinton, faced with "a bunch of bad options," ruled out U.S. ground forces and chose air power.[128] The NATO bombing campaign, Papa Bear, unleashed even more cruelties in Kosovo, as the Serbs systematically burned, looted, raped, and forced 800,000 Muslim refugees to flee to neighboring Albania and Macedonia. Pounded by air attacks, encircled by hostile nations, and suffering a NATO-imposed oil embargo, Milosevic relented in early June under an agreement to withdraw his forces from Kosovo, permit the return of refugees, accept a NATO security presence, and grant greater autonomy to Kosovo. The International War Crimes Tribunal at The Hague indicted and later tried Milosevic and his top aides for war crimes against the peoples of Kosovo and Bosnia.

Despite disagreements over Kosovo, America's NATO allies invoked Article V for collective defense after the terrorist attacks of September 2001, but the Bush administration declined offers of military assistance in Afghanistan. The subsequent fissures over the invasion of Iraq, as well as the projected expansion of both NATO and EU membership, raised questions about the future of the Atlantic alliance: Could an expanded Europe, including Russia, forge a new partnership with the United States, or was divorce likely?

Hope and Tragedy in Africa

Nelson Mandela (b. 1918).
A founder of the African National Congress (ANC), this attorney and member of the Xhosa tribe was a young man when the white South African government jailed him in November 1962. Following his release from prison in February 1990, Mandela gave the black-nationalist salute. (Reuters/Bettmann)

As communism collapsed in Eastern Europe, apartheid began its descent in South Africa. As with change in Europe, the main impetus for reversing decades of social, political, and economic discrimination came from within—in this case, from within a nation of 35 million blacks, people of mixed race, and Asians ruled by 6.7 million whites. The United States played a modest role in nurturing the process.

One of the last diplomatic achievements of the Reagan administration, the mediation of the Namibia-Angola agreement in 1988, prepared the way. These accords established independence for Namibia and called for the staged withdrawal of Cuban and South African troops from Angola. South Africa's antiapartheid organizations now found it increasingly difficult to obtain outside assistance and weapons to mount guerrilla campaigns inside South Africa. Harsh measures by Pretoria's security police also neutralized most armed black nationalist activity. Thus when South Africa's white leaders, P. W. Botha and his successor, F. W. de Klerk, recommended negotiating an end to apartheid, beleaguered black activists responded positively.

The Bush administration pressed Pretoria to negotiate by maintaining economic sanctions against South Africa. From 1986 to 1989, sanctions cost South Africa $32 billion to $40 billion. When de Klerk became president in September 1989, reforms quickly followed. He lifted prohibitions against dissent, stopped executions, freed selected political prisoners, legalized banned organizations such as the African National Congress (ANC), and desegregated beaches and some housing areas. He offered to talk with black leaders to devise a new constitution in which blacks would share governing power. De Klerk also released the political prisoner and ANC leader Nelson Mandela in February 1990. When the gray-haired, seventy-one-year-old Mandela, the symbol of resistance to apartheid, walked out of a prison near Cape Town, he raised his right arm in the black nationalist salute.

Twenty-six parties entered serious talks for a democratic South Africa in early 1993. Four straight years of zero economic growth helped spur compromises. Agreement finally came in September 1993, and South Africa's first all-race elections were held in April 1994. The ANC handily won, and Mandela became South Africa's first black president. After the parliament drew up a constitution, the U.S. Congress repealed sanctions. Mandela and de Klerk shared the Nobel Peace Prize in 1993. Mandela's regime welcomed U.S. aid and investment. Firms that had previously disinvested, such as Ford, Honeywell, General Electric, Sara Lee, and Citibank, quickly returned, and Coca-Cola and Pepsi "zoomed" into South Africa to compete "in their global cola war."[129] By 1996 more than 500 U.S. companies were operating in South Africa, with a total asset value of $3.5 billion. A Truth and Reconciliation Commission attempted to heal the past. Overshadowing South Africa and much of sub-Saharan Africa, however, was the growing HIV/AIDS pandemic. In 2000, a U.S. National Intelligence Estimate predicted a "demographic catastrophe over the next twenty years" with possibly a quarter of southern Africa's population dying from the disease, thus raising the likelihood of "revolutionary wars, ethnic wars, genocides, and disruptive regime transitions."[130] With the percentage of adults living with the virus surging from 2 to 20 percent in the first years of the new century, President George W. Bush visited South Africa and Botswana in July 2003 and

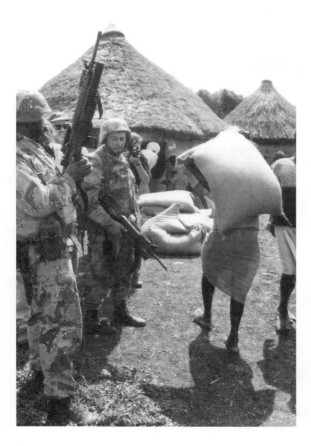

U.S. Marines in Somalia.
Armed with M-16A2 5.56mm rifles
equipped with grenade launchers,
these marines escorted relief workers
in December 1991 as they delivered
sacks of grain to a Somalian village
during Operation Restore Hope. "We
had a good plan for going in. But we
didn't have such a good plan for
getting out," one marine observed.
(Courtesy of U.S. Navy/Department of
Defense, Still Media Records Center)

pledged $15 billion in the global fight against AIDS. Because AIDS killed mainly adults between twenty and forty-five years old, Africa's children faced a grim future.

Ghastly television pictures of emaciated children had helped spur U.S. intervention in Africa a decade earlier. In December 1992, after he had lost the election to Clinton, George Bush senior ordered 28,150 U.S. troops to the Horn of Africa on a humanitarian mission to feed the starving population of civil-war-torn Somalia. Somalia ranked as "a tragedy of major proportions," Acting Secretary of State Eagleburger emphasized, "and, underline this, *one that we had to do something about.*"[131] Deploying troops despite Pentagon misgivings, Bush hoped that U.S. forces could restore order, move relief supplies to desperate Somalis, and then turn peacekeeping duties over to the United Nations.

Bush's Operation Restore Hope succeeded at first. U.S. marines landed with reporters and camera crews waiting on the beach. U.S. officials initiated cooperative relations with the most powerful Somali warlord, General Mohamed Farah Aidid, who controlled Mogadishu. Relief operations fed the hungry, and mediation efforts progressed, with clan leaders agreeing to negotiate national reconciliation.

President Clinton began to pull U.S. forces out. With starvation stopped, the United Nations tried to restore political stability to the country. The Clinton administration left 8,000 U.S. logistical troops in Somalia, along with a 1,000-person quick-reaction force. Such attempts at nation-building, even under UN auspices, aroused nationalist resentment. In mid-1993 Aidid's forces attacked Pakistani peacekeeping troops, killing twenty-four. U.S. forces under UN command tried unsuccessfully to kill Aidid in a "decapitation mission."[132]

In early October, nineteen U.S. Army Rangers died in a bloody firefight deep within "Indian country," as the U.S. commander put it.[133] A shocked Clinton watched television pictures of dead U.S. soldiers being dragged through the streets of Mogadishu by seemingly jubilant Somalis. "I can't believe we're being pushed around by these two-bit pricks," he told aides. Clinton quickly retreated from nation building in Somalia, convinced that public opinion opposed the sacrifice of "one American life."[134] He withdrew all U.S. forces by April 1994, leaving the mission to the UN. Critics identified a new syndrome—"Vietmalia, combining *Vietnam* and *Somalia*."[135] Somalia remained tumultuous.

Just a month after U.S. personnel departed Somalia, mass killing erupted in the central African republic of Rwanda. A suspicious April 1994 plane crash that killed the presidents of Rwanda and Burundi, both members of the dominant Hutu majority, touched off massacres of the Tutsi minority that left more than 800,000 dead in eighty-nine days. With macabre television images reinforcing American stereotypes about "backward" and "savage" Africans, the Clinton administration resisted proposals for vigorous intervention, concentrated on evacuating U.S. citizens and reducing UN peacekeeping forces, and even instructed officials to avoid the term *genocide*.[136] "I was sorry about the Rwandans," said the State Department officer in charge, "but my job was to get our folks out."[137] Not until the massacres had ended did Clinton order U.S. troops in July to secure the airport in Kigala so that relief supplies could flow directly to Rwanda and stem the flood of refugees into neighboring Burundi, Tanzania, and Zaire.

The Rwanda massacres embarrassed Washington ("not even a sideshow—a no-show," confessed Anthony Lake).[138] On visiting Africa in 1998, President Clinton apologized for not "calling these crimes by their rightful name: genocide."[139] Washington helped create the African Crisis Response Initiative, designed to assist African countries to organize joint forces for rapid intervention in the future. Despite such plans, further fighting flared between Hutus and Tutsis in Burundi in 1996, and the next year a revolt, backed by Rwanda, Uganda, and Eritrea, toppled long-time U.S. client Mobutu Sese Seko in Zaire (renamed the Democratic Republic of Congo). "Caught with our pants down," Washington recognized the new government of Laurent Kabila, whose troops promptly slaughtered thousands of Hutu *genocidaires* exiled in the eastern provinces.[140] Over the next five years the Democratic Republic of the Congo suffered some 3.3 million "excess deaths" from combat and from "easily treatable diseases and malnutrition" exacerbated by the country's collapsing health system and economy.[141] The second Bush administration disingenuously blamed the United Nations for having "failed to act once again."[142]

U.S. relations also fared badly with Sudan, whose Islamist regime temporarily sheltered Osama bin Laden during the mid-1990s. Washington fired cruise missiles at a Sudanese pharmaceutical plant in August 1998 in retaliation for deadly terrorist attacks by Al-Qaeda on U.S. embassies in Kenya and Tanzania. American missiles also struck targets in Afghanistan, apparently just missing bin Laden. Skeptics, however, depicted these strikes as Clinton's "greatest foreign policy blunder," insinuating that the president, facing impeachment, was following a *"Wag the Dog"* strategy—so named for a contemporary movie in which a president foments a phony war to deflect attention from a sex scandal.[143]

Elsewhere in Africa the U.S. record was mixed. Washington maintained close ties with General Sani Abachi's repressive military regime in Nigeria, which exported $6.3 billion in oil, gas, and other commodities to the United States in 1997, making it the fifth largest supplier of foreign oil. Abachi's death in 1998 began a tumultuous transition to civilian rule. Although civil wars destabilized former Cold War clients such as Liberia, Sudan, Somalia, and Zaire (Congo), recent targets of U.S. assistance (South Africa, Ghana, Ethiopia, Mozambique, Uganda, and Mali) made significant political and economic progress in the 1990s. In 1996 the Botswanan ambassador hosted a dinner in Washington to give thanks for $203 million in U.S. aid, sent over three decades, which enabled his country to "graduate" from the foreign-assistance rolls.[144] That same year American trade with the eleven countries of southern Africa totaled $9 billion, the equivalent of U.S. trade with Russia and former Soviet republics. During a six-nation visit in March 1998, President Clinton hailed the "beginning of a new African Renaissance," but Congress killed his proposed Africa Trade and Investment Act.[145] Despite combined economic growth rates of 2.9 percent in 2002 (higher than the world average) and notwithstanding plans for continentwide cooperation through the new African Union, Africa's future depended on solutions to the AIDS crisis and ending civil wars. Nelson Mandela's condemnation of the war against Iraq "in no uncertain terms" indicated that the Bush administration's obsession with terrorism risked a dangerous replay of Cold War disregard for African priorities.[146] The belated and token intervention of U.S. marines into war-torn Liberia and their quick withdrawal in October 2003 underscored Washington's ambivalence.

Markets, Invasions, and Implosions in Latin America

The first Bush administration only slowly reversed past policies toward Latin America. The president himself held traditional proprietary North American ideas about the region, and he had helped devise and administer Reagan's interventionism. The Western Hemisphere seemed to be advancing from military regimes to popularly elected governments (as in Argentina, Chile, and Brazil). Narcotics continued to flow into the profitable U.S. marketplace despite expensive antidrug operations; the Latin American debt, rampant inflation, and sluggish growth rates imperiled economies; a graying Fidel Castro still bedeviled Washington; an escalating crisis with Panama threatened further instability in the Caribbean. But after the Sandinistas lost elections in 1990 to U.S.-backed Violeta Barrios de Chamorro and her National Opposition Union, the civil war in Nicaragua finally ended. The civil war in El Salvador was stopped under a UN-brokered agreement in 1992, leaving Central America with staggering costs of reconstruction and reconciliation and tens of thousands dead. Latin America's economic linkage with the United States nonetheless remained strong: in 1990 40 percent of the region's exports flowed to the United States.

Bush's and Clinton's sponsorship of NAFTA, as well as the agreement to implement a Free Trade Area of the Americas (FTAA) by 2005, held the promise of a more prosperous Latin America. "A rising tide lifts all boats," Clinton said at the Summit of the Americas in 1994, whereupon the prime minister of Barbados reminded him that "a rising tide can . . . overturn small boats."[147] Disagreements over farm subsidies, as well as financial crises in Brazil and Argentina, slowed integration so that only a U.S.-Chile free-trade agreement was achieved by late 2003.

Debts posed a major obstacle to economic stability. In 1990, Latin American countries owed more than $400 billion (total Third World debt stood at more than $1.3 trillion). Brazil, Mexico, and Argentina owed the most, and much of it to U.S. banks. The debt crisis hurt the United States. As debtors struggled to meet debt-service payments, they trimmed their imports; U.S. exports then slumped by billions of dollars, and North American jobs were lost. Latin migrants trying to escape grinding poverty pressed against U.S. immigration gates. The narcotics trade expanded as poor farmers and laborers turned to lucrative drug crops for income. Because health services and educational outlays had to be reduced and economic-development projects scuttled throughout Latin America, political unrest spread.

Secretary of the Treasury Nicholas F. Brady instituted a program in 1989 that provided for some debt relief and lower interest rates. Several agreements between commercial banks and Latin American governments, and backed by the International Monetary Fund, cut debt burdens by about one-third. In return, Latin American debtors accepted market-opening requirements—controlling inflation, attracting foreign investment, and reducing trade restrictions. As Latin American governments in the early 1990s instituted reforms to improve "investor confidence" and advanced regional economic integration based on a "free trade" philosophy, "swelling flows of foreign direct investment" helped ease the debt crisis and raised hopes that the hemisphere's groaning poverty and environmental deprivation could find relief.[148] Spurred by NAFTA and planning for the Free Trade Area of the Americas, Latin American exports grew from an average 4.5 percent during the 1980s to 9.9 percent in the 1990s, while foreign investments leaped from $6.7 billion in 1990 to $22.4 billion in 1996. Political corruption and a growing fiscal crisis, however, triggered an "implosion" in Argentina in December 2001 when that country defaulted on its $140 billion foreign debt; the financial meltdown threatened to infect Uruguay, Paraguay, and even Brazil.[149] Latin America in 2002 suffered its worst economic performance in two decades, with a negative growth rate of 1.1 percent. Not until the summer of 2003—after the war against Iraq that several Latin American countries opposed—did the Bush administration encourage the IMF to restructure Argentina's debt repayments.

When President Carlos Salinas of Mexico proposed a free trade agreement with Washington in 1990, he reversed more than a century of "building walls to keep out U.S. goods, investment, and influence."[150] Embraced by the Bush administration, signed by Canada, Mexico, and the United States in 1992, approved by Congress in

1993, the resulting North American Free Trade Agreement created the world's largest free trade bloc, comprising 370 million people with a combined gross domestic product of $6.5 trillion. President Clinton subsequently negotiated side agreements with Mexico to protect workers' rights and environmental standards, and he mobilized an effective lobbying effort that included former presidents and secretaries of state. Notwithstanding a Mexican financial crisis in 1994, bilateral trade rose by $17 billion annually between 1993 and 1996, with a $7 billion net surplus for U.S. exports. Statistics revealed 100,000 U.S. jobs lost due to NAFTA by 1997, but unemployment rates reached historic lows as the revived U.S. economy created 2.5 million new jobs per year in the mid-1990s. U.S. direct investments in Mexico averaged $3.1 billion annually after 1994. Mexico even paid back, with interest, $13.5 billion loaned by the U.S. Treasury in 1995 as part of the $50 billion financial package to rescue the Mexican peso. Despite continuing bilateral problems with drugs and illegal immigration, NAFTA promised to expand an already burgeoning "Mexamerica," the 2,000-mile border society where two cultures blended "like reluctant lovers in the night, embracing for fear that letting go could only be worse."[151]

THE AMERICAN ADDICTION

The American Addiction. This political cartoon from a Honduran newspaper reflected the Latin American perspective that the drug crisis in the United States stemmed not from the production of cocaine in Latin America but from the consumption of dangerous drugs in North America. Could the cartoonist also be suggesting that the drug trade was destroying Latin America? (McDonald/Diario El Heraldo, San Pedro Sula, Honduras)

Many Americans believed that the flourishing drug trade endangered international stability and hence U.S. security. President Clinton called narcotrafficking "an unusual and extraordinary threat to . . . national security."[152] Between 1985 and 1995 the world production of opium and coca leaves roughly tripled, as drug prices dropped and U.S. prisons filled to capacity with people convicted of drug-related crimes. With 489 million people, 128 million passenger cars, 11.5 million trucks, and 2.2 million railroad cars passing through U.S. border inspections per year, actually finding drugs was "like trying to catch minnows at the base of Niagara Falls."[153]

The United States spent upwards of $3 billion a year in a supply-side war against foreign sources and middlemen. In 1986, for example, American troops and army Blackhawk helicopters helped the Bolivian military swoop down on jungle cocaine laboratories. Under Bush and Clinton, U.S. counternarcotics aid flowed to the Andean nations of Peru, Bolivia, and Colombia, but Washington also increasingly stressed the importance of staunching demand inside the United States itself. This apparent change stemmed in part from pressure from Latin Americans who feared new U.S. interventionism; they had grown bitter over the drug issue, because they contended that North Americans unfairly blamed them for the problem. "No one is forcing the gringos to snort coke, so let Washington deal with it," they seemed to say.[154] For example, an estimated 72 million Americans (34 percent of the population) had used illegal drugs, while only 3.9 percent of Mexico's population had done the same.

Mexico had become a major source of marijuana and heroin and a major highway for South American cocaine shipments destined for the United States. From Bolivia, Peru, and Colombia came coca, which was processed into cocaine and crack. (Tons of opium/heroin also entered the United States from the "Golden Triangle" of Burma, Thailand, and Laos and the "Golden Crescent" of Iran, Afghanistan, and Pakistan.) Any nation that came into contact with the drug trade became exposed to corruption, drug addiction, violence, and death. Illegal drug money bribed politicians in some Latin American states. In Colombia the sharpshooters of the militarized drug cartels assassinated judges, journalists, police officers, and public officials. "Narcoterrorism" destabilized Peru: Leftist guerrillas called the *Sendero Luminoso* (Shining Path) used the drug trade to help finance their rebellion.[155] Drug profits, not reinvested in long-term development, distorted regional economies; the "laundering" of "narcodollars" befouled banking systems. Colombia took courageous steps to defeat the drug lords of the Medellín and Cali cartels, only to produce the "hydra effect" of more dispersed operations and new drug fiefdoms in Mexico, Venezuela, and Brazil.[156] By 1998, 75% of the cocaine entering the United States arrived through Mexico. Of the five to seven tons of illegal drugs crossing the southwest border every day, authorities confiscated only an estimated 15 percent.

The arrest in 2002 of the principal Mexican drug lord Benjamin Arellano Felix did little to stem the traffic. "It would stop being a business if the United States didn't want drugs," said Arellano.[157] Nor did Washington's direct participation in Plan Colombia reap much benefit. Despite $700 million per year in U.S. military aid after 1998, the Colombian government's war against narco-trafficking guerrillas had the reverse effect of increasing the production of coca and poppies (heroin). Farther south, the triborder region of Paraguay, Argentina, and Brazil had become by 2003 "the world's new Libya," where drug lords and terrorists with "widely disparate ideologies" met to "swap tradecraft."[158] Narcotics had become "a shared tragedy for both halves of the hemisphere."[159]

The drug issue became central to Panamanian–United States relations. After the United States signed the 1978 canal treaties with Panama's military government (see pages 417–418), the Carter administration tried to nudge the country toward civilian rule. But the military solidified its hold. In 1983 General Manuel Antonio Noriega took power. As the intelligence chief of the Panama Defense Forces, he had come to know Panama's thriving world of drug trafficking. As Panamanian banks laundered drug money, Noriega became a millionaire by cutting deals with Colombia's cocaine barons. By the late 1980s his dictatorial rule and drug-running had stirred anger in North Americans eager to blame the swaggering Panamanian for U.S. drug problems.

Little did the American people know that official Washington and Noriega had long been covert allies. As a young officer in the 1960s, Noriega received regular payments from the CIA; during the 1980s he helped train the *contras*. Thus Washington turned a blind eye to his drug trafficking until 1988, when two Florida grand juries indicted the dictator for shipping Colombian drugs to the United States. Washington froze Panamanian assets in the United States and offered Noriega a safe haven in Spain; the defiant Panamanian strongman stirred anti-*yanqui* rallies in the fall of 1989. Harassing incidents in Panama, including the wife of a U.S. soldier allegedly "threatened with rape," soon grabbed headlines.[160] "This president is going to do something," snapped Bush, who ordered an invasion.[161] General Powell called Noriega "a dope-sniffing, voodoo-loving thug."[162]

In the early hours of December 20, 1989, Operation Just Cause commenced. The invasion of Panama by 22,500 troops proved a violent success. A billion dollars' worth of property in Panama City was damaged and 516 Panamanians died. Only 23 American soldiers perished. The resistance had been greater than anticipated. Pandering to racial stereotypes, the U.S. press misreported lurid details about Noriega: "Vats of blood. Animal entrails. . . . More than 100 pounds of cocaine."[163] The cocaine turned out to be tamales. When U.S. troops finally located Noriega in the Vat-

General Colin Powell's Briefing on Panama. Born in New York City in 1937, Powell earned a B.S. degree from the City University of New York before he began his military career. In 1987–1989 the army general served as assistant to the president for national security affairs, and in 1989 he was named chair, Joint Chiefs of Staff. Here he gives a briefing, on December 20, 1989, shortly after U.S. troops attacked Panama. An admiring Japanese journalist compared Powell to a samurai warrior who combined taciturnity with stoicism. He became secretary of state in 2001. (Department of Defense)

ican Embassy in Panama City, the psychological operations team resorted to rock-and-roll music boomed over loudspeakers to induce surrender. Among the musical messages played were "Born to Run," "Crying in the Chapel," "I Fought the Law and the Law Won," and "We Gotta Get Outta This Place."[164] On January 4, 1990, Manuel Antonio Noriega became a federal prisoner in Miami awaiting trial on drug charges. Foiled in his efforts to reveal CIA secrets and embarrass President Bush, Noriega was convicted of cocaine smuggling in April 1992 and went to prison.

Bush's popularity shot up after the military invasion of Panama. Democrats and Republicans alike cheered even though Bush had not consulted Congress. Critics, however, lambasted the administration for violating the UN Charter and the Organization of American States Charter, which contain nonintervention provisions. The OAS censured the United States, and only a U.S. veto prevented passage of a UN Security Council resolution condemning the invasion. The invasion nonetheless accustomed Latin Americans and the U.S. public to the military's growing role in the drug war—"the only one [war] we've got," as one general put it.[165]

The U.S. military also intervened in poverty-stricken Haiti to restore a deposed president. Elected in 1990, the Reverend Jean-Bertrand Aristide fled nine months later when Haitian military leaders resisted his plans for demilitarization and social reform. With Aristide exiled to the United States, a junta headed by General Raul Cedras terrorized and tortured political opponents. As thousands of Haitians tried to escape on makeshift boats, both Bush and Clinton, fearing an immigration crisis, denounced the junta but ordered the U.S. Coast Guard to turn back refugees seeking asylum. "A total fuck-up," recalled Anthony Lake, as the Pentagon hesitated to use force so soon after the Somalia debacle, and the Congressional Black Caucus charged racism because Washington granted asylum to Cubans fleeing Castro but not to Haitians.[166]

Despite strong public opposition to intervention, Clinton decided to deploy force in late summer 1994. With a 20,000-strong invasion force set to land within thirty-six hours, a negotiating team headed by Jimmy Carter and General Colin

Cuban Refrain. The cartoonist Mike Peters captures the words of nine U.S. presidents who thought they could overthrow Cuba's defiant leader. Forty years after his accession to power in 1959, an unrepentant Fidel Castro still vowed "Socialism or death" and accused Wall Street capitalists of playing "Russian roulette" with the world economy. The price of free markets, he claimed, is paid in human misery, child labor, prostitution, and drug traffic. (© 1994 Mike Peters/Dayton Daily News)

Powell persuaded the junta to step down to avert bloodshed. Operation Uphold Democracy disarmed the Haitian military, returned Aristide to power, failed to create "a secure and stable environment," then left on schedule in April 1995.[167] "Nine million Haitians [living] off our shores, . . . all want to be your neighbor," the mission commander warned.[168] With Haiti's living standards remaining the poorest in the hemisphere, another coup in early 2004 prompted the U.S. once again to restore order.

As for Cuba, the end of the Cold War caused Castro's Cuba to retrench but not repent, as it repatriated its military forces from abroad and began to adapt to world markets. While hosting an international symposium on the history of the missile crisis in 1992, Castro announced that Cuba would no longer give military support to revolutionary movements. Cuba was "desovietized forever."[169] The end of Soviet subsidies produced tremendous economic hardship in Cuba, thereby increasing the number of Cubans fleeing in makeshift rafts across the Florida Straits. After thirty-seven refugees drowned when Cuban authorities sank their hijacked boat in August 1994, rioting in Havana prompted Castro to denounce the United States for encouraging hijackers; henceforth Cuban police would not stop people from leaving so long as they did not hijack boats or planes. More than 35,000 departed in the next month.

Recalling the Mariel boatlift of 1980, the president consulted with the conservative anti-Castro Cuban American National Foundation (CANF), which persuaded Clinton to "demagnetize" the United States by barring entry to the *balseros* (rafters).[170] Clinton then reached an agreement with Havana that increased to 20,000 the legal immigrants permitted into the United States annually, required Cuba to halt illegal immigration, and placed refugees under detention at the Guantánamo naval base and in Panama. A subsequent agreement in May 1995 allowed the detainees to enter the United States. To discourage a new exodus, Washington promised to return all future boat people to Cuba.

Cooperation between Cuban and U.S. authorities in resolving the refugee problem ended abruptly. Three civilian aircraft piloted by a Cuban-American group called Brothers to the Rescue flew toward Cuba in Feburary 1996 in search of boat people. Because the Brothers organization had been warned about previous violations of Cuban air space, Cuban MiGs gave chase and shot down two of the planes, killing four crew members. "This is not *cojones* [testicles]," Madeleine Albright lectured Havana, "this is cowardice."[171]

Congress quickly passed the Helms-Burton bill by large majorities, and Clinton signed it into law on the eve of the Florida primary. The legislation not only allowed U.S. citizens (including naturalized Cuban-Americans) to sue foreign companies that did business using properties confiscated by the Castro regime; it also barred any relaxation of sanctions until a democratic government ruled in Cuba. "Adiós, Fidel," bragged Senator Jesse Helms of North Carolina.[172] Although such blatant Yankee economic interference did discourage foreign investment, Mexico, Canada, and the EU protested the measure for interrupting their lucrative trade with and investment in Cuba. When the EU claimed that Helms-Burton violated the rules of the new World Trade Organization, Clinton temporarily suspended suits against foreign firms while maintaining the punishing embargo. Castro continued to rail about North America's "canned culture" invasion that "transmits poisonous messages . . . to all families, to all homes, to all children."[173]

Clinton instituted a modest thaw in early 1999 by authorizing U.S. citizens to send at least $1,200 a year to Cuban families, increasing passenger flights to and from Cuba, and allowing food sales to nongovernmental enterprises on the island. Additional Clinton reforms ran afoul of the legal-political controversies surrounding six-year-old refugee Elian Gonzalez, rescued off the Florida coast and eventually returned to his Cuban father in spring 2000 against the angry protests of Cuban Americans. Florida's decisive role in George W. Bush's disputed electoral victory that fall returned Cuban policy to Republican hard-liners. "A façade [and] all cosmetics," sniffed Washington when Castro offered to cooperate after 9/11 in the war against terrorism and in the housing of Taliban and Al-Qaeda prisoners at the Guantánamo Bay naval base.[174] In fall 2003, with a political eye toward the Cuban-American vote in the next presidential election, Bush tightened sanctions against Castro, prompting a Cuban diplomat to counter that Bush should "stop acting like a cowboy."[175] The U.S. Chamber of Commerce and key corporations nonetheless continued to press Washington to end the embargo.

Mideast Quagmires: Gulf Wars and the Arab-Israeli Peace Process

The invasion of Kuwait by Iraq on August 2, 1990, led to a significant exercise of U.S. power. Instead of paying back billions of dollars in loans received from Kuwait during the eight-year war between Iran and Iraq, Iraq's dictator, Saddam Hussein used old territorial claims and invasion to annex Kuwait in the name of all "zealous Arabs who believe in one Arab nation."[176] Washington feared that Hussein might next invade Saudi Arabia and thus control 40 percent of the world's oil. Exhorted

World Orders, Old and New.
In 1991, as the United States fought the Persian Gulf War, the cartoonist Jim Borgman linked past (Theodore Roosevelt) and present (George H. W. Bush) to suggest that the United States still saw itself as—and acted like—an international policeman. Not much had changed, it seemed to many Americans, since the early twentieth-century days of the Roosevelt Corollary and the Big Stick. (Jim Borgman, Cincinnati Enquirer © 1991. Reprinted with special permission of King Features Syndicate)

by Prime Minister Margaret Thatcher not "to go wobbly," the senior Bush pledged: "This will not stand."[177] He organized an international coalition of thirty countries to liberate Kuwait. By November the UN had imposed economic sanctions and demanded Iraqi withdrawal. Bush initially sent some 200,000 American troops as part of a multinational peacekeeping force to defend Saudi Arabia (Operation Desert Shield). In early November he increased the expeditionary force to more than 500,000; contingents from other allied countries brought the troop level to 700,000. The Security Council commanded Iraq to evacuate Kuwait by January 15, 1991, or else face military attack.

"Maybe I'll turn out to be a Teddy Roosevelt," mused Bush in the first weeks of the crisis.[178] "It must be done as massively and decisively as possible," the Vietnam-conscious JCS chair Powell advised.[179] Bush did not announce the offensive buildup until after the November mid-term elections. UN sanctions cut off 90 percent of Iraq's imports and 97 percent of its exports. Iraq replied that it would consider withdrawal from Kuwait only if the United States forced Israel to relinquish its occupied territories.

When Bush asked for authorization to send U.S. troops into combat under a UN resolution, Congress debated for four days. Senator George Mitchell of Maine cited the risks: "an unknown number of casualties and deaths, billions of dollars spent, a greatly disrupted oil supply and oil price increases, the possible long-term American occupation of Iraq, long-lasting Arab enmity against the United States, a possible return to isolationism at home."[180] Senator Robert Dole of Kansas rebutted that "Saddam . . . may think he's going to be rescued, maybe by Congress."[181] Despite mass protests chanting "hell no, we won't go—we won't fight for Texaco," a majority in both houses narrowly approved Bush's request to use force.[182]

Burning Oil Fields in Kuwait.
Months after Operation Desert Storm freed Kuwait from Iraqi rule, oil fields blazed, creating an environmental disaster. Some oil facilities were hit in the fighting. Retreating Iraqi forces also torched Kuwait's oil industry. Soot and unburned crude oil billowed into the air and then polluted soils, vegetation, and Persian Gulf waters. (U.S. Navy/Department of Defense, Still Media Records Center)

Described by one critic as a "Pentagon trade show with live ammunition," Operation Desert Storm began with a spectacular aerial bombardment of Iraq and Kuwait on January 16.[183] For five weeks satellite television coverage via Cable News Network (CNN) enabled Americans to watch Tomahawk cruise missiles hit Iraqi targets and U.S. Patriot missiles intercept Iraqi Scud missiles. Bush and Baker masterfully kept the coalition intact, persuading Israel not to retaliate after Iraqi Scud attacks and keeping Gorbachev "steadfast" as allied bombs devastated Russia's erstwhile client. Finally, on February 23, hundreds of thousands of allied ground forces invaded Kuwait and eastern Iraq. Iraqi troops scrambled to leave Kuwait, blowing up as many as 800 oil wells as they retreated. Allied aircraft flew hundreds of sorties along the "Highway of Death" from Kuwait City to Basra. After only one hundred hours of fighting on the ground, Iraq accepted a UN-imposed cease-fire. An exultant Bush proclaimed: "By God, we've kicked the Vietnam syndrome once and for all."[184]

Estimates vary, but Iraq's casualties numbered at least 25,000 military dead. U.S. forces suffered only 148 deaths and 458 wounded, but 140,000 service personnel were exposed to low levels of the nerve agent sarin; by 2002 more than half of Gulf War veterans had sought medical care or filed disability claims. The Iraqi people, "relegated to a preindustrial age," had to battle cholera and typhoid fever.[185]

The Gulf War was "like teenage sex," one senator brashly quipped. "We got in too soon and out too soon."[186] Bush did not order troops to Baghdad to capture Saddam Hussein because he wanted to maintain Iraq as buffer to still-hostile Iran.

Bush hoped that the Iraqi military or disgruntled associates in the Ba'ath party would oust Saddam in a coup. Yet when Kurds in northern Iraq and Shi'ites in the south rebelled, Bush did little to help. Saddam Hussein crushed both rebellions. Public pressure persuaded Bush to send thousands of U.S. troops to northern Iraq, where the United Nations designated a "no-fly" zone prohibiting Iraqi aircraft from attacking Kurds. Hussein's survival left a sour taste for Americans who wanted a clearcut victory.

Under Security Council Resolution 687, Iraq had to accept the inviolability of the boundary with Kuwait; tolerate the presence of UN peacekeepers on its borders; and fully disclose all chemical, biological, and nuclear weapons, including missiles, and cooperate in their destruction. Bush had boasted during the air war that "our pinpoint attacks have put Saddam out of the nuclear bomb-building business for a long time to come."[187] What allied bombs had missed, UN inspectors tried to locate. Saddam Hussein's scientists and engineers had built nuclear facilities that were within months of producing nuclear weapons when the Gulf War began. Inspectors found and destroyed more than 100 Scud missiles, 70 tons of nerve gas, and 400 tons of mustard gas.

Saddam Hussein nonetheless continued to bedevil Washington. In retaliation for an apparent Iraqi assassination plot against former president Bush, Clinton ordered missile attacks on Baghdad in 1993. He sent 36,000 troops to Kuwait the following year to deter Iraqi military movements southward, then bombed Iraq again in 1996 when Hussein crushed a Kurdish revolt in northern Iraq. UN sanctions to force removal of all weapons of mass destruction reportedly contributed to the deaths of many Iraqi civilians, including as many as half a million children. Asked about the human costs, Secretary Albright replied that "the price is worth it."[188] Baghdad played a six-year shell game by interfering with UN inspectors as they searched for chemical weapons and biological stores of anthrax, botulinum, and aflatoxin. "When we go to a site," the American UN inspector Scott Ritter declared to his colleagues, "we're gonna raise our tails and we're gonna spray urine all over their walls."[189] The Iraqi government protested UN inspection teams' zealotry and their sharing of intelligence data with U.S. officials—information later used to target sites for U.S. air strikes. In February and November 1998 the United States rushed forces to the Persian Gulf, each time deferring attack when Iraq promised complete access for inspectors.

When Saddam Hussein again stiff-armed UN inspectors on the eve of Clinton's impeachment in December 1998, the president launched Operation Desert Fox, a joint Anglo-American bombing campaign aimed at "degrading" Iraq's military capabilities.[190] Several hundred Tomahawk missiles (more than in the Gulf War) fired over a period of four days set back Iraq's weapons program by "a year or more," but also provoked criticism from China, Russia, and France.[191] Until Clinton left office he weighed options for "regime change" in Iraq, but the war in Kosovo and renewed violence between Israelis and Palestinians in autumn 2000 diverted his attention.[192] Meanwhile, Saddam Hussein defied the new UN Monitoring and Verification Commission (UNMOVIC). The second Bush administration, notwithstanding Pentagon hawks with "an almost obsessive fixation" on toppling Saddam, did little more than propose "smart sanctions" until the 9/11 attacks seemed to suggest links between terrorism and so-called rogue regimes.[193] Planning for the invasion of Iraq quickly followed.

Not surprisingly, both wars against Iraq impacted the Arab-Israeli peace process. When the elder Bush took office in 1989, *intifada* deaths had mounted, a new conservative Likud government in Israel vowed never to relinquish the occupied territories, and radical Palestinian factions continued their *jihad* against the Jewish state. Secretary Baker pressed both sides but especially implored Israel: "Forswear annexation. Stop settlement activity."[194] The end of the Cold War and Gulf War actually improved the diplomatic climate. No longer subsidized by the Soviet Union, Yasir Arafat also alienated oil-rich Saudi Arabia and the Gulf emirates by his

PLO-Israeli Agreement. On September 13, 1993, President Clinton acted as stage manager on the South Lawn of the White House when Israeli prime minister Yitzhak Rabin (left), and Palestine Liberation Organization chair Yasir Arafat (right), signed a historic accord for Palestinian self-rule in the Gaza Strip and Jericho—first steps, perhaps, toward a Palestinian homeland. After Rabin and Arafat affixed their signatures, Clinton shook hands with both men and then stepped back and gestured with his arms. Arafat reached his hand out, and after several long seconds, Rabin responded. (The White House)

ill-fated backing of Iraq during the 1991 war. When Israel showed restraint in the face of Iraqi missile attacks and Washington promised an expanded peace process after the war, Arafat chose to negotiate despite his fear of becoming "a male bee that fertilizes once and then dies."[195] Eight trips to the Mideast by Baker in 1991 led to multilateral negotiations in Madrid in 1992. Bush's withholding of $10 billion in loan guarantees because of expanded Israeli settlements helped to elect a more flexible Labor government under Yitzhak Rabin in July 1992.

A breakthrough came the next year after secret meetings between Israeli and PLO representatives in Norway. In September 1993, Rabin and Arafat signed in Washington a declaration of principles for eventual Palestinian self-rule in the Gaza Strip and in the Jericho area of the West Bank. In May 1994, Palestinian autonomy began when Israeli forces withdrew from Gaza and Jericho. Israel and Jordan signed a peace accord in July after the United States agreed to forgive Jordan's foreign debt, but Syria refused to make peace despite a visit by Clinton to Damascus.

Rabin's assassination in November 1995, Palestinian terrorist bombings, and the election of hard-line prime minister Benjamin Netanyahu in 1996 slowed the peace process. Except for relinquishing Hebron in 1997, Netanyahu vetoed further withdrawals. At a nine-day summit in Maryland in October 1998, Arafat and Netanyahu did agree to some Israeli pullbacks in return for changes in the PLO Charter calling for Israel's destruction. Ehud Barak's electoral victory in spring 1999, followed by secret Israeli-PLO negotiations in Stockholm, set the stage for what was supposed to be a final peace agreement at Camp David in July 2000. Despite Israel's apparent willingness to cede some 97 percent of the West Bank, the Camp David summit foundered over details and bad personal chemistry between Arafat and Barak. The

Likud leader Ariel Sharon's visit in September to Jerusalem's Temple Mount, a disputed area, ignited Palestinian clashes that quickly turned into a second *intifada*. The violence increased after Sharon became prime minister in early 2001. Viewing Sharon as an ally in the war against terrorism, George W. Bush did not personally intercede until after the successful invasion of Iraq, when he arranged in June 2003 a summit between Sharon and the new Palestinian prime minister Mahmoud Abbas. No sooner had Bush promised to "ride herd" on the resulting "road map" than escalating violence on both sides derailed the process.[196] In 2004, Palestinian suicide bombings against Israelis, Israeli assassinations of Palestinian leaders, and Sharon's insistence on retaining Jewish settlements in occupied territory kept the levels of death and destruction high.

Feuding and Trading with China, Vietnam, and Japan

Human rights and trade issues continued to dominate U.S. relations with Asia under the Bushes and Clinton. During the night of June 3–4, 1989, Chinese soldiers and tanks stormed into Beijing's Tiananmen Square. The epicenter of Chinese life "became a killing field" in which hundreds—perhaps thousands—of demonstrators lay dead.[197] For weeks unarmed students had been holding peaceful prodemocracy rallies and appealing for talks with government leaders. China's octogenarian rulers, however, in contrast to their counterparts in much of Eastern Europe, chose repression over constructive change. The most powerful leader in the Chinese government, Deng Xiaoping, saw the students' call for political liberalization to match economic reforms as an attempt "to create chaos under the heavens."[198] Deng thereupon crushed the prodemocracy movement, purged reformers from the government, and ordered the arrest and execution of protesters. With Tiananmen "a record-breaking world event on television," world opinion became outraged.[199]

Bush signaled China that he wanted to keep relations intact, "but it's hard when they are executing people."[200] Washington suspended weapons sales and deferred new World Bank loans to China but continued Beijing's most-favored-nation trade status. Convinced that global security required stable and friendly Sino–American ties, Bush sent Brent Scowcroft secretly to Beijing on June 30 with the message that "we can do a lot more for them when they aren't killing their own people."[201]

Critics charged that the United States was shortsightedly siding with China's elderly clique while alienating the nation's younger, progressive, future leaders. Bush cheered such leaders in Prague but snubbed them in Beijing. The debate centered on a classic question: When calls for human rights and calculations of global power politics collide, must either give way?

Despite China's negative record on human rights, its economy boomed during the 1990s. U.S. trade with China reached $33.1 billion in 1992, with an $18.3 billion surplus in China's favor; by 1997 the figures climbed to $63 billion and $39.5 billion. "The China market is a big cake," noted one Chinese diplomat. "Come early and get a big piece."[202] The Clinton administration renewed China's most-favored-nation trading privileges in June 1993 after the Beijing government released several prominent dissidents. Beijing's establishment of diplomatic ties with South

Prodemocracy Courage, Tiananmen Square, Beijing, China. In early 1989 university students and sympathizers camped in Beijing's great square. They made hopeful speeches about democracy and even built a towering replica of the Statue of Liberty. Drawing inspiration from Poland's Solidarity movement, the young prodemocracy activists pleaded with their nation's aged leaders to liberalize China's politics. In June the military swept into the square. After the massacre, one person—probably a student—braved tanks in a sobering example of the classic contest between the courageous individual and the powerful state. (AP/Wide World Photos)

Korea in 1992, its growing trade with Seoul, and its pressure on North Korea to permit international nuclear inspection also pleased Washington. When Clinton again granted China most-favored-nation status in 1994, he frankly declared that human rights and trade issues were henceforth delinked.

Tensions nonetheless increased after a visit by Taiwan's president to his Cornell University alma mater in May 1995. Accusing Washington of a plot to "divide, weaken, and contain China," Beijing precipitated a crisis in March 1996 by firing three ballistic missiles close to Taiwan and conducting military exercises in the Taiwan Strait.[203] Secretary of Defense William Perry warned of "grave consequences" if any missiles struck Taiwan, and two U.S. carrier task forces steamed ostentatiously toward the region.[204] "Bullshit that the U.S. will intervene," said a Chinese official. "You did nothing in 1954 and 1958 . . . You are bluffing."[205] Both sides soon backed off, as the United States reaffirmed its support of "one China," and the Chinese agreed not to sell nuclear technology to states that supported terrorism. Despite Republican charges ("donorgate") that Chinese agents had attempted to "buy" the 1996 U.S. elections by funneling money to Democratic candidates, a week-long state visit to the United States by Chinese president Jiang Zemin in October 1997 produced a "constructive strategic partnership."[206]

The United States and China cooperated to help defuse a crisis between India and Pakistan over nuclear testing the following year.[207] The second Bush administration reignited tensions in early 2001 when a U.S. surveillance aircraft collided with a Chinese jet and crash-landed on Hainan Island. No sooner did Bush apologize than he announced arms sales and "whatever it takes to help Taiwan defend itself."[208] Again 9/11 altered the landscape, as Bush made two fruitful trips to China and President Jiang Zemin visited Bush's Texas ranch in October 2002. With China becoming a full member of the World Trade Organization, Secretary Powell promised the "three Cs"—a "candid, constructive, and cooperative relationship."[209] Although Beijing opposed the war against Iraq, it cooperated in containing North Korea's nuclear threat. The instant popularity of seven-foot-five-inch Yao Ming as a member of the Houston Rockets basketball team also enhanced China's image in the United States, as did the choice of Beijing as host for the 2008 Olympic Games.

U.S. relations with Vietnam also improved. In fall 1992, President Bush announced the "last chapter of the Vietnam War" after protracted negotiations to reach a full accounting of the 2,265 U.S. military personnel still listed as missing in action (MIAs).[210] Satisfied that Hanoi officials had tried to identify and return all remains, the Clinton administration lifted the nineteen-year-old trade embargo in February 1994. Within hours PepsiCo erected a giant, inflated can of soda in the middle of Ho Chi Minh City and gave away 40,000 cans of the international soft drink. Caterpillar, Otis, and other companies hoped to win contracts worth billions of dollars to repair Vietnam's infrastructure. General Electric set up offices two blocks from the infamous "Hanoi Hilton" prison.[211] Despite a devastating war and two decades of isolation, many of the 71 million Vietnamese apparently retained a certain attraction to things American. "English is the language of money, the language of our future," said a Vietnamese diplomat.[212] Hanoi undoubtedly saw a strong U.S. economic presence as a possible counter to its giant neighbor China.

President Clinton established full diplomatic relations in July 1995, and his appointment as ambassador of Pete Peterson, a former prisoner of war in North Vietnam for seven years, proved "a political masterstroke" in defusing much of the resentment against normalization.[213] Ironically, the economic growth fueled by foreign investment ($8.6 billion in 1996) most benefited the south near Ho Chi Minh City where Nike and other companies utilized infrastructure left by the Americans. Just as joint historical symposia on the Vietnam War helped to reconcile the past, so did Colin Powell's visit to Hanoi in 2001 wherein the former U.S. soldier wowed his hosts by "brandishing a toy six-gun" and singing the country classic "El Paso" during an off-the-record talent show.[214]

Trade issues also dominated the Japanese-American relationship. Anti-Americanism in Japan and "Japan bashing" (*Nihon tataki*) in the United States bedeviled the world's two major economies.[215] In 1990 the world's ten largest banks had headquarters in Japan. Japan's biggest company, NTT, was more than twice the size of America's leading corporation, IBM. The best-selling car in America in 1989 was the Honda Accord. Many Americans especially worried that the dollar-rich Japanese were buying up too many businesses in the United States. By 1990 Japanese interests controlled 25 percent of California's banking assets and owned almost half of downtown Los Angeles. When Japanese firms acquired the MCA and Columbia movie studios in the early 1990s, it seemed that Godzilla was mounting a cultural invasion.

Predictions of Japan's global economic hegemony fizzled. The Japanese variant of capitalism, characterized by government management of the economy and close ties among corporate "families" of manufacturers, suppliers, exporters, and banks, proved ill adapted to globalization. Japan's highly structured society encouraged high production and savings from its citizens but discouraged bold Japanese entrepreneurs equivalent to America's Ted Turner or Bill Gates. Japanese investments in Hollywood soured because industrial know-how had little relevance to a field such as entertainment. As the New York stock exchange soared in the mid-1990s, Tokyo's Nikkei average slumped to half the levels of the late 1980s. U.S. exports to Japan jumped from $27 billion in 1986 to $47.8 billion in 1992 to $66 billion in 1997, even though the trade deficit (in Japan's favor) still hovered around $50 billion in the mid-1990s. McDonald's ranked as Japan's largest restaurant chain by 1995 and Apple Computer became the second largest vendor of personal computers. After Japanese banking losses during the Asian financial crisis of 1997–1998, the $8 trillion U.S. economy stood roughly twice as large as Japan's. Nonetheless, Tokyo still maintained large trade surpluses, with every dollar earned adding to Japan's huge foreign investments. "Japan is still the main source of long-term capital for the world today," noted a long-time Asia watcher, "and the United States is still the largest debtor nation."[216]

Washington much valued Japan's close military alliance with the United States and its shouldering of more of the mutual defense costs. American officials praised Tokyo for applying Japanese funds to relieve the international debt problem and for providing economic assistance to developing nations such as the Philippines. North Korea's nuclear ambitions and China's potential menace to Taiwan reinforced Tokyo's desire for continuing military ties even in the absence of a Soviet enemy. Relations were temporarily strained by the rape of a twelve-year-old girl on Okinawa by three U.S. servicemen in 1995, and in 2001 when the nuclear submarine *Greenville* accidentally rammed a Japanese fishing boat and killed nine. Apologies for such incidents helped to maintain the U.S.-Japan security alliance ("the bedrock for peace and prosperity in the Pacific"), including Tokyo's $40 billion per year self-defense forces (plus paying 70 percent of burden sharing for U.S. troops in Japan).[217] As the new millennium began, many Americans still held ambivalent attitudes about their erstwhile enemy and long-time ally—as "miracle and menace, docile and aggressive, fragile blossom and Tokyo Rose."[218] Nonetheless, the addition to major league baseball of such talented Japanese players as Hideo Nomo, Hideki Matsui, and Ichiro Suzuki thrilled fans in both countries.

Global Bewilderments and Opportunities

"Gosh, I miss the Cold War," President Clinton half-joked after American soldiers were killed in Somalia.[219] Indeed, the post–Cold War era seemed less manageable than the bipolar system that had preceded it—so full of "terrorists," so rife with religious, tribal, and ethnic tensions, so overarmed, so wracked by economic catastrophes, so divided on the basis of gender, so plagued by illicit drugs, crime, and AIDS, so threatened by the proliferation of nuclear weapons and the deterioration of the natural environment, so burdened by overpopulation and famines, so disunited just when it appeared that the United Nations had emerged as a major builder of coalitions.

Arms sales accelerated across the post–Cold War world. Surface-to-surface missiles were showing up in the world arms market. So were U.S. Stinger missiles that the Reagan administration had given in the 1980s to radical islamic rebels in Afghanistan. After the Soviet withdrawal, Reagan's Afghan "freedom fighters" used the weapons against their rivals, became traffickers in heroin, trained *jihad* terrorists and assassins, and suppressed the rights of indigenous Afghan women. The United States continued as the world's leading arms merchant, exporting $15 billion in

World Arms Exports, 1992–1994

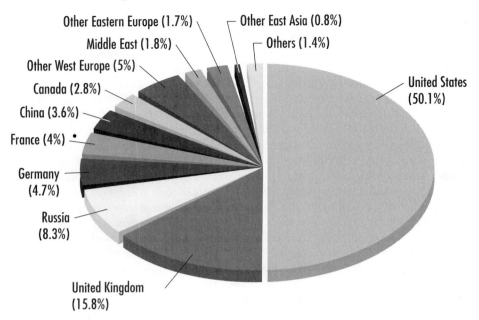

Other Eastern Europe (1.7%)
Middle East (1.8%)
Other West Europe (5%)
Canada (2.8%)
China (3.6%)
France (4%)
Germany (4.7%)
Russia (8.3%)
United Kingdom (15.8%)
Other East Asia (0.8%)
Others (1.4%)
United States (50.1%)

Source: U.S. Arms Control and Disarmament Agency

weapons each year as Third World governments lined up to buy Patriot missiles with money better spent on health and education.

Other weapons posed deadly threats. The release of sarin gas into the Tokyo subway by a Japanese religious cult in 1995 and the mysterious deaths of five American anthrax victims after 9/11 raised the chilling specter of biological and chemical terrorism. With biological weapons banned since 1972, the 1993 Chemical Convention (ratified by Washington in 1997) required signatories to destroy all chemical weapons by the year 2005 and to submit to rigorous inspection. More than one hundred nations in 1997 signed a treaty banning antipersonnel land mines. The American activist Jody Williams shared the Nobel Peace Prize for her work in behalf of the treaty, but President Clinton refused to sign it because U.S. troops in Korea relied on mines to protect against a North Korean attack.

Nuclear proliferation remained a grave threat to all nations. Even though Brazil and Argentina signed a pact never to build nuclear weapons and South Africa dismantled its nuclear weapons after 1993, Israel, Pakistan, and India had all joined the nuclear club, and others such as Iran, Iraq, and North Korea aspired to do so. Pakistan dismissed its chief scientist in early 2004 for illegally sharing nuclear technology with Iran and Libya, shortly after both countries agreed to curtail their weapons programs and accept UN inspections. In an earlier episode that one official called "far more frightening than the Cuban Missile Crisis," only eleventh hour U.S. pressure reportedly forestalled a Pakistani nuclear strike against India in May 1990.[220] As for the former Soviet republics, Congress provided nearly $1.5 billion to help Russia, Belarus, Ukraine, and Kazakhstan dismantle much of the former Soviet nuclear arsenal and safeguard the remaining nuclear materials inside Russia. In a "Megatons to Megawatts" arrangement, President Clinton promised to buy from Russia 500 metric tons of highly enriched uranium over a 20-year period for $12 billion, and in 1994 U.S. nuclear technicians in Project SAPPHIRE spirited out of Kazakhstan some 600 kilograms of uranium to prevent its theft or sale.[221] Calling nonproliferation "one of our nation's highest priorities," the Clinton administration did what it could to prevent "nuclear yardsales" and to maintain nuclear security inside Russia.[222]

The discovery that North Korea had accumulated enough plutonium from its Yongbyon reactor to make several atomic bombs spawned a short-lived crisis in the early 1990s. Pyongyang refused to cooperate with the International Atomic Energy Agency and threatened to withdraw from the Nuclear Proliferation Treaty (NPT), which North Korea had signed in 1985. As Clinton's generals made plans for a preemptive "surgical strike" and a second Korean war "whose costs would far exceed" the first, a "private" visit by former president Jimmy Carter to North Korea in October 1994 brokered an agreement whereby North Korea agreed to halt its nuclear weapons program and submit to international inspection; in return the United States promised $4 billion in energy aid.[223] The matter remained quiescent until autumn 2002, when North Korea admitted to cheating on nuclear weapons, withdrew from the NPT, and threatened to turn Seoul into a "sea of fire" unless the United States

A North Korean Nuclear Threat? This cartoon depicts North Korean dictator Kim Jong II "flashing" a nuclear threat against Uncle Sam in late 2002. Although President George W. Bush had publicly declared his loathing of Kim, a "pygmy" who was "starving his own people" in "a Gulag the size of Houston," Washington's ensuing war against Iraq kept the Korean crisis on the back burner for the next year. North Korea's 1-million-man army and potential nuclear capability also reinforced the scholar Leon Sigal's maxim that "you don't want to get into a pissing match when the other guy has a full bladder." (Dan Wasserman, Copyright © 2002, Tribune Media Services. Reprinted with permission.)

signed a non-aggression pact.[224] In subsequent negotiations among the United States, China, Russia, Japan, and South Korea aimed at offering Pyongyang a "multilateral security pledge," George W. Bush, for once, extolled the virtues of "a collective voice trying to convince a leader to change behavior."[225]

"Until now the cold war provided an alibi" to avoid tackling many global issues, wrote a leading analyst. "No longer."[226] The deterioration of the international environment and deteriorating public health not only endangered economic prosperity; it also threatened to undermine international stability. A sample of recent data revealed problems:

- The director general of the World Bank noted in 2002 that growing global poverty ticked like "a time bomb lodged against the heart of liberty."[227]
- Every year, 8 million people die of AIDS, tuberculosis, and malaria, predominantly in poor countries—"approximately one Holocaust each year."[228]
- Without effective curtailment of greenhouse gases, average global temperatures will increase between 2 and 6.5 degrees Fahrenheit by the end of the twenty-first century.
- Americans use about one-third of all chlorofluorocarbons (CFCs) in the world—the chemical most responsible for depletion of the ozone layer that shields the earth from the sun's deadly ultraviolet rays.
- In 2002, about 42 million people were living with HIV/AIDS. 45 million more will become infected by 2010. 3.2 million died of AIDS in 2002.
- Industrial countries produce more than 90 percent of the 400 million tons of hazardous waste entering the biosphere each year.
- "World food production will have to increase by more than 75% over the next thirty years to keep pace with population growth," a UN official has estimated.[229]
- With an estimated 2.7 children dying every year of infectious diseases preventable by vaccines, multi-billionaire Bill Gates has committed $1.4 billion to support the Global Alliance for Vaccines and Immunizations.
- "Tropical forests cover only 7 percent of Earth's land surface," according to the World Resources Institute, "but they contain more than half of all living species. Yet these forests are being cut and cleared at a very rapid rate—an area of about 40 million acres (about the size of the state of Washington) every year."[230]

As evidenced by "collapsing fisheries, falling water tables, shrinking forests, dying lakes, crop-withering heat waves, and disappearing species," the world faced a host of borderless issues.[231] The catapulting growth in population meant a greater use of scarce resources, more pollution, more disease, and more famines such as those that wracked Africa in the 1980s and 1990s. Overgrazing and tree-cutting in many parts of the Third World, as in Bangladesh, produced quick runoffs of rainfalls and flooding, washing away precious topsoil and killing many. In turn, these ecological/economic problems generated political instability and social disintegration. Food riots and migrations of refugees challenged governments. Yet the first Bush administration vetoed monies for the UN Population Fund in 1989 because the agency supported birth-control programs that allowed abortions. Because Washington did not want the 1982 Convention on the Law of the Sea to restrict

Deforestation of the Amazon.   The burning of tropical forests in order to open land to farming, grazing, and settlement has eliminated hundreds of plant and animal species. The clearing has also accelerated soil erosion and filled the atmosphere with carbon dioxide, one of the greenhouse gases causing global warming. In the years 1981–1990, more than 40 million acres of tropical forests were lost each year. The photograph on the left was taken by Skylab 2 in 1973 on a partly cloudy day in the Amazon basin. The photograph on the right, taken by the crew of the space shuttle *Discovery* in 1988, reveals the effects of burning as thick smoke covers the same area. (Courtesy of NASA)

private American business, not until fall 1997 did President Clinton transmit the treaty to the Senate, where it still remains pending.

If "all of your people want to get rich in exactly the same way we got rich," President Clinton admitted to China's president in 1996, "we won't be breathing very well" and will face "irreparable damage to the global environment."[232] Yet less developed countries resented lectures from industrial nations that had perpetrated environmental wrongs for decades. And, "you can't have an environmentally healthy planet in a world that is socially unjust," noted the president of Brazil at the 1992 Earth Summit in Rio de Janeiro.[233] At that summit, attended by 178 nations, Bush spoke against strong environmental protection rules, charging that they would cost jobs. He refused to sign the Biodiversity Treaty designed to slow the loss of endangered species. Clinton, however, signed the treaty in 1993 (it still remains pending in the Senate).

"We do not have generations," noted the Worldwatch Institute's Lester R. Brown. "We only have years in which to turn things around."[234] Pressure from environmentalists forced the U.S. tuna industry to stop using fish–netting techniques that killed 100,000 dolphins annually. Entertainers regularly supported environmental causes, most notably the rock star Bono's tour in 2002 to publicize relief for debt-ridden, AIDS-stricken African nations. The Clean Air Act of 1990 took steps to reduce acid rain and toxic wastes in the air. Washington also began "debt-for-nature swaps" wherein Third World nations willing to undertake major programs to protect the environment enjoyed some debt reduction.[235]

The UN Environmental Program kept "global commons" issues alive. Eighty-six nations agreed at Helsinki in mid-1989 to phase out the manufacture and use of ozone-destroying chemicals by the year 2000; by 1994 their efforts had reduced by half the *increase* in the concentration of CFCs in the atmosphere. Through the efforts of the World Health Organization (WHO), infectious diseases such as small-pox and malaria have nearly been eliminated. Combating the global spread of AIDS is the organization's next daunting task. Genetic-engineering programs funded by the World Bank hope to launch a "gene revolution" to improve farm productivity.[236] A conference in Kyoto in 1997 attended by 166 countries agreed to a Global Warming Convention under which developed nations must reduce carbon dioxide, methane, and other greenhouse gas emissions by 6 to 8 percent below their 1990 levels. Despite approval by Clinton, the younger Bush withdrew from the pact in 2001, saying that "we will not do anything that harms our economy, because first things first are the people who live in America."[237]

In early 1994 the State Department focused for the first time on the treatment of women in its annual human-rights report. Its grim findings included forced sterilizations and abortions in China; coerced prostitution in Thailand and Burma; females spending one-third as much time in school as males in Zaire; "dowry deaths" in India (husbands killing their wives because of insufficient dowries); laws making adultery illegal for women but not for men in Morocco and the Republic of the Congo. The United Nations reported in 2000 that two-thirds of the world's 876 million illiterate people are female. Worldwide, women held only 14 percent of top managerial jobs, 10 percent of seats in national legislatures, and 6 percent of cabinet-level posts. In 1996, U.S. courts granted asylum to a nineteen-year-old woman who had fled her native Togo to avoid having "my woman's parts . . . scraped off"; the United States thus joined Canada in making genital mutilation (2 million victims per year) and other gender-based abuses grounds for asylum.[238] With UN conventions on the rights of women still unratified by the United States, the State Department in November 2001 indicted Afghanistan's Taliban regime for "egregious acts of violence against women, including rape, abduction, and forced marriage."[239] Indeed, Osama bin Laden had exposed his own gender bias in 1998 by calling for holy war in part because Mecca's sacred sites in Saudi Arabia had been defiled by "American women soldiers . . . these American and Jewish prostitutes."[240]

Because "information, ideas, and money now pulse across the planet at light speed," international communications issues assumed new importance.[241] Since the 1970s, developing nations had been calling for a "New Information Order" in which the powerful developed nations would have to democratize access to information and to report news accurately and fairly. Third World critics charged that the control of information by developed nations—especially the United States—created dependency and retarded economic growth. Because of its remote-sensing satellites, the United States allegedly could marshal greater information (data on weather and market conditions, mineral deposits, and agricultural output) than weaker states in negotiations on tariffs and other issues. Through the International Telecommunications Satellite Consortium (INTELSAT), founded in 1964 to coor-

American Decline, American Ignorance. Peter C. Vey's cartoon speaks to a major point that "declinists" made to explain why U.S. power slipped: The American educational system needed reform. American students were ignorant of the wider world. A 1989 Gallup poll discovered that 14 percent of the American respondents could not pick out the United States on a world map and that 50 percent did not know that the Sandinistas and U.S.-backed *contras* were battling in Nicaragua. A 1990 Gallup survey found that one-third of the interviewees did not know whether the United States had fought on the side of the South Vietnamese or North Vietnamese in America's longest war. (P. C. Vey, reprinted from the *New York Times*)

dinate the use of satellites, the United States has also preserved control of the majority of the electromagnetic spectrum for itself and its allies. By 1999, Time Warner, the world's largest TV producer and distributor, was selling thousands of hours of programs to 175 countries. Such dominance helped, for example, to increase sales of sneakers to China through video images of Michael Jordan slam-dunking ("*kou qui*") a basketball.[242] An international agreement in 1997 opened the $600 billion global telephone market to greater competition, with U.S. companies poised to increase their one-third share. Although most software, search engines, and 90 percent of the 610 billion e-mail messages on the World Wide Web were in English by 2000, experts predicted that "Internet traffic in languages other than English" will predominate "within the next few years."[243] Electronic commerce (or "e-business") totaled $145 billion in 1999 and was expected to reach $7.29 trillion worldwide by 2004.[244]

Powerful governments found it impossible to silence opponents who had easy access to the new technology. In 1989 protesting Chinese students listened to Voice of America radio broadcasts to follow events throughout China and used fax machines to communicate with the outside world. International revulsion against the Chinese crackdown was so extensive largely because the ghastly events appeared on worldwide television. In an "anomaly of history" in 1989, East Europeans "watched the revolution on CNN relayed by a Russian satellite and mustered the courage to rebel against their own sovereigns."[245] Nor could Islamic censorship in Iran suppress the "tide of godlessness" represented by bootleg videocassettes of "Baywatch" and

Titanic.[246] In 2000 a young hacker from the Philippines launched a virus that cost some $15 billion in damages in the United States alone. Computers seized after 9/11 revealed Al-Qaeda plans to destroy U.S. dams and power grids by attacking the computer systems that controlled them—a form of "e-jihad," or holy war on-line.[247]

Globalization (roughly defined as the process of integrating peoples politically, culturally, and economically into a larger community) made foreign relations less foreign. "The world has invaded us and we have invaded it," said one State Department official.[248] The impact of NAFTA on both St. Joseph, Missouri, and Racine, Wisconsin, for example, was the loss of manufacturing jobs when textiles and refrigeration plants relocated to Mexico, and the addition of employees by high-tech firms eager to take advantage of the booming export market. Even college sports became globalized, as the popularity of National Basketball Association basketball, enhanced by the televised triumphs of America's "Dream Team" in the 1992 Olympics, attracted nearly 300 student athletes from 59 countries to accept basketball scholarships at American universities by 1998. Street protests against the effects of globalization began with the "Battle in Seattle" in 1999 and were repeated at subsequent economic summits.[249] Many critics saw globalization as "neoimperialism wearing Bill Gates's face and Mickey Mouse's ears," exploiting "women, minorities, the poor, and developing regions. It fouls ecosystems, displaces local cultures . . . and deepens the divide (digital and otherwise) between the global haves and have-nots."[250] Even as the "iconography of America" grew increasingly "international," with Italian jeans manufacturers advertising "their wares in Germany on posters depicting Monument Valley" and the German cigarette brand West evoking frontier images of "a beckoning yonder" of America as "the very site of freedom and space," a French sheep farmer became a national hero in 1999 by destroying a McDonald's restaurant to "protect culinary sovereignty."[251] Yet the widespread popularity of the Japanese game Pokemon suggested "true cultural globalization, not just Americanization."[252] For good or ill, contemporary globalization grew "farther, faster, cheaper and deeper."[253]

As the United States faced what the veteran analyst George F. Kennan called the global "bewilderments" of the new millennium, it also had to deal with pressing domestic problems.[254] Americans ballyhooed victory in the Cold War and the triumph of capitalism, but "why doesn't it feel better?" asked one journalist.[255] The United States in 1998 trailed twenty-two other leading industrialized nations in high school graduation rates. Even with a revived economy and balanced budget by 2000, America continued to suffer domestic troubles: an increasing division between rich and poor; millions unable to afford medical insurance and adequate health care; workers losing jobs as corporations "outsourced" abroad. Moreover, suggested one observer, "a nation prey to drugs, guns, and violence" and "torn by racial tension" might become "a weak player on the world stage."[256] Clinton warned that the "currency of national strength in this new era will be denominated not only in ships and tanks and planes, but in diplomas and patents and paychecks."[257]

As demonstrated after 9/11, however, America's military might and global reach grew ever more predominant. Even during the Clinton years ("a decade of Prometheus playing pygmy," according to one pundit), the defense budget remained on "Cold War autopilot" ($270 billion in 1999) and the Pentagon developed new weapons systems and strategies for use against "rogue" states and terrorists.[258] The air force emphasized "stealth" aircraft that could deliver "smart" bombs and missiles without alerting enemy radar. The navy reluctantly planned new generations of cruise-missile ships to replace the aging supercarriers whose aviators were vulnerable to capture by foes who could manipulate the global media. The army forced itself to stress hand-to-hand combat by small units of "Rangers" at some cost to historically preferred large-scale battles of maneuver by division and corps. Most important, the Marine Corps rose to a new level of parity with the other services as the arm that could most readily attack from the sea with ship-based helicopters, close air-support jets, tanks, and troops. Dubbed Tomahawk Diplomacy after the American cruise missile of choice, the new strategy smacked of nineteenth-century "gunboat diplomacy"—the arbitrary application of military and naval force against less "civilized" people to teach them proper behavior. The military increasingly took on the roles of peacekeepers and nation builders in such faraway places as Somalia, Haiti, Afghanistan, and Iraq.

The second Bush administration added its own impetus to this "revolution in military affairs."[259] Secretary Rumsfeld's spurring of the military bureaucracy to move faster and assume more risks seemed to resemble "a hostile takeover."[260] The younger Bush worried less about U.S. casualties and preferred "boots on the ground" (in the new jargon) to putting "a million-dollar missile on a five-dollar tent."[261] Not only did the Bush team wage two victorious wars halfway around the world in two years, but it also forged military ties and base agreements with former Soviet clients from Eastern Europe to Central Asia. All told, some half million uniformed and civilian personnel served in 725 military installations abroad under Bush. In 2003, U.S. Army Special Operations Command deployed in sixty-five countries—from training Nepalese troops to fight Maoist rebels to pursuing Abu Sayaf guerrillas in the Philippines to helping Colombian soldiers in their war against narco-traffickers. "Homeland security" (including a new Cabinet-level department) became part of national security, as Congress passed the Patriot Act in autumn 2001 that expanded the federal government's power to conduct electronic surveillance, hold military trials for suspected terrorists, and other activities that arguably infringed on basic civil rights. Further, the new Bush Doctrine of military preemption, including the possible first use of nuclear weapons, against emergent threats "before they are fully formed" caused as much "shock and awe" as did the invasion of Iraq.[262] The president pledged to maintain "military strengths beyond challenge."[263] Indeed, with the United States producing 23 percent of the gross world product and controlling more than twice the resources of any two countries, U.S. military power overshadowed all potential rivals for the near term, perhaps prolonging what political scientists call a "unipolar moment" through "command of the commons" (seas, space, and air).[264] With the U.S. economy serving as the engine of globalization, with American products from velcro to videos to Viagra popular everywhere, America's soft power matched its hard power.

Such extraordinary power prompted observers to ruminate, both positively and negatively, about an American global empire. "If people want to say we are an imperial power, fine," wrote the neoconservative editor of *The Weekly Standard*.[265] Others acknowledged an "informal" empire "richly equipped with imperial paraphernalia:

John Kerry (b. 1943). A graduate of Yale University (1966), Kerry served as a naval officer in Vietnam where he won the Silver Star and other combat medals. Speaking for the Vietnam Veterans Against the War in 1971, he queried: "How do you ask a man to be the last man to die for a mistake?" As U.S. senator from Massachusetts after 1984, Kerry opposed the Reagan administration's policies in Central America and worked with fellow Vietnam War veteran Senator John McCain (Republican, Arizona) to normalize diplomatic relations with Vietnam in the 1990s. As the Democratic nominee for president in 2004, Kerry criticized George W. Bush's foreign policies as "arrogant, inept, and reckless." (© EPA/William Philpott/AP World Wide Photos)

troops, ships, planes, bases, proconsuls, local collaborators, all spread around the luckless planet."[266] The second Bush administration's haughty, go-it-alone style led many, including allies, to see Uncle Sam as the playground bully; the French coined the pejorative label "hyperpower" and pinned it on Washington.[267] Even some who cheered Bush's attempt to reorder the Middle East worried about its "excessively military cast. Delighted to own the biggest hammer on the planet, policymakers tend to treat every problem as if it were a nail."[268] Still others argued that Americans "don't really have what it takes to rule the world," that Americans are much better at conquering than "running a screwed-up sun-scorched sandpit like Iraq."[269] Diplomacy receded as a method to resolve differences, and the Bush administration frequently ignored or bypassed the United Nations as a body that offered "false comfort" to U.S. interests.[270] When the occupation of Iraq became "untidy," in Rumsfeld's words, Bush's appeal to the United Nations to help the "young democracy" met a "chilly" reception.[271]

"We are the only country capable of projecting power globally and often the only one with impartial standing to mediate disputes," Clinton's national security adviser Sandy Berger had written prophetically in 2000. "If we fail to support our friends, . . . we will find ourselves alone when we need them. Indeed, nations will increasingly coalesce against us."[272] A British journalist at the same time wrote similarly of the "paradox" of American power—"too great to be challenged by any other state, yet not great enough to solve problems such as global terrorism and nuclear proliferation."[273] After 9/11, nervous Americans pondered and debated such advice, mindful of both the good and bad consequences of their behavior—much as they had done throughout their history.

FURTHER READING FOR THE PERIOD SINCE 1989

Some works listed in Chapter 11 also cover topics in this period.

For studies of 9/11 and after, see Tariq Ali, *Bush in Babylon* (2003); Sara Beck and Malcolm Downing, eds., *The Battle for Iraq* (2003); Stephen Brill, *After* (2003); Steve Coll, *Ghost Wars* (2004); Anthony H. Cordesman, *Terrorism, Asymmetric Warfare, and Weapons of Mass Destruction* (2001) and *The Gulf War* (2003); Richard Crockett, *America Embattled* (2003); Mary L. Dudziak, ed., *September 11 in History* (2003); Norman Friedman, *Terrorism, Afghanistan, and America's New Way of War* (2003); Rohan Gunaratna, *Inside Al Qaeda* (2002); David Harvey, *The New Imperialism* (2003); Dilip Hiro, *War Without End* (2002); Gilles Kepel, *Jihad* (2002); Bruce Lincoln, *Holy Terrors* (2003); Sandra Mackey, *The Reckoning* (2002); Williamson Murray and Robert H. Scoles, Jr., *The Iraq War* (2003); Kenneth M. Pollock, *The Coming Storm* (2002); David S. New, *Holy War* (2002); Ahmed Rashid, *Jihad* (2002) and *Taliban* (2001); and Bob Woodward, *Bush at War* (2002) and *Plan of Attack* (2004).

Studies that emphasize the Bush-Clinton-Bush years and characteristics of the post–Cold War world include William C. Berman, *America's Right Turn* (1994) and *From the Center to the Edge* (2001) (Clinton); Michael Beschloss and Strobe Talbott, *At the Highest Levels* (1993); Meena Bose and Rosanna Perotti, eds., *From Cold War to World Order* (2002); Fraser Cameron, *US Foreign Policy After the Cold War* (2002); Colin Campbell and Bert A. Rockman, *The Bush Presidency* (1991); James E. Cronin, *The World the Cold War Made* (1996); Ivo H. Daalder and James M. Lindsay, *American Unbound* (2003); Michael Dobbs, *Madeleine Albright* (1999); H. Richard Frimen, *NarcoDiplomacy* (1996); Raymond Garthoff, *The Great Transition* (1994); John Robert Greene, *The Presidency of George Bush* (2000); Fred Greenstein, ed., *The George W. Bush Presidency* (2003); William Greider, *Fortress America* (1998); Mark Hertsgaard, *The Eagle's Shadow* (2002); Michael Hirsh, *At War with Ourselves* (2003); William G. Hyland, *Clinton's World* (1999); Stanley Hoffmann, *World Disorders* (1999); Chalmers Johnson, *The Sorrows of Empire* (2004); Haynes Johnson, *The Best of Times* (2001) (Clinton); Joe Klein, *The Natural* (2002) (Clinton); Paul Krugman, *The Great Unraveling* (2003); Charles Kupchan, *The End of the American Era* (2002); Lewis Lapham, *Theater of War* (2002); Robert J. Lieber, ed., *Eagle Adrift* (1997); Michael Mandelbaum, *The Dawn of Peace in Europe* (1997); Robert S. Litwak, *Rogue States and U.S. Foreign Policy* (2000); James Mann, *The Rise of the Vulcans* (2004); Joseph S. Nye, *The Paradox of American Power* (2002); Herbert S. Parmet, *George Bush* (1998); John G. Ruggie, *Winning the Peace* (1996); James M. Scott, *After the End* (1999); Paul B. Stares, *Global Habit* (1996) (drugs); Ronald Steel, *Temptations of a Superpower* (1995); Jessica Stern, *The Ultimate Terrorists* (1999); Ron Suskind, *The Price of Loyalty* (2004); Kenneth W. Thompson, ed., *The Bush Presidency* (1998); Emmanuel Todd, *After the Empire* (2004); and Robert W. Tucker and David C. Henrickson, *The Imperial Temptation* (1992).

For the dramatic changes in the Soviet Union and Eastern Europe, for why the Cold War ended, and for the consequences of these changes for U.S. foreign relations, see Timothy Garton Ash, *The Uses of Adversity* (1989) and *The Magic Lantern* (1990); Ronald D. Asmus, *Opening NATO's Door* (2002); Anders Åslund, *Gorbachev's Struggle for Economic Reform* (1989); Archie Brown, *The Gorbachev Factor* (1996); Stephen F. Cohen, *Failed Crusade* (2000); Laurent Cohen-Tanugi, *An Alliance at Risk* (2003) (NATO); Dusko Doder and Louise Branson, *Gorbachev* (1990); Andrew Felkey, *Yeltsin's Russia and the West* (2002); John Lewis Gaddis, *The United States and the End of the Cold War* (1992); Carlotta Gall and Thomas de Waal, *Chechnya* (2002); Matthew Evangelista, *Unarmed Forces* (1999); Michael Hogan, ed., *The End of the Cold War* (1992); Jerry F. Hough, *Democratization and Revolution in the U.S.S.R., 1985–1991* (1997); Robert G. Kaiser, *Why Gorbachev Happened* (1991);

William W. Kaufmann, *Glasnost, Perestroika, and U.S. Defense Spending* (1990); Charles W. Kegley, Jr., ed., *The Long Postwar Peace* (1991); Richard Lebow and Janice Gross Stein, *We All Lost the Cold War* (1993); Allen Lynch, *The Cold War Is Over—Again* (1992); Michael Mandelbaum, ed., *Central Asia and the World* (1994) (former Soviet republics); Michael McCgwire, *Perestroika and Soviet National Security* (1991); Thomas G. Paterson, *On Every Front* (1992); David Remnick, *Lenin's Tomb* (1993); Robert Service, *Russia* (2003); William C. Wohlforth, *Cold War Endgame* (2003); Christopher I. Xenakis, *What Happened to the Soviet Union* (2002); and Ivan Zasoursky, *Media and Power in Post-Soviet Russia* (2002).

For Germany and reunification, see Timothy Garton Ash, *In Europe's Name* (1993); Dan Diner, *German Anti-Americanism* (1995); Michael A. Freney and Rebecca S. Hartley, *United Germany and the United States* (1991); Charles S. Maier, *Dissolution* (1997) (East Germany); and Stephen F. Szabo, *The Diplomacy of German Unification* (1992).

For the wars in the former Yugoslavia and the international response, see Michael E. Brown, ed., *The International Dimensions of Internal Conflict* (1996); Norman Cigar and Paul Williams, *Indictment at the Hague* (2002); Donald C. F. Daniel et al., *Coercive Inducement and the Containment of International Crises* (1999); James Gow, *The Triumph of the Lack of Will* (1997); John Hagan, *Justice in the Balkans* (2003); David Halberstam, *War in a Time of Peace* (2001); James Mayall, ed., *The New Interventionism* (1996); Matthew McAllester, *Beyond the Mountains of the Damned* (2002) (Kosovo); Miron Rezan, *Europe's Nightmare* (2001) (Kosovo); Cees Wiebes, *Intelligence and War in Bosnia, 1992–1995* (2003); and Susan L. Woodward, *Balkan Tragedy* (1995).

For the thesis that the United States has suffered decline, see Michael A. Bernstein and David E. Adler, eds., *Understanding American Economic Decline* (1994); David P. Calleo, *Beyond American Hegemony* (1987); Jim Hanson, *The Decline of the American Empire* (1993); Paul Kennedy, *The Rise and Fall of the Great Powers* (1987); Thomas J. McCormick, *America's Half-Century* (1995); Walter Russel Mead, *Mortal Splendor* (1987); and Michael E. Porter, *The Competitive Advantage of Nations* (1990). Critics of the declinist thesis are Henry Nau, *The Myth of America's Decline* (1990); Joseph S. Nye, Jr., *Bound to Lead* (1990); and Richard Rosecrance, *America's Economic Resurgence* (1990).

The spread of nuclear weapons and efforts at nonproliferation are explored in Ronald J. Bee, *Nuclear Proliferation* (1995); William E. Burrows and Robert Windrem, *Critical Mass* (1994); Ronald E. Powaski, *Return to Armageddon* (2000); Stephen I. Schwartz, ed., *Atomic Audit* (1998); Leon V. Sigal, *Disarming Strangers* (1998) (North Korea); and Raju Thomas, *The Nuclear Nonproliferation Regime* (1997).

International economic issues are discussed in C. Fred Bergsten, *Dilemmas of the Dollar* (1996); Alfred E. Eckes, Jr., and Thomas W. Zeiler, *Globalization and the American Century* (2003); Barry Eichengreen and Peter H. Lindert, eds., *The International Debt Crisis in Historical Perspective* (1990); Otis L. Graham, *Losing Time: The Industrial Policy Debate* (1992); George W. Grayson, *The North American Free Trade Agreement* (1995); Ricardo S. Grinspun and Maxwell A. Cameron, eds., *The Political Economy of North American Free Trade* (1993); Gary G. Hufbauer and Jeffrey J. Schott, *NAFTA* (1993); Kent Jones, *Who's Afraid of The WTO* (2003); Mary Cusimano Love, ed., *Beyond Sovereignty* (2003); Patrick Low, *Trading Free* (1993); John R. MacArthur, *The Selling of Free Trade* (2002); William A. Orme, Jr., *Understanding NAFTA* (1996); Louis W. Pauly, *Who Elected the Bankers?* (1997); Stephen J. Randall and Herman W. Konrad, eds., *NAFTA in Transition* (1995); Maryse Robert, *Negotiating NAFTA* (2002); Peter Singer, *One World: The Ethics of Globalization* (2002); Robert Solomon, *Money on the Move* (1999); and Joseph E. Stiglitz, *Globalization and Its Discontents* (2002) and *The Roaring Nineties* (2003).

Environmental issues are explored in Richard E. Benedick, *Ozone Diplomacy* (1998); Lee-Anne Broadhead, *International Environmental Politics* (2002); David E. Fisher, *Fire and Ice* (1990); Laurie Garrett, *Microbes Versus Mankind* (1997); Thomas F. Homer-Dixon, *Environmental Scarcity and Global Security* (1993); Alexander King and Bertrand Schneider, *The First Global Revolution* (1991); Paul Klugman, *The Age of Diminished Expectations* (1990); Jeremy Leggett, *Carbon War* (2001) (Global Warming); Ralph B. Levering and Miriam L. Levering, *Citizen Action for Global Change* (1999); Jim MacNeill et al., *Beyond Interdependence* (1991); Jessica T. Mathews, *Preserving the Global Environment* (1990); George D. Moffett, *Global Population Growth* (1994); and Donald Worster, ed., *The Ends of the Earth* (1989).

For refugees and relief and immigration policy, see Frank B. Bean et al., *At the Crossroads* (1998) (Mexico); John F. Hutchinson, *Champions of Charity* (1996) (Red Cross); Gil Loescher, *Beyond Charity* (1993);

Michael S. Teitelbaum and Myron Weiner, eds., *Threatened Peoples, Threatened Borders* (1995); and Reed Ueda, *Postwar Immigrant America* (1994).

For cultural relations, communications, and globalization see Royce J. Ammon, *Global Television and the Shaping of World Politics* (1999); Wilson Dizard, Jr., *Digital Diplomacy* (2001); Thomas L. Friedman, *The Lexus and the Olive Tree* (1999); Richard F. Kuisel, *Seducing the French: The Dilemma of Americanization* (1993); Frank Ninkovich, *U.S. Information Policy and Cultural Diplomacy* (1996); Aviad E. Raz, *Riding the Black Ship: Japan and Tokyo Disneyland* (1999); James L. Watson, ed., *Golden Arches East* (1998); and Donald Wilhelm, *Global Communications and Political Power* (1990).

For Japan, China, and Asia, see Zachary Abuza, *Militant Islam in Southeast Asia* (2003); Chu-yuan Cheng, *Behind the Tiananmen Massacre* (1990); Stephen D. Cohen, *Cowboys and Samurai* (1991); Warren I. Cohen, ed., *Pacific Passage* (1996); Bruce Cumings, *Divided Korea* (1995); Craig C. Garby and Mary Brown Bullock, eds., *Japan* (1994); Sheila K. Johnson, *The Japanese Through American Eyes* (1990); Paul Klugman, ed., *Trade with Japan* (1992); Walter LaFeber, *The Clash* (1997) (Japan); David M. Lampton, *Same Bed, Different Dreams* (2000) (U.S.-China); Edward J. Lincoln, *Japan's Unequal Trade* (1990); Robert S. McMahon, *The Limits of Empire* (1999) (Southeast Asia); Andrew Nathan and Perry Link, eds., *The Tiananmen Papers* (2001); Michael O'Haulon and Mike Mochizuki, *Crisis on the Korean Peninsula* (2003); Kenneth Pyle, *The Japanese Question* (1992); Michael Schaller, *Altered States* (1997) (Japan); Patrick Smith, *Japan* (1997); and Robert L. Suettinger, *Beyond Tiananmen* (2004).

For Africa, including intervention in Somalia, see the Brown, Daniel, and Mayall books cited above, and Michael Barnett, *Eyewitness to a Genocide* (2003) (Rwanda); Michael Clough, *Free at Last?* (1992); John L. Hirsch and Robert B. Oakley, *Somalia and Operation Restore Hope* (1995); Heidi Holland, *The Struggle* (1990) (ANC in South Africa); Jeffrey A. Lefebvre, *Arms for the Horn* (1991) (Ethiopia and Somalia); Fatima Meer, *Higher Than Hope* (1990) (Mandela); Robert K. Massie, *Loosing the Bonds* (1998) (South Africa); Larry Minear and Thomas G. Weiss, *Humanitarian Politics* (1995); Samantha Power, *"A Problem from Hell"* (2002) (Genocide); Peter J. Schraeder, *United States Foreign Policy Toward Africa* (1994); and Jonathan Stevenson, *Losing Mogadishu* (1995).

The Palestinian question, Israel, and the Middle East are discussed in Richard J. Chasdi, *Tapestry of Terror* (2002); Deborah J. Gerner, *One Land, Two Peoples* (1990); F. Robert Hunter, *The Palestinian Uprising* (1991); Burton I. Kaufman, *The Arab Middle East and the United States* (1996); David McDowall, *Palestine and Israel* (1990); Tim Niblock, *"Pariah States" and Sanctions in the Middle East* (2002); William B. Quandt, *Peace Process* (1993); Yezid Sayigh, *Armed Struggle and the Search for State* (1997); David Schoenbaum, *The United States and the State of Israel* (1993); Bernard Wasserman, *Israelis and Palestinians* (2003); and Eyal Zisser, *Assad's Legacy: Syria in Transition* (2002).

Iraqi-U.S. relations and the Persian Gulf War and its impact are the subject of Deborah Amos, *Lines in the Sand* (1992); Rick Atkinson, *Crusade* (1993); Lawrence Freedman and Efraim Karsh, *The Gulf Conflict* (1993); Stephen R. Graubard, *Mr. Bush's War* (1992); Khihir Hamza, *Saddam's Bombmaker* (2000); Avigdor Haselkorn, *The Continuing Storm: Iraq, Poisonous Weapons, and Deterrence* (1999); Efraim Karsh and Inari Rautsi, *Saddam Hussein* (1991); Jean E. Krasno and James D. Sutterlin, *The United Nations and Iraq* (2002); John R. MacArthur, *Second Front* (1992) (censorship); Ken Matthews, *The Gulf Conflict and International Relations* (1993); Judith Miller and Laurie Mylroie, *Saddam Hussein* (1990); Morris M. Mottale, *The Origins of the Gulf Wars* (2001); John Mueller, *Policy and Opinion in the Gulf War* (1994); Joseph S. Nye, Jr., and Roger K. Smith, eds., *After the Storm* (1992); Michael A. Palmer, *Guardians of the Gulf* (1992); Geoff Simons, *Targeting Iraq* (2002); Jean Edward Smith, *George Bush's War* (1992); Philip M. Taylor, *War and the Media* (1992); and Kenneth R. Timmerman, *The Death Lobby: How the West Armed Iraq* (1991).

For U.S. relations with Latin America, see Jan S. Adams, *A Foreign Policy in Transition* (1992) (Central America); Sergio Aguayo, *Myths and (Mis)Perceptions* (1998) (Mexico); Peter Andreas, *Border Games* (2000) (Mexico); John Booth and Thomas Walker, *Understanding Latin America* (1993); Maxwell A. Cameron and Brian W. Tomlin, *The Making of NAFTA* (2001); Richard Crandall, *Driven by Drugs* (2002) (Colombia); Timothy J. Dunn, *The Militarization of the U.S.-Mexico Border* (1996); H. Michael Erisman, *Cuba's Foreign Relations in a Post–Soviet World* (2002); Guy Gugliotta and Jeff Leen, *Kings of Cocaine* (1989); Susanne Jonas, *The Battle for Guatemala* (1991); Walter LaFeber, *Inevitable Revolutions* (1993); Juan J. Lopez, *Democracy Delayed* (2002) (Cuba); Abraham F. Lowenthal, *Partners in Conflict* (1990); Abraham F. Lowenthal and Katrina Burgess, eds., *The California-Mexico Connection* (1993); Donald J. Mabry, ed., *The Latin American Narcotics Trade and U.S.*

National Security (1989); Christopher Mitchell, ed., *Western Hemisphere Immigration and United States Foreign Policy* (1992); Morris Morley and Christopher McGillion, *Unfinished Business* (2002) (Cuba); Robert A. Pastor, *Whirlpool* (1992), *Integration with Mexico* (1993), and *Exiting the Whirlpool* (2001); Leigh A. Payne, *Uncivil Movements: The Armed Right Wing and Democracy in Latin America* (2000); Brenda Gayle Plummer, *Haiti and the United States* (1992); Susan K. Purcell and Robert M. Immerman, ed., *Japan and Latin America in the New Global Order* (1992); W. Dirk Raat, *Mexico and the United States* (1996); Joaquin Roy, *Cuba, the United States, and the Helms-Burton Doctrine* (2000); Bert Ruiz, *The Colombian Civil War* (2002); Lars Schoultz, *Beneath the United States* (1998); Peter D. Scott and Jonathan Marshall, *Cocaine Politics* (1991); Peter H. Smith, *Talons of the Eagle* (1996); Howard J. Wiarda, *American Foreign Policy Toward Latin America in the 80s and 90s* (1992); and Sidney Weintraub et al., eds., *U.S.-Mexican Industrial Integration* (1991).

For Panama and the war against Noriega, consult Kevin Buckley, *Panama* (1991); John Dinges, *Our Man in Panama* (1990); Frederick Kempe, *Divorcing the Dictator* (1990); John Lindsey-Poland, *Emperors in the Jungle* (2003); R. M. Koster and Guillermo Sanchez, *In The Time of the Tyrants* (1990); Walter LaFeber, *The Panama Canal* (1989); and Margaret E. Scranton, *The Noriega Years* (1991).

See also the General Bibliography, Robert L. Beisner, ed., *Guide to American Foreign Relations Since 1600* (2003), and the following notes.

For a comprehensive survey of foreign-relations topics, see the articles in the four-volume *Encyclopedia of U.S. Foreign Relations* (1997), edited by Bruce W. Jentleson and Thomas G. Paterson.

NOTES TO CHAPTER 12

1. David Frum, *The Right Man* (New York: Random House, 2003), p. 114.
2. Quoted in *Hartford Courant,* August 30, 2003.
3. John Updike, "Comment," *The New Yorker, LXXVII* (September 24, 2001), 28.
4. Quoted in "Mayor of the World," *Time, CLVIII* (December 31, 2001/January 7, 2002), 44.
5. Port Authority transcripts quoted in *Hartford Courant,* August 29, 2003.
6. David Von Drabble in *Washington Post National Weekly Edition,* September 17–23, 2001.
7. Quoted in Nicholas Lemann, "The Options," *The New Yorker, LXXVII* (October 1, 2001), 72.
8. Quoted in Bob Woodward, *Bush at War* (New York: Simon & Schuster, 2002), p. 18.
9. Quoted in Walter LaFeber, "The Bush Doctrine," *Diplomatic History, XXVI* (Fall 2002), 143.
10. Quoted in Woodward, *Bush at War,* p. 7.
11. CIA official quoted in *Washington Post National Weekly Edition,* May 27–June 2, 2002.
12. Quoted in Woodward, *Bush at War,* p. 3.
13. Osama bin Laden quoted in Kathleen Hall Jamieson and Paul Waldman, *The Press Effect* (New York: Oxford University Press, 2003), p. xi.
14. Maryann Cusimano Love, "Global Problems, Global Solutions," in Maryann Cusimano Love, ed., *Beyond Sovereignty* (Belmont, Calif.: Thompson-Wadsworth, 2003), p. 2.
15. Quoted in Woodward, *Bush at War,* p. 211.
16. Quoted in Frances FitzGerald, "George Bush and the World," *New York Review of Books,* September 26, 2002, p. 80.
17. Stephen M. Walt, "Beyond bin Laden," *International Security, XXVI* (Winter 2001/2002), 57–58.
18. Quoted in Joseph S. Nye, Jr., "U.S. Power and Strategy After Iraq," *Foreign Affairs, LXXXII* (July/August 2003), 61.
19. Quoted in FitzGerald, "Bush and the World," p. 85.
20. Quoted in Elizabeth Drew, "Hung Up in Washington," *New York Review of Books,* February 12, 2004, p. 18.
21. Quoted in Woodward, *Bush at War,* p. 81.
22. Quoted in Frum, *Right Man,* p. 239.
23. Rumsfeld quoted in Spencer Ackerman and John B. Judis, "The First Casualty," *The New Republic, CCXXVII* (June 30, 2003), 14.
24. Michael Ignatieff, "Why Are We in Iraq? (And Liberia? And Afghanistan?)," *New York Times Magazine* (September 7, 2003), p. 71.
25. Bush, Rumsfeld, and Rice quoted in Ackerman and Judis, "First Casualty," pp. 14, 17.; Tenet quoted in Bob Woodward, *Plan of Attack* (New York: Simon & Schuster, 2004), p. 249.
26. Quoted in Michael Dunne, "The United States, the United Nations, and Iraq," *International Affairs, LXXIX* (March 2003), 271.
27. Quoted in Woodward, *Plan of Attack,* p. 294.
28. Quoted in William Finnegan, "Marches and Parades," *The New Yorker, LXXIX* (May 19, 2003), 33.
29. Quoted in Dana H. Allin, Philip H. Gordon, and Michael O'Hanlon, "The Democratic Party and Foreign Policy," *World Policy Journal, XIX* (Spring 2003), 12.
30. Quoted in Samuel F. Wells, Jr., "The Transatlantic Illness," *Wilson Quarterly, XXVII* (Winter 2003), 42.
31. Max Boot, "The New American Way of War," *Foreign Affairs, LXXXII* (July/August 2003), 44.
32. Quoted in Williamson Murray and Robert H. Scales, Jr., *The Iraq War* (Cambridge: Harvard University Press, 2003), p. 110.
33. Nye, "U.S. Power," p. 60.
34. Michael Cox, "Martians and Venutians in the New World Order," *International Affairs, LXXIX* (Spring 2003), 523–532.
35. Condoleezza Rice and Paul Wolfowitz quoted in Mark Danner, "Iraq: The New War," *New York Review of Books,* September 25, 2003, pp. 90–91; Bush quoted in Ron Suskind, *The Price of Loyalty* (New York: Simon & Schuster, 2004), p. 187.
36. Paul Bremer quoted in *New York Times,* December 15, 2003; David Kay quoted *Ibid.,* February 1, 2004.

37. General John Abizaid quoted in Danner, "Iraq," p. 88; *New York Times,* October 22, 2003.

38. Arthur M. Schlesinger, Jr., "Eyeless in Iraq," *New York Review of Books,* October 23, 2003, p. 26.

39. Diplomat quoted in *Newsweek, CLII* (October 6, 2003), 37; James Fallows, "Blind into Baghdad," *The Atlantic Monthly, CCIXIII* (January/February 2004), 90.

40. Nicholas Lemann, "Comment: Real Reasons," *The New Yorker, LXXIX* (September 22, 2003), 82.

41. Quoted in *Hartford Courant,* September 8, 2003.

42. Jeffrey Bell quoted in Josiah M. Marshall, "Practice to Deceive," *The Washington Monthly, XXXVII* (April 2003), 29.

43. Todd Gitlin, "America's Age of Empire," *Mother Jones, XXVIII* (January/February 2003), 36.

44. Cheney quoted in William K. Tabb, "Two Wings of the Eagle," *Monthly Review, LV* (Summer 2003), 80.

45. Roger Lapham, *Theater of War* (New York: New Press, 2002), p. 28.

46. Richard N. Haas quoted in Joseph S. Nye, *The Paradox of American Power* (New York: Oxford University Press, 2002), p. 159.

47. Quoted in George Bush and Brent Scowcroft, *A World Transformed* (New York: Knopf, 1998), p. 151.

48. Quoted in Hans-Hermann Hertle, "The Fall of the Wall," *Cold War International History Project Bulletin,* nos. 11–12 (Fall/Winter 2001), 136.

49. Quoted in *Time, CXXXIV* (November 20, 1989), 29.

50. *Ibid.,* p. 25.

51. Quoted in *Washington Post National Weekly Edition,* January 1–7, 1990.

52. Marina Sylvanskaya quoted in Jacques Levesque, "Soviet Approaches to Eastern Europe at the Beginning of 1989," *Cold War International History Project Bulletin,* nos. 12–13 (Fall/Winter 2001), 51.

53. Quoted in Richard Ned Lebow and Janice Gross Stein, "Reagan and the Russians," *The Atlantic Monthly, CCLXXIII* (February 1994), 36.

54. Quoted in Vladislav M. Zubok, "Gorbachev and the End of the Cold War," in William C. Wohlforth, ed., *Cold War Endgame* (University Park: Penn. State University Press, 2003), p. 324.

55. Quoted in Jim Hoagland, "Europe's Destiny," *Foreign Affairs: America and the World,* 1989/90, *LXIX* (1990), 38.

56. Anatoly Chernaev quoted in Vladislav M. Zubok, "New Evidence on the End of the Cold War," *Cold War International History Project,* nos. 12–13 (Fall/Winter 2001), 6.

57. Quoted in *Time, CXXXV* (January 1, 1990), 53.

58. Zubok, "New Evidence," p. 11.

59. Quoted in Mikhail Gorbachev, *Memoirs* (New York: Doubleday, 1996), p. 525.

60. Quoted in Michael Beschloss and Strobe Talbott, *At the Highest Levels* (Boston: Little, Brown, 1993), p. 134.

61. Vyacheslav Dashichev quoted in Archie Brown, *The Gorbachev Factor* (New York: Oxford University Press, 1996), p. 245.

62. Richard J. Barnet, "Reflections: After the Cold War," *The New Yorker, LXV* (January 1, 1990), 66.

63. Quoted in Elizabeth Drew, "Letter from Washington," *ibid., LXV* (November 22, 1989), 122.

64. Entry, George H. W. Bush, "China (Peking) Diary, 1974–75," George H. W. Bush Library, College Station, Texas.

65. Quoted in Beschloss and Talbott, *Highest,* p. 205.

66. Margaret Thatcher, *The Downing Street Years* (New York: Harper-Collins, 1993), p. 783.

67. Quoted in Beschloss and Talbott, *Highest,* p. 41.

68. David Halberstam, *War in a Time of Peace* (New York: Scribners, 2001), p. 65.

69. Senior official quoted in Elizabeth Drew, *On the Edge* (New York: Simon & Schuster, 1994), p. 138.

70. Quoted in Strobe Talbott, *The Russian Hand* (New York: Random House, 2002), p. 407.

71. Brian Urquhart in "The Talk of the Town," *The New Yorker, LXXII* (December 2, 1996), 45.

72. Quoted in *New York Times,* December 23, 1992.

73. Halberstam, *War in Time of Peace,* p. 175.

74. Mark Danner, "Marooned in the Cold War," *World Policy Journal, XIV* (Fall 1997), 11.

75. Quoted in Jussi M. Hanhimaki, "Global Visions and Parochial Politics," *Diplomatic History, XXVII* (September 2003), 440.

76. Quoted in Halberstam, *War in a Time of Peace,* p. 243.

77. Quoted in *Washington Post National Weekly Edition,* July 4, 1997.

78. Martin Walker, "The Clinton Doctrine," *The New Yorker, LXXII* (October 7, 1996), 7.

79. Quoted in *Hartford Courant,* December 16, 1993.

80. Douglas Brinkley, "Democratic Enlargement: The Clinton Doctrine," *Foreign Policy,* no. 106 (Spring 1997), 125.

81. Quoted in Joe Klein, *The Natural* (New York: Doubleday, 2002), p. 11.

82. Robert Kagan, "The Benevolent Empire," *Foreign Policy,* no. 111 (Summer 1998), 25.

83. Quoted in John T. Rourke, *International Politics on the World Stage* (New York: Dushkin/McGraw-Hill, 1999; 7th ed.), p. 476.

84. George W. Bush quoted in William Finnegan, "The Economics of Empire," *Harper's Magazine, CCCVI* (May 2003), 41.

85. Richard Brookhiser, "The Mind of George W. Bush," *The Atlantic Monthly, CCLXXXIX* (April 2003), 59.

86. Quoted in Woodward, *Bush at War,* p. 137; quoted in Michael J. Mazarr, "George W. Bush, Idealist," *International Affairs, LXXIX* (June 2003), 503.

87. Quoted in David Remnick, "After the War," *The New Yorker, LXXIX* (March 31, 2003), 29.

88. Eliot Cohen quoted in *Washington Post National Weekly Edition,* December 25, 2000/January 1, 2001.

89. Quoted in Michael Hirsh, *At War with Ourselves* (New York: Oxford University Press, 2003), p. 52.

90. Quoted *Ibid.,* p. 54.

91. Woodward, *Bush at War,* p. 322; Powell quoted in *Washington Post National Weekly Edition,* April 7–13, 2003.

92. Quoted in Hendrik Hertzberg, "Blixkrieg," *The New Yorker, LXXIX* (February 10, 2003), 33.

93. Bush quoted in Woodward, *Bush at War,* p. 256.

94. Former official quoted in Seymour M. Hersh, "The Iraq Hawks," *The New Yorker, LXXVII* (December 24 & 31, 2001), 59.

95. Fred I. Greenstein, "Ronald Reagan, Mikhail Gorbachev, and the End of the Cold War," in William C. Wohlforth, ed., *Witnesses to the End of the Cold War* (Baltimore: Johns Hopkins University Press, 1996), p. 216.

96. Arnold L. Horelick, "U.S.–Soviet Relations," *Foreign Affairs: America and the World, 1989/90, LXIX* (1990), 54–55.

97. Quoted in *New York Times,* April 9, 1989.

98. Jack Matlock quoted in John Robert Greene, *The Presidency of George Bush* (Lawrence: University Press of Kansas, 2000), p. 90.

99. Quoted in Zubok, "New Evidence," p. 14.

100. Quoted in *New York Times,* August 5, 1990.

101. John B. Dunlap, "The August 1991 Coup and Its Impact on Soviet Politics," *Journal of Cold War Studies, V* (Winter 2003), 112.

102. Quoted in Charles William Maynes, "A Workable Clinton Doctrine," *Foreign Policy*, no. 93 (Winter 1993/1994), 3; Paul D. Wolfowitz, "Clinton's First Year," *Foreign Affairs*, LXXIII (January/February 1994), 41.

103. Talbott quoted in Stephen F. Cohen, *Failed Crusade* (New York: Norton, 2000), pp. 7, 250.

104. Stephen Handelman, *Comrade Criminal* (New Haven: Yale University Press, 1994); Jonathan Haslam, "Russia's Seat at the Table," *International Affairs*, LXXIV (January 1998), 125.

105. Quoted in Raymond Garthoff, "The United States and the New Russia," *Current History*, XCVI (October 1997), 307.

106. Jeremy Taylor, "Russia Is Finished," *The Atlantic Monthly*, CCLXXXVII (May 2001), 52.

107. Quoted in Simon Serfaty, "Europe Enlarged, America Detached?" *Current History*, CII (March 2003), 101.

108. Alexander Bessmertnykh quoted in Thomas M. Nichols, "Russia's Turn West," *World Policy Journal*, XIX (Winter 2002/2003), 4.

109. Jim Hoagland, "Europe's Destiny," *America and the World, 1989/90*, p. 41.

110. Bush aide quoted in Frank Costigliola, "An 'Arm Around the Shoulder': The United States, NATO, and German Unification, 1989–1990," *Contemporary European History*, III (March 1994), 88.

111. Richard Helms in *Hartford Courant*, March 4, 1990.

112. Brent Scowcroft quoted in James Chace, "New World Disorder," *New York Review of Books*, December 17, 1998, p. 60.

113. Stanley Hoffmann, "Bush Abroad," *New York Review of Books*, November 5, 1992, p. 54.

114. Thatcher, *Downing Street*, p. 797.

115. John S. Duffield, *World Power Forsaken: German Security After Unification* (Stanford: Stanford University Press, 1998), p. viii.

116. Hans-Dietrich Gentscher, *Rebuilding a House Divided* (New York: Broadway, 1998), p. 361.

117. Condoleezza Rice, Gerhard Schroeder, and Herta Daubler-Gmein quoted in Martin Walker, "The Winter of Germany's Discontent," *World Policy Journal*, XIX (Winter 2002/03), 2–3.

118. Quoted in James Goldgeier, "NATO Expansion: Anatomy of a Decision," *The Washington Quarterly*, XXI (Winter 1998), 94.

119. U.S. diplomat quoted in Haslam, "Russia's Seat," p. 124.

120. William Perry quoted in Victor Israelyan, "Don't Tease a Wounded Bear," *The Washington Quarterly*, XXI (Winter 1998), 53; Kennan quoted in *New York Times*, February 5, 1997.

121. Brent Scowcroft quoting Baker in Michael Kelly, "Surrender and Blame," *The New Yorker*, LXX (December 19, 1994), 45.

122. Andrew Bell Fialkoff, "A Brief History of Ethnic Cleansing," *Foreign Affairs*, LXXII (Summer 1993), 120.

123. Warren Christopher quoted in Samantha Power, *"A Problem from Hell"* (New York: BasicBooks, 2002), p. xii.

124. Quoted in John Newhouse, "No Exit, No Entrance," *The New Yorker*, LXIX (June 28, 1993), 46.

125. Colin L. Powell, *My American Journey* (New York: Random House, 1995), pp. 576–577.

126. Clinton quoted in Power, *"Problem from Hell,"* p. 437.

127. Richard Holbrooke, "Why We Are in Bosnia," *The New Yorker*, LXXIV (May 18, 1998), 63.

128. Clinton quoted in Eric Moskowitz and Jeffrey S. Lantis, "The War in Kosovo," in Ralph G. Carter, ed., *Contemporary Cases in U.S. Foreign Policy* (Washington, D.C.: CQ Press, 2002), p. 81.

129. Robert K. Massie, *Loosing the Bonds* (New York: Doubleday, 1998), p. 689.

130. National Intelligence Estimate quoted in *Washington Post National Weekly Edition*, May 8, 2000.

131. Quoted in *Washington Post National Weekly Edition*, December 14–20, 1992.

132. Quoted in *Washington Post National Weekly Edition*, October 18–24, 1993.

133. General Thomas Montgomery quoted in Daniel P. Bolger, *Savage Peace* (Novato, Calif.: Presidio Press, 1995), p. 314.

134. Quoted in George Stephanopoulos, *All Too Human* (Boston: Little, Brown, 1999), p. 214.

135. Quoted in Halberstam, *War in a Time of Peace*, p. 265.

136. Quoted in David F. Gordon and Howard Wolpe, "The Other Africa," *World Policy Journal*, XV (Spring 1998), 52.

137. Prudence Bushnell quoted in Power, *"Problem from Hell,"* p. 351.

138. Quoted in *ibid.*, p. 344.

139. Quoted in *Hartford Courant*, March 26, 1998.

140. State Department official quoted in Frank Smyth, "A New Game," *World Policy Journal*, XV (Summer 1998), 90.

141. International Rescue Committee quoted in "Primary Sources," *The Atlantic Monthly* (July/August 2003), 38.

142. Ari Fleischer quoted in Philip Gourevitch, "The Congo Test," *The New Yorker*, LXXIX (June 2, 2003), 34.

143. David Benjamin and Stephen Simon quoted in *Washington Post National Weekly Edition*, January 7–13, 2002.

144. Quoted in Gordon and Wolpe, "Other Africa," 58.

145. Quoted in *Washington Post National Weekly Edition*, December 21–28, 1998.

146. Quoted in Salih Booker, William Minter, and Ann-Louise Colgan, "America and Africa," *Current History*, CII (May 2003), 196.

147. Quoted in *New York Times*, December 12, 1994.

148. Inter-American Dialogue, *Convergence and Community* (Washington, D.C.: Aspen Institute, 1992), p. 9.

149. Michael Shifter, "Latin America's New Political Leaders," *Current History*, CII (February 2003), 55.

150. Pastor, "Clinton Administration," p. 101.

151. Tom Miller, *On the Border* (1981), quoted in W. Dirk Raat, *Mexico and the United States* (Athens: University of Georgia Press, 1992), p. 173.

152. Quoted in Sewall H. Menzel, *Cocaine Quagmire* (New York: University Press of America, 1997), p. 153.

153. Stephen Flynn, "America the Vulnerable," *Foreign Affairs*, LXXXI (January/February 2002), 75.

154. Patrick Lloyd Hatcher, "The Unwinnable War on the Drug Trade," *Orbis*, XLI (Fall 1997), 659.

155. Quoted in William O. Walker III, "Drug Control and National Security," *Diplomatic History*, XII (Spring 1988), 188.

156. Eva Bertram and Kenneth Sharpe, "The Unwinnable Drug War," *World Policy Journal*, XIII (Winter 1996/1997), 45.

157. Quoted in *Washington Post National Weekly Edition*, November 11–17, 2002.

158. Jessica Stern, "The Protean Enemy," *Foreign Affairs*, LXXXII (July/August 2003), 32.

159. Sol M. Linowitz, "Latin America," *Foreign Affairs*, LXVII (Winter 1988/1989), 56.

160. John Lindsay-Poland, *Emperors in the Jungle* (Durham: Duke University Press, 2003), p. 115.

161. Editors of *The New Republic, Bushisms,* (New York: Workman, 1992), p. 65.

162. Powell quoted in Douglas Little, *American Orientalism* (Chapel Hill: University of North Carolina Press, 2002), p. 253.

163. *Los Angeles Times* quoted in Lindsay-Poland, *Emperors*, p. 120.

164. Public Affairs After Action Report, December 20, 1989–January 31, 1990, National Security Archive, Washington, D.C.

165. General Maxwell Thurman quoted in Lindsay-Poland, *Emperors*, p. 117.

166. Quoted in Klein, *The Natural*, p. 73.

167. Quoted in Tracy Kidder, "The Siege of Mirebalais," *The New Yorker, LXXI* (April 17, 1995), 84.

168. Admiral Paul Miller quoted in Stephanopoulos, *All Too Human*, p. 309.

169. Jorge Domínguez, "U.S.-Cuban Relations: From the Cold War to the Colder War," *Journal of Interamerican Studies and World Affairs, XXXIX* (Fall 1997), 54.

170. Quoted in William M. LeoGrande, "From Havana to Miami," *ibid., XL* (Spring 1998), 77.

171. Quoted in Ann Blackman, *Seasons of Her Life* (New York: Charles Scribner's Sons, 1998), p. 246.

172. Quoted in Wayne S. Smith, "Our Dysfunctional Cuban Embargo," *Orbis, XLII* (Fall 1998), 537.

173. Quoted in *Washington Post National Weekly Edition*, November 30, 1998.

174. Vicki Huddleston quoted in Morris Morley and Chris McGillion, *Unfinished Business* (New York: Cambridge University Press, 2002), p. 199.

175. Dagoberto Rodriguez quoted in *Miami Herald*, October 10, 2003.

176. Quoted in Deborah Amos, *Lines in the Sand* (New York: Simon & Schuster, 1992), p. 82.

177. Quoted in Michael Howard, "The Prudence Thing," *Foreign Affairs, LXXVII* (November/December 1998), 131.

178. Quoted in John T. Rourke, *Presidential Wars and American Democracy* (Washington, D.C.: Paragon, 1993), p. 14.

179. Quoted in Pierre Salinger and Eric Laurent, *Secret Dossier* (New York: Penguin, 1991), p. 110.

180. Quoted in Freedman and Karsh, *Gulf*, p. 293.

181. Quoted in Rourke, *Presidential Wars*, p. 59.

182. Quoted in Greene, *Presidency of George Bush*, p. 123.

183. Lapham, *Theater of War*, p. 132.

184. Quoted in Dunne, "United States . . . and Iraq," p. 264.

185. Quoted in Robert W. Tucker and David C. Hendrickson, *The Imperial Temptation* (New York: Council on Foreign Relations Press, 1992), p. 76.

186. Thomas Harkin quoted in *Hartford Courant*, March 20, 2003.

187. Quoted in Rick Atkinson, *Crusade* (Boston: Houghton Mifflin, 1993), p. 496.

188. Quoted in Ussama Makdisi, "'Anti-Americanism' in the Arab World,'" *Journal of American History, LXXXIX* (September 2002), 556.

189. Quoted in Peter J. Boyle, "Scott Ritter's Private War," *The New Yorker, LXXIV* (November 9, 1998), 66.

190. Quoted in *New York Times*, December 17, 1998.

191. William Cohen quoted in *Newsweek, CXXXII* (December 28, 1998), 48.

192. Quoted in Kenneth M. Pollock, *The Threatening Storm* (New York: Random House, 2002), p. 94.

193. Quoted *Ibid.*, p. 106.

194. James Baker, "Principles and Pragmatism," May 22, 1989, Department of State Current Policy no. 1176.

195. Quoted in Yezid Sayigh, *Armed Struggle and the Search for State* (New York: Oxford University Press, 1997), p. 654.

196. Quoted in *New York Times*, June 15, 2003.

197. Baker, *Politics of Diplomacy*, p. 103.

198. Quoted in Roderick MacFarquhar, "The End of the Chinese Revolution," *New York Review of Books*, July 20, 1989, p. 8.

199. John K. Fairbank, "Why China's Rulers Fear Democracy," *ibid.*, September 28, 1989, p. 33.

200. Entry of June 20, 1989, Bush and Scowcroft, *World Transformed*, p. 102.

201. Lawrence Eagleburger quoted in Baker, *Politics of Diplomacy*, p. 110.

202. Quoted in Lampton, *Same Bed*, p. 40.

203. Quoted in Jonathan D. Pollock, "The United States and Asia in 1996," *Asian Survey, XXXVII* (January 1997), 97.

204. William Perry quoted *ibid.*

205. Quoted in Lampton, *Same Bed*, 52.

206. Quoted in Lucien W. Pye, "The United States and Asia in 1997," *Asian Survey, XXXVII* (January 1998), 99; quoted in Yoichi Funabashi, "Tokyo's Depression Diplomacy," *Foreign Affairs, LXXVII* (November/December 1998), 32.

207. Quoted in Ted Galen Carpenter, "Roiling Asia," *Foreign Affairs, LXXVII* (November/December 1998), 4.

208. Quoted in Elizabeth Economy, "Changing Course on China," *Current History, CII* (September 2003), 246.

209. Quoted in Oleksandr Gladky, "American Foreign Policy and U.S. Relations with Russia and China," *World Affairs, CLXVI* (Summer 2003), 7.

210. Quoted in Robert B. Oxnam, "Asia & Pacific Challenges," *Foreign Affairs: America and the World 1992–93, LXXII* (January 1993), 71.

211. *Washington Post National Weekly Edition*, August 8–14, 1994.

212. Quoted in *New York Times*, February 6, 1994.

213. Robert J. McMahon, *The Limits of Empire* (New York: Columbia University Press, 1999), p. 224.

214. John T. Rourke, *International Politics on the World Stage*, 9th ed. (New York: McGraw-Hill, 2003), p. 288.

215. Quoted in James Fallows, "Getting Along with Japan," *The Atlantic Monthly, CCLXIV* (December 1989), 55.

216. Chalmers Johnson quoted in *Washington Post National Weekly Edition*, August 24, 1998.

217. George W. Bush quoted in Elinor Sloan, "Beyond Primacy," *International Journal, LXIII* (Spring 2003), 309.

218. Bruce Cumings quoted in Benjamin Schwartz, "Why America Thinks It Has to Run the World," *The Atlantic Monthly, CCLXXVII* (June 1996), 94.

219. Quoted in *Washington Post National Weekly Edition*, October 25–31, 1993.

220. Richard Kerr quoted in Seymour Hersh, "On the Nuclear Edge," *The New Yorker, LXIX* (March 29, 1993), 55.

221. Quoted in Arjun Makhijani et al., "Dismantling the Bomb," in Stephen I. Schwartz, ed., *Atomic Audit* (Washington, D.C.: Brookings, 1998), p. 346.

222. Quoted in Josiah M. Marshall, "The Power Rangers," *The New Yorker, LXXIX* (February 2, 2004), 88.

223. Carter Diary quoted in Douglas Brinkley, *The Unfinished Presidency* (New York: Viking, 1998), p. 399.

224. Quoted in Roland Bleiker, "A Rogue is a Rogue is a Rogue," *International Affairs, LXXIX* (July 2003), 724.

225. Anthony Lake, "Confronting Backlash States," *Foreign Affairs, LXXIII* (March/April 1994), 45.

226. Strobe Talbott in *Time, CXXXV* (January 1, 1990), 72.

227. Mike Moore quoted in Bruce R. Kuniholm, "9/11, the Great Game, and the Vision Thing," *Journal of American History, LXXXIX* (September 2002), 437.

228. Maryann Cusimano Love, "Mind the Gaps," in Love, *Beyond Sovereignty*, p. 323.

229. Jacques Diouf quoted in *Great Decisions, 1997* (New York: Foreign Policy Association, 1997), p. 59.

230. World Resources Institute, *Environmental Almanac* (Boston: Houghton Mifflin, 1992), p. 13.

231. Lester R. Brown, "The Acceleration of History," in Worldwatch Institute, *State of the World 1996* (New York: Norton, 1996), p. 4.

232. Quoted in *New York Times*, April 17, 1996.

233. Quoted in Rourke, *International Politics* (9th ed.), p. 47.

234. Quoted in *Time, CXXXIII* (January 2, 1989), 30.

235. James Baker, "Diplomacy for the Environment," February 26, 1990, Department of State Current Policy no. 1254.

236. Harlan Cleveland, *Birth of a New World* (San Francisco: Jossey-Bass, 1993), p. 46.

237. Quoted in Charles A. Kupchan, "The Rise of Europe," *Political Science Quarterly, CXVIII* (Summer 2003), 223.

238. Fauziya Kassindja quoted in Rourke, *International Politics* (9th ed.), p. 514.

239. Quoted in Emily S. Rosenberg, "Rescuing Women and Children," *Journal of American History, LXXXIX* (September 2002), 456.

240. Quoted in J. Ann Tickner, "Feminist Perspectives on 9/11," *International Studies Perspectives, III* (2002), 333.

241. Anthony Lake quoted in Brinkley, "Democratic," p. 117.

242. Quoted in Rourke, *International Politics*, p. 192.

243. Barbara Wallraff, "What Global Language?" *The Atlantic Monthly, CCLXXXVIII* (November 2000), 61.

244. Richard A. Love, "The Cyberthreat Continuum," in Love, *Beyond Sovereignty*, p. 198.

245. Walter B. Wriston, "Bits, Bytes, and Diplomacy," *Foreign Affairs, LXXVI* (September/October 1997), 175.

246. Quoted in *Washington Post National Weekly Edition,* December 14, 1998.

247. Love, "Cyberthreat Continuum," p. 196.

248. L. Craig Johnstone quote in Love, "Global Problems," p. 10.

249. Quoted in Nye, *Paradox*, p. 100.

250. Love, "Global Problems," p. 5.

251. Rob Kroes, "American Empire and Cultural Imperialism," in Thomas Bender, ed., *Rethinking American History in a Global Age* (Berkeley: University of California Press, 2002), pp. 303–304; *New York Times*, August 29, 1999.

252. Thomas Zeiler, "Globalization," in Alexander DeConde et al., *Encyclopedia of American Foreign Policy, 3 vols.* (New York: Scribner's, 2002), *II*, 146.

253. Thomas Friedman, *The Lexus and the Olive Tree* (New York: Farrar, Straus and Giroux, 1999), pp. 7–8.

254. George F. Kennan, "Correspondence," *World Policy Journal, XV* (Spring 1998), 107.

255. Maureen Dowd in *New York Times,* March 4, 1990.

256. Ronald Steel, "The Domestic Core of Foreign Policy," *The Atlantic Monthly, CCLXXV* (June 1995), 86.

257. Quoted in Jonathan Clarke, "The Conceptual Poverty of U.S. Foreign Policy," *ibid., CCLXXII* (September 1993), 62.

258. Charles Krauthammer quoted in Nye, *Paradox*, p. 2; quoted in Robert Worth, "Clinton's Warriors," *World Policy Journal, XV* (Spring 1998), 47.

259. Quoted in *Washington Post National Weekly Edition*, April 26–May 4, 2003.

260. Quoted in Marshall, "The Power Rangers," p. 86.

261. Bush quoted in Woodward, *Bush at War*, p. 63.

262. Bush quoted in Sloan, "Beyond Primacy," 309.

263. Quoted in Hirsh, *At War with Ourselves*, p. 17.

264. Barry R. Posen, "Command of the Commons," *International Security, XXVIII* (Summer 2003), 7.

265. William Kristol quoted in Nye, "U.S. Power," 64.

266. Arthur M. Schlesinger, Jr., quoted in Brian Urquhart, "World Order and Mr. Bush," *New York Review of Books*, October 9, 2003, p. 10.

267. Hubert Vedrine quoted in *Washington Post National Weekly Edition,* November 22, 1999.

268. Andrew J. Bacevich in *Washington Post National Weekly Edition,* April 28–May 4, 2003.

269. Niall Ferguson, "The Empire Slinks Back," *New York Times Magazine,* April 27, 2003, pp. 52, 54.

270. Cheney and Rumsfeld quoted in Nye, "U.S. Power," p. 64.

271. Rumsfeld quoted in Boyer, "War Machine, 71; Bush quoted in Elizabeth Kolbert, "Solo Act," *The New Yorker, LXXIX* (October 6, 2003), 43.

272. Quoted in *Washington Post National Weekly Edition*, November 13, 2000.

273. Sebastian Mallaby quoted in Nye, *Paradox*, p. 40.

Makers of American Foreign Relations

Presidents	Secretaries of State	Chairs of the Senate Foreign Relations Committee
George Washington (1789–1797)	Thomas Jefferson (1790–1793) Edmund Randolph (1794–1795) Timothy Pickering (1795–1797)	
John Adams (1797–1801)	Timothy Pickering (1797–1800) John Marshall (1800–1801)	
Thomas Jefferson (1801–1809)	James Madison (1801–1809)	
James Madison (1809–1817)	Robert Smith (1809–1811) James Monroe (1811–1817)	James Barbour (1816–1817)
James Monroe (1817–1825)	John Quincy Adams (1817–1825)	James Barbour (1817–1818) Nathaniel Macon (1818–1819) James Brown (1819–1820) James Barbour (1820–1821) Rufus King (1821–1822) James Barbour (1822–1825)
John Quincy Adams (1825–1829)	Henry Clay (1825–1829)	Nathaniel Macon (1825–1826) Nathan Sanford (1826–1827) Nathaniel Macon (1827–1828) Littleton W. Tazewell (1828–1829)
Andrew Jackson (1829–1837)	Martin Van Buren (1829–1831) Edward Livingston (1831–1833) Louis McLane (1833–1834) John Forsyth (1834–1837)	Littleton W. Tazewell (1829–1832) John Forsyth (1832–1833) William Wilkins (1833–1834) Henry Clay (1834–1836) James Buchanan (1836–1837)
Martin Van Buren (1837–1841)	John Forsyth (1837–1841)	James Buchanan (1837–1841)
William H. Harrison (1841)	Daniel Webster (1841)	William C. Rives (1841)
John Tyler (1841–1845)	Daniel Webster (1841–1843)	William C. Rives (1841–1842)

Makers of American Foreign Relations *(continued)*

Presidents	Secretaries of State	Chairs of the Senate Foreign Relations Committee
	Abel P. Upshur (1843–1844) John C. Calhoun (1844–1845)	William S. Archer (1842–1845)
James K. Polk (1845–1849)	James Buchanan (1845–1849)	William Allen (1845–1846) Ambrose H. Sevier (1846–1848) Edward A. Hannegan (1848–1849) Thomas H. Benton (1849)
Zachary Taylor (1849–1850)	John M. Clayton (1849–1850)	William R. King (1849–1850)
Millard Fillmore (1850–1853)	Daniel Webster (1850–1852) Edward Everett (1852–1853)	Henry S. Foote (1850–1851) James M. Mason (1851–1853)
Franklin Pierce (1853–1857)	William L. Marcy (1853–1857)	James M. Mason (1853–1857)
James Buchanan (1857–1861)	Lewis Cass (1857–1860) Jeremiah S. Black (1860–1861)	James M. Mason (1857–1861)
Abraham Lincoln (1861–1865)	William H. Seward (1861–1865)	Charles Sumner (1861–1865)
Andrew Johnson (1865–1869)	William H. Seward (1865–1869)	Charles Sumner (1865–1869)
Ulysses S. Grant (1869–1877)	Elihu B. Washburne (1869) Hamilton Fish (1869–1877)	Charles Sumner (1869–1871) Simon Cameron (1871–1877)
Rutherford B. Hayes (1877–1881)	William M. Evarts (1877–1881)	Hannibal Hamlin (1877–1879) William W. Eaton (1879–1881)
James A. Garfield (1881)	James G. Blaine (1881)	Ambrose E. Burnside (1881) George F. Edmunds (1881)
Chester A. Arthur (1881–1885)	Frederick T. Frelinghuysen (1881–1885)	William Windom (1881–1883) John F. Miller (1883–1885)
Grover Cleveland (1885–1889)	Thomas F. Bayard (1885–1889)	John F. Miller (1885–1887) John Sherman (1887–1889)
Benjamin Harrison (1889–1893)	James G. Blaine (1889–1892) John W. Foster (1892–1893)	John Sherman (1889–1893)
Grover Cleveland (1893–1897)	Walter Q. Gresham (1893–1895) Richard Olney (1895–1897)	John T. Morgan (1893–1895) John Sherman (1895–1897)
William McKinley (1897–1901)	John Sherman (1897–1898) William R. Day (1898) John Hay (1898–1901)	William P. Frye (1897) Cushman K. Davis (1897–1901)
Theodore Roosevelt (1901–1909)	John Hay (1901–1905) Elihu Root (1905–1909) Robert Bacon (1909)	William P. Frye (1901) Shelby M. Cullom (1901–1909)
William Howard Taft (1909–1913)	Philander C. Knox (1909–1913)	Shelby M. Cullom (1909–1913)

Makers of American Foreign Relations *(continued)*

Presidents	Secretaries of State	Chairs of the Senate Foreign Relations Committee
Woodrow Wilson (1913–1921)	William Jennings Bryan (1913–1915) Robert Lansing (1915–1920) Bainbridge Colby (1920–1921)	Augustus O. Bacon (1913–1915) William J. Stone (1915–1919) Henry Cabot Lodge (1919–1921)
Warren G. Harding (1921–1923)	Charles E. Hughes (1921–1923)	Henry Cabot Lodge (1921–1923)
Calvin Coolidge (1923–1929)	Charles E. Hughes (1923–1925) Frank B. Kellogg (1925–1929)	Henry Cabot Lodge (1923–1924) William E. Borah (1925–1929)
Herbert C. Hoover (1929–1933)	Henry L. Stimson (1929–1933)	William E. Borah (1929–1933)
Franklin D. Roosevelt (1933–1945)	Cordell Hull (1933–1944) Edward R. Stettinius, Jr. (1944–1945)	Key Pittman (1933–1940) Walter F. George (1940–1941) Tom Connally (1941–1945)

Presidents	Secretaries of State	Chairs of the Senate Foreign Relations Committee	Secretaries of Defense	Assistants to the President for National Security Affairs
Harry S. Truman (1945–1953)	Edward R. Stettinius, Jr. (1945) James F. Byrnes (1945–1947) George C. Marshall (1947–1949) Dean G. Acheson (1949–1953)	Tom Connally (1945–1947) Arthur H. Vandenberg (1947–1949) Tom Connally (1949–1953)	James V. Forrestal (1947–1949) Louis A. Johnson (1949–1950) George C. Marshall (1950–1951) Robert A. Lovett (1951–1953)	
Dwight D. Eisenhower (1953–1961)	John F. Dulles (1953–1959) Christian A. Herter (1959–1961)	Alexander Wiley (1953–1955) Walter F. George (1955–1957) Theodore F. Green (1957–1959) J. William Fulbright (1959–1961)	Charles E. Wilson (1953–1957) Neil H. McElroy (1957–1959) Thomas S. Gates, Jr. (1959–1961)	Robert Cutler (1953–1955 & 1957–1958) Dillon Anderson (1955–1956) William H. Jackson (1956) Gordon Gray (1958–1961)
John F. Kennedy (1961–1963)	Dean Rusk (1961–1963)	J. William Fulbright (1961–1963)	Robert S. McNamara (1961–1963)	McGeorge Bundy (1961–1963)
Lyndon B. Johnson (1963–1969)	Dean Rusk (1963–1969)	J. William Fulbright (1963–1969)	Robert S. McNamara (1963–1968) Clark M. Clifford (1968–1969)	McGeorge Bundy (1963–1966) Walt W. Rostow (1966–1969)

Makers of American Foreign Relations *(continued)*

Presidents	Secretaries of State	Chairs of the Senate Foreign Relations Committee	Secretaries of Defense	Assistants to the President for National Security Affairs
Richard M. Nixon (1969–1974)	William P. Rogers (1969–1973) Henry A. Kissinger (1973–1974)	J. William Fulbright (1969–1974)	Melvin R. Laird (1969–1973) Elliot L. Richardson (1973) James R. Schlesinger (1973–1974)	Henry A. Kissinger (1969–1974)
Gerald R. Ford (1974–1977)	Henry A. Kissinger (1974–1977)	J. William Fulbright (1974–1975) John Sparkman (1975–1977)	James R. Schlesinger (1974–1976) Donald Rumsfeld (1976–1977)	Henry A. Kissinger (1974–1975) Brent Scowcroft (1975–1977)
James E. Carter (1977–1981)	Cyrus R. Vance (1977–1980) Edmund Muskie (1980–1981)	John Sparkman (1977–1979) Frank Church (1979–1981)	Harold Brown (1977–1981)	Zbigniew Brzezinski (1977–1981)
Ronald W. Reagan (1981–1989)	Alexander M. Haig, Jr. (1981–1982) George P. Shultz (1982–1989)	Charles Percy (1981–1985) Richard G. Lugar (1985–1987) Claiborne Pell (1987–1989)	Caspar Weinberger (1981–1987) Frank C. Carlucci (1987–1989)	Richard Allen (1981) William P. Clark, Jr. (1981–1983) Robert C. McFarlane (1983–1985) John M. Poindexter (1985–1986) Frank C. Carlucci (1986–1987) Colin L. Powell (1987–1989)
George H. W. Bush (1989–1993)	James A. Baker III (1989–1992) Lawrence Eagleburger (1992–1993)	Claiborne Pell (1989–1993)	Richard B. Cheney (1989–1993)	Brent Scowcroft (1989–1993)
William J. Clinton (1993–2001)	Warren M. Christopher (1993–1997) Madeleine K. Albright (1997–2001)	Claiborne Pell (1993–1995) Jesse Helms (1995–2001)	Les Aspin (1993–1994) William J. Perry (1994–1997) William S. Cohen (1997–2001)	Anthony Lake (1993–1996) Samuel R. Berger (1996–2001)
George W. Bush (2001–)	Colin L. Powell (2001–)	Joseph L. Biden, Jr. (2001–2003) Richard G. Lugar (2003–)	Donald Rumsfeld (2001–)	Condoleezza Rice (2001–)

General Bibliography

General Reference Works

See also "Overviews of Relations with Countries, Regions, and Other Places of the World" and "Overviews of Subjects," both below, and your library's computer-based sources. Comprehensive bibliographies also appear in Robert L. Beisner, ed., *Guide to American Foreign Relations Since 1600* (2003) and Bruce W. Jentleson and Thomas G. Paterson, eds., *Encyclopedia of U.S. Foreign Relations* (1997).

Annual Surveys: *Facts on File* (1941–); *Human Development Report* (1990–); *Keesing's Record of World Events* (also titled *Keesing's Contemporary Archives*) (1931–); London Institute of World Affairs, *The Yearbook of World Affairs* (1947–); Alan F. Pater and Jason R. Pater, eds., *What They Said In . . .: The Yearbook of World Opinion* (1971–); *Political Handbook of the World* (1928–); *The Statesmen's Year-Book World Gazetteer* (1864–); United Nations, *Demographic Yearbook* (1948–); *The World Bank Atlas* (1967–); *World Development Report* (1978–). See also "Statistics."

Atlases and Gazetteers: Ewan W. Anderson and Don Shewan, *An Atlas of World Political Flashpoints* (1993); Andrew Boyd, *An Atlas of World Affairs* (1998); Saul B. Cohen, *Columbia Gazetteer of the World* (1998); Rodger Doyle, *Atlas of Contemporary America* (1994); Robert Ferrell and Richard Natkiel, *Atlas of American History* (1987); *Hammond Atlas of the World* (1992); Eric Homberger, *The Penguin Historical Atlas of North America* (1995); Michael Kidron and Ronald Segal, *The State of the World Atlas* (1995); Catherine Mattson and Mark T. Mattson, *Contemporary Atlas of the United States* (1998); David Munro, ed., *Chambers World Gazetteer* (1988); *National Geographic Atlas of the World* (1992); Richard Natkiel et al., eds., *Atlas of the Twentieth Century* (1982); *The New York Times Atlas of the World* (1992); *Oxford Atlas of the World* (2000); Rand McNally, *Today's World* (1996); Dan Smith, *The State of War and Peace Atlas* (1997); Dean Smith and Michael Kidron, *The State of the World Atlas* (1999); U.S. Military Academy, *West Point Atlas of American Wars* (1997).

Bibliographies: Samuel Flagg Bemis and Grace Gardner Griffin, *Guide to the Diplomatic History of the United States, 1775–1921* (1935); Richard Dean Burns, ed., *A Guide to American Foreign Relations Since*

1700 (1982); Congressional Information Service, *American Foreign Policy Index* (1994–); Council on Foreign Relations, *Foreign Affairs Bibliography* (1933–1972); Byron Dexter, ed., *The Foreign Affairs 50-Year Bibliography* (1972); Frank Freidel, ed., *Harvard Guide to American History* (1974); Mary Beth Norton, ed., *Guide to Historical Literature* (1995); Francis P. Prucha, *Handbook for Research in American History* (1987). The journal *Diplomatic History* regularly publishes articles that review the historiography of major topics and periods and provide extensive bibliographical guidance. The *Journal of American History* regularly lists recent publications. Journals such as *Foreign Affairs* and *Political Science Quarterly* regularly publish reviews of recent books.

Biographical Aids: John S. Bowman, *The Cambridge Dictionary of American Biography* (1995); Asa Briggs, *A Dictionary of Twentieth Century World Biography* (1990); Mari Jo Buhle et al., eds., *The American Radical* (1994); David Crystal, ed., *The Cambridge Biographical Encyclopedia* (1994); *Current Biography* (1940–); *Dictionary of American Biography* (1928–); *Encyclopedia of World Biography* (1998); John A. Garraty and Mark C. Carnes, eds., *American National Biography* (1999); John Garraty and Jerome L. Sternstein, eds., *The Encyclopedia of American Biography* (1996); *International Who's Who* (1935–); Bernard K. Johnpoll and Harvey Klehr, eds., *Biographical Dictionary of the American Left* (1986); Warren F. Kuehl, ed., *Biographical Dictionary of Internationalists* (1983); *National Cyclopedia of American Biography* (1898–); Alan Palmer, *Who's Who in Modern History* (1980); Philip Rees, *Biographical Dictionary of the Extreme Right Since 1890* (1991); Frank W. Thackery and John E. Findling, eds., *Statesmen Who Changed the World* (1993); U.S. Department of State, *Biographic Register* (1860–1974) and *Foreign Service List* (1929–); *Who Was Who in America* (1963–); *Who's Who in America* (1899–); *Who's Who in the World* (1971–).

Chronologies: Lester H. Brune, *Chronological History of U.S. Foreign Relations* (2002); Gorton Carruth, *The Encyclopedia of American Facts and Dates* (1993) and *The Encyclopedia of World Facts and Dates* (1993); Council on Foreign Relations, *Foreign Affairs Chronology, 1978–1989* (1990) and *The United States in World Affairs* (1932-1972); Robert H. Ferrell and John S. Bowman, eds., *The Twentieth Century* (1984);

Bernard Grun, *The Timetables of History* (1991); John E. Jessup, *A Chronology of Conflict and Resolution, 1945–1985* (1989); Thomas Parker and Douglas Nelson, *Day by Day: The Sixties* (1983); Royal Institute of International Affairs, *Survey of International Affairs, 1920–1963* (1972–1977); Laurence Urdang, ed., *The Timetables of American History* (1996). See also "Annual Surveys."

Documentary Collections and Series: Martin P. Claussen, ed., *The National State Papers of the United States: Texts of Documents (1789–1817)* (1980–); Council on Foreign Relations, *Documents on American Foreign Relations, 1938/1939–1970* (1939–1973); Royal Institute of International Affairs, *Documents on International Affairs, 1928–1963* (1929–1973); Arthur M. Schlesinger, Jr., ed., *The Dynamics of World Power: A Documentary History of U.S. Foreign Policy, 1945–1973* (1973); U.S. Congress, *American State Papers* (1852–1859); U.S. Department of State, *A Decade of American Foreign Policy: Basic Documents, 1941–1949* (1985), *American Foreign Policy: Basic Documents, 1950–1955* (1957), *American Foreign Policy: Basic Documents, 1977–1980* (1983–1986), *American Foreign Policy: Current Documents, 1956–1967* (1956–1967), *American Foreign Policy: Current Documents, 1981–* (1984–), *Bulletin* (1938–), *Dispatch* (1990–), *Foreign Relations of United States, 1861–* (1862–), and *Press Conferences of the Secretaries of State, 1922–1974* (n.d.); *Vital Speeches of the Day* (1934–).

Encyclopedias and Dictionaries: Alexander DeConde et al., eds., *Encyclopedia of American Foreign Policy* (2002); John Drexel, ed., *The Facts on File Encyclopedia of the 20th Century* (1991); Graham Evans and Jeffrey Newnham, *The Penguin Dictionary of International Relations* (1999); John M. Farragher, ed., *The American Heritage Encyclopedia of American History* (1998); John E. Findling, *Dictionary of American Diplomatic History* (1989); Charles W. Freeman, Jr., *The Diplomat's Dictionary* (1997); Jack P. Greene, ed., *Encyclopedia of American Political History* (1984); Kenneth L. Hill, *Encyclopedia of Conflicts Since World War II* (1998); Bruce W. Jentleson and Thomas G. Paterson, eds., *Encyclopedia of U.S. Foreign Relations* (1997); Stanley I. Kutler, ed., *Encyclopedia of the United States in the Twentieth Century* (1995); Richard B. Morris et al., *Encyclopedia of American History* (1996); Cathal J. Nolan, *The Greenwood Encyclopedia of International Relations* (2002); James H. Olson, *Historical Dictionary of the Great Depression* (2001); Jerry K. Sweeney et al., *America and the World, 1776–1998* (2000).

Statistics: Erik W. Austin and Jerome C. Clubb, *Political Facts of the United States Since 1789* (1986); International Monetary Fund, *International Financial Statistics* (1948–); George T. Kurian, ed., *The Illustrated Book of World Rankings* (1996); Robert D. Schulzinger, ed., *A Companion to American Foreign Relations* (2003); Victor Showers, *World Facts and Figures* (1989); Ruth L. Sivard, *World Military and Social Expenditures* (1974–); Charles L. Taylor and David A. Jodice, *World*

Handbook of Political and Social Indicators (1983); United Nations, *Demographic Yearbook* (1948–), *Report on the World Social Situation* (1952–), and *Statistical Yearbook* (1948–); U.S. Agency for International Development, *United States Overseas Loans and Grants and Assistance from International Organizations, July 1, 1945–Sept. 30, 1980* (1981); U.S. Bureau of the Census, *Historical Statistics of the United States* (1975) and *Statistical Abstract of the United States* (1878–); U.S. Central Intelligence Agency, *Handbook of International Economic Statistics* (1971–) and *The World Factbook* (1981–); World Bank, *World Tables* (1974–); World Resources Institute, *World Resources* (1990–). See also "Annual Surveys."

Overviews of Relations with Countries, Regions, and Other Places of the World, Including Atlases and Gazetteers (A), Annual Surveys and Chronologies (AS), Bibliographies (B), Biographical Aids (BA), Chronologies (C), Encyclopedias and Dictionaries (E), and Statistics (S)

Afghanistan: M. Hassar Kakar, *Afghanistan: The Soviet Invasion and the Afghan Response* (1995); William Maley, ed., *Fundamentalism Reborn* (2002); Nancy P. Newell and Richard S. Newell, *The Struggle for Afghanistan* (1981); Leon B. Poullada, *The Kingdom of Afghanistan and the United States, 1828–1973* (1995); Ahmed Rashid, *Taliban* (2001); Jeffrey J. Roberts, *The Origins of the Conflict in Afghanistan* (2002); Barnet Rubin, *The Fragmentation of Afghanistan* (2002).

Africa: Chris Cook and David Killinway, *African Political Facts Since 1945* (1991) (E); Peter Duignan and Lewis H. Gann, *The United States and Africa* (1987); Piero Gleijeses, *Conflicting Missions* (2001); Dennis Hickey and Kenneth White, *An Enchanting Darkness* (1993); Lawrence C. Howard, *American Involvement in Africa South of the Sahara, 1800–1860* (1988); Henry F. Jackson, *From the Congo to Soweto* (1982); Zaki Laidi, *The Superpowers and Africa* (1990); Colin Legum, ed., *Africa Contemporary Record* (1968–) (AS); Michael McCarthy, *Dark Continent* (1983); Lysle E. Meyer, *The Farther Frontier* (1992); Thomas Noer, *Cold War and Black Liberation* (1985); Anthony G. Pazzanita and Tony Hodges, *Historical Dictionary of Western Sahara* (1994) (E); Peter J. Schraeder, *United States Foreign Policy Toward Africa* (1994); Elliot P. Skinner, *African-Americans and U.S. Policy Toward Africa, 1850–1924* (1992); U.S. Library of Congress, *The United States and Sub-Saharan Africa* (1984) (B). See also countries.

Alaska: Paul S. Holbo, *Tarnished Expansion* (1983); Ronald J. Jensen, *The Alaska Purchase* (1975); Walter A. McDougall, *Let the Sea Make a Noise* (1993). See also Kushner and Saul in "Russia and the Soviet Union."

Albania: William B. Bland, *Albania* (1988) (B).

Algeria: Charles-Robert Ageron, *Modern Algeria* (1992); Matthew Connelly, *A Diplomatic Revolution* (2002); Martin Stone, *The Agony of Algeria* (1997); Irwin W. Wall, *France, the United States, and the Algerian War* (2001). See also "North Africa."

Angola: Richard Black, *Angola* (1992) (B); Susan H. Broadhead, *Historical Dictionary of Angola* (1992) (E); Thomas Collelo, ed., *Angola* (1990); Fernando A. Guimãres, *The Origins of the Angolan Civil War* (1998); Lawrence W. Henderson, *Angola* (1979); John A. Marcum, *The Angolan Revolution* (1969, 1978); Kenneth Mokoena and Nicole Gaymon, eds., *The Angola Crises* (1991); Inge Tvedten, *Angola* (1997). See also "Africa."

Antarctica: Peter J. Beck, *The International Politics of Antarctica* (1986); Robert Headland, *Chronological List of Antarctic Expeditions* (1989) (E and C); Christopher C. Joyner and Ethel R. Theis, *Eagle over the Ice* (1997); Frank G. Klotz, *America on the Ice* (1990); Jeffrey D. Myhre, *The Antarctic Treaty System* (1986); John Stewart, *Antarctica* (1990) (E); Gilligan D. Triggs, ed., *The Antarctic Treaty Regime* (1987).

Arab World: See "Israel, Palestine, and Arab-Israeli Conflict" and "Middle East."

Arctic: Elizabeth B. Elliot-Meisel, *Arctic Diplomacy: Canada and the United States in the Northwest Passage* (1998); Clive Holland, *Arctic Exploration and Development* (1993) (E). See also "Canada."

Argentina: Alan Biggs, *Argentina* (1991) (B); Deborah Norden and Robert Guillermo Russell, *The United States and Argentina* (2002); Harold F. Peterson, *Argentina and the United States* (1964); David Rock, *Argentina* (1985); David Sheinin, *Searching for Authority* (1998); Joseph Tulchin, *Argentina and the United States* (1990); Arthur P. Whitaker, *The United States and the Southern Cone* (1976). See also "Latin America."

Armenia: Vrej Nerses Neressian, *Armenia* (1993) (B).

Asia and Pacific Islands: Alexander Besher, *The Pacific Rim Almanac* (1991) (E); Jessica S. Brown et al., eds., *The United States in East Asia* (1985) (B); Frederica M. Bunge and Melinda W. Cooke, eds., *Oceania* (1985); I. C. Campbell, *A History of the Pacific Islands* (1989); Warren I. Cohen, *The Asian American Century* (2002); Donald Denoon and Stewart Firth, eds., *The Cambridge History of the Pacific Islanders* (1997); John C. Dorance, *The United States and the Pacific Islands* (1992); Norman Douglas and Ngaire Douglas, eds., *Pacific Islands Yearbook* (1932–) (AS); Arthur P. Dudden, *The American Pacific* (1992); Ainslie T. Embree, *Encyclopedia of Asian History* (1988) (E); Gerald Fry, *Pacific Basin and Oceania* (1987) (B); Roger W. Gale, *The Americanization of Micronesia* (1979); Arrell M. Gibson, *Yankees in Paradise* (1993); David Hanlon, *Remaking Micronesia* (1998); Donald D. Johnson, *The United States in the Pacific* (1995); James I. Matray, *Encyclopedia of U.S.–East Asian Relations* (2002) (E); John C. Perry, *Facing West* (1994); Deryck Scarr, *The History of the Pacific Islands* (1990); Gerald Segal, *Rethinking the Pacific* (1990); David Shavit, *The United States in Asia* (1990) (E); Roger C. Thompson, *The Pacific Rim Since 1945* (1994); Howard Willens and Deanne C. Seimar, *National Security and Self-determination* (2000) (Micronesia). See also countries and "Vietnam and Southeast Asia."

Australia: Glen St. John Barclay, *Friends in High Places* (1985); Philip Bell, *Implicated* (1993); Norman Harper, *A Great and Powerful Friend* (1987); Joseph Siracusa and Yeong-Han Cheong, *America's Australia, Australia's America* (1997). See also "Asia and Pacific Islands."

Austria: William Bader, *Austria Between East and West* (1966); Audrey K. Cronin, *Great Power Politics and the Struggle over Austria, 1945–1955* (1986); Barbara Jelavich, *Modern Austria* (1988); Mellany A. Sully, *A Contemporary History of Austria* (1990); Reinhold Wagnleitner, *Coca-Colonization and the Cold War* (1994). See also "Europe."

Azerbaijan: Ian Bremmer and Ray Taras, eds., *Nations and Politics in the Soviet Successor States* (1993). See also "Russia and the Soviet Union."

The Bahamas: Paul G. Boultbee, *The Bahamas* (1989) (B).

Bahrain: F. Gregory Gauss, *Oil Monarchies* (1994). See also "Middle East" and "Persian Gulf."

Baltic States: Walter C. Clemens, Jr., *Baltic Independence and Russian Empire* (1991); David Flint, *The Baltic States* (1992); Kristian Gerner, *The Baltic States and the End of the Soviet Empire* (1993); Walter R. Iwaskiw, ed., *Estonia, Latvia, and Lithuania* (1996); Anatol Lieven, *The Baltic Revolution* (1993); Inese A. Smith and Marita V. Grunts, *The Baltic States* (1993). See also "Estonia."

Bangladesh: See Brown in "India."

Belarus: Helen Fedor, *Belarus and Moldova* (1995).

Belgium: Jonathan E. Helmreich, *United States Relations with Belgium and the Congo* (1998); Frank E. Hugget, *Modern Belgium* (1969). See also "Europe."

Belize: O. Nigel Bolland, *Belize* (1996). See also Merrill in "Guyana."

Berlin: See "Germany and Berlin."

Bhutan: See "Nepal."

Bolivia: Rex A. Hudson and Dennis M. Haggerty, eds., *Bolivia* (1991); Kenneth D. Lehman, *Bolivia and the United States* (1999); Waltraud Q. Morales, *Bolivia* (1992); J. W. Wilkie, *The Bolivian Revolution and U.S. Aid Since 1952* (1969). See also "Latin America" and Pike in "Peru."

Bosnia–Herzegovina: Noel Malcolm, *Bosnia* (1994). See also "Yugoslavia."

Brazil: Jan Black, *United States Penetration of Brazil* (1977); Elizabeth A. Cobbs, *The Rich Neighbor Policy: Rockefeller and Kaiser in Brazil* (1992); John Dickenson, ed., *Brazil* (1997) (B); Gerald K. Haines, *The Americanization of Brazil* (1989); Stanley Hilton, *Brazil and the Great Powers* (1975); Rex A. Hudson, ed., *Brazil* (1998); Frank McCann, *The Brazilian-American Alliance, 1937–1945* (1973); Joseph Smith, *Unequal Giants* (1991); Steven C. Topik, *Trade and Gunboats* (1996); W. Michael Weis, *Cold Warriors and Coups d'État* (1993). See also "Latin America."

Bulgaria: Glenn A. Curtis, ed., *Bulgaria* (1993). See also "Europe."

Burma: See "Myanmar."

Burundi: Morna Daniels, *Burundi* (1992) (B). See also "Africa."

Cambodia: MacAlister Brown and Joseph J. Zasloff, *Cambodia Confronts the Peacemakers, 1979–1998* (1998); David P. Chandler, *The Tragedy of Cambodian History* (1991); Michael Haas, *Cambodia, Pol Pot, and the United States* (1991); Henry Kamm, *Cambodia* (1998); Ben Kiernan, *How Pol Pot Came to Power* (1985) and *The Pol Pot Regime* (1996); Russell R. Ross, ed., *Cambodia* (1990); William Shawcross, *The Quality of Mercy* (1984) and *Sideshow* (1979). See also "Southeast Asia."

Cameroon: Julius A. Amin, *The Peace Corps in Cameroon* (1992); Mark DeLancey, *Cameroon* (1986) (B); Mark DeLancey and H. Mbella Mokeba, *Historical Dictionary of Cameroon* (1990) (E). See also "Africa."

Canada: David J. Bercuson and J. L. Granatstein, *The Collins Dictionary of Canadian History* (1988) (E); Robert Bothwell, *Canada and the United States* (1992); Charles Doran, *Forgotten Partnership* (1984); John Findlay and Ken S. Coates, eds., *Parallel Destinies* (2002); J. L. Granatstein and Robert Bothwell, *Pirouette* (1990); J. L. Granatstein and Norman Hillmer, *For Better or For Worse* (1992); Archie Hobson, *The Cambridge Gazetteer of the United States and Canada* (1996) (A); Lansing Lamont and Duncan Edmonds, eds., *Friends So Different*

(1989); Seymour Martin Lipset, *Continental Divide* (1990); Lawrence Martin, *The Presidents and the Prime Ministers* (1982); Graeme S. Mount, *Invisible and Inaudible in Washington* (1999); Denis Smith, *Diplomacy of Fear* (1988); Reginald C. Stuart, *United States Expansionism and British North America 1775–1871* (1988); John H. Thompson and Stephen J. Randall, *Canada and the United States* (1998). See also "Great Britain."

Caribbean: Charles D. Ameringer, *The Caribbean Legion* (1974); David Healy, *Drive to Hegemony* (1988); Roger Hughes, *The Caribbean* (1987) (B); Lester D. Langley, *The United States and the Caribbean, 1900–1970* (1980) and *The United States and the Caribbean in the Twentieth Century* (1989); Sandra W. Meditz and Dennis M. Hanratty, eds., *Islands of the Commonwealth Caribbean* (1989); Robert F. Smith, *The Caribbean World and the United States* (1994). See also "Central America," "Latin America," and countries.

Central African Republic: Pierre Kalck, *Historical Dictionary of the Central African Republic* (1992) (E). See also "Africa."

Central America: Tom Barry, *Central America Inside Out* (1991) (C and E); Leslie Bethel, ed., *Central America Since Independence* (1991); Morris J. Blachman et al., eds., *Confronting Revolution* (1986); John Booth and Thomas Walker, *Understanding Central America* (1993); John Coatsworth, *Central America and the United States* (1994); Kenneth M. Coleman and George C. Herring, eds., *Understanding the Central American Crisis* (1991); John E. Findling, *Close Neighbors, Distant Friends* (1987); Kenneth J. Grieb, *Central America in the Nineteenth and Twentieth Centuries* (1988) (B); Walter LaFeber, *Inevitable Revolutions* (1993); Thomas M. Leonard, *Central America and the United States* (1991) and *Central America and U.S. Policies, 1820s–1980s* (1985) (B); Thomas D. Schoonover, *The United States in Central America, 1860–1911* (1991); Ralph L. Woodward, *Central America* (1985). See also "Caribbean," "Latin America," and individual countries.

Chad: Thomas Collelo, ed., *Chad* (1990); Samuel Decalo, *Historical Dictionary of Chad* (1987) (E). See also "Africa."

Chile: Michael Francis, *The Limits of Hegemony* (1977); David Mares and Francisco Rosas Arevena, *United States and Chile* (2001); Michael Monteon, *Chile in the Nitrate Era* (1982); Heraldo Munoz and Carlos Portales, *Elusive Friendship* (1991); Fredrick B. Pike, *Chile and the United States, 1880–1962* (1963); William F. Sater, *Chile and the United States* (1990); Paul E. Sigmund, *The United States and Democracy in Chile* (1993). See also "Latin America" and Whitaker in "Argentina."

China (and Taiwan): Gordon Chang, *Friends and Enemies* (1990); Warren I. Cohen, *America's Response to China* (2000); Jacques Downs,

The Golden Ghetto (1997); Rosemary Foot, *The Practice of Power* (1995); Jonathan Goldstein et al., eds., *America Views China* (1991); Harry Harding, *A Fragile Relationship* (1992); Michael H. Hunt, *The Making of a Special Relationship* (1983); Chen Jian, *Mao's China and the Cold War* (2001); Arnold Xiangze Jiang, *The United States and China* (1988); Noam Kochavi, *A Conflict Perpetuated* (2002); David M. Lampton, *Same Bed Different Dreams* (2000); Wei-chin Lee, *Taiwan* (1990) (B); Ernest R. May and John K. Fairbank, eds., *America's China Trade in Historical Perspective* (1986); Robert S. Ross, *Negotiating Cooperation* (1995); Michael Schaller, *The United States and China in the Twentieth Century* (1990); David Shambaugh, *Beautiful Imperialist* (1991); *Taiwan, Hong Kong, and the United States* (1994); Qiang Zhai, *China and the Vietnam Wars* (2000); Shu Guang Zhang, *Deterrence and Strategic Culture* (1992). See also "Asia and Pacific Islands."

Colombia: David Bushnell, *The Making of Modern Colombia* (1993); Robert H. Davis, *Colombia* (1990) (B); Dennis M. Hanratty and Sandra W. Meditz, eds., *Colombia* (1990); Richard L. Lael, *Arrogant Diplomacy* (1987); Stephen J. Randall, *Colombia and the United States* (1992) and *The Diplomacy of Modernization* (1977); Bert Ruiz, *Colombia's Civil War* (2002). See also "Latin America" and "Panama (and Panama Canal)."

Comoros: See "Indian Ocean."

Congo (Brazzaville): See "Africa."

Congo (Kinshasa): David N. Gibbs, *The Political Economy of Third World Intervention* (1991); Madeline G. Kalb, *The Congo Cables* (1982); Sean Kelly, *America's Tyrant: The CIA and Mobutu of Zaire* (1993); Sandra W. Meditz and Tim Merrill, eds., *Zaire* (1994); Michael G. Schatzberg, *Mobutu or Chaos* (1991); Crawford Young and Thomas Turner, *The Rise and Decline of the Zairian State* (1985). See also "Africa" and Helmreich in "Belgium."

Costa Rica: Theodore S. Creedman, *Historical Dictionary of Costa Rica* (1991) (E); Kyle Longley, *The Sparrow and Hawk* (1997); Charles L. Stansifer, *Costa Rica* (1991) (B). See also "Central America" and "Latin America."

Cuba: James G. Blight and Philip Brenner, *Sad and Luminous Days* (2002); James G. Blight et al., *Cuba on the Brink* (2002); Ronald H. Chilcote and Sheryl Lutjens, eds., *Cuba, 1953–1978* (1986) (B); Juan del Aguilar, *Cuba* (1988); Jorge Domínguez, *To Make the World Safe for Revolution* (1989); Jesse J. Dossick, ed., *Cuba, Cubans, and Cuban-Americans, 1902–1991* (1992) (B); José M. Hernández, *Cuba and the United States: Intervention and Militarism, 1868–1933* (1993); Morris H. Morley, *Imperial State and Revolution* (1987); Morris Morley and Christopher

McGillon, *Unfinished Business* (2002); Thomas G. Paterson, *Contesting Castro* (1994); Louis A. Pérez, Jr., *Cuba* (1995), *Cuba* (1988) (B), and *Cuba and the United States* (2003); Sheldon M. Stern, *Averting the "Final Failure"* (2003); Jaime Suchlicki, *Historical Dictionary of Cuba* (1988) (E); Victor Anders Triay, *Fleeing Castro* (1998). See also "Caribbean," "Latin America," and "Spanish-American-Cuban-Filipino War."

Cyprus: Tozun Bahcheli, *Greek-Turkish Relations Since 1955* (1990); Henry A. Richter, *Greece and Cyprus Since 1920* (1991) (B); Eric Solsten, ed., *Cyprus* (1991). See also Stearns in "Greece."

Czech Republic (and Czechoslovakia): David Short, *Czechoslovakia* (1986) (B); Gordon Skilling, *Czechoslovakia* (1991); Walter Ullmann, *The United States in Prague, 1945–1948* (1978); Betty Miller Unterberger, *The United States, Revolutionary Russia, and the Rise of Czechoslovakia* (1989). See also "Eastern Europe."

Dominican Republic: G. Pope Atkins and Larman C. Wilson, *The Dominican Republic and the United States* (1998) and *The United States and the Trujillo Regime* (1972); Ian Bell, *The Dominican Republic* (1981); Bruce J. Calder, *The Impact of Intervention* (1984); Eric Thomas Chester, *Rag-Tags, Scum, Riff-Raff, and Commies* (2001); Piero Gleijeses, *The Dominican Crisis* (1978); Richard A. Haggerty, ed., *Dominican Republic and Haiti* (1991); Eric P. Roorda, *The Dictator Next Door* (1998); Kai Schoenhals, *Dominican Republic* (1990) (B); Howard J. Wiarda, *The Dominican Republic* (1992). See also "Caribbean" and "Latin America."

Eastern Europe: Robert F. Byrnes, *U.S. Policy Toward Eastern Europe and the Soviet Union* (1989); Stephen A. Garrett, *From Potsdam to Poland* (1986); Bennett Kovrig, *Of Walls and Bridges* (1991); Geoffrey Swain and Nigel Swain, *Eastern Europe Since 1945* (1993). Also see "Russia and the Soviet Union," "Europe," and countries.

Ecuador: David Corkill, *Ecuador* (1989) (B); Dennis M. Hanratty, ed., *Ecuador* (1991); David W. Schodt, *Ecuador* (1987). See also "Latin America" and Pike in "Peru."

Egypt: Gregory L. Aftandilian, *Egypt's Bid for Arab Leadership* (1993); Geoffrey Aronson, *From Sideshow to Center Stage* (1986); William J. Burns, *Economic Aid and American Policy Toward Egypt, 1955–1981* (1985); Peter L. Hahn, *The United States, Great Britian, and Egypt, 1945–1956* (1991); Ragai N. Makar, *Egypt* (1988) (B); Helen C. Metz, ed., *Egypt* (1991); Gail E. Meyer, *Egypt and the United States* (1980); William B. Quandt, *The United States and Egypt* (1990). See also "Israel, Palestine, and Arab-Israeli Conflict" and "Middle East."

El Salvador: America's Watch, *El Salvador's Decade of Terror* (1991); Cynthia Arnson, *El Salvador* (1982); Enrique A. Baloyra, *El Salvador*

in Transition (1982); Martin Diskin and Kenneth Sharpe, *The Impact of U.S. Policy in El Salvador, 1979–1986* (1986); Richard A. Haggerty, ed., *El Salvador* (1990); T. S. Montgomery, *Revolution in El Salvador* (1982); Ralph Lee Woodward, *El Salvador* (1988) (B). See also "Central America" and "Latin America."

Estonia: Toivo U. Raun, *Estonia and the Estonians* (1991). See also "Baltic States."

Ethiopia: David A. Korn, *Ethiopia, the United States, and the Soviet Union* (1986); Jeffrey S. Lefebvre, *Arms for the Horn* (1991); Harold G. Marcus, *Ethiopia, Great Britain, and the United States, 1941–1974* (1983); Thomas P. Ofcansky, ed., *Ethiopia* (1993); Chris Prouty and Eugene Rosenfeld, *Historical Dictionary of Ethiopia* (1994) (E). Also see "Africa."

Europe: Peter Coffey, *The EC and the United States* (1993); *The Economist Atlas of the New Europe* (1992) (A); Nicholas V. Gianaris, *The European Community and the United States* (1991); Jeffrey Glen Giauque, *Grand Designs and Visions of Unity* (2002); John L. Harper, *American Visions of Europe* (1994); Ethan B. Kapstein, *The Insecure Alliance* (1990); John Killick, *The United States and European Integration, 1945–1960* (1998); Geir Lundestad, *"Empire" by Integration* (1998); Jacques Portes, ed., *Europe and America* (1987); Kevin Ruane, *The Rise and Fall of the European Defense Community* (2000); Thomas A. Schwartz, *Lyndon Johnson and Europe* (2003); Marc Trachtenberg, ed., *Between Empire and Alliance* (2003) and *A Constructed Peace* (1999); Pascaline Winand, *Eisenhower, Kennedy, and the United States of Europe* (1993). See also "Eastern Europe," "North Atlantic Treaty Organization (NATO)," countries, and wars.

Finland: Jussi M. Hanhimäki, *Containing Coexistence* (1997); Max Jacobson, *Finnish Neutrality* (1969); Robert Rinehart, ed., *Finland and the United States* (1993); Eric Solsten and Sandra W. Meditz, *Finland* (1990). See also "Europe" and "Scandinavia."

France: Henry Blumenthal, *A Reappraisal of Franco-American Relations, 1830–1871* (1959), *France and the United States* (1970), and *Illusion and Reality in Franco-American Diplomacy, 1914–1945* (1986); Charles Cogan, *Oldest Allies, Guarded Friends* (1994); Frank Costigliola, *The Cold Alliance* (1992); William Hitchcock, *France Restored* (2001); Robert O. Paxton and Nicholas Wahl, eds., *De Gaulle and the United States, 1930–1970* (1994); Jacques Portes, *Fascination and Misgiving: The United States in French Opinion* (2000); Irwin M. Wall, *The United States and the Making of Postwar France* (1991); Marvin Zahniser, *Uncertain Friendship* (1975) and *Then Came Disaster* (2002). See also "Europe."

Gabon: David E. Gardinier, *Historical Dictionary of Gabon* (1994) (E). See also "Africa."

Germany and Berlin: David E. Barclay and Elisabeth Glaser-Schmidt, eds., *Transatlantic Image and Perceptions* (1997); Steven Casey, *Cautious Crusade* (2001); Hans W. Gatzke, *Germany and the United States* (1980); William Glenn Gray, *Germany's Cold War* (2003); Wolfram F. Hanrieder, *Germany, America, Europe* (1989); Manfred Jonas, *The United States and Germany* (1984); Margrit Krewson, *German-American Relations* (1995) (B); James McAlister, *No Exit* (2002); Roger P. Morgan, *The United States and West Germany, 1945–1973* (1974); Frank Ninkovich, *Germany and the United States* (1995); M. E. Sarotte, *Dealing with the Devil* (2001); Hans-Jürgen Schröder, ed., *Confrontation and Cooperation* (1993); Thomas A. Schwartz, *America's Germany* (1991); Eric Solsten, ed., *Germany* (1996); Ian Wallace, *Berlin* (1993) (B); Peter Wyden, *Wall* (1989). See also "Europe," "Holocaust," "War Crimes and Trials," "World War I," and "World War II."

Ghana: LaVerde Berry, ed., *Ghana* (1995); Daniel McFarland, *Historical Dictionary of Ghana* (1985). See also "Africa."

Great Britain: C. J. Bartlett, *"The Special Relationship"* (1992); Charles S. Campbell, *From Revolution to Rapprochement* (1974); David Dimbleby and David Reynolds, *An Ocean Apart* (1989); Alan P. Dobson, *Anglo-American Relations in the Twentieth Century* (1995); Robert M. Hathaway, *Great Britain and the United States* (1990); David A. Lincove and Gary R. Treadway, eds., *The Anglo-American Relationship* (1988) (B); William Roger Louis and Hedley Bull, eds., *The Special Relationship* (1986); Jonathan Hollowell, ed., *Twentieth Century Anglo-American Relations* (2001); B. J. C. McKercher, *Transition of Power* (1999); John Moser, *Twisting the Lion's Tail* (1999); Anne Orde, *The Eclipse of Great Britain* (1996); Richie Ovendale *Anglo-American Relations in the Twentieth Century* (1998); David Reynolds, *Britannia Overruled* (2000). See also "Canada" and "War of 1812."

Greece: Louis Cassimatis, *American Influence in Greece, 1917–1929* (1988); Theodore A. Couloumbis, *The United States, Greece, and Turkey* (1983); Theodore A. Couloumbis and John O. Iatrides, eds., *Greek-American Relations* (1980); Glenn E. Curtis, ed., *Greece* (1995); John O. Iatrides, ed., *Ambassador MacVeagh Reports: Greece, 1933–1947* (1980); Jon V. Kofas, *Intervention and Underdevelopment: Greece During the Cold War* (1989); Monteagle Stearns, *Entangled Allies* (1991); Lawrence S. Wittner, *American Intervention in Greece, 1943–1949* (1982). See also "Europe" and Richter in "Cyprus."

Grenada: Peter M. Dunn and Bruce W. Watson, eds., *American Intervention in Grenada* (1985); Gordon K. Lewis, *Grenada* (1987); Kai P. Schoenhals and Richard A. Melanson, eds., *Revolution and Intervention in Grenada* (1985). See also "Caribbean."

Guam: Timothy P. Maga, *Defending Paradise* (1988); Earl S.

Pomeroy, *Pacific Outpost* (1951); Robert F. Rogers, *Destiny's Landfall* (1995). See also "Asia and Pacific Islands."

Guatemala: Nick Cullather, *Secret History* (1999); Paul J. Dosal, *Doing Business with the Dictators: A Political History of United Fruit in Guatemala, 1899–1944* (1993); Piero Gleijeses, *Shattered Hope* (1991); Jim Handy, *Gift of the Devil* (1985); Richard Immerman, *The CIA in Guatemala* (1982); Stephen M. Streeter, *Managing the Counterrevolution* (2001). See also "Central America" and "Latin America."

Guyana: Tim Merrill, ed., *Guyana and Belize* (1993). See also "Latin America."

Haiti: Frances Chambers, *Haiti* (1983) (B); David Nicholls, *From Dessalines to Duvalier* (1979); Brenda Gayle Plummer, *Haiti and the United States* (1992); Mary Renda, *Taking Haiti* (2001); Robert I. Rotberg, *Haiti* (1971). See also "Caribbean," "Latin America," and Haggerty and Logan in "Dominican Republic."

Hawai'i: Helena G. Allen, *The Betrayal of Queen Lilioukalani* (1982); Ralph S. Kuykendall, *The Hawaiian Kingdom* (1938–1967); Nancy Morris and Love Dean, *Hawai'i* (1992) (B); Merze Tate, *The United States and the Hawaiian Kingdom* (1965). See also "Asia and Pacific Islands."

Honduras: Alison Acker, *Honduras* (1988); Pamela F. Howard-Reguindin, *Honduras* (1992) (B); Harvey Meyer and Jessie Meyer, *Historical Dictionary of Honduras* (1994) (E). See also "Central America."

Hong Kong: See Tucker in "China (and Taiwan)."

Hungary: Stephan R. Burant, ed., *Hungary* (1990). See also "Eastern Europe" and "Europe."

Iceland: Donald E. Neuchterlein, *Iceland* (1975). See also "Scandinavia."

India: William J. Barnds, *India, Pakistan, and the Great Powers* (1972); H. W. Brands, *India and the United States* (1990); W. Norman Brown, *The United States and India, Pakistan, and Bangladesh* (1972); Srinivas M. Chary, *The Eagle and the Peacock* (1994); Kenton J. Clymer, *Quest for Freedom* (1995); James Heitzman and Robert L. Worden, eds., *India* (1996); Gary R. Hess, *America Encounters India, 1941–1947* (1971); Harold R. Issacs, *Images of Asia* (1958); Dennis Kux, *India and the United States* (1992); Robert J. McMahon, *The Cold War on the Periphery* (1994); Dennis Merrill, *Bread and the Ballot* (1990); Norman D. Palmer, *The United States and India* (1984); Andrew Rotter, *Comrades at Odds* (2000); Santosh C. Saha, *Indo-U.S. Relations, 1947–1988* (1990) (B). See also "Asia and Pacific Islands" and Wolpert in "Afghanistan."

Indian Ocean: Helen C. Metz, ed., *Indian Ocean: Five Island Countries* (1995). See also "Africa."

Indonesia: Theodore Friend, *Indonesian Destinies* (2003); Paul F. Gardner, *Shared Hopes, Separate Fears* (1997); Michael Leifer, *Indonesia's Foreign Policy* (1983); Robert J. McMahon, *Colonialism and Cold War* (1981); Andrew Roadnight, *United States Policy Toward Indonesia in the Truman and Eisenhower Years* (2002); Robert L. Worden, ed., *Indonesia* (1993). See also "Asia and Pacific Islands."

Iran: James A. Bill, *The Eagle and the Lion* (1988); Richard W. Cottam, *Iran and the United States* (1988); Mark J. Gasiorowski, *U.S. Foreign Policy and the Shah* (1991); Sīrūs Ghanī, *Iran and the West* (1987) (B); James F. Goode, *The United States and Iran, 1946–51* (1989); Nikki R. Keddie and Mark J. Gasiorowski, eds., *Neither East nor West* (1990); Mark H. Lytle, *The Origins of the Iranian-American Alliance, 1941–1953* (1987); Rouhollah K. Ramazani, *The United States and Iran* (1982); Barry Rubin, *Paved with Good Intentions* (1980); Kuross A. Samii, *Involvement by Invitation* (1987); Abraham Yeselson, *United States–Persian Diplomatic Relations, 1883–1921* (1956). See also "Middle East" and "Persian Gulf."

Iraq: Rick Atkinson, *Crusade* (1993); Lawrence Freedman and Efraim Karsh, *The Gulf Conflict, 1990–1991* (1993); Bruce Jentleson, *With Friends like These* (1994); Sandra Mackey, *The Reckoning* (2002); Helen C. Metz, ed., *Iraq* (1990); Morris M. Mottale, *The Origins of the Gulf Wars* (2001); Geoff Simons, *Targeting Iraq* (2002); William Stivers, *Supremacy and Oil* (1982). See also "Middle East" and "Persian Gulf."

Ireland: Donald H. Akenson, *The United States and Ireland* (1973); Thomas N. Brown, *Irish-American Nationalism, 1870–1890* (1966); Francis M. Carroll, *American Opinion and the Irish Question, 1910–1923* (1978); Sean Cronin, *Washington's Irish Policy, 1916–1986* (1987); Troy D. Davis, *Dublin's American Policy* (1998); Alan J. Ward, *Ireland and Anglo-American Relations, 1899–1921* (1969). See also "Europe" and "Great Britain."

Israel, Palestine, and Arab-Israeli Conflict: George W. Ball and Douglas B. Ball, *The Passionate Attachment* (1992); Abraham Ben-Zvi, *The United States and Israel* (1994); Ian J. Bickerton and Carla L. Klausner, *A Concise History of the Arab-Israeli Conflict* (1998); Herbert Druks, *The Uncertain Friendship* (2001); William Roger Louis and Robert W. Stookey, eds., *The End of the Palestine Mandate* (1986); Camille Mansour, *Beyond Alliance* (1994); Donald Neff, *Fallen Pillars: U.S. Policy Towards Palestine and Israel Since 1945* (1995); Ilan Pappe, *The Israel/Palestine Question* (1999); William B. Quandt, *Peace Process* (1993); John Quigley, *Palestine and Israel* (1990); Bernard Reich, ed., *An Encyclopedia of the Arab-Israeli Conflict* (1996) (E) and *The United*

States and Israel (1984); Cheryl Rubenberg, *Israel and the American National Interest* (1986); David Schoenbaum, *The United States and the State of Israel* (1993); Mohammed K. Shadid, *The United States and the Palestinians* (1981); Charles D. Smith, *Palestine and the Arab-Israeli Conflict* (1992); Steven Spiegel, *The Other Arab-Israeli Conflict* (1985); Michael W. Suleiman, ed., *U.S. Policy on Palestine* (1995); Mark Tessler, *A History of the Israeli-Palestinian Conflict* (1994); Edward Tivnan, *The Lobby* (1987). See also "Middle East."

Italy: Alessandro Brogi, *A Question of Self-esteem* (2002); Alexander DeConde, *Half-Bitter, Half-Sweet* (1971); H. Stuart Hughes, *The United States and Italy* (1979); James E. Miller, *The United States and Italy, 1940–1950* (1986); David F. Schmitz, *The United States and Fascist Italy, 1922–1940* (1988); Leo J. Wollemborg, *Stars, Stripes, and Italian Tricolor* (1990). See also "Europe."

Jamaica: See "Caribbean."

Japan: Sadao Asada, *Japan and the World* (1989) (B); Michael A. Barnhart, *Japan and the World Since 1868* (1995); John H. Boyle, *Modern Japan: The American Nexus* (1993); Roger Buckley, *US-Japan Alliance Diplomacy, 1945–1990* (1992); Donald E. Dolan and Robert L. Worden, eds., *Japan* (1992); John K. Emmerson and Harrison M. Holland, *The Eagle and the Rising Sun* (1988); Akira Iriye and Robert A. Wampler, eds., *Partnership* (2001); Walter LaFeber, *The Clash* (1997); Rita E. Neri, *U.S. and Japan Foreign Trade* (1988) (B); Charles E. Neu, *The Troubled Encounter* (1975); Ian Nish, *Japanese Foreign Policy in the Interwar Period* (2002); Michael Schaller, *Altered States* (1997) and *The American Occupation of Japan* (1985); Sayuri Shimizu, *Creating People of Plenty* (2001). See also "Asia and Pacific Islands," "War Crimes and Trials," and "World War II."

Jordan: Madiha Rashid al-Madfai, *Jordan, the United States, and the Middle East Peace Process* (1993); Helen C. Metz, ed., *Jordan* (1991). See also "Middle East."

Kazakhstan: Glenn E. Curtis, *Kazakhstan, Kyrgyzstan, Tajikistan, Turkmenistan, and Uzbekistan* (1997); Michael Mandelbaum, ed., *Central Asia and the World* (1994).

Kenya: See "Africa" and Lefebvre in "Ethiopia."

Korea and Korean War: Jongsuk Chay, *Diplomacy of Asymmetry* (1990); Bruce Cumings, *Korea's Place in the Sun* (1997) and *The Origins of the Korean War* (1981, 1990); Paul M. Edwards, *The Korean War* (1998) (B); Burton I. Kaufman, *The Korean War* (1997); Yun-Bok Lee and Wayne Patterson, eds., *Korean-American Relations, 1866–1997 (1998)*; Mitchell B. Lerner, *The "Pueblo" Incident* (2002); Peter Lowe, *The Korean War* (2000); Donald S. Macdonald, *U.S.-Korean Relations* (1992);

James I. Matray, ed., *Historical Dictionary of the Korean War* (1991) (E); Keith McFarland, *The Korean War* (1986) (B); Andrew C. Nahm, *Historical Dictionary of the Republic of Korea* (1993) (E); Stanley Sandler, *The Korean War* (1995) (E); Andrea M. Savada, ed., *North Korea* (1994) and *South Korea* (1992); Andre Schmid, *Korea Between Empires* (2002); Leon V. Sigal, *Disarming Strangers* (1998); William Stueck, *The Korean War* (1995) and *Rethinking the Korean War* (2002); Harry G. Summers, Jr., *Korean War Almanac* (1990) (C and E); Spencer Tucker, *Encyclopedia of the Korean War* (E) (2000). See also "Asia and Pacific Islands."

Kuwait: Abdul-Reda Assiri, *Kuwaiti Foreign Policy* (1990); Jill Crystal, *Kuwait* (1992) and *Oil and Politics in the Gulf* (1995). See also "Middle East" and "Persian Gulf."

Kyrgyzstan: See "Kazakhstan."

Laos: Timothy N. Castle, *At War in the Shadow of Vietnam* (1993); Helen Cordell, *Laos* (1993) (B); Arthur J. Dommen, *Laos* (1985); Jane Hamilton-Merritt, *Tragic Mountains* (1993); Andrea M. Savada, ed., *Laos* (1995); Charles A. Stevenson, *The End of Nowhere* (1972). See also "Vietnam and Southeast Asia."

Latin America: G. Pope Atkins, *Encyclopedia of the Inter-American System* (1997) (E) and *Latin America in the International System* (1995); John A. Britton, *The United States and Latin America* (1997) (B); Peter Calvert, *The International Politics of Latin America* (1994); David W. Dent, *U.S.–Latin American Policymaking* (1995) (B); Mark T. Gilderhus, *The Second Century* (2000); Jack W. Hopkins, ed., *Latin America and Caribbean Contemporary Record* (1983–) (AS); John J. Johnson, *A Hemisphere Apart* (1990); Lester D. Langley, *America and the Americas* (1989); Thomas M. Leonard, ed., *United States–Latin American Relations, 1850–1903* (1999); Kyle Longley, *In the Eagle's Shadow* (2002); Abraham F. Lowenthal, ed., *Exporting Democracy* (1991); Carlos Marichal, *A Century of Debt Crises in Latin America* (1988); Alan McPherson, *Yankee No!* (2003); Michael C. Meyer, ed., *Supplement to a Bibliography of United States–Latin American Relations Since 1810* (1979) (B); Nancy Mitchell, *The Danger of Dreams* (1999); Fredrick B. Pike, *The United States and Latin America* (1992); David M. Pletcher, *The Diplomacy of Trade and Investment* (1998); Lars Schoultz, *Beneath the United States* (1998); David Shavit, *The United States in Latin America* (1992) (E); Peter H. Smith, *Talons of the Eagle* (1996); Barbara Stallings, *Banker to the Third World* (1988); Barbara A. Tenenbaum, ed., *Encyclopedia of Latin American History and Culture* (1995) (E); David F. Trask et al., *A Bibliography of United States–Latin American Relations Since 1810* (1968) (B). See also "Caribbean," "Central America," "Communications," "Monroe Doctrine," "Pan Americanism," and countries.

Latvia: See "Baltic States."

Lebanon: C. H. Bleaney, *Lebanon* (1991) (B); Thomas L. Friedman, *From Beirut to Jerusalem* (1989); Irene Gendzier, *Notes from the Minefield* (1997); Dilip Hiro, *Lebanon* (1993); Itamar Rabinovich, *The War for Lebanon, 1970–1985* (1986). See also "Middle East."

Liberia: D. Elwood Dunn, *The Foreign Policy of Liberia During the Tubman Era, 1944–1971* (1979); Katherine Harris, *The United States and Liberia* (1985); Hassan B. Sisay, *Big Powers and Small Nations* (1985); Charles M. Wilson, *Liberia* (1985). See also "Africa."

Libya: Scott L. Bills, *The Libyan Arena* (1995); Mahmoud G. ElWarfally, *Imagery and Ideology in U.S. Policy Toward Libya, 1969–1982* (1988); P. Edward Haley, *Qaddafi and the United States Since 1969* (1984); Dirk Wandewalle, ed., *Qadhafi's Libya* (1995). See also "Africa" and "Middle East."

Lithuania: Saulius Sužiedelis, *Historical Dictionary of Lithuania* (1997) (E). See also "Baltic States."

Madagascar: Hilary Budt, *Madagascar* (1993) (B). See also "Africa" and "Indian Ocean."

Malaysia: James W. Gould, *The United States and Malaysia* (1969). See also "Asia and Pacific Islands."

Maldives: See "Indian Ocean."

Mauritania: Robert E. Handloff, ed., *Mauritania* (1990). See also "Africa."

Mauritius: Larry Bowman, *Mauritius* (1991). See also "Indian Ocean."

Mexico: Peter Andreas, *Border Games* (2000); Leslie Bethel, ed., *Mexico Since Independence* (1991); Jorge Domínguez and Rafael Fernandez de Castro, *United States and Mexico* (2001); Donald S. Frazier, ed., *The United States and Mexico at War* (1998) (E); John M. Hart, *Empire and Revolution* (2002); Lester D. Langley, *Mexico and the United States* (1991); David E. Lorey, ed., *United States–Mexico Border Statistics Since 1900* (1990) (S) and *The U.S.–Mexican Border in the Twentieth Century* (2000); Jacqueline Mazza, *Don't Disturb the Neighbors* (2001); Robert A. Pastor and Jorge G. Castañeda, *Limits to Friendship* (1988); George D. C. Philip, *Mexico* (1993) (B); W. Dirk Raat, *Mexico and the United States* (1997); Daniela Spenser, *The Impossible Triangle* (1999); Norman E. Tutorow, ed., *The Mexican-American War* (1981) (B); Josefina Vázquez and Lorenzo Meyer, *The United States and Mexico* (1985); David J. Weber, *The Mexican Frontier, 1821–1846* (1982). See also "Latin America."

Micronesia: See "Asia and Pacific Islands."

Middle East: Robert J. Allison, *The Crescent Observed: The United States and the Muslim World, 1776–1815* (1995); Warren Bass, *Support Any Friend* (2003); Thomas A. Bryson, *American Diplomatic Relations with the Middle East, 1784–1975* (1977) and *U.S.–Middle East Diplomatic Relations* (1979) (B); Uriel Dann, ed., *The Great Powers in the Middle East, 1919–1939* (1988); John A. DeNovo, *American Interests and Policies in the Middle East, 1900–1939* (1963); T. G. Fraser, *The USA and the Middle East Since World War 2* (1989); Martin Gilbert, *Atlas of the Arab-Israeli Conflict* (1993) (A); Burton I. Kaufman, *The Arab Middle East and the United States* (1996); Colin Legum et al., eds., *Middle East Contemporary Survey* (1978–) (AS); George Lenczowski, *American Presidents and the Middle East* (1989); Douglas Little, *American Orientalism* (2003); Melani McAllister, *Epic Encounters* (2001); David Shavit, *The United States in the Middle East* (1988) (E); Sanford R. Silverburg and Bernard Reich, *U.S. Foreign Policy and the Middle East/North Africa* (1989) (B); Reeva S. Simon et al., eds., *The Encyclopedia of the Modern Middle East* (1996) (E); Kenneth Stein, *Heroic Diplomacy* (1999); William Stivers, *America's Confrontation with Revolutionary Change in the Middle East, 1948–83* (1986); Alan R. Taylor, *The Superpowers and the Middle East* (1991). See also "Biological and Chemical Warfare," "Israel, Palestine, and Arab-Israeli Conflict," "Persian Gulf," and countries.

Moldova: See "Belarus."

Mongolia: Robert C. Worden and Andrea M. Savada, eds., *Mongolia* (1991).

Morocco: Leon B. Blair, *Western Window in the Arab World* (1970); Luella J. Hall, *The United States and Morocco, 1776–1956* (1961). See also "Africa" and "North Africa."

Mozambique: Mario Azevedo, *Historical Dictionary of Mozambique* (1991) (E); Maraget Hall and Tom Young, *Confronting Leviathan* (1997); Malyn Newitt, *A History of Mozambique* (1995). See also "Africa."

Myanmar: John F. Cady, *The United States and Burma* (1976); Patricia M. Herbert, *Burma* (1991) (B). See also "Vietnam and Southeast Asia."

Namibia: John J. Grotpeter, *Historical Dictionary of Namibia* (1994) (E). See also "Africa."

Nepal: Andrea M. Savada, ed., *Nepal and Bhutan* (1993).

Netherlands: Doeko Bosscher et al., eds., *American Culture in the Netherlands* (1996); Hans Loeber, ed., *Dutch-American Relations,*

1945–1969 (1992); J. W. Schulte Nordholt and Robert P. Swierenga, eds., *A Bilateral Centennial: A History of Dutch-American Relations, 1783–1982* (1982); Gertrude Reichenbach-Consten and Abraham Noordergraaf, eds., *Two Hundred Years of Netherlands-American Interaction* (1985); Cornelius van Minnen, *American Diplomats in the Netherlands, 1815–50* (1993). See also "Europe."

New Zealand: See "Australia."

Nicaragua: Karl Berman, *Under the Big Stick* (1986); E. Bradford Burns, *Patriarch and Folk* (1991); Paul C. Clark, Jr., *The United States and Somoza* (1992); Michael D. Gambone, *Eisenhower, Somoza, and the Cold War in Nicaragua* (1997); Peter Kornbluh, *Nicaragua* (1987); Tim L. Merrill, ed., *Nicaragua* (1994); Morris H. Morley, *Washington, Somoza, and the Sandinistas* (1994); Neil Narr, *Sandinista Nicaragua* (1990) (B); Robert Pastor, *Condemned to Repetition* (1987); Thomas W. Walker, *Nicaragua* (1991), ed., *Reagan Versus the Sandinistas* (1987), and ed., *Revolution and Counterrevolution in Nicaragua* (1991); Knut Walter, *The Regime of Anastasio Somoza* (1993); Ralph Lee Woodward, *Nicaragua* (1994) (B). See also "Central America" and "Latin America."

Nigeria: Bassey E. Ate, *Decolonization and Dependence* (1987); Helen C. Metz, ed., *Nigeria* (1992); Robert B. Shepard, *Nigeria, Africa, and the United States* (1991); Joseph E. Thompson, *American Policy and African Famine* (1990). See also "Africa."

North Africa: Charles F. Gallagher, *The United States and North Africa* (1963); Richard S. Parker, *North Africa* (1984). See also "Africa."

North Korea: See "Korea and Korean War."

Norway: Mats Berdal, *The United States, Norway, and the Cold War* (1997); Wayne S. Cole, *Norway and the United States* (1989); Ronald C. Popperwell, *Norway* (1972); Sigmund Skard, *The United States in Norwegian History* (1976); Rolf Tamnes, *The United States and the Cold War in the High North* (1991). See also "Europe" and "Scandinavia."

Oceania: See "Asia and Pacific Islands."

Oman: Joseph A. Kechichian, *Oman and the World* (1995). See also "Middle East" and "Persian Gulf."

Pacific Islands: See "Asia and Pacific Islands."

Pacific Rim: See "Asia and Pacific Islands."

Pakistan: Peter R. Blood, ed., *Pakistan* (1995); Dennis Kux, *The United States and Pakistan, 1947–2000* (2001); Iftikhar Malik, *U.S.–South Asian Relations, 1940–1947* (1991); Shirin Tahir-kheli, *The United States and Pakistan* (1982); David D. Taylor, *Pakistan* (1990) (B); M. S. Venkataramani, *The American Role in Pakistan, 1947–1958* (1982). See also Wolpert in "Afghanistan" and Barnds and McMahon in "India."

Palestine: See "Israel, Palestine, and Arab-Israeli Conflict."

Panama (and Panama Canal): Michael L. Conniff, *Panama and the United States* (1992); David N. Farnsworth and James W. McKenney, *U.S.-Panama Relations, 1903–1978* (1983); Walter LaFeber, *The Panama Canal* (1990); Thomas M. Leonard, *Panama, the Canal, and the United States* (1993) (B); John Lindsay-Poland, *Emperors in the Jungle* (2003); John Major, *Prize Possession* (1993); David McCullough, *The Path Between the Seas* (1977). See also "Latin America."

Paraguay: Anibal Miranda, *United States–Paraguay Relations* (1990); Riordan Roett and Richard S. Sacks, *Paraguay* (1991). See also "Latin America" and Whitaker in "Argentina."

Persian Gulf: Bruce R. Kuniholm, *The Persian Gulf and United States Policy* (1984) (B); Charles A. Kupchan, *The Persian Gulf and the West* (1987); Helen C. Metz, ed., *Persian Gulf States* (1993); Michael A. Palmer, *Guardians of the Gulf* (1992). See also "Middle East" and Cottam in "Iran."

Peru: Lawrence A. Clayton, *Peru and the United States* (1999); Rex A. Hudson, ed., *Peru* (1993); Cynthia McClintock and Fabian Vallas, *The United States and Peru* (2002); Fredrick B. Pike, *The United States and the Andean Republics* (1977); Ronald B. St. John, *The Foreign Policy of Peru* (1992). See also "Latin America."

Philippines: Teodoro A. Agoncillo, *A Short History of the Philippines* (1969); David H. Bain, *Sitting in Darkness* (1984); H. W. Brands, *Bound to Empire* (1992); Nick Cullather, *Illusions of Influence* (1994); Ronald E. Dolan, ed., *Philippines* (1993); Julia Go and Anne L. Foster, eds., *The American Colonial State in the Philippines* (2003); Stanley Karnow, *In Our Image* (1989); Brian M. Linn, *The Philippine War* (2000); Glenn A. May, *Battle for Batangas* (1991); Jim Richardson, *Philippines* (1989) (B). See also "Asia and Pacific Islands" and "Spanish-American-Cuban-Filipino War."

Poland: Debra J. Allen, *The Oder-Neisse Line* (2003); Glenn E. Curtis, ed., *Poland* (1994); Richard Lukacs, *Bitter Legacy* (1982); Helene Sjursen, *The United States, Western Europe, and the Polish Crisis* (2003); Piotr Wandycz, *The United States and Poland* (1980). See also "Eastern Europe" and "Europe."

Portugal: Scott B. MacDonald, *European Destiny, Atlantic Transformations* (1993); Kenneth Maxwell and Michael H. Haltzel, eds., *Portugal* (1990); Eric Solsten, ed., *Portugal* (1994). See also "Europe."

Puerto Rico: Laura Briggs, *Reproducing Empire* (2002); Raymond Carr, *Puerto Rico* (1984); Arturo Morales Carríon, *Puerto Rico* (1984); Elena E. Cevallos, *Puerto Rico* (1985) (B); Truman B. Clark, *Puerto Rico and the United States, 1917–1933* (1975); Ronald Fernandez, *The Disenchanted Island* (1996); A. W. Maldonado, *Teodora Moscoso and Puerto Rico's Operation Bootstrap* (1997); José Trías Monge, *Puerto Rico* (1997). See also "Caribbean."

Qatar: See "Persian Gulf."

Romania: Ronald D. Bachman, ed., *Romania* (1990); Joseph F. Harrington and Bruce J. Courtney, *Tweaking the Nose of the Russians* (1991). See also "Eastern Europe."

Russia and the Soviet Union: N. N. Bolkhovitinov and J. Dane Hartgrove, *Russia and the United States* (1987) (B); Peter G. Boyle, *American-Soviet Relations* (1993); Archie Brown et al., eds., *The Cambridge Encyclopedia of Russia and the Soviet Union* (1994) (E); Donald Davis and Eugene P. Trani, *The First Cold War* (2000); Philip J. Funigiello, *American-Soviet Trade in the Cold War* (1988); John Lewis Gaddis, *Russia, the Soviet Union, and the United States* (1990); Raymond L. Garthoff, *Détente and Confrontation* (1985) and *The Great Transition* (1994); Hope M. Harrison, *Driving the Soviets up the Wall* (2003); Walter LaFeber, *America, Russia, and the Cold War* (2002); James K. Libbey, *American-Russian Economic Relations* (1989) (B); J. D. Parks, *Culture, Conflict, and Coexistence: American-Soviet Cultural Relations, 1917–1958* (1983); Norman E. Saul, *Concord and Conflict: The United States and Russia, 1867–1914* (1996), *The United States and Russia, 1763–1867* (1991), and *War and Revolution* (2002); David Shavit, *United States Relations with Russia and the Soviet Union* (1993) (E). See also "Baltic States," "Cold War," "Eastern Europe," and "Europe."

Rwanda: Learthen Dorsey, *Historical Dictionary of Rwanda* (1994) (E). See also "Africa."

Samoa (American): J. A. C. Gray, *Amerika Samoa* (1960); Paul Kennedy, *The Samoan Tangle* (1974); George H. Ryden, *The Foreign Policy of the United States in Relation to Samoa* (1933). See also "Asia and Pacific Islands."

Saudi Arabia: Irvine H. Anderson, *Aramco, the United States, and Saudi Arabia* (1981); Peter T. Hart, *Saudi Arabia and the United States* (1999); (1998); Helen C. Metz, ed., *Saudia Arabia* (1993); Aaron D. Miller, *Search for Security: Saudi Arabian Oil and American Foreign Policy, 1939–1949* (1980); Nadav Safran, *Saudi Arabia* (1986). See also "Middle East."

Scandinavia: Jussi M. Hanhimäki, *Scandinavia and the United States* (1997); Geir Lundestad, *America, Scandinavia, and the Cold War* (1980); Franklin D. Scott, *Scandinavia* (1975) and *The United States and Scandinavia* (1950). See also "Europe" and countries.

Senegal: R. M. Dilley and J. S. Eades, *Senegal* (1994) (B). See also "Africa."

Serbia: See "Yugoslavia."

Seychelles: See "Indian Ocean."

Singapore: Barbara L. LePoer, ed., *Singapore* (1991).

Slovenia: See "Yugoslavia."

Somalia: John L. Hirsch and Whert B. Oakley, *Somalia and Operation Restore Hope* (1995); Helen C. Metz, ed., *Somalia* (1993). See also "Africa" and Lefebvre in "Ethiopia."

South Africa: James Barber and John Barratt, *South Africa's Foreign Policy* (1990); Thomas Borstelmann, *Apartheid's Reluctant Uncle* (1993); Rita M. Byrnes, ed., *South Africa* (1997); Christopher Coker, *The United States and South Africa, 1968–1985* (1986); Jeffrey V. Davis, *South Africa* (1994) (B); Terrell D. Hale, *United States Sanctions and South Africa* (1993) (B); Richard W. Hull, *American Enterprise in South Africa* (1990); C. T. Keto, *American–South African Relations, 1784-1980* (1985) (B); Y. G. M. Lulat, *U.S. Relations with South Africa* (1991) (B); Robert K. Massie, *Loosing the Bonds* (1997); William Minter, *King Soloman's Mines Revisited* (1986); Thomas J. Noer, *Briton, Boer, and Yankee* (1978) and *Cold War and Black Liberation* (1985). See also "Africa."

Southeast Asia: See "Vietnam and Southeast Asia."

Spain: Michael Alpert, *A New International History of the Spanish Civil War* (1998); Rodrigo Botero, *Ambivalent Embrace* (2001); Thomas Chavez, *Spain and the Independence of the United States* (2002); James W. Cortada, *Two Nations over Time* (1978), and ed., *Spain in the Twentieth-Century World* (1980); Robert W. Kern, *Historical Dictionary of Modern Spain* (1990) (E); Boris N. Liedtke, *Embracing a Dictatorship* (1998). See also "Europe" and "Spanish-American-Cuban-Filipino War."

Sri Lanka: Russell R. Ross and Andrea M. Savada, eds., *Sri Lanka* (1990).

Sudan: Carolyn Fkuehr-Lobban et al., *Historical Dictionary of Sudan* (1992) (E); Helen C. Metz, ed., *Sudan* (1992); Peter Woodward, *Sudan* (1989). See also "Africa."

Sweden: Sture Kindmark and Tore Tallroth, eds., *Swedes Looking West* (1983). See also "Europe" and "Scandinavia."

Switzerland: Heinze K. Meier, *Friendship Under Stress: U.S.–Swiss Relations, 1900–1950* (1970) and *The United States and Switzerland in the Nineteenth Century* (1963). See also "Europe."

Syria: David W. Lesch, *Syria and the United States* (1992); Moshe Ma'oz, *Syria and Israel* (1995); Andrew Rathwell, *Secret War in the Middle East* (1995); Bonnie Saunders, *The United States and Arab Nationalism* (1996); Eyal Zisser, *Assad's Legacy* (2002). See also "Middle East."

Taiwan (Formosa): See "China (and Taiwan)."

Tajikistan: See "Kazakhstan."

Tanzania: See "Africa."

Thailand: Richard Aldrich, *The Key to the South* (1993); Barbara L. LePoer, ed., *Thailand* (1989); Robert J. Muscat, *Thailand and the United States* (1990). See also "Vietnam and Southeast Asia."

Trieste: Bogdan C. Novak, *Trieste, 1941–1954* (1970); Roberto Rabel, *Between East and West* (1988). See also "Italy."

Trinidad and Tobago: See "Caribbean."

Tunisia: See "North Africa."

Turkey: David J. Alvarez, *Bureaucracy and Cold War Ideology* (1980); George S. Harris, *Troubled Alliance* (1972); Harry H. Howard, *Turkey, the Straits, and U.S. Policy* (1974); Helen C. Metz, ed., *Turkey* (1996). See also "Europe" and Couloumbis and Stearns in "Greece."

Turkmenistan: See "Kazakhstan."

Uganda: Rita M. Byrnes, ed., *Uganda* (1992). See also "Africa."

Ukraine: Lubomyr A. Hajda, ed., *Ukraine in the World* (1998); Steven Woehrel, *Ukraine* (1994). See also "Russia and the Soviet Union."

United Arab Emirates: See "Middle East" and "Persian Gulf."

Uzbekistan: See "Kazakhstan."

Uruguay: Kitty L. Drummond, *Relations Between Uruguay and the United States* (1936); Rex A. Hudson and Sandra W. Meditz, eds., *Uruguay* (1992); Martin Weinstein, *Uruguay* (1987). See "Latin America" and Whitaker in "Argentina."

Venezuela: Judith Ewell, *Venezuela and the United States* (1996); Janet Kelley and Carlos A. Romero, *United States and Venezuela* (2001); Sheldon B. Liss, *Diplomacy and Independence* (1978); Stephen G. Rabe, *The Road to OPEC* (1982); Darlene Rivas, *Missionary Capitalist* (2002). See also "Latin America" and "Oil."

Vietnam and Southeast Asia: David L. Anderson, ed., *Shadow on the White House* (1993); David Anderson, *The Columbia Guide to the Vietnam War* (2002) (E); Pierre Asselin, *A Bitter Peace* (2002); Larry Berman, *No Peace, No Honor* (2001); John S. Bowman, ed., *The Vietnam War* (1986) (C); Robert Brigham, *Guerrilla Diplomacy* (1998); Lester H. Brune and Richard Dean Burns, eds., *America and the Indochina Wars, 1945–1990* (1991) (B); Peter Busch, *All the Way with JFK* (2003); Robert Buzzanco and Marilyn Young, eds., *A Companion to the Vietnam War* (2002) (E); Philip E. Catton, *Diem's Final Failure* (2002); William J. Duiker, *Historical Dictionary of Vietnam* (1989) (E); Frances Fitzgerald, *Fire in the Lake* (1972); H. Bruce Franklin, *Vietnam and Other American Fantasies* (2002); Lloyd C. Gardner, *Approaching Vietnam* (1988); George C. Herring, *America's Longest War* (2000); Gary R. Hess, *Vietnam and the United States* (1998); George McT. Kahin, *Intervention* (1986); David Kaiser, *American Tragedy* (2000); Gabriel Kolko, *Anatomy of a War* (1985); Stanley I. Kutler, ed., *Encyclopedia of the Vietnam War* (1995) (E); Frederik Logevall, *Choosing War* (1999); Robert J. McMahon, *The Limits of Empire* (1999); Charles E. Neu, *After Vietnam* (2000); James S. Olson, *Dictionary of the Vietnam War* (1988) (E) and *The Vietnam War* (1993) (B); Andrew J. Rotter, *The Path to Vietnam* (1987); Robert D. Schulzinger, *A Time for War* (1997); Harry G. Summers, Jr., *Vietnam War Almanac* (1985) (C); Randall B. Woods, ed., *Vietnam and the American Political Tradition* (2003); Marilyn Young, *The Vietnam Wars* (1991). See also "Asia and Pacific Islands," "Military, U.S. Army, and Wars," and "Peace Movements."

Virgin Islands and West Indies: William W. Boyer, *America's Virgin Islands* (1983); Cary Fraser, *Ambivalent Anti-Colonialism* (1994); Verna P. Moll, *Virgin Islands* (1991) (B); Andrew Jackson O'Saughnessy, *An Empire Divided* (2000); Stephen J. Randall and Graeme Malent, *The Caribbean Basin* (1998); Charlie Witham, *Bitter Rehearsal* (2002). See also "Caribbean."

Yemen: Ahmed Nomen Al-Madhaqi, *Yemen and the USA* (1994); Fred Halliday, *Revolution and Foreign Policy* (1989). See also "Middle East."

Yugoslavia: Leonard Cohen, *Broken Bonds* (1993); Misha Glenny, *The Balkans* (2000); Lorraine M. Lees, *Keeping Tito Afloat* (1997); Miron Rezan, *Europe's Nightmare* (2001); Ivo Tasovic, *American Policy and Yugoslavia, 1939–1941* (1999); Susan Woodward, *Balkan Tragedy* (1995). See also "Eastern Europe."

Zambia: See "Africa."

Zimbabwe: Andrew DeRoche, *Black, White, and Chrome* (2001); Gerald Horne, *From the Barrel of a Gun* (2001); R. Kent Rasmussen, *Historical Dictionary of Zimbabwe* (1990) (E). See also "Africa."

Overviews of Subjects, Including Atlases (A), Annual Surveys (AS), Bibliographies (B), Biographical Aids (BA), Chronologies (C), Encyclopedias (E), and Statistics (S)

African Americans: Carol Anderson, *Eyes Off the Prize* (2003); Thomas Borstelmann, *The Cold War and the Color Line* (2001); Chris Dixon, *African America and Haiti* (2000); Mary Dudziak, *Cold War Civil Rights* (2000); Robert Gallicho, *The African American Encounter with Japan and China* (2001); Gerald Horne, *Black and Red* (1986); Michael L. Krenn, *Black Diplomacy* (1998); Azza Salema Layton, *International Relations and Civil Rights* (2000); James H. Meriwether, *Proudly We Can Be Africans* (2002); Brenda Gayle Plummer, *Rising Wind* (1996); "Symposium: African Americans and U.S. Foreign Relations," *Diplomatic History, XX* (Fall 1996); Lamin Sanneh, *Abolitionists Abroad* (2000); Penny von Eschen, *Race Against Empire* (1997). See also "Race and Racism" and Skinner in "Africa."

AIDS Pandemic: J. Mann, Daniel Tarantola, and T. Netter, eds., *AIDS in the World* (1992, 1996); Matthew Smallman-Raynor et al., *Atlas of AIDS* (1992). See also "Health Organizations."

Air Force and Air Power: Charles D. Bright, ed., *Historical Dictionary of the U.S. Air Force* (1992) (E); Alan P. Dobson, *Peaceful Air Warfare* (1991); Richard P. Hallion, *The Literature of Aeronautics, Astronautics, and Air Power* (1984) (B); John B. Rae, *Climb to Greatness* (1968); Michael S. Sherry, *The Rise of American Air Power* (1987); Jeffrey S. Underwood, *The Wings of Democracy* (1991); Bruce W. Watson and Susan W. Watson, *The United States Air Force* (1992) (E). See also "Military, U.S. Army, and Wars" and specific wars.

Alliance for Progress: Jerome Levinson and Juan de Onís, *The Alliance That Lost Its Way* (1970); L. Ronald Scheman, ed., *The Alliance for Progress* (1988). See also "Latin America."

American Revolution: Richard Blanco, ed., *The American Revolution* (1993) (E); Mark M. Boatner III, *Encyclopedia of the American Revolution* (1974) (E); Lester J. Cappon, ed., *Atlas of Early American History: The Revolutionary Era, 1760–1790* (1976) (A); John M. Faragher, ed., *The Encyclopedia of Colonial and Revolutionary America* (1990) (E); Jack P. Greene and J. R. Pole, eds., *The Blackwell Encyclopedia of the American Revolution* (1991) (E); John W. Raimo, ed., *Bio-*

graphical Directory of American Colonial and Revolutionary Governors, 1607–1789 (1980) (BA).

Anti-Americanism: "Anti-Americanism," *The Annals,* May 1988; Dan Diner, *German Anti-Americanism* (1995); Rob Kroes and Maarten van Rossem, eds., *Anti-Americanism in Europe* (1986); Denis Lacorne et al., eds., *The Rise and Fall of Anti-Americanism* (1990); Richard Pells, *Not Like Us* (1997); Alvin Z. Rubenstein and Donald E. Smith, eds., *Anti-Americanism in the Third World* (1985); David Strauss, *Menace in the West: The Rise of French Anti-Americanism in Modern Times* (1978).

Anticommunism and McCarthyism: Jeff Broadwater, *Eisenhower and the Anti-Communist Crusades* (1992); Peter H. Buckingham, *America Sees Red* (1987) (B); Richard M. Fried, *Nightmare in Red* (1990); Robert Griffith, *The Politics of Fear* (1987); Joel Kovel, *Red Hunting in the Promised Land* (1994); Stanley I. Kutler, *The American Inquisition* (1982); David K. Johnson, *The Lavender Scare* (2003); Richard G. Powers, *Not Without Honor* (1995); Athan Theoharis, *Chasing Spies* (2002); Stephen J. Whitfield, *The Culture of the Cold War* (1996). See also "Cold War."

ANZUS Pact: David W. McIntyre, *Background to the Anzus Pact* (1995). See also "Australia."

Arab-Israeli Conflict: See "Israel, Palestine, and Arab-Israeli Conflict" and "Middle East."

Arms Control: See "Disarmament and Arms Control."

Arms Sales and Trade: Michael Broszka and Thomas Ohlson, *Arms Transfers to the Third World* (1987); Michael T. Klare, *American Arms Supermarket* (1984); Edward J. Laurence, *The International Arms Trade* (1992); Andrew J. Pierre, *The Global Politics of Arms Sales* (1982). See also "Military, U.S. Army, and Wars."

Assassination: Carl Sifakis, *Encyclopedia of Assassinations* (1991) (E).

Atlantic Charter: Douglas Brinkley and David Facey-Crowther, eds., *The Atlantic Charter* (1994); Theodore A. Wilson, *The First Summit* (1991). See also "World War II."

Biological and Chemical Warfare: G. M. Burck and Charles C. Flowerree, *International Handbook on Chemical Weapons Proliferation* (1991) (E); Anthony H. Cordesman, *Weapons of Mass Destruction in the Middle East* (1991); Arthur J. Dommen et al., *The United States and Biological Warfare* (1999); Stephen Endicott and Edward Hagerman, *The United States and Biological Warfare* (1999); Sheldon H. Harris, *Factories of Death* (1994); John Norris and Will Fowler, *NBC: Nuclear, Biological, and Chemical Warfare on the Modern Battlefield* (1998) (E); Amy E. Simpson, ed., *The Chemical Weapons Convention Handbook* (1993).

Bricker Amendment: Duane Tananbaum, *The Bricker Amendment Controversy* (1988). See also "Congress (House and Senate)."

Bureaucracy: Graham Allison, *Essence of Decision* (1971); I. M. Destler, *Presidents, Bureaucrats, and Foreign Policy* (1974); Louis Galambos, ed., *The New American State* (1987); Morton H. Halperin, *Bureaucratic Politics and Foreign Policy* (1974); Irving L. Janis, *Groupthink* (1983); James Q. Wilson, *Bureaucracy* (1989). See also "President (General)."

Business: See "Economic Relations and Business."

Central Intelligence Agency (CIA): See "Intelligence, CIA, and Covert Action."

Chemical Warfare: See "Biological and Chemical Warfare."

Civil Defense: Laura McEnany, *Civil Defense Begins at Home* (2000); Kenneth D. Rose, *One Nation Underground* (2001).

Civil War (American): Mark M. Boatner III, *The Civil War Dictionary* (1988) (E); D. P. Crook, *The North, the South, and the Powers* (1974); Richard N. Current, ed., *Encyclopedia of the Confederacy* (1993) (E); David S. Heidler et al., *Encyclopedia of the American Civil War* (2000) (E); John T. Hubbell and James W. Geary, eds., *Biographical Dictionary of the Union* (1995) (BA); David C. Roller and Robert W. Twyman, eds., *The Encyclopedia of Southern History* (1979) (E); Jon L. Wakelyn, ed., *Biographical Dictionary of the Confederacy* (1977) (BA); Steven E. Woodworth, ed., *The American Civil War* (1996) (B).

Cold War: Thomas S. Arms, *Encyclopedia of the Cold War* (1994) (E); H. W. Brands, *The Devil We Knew* (1993); John Lewis Gaddis, *We Now Know* (1997); Michael Kort, *The Columbia Guide to the Cold War* (2001) (E); Walter LaFeber, *America, Russia, and the Cold War* (2001); Ralph B. Levering et al., *Debating the Origins of the Cold War* (2002); Wilford Loth, *Overcoming the Cold War* (2002); Thomas J. McCormick, *America's Half-Century* (1995); Robert J. McMahon, *The Cold War* (2003); Richard Schwartz, *Cold War Culture* (E) (1998); Joseph Smith and Simon Davis, *Historical Dictionary of the Cold War* (E) (2000); *Thomas G. Paterson,* Meeting the Communist Threat (1988) and *On Every Front* (1992). See also "Disarmament and Arms Control," "Nuclear Arms," "Russia and the Soviet Union," and "Threat Perception and Calculation."

Communications: James L. Baughman, *The Republic of Mass Culture* (1992); Menahem Blondheim, *New Over the Wires* (1994); David H. Culbert, *News for Everyman* (1976) (radio); Wilson Dizard, Jr., *Digital Diplomacy* (2001); Paul R. Edwards, *The Closed World* (1996)

(computers); Howard H. Frederick, *Global Communications and International Relations* (1992); Bradley S. Greenberg, ed., *Communication and Terrorism* (2001); Julian Hale, *Radio Power* (1975); Daniel R. Headrick, *The Invisible Weapon: Telecommunications and International Politics, 1851–1945* (1991); David Paull Nickles, *Under the Wire* (2003); James G. Savage, *The Politics of International Telecommunications Regulation* (1989); James Schwoch, *The American Radio Industry and Its Latin American Activities* (1990); Philip M. Taylor, *Global Communications* (1997). See also "Cultural Relations."

Congress (House and Senate): Betty Austin, *J. William Fulbright* (1995) (B); Stephen G. Christianson, *Facts About the Congress* (1996); Congressional Quarterly, *Biographical Directory of the American Congress* (1997) (BA) and *Congress and the Nation, 1945–1984* (1965–1985) (E); Robert U. Goehlert and John R. Sayre, *The United States Congress* (1981) (B); Barbara Hinckley, *Less Than Meets the Eye* (1994); James M. Lindsey, *Congress and the Politics of U.S. Foreign Policy* (1994); James A. Robinson, *Congress and Foreign Policy-Making* (1967); John Rourke, *Congress and the Presidency in U.S. Foreign Policymaking* (1983); Goran Rystad, ed., *Congress and American Foreign Policy* (1982); John Spanier and Joseph Nogee, eds., *Congress, the Presidency, and Foreign Policy* (1980); U.S. Congress, *Biographical Directory of the United States Congress, 1774–1989* (1989) (BA); Gerald F. Warburg, *Conflict and Consensus* (1989); Stephen R. Weissman, *A Culture of Deference* (1995). See also "Constitution and Constitutional Interpretation," "President (General)," and "War Powers."

Conservation: See "Environment."

Constitution and Constitutional Interpretation: David G. Adler and Larry N. George, eds., *The Constitution and American Foreign Policy* (1996); Henry B. Cox, *War, Foreign Affairs, and Constitutional Power, 1829–1901* (1984); Louis Fischer, *Constitutional Conflicts Between the President and Congress* (1985); Thomas M. Franck and Michael J. Glennon, *Foreign Relations and National Security Law* (1993); Louis Henkin, *Constitutionalism, Democracy, and Foreign Affairs* (1990) and *Foreign Affairs and the Constitution* (1972); Harold Honggju Koh, *The National Security Constitution* (1990); Leonard W. Levy et al., eds., *Encyclopedia of the American Constitution* (1986) (E); Gordon Silberstein, *Imbalance of Powers* (1997); Joan E. Smith, *The Constitution and American Foreign Policy* (1989); Abraham Sofaer, *War, Foreign Affairs, and Constitutional Power* (1976). See also "War Powers."

Containment: Terry L. Deibel and John Lewis Gaddis, eds., *Containment* (1986); John Lewis Gaddis, *Strategies of Containment* (1982); Charles Gati, ed., *Caging the Bear* (1974); Deborah Larson, *Origins of Containment* (1985). See also "Cold War."

Counterinsurgency: Benjamin R. Beede, *Intervention and Counterinsurgency* (1984) (B); Douglas S. Blaufarb, *The Counterinsurgency Era* (1977); Larry E. Cable, *Conflict of Myths* (1986); Anthony James Joes, *America and Guerrilla Warfare* (2000); Michael T. Klare and Peter Kornbluh, eds., *Low-Intensity Warfare* (1988); Michael McClintock, *Instruments of Statecraft* (1992); D. Michael Shafer, *Deadly Paradigms* (1988). See also "Intelligence, CIA, and Covert Action."

Credibility: Robert J. McMahon, "Credibility and World Power," *Diplomatic History, XV* (Fall 1991), 455-471; Jonathan Mercer, *Reputation and International Politics* (1996).

Cultural Relations: Christian G. Appy, ed., *Cold War Constructions* (2000); Jongsuk Chay, ed., *Culture and International Relations* (1990); Heidi Fehrenbach and Uta G. Poiger, eds., *Transactions, Transgressions, and Transformations* (2000); Jessica C. E. Gienow-Hecht, *Transmission Impossible* (1999); Petra Goedda, *GIs and Germans* (2003); Morrell Heald and Lawrence S. Kaplan, *Culture and Diplomacy* (1977); Akira Iriye, *Cultural Internationalism and World Order* (1997); Robert D. Johnson, ed., *On Cultural Ground* (1994); Gilbert M. Joseph el al., eds., *Close Encounters of Empire* (1998); Amy Kaplan and Donald E. Pease, eds., *Cultures of United States Imperialism* (1993); Rob Kroes, *If You've Seen One You've Seen the Mall* (1996); Peter J. Kuznick and James Gilbert, eds., *Rethinking Cold War Culture* (2001); Frank Ninkovich, *The Diplomacy of Ideas* (1981); Naima Prevots, *Dance for Export* (1998); Uta G. Poiger, *Jazz, Rock, and Rebels* (2000); Yale Richmond, *Cultural Exchange and the Cold War* (2003); Emily Rosenberg, *Spreading the American Dream* (1982); Frances Sauders, *The Cultural Cold War* (1999); Anthony Smith, *The Geopolitics of Information* (1980); Reinhold Wagnleitner and Elaine T. May, eds., *"Here, There, and Everywhere": The Foreign Politics of American Popular Culture* (2000); . See also "Communications," "Films, Television, and Cultural Expansion," "Philanthropy and Foundations," and "Propaganda and Public Diplomacy."

Decline Thesis: David P. Calleo, *Beyond American Hegemony* (1987); Paul Kennedy, *The Rise and Fall of the Great Powers* (1987); Henry Nau, *The Myth of America's Decline* (1990); Joseph P. Nye, Jr., *Bound to Lead* (1990).

Decolonization: Franz Ansprenger, *The Dissolution of Colonial Empires* (1989); Prosser Gifford and William Roger Louis, eds., *Decolonization and African Independence* (1988); D. A. Low, *Eclipse of Empire* (1991); David Ryan and Victor Pugong, eds., *The United States and Decolonization* (2000); Brian Urquhart, *Decolonization and World Peace* (1989).

Defense: See "Military, U.S. Army, and Wars," "Nuclear Arms," and particular wars.

Department of State, Foreign Service, and Diplomatic Practice: W. Wendell Blancke, *The Foreign Service of the United States* (1969); Robert U. Goehlert and Elizabeth Hoffmeister, *The Department of State and American Diplomacy* (1986) (B); Warren F. Ilchman, *Professional Diplomacy in the United States, 1779–1939* (1961); Charles S. Kennedy, *The American Consul* (1990); Henry E. Mattox, *The Twilight of Amateur Diplomacy* (1989); Robert H. Miller et al., *Inside an Embassy* (1992); Cathal Nolan, ed., *Notable U.S. Ambassadors Since 1775* (1998); Elmer Plischke, *United States Diplomats and Their Mission* (1979); and *U.S. Department of State* (1999); Martin Weil, *A Pretty Good Club* (1978); Richard H. Werking, *The Master Architects* (1977). See also "President (General)."

Dependency: Fernando Henrique Cardoso and Enzo Faletto, *Dependency and Development in Latin America* (1979); Andre Gunder Frank, *Capitalism and Underdevelopment in Latin America* (1967); Vincent A. Mahler, *Dependency Approaches to International Political Economy* (1980); Robert A. Packenham, *The Dependency Movement* (1992). See also "World-System Analysis."

Deterrence: Alexander L. George and Richard Smoke, *Deterrence in American Foreign Policy* (1974); Ted Hopf, *Peripheral Visions* (1994); Robert Jervis et al., *Psychology and Deterrence* (1985). Also see "Cold War" and "Nuclear Arms."

Dictatorships: H. E. Chehabi and Juan J. Linz, *Sultanistic Regimes* (1998); David F. Schmitz, *Thank God They're on Our Side* (1999).

Diplomatic Immunity: Linda S. Frey and Marsha L. Frey, *The History of Diplomatic Immunity* (1999).

Disarmament and Arms Control: Sheikh Rustum Aki, *The Peace and Nuclear War Dictionary* (1989) (E); Stephen E. Atkins, *Arms Control and Disarmament* (1989) (B); Richard Dean Burns, ed., *Encyclopedia of Arms Control and Disarmament* (1993) (E); Jeffrey M. Elliot and Robert Reginald, *The Arms Control, Disarmament, and Military Security Dictionary* (1989) (E); Milton S. Katz, *Ban the Bomb* (1986); Kendrick Oliver, *Kennedy, MacMillan, and the Nuclear Test Ban Treaty, 1961–63* (1998); Henry D. Sokoloski, *Best of Intentions* (2001); Stockholm International Peace Research Institute, *SIPRI Yearbook: International Armaments and Disarmament* (1969– (AS and S); United Nations, *Disarmament Yearbook* (1976– (AS); Lawrence S. Wittner, *The Struggle Against the Bomb* (1993–2003). See also "Cold War," "Nuclear Arms," and "Peace Movements."

Dollar Diplomacy: Emily S. Rosenberg, *Missionaries to the World* (1999); Cyrus Veeser, *A World Safe for Capitalism* (2002). See also "Economic Relations and Business."

Domino Theory: Frank Ninkovich, *Modernity and Power* (1994).

Drug Trafficking: Bruce M. Bagley, ed., *Drug Trafficking Research in the Americas* (1997) (B); Ted Galen Carpenter, *Bad Neighbor Policy* (2003); Richard Crandall, *Driven by Drugs* (2002); Donald J. Mabry, ed., *The Latin American Narcotics Trade and U.S. National Security* (1989); Scott B. MacDonald and Bruce Zagaris, eds., *International Handbook on Drug Control* (1992) (E); Katherine Meyer and Terry Parssinen, *Webs of Smoke* (2002); Peter Dale Scott, *Drugs, Oil, and War* (2002); Arnold H. Taylor, *American Diplomacy and the Narcotics Traffic, 1900–1931* (1969); William O. Walker III, *Drug Control in the Americas* (1981), ed., *Drugs in the Western Hemisphere* (1996), and *Opium and Foreign Policy* (1991).

Economic Relations and Business: William H. Becker and Samuel F. Wells, eds., *Economics and World Power* (1984); Alfred E. Eckes, Jr., *Opening America's Market* (1995); Dana Frank, *Buy American* (1999); Michael J. Freeman, *Atlas of World Economy* (1991) (A); Fancis J. Gavin, *Gold, Dollars, and Power* (2003); Carolyn Gibson, *The McGraw-Hill Dictionary of International Trade* (1994) (E); Robert Gilpin, *Global Political Economy* (2002); Judith Goldstein, *Ideas, Interests, and American Trade Policy* (1993); John N. Ingham, *Biographical Dictionary of American Business Leaders* (1983) (BA); John N. Ingham and Lyness B. Feldman, *Contemporary American Business Leaders* (1990) (BA); Edward S. Kaplan and Thomas W. Ryley, *Prelude to Trade Wars: American Trade Policy, 1890–1922* (1994); Diane Kunz, *Butter and Guns* (1997); Thelma Liesner, *One Hundred Years of Economic Statistics* (1989) (S); Wahib Nasrallah, *United States Corporation Histories* (1991) (B); Timothy O'Donnell et al., eds., *World Economic Data* (1991) (S); James S. Olsen, *Dictionary of American Economic History* (1992) (E); Robert Soloman, *Money on the Move* (1999); Joan E. Spero and Jeffrey A. Hart, *The Politics of International Economic Relations* (1997); United Nations, *International Trade Statistics Yearbook* (1985– (AS and S), *World Economic Survey* (1955– (AS and S), and *Yearbook of International Trade Statistics* (1950–1982) (AS and S); Herman Van Der Wee, *The Search for Prosperity: The World Economy, 1945–1977* (1977); Malcolm Warner, ed., *International Encyclopedia of Business and Management* (1996) (E); Mira Wilkins, *The Emergence of Multinational Enterprise* (1970) and *The Maturing of Multinational Enterprise* (1975); Thomas W. Zeiler, *Free Trade, Free World: The Advent of GATT* (1999). See also "Dollar Diplomacy," "Economic Sanctions and Export Controls," "Export-Import Bank," "Minerals," "North American Free Trade Agreement (NAFTA)," "Tariffs and Protectionism," and Funigiello in "Russia and the Soviet Union."

Economic Sanctions and Export Controls: Margaret P. Doxey, *Economic Sanctions and International Enforcement* (1980); Gary C. Hufbauer and Jeffrey J. Schott, *Economic Sanctions Reconsidered* (1990); William J. Long, *U.S. Export Control Policy* (1989); Donald Losman,

International Economic Sanctions (1979); Homer E. Moyer, Jr., and Linda L. Mabry, *Export Controls as Instruments of Foreign Policy* (1988); Sidney Weintraub, ed., *Economic Coercion and U.S. Foreign Policy* (1982); Thomas G. Weiss, *Political Gain and Civilian Pain* (1998). See also "Economic Relations and Business" and "Tariffs and Protectionism."

Environment: Scott Barrett, *Environment and Statecraft* (2003); Lee-Anne Broadhead, *International Environmental Politics* (2002); Robert Broadman, *International Organization and the Conservation of Nature* (1981); Lester R. Brown et al., *State of the World* (1984–) (AS); Lynton K. Caldwell, *International Environmental Policy* (1990); André R. Cooper, Sr., ed., *Cooper's Comprehensive Environmental Desk Reference* (1996) (E); Kurkpatrick Dorsey, *The Dawn of Conservation Diplomacy* (1999); Fridtjof Nansen Institute (Norway), *Green Globe Yearbook* (1992–) (AS); John McCormick, *The Global Environment* (1995) and *Reclaiming Paradise: The Global Environmental Movement* (1989); Organisation for Economic Co-operation and Development, *The State of the Environment* (1991) (E and S); Robert Paehlke, ed., *Conservation and Environmentalism* (1995) (E); Kirkpatrick Sale, *The Green Revolution* (1993); Philip Shabecoff, *Earth Rising* (2000); Richard P. Tucker, *Insatiable Appetite* (2000); World Resources Institute, *Environmental Almanac* (1992) (E); World Resources Institute (or International Institute for Environment and Development), *World Resources* (1976–). See also "Law of the Sea."

Ethics: Gerald Elfstrom, *Ethics for a Shrinking World* (1990); J. E. Hare and Carey B. Joynt, *Ethics and International Affairs* (1982); Dorothy V. Jones, *Code of Peace* (1991); Kenneth W. Thompson, ed., *Ethics and International Relations* (1985) and *Moral Dimensions of American Foreign Policy* (1984).

Ethnic Conflict: David Callahan, *Unwinnable Wars* (1997); Human Rights Watch, *Slaughter Among Neighbors* (1995); David A. Lake and Donald Rothchild, eds., *The International Spread of Ethnic Conflict* (1998). See also countries.

Ethnic Groups and Immigration: Mohammed E. Ahrari, ed., *Ethnic Groups and U.S. Foreign Policy* (1987); Gerald Chaliand and Jean-Pierre Rageau, *The Penguin Atlas of Diasporas* (1995) (A); Francesco Cordasco, ed., *Dictionary of American Immigration History* (1990) (E); Alexander DeConde, *Ethnicity, Race, and American Foreign Policy* (1992); Izumi Hirobe, *Japanese Pride, American Prejudice* (2001); David M. Reimers, *Still the Golden Door: The Third World Comes to America* (1992); Abdul Aziz Said, ed., *Ethnicity and U.S. Foreign Policy* (1977); Tony Smith, *Foreign Attachments* (2000); Stephen Thernstrom, ed., *Harvard Encyclopedia of American Ethnic Groups* (1980) (E); Robert W. Tucker et al., eds., *Immigration and U.S. Foreign Policy* (1990). See also "Refugees."

Exceptionalism: David K. Adams and Cornelius A. van Minnen, eds., *Reflections on American Exceptionalism* (1994). See also "Ideology."

Executive Agreements: Lawrence Margolis, *Executive Agreements and Presidential Power in Foreign Policy* (1986); Wallace M. McClure, *International Executive Agreements* (1941). See also "President (General)."

Export-Import Bank: Frederick C. Adams, *Economic Diplomacy* (1976); Richard E. Feinberg, *Subsidizing Success* (1982); Rita M. Rodriquez, ed., *The Export-Import Bank at Fifty* (1987). See also "Economic Relations and Business."

Extraterritoriality: Wesley R. Fishel, *The End of Extraterritoriality* (1952); Dietr Lange and Gary Born, eds., *The Extraterritorial Application of National Laws* (1987); Elaine Scully, *Bargaining with the State from Afar* (2001). See also "International Law and Hague Conferences."

Films, Television, and Cultural Expansion: Royce J. Ammon, *Global Television and the Shaping of World Politics* (1999); Robert Burgoyne, *Film Nation* (1997); David A. Cook, *Lost Illusions* (2000); Thomas Doherty, *Projections of War* (1999); Susan Jeffords, *Hard Bodies* (1993); James F. Larson, *Global Television and Foreign Policy* (1988); Thomas J. Saunders, *Hollywood in Berlin* (1994); Kristin Thompson, *Exporting Entertainment* (1985); Robert Brent Toplin, *Reel History* (2002). See also "Communications" and "Cultural Relations."

Food Diplomacy and Relief: Nicole Ball, ed., *World Hunger* (1981) (B); Raymond F. Hopkins and Donald J. Puchala, *Global Food Interdependence* (1980); Don Paarlberg, *Toward a Well-Fed World* (1988); Vernon W. Ruttan, ed., *Why Food Aid?* (1993); Hans W. Sinder et al., *Food Aid* (1987); Ross B. Talbott, *The Four World Food Agencies in Rome* (1990). See also "Foreign Aid" and "Humanitarian Relief and Intervention."

Foreign Aid: David Baldwin, *Economic Development and American Foreign Policy, 1943–1962* (1966); Herbert Feis, *Foreign Aid and Foreign Policy* (1964); David H. Lumsdaine, *Moral Vision in International Politics: The Foreign Aid Regime, 1949–1989* (1993); Robert A. Packenham, *Liberal America and the Third World* (1973); Roger Riddell, *Foreign Aid Reconsidered* (1987); Vernon W. Ruttan, *United States Development Assistance Policy* (1995). See also "Food Diplomacy and Relief."

Foreign Investment in the United States: Mira Wilkins, *The History of Foreign Investment in the United States to 1914* (1989). See also "Economic Relations and Business."

Foreign Service: See "Department of State, Foreign Service, and Diplomatic Practice."

French and Indian War: Fred Anderson, *Crucible of War* (2001); Frank W. Brecher, *Losing a Continent* (1998); Seymour I. Schwartz, *The French and Indian War, 1754–1763* (1995) (E). See also "Military, U.S. Army, and Wars."

Fulbright Program: Walter Johnson and Francis Collegan, *The Fulbright Program* (1965); Leonard Sussman, *The Culture of Freedom* (1992). See also "Cultural Relations."

Genocide: Israel Charney, ed., *Genocide* (1988) (B); Leo Kuper, *Genocide* (1981); Lawrence J. LeBlanc, *The United States and the Genocide Convention* (1991); Samantha Power, *The Problem from Hell* (2002); Charles B. Stroozier and Michael Flynn, eds., *Genocide, War, and Human Survival* (1996). See also "Holocaust," "Humanitarian Relief and Intervention," and "War Crimes and Trials."

Good Neighbor Policy: David Green, *The Containment of Latin America* (1971); Fredrick B. Pike, *FDR's Good Neighbor Policy* (1995); Bryce Wood, *The Dismantling of the Good Neighbor Policy* (1985) and *The Making of the Good Neighbor Policy* (1961). See also "Latin America."

Guano: Jimmy M. Skaggs, *The Great Guano Rush* (1994).

Health and Medical History of Leaders: Kenneth R. Crispell and Carlos F. Gomez, *Hidden Illness in the White House* (1988); Robert H. Ferrell, *Ill-Advised* (1992); Robert E. Gilbert, *The Mortal Presidency* (1992); Bert E. Park, *Ailing, Aged, Addicted* (1993) and *The Impact of Illness on World Leaders* (1986). See also "President (General)" and "President (By Administration)."

Health Organizations: Kelly Lee, *Historical Dictionary of the World Health Organization* (1998) (E); Javid Siddiqi, *World Health and World Politics* (1994); Paul Weindling, ed., *International Health Organizations and Movements* (1995).

Holocaust: Yehudi Bauer, *Rethinking the Holocaust* (2001); Richard Breitman, *Official Secrets* (1998); Richard Breitman and Alan M. Kraut, *American Refugee Policy and European Jewry* (1987); Henry L. Feingold, *Bearing Witness* (1995); Martin Gilbert, *Auschwitz and the Allies* (1981); Israel Gutman, ed., *Encyclopedia of the Holocaust* (1990) (E); Deborah E. Lipstadt, *Beyond Belief* (1993); Michael R. Marrus, *The Holocaust in History* (1987); David Wyman, *The Abandonment of the Jews* (1984) and *Paper Walls* (1968). See also "Genocide," "Germany and Berlin," "War Crimes and Trials," and "World War II."

Hostage-Taking: Russell D. Buhite, *Lives at Risk* (1995); David P. Houghton, *U.S. Foreign Policy and the Iran Hostage Crisis* (2001); Russell Lee Moses, *Freeing the Hostages* (1996).

Humanitarian Relief and Intervention: Robert C. DiPrizo, *Armed Humanitarians* (2002); Larry Minear and Thomas G. Weiss, *Humanitarian Politics* (1995); Robert I. Rotberg and Thomas G. Weiss, eds., *From Massacres to Genocide* (1996). See also "Ethnic Conflict," "Genocide," "Human Rights," and countries.

Human Rights: America's Watch Staff (periodic reports on Latin American countries); Amnesty International, *The Amnesty International Report* (1977– (AS); Peter R. Baehr, *The Role of Human Rights in Foreign Policy* (1994); Jack Donnelly and Rhoda E. Howard, eds., *International Handbook of Human Rights* (1987) (E); Charles Humana, *World Human Rights Guide* (1992); Human Rights Watch, *World Report* (1983– (AS); Natalie Kaufman, *Human Rights Treaties and the Senate* (1990); William Korey, *The Promises We Keep* (1993); Edward Lawson, *Encyclopedia of Human Rights* (1991) (E); A. Glenn Mower, *Human Rights and American Foreign Policy* (1987) and *The United States, the United Nations, and Human Rights* (1979); A. H. Robertson and J. G. Merrills, *Human Rights in the World* (1997) (B); Lars Schoultz, *Human Rights and United States Policy Toward Latin America* (1981); Kenneth W. Thompson, ed., *The Moral Imperatives of Human Rights* (1980); Sandy Vogelgesang, *American Dream, American Nightmare* (1980). See also "Holocaust," "Humanitarian Relief and Intervention," and "War Crimes and Trials."

Ideology: Richard J. Barnet, *Roots of War* (1972); Arthur A. Ekirch, Jr., *Ideas, Ideals, and American Diplomacy* (1966); John Fousek, *To Lead the Free World* (2002); Michael H. Hunt, *Ideology and U.S. Foreign Policy* (1987); Christina Klein, *Cold War Orientalism* (2003); Michael E. Latham, *Modernization as Ideology* (2000); Ron Robin, *The Making of the Cold War Enemy* (2001); E. L. Tuveson, *Redeemer Nation* (1968); William A. Williams, *The Tragedy of American Diplomacy* (1962). See also "Manifest Destiny" and "Race and Racism."

Immigration: See "Ethnic Groups and Immigration."

Imperialism: Michael B. Brown, *The Economics of Imperialism* (1974); Philip Darby, *Three Faces of Imperialism* (1987); Michael Doyle, *Empires* (1986); Niall Ferguson, *Empire* (2003); Peter L. Hahn and Mary Ann Heiss, eds., *Empire and Revolution* (2001); Eric Hinderaker, *Elusive Empires* (1997); Amy Kaplan, *The Anarchy of Empire in the Making of U.S. Culture* (2002); Gabriel Kolko, *The Roots of American Foreign Policy* (1969); Frank Ninkovich, *The United States and Imperialism* (2001); Tony Smith, *The Pattern of Imperialism* (1981). See also "Dependency" and "World-System Analysis."

Indians (Native Americans): Brian W. Dippie, *The Vanishing American* (1982); Michael Green, *The Politics of Indian Removal* (1982); Barry Klein, ed., *Reference Encyclopedia of the American Indian* (1993)

(E); Calvin Martin, ed., *The American Indian and the Problem of History* (1986); Jane T. Merritt, *At the Crossroads* (2003); Francis Paul Prucha, *Atlas of American Indian Affairs* (1990) (A) and *The Indian in American Society* (1985); Jayme Sokolow, *The Great Encounter* (2002); Paul Stuart, *Nation Within a Nation* (1987) (S); Carl Waldman, *Atlas of the North American Indian* (1985) (A); Anthony F. C. Wallace, *Jefferson and the Indians* (2001); Philip Weeks, *"They Made Us Many Promises"* (2002).

Intelligence, CIA, and Covert Action: David Alvarez, *Secret Messages* (2000); Christopher Andrew, *For the President's Eyes Only* (1995); James Bamford, *Body of Secrets* (2001); Paul W. Blackstock and Frank L. Schaf, eds., *Intelligence, Espionage, Counterespionage, and Covert Operations* (1978) (B); Marjorie W. Cline et al., *Scholar's Guide to Intelligence Literature* (1983) (B); George C. Constantinides, *Intelligence & Espionage* (1983) (B); Arthur B. Darling, *The Central Intelligence Agency* (1990); Rhodri Jeffreys-Jones, *The CIA and American Democracy* (2003) and *Cloak and Dollar* (2002); Rhodri Jeffreys-Jones and Andrew Lownie, eds., *North American Spies* (1991); Loch K. Johnson, *America's Secret Power* (1989), *A Season of Inquiry* (1985), *Secret Agencies* (1996), and *Bombs, Bugs, Drugs, and Thugs* (2000); Stephen F. Knott, *Secret and Sanctioned* (1996); Mark Lowenthal, *U.S. Intelligence* (1992); Thomas Mahnken, *Uncovering the Ways of War* (2002); Ernest R. May, ed., *Knowing One's Enemies* (1985); Gregory Mitrovich, *Undermining the Kremlin* (2000); Neal H. Petersen, *American Intelligence, 1775–1990* (1992) (B); Walter Pforzheimer, *Bibliography of Intelligence Literature* (1985) (B); Thomas Powers, *Intelligence Wars* (2003); John Prados, *The Presidents' Secret Wars* (1986); John Ranelagh, *The Agency* (1986); Frank J. Smist, Jr., *Congress Oversees the United States Intelligence Community* (1994); Jeffrey T. Richelson, *A Century of Spies* (1995) and *The U.S. Intelligence Community* (1995); Bradley F. Smith, *The Shadow Warriors* (1983); William Taubman, *Secret Empire* (2003); Evan Thomas, *The Very Best Men* (1995); Gregory F. Treverton, *Covert Action* (1987); Robin W. Winks, *Clock & Gown* (1987). See also "Assassination."

International Finance: See "International Monetary Fund and System" and "World Bank."

International Law and Hague Conferences: Robert L. Bledsoe and Boleslaw A. Boczek, *The International Law Dictionary* (1987) (E); Calvin D. Davis, *The United States and the First Hague Conference* (1962) and *The United States and the Second Hague Conference* (1976); Ingrid Delupis, ed., *Bibliography of International Law* (1975) (B); Richard Falk et al., eds., *International Law* (1985); James Fox, *Dictionary of International and Comparative Law* (1991) (E); Daniel P. Moynihan, *The Law of Nations* (1990). See also "Law of the Sea."

International Monetary Fund and System: Margaret G. DeVries, *The IMF in a Changing World* (1986); Barry Eichengreen, *Glob-*

alizing Capital (1996); Harold James, *International Monetary Cooperation Since Bretton Woods* (1996); Mary E. Johnson, *The International Monetary Fund* (1993) (B); Robert Soloman, *Money on the Move* (1999); Brian Tew, *The Evolution of the International Monetary Fund, 1945–81* (1982).

International Organizations: Sheikh Ali, *The International Organization and World Order Dictionary* (1992) (E); John Boli and George M. Thomas, eds., *Constructing World Culture* (1999); George W. Baer, ed., *International Organizations, 1918–1945* (1981) (B); Akira Iriye, *Global Community* (2002); Edward C. Luck, *Mixed Messages* (1999); Edward J. Osmanczyk, *The Encyclopedia of the United States and International Organizations* (1990) (E); Hans-Albrecht Schraepler, *Directory of International Organizations* (1996); Union of International Associations, *Yearbook of International Organizations* (1948–) (AS). See also specific organizations.

Isolationism: Selig Adler, *The Isolationist Impulse* (1957); Wayne S. Cole, *Roosevelt and the Isolationists* (1983); Justus D. Doenecke, *Anti-Intervention* (1987) (B) and *Storm on the Horizon* (2001); Thomas N. Guinsburg, *The Pursuit of Isolationism in the United States Senate* (1982); Manfred Jonas, *Isolationism in America, 1935–1941* (1966).

Journalism and Media: James L. Baughman, *Henry R. Luce and the Rise of the American News Media* (1988); Gerd Horten, *Radio Goes to War* (2002); Joseph P. McKerns, ed., *Biographical Dictionary of American Journalism* (1989) (BA); Brigitte Lebens Nacos, *The Press, Presidents, and Crises* (1990); Johanna Neuman, *Lights, Camera, War* (1995); David D. Permutter, *Photojournalism and Foreign Policy* (1998); Arch Puddington, *Broadcasting Freedom* (2000); Michael Schudson, *The Power of News* (1995); Simon Serfaty, *The Media and Foreign Policy* (1990); Michael S. Sweeney, *Secrets of Victory* (2000); William H. Taft, ed., *Encyclopedia of Twentieth-Century Journalists* (1986) (BA); John Tebbel and Sarah Miles Watts, *The Press and the Presidency* (1985). See also "Film, Television, and Cultural Expansion" and "Public Opinion."

Korean War: See "Korea and Korean War."

Labor: Philip S. Foner, *U.S. Labor Movement and Latin America* (1988); Ronald Radosh, *American Labor and United States Foreign Policy* (1969); Federico Romero, *The United States and the European Trade Union Movement, 1944–1951* (1992).

Law of the Sea: Jack N. Barkenbus, *Deep Seabed Resources* (1979); Ann L. Hollick, *U.S. Foreign Policy and the Law of the Sea* (1981); Ralph B. Levering and Miriam L. Levering, *Citizen Action for Global Change* (2002); D. P. O'Connell, *The International Law of the Sea* (1982); Clyde Sanger, *Ordering the Oceans* (1987); United Nations, *The Law of the Sea* (1991) (B). See also "Environment" and "International Law and Hague Conferences."

League of Nations: Denna F. Fleming, *The United States and the League of Nations* (1932); Warren F. Kuehl, *Seeking World Order* (1969); F. S. Northedge, *The League of Nations* (1986). See also "International Organizations" and "United Nations."

Low Intensity Warfare: See "Counterinsurgency."

Manifest Destiny: Thomas R. Hietala, *Manifest Design* (2003); Reginald Horsman, *Race and Manifest Destiny* (1981); Linda S. Hudson, *Mistress of Manifest Destiny* (2001); Robert W. Johannsen, ed., *Manifest Destiny* (1998); Robert E. May, *Manifest Destiny's Underworld* (2002); Christopher Morris and Sam W. Haynes, eds., *Manifest Destiny and Empire* (1998); Anders Stephanson, *Manifest Destiny* (1995); Albert K. Weinberg, *Manifest Destiny* (1935). See also "Ideology."

Marshall Plan: John Bledsoe Bonds, *Bipartisan Strategy* (2002); Michael J. Hogan, *The Marshall Plan* (1987); Alan S. Milward, *The Reconstruction of Western Europe, 1945–51* (1984); Martin A. Schein, ed., *The Marshall Plan* (2001); Imanuel Wexler, *The Marshall Plan Revisited* (1983). See also "Europe" and "Foreign Aid."

Marine Corps: Allan R. Millett, *Semper Fidelis* (1980). See also "Military, U.S. Army, and Wars" and specific wars.

McCarthyism: See "Anticommunism and McCarthyism."

Media: See "Journalism and Media."

Merchant Marine: John A. Butler, *Sailing on Friday* (1997); Rene De La Pedraja, *A Historical Dictionary of the U.S. Merchant Marine and Shipping Industry* (1994) (E).

Military, U.S. Army, and Wars: William M. Arkin et al., *Encyclopedia of the U.S. Military* (1990) (E); Benjamin R. Beede, *Military and Strategic Policy* (1990) (B); John W. Chambers, *To Raise an Army* (1987); E. Ernest Dupuy and Trevor N. Dupuy, *The Harper Encyclopedia of Military History* (1993) (E); John C. Fredriksen, *Shield of the Republic/Sword of Empire* (1990) (B); Kenneth J. Hagan and William R. Roberts, eds., *Against All Enemies* (1986); Robin Higham and Donald J. Mrozek, eds., *A Guide to the Sources of United States Military History* (1975–) (B); International Institute for Strategic Studies, *Strategic Survey* (1966–) (AS) and *The Military Balance* (1959/1960–) (AS); *International Military and Defense Encyclopedia* (1993) (E); John E. Jessup and Louise B. Ketz, eds., *Encyclopedia of the American Military* (1994) (E); Allan R. Millett and Peter Maslowski, *For the Common Defense* (1994); Jay M. Shafritz et al., eds., *Dictionary of Military Science* (1989); Roger J. Spiller and Joseph G. Dawson III, eds., *Dictionary of American Military Biography* (1984) (BA); Jerry K. Sweeney, ed., *A Handbook* *of American Military History* (1996) (E); Herbert K. Tillema, *International Armed Conflict Since 1945* (1991) (B); Peter G. Tsouras et al., *The United States Army* (1991) (E); U.S. Military Academy, *The West Point Atlas of American Wars, 1689–1953* (1959) (A); Cynthia Watson, *U.S. National Security Policy Groups* (1990) (E); Russell F. Weigley, *The American Way of War* (1973) and *History of the United States Army* (1984). See also "Marine Corps," "Navy and Sea Power," and wars.

Minerals: Alfred E. Eckes, *The United States and the Global Struggle for Minerals* (1979); Jordan E. Helmreich, *Gathering Rare Ores* (1986); Ronnie Lipschutz, *When Nations Clash* (1989). See also "Economic Relations and Business."

Missionaries: Henry Bowden, *Dictionary of American Religious Biography* (1993) (BA); John K. Fairbank, ed., *The Missionary Enterprise in China and America* (1974); Gael Graham, *Gender, Culture, and Christianity* (1995); Patricia Hill, *The World Their Household* (1985); Jane Hunter, *The Gospel of Gentility* (1984); William R. Hutchison, *Errand to the World* (1987); Paul A. Varg, *Missionaries, Chinese, and Diplomats* (1958). See also "Cultural Relations" and "Ideology."

Monroe Doctrine: James E. Lewis, Jr., *The American Union and the Problem of Neighborhood* (1998); Ernest R. May, *The Making of the Monroe Doctrine* (1975); Dexter Perkins, *A History of the Monroe Doctrine* (1963); Gaddis Smith, *The Last Years of the Monroe Doctrine* (1994). See also "Latin America."

Nation–Building: James Dobbins et al., *America's Role in Nation-Building* (2003).

National Security Council: Gerry Andrianopoulos, *Kissinger and Brzezinski* (1991); John Prados, *Keepers of the Keys* (1991); Bromley K. Smith, *Organizational History of the National Security Council During the Kennedy and Johnson Administrations* (1988).

Navy and Sea Power: George W. Baer, *One Hundred Years of Sea Power* (1994); James C. Bradford, *Admirals of the New Steel Navy* (1990), *Captains of the Old Steam Navy* (1986), and *Command Under Sail* (1985); William B. Cogan, *Dictionary of Admirals of the United States Navy* (1989) (BA); Paolo E. Coletta, *A Selected and Annotated Bibliography of American Naval History* (1988) (B); Paolo E. Coletta et al., eds., *American Secretaries of the Navy* (1980) (BA); Michael J. Crawford and Christine F. Hughes, *The Reestablishment of the Navy, 1787–1801* (1995) (B); Kenneth J. Hagan, ed., *In Peace and War* (1984) and *This People's Navy* (1991); John B. Hattendorf and Lynn C. Hattendorf, *A Bibliography of the Works of Alfred Thayer Mahan* (1986) (B); David F. Long, *Gold Braid and Foreign Relations* (1988); Barbara A. Lynch and John E. Vajda, *United States Naval History* (1993)

(B); Franklin D. Margiotta, ed., *Brassey's Encyclopedia of Naval Forces and Warfare* (1996) (E); Nathaniel Philbrick, *Sea of Glory* (2003); Jack Sweetman, ed., *American Naval History* (1984) (C); Bruce W. Watson and Susan M. Watson, *The United States Navy* (1991) (E). See also "Military, U.S. Army, and Wars" and wars.

Neutralism and Nonalignment: H. W. Brands, *The Specter of Neutralism* (1989); K. C. Chaudhary, *Non-aligned Summitry* (1988); Steven R. David, *Choosing Sides* (1991); Richard L. Jackson, *The Non-aligned, the UN, and the Superpowers* (1983); Lawrence W. Martin, ed., *Neutralism and Nonalignment* (1962).

Nobel Peace Prize: Irwin Abrams, *The Nobel Peace Prize and the Laureates* (1988); Oaula McGuire, ed., *Nobel Prize Winners Supplement* (1992); Tyler Wasson, ed., *Nobel Prize Winners* (1987). See also "Peace Movements."

Nonproliferation (Nuclear): See "Cold War" and "Nuclear Arms."

North American Free Trade Agreement (NAFTA): Maxwell A. Cameron and Brian W. Tomlin, *The Making of NAFTA* (2001); Allan Metz, *A NAFTA Bibliography* (1996) (B); John R. Macarthur, *The Selling of "Free Trade"* (2002); William A. Orme, Jr., *Understanding NAFTA* (1996); Maryse Robert, *Negotiating NAFTA* (2002); Jerry M. Rosenberg, *Encyclopedia of the North American Free Trade Agreement* (1984) (E). See also "Canada" and "Economic Relations and Business."

North Atlantic Treaty Organization (NATO): Ronald A. Asmus, *Opening NATO's Door* (2002); Timothy Ireland, *Creating the Entangling Alliance* (1981); Robert S. Jordan, Jr., ed., *Generals in International Politics* (1987); Lawrence S. Kaplan, *The Long Entanglement: NATO's First Fifty Years* (1999) and *NATO & the United States* (1994); Augustus R. Norton et al., *NATO* (1985) (B); S. V. Papacosma et al., *NATO After Fifty Years* (2001); Joseph Smith, ed., *The Origins of NATO* (1990). See also "Cold War," "Europe," and "Nuclear Arms."

Nuclear Arms: Timothy Botti, *Ace in the Hole* (1996); Paul Boyer, *By the Bomb's Early Light* (1985); McGeorge Bundy, *Danger and Survival* (1990); Campbell Craig, *Destroying the Village: Eisenhower and Nuclear Arms* (1998); Robert A. Divine, *The Sputnik Challenge* (1993); Lawrence Freedman, *The Evolution of Nuclear Strategy* (1989); Gregg Herken, *Counsels of War* (1985); David Holloway, *The Soviet Union and the Arms Race* (1984); Robert S. Morris, *Racing for the Bomb* (2002); John Newhouse, *War and Peace in the Nuclear Age* (1989); Septimus Paul, *Nuclear Rivals* (2000); William G. M. Pearson, *The Nuclear Arms Race* (1989) (E); Ronald E. Powaski, *March to Armageddon* (1987) and *Return to Armageddon* (2000); Scott D. Sagan, *The Limits of Safety* (1993); Stephen I. Schwartz, ed., *Atomic Audit* (1998); S. S. Schweber,

In the Shadow of the Bomb (2000); Richard Smoke, *National Security and the Nuclear Dilemma* (1987); Spencer R. Weart, *Nuclear Fear* (1988); Allan M. Winkler, *Life Under a Cloud* (1993). See also "Cold War," "Disarmament and Arms Control," and "Space and Satellites."

Oil: M. A. Adelman, *The Genie out of the Bottle* (1995); Jeremy Leggett, *Carbon War* (2002); Gerald D. Nash, *United States Oil Policy, 1890–1964* (1968); David S. Painter, *Oil and the American Century* (1986); Stephen J. Randall, *United States Foreign Oil Policy, 1919–1984* (1985); Anthony Sampson, *The Seven Sisters* (1991); Fiona Venn, *Oil Diplomacy in the Twentieth Century* (1986); Daniel Yergin, *The Prize* (1991). See also "Mexico," "Middle East," "Minerals," "Organization of Petroleum Exporting Countries (OPEC)," "Venezuela," and Anderson and Miller in "Saudi Arabia."

Olympics: Allen Guttmann, *The Games Must Go On* (1984) and *The Olympics* (1992); Christopher R. Hill, *Olympic Politics* (1996); David Wallechinsky, *The Complete Book of the Summer Olympics* (1996) (E) and *The Complete Book of the Winter Olympics* (1993) (E). See also "Sports."

Organization of American States (OAS): David Sheinin, *The Organization of American States* (1996) (B). See also "Latin America" and "Pan-Americanism."

Organization of Petroleum Exporting Countries (OPEC): M. E. Ahrari, *OPEC* (1986); Albert L. Danielson, *The Evolution of OPEC* (1982); Ian Skeet, *OPEC* (1988). See also "Oil" and Rabe in "Venezuela."

Pan Americanism: J. Floyd Mecham, *The United States and Inter-American Security, 1889–1960* (1961); David Sheinin, ed., *Beyond the Ideal* (2000). See also "Latin America."

Peace Corps: Fritz Fischer, *Making Them Like Us* (1998); Elizabeth Cobbs Hoffman, *All You Need Is Love* (1998); T. Zane Reeves, *The Politics of the Peace Corps & Vista* (1988); Gerald T. Rice, *Bold Experiment* (1985); Robert Ridinger, *The Peace Corps* (1989) (B): D. David Searles, *The Peace Corps Experience* (1997). See also "Cultural Relations."

Peacekeeping: Jane Boulden, *Peace Enforcement* (2002); Paul F. Diehl, *International Peacekeeping* (1993); William J. Durch, ed., *The Evolution of UN Peacekeeping* (1993); Frederick H. Fleitz, Jr., *Peacekeeping Fiascoes of the 1990s* (2002); Alan James, *Peacekeeping in International Politics* (1990); See also "United Nations."

Peace Movements: Harriet Hyman Alonso, *Peace as a Woman's Issue* (1993); Charles Chatfield, *The American Peace Movement* (1992); Charles DeBenedetti, ed., *Peace Heroes in Twentieth Century America*

(1986) and *The Peace Reform in American History* (1980); Matthew Evangelista, *Unarmed Forces* (1999); Michael S. Foley, *Confronting the War Machine* (2003); Catherine Foster, *Women for All Seasons* (1989); Charles F. Howlett, *The American Peace Movement* (1990) (B); Rhodri Jeffreys-Jones, *Peace Now!* (1999); Harold Josephson et al., eds., *Biographical Dictionary of Modern Peace Leaders* (1985) (BA); Robert Kleidman, *Organizing for Peace: Neutrality, the Test Ban, and the Freeze* (1993); Elvin Laszlo and Jong Youl Yoo, eds., *World Encyclopedia of Peace* (1986) (E); Robert S. Meyer, *Peace Organizations Past and Present* (1988) (E); David S. Patterson, *Toward a Warless World* (1976); Nancy L. Roberts, *American Peace Writers, Editors, and Periodicals* (1991) (BA); Lawrence S. Wittner, *Rebels Against War* (1984) and *The Struggle Against the Bomb* (1993–2003); Valarie H. Ziegler, *The Advocates of Peace in Antebellum America* (1992). See also specific wars.

Pearl Harbor, 1941: Stanley L. Falk, "Pearl Harbor," *Naval History* (1988) (B); Richard F. Hill, *Hitler Attacks Pearl Harbor* (2002); Robert W. Love, Jr., ed., *Pearl Harbor Reexamined* (1990); Martin V. Melosi, *The Shadow of Pearl Harbor* (1977); Frank P. Mintz, *Revisionism and the Origins of Pearl Harbor* (1985); James W. Morley, ed., *The First Confrontation* (1995); Gordon W. Prange, *Pearl Harbor* (1986); Myron J. Smith, Jr., *Pearl Harbor* (1991) (B). Also see "World War II."

Philanthropy and Foundations: Robert Arnove, *Philanthropy and Cultural Imperialism* (1980); Edward H. Berman, *The Influence of the Carnegie, Ford, and Rockefeller Foundations on American Foreign Policy* (1983); Marcos Cueto, ed., *Missionaries of Science: The Rockefeller Foundation and Latin America* (1994); Merle Curti, *American Philanthropy Abroad* (1963); Robert L. Daniel, *American Philanthropy in the Near East, 1820–1960* (1970); Raymond Fosdick, *The Story of the Rockefeller Foundation* (1989). See also "Cultural Relations" and Cobbs in "Brazil."

Population: *The Encyclopedia of Global Population and Demographics* (1998) (E); William Peterson and Renee Peterson, *Dictionary of Demography* (1986) (E).

President (General): James Barber, *The Presidential Character* (1992); Meena Bose, *Shaping and Signaling Presidential Policy* (1998); E. S. Corwin, *The President* (1957); Alexander DeConde, *Presidential Machismo* (2000); Robert A. Divine, *Foreign Policy and U.S. Presidential Elections, 1940–1960* (1974); Robert U. Goehlert and Fenton S. Martin, *The Presidency* (1985) (B); Louis Gould, *The Modern American Presidency* (2003); Mark Grossman, *Encyclopedia of the United States Cabinet* (E) (2000); Gary Hess, *Presidential Decisions for War* (2001); George T. Kurian, *A Historical Guide to the U.S. Government* (1997) (E); Leonard W. Levy and Louis Fisher, eds., *Encyclopedia of the American Presidency* (1993) (E); Theodore Lowi, *The Personal President* (1985); John E. Mueller, *War, Presidents, and Public Opinion* (1973); Richard E. Neustadt,

Presidential Power and the Modern Presidents (1990); Arthur M. Schlesinger, Jr., *The Imperial Presidency* (1973); Robert Sobel, ed., *Biographical Directory of the United States Executive Branch, 1774–1977* (1977) (BA). See also "Bureaucracy," "Congress (House and Senate)," "Constitution and Constitutional Interpretation," "Health and Medical History of Leaders," and "War Powers."

Privateering: Donald B. Chidsey, *The American Privateers* (1962); Reuben E. Stivers, *Privateers and Volunteers* (1975); Carl E. Swanson, *Predators and Prizes* (1991). See also "Navy and Sea Power."

Propaganda and Public Diplomacy: Leo Bogart, *Premises for Propaganda* (1976) (USIA); Nicholas Cull, *Selling War* (1995); Robert Cole, *The Encyclopedia of Propaganda* (1997) (E); Robert E. Elder, *The Information Machine* (1968); Walter Hixson, *Parting the Curtain* (1997); David F. Krugler, *The Voice of America and the Domestic Propaganda Battles, 1945–1953* (2000); Alexandre Lauien, *The Voice of America* (1988); Clayton D. Laurie, *The Propaganda Warriors* (1996); Gifford Malone, *Political Advocacy and Cultural Communication* (1988); Jarol B. Manheim, *Strategic Public Diplomacy and American Foreign Policy* (1994); Sig Mickelson, *America's Other Voice* (1983); Michael Nelson, *War of the Black Heavens: The Battles of Western Broadcasting in the Cold War* (1997); Holly C. Shulman, *The Voice of America* (1990); Thomas C. Sorensen, *The Word War* (1968); Allen M. Winkler, *The Politics of Propaganda* (1978). See also "Communications," "Cultural Relations," and "Fulbright Program."

Public Opinion: Eric Alterman, *Who Speaks for America* (1998); Richard J. Barnet, *The Rockets' Red Glare* (1990); Bernard C. Cohen, *The Public's Impact on Foreign Policy* (1973); H. Schuyler Foster, *Activism Replaces Isolationism: U.S. Public Attitudes, 1940–1975* (1983); George Gallup, *The Gallup Poll: Public Opinion* (1972– (AS and S); Ole R. Holsti, *Public Opinion and American Foreign Policy* (1996); Ralph B. Levering, *The Public and American Foreign Policy* (1978); David D. Newsom, *The Public Dimension of Foreign Policy* (1996); Melvin Small, *Democracy and Diplomacy* (1996). Robert Sobel, *The Impact of Public Opinion on U.S Foreign Policy Since Vietnam* (2001). See also "Journalism and Media" and "President (General)."

Race and Racism: Kate A. Baldwin, *Beyond the Color Line and Iron Curtain* (2002); Michael L. Krenn, ed., *Race and U.S. Foreign Policy* (1998); Yukiko Koshiro, *Transpacific Racisms* (1999); Paul Gordon Lauren, *Power and Prejudice* (1988); Hazel M. McFerson, *The Racial Dimension of American Overseas Colonial Policy* (1997); Brenda Gayle Plummer, ed., *Window on Freedom* (2003); George E. Shepherd, ed., *Racial Influence on American Foreign Policy* (1971); Jay A. Sigler, ed., *International Handbook on Race and Race Relations* (1987) (E). See also "African Americans," "Ethnic Groups and Immigration," "Ideology," and "Manifest Destiny."

Recognition Policy: Thomas M. Franck, *The Power of Legitimacy Among Nations* (1990); L. Thomas Galloway, *Recognizing Foreign Governments* (1978).

Red Cross: Nicholas O. Berry, *War and the Red Cross* (1997); Pierre Bossier, *From Solferino to Tsushima* (1985); John F. Hutchinson, *Champions of Charity* (1996). See also "Humanitarian Relief and Intervention."

Refugees: Anna Bramwell, ed., *Refugees in the Age of Total War* (1988); Gil Loescher, *Beyond Charity* (1993); Gil Loescher and John A. Scalan, *Calculated Kindness* (1986); J. Bruce Nichols, *The Uneasy Alliance: Religion, Refugee Work, and U.S. Foreign Policy* (1988); Michael S. Teitelbaum and Myron Weiner, eds., *Threatened Peoples, Threatened Borders* (1995); U.S. Committee on Refugees, *World Refugee Survey* (1980– (AS). See also "Ethnic Groups and Immigration," "Holocaust," and "Humanitarian Relief and Intervention."

Rivers: *Rand McNally Encyclopedia of World Rivers* (1980) (E).

Scientists and Science: Robert Gilpin and Christopher Wright, eds., *Scientists and National Policy-making* (1964); Greta Jones, *Science, Politics and the Cold War* (1988); Clarence Lasby, *Operation Paperclip* (1971); Joseph Rotblat, ed., *Scientists, the Arms Race, and Disarmament* (1982); Alice K. Smith, *A Peril and a Hope: The Scientists' Movement in the United States, 1945–47* (1965). See also "Nuclear Arms."

Sectionalism: Peter Trubowitz, *Defining the National Interest* (1998). See also "The South (U.S.)."

Self-Determination: Antonio Cassese, *Self-Determination of Peoples* (1995); David B. Knight and Maureen Davies, *Self-Determination* (1988) (B).

Slave Trade and Slavery: William Dusinberre, *Slavemaster President* (2003); Don E. Fehrenbacher, *The Slaveholding Republic* (2001); Randall Miller and John Smith, eds., *Dictionary of Afro-American Slavery* (1988) (E); Junius P. Rodriguez, ed., *The Historical Encyclopedia of World Slavery* (1997) (E).

The South (U.S.): Joseph A. Fry, *Dixie Looks Abroad* (2002); Alfred Hero, *The Southerner and World Affairs* (1965); Charles O. Lerche, *The Uncertain South* (1964); Tim Mathewson, *A Proslavery Foreign Policy* (2003); Tennant S. McWilliams, *The New South Faces the World* (1988).

Space and Satellites: William E. Burrows, *Deep Black* (1986); Walter A. McDougall, *The Heavens and the Earth* (1985); Jeffrey T.

Richelson, *America's Secret Eyes in Space* (1990); Paul B. Stares, *The Militarization of Space* (1985). See also "Nuclear Arms."

Spanish-American-Cuban-Filipino War: Benjamin R. Beede, ed., *The War of 1898 and U.S. Interventions, 1899–1934* (1994) (B); James C. Bradford, ed., *Crucible of Empire* (1993); Jerry Keenan, ed., *Encyclopedia of the Spanish-American and Philippine-American War* (E) (2001); Louis A. Peréz, Jr., *The War of 1898* (1998); Anne C. Venzon, *The Spanish-American War* (1990) (B). Also see "Cuba," "Military, U.S. Army, and Wars," and "Spain."

Sports: Allen Guttmann, *Games and Empires* (1994); Walter LaFeber, *Michael Jordan and the New Global Capitalism* (2002). See also "Olympics."

Summit Conferences: Keith Eubank, *The Summit Conference* (1966); Elmer Plischke, *Diplomat in Chief* (1986) and *Summit Diplomacy* (1958); Robert D. Putnam and Nicholas Bayne, *Hanging Together: The Seven-Power Summits* (1984); Gordon R. Weihmiller and Dusko Doder, *U.S.-Soviet Summits* (1986). See also "Cold War."

Tariffs and Protectionism: David A. Lake, *Power, Protection, and Free Trade* (1988); James M. Lutz, *Protectionism* (1988) (B); Robert A. Pastor, *Congress and the Politics of U.S. Foreign Economic Policy, 1929–1976* (1980); Sidney Ratner, *The Tariff in American History* (1972); Frank W. Taussig, *Tariff History of the United States* (1931); Tom E. Terrill, *The Tariff, Politics, and American Foreign Policy, 1874–1901* (1973); Paul Wolman, *Most Favored Nation* (1992); Thomas Zeiler, *American Trade and Power in the 1960s* (1992). See also "Economic Relations and Business" and "Economic Sanctions and Export Controls."

Telecommunications: See "Communications."

Terrorism: Stephen Brill, *After* (2003); Richard J. Chasdi, *Tapestry of Terror* (2002); Anthony H. Cordesman, *Terrorism, Asymmetric Light Warfare, and Weapons of Mass Destruction* (2001); Martha Crenshaw and John Pimlott, eds., *Encyclopedia of World Terrorism* (1996) (E); Richard Crockett, *American Embattled* (2003); Christopher Dobson and Ronald Payne, *The Never Ending War* (1987); Norman Friedman, *Terrorism, Afghanistan, and America's New Way of War* (2003); Rohan Gunaratna, *Inside Al Qaeda* (2002); Dilip Hiro, *War Without End* (2002); Giles Kepel, *Jihad* (2002); Robert Kumamoto, *International Terrorism and American Foreign Relations, 1945–1976* (1999); Walter Laqueur, *The Age of Terrorism* (1987); Edward F. Mickolus et al., *International Terrorism in the 1980s* (1989) (C), *Terrorism, 1988–1991* (1993) (C), and *Transnational Terrorism . . . , 1968–1979* (1980) (C); Suzanne R. Ontiveros, *Global Terrorism* (1986) (B); Ahmed Rashid, *Jihad* (2002; Barry Rubin, ed., *The Politics of Terrorism* (1990); Jeffrey D. Simon, *The Ter-*

rorist Trap (1994); Jessica Stern, *The Ultimate Terrorists* (1999); John R. Thackrah, *Encyclopedia of Terrorism and Political Violence* (1987) (E).

Threat Perception and Calculation: Noel E. Firth and James H. Noren, *Soviet Defense Spending: A History of CIA Estimates, 1950–1990* (1998); Robert H. Johnson, *Improbable Dangers* (1994). See also "Cold War."

Think Tanks: Donald E. Abelson, *American Think-Tanks and Their Role in US Foreign Policy, 1976–88* (1996); Peter Grose, *Continuing the Inquiry* (1996); David M. Ricci, *The Transformation of American Politics* (1993); Robert D. Schulzinger, *The Wise Men of Foreign Affairs: The History of the Council on Foreign Relations* (1984); Christopher Simpson, ed., *Universities and Empire: Money and Politics in the Social Sciences During the Cold War* (1999); Bruce L. R. Smith, *The Rand Corporation* (1966); James A. Smith, *The Idea Brokers* (1991); Michael Wala, *The Council on Foreign Relations and American Foreign Policy in the Early Cold War* (1994).

Tourism and Travel: James Clifford, *Routes* (1997); Foster Rhea Dulles, *Americans Abroad* (1964); Cynthia Enloe, *Bananas, Beaches, and Bases* (1990); Maxine Fieffer, *Tourism in History* (1985); Marie-Franáoise Lanfant et al., *International Tourism* (1995); Sara Mills, *Discourses of Difference* (1991); Margaritte S. Shaffer, *See America First* (2001); David Spurr, *The Rhetoric of Empire* (1993); John Urry, *The Tourist Gaze* (1990).

Trade: See "Economic Relations and Business," "Economic Sanctions and Export Controls," "Tariffs and Protectionism," "United States Trade Representative," and "World Trade Organization (WTO)."

United Nations: Joseph P. Baratta, *Strengthening the United Nations* (1987) (B); Robert A. Divine, *Second Chance* (1967); Seymour M. Finger, *American Ambassadors at the United Nations* (1987); Thomas M. Frank, *Nation Against Nation* (1985); Robert F. Gorman, *Great Debates at the United Nations* (2001); Max Harrelson, *Fires All Around the Horizon* (1989); Robert C. Hilderbrand, *Dumbarton Oaks* (1990); Evan Luard and Derek Herter, *The United Nations* (1993); Kumiko Matsuura et al., *Chronology and Fact Book of the United Nations, 1941–1991* (1992) (C); Edmund Jan Osmanczyk, *The Encyclopedia of the United Nations and International Relations* (1990) (E); Gary B. Ostrower, *The United States and the United Nations* (1998); William Preston, Jr., et al., *Hope and Folly* (1989) (UNESCO); Caroline Pruden, *Conditional Partners* (1998). See also "International Organizations," "League of Nations," and "Peacekeeping."

United States Trade Representative: Steve Dryden, *Trade Warriors* (1995). See also "Economic Relations and Business."

Vietnam War: See "Vietnam and Southeast Asia."

War Crimes and Trials: Omar Bartov et al., eds., *Crimes of War* (2002); Gary Jonathan Bass, *Stay the Hand of Vengeance* (2002); Norman Cigar and Paul Williams, *Indictment at the Hague* (2002); Richard L. Lael, *The Yamashita Precedent: War Crimes and Command Responsibility* (1982); John R. Lewis, *Uncertain Judgment* (1979) (B); Timothy Maga, *Judgment at Tokyo* (2002); Philip R. Piccigallo, *The Japanese on Trial* (1979); Telford Taylor, *Nuremberg and Vietnam* (1970); Norman E. Tutorow, ed., *War Crimes, War Criminals, and War Crimes Trials* (1986) (B). See also "Germany and Berlin," "Holocaust," "Human Rights," and "Japan."

War of 1812: John C. Fredriksen, *Free Trade and Sailors' Rights* (1985) (B); Dwight L. Smith, *The War of 1812* (1985) (B). See also "Military, U.S. Army, and Wars."

War Powers: Louis Fischer, *Presidential War Power* (1995); Christopher N. May, *In the Name of War* (1989); Gary M. Stein and Morton H. Halperin, eds., *The U.S. Constitution and the Power to Go to War* (1994); John H. Sullivan, *The War Powers Resolution* (1982); Francis D. Wormuth and Edwin B. Firmage, *To Chain the Dog of War* (1989). See also "Congress (House and Senate)," "Constitution and Constitutional Interpretation," and "President (General)."

West (U.S.) and Frontier: William A. Beck and Ynez D. Haase, *Historical Atlas of the American West* (1989) (A); William Goetzmann and Glyndwr Williams, *The Atlas of North American Exploration* (1992) (A); J. Norman Heard, *Handbook of the American Frontier* (1987) (E); Adrian Johnson, *America Explored* (1974) (E); Howard R. Lamar, ed., *The New Encyclopedia of the American West* (1998) (E); Patricia Nelson Limerick et al., eds., *Trials* (1991); Clyde A. Milner III et al., eds., *The Oxford History of the American West* (1994) (E); Charles Phillips and Alan Axelrod, eds., *Encyclopedia of the American West* (1996) (E); Dan L. Thrapp, *The Encyclopedia of Frontier Biography* (1988– (BA).

Whaling: Daniel Francis, *A History of World Whaling* (1990); Alexander Sarbuck, *History of the American Whale Fishery* (1989). See also "Environment."

Women and Gender Issues: Homer L. Calkin, *Women in the Department of State* (1978); Edward P. Crapol, ed., *Women and American Foreign Policy* (1992); Robert Dean, *Imperial Brotherhood* (2001); John A. Edens, *Eleanor Roosevelt* (1994) (B); Rebecca Grant and Kathleen Newland, eds., *Gender and International Relations* (1991); Kristin Hoganson, *Fighting for American Manhood* (1998); Maria Hohn, *GIs and Frauleins* (2002); Human Rights Watch, *Global Report on Women's Human Rights* (1995); Susan Jeffords, *The Remasculinization of America* (1989); Rhodri Jeffreys-Jones, *Changing Differences* (1995); Nancy W. McGlen and Meredith Reid Sarkes, *Women in Foreign Policy* (1993); Katherine H. S. Moon, *Sex Among Allies* (1997); Margaret Paton-Walsh, *Our War Too* (2002); Linda Schott, *Reconstructing Women's Thoughts* (1997); Kim Townsend, *Manhood at* Harvard (1996); Mari Yoshihara, *Embracing the East: White Women and American Orientalism* (2003). See also "Peace Movements."

World Bank: Devesh Kapur et al., *The World Bank* (1997).

World Cities: Immanuel Ness, *Encyclopedia of World Cities* (1998).

World Court: Michael Dunne, *The United States and the World Court, 1920–1935* (1988); D. F. Fleming, *The United States and the World Court* (1945); Shabtai Rosenne, *The World Court* (1989) (E). See also "International Law and Hague Conferences."

World's Fairs: John E. Findling, ed., *Historical Dictionary of World's Fairs and Expositions* (1990); Robert H. Haddow, *Pavilions of Plenty* (1997); Robert W. Rydell, *All the World's a Fair* (1987) and *World of Fairs* (1993); Robert W. Rydell and Nancy Gwinn, eds, *Fair Representations* (1994). See also "Cultural Relations" and "Propaganda and Public Diplomacy."

World Health Organization: See "Health Organizations."

World-System Analysis: Thomas J. McCormick, *America's Half-Century* (1995); Immanuel Wallerstein, *Geopolitics and Geoculture* (1991), *The Modern World-System* (1974), *Politics of the World-Economy* (1984), and *World Inequality* (1975). See also "Dependency."

World Trade Organization (WTO): Bernard Hoekman and Michel Kostecki, *The Political Economy of the World Trading System* (1996). Also see "Economic Relations and Business."

World War I: Arthur Banks, *A Military History Atlas of the First World War* (1975) (A); Martin Gilbert, *Atlas of World War I* (1994) (A); Holger H. Herwig and Neil M. Heyman, *Biographical Dictionary of World War I* (1982) (BA); George T. Kurian, *Encyclopedia of the First World War* (1990) (E); Stephen Pope and Elizabeth-Anne Wheal, *The Dictionary of the First World War* (1995) (E); Anne C. Venzon, ed., *The United States and the First World War* (1995) (B). See also "Military, U.S. Army, and Wars."

World War II: Marcel Baudot et al., eds., *The Historical Encyclopedia of World War II* (1980) (E); I. C. B. Dear and M. R. D. Foot, eds., *The Oxford Companion to World War II* (1995) (E); John Keegan, ed., *The Times Atlas of the Second World War* (1989) (A) and *World War II* (2000) (E); Williamson Murray and Allen Millet, *A War to Be Won* (2000); Norman Polmar and Thomas B. Allen, *World War II* (1991) (E); John J. Sbrega, *The War Against Japan* (1989) (B); U.S. Military Academy, *Campaign Atlas to the Second World War* (1980) (A); Peter Young, ed., *Atlas of the Second World War* (1973) (A); Gerhard Weinberg, *A World at Arms* (1995); David T. Zabecki, *World War II in Europe* (1997) (E). See also "Military, U.S. Army, and Wars."

Index

Italic page numbers indicate maps, photos, illustrations, or captions.

Abachi, Sani, 485
Abbas, Mahmoud, 496
ABC powers, 50. *See also* Argentina;
     Brazil; Chile
ABC television, 436
Abraham Lincoln (aircraft carrier), 465
Abraham Lincoln brigade, 126
Abrams, Creighton, *320*
Acheson, Dean, 213, 229, *247, 267,*
     248, 287; on China, 253; Cuban
     missile crisis and, 338, 339; as
     Johnson's advisor, *316,* 320, 347;
     Korean War and, 266, 270, 274;
     McCarthy and, 280
Achille Lauro (cruise ship), 449
Addams, Jane, 20, 83, 120
Ad Hoc Task Force on Vietnam, 320
Afghanistan, 299, 487; Al-Qaeda in,
     462; arms sales to, 499; bombing
     of, 485; Central Intelligence
     Agency in, 428, 429, 433; loans
     to, 246; Soviets in, 385, 421, 428,
     441, 442, 452, 468; Taliban
     regime in, 464, 504; U.S. invasion
     of, 481, 507
Africa, 333; AIDS in, 482–483, 485,
     503; Cold War in, 386; famine in,
     388, *389,* 450, 502; Italian
     colonies in, 125; Kennedy and,
     327; nationalism in, 424–425; in
     1945, map, *296;* Soviets in, 426;
     trade with, 384–385, 424, 426; in
     2000, map, *297. See also specific*
     countries and regions
African Americans. *See* Black Americans
African Crisis Response Initiative, 484
African National Congress (ANC),
     482, 482

African Union, 485
Africa Trade and Investment Act, 485
Agent Orange, 353, 401
Agnew, Spiro, 380, *385,* 392
Aguinaldo, Emilio, 18, *21,* 21–22
Aidid, Mohamed Farah, 483–484
AIDS. *See* HIV/AIDS
Aircraft, 159, 282; A-20 ("Boston")
     bomber, 133; B-1 bomber, 375;
     B-29 bomber, 222, *223,* 238,
     269; B-52 bomber, 274, 318, 319,
     339, 374, 392, 394, 395; Berlin
     airlift and, 238, *239;* C-130 Her-
     cules transport, 412; Cuban MiGs,
     491; F-4 Phantom jets, 379; F-86
     Sabre jets, *272;* Japanese, 184,
     225; Korean Air Lines 007,
     438–439; long-range bombers,
     374; MiG-15 fighter jets, *272,*
     340, 383; sales of, to World War II
     belligerents, 107–108, 109, 110,
     132; Soviet, *272,* 338, 340, 341,
     376, 383, 427; stealth bombers,
     432, 507; strategic bombers, 428,
     436; surveillance over China, 497;
     in 9/11 (2001) terrorist attacks,
     462; terrorists and, 449; U-2 spy
     planes, 284, 287, *290,* 291, 326,
     329, 374, 384
Aircraft carriers, *209,* 349
Air force, 107, 109, 133, 166; Chinese,
     148, 192; German, 108; stealth
     aircraft and, 506–507; Strategic
     Air Command, 274, 287, *291*
Air Force One (film), 462
Akhromeyev, Sergei, *469*
Alaska boundary dispute, 57
Albania, 481

Albiza Campos, Pedro, 162
Albright, Madeleine K., 473, *474,* 491,
     494; Balkan crisis and, 481
Alcohol, U.S. soldiers and, 85
Aldrich, Nelson, 20
Algeria, 287
Allen, George, 304
Allen, Richard V., 434
Allende, Salvador, *383,* 383
Alliance for Progress, 328, 333–334,
     334, 347
Allies, World War I, 74, 75–76, 80,
     86–87; Atlantic Charter and, 175;
     debts of, 101, 116, 119; peace
     and, 88, 90
Allies, World War II, 121, 177, 181; at
     Atlantic Charter Conference,
     173–176; Japanese containment
     and, map, *207;* at Potsdam Con-
     ference, 210–211; strategy of, 187,
     188, 191; at Yalta Conference,
     202–206. *See also* France; Great
     Britain; Soviet Union
Allison, Graham, 398
Al-Qaeda, 462–463, 464, 467, 491, 506
Alsace-Lorraine, 80
Amazon, deforestation of, *503*
Ambrose, Stephen E., *278*
American Asiatic Association, 24, 25
American Century (magazine), 186
American Committee for the Out-
     lawry of War, 120
American Federation of Labor, 123,
     196
America First Committee, 178, 181
American Historical Association, 28
Americanization, 116, 143, 248,
     305–306

American Legion, 123
American Locomotive Company, 76
American Medical Association, 436
American Peace Commission, 88
American Relief Administration, 123
American Tragedy, An (Dreiser), 124
American Union Against Militarism, 83
AM/LASH (CIA program), 341
Amnesty International, 430
Anaconda Copper, 115, 383
Andropov, Yuri, 439
Anglo-Iranian Oil Company, 409
Anglo-Japanese alliance (1902), 52, 57
Anglophobia, 74. *See also* Great Britain
Angola, 384, 451; Central Intelligence Agency in, 385, 433, 450; Cuban/Soviet influence in, 385, 425, 426, 442, 450, 482; Portugal and, 384, 385
Anti-ballistic missile (ABM) system, 374, 375, 376
Anti-ballistic missile (ABM) treaty, 477
Anti-Comintern Pact, 127
Anticommunism. *See* McCarthyism; Red Scare
Anti-imperialism, 4, 9–10, 11, 19–20, 43, 146; women's organizations and, 39–40
Anti-Imperialist League, 19
Anti-Semitism, 195, 241–242, 448. *See also* Jews
Antiwar movement: Gulf War and, 492; during interwar years, 120–122, 129, 130; invasion of Iraq and, 464–465; Vietnam War and, 353–355, *355. See also* Pacifist organizations
ANZUS Pact, 274
Apartheid, 254, 384, 386, 451, 453; end of, 482
Apocalypse Now (film), 399
Appeasement policy, 108, 126, 130, 131
Apple Computer, 499
Aquino, Benigno S., 452
Aquino, Corazon, 452
Arabian-American Oil Company (Aramco), 209
Arabic (ship), 78, 80

Arabs: conflicts with Israel, 300, 372, *378,* 379, 380, 421, 422; founding of Israel and, 241–242; Nasserite, 302; nationalism and, 299, 377, 447; peace talks with Israel, 494; purchase of U.S. properties by, 387; stereotypes of, 299. *See also* Middle East; *specific countries*
Arafat, Yasir, 379, 448, 494; Iranian hostages and, 411; PLO-Israeli agreement and, 495, *495*
Arango, José Augustín, 34
Arbenz Guzmán, Jacobo, 303, 304
Arellano Felix, Benjamin, 488
Argentina, 50, 151, 208, 500; debt of, 44; drug trade in, 488; financial crisis in, 486; Germany and, 166; human rights in, 421, 430, 431; military aid to, 254; Pan Americanism and, 165, 166; terrorism in, 371; United Nations' membership of, 200; U.S. hegemony and, 167
Arias Sánchez, Oscar, 446
Aristide, Jean-Bertrand, 489, 490
Aristocracy, 40
Armour company, 101
Arms embargoes, 50, 132, 176; of Bosnia, 481; of Iraq, 476; of Italy, 126; of South Africa, 384; of Spain, 131; of World War II belligerents, 110, 130, 133
Arms limitation: Eisenhower and, 278–279; Geneva Summit (1955), 283–284; interwar conferences for, 120–122; Rapacki plan for, 288, 307; Washington Naval Conference, 122, 140, 143, 144–145. *See also* Strategic Arms Limitation Talks
Arms manufacturers, 129. *See also* Military–industrial complex
Arms race, 278, 307; post-World War I, 120. *See also* Cold War; Military buildup; Missiles; Nuclear weapons
Arms sales, 499–500; to belligerents, World War II, 107–108, 109, 110, 132–133, 176, 177; Carter era, 421, 430–431; to East Africa, 386; to Egypt, 377; to Iran, 372, 382,

409–410, 413, 446; to Israel, 302, 379, 382; to Latin America, 208; to Pakistan, 374, 429; to Saudi Arabia, 372, 447; to South Africa, 451; Soviet deals, 149, 377, 421; to Taiwan, 497; to Third World, 499–500. *See also* Military aid
Armstrong, Anne, 371
Army, 60, 133; blacks in, 17, 85; Chinese, 268–270; Cuba and, 44; doughboys, World War I, 85–87; in Formosa, 250; Green Berets, 329, 332, *342,* 412; intervention in Russia, 97–98; in Korea, 268, 269–270; Mexican revolution and, 51; North Korean, 273; Rangers, 412, 484, 507; Rough Riders, 16, 17; Special Operations Command, 507; women in, 84; before World War I, 82; World War I expansion of, 83–84. *See also* Red (Soviet) Army
Army Appropriation Bill (1901), 43
Army of the Republic of Vietnam (ARVN), 348, *351,* 392, 396, 401
Arnold, Henry, 107, 108, 110
Asia: Co-Prosperity Sphere in, 147, 182; financial crisis in, 475, 499; great powers in, map, *26;* Japanese power in, 145; nationalism in, 166, 212; U.S. interests in, 55, 117, 249; U.S. military in, 368; after World War II, 209, map, *251;* World War II deaths in, 211. *See also* Indochina; Southeast Asia; *specific countries*
Asia Pacific Economic Cooperation Forum, 475
Assassinations: of Benigno Aquino, 452; Central Intelligence Agency and, 337, 398; of Kennedy, 346; of Rabin, 495; of Sadat, 448
Associated Press, 116
Aswan Dam (Egypt), 299, 301
Atlanta Constitution, 225
Atlantic Charter Conference, *172,* 173–176, 186, 187, 198
Atomic bomb, 228; development of, 213, 237–238, 307; diplomacy and, 226, 234; in Hiroshima and Nagasaki, 211, *221,* 222–225,

223, 226, 227, 400; in Korean War, 271; Manhattan Project and, 222, 224, 225, 226; Soviet development of, 247, 256; testing, 210, 226, 248, 294. *See also* Nuclear weapons

"Atoms for Peace" speech, 279

Attlee, Clement, 270

Auchincloss, Louis, *90*

Auschwitz extermination camp, 198

Australia, 209, 401; in ANZUS pact, 274; in Southeast Asia Treaty Organization, 292, 324

Austria, 90, 128, 195, 196, *232;* aid to, 199; Cold War neutrality of, 282; German annexation of, 128

Austro-Hungarian Empire, 74, 87, 88, 100; collapse of, 89–90, *92*

Authoritarian regimes, 433–434, 451

Aviation industry, 108, 109. *See also* Aircraft

Axis, World War II, 175, 176, 181, 183, 187; demilitarization of, 200; Latin America and, 166, 167, 208; Rome-Berlin, 127. *See also* Germany; Italy; Japan

Ba'ath party (Iraq), 493

Baez, Joan, 354

Baghdad Pact, 282, 298, 300, 307

Bailey, Josiah, 181

Baker, James A., III, *469,* 471, 473, 476; Arab-Israeli conflict and, 494, 495; Balkan crisis and, 480; Gulf War and, 493

Baker, Josephine, *298*

Baker, Mark, 399

Baker, Newton, 85

Baker, Ray Stannard, 96

Balance of power, 27, 28, 39, 58, 228, 371

Balch, Emily Green, 120

Baldwin, Stanley, 115

Balfour, Sir Arthur, 44

Balkans, 180, 206, 480. *See also specific countries*

Ball, George W., 339, 350, 351, 448; Iran and, 410

Baltic states, 189, 469, 471. *See also specific state or country*

Bandung Conference (1955), 293, 299

Bangladesh, 373–374, 502

Banking, 157, 159, 372, 410, 479, 482; in China, 54; development and, 276, 305, 446; in Haiti, 46; World War I loans and, 101. *See also* Export-Import Bank; Inter-American Bank; World Bank

Bao Dai, emperor of Vietnam, 323, 324

Barak, Ehud, 495, 496

Barnet, Richard J., 398

Baruch, Bernard, 237

Baruch Plan, 237, 238

Baseball, *373,* 384, 499

Batista, Fulgencio, *161,* 161–162, 302–303; overthrow of, 305, 335

Battle Cry of Peace (film), 83

Bayh, Birch, 431

Bay of Pigs invasion (1961), 336–337, *337,* 343

Beard, Charles, 129

Beaulac, Willard L., *334*

Beaupré, Arthur N., 37

Beckwith, Charlie, 412

Begin, Menachem, 421–422, 447–448

Beirut (Lebanon) bombing of, 448

Belarus, 501

Belgium, 126, 144, 203; Congo and, 334, 335; Ruhr Valley seizure by, 119–120; in World War I, 74, 75, 80

Bell, J. Franklin, 22

Bemis, Samuel Flagg, 79–80

Benelux nations, 246. *See also* Belgium; Luxembourg; Netherlands

Benes, Eduard, 233

Ben-Gurion, David, *242*

Bennett, W. Tapley, 348

Berger, Samuel R., 474, 508–509

Berle, Adolf A., 166, 205

Berlin, 331–332, 377; airlift to, 238–239, *239;* crisis in, 288–290; East, 282, 288; West, 289–290, 330, 332, 467

Berlin Wall, *331,* dismantling of, 467, 469

Bernstorff, Johann von, 72, 78

Berra, Yogi, 471

Bethlehem Steel (company), 76, 386

Bethmann-Hollweg, Theobold von, 71–72, 75

Beveridge, Albert, 4, 20, 28

Bevin, Ernest, 244

Bidault, Georges, 244

Big Parade, The (film), 100

Bikini atomic test, 248, 294

Bin Laden, Osama, 462–463, *464,* 504; in Sudan, 484–485

Biological weapons, 493, 494, 500

Bipartisanship, 255–256

Bismarck (battleship), 177

Bix, Herbert, *226*

Black Africans, apartheid and, 254, 384, 386, 451, 453, 482

Black Americans, 335, *353;* in government, 384, 416, 489; invasion of Ethiopia and, 131; in military, 17, 85, 253; racism against, 85, 253, 255, 297–298; school segregation and, 297–298

Black Chamber code-breakers, 144

Black Hand, 74

Black Power, *353*

Black Sunday (film), 462

Black Tom munitions factories, 81

Blaine, James G., 121, 165

Blight, David W., *17,* 17

Bliss, Tasker, 88

Boaz, Franz, 159

Bodies of Memory (Igarashi), *249*

Boer War (1899–1902), 28

Bohlen, Charles E., 115

Bok, Edward, 120

Bolivia, 101, 208; aid to, 421; drug trade in, 487

Bolshevism, 90, 96–99, 101, 119, 122, 123; Asia and, 145, 146; Coolidge and, 112, 157. *See also* Soviet Union (USSR)

Bolton, Herbert E., 163

Bombers. *See* Aircraft

Bombing: of Afghanistan, 485; of Beirut, 448; of Cambodia, 392–393; of China, by Nationalists, 292; of Dresden, 211–212, 225; of France, *212;* of Guatemala City, 304; of Hiroshima and Nagasaki, 211, 222–225, *226,* 227; of Iraq, 493, 494; of Lebanon, by Israel, 447–448; of Libya, 449–450;

of North Vietnam, 394, 395, 399; Palestinian terrorists, 495, 496; of Serbia, by NATO, 481; of Shanghai, 148, *149;* of Southeast Asia, 371, 400; of Sudan, 484–485; of Tokyo, 212, 225; of Vietnam, 318–319, 320, 321, 323, 350, 351, 374

Bono (rock star), 503

Borah, William E., 113, 121, *139,* 144, 147; anti-war sentiment of, 93–94, 121, 129, *354;* Latin America and, 152; Manchurian Crisis and, 142

Borgman, Jim, *492*

Borno, Louis, 160

Born on the Fourth of July (Kovic), 399

Borodin, Michael, 146, 147

Borstelmann, Thomas, 335

Bosch, Juan, 347

Bosnia, 61, 74, 479

Bosnia-Herzegovina, 480–481

Botha, P. W., 482

Botswana, 482, 485

Boxer Rebellion (China), 27, 51, 54

Boy Scouts of America, 61

Bradley, Omar, 270

Brady, Nicholas F., 486

Brandegee, Frank, 91

Brandt, Willy, *331, 376*

Brazil, 50, 154, 208, 500; debt of, 486; drug trade in, 488; financial crisis in, 486; Germany and, 166; human rights in, 431; loans to, 475; military coup in, 347; political upheaval in, 167

Brest-Litovsk, Treaty of (1918), 86, 96

Bretton Woods Agreement Act (1945), 199, 386, 387

Brezhnev, Leonid, 371, 374, 384, 386; death of, 439; Strategic Arms Limitation Talks and, 375

Brezhnev Doctrine, 469

Briand, Aristide, 121

Bricker, John, 307

Bricker Amerndment, 307

Bridges, Styles, 252

Brinkley, David, 236, 275, 319

Brinkmanship, 280, 293

Britain. *See* Great Britain

British Aggressions in Venezuela, or the Monroe Doctrine on Trial (pamphlet), 5

British Guiana, 5

Brothers to the Rescue, 491

Brown, Lester, 503

Brussels Treaty (1948), 246

Brussels World's Fair (1958), 298

Bryan, C. D. B., 399

Bryan, William Jennings, 41, *49,* 59, 76, 83; as anti-imperialist, 19, 20; China and, 54; Dominican Republic and, 46; *Lusitania* and, 68, 71, 72, *77,* 79; Nicaragua and, 48; as presidential candidate, 13

Bryan-Chamorro Treaty (1916), 48

Brzezinski, Zbigniew, *415,* 415–416, 430, 431; Iran and, 410, 411, 412; Middle East peace and, 421–422; Panama Canal and, 418; Soviet hardline and, 426, 428, 429; Trilateral Conmmission and, 414

Bucareli Agreements (1923), 163

Buchenwald concentration camp, 195, *197*

Buck, Pearl, 145, *252*

Buddhists, Vietnam War and, *345,* 345–346, 401

Buenos Aires Conference (1936), 166

Bulgaria, 87, *92,* 231, 479; fall of communism in, 468; after World War II, 206, 207

Bulletin of the Atomic Scientists, 256

Bullitt, William C., 98, 99, 114, 125

Bunau-Varilla, Philippe, 35, 37

Bundy, McGeorge, 329, 338, 350

Bunker, Ellsworth, 317, 417

Burdick, Eugene, 297

Burma, 191, 212, 228, 299, 487, 504

Burundi, 484

Bush, Barbara, *469*

Bush, George H. W., 370, 467, *469, 490,* 502; China and, 496; on environmental issues, 453; Gorbachev and, 476; Gulf War and, *492,* 492–494; Iran-Contra affair and, 436; Latin America and, 485; New World Order of, *492;* North American Free Trade Agreement and, 486–487; Panama invasion

and, 488, 489; Somalian civil war and, 483; Vietnam and, 498

Bush, George W., 484; AIDS in Africa and, 482–483; cabinet of, 475–476; China and, 497; Cuba and, 491; global warming and, 504; Iraq invasion and occupation, 465–467, 479, 494; Middle East and, 508; North Korea and, *501, 502;* preemptive war doctrine, 464, 467, 507; Putin and, 477; 9/11 terrorist attacks and, 462, *463,* 464; war on terrorism of, 464, 467, 477, 496, 507

Bush Doctrine, 462, 507

Business: corporatism, 111, 153; e-business, 505; expansion of, 130; Japanese purchase of, 498; multinational corporations, 386, 391, 417, 418; Nazi collaboration with, 116, 128, 130; Sino-Soviet détente and, 371; in South Africa, 425, 482; in Vietnam, 498; World War I and, 129, 130

Butler, Smedley D., 159

Byrd Amendment (1971), 384, 425

Byrnes, James F., *227,* 234, 235

Byroade, Henry, 300

C. Turner Joy (destroyer), 349

Cable, John, 107

Cable News Network (CNN), 493, 505

Cagney, James, 256

Cairo Conference (1943), *192,* 192

Calder, Bruce, 46

California, racism in, 53, 55

Calley, William, 353, 393

Cambodia, 324, 399; Central Intelligence Agency in, 433; food aid for, 389; French and, 321; genocide in, 397; Khmer Rouge in, 392, 393, 397; *Mayaguez* incident and, 398; U.S. thrust into, 392–393, 397

Camp David, 290–291, 421–422, *469,* 495

Canada, 41, 108, 246; Alaska boundary and, 57; Cuba and, 447, 491; environmental concerns in, 453; free trade agreements and, 453, 486

Canal Zone. *See* Panama Canal
Can Lao (Vietnam), 326
Cannon, Joe, 2
Caperton, William B., 46, 158
Caputo, Philip, 353, 399
Cárdenas, Lázaro, *164,* 164, 165
Caribbean region, 442; Good Neigh-
    bor Policy in, 157; U.S. interests
    in, 9; U.S. interventions in, *47,*
    152, *154,* 254; U.S. power in, 10,
    60, 75, 143, 151, 334. *See also*
    Latin America; Central America;
    specific countries
Carlucci, Frank C., 435
Carnegie, Andrew, 19, 22, 28, 165
Carnegie Endowment for International
    Peace, 120
Carranza, Venustiano, 48, 49, 50–51
Carson, Rachel, 390
Cartagena (ship), 34
Carter, Jimmy, 444, 501; Africa and,
    424–425; cabinet of, *415,*
    415–416; China and, 417; Cuba
    and, 420–421, *490;* Haiti and,
    489; human rights and, 410, 416,
    417, 430–431; Iranian hostage cri-
    sis and, 409, *410,* 410–414; Latin
    America and, 418–420, 421; Mid-
    dle East and, 421–424; Panama
    and, 417–418, 488; political style
    of, 414; Soviet Union and, 415,
    417, 425–426, 427–429
Carter Doctrine, 417, 429
Casablanca Conference (1943),
    188
Casey, William J., 434, 445, 446
Castillo Armas, Carlos, 303, 304
Castro, Cipriano, 44
Castro, Fidel, 384, 419–420, 446–447,
    485, *490;* Bay of Pigs invasion
    and, 336–337, *337;* Carter and,
    420; Central Intelligence Agency
    plots against, 277, 335, 336, 337,
    341, 398; Cuban revolution and,
    305, 335–336; Mariel exodus
    (1980) and, 421, 447, 490; missile
    crisis (1962) and, 338–340. *See
    also* Cuba
Castro, Raúl, 338
Caterpillar corporation, 498

Catt, Carrie Chapman, 120
Ceausescu, Nicolae, 468
Cedras, Raul, 489
Celler, Emanuel, 196
Central America, 143, 151; civil wars
    in, 485–486; communism in, *443,*
    446; German investment in, 39,
    109; Reagan and, 442–447, 453;
    underdevelopment in, 443;
    United Fruit Company and, 41,
    155; U.S. intervention in, 46–48.
    See also Caribbean, Latin America;
    specific countries
Central Intelligence Agency (CIA),
    191, 367, 389; in Afghanistan,
    428, 429, 433; in Angola, 385,
    433, 450; assassination plots of,
    276–277, 337, 341, 398; and
    Balkan crisis, 480; in Cambodia,
    433; in Central America,
    303–304, 442; in Chile, 383, 434;
    in Congo, 276, 335; creation of,
    213, 246; Cuba and, 277, 335,
    336, 337, 341, 384; in Ethiopia,
    433, 450; expansion of, 308; Free
    Europe Committee and, *284;* in
    Guatemala, 277, 307; in Indone-
    sia, 277; interventions by, 414; in
    Iran, 277, 307; Iran-Contra affair
    and, 435–436; Iranian hostage cri-
    sis and, 409, 411; Kissinger and,
    371; in Laos, 342, 343; in
    Nicaragua, 418, 433, 444–445;
    Noriega and, 488, 489; in Philip-
    pines, 277; Radio Free Europe
    and, 286; under Reagan, 433,
    434; Syria and, 302; U-2 spy plane
    mission, 291; Vietnam and, 307,
    317, 325, 350, 353, 396
Central Powers, in World War I. *See*
    Austro-Hungary; Germany;
    Turkey
Ceylon (Sri Lanka), 212
Chad, famine in, *389*
Chamberlain, Joseph, 28
Chamberlain, Neville, 110, 127, 130;
    appeasement and, 108, 126, 130,
    131, 206
Chamorro, Violeta Barrios de, 446, 485
Chaplin, Charlie, *126*

Chapultepec, Act of (1945), 201, 208,
    210
Charles, Ray, 451
Charter 77, 377
Chase Manhattan Bank, 372, 410
Château-Thierry, battle of, 86, 87
Chechnya, war in, 477
Checkpoint Charlie, 331
Chemical Convention (1993), 500
Chemical weapons, 432, 493, 494,
    500; in Vietnam, 353, 401; World
    War I, 85, *87*
Chemidlin, Paul, 107
Cheney, Richard, 464, 467
Chennault, Claire Lee, 148, 192
Chernenko, Konstantin, 439
Chernobyl nuclear disaster, 440
Chiang Kai-shek. *See* Jiang Jieshi
Chile, 50, 101, 166, 208, 383–384; au-
    thoritarianism in, 434; Central In-
    telligence Agency in, 383, 434;
    copper in, 115, 153, 155, 383;
    economy of, 383; Peru and, 152;
    political upheaval in, 167; U.S.
    trade agreement with, 486
China, 24–26, 191–195; aid to, 151,
    182, 184, 199, 251; cigarette sales
    in, *25;* civil war in, 248, 249–252;
    communists in, 146–147,
    148–149; immigration from, 192;
    Japan and, 25, 124, 131, 132,
    148–151, 182; Liaodong Province,
    24, 53; loans to, 132, 150, 429;
    Manchuria and, 51–52, 140–142,
    152, 183; nationalism in, 101,
    140, 146; Open Door for, 10, 25,
    27, 51–52, 54, 144, 191; Philip-
    pines and, 145; revolution in, 54,
    115; Russia and, 51–52; Shandong
    province, 25, 55, 89, 144, 145;
    trade with, 146; United Nations
    and, 199, 200, 205; U.S. interests
    in, 209; war with Japan, 124, 131,
    132, 202; World War I peace and,
    89; World War II deaths in, 211.
    See also Nationalist China; People's
    Republic of China (PRC)
China Aid Act (1948), 251
China Incident, 148, 149
China Lobby, 252, 308

China White Paper, 252

Chlorofluorocarbons (CFCs), 502, 504

Chomsky, Noam, 353

Christian-Muslim rivalry, in Lebanon, 302

Christopher, Warren M., 473, 474

Church, Frank, *354, 383,* 398, 428, 431

Churchill, Randolph, 61

Churchill, Winston S., 61, *109,* 178, 202, *236, 246,* 283; Atlantic Charter and, *172,* 173–176, *175,* 180; atomic bomb and, 226; British empire and, 206, 322–323; at Cairo Conference, *192,* 192; China and, 191, 192; "Iron curtain" speech of, 236; Lend-Lease and, 173, 178; Middle East and, 209; Pearl Harbor attack and, *185,* 185; percentage agreement with Stalin, 206–207; at Potsdam Conference, 210, 211; on Soviet threat to Greece, 240; United Nations and, 200; World War II strategy and, 186–187, 188, 189; at Yalta Conference, 202, *204,* 204–206

Citibank, 482

City of Memphis (ship), 81

Civil Service Loyalty Review Board, 280

Civil wars: in Africa, 385, 424, 425, 485; in Angola, 450; in China, 147, 148–149, 191, 248, 249, 274; in Congo, 334–335, 484, 485; in East Timor, 398; in Ethiopia, 450; in Greece, 239, 240, 241; in Laos, 342–344; in Lebanon, 302, 381, 447; in Nicaragua, 485; in Nigeria, 424; in El Salvador, *433,* 443–444, 485–486; in Somalia, 483–484; in Spain, 127, 130, 131; in Zimbabwe/Rhodesia, 425. *See also* Korean War; Vietnam War

Clark, William, 434

Clay, Lucius, *234,* 238, 331

Clayton-Bulwer Treaty (1850), 35

Clean Air Act (1990), 503

Clemenceau, Georges, 85, 89, 91, *93*

Cleveland, Grover, *11,* 11, 18, 28;

Cuba and, 12, 13; Venezuelan crisis and, 5–8, *6, 7, 9*

Clifford, Clark, 240, 242, 319, 320

Clinton, William J., 473, *474, 480, 495,* 503; Africa and, 485; and arms proliferation, 501; Balkan crisis and, 480–481; cabinet of, 473–474; China and, 496, 497; Cuba and, *490,* 490–491; on domestic troubles, 506; global warming and, 504; Haiti and, 490; Kosovo and, 481; NATO expansion and, 479; North Korea and, 500, 501; Russia and, 473, 477, 501; Rwanda genocide and, 484; Somalia and, 484, 499; trade agreements and, 474–475, 486, 487; united Germany and, 479; Vietnam and, 498

Closing Circle, The (Commoner), 390

CNN (Cable News Network), 493, 505

Coca-Cola Company, *294,* 386, *431,* 482

Coca-colonization, 245, *294*

Cocaine trade, *487,* 487, 488, 489

Cock-eyed World (film), 157

Cody, Buffalo Bill, 27, 61

Cold War, 231, 323, 452, 467; Africa and, 386; Americanization, 305–306; Berlin crisis and, 238–239; brinkmanship, 280, 293; China and, 249–253; Cuban missile crisis and, 338–342; and détente, 291, 372; Dulles and, 275, 278–281; Eastern Europe and, 231–235; economic troubles and, 441; Eisenhower and, 307–308, 329; emerging culture of, 253–256; end of, 479, 490, 499; in Europe, 243–248; Germany in, 238; globalization of; Gorbachev and, *440;* Iranian crisis and, 236–237; Japan and, 248–249; Kennedy and, 346; Khrushchev and, 282–286, 290–291, 299; Korean War and, 265–274; military-industrial complex and, *427;* nonalignment in, 296, 299, 342; race and, 297–298; Truman Doctrine and, 239–241, 252, 442; U-2 crisis and, 291; Vietnam and, 326, 348. *See also* Arms race; Communism; Containment; Military buildup; Soviet Union

Colleges. *See* Universities and colleges

Colombia, 154, 446; drug trade in, 487, 488; isthmian canal and, 34–38, 60

Colonialism, 187, 299, 306; in Africa, 424; Coca-colonization, 245, *294;* corporate, 153; French, in Indochina, 321, 323. *See also* Imperialism

Columbia Pictures, 498

Coming Home (film), 399

Commager, Henry Steele, 398

Commerce. *See* Trade

Commerce Department, 116

Commission on Foreign Economic Policy, 276

Commission on Strategic Forces, 436

Committee of Americans for the Canal Treaties, 418

Committee on the Present Danger, 431, 434

Committee to Defend America by Aiding the Allies, 178

Commoner, Barry, 390

Commonwealth of Independent States, 471. *See also* Russia; *and specific former Soviet Republics*

Communications, international, 116, 504–506. *See also* Propaganda

Communism, 347; in Central America, *443,* 446; CIA and, 191; in Cuba, 336; Dulles and, 99, 279, 280, 300, 308; in Eastern Europe, 231, 233–234; Eisenhower and, 279–280, 302; end of, in Eastern Europe, 468, 469; end of, in Russia, 471; in Greece, 240; Korean War and, 270, 271; in Laos, 342; in Latin America, 157, 303–305; in Middle East, 302; NSC-68 and, 247–248; in Philippines, 451; in Poland, 208; Reagan and, *443;* Red Fascism and, 231, *233;* Third World and, 296, 297, 299–300, 326; in Vietnam, 321, 323, 324,

325, 348, 395. *See also* Cold War; Containment policy; Mao Zedong; People's Republic of China; Soviet Union; Stalin, Joseph

Comprehensive Nuclear Test Ban Treaty (1999), 473

Computer viruses, 505–506

Concentration camps, 195, *197*

Conference on Security and Cooperation (1975), 377

Conference on the Human Environment (1972), 390

Congo (Zaire), 80, 276, 385, 386, 424, 504; civil war in, 334–335, 484, 485; Democratic Republic of, 484

Congress: 18, 131; bipartisanship in, 255; Black Caucus, 384, 489; Byrd Amendment, 384, 425; China Lobby in, 252, 308; Cold War and, 307–308; Cuba and, 2, 3–4, 5, 13, 15; Formosa Resolution, 292, 293; Gulf War and, 492; immigration reform by, 420; Iran-Contra scandal and, 435; Jewish refugees and, 196; League of Nations and, 91, 93–94, 99; Lend-Lease and, 178–179; Marshall Plan and, 244; Neutrality Acts and, 130, 131–132, 181; Nicaraguan *contras* and, 445, 446; Panama Canal and, 35–37, 58; Puerto Rico and, 60; Republican control of, 473; on Salvadoran death squads, 444; South Korea and, 273; tariff reduction by, 119; Venezuelan crisis and, 7, 8, 9; Vietnam War and, 324, 350, 355, 395, 396; War Debt Commission, 119; war powers of, 370; World War I and, 79, 81; World War II and, 186. *See also* Senate

Congress of Cultural Freedom, 246

Connally, John, 387

Connally, Tom, 267

Conrad, Paul, *318*

Conservatives, 418, 431

Constitutionalists (Mexico), 48, 50, 51

Consumerism, 305

Contadora group, 446

Containment policy, 249, 255, 326, 371; under Carter, 416–417, 425, 429; under Eisenhower-Dulles, 275, 279–280, 288, 302, 306; in Middle East, 382, 417; post-World War II, 243, *245,* 247; Third World and, 296; Vietnam War and, 355, 398. *See also* Cold War

Contras (Nicaragua), 435, 442, 445–446

Conventional Forces in Europe (CFE) negotiations, 476

Coolidge, Calvin, 112, 157, 163, 165

Cooper-Church Amendment (1964), 393

Copper, Chilean, 115, 153, 155, 383

Corporatism, 111, 153

Corporations, multinational, 386, 391, 417, 418. *See also* specific corporations

Costa Rica, 445, 446

Costigliola, Frank, 125

Cotton trade, 124, 301, 429

Coughlin, Charles E., 129, 196

Croatia, 480, 481

Cromwell, William Nelson, 35, 36, 37

Cronkite, Walter, 319

Cruise, Tom, 450

Cruise missiles, 375, 376, 427, 432, 437, *441,* 484–485; Tomahawk, 493, 494, 507

Cuba: Angola and, 385, 420–421, 425, 442, *490;* Bay of Pigs invasion and, 336–337; Brothers to the Rescue and, 491; Carter and, 420–421; Central Intelligence Agency and, 277, 335, 336, 337, 341, 384; embargo of, 336, 337, 384, 491; immigration from, 421, 490–491; independence of, 4, 11–16; Josephine Baker in, *298;* Machado regime in, 161, 165; Mexico and, 420; missile crisis and, 337–342, *339,* Namibia and, 451; nationalism in, 161–162, 305, 307; under Platt Amendment, 40, 42–44, 48, 60, 161; political upheaval in, 167, 307; Reagan and, 444, 446–447; revolution in, 335–337; Soviet aid to,

336, 420, 428, 490; Spanish-American-Cuban-Filipino War and, 2; sugar and, 11, 12, 41, 43–44, 153, 155, 161, 334, *337;* U.S. interests in, 2–5, 335. *See also* Castro, Fidel

Cuban American National Foundation (CANF), 490

Cubela Secades, Rolando, 341

Cultural exchanges: economic expansion and, 115–119; Fulbright Program, 246; jazz tours of Soviet bloc, 285; with Mexico, 163

Cultural relations, 61; Britain and, 54–59, 173; China and, 27, 147, 367–368, 431; Cuba and, 42–44, 161–162, *289,* 384; Europe and, 116, 128–129, 437–438; Latin America and, 154, 159; Japan and, 248–249, *249,* 295, 495; Mexico and, 51, 163; Philippines and, 23–24; Soviet Union and, 98–99, 186, 284–285, 305–306

Cultural stereotypes, 163, 298–299

Culture: American invasion and, 173; Americanization and, 116, 128–129, 143, 248, 305–306, 437–438, 505–506; globalization of, 506; Western Europe, 305. *See also* Films

Culver, John, 431

Cunard Line, 68

Curtin, John, 209

Cyprus, 347, 479

Czech legion, 98

Czechoslovakia, 90, *92,* 195, 235, 244, 377; arms deal with Egypt, 300, 301; division of, 479; East German refugees in, 468; fall of communism in, 468; German annexation of, 108, 127–128, 131–132; Guatemala and, 304; Soviet Union and, 203, 231, 233, 347. *See also* Slovak Republic

Czech Republic, *471,* 479

Dachau concentration camp, 195

Daniels, Josephus, *164,* 164

Darlan, Jean-François, 188

Dartiguenave, Philippe Sudre, 160
Darwinism, 39, 56
Davies, John Paton, 145, 194, 250, 281
Davies, Joseph E., 125, *157*
Davis, Nathaniel, 385
Dawes, Charles G., 120
Dawes Plan (1924), 120
Day, William R., 18
Day After, The (film), 436
Dayton Accords, 481
Death squads, 444
Debs, Eugene, 99
Debt: Argentine, 44; Haitian, 159; Jordanian, 495; Latin American, 486; Philippine, 452, 499; post-World War I, 101, 116, 119; Third World, 386, 452, 454, 503–504. *See also* Loans
Declaration of Panama (1939), 166, 208
Declaration of the United Nations (1942), 175
Deer Hunter, The (film), 399
Defense Department, 246, 279, 287; Korean War and, 274; *Pentagon Papers and,* 393
Deforestation, 502, *503*
De Gaulle, Charles, 307, 344, 346
De Klerk, F. W., 482
De Lesseps, Ferdinand, 35
Delivery vehicles, for nuclear weapons, 376, 427, 477
De Lôme, Enrique Dupuy, 4, 16
Democracy, 249, 417; prosperity and, 229
Democratic Party, 41, 88, 114, 133; Cold War and, 308; Geneva summit and, 283; League of Nations and, 95; prosperity and, 111; Venezuela crisis and, 5–6
Democratic People's Republic of Korea. *See* North Korea
Democratic Republic of Congo, 484
Democratic Republic of Vietnam (DRV), 322, 324. *See also* North Vietnam
Deng Xiaoping, 496
Denmark, 60, 76
Denver (ship), 43
Deployment of weapons, 376

Depression, 6, 9. *See also* Great Depression
Détente: Carter and, 414; with China, 366, 371, *373,* 391; Cold War and, 291; Cuba and, 384; Ford and, 385; Kissinger and, 372–373, 374; McCarthyism and, 307; Middle East and, 380; SALT-I and, 372; with Soviet Union, 282, 285, 371, 374, 376, 391; Vietnam War and, 391, 397, 400
Detzer, Dorothy, 121, 130
Developing nations. *See* Third World; *specific countries and regions*
Dewey, George, 17, 18, 21, 44
Dewey, John, 82
Dewey, Thomas E., 200
Díaz, Adolfo, 47–48
Díaz, Porfirio, 48
Diem, Ngo Dinh, 324–326, *325,* 344, 346
Dienbienphu, battle at, 323–324
Diplomacy, 4, 9, 10; atomic, 234; cultural, *306;* dollar, 40–41, 43, 45, 54, 58, *246;* preventive, 416; Tomahawk, 507
Disarmament conferences, in interwar years, 120–122. *See also* Arms limitation; Washington Naval Conference
Discovery (space shuttle), *503*
Disease: flu epidemic, 85; HIV/AIDS, 405, 482–483, 485, 502, *503;* venereal, 85–86; World Health Organization and, 246, 504; yellow fever, 16, 116, 154
Dispatches (Herr), 399
Displaced persons. *See* Refugees
Dobrynin, Anatoly, 394, 426, 439
Dodd, Christopher, 442–443
Dodd, William E., 127
Dole, Robert, 492
Dollar devaluation, 387–388
Dollar diplomacy, 40–41, 43, 45, 54, 58, *246*
Dominican Republic, 383; human rights in, 421; Jewish refugees to, 197; political upheaval in, 167; U.S. interests in, 45–46, 153,

208; U.S. troops in, 156–157, 347–348
Domino theory, 240, 254, 306, 324, 431; Third World and, 274, 280, 442
Doughboys, in Europe, 85–87. *See also* World War I
Douglas, William O., 324
Douglas Company, 107, 108
Dow Chemical, 353
Dower, John W., 249
Draft, 83–84, 177, 178
Drago, Luis M., 44
Dresden, bombing of, 211–212, 225
Drought, James M., 183
Dr. Strangelove (film), *370*
Drug trade, Latin American, 485, 486, *487,* 487–489
Duarte, José Napoleón, 443–444
Du Bois, W. E. B., 201
Dubrow, Elbridge, 326
Dudziak, Mary, *298*
Duiker, William, *322*
Duke, James B., 25
Dulles, Allen W., 99, 276, 336
Dulles, Foster Rhea, 280
Dulles, John Foster, 253, *279, 281,* 281, 282, *325;* anticommunist stance of, 99, 279, 280, 300, 308; brinkmanship and, 280, China and, 292, 293, 306, 365; Cold War and, 275, 278–283; death of, 296; on Japan, 295; Korean War and, 266; Latin American nationalism and, 303, 304; Middle East and, 301, 302; purge of State Department by, *281;* on racial strife, 298; on Sino-Soviet split, 292
Dumbarton Oaks Conference (1944), 199–200
Du Pont, 123, 130
Dutch East Indies, 101, 182
Duvalier, "Baby Doc," 160, 452
Duvalier, François "Papa Doc," 160

Eagleburger, Lawrence, 473, 483
Earth Day, 390
Earth Summit (Rio, 1992), 503
Earthwatch, 390

East Berlin, 282, 289

Eastern Europe, 210, 505; aid to, 199, 479; anti-Soviet propaganda for, *284;* boundaries of, 187, 189; communism in, 231–235, 275; détente and, 372; dissidents in, 453; European Union and, 479; fall of communism in, 468, 469–471; human rights in, 377; Marshall Plan and, 244; nationalism in, 286–287, 417; Rapacki Plan for, 288; revolution in, 471–475; self-determination in, 300; Soviet troops in, 228, 282, 469; Soviet Union and, 189, 199, 207, 208, 226, 254, 452; trade with, 233, 276; Warsaw Pact of, 247, 286; after World War II, 246. *See also specific countries*

East Germany, 238, 330–331; Berlin crisis and, 289; German reunification and, 478; opening of Berlin Wall and, 467–468, 469; refugees from, 330, 331, 468

East Timor, 398

Economic aid. *See* Foreign aid

Economic Conference (London), 118

Economic cooperation, 113, 177

Economic Cooperation Act (1948), 244, 245

Economic depression, 6, 9. *See also* Great Depression

Economic nationalism, 118, 119, 161, 303

Economic sanctions: against Cuba, 383, 384, 420, 447; against Iraq, 492, 494; against Italy, 126; against Japan, 142, 148, 149, 151, 181, 182, 184; against Nicaragua, 446; against Rhodesia, 384, 425; against Serbia-Montenegro, 480; against South Africa, 384, 424, 425, 451, 482. *See also* Trade embargoes

Economist (magazine), 228

Economists, 153

Economy: Arab oil embargo and, 380; Asian financial crisis (1997–1998), 475; Chilean, 383; China trade and, 366; Chinese trade and, 496;

cultural expansion and, 115–119; European recovery, 210, 305; German, 238; globalization and, 507; global recession (1970s), 386; Japanese, 295, 305, 387, 498–499; Latin American, 153, 334, 486; Mexican, 487; Russian collapse, 477; South African, 482; Soviet, 122–124, *124*, 440, 441, 468; Third World and, 386–387, 388, 433; U.S. loss of competitive edge in, 387; U.S. military spending and, 453; U.S. share of World (1925–1929), *117;* Vietnamese, 498; Vietnam War and, 320; after World War I, 101; after World War II, 212–213, 229, 244

Ecuador, 383

Eden, Anthony, *125,* 176

Edge Act (1919), 101, 116

Edison, Thomas A., 16

Egypt, 302, 377, 379, 429; Anglo-French invasion of, 58, 286, 301; Czech arms deal with, 300, 301; Israel and, 300, 301, 380, 381, 421–422; Soviet Union and, 299, 380; in United Arab Republic, 302

Egyptian-Israeli Peace Treaty (1979), 421–422, *422,* 424

Einstein, Albert, 129, 221, 225

Eisenhower, Dwight D., 99, *197, 278,* 279–280, 295, *299;* Americanization and, 305; Berlin crisis and, 289–291; Castro and, 336, *337, 490,* Central Intelligence Agency and, 276–278; Cold War and, 307–308, 329; Eastern Europe and, 286, 287; Korean War and, 274, 275; Laos and, 342; Latin American nationalism and, 304, 305; military buildup under, 277–279, 281, *289, 427;* personal style of, 275–276; racism and, 298; Suez crisis and, 301–302; Taiwan Strait crisis and, 292, 293; U-2 crisis and, 291; Vietnam and, 323–324, 325, *325, 396;* World War II and, 187, *197,* 212, 276

Eisenhower Doctrine, 280, 302, 306

Eisenstein, Sergei, 124

Electronic business, 505

Eliot, Charles W., 19

Ellsberg, Daniel, 393

El Salvador, 165, 420, 442, 446; civil war in, *433,* 443–444, 485–486

Embargoes. *See* Arms embargoes; Economic sanctions; Naval blockades; Trade embargoes

Emigration, Jewish, from Soviet Union, 372, 426. *See also* Immigration; Refugees

Energy conservation, 430

Englebrecht, Helmuth, 129

Englehardt, Tom, *252*

English language, 505

Enola Gay (bomber), 222, *223*

Entebbe, Uganda, 382, 411

Environmental issues, 57; books about, 390; global concern on, 390–391, 453, 502, 503–504; in post-Cold War era, *493*

Environmental Protection Agency (EPA), 390

Eritrea, 126, 484

Erlich, Paul, 390

Espionage and Sedition Acts, 99

Essen, Germany, *245*

Essence of Decision (Allison), 398

Estonia, 90, *92,* 469, 479

Estrada Palma, Tomás, 43

Ethiopia, 333, 425, 485; Central Intelligence Agency in, *433,* 450; Italian invasion of, *125,* 126, 130, 131; Soviet/Cuban influence in, 420, 425, 426, 450

"Ethnic cleansing," 480, 481. *See also* Genocide

Ethnic conflicts: in Balkans, 480–481; Hutu-Tutsi in Africa, 484

Europe: Americanization of, 116; anti-nuclear protests in, 436–437, 441; Cold War in, 243–248, 306; détente in, 376; line of defense in, 108–109; Soviet Union and, 122; terrorism in, 379; trade with, 229; U.S. tariffs and, 117; World War I, map, *75,* 100–101, 109; World War I debt of, 119; before World

War II, map, *92;* after World War
II, map, *232. See also* Eastern Eu-
rope; North Atlantic Treaty Orga-
nization (NATO); Western
Europe; *specific countries*
European Advisory Commission, 188
European Central Bank, 479
European Common Market, 388
European Community (EC), 479, 480
European Defense Community (EDC),
282
European Monetary Union, 479
European Recovery Program (ERP).
See Marshall Plan
European Union (EU), 479, 481, 491
Evans, Robley D., 61
Everything We Had (Santolini), 399
Exodus (ship), 241
Expansion, 19; in Asia, 249; Cold War
and, 255; commerce and, 14; eco-
nomic, 229; during interwar years,
130; Japanese, during interwar
years, 146, *150;* Soviet, 426, 431;
Vietnam War and, 397. *See also*
Colonialism; Imperialism
Explorer I (satellite), 287
Export-Import Bank, 119, 276
Export-Import Bank loans: to
Afghanistan, 246; to Chile, 383; to
China, 429; to Cuba, 161; to
Czechoslovakia, 235; to Greece,
240; to Haiti, 160; to Latin Amer-
ica, 152, 155, 208; to Mexico,
165; to South Africa, 425; to So-
viet Union, 124
Extraterritoriality, 146, 192
Exxon, 383, 391, 425

Falaba (ship), 78, 79
Fairs. *See* World's fairs.
Famine, in Africa, 388, *389,* 450
Farabundo Martí Front for National
Liberation (FMLN), 444
I.G. Farben Company, 130
Farouk, king of Egypt, 300
Fascism, 130, 231, *233. See also* Nazi
Germany; Italy
FBI (Federal Bureau of Investigation),
165, 392

Federal Republic of Germany. *See* West
Germany
Federal Republic of Yugoslavia. *See*
Yugoslavia
Fellowship of Reconciliation, 120
Ferebee, Thomas, 222
Ferrell, Robert H., *204*
Fields of Fire (Webb), 399
Films, 16, 83, 128, *149,* 166, 198, 450,
485; Americanization and, 116;
about Cuba, 161–162; Cold War
and, 255, 256, 305; about Haiti,
159; in Japan, 248, 294; Japanese
investment in, 498; Mexican
stereotypes in, 163; about
Nicaragua, 157; Soviet-American
relations and, *124,* 124, 305; ter-
rorist actions in, 462; about Viet-
nam War, 397, 399; about World
War II, 186
Finland, *92,* 120, 177, 254; Soviet
Union and, 90, 96, 231
Firestone corporation, 425
First strike, nuclear weapons, 376, 436,
439
Fischer, Fritz, *333*
Fisher, John, 58
Fisheries disputes, 57; dolphin killing
and, 503; tuna war, 383
Five Power Treaty (1922), 144
Flack, Roberta, 451
Flagg, James Montgomery, *154, 186*
Fletcher, Henry P., 60
Flight (film), 157
Flu epidemic (1918), 85
Flying Tigers (China), 148, 192
Food: famine in Africa, 388, *389,* 450,
502; Food for Peace Program, 276;
Indian self-sufficiency in, 453;
population growth and, 502; World
Food Conference (1974), 389
Foraker Act (1900), 60
Forbes, W. Cameron, 160
Ford, Gerald R., 369, 382, *385, 396,*
414, 418; Africa and, 385; Cuba
and, 384, *490;* Strategic Arms
Limitation Talks and, 375, 377
Ford, Henry, 83, 116, 123, 128
Forde, Henry, 421
Ford Motor Company, 391, 425, 482

Fordney-McCumber Act (1922), 117
Foreign Affairs (journal), 156, 243, 371
Foreign aid, 229, 389–390; to Angola,
370; to Bolivia, 421; to Botswana,
485; to Cambodia, 370, 389; Cold
War rivalry in, 307; to Eastern
Europe, 199, 479; to Egypt, 301,
421; to El Salvador, 444; to Haiti,
490; increase in, 276, 387; to India, 332; to Israel, 300, 421, 448;
Japanese, 452, 499; to Latin America, 302, 304, 417; linked to human rights, 416; to Nicaragua,
420, 444; to Philippines, 452; to
Poland, 199, 286; to Russia, 477,
478; to South Korea, 273, 274,
389; to South Vietnam, 370, 389,
392; Soviet, to Egypt, 302; Soviet,
to India, 299; Soviet, to Indonesia, 299; to Taiwan, 292; to Third
World, 299; to Turkey, 370; World
War I, 76; to Yugoslavia, 286. *See
also* Export-Import Bank; Lend-
Lease aid; Loans; Military aid
Foreign Corrupt Practices Act (1977),
391
Foreign investment, 387; in Africa,
385, 386, 424; in Cuba, 491; in
interwar years, 116–117, 118,
147; Japanese, 140, 499; in Latin
America, 153, 154, 302, 382–383,
417, 418, 486; in Mexico, 50,
487; in Nicaragua, 158; in Philip-
pines, 143, 452; in South Africa,
451; in Third World, 295; in Viet-
nam, 498
Foreign policy public, 11
Forests, 502, *503*
Formosa. *See* Taiwan
Forrestal, James V., 235, 240
Fortas, Abe, *347*
Fortuny, José Manuel, 303
Four Policemen, 189, 194
Four Power Treaty (1922), 144
Fourteen Points, 87–88, 92
Fourth World, 386
Fousek, John, *185*
France, 111, 141, 282, 307, 508; air-
craft sales to, 107–108, 109, 110,
132; Algeria and, 287; alliance

with, 292; appeasement policy of, 108, 126, 127; arms sales to, 176, 177; Balkan crisis and, 480; Brussels Treaty and, 246; colonies of, 182; disarmament and, 144; Geneva summit and, 283; Germany and, 156, 238; Great Britain and, 58; Haiti and, 46; Indochina and, 24, 89, 101, 174, 187, 228; invasion of Egypt by, 286; Kellogg-Briand Pact and, 121–122; mandate system and, 89; Marshall Plan and, 245; Morocco and, 58; nuclear forces of, 438; nuclear weapons of, 347; Ruhr valley seizure by, 119–120; Southeast Asia Treaty Organization and, 324; Soviet Union and, 122; Spanish civil war and, 127; United Nations and, 200, 205; Vietnam and, 212, 254, 279, 321, 323–324; World War I and, 73, 74, 75, 76, 80, 100; World War I peace and, 88, 89, 90; after World War II, 205; World War II and, 177, 187, 198

France, Anatole, 80
Francis, David, 96
Franco, Francisco, 127, 131
Frankfurter, Felix, 196, 197
Franz Ferdinand, archduke of Austria-Hungary, 74
Free elections, 233, 289
Free Europe Committee, *284*
Free South Africa Movement, 451
Free Trade Area of the Americas, 475, 486
Friedman, Thomas, *472*
Friendly Fire (Bryan), 399
Frost, Robert, 256
Fulbright, J. William, 246, 253, 255, 328, 336; Vietnam and, *354,* 355
Fulbright Program, 246

Gabon, 424
Gadhafi, Moammar, 382, 449–450
Gaither Report, 287
Galbraith, John Kenneth, 340
Gambia, 187

Gandhi, Mahatma, 101
Garbo, Greta, 125
Gardner, Lloyd C., 206
Garment, Leonard, *379*
Gas warfare, 85, *87,* 432, 493, 494. *See also* Chemical weapons
Gates, Bill, 502, 506
Gaza. *See* West Bank and Gaza
Gbedemah, K. A., 298
Gender: 4, 20, 28, 52–53, 81, 85, *86,* 203, *234,* 249, 289–291, *300,* 382, 414, 436, 466, *501,* 504; cultural bias and, 298–299. *See also* Masculine ethos
Gender stereotypes: cultural bias and, 298–299; masculinity, 153, *242,* 299
General Agreement on Tariffs and Trade (GATT), 388, 475
General Electric, 115, 123, 425, 482, 498
General Motors, 116, 391, 425
Genet, Charles Clinton, 85
Geneva Conference on Indochina (1954), 292, 324, 325, 345, 356
Geneva Disarmament Conference, 122
Geneva summit meeting (1955), 283–285
Genocide: Balkan ethnic cleansing, 480, 481; Cambodian, 397, 430; Nazi Holocaust, 195–198; in Rwanda, 484
Gentscher, Hans-Dietrich, 479
George V, King of England, 69
George Washington (ship), 89, 96
Gerard, James W., 79
German Democratic Republic (GDR). *See* East Germany
Germany, 27, 28, 53, 60, 125–129; air force of, 108; alliance with Italy, 127; Al-Qaeda in, 463; appeasement policy toward, 108, 126; atomic bomb and, 225; Bolsheviks and, 96; bombing of Dresden, 211–212; China and, 24; France and, 156, 238; Great Britain and, 238; Haiti and, 46; Holocaust and, 195, 197–198; invasion of Czechoslovakia by, 127, 131–132; Latin America and, 44–45, 109, 166, 208; *Lusitania* and, 51, 68,

70, 71–72, 77; Mexico and, 50, 51, 81, 82; Morocco and, 58; pact with Japan, 127, 148, 182; Poland and, 110, 127–128, 133, 176, 208; rearmament of, 122, 126; rehabilitation of, 111, 238; reunification of, 283–284, 468, 476, *478,* 478; Rhineland, 89, 111, 126; Russia and, 96; Soviet Union and, 122, 127–128, 228; Spanish civil war and, 127; submarine warfare of, 68–72, 77, 78–80, 81, 82, 174, 179; threat from, 38–39, 108, 118–119, 182; trade with Soviet bloc by, 429; transformations, map, *470;* U.S. businesses and, 116; U.S. invasion of Iraq and, 465; World War I and, 73–76, 86, 87; World War I peace and, 88, 89–90, 91, *92;* World War I reparations and, 119; World War II and, 177, map, *179,* 183, 186, 188; World War II deaths in, 211–212; World War II peace and, 189, 201–202, 205, 210–211, *232. See also* Berlin; East Germany; Nazis; West Germany
Ghana, *327,* 335, 485
Giap, Vo Nguyen, 318, 319, 356
Gilbert, Prentiss B., 122
Gillespie, Dizzy, 285
Gillette corporation, 386
Gilpatrick, Roswell, 329
Glasgow, Ellen, 100
Glasnost (Soviet policy), 440, 469
Global Alliance for Vaccines and Immunizations, 502
Globalization, 475, 498; of Cold War, 305–308; communications and, 116, 504–506; as neoimperialism, 506; U.S. economy as engine of, 507
Global warming, 453, 502, *503,* 504
Godzilla (film), 294
Goedde, Petra, *239*
Gold crisis, 320, 387
Goldman, Emma, 83
Goldwater, Barry, *328,* 348, *369,* 395, 445
Gómez, Máximo, 12

Gompers, Samuel, 19, 99
Gomulka, Wladyslaw, 286
Gondra Treaty (1923), 165
Gone with the Wind (film), 128
Gonzalez, Elian, 491
Goodacre, Glenna, *400*
Good Earth, The (Buck), 145, *252*
Good Neighbor Policy, 152–154, 167,
    303; in Cuba, 161; in Dominican
    Republic, 157; in Mexico, 164,
    208; in Nicaragua, 158; Pan
    Americanism and, 165
Goodwin, Richard, *334*
Goodyear corporation, 101
Gorbachev, Mikhail S., 453, *469,* 471,
    493; coup against, 477; Reagan
    and, 439–442, *440;* 1989 revolu-
    tions and, 469; Soviet arms reduc-
    tions and, 468–469, 476; united
    Germany and, *478*
Gorbachev, Raisa M., *469*
Gore, Thomas P., 79
Graham, Billy, 436
Graham, Martha, *306*
Grayson, Cary, 95
Great Britain, 60, 72, 132, 182, 195;
    alliance with, 292; Al-Qaeda in,
    463; American cultural invasion
    of, 173; appeasement policy of,
    108, 126, 130; arms sales to, 107,
    176, 177; atomic bomb of, 307;
    Baghdad Pact and, 300; Balkan
    crisis and, 480; Boer War and, 28;
    Brussels Treaty and, 246; Canadian
    border disputes and, 57; China
    and, 24–25, 54; Cuba and, 447;
    disarmament and, 121–122, 144;
    empire of, 61, 212, 228, 323;
    France and, 58; Geneva summit
    and, 283; German partition and,
    238; Greece and, 206, 211; India
    and, 101, 130; Indochina and,
    323, 324; invasion of Egypt by,
    286; invasion of Iraq by, 465; Iran-
    ian oil crisis and, 236, 237; Israel
    and, 241; Japan and, 52, 57; Jewish
    refugees and, 197; Korean War
    and, 270; Latin America and, 6,
    38; Lend-Lease to, 173, 174,
    178–179; loan to, 237; mandate

system and, 89; Mexico and, 50;
    Middle East and, 209, 287; naval
    blockade, World War I, 76–79; nu-
    clear forces of, 438; Panama Canal
    and, 35; rapprochement with, 40,
    55–58; Spanish civil war and, 127;
    Suez crisis and, 301, 302; trade of,
    115, 174; U.S. neutrality and,
    75–76; Venezuela crisis and, 5, 44;
    World War I and, 73, 74, 75–76,
    80, 88; World War I deaths, 100,
    211; World War I debts of, 119;
    World War II aftermath, 199, 205,
    212; World War II strategies and,
    187; Zimbabwe/Rhodesia and,
    425
Great Depression, 111, 112, 123, 140,
    155; global effects of, 117–118,
    118, 154, 166
Greater East Asia Co-Prosperity
    Sphere, 147, 182
Great Society, 347, 351
Greece, 199, 282; civil war in, 240,
    241; Great Britain and, 206, 211;
    Turkey and, 239, 347
Green Berets, 329, 332, *342,* 412
Greenhouse gas emissions, 453, 502,
    504
Greenpeace, 390
Greenville (submarine), 499
Greer (destroyer), 174, 180
Grenada, U.S. invasion of, 447
Gresham, Walter Q., 11
Grew, Joseph C., 60, 181, 182, 185
Grey, Sir Edward, 58, 78
Gromyko, Andrei, 293, *434,* 441
Grossman, Robert, *369*
Grosvenor, Edwin A., 28
Group of 77, 388
Groves, Leslie, 222, 225
Grow, Robert W., 237
Gruening, Ernest, 350
Guam, 144
Guangzhou Bay (China), 24
Guantánamo Bay naval base, 43, 339,
    490, 491
Guatemala, 303, 304; Central Intelli-
    gence Agency in, 277, 307; hu-
    man rights in, 421, 431; U.S.
    interests in, 153, 208, 442

Guerin, Fritz W., *17*
Guevara, Che, 338
Guiliani, Rudolph, 462
Gulag Archipelago (Solzhenitsyn), 377
Gulflight (ship), 79
Gulf War (1991), 464, 465, 479,
    492–494
Guomindang (China), 145, 146, 147,
    148, 252; supply routes to, 182;
    U.S. China policy and, 191, 194

Hague, the. *See* World Court
Hague Peace Conference (1907), 59
Haig, Alexander M., Jr., *433,* 434, 444
Haiti, 45, 46, 452; human rights in,
    421; U.S. interests in, 153; U.S.
    occupation of, 156, 158–160,
    160, 489–490, 507
Haitian National Bank, 46
Halberstam, David, *322*
Halifax, Lord, *106,* 197
Hamm, Clifford, *159*
Hanighen, Frank, 129
Harding, Warren G., 95, *112,* 112,
    144, 156
Harriman, E. H., 54
Harriman, W. Averell, 123, *237,* 343,
    346; Carter and, 418; on Soviet
    Union, 208, 210, 230; Truman
    and, 228
Hart, Frederick, *400*
Harvard University, 61
Hatfield, Mark O., 446
Havana Conference (1928), 165
Havel, Václav, 377, *471*
Hawai'i, 53; annexation of, 6, 11, 15,
    18, 27
Hay, John M., 25, 40, 59; Open Door
    notes and, *27,* 27, 51, 54; Panama
    Canal and, 34–37
Hay-Bunau-Varilla Treaty (1903), 35
Hay-Herrán Treaty (1903), 36–37, 700
Hay-Pauncefote Treaty (1900), 35
Hearst, William Randolph, 4, 16, 114
Helms, Jesse, 491
Helms, Richard, 383
Helms-Burton Act, 491
Helsinki conferences (1975), 375, 377
Hemingway, Ernest, *100*

Henry, prince of Prussia, 61
Hepburn Bill (1902), 35
Heroin trade, 487
Herr, Michael, 399
Herrán, Thomás, 36
Hilderbrand, Robert, 200
Hindenburg, Paul von, 87
Hippisley, Alfred, 25
Hirohito, emperor of Japan, *226,* 227, 248, *249*
Hiroshima, bombing of, 211, 222–225, *226,* 227
Hiss, Alger, 202, 266, 270
Hitler, Adolf, 125–126,*126,* 127, 129, 132, 181, 185, 186, 187; Allied unity and, 175, 180, 188; appeasement policy toward, 108, 126, 128 *blitzkrieg* of, 133, 177; German rearmament under, 122; Jews and, 174, 195, 197, 198; Latin America and, 166; Soviet invasion and, 125; Stalin compared to, 231; view of America by, 128–129. *See also* Nazis
HIV/AIDS, 502, 504; in Africa, 482–483, 485, 503
Hmong clans (Laos), 343–344
Hoar, George F., 4, 19, 20
Hobart, Garrett, 3
Ho Chi Minh, *322,* 325, 346, 348, 356, 401; French and, 89, 101, 321–322, 323, 324; Nixon and, 391, 392; Tet offensive and, *318,* 319
Ho Chi Minh Trail, *352,* 356
Hoffman, Paul, 244
Hogan, Michael J., 244
Hoganson, Kristin, *14*
Holbrooke, Richard, 479, *480,* 481
Hollywood movies. *See* Films
Holocaust, 195–198
Homeland security, 507
Honduras, 153, 442, 445
Honecker, Erich, 468
Honeywell corporation, *427,* 482
Hong Kong, 25
Hoover, Herbert, 75, 112–113, *113, 129, 158;* economic nationalism and, 118; Haiti and, 160; Manchurian crisis and, 140, 141,

142, 143; oil reserves and, 155; postwar Germany and, 238; on Soviet Union, 122
Hoover, J. Edgar, *164,* 165
Hopkins, Harry, 176, 187, 205, *210,* 210
Hornbeck, Stanley K., 141, 183
House, Edward M., 70, 74, *78,* 79; World War I peace and, 89, 98
House-Grey Memorandum (1916), 78
Hubbard, John, 34
Huerta, Victoriano, 48–50, 58
Hughes, Charles Evans, *112,* 113, 122, 156, 165; at Washington Conference, 148
Hughes, Langston, 131
Huguang Railroad, 54
Hull, Cordell, *114,* 114, 131, *132,* 180, 183, 184; Atlantic Charter and, 174, 176; embargo of Japan and, 149, 150–151; on Haiti, 158–159; on Jewish refugees, 196, 198; Latin America and, 155, 165, 166; Soviet Union and, 126; tariff reduction and, 119; World War II peace and, 189, 200, 202
Human rights, 78, 384; authoritarianism and, 434; Bricker Amendment on, 307; Carter and, 410, 417, 421, 425, 430–431; in China, 496, 497; in El Salvador, 444; European conference on, 377; U.N. Declaration on, 255; women's rights and, 504
Human Rights Watch, *465*
Humphrey, Hubert, *320, 347,* 356
Hungary, 468, 479; revolution in, 98, 286–287; Soviet Union and, 203, 207, 209, 231, 233, 301; war refugees in, 195, 198; after World War I, 90, *92*
Hunt, Michael H., 56
Hurley, Patrick J., *193,* 193, 195, 250
Hu Shi, 147
Hussein, king of Jordan, 277, 302, 379, 424
Hussein, Saddam, *450,* 464, 465; capture of, 466; invasion of Kuwait by, 491–492, 493
Hussein, Qusay, *466*
Hussein, Uday, *466*

Hutu-Tutsi rivalry (Rwanda), 484
Hydrogen bomb, 256, 294. *See also* Atomic bomb

IBM (International Business Machines), 120, 386, 498
Iceland, 180, 440
Igarashi, Yoshikuni, *249*
Illinois (ship), 81
Immigration: Chinese, 192; Cuban, 446–447, 490–491; Haitian, 489; illegal, from Mexico, 420; Japanese, 53, 148; Jewish, 195–197, 372, 426; quota system, 115, 195. *See also* Refugees
Immigration Act (1924), 148
Immigration Reform and Control Act (1986), 420
Imperialism, 130, 147, 301; reaction to, 4, 9–10, 11, 19–20. *See also* Colonialism; Expansion
Independent internationalism, 110–115, 143
India, 209, 299; aid to, 332; British in, 101, 130, 212, 228; food self-sufficiency in, 453; independence of, 58; nuclear arms of, 347, 388, 430, 497, 500; Pakistan and, 332, 500; Soviet Union and, 374; women's rights in, 504
Indochina, 292; environmental damage in, 390; French in, 24, 89, 101, 174, 187, 228, 277, 322; Japanese in, 174; military aid to, 267, 396; Vietnam War and, 400; after World War II, 248. *See also* Southeast Asia; *specific countries*
Indonesia, 211, 248, 277; Dutch and, 212, 228; East Timor and, 398; human rights in, 431; Soviet aid to, 299
Industry, environment and, 390. *See also* Business; Military-industrial complex; Trade; *specific industries*
Information, global revolution in, 504–506
Inland Fisheries Treaty (1908), 57
In Retrospect (McNamara), *328*
Insular Cases (1901–1904), 60

Intelligence, 183, *184. See also* Central
Intelligence Agency; U-2 spy
planes
Inter-American Defense College, 382
Inter-American Development Bank,
276, 305, 446
Intercontinental ballistic missiles
(ICBMs), 287, *288, 289, 290,*
329; defined, 376; limitations on,
374, 375, 376, 426, 427, 428,
477; vulnerability of, 436
Intergovernmental Committee on
Refugees, 196
Intergovernmental organizations
(IGOs), 390
Intermediate-range ballistic missiles
(IRBMs), 287
Intermediate-range nuclear forces
(INFs), 376, 437–438
Intermediate-Range Nuclear Forces
(INF) Treaty (1987), 440–441,
441
International Atomic Energy Agency,
279, 501
International Bank for Reconstruction
and Development. *See* World
Bank
International Business Machines
(IBM), 120, 386, 498
International communications issues,
504–506
International competition, 20
International Fund for Agricultural
Development, 389
International Harvester, 123
Internationalists, 93, 95, 110–115, 143
International Ladies Garment Union,
123
International Monetary Fund (IMF),
199, 213, 243, 475; Latin America
and, 486; regulation by, 388
International Non-Intervention Com-
mittee, 127
International Telecommunications
Satellite Consortium (INTEL-
SAT), 504
International Telephone and Telegraph
(ITT), 116, 155, 383
Internet, 463
Interwar years (1920–1939), 106–133;

appeasement policy in, 108, 126;
arms sales to belligerents in,
107–108, 109, 110, 132–133;
China in, 115, 124, 131, 132,
145–147; economic and cultural
expansion in, 115–119; Germany
in, 108, 109, 110, 119, 126–129,
131–132; independent internationalism in, 110–115; isolationism and neutrality in, 109,
129–130; Japan in, 108, 115, 122,
123, 131, 132, 147–151; Latin
America in, 151–156; Mexico in,
163–165; Pan Americanism in,
165–166, 177; peace initiatives in,
120–122; U.S.-Soviet relations in,
115, 122–125
Intifada (Palestinian uprising), 448, 494,
496
Investment. *See* Foreign investment
Iran, 211, 302, 377, 464, 487; alliance
with, 382, 410; arms sales to, 372,
382, 409–410, 413, 446; Azerbaijan and, 236, 237; Baghdad Pact
and, 300; censorship in, 505; Central Intelligence Agency in, 277,
307; hostage crisis in, *408,*
409–413, *413;* human rights in,
410, 431; Iran-Contra affair and,
434–435; nuclear arms and, 500;
oil in, 209, 236, 237, 409, 412;
Soviet Union and, 236–237; war
with Iraq, 412, 421, 450
Iran-Contra scandal, 434–436, 446,
453
Iraq, 302, 413; Baghdad Pact and, 300;
Coalition Provisional Authority
in, 467; economic sanctions
against, 492, 494; George W. Bush
and, 464, *465;* Gulf War and,
464, 479, 492–494; invasion of
Kuwait by, 476, 491–492; Kurds
in, 371, 493, 494; nuclear arms
and, 500; oil in, 209; state-sponsored murder in, *465;* U.S. invasion and occupation of, 464–467,
479, 481, 507, 508; war with Iran,
412, 421, 450; weapons of mass
destruction in, 464, 466, 494
Ireland, 195

Irish Americans, 74
Irish Easter Rebellion (1916), 80
Iron and steel production, 10
"Iron curtain" speech (Churchill), 236
Ishii, Kikujiro, 55
Islamic fundamentalism, 428, 467, 505
Isolationism, 109, 128, 129–130, 149,
181, 186. *See also* Neutrality
Isolationists, *139,* 149, 176, 178
Israel, 198, 377, 447–448; aid to, 300,
421, 448; Arab conflicts with, 300,
494; creation of, *242,* 241–243;
Egypt and, 300, 301, 380, 381,
421–422, *422;* nuclear weapons
of, 500; stereotypes of, 299;
Uganda hostages and, 411;
weapons sales to, 302, 379, 382
Italy, 144, *330;* alliance with Germany,
127; invasion of Ethiopia by, 126,
130, 131; Latin America and, 166;
menace from, 108, 118–119; post-
World War II, 208–209; rearmament of, 122; refugees in, 195,
198, 199; Spanish civil war and,
127; World War I and, 74, 88, 89;
World War II and, 182, 187, 188
ITT (International Telephone and Telegraph), 116, 155, 383
Iwo Jima, 248

Jackson, Henry M., *197,* 428
Jackson, Jesse, *437*
Jacobson, Eddie, 242
Jamaica, 58
James, Jack, 266
James, William, 22
Japan, 60, 307; alliance with, 274,
293–295, 499; Allies' containment
of, map, *207;* anti-Americanism
in, 498; Asian expansion of, 52,
147–151, map, *150;* bombing of,
221, 222–225, *226;* China and,
25, 123, 131, 132, 148–151, 182,
191, 193; economic sanctions of,
142, 148, 149, 151, 181, 182,
184; economy of, 295, 305, 387;
foreign investments of, 499; German pact with, 127, 148; Great
Britain and, 52, 57; Indochina

and, 174; interwar years (1920–1939), 147–151; Korea and, 24, 52, 53, 452; Latin America and, 166; Manchuria and, 122, 140–142, *141,* 152, 166, 183; menace from, 108, 118–119; oil needs of, 142, 147, 182, 183, 380; Pacific war and, 203–204; People's Republic of China and, *364,* 367, 373; Soviet Union and, 189; trade with, 148, 387, 388, 452, 454; Tripartite Pact and, 182, 184; U.S. influence in, 368; U.S. occupation of, 248–249, 294; Washington Conference and, 143, 144; World War I and, 74; World War II and, 181–186, 188, 205, *207,* 227; after World War II, 211

Jefferson, Thomas, 20, 434
Jenner, William E., 267
Jerome, Jenny, 61
Jespersen, T. Christopher, *396*
Jewish Welfare Board, 85
Jews: anti-Semitism and, 195, 241, 448; creation of Israel and, *242,* 241–242; Holocaust and, 195–198; masculinity and, *242,* 299; Nazis and, 109, 126, 127, 132, 174; Soviet emigrants, 372, 426. *See also* Israel
Jiang, Madame (Meiling Soong), 147, *192*
Jiang Jieshi (Chiang Kai-shek), 182, 185, 191, 205, 251, *252,* 280; communists and, 146–147, 148–149; Japan and, 140; Korean War and, 271, 273, 274; Stilwell and, 192–193; Taiwan Strait crisis and, 292–293; "two Chinas" policy and, 308; U.S. support for, *192,* 194, 249, 250, 292, 307, 365
Jiang Zemin, 497
Jiaozhou (Kiaochow), 24, 55
Jihad (Muslim holy war), *464,* 494, 505
Jim Crow, 297. *See also* Racism
Jingoism, 3, 9, 11, 74
Jinmen (Quemoy), 292–293
Johnson, Hiram, 94, 97, *129,* 178
Johnson, James Weldon, 158

Johnson, Lyndon, *316,* 329, 341, 417, *490;* Dominican Republic and, 347–348; on Peace Corps, 332–333; personal style of, 346–347, *347;* Tet offensive and, 317, *318,* 319; Vietnam War and, *320,* 321, 344, 348–350, 351, 355–356, *396,* 398
Joint Chiefs of Staff, 293; Cuba and, 337, 339; directive 1067, 202, 210; Iran hostage crisis and, 411; Korean War and, 270; Laos and, 343; Vietnam and, 350
Jones, Thomas K., *437*
Jones Act of 1916, 24
Jones Act of 1917, 162
Jordan, 302, 381, 447; Israel peace accord and, 494
Jordan, David Starr, 19
Jordan, Michael, 505
Judd, Walter, 252

Kabila, Laurent, 484
Kaiser Aluminum, 386
Kamikaze air attacks, 225
Karski, Jan, 197
Katsura, Taro, 53
Katyn (Poland) massacre, 188
Kaunda, Kenneth, 425
Kazakhstan, 501
Kearny (destroyer), 181
Kelley, Jay W., 277
Kellogg, Frank B., 94, 113, 121, 152
Kellogg-Briand Pact (1928), 121–122, 140, 142, 148
Kemmerer, Edward, 153
Kennan, George F., 235, 247, 355, 479; anti-nuclear movement and, 436; containment policy and, *243,* 243, 288, 429; on new millennium, 506; Potsdam accord and, 211; on Soviet threat, 115, 125, 228
Kennedy, John F., 308, *326,* 356; Africa and, *327;* Alliance for Progress and, 328, 333–334; Berlin crisis and, 330–332, 467; Cuba and, 336–337, 338–341, *490;* Laos and, 342–344; military buildup

under, 329, 331; policy style of, 326–328; Third World and, 326, 332–333; Vietnam and, 324, 326, 332, 343–346, *398*
Kennedy, Joseph P., 327
Kennedy, Robert F., 319, 329, 337, 355; Cuban missile crisis and, 338, 340
Kent, Bruce, 120
Kenya, 386, 429
Kerensky, Alexander, 96
Kerry, John, *508*
Khanh, Nguyen, 348
Khe Sanh, battle for, 318–319
Khmer Rouge, 392, 393, 397, 430
Khomeini, Ruhollah, 409, 410, 411, 413, 450
Khrushchev, Nikita S., 99, *282,* 293; Cold War diplomacy of, 282, 287, *289,* 290–291, 299; Cuba and, *337,* 338, 339–341; debate with Nixon, *283,* 285, 305, 326; deStalinization and, 287; Kennedy and, 329–332; U-2 crisis and, *290,* 291
Kimball, Jeffrey, 397
Kim Il Sung, 271–272, 273
Kim Jong Il, *501*
King, Ernest, 187
King, Martin Luther, Jr., 354
King, W. L. Mackenzie, 208
Kirkpatrick, Jeane, 433, 434, 451
Kissinger, Henry A., *369,* 369–371, *370,* 375, 377, *379,* 418; Africa and, 385, 386; Cuba and, 384; détente and, 372–373, 374; on foreign aid, 389–390; Iran and, 410; *Mayaguez* incident and, 398; Middle East and, 382; Nixon's visit to China and, 365–366, *366,* 367, 368; on ocean mining, 391; personal style of, 369–370; Pinochet and, 384; shuttle diplomacy of, 381; Vietnam War and, 392, 393, 394–395, 396
Kitchen debate, *283,* 305, 326
Kitchin, Claude, 81, 83
Knapp, Harry, 156
Knowland, William E., 293
Knox, Frank, 177

Knox, Philander C., *35,* 40, 45, 47, 54

Kohl, Helmut, 468, 478, 479

Kolchak, A. V., 98

Konoe, Fumimaro, 182, 183

Korea, Japan and, 24, 52, 53, 248. *See also* North Korea; South Korea

Korean Air Lines Flight 007, 438–439

Korean War, 248, 265–274, map, *269;* casualties in, 271; China and, *265,* 268, 269–270, 271, 272–273, 274, 292; Japan and, 295; MacArthur and, 266, 267, 268, 269–270; peace talks for, 271, 292; Soviet Union and, 267, 268, 270–273, 282; U.S. entry in, 268–270; Vietnam and, 323

Kosovo conflict, 479, *480,* 481, 494

Kosygin, Alexei, 347, 380

Kovic, Ron, 399

Krenz, Egon, 468

Kristallnacht, 195

Kuhn, Bowie, 384

Kun, Bela, 98

Kung, H. H., 147

Kurds: in Iran, 409; in Iraq, 371, 493, 494

Kuwait, 494; Iraqi invasion of, 476, 491–492, *493*

Kyoto Global Warming Convention (1997), 504

LaFollette, Robert M., 39, 81, 83, *84,* 94

Lake, Anthony, 393, 474, 479, 484

Lambert, Jack, *230*

Land mines treaty, 500

Langley (aircraft carrier), *209*

Lansdale, Edward, 325, 338

Lansing, Robert, 41, 72, 74, 76, 80; Asia and, 55; World War I peace and, 88, 98

Lantaff, Paul, 304

Laos, 324, 342–344, 393, 397, 487; Central Intelligence Agency in, 342, 343; French and, 321; refugees from, 399

Latham, Michael E., 332

Latin America, 114, 116, 197, 307; Alliance for Progress and, 328, 333–334, *334,* 347; alliances with, 201; anticommunism in, 254, 300; Britain and, 6, 38; Carter administration and, 417–421; communists in, 157, 303–305; debt of, 486; drug trade in, 485, 486, *487,* 487–489; economic expansion and, 41, 117; foreign investment in, 153, 154, 302, 382–383, 417, 418, 486; Germany and, 44–45, 109, 166; Good Neighbor Policy, 152–154, 167; Great Britain and, 6, 38; nationalism in, 302–305; Pan Americanism and, 165–166, 177; racism in, 55; trade with, 154, 155–156, 417, 486; U.S. interests in, 38, 58, 96, 101, 111, 147, 382–383; U.S. intervention in, 130, map, *419,* 485, 487; U.S. power in, 143, 348. *See also* Caribbean; Central America; *specific countries*

Latvia, 90, *92,* 469, 479

Law of the Sea Conference (1970), 390–391

Law of the Sea Treaty (1982), 433, 502–503

Lea, Tom, *203*

League of Nations, 92–96, 113, 189; appeasement policy and, 126; Congress and, 91, 93–94, 99; Italy and, 126; Manchurian crisis and, 141, 142; pacifism and, 120, 122; Soviet Union in, 122; Wilson and, 89, 90–91, 93, 112

Leahy, William D., 224

Lebanon, 279, 302, 424, 453; civil war in, 381, 421, 447; hostages in, 434; Palestine Liberation Organization in, 447–448

Lederer, William J., 296

Le Duc Tho, 370, 394, 395

Lee, Fitzhugh, 2, 13, 15

LeMay, Curtis, 351

Lemmon, Jack, 383

Le Monde (newspaper), 245

Lend-Lease aid, 186; to Britain, 173, 178; to China, 193, 250; to Soviet Union, *180,* 180, 188, 190, 209, 210, 236

Lend-Lease Bill, 178–179

Lenin, Vladimir Ilyich, 96, *97,* 98, 122

Less developed countries (LDCs), 386. *See also* Third World

Levinson, Salmon, 121

Lewis, Robert, 222

Lewis, Ross, *288*

Liaodong Province (China), 24, 53

Liberia, 58, 485

Libya, 449–450, 500

Life magazine, 186, 252

Lima Conference (1938), 166, 208

Limited Test Ban Treaty (1963), 341

Lin Bao, 355

Lind, John, 49

Lindbergh, Charles, *152,* 164

LINEBACKER (bombing raids), 394, 395

Lippmann, Walter, 153, 248, 289, 399; on Soviet containment, 243

Lithuania, 80, 90, *92,* 469, 479

Liu Shaoqi, *265*

"Little Boy" (atomic bomb), *223*

Litvinov, Maxim, *124,* 124, *237*

Lloyd George, David, 73, *89,* 99

Loans: to belligerents, World War II, 101, 130; to Brazil, 475; to China, 132, 192, 496; defaulted, 120; to Great Britain, 237; to Mexico, 165, 475, 486; to Russia, 475, 477. *See also* Debt; Export-Import Bank; Foreign aid; World Bank

Locarno Treaty (1925), 121

Lockhart, Bruce, 99

Lockheed Aircraft, 391

Lodge, Henry Cabot, 4, 20, 23, 57; League of Nations and, 91, 93, *94*

Lodge, Henry Cabot, Jr., 346, 348.

London Conference of Foreign Ministers, 233–234

Long, Breckinridge, 197

Long, John D., 2

Long March (China), 149

Lon Nol, 392, 393

Loomis, Francis B., 34

López Portillo, José, 420

Lovett, Robert, 338

Low, David, *132*

Lowenthal, Max, 242

Luce, Henry R., 186, 252

Lucky Dragon (fishing boat), 294
Ludlow, Louis, 129, 130
Lumumba, Patrice, 276, 334–335
Lusitania (ship), 51, 55, *67,* 68–72, *69, 70, 71, 77,* 77, 78, 79
Lyons, Eugene, 125
Lytton Commission, 141, 142

Maastricht Treaty (1993), 479
MacArthur, Douglas, 187, 205, 343; Korean War and, 266, 267, 268, 269–270, *270;* occupation of Japan and, 248, 249, *249*
McCain, John, *508*
McCarthy, Eugene, 319, 320, 355
McCarthy, Joseph, 250, 256, 266, 279–280, *280,* 308; State Department and, 250, 270, 281, *281*
McCarthyism, 256, 267, 274, 281, 287, 307
McCormack, John W., 178
McCoy, Frank R., 23, 60, 158
MacDonald, James G., *242*
McDonald's restaurants, *472,* 499, 506
Macedonia, 481
McFarlane, Robert C., 434, 435
McGovern, George, 366, 431
Machado, Gerardo, 161, 165
Machiya, Michihiko, 223
McKinley, William, 2–5, *3,* 9, 11, *14,* 14–16, 18–21, 24, 28, 35; China and, 27; Cuba and, 42; Philippines and, 20, 21, 27; Spanish-American-Cuban-Filipino War and, 13–16
McKinley Tariff (1890), 14
McLaglen, Victor, 157
McLemore, Jeff, 79
McLeod, Scott, 280
MacMillan, Harold, 302
McNamara, Robert Strange, 347; Cuban missile crisis and, 337, 338, 339, 341; Vietnam War and, 319, *328,* 346, 348, 350, 351, 355
McNaughton, John, *316*
Madame Secretary (Albright), *474*
Maddox (destroyer), 349
Madero, Francisco I., 48
Madman strategy, 368, 391

Maginot Line, 126
Magoon, Charles E., 43
Mahan, Alfred Thayer, 39, 41
Maine (battleship), *1,* 2, 3, 4, *15*
Making Them Like Us (Fischer), *333*
Malta, 479
Manchuria, 149, 249, 252, 253; crisis in, 121, 140–143; Japan and, 54, 140–143, 147, 152, 166, 183; Russia and, 51–52; Soviet Army in, 205, 227, 250
Mandate system, 89, 90
Mandela, Nelson, 482, *482,* 485
Manhattan Project, 222, 224, 225, 226
Mann, Thomas, 305, 347, 348
Mansfield, Mike, 324, *354*
Mao Zedong, *193,* 193, 194, *252,* 254, *293,* 355, 371, *373;* Chinese civil war and, 147, 148–149, 191, 249, 251–252, 274; Korean War and, *265,* 268, 273; Nixon and, 365, 367; Republic of China and, 293; Stalin and, 205, 249–250. *See also* People's Republic of China (PRC)
Marco Polo Bridge incident, 148
Marcos, Ferdinand, 451–452
Mariel boatlift (1980), 421, 447, 490
MARIGOLD (peace initiative), 356
Marines, *154,* 507; in Cuba, 44; in Dominican Republic, 45, 46, 156–157; in Haiti, 46, 47–48, 158–160, *160;* in Lebanon, 448; in Mexico, 50; in Nicaragua, 157, *159;* in Somalia, *483,* 483; in Vietnam, *343*
Marshall, George C., 146, 174, 228, 242; China and, 250; European recovery plan of, 235, 244–245; Korean War and, 268; World War II and, 178, 185, 188
Marshall, James, 95
Marshall Islands, 248
Marshall Plan, 235, 244–245
Mart, Michelle, *242*
Martens, Ludwig, 99
Martí, José, 12, 44
Masaryk, Jan, 233
Masaryk, Thomas, 98, 100
Masculine ethos, 153; Jews and, *242,* 299

Mastny, Vojtech, 233
Matsui, Hideki, 499
Matsuoka, Yosuke, 182, 183
Mayaguez (ship), 398
May Fourth Movement (China), 89
Mayo, Henry T., 50
May 30th Movement (China), 146
Mazu (Matsu), 292–293
MCA (corporation), 498
Mead, Lucia True Ames, 20
Meany, George, 418
Mehta, G. L., 297
Meir, Golda, *379*
Mendès-France, Pierre, 324
Merchant Marine Act (1920), 116
Merchants of Death (Englebrecht & Hanighen), 129
Messersmith, George, 196
Meuse-Argonne offensive, 87
Mexico, 157, 166, 446; Cuba and, 383, 491; drug trade in, 487, 488; financial bailout of, 475; Germany and, 50, 51, 81, 82; Good Neighbor Policy in, 164, 208; immigrants from, 420; loans to, 165, 475, 486; nationalism and, 60, 165; Nicaragua and, 420; North American Free Trade Agreement and, 486–487, 506; oil production in, 48, 50, 163, 164, 420; revolution in, 48–51, 163; Spanish civil war and, 127; trade with, 487; U.S. influence in, 58, 151
Mexico City, 50, 163
Micronesia, 248
Middle East, 209, 306, 377–382, *449;* arms sales to, 421; Bush plan for, 508; Carter Doctrine and, 417, 429; Eisenhower Doctrine and, 302; Great Britain and, 209, 287; mandate system and, 89; map, *378, 449;* nationalism in, 299, 300–302; peace process in, 386, 453; Soviets in, 426; U.S. interests in, 116, 117, 299; U.S. intervention in, 280. *See also* Arabs; Muslims; *specific countries*
Midway Island, 148
Migratory Bird Treaty (1916), 57
Mikolajczyk, Stanislas, 204

Miles, Nelson A., 18
Military: American, in Britain, 173; draft, 83–84, 177–178; Iranian, 410; Japanese, 294; nation building by, 507; Nixon's reduction of, 372; problems in, 401; rearmament, for World War II, 108, 174; Rhineland occupation and, 111; Tomahawk diplomacy of, 507; World War I preparedness, 82–83. *See also* Air force; Arms limitation; Arms race; Army; Defense Department; Joint Chiefs of Staff; Marines; Navy
Military aid, 276; to Angola, 385; to Argentina, 254; Axis powers to Spain, 127; to Chile, 383; to China, 250–251; Chinese, to North Vietnam, 325, 355; to *contras*, 45–446, 435, 442; to El Salvador, 443, 444; to Europe, 247; to Greece, 241; human rights violations and, 431; to Indochina, 267, 396; to Latin America, 304, 421; to Nationalist China (Taiwan), 292; to Nicaragua, 418, 445–446; to North Atlantic Treaty Organization, 255; to Philippines, 267; to South Korea, 273; to South Vietnam, 323, 325, 343, 345; Soviet, to Cuba, 337–341; Soviet, to North Vietnam, 325; to Taiwan, 430. *See also* Arms sales
Military bases, 177, 329; in Central America, 208; in Cuba, 43, 339; in Egypt, 429; in former Soviet bloc, 507; in Haiti, *160*, 160; in Japan, 249, 294, 452; in Kenya, 429; in Morocco, 274; in Oman, 429; at Pearl Harbor, 144, 148; in Philippines, 452; in Saudi Arabia, 274; in Somalia, 425, 429; in Spain, 274; on Taiwan, 430; in Vietnam, 317, 396
Military buildup: under Carter, 429, 430; under Eisenhower, 277–279, 281; under Johnson, 320; under Kennedy, 329, 331; in Korean War, 274; in Nazi Germany, 126; under Reagan, 432, 452, 453,

468; Soviet, 441. *See also* Arms race
Military-industrial complex, 99, 213, 279, *427*
Military preemption, doctrine of, 464, 467, 507
Mills, Stephanie, 451
Millspaugh, Arthur C., 237
Milosevic, Slobodan, 481
Missiles: arms race and, 287–288, *289*, 329; Chinese, 497; in Cuba, 337–342; glossary of, 376; in Gulf War, 493; intermediate range nuclear forces, 287, 376, 440–441; Iraqi, 450; Iraqi Scud missiles, 493, 494; Jupiter, *330*, 340; Midgetman program, 432; Minuteman, *291*; Missile experimental (MX), 376, 427, *428*, 432; Multiple independently targetable reentry vehicles (MIRVs), 374, 375, 376, 427, 477; Patriot missiles, 493, 500; Pershing missiles, 428, 437, 438, *441*; Soviet, 287, *337*, 338–341, 413, 437–438, *441*; Strategic Arms Limitation Talks and, 426; submarine launched ballistic (SLBMs), *330*, 374, 375, 376, 427, 428, 477; surface-to-air (SAMs), 338, 376, 379; Titan II missile, *277*; world market for, 499. *See also* Cruise missiles; Intercontinental Ballistic Missiles; Intermediate Range Ballistic Missiles
Missing (film), 383
Missionaries, 4; in China, 24, 27, *52*, 146
Mission to Moscow (film), 186
Mitchell, George, 492
Mitterand, François, 432
MKULTRA (CIA program), 277
Mobil corporation, 425
Mobutu Sese Seko, 484
Molotov, V. M., 187, 194, 204, *228*, 228, *230*, 241, *243*; on Dulles, *279*; at London conference, 234; Marshall Plan and, 244; meeting with Truman, 211, 230; Yalta and, 233

Mondale, Walter, 424, 432
Monetary system, 387–388. *See also* Bretton Woods
Mongolia, 149, 253, 367
Monnet, Jean, 108
Monocacy (gunboat), *146*
Monroe, James, 45
Monroe, Marilyn, 305, 328
Monroe Doctrine, 12, 91, *337*; Roosevelt Corollary to, 28, 44–45, 151, 157, *492*; Venezuela crisis and, 5, 6, 7, 9
Montevideo Conference (1933), 165
Moral Equivalent of War (MEOW), 430
Morgan, J. P., 54, 76
J. P. Morgan Company, 76, 120, 163
Morgenthau, Henry, Jr., 114, *202*, 202, 353; on arms sales to belligerents, 107, 108, 110; on Jewish refugees, 196, 198
Morgenthau Plan, 202, 210, 238
Morocco, 58, 198, 274; human rights in, 431, 504
Moro National Liberation Front, 452
Moros (Philippines), 23–24
Morris, Edmund, *435*
Morrow, Dwight W., *152*, 163–164
Morse, Wayne, 350, *354*
Moscow: Conference (1945), 188, 189, 233; exhibition (1959), *283*, 305; Youth Festival (1957), 285
Mossadegh, Mohammed, 300, 408
Most-favored-nation status, 147, 496, 497
Motion pictures. *See* Films (Hollywood movies)
Motorola corporation, 295
Muccio, John J., 266
Mugabe, Robert, 425
Mukden incident, 140, 141
Multinational corporations, 386, 391; Latin America and, 417, 418
Multiple independently targetable reentry vehicle (MIRV), 374, 375, 376, 427, 477
Munich Conference (1938), 108, 128, 131–132, 327
Muños Marín, Luis, 162
Murrow, Edward R., 227

Musashi (warship), 148

Muslims, 413; in former Yugoslavia, 480, 481; holy war of *(jihad), 464,* 494, 505; in Iran, 409; Islamic fundamentalism, 428, 467, 505; Lebanon civil war and, 302, 448; Moros, in Philippines, 23–24, 452; Shi'ite, 450, 493. *See also* Arabs

Mussolini, Benito, *126,* 126, 133

Mutual Defense Assistance Bill, 247

Mutually assured destruction (MAD), 374, 375, 376

Mutual Security Administration, 245, 276

Mutual Security Treaty, 294

My Lai massacre, 353, 393

Nagasaki, atomic bombing of, 211, *221,* 222–225, 227

Nagy, Ferenc, 231, 233

Nahl, Perham, *33*

Naimark, Norman, *234*

Nam (Baker), 399

Namibia, 451, 482; South Africa and, 424, 450

Nanjing, 148

Nash, Paul, *100*

Nashville (ship), 34, 37

Nasser, Gamal Abdel, 299, 300, *301,* 301–302

Nathan, James, 341

National Aeronautics and Space Administration (NASA), 287, 291

National Association of Manufacturers, 6

National Basketball Association, 498, 506

National City Bank, 157, 159

National Council for the Prevention of War, 121

National Defense Act (1916), 83

National Defense Education Act (1958), 287–288

National Endowment for Democracy, 434

National Intelligence Estimate, 482

Nationalism, 4, 229, 307; African, 424–425; Arab, 299–300, 377,

447; Asian, 166; communism and, 248, 274; Cuban, 161–162; Eastern European, 286–287, 417; economic, 118, 119, 161, 303; Greek, 240; Laotian, 342; Latin American, 153, 166, 167, 302–305, 334, 347, 417–421; Mexican, 49, 165; in Middle East, 300–302; Nicaraguan, 418–419; Panamanian, 417–418; Puerto Rican, 162; Russian, 228; in Somalia, 484; in Spain, 127; Third World, 295, 299–300, 302, 307, 355, 416; U.S. insensitivity to, 60; Vietnamese, 321, 323, 326, 345; after World War I, 89–90, 101

Nationalist China, 146, 193, 250, 271, 308; Taiwan Strait crisis and, 292–293. *See also* Taiwan

National Liberation Front (EAM, Greece), 240, 241

National Liberation Front (NLF) (North Vietnam), 326, 344, 345, 348, 350, 351; Nixon Doctrine and, 392; peace terms and, 395; Tet offensive and, 317–319, *349,* 356

National Origins Act (1924), 195

National security, 255

National Security Council (NSC), 331, 430; creation of, 245–246; Cuba and, 338–339, 341; Iran hostage crisis and, 411; Paper 68 (NSC-68), 247–248, 271, 274, 427; under Reagan, 434; Southern Africa and, 384; Vietnam and, *320,* 324

National Student Association, 277

Nation building, *332,* 333, 507; in Africa, 334–335, 484; in Vietnam, 345

Nation (magazine), 156, 160

Naval blockades: of Vietnam, 394; World War I, 76–79

Naval War College, 39, 148

Navy, 9, 17, 28, 133, 180; aircraft carriers, *209,* 349; Anglo-American cooperation, 177; arms race and, *59,* 144; British, 68, 126; Chinese guerrillas and, 191; in Dominican Republic, 46; German, 126, 180;

Great White Fleet, 61; Guantánamo Bay base, 43, 339, 490, 491; Haiti and, 46; Japanese, 144, 148; in Mediterranean, 240, 302; Pacific expansion of, 53, 144, 182, *209;* Panama Canal and, 37, 38; Pearl Harbor and, 184–185, *185;* Seventh Fleet, 268, 273, 292, 343, 365; Six Fleet, 302; Washington conference and, 122, 144–145; World War I expansion, 83. *See also* Marines; Submarines; *and specific ships*

Navy Act of 1896, 9

Nazis, 128, 175, 176, 180, *233;* business collaboration with, 116, 128, 130. *See also* Germany, World War II and; Hitler, Adolf

Nazi-Soviet Pact (1939), 125, 182, 469

NBC news program, 319

Nehru, Jawaharlal, *299,* 299

Netanyahu, Benjamin, 495

Netherlands (Dutch), 76, 144; empire of, 101, 182; Indonesia and, 212, 228

Neutrality and Neutralism, 129–130; Austria, in Cold War, 282; Cold War nonalignment, 296, 299, 342; Latin American, 165; nonentanglement and, 129, 131; in World War I, 72, 73–76, 165

Neutrality Acts (1935, 1936, 1937), 108, 111, 130, 131, 132–133, 182; revision of, 176–177, 181

Neutron bomb, 376, 432

Nevins, Allan, 213

New Deal, 118, 130, 148, 162–163

Newfoundland fisheries, 57

New Information Order, 504–505

New International Economic Order, 388

New Mexico, 210, 226

New Panama Canal Company, 35, 37

New People's Army (Philippines), 451

Newspapers, yellow press, 11

New York, 9/11 terrorist attacks in, *461,* 462

New York Journal, 4, 16

New York Peace Society, 120

New York (ship), 68

New York Times, 123, 393
New York World, 4, 8, 37
New Zealand, 209, 274, 401; in Southeast Asia Treaty Organization, 292, 324
Ngoc, Nguyen, 319
Nhu, Madame, 346
Nhu, Ngo Dinh, 326, 346
Nicaragua, 46–48, 155, 444–446; Central Intelligence Agency in, 418, 433, 444–445; civil war in, 485; Panama Canal and, 35; Sandanistas in, 418, 420, 442, 444, 446; U.S. aid to *contras* in, 435, 442, 445–446; U.S. military intervention in, 147, 157–158, 165, 418, 420
Nicholas II, tsar of Russia, 96
Nigeria, 424, 485; oil production in, 386, 424, 485
Nike (shoe manufacturer), 498
Nimitz, Chester, 205
Nimitz (supercarrier), 412
Nine Power Treaty (1922), 143, 144
Ninotchka (film), 125
Nitze, Paul, 247, 338, 427, 431
Nixon, Richard M., *275,* 295, 356, 375; Cuba and, 384, *490;* debate with Khrushchev, *283,* 305, 326; détente and, 372, 373; dollar devaluation and, 387–388; environment and, 390; Kissinger and, *369, 370,* 370, 371; Middle East and, *379,* 380, 382; personal style of, 368–369; tour of Latin America by, 304, 305; trip to China, *364,* 365–368, *366, 373,* 393; Vietnam and, 374, 391–397, *394, 396,* 400
Nixon Doctrine, 377, 392
Nkrumah, Kwame, *327*
Nobel Peace Prize, 471, 472, 482, 500
Nomo, Hideo, 499
Nomura, Kichisaburo, 183
Nonalignment, 296, 299
Nonentanglement, 59, 129, 131. *See also* Isolationism; Neutrality
Nongovernmental organizations (NGOs), 390
Nonintervention pledge, 165–166
Noriega, Manuel Antonio, 488–489
Norris, Chuck, 399

Norris, George, 81, 94, 129, *149,* 151
North, Oliver, 435, 446
North Africa, 187, 188. *See also specific country*
North American Free Trade Agreement (NAFTA), 474, 486, 506
North Atlantic Treaty Organization (NATO), 255, 302, 426, 476; America joining, 246–247; Balkan crisis and, 480, 481; defense spending of, 288, 436; expansion of, 479; nuclear weapons and, 329, 437–438, *439;* Soviet Union and, 246–247; united Germany in, 476, *478,* 479; West Germany in, 247, 282, 286
North Korea, *265,* 464, 500; China and, 268–270, 271; invasion of South Korea by, 266–268; Korean War and, 266–273; nuclear weapons of, 497, 500, 501, *501; Pueblo* affair and, 319, 411. *See also* Korean War
North Pacific Fur Seal Convention (1911), 57
North Vietnam, 326, 348, 391; bombing of, 394, 395, 399; Cambodia and, 392–393; Chinese aid to, 325, 355; Laos and, 343; peace talks with, 356, 366; Tonkin Gulf and, 349, 350. *See also* Ho Chi Minh; Vietnam War
Novgorod automobile factory, 123
Novikov, Nikolai, 238
NTT (Japanese firm), 498
Nuclear arms race, 226, *288;* glossary for, *376. See also* Arms race
Nuclear nonproliferation, 237–238, 287, 307, 347, 464, 493–494, 500–502. *See also* Nuclear Nonproliferation Treaty; nuclear weapons
Nuclear Nonproliferation Treaty (1968), 347, 501
Nuclear weapons, 226, 500–501; brinkmanship, 280, 293; Chinese development of, 292, 293; Cuban missile crisis and, 337–341; delivery vehicles for, 376, 427; in Europe, 287; first strike of, 376,

436, 439; former Soviet Union, 501; freeze on, 376, 436; Indian development of, 347, 388, 497; in Iraq, 464, 493, 494; Korean War and, 270; limitations on, 277–279, 341, 477; nonproliferation of, 347, 366, 430, 501; proliferation of, 256, 282, 308, 329, 500; protests against, 294, 390, 436–437, 441; Reagan and, 436–438, *439;* Strategic Arms Limitation Talks (SALT), 372, 374–376, 426, 427–429; Taiwan Strait crisis and, 293; testing of, 291, 341, 436, 440; Vietnam and, 350, 391–392, 400. *See also* Atomic bomb; Missiles
Nuremberg Laws, 195
Nye, Gerald P., 107, 109, 110, 129, 130
Nyerere, Julius, 388

Obasanjo, Olusegun, president of Nigeria, 425
Obregón, Alváro, 163
Ocean resources, 390–391. *See also* Fisheries disputes
Office of Strategic Services (OSS), 192, *193,* 213, 321
Office of War Information, *225*
Oil industry and trade: Chinese, 429; embargo (1973), 380–381, 389; environment and, 390; Iranian, 209, 236, 237, 409, 412; Italy and, 131; Japanese imports, 142, 147, 182, 183, 184; Kuwaiti, *493;* Mexican, 48, 50, 163, 164, 420; Middle Eastern, 209, 236, 237, 301, 382; nationalization of, 383; Nigerian, 386, 424, 485; Organization of Petroleum Exporting Countries and, 372, 380, *381,* 383, 386; Peruvian, 383; Saudi, 380, 421, 494; U.S. import of, 387, 421; Venezuelan, 153, 154, 163, 208. *See also* Standard Oil Company
O'Jays, the, 451
Okinawa, 140, 248, 249; battle for, *224*
Olney, Richard, 5, 6, 8, 12, 13
Olympia (warship), 17

Olympic Games, 61, 127, 379, 429, 498, 506
Oman, 429
Omnibus Trade and Competitiveness Act (1988), 452
O'Neill, Paul, *463*
Open Door notes, 25, 51, 54
Open Door policy, 117, 151, 211; in China, 10, 25, 27, 51–52, 54, 55, 144, 145, 151, 191; during Cold War, 233, 255; Manchurian crisis and, 140, *141,* 142, 143; Roosevelt and, 41, 60; Wilson and, 73, 82
Operation AJAX, 409
Operation Castration, 336
Operation Desert Fox, 494
Operation Desert Shield, 492
Operation Desert Storm, *493,* 493
Operation Eagle Claw, 412
Operation Iraqi Freedom, 465–466
Operation Just Cause, 488–489
Operation MAGIC, 183, *184,* 185
Operation Mongoose, 337, 338
Operation Northwoods, 337
Operation OVERLORD, 187, 188, 189
Operation Poor Richard, 304
Operation Restore Hope, *483,* 483–484
Operation Rolling Thunder, 350
Operation TORCH, 187
Operation Uphold Democracy, 490
Operation Vittles, *239*
Opium trade, 487
OPLAN 34-A (covert operation), 348, 349
ORANGE (war plan), 166
Oregon (ship), 39
Organization of American States (OAS), 302, 303, 333, 384, 489
Organization of Petroleum Exporting Countries (OPEC), 372, 380, *381,* 383, 386
Orinoco River, 5, 8
Orlando, Vittorio, 89
Orozco, José Clemente, 163
Ortega Saavedra, Daniel, 446
Oscar II (ship), 83

Osipovich, Gennadi, 439
Osrin, Ray, *366*
Ostpolitik, 331, 376
Otis corporation, 498
Ouimet, Francis, 61

Pacific Ocean: line of defense in, 108, 151, 182; World War II in, 184–185, 203–204, 205, *209;* post–World War II, 248, map, *251. See also specific islands*
Pacifist organizations, 186; during interwar years, 120–122, 129, 130; women in, *81,* 83, 120, 129, 130; World War I and, 83, 87. *See also* Antiwar movement; Nuclear weapons, protests against
Page, Walter Hines, 74, 81
Paine, Tom, 434
Pakistan, 274, 365, 413, 487; arms sales to, 374, 429; Baghdad Pact and, 298, 300; Bangladesh and, 373–374; India and, 332, 500; Japanese aid to, 452; nuclear arms of, 497, 500; in Southeast Asia Treaty Organization, 292, 324
Palestine, Jewish state in, 197, 198, 241. *See also* Israel
Palestine Liberation Organization (PLO), 379, 380, 416, 424; Arab-Israeli peace and, *495,* 496; bases in Lebanon, 447–448; Iranian hostages and, 411
Palestinians, *intifada* (uprising) by, 448, 494, 496; in Lebanon, 448; as refugees, 300, 379, 381; in West Bank and Gaza, 422, 424, 448
Palme, Olof, 395
Palmer, A. Mitchell, *99*
Panama, 34–38, 60, 254, 446; canal zone and, 347, 417–418; crisis in, 485; Declaration of (1939), 166, 208; nationalism in, 305; U.S. invasion of, 488–489, *489*
Panama Canal, *33,* 57, 58, 59–60, 305, 347; Carter and, 417–418; map, *36;* neutrality of, 417; site selection for, 35–38, *38*
Panama-Pacific Exhibition, *33*

Pan American Conferences (1923–1938), 165–166
Pan American Conference (1939), 177
Panay (gunboat), 149
Panther (ship), 46
Papachristou, Judith, 20
Paraguay, 420, 486, 488
Paramount Pictures, 124
Paris, peace negotiations (1969–1973), 392, 393, 395
Paris, Treaty of (1899), 21
Paris, Treaty of (1919), 91, 98
Paris Peace Conference (1946), 233–234
Paris summit meeting (1960), 290–291
Park, Bert E., 94
Pathet Lao, 343–344
Patriot Act (2001), 507
Paul, Alice, 99
Paul, Randolph, 198
Pauncefote, Julian, 35
Peace Corps, *327,* 332–333
Pearl Harbor, 144, 148, 184–186, *185, 186, 209,* 225, 227
Pentagon, 350, 353, 375, *427;* Balkan crisis and, 480; new weapons systems of, 506–507; occupation of Iraq and, 467; under Reagan, 432; 9/11 (2001) terrorist attack on, 462, 463. *See also* Defense Department; Joint Chiefs of Staff
Pentagon Papers, 393
People's Republic of China (PRC), 306; aid to North Vietnam by, 325, 355; Carter and, 417; Congo and, 335; détente with, 366, 371, *373,* 391; hard-line toward, 308; Johnson and, 347; Korean War and, *265,* 268, 269–270, 271, 272–273, 274; Nixon's trip to, *364,* 365–368, *366,* 393; nonrecognition of, 252, 253, 254, 307; nuclear weapons of, 307, 366; Soviet Union and, 252–253, 291–293, 365, 372; Taiwan Strait crisis and, 292–293; threat to Taiwan by, 497, 499; Tiananmen Square massacre, 496, *497;* trade with, 386, 429, 496–497, 505; U.S. interests in, 426; U.S.

invasion of Iraq and, 465; Vietnam and, 321, 324, 344, 355, 400. *See also* Mao Zedong
PepsiCo, 372, 482, 498
Percentages agreement, 206–207
Perestroika (Soviet policy), 440, 469
Pérez, Louis A., Jr., 3, *15*
Pérez Jiménez, Marcos, 304
Perkins, Dexter, *11*
Permanent Court of International Justice. *See* World Court
Perón regime, 254
Perry, William, 497
Pershing, John J., 24, 51, 84, 85
Peru, 167, 383; Chile and, 152; narcoterrorism in, 487–488
Peters, Mike, *490*
Peterson, Pete, 498
Petroleum. *See* Oil industry and trade
Peurifoy, John, 303
Philippine Islands, 28, 53, 60, 166, 292, 505; authoritarian regimes in, 433, 451–452; Central Intelligence Agency, 277; economic expansion and, 117; human rights in, 431; military aid to, 267; Moros in, 23–24, 452; Southeast Asia Treaty Organization and, 324; Spanish-American-Cuban-Filipino War and, 16–17, 18; U.S. control of, 20, 322; U.S. investment in, 143, 452; U.S. protection of, 144, 145; World War II deaths in, 204, 211; World War II in, 184
Phillips, Cabell, *280*
Phillips, William, 60
Phoenix program, 353
Pike, Fredrick, 154
Ping-Pong diplomacy, 365
Pinochet, Augusto, 384
Pittman, Key, 132, 133
Plan Colombia, 488
Plan of San Diego, 51
Platt Amendment (1934), 40, 42–44, 48, 60, 161
Poindexter, John M., 434, 435
Point Four Program, 246, 254
Pokemon (computer game), 506
Poland, 80, 90, *92,* 200, 479; aid to, 199, 286; boundary with Ger-

many, 211, 376–377; fall of communism in, 468; German invasion of, 110, 127–128, 133, 176; Holocaust in, 195, 197–198; nationalism in, 286, 287; Solidarity in, 377, 438, *497;* Soviet Union and, 128, 188, 203, 208, 231; World War II and, 189, 211; Yalta agreement on, 202–203, 204–205, 210, 233
Pollution. *See* Environmental issues
Pompidou, Georges, 374
Ponce (Puerto Rico) Massacre, 162
Popular Movement for the Liberation of Angola (MPLA), 385
Population Bomb (Erlich), 390
Population growth, 388, 453, 502
Portsmouth Conference (1905), 40
Portugal, 144, 299, 398; Angola and, 384, 385
Potsdam Conference (1945), 210–211, 226, *227,* 231, 238
Potter, David, 295
Poverty, 502. *See also* Third World
Powell, Colin, 353, 401, 497; Balkan crisis and, 481; Bush and, 475, 476; Gulf War and, 492; Haiti and, 489–490; Panama invasion and, 488, *489;* Reagan administration and, 435, 445, 448; Vietnam and, 498
Power, balance of, 27, 28, 39, 58, 228, 371
Powers, Francis Gary, 291
President's Committee on Civil Rights, 255
Presley, Elvis, 173
Prevots, Naima, *306*
Prince of Wales (ship), *172,* 173
Prisoners of War (POWs), 271
Proctor, Redfield, 2
Profiles in Courage (Kennedy), *326*
Progressive era, 39, 73
Project Paperclip, 238
Project SAPPHIRE, 501
Propaganda, 175; anti-American, 246, 283, 305, 420; anti-Soviet, 97, *265, 284,* 284, 303; CIA and, 325, 385; communist, 124–125, 254; free enterprise, 434; pro-

Western, 300, 447; USIA and, 274, 276; wartime, 129, 189, 209. *See also* Voice of America
Prosperity and democracy, 229
Prostitution, U.S. soldiers and, 85
Public health, 116. *See also* Disease
Public opinion, 11, 18
Pueblo (spy ship), 319, 411
Puerto Rico, 18, 60, *162,* 162–163
Pulitzer, Joseph, 4
PURPLE (code machine), *184*
Putin, Vladimir, 477
Pyle, Ernie, *203*

Qualia, Tom, *333*
"Quarantine speech" (Roosevelt), 131, 149
Quebec Conference (1944), 202
Quemoy (Jinmen), 292–293

Rabin, Yitzhak, 495, *495*
Race riots (1919), 99
Racism and race, 28; African apartheid, 254, 386, 424–425; against black Americans, 84, 85, 253, 255, *353;* Cold War and, 297–298; and cultural stereotypes; against Filipinos, 21, 23; against Haitians, 158–159, 489; against Japanese, 53, 55; against Jews, 125–126. *See also* Anti-Semitism; and nation building in Africa, 335; pseudoscientific thinking about, 39, 55–56; in Vietnam, 401
Radford, Arthur, 323
Radio Corporation of America (RCA), 116
Radio Free Europe, 276, 286
Radio Liberty, 276
Radio Martí, 447
Railroads, 98; in China, 54, 140
RAINBOW (war plan), 166
Rambo (film series), 397
Rangers, 412, 484, 507
Rankin, Jeannette, *81,* 186
Rapacki, Adam, 288
Rapacki Plan, 288, 289, 307
Rather, Dan, 367

Raw materials, 321; U.S. import of, 229, 255, 387, 424, 425

Ray, Ted, 61

Reagan, Nancy, *434*

Reagan, Ronald, 399, *432, 434,* 467, 482, 485; Afghanistan and, 499; Africa and, 450–451; beliefs of, 432–434; Bush and, 471; cabinet of, 434; Central America and, 442–447, *443;* Cuba and, 444, 446–447, *490;* El Salvador and, 443–444; Gorbachev and, *440;* Iran-Contra affair and, 434–436, *435;* Iranian hostage crisis and, 412, 413; Iran-Iraq war and, 450; Japan and, 452; legacy of, 452–454; Libyan terrorism and, 449–450; Middle East and, 447–449; military buildup under, 432, 452, 453, 468; Nicaragua and, 444–446; on Panama Canal, 417, 418; personal style of, 431–432; Philippines and, 451–452; Soviet Union and, 432; Third World and, 442

Reagan Doctrine, 433

Reciprocal Trade Agreements Act (1934), 119, 156

Reciprocity Treaty (1902), 43

Reconstruction Finance Corporation, 124

Red Fascism, 231, *233. See also* Communism

Red Scare, 96–99. *See also* Bolshevism; communism; McCarthyism

Red (Soviet) Army, 188, 203, 208, 241; in Afghanistan, 428; cut backs in, 468–469; in Eastern Europe, 228, 282–284, 469; in Hungary, *285,* 286; in Manchuria, 205, 227, 250; in Romania, 231

RED SOX/RED CAP (CIA program), 286

Reed, James, 93

Reeves, Richard, *369*

Refugees: Cuban, 490–491; East German, 330, 331, 468; ethnic Albanian, 481; Haitian, 489; Hungarian, 286; Palestinian, 300, 379, 381; Rwandan, 484; Vietnamese,

396–397, 399; World War II, 195–197

Reid, Whitelaw, 59

Rekjavík summit (1986), 440

Renda, Mary, *160*

Report to the Secretary on the Acquiescence of This Government in the Murder of the Jews, 198

Republican Party, 88, 111, 275; control of Congress by, 473; Cuba and, 491; imperialism and, 20; Reagan era, 431; support for dictatorial regimes, 414

Republic of the Congo, 504. *See also* Zaire (Congo)

Republic of Vietnam, 325. *See also* South Vietnam

Reuben James (destroyer), 181

Revolutions: anticolonial, 295; Cuban, 335–337; Eastern European, 468–471, 505; Hungarian, 98, 286–287; Mexican, 48–51, 163; Russian, 81, 96

Reza Shah Pahlavi, Mohammad, 382, 409–411, 412, 413

Rhee, Syngman, 271, 273

Rhineland, 89, 111, 126

Rhodesia. *See* Zimbabwe/Rhodesia

Ribbentrop, Joachim von, *127*

Ricarte, Artemio, 24

Rice, Condoleezza, 463, 464, 475, 476

Ridgeway, Matthew, 323

Rio de Janeiro Conference (1942), 208

Rio Earth Summit (1992), 503

Rio Pact (1947), 302

Ripka, Hubert, 235

Ritter, Scott, 494

Road to Rio (film), 166

Roberts, Grace, *52*

Robin, Ron, *265*

Robins, Raymond, 96

Rockefeller, David, 410, 414

Rockefeller, Nelson A., 154, *155,* 166, 383

Rockefeller Foundation, 116, 147, 154

Rockhill, William H., 25

Rogers, Will, 119, 124, 141, 164

Rogers, William P., 367, 370

Rogers Act (1924), 115

Roman Catholic bishops, 436

Romania, 90, *92,* 195, 479; fall of communist regime in, 468; Soviet dominance in, 203, 205, 208, 209, 231

Rome-Berlin Axis, 126. *See also* Axis

Roosevelt, Eleanor, 120, 255

Roosevelt, Franklin D., *49,* 111, 122, 156; on arms sales to belligerents, *106,* 107–109, *109,* 110; at Atlantic Charter conference, *172,* 173–176, 198; atomic bomb and, 226; at Cairo Conference, *192;* China and, 51, 182, 191, 192, 194–195; entry into World War II and, 109–110, 186; foreign policy style of, *106,* 113–114; Good Neighbor Policy and, 152–154, 161; Haiti and, 160; Indochina and, 322–323; Japan and, 150, 183, 186; Jewish refugees and, 195, 196, 198; Lend-Lease and, 173, 174, 178–180, 188; Mexico and, 165; Middle East and, 209; at Moscow Conference, 188, 189; naval buildup under, 151, 180; neutrality and, 129–132, *132;* New Deal of, 118, 130, 148, 162–163; Nicaragua and, 158; "quarantine" speech of, 131, 149; repudiation of isolationism by, 177, 178, 181; Soviet Union and, *124,* 124, 148; United Nations and, 200–201; at Yalta Conference, 194, 202–203, *204,* 204–206

Roosevelt, Theodore, 41, 55, 58, 59, *492;* Anglo-American entente and, 56, 57, 58; "big stick" policy of, 39, 113, 414; Cuba and, 2, 3, 16, 17, 43; as imperialist, 4, 8, 10, 18, 20, 27; Japan and, 52–54, 55; *Lusitania* and, 70; Monroe Doctrine and, 28, 44–45; Panama Canal and, *35,* 35–38; personal style of, 40; Philippines and, 24; World War I and, 82, 83

Roosevelt, Theodore, Jr., 162

Roosevelt Corollary, 157, *492. See also* Monroe Doctrine

Root, Elihu, 40, 46, *54,* 57, 61, 113; Cuba and, 40, 42–43

Roots of War (Barnet), 398
Root-Takahira declaration (1908), 54
Rosenberg, Emily, 24
Rosskam, Edwin, *162*
Rostow, Walter, 336, 342, 344, 346, 356
Rotary International, 154
Rotter, Andrew, *300*
Rough Riders, 16, 17, *42*
Ruhr Valley, 119–120, 202
Rumor of War, A (Caputo), 353, 399
Rumsfeld, Donald, *450,* 464, 476, 507; on occupation of Iraq, 466, 467
Rusk, Dean, 253, *316,* 320, 347, 431; Cuban missile crisis and, 336, 338, 340; on Kennedy, 327; Vietnam War and, 328–329, 345, 346, 349, 350–351, 355
Russia, 27; China and, 24, 51–52; economic collapse in, 477; Japan and, 52, 53; loans to, 475, 477; nationalism in, 228; North Atlantic Treaty Organization and, 479; nuclear weapons in, 501; revolution in, 81, 96; transformations in, map, *470;* U.S. invasion of Iraq and, 465; World War I and, 74, 86, 89, 90, *92,* 100. *See also* Bolshevism; Soviet Union (USSR)
Russo-Japanese War, 140
Rwanda, genocide in, 484

Sadat, Anwar el-, 380, 381, 382, 421, 422, 448
St. Louis (ship), 196
St. Louis World's Fair, *23,* 24
Sakhalin Island, 144, 205
Sakharov, Andrei, 426
Salinas, Carlos, 486
Salisbury, Lord, *7, 7,* 8
Sam, Guillaume, 46
Sam Rayburn (submarine), *330*
Sandinista National Liberation Front (FSLN), 418, 420, 442, 485
Sandino, César Augusto, 157, *158,* 418
Sands of Iwo Jima (film), 255
San Francisco Conference (1945), 200
San Francisco Examiner, 53

San Francisco School Board, 53
San Juan Hill, battle for, 17
San Martín, Ramón Grau, 161
Santoli, Al, 399
Santos Zelaya, José, 46–47
Sarajevo, Bosnia, 61, 74
Sara Lee corporation, 482
Satellites: communications, 504–505; launches of, 287–288, *288*
Saudi Arabia, 209, 301, 302, 413, 464; arms sales to, 372, 447; Gulf War and, 491, 492; oil in, 380, 421, 494; U.S. military base in, 274, 429; women's rights in, 504
SAVAK (Iranian secret police), 409
Scali, John, 340
Schindler's List (film), 198
Schlesinger, Arthur M., Jr., 327. 328, 336, 353
Schmidt, Helmut, 429
School segregation, 297–298
Schoultz, Lars, *38*
Schrecker, Ellen, *280*
Schroeder, Gerhard, 479
Schuler, Friedrich E., 164
Schwartz, Thomas A., *245*
Schweiger, Walter, 68–69, *70,* 77
Scowcroft, Brent, *469,* 473, 496
Scruggs, William L., 5, 8
Scully, Eileen, 54
Second strike, 374, 376
Security Council, United Nations, 200, 205, 465; Gulf War and, 492, 493; Korean War and, 273
Seeger, Pete, 354
Seibel, Fred O., *106*
Selassie, Haile, 126
Selective Service Act (1917), 83–84
Selective Service Act (1940), 177–178
Sellers, Peter, *370*
Senate: ABM treaty and, 375; Foreign Relations Committee, 133; Kellogg-Briand Pact and, 121; Military Affairs Committee, 107, 108; Republican control of, 431; treaty-making power of, 307, 418; Vietnam War and, 393. *See also* Congress
Sendero Luminoso (Shining Path), 488

September 11 (9/11) terrorist attacks, *461,* 462–464, 494
Serbia-Montenegro, 480–481
Service, John S., 193, 194, 250
Shah of Iran. *See* Reza Shah Pahlavi, Mohammad
Shandong province (China), 25, 55, 89, 144, 145
Shanghai, bombing of, 148, *149*
Sharon, Ariel, 496
Sherman, John, 14
Sherry, Michael, 110, *120*
Shevardnadze, Eduard, 441, *469,* 471, 476
Shi'ite Muslims, 450, 493
Shining Path (Peru), 488
Shotwell, James T., 121
Shriver, Sargent, *333*
Shultz, George P., 434, 435, *436,* 448
Siberia, 97, 98, 144
Sicily, 187
Sigal, Leon, *501*
Sigsbee, Charles, *1*
Silent Spring (Carson), 390
Silk Stockings (film), 305
Simon Bolivar (film), 166
Singer Sewing Company, 41
Sino-Japanese War, 24
Six Crises (Nixon), 367
Six-Day War (1967), 379
Slovakia, 479
Slovenia, 479, 480
Smith, Ian, 384, 425
Smith, Jacob, 22
Smithsonian agreement, 387–388
Smoot-Hawley Tariff (1930), 117, 161
Snow, Edgar, 365
Sola, Vazquez de, *394*
Solidarity (Poland), 377, 438, *497*
Solzhenisyn, Aleksandr, 377
Somalia, 126, 429, *483,* 483–484; civil war in, 485; Soviets and, 425, 426; U.S. intervention in, 499, 507
Somoza Debayle, Anastasio, 420
Somoza family, 418
Somoza García, Anastasio, *155,* 158
Soong, Meiling (Madame Jiang), 147, *192*
Soong, T. V., 147

South Africa, 385, 485; apartheid in, 254, 384, 386, 424–425, 451, 453; authoritarianism in, 434; Boer War in, 28; majority rule in, 482; Namibia and, 424, 450; nuclear weapons of, 500; trade and investment in, 424, 425, 482; white minority rule in, 386, 424, 425

South America, 101, 155; German investment in, 39, 109. *See also* Latin America

Southeast Asia: bombing of, 371; Cold War in; Japan and, 147, 174, 182, 185; military aid to, 397; U.S. interests in, 322; Vietnam War and, map, *352. See also* Indochina; *specific countries*

Southeast Asia Treaty Organization (SEATO), 282, 292, 299, 324

South Korea: aid to, 273, 389; authoritarianism in, 434; China and, 496–497; human rights in, 431; Japan and, 452; North Korean invasion of, 266–268, 271, 273; Soviet Union and, 438–439; U.S. ties to, 368, 401. *See also* Korean War

South Manchuria Railway, 140

South Vietnam, 307, 345, 348; aid to, 370, 389, 392; Vietcong in, 344, 353. *See also* Vietnam

South Vietnamese Army (ARVN), 317–320

South West African People's Organization (SWAPO), 451

Souvanna Phouma, 342, 343

Soviet Union (USSR), 115, 141, 186; Afghanistan and, 385, 421, 428, 441, 442, 452; aircraft/bombers of, *272,* 338, 340, 341, 376, 383, 427; in Angola and Ethiopia, 420–421, 425; anti-Bolshevism and, 96–99; armament spending in, 282; Atlantic Charter and, 175, 176; atomic bomb and, 226, 237–238, 247; Austria and, 282; Berlin and, 289–291, 377; Carter administration and, 415, 417, 425–426, 427–429; Central America and, 442–443; China and, 194, 252–253, 291–293, 365, 366, 367, 368, 372; Cold War rivalry with U.S., 228, 231, 307; Congo and, 335; containment of (*See* Containment policy); Cuba and, 336, 420, 490; Czechoslovakia and, 98, 203, 231, 233, 347, 348; détente and, 282, 285, 371, 374, 376, 391; disintegration of, 471; Eastern Europe and, 189, 199, 207, 209, 231, 233, 301; economy of, 441; Egypt and, 377; Eisenhower and, 212, 278–279; expansion of, 426, 431; Finland and, 177; Ford plant in, 116; Geneva summit and, 283; Germany and, 122, 125, 127–128; under Gorbachev, 439–442, 468–469; grain sales to, 414; Greece and, 240, 241; human rights in, 417; Hungary and, 203, 207, 209, 231, 233; India and, 374; during interwar years, 111, 122–125; Iran and, 236–237; isolation of, 145; Japan and, 146, 147, 148, 149, 248, 249; Jewish emigration from, 372, 426; Johnson and, 347; Korea Air Lines 007 and, 438–439; Korean War and, 267, 268, 270–273, 282; Latin America and, 303; Lend-Lease aid to, 180, 188, 209, 210, 236; Marshall Plan and, 235, 244; Middle East and, 242–243, 380, 382; missiles of, 287, 329, 413; Namibia and, 451; national liberation and, 377, 386; Nazi pact with, 125, 182, 469; North Atlantic Treaty Organization and, 246–247; Poland and, 128, 188, 202, 208, 231; Potsdam accords and, 210–211; Reagan and, 432, 436, 437–438, 439–442, 452–453; 1989 revolutions and, 468–471, 505; Spanish civil war and, 127; Strategic Arms Limitation Talks and, 374–376, 426, 427–429; Syria and, 380, 421; Taiwan Strait crisis and, 293; Third World and, 299; trade with, 386, 429, 438; transformations, map, *470;* Turkey and, 240–241; U-2 crisis and, *290,* 291; United Nations and, 200, 201; U.S. propaganda and, 282–284; Vietnam War and, 324, 400; Warsaw Pact and, 247; Watergate scandal and, 369; West Germany and, 285, 288–290, 376–377; World War II and, 198, 212; Yalta Conference and, 202–206, 230. *See also* Cold War; Red (Soviet) Army; Russia; Stalin, Joseph

Soweto, 386

Space exploration, 374

Spacek, Sissy, 383

Spain, 274, 463; civil war in, 127, 130, 131; Cuba and, 2–5, 12, 13

Spanish-American-Cuban-Filipino War, 10, 16–18, 28, 39; events leading to, 13–16

Special Forces, 344. *See also* Green Berets; Rangers

Speck von Sternburg, Hermann, 44–45

Spellman, Francis Cardinal, 324

Spielberg, Steven, 198

Spock, Benjamin, 354

Sputnik (satellite), 287

Stalin, Joseph, 125, 187, *228,* 237, 255; Atlantic Charter and, 176; Berlin blockade and, 238; China and, 149, 249–250, 252, 280–281; Cold War and, 228, 248; compared to Hitler, 231; death of, 271, 278, 280; denouncement of, 286; Eastern Europe and, 231, 233, 234, 244; on German containment, 188; Greek communists and, 240; Korean War and, *265,* 268, 269, 271–273; Lend-Lease and, 190, 210; as obstructionist, 253–254; pact with Hitler, 125, *127;* percentage agreement and, 206–207; at Potsdam Conference, 210, 211, 231; purges of, 125; at Teheran Conference, 189; on Truman, *230;* Warsaw uprising and, 208; at Yalta Conference, 194, 202, 204–206, 241

Stalingrad, siege of, 188

Stallone, Sylvester, 399
Standard Oil Company, 41, 48, 130, 149, 154, 164
Stark, Harold R., 177
Stark (frigate), 450
"Star Wars" (SDI), 376, 438, *439,* 440, 476
State, U.S. Department of, 99, 199, 210; Africa and, 385; Brzezinski and, 416, 430; China and, 192; on Cuban/Soviet threat, 442; defense establishment and, 213; Dominican Republic and, 156; Egypt and, 301; elite inner circle of, 60–61; Guatemala and, 303; Haiti and, 46; Iranian crisis and, 237; Israel and, 242; Jewish refugees and, 196, 197, 198; Korean War and, 266, 270; Latin America and, 334; *Lusitania* disaster and, 68; McCarthyism and, 250, 270, 281; Nicaragua and, 47, 48; nuclear arms race and, 428; occupation of Iraq and, 467; Pakistan and, 374; Panama Canal and, 36; race and, 298; Roosevelt and, 114, 132; Southeast Asia and, 323; Soviet affairs and, 115, 123; U-2 spy plane and, 291; women's rights, 504; World War I reparations and, 119
Steel, Ronald, 398
Steffens, Lincoln, 98
Stereotypes, and cultural bias, 163, 298–299
Stettinius, Edward R., Jr., 200, 208
Stevenson, Adlai E., 275, 339, *340*
Stillman, Edmund, 398
Stilwell, Joseph W., 191, *192,* 192–193
Stimson, Henry L., 61, *113,* 113, 121, 202, 329; atomic diplomacy and, 234; Japan and, 183; Manchurian crisis and, *139,* 140–142, 143, 152; Nicaragua and, 158; post-World War II Europe and, 233; as Secretary of War, 177, 178; Soviet Union and, 123, 148
Stimson Doctrine, 142
Stockdale, James B., 349
Straight, Willard, 54, 60
Strategic Air Command, 274, *277,* 287

Strategic Arms Limitation Talks (SALT), 431; under Carter, 426, 427–429; under Ford, 375–376; under Nixon, 372, 374–375
Strategic Arms Limitation Treaty (1972), 372
Strategic Arms Reduction Talks (START), 438, 476, 477
Strategic Defense Initiative (SDI-Star Wars), 376, 438, *439,* 440, 476
Strategic weapons, 376, 477
Stuart, J. Leighton, 252
Submarine-launched ballistic missiles (SLBMs), *330,* 374, 375, 376, 436, 437; limitations on, 427, 428, 477
Submarines, 51, *330,* 499; *Lusitania* disaster and, 68–72, 79; Soviet, 340; Trident series, 375, 427, 432; World War I, 78–80, 81, 82; World War II, 174, 179, 181
Sudan, 450; bombing of, 484–485
Suez crisis, 300, 301–302
Sugar trade: Cuban, 11, 12, 41, 43–44, 153, 155, 161, 334, 336, *337;* Haitian, 159; Puerto Rican, 162
Suharto, Kemusu, 398
Sullivan, Leon H., 425
Sullivan, William, 410
Sullivan Principles, 425
Summers, Lawrence, 475
Summit of the Americas (1994), 486
Sunday, Billy, 81
SUNFLOWER (peace initiative), 356
Sun Zhongshan (Sun Yat-Sen), 101, 145, 146
Supreme Court, 60, 297, 393
Surface-to-air missiles (SAMs), 338, 376, 379
Suri, Jeremy, 371
Sussex (ship), 79–80
Suzuki, Ichiro, 499
Suzuki, Kantaro, 227
Sweden, 198
Swift, Ann, 409
Swift company, 101
Switzerland, 198
Syria, 301, 302, 379, 381, 424; Arab-Israeli conflict and, 495; Lebanon and, 447, 448

Tactical nuclear weapons, 376
Taft, Robert, 246–247, 267
Taft, William Howard, 43, 45, 47, 48, 58; China trade and, 54, 55; Philippines and, *22, 23,* 40
Taft-Katsura memorandum, 53
Taiwan (Formosa), 24, 192, 252, 292, 307; arms sales to, 497; Army Advisory Group on, 250; Chinese threat to, 497, 499; human rights in, 431; Korean War and, 268, 273, 274; People's Republic of China and, 292–293; Taiwan Strait crisis and, 292–293; U.S. commitment to, 367, 368, 430. *See also* Jiang Jieshi; Nationalist China
Taiwan Strait crisis, 292–293
Takahira, Kogoro, 52, 54
Taking Haiti (Renda), *160*
Talbott, Strobe, 477
Taliban, 464, 491, 504
Tang Wensheng, 367
Tanzania, 385, 484
Tariffs, 14, 186; Chinese, 147; General Agreement on Trade and, 388, 475; interwar years' policy, 117, 118–119; Japanese, 452; reduction in, 276, *326,* 388, 417
Taxation, 116, 163
Taylor, Maxwell, 344, 397, 418
Technology transfer, 417
Teheran, hostage crisis in (1979–1981), *408,* 409–413
Teheran Conference (1943), 189
Teller Amendment, 3–4
Temptations, the, 451
Tenet, George L., 462, 464
Terrorism, 497, 500; in Argentina, 371; in Europe, 379; hijackings, 449, 462–463; Iran hostage crisis, *408,* 409–413; Libyan-sponsored, 449; Palestinian, 495; September 11 (2001), *461,* 462–464, 494; in Uganda, 382; war on, 464, 467, 477, 496, 507; world trade and, 475
Tet offensive, 317–320, *349, 352,* 356, 397
Texaco (Texas Oil Company), 48
Texas, 51